COORDINATED RESEARCH IN CRIMINAL LAW AND PRACTICE FROM WEST

WEST'S CRIMINAL PRACTICE SERIES

Search and Seizure
Wayne R. LaFave

Substantive Criminal Law
Wayne R. LaFave and Austin W. Scott, Jr.

Criminal Law Defenses
Paul H. Robinson

Criminal Procedure
Wayne R. LaFave and Jerold H. Israel

Federal Sentencing Law and Practice
Thomas W. Hutchison and David Yellen

Federal Criminal Practice: Prosecution and Defense
Harry I. Subin, Chester L. Mirsky and Ian S. Weinstein

Federal Criminal Law and Related Actions: Crimes, Forfeiture, the False Claims Act and RICO
Sarah N. Welling, Sara Sun Beale and Pamela H. Bucy

Federal Practice and Procedure
Vols. 1, 2, 3 and 3A – Criminal
Charles Alan Wright

Federal Jury Practice and Instructions
Volumes 1 and 2 – Civil and Criminal
Hon. Edward J. Devitt, Hon. Charles B. Blackmar,
Michael A. Wolff and Kevin F. O'Malley

Federal Criminal Code and Rules Pamphlet

Federal Sentencing Guidelines Manual
United States Sentencing Commission

WEST'S STATE PRACTICE SERIES

West has the following specialized criminal practice and procedure volumes in the state practice series:

Arizona Criminal Procedure Forms

California Criminal Trialbook

COORDINATED RESEARCH FROM WEST

California Jury Instructions – Criminal

Colorado Jury Instructions – Criminal

Connecticut Criminal Jury Instructions

Illinois Criminal Practice and Procedure

Illinois Pattern Jury Instructions – Criminal

Indiana Criminal Procedure

Iowa Criminal Law and Procedure

Kansas Criminal Code and Code of Criminal Procedure

Kentucky Criminal Practice and Procedure

Kentucky Substantive Criminal Law

Massachusetts Criminal Practice and Procedure

Massachusetts Criminal Law

Michigan Criminal Law

Minnesota Criminal Law and Procedure

Mississippi Model Jury Instructions – Civil and Criminal

Missouri Criminal Practice and Procedure

New Jersey Criminal Practice and Procedure

New Jersey Criminal Law

McKinney's Forms for NY Laws – Criminal Procedure

Pennsylvania Criminal Procedure Forms and Commentary

Tennessee Criminal Practice and Procedure

Texas Criminal Forms

Washington Criminal Practice and Procedure

Washington Criminal Law

———

WESTLAW CRIMINAL JUSTICE DATABASES

FCJ–FSG Federal Sentencing Guidelines
FSLP Federal Sentencing Law and Practice
CJ–SCJ ABA Standards for Criminal Justice
CJ–CJA Criminal Justice Abstracts
WTH–CJ WESTLAW Highlights – Criminal Justice
CJ–TP Law Reviews, Texts and Journals

———

To order any of these West Criminal Law and Practice tools, call your West Representative or 1–800–344–5009.

FEDERAL CRIMINAL LAW AND RELATED ACTIONS:

Crimes, Forfeiture, the False Claims Act and RICO

By

SARAH N. WELLING
Wendell H. Ford Professor
University of Kentucky College of Law

SARA SUN BEALE
Professor
Duke University School of Law

PAMELA H. BUCY
Frank M. Bainbridge Professor
University of Alabama School of Law

Volume 2

Chapters 17–33
Tables and Index

CRIMINAL PRACTICE SERIES

ST. PAUL, MINN.
West Group
1998

WESTLAW® ELECTRONIC RESEARCH GUIDE

WESTLAW, Computer–Assisted Legal Research

WESTLAW is part of the research system provided by West Group. With WESTLAW, you find the same quality and integrity that you have come to expect from West books. For the most current and comprehensive legal research, combine the strengths of West books and WESTLAW.

WESTLAW Adds to Your Library

Whether you wish to expand or update your research, WESTLAW can help. For instance, WESTLAW is the most current source for case law, including slip opinions and unreported decisions. In addition to case law, the online availability of statutes, statutory indexes, legislation, court rules and orders, administrative materials, looseleaf publications, texts, periodicals, news and business information makes WESTLAW an important asset to any library. Check the online WESTLAW Directory or the print WESTLAW Database Directory for a list of available databases and services. Following is a brief description of some of the capabilities that WESTLAW offers.

Natural Language Searching

You can search most WESTLAW databases using WIN®, the revolutionary Natural Language search method. As an alternative to formulating a query using terms and connectors, WIN allows you to simply enter a description of your research issue in plain English:

> What is the government's obligation to warn military
> personnel of the danger of past exposure to radiation?

WESTLAW then retrieves the set of documents that have the highest statistical likelihood of matching your description.

Retrieving a Specific Document

When you know the citation to a case or statute that is not in your library, use the Find service to retrieve the document on WESTLAW. Access Find and type a citation like the following:

> 181 ne2d 520
> in st 27-1-12-1

Updating Your Research

You can use WESTLAW to update your research in many ways:

- Retrieve cases citing a particular statute.

- Update a state or federal statute by accessing the Update service from the displayed statute using the Jump marker.

- Retrieve newly enacted legislation by searching in the appropriate legislative service database.

- Retrieve cases not yet reported by searching in case law databases.

- Read the latest U.S. Supreme Court opinions within an hour of their release.

- Update West digests by searching with topic and key numbers.

Determining Case History and Retrieving Citing Cases

KeyCite$_{SM}$, the new citation research service developed by West Group and made available through the WESTLAW computer-assisted legal research service, integrates all the case law on WESTLAW, giving you the power to

- trace the history of a case;

- retrieve a list of all cases on WESTLAW that cite a case; and

- track legal issues in a case.

Citing references from the extensive library of secondary sources on WESTLAW, such as ALR® annotations and law review articles, are covered by KeyCite as well. You can use these citing references to find case discussions by legal experts.

Now, in this one service on WESTLAW, you receive

- the case-verification functions of Insta-Cite®;

- the case-citing functions of Shepard's® and Shepard's PreView®; and

- the currentness of QuickCite®.

In addition, KeyCite is completely integrated with West's Key Number System so that it provides the tools for navigating the case law databases on WESTLAW. Only KeyCite combines the up-to-the-minute case-verification functions of an online citator service with the case-finding tools needed to find relevant case law.

Additional Information

For more detailed information or assistance, contact your WESTLAW account representative or call 1-800-REF-ATTY (1-800-733-2889).

SUMMARY OF CONTENTS

SUMMARY OF CONTENTS

TABLE OF CONTENTS

Volume 1

PART I. GENERAL DOCTRINES

CHAPTER 1. JURISDICTION

CHAPTER 2. INCHOATE LIABILITY

TABLE OF CONTENTS

TABLE OF CONTENTS

TABLE OF CONTENTS

TABLE OF CONTENTS

TABLE OF CONTENTS

TABLE OF CONTENTS

TABLE OF CONTENTS

TABLE OF CONTENTS

CHAPTER 10. ENVIRONMENTAL CRIMES

TABLE OF CONTENTS

TABLE OF CONTENTS

TABLE OF CONTENTS

TABLE OF CONTENTS

TABLE OF CONTENTS

CHAPTER 16. HOMICIDE

TABLE OF CONTENTS

Volume 2

CHAPTER 17.   MAIL AND WIRE FRAUD

TABLE OF CONTENTS

TABLE OF CONTENTS

CHAPTER 18. MONEY LAUNDERING AND CURRENCY REPORTING CRIMES

TABLE OF CONTENTS

TABLE OF CONTENTS

TABLE OF CONTENTS

CHAPTER 19. OBSTRUCTION OF JUSTICE; THE VICTIM AND WITNESS PROTECTION ACT

TABLE OF CONTENTS

TABLE OF CONTENTS

TABLE OF CONTENTS

TABLE OF CONTENTS

CHAPTER 23. TAX FRAUD

TABLE OF CONTENTS

TABLE OF CONTENTS

TABLE OF CONTENTS

PART V. FORFEITURE

CHAPTER 28. CIVIL FORFEITURE

TABLE OF CONTENTS

TABLE OF CONTENTS

TABLE OF CONTENTS

TABLE OF CONTENTS

TABLE OF CONTENTS

FEDERAL CRIMINAL LAW AND RELATED ACTIONS

Crimes, Forfeiture, the False Claims Act and RICO

Volume 2

PART II—Continued

CRIMES.

CHAPTER 17

MAIL AND WIRE FRAUD

Table of Sections

1

WESTLAW ELECTRONIC RESEARCH

See WESTLAW Electronic Research Guide preceding the Summary of Contents.

§ 17.1 Introduction

The mail fraud statute was enacted in 1872 pursuant to Congress's authority over the mails.[1] It is the oldest federal criminal statute being used extensively to prosecute crimes that are within the province of state and local law enforcement. Although many fraud and related types of cases are being prosecuted today under other specific federal statutes, the mail fraud caseload remains large. The durability of the crime of mail fraud—despite the enactment over the years of a series of related, more specific criminal statutes—is largely explained by the unusual flexibility that the courts have accorded it. As one former federal prosecutor explained:

§ 17.1

1. Article I, Section 8 of the Constitution authorizes Congress to "establish Post Offices and Post roads," and this provision has been treated as the authority for the operation and regulation of the postal system. *See* McCulloch v. Maryland, 17 U.S. (4 Wheat.) 316, 417, 4 L.Ed. 579 (1819). The constitutionality of the mail fraud act rests on this provision (and on the Necessary and Proper Clause). In Badders v. United States, 240 U.S. 391, 393, 36 S.Ct. 367, 60 L.Ed. 706 (1916), the Court held that Congress has the authority to prohibit any act of mailing "done in furtherance of a scheme that [Congress] regards as contrary to public policy, whether it can forbid the scheme or not."

The constitutional issues raised by the passage of the act are discussed in § 1.4, and in Sara Sun Beale, *Mail: Federal Mail Fraud Act*, 3 ENCYCLOPEDIA OF CRIMINAL JUSTICE, 1015, 1015–16 (1983), and Jed S. Rakoff, *The Federal Mail Fraud Statute (Part I)*, 18 DUQ.L.REV. 771 (1980). The latter also provides an excellent account of the legislative history, the early judicial decisions construing the act, and later revisions in its language. The Supreme Court discussed the early legislative history of the act in Durland v. United States, 161 U.S. 306, 16 S.Ct. 508, 40 L.Ed. 709 (1896), and McNally v. United States, 483 U.S. 350, 107 S.Ct. 2875, 97 L.Ed.2d 292 (1987). More recent revisions to the statute are discussed in Peter J. Henning, *Maybe It Should Just Be Called Federal Fraud: The Changing Nature of the Mail Fraud Statute*, 36 B.C.L.REV. 435 (1995).

To federal prosecutors of white collar crime, the mail fraud statute is … our true love. We may flirt with RICO, show off with 10b–5, and call the conspiracy law "darling," but we always come home to the virtues of 18 U.S.C. § 1341, with its simplicity, adaptability, and comfortable familiarity.[2]

Of course, a "flirtation" with RICO need not compromise at all the relationship with mail fraud, which is frequently used as predicate offense in RICO cases. Indeed, a number of the lower court opinions defining the scope of the mail fraud statute have been issued in civil RICO cases.

The mail fraud act is codified as 18 U.S.C. § 1341 (1994). It currently provides:

> Whoever, having devised or intending to devise any scheme or artifice to defraud, or for obtaining money or property by means of false or fraudulent pretenses, representations, or promises, or to sell, dispose of, loan, exchange, alter, give away, distribute, supply, or furnish or procure for unlawful use any counterfeit or spurious coin, obligation, security, or other article, or anything represented to be or intimated or held out to be such counterfeit or spurious article, for the purpose of executing such scheme or artifice or attempting so to do, places in any post office or authorized depository for mail matter, any matter or thing whatever to be sent or delivered by the Postal Service, or deposits or causes to be deposited any matter or thing whatever to be sent or delivered by any private or commercial interstate carrier, or takes or receives therefrom, any such matter or thing, or knowingly causes to be delivered by mail or such carrier according to the direction thereon, or at the place at which it is directed to be delivered by the person to whom it is addressed, any such matter or thing, shall be fined under this title or imprisoned not more than five years, or both. If the violation affects a financial institution, such person shall be fined not more than $1,000,000 or imprisoned not more than 30 years, or both.

In 1952 Congress responded to the problem of radio frauds by enacting a wire fraud statute, 18 U.S.C. § 1343, to parallel the mail fraud act.[3] Section 1343, which was later amended to include television frauds, now provides:

> Whoever, having devised or intending to devise any scheme or artifice to defraud, or for obtaining money or property by means of false or fraudulent pretenses, representations, or promises, trans-mits or causes to be transmitted by means of wire, radio, or television communication in interstate or foreign commerce, any writings, signs, signals, pictures, or sounds for the purpose of executing such scheme or artifice, shall be fined under this title or

---

2. *Ibid.*

3. The wire fraud statute was enacted as § 18(a) of the Communications Act of 1952, Pub.L.No. 82–554, 66 Stat. 722. The legislative history reflects a focus on fraud by radio. *See* Conf.Rep. 82–2426, 82nd Cong., 2d Sess., *reprinted in* 1952 U.S.C.C.A.N. 2234, 2256, 2262.

imprisoned not more than five years, or both. If the violation affects a financial institution, such person shall be fined not more than $1,000,000 or imprisoned not more than 30 years, or both.

Most often, mail and wire fraud prosecutions are initiated where the facts show a classic case of fraud—conduct amounting to the crime of obtaining property by false pretenses. However, the statutes are increasingly being used to prosecute conduct not amounting to traditional criminal fraud but which may involve other crimes such as bribery or extortion. In other cases, mail and wire fraud have been used to prosecute conduct that does not show fraud in a classic sense and does not violate any other provision of the state or federal penal laws. The conduct involved may take place in a commercial or corporate setting or involve a state or local government official; increasingly mail and wire fraud are being used to prosecute various forms of commercial bribery and political corruption. Congress indicated its approval of these nontraditional uses of the mail and wire fraud statutes by enacting 18 U.S.C. § 1346 (1994), which states that for purposes of the mail, wire, and bank fraud statutes, "the term 'scheme or artifice to defraud' includes a scheme or artifice to deprive another of the intangible right of honest services."

Library References:

C.J.S. Postal Service and Offenses Against Postal Laws § 23; Telegraphs, Telephones, Radio, and Television § 116–123.
West's Key No. Digests, Postal Service ☞35; Telecommunications ☞362.

§ 17.2   The Relationship Between the Mail and Wire Fraud Statutes

Because the wire fraud statute was modeled on the mail fraud statute, they are generally given the same interpretation and the cases decided under one statute are generally applicable to the other.[1] Howev-

---

§ 17.2

1. *D.C. Circuit:* United States v. Lemire, 720 F.2d 1327, 1234–35 n. 6 (D.C.Cir. 1983) (elements of two statutes are "identical" and "cases construing mail fraud apply to the wire fraud statute as well.")

First Circuit: United States v. Czubinski, 106 F.3d 1069, 1076 n. 10 (1st Cir.1997) (observing that "[i]dentical standards apply in determining the 'scheme to defraud' element under the mail and wire fraud statutes"); United States v. Pietri Giraldi, 864 F.2d 222, 224 (1st Cir.1988); United States v. Castillo, 829 F.2d 1194, 1198 (1st Cir. 1987) (wire fraud statute was patterned upon mail fraud act, statutes are "in pari passu," and therefore "in general, caselaw construing § 1341 is instructive for purposes of § 1343"); United States v. Fermin Castillo, 829 F.2d 1194, 1198 (1st Cir.1987).

Second Circuit: Colony at Holbrook, Inc. v. Strata G.C., Inc., 928 F.Supp. 1224, 1231 (E.D.N.Y.1996) (elements of wire and mail fraud "are essentially the same"); Lou v. Belzberg, 728 F.Supp. 1010, 1025 n. 4 (S.D.N.Y.1990) (noting that "[c]ases dealing with the mail fraud statute are also applicable to the wire fraud statute," and that "the requisite elements for a scheme to defraud are shared under both statutes.")

Third Circuit: United States v. Bentz, 21 F.3d 37, 40 (3d Cir.1994).

Fourth Circuit: United States v. Re-Brook, 58 F.3d 961, 966 n. 6 (4th Cir.1995) (noting that wire fraud and mail fraud statutes are " 'given a similar construction and are subject to the same substantive analysis' ") (citation omitted); John C. Holland Enterprises, Inc. v. J.P. Mascaro & Sons, Inc., 653 F.Supp. 1242, 1249 (E.D.Va.) (civil RICO case based upon predicate mail fraud)

er, there is one important exception: the courts have given the jurisdictional provisions of the wire fraud statute an interpretation that restricts it to interstate cases, though no such restriction is found in the mail fraud decisions.[2] Since these provisions are generally read in tandem and decisions under the two statutes are interchangeable, we will not generally draw any distinction between them. Though we shall refer frequently to the "mail and wire fraud statutes," for the sake of brevity we shall sometimes refer only to "mail fraud," using that phrase generically to include wire fraud as well (except in the case of the jurisdictional issue noted above).

Library References:

C.J.S. Postal Service and Offenses Against Postal Laws § 23; Telegraphs, Telephones, Radio, and Television § 116–123.

West's Key No. Digests, Postal Service ☞35; Telecommunications ☞362.

§ 17.3 The Federal Courts' Approach to the Construction of the Mail and Wire Fraud Statutes

In a case decided a century ago the Supreme Court set the pattern for construction of the mail fraud act (and subsequently the wire fraud act). The question in the case was whether the mail fraud statute followed the common law rule, which was that only misrepresentations as to present or past facts constituted a basis for a charge of obtaining property by false pretenses. This was the prevailing rule in the United States at the time the case was decided. Consequently, in most state courts a person could not be convicted of obtaining property by false pretenses if he had only made a false promise, *i.e.* stated an intention to pay money at some future date without intending in fact to make the payment.[1] In *Durland v. United States*[2] the Supreme Court held that the

(commenting that because "the requisite elements of a 'scheme to defraud' under the wire fraud statute are the same as those under the mail fraud statute, the cases construing one have been held applicable to the other"), *aff'd*, 829 F.2d 1120 (4th Cir.1987) (Table).

Fifth Circuit: United States v. Allen, 76 F.3d 1348, 1362–63 (5th Cir.), *cert. denied*, ___ U.S. ___, 117 S.Ct. 121, 136 L.Ed.2d 71 (1996); United States v. Herron, 825 F.2d 50, 54 n. 5 (5th Cir.1987) (noting the "wire and mail fraud statute employ the same 'scheme or artifice to defraud' language, and the construction of either statute informs the application of the other"); United States v. Bruno, 809 F.2d 1097, 1104 (5th Cir.1987) (noting that the elements of the statute are identical, and that "cases construing mail fraud apply to the wire fraud statute as well.")

Sixth Circuit: Cf. Hofstetter v. Fletcher, 905 F.2d 897, 902 (6th Cir.1988) (noting that "wire fraud language should be inter-

preted with the same breadth as the analogous language in the mail fraud statute.")

Seventh Circuit: United States v. Briscoe, 65 F.3d 576, 583 (7th Cir.1995); United States v. Kuecker, 740 F.2d 496, 504 (7th Cir.1984) (noting that "the prerequisites for establishing intent to defraud are identical for both wire and mail fraud.")

Ninth Circuit: Belt v. United States, 868 F.2d 1208, 1211 (9th Cir.1989) ("statutes are given a similar construction and are subject to the same substantive analysis.")

2. For a discussion of jurisdiction under these statutes, see §§ 17.27–17.31.

§ 17.3

1. *See generally*, Arthur R. Pearce, *Theft by False Promises*, 101 U.Pa.L.Rev. 967 (1953). In modern times, there has been movement in the direction of making false promises the subject of criminal prosecution. *See, e.g.*, People v. Ashley, 42 Cal.2d

mail fraud statute was not limited to the common law conception of fraud prevailing at the time of the statute's enactment. The Court looked to "the evil sought to be remedied" by the statute and concluded:

> It is common knowledge that nothing is more alluring than the expectation of receiving large returns on small investments. Eagerness to take the chances of large gains lies at the foundation of all lottery schemes, and, even when the matter of chance is eliminated, any scheme or plan which holds out the prospect of receiving more than is parted with appeals to the cupidity of all.
>
> In the light of this the statute must be read, and so read it includes everything designed to defraud by representations as to the past or present, or suggestions and promises as to the future.... It was with the purpose of protecting the public against all such intentional efforts to despoil, and to prevent the postoffice from being used to carry them into effect, that this statute was passed; and it would strip it of value to confine it to such cases as disclosed an actual misrepresentation as to some existing fact, and exclude those in which is only the allurement of a promise.[3]

In one sense *Durland* merely anticipated a desirable change in the scope of fraud that was ultimately adopted by the states as well. In another sense, however, *Durland* was a much more radical decision, since it cut the mail fraud statute loose from its common law moorings and established that federal mail fraud was not limited to the scope of frauds punishable under state law. It also set forth a broad vision of the protective function of the act. Consequently, the federal courts have given the concept of fraud in both the mail and wire fraud acts a broad and flexible reading.

Some of the decisions interpreting the mail fraud act have given it such a broad interpretation that it raises vagueness concerns. For example, in one case the Fifth Circuit commented that the act does not use the term defraud in a technical sense; rather it "puts its imprimatur on the accepted moral standards and condemns conduct which fails to match the 'reflection of moral uprightness, of fundamental honesty, fair play and right dealing in the general and business life of members of society.' "[4]

In *McNally v. United States*[5] the Supreme Court issued a decision that seemed to sound a new note, indicating that without clearer instructions from Congress the mail and wire fraud statutes should not be applied by federal prosecutors attempting to police the ethics of state

---

246, 267 P.2d 271 (1954); MODEL PENAL CODE § 223.3 (Proposed Official Draft) (1962); N.Y.Penal Law § 155.05(2)(d) (1967).

2. 161 U.S. 306, 16 S.Ct. 508, 40 L.Ed. 709 (1896).

3. *Supreme Court:* Durland v. United States, 161 U.S. 306, 313–14, 16 S.Ct. 508, 511, 40 L.Ed. 709 (1896).

4. *Fifth Circuit:* Blachly v. United States, 380 F.2d 665, 671 (5th Cir.1967) (citation omitted).

For a discussion of the vagueness/due process issue, see § 17.26.

5. 483 U.S. 350, 107 S.Ct. 2875, 97 L.Ed.2d 292 (1987).

and local government officials. The Court stated that "[r]ather than construe the statute in a manner that leaves its outer boundaries ambiguous and involves the Federal Government in setting standards of disclosure and good government for local and state officials," it would read the mail fraud statute as limited in scope to the protection of property rights.[6] The Court concluded that if Congress wished to go further, "it must speak more clearly than it has."[7]

The effect of *McNally* was soon nullified, however, when Congress accepted the Court's invitation to "speak more clearly" and passed 18 U.S.C. § 1346, which was intended to reverse the decision in *McNally*. Section 1346 endorsed the lower court decisions that had created the intangible rights theory under which the mail and wire fraud statutes had been used to prosecute political corruption that was said to defraud citizens of the honest services of government officials. Section 1346 provides that in mail, wire, and bank fraud cases "the term 'scheme or artifice to defraud' includes a scheme or artifice to deprive another of the intangible right of honest services."

§ 17.4   Elements of a Mail or Wire Fraud Charge

The elements of a mail or wire fraud charge are (1) a scheme to defraud or to obtain property by false pretenses, (2) fraudulent intent, and (3) a mailing or use of wire, radio, or television communications for the purpose of executing the fraudulent scheme. There is a significant overlap in the proof of elements (1) and (2). It is important to note that these statutes do not criminalize fraud, but rather define the offense as a mailing or wire communication made in furtherance of a fraudulent scheme. For that reason, there is no requirement that the fraud be successful or that the victim be deceived. In essence, the statute criminalizes an attempt to defraud by using either the mails or wire communications.[1]

Library References:

    C.J.S. Postal Service and Offenses Against Postal Laws § 23; Telegraphs, Telephones, Radio, and Television § 116–123.

    West's Key No. Digests, Postal Service ⊙⊸35; Telecommunications ⊙⊸362.

§ 17.5   Scheme to Defraud—In General

Although the concept of scheme to defraud is the core element of mail and wire fraud, it is not defined in the statute. Moreover, as noted above, the Supreme Court decided at an early date that the mail fraud statute would not be limited to the common law concept of fraud, but rather would be given a flexible interpretation in order to reach all attempts to use the mails take advantage of the public.[1]

6. 483 U.S. at 360, 107 S.Ct. at 2881.

7. 483 U.S. at 360, 107 S.Ct. at 2881.

§ 17.4

1. For a general discussion of this point, *see* § 17.8.

§ 17.5

1. *See* § 17.3.

Nonetheless, the statute does not forbid every misuse of the mail, but only those that involve an element of fraud, however broadly that may be defined. For example, before the passage of the federal kidnapping statute, the government sought to prosecute blackmail and kidnapping cases under the mail fraud statute where the mails were used to communicate the threats or demands for ransom.[2] Some lower courts upheld these prosecutions on the view that any scheme to obtain another's "money wrongfully, without giving him any equivalent for it, is a scheme to defraud."[3] In *Fasulo* v. *United States*[4] the Supreme Court rejected the notion that "every scheme that in its necessary consequences is calculated to injure another or to deprive him of his property wrongfully" is mail fraud,[5] holding that "the use of the mails for the purpose of obtaining money by means of threats of murder or bodily harm" is not a "scheme to defraud" within the meaning of the mail fraud act.[6] Though it expressly declined to give a comprehensive definition of the phrase "scheme to defraud," the Court noted that an attempt to obtain money by intimidation does not involve "anything in the nature of deceit or fraud as known to the law or generally understood."[7]

The Supreme Court has repeatedly reiterated the central role of deception in the concept of fraud. Most recently, in *Carpenter v. United States*[8] the Court noted that "the words 'to defraud' in the mail fraud statute have the 'common understanding' of 'wronging one in his property rights by dishonest methods or schemes,' and 'usually signify the deprivation of something of value by trick, deceit, chicane or overreaching.'" In affirming the mail fraud conviction of a Wall Street Journal employee who had executed a scheme to misuse the newspaper's confidential information for personal profit, the Court relied on the employee's deception in covering up the scheme.[9] Although the *Carpenter* Court referred to schemes to defraud as *usually* involving "trick, deceit, chicane, or overreaching," it is probably more accurate to say that such schemes must always involve some form of deception or deceit to come within the scope of the mail or wire fraud statutes. This proposi-

2. For a discussion of these prosecutions, see Jed S. Rakoff, *The Federal Mail Fraud Statute (Part I)*, 18 Duq.L.Rev. 771, 802–806 (1980).

3. *Sixth Circuit:* United States v. Horman, 118 F. 780, 781 (S.D.Ohio), aff'd, 116 F. 350 (6th Cir.1902).

4. 272 U.S. 620, 47 S.Ct. 200, 71 L.Ed. 443 (1926).

5. 272 U.S. at 628–29, 47 S.Ct. at 201–02.

6. 272 U.S. at 625, 47 S.Ct. at 201.

7. 272 U.S. at 628–29, 107 S.Ct. at 201–02.

8. 484 U.S. 19, 27, 108 S.Ct. 316, 321, 98 L.Ed.2d 275 (1987) (quoting McNally v. United States, 483 U.S. 350, 358, 107 S.Ct. 2875, 2880, 97 L.Ed.2d 292 (1987), and Hammerschmidt v. United States, 265 U.S. 182, 188, 44 S.Ct. 511, 512, 68 L.Ed. 968 (1924)).

9. *Supreme Court*: Carpenter v. United States, 484 U.S. 19, 28, 108 S.Ct. 316, 321, 98 L.Ed.2d 275 (1987). The Court noted that during the course of the four month scheme, the defendant continued in the employ of the newspaper, "all the while pretending to perform his duty of safeguarding [the paper's confidential information]." *Id.* Further, the defendant had reported leaks of confidential information unrelated to his scheme, demonstrating not only his recognition of the information as confidential, but also "his deceit as he played the role of a loyal employee." *Id.*

tion has been both implied by the Supreme Court and stated quite clearly by some of the lower courts.[10]

Indeed the deception requirement is helpful in sufficiently narrowing the term "scheme to defraud" so as to fend off challenges to the mail fraud statute as unconstitutionally vague.[11] A number of lower court opinions describe the concept scheme to defraud in sweeping terms including "moral uprightness," "fundamental honesty," or "fair play and right dealing in the general and business life of members of society."[12] Other courts have criticized the use of broad language such as "morality" and "fair play," and cautioned that it should not be taken literally.[13] One limitation on these sweeping concepts is the understanding that the mail and wire fraud statutes do not reach every business practice that does not fulfill expectations or every breach of a business contract, but only practices calculated to deceive.[14]

10. *Supreme Court*: Fasulo v. United States, 272 U.S. 620, 629, 47 S.Ct. 200, 202, 71 L.Ed. 443 (1926) (noting that a scheme to obtain money by intimidation was not a scheme to defraud since it did not involve "anything in the nature of deceit or fraud as known to the law or generally understood.")

First Circuit: McEvoy Travel Bureau, Inc. v. Heritage Travel, Inc., 904 F.2d 786, 791 (1st Cir.1990) (civil RICO claim based on alleged predicate acts of mail fraud) (noting that a scheme to defraud "must be intended to deceive another, by means of false or fraudulent pretenses, representations, promises, or other deceptive conduct.")

Second Circuit: McLaughlin v. Anderson, 962 F.2d 187, 192 (2d Cir.1992) (civil RICO claim based on alleged predicate acts of mail fraud) ("The mail fraud statute requires some element of deception.")

Third Circuit: Kehr Packages, Inc. v. Fidelcor, Inc., 926 F.2d 1406, 1415 (3d Cir. 1991) (civil RICO case with predicate acts of mail fraud) (fraud involves fraudulent misrepresentations or omissions calculated to deceive).

Fifth Circuit: United States v. Kreimer, 609 F.2d 126, 128 (5th Cir.1980) (noting that the statute "implicates only plans calculated to deceive").

Eighth Circuit: United States v. Goodman, 984 F.2d 235, 239–40 (8th Cir.1993) (difference between legal promotion and mail fraud is "affirmative misrepresentation or active concealment manifesting intent to deceive").

Ninth Circuit: United States v. Bohonus, 628 F.2d 1167, 1172 (9th Cir.1980) ("The fraudulent scheme need not be one which includes an affirmative misrepresen-

tation of fact, since it is only necessary for the government to prove that the scheme was calculated to deceive persons of ordinary prudence.")

11. For a general discussion of vagueness concerns in connection with the mail and wire fraud statutes, see § 17.26.

12. *Third Circuit:* United States v. Boffa, 688 F.2d 919, 926 (3d Cir.1982).

Fifth Circuit: United States v. Curry, 681 F.2d 406, 410 (5th Cir.1982); United States v. Kreimer, 609 F.2d 126, 128 (5th Cir.1980).

Sixth Circuit: United States v. Fischl, 797 F.2d 306, 311 (6th Cir.1986).

Eighth Circuit: United States v. Nelson, 988 F.2d 798, 803 (8th Cir.1993).

Ninth Circuit: United States v. Bohonus, 628 F.2d 1167, 1171 (9th Cir.1980).

13. *Seventh Circuit:* In re EDC, Inc., 930 F.2d 1275, 1281 (7th Cir.1991) (Posner, J.) (describing such formulations as "extravagant rhetoric" and "hyperbole," and noting that they "must be taken with a grain of salt"); United States v. Holzer, 816 F.2d 304, 309 (7th Cir.1987) (Posner, J.) (noting that such broad language "cannot have been intended, and must not be taken, literally"), *judgment vacated on other grounds*, 484 U.S. 807, 108 S.Ct. 53, 98 L.Ed.2d 18 (1987).

Eleventh Circuit: United States v. Brown, 79 F.3d 1550, 1556 (11th Cir.1996) (criticizing this broad language and quoting Judge Posner's comment in *Holzer* (see above) that it "'cannot have been intended, and must not be taken, literally.'")

14. *E.g.,*

Fifth Circuit: United States v. Kreimer, 609 F.2d 126, 128 (5th Cir.1980).

Library References:

C.J.S. Postal Service and Offenses Against Postal Laws § 23; Telegraphs, Telephones, Radio, and Television § 116–123.

West's Key No. Digests, Postal Service ⇐35; Telecommunications ⇐362.

§ 17.6 Scheme to Defraud—The Distinction Between Schemes to Defraud and False Pretenses

The mail and wire fraud statutes are both worded in the disjunctive, reaching a "scheme or artifice to defraud" *or* one to "obtain money or property by false or fraudulent pretenses, representations, or promises."[1] Although the two clauses overlap to a significant degree and many decisions lump them together, some lower courts have relied on the disjunctive structure to justify distinguishing between the two prongs of the statute. The Supreme Court rejected one proffered distinction between the two clauses in *McNally v. United States,*[2] but that decision rested less on the statutory language than on the Court's reluctance to allow the statute to be employed to prosecute state and local political corruption.[3]

McNally does not necessarily undermine a different distinction drawn by some lower courts, which require an affirmative misrepresentation in cases brought under the false-pretenses prong of the statute but not under the scheme-to-defraud prong.[4] As the Tenth Circuit explained:

Ninth Circuit: Cf. United States v. Bohonus, 628 F.2d 1167 (9th Cir.1980) (rejecting vagueness challenge in part because mail fraud requires specific intent to deceive).

§ 17.6

1. The text of each act is reprinted in § 17.1.

2. 483 U.S. 350, 107 S.Ct. 2875, 97 L.Ed.2d 292 (1987). In *McNally* the Court rejected the government's argument that the scheme to defraud prong of the statute—in contrast to the false pretenses prong—did not require that the victim be deprived of any "money or property," and hence that the scheme to defraud prong reached schemes aimed at defrauding the public of its intangible right to good government. Congress subsequently adopted 18 U.S.C. § 1346 to overrule the *McNally* decision and make clear its intention that the mail and wire fraud statutes reach deprivations of honest services. For a discussion of the application of the mail and wire fraud statutes to political corruption cases under the intangible rights doctrine, see § 17.19.

3. The Court refused to "construe the statute in a manner that leaves its outer boundaries ambiguous and involves the Federal Government in setting standards of

disclosure and good government for local and state officials." 483 U.S. at 360, 107 S.Ct. at 2881.

4. *First Circuit:* United States v. Goldberg, 913 F.Supp. 629, 636–37 (D.Mass. 1996).

Second Circuit: United States v. Ashley, 905 F.Supp. 1146, 1155 (E.D.N.Y.1995). *See also* United States v. Margiotta, 688 F.2d 108, 121 (2d Cir.1982) (clauses should be interpreted as independent of one another).

Third Circuit: United States v. Rafsky, 803 F.2d 105, 108 (3d Cir.1986).

Seventh Circuit: United States v. Doherty, 969 F.2d 425, 429 (7th Cir.1992) ("a course of conduct not involving any factual misrepresentation can be prosecuted as a 'scheme to defraud' under the mail and wire fraud statutes").

Eighth Circuit: Murr Plumbing, Inc. v. Scherer Bros. Fin. Servs. Co., 48 F.3d 1066, 1069 & n. 6 (8th Cir.1995).

Tenth Circuit: United States v. Cochran, 109 F.3d 660, 664 (10th Cir.1997); United States v. Kennedy, 64 F.3d 1465, 1475–76 & n. 10 (10th Cir.1995); United States v. Cronic, 900 F.2d 1511, 1513 (10th Cir.1990).

The offense of a scheme to defraud focuses on the intended end result, not on whether a false representation was necessary to effect the result. Schemes to defraud, therefore, may come within the scope of the statute even absent an affirmative misrepresentation.[5]

The requirement for an affirmative misrepresentation if the defendant is charged under the false pretenses prong means that the language of the indictment may be significant. Although the federal courts give the concept of affirmative misrepresentation a fairly broad interpretation, the experience under the bank fraud statute demonstrates convictions that would have been upheld under the defraud prong may be reversed if they are brought only under the false pretenses prong.[6]

Although some courts have emphasized the distinction between the clauses, most opinions lump the clauses together without discussion in both mail and wire fraud cases, and the courts' analysis tends to focus on the requirements of the defraud clause. In contrast, the distinction between the clauses seems to be more rigorously observed in the bank fraud cases. This may reflect a small difference between the text of the bank fraud act and the wire and mail fraud statutes. Although Congress tracked the language of mail fraud act when it enacted the bank fraud act, it numbered the defraud prong of the statute and the false pretenses as separate subsections, emphasizing their distinctiveness on the face of the statute.

§ 17.7   Scheme to Defraud—Materiality

Although materiality is not mentioned in either the mail or wire fraud statutes, the federal courts have generally held that these statutes reach only misrepresentations or nondisclosures that are material. This issue arises in several contexts. Many federal courts have ruled that politicians have a fiduciary duty to the public to reveal material information and that private employees have a fiduciary duty to their employers to reveal material information. These aspects of the materiality requirement are discussed below in connection with the honest services requirement imposed by 18 U.S.C. § 1346.[1] The question addressed in this section is the applicability of the materiality requirement to other commercial transactions where there is no claim of a duty of honest services. Much of the litigation regarding the materiality requirement has focused on how to distinguish material misrepresentations from mere puffing, and whether the concept of materiality includes a reasonableness requirement.

5. *Tenth Circuit:* United States v. Cronic, 900 F.2d 1511, 1513 (10th Cir. 1990).

6. For a discussion of this issue in the context of bank fraud, see § 6.2.

§ 17.7

1. *See* § 17.19(A)(ii), § 17.19(B).

A. DISTINGUISHING PUFFING FROM THE MAKING OF MATERIAL MISREPRESENTATIONS

It is generally accepted that a seller can puff up an item and that mere puffing does not constitute a material misrepresentation under the mail or wire fraud statutes.[2] A number of cases address the line between permissible puffing and material misrepresentations. The Supreme Court first addressed this issue in *United States v. New So. Farm & Home Co.*,[3] in which it held that assigning qualities to an article that the article does not possess is a material misrepresentation, not puffing:

> [W]hen a proposed seller ... assigns to the article qualities which it does not possess, does not simply magnify in opinion the advantages which it has, but invents advantages and falsely asserts their existence, he transcends the limits of 'puffing' and engages in false representations and pretenses. An article alone is not necessarily the inducement and compensation for its purchase. It is in the use to which it may be put, the purpose it may serve; and there is deception and fraud when the article is not of the character or kind represented and hence does not serve the purpose.[4]

The Court further defined puffing in *Reilly v. Pinkus*[5] (an action by the postmaster to forbid delivery of mail related to a fraudulent scheme), where it stated that a representation exceeds puffing and becomes material when the buyer is "entitled to rely" on it. In *Reilly*, the Court found that an ad for a diet aid stating that the product could be used by people with heart and kidney problems was a material misrepresentation in light of evidence that the product might be particularly dangerous for persons with heart or kidney problems.

The lower courts have employed two approaches to limit the concept of puffing and distinguish it from fraud. First, some courts have indicated that puffing is limited to expressions of opinion, and that false statements of fact cannot be characterized as mere puffing.[6] Even if an

2. *See, e.g.,*

Supreme Court: Reilly v. Pinkus, 338 U.S. 269, 274, 70 S.Ct. 110, 113, 94 L.Ed. 63 (1949).

Second Circuit: Gottlieb v. Schaffer, 141 F.Supp. 7, 15–16 (S.D.N.Y.1956).

Third Circuit: United States v. Pearlstein, 576 F.2d 531, 540 (3d Cir.1978).

Sixth Circuit: Henderson v. United States, 202 F.2d 400, 404 (6th Cir.1953).

Seventh Circuit: Associates in Adolescent Psychiatry v. Home Life Ins. Co., 941 F.2d 561, 570 (7th Cir.1991); United States v. Shelton, 669 F.2d 446, 465 (7th Cir. 1982); United States v. Serlin, 538 F.2d 737, 744 (7th Cir.1976).

Eighth Circuit: Rosenberger v. Harris, 136 Fed. 1001, 1002 (W.D.Mo.1905), *rev'd on other grounds*, 145 Fed. 449 (8th Cir. 1906).

Ninth Circuit: United States v. Gay, 967 F.2d 322, 329 (9th Cir.1992); In re All Terrain Vehicle Litig., 771 F.Supp. 1057, 1061 (C.D.Cal.1991), *aff'd*, 979 F.2d 755 (9th Cir.1992).

Tenth Circuit: United States v. Themy, 624 F.2d 963, 968 (10th Cir.1980).

Eleventh Circuit: United States v. Simon, 839 F.2d 1461, 1468 (11th Cir.1988).

3. 241 U.S. 64, 36 S.Ct. 505, 60 L.Ed. 890 (1916).

4. 241 U.S. 64, 71, 36 S.Ct. 505, 507, 60 L.Ed. 890 (1916).

5. 338 U.S. 269, 274, 70 S.Ct. 110, 113, 94 L.Ed. 63 (1949).

6. *Seventh Circuit*: United States v. Shelton, 669 F.2d 446, 465 (7th Cir.1982).

Eighth Circuit: United States v. Cain, 121 F.3d 385, 388 (8th Cir.1997).

Ninth Circuit: United States v. Gay, 967 F.2d 322, 329 (9th Cir.1992).

Tenth Circuit: United States v. Themy, 624 F.2d 963, 968 (10th Cir.1980).

expression that leases are "very valuable" might be puffing, false statements that specify the value as up to $4 million and further falsely state that Arco, Getty, and Texaco had paid millions for the leases were not mere puffing.[7] On the other hand, a statement that a company is "nationally known" and its product is "among the finest writing instruments in the world" was treated as mere puffing.[8] Second, some courts have characterized puffing as enthusiastic overselling, and emphasized the link between the defense of puffing and the requirement of fraudulent intent. These courts have held that an instruction on good faith is sufficient to encompass a defense of puffing.[9]

B. IMPORTING A REASONABLENESS STANDARD INTO THE CONCEPT OF MATERIALITY

As noted above,[10] in *Reilly v. Pinkus* the Supreme Court suggested that fraud exists where the buyer is "entitled to rely" on the representation. The idea that a buyer is entitled to rely on some representations— and not on others—is closely related to the reasonableness standard that some circuits have read into the materiality requirement.

The federal circuits are split on the question whether "reasonableness" is an element of materiality under the mail and wire fraud statutes. The Fifth, Sixth, Tenth and Eleventh circuits have adopted a reasonableness requirement, holding that a seller's misrepresentation is material only if a reasonable person would have relied on it.[11] Cases not involving sellers in the Third and Eighth circuits also indicate that the circuits would adopt the reasonableness standard in a seller's case.[12] The First, Second, and D.C. circuits, in contrast, have held that a misrepresentation is material even if only the most gullible would have been deceived.[13] The precedent in the Ninth circuits is split, but much of the

---

Eleventh Circuit: United States v. Simon, 839 F.2d 1461, 1468 (11th Cir.1988).

7. *Eleventh Circuit:* United States v. Simon, 839 F.2d 1461, 1468 (11th Cir.1988).

8. *Third Circuit:* United States v. Pearlstein, 576 F.2d 531, 540 (3d Cir.1978).

9. *Seventh Circuit:* United States v. Shelton, 669 F.2d 446, 465 (7th Cir.1982).

Ninth Circuit: United States v. Gay, 967 F.2d 322, 329 (9th Cir.1992).

10. *See* § 17.7(A).

11. *Fifth Circuit:* United States v. Townley, 665 F.2d 579, 585 (5th Cir.1982).

Sixth Circuit: Blount Fin. Servs., Inc. v. Walter E. Heller and Co., 819 F.2d 151, 153 (6th Cir.1987).

Tenth Circuit: United States v. White, 673 F.2d 299, 302 (10th Cir.1982).

Eleventh Circuit: United States v. Brown, 79 F.3d 1550, 1557 (11th Cir.1996).

12. *Third Circuit:* Zoria v. Mazzocone, 1996 WL 165509 *2 (E.D.Pa.1996), holding that mail and wire fraud schemes "must involve fraudulent misrepresentations or omissions designed to deceive persons of ordinary prudence," *citing to* United States v. Pearlstein, 576 F.2d 531, 535 (3d Cir.1978).

Eighth Circuit: United States v. Wicker, 80 F.3d 263, 265 (8th Cir.1996); United States v. Goodman, 984 F.2d 235, 240 (8th Cir.1993).

13. *D.C. Circuit:* United States v. Maxwell, 920 F.2d 1028, 1036 (D.C.Cir. 1990).

First Circuit: United States v. Brien, 617 F.2d 299, 311 (1st Cir.1980).

Two First Circuit cases, United States v. Faulhaber, 929 F.2d 16, 18 (1st Cir.1991) and United States v. Lopez, 71 F.3d 954, 962 (1st Cir.1995), agree that a material statement is one that could persuade a reasonable person, and conclude that accordingly mail fraud has no materiality requirement since it reaches misrepresentations

most recent precedent adopts the "reasonable person" standard.[14]

In *United States v. Goodman*,[15] the Eighth Circuit explained that the reasonableness requirement is necessary to keep the mail fraud act from sweeping too broadly and giving prosecutors too much discretion. The court said:

> "Without some objective evidence demonstrating a scheme to defraud, all promotional schemes to make money, even if 'sleazy' or 'shrewd,' would be subject to prosecution on the mere whim of the prosecutor. More is required under our criminal law. Perhaps the naive and gullible consumer needs more protection from the wily promoter than the sophisticated customer. But in today's society, criminal prosecution cannot be used to punish those who run promotional schemes to make money simply because some persons are more susceptible to try their luck than a more prudent recipient of the mail. If purchase by the naive and imprudent consumer be the test to prosecute promoters, most state and charitable lotteries, as well as promotions using 900 numbers to solicit 'lonely hearts,' could be criminally liable."

The First and D.C. circuits, in contrast, have taken the view that the mail and wire fraud statutes aim to protect people—all people—and therefore even an unreasonable misrepresentation is cognizable as fraud. As the First Circuit explained in *United States v. Brien*:[16]

> If a scheme to defraud has been or is intended to be devised, it makes no difference whether the persons the schemers intended to defraud are gullible or skeptical, dull or bright. These are criminal statutes, not tort concepts.... We discern no intention on the part of Congress to differentiate between schemes that will ensnare the ordinary prudent investor and those that attract only those with lesser mental acuity. Therefore, the court upheld a district court's jury instruction that "It is immaterial whether only the most gullible would have been deceived by the techniques involved. Section 1341 protects the naive as well as the worldly-wise, and the former are more in need of protection than the latter."[17]

Similar reasoning is found in the opinions of other courts.[18]

that deceive only the gullible. However, for the sake of clarity, we are dividing the circuits by whether the material misrepresentation is capable of influencing a reasonable person and whether the material misrepresentation is capable of influencing just the most gullible people.

Second Circuit: Gottlieb v. Schaffer, 141 F.Supp. 7, 16 (S.D.N.Y.1956).

14. In the Ninth Circuit, the gullibility standard was prevalent in cases in the 1960s. *See, e.g.,* Lustiger v. United States, 386 F.2d 132, 136 n. 3 (9th Cir.1967); Lemon v. United States, 278 F.2d 369, 373 (9th Cir.1960). But when the Ninth Circuit addressed this issue again in 1991, it approved the use of the reasonableness standard. In re All Terrain Vehicle Litig., 771 F.Supp. 1057, 1061 (C.D.Cal.1991), *aff'd,* 979 F.2d 755 (9th Cir.1992).

15. 984 F.2d 235, 240 (8th Cir.1993).

16. 617 F.2d 299, 311 (1st Cir.1980).

17. This instruction followed word-for-word the holding of the Ninth Circuit in Lemon v. United States, 278 F.2d 369, 373 (9th Cir.1960).

18. *See, e.g.,*

D.C. Circuit: United States v. Maxwell, 920 F.2d 1028, 1036 (D.C.Cir.1990).

Some Seventh Circuit cases have held that the mail fraud statute protects the gullible against frauds directed against them, but other cases in the same circuit have defined fraud in terms of representations or omissions calculated to deceive a reasonable person. In *United States v. Coffman*[19] the court explored the basis for each line of precedent and sought to reconcile them. Writing for the court, Judge Posner commented that if the statements in many opinions limiting mail and wire fraud to representations calculated to deceive ordinary persons were taken literally, they would "invite con men to prey on people of below-average intelligence, who are anyway the biggest targets of such criminals and hence the people most needful of the law's protection."[20] He noted that "[i]t would be very odd for the law to protect only those who, being able to protect themselves, do not need the law's protection."[21] The *Coffman* opinion attempted to reconcile the two lines of precedent by emphasizing the two purposes served by the reasonableness requirement, neither of which, the court concluded, "has anything to do with declaring open season on the people most likely to be the targets of fraud."[22] First, the reasonableness enquiry serves as circumstantial evidence of intent to defraud. Second, the reasonableness enquiry is intended to help identify the boundary between fraud and sharp dealing. Since almost all sellers engage in a certain amount of puffing and all buyers (even those who are gullible) know this, the law does not criminalize "business conduct that is customary rather than exceptional and relatively harmless."[23] Since this behavior is so normal and commonplace, it does not fool anyone and is not made criminal.

In circuits where reasonableness is required, one major factor in determining the reasonableness of the victims' reliance is the ease with which they could have verified the misrepresentations. For example, the Sixth Circuit held that a financier did not make a material misrepresentation to a consumer loan company by failing to disclose it could have charged a lower prime interest rate. The court commented that "[a]n ordinary and prudent business person in the financial field would not have merely accepted [the defendant's] quotation of the prime rate, but would have verified the rate independently."[24] In the court's view, the

Seventh Circuit: United States v. Sylvanus, 192 F.2d 96, 105 (7th Cir.1951). *See also* United States v. Coffman, 94 F.3d 330 (7th Cir.1996), discussed *infra*.

Ninth Circuit: Lemon v. United States, 278 F.2d 369, 373 (9th Cir.1960).

19. 94 F.3d 330 (7th Cir.1996).

20. 94 F.3d at 333.

21. 94 F.3d at 333.

22. 94 F.3d at 334.

23. 94 F.3d at 334.

24. *Sixth Circuit:* Blount Fin. Servs., Inc. v. Walter E. Heller & Co., 819 F.2d 151, 153 (6th Cir.1987) (civil RICO action predicated on a claim of mail fraud).

Similarly, in Associates in Adolescent Psychiatry v. Home Life Insurance Co., 941 F.2d 561, 570–71 (7th Cir.1991), the plaintiff brought RICO charges predicated on the claim that the defendant had fraudulently represented "that the Flexible Annuity offered rates of return equal to the highest in the market." The Seventh Circuit rejected this argument on the ground that "[n]o prudent person would treat as gospel statements such as those" and thus the statements were puffery. The court noted that "[t]he relation between the rates offered on the Flexible Annuity and those available on other investments can be checked by a quick look a the *Wall Street Journal* or the *Chicago Tribune*." This opinion may have

victim's reliance and inaction were unreasonable. The Eleventh Circuit used similar reasoning to reverse the mail fraud conviction of a Florida builder who had exaggerated the value of the homes he constructed. The court concluded that the misrepresentations were not material because a reasonable buyers who had traveled to Florida to visit the homes could easily verify the builder's representations by checking with other real estate agents or reviewing the real estate ads in local publications.[25]

C. REPRESENTATIONS THAT DO NOT GO TO THE VALUE OF THE BARGAIN

One other distinction was laid out by the Second Circuit in *United States v. Regent Office Supply Co.*[26] The court said a misrepresentation that does not go to "the value of the bargain"—meaning the quality, adequacy or price of the goods—is not material. The court concluded that no fraud existed in *Regent* because the buyer got exactly the goods he expected. It was immaterial that the seller was selling for a reason other than what he told the buyer.

§ 17.8 Scheme to Defraud—The Role of Loss to the Victim and Gain to the Defendant

The classic paradigm of fraud involves the defendant's use of deceit to obtain money or property from the victim, where the victim's loss is the defendant's gain.[1] But the mail and wire fraud statutes do not criminalize fraud. Instead, they criminalize the use of the mails or interstate wire communications to further a scheme to defraud or to obtain money or property by false pretenses. Accordingly, it is well-settled across the circuits that neither mail or wire fraud requires that the defendant's fraudulent scheme succeed, and thus there is no requirement that the government prove an actual loss to the victim or actual gain to the defendant.[2] On the other hand, mail and wire fraud do

been superseded within the circuit by United States v. Coffman, 94 F.3d 330 (7th Cir.1996), which is discussed in the text above.

25. *Eleventh Circuit*: United States v. Brown, 79 F.3d 1550, 1557 (11th Cir.1996).

26. 421 F.2d 1174, 1182 (2d Cir.1970).

§ 17.8

1. As discussed at greater length in §§ 17.3 and 17.19, 18 U.S.C. § 1346 expanded the definition of mail and wire fraud to include the deprivation of honest services, as well as money or property.

2. *See, e.g.,*

Second Circuit: United States v. Brennan, 938 F.Supp. 1111, 1127 (E.D.N.Y. 1996) (citing United States v. Starr with approval); Polycast Tech. Corp. v. Uniroyal, 728 F.Supp. 926, 946 (S.D.N.Y.1989) (hold-

ing that harm to victim or gain to defendant is unnecessary); United States v. Starr, 816 F.2d 94, 98 (2d Cir.1987) (holding that harm to victim is not necessary).

Third Circuit: United States v. Sokolow, 91 F.3d 396, 406 (3d Cir.1996) (holding that no loss by the victim is necessary); United States v. Copple, 24 F.3d 535, 544 (3d Cir.1994) (same).

Fifth Circuit: United States v. Goss, 650 F.2d 1336, 1343 (5th Cir. Unit A 1981) (holding that no loss by the victim is necessary).

Sixth Circuit: Epstein v. United States, 174 F.2d 754, 766 (6th Cir.1949) (holding that no loss by the victim is necessary).

Seventh Circuit: United States v. Ross, 77 F.3d 1525, 1543 (7th Cir.1996) (holding that gain by the defendant is not necessary).

require an intent to defraud and the use of the mails or wire communications to further a fraudulent scheme. The question is what role loss to the victim and gain to the defendant play in defining the concepts of scheme to defraud and fraudulent intent under the mail and wire fraud statutes. If the defendant's scheme contemplates a loss to the victim but no corresponding gain to the defendant, is that mail or wire fraud? What if the defendant's scheme will enrich him or her, but the victim will suffer no loss of money, property, or honest services? The Supreme Court has not ruled on these issues, and the lower courts have taken a variety of approaches.

A number of courts have stated that the mail and/or wire fraud statutes require a scheme that contemplates a loss to the victim.[3] These courts treat the use of deceit to cause a loss to a victim as an essential component of the concepts of fraud and fraudulent intent. As the Second Circuit explained, " '[m]isrepresentations amounting only to deceit are insufficient to maintain a mail or wire fraud prosecution.' ... 'Instead, the deceit must be coupled with a contemplated harm to the victim.' "[4] The application of this standard is straightforward in cases where the prosecution alleges a scheme to deprive the victim of money or property, but more difficult where the prosecution is premised on an honest services theory. A number of cases seem to treat a deprivation of honest

Eighth Circuit: United States v. Solomonson, 908 F.2d 358, 364 (8th Cir.1990) (holding that loss by the victim is unnecessary); United States v. Gaskill, 491 F.2d 981, 984 (8th Cir.1974) (holding that neither loss by the victim nor gain by the defendant is necessary).

Ninth Circuit: United States v. Bonallo, 858 F.2d 1427, 1433 (9th Cir.1988) (holding that neither loss by the victim nor gain by the defendant is necessary); Schreiber Distrib. Co. v. Serv–Well Furniture Co., 806 F.2d 1393, 1400 (9th Cir.1986) (same).

Tenth Circuit: United States v. Stewart, 872 F.2d 957, 960 (10th Cir.1989) (holding that loss by the victim is unnecessary); United States v. Marchese, 838 F.Supp. 1424, 1428 (D.Colo.1993) (holding that loss by the victim in unnecessary); Greyhound Fin. Corp. v. Willyard, 1989 WL 201094 *15 (D.Utah 1989) (holding that neither loss by the victim nor gain by the defendant is necessary).

Eleventh Circuit: United States v. Goss, 650 F.2d 1336, 1343 (5th Cir. Unit A 1981) (holding that no loss by the victim is necessary); United States v. Mills, 1996 WL 634207 *16 (S.D.Ga.1996) (holding that gain by defendant is unnecessary).

District of Columbia Circuit: United States v. Maxwell, 920 F.2d 1028, 1036 (D.C.Cir.1990) (holding that loss by victim is unnecessary).

3. *First Circuit:* United States v. Sawyer, 85 F.3d 713, 725 (1st Cir.1996).

Second Circuit: United States v. Gabriel, 125 F.3d 89 (2d Cir.1997); United States v. Zagari, 111 F.3d 307, 327 (2d Cir.), *cert. denied*, ___ U.S. ___, 118 S.Ct. 445, 139 L.Ed.2d 381 and ___ U.S. ___, 118 S.Ct. 455, 139 L.Ed.2d 390 (1997); United States v. Dinome, 86 F.3d 277, 283 (2d Cir.1996); United States v. D'Amato, 39 F.3d 1249, 1257 (2d Cir.1994).

Third Circuit: Schuylkill Skyport Inn v. Rich, 1996 WL 502280 *17 (E.D.Pa.1996), citing United States v. Bronston, 658 F.2d 920, 927 (2d Cir.1981).

Fifth Circuit: United States v. Blocker, 104 F.3d 720, 730 (5th Cir.1997); United States v. Jimenez, 77 F.3d 95, 97 (5th Cir. 1996).

Eighth Circuit: United States v. Jain, 93 F.3d 436, 441–42 (8th Cir.1996), *cert. denied*, ___ U.S. ___, 17 S.Ct. 2452, 138 L.Ed.2d 210 (1997).

Ninth Circuit: United States v. Lewis, 67 F.3d 225, 232 (9th Cir.1995); United States v. Simas, 937 F.2d 459, 462–63 (9th Cir.1991).

Tenth Circuit: United States v. Stewart, 872 F.2d 957, 960 (10th Cir.1989).

4. *Second Circuit:* United States v. D'Amato, 39 F.3d 1249, 1257 (2d Cir.1994) (citations omitted).

services or breach of fiduciary duty—by itself—as insufficient to demonstrate the requisite injury.[5] These cases look for evidence that the breach of honest services could have harmed the victim in some significant way. In these cases the issue of loss to the victim is bound up with the definition of the breach of honest services.[6]

Other courts do not regard loss to the victim as crucial where the aim of the scheme is gain to the defendant. Some courts have stated that the mail or wire fraud statutes require proof that the defendant intended to use fraud or false pretenses *either* to enrich himself *or* to cause a loss to the victim.[7] These courts would allow a prosecution to proceed if the defendant could show that he would be enriched by his fraudulent scheme, even though no victim would suffer a corresponding loss. A few other courts have simply stated that a scheme to benefit the defendant is sufficient.[8]

At least one court has concluded that the concept of fraud under the mail and wire fraud statutes requires a transfer where the victim's loss is the defendant's gain. In *United States v. Walters*[9] the Seventh Circuit reversed the conviction of a sports agent whose secret contracts with collegiate athletes violated NCAA rules. The government had argued that the agent had defrauded the universities for whom these athletes played, which had provided scholarships in the belief that the athletes were eligible to play under the NCAA rules. The court rejected the government's argument:

> According to the United States, neither an actual nor a potential transfer of property from the victim to the defendant is essential. It is enough that the victim lose; what (if anything) the schemer hopes

---

5. *See, e.g.,*

First Circuit: United States v. Sawyer, 85 F.3d 713, 725 (1st Cir.1996).

Second Circuit: United States v. D'Amato, 39 F.3d 1249, 1257 (2d Cir.1994).

Eighth Circuit: United States v. Jain, 93 F.3d 436, 441–42 (8th Cir.1996), *cert. denied,* ___ U.S. ___, 17 S.Ct. 2452, 138 L.Ed.2d 210 (1997).

6. For a further discussion of the honest services theory of mail and wire fraud, see § 17.19.

7. *First Circuit:* United States v. Dockray, 943 F.2d 152, 154 (1st Cir.1991).

Fifth Circuit: United States v. St. Gelais, 952 F.2d 90, 96 (5th Cir.1992); United States v. Judd, 889 F.2d 1410, 1414 (5th Cir.1989).

Seventh Circuit: United States v. Briscoe, 65 F.3d 576, 585 (7th Cir.1995) (stating that defendant must intend to cause "loss" to the victim or financial gain to self). *See also* United States v. Ross, 77 F.3d 1525, 1543 (7th Cir.1996) (personal benefit not necessary to demonstrate intent; intent to cause "actual or potential loss" by the vic-

tims is enough). But see United States v. Walters, 997 F.2d 1219 (7th Cir.1993), discussed in the text accompanying nn.9–11.

Ninth Circuit: United States v. Lewis, 67 F.3d 225, 233 (9th Cir.1995) (saying financial gain by defendant or financial loss by "another" is sufficient); United States v. Cloud, 872 F.2d 846, 852 (9th Cir.1989).

Eleventh Circuit: United States v. Cross, 928 F.2d 1030, 1044 (11th Cir.1991).

8. *Fifth Circuit:* United States v. Curry, 681 F.2d 406, 417 (5th Cir.1982) (personal financial gain by the defendant is sufficient).

Eleventh Circuit: United States v. Mills, 1996 WL 634207 (S.D.Ga.) ("a showing of personal benefit is not required to demonstrate intent to defraud. It is enough that the defendant intended to cause actual or potential loss to the victims of the fraud, whether to enrich himself, another, or no one" (quotations and citations omitted)). *See also* United States v. Cross, 928 F.2d 1030, 1044 (11th Cir.1991).

9. 997 F.2d 1219 (7th Cir.1993).

to gain plays no role in the definition of the offense. We asked the prosecutor at oral argument whether on this rationale practical jokes violate § 1341. A mails B an invitation to a surprise party for their mutual friend C. B drives his car to the place named in the invitation. But there is no party; the address is a vacant lot; B is the butt of a joke. The invitation came by post; the cost of gasoline means that B is out of pocket. The prosecutor said that this indeed violates § 1341, but that his office pledges to use prosecutorial discretion wisely.

Many people will find this position unnerving (what if the prosecutor's policy changes, or A is politically unpopular and the prosecutor is looking for a way to nail him?). Others, who obey the law out of a sense of civic obligation rather than the fear of sanctions, will alter their conduct no matter what policy the prosecutor follows. Either way, the idea that practical jokes are federal felonies would make a joke of the Supreme Court's assurance that § 1341 does not cover the waterfront of deceit.[10]

Concluding "that both the 'scheme or artifice to defraud' clause and the 'obtaining money or property' clause of § 1343 contemplate a transfer of some kind," the court held that "only a scheme to obtain money or other property from the victim by fraud violates § 1341," and that "[l]osses that occur as byproducts of a deceitful scheme do not satisfy the statutory requirement."[11]

Professor Craig Bradley has argued that the legislative history of the mail fraud establishes that the first prong of the Act—the defraud prong—requires a scheme to cause both loss to the victim and corresponding gain to the defendant, but the second clause does not. Bradley concedes that in light of the common law understanding of fraud, "Congress almost surely contemplated a classic fraud in which the victim is induced by false representations to hand over money or tangible property to the defendant and the victim's loss is the defendant's gain."[12] On the other hand, Bradley argues that the false pretenses prong of the statute is not so limited, and that it properly applies to a scheme intended to produce an economic gain to the defendant, even if the victim suffered no economic loss.[13] Since the wire fraud act was modeled on the mail fraud act, Professor Bradley's argument would probably require a parallel construction of the wire fraud statute.

10. 997 F.2d at 1224.

11. 997 F.2d at 1227.

12. Craig M. Bradley, *Mail Fraud After* McNally *and* Carpenter: *The Essence of Fraud*, 79 J.CRIM.L. & CRIMINOLOGY 573, 594 (1988). The main focus of Professor Bradley's article is the limitation imposed by the Supreme Court's holding in *McNally*, and the requirement that the prosecution establish a scheme to deprive the victim of money or property (and not merely the de-privation of some intangible services). The enactment of 18 U.S.C. § 1346 overrules *McNally*, and permits the prosecution of mail and wire fraud cases based upon the fraudulent deprivation of honest services. Although Bradley was not examining the precise question at issue here, his analysis is nonetheless instructive.

13. 79 J.CRIM.L. & CRIMINOLOGY at 608–13.

§ 17.9 Schemes to Deprive The Victim of Property—In General

The mail and wire fraud statutes encompass schemes to defraud the victim of "money or property," and the question what constitutes property for this purpose has been heavily litigated. This issue was most pressing before Congress explicitly extended the mail and wire fraud statutes to schemes to defraud the victim of honest services in 18 U.S.C. § 1346 (1994).[1] In cases arising after the passage of § 1346,[2] the definition of property becomes critical where the facts cannot be cast as a breach of honest services. Such cases arise, for example, when all of the persons involved in the scheme are outsiders who clearly hold no position of trust and owe no special duty to the victim.

Library References:

C.J.S. Postal Service and Offenses Against Postal Laws § 23; Telegraphs, Telephones, Radio, and Television § 116–123.
West's Key No. Digests, Postal Service ⟹35; Telecommunications ⟹362.

§ 17.10 Schemes to Deprive The Victim of Property—The Supreme Court's Treatment of the Property Issue

The Supreme Court considered the definition of property in its opinions in *McNally v. United States*[1] and *Carpenter v. United States*.[2] In *McNally*, the Court touched on the issue in passing, commenting that one of its prior decisions held that the phrase scheme to defraud " 'is to be interpreted broadly insofar as property rights are concerned.' "[3] In *Carpenter* the Court held that the mail and wire fraud statutes encompass deprivations of both tangible and intangible property,[4] and that the *Wall Street Journal*'s interest in the confidentiality and timing of one of its columns was property for this purpose. In making this determination, the Court cited a range of authorities. Although it relied mainly on its own prior decisions holding that confidential information (including news) is treated as property,[5] the Court also cited a general treatise on

§ 17.9

1. By enacting § 1346 Congress intended to overrule McNally v. United States, 483 U.S. 350, 107 S.Ct. 2875, 97 L.Ed.2d 292 (1987), and reinstate the case law recognizing that the mail and wire fraud statutes reached the intangible right of honest services. For a discussion of § 1346 and the honest services case law, see § 17.19.

2. Section 1346 was enacted on November 18, 1988. For a discussion of its legislative history, see § 17.19 n.3.

§ 17.10

1. 483 U.S. 350, 107 S.Ct. 2875, 97 L.Ed.2d 292 (1987).

2. 484 U.S. 19, 108 S.Ct. 316, 98 L.Ed.2d 275 (1987).

3. 483 U.S. at 356, 107 S.Ct. at 2879 (quoting Durland v. United States, 161 U.S. 306, 16 S.Ct. 508, 40 L.Ed. 709 (1896)).

4. 484 U.S. at 25, 108 S.Ct. at 320.

5. 484 U.S. at 26, 108 S.Ct. 320 (*citing* Ruckelshaus v. Monsanto Co., 467 U.S. 986, 104 S.Ct. 2862, 81 L.Ed.2d 815 (1984): Dirks v. SEC, 463 U.S. 646, 653 n. 10, 103 S.Ct. 3255, 3261 n. 10, 77 L.Ed.2d 911 (1983); International News Service v. Associated Press, 248 U.S. 215, 236, 39 S.Ct. 68, 71, 63 L.Ed. 211 (1918); and Board of Trade of Chicago v. Christie Grain & Stock Co., 198 U.S. 236, 250–51, 25 S.Ct. 637, 639–40, 49 L.Ed. 1031 (1905)). *See also* 484 U.S. at 27, 108 S.Ct. at 321 (*citing* Snepp v. United States, 444 U.S. 507, 515 n. 11, 100 S.Ct. 763, 769 n. 11, 62 L.Ed.2d 704 (1980) (per

corporate law[6] and New York state authority.[7]

Taken together, *McNally* and *Carpenter* indicate that the mail fraud and wire statutes are not limited to schemes involving tangible property, and that intangible rights that have been recognized as property rights for other purposes may also fall within the purview of these statutes. They provide little guidance, however, on the analysis that the lower courts should follow in determining whether other types of interests should be characterized as property for this purpose.

§ 17.11 Schemes to Deprive The Victim of Property—An Overview of the Lower Courts' Approach

No single analytical approach is dominant in the lower courts. Most opinions follow traditional real-property analysis,[1] though there are some opinions that rely on state statutes or on tort or contract analysis.[2] In determining what rights should be treated as property for this purpose, some courts have relied on the rule of lenity, which counsels that ambiguous criminal statutes should be construed in favor of the defendant.[3] Other lower courts, in contrast, have concluded that a broad construction of property accords with the Supreme Court's decisions in *McNally* and *Carpenter* and with the subsequent enactment of 18 U.S.C. § 1346.[4] There is also some disagreement about the role of state law.

curiam) for the proposition that even in the absence of a written trust agreement an employee has a fiduciary obligation to protect confidential information gained in the course of his employment).

6. 484 U.S. at 26, 108 S.Ct. at 320 (*citing* 3 W. FLETCHER, CYCLOPEDIA OF LAW OF PRIVATE CORPORATIONS § 857.1 (rev.ed.1986)).

7. 484 U.S. at 27–28, 108 S.Ct. at 321 (describing Diamond v. Oreamuno, 24 N.Y.2d 494, 497, 301 N.Y.S.2d 78, 80, 248 N.E.2d 910 (1969) as holding that a person who acquires information in a confidential relationship with another is not free to exploit the information for his personal benefit, but must account to his principal for any profits derived from such exploitation).

§ 17.11

1. *See, e.g.,*

First Circuit: United States v. Bucuvalas, 970 F.2d 937, 945 (1st Cir.1992).

Second Circuit: United States v. Evans, 844 F.2d 36 (2d Cir.1988).

Third Circuit: United States v. Martinez, 905 F.2d 709, 714 (3d Cir.1990).

Fifth Circuit: United States v. Salvatore, 110 F.3d 1131, 1139 (5th Cir.), *cert. denied,* ___ U.S. ___, 118 S.Ct. 441, 139 L.Ed.2d 378 (1997); United States v. Cleveland, 951 F.Supp. 1249, 1261 (E.D.La.1997).

2. *Third Circuit:* United States v. Henry, 29 F.3d 112, 116 (3d Cir.1994) (Weis, J., dissenting) (fact that bank that lost right to fair bidding opportunity would have cause of action for tortious interference with contractual rights demonstrates that this is an enforceable property interest for purposes of mail and wire fraud).

3. *See, e.g.,*

First Circuit: United States v. Boots, 80 F.3d 580, 588–89 (1st Cir.), *cert. denied,* ___ U.S. ___, 117 S.Ct. 263, 136 L.Ed.2d 188 (1996).

Second Circuit: United States v. Evans, 844 F.2d 36, 42 (2d Cir.1988).

Ninth Circuit: United States v. Bruchhausen, 977 F.2d 464, 468 (9th Cir.1992).

4. The Third and Fifth circuits have said that a broad construction of the mail fraud statute is indicated by Congress' 1988 enactment of 18 U.S.C. § 1346, which said that property under the mail fraud statute should be construed to include honest government services.

Third Circuit: United States v. Martinez, 905 F.2d 709, 715 (3d Cir.1990).

Fifth Circuit: United States v. Salvatore, 110 F.3d 1131, 1140 n. 1 (5th Cir.), *cert. denied,* ___ U.S. ___, 118 S.Ct. 441, 139 L.Ed.2d 378 (1997 1997); United States v. Cleveland, 951 F.Supp. 1249, 1259 n. 6 (E.D.La.1997).

Although most of the federal courts have relied on state authorities and some decisions treat state law as dispositive of the question whether a particular interest is property,[5] at least one judge has argued that federal law alone should govern what interests are "property" for purposes of the mail and wire fraud statutes.[6] There is also precedent going both ways on the question whether there is an implied de minimis threshold for the value of the property that can trigger a mail or wire fraud prosecution. [7]

Courts have been asked to characterize a wide variety of rights as property for purposes of the mail or wire fraud statute, including frequent flyer mileage,[8] market share,[9] union ballots[10] and employees' rights under a collective bargaining agreement,[11] shareholder rights to the information necessary to monitor the behavior of the corporation and its officers,[12] the right to control one's exposure to tort liability,[13] a

---

5. *See, e.g.,*

Fifth Circuit: United States v. Salvatore, 110 F.3d 1131, 1141 (5th Cir.), *cert. denied,* ___ U.S. ___, 118 S.Ct. 441, 139 L.Ed.2d 378 (1997).

Seventh Circuit: Borre v. United States, 940 F.2d 215, 221 (7th Cir.1991).

6. *Seventh Circuit:* Borre v. United States, 940 F.2d 215, 225 (7th Cir.1991) (Easterbrook, J., concurring and dissenting).

7. Compare:

D.C. Circuit: United States v. Madeoy, 912 F.2d 1486, 1492 (D.C.Cir.1990) (rejecting de minimis analysis).

Second Circuit: United States v. Schwartz, 924 F.2d 410 (2d Cir.1991) (applying de minimis requirement to conclude that paper and ink of single unissued permit are not property).

Eighth Circuit: United States v. Granberry, 908 F.2d 278 (8th Cir.1990) (applying de minimis requirement to conclude that paper and ink of single unissued permit are not property).

Ninth Circuit: United States v. Kato, 878 F.2d 267, 271 (9th Cir.1989) (Noonan, J., dissenting) (proper to treat paper and ink of a permit as property).

8. *Fifth Circuit:* United States v. Loney, 959 F.2d 1332 (5th Cir.1992) (frequent flyer coupons are property, and scheme was also intended to deprive airline of revenues).

Tenth Circuit: United States v. Schreier, 908 F.2d 645, 647 (10th Cir.1990) (manipulation of frequent flyer mileage created liability on part of airline resulting in misappropriation of airline's property).

For a more extended discussion of cases involving frequent flyer coupons and mileage, see § 17.17.

9. *Ninth Circuit:* Lancaster Community Hosp. v. Antelope Val. Hosp. Dist., 940 F.2d 397, 405–06 (9th Cir.1991) (scheme to increase one's market share at expense of another is too amorphous to be property, and customers are not property).

10. *D.C. Circuit:* United States v. DeFries, 43 F.3d 707, 709 (D.C.Cir.1995).

11. *Second Circuit:* United States v. Rastelli, 870 F.2d 822, 830–31 (2d Cir.1989) (economic benefits under collective bargaining agreement are property rights).

Third Circuit: See United States v. Boffa, 688 F.2d 919, 930 (3d Cir.1982) (holding that scheme to deprive employees of economic benefits under collective bargaining agreement "lies squarely within the ambit of the mail fraud statute"). Although some later cases read *Boffa* as exclusively an honest services prosecution, this portion of the opinion seems to treat the contractual rights under the collective bargaining agreement as property.

Sixth Circuit: United States v. S & Vee Cartage Co., Inc., 704 F.2d 914, 921 (6th Cir.1983) (upholding corporation's conviction for mail fraud and other offenses based upon scheme to defraud pension fund and employees of contributions required by collective bargaining agreement).

12. *Second Circuit:* United States v. Wallach, 935 F.2d 445, 464–66 (2d Cir.1991) (holding that shareholders have a property right in information necessary to monitor corporation).

For a discussion of the question whether the right to control the risk of loss or to make informed decisions is property, see § 17.16.

college's right to allocate athletic scholarships on the basis of truthful information,[14] and the government's right to collect taxes and fees for postal services.[15]

One of the most hotly litigated issues is the application of the mail fraud and wire statutes to fraudulent schemes to obtain government licenses and permits. The reported cases have involved everything from licenses for school bus drivers[16] and physicians[17] to arms export licenses.[18] Because the nature of the property interests encompassed by the mail and wire fraud statutes has been litigated most extensively in cases involving unissued licenses, the license cases discuss many of the theories and arguments that may be relevant to other kinds of legal interests. Accordingly, we discuss the license cases at some length, and we suggest that counsel concerned with other kinds of legal interests review our discussion of the license cases as well.

§ 17.12   Schemes to Deprive The Victim of Property—Licenses Before Issuance

The circuit courts of appeal are split on the question whether licenses procured by fraud were "property" while still in the hands of the government.[1] Three circuits (and some judges within other circuits) have taken the view that licenses are government property before their issuance.[2] Other circuits hold that the government has only a regulatory

13. *Eighth Circuit:* United States v. Granberry, 908 F.2d 278, 280 (8th Cir.1990) (ability to avoid tort liability that might arise from hiring a person who had been convicted of murder to drive school buses is not property).

For a discussion of the question whether the right to control the risk of loss or to make informed decisions is property, see § 17.16.

14. *Seventh Circuit:* United States v. Walters, 775 F.Supp. 1173, 1179 (N.D.Ill. 1991). The defendant's convictions were subsequently reversed because the government failed to prove that mailing element and also failed to prove that the defendant obtained the property of which the victim was deprived. United States v. Walters, 997 F.2d 1219 (7th Cir.1993). For an interesting discussion and critique of the use of the mail fraud act to target sports agents and "clean up" college sports, see Landis Cox, Note, *Targeting Sports Agents with the Mail Fraud Statute: United States v. Norby Walters & Lloyd Bloom*, 41 DUKE L.J. 1157 (1992).

The government's theory here is similar to its argument in other cases that the right to information necessary to make informed decisions is a property right. For a discussion of the question whether the right to control the risk of loss or to make informed decisions is property, see § 17.16.

15. *Second Circuit:* United States v. Gelb, 881 F.2d 1155, 1162 (2d Cir.1989) (Postal Service has property interest in postage).

Seventh Circuit: Ginsburg v. United States, 909 F.2d 982, 987 (7th Cir.1990) (federal government has property right to income taxes).

For a more extended discussion of the question whether government revenues are property, see § 17.18.

16. *Eighth Circuit:* United States v. Granberry, 908 F.2d 278 (8th Cir.1990) (unissued license to drive school bus is not property).

17. *Third Circuit:* United States v. Martinez, 905 F.2d 709 (3d Cir.1990) (medical license is property).

18. *Second Circuit:* United States v. Schwartz, 924 F.2d 410 (2d Cir.1991) (arms export licenses are not property).

§ 17.12

1. For a useful overview and analysis of the cases, see Donna M. Maus, Note, *License Procurement and the Federal Mail Fraud Statute*, 58 U.CHI.L.REV. 1125 (1991).

2. *First Circuit:* United States v. Bucuvalas, 970 F.2d 937 (1st Cir.1992).

Second Circuit: See United States v. Novod, 923 F.2d 970 (2d Cir.), *modified on*

interest until it issues a license, which then becomes property in the licensee's hands.[3]

A. OPINIONS CHARACTERIZING UNISSUED LICENSES AS PROPERTY

The courts that have concluded that unissued licenses are property have followed several different lines of analysis. Some of the courts have emphasized a traditional property analysis, beginning with the notion that the law views property as "a bundle of rights," including the right to use, possess, control and sell.[4] As the Fifth Circuit explained, "Necessarily encompassed within the right to use and dispose of an object is the right to control that object—and in the case of licenses, the right to control their issuance."[5] Since licenses are "things of value," and since something the government controls and values is deemed property, licenses are property.[6] Other courts have reasoned that if a license is

other grnds, 927 F.2d 726 (2d Cir.1991); United States v. Berg, 710 F.Supp. 438 (E.D.N.Y.1989), rev'd, United States v. Schwartz, 924 F.2d 410 (2d Cir.1991); United States v. Turoff, 701 F.Supp. 981 (E.D.N.Y.1988). Other Second Circuit cases are to the contrary. See nn.17, 18 & 21 infra.

Third Circuit: United States v. Martinez, 905 F.2d 709 (3d Cir.1990).

Fifth Circuit: United States v. Salvatore, 110 F.3d 1131 (5th Cir.), cert. denied, ___ U.S. ___, 118 S.Ct. 441, 139 L.Ed.2d 378 (1997); United States v. Cleveland, 951 F.Supp. 1249 (E.D.La.1997).

Ninth Circuit: United States v. Kato, 878 F.2d 267, 271 (9th Cir.1989) (Noonan, J., dissenting).

3. Second Circuit: United States v. Evans, 844 F.2d 36 (2d Cir.1988); United States v. Schwartz, 924 F.2d 410 (2d Cir. 1991).

Sixth Circuit: United States v. Murphy, 836 F.2d 248 (6th Cir.1988); Blanton v. United States, 1988 WL 182378 (M.D.Tenn. 1988).

Seventh Circuit: Toulabi v. United States, 875 F.2d 122 (7th Cir.1989).

Eighth Circuit: United States v. Granberry, 908 F.2d 278 (8th Cir.1990).

Ninth Circuit: United States v. Kato, 878 F.2d 267 (9th Cir.1989).

4. See, e.g.,

First Circuit: United States v. Bucuvalas, 970 F.2d 937, 945 (1st Cir.1992).

Third Circuit: United States v. Martinez, 905 F.2d 709, 714 (3d Cir.1990).

Fifth Circuit: United States v. Salvatore, 110 F.3d 1131, 1139 (5th Cir.), cert. denied, ___ U.S. ___, 118 S.Ct. 441, 139 L.Ed.2d 378 (1997); United States v. Cleveland, 951 F.Supp. 1249, 1261 (E.D.La.1997).

Sixth Circuit: Cf. United States v. Frost, 125 F.3d 346, 367 (6th Cir.1997) (using bundle or rights analysis to support conclusion that university has a property right in unissued degrees which its faculty have a fiduciary duty to protect, but distinguishing unissued licenses), petitions for cert. filed, U.S., Mar. 14, 1998 (Nos. 97–1549, 97–8295, 97–8305, 97–8328, and 97–8374).

For a decision of the Supreme Court applying the bundle of rights analysis to the definition of property in another context, see Loretto v. Teleprompter Manhattan CATV Corp., 458 U.S. 419, 435, 102 S.Ct. 3164, 3175, 73 L.Ed.2d 868 (1982).

5. Fifth Circuit: United States v. Salvatore, 110 F.3d 1131, 1140 (5th Cir.), cert. denied, ___ U.S. ___, 118 S.Ct. 441, 139 L.Ed.2d 378 (1997).

6. Fifth Circuit: United States v. Cleveland, 951 F.Supp. 1249, 1261 (E.D.La. 1997), quoting McNally v. United States, 483 U.S. 350, 358, 107 S.Ct. 2875, 2880, 97 L.Ed.2d 292 (1987). The Fifth Circuit made a similar analogy in United States v. Loney, 959 F.2d 1332, 1335 (5th Cir.1992), saying that although frequent-flyer coupons have no inherent value to airlines, airlines do value the ability to decide to whom to issue such coupons. Therefore, airlines' right to control issuance of the coupons means that the coupons are property when in the possession of the airlines. For a discussion of frequent-flyer coupons, see § 17.17.

property in the hand of the licensee, it must also be property in the hand of the issuing agency. As one district court commented that "[t]o hold, as some courts have, . . . that such valuable property vanishes when held in the hands of the issuer strikes the Court as preposterous."[7] Another district court was equally harsh, commenting that a "distinction between an unissued and issued license belongs in the realm of metaphysics, not in a common sense application of the law. . . . The Court finds no reason to make distinctions of such pointless subtlety."[8]

Several of the opinions holding that unissued licenses are property rely heavily on comparisons with the Supreme Court's decision in *Carpenter*.[9] For example, the First Circuit concluded that the city of Boston's property right to control dissemination of its liquor and entertainment licenses was analogous to the *Wall Street Journal's* property right to control dissemination of the confidential information gathered by its columnists.[10] Similarly, a panel opinion in the Second Circuit argued that the property lost by the State, a waste dump permit, was "akin to what the *Journal* lost in *Carpenter*: the right to control a substantial 'asset' central to its organizational mission."[11] Indeed, licenses and other forms of government largess were considered government property long before legal recognition was accorded to the property rights of the licensee or recipient.[12]

A few opinions have concluded that a physical license or permit is property for purposes of mail or wire fraud. Although some courts have concluded that the physical permit—paper and ink—has a de minimis value that does not rise to the level of property for this purpose,[13] the D.C. Circuit and individual judges in other circuits have agreed that a permit can be tangible property under the mail and wire fraud statutes.[14]

---

7. *Second Circuit*: United States v. Berg, 710 F.Supp. 438, 444 (E.D.N.Y.1989). The district court's opinion was reversed on appeal, 924 F.2d 410 (2d Cir.1991). For other Second Circuit cases, see n.2 *supra*.

8. *Fifth Circuit*: United States v. Cleveland, 951 F.Supp. 1249, 1260 (E.D.La. 1997).

9. *Second Circuit*: United States v. Novod, 923 F.2d 970, 975 (2d Cir.), *modified on other grnds*, 927 F.2d 726 (2d Cir. 1991).

Third Circuit: United States v. Martinez, 905 F.2d 709, 714–715 (3d Cir.1990).

Fifth Circuit: United States v. Salvatore, 110 F.3d 1131, 1140 (5th Cir.), *cert. denied*, ___ U.S. ___, 118 S.Ct. 441, 139 L.Ed.2d 378 (1997).

10. *First Circuit:* United States v. Bucuvalas, 970 F.2d 937, 945 (1st Cir.1992).

11. *Second Circuit*: United States v. Novod, 923 F.2d 970, 975 (2d Cir.), *modified on other grnds*, 927 F.2d 726 (2d Cir. 1991).

12. A number of courts have cited Charles Reich, *The New Property*, 73 YALE L.J. 733, 778 (1964), in connection with this point. *See:*

Second Circuit: United States v. Berg, 710 F.Supp. 438, 444 (E.D.N.Y.1989), *rev'd* United States v. Schwartz, 924 F.2d 410 (2d Cir.1991); United States v. Turoff, 701 F.Supp. 981, 989 (E.D.N.Y.1988). As indicated by its reversal in Berg, the Second Circuit has concluded that unissued licenses are not property. *See* nn.17, 18, & 21.

Fifth Circuit: United States v. Salvatore, 110 F.3d 1131, 1141 (5th Cir.), *cert. denied*, ___ U.S. ___, 118 S.Ct. 441, 139 L.Ed.2d 378 (1997); United States v. Cleveland, 951 F.Supp. 1249, 1261 (E.D.La.1997).

13. *Second Circuit:* United States v. Schwartz, 924 F.2d 410, 416 (2d Cir.1991).

Eighth Circuit: United States v. Granberry, 908 F.2d 278, 280 (8th Cir.1990).

14. *D.C. Circuit:* United States v. DeFries, 43 F.3d 707, 709 (D.C.Cir.1995).

Second Circuit: United States v. Novod, 923 F.2d 970, 974 (2d Cir.), *modified on*

The D.C. Circuit reasoned that "[t]he mail fraud statute speaks only of 'money or property' generally, not of property above a certain value."[15]

Finally, the Third Circuit suggested an entirely different line of analysis which obviates the need to determine whether the *unissued* license is property. Since a license is property once it is in the hands of the licensee, the court found it unnecessary to consider if a license was property while still in the government's hands. The court reasoned that "[t]he statute, which proscribes 'obtaining money or property,' is broad enough to cover a scheme to defraud a victim of something that takes on value only in the hands of the acquirer as well as a scheme to defraud a victim of property valuable to the victim but valueless to the acquirer."[16] This analysis raises the question whether the statutes require a loss to the victim as well as a gain to the defendant. For a general discussion of this issue, see § 17.8.

B. OPINIONS CONCLUDING THAT UNISSUED LICENSES ARE NOT PROPERTY

The courts that have found that unissued licenses do not qualify as property for purposes of the mail and wire fraud statutes have emphasized that the government's role is that of a regulator, not a property owner. For example, the Second Circuit rejected the government's claim that an arms sale permit was property under the mail and wire fraud statutes.[17] Beginning with the premise that the weapons were the property in question, the court then followed a traditional property analysis, considering the common law concepts of possession and alienation. Three principal factors weighed against the conclusion that the permit was property. First, possession is a key indicator of property ownership, and there was never any expectation that the government would possess the weapons. Second, traditional property law disfavors restraints on sale, and accordingly the government's ability to restrain sale of weapons is not akin to a traditional property interest. Finally, the court said traditional property law is governed by supply-and-demand, while international arms sales are governed instead by foreign and human-rights policy; therefore, again, the government's interest is not a traditional property interest. The court concluded that "[a] law prohibiting a particular use of a commodity that the government does not use or possess ordinarily does not create a property right."[18]

other grnds, 927 F.2d 726 (2d Cir.1991) (dump permit is tangible thing); United States v. Turoff, 701 F.Supp. 981 (E.D.N.Y. 1988) (taxi medallions are tangible property). *But see* United States v. Schwartz, 924 F.2d 410, 416 (2d Cir.1991).

    Ninth Circuit: United States v. Kato, 878 F.2d 267, 271 (9th Cir.1989) (Noonan, J., dissenting).

    15. *D.C. Circuit:* United States v. De-Fries, 43 F.3d 707, 709 (D.C.Cir.1995). The court also noted that *McNally* holds that

the mail fraud statute protects only traditional forms of property, but does not indicate that the property has to meet a threshold value amount. *Id.*

    16. *Third Circuit:* United States v. Martinez, 905 F.2d 709, 713 (3d Cir.1990).

    17. *Second Circuit:* United States v. Evans, 844 F.2d 36 (2d Cir.1988).

    18. *Second Circuit:* United States v. Evans, 844 F.2d 36, 42 (2d Cir.1988).

The Seventh Circuit also emphasized the regulatory character of the government's interest in an unissued license. The court observed that from the government's perspective a chauffeur's license is "a promise not to interfere, not a sliver of property."[19] The court noted that taxi driving is not something made possible by dint of public resources, that there was no cap on licensed taxi drivers, and the license merely indicated that the driver had passed a geography test and paid a license fee. All the city did was to promise not to interfere with the driver's ability to work. Accordingly, the government's interest was regulatory in character, not a property interest.

Several other courts have also held, without extensive analysis, that various types of licenses and permits are not property for purposes of mail or wire fraud before issuance.[20] Courts that have refused to characterize unissued licenses as property have rejected the argument that the paper licenses themselves are property, calling their worth "de minimis."[21]

§ 17.13 Schemes to Deprive The Victim of Property— Schemes Involving Unissued Government Franchises

The question of whether a franchise is property when in the government's control has been litigated in only a few cases. The Fifth, Seventh and Eleventh Circuits have relied upon state law and traditional property concepts to conclude that a franchise is property under the mail and wire fraud statutes. A district court in the Eighth Circuit has held that the government has only a regulatory and not a property interest.

For example, in considering whether a cable TV franchise was property before its issuance, the Seventh Circuit relied upon Illinois common law, which had characterized franchises as "a royal privilege" given from government to citizen. The court noted that "a cable television franchise represents far more than a mere 'promise not to interfere' by the government" because of the government's ongoing interest in the franchise.[1] Similarly, in discussing video poker licenses, which it also termed a franchise, the Fifth Circuit noted that the state had "a direct

19. *Seventh Circuit*: Toulabi v. United States, 875 F.2d 122 (7th Cir.1989).

20. *Sixth Circuit*: United States v. Murphy, 836 F.2d 248, 254 (6th Cir.1988) (bingo license procured by fraud not property); Blanton v. United States, 1988 WL 182378 (M.D.Tenn.1988) (liquor license not property in government's hands).

Eighth Circuit: United States v. Granberry, 908 F.2d 278 (8th Cir.1990) (license to drive school bus not property).

21. *Second Circuit*: United States v. Schwartz, 924 F.2d 410, 418 (2d Cir.1991) (holding that "the value of the paper, ink and seal at issue is plainly inconsequential and—as *McNally* held ... 'to defraud'

meant depriving individuals or the government of something of value....")

Eighth Circuit: United States v. Granberry, 908 F.2d 278, 280 (8th Cir.1990) (holding that the value of an unissued bus driver license is "negligible" apart from the legal entitlement it represents).

§ 17.13

1. *Seventh Circuit:* Borre v. United States, 940 F.2d 215, 221 (7th Cir.1991) (quoting and distinguishing Toulabi v. United States, 875 F.2d 122, 125 (7th Cir. 1989)).

and significant financial stake," not merely a regulatory interest, since it would be paid a percentage of the revenues, like any other franchisor.[2]

In contrast, a district court in Missouri concluded that a franchise is not property prior to its issuance.[3] Relying on decisions from other circuits holding that the government's right to issue licenses based on good information is an intangible, non-property right,[4] the court held that " 'until an ordinance granting a franchise is accepted, the franchise lacks the essential elements of a contract . . . [and] is a mere proposition.' "[5] The court reasoned that the mere contemplation of an ongoing contractual relationship did not qualify as a property right protected by the mail and wire fraud statutes, and that the government's traditional right to control its "property" was not implicated because the government had no property.[6]

§ 17.14   Schemes to Deprive The Victim of Property—The Right to a Fair Bidding Opportunity

The two courts that have addressed this issue both held that the right to a fair bidding opportunity is not property under the mail fraud statute because the law traditionally has not recognized and enforced chance or opportunity as a property right.[1] The issue did divide a panel of the Third Circuit. The majority concluded that even though the right to a fair opportunity to bid for the right to serve as a depository was valuable to the competing banks, "it is not a traditionally recognized, enforceable property right."[2] This holding provoked a strong dissent by Judge Weis, who argued that the banks' ability to profit from serving as a depository for more than $34 million was a "substantial property right."[3] Commenting that the wire fraud statute should be broadly interpreted, Judge Weis concluded the bank that submitted the highest legitimate bid had an enforceable proprietary interest as demonstrated by the fact that it would have a civil remedy for tortious interference with prospective contractual relationships.

2. *Fifth Circuit:* United States v. Salvatore, 110 F.3d 1131, 1141 (5th Cir.), *cert. denied*, ___ U.S. ___, 118 S.Ct. 441, 139 L.Ed.2d 378 (1997).

3. *Eighth Circuit*: United States v. Slay, 717 F.Supp. 689, 692–93 (E.D.Mo. 1989).

4. *Sixth Circuit:* United States v. Murphy, 836 F.2d 248 (6th Cir.1988) (holding that bingo licenses are not property in the government's hands).

Ninth Circuit: United States v. Dadanian, 856 F.2d 1391 (9th Cir.1988) (holding that a gambling license is not property in the government's hands).

5. 717 F.Supp. 689, 693 (E.D.Mo. 1989) (citing 12 E. McQuillin, Municipal Corporations § 34.06 at 23).

6. 717 F.Supp. 689, 694 (E.D.Mo. 1989).

§ 17.14

1. *Third Circuit:* United States v. Henry, 29 F.3d 112 (3d Cir.1994).

Fourth Circuit: United States v. Berlin, 707 F.Supp. 832, 835 (E.D.Va.1989) (holding that companies have no cognizable property right in a contract to be awarded by the government, and "the opportunity to compete on a level playing field for a chance" to gain such a property right is not a "traditional property right").

2. *Third Circuit:* United States v. Henry, 29 F.3d 112, 115 (3d Cir.1994).

3. 29 F.3d at 116 (Weis, J., dissenting).

§ 17.15 Schemes to Deprive The Victim of Property—The Ability to Control Use of a Product After it is Sold

In several cases involving the sale or arms or high technology the government argued that the right to control a product after its sale is a property interest under the mail and wire fraud statutes.[1] In general, the courts have resisted the government's urging to characterize as property the government's ability to decide whether to give the necessary permission to sell arms or private companies' ability to choose to whom to sell their weapons or technology. As noted above, in the cases involving permits for the sale of arms, the courts have characterized the government's interest as a regulatory rather than a property interest.[2]

The few lower court decisions involving private contracts send conflicting signals. In a case involving a buyer who duped the manufacturer of high technology and then resold the technology to Soviet Bloc countries, the Ninth Circuit held that there is no established property right in the ultimate destination of one's products.[3] The court distinguished the well established right to control confidential business information, which is property for purposes of the mail and wire fraud statutes.[4] Particularly in light of the rule of lenity, the court refused to treat the manufacturer's interest as a property right that could support a mail or wire fraud prosecution.[5] In a concurring opinion, Judge Fernandez disagreed with the court's analysis on this point, arguing that "[t]he strictures an owner puts on his willingness to sell an item are not mere ephemera. When a prospective buyer lies in order to evade those strictures, a fraud has been committed upon the owner of the item just as surely as if the buyer had issued a rubber check. This is not an exotic proposition."[6] The Second Circuit's position seems closer to that of Judge Fernandez than to that of the Ninth Circuit majority. The court recognized that a company does have a property right in the ability to control what happens to its products after sale if it has contracted for such control.[7] The manufacturer in the case before it had specifically provided in the contract that its product would not be exported illegally after sale. Accordingly, even though the manufacturer was paid for its

---

§ 17.15

1. *Second Circuit:* United States v. Schwartz, 924 F.2d 410 (2d Cir.1991); United States v. Evans, 844 F.2d 36 (2d Cir. 1988).

Ninth Circuit: United States v. Bruchhausen, 977 F.2d 464 (9th Cir.1992).

2. *See* § 17.12(B).

3. *Ninth Circuit:* United States v. Bruchhausen, 977 F.2d 464 (9th Cir.1992). *But cf.* United States v. Volpe, 863 F.Supp. 1120, 1130 (N.D.Cal.1994) (distinguishing case where defendant fraudulently mislead defendant insurer about identity of in-

sureds, thereby inducing insurer to provide coverage to individuals it would not otherwise have insured), *order vacated on other grnds*, 943 F.Supp. 1211 (N.D.Cal.1996).

4. This point was settled by the Supreme Court in Carpenter v. United States, 484 U.S. 19, 108 S.Ct. 316, 98 L.Ed.2d 275 (1987). For a discussion of *Carpenter*, see § 17.10.

5. 977 F.2d at 468.

6. 977 F.2d at 469 (Fernandez, J., dissenting).

7. *Second Circuit:* United States v. Schwartz, 924 F.2d 410, 421 (2d Cir.1991).

product, it received less than it bargained for when the defendant smuggled the goods illegally.

§ 17.16   Schemes to Deprive The Victim of Property—Right to Control the Risk of Loss or to Make Informed Decisions

Several cases have considered the right to control the risk of loss or to make informed decisions. These cases send conflicting signals, and may reflect either the influence of particular facts or differences among the courts that decided the cases. The courts that have upheld prosecutions on the basis of a right to control liability do not seem to have recognized the tremendous expansive potential of this theory, or to have established any real limiting principles.

Some opinions have concluded that the deprivation of information that might have value in assessing the desirability of a business transaction is not a property interest for purposes of mail or wire fraud. For example, the Ninth Circuit held that a bank's right to make informed lending choices is not a property right for this purpose.[1] Similarly, in a case involving a buyer's resale of arms to Soviet bloc countries, Judge Fernandez of the Ninth Circuit commented that "the right of a manufacturer to make decisions based upon truthful information is too ethereal to be a property right for the purpose of the wire fraud statute."[2] A decision of the Third Circuit also commented that the "loss of control argument . . . is too amorphous to constitute a violation of the mail fraud statute as currently written."[3]

Other decisions, in contrast, recognize that the right to information relevant to a business decision or the right to limit the risk of loss are valuable rights that should be treated as property for purposes of the mail and wire fraud statutes.

For example, the Seventh Circuit upheld the mail fraud conviction of a futures and options trader who deprived the clearing firm with whom he dealt of "the right to control its risk of loss, which had a real and substantial value."[4] The defendant pointed out that his actions in leading the firm to believe his trades would pose little risk did not even violate his contract with the clearing firm. It seems likely that the court was influenced by the fact that the scheme involved trading on the floor of the Chicago Board of Trade, a nationally important commercial institution, and massive trades that cost one of the firms that the defendants had duped $8.5 million, $2 million more than its net worth.[5]

§ 17.16

1. *Ninth Circuit:* United States v. Lewis, 67 F.3d 225, 232–33 (9th Cir.1995).

2. *Ninth Circuit:* United States v. Bruchhausen, 977 F.2d 464, 469 (9th Cir. 1992) (Fernandez, J., concurring). *See id.* at 469 (Kozinski, J., concurring) (joining Fernandez as well as majority opinion).

3. *Third Circuit:* United States v. Zauber, 857 F.2d 137, 147 (3d Cir.1988).

Accord United States v. Johns, 742 F.Supp. 196, 214 (E.D.Pa.1990).

4. *Seventh Circuit:* United States v. Catalfo, 64 F.3d 1070, 1077 (7th Cir.1995), *cert. denied*, 517 U.S. 1192, 116 S.Ct. 1683, 134 L.Ed.2d 784 (1996).

5. The same court also upheld mail fraud convictions of brokers and traders of soybean futures who shifted or altered the economic risk to their customers by picking

Similar decisions can be found in other circuits. A decision from the Eighth Circuit also found that the government had a property right in its ability to control potential liability. Although it rejected the prosecution's argument that a bus driver's license was property in the government's hands, the court found that the defendant's fraudulent scheme had deprived the government of its right to avoid tort liability for allowing a convicted murderer to drive school busses.[6] Another decision from the same circuit held that deprivation of the victim's right to control its own spending can be the basis of a mail fraud conviction.[7]

The Second Circuit found a right to information to be a property right in a case involving management's cover up of the purposes for which certain expenses had been paid. The court concluded that the right of shareholders to inspect company books and to be informed of the information necessary to monitor the behavior of the corporation and its officers was a property right for purposes of the mail and wire fraud statutes, and that the misleading entries on the corporate books had defrauded the shareholders of this right.[8] The court commented the right to control language was too broad, and that the cases actually limited the application of the theory to instances where "some person or entity has been deprived of potentially valuable economic information."[9] Since the case before it involved the use of the mails to submit false invoices and other inaccurate information intended to misrepresent the nature of the transactions involved, which obscured the value of the stock and deprived the shareholders and the corporation of the opportunity to make informed decisions, it involved a deprivation of property under the mail fraud act.[10] The court upheld the defendants' convictions despite the fact that all of the officers and directors of the corporation had agreed to the payments and knew of the misleading way they were being billed.

§ 17.17 Schemes to Deprive The Victim of Property—Frequent–Flyer Coupons and Mileage

Several courts have held that frequent flyer coupons are property for purposes of the mail and wire fraud statutes. For example, the Fifth Circuit held that the coupons are property, noting that "[t]here is no question that a flight award coupon is 'something of value,' for it can be used to obtain free flight tickets."[1] The court then added in a footnote that "If such coupons did not represent something of value, one wonders why Loney went to such trouble to obtain and sell them."[2] The court

---

customer prices and opposing traders, and depriving their customers of the opportunity to obtain a better price. United States v. Ashman, 979 F.2d 469, 476–79 (7th Cir. 1992).

6. *Eighth Circuit:* United States v. Granberry, 908 F.2d 278, 280 (8th Cir. 1990).

7. *Eighth Circuit:* United States v. Shyres, 898 F.2d 647, 652 (8th Cir.1990).

8. *Second Circuit:* United States v. Wallach, 935 F.2d 445, 464–66 (2d Cir. 1991).

9. 935 F.2d at 462–63.

10. 935 F.2d at 463–64.

§ 17.17

1. *Fifth Circuit:* United States v. Loney, 959 F.2d 1332, 1335 (5th Cir.1992).

2. 959 F.2d 1332, 1335 n. 8 (5th Cir. 1992).

rejected the idea that the rule of lenity should apply, saying the Supreme Court decision in *McNally v. United States*[3] commands a broad construction of property. Similarly, the Tenth Circuit held that travel agents who credited miles earned by other passengers to a fictitious passenger account and then exchanged those miles for frequent flyer coupons had defrauded the airline of property.[4] The court rejected the defense claim that the airlines had not been deprived of property because the coupons had no value while still in the airlines' hands. It noted that when the agents claimed the mileage for the fictitious ticketholder, they imposed upon the airline a liability that would not otherwise exist. In acquiring the mileage, the court concluded, the agents imposed liability on the airline and obtained property for themselves. In a case involving a similar scheme by travel agents, the Ninth Circuit agreed that the defendants had fraudulently deprived the airline of a property right in things of value which resulted in the imposition of liabilities that the airline would not otherwise have borne.[5] The court distinguished an earlier decision in which it held, in a different context, that frequent flyer award coupons are contractual rights rather than property rights per se.[6]

§ 17.18   Schemes to Deprive The Victim of Property—Loss of Revenue

Employing state law and the traditional property law conceptions of "control," the lower courts have found a property interest where the government actually lost revenues or incurred liabilities, but not where a government employee took bribes without reducing the revenues owed to the government. Two Seventh Circuit cases held that the government was deprived of a property interest when its revenues were reduced by fraud. One case held that a scheme to reduce tax assessments deprived the county of property tax revenue in which the county had a property interest under state law, and that state law was dispositive on the question of whether defrauded taxes are property under the mail fraud statute.[1] Similarly, where a deputy sheriff made private deals with debtors and received part of the proceeds of property that he was supposed to sell for delinquent taxes, the court concluded that the government's right to seize and sell a delinquent taxpayer's property and its corresponding right to any revenue from the sale were property rights.[2] The D.C. Circuit held that a government guarantee to pay a lender if a borrower defaults on a loan "is a 'property interest,' not an 'intangible right' under *McNally* and *Carpenter* because it involves the

---

3. 483 U.S. 350, 107 S.Ct. 2875, 97 L.Ed.2d 292 (1987).

4. *Tenth Circuit:* United States v. Schreier, 908 F.2d 645 (10th Cir.1990).

5. *Ninth Circuit:* United States v. Mullins, 992 F.2d 1472, 1476–77 (9th Cir. 1993).

6. *Ninth Circuit:* United States v. Mullins, 992 F.2d 1472, 1476–77 (9th Cir.

1993) (distinguishing TransWorld Airlines, Inc. v. American Coupon Exch., Inc., 913 F.2d 676 (9th Cir.1990)).

§ 17.18

1. *Seventh Circuit:* United States v. Doe, 867 F.2d 986, 989 (7th Cir.1989).

2. *Seventh Circuit:* United States v. Folak, 865 F.2d 110, 113–14 (7th Cir.1988).

Government's 'control over how its money [is] spent.' "[3] The court also noted that the commitment to guarantee a loan created a significant liability which could, in fact, cost the government money.[4]

In contrast, in another case where a state judge received bribes the Seventh Circuit held that the state had not been deprived of any property interest.[5] The court noted that the state's justice was not for sale and it did not lose any expected revenues because of the scheme. In contrast to the bribes paid to the deputy sheriff in the case noted above,[6] which were paid from sales proceeds that belonged exclusively to the state, the moneys paid to the judge as bribes were entirely illegitimate and the state had no property interest in them.

§ 17.19 Schemes to Deprive The Victim of Property—Honest Services

In 1988 Congress enacted 18 U.S.C. § 1346, which provides that the mail, wire and bank fraud statutes encompass schemes to defraud another of "the intangible right of honest services."[1] Section 1346 was passed in response to the Supreme Court's decision in *McNally v. United States,*[2] which had held that the mail fraud statute reached only reach schemes to deprive the victims of money or property.[3]

3. *D.C. Circuit:* United States v. Madeoy, 912 F.2d 1486, 1492 (D.C.Cir.1990) (citing McNally v. United States, 483 U.S. 350, 360, 107 S.Ct. 2875, 2881, 97 L.Ed.2d 292 (1987)).

4. 912 F.2d at 138–39.

5. *Seventh Circuit*: United States v. Holzer, 840 F.2d 1343 (7th Cir.1988).

6. *Seventh Circuit:* United States v. Folak, 865 F.2d 110, 113–14 (7th Cir.1988).

§ 17.19

1. Section 1346 provides in full: "For the purposes of this chapter, the term 'scheme or artifice to defraud' includes a scheme or artifice to deprive another of the intangible right of honest services."

2. 483 U.S. 350, 107 S.Ct. 2875, 97 L.Ed.2d 292 (1987).

3. Section 1346 was enacted as an amendment to the Anti–Drug Abuse Act of 1988, Pub. L. No. 100–690, § 7603(a), 102 Stat. 4508. The legislative history of the statute is quite sparse. In United States v. Brumley, 79 F.3d 1430, 1436 (5th Cir. 1996), a panel of the Fifth Circuit described the legislative record:

The specific text of what has become 18 U.S.C. § 1346 was never referred to any committee of either the House or the Senate, was never the subject of any committee report from either the House or the Senate, and was never the subject of any floor debate reported in the Congres-

sional Record. There are only two items of legislative history pertinent to the text of § 1346 as actually passed. First, there are remarks on the floor by Representative Conyers regarding various items in the Omnibus Drug bill including the section that would add a new § 1346....

. . . .

Second, after the passage of the Omnibus Drug Bill, the Senate Judiciary Committee prepared and entered into the Congressional Record a report regarding all of the provisions in the Anti–Drug Abuse Act of 1988 which were within the jurisdiction of the Senate Judiciary committee for the purpose of detailing "Congress' intent in enacting these provisions."

Representative John Conyers, the floor sponsor of the amendment, stated that it was "intended merely to overturn the *McNally* decision" and that "[n]o other change in the law is intended." 134 CONG. REC. H11,108–01 (daily ed. Oct. 21, 1988) (statement of Rep. Conyers). Representative Conyers also noted that the amendment applies to wire as well as mail fraud. *Ibid.* The Senate Judiciary Committee's section-by-section commentary stated that the "intent [of § 1346] is to reinstate all of the pre-*McNally* case law pertaining to the mail and wire fraud statutes without change." 134 CONG. REC. S17,360–02 (daily ed. Nov. 10, 1988).

With one notable exception, the lower courts have agreed that in enacting § 1346 Congress overruled *McNally*[4] and endorsed or reinstated the pre-*McNally* cases that defined the concept of honest services.[5]

A number of courts and commentators have discussed the legislative history. Professor Geraldine Szott Moohr made the interesting point that Representative Conyers ultimately voted against the bill, which casts some doubt on the weight to be given to his interpretation of the amendment. Geraldine Szott Moohr, *Mail Fraud and the Intangible Rights Doctrine: Someone to Watch Over Us*, 31 HARV. J. LEGIS. 153, 169 n.69 (1994). The *Brumley* panel, which discounted the statement of Conyers and the after the fact description of the Senate Judiciary Committee, also detailed Congress' failure to enact other bills intended to respond to *McNally*. 79 F.3d at 1437–39. Although the en banc court disagreed with the panel's conclusion that § 1346 did not overrule *McNally*, 116 F.3d 728, the panel opinion still contains a useful recitation of the legislative action on each of the bills proposed as responses to *McNally*. The Supreme Court denied certiorari, ___ U.S. ___, 118 S.Ct. 625, 139 L.Ed.2d 606 (1997). For a discussion of discussion of the opinions in *Brumley*, see the text *infra* accompanying notes 6–8.

4. *D.C. Circuit*: United States v. DeFries, 43 F.3d 707, 709 n. 1 (D.C.Cir.1995).

First Circuit: United States v. Czubinski, 106 F.3d 1069, 1076 (1st Cir.1997).

Third Circuit: United States v. Martinez, 905 F.2d 709, 715 (3d Cir.1990).

Fourth Circuit: United States v. Bryan, 58 F.3d 933, 940–41 n. 1 (4th Cir.1995).

Fifth Circuit: United States v. Holley, 23 F.3d 902, 910 (5th Cir.1994).

Sixth Circuit: United States v. Frost, 125 F.3d 346, 364 (6th Cir.1997), *petitions for cert. filed*, U.S., Mar. 14, 1998 (Nos. 97–1549, 97–8295, 97–8305, 97–8328, and 97–8374); United States v. Ames Sintering Co., 927 F.2d 232, 235 (6th Cir.1990).

Seventh Circuit: United States v. Catalfo, 64 F.3d 1070, 1077 n. 5 (7th Cir.1995), *cert. denied*, 517 U.S. 1192, 116 S.Ct. 1683, 134 L.Ed.2d 784, (1996).

Eighth Circuit: United States v. Blumeyer, 114 F.3d 758, 765 (8th Cir.), *cert. denied*, ___ U.S. ___, 118 S.Ct. 350, 139 L.Ed.2d 272 (1997); United States v. Granberry, 908 F.2d 278, 281 n. 1 (8th Cir.1990).

Ninth Circuit: United States v. Dischner, 974 F.2d 1502, 1518 n. 16 (9th Cir. 1992); United States v. Frega, 933 F.Supp. 1536, 1546–47 (S.D.Cal.1996).

Eleventh Circuit: United States v. Waymer, 55 F.3d 564, 568 n. 3 (11th Cir.1995), *cert. denied*, 517 U.S. 1119, 116 S.Ct. 1350, 134 L.Ed.2d 519 (1996).

5. *D.C. Circuit:* United States v. Sun–Diamond Growers of Cal., 941 F.Supp. 1262 (D.D.C.1996) (Congress wanted to reinstate all pre-*McNally* case law without change).

First Circuit: United States v. Czubinski, 106 F.3d 1069, 1076 (1st Cir.1997) (§ 1346 "restores" mail and wire fraud statutes to the pre-*McNally* application); United States v. Sawyer, 85 F.3d 713, (1st Cir.1996) (§ 1346 "reinstate[s] the reasoning of pre-*McNally* case law holding the mail fraud statute reached schemes to defraud individuals of the intangible right to honest services of government officials").

Third Circuit: See United States v. D'Alessio, 822 F.Supp. 1134, 1148 (D.N.J. 1993) (pre-*McNally* case law has "persuasive effect" in prosecutions under § 1346). *Cf.* United States v. Bissell, 954 F.Supp. 841, 861 (D.N.J.1996) (Congress intended to "restore" mail fraud statute to its pre-*McNally* scope, and post-*McNally* cases are consistent with accepted pre-*McNally* interpretation of the statute).

Fourth Circuit: United States v. Bryan, 58 F.3d 933, 942 (4th Cir.1995) (in the wake of § 1346 pre-*McNally* cases have "persuasive" effect).

Fifth Circuit: Cf. United States v. Gray, 96 F.3d 769, 774 (5th Cir.1996) (noting that parties "properly" looked to pre-*McNally* precedents), *cert. denied*, ___ U.S. ___, 117 S.Ct. 1275, 137 L.Ed.2d 351 (1997).

Sixth Circuit: United States v. Frost, 125 F.3d 346, 364 (6th Cir.1997) (Congress intended § 1346 to "reinstate" the doctrine of intangible rights to honest services), *petitions for cert. filed*, U.S., Mar. 14, 1998 (Nos. 97–1549, 97–8295, 97–8305, 97–8328, and 97–8374).

Seventh Circuit: United States v. Bolden, 1997 WL 473240 * 3 (N.D.Il.1997) (Congress intended § 1346 to "restore the law to its state prior to *McNally*") (not reported in F.Supp.).

Eighth Circuit: United States v. Blumeyer, 114 F.3d 758, 765 (8th Cir.), *cert. denied*, ___ U.S. ___, 118 S.Ct. 350, 139 L.Ed.2d 272 (1997) (§ 1346 "restored the 'vitality' " of the court's pre-*McNally* cases).

The Fifth Circuit is the sole exception. A panel decision in *United States v. Brumley*[6] reached the surprising conclusion that the adoption of § 1346 was not intended to reverse *McNally*, and that even as amended the mail and wire fraud statutes do not reach a scheme by state government officials to deprive the citizens of their faithful service.[7] Although the en banc court reversed, holding that § 1346 does indeed encompass the honest services of state and local government officials, the en banc opinion also emphasized the diversity among pre-*McNally* decisions and stated that some of those decisions were too broad to be read literally.[8] Accordingly, unless the Supreme Court provides further clarification, counsel should consult both pre-and post-*McNally* cases in researching honest services charges under § 1346, and should also recognize that the Fifth Circuit may be particularly receptive to arguments that would narrow some of the more sweeping pre-*McNally* precedents.

18 U.S.C. § 1346 defines the term "scheme or artifice to defraud" to include a scheme or artifice to deprive *another* of the intangible right of honest services.[9] Although the Fifth Circuit's panel opinion in *United States v. Brumley* [10]held that this language did not include state agencies victimized by official corruption, that decision was repudiated by the en banc court[11] and has not been followed elsewhere. Aside from that one

Ninth Circuit: Pharmacare v. Caremark, 965 F.Supp. 1411, 1418 (D.Haw. 1996) (civil RICO case predicated on mail fraud) (§ 1346 nullified *McNally* and "reinstituted the pre-*McNally* jurisprudence").

6. 79 F.3d 1430 (5th Cir.1996).

7. The panel noted that *McNally* "made it absolutely clear that Congress 'must speak more clearly than it has,' " to extend the statute in a manner that would leave its outer boundaries ambiguous and involve the federal courts in setting standards of disclosure and good government for state officials. 79 F.3d at 1434. The panel concluded, in essence, that Congress had not spoken clearly enough to meet this standard in § 1346. *See* 79 F.3d at 1437, 1439.

The key language in § 1346 states that mail and wire fraud include "a scheme or artifice to deprive *another* of the intangible right to honest services." The statute did not define "another." Although the court did not rest its decision on this point, it noted that "another" could be construed to be parallel to the introductory term "whoever," which is defined in 1 U.S.C. § 1 to include individuals, associations, and corporations, but not a state, or all of the citizens within a state or local government unit. 79 F.3d at 1435. The court found that § 1346 had been inserted into the Omnibus Drug Bill on the same day the bill was passed,

and that the legislative history was "minimal." It found unpersuasive both the section-by-section explanation cited supra in note 3, which was prepared after enactment, and a statement to the same effect by Representative Conyers on the floor of the House. Indeed, the court noted that Representative Conyers did not even vote for the bill ultimately enacted. 79 F.3d at 1437 n.6. The court gave great weight to the fact that the same Congress considered and failed to enact two other bills that expressly spoke to the conduct of public officials which defrauded the public of the right to good government. 79 F.3d at 1437–39. The court concluded that the House of Representatives had refused to go along with a Senate bill that would have achieved the objective of overturning *McNally*. Instead, the only legislation passed was § 1346, which the court called "a last minute, 'bobtailed' compromise." 79 F.3d at 1439.

8. *Fifth Circuit:* United States v. Brumley, 116 F.3d 728, 733 (5th Cir.), *cert. denied*, ___ U.S. ___, 118 S.Ct. 625, 139 L.Ed.2d 606 (1997).

9. 18 U.S.C. § 1346 (emphasis added).

10. *Fifth Circuit:* United States v. Brumley, 79 F.3d 1430 (5th Cir.1996).

11. *Fifth Circuit:* United States v. Brumley, 116 F.3d 728, 731–32 (5th Cir. 1997) (en banc) (holding that the term "another" defines the range of victims and that

exception, the lower courts have broadly interpreted the class of victims under § 1346 to include government entities, citizens, and states (as well as private employers).[12]

A. THE APPLICATION OF § 1346 TO PUBLIC OFFICIALS AND GOVERNMENT EMPLOYEES

In general the lower courts have had little trouble defining the core of the prohibition in § 1346. There is general agreement that § 1346 is applicable to cases involving serious public corruption, i.e., the bribery of public officials or the failure of public decision-makers to disclose serious conflicts of interest.[13] As one court explained, the cases in which the

both a government entity and citizens as a body politic qualify as "another" and can be the victims of a scheme to deprive another of the intangible right of honest services), *cert. denied*, ___ U.S. ___, 118 S.Ct. 625, 139 L.Ed.2d 606 (1997).

12. *Ninth Circuit:* United States v. Frega, 933 F.Supp. 1536, 1546 (S.D.Cal. 1996) (holding that "another" can easily be read to include a state citizen, who would be the victim of public corruption fraud).

Eleventh Circuit: United States v. Castro, 89 F.3d 1443, 1456 (11th Cir.1996) (holding that neither the plain language of § 1346 nor its legislative history supports limiting the scope of the term "another" to exclude governmental entities such as a state), *cert. denied*, ___ U.S. ___, 117 S.Ct. 965, 136 L.Ed.2d 850 (1997).

See generally the cases cited supra in notes 4 and 5.

13. *First Circuit:* United States v. Sawyer, 85 F.3d 713, 722 (1st Cir.1996). *See also* United States v. Czubinski, 106 F.3d 1069, 1076 (1st Cir.1997) (dicta).

Third Circuit: See United States v. Mangiardi, 962 F.Supp. 49, 51 (M.D.Pa. 1997) (indictment does not support a charge of mail fraud intended to deprive citizens of the honest services of a public official where no official is alleged to have been bribed or to have profited personally from the activities of defendants); United States v. Bissell, 954 F.Supp. 841, 861–62 (D.N.J.1996) (indictment sufficiently alleged scheme to deprive citizens of county prosecutor's honest services where prosecutor maintained undisclosed business relationships with adversary of office of county prosecutor, threatened to frame owner of distribution company, obstructed justice, and perjured himself).

Fourth Circuit: See United States v. ReBrook, 58 F.3d 961, 966 (4th Cir.1995)

(upholding wire fraud conviction of attorney for state lottery who misappropriated confidential nonpublic information); United States v. Bryan, 58 F.3d 933, 941–42 (4th Cir.1995) (upholding mail and wire fraud convictions of state lottery director who rigged process of awarding government contracts and used confidential, non-public information to purchase securities of companies doing business with the lottery).

Fifth Circuit: United States v. Brumley, 116 F.3d 728 (5th Cir.1997) (affirming wire and mail fraud convictions of state workers compensation official who solicited and received undisclosed "loans" from attorneys representing claimants), *cert. denied*, ___ U.S. ___, 118 S.Ct. 625, 139 L.Ed.2d 606 (1997).

Seventh Circuit: United States v. Bolden, 1997 WL 473239, at *1–2 (N.D.Ill. 1997) (indictment sufficiently alleged scheme to deprive Chicago and its citizens of Commissioner's honest services by failing to disclose conflict of interest in hiring a person in order to further a scheme to generate revenue and conceal that financial interest).

Eighth Circuit: United States v. Blumeyer, 114 F.3d 758, 766 (8th Cir.), *cert. denied*, ___ U.S. ___, 118 S.Ct. 350, 139 L.Ed.2d 272 (1997) (upholding mail and wire fraud convictions of state legislator who concealed his interest in and receipt of payments from a company with business before his legislative committee). *Cf.* United States v. Walker, 97 F.3d 253, 255 (8th Cir.1996) (upholding mail fraud conviction based upon mailing false campaign finance disclosure report designed to disguise source of campaign funds).

Ninth Circuit: United States v. Frega, 933 F.Supp. 1536, 1539 (S.D.Cal.1996) (denying motion to dismiss indictment where attorney gave judges gifts with intent to influence or reward them in regard to cases

deprivation of honest services has been found typically involve "either bribery of the official or her failure to disclose a conflict of interest resulting in personal gain."[14] Another court explained that "[w]hen official action is corrupted by secret bribes or kickbacks, the essence of the political contract is violated."[15]

i. Bribery

It is generally agreed that a public official's receipt of a bribe constitutes a breach of honest services, and accordingly that such a breach can give rise to a mail or wire fraud violation if the requisite jurisdictional nexus can be shown. In a prosecution involving the former governor of Maryland the Fourth Circuit explained the connection between bribery and fraud:

> [T]he fraud involved in the bribery of a public official lies in the fact that the public official is not exercising his independent judgment in passing on official matters. A fraud is perpetrated upon the public to whom the official owes fiduciary duties, e. g., honest, faithful and disinterested service. When a public official has been bribed, he breaches his duty of honest, faithful and disinterested service. While outwardly purporting to be exercising independent judgment in passing on official matters, the official has been paid for his decisions, perhaps without even considering the merits of the matter. Thus, the public is not receiving what it expects and is entitled to, the public official's honest and faithful service.[16]

According to this theory, the receipt of the bribe constitutes the fraudulent deprivation of honest services, and it is not necessary to show that the public suffered any financial loss because of the fraud. For example, in a pre-*McNally* case the Seventh Circuit ruled that a judge's receipt of bribes is a fraud on the public, even if there was no evidence that he ruled differently in a case because of a bribe or that either the public or any litigant suffered any loss.[17] As a fiduciary, the judge had a

in which he was counsel of record and in which they were presiding).

Eleventh Circuit: United States v. Lopez–Lukis, 102 F.3d 1164, 1165–66 (11th Cir.1997) (reversing dismissal of count in indictment charging scheme to deprive electorate of legislator's honest services by selling control of legislative body and selling her vote); United States v. Paradies, 98 F.3d 1266, 1271–76 (11th Cir.1996) (holding that scheme to bribe city council member to buy favorable votes clearly falls within § 1346); United States v. Castro, 89 F.3d 1443, 1447 (11th Cir.1996) (upholding mail fraud conviction of state judge who accepted kickbacks in return for appointments), *cert. denied,* ___ U.S. ___, 117 S.Ct. 965, 136 L.Ed.2d 850 (1997).

14. *First Circuit:* United States v. Sawyer, 85 F.3d 713, 724 (1st Cir.1996).

15. *Eighth Circuit:* United States v. Jain, 93 F.3d 436, 442 (8th Cir.1996), *cert. denied,* ___ U.S. ___, 117 S.Ct. 2452, 138 L.Ed.2d 210 (1997).

16. *Fourth Circuit:* United States v. Mandel, 591 F.2d 1347, 1362 (4th Cir.) (citation omitted), *aff'd per curiam by equally divided court,* 602 F.2d 653 (4th Cir.1979) (en banc), *coram nobis granted in light of* McNally, 862 F.2d 1067 (4th Cir.1988). The passage of 18 U.S.C. § 1346 effectively reinstates the court's decision for conduct arising after the passage of that provision. *See* text accompanying n.5 *supra.*

17. *Seventh Circuit:* United States v. Holzer, 816 F.2d 304, 307–08 (8th Cir. 1987), *vacated and remanded for reconsideration in light of* McNally, 484 U.S. 807, 108 S.Ct. 53, 98 L.Ed.2d 18 (1987), *rev'd in part,* 840 F.2d 1343 (7th Cir.1988). The passage of 18 U.S.C. § 1346 reinstates the

duty toward the public, and his deliberate concealment of his solicitation and acceptance of bribes was a violation of that fiduciary duty. Similarly, despite the fact that the state and the public suffered no financial loss the same court upheld the conviction of the former governor of Illinois for taking bribes to support legislation beneficial to horse racing interests.[18]

The enactment of § 1346 provides strong support for the view that it is the deprivation of the honest service by the government official—regardless of any financial loss—that constitutes the fraud under either the mail or wire fraud statute. Under *McNally* fraud by a public official was covered by the mail fraud act if the prosecution could establish a deprivation of money or property. Section 1346 was passed to enlarge the sweep of the mail fraud act to cases, such as *McNally* itself, where there was a breach of a fiduciary duty that could not be tied to any financial or property loss to the public.

ii.   The Duty to Disclose Material Information

About half of the circuits have endorsed the view that in the case of public officials the duty of honest services includes a fiduciary's duty to disclose material information.[19] The fiduciary duty to disclose is also noted in Justice Steven's dissent in *McNally*,[20] which describes the pre-*McNally* case law that Congress sought to reinstate through § 1346. This formulation obviously requires the courts to determine what information is material within the meaning of the mail and wire fraud statute, so as to require disclosure as part of the duty of honest services.

A number of courts have considered whether the disclosure of particular information was material. For example, *United States v. Waymer*[21] involved the mail fraud conviction of a school board member who failed to disclose that he received a 15 percent kickback from the contractor who provided pest control services to the Atlanta school

original panel opinion for conduct arising after the passage of that provision. *See* text accompanying n.5 *supra*.

18. *Seventh Circuit:* United States v. Isaacs, 493 F.2d 1124 (1974).

19. *First Circuit:* United States v. Sawyer, 85 F.3d 713, 724 (1st Cir.1996); United States v. Silvano, 812 F.2d 754, 759 (1st Cir.1987).

Second Circuit: United States v. Mittelstaedt, 31 F.3d 1208, 1217 (2d Cir.1994).

Fourth Circuit: See, e.g., United States v. Mandel, 591 F.2d 1347, 1362 (4th Cir.) (citation omitted), *aff'd per curiam by equally divided court,* 602 F.2d 653 (4th Cir.1979) (en banc), *coram nobis granted in light of* McNally, 862 F.2d 1067 (4th Cir. 1988). The passage of 18 U.S.C. § 1346 effectively reinstates the court's decision for conduct arising after the passage of that provision. *See* text accompanying n.5 *supra*.

Seventh Circuit: United States v. Holzer, 816 F.2d 304, 307–08 (7th Cir. 1987), *vacated and remanded for reconsideration in light of* McNally, 484 U.S. 807, 108 S.Ct. 53, 98 L.Ed.2d 18 (1987), *rev'd in part,* 840 F.2d 1343 (7th Cir.1988). The passage of 18 U.S.C. § 1346 reinstates the original panel opinion for conduct arising after the passage of that provision. *See* text accompanying n.5 *supra*.

Eleventh Circuit: United States v. Waymer, 55 F.3d 564, 571 (11th Cir.1995), *cert. denied,* 517 U.S. 1119, 116 S.Ct. 1350, 134 L.Ed.2d 519 (1996); United States v. O'Malley, 707 F.2d 1240, 1247 (11th Cir.1983).

20. 483 U.S. 350, 371, 107 S.Ct. 2875, 2887, 97 L.Ed.2d 292 (1987) (Stevens, J., dissenting).

21. 55 F.3d 564 (11th Cir.1995), *cert. denied,* 517 U.S. 1119, 116 S.Ct. 1350, 134 L.Ed.2d 519 (1996).

system. He performed no services in exchange for the payments in question. On appeal the defendant argued that he had made sufficient disclosure by informing an associate school superintendent in writing that he was doing consulting work for the contractor. The court rejected this claim, holding that information that a contractor is paying 15 percent of the contract fees to a board member who provides no services in return "so obviously smacks of impropriety that it can hardly be characterized as a minor detail of which the Board need not be appraised."[22] Indeed, had the board known that the contract price was inflated to include a 15 percent kickback, it likely would have ordered the contract rebid.

Another decision that discusses the materiality requirement involved a judge who took payments referred to as "loans," though they were never repaid, from attorneys who practiced before him. In *United States v. Holzer*[23] the court concluded that the judge had a fiduciary duty to disclose these transactions because they gave rise to the inference that his rulings might be affected. The court stated that "[a] judge ... need not, in a case to which Sears Roebuck is a party, disclose that he is a customer of Sears.... A judge is not 'grateful' to Sears Roebuck for selling him a lawnmower at the market price of lawnmowers. It is when the other party to the transaction is doing him a favor that an inference of gratitude, or an inference that a *quid pro quo* can be expected, may arise and make the failure to disclose the transaction ... material."[24]

The results in *Waymer* and *Holzer* seem correct, but they also suggest the beginning of a slippery slope in determining materiality. The defendant in *Waymer* did disclose that he had a business relationship with the contractor. Suppose the facts had been slightly different, and he had performed some services which the government claims served as little more than window dressing for a kickback. What disclosure would be required? Would it be sufficient to disclose the amount of the payments? Would it be necessary also to state the nature of the services provided? The number of hours spent on the provision of those services? Obviously a more expansive definition of materiality will encourage public officials to provide greater disclosure, but it would certainly be preferable to set out clear disclosure requirements in advance rather than to determine them after the fact in a criminal prosecution. Moreover, such requirements might well vary depending on the position of the official involved, and the degree of disclosure that is desirable involves matters of policy that might better be decided at the state and local level.

The First and Second circuits have suggested a limiting principle for the fiduciary duty to disclose, holding that a misrepresentation or

22. 55 F.3d at 572.

23. 816 F.2d 304 (7th Cir. 1987), *vacated and remanded for reconsideration in light of* McNally, 484 U.S. 807, 108 S.Ct. 53, 98 L.Ed.2d 18 (1987), *rev'd in part*, 840 F.2d 1343 (7th Cir.1988). The passage of 18 U.S.C. § 1346 reinstates the original panel opinion for conduct arising after the passage of that provision. *See* text accompanying n.5 *supra*.

24. 816 F.2d at 307–08.

omission of material information is cognizable under the mail or wire fraud statutes only when it could result in harm to the public.[25] The other circuits do not specifically require this "public harm" element.[26] However, the *Waymer* court implicitly focused on the harm to the public when it noted that the school board would likely have rebid the contracts to get a lower price if it had known that a 15 percent kickback was being paid. *Waymer* suggests that even circuits that do not explicitly require a showing of harm to the public nonetheless include this in the concept of materiality.

iii. The Relevance of State Law

Since mail and wire fraud prosecutions almost invariably involve state and local (rather than federal) officials, three issues involving the relevance of state law have emerged: (1) whether state law defines the parameters of the duties owed by these officials, (2) whether the breach of a duty to provide services rooted in state law must violate the criminal law of the state in order to provide a predicate for an honest services prosecution under § 1346, and (3) whether a violation of a duty imposed under state law necessarily establishes a deprivation of honest services under § 1346.

a. Does State or Federal Law Define the Scope of the Honest Services Required by § 1346?

A split among the circuits has developed on this issue. Most of the circuits that have considered the question have ruled that it is not necessary to find a basis in state law for aspects of the duty of honest services under § 1346.[27] When federal law provides the definition of honest services, it creates a uniform national standard, rather than a patchwork of varying state standards incorporated and enforced under the mail and wire fraud statutes. This position is broadly consistent with the Supreme Court's recognition in *Durland v. United States*[28] that the

25. *See, e.g.,*

First Circuit: United States v. Silvano, 812 F.2d 754, 759 (1st Cir.1987).

Second Circuit: United States v. Mittelstaedt, 31 F.3d 1208, 1217 (2d Cir.1994).

26. *See, e.g.,*

Seventh Circuit: United States v. Holzer, 816 F.2d 304, 307–08 (7th Cir. 1987), *vacated and remanded for reconsideration in light of* McNally, 484 U.S. 807, 108 S.Ct. 53, 98 L.Ed.2d 18 (1987), *rev'd in part,* 840 F.2d 1343 (7th Cir.1988). The passage of 18 U.S.C. § 1346 reinstates the original panel opinion for conduct arising after the passage of that provision. *See* text accompanying n.5 *supra.*

Eleventh Circuit: United States v. Waymer, 55 F.3d 564, 571 (11th Cir.1995), *cert. denied,* 517 U.S. 1119, 116 S.Ct. 1350, 134 L.Ed.2d 519 (1996); United States v. O'Malley, 707 F.2d 1240, 1247 (11th Cir.1983).

27. *First Circuit:* United States v. Sawyer, 85 F.3d 713, 719 (1st Cir.1996); United States v. Goldberg, 928 F.Supp. 89, 93 (D.Mass.1996).

Third Circuit: United States v. Bissell, 954 F.Supp. 841, 862 (D.N.J.1996); United States v. Caruso, 948 F.Supp. 382, 387 (D.N.J.1996).

Fourth Circuit: United States v. Bryan, 58 F.3d 933, 941 (4th Cir.1995); United States v. ReBrook, 58 F.3d 961, 967 (4th Cir.1995).

Ninth Circuit: United States v. Frega, 933 F.Supp. 1536, 1547–48 (S.D.Cal.1996).

28. *Supreme Court:* Durland v. United States, 161 U.S. 306, 16 S.Ct. 508, 40 L.Ed. 709 (1896).

concept of mail fraud should be permitted to evolve, with the federal courts adapting it to protect the public from every variety of fraud, unhampered by common law concepts. Just as the Supreme Court refused to restrict the concept of mail fraud to common law concepts, most of the lower courts have refused to restrict the mail and wire fraud statutes to the concept of honest services defined by state law. Their position finds support in Justice Stevens' dissenting opinion in *McNally*, where he stated "[o]f course 'the fact that a scheme may or may not violate State law does not determine whether it is within the proscriptions of the federal statute.' The mail fraud statute is a self-contained provision, which does not rely on any state enactments for its force."[29] The enactment of § 1346 overruled *McNally*, reinstating the pre-*McNally* cases described in Justice Steven's dissenting opinion and evincing general Congressional support for Steven's interpretation of the mail fraud act. This point cannot be taken too far, however, since Congress did not have before it the question whether the scope of honest services should be drawn from state law sources.

In contrast, the Fifth Circuit explicitly requires that honest services be defined as duties set out in state law. In *United States v. Brumley*[30] the en banc court relied on the plain language of the statute, legislative history, and principles of federalism in holding that a federal prosecutor must prove that conduct of a state official breached a duty respecting the provision of services owed to the official's employer under state law. Although the court recognized that § 1346 draws upon federal criminal law to define the scheme or artifice to defraud elements, the court held that § 1346 defines honest services by reference to duties found in state law.[31] The court explained:

> We begin with the plain language of the statute. There are two words—"honest" and "services." We will not lightly infer that Congress intended to leave to courts and prosecutors, in the first instance, the power to define the range and quality of services a state employer may choose to demand of its employees. We find nothing to suggest that Congress was attempting in § 1346 to garner to the federal government the right to impose upon states a federal vision of appropriate services—to establish, in other words, an ethical regime for state employees. Such a taking of power would sorely tax separation of powers and erode our federalist structure. Under the most natural reading of the statute, a federal prosecutor must prove that conduct of a state official breached a duty respecting the provision of services owed to the official's employer under state law. Stated directly, the official must act or fail to act contrary to the requirements of his job under state law. This means that if the official does all that is required under state law, alleging that the

---

29. *Supreme Court:* McNally v. United States, 483 U.S. 350, 377, 107 S.Ct. 2875, 2890, 97 L.Ed.2d 292 (1987) (Stevens, J., dissenting) (citation omitted).

30. 116 F.3d 728, 733–35 (5th Cir.) (en banc), *cert. denied,* ___ U.S. ___, 118 S.Ct. 625, 139 L.Ed.2d 606 (1997).

31. 116 F.3d at 734.

services were not otherwise done "honestly" does not charge a violation of the mail fraud statute. The statute contemplates that there must first be a breach of a state-owed duty. . . .

. . .

. . . Despite its rhetorical ring, the rights of citizens to honest government have no purchase independent of rights and duties locatable in state law. To hold otherwise would offer § 1346 as an enforcer of federal preferences of "good government" with attendant potential for large federal inroads into state matters and genuine difficulties of vagueness.[32]

b. Is a Violation of a State Criminal Law a Prerequisite for an Honest Services Prosecution?

Although the Fifth Circuit has left open the question whether a breach of a duty to perform must also violate the criminal law of the state,[33] the other courts that have considered the question have all declined to require proof of a state criminal violation in order to sustain a conviction for honest services fraud.[34]

c. Does a State Official's Violation of a State Law Automatically Establish a Violation of § 1346?

Only a few decisions have explored the third question, which is whether a state law violation automatically establishes a violation of § 1346. The most extended treatment of this issue is found in *United States v. Sawyer*,[35] where the First Circuit held that a lobbyist's violation of the state gift statute was insufficient, by itself, to establish a scheme to defraud the public of its intangible right to honest services. The court held that the lobbyist's intentional violations of the gift statute were not sufficient without proof that the intent behind the violations was the deprivation of honest services.[36] The court warned against allowing the

---

32. 116 F.3d at 734–35.

33. *Fifth Circuit:* United States v. Brumley, 116 F.3d 728, 734 (5th Cir.1997) (en banc), *cert. denied,* ___ U.S. ___, 118 S.Ct. 625, 139 L.Ed.2d 606 (1997).

34. *First Circuit:* United States v. Sawyer, 85 F.3d 713, 719 (1st Cir.1996) (proof of a state law violation is not required for conviction of honest services fraud); United States v. Goldberg, 928 F.Supp. 89, 93 (D.Mass.1996) (violation of state ethics law, without more, does not establish mail fraud violation).

Third Circuit: United States v. Bissell, 954 F.Supp. 841, 862 (D.N.J.1996) (one need not violate a state law or regulation to be liable for mail fraud); United States v. Caruso, 948 F.Supp. 382, 387 (D.N.J.1996)

(indictment charged defendant with each element of federal mail fraud even where defendant could not be convicted under state law of larceny).

Fourth Circuit: United States v. Bryan, 58 F.3d 933, 941 (4th Cir.1995) (when fraud conviction is based on the deprivation of the right to intangible services as opposed to the deprivation of property or money, the mail fraud statute contains no independent criminal violation requirement).

Ninth Circuit: United States v. Frega, 933 F.Supp. 1536, 1547–48 (S.D.Cal.1996) (§ 1346 need not reference state law to define fraudulent conduct).

35. 85 F.3d 713, 730–31 (1st Cir. 1996).

36. 85 F.3d at 728–29.

jury to assume that any violation of state law automatically amounts to a federal crime.[37] In dicta the en banc majority in *Brumley* agreed with this result, though for different reasons. The Fifth Circuit judges who made up the majority in *Brumley* reasoned that § 1346 requires an actual breach of a state-owed duty by a state employee, whereas the gratuities statute reaches cases where there is no more than an appearance of corruption.[38] In the Fifth Circuit's view, a deprivation of honest services requires proof that an employee consciously acted in a manner that was not in the best interest of his employer, something closer to bribery than to a mere gratuities violation.

B. THE APPLICATION OF § 1346 TO THE PRIVATE SECTOR

Prior to the *McNally* decision the lower courts had applied the intangible rights theory of mail fraud to cases arising in the private sector, including cases of commercial bribery, corporate misconduct, unethical professional behavior, and misconduct relating to the sale of securities.[39] Since § 1346 simply announces that the mail and wire fraud statutes encompass a scheme to defraud the victim of "the right of honest services," the lower courts have recognized that this applies to the private as well as the public sector.[40]

37. 85 F.3d at 731.

38. *Fifth Circuit:* United States v. Brumley, 116 F.3d 728, 734 (5th Cir.1997) (en banc), *cert. denied*, ___ U.S. ___, 118 S.Ct. 625, 139 L.Ed.2d 606 (1997).

39. *See, e.g.,*

Second Circuit: United States v. Carpenter, 791 F.2d 1024, 1034 (2d Cir.1986), *cert. granted*, 479 U.S. 1016, 107 S.Ct. 666, 93 L.Ed.2d 275 (U.S.N.Y.1986) (upholding conviction of Wall Street Journal reporter, inter alia, because of breach of fiduciary duty by concealment of information he had duty to report regarding his own trading and his leaks to others of employer's confidential information), *aff'd*, 484 U.S. 19, 108 S.Ct. 316, 98 L.Ed.2d 275 (1987) (upholding conviction after *McNally* on the basis of finding that defendant deprived his employer of intangible property right in confidentiality of the contents and timing of defendant's column); United States v. Siegel, 717 F.2d 9 (2d Cir.1983) (upholding application of mail fraud statute to corporate officers' failure to disclose off-the-books cash sales, some or all of which were used for payoffs to secure labor peace); United States v. Bronston, 658 F.2d 920 (2d Cir.1981) (upholding conviction of prominent attorney for undisclosed conflict of interest through secret representation of client whose interests were adverse to other clients of the firm); United States v. Von Barta, 635 F.2d

999 (2d Cir.1980) (upholding indictment of bond salesman and trader for defrauding his employer of his honest services by failing to disclose that he was trading on behalf of a bogus undercapitalized company he had created).

Seventh Circuit: United States v. George, 477 F.2d 508 (7th Cir.1973) (upholding purchasing agent's conviction for receiving kickbacks).

For a discussion of the development of this line of cases, see Michael R. Dreeben, *Insider Trading and Intangible Rights: Redefinition of the Mail Fraud Statute*, 26 AM. CRIM. L. REV. 181, 185–87 (1988).

40. *Fifth Circuit:* United States v. Gray, 96 F.3d 769, 773–74 & n. 8 (5th Cir.1996) (upholding application of § 1346 to Baylor basketball coaches' breach of fiduciary duty to employer), *cert. denied*, ___ U.S. ___, 117 S.Ct. 1275, 137 L.Ed.2d 351 (1997).

Sixth Circuit: United States v. Frost, 125 F.3d 346, 365–66 (6th Cir.1997), *petitions for cert. filed*, U.S., Mar. 14, 1998 (Nos. 97–1549, 97–8295, 97–8305, 97–8328, and 97–8374).

Eighth Circuit: United States v. Jain, 93 F.3d 436, 441 (8th Cir.1996), *cert. denied*, ___ U.S. ___, 117 S.Ct. 2452, 138 L.Ed.2d 210 (1997).

Although they do not raise the First Amendment issues posed by mail fraud prosecutions in the public sector, honest services prosecutions in the private sector raise other troubling issues.

● Some prosecutions demonstrate the potential for both overlap and divergence between the case law developed under the mail and wire fraud statutes on the one hand, and the law that has developed under other specialized statutory regimes, such as the federal securities laws. The securities laws reflect various limitations intended to strike "a delicate balance between fairness to investors and the realities of the market," but there are no parallel limitations on prosecutions under the mail and wire fraud statutes.[41]

● Other cases involve behavior that is normally regulated only by state corporate law. Congress has never attempted to regulate intra-corporate affairs, and the Supreme Court has declined to interpret the federal securities laws as creating a general rule of federal fiduciary duties. Critics charge that federal mail and wire fraud prosecutions could displace the varied rules that different states developed to attract corporate charters and inhibit desirable experimentation. Allowing federal law developed in mail fraud prosecutions to define these duties may undermine the efficiency of the state regimes that are currently based upon a sound view of the economic function of the modern corporation, shifting decision making about the best rule of corporate law to individual federal prosecutors and juries, acting after the fact.[42]

● The extension of § 1346 to the private sector raises the specter of the over criminalization of private relationships that could turn "every breach of contract or every misstatement made in the course of dealing" into a crime.[43] Taken to its furthest extreme, "every civil wrong is potentially indictable."[44]

41. *See* Michael R. Dreeben, *Insider Trading and Intangible Rights: Redefinition of the Mail Fraud Statute*, 26 AM. CRIM. L. REV. 181, 209–14 (1988). This problem arises from the general breadth of the mail fraud statute, not merely from the honest services provision in § 1346. Even before the enactment of § 1346 the Supreme Court unanimously upheld a mail fraud conviction on the theory that there had been a fraudulent deprivation of an intangible property right, while at the same time dividing four to four on the question whether the same conduct constituted a violation of the securities laws. Carpenter v. United States, 484 U.S. 19, 108 S.Ct. 316, 98 L.Ed.2d 275 (1987).

42. *See* Peter R. Ezersky, Note, *Intra-Corporate Mail and Wire Fraud: Criminal Liability for Fiduciary Breach*, 94 YALE L.J. 1427 (1985).

43. *Tenth Circuit:* United States v. Cochran, 109 F.3d 660, 667 (10th Cir. 1997).

44. As the court explained in United States v. Frost, 125 F.3d 346, 368 (6th Cir.1997), *petitions for cert. filed*, U.S., Mar. 14, 1998 (Nos. 97–1549, 97–8295, 97–8305, 97–8328, and 97–8374):

This refusal to carry the intangible rights doctrine to its logical extreme stems from a need to avoid the over-criminalization of private relationships: "[I]f merely depriving the victim of the loyalty and faithful service of his fiduciary constitutes mail fraud, the ends/means distinction is lost. Once the ends/means distinction is abolished and disloyalty alone becomes the crime, little remains before every civil wrong is potentially indictable." Lemire, 720 F.2d at 1336 n. 11 (quoting John C. Coffee, Jr., *From Tort to Crime: Some Reflections on the Criminalization of Fiduciary Breaches and the*

• In the employment context, a broad application of § 1346 threatens to create a "a draconian personnel regulation" that would transform workplace violations into felonies.[45] A broad reading of § 1346 could bring about "a significant reallocation of the social control between employer and employee in favor of the former," with the danger being especially acute in service industries, such as law, investment banking, advertising, and other consulting businesses.[46]

In light of these considerations, many of the lower court opinions express concern about limiting the scope of honest services prosecutions, and some courts now require the government to prove more than an employer's loss of loyalty and fidelity. The opinions reflect several slightly different approaches, although they boil down to some consideration of the potential harm to the victim.[47]

Some circuits have held that a breach of a fiduciary duty constitutes mail or wire fraud in the private sector only if " 'the defendant might reasonably have contemplated some concrete business harm to his employer stemming from his failure to disclose the conflict along with any other information relevant to the transaction.' "[48] This approach has been characterized as an emphasis on the employee's intent and on the foreseeability of economic harm.[49]

Other circuits have taken a different approach, requiring that the breach of honest services must involve a "material" misrepresentation

Problematic Line Between Law and Ethics, 19 AM. CRIM. L.REV. 117, 167 (1981)).

45. *Tenth Circuit:* United States v. Jain, 93 F.3d 436, 442 (10th Cir. 1996), *cert. denied,* ___ U.S. ___, 117 S.Ct. 2452, 138 L.Ed.2d 210 (1997).

46. *See* John Coffee, *Hush: The Criminal Status of Confidential Information after McNally and Carpenter and the Enduring Problem of Overcriminalization,* 26 Am. Crim. L. Rev. 121 (1988). Professor Coffee argues that *"Carpenter's* doctrinal innovation—the idea that divulging confidential information of ones's employer amounts to embezzlement—has the ability to chill employee mobility and increase the social control that employers have over employees." *Id.* at 123. Under his analysis a broker at a securities firm who is fired because of his low sales volume could be told that all information regarding the firm's clients is a trade secret, and prohibited from contacting his former clients under pain of a criminal prosecution. *Ibid.* The same analysis could be applied to an associate who left the employ of a law firm.

47. Despite the similarity of the language used in the various opinions, at least some courts perceive a difference between the approaches. This point is explicit in the Sixth Circuit's discussion in United States

v. Frost, 125 F.3d 346, 368–69 (6th Cir. 1997), *petitions for cert. filed,* U.S., Mar. 14, 1998 (Nos. 97–1549, 97–8295, 97–8305, 97–8328, and 97–8374) where the court concludes that the difference in the two standards may be "slight," but that the focus on intent of employee is preferable to the materiality enquiry.

48. *Sixth Circuit:* United States v. Frost, 125 F.3d 346, 368 (6th Cir.1997), *petitions for cert. filed,* U.S., Mar. 14, 1998 (Nos. 97–1549, 97–8295, 97–8305, 97–8328, and 97–8374) (citation omitted).

Accord:

D.C. Circuit: United States v. Sun–Diamond Growers of Calif., 138 F.3d 961, 973–74 (D.C.Cir.1998) (sufficient to show defendant could have anticipated scheme " 'posed an independent business risk to the employee's corporate employer.' ") (citation omitted); United States v. Lemire, 720 F.2d 1327, 1337 (D.C.Cir.1983).

49. In United States v. Sun-Diamond Growers of Calif., 138 F.3d 961, 974 (D.C.Cir.1998), the court emphasized that it required only that harm to the victim be within defendant's reasonable contemplation, and not that defendant intend such harm.

or omission.[50] Some courts define materiality has having a natural tenancy to influence or the capability of influencing decision makers.[51] However, materiality may also include foreseeability from the employee's vantage point: materiality has been defined in this context as existing whenever an employee has reason to believe the information would lead a reasonable employer to change its business conduct.[52]

It should be noted that honest services cases from the private sector may also turn on other elements of the mail and wire fraud offenses, particularly fraudulent intent and gain to the defendant and/or loss to the victim.[53]

§ 17.20   Mens Rea: Intent to Defraud—In General

Although the mail and wire fraud statutes are silent on the question of mens rea, intent to defraud is recognized as a central element of both statutes.

Library References:

C.J.S. Postal Service and Offenses Against Postal Laws § 23; Telegraphs, Telephones, Radio, and Television § 116–123.
West's Key No. Digests, Postal Service ⬤—35; Telecommunications ⬤—362.

§ 17.21   Mens Rea: Intent to Defraud—Specific Intent

Mail and wire fraud are generally classified as specific intent offenses that require intent to defraud.[1] Although few opinions attempt to

50. *Second Circuit*: United States v. Bronston, 658 F.2d 920, 927 (2d Cir.1981).

Fifth Circuit: United States v. Gray, 96 F.3d 769, 775 (5th Cir.1996), *cert. denied,* ___ U.S. ___, 117 S.Ct. 1275, 137 L.Ed.2d 351 (1997).

Eighth Circuit: United States v. Brown, 540 F.2d 364, 375 (8th Cir.1976).

Tenth Circuit: United States v. Cochran, 109 F.3d 660, 667 (10th Cir. 1997); United States v. Jain, 93 F.3d 436, 442 (8th Cir. 1996), *cert. denied,* ___ U.S. ___, 117 S.Ct. 2452, 138 L.Ed.2d 210 (1997).

51. *Tenth Circuit*: United States v. Cochran, 109 F.3d 660, 667 n. 3 (10th Cir. 1997).

52. *Fifth Circuit:* United States v. Gray, 96 F.3d 769, 775 (5th Cir. 1996) (misrepresentation is material in the context of private activity "whenever 'an employee has reason to believe the information would lead a reasonable employer to change its business conduct' "), *cert. denied,* ___ U.S. ___, 117 S.Ct. 1275, 137 L.Ed.2d 351 (1997) (citation omitted).

Tenth Circuit: United States v. Jain, 93 F.3d 436, 442 (10th Cir. 1996) (concluding that physician's failure to disclosure his receipt of referral fees was not material in

absence of evidence that patients are concerned about fees that did not affect either the price or quality of the medical services they receive), *cert. denied,* ___ U.S. ___, 117 S.Ct. 2452, 138 L.Ed.2d 210 (1997).

53. For a more general discussion of fraudulent intent, see § 17.21, and for a discussion of the requirement of gain to the defendant or loss to the victim, see § 17.8.

§ 17.21

1. *D.C. Circuit*: United States v. Winstead, 74 F.3d 1313, 1317 (D.C.Cir.1996).

First Circuit: United States v. Sawyer, 85 F.3d 713, 723 (1st Cir.1996).

Second Circuit: United States v. Wallach, 935 F.2d 445, 461 (2d Cir.1991).

Third Circuit: United States v. Copple, 24 F.3d 535, 544 (3d Cir.1994).

Fourth Circuit: United States v. Ham, 998 F.2d 1247, 1254 (4th Cir.1993).

Fifth Circuit: United States v. Walters, 87 F.3d 663, 667 (5th Cir.1996), *cert. denied,* ___ U.S. ___, 117 S.Ct. 498, 136 L.Ed.2d 390 (1996).

Sixth Circuit: United States v. Frost, 125 F.3d 346, 354 (6th Cir.1997), *petitions*

define fraudulent intent, it boils down to the intent to employ deception or deceit in order to take advantage of—or defraud—the victim. As one court explained, "Mail and wire fraud, just like common law fraud, . . . entail '[a]n intention to induce the [victim] to act or to refrain from action in reliance upon the misrepresentation.' "[2] Some courts use the terms "defraud" and "deceive" interchangeably, suggesting that they are synonymous.[3] Although the paradigm of fraudulent intent is the deliberate misrepresentation of a material fact with the intent to induce the victim to act in reliance, a fraudulent scheme need not include a specific false representation if the plan as a whole evidences the requisite deception or deceit.[4] Accordingly, the intent required for a scheme to

for cert. filed, U.S., Mar. 14, 1998 (Nos. 97–1549, 97–8295, 97–8305, 97–8328, and 97–8374).

Seventh Circuit: United States v. Vest, 116 F.3d 1179, 1183 (7th Cir.1997), *cert. denied,* __ U.S. __, 118 S.Ct. 1058, 140 L.Ed.2d 120 (1998).

Eighth Circuit: United States v. Blumeyer, 114 F.3d 758, 767 (8th Cir.), *cert. denied,* __ U.S. __, 118 S.Ct. 350, 139 L.Ed.2d 272, and __ U.S. __, 118 S.Ct. 586, 139 L.Ed.2d 423 (1997).

Ninth Circuit: United States v. Lewis, 67 F.3d 225, 232 (9th Cir.1995).

Tenth Circuit: United States v. Migliaccio, 34 F.3d 1517, 1523 (10th Cir.1994).

Eleventh Circuit: United States v. Paradies, 98 F.3d 1266, 1283 (11th Cir.1996), *cert. denied,* __ U.S. __, 117 S.Ct. 2483, 138 L.Ed.2d 992 (1997), and __ U.S. __, 118 S.Ct. 598, 139 L.Ed.2d 487 (1997).

2. *Eleventh Circuit:* Pelletier v. Zweifel, 921 F.2d 1465, 1499 (11th Cir.1991), citing the elements of common-law fraud from PROSSER AND KEETON ON TORTS 728 (5th ed.1984).

3. *Supreme Court:* Hammerschmidt v. United States, 265 U.S. 182, 188, 44 S.Ct. 511, 512, 68 L.Ed. 968 (1924) ("The words 'to defraud' commonly signify the deprivation of something of value by trick, deceit, chicane, or overreaching.")

Second Circuit: United States v. Altman, 48 F.3d 96, 101 (2d Cir.1995).

Fifth Circuit: United States v. Walters, 87 F.3d 663, 664 (5th Cir.1996), cert. denied, __ U.S. __, 117 S.Ct. 498, 136 L.Ed.2d 390 (1996).

Sixth Circuit: United States v. Smith, 39 F.3d 119, 121–22 (6th Cir.1994) ("A defendant does not commit mail fraud unless he possesses the specific intent to deceive or defraud."); Bender v. Southland Corp., 749 F.2d 1205, 1216 (6th Cir.1984) ("A scheme to defraud must involve intentional fraud, consisting in deception intentionally practiced . . .").

Ninth Circuit: United States v. Simas, 937 F.2d 459, 462–63 (9th Cir.1991) (defining "intent to defraud" as the "specific intent to deceive.")

Eleventh Circuit: United States v. Paradies, 98 F.3d 1266, 1284 (11th Cir.1996), *cert. denied,* __ U.S. __, 117 S.Ct. 2483, 138 L.Ed.2d 992 (1997) and __ U.S. __, 118 S.Ct. 598, 139 L.Ed.2d 487 (1997).

4. The mail fraud statute contains two clauses, the defraud prong and the false pretenses prong. See § 17.6 for a discussion of the difference between the clauses. For cases holding that a scheme to defraud need not contain a false representation, see:

First Circuit: United States v. Goldberg, 913 F.Supp. 629, 636–37 (D.Mass. 1996).

Second Circuit: United States v. Ashley, 905 F.Supp. 1146, 1155 (E.D.N.Y.1995). *See also* United States v. Margiotta, 688 F.2d 108, 121 (2d Cir.1982) (clauses should be interpreted as independent of one another).

Third Circuit: United States v. Rafsky, 803 F.2d 105, 108 (3d Cir.1986).

Seventh Circuit: United States v. Doherty, 969 F.2d 425, 429 (7th Cir.1992) ("a course of conduct not involving any factual misrepresentation can be prosecuted as a 'scheme to defraud' under the mail and wire fraud statutes").

Eighth Circuit: Murr Plumbing, Inc. v. Scherer Bros. Fin. Servs. Co., 48 F.3d 1066, 1069 & n. 6 (8th Cir.1995).

Tenth Circuit: United States v. Cochran, 109 F.3d 660, 664 (10th Cir.1997); United States v. Kennedy, 64 F.3d 1465, 1475–76 & n. 10 (10th Cir.1995); United States v. Cronic, 900 F.2d 1511, 1513 (10th Cir.1990).

defraud is the intent to deceive.[5] The intent to defraud requirement of mail fraud includes deliberately deceptive nondisclosures, the knowing concealment of information that one is under a duty to disclose.[6] As one court explained, "direct misrepresentations are only one form of fraud. Deceptive nondisclosures such as enticing a victim into taking steps . . . based on ignorance of a defendant's scheme to cheat or steal are covered by 18 U.S.C. §§ 1341 and 1343."[7]

There is some authority holding that intent to defraud does not require that the defendant have an evil motive.[8] There is also case law holding that the intent to defraud does not require the government to show that the defendant intended to violate the law.[9]

5. *See, e.g.,*

Third Circuit: Genty v. Resolution Trust Corp., 937 F.2d 899, 908 (3d Cir. 1991) ("the defendant must have knowledge of the illicit objectives of the fraudulent scheme and willfully intend that those larger objectives be achieved"); United States v. Pearlstein, 576 F.2d 531, 541 (3d Cir.1978) ("the evidence must indicate that the defendants had knowledge of the fraudulent nature of the . . . operation and willfully participated in the scheme with the intent that its illicit objectives be achieved").

Fifth Circuit: United States v. Gray, 105 F.3d 956, 968 (5th Cir.1997) (approving jury instruction that "acting with the intent to defraud 'means to act knowingly and with the intention or purpose to deceive or to cheat.' "), *cert. denied*, ___ U.S. ___, 117 S.Ct. 1326, 137 L.Ed.2d 487 (1997) *and* ___ U.S. ___, 117 S.Ct. 1856, 137 L.Ed.2d 1057 (1997); United States v. Jimenez, 77 F.3d 95, 97 (5th Cir.1996) (defendant must act "knowingly with the specific intent to deceive for the purpose of causing pecuniary loss to another or bringing about financial gain to himself").

Sixth Circuit: Bender v. Southland Corp., 749 F.2d 1205, 1216 (6th Cir.1984) (holding that a mail fraud scheme "must involve: [I]ntentional fraud, consisting in deception intentionally practiced to induce another to part with property.")

Seventh Circuit: United States v. Grandinetti, 891 F.2d 1302, 1306 (7th Cir.1989) (explaining the required mens rea as "knowing, intentional, or purposeful participation"); United States v. Kuecker, 740 F.2d 496, 499 (7th Cir.1984) (upholding jury instruction that acting with "intent to defraud" is the same as acting "with intent to deceive or cheat.")

6. *See, e.g.,*

Second Circuit: United States v. Altman, 48 F.3d 96, 101 (2d Cir.1995) ("The

concealment by a fiduciary of material information which he is under a duty to disclose to another under circumstances where the nondisclosure could or does result in harm to the other is a violation of the [mail fraud] statute.") (quoting United States v. Bronston, 658 F.2d 920, 926 (2d Cir.1981)); United States v. Bryser, 838 F.Supp. 124 (S.D.N.Y.1993) ("Direct misrepresentations are only one form of fraud. . . . Deceptive nondisclosures such as enticing a victim into taking steps (such as, here, placing money with what appears to be an honest safekeeping enterprise) based on ignorance of a defendant's scheme to cheat or steal are covered by 18 U.S.C. §§ 1341 and 1343.")

Sixth Circuit: United States v. Frost, 125 F.3d 346 (6th Cir.1997), *petitions for cert. filed*, U.S., Mar. 14, 1998 (Nos. 97-1549, 97-8295, 97-8305, 97-8328, and 97-8374).

D.C. Circuit: United States v. Winstead, 74 F.3d 1313 (D.C.Cir.1996) (defendant convicted of mail fraud for failing to disclose employment while receiving disability payments) ("The term false or fraudulent pretenses, representations or promises . . . includes the knowing concealment of facts that are material or important to the matter in question, and that were made or used with the intent to defraud.").

7. *Second Circuit*: United States v. Bryser, 838 F.Supp. 124, 130 (S.D.N.Y. 1993).

8. *Second Circuit*: United States v. Simon, 425 F.2d 796, 808-09 (2d Cir.1969); United States v. Savran, 755 F.Supp. 1165 (E.D.N.Y.1991).

Third Circuit: United States v. Weingold, 844 F.Supp. 1560, 1574 (D.N.J.1994).

9. *Second Circuit*: United States v. Porcelli, 865 F.2d 1352, 1358 (2d Cir.1989).

Seventh Circuit: But see United States v. Bryza, 522 F.2d 414, 420 (7th Cir.1975)

Library References:

C.J.S. Postal Service and Offenses Against Postal Laws § 23; Telegraphs, Telephones, Radio, and Television § 116–123.

West's Key No. Digests, Postal Service ⟺35; Telecommunications ⟺362.

§ 17.22 Mens Rea: Intent to Defraud—Good Faith and Reliance on the Advice of Counsel

Good faith is a complete defense to the charge of mail or wire fraud because it negates the crucial element of fraudulent intent.[1] As one court

("The burden is on the government to establish beyond a reasonable doubt that the defendant not only knowingly performed acts which the law forbids, but that he did the acts with intent to violate the law.").

Eighth Circuit: United States v. Wicker, 80 F.3d 263, 267 (8th Cir.1996) (holding that the critical inquiry is not whether the defendant intended to break the law, but whether he intended to defraud the victims of his scheme).

Eleventh Circuit: United States v. Paradies, 98 F.3d 1266, 1284 (11th Cir.1996) (upholding district court's refusal to instruct jury that defendants must know their conduct violated the law; government need only prove that the defendant had the intent to deceive), *cert. denied*, ___ U.S. ___, 117 S.Ct. 2483, 138 L.Ed.2d 992 (1997), and ___ U.S. ___, 118 S.Ct. 598, 139 L.Ed.2d 487 (1997). *See also* United States v. Hooshmand, 931 F.2d 725, 731 (11th Cir. 1991); Pelletier v. Zweifel, 921 F.2d 1465, 1499 (11th Cir.1991); United States v. Williams, 728 F.2d 1402, 1404 (11th Cir. 1984).

§ 17.22

1. *See, e.g.,*

First Circuit: United States v. Dockray, 943 F.2d 152, 154 (1st Cir.1991) ("absolute defense"); United States v. Abrahams, 466 F.Supp. 552, 555 (D.Mass.1978).

Second Circuit: United States v. Somerstein, 971 F.Supp. 736, 741 (E.D.N.Y.1997); Volmar Distribs. v. New York Post Co., 899 F.Supp. 1187, 1191 (S.D.N.Y.1995); United States v. Winans, 612 F.Supp. 827, 847 (S.D.N.Y.1985) ("complete defense"), *affirmed in part*, 791 F.2d 1024, *affirmed on other grounds sub nom.* Carpenter v. United States, 484 U.S. 19, 108 S.Ct. 316, 98 L.Ed.2d 275 (1987); United States v. Sheiner, 273 F.Supp. 977, 982–83 (S.D.N.Y.1967).

Third Circuit: United States v. Sokolow, 1994 WL 613640 *2 (E.D.Pa.1994), *affirmed*, 91 F.3d 396 (3d Cir.1996); United States v. Pitts, 1992 WL 13017 (E.D.Pa. 1992); United States v. March, 251 F.Supp.

642, 645 (M.D.Pa.1966) ("complete defense").

Fourth Circuit: United States v. Mandel, 415 F.Supp. 997, 1010 (D.Md.1976), *vacated on other grounds*, 862 F.2d 1067 (4th Cir.1988).

Fifth Circuit: United States v. Cavin, 39 F.3d 1299, 1310 (5th Cir.1994) ("A good faith defense is 'the affirmative converse of the government's burden of proving ... intent to commit a crime.' Acquittal is not optional upon a finding of good faith ... because a finding of good faith precludes a finding of fraudulent intent." (Citations omitted)).

Sixth Circuit: Henderson v. United States, 202 F.2d 400, 404 (6th Cir.1953) ("complete defense").

Seventh Circuit: United States v. Ashman, 979 F.2d 469, 480 (7th Cir.1992) ("complete defense"); United States v. Walters, 913 F.2d 388, 391 (7th Cir.1990) (same), *rev'd on other grounds*, 997 F.2d 1219 (7th Cir.1993); United States v. Martin–Trigona, 684 F.2d 485, 492 (7th Cir. 1982) (same); United States v. Rothman, 567 F.2d 744, 751 (7th Cir.1977) (same).

Eighth Circuit: United States v. Behr, 33 F.3d 1033 (8th Cir.1994) (approving the following jury instruction: "The good faith of a defendant is a complete defense to the charges of conspiracy and mail fraud ... because good faith on the part of the defendant is, simply, inconsistent with the intent to defraud ..."); United States v. Bishop, 825 F.2d 1278, 1283 (8th Cir.1987) ("complete defense"); United States v. Sherer, 653 F.2d 334, 337 (8th Cir.1981) (same).

Ninth Circuit: Pedrina v. Chun, 906 F.Supp. 1377, 1422–23 (D.Haw.1995) ("good faith generally constitutes a complete defense to any crime which requires fraudulent intent"), *aff'd*, 97 F.3d 1296 (9th Cir.1996), *cert. denied*, ___ U.S. ___, 117 S.Ct. 2441, 138 L.Ed.2d 201 (1997).

Tenth Circuit: United States v. Smith, 13 F.3d 1421, 1425–26 (10th Cir.1994) ("complete defense"); United States v. Mi-

explained, "[t]he good faith of a defendant is a complete defense to the charge of mail fraud because good faith is simply inconsistent with the intent to obtain money or property by means of false or fraudulent pretenses, representations, or promises."[2] Good faith has been defined as "a belief or opinion honestly held, an absence of malice, or ill will, and an intention to avoid taking unfair advantage of another."[3]

Although defendants frequently argue that their reliance on the advice of counsel establishes good faith, reliance on counsel is not in itself a defense. Rather, the courts treat reliance on counsel as an indication of good faith that the jury may consider.[4]

gliaccio, 34 F.3d 1517, 1524 (10th Cir.1994) (same).

Eleventh Circuit: United States v. Goss, 650 F.2d 1336, 1344–45 (5th Cir. Unit A 1981) ("complete defense").

District of Columbia: Deaver v. United States, 155 F.2d 740, 744 (D.C.Cir.1946).

2. *Tenth Circuit*: United States v. Migliaccio, 34 F.3d 1517, 1524 (10th Cir.1994) (holding that "[s] person who acts or causes another to act, on a belief or opinion honestly held, is not punishable under the mail fraud statute merely because the belief or opinion turns out to be inaccurate, incorrect, or wrong. An honest mistake in judgment or error in management does not rise to the level of intent to defraud.")

3. *Tenth Circuit*: United States v. Migliaccio, 34 F.3d 1517, 1524 (10th Cir.1994).

4. *See, e.g.,*

D.C. Circuit: United States v. Finance Comm. to Re-Elect the President, 507 F.2d 1194, 1198 (D.C.Cir.1974) (commenting that "advice of counsel is not an absolute defense," noting appellant's contention that the defense has two elements—(1) full disclosure to counsel; (2) unbiased and competent counsel—and concluding the defendant did make full disclosure); United States v. McMillan, 114 F.Supp. 638, 642–43 (D.C.Cir.1953).

Second Circuit: United States v. Winans, 612 F.Supp. 827, 848 (S.D.N.Y.1985) ("Reliance on the advice of counsel is not an absolute defense, but is one factor to be considered in assessing good faith and intent. Essential to any claim based on reliance on counsel is that the attorney must have been fully informed of all the relevant facts.... Any attorney whose advice is later used to establish good faith must have been 'unbiased and competent.'") (citations omitted), *affirmed in part*, 791 F.2d 1024, *affirmed on other grounds sub nom.* Carpenter v. United States, 484 U.S. 19, 108 S.Ct. 316, 98 L.Ed.2d 275 (1987).

Third Circuit: United States v. Pitts, 1992 WL 13017 *4 (E.D.Pa.1992) ("A defense of good faith reliance on counsel applies only when a defendant has made full and honest disclosure of all material facts to the attorney whose counsel is being sought.... The basis of the advise [sic] of counsel defense is that good faith reliance on advise [sic] of counsel negates intent.").

Fourth Circuit: Dan River v. Icahn, 701 F.2d 278, 291 (4th Cir.1983) ("while not an absolute defense, reliance upon legal counsel is evidence of good faith which rebuts inferences of criminal intent"); United States v. Painter, 314 F.2d 939, 943 (4th Cir.1963); Linden v. United States, 254 F.2d 560, 568 (4th Cir.1958) ("That the defendants proceeded under advice of a lawyer is a fact to be considered together with other facts in determining the question of the defendants' good faith, but legal advice does not under all circumstances constitute an impregnable wall of defense. To hold otherwise would be to say that no matter how violative of law a defendant's conduct may be, regardless of consciousness of wrongdoing on his part and his adviser's, the advice confers immunity.").

Fifth Circuit: Kroll v. United States, 433 F.2d 1282, 1285–86 (5th Cir.1970); Shale v. United States, 388 F.2d 616, 618 (5th Cir.1968) ("no automatic defense").

Seventh Circuit: United States v. Walters, 913 F.2d 388, 392 (7th Cir.1990) (finding reversible error in trial court's failure to provide an advice-of-counsel instruction to the jury as a theory of defense), *rev'd on other grounds*, 997 F.2d 1219 (7th Cir. 1993).

Ninth Circuit: Pedrina v. Chun, 906 F.Supp. 1377, 1423 (D.Haw.1995) ("Reliance on the advice of counsel is a circumstance indicating good faith which the trier of fact is entitled to consider on the issue of fraudulent intent. A claim of good faith reliance on counsel requires that the advice be obtained after full disclosure of all the

When a defendant claims that reliance on the advice of counsel negates any implication of fraudulent intent, the courts look carefully at the circumstances under which the legal advice was provided. In order to negate intent, it is generally necessary to show that the defendant informed the attorney fully of all material facts[5] and consulted the attorney for his or her legal advice, not to ensure the success of the scheme.[6] Some courts have noted that this defense requires reliance on the advice of an unbiased and competent attorney who is not a participant in the scheme.[7]

Library References:

C.J.S. Postal Service and Offenses Against Postal Laws § 23; Telegraphs, Telephones, Radio, and Television § 116–123.

West's Key No. Digests, Postal Service ⚖35; Telecommunications ⚖362.

§ 17.23 Mens Rea: Intent to Defraud—Reckless Disregard for Truth or Falsity

Despite the general recognition that the mail and wire fraud statutes require specific intent, a number of the lower courts nonetheless

facts to which the advice pertains. The defendant must also show that he actually relied on the advice, believing it to be correct. Reliance on advice of counsel will not shield a party who simply confers with an attorney as one would confer with any business associate. It will also not shield defendants who retain counsel to insure the success of their fraudulent schemes, rather than to secure legal advice." (Citations omitted)), *aff'd*, 97 F.3d 1296 (9th Cir. 1996), *cert. denied*, ___ U.S. ___, 117 S.Ct. 2441, 138 L.Ed.2d 201 (1997); United States v. Shewfelt, 455 F.2d 836, 839 (9th Cir.1972).

Tenth Circuit: Rea v. Wichita Mortgage Corp., 747 F.2d 567, 576 (10th Cir.1984).

Eleventh Circuit: United States v. Parker, 839 F.2d 1473, 1482 n. 6 (11th Cir. 1988) ("To succeed with a defense of good faith reliance on the advice of counsel, the defendant must show that 1) he fully disclosed all relevant facts to his counsel and 2) he relied in good faith on his counsel's advice.")

5. *D.C. Circuit*: United States v. Finance Comm. to Re-Elect the President, 507 F.2d 1194, 1198 (D.C.Cir.1974).

Second Circuit: United States v. Winans, 612 F.Supp. 827, 847 (S.D.N.Y.1985), *affirmed in part*, 791 F.2d 1024 (2d Cir.), *affirmed on other grounds sub nom.* Carpenter v. United States, 484 U.S. 19, 108 S.Ct. 316, 98 L.Ed.2d 275 (1987).

Third Circuit: United States v. Pitts, 1992 WL 13017 * 4 (E.D.Pa.1992).

Fourth Circuit: United States v. Painter, 314 F.2d 939, 943 (4th Cir.1963).

Fifth Circuit: Shale v. United States, 388 F.2d 616, 618 n. 2 (5th Cir.1968).

Seventh Circuit: *See* United States v. Walters, 913 F.2d 388, 391–92 (7th Cir. 1990) (if defendant presented evidence that he provided his attorney with all material evidence known to him, he is entitled to have jury instructed on advice of counsel/good faith defense).

Ninth Circuit: Pedrina v. Chun, 906 F.Supp. 1377, 1423 (D.Haw.1995), *affirmed other grounds*, 97 F.3d 1296 (9th Cir.), *cert. denied*, ___ U.S. ___, 117 S.Ct. 2441, 138 L.Ed.2d 201 (1997).

Eleventh Circuit: United States v. Parker, 839 F.2d 1473, 1482 n. 6 (11th Cir. 1988); United States v. Conner, 752 F.2d 566, 574 (11th Cir.1985).

6. *Ninth Circuit*: Pedrina v. Chun, 906 F.Supp. 1377, 1423 (D.Haw.1995), *affirmed other grounds*, 97 F.3d 1296 (9th Cir.), *cert. denied*, ___ U.S. ___, 117 S.Ct. 2441, 138 L.Ed.2d 201 (1997).

Eleventh Circuit: United States v. Conner, 752 F.2d 566, 574 (11th Cir.1985).

7. *D.C. Circuit*: United States v. Finance Comm. to Re-Elect the President, 507 F.2d 1194, 1198 (D.C.Cir.1974).

Second Circuit: United States v. Winans, 612 F.Supp. 827, 847 (S.D.N.Y.1985), *affirmed in part*, 791 F.2d 1024 (2d Cir.), *affirmed on other grounds sub nom.* Carpenter v. United States, 484 U.S. 19, 108 S.Ct. 316, 98 L.Ed.2d 275 (1987).

hold that these statutes reach not only those defendants who intentionally misrepresent, but also defendants who make representations with a reckless disregard for truth or falsity.[1] The courts that apply this reckless disregard standard have taken the standard from civil fraud cases, as well as from cases involving securities fraud and bank fraud.[2] The courts which hold that reckless disregard as to truth or falsity is sufficient for mail or wire fraud often explain that reckless disregard is legally equivalent to intentional misrepresentation.[3] The Second Circuit has explained, "If the defendants acted willfully and purposely with an evil intent, or with a reckless indifference to the truth, then they are chargeable with the requisite knowledge and criminal intent."[4] As support for this principle, the court quoted the following statement by Judge Learned Hand:

> [A]lthough a man might not be charged for his honest beliefs, however imbecile they might be, it was not necessary to show that he disbelieved what he said. Some utterances are in such form as to imply knowledge at first hand, and the utterer may be liable, even though he believes them, if he has no knowledge on the subject. And all unconditional utterances, intended to be taken seriously, imply at

§ 17.23

1. *Second Circuit*: United States v. Sheiner, 273 F.Supp. 977, 983 (S.D.N.Y. 1967).

Third Circuit: United States v. Universal Rehabilitation Servs. Inc., 1996 WL 297575 *1 (E.D.Pa.1996); United States v. Coyle, 63 F.3d 1239, 1243 (3d Cir.1995); United States v. Boyer, 694 F.2d 58, 59 (3d Cir.1982).

Fifth Circuit: United States v. Quadro Corp., 928 F.Supp. 688, 696 (E.D.Tex.1996), *aff'd*, 127 F.3d 34 (5th Cir.1997).

Eighth Circuit: United States v. Marley, 549 F.2d 561, 563 (8th Cir.1977); United States v. Henderson, 446 F.2d 960 (8th Cir.1971).

Ninth Circuit: Irwin v. United States, 338 F.2d 770, 772 (9th Cir.1964).

Tenth Circuit: United States v. Prows, 118 F.3d 686, 691 (10th Cir.1997).

2. *Third Circuit:* Kronfeld v. New Jersey Nat'l Bank, 638 F.Supp. 1454, 1465 (D.N.J.1986) (intent standard under mail and wire fraud statutes is identical to scienter standard in 10(b)[of the Securities and Exchange Act of 1934] actions); United States v. Boyer, 694 F.2d 58, 59 (3d Cir. 1982) (citing McLean v. Alexander, 599 F.2d 1190, 1196 (3d Cir.1979) for the proposition that "the scienter required to sustain a claim under Section 10(b) [of the Securities Exchange Act of 1934] included misrepresentations made knowingly or willfully, or with reckless disregard for their truth or

falsity, or without a genuine belief in their truth."). Although noting that the standard of proof for civil liability in fraud is lower than the proof beyond a reasonable doubt required for a criminal conviction, the court concluded that "there is no reason to suppose that in enacting criminal statutes prohibiting mail or securities fraud that Congress intended that the substantive element of the offense—the scienter—should be different than for civil liability for fraud." *Id.*

3. *Third Circuit*: United States v. Boyer, 694 F.2d 58, 59 (3d Cir.1982) (holding that reckless indifference is the equivalent of intentional misrepresentation "because you may not recklessly represent something as true which is not true, even if you don't know it, if the fact that you don't know it is due to reckless conduct on your part.").

Eighth Circuit: Baker v. United States, 115 F.2d 533, 541 (8th Cir.1940) ("The charge that the representations were false was the legal equivalent of a charge that they were made in reckless disregard of the truth."); United States v. Henderson, 446 F.2d 960, 966 (8th Cir.1971) ("Such irresponsibility [reckless disregard] can rise to the level of criminal conduct.") (citing Elbel v. United States, 364 F.2d 127, 134 (10th Cir.1966); United States v. Meyer, 359 F.2d 837, 839 (7th Cir.1966)).

4. *Second Circuit*: United States v. Sheiner, 273 F.Supp. 977, 982 (S.D.N.Y. 1967) (citing Irwin v. United States, 338 F.2d 770, 774 (9th Cir.1964)).

least a belief, and, if the utterer does not believe them, they are false, though his mind be quite indeterminate as to their truth.[5]

Courts have often applied the reckless disregard standard when it was clear that the defendant had a duty to ascertain whether the facts that he was asserting were true or false.[6]

Although it is difficult to see how the reckless disregard standard can be reconciled with the concept of fraud as a specific intent crime, few courts have addressed this issue.[7] The reckless disregard standard also effectively restricts the good faith defense. If a defendant's misrepresentations were made in subjective good faith, but he acted with reckless disregard for the truth, he will have no defense in a court that treats reckless disregard as sufficient.[8]

Library References:

C.J.S. Postal Service and Offenses Against Postal Laws § 23; Telegraphs, Telephones, Radio, and Television § 116–123.
West's Key No. Digests, Postal Service ☞35; Telecommunications ☞362.

§ 17.24 Mens Rea: Intent to Defraud—Intent to Cause Harm or Injury

Many of the lower courts have held that fraudulent intent is not present unless the defendant intended or foresaw that his deceit or misrepresentation would result in harm or injury.[1] This interpretation of

5. *Second Circuit*: Knickerbocker Merchandising Co. v. United States, 13 F.2d 544, 545 (2d Cir.1926).

6. *Supreme Court*: Spurr v. United States, 174 U.S. 728, 735, 19 S.Ct. 812, 815, 43 L.Ed. 1150 (1899) ("If an officer certifies a check with the intent that the drawer shall obtain so much money out of the bank, when he has none there, such officer not only certifies unlawfully, but the specific intent to violate the statute may be imputed. And so evil design may be presumed if the officer purposely keeps himself in ignorance of whether the drawer has money in the bank or not, or is grossly indifferent to his duty in respect to the ascertainment of that fact.").

Eighth Circuit: United States v. Henderson, 446 F.2d 960, 966 (8th Cir. 1971) ("It is well established that ignorance of inculpatory facts due to a reckless disregard is no more a defense than ignorance of inculpatory law.").

7. The argument that the reckless disregard lowers the standard of specific intent was discussed and rejected in United States v. Boyer, 694 F.2d 58 (3d Cir.1982). In rejecting the argument, the court was heavily influenced by the scienter requirement for securities fraud, and it commented that it found no reason to think Congress

intended the standards for fraud to be different. 694 F.2d at 59.

8. *Third Circuit: See* United States v. Boyer, 694 F.2d 58, 59–60 (3d Cir.1982).

§ 17.24

1. *Second Circuit*: United States v. Zagari, 111 F.3d 307, 327 (2d Cir.1997) ("To establish the existence of a scheme to defraud, the government must present proof that the defendants possessed a fraudulent intent.... [T]he government is not required to show that the intended victim was actually defrauded [but] need only show that the defendants contemplated some actual harm or injury.") (quoting United States v. Wallach, 935 F.2d 445, 461 (2d Cir.1991)), *cert. denied*, ___ U.S. ___, 118 S.Ct. 445, 139 L.Ed.2d 381 (1997); United States v. Somerstein, 971 F.Supp. 736, 741 (E.D.N.Y.1997) ("The government must show that some actual harm or injury was contemplated by the schemer.").

Fifth Circuit: United States v. Blocker, 104 F.3d 720, 730 (5th Cir.1997) ("The intent to defraud for purposes of mail fraud requires intent to deceive and to cause some harm to result from the deceit."); United States v. Jimenez, 77 F.3d 95, 97 (5th Cir.1996).

Ninth Circuit: United States v. Simas, 937 F.2d 459, 462–63 (9th Cir.1991); United

mens rea parallels the case law holding that injury to the victim is an essential component of the concept of scheme to defraud.[2] When the "necessary result" of the actor's scheme is to injure others, fraudulent intent may be inferred from the scheme itself and this requirement poses no additional obstacle for the government.[3] Similarly, if the government can demonstrate loss by a victim of the alleged fraud, then that evidence of loss may be treated as evidence of the schemer's intent to defraud.[4] However, where there has been no actual injury and harm to the victim was not a necessary result of the scheme, the government may be required to produce independent evidence to show this aspect of the defendant's fraudulent intent.[5]

Library References:

C.J.S. Postal Service and Offenses Against Postal Laws § 23; Telegraphs, Telephones, Radio, and Television § 116–123.

West's Key No. Digests, Postal Service ☜35; Telecommunications ☜362.

§ 17.25   Mens Rea: Intent to Defraud—Proof of Intent

The intent to defraud does not have to be proven by direct evidence. On the contrary, it may be inferred from circumstantial evidence,[1] and it will often be the case that the requisite intent to defraud may be established by inference from facts and circumstances surrounding a transaction.[2]

Library References:

C.J.S. Postal Service and Offenses Against Postal Laws § 23; Telegraphs, Telephones, Radio, and Television § 116–123.

West's Key No. Digests, Postal Service ☜35; Telecommunications ☜362.

§ 17.26   Vagueness Objections to Broad Interpretations of the Mail and Wire Fraud Statutes

One element of the Due Process clauses of the Fifth and Fourteenth Amendments is a proscription against "vague" criminal statutes.[1] The

States v. Lewis, 67 F.3d 225, 232 (9th Cir. 1995).

2. For a discussion of this aspect of scheme to defraud, see § 17.8.

3. *Second Circuit*: United States v. Somerstein, 971 F.Supp. 736, 741 (E.D.N.Y. 1997)

4. *Third Circuit*: United States v. Sokolow, 91 F.3d 396 (3d Cir.1996), cert. denied, ___ U.S. ___, 117 S.Ct. 960, 136 L.Ed.2d 846 (1997).

5. *Id.*

§ 17.25

1. *Second Circuit*: United States v. Zagari, 111 F.3d 307, 327 (2d Cir.1997), *cert. denied*, ___ U.S. ___, 118 S.Ct. 445, 139 L.Ed.2d 381 (1997) (citing United States v. Gelb, 700 F.2d 875, 880 (2d Cir.1983)).

Eleventh Circuit: United States v. Hawkins, 905 F.2d 1489, 1496 (11th Cir.1990) ("The government need not produce direct proof of scienter in a [mail] fraud case; circumstantial evidence of criminal intent can suffice.").

2. *Eighth Circuit*: United States v. Blumeyer, 114 F.3d 758, 766 (8th Cir.1997), *cert. denied*, ___ U.S. ___, 118 S.Ct. 350, 139 L.Ed.2d 272 (1997), and ___ U.S. ___, 118 S.Ct. 586, 139 L.Ed.2d 423 (1997); United States v. Behr, 33 F.3d 1033, 1035 (8th Cir.1994); United States v. Clausen, 792 F.2d 102, 105 (8th Cir.1986); United States v. Sedovic, 500 F.Supp. 515 (E.D.Mo.1980).

§ 17.26

1. For a general discussion of the void for vagueness doctrine as applied in criminal cases, see 1 WAYNE LaFAVE & AUSTIN

Supreme Court has held that the void for vagueness doctrine " 'requires that a penal statute define the criminal offense with sufficient definiteness that ordinary people can understand what conduct is prohibited and in a manner that does not encourage arbitrary and discriminatory enforcement.' "[2]

Given the breadth of the mail and wire fraud statutes, especially as extended by 18 U.S.C. § 1346, some judges and legal commentators have suggested that the mail and wire fraud statutes cannot meet this standard.[3] The statutes plainly allow enormous leeway for prosecutorial discretion, and there is scholarly support for the view that some mail fraud prosecutions have been politically motivated.[4]

Despite the concerns expressed by academics, and occasionally in judicial opinions, most of the lower court decisions have dispatched vagueness claims with little difficulty.[5]

Some of the cases have focused on the breadth of the general concept of fraud as it has been construed under the mail and wire fraud statutes. A 1997 decision from the Sixth Circuit reviewed the reasons lower courts have given for rejecting vagueness objections to the flexible and expansive reading the federal courts have given to the concept of fraud under the mail and wire fraud statutes:

> "Section 1341 has withstood repeated challenges which have raised the claim that it does not provide fair notice and warning of the conduct proscribed by the statute. The broad language of the stat-

SCOTT, JR., SUBSTANTIVE CRIMINAL LAW § 2.3 (1986), and John C. Jeffries, *Legality, Vagueness, and the Construction of Penal Statutes*, 71 VA. L. REV. 189 (1985).

2. *Supreme Court:* Posters 'N' Things, Ltd. v. United States, 511 U.S. 513, 525, 114 S.Ct. 1747, 1754, 128 L.Ed.2d 539 (1994), *quoting* Kolender v. Lawson, 461 U.S. 352, 357, 103 S.Ct. 1855, 1858, 75 L.Ed.2d 903 (1983).

3. Craig M. Bradley, *Foreword: Mail Fraud after* McNally *and* Carpenter: *The Essence of Fraud*, 79 J. CRIM. L. & CRIMINOL-OGY, 573, 620–21 (1988); Ellen S. Podgor, *Mail Fraud: Opening Letters*, 43 S.C. L. REV. 236–39, 267–71 (1992).

The leading judicial statement of these concerns is Judge Ralph Winter's opinion in United States v. Margiotta, 688 F.2d 108, 139–41 (2d Cir.1982) (Winter, J., concurring and dissenting). More recently, in Emery v. American General Finance, Inc., 71 F.3d 1343, 1346 (7th Cir.1995), the court collected a number of other cases in which similar concerns had been expressed. *See also* McNally v. United States, 483 U.S. 350, 360, 107 S.Ct. 2875, 2881, 97 L.Ed.2d 292 (1987), in which a majority of the Court limited the scope of the mail fraud statute to property rights, "[r]ather than to construe the statute in a manner that leaves its outer boundaries ambiguous and involves the Federal Government in setting standards of disclosure and good government for local and state officials." Since § 1346 amended the statute to incorporate the honest services theory upon which the government relied in *McNally*, critics argue that the outer boundaries of the statutes are now "ambiguous."

4. *See* Gregory H. Williams, *Good Government by Prosecutorial Decree: The Use and Abuse of the Mail Fraud Statute*, 32 ARIZ. L. REV. 137, 147–48 (1990) (describing political motivation for prosecutions of Preston Tucker and former Illinois governor Otto Kerner, whom Richard Nixon held responsible for his loss to John Kennedy in 1960 presidential election).

5. Several courts have dismissed vagueness claims out of hand. *See, e.g.,*

Fourth Circuit: United States v. Condolon, 600 F.2d 7, 9 (4th Cir.1979).

Seventh Circuit: United States v. Feinberg, 535 F.2d 1004, 1010 (7th Cir.1976). *Feinberg* was followed without discussion in United States v. Brocksmith, 991 F.2d 1363, 1366 n. 1 (7th Cir.1993), and United States v. Suter, 755 F.2d 523, 527 n. 5 (7th Cir.1985).

ute, intended by Congress to be sufficiently flexible to cover the wide range of fraudulent schemes mankind is capable of devising, is not unconstitutionally vague because § 1341 contains the requirement that the defendant must have acted willfully and with a specific intent to defraud."

Indeed, the law traditionally has conceived of "fraud" in general as a necessarily fluid concept; as one court has observed, fraud "is as old as falsehood and as versable as human ingenuity." "That there may be marginal cases in which it is difficult to determine the side of the line on which a particular fact situation falls is no sufficient reason to hold the language too ambiguous to define a criminal offense." Moreover, the case law provides innumerable illustrations of how an individual clearly may perpetrate a "scheme to defraud," thereby belying the claim that § 1341 has no valid application.[6]

This passage touches on three key points relied upon by other courts: (1) a recognition that a flexible definition is necessary to respond to new forms of fraud, which evolve constantly,[7] (2) the notion that prior decisional law clarifies somewhat the scope of the mail and wire fraud statutes,[8] and (3) a reliance on the element of specific intent to narrow the reach of the statutes to cases of deliberate wrongdoing, which provides its own notice.[9]

Since the adoption of § 1346, several lower courts have considered vagueness challenges in mail and wire fraud cases premised on claims that state or local government officials deprived the public of their honest services. Two features of such cases are relevant to the analysis

---

6. *Sixth Circuit:* United States v. Frost, 125 F.3d 346, 370 (6th Cir.1997), *petitions for cert. filed*, U.S., Mar. 14, 1998 (Nos. 97–1549, 97–8295, 97–8305, 97–8328, and 97–8374) (citations omitted).

7. One of the most well known statements of this position is Chief Justice Burger's often-cited statement that a flexible definition of fraud is necessary in order to cope with "the new varieties of fraud that the ever-inventive American 'con artist' is sure to develop." United States v. Maze, 414 U.S. 395, 407, 94 S.Ct. 645, 651, 38 L.Ed.2d 603 (1974) (Burger, C.J., dissenting).

8. *First Circuit:* United States v. Young, 955 F.2d 99, 104 (1st Cir.1992) (rejecting vagueness claim with comment that "[w]e see nothing vague, however, about legal terminology used for nearly two hundred years.")

Ninth Circuit: United States v. Bohonus, 628 F.2d 1167, 1173–74 (9th Cir.1980) (numerous prior decisions "afforded the defendant reasonable notice that his conduct might well fall within the proscription of the mail fraud statute.")

9. *Seventh Circuit:* Emery v. American General Finance, Inc., 71 F.3d 1343, 1346 (7th Cir.1995) (commenting that consistent with concern regarding vagueness, court's recent cases make it clear that all the mail fraud statute punishes is "deliberate fraud.")

Ninth Circuit: United States v. Bohonus, 628 F.2d 1167, 1173–74 (9th Cir.1980).

Tenth Circuit: United States v. Stewart, 872 F.2d 957, 959 (10th Cir.1989).

Eleventh Circuit: United States v. Conner, 752 F.2d 566, 574 (11th Cir.1985).

The lower courts have relied on a series of Supreme Court decisions holding that a scienter element can mitigate a law's vagueness. *See, e.g.*, Posters 'N' Things, Ltd. v. United States, 511 U.S. 513, 525, 114 S.Ct. 1747, 1754, 128 L.Ed.2d 539 (1994); Village of Hoffman Estates v. Flipside, Hoffman Estates, 455 U.S. 489, 499, 102 S.Ct. 1186, 1193, 71 L.Ed.2d 362 (1982); Colautti v. Franklin, 439 U.S. 379, 395, 99 S.Ct. 675, 685, 58 L.Ed.2d 596 (1979); Screws v. United States, 325 U.S. 91, 101–02, 65 S.Ct. 1031, 1035, 89 L.Ed. 1495 (1945) (plurality opinion).

of vagueness claims. First, it is well settled that statutory ambiguity is especially problematical when it may chill speech or other activities protected by the First Amendment.[10] Second, where the defendants are state or local officials, political considerations may provide a motivation for discriminatory enforcement of a statute that gives prosecutors too much leeway. It may therefore seem surprising that vagueness claims have been equally unsuccessful in honest services prosecutions.

Although no case under § 1346 has reached the Supreme Court, several lower courts have rejected vagueness challenges to honest services prosecutions brought under § 1346. As noted above,[11] the courts have generally agreed that certain forms of conduct fall within the ambit of honest services under § 1346, particularly bribery, the receipt of kickbacks, and the failure to disclose serious conflicts of interest. Accordingly, where the government has proved conduct of this nature, a vagueness challenge will ordinarily be rejected on the ground that the defendant had ample notice of the criminality of his conduct.[12] For example, the Eleventh Circuit rejected a vagueness challenge to a city councilman's honest services conviction. It noted that the pre-*McNally* cases had uniformly construed the mail fraud statute to cover the situation where public officials received bribes,[13] concluded that "[it] should be plain to ordinary people that offering and accepting large sums of money in return for a city councilman's vote is the type of conduct prohibited by the language of § 1346."[14] Similarly, a district court in the Ninth Circuit rejected a vagueness claim on the grounds that a person of reasonable intelligence would know that a sitting judge's acceptance of bribes would constitute a criminal offense.[15] Courts rejecting vagueness challenges to § 1346 have also emphasized the importance of the requirement of specific intent to commit a fraud.[16]

10. For a scholarly discussion of vagueness objections to honest services prosecutions, see John C. Coffee, Jr., *The Metastasis of Mail Fraud: The Continuing Story of the Evolution of White–Collar Crime*, 21 Am. Crim. L. Rev. 1, 7–10, 13–17 (1983); Gregory H. Williams, *Good Government by Prosecutorial Decree: The Use and Abuse of the Mail Fraud Statute*, 32 Ariz. L. Rev. 137, 150–53 (1990).

11. See § 17.19.

12. *Fourth Circuit: See* United States v. Bryan, 58 F.3d 933, 942 (4th Cir.1995) (rejecting vagueness challenge on the ground that the director of a state lottery should have known that he was acting unlawfully in fraudulently manipulating government contracts and using confidential, non-public information to purchase the securities of companies doing business with the lottery).

13. *Eleventh Circuit:* United States v. Paradies, 98 F.3d 1266, 1283 n. 30 (11th Cir.1996), *cert. denied,* ___ U.S. ___, 117 S.Ct. 2483, 138 L.Ed.2d 992 (1997), and ___

U.S. ___, 118 S.Ct. 598, 139 L.Ed.2d 487 (1997).

14. *Eleventh Circuit:* United States v. Paradies, 98 F.3d 1266, 1283 (11th Cir. 1996), *cert. denied,* ___ U.S. ___, 117 S.Ct. 2483, 138 L.Ed.2d 992 (1997), and ___ U.S. ___, 118 S.Ct. 598, 139 L.Ed.2d 487 (1997).

15. *Ninth Circuit:* United States v. Frega, 933 F.Supp. 1536, 1547 (S.D.Cal. 1996).

16. *Fifth Circuit: Cf.* United States v. Gray, 96 F.3d 769, 776–77 (5th Cir.1996) (rejecting vagueness challenge by mens' basketball coaches at Baylor University who executed a fraudulent scheme to establish academic eligibility for five transfer students to play basketball despite their knowledge of NCAA rules and of Baylor's requirement that coaches notify school of any NCAA violation), *cert. denied,* ___ U.S. ___, 117 S.Ct. 1275, 137 L.Ed.2d 351 (1997).

Ninth Circuit: United States v. Frega, 933 F.Supp. 1536, 1547 (S.D.Cal.1996) (holding that § 1346 was not unconstitu-

It should be noted that to date the government has been relatively cautious in its use of § 1346. It is by no means clear that the cases upholding § 1346 in prosecutions involving bribes and kickbacks provide any indication of how the courts would resolve a vagueness challenge to a prosecution at the outer limits of the honest services theory.[17]

§ 17.27   Jurisdiction—In General

Although the mail and wire fraud statutes are otherwise parallel, they are distinguished by their jurisdictional elements.

The jurisdictional language of the mail fraud act, 18 U.S.C. § 1341 (1994), is convoluted. It provides that a person who has devised a scheme or artifice to defraud commits an offense if he—

> "for the purpose of executing such scheme or artifice or attempting so to do, places in any post office or authorized depository for mail matter, any matter or thing whatever to be sent or delivered by the Postal Service,"

> "or takes or receives therefrom, any such matter or thing,"

> "or knowingly causes to be delivered by mail ... according to the direction thereon, or at the place at which it is directed to be delivered by the person to whom it is addressed, any such matter or thing."

The statute thus covers depositing mail, receiving mail, and knowingly causing mail to be delivered by third parties, if the mailing is "for the purpose of executing such scheme or artifice to defraud." Moreover, although § 1346 is captioned—and popularly known—as the mail fraud statute, an amendment in 1994 extended its scope to the use of the private or commercial interstate carriers, such as United Parcel Service and Federal Express.[1]

tionally vague where the Government alleged a specific intent to defraud the people of California by depriving them of their right to the honest services).

Eleventh Circuit: United States v. Castro, 89 F.3d 1443, 1449 (11th Cir.1996) (holding that the term "honest services" in the mail fraud statute is not unconstitutionally vague because it requires a specific intent to defraud), *cert. denied,* ___ U.S. ___, 117 S.Ct. 965, 136 L.Ed.2d 850 (1997); United States v. Paradies, 98 F.3d 1266, 1283 (1996) (vagueness challenge must fail because evidence was overwhelming that these defendants intended to defraud the citizens of honest services), *cert. denied,* ___ U.S. ___, 117 S.Ct. 2483, 138 L.Ed.2d 992 (1997), and ___ U.S. ___, 118 S.Ct. 598, 139 L.Ed.2d 487 (1997); United States v. Waymer, 55 F.3d 564, 568–69 (11th Cir.1995) (holding that § 1346 was not unconstitutionally vague as applied because the Government had carried its burden of proving

specific intent to commit a fraud), *cert. denied,* 517 U.S. 1119, 116 S.Ct. 1350, 134 L.Ed.2d 519 (1996).

17. For example, what if a candidate mails a political brochure or appears in a TV ad making a campaign promise the candidate did not intend to carry out? *See* United States v. Margiotta, 688 F.2d 108, 141 (2d Cir.1982) (Winter, J., concurring and dissenting). *See also* Ellen S. Podgor, *Mail Fraud: Opening Letters,* 43 S.C. L. REV. 223, 238–39 (1992) (hypothesizing a mail fraud prosecution based upon George Bush's statement "Read my lips: no new taxes").

§ 17.27

1. As amended by the Violent Crime Control and Law Enforcement Act of 1994, Pub.L. No. 103–322, § 250006, 108 Stat. 1796, 2087, the statute provides that it is a crime if one who has devised a scheme to defraud "deposits or causes to be deposited

The wire fraud statute, 18 U.S.C. § 1343 (1994), provides that a person who has devised a scheme or artifice to defraud commits an offense if he "transmits or causes to be transmitted by means of wire, radio, or television communication in interstate or foreign commerce, any writings, signs, signals, pictures, or sounds for the purpose of executing such scheme or artifice." This provision has been applied to telephone calls,[2] wire fund transfers,[3] faxes[4] and other transmissions via wire,[5] microwave,[6] or satellite.[7] Although the interpretation of the mail and wire fraud acts is generally parallel, one important distinction is noted in § 17.29.

§ 17.28 Jurisdiction—The Connection Between the Fraudulent Scheme and the Mailing or Wire Transmission

The Supreme Court has explored the issue of the requisite connection between the scheme to defraud and the mailing in a series of cases.[1] In *Schmuck v. United States*[2] the Court summarized its prior decisions, stating:

"The federal mail fraud statute does not purport to reach all frauds, but only those limited instances in which the use of the mails is a part of the execution of the fraud, leaving all other cases to be dealt with by appropriate state law." To be part of the execution of the fraud, however, the use of the mails need not be an essential element of the scheme. It is sufficient for the mailing to be "incident to an essential part of the scheme,"or "a step in [the] plot."[3]

The standard articulated in *Schmuck* is consistent with the language of § 1341, which requires a mailing "for the purpose of executing such

any matter or thing whatever to be sent or delivered by any private or commercial interstate carrier, ... or knowingly causes to be delivered ... by such carrier...." 18 U.S.C. § 1341 (1994).

2. *See, e.g.,*

First Circuit: United States v. Cassiere, 4 F.3d 1006, 1012 (1st Cir.1993).

3. *See, e.g.,*

Fourth Circuit: United States v. Aramony, 88 F.3d 1369–74 (4th Cir.1996).

Fifth Circuit: United States v. Allen, 1348, 1362 (5th Cir.1996).

Ninth Circuit: United States v. Rude, 88 F.3d 1538, 1544 (9th Cir.1996).

4. *First Circuit:* United States v. Lopez, 71 F.3d 954, 961 (1st Cir.1995); United States v. Cassiere, 4 F.3d 1006, 1012 (1st Cir.1993).

5. *First Circuit:* United States v. Fermin Castillo, 829 F.2d 1194, 1197 (1st Cir. 1987) (telexes).

Eighth Circuit: United States v. Gaultier, 727 F.2d 711, 716 (8th Cir.1984).

6. *Eighth Circuit:* United States v. Gaultier, 727 F.2d 711, 716 (8th Cir.1984); United States v. Bohr, 581 F.2d 1294, 1303 (8th Cir.1978).

7. *Eighth Circuit:* United States v. Gaultier, 727 F.2d 711, 716 (8th Cir.1984).

§ 17.28

1. For a critical analysis of these cases concluding that the Court has flip-flopped between narrow and broad readings of the mailing element, see Peter J. Henning, *Maybe It Should Just Be Called Federal Fraud: The Changing Nature of the Mail Fraud Statute*, 36 B.C. L.Rev. 435, 450–60 (1995).

2. 489 U.S. 705, 109 S.Ct. 1443, 103 L.Ed.2d 734 (1989).

3. 489 U.S. 705, 710–711, 109 S.Ct. 1443, 1447–48, 103 L.Ed.2d 734 (citations and footnote omitted).

scheme or artifice." While not requiring that the mailing be an essential part of the scheme, the Court did require that the mailing be a part of the execution of the scheme, a step in the plot. These principles apply to wire fraud cases as well as mail fraud cases.[4]

The application of this standard in *Schmuck* demonstrates, however, that a mailing or wire transmission that is quite peripheral to a fraudulent scheme may nonetheless trigger federal jurisdiction under the mail and wire fraud acts. The scheme to defraud in *Schmuck* involved rolling back car odometers and selling the vehicles at inflated prices to retail dealers, who in turn sold the cars to unwitting consumers. Schmuck's scheme had been in operation for 15 years at the time he was prosecuted for mail fraud. The government alleged that the requisite mailing occurred when retail dealers mailed the title registration materials for a vehicle to the state. Even though the registration-form mailings did not contribute directly to the duping of either retail dealers or their customers, and indeed occurred *after* Schmuck had obtained payment, the Supreme Court upheld Schmuck's mail fraud conviction by a 5–to–4 vote. The majority emphasized that the scheme was an ongoing venture. A rational jury "could have found that the title registration mailings were part of the execution of the fraudulent scheme," because the retail dealers' willingness to purchase cars from Schmuck depended on their ability to transfer title when they resold the cars.[5] Since the registration form-mailings were essential for the passage of title, the majority concluded that the mailings were incident to an essential part of the scheme.[6]

The dissenters in *Schmuck* argued that the Court's prior decisions had established that a mailing made after a scheme reaches fruition does not in any way execute or further the scheme, and hence does not satisfy the mail fraud statute.[7] The dissenters emphasized that the mail fraud act extends federal jurisdiction only to "mail fraud, not mail and fraud."[8] Only a mailing "in furtherance of the fraud" triggers the mail fraud statute.[9] As a critic of *Schmuck* has noted, the mailings "bore no relationship to the odometer tampering at the root of the fraud," and were "a happenstance of the state's registration system . . . completely

---

4. *Fifth Circuit*: United States v. Allen, 76 F.3d 1348, 1362–63 (5th Cir.1996).

5. 489 U.S. at 712, 109 S.Ct. at 1448.

6. 489 U.S. at 712, 109 S.Ct. at 1448.

7. In *United States v. Maze*, 414 U.S. 395, 94 S.Ct. 645, 38 L.Ed.2d 603 (1974), the Supreme Court reversed a mail fraud conviction based on the use of a stolen credit card because the scheme reached fruition when the defendant received the goods and services, long before the merchants mailed the receipts to the credit card company for reimbursement. Similarly, in *Kann v. United States*, 323 U.S. 88, 95, 65 S.Ct. 148, 151, 89 L.Ed. 88 (1944), the

Court concluded that mail fraud charges could not be based upon a bank's submission of checks to another bank for payment, because the fraudulent scheme had already reached fruition when the defendant cashed the checks obtained through the fraud. Theses cases, the dissenters argued, were indistinguishable from *Schmuck* and required the conclusion that there had been no violation of the mail fraud statute.

8. 489 U.S. at 722–723, 109 S.Ct. at 1453–54 (Scalia, J., dissenting).

9. 489 U.S. at 722–723, 109 S.Ct. at 1453–54 (Scalia, J., dissenting).

unaffected by the defendant's actions."[10]

At one level, the difference between the majority and dissent in *Schmuck* turns largely on how the "scheme to defraud" is defined. The majority defined the scheme in *Schmuck* as a large scale multi-year operation encompassing the sale of more than 150 cars, which required the mailing of each car's title.[11] In contrast, it defined the scope of the schemes in prior cases more narrowly. For example, in *Maze* and *Kann* the Court treated each separate use of a stolen credit card as a separate scheme that reached fruition when the defendant received the goods or services he purchased with the credit card.[12] Thus mailings that occurred after the defendant paid with the stolen card were not in furtherance of the fraudulent scheme, which was already complete. The dissenters argued that the fraud committed by Schmuck "was complete with respect to each car when petitioner pocketed the dealer's money," and "[a]s far as each particular transaction was concerned, it was as inconsequential to him whether the dealer resold the car as it was to the defendant in *Maze* whether the defrauded merchant ever forwarded the charges to the credit card company."[13] The dissenters noted that in each of the prior cases the Court had an opportunity to combine the individual transactions into a prior scheme, but it nonetheless found that no mail fraud had occurred.[14]

Schmuck holds that the mailing must be in furtherance of the fraud, even though it need not be essential to the scheme's success. Many of the lower courts refer to this as the requirement that the mailing be *closely related* to the fraudulent scheme.[15] If the defendant receives goods or money through the mails as part of the fraudulent scheme, that is clearly sufficient to satisfy the jurisdictional requirement.[16] In the wake of *Schmuck*, one lower court has candidly acknowledged that the mailing requirement is "fairly easy to satisfy" in most cases,[17] and other courts have strained to find the requisite mailing where the connection between the fraud and the mailing was tenuous at best.[18]

10. Peter J. Henning, *Maybe It Should Just Be Called Federal Fraud: The Changing Nature of the Mail Fraud Statute*, 36 B.C.L.Rev. 435, 458 (1995).

11. 489 U.S. at 711, 109 S.Ct. at 1448.

12. 489 U.S. at 714, 109 S.Ct. at 1449.

13. 489 U.S. at 723, 109 S.Ct. at 1454 (Scalia. J., dissenting).

14. 489 U.S. at 723–24, 109 S.Ct. at 1454 (Scalia, J., dissenting).

15. *First Circuit:* United States v. Morrow, 39 F.3d 1228, 1237 (1st Cir.1994); United States v. Silvano, 812 F.2d 754, 760 (1st Cir.1987).

Third Circuit: United States v. Coyle, 63 F.3d 1239, 1244 (3d Cir.1995); United States v. Frey, 42 F.3d 795, 798 (3d Cir.1994).

Sixth Circuit: United States v. Griffith, 17 F.3d 865, 873 (6th Cir.1994).

Ninth Circuit: United States v. Hubbard, 96 F.3d 1223, 1228 (9th Cir.1996).

16. *E.g.,*

Supreme Court: Pereira v. United States, 347 U.S. 1, 9, 74 S.Ct. 358, 362, 98 L.Ed. 435 (1954).

Fifth Circuit: United States v. Pepper, 51 F.3d 469, 474 (5th Cir.1995).

17. *Seventh Circuit:* United States v. Hickok, 77 F.3d 992, 1004 (7th Cir.), *cert. denied*, 517 U.S. 1200, 116 S.Ct. 1701, 134 L.Ed.2d 800 (1996).

18. *E.g.,*

First Circuit: United States v. Morrow, 39 F.3d 1228, 1237 (1st Cir.1994) (holding letter of acknowledgment from insurance

Several important points emerge from the Supreme Court's opinions in *Schmuck* as well as its earlier decisions.

A. INNOCENT MAILINGS OR WIRE TRANSMISSIONS

The mailings or wire transmissions need not themselves be false or fraudulent.[19] In *Schmuck* the defendant argued that routine mailings that are innocent in themselves cannot supply the mailing element of the mail fraud offense. The Court observed that in *Parr v. United States*[20] it had "specifically acknowledged that 'innocent' mailings—ones that contain no false information—may supply the mailing element."[21] The Court also noted that in other cases it had "found the elements of mail fraud to be satisfied where the mailings have been routine."[22]

B. MAILINGS AFTER THE DEFENDANT RECEIVED THE VICTIM'S PROPERTY

As the lower courts have recognized,[23] the Supreme Court's decision in *Schmuck* makes it clear that a mailing that occurs after the defendant receives the victim's money or property may provide a sufficient basis for

company that it had received defendant's claim was " 'incidental' to an essential element in the scheme, namely, the criss-cross of mailings that would reasonably be expected when false claims are submitted to insurance companies, are processed, and are ultimately paid, thereby making the fraud successful.")

Eighth Circuit: United States v. Reed, 47 F.3d 288, 290–91 (8th Cir.1995) (upholding conviction of accountant who embezzled from client funds based upon bank's mailing to defendant of monthly statement for account).

Ninth Circuit: United States v. Stein, 37 F.3d 1407, 1408 (9th Cir.1994) (upholding conviction based upon mailing of consent order defendant had signed under threat of SEC investigation since it delayed detection of scheme).

19. *First Circuit:* United States v. Morrow, 39 F.3d 1228, 1237 (1st Cir.1994).

Third Circuit: United States v. Frey, 42 F.3d 795, 798 (3d Cir.1994).

Fifth Circuit: United States v. Tencer, 107 F.3d 1120, 1125 & n. 1 (5th Cir.), *cert. denied,* ___ U.S. ___, 118 S.Ct. 390, 139 L.Ed.2d 305 (1997).

Seventh Circuit: United States v. Hickok, 77 F.3d 992, 1004 (7th Cir.), *cert. denied,* 517 U.S. 1200, 116 S.Ct. 1701, 134 L.Ed.2d 800 (1996).

Eighth Circuit: United States v. Pemberton, 121 F.3d 1157, 1170–71 (8th Cir. 1997), *cert. denied,* ___ U.S. ___, ___, 118 S.Ct. 1046, 1047, 140 L.Ed.2d 111 (1998); United States v. Nelson, 988 F.2d 798, 804 (8th Cir.1993).

Eleventh Circuit: United States v. Waymer, 55 F.3d 564, 569 (11th Cir.1995), *cert. denied,* 517 U.S. 1119, 116 S.Ct. 1350, 134 L.Ed.2d 519 (1996).

20. 363 U.S. 370, 390, 80 S.Ct. 1171, 1183, 4 L.Ed.2d 1277 (1960).

21. *Supreme Court:* Schmuck v. United States, 489 U.S. 705, 714, 109 S.Ct. 1443, 1449, 103 L.Ed.2d 734 (1989).

22. *Supreme Court:* Schmuck v. United States, 489 U.S. 705, 714, 109 S.Ct. 1443, 1449, 103 L.Ed.2d 734 (1989) (citing Carpenter v. United States, 484 U.S. 19, 28, 108 S.Ct. 316, 321, 98 L.Ed.2d 275 (1987), which held that the routine mailing of newspapers to subscribers could fulfill the mailing requirement).

23. *First Circuit:* United States v. Lopez, 71 F.3d 954, 961 (1st Cir.1995) (upholding convictions based upon wire communications three years after defendant received victim's funds).

Second Circuit: United States v. Slevin, 106 F.3d 1086, 1089 (2d Cir.1996).

Fifth Circuit: United States v. Allen, 76 F.3d 1348, 1362 (5th Cir.1996).

Tenth Circuit: United States v. Dunning, 929 F.2d 579, 580 (10th Cir.1991); United States v. Kelley, 929 F.2d 582, 584 (10th Cir.1991).

a mail or wire fraud prosecution if it can still be said that the mailing was part of the execution of the fraudulent scheme.

Some lower court decisions where the timing of the mailing is an issue turn on the court's characterization of the scope of the fraudulent scheme. Taking their cue from the majority in *Schmuck*, many of the lower courts have been willing to take a big picture view, finding a single ongoing scheme involving many victims, rather than a series of smaller schemes that reached fruition before mailing.[24] Once the fraud is characterized with this big picture view, it is easy to see that the receipt of property from one or more of the victims does not bring the scheme to a close, and that later mailings, as in *Schmuck*, may further the overall scheme. Some of these cases involve mailings made long after the defendant had obtained the object of the fraudulent scheme.[25]

C. POST-FRAUD ACCOUNTING

On the other hand, *Schmuck* reaffirmed the rule that a mailing that is no more than "post fraud accounting among the potential victims of the ... scheme" does not facilitate the scheme and is not sufficient to satisfy the mailing requirement.[26] Although most mail fraud convictions are upheld, the lower courts reverse an occasional case on the grounds that the mailings boiled down to no more than such a post-fraud accounting.[27]

D. MAILINGS TO CONCEAL THE FRAUD
OR LULL THE VICTIMS

Another line of cases involves conduct designed to prevent or delay discovery of the scheme or complaints to the authorities. As the Supreme Court explained in *United States v. Lane*,[28] "[m]ailings occurring after

24. *Second Circuit*: United States v. Slevin, 106 F.3d 1086, 1089 (2d Cir.1996).

Third Circuit: United States v. Frey, 42 F.3d 795, 798 (3d Cir.1994).

Sixth Circuit: United States v. Montgomery, 980 F.2d 388, 393 (6th Cir.1992).

Seventh Circuit: United States v. Biesiadecki, 933 F.2d 539, 545–546 (7th Cir. 1991).

Tenth Circuit: United States v. Massey, 48 F.3d 1560, 1566–67 (10th Cir.1995).

Ninth Circuit: United States v. Hubbard, 96 F.3d 1223, 1228 (9th Cir.1996).

25. *E.g.,*

First Circuit: United States v. Lopez, 71 F.3d 954, 961 (1st Cir.1995) (attempts to conceal three years after defendant obtained victim's property were in furtherance of fraudulent scheme).

26. *Supreme Court:* Schmuck v. United States, 489 U.S. 705, 714, 109 S.Ct.

1443, 1449, 103 L.Ed.2d 734 (1989) (distinguishing prior decisions where the Court had found that the mailing did not facilitate the fraud).

27. *Fifth Circuit:* United States v. Vontsteen, 872 F.2d 626, 629 (5th Cir. 1989).

Eleventh Circuit: United States v. Smith, 934 F.2d 270, 272 (11th Cir.1991); United States v. Mills, 1996 WL 634207 *17–*19 (S.D.Ga.1996), *affirmed in part, reversed in part*, 138 F.3d 928 (11th Cir. 1998).

28. 474 U.S. 438, 451–52, 106 S.Ct. 725, 733, 88 L.Ed.2d 814 (1986), quoting United States v. Maze, 414 U.S. 395, 403, 94 S.Ct. 645, 650, 38 L.Ed.2d 603 (1974). *See also* United States v. Sampson, 371 U.S. 75, 81, 83 S.Ct. 173, 176, 9 L.Ed.2d 136 (1962).

receipt of the goods obtained by fraud are within the statute if they were 'designed to lull the victims into a false sense of security, postpone their ultimate complaint to the authorities, and therefore make the apprehension of the defendants less likely than if no mailings had taken place.' " Accordingly, many decisions in the lower courts recognize that mail and wire fraud convictions may rest on conduct designed to lull the victims and allay their suspicions, or to conceal the fraud.[29]

E. MAILINGS THAT INCREASE THE CHANCES OF DETECTION

The majority in *Schmuck* rejected the defendant's contention that the mailing element in prosecutions under 18 U.S.C. § 1341 cannot be satisfied by mailings that ultimately contribute to the discovery of the fraudulent scheme. They held:

> The relevant question at all times is whether the mailing is part of the execution of the scheme *as conceived by the perpetrator at the time*, regardless of whether the mailing later, through hindsight, may prove to have been counterproductive and return to haunt the perpetrator of the fraud.[30]

The italicized language adopts a subjective standard, looking at whether the defendant intended the mailing to assist the fraudulent scheme rather than at the actual impact of the mailing. This subjective standard appears to have been a break from prior precedents, which applied an objective standard, holding that the jurisdictional requirement could not be met by a mailing that was counterproductive to the fraudulent

---

29. *First Circuit:* United States v. Lopez, 71 F.3d 954, 961 (1st Cir.1995) (attempts to conceal three years after defendant obtained victim's property were in furtherance of fraudulent scheme); United States v. Morrow, 39 F.3d 1228 (1st Cir. 1994) (concluding defendant's mailing in response to police request was intended to conceal fraud and sufficiently related to the scheme); United States v. Young, 955 F.2d 99, 108 (1st Cir.1992).

Second Circuit: United States v. Slevin, 106 F.3d 1086, 1089 (2d Cir.1996).

Third Circuit: United States v. Coyle, 63 F.3d 1239, 1244 (3d Cir.1995).

Fifth Circuit: United States v. Allen, 76 F.3d 1348, 1362 (5th Cir.1996).

Sixth Circuit: United States v. Griffith, 17 F.3d 865, 873 (6th Cir.1994).

Seventh Circuit: United States v. Ashman, 979 F.2d 469, 483 (7th Cir.1992); United States v. Biesiadecki, 933 F.2d 539, 545–546 (7th Cir.1991); United States v. Anderson, 809 F.2d 1281, 1287 (7th Cir. 1987) (mailing of refund check was effort by defendant to keep recipient from asking too many questions and thus to conceal the scheme of fixing tickets for driving under the influence of alcohol).

Eighth Circuit: United States v. Lefkowitz, 125 F.3d 608, 615–616 (8th Cir. 1997), *cert. denied,* ___ U.S. ___, 118 S.Ct. 1527, 140 L.Ed.2d 678 (1998); United States v. Pemberton, 121 F.3d 1157, 1170–71 (8th Cir.1997), *cert. denied,* ___ U.S. ___, ___, 118 S.Ct. 1046, 1047, 140 L.Ed.2d 111 (1998).

Ninth Circuit: United States v. Rude, 88 F.3d 1538, 1544 (9th Cir.1996); United States v. Stein, 37 F.3d 1407, 1408 (9th Cir.1994) (mailing to lull investors into "a false sense of security" was sufficiently related to securities-fraud scheme, even though the mailing served to expose Stein's "improper securities dealings").

Tenth Circuit: United States v. Massey, 48 F.3d 1560, 1566–67 (10th Cir.1995).

30. *Supreme Court:* Schmuck v. United States, 489 U.S. 705, 715, 109 S.Ct. 1443, 1450, 103 L.Ed.2d 734 (1989) (emphasis added).

scheme.[31]

This issue arises in various contexts, such as enquiries related to fraudulent claims for insurance, filings required in connection with trust funds of accounts that the defendant has looted, and investigations of defendant's qualification to serve as a surety. Mailings by the defendant pose no problem, since it is ordinarily clear that he or she intended the mailings to facilitate the scheme to defraud, even if their actual effect was counterproductive. The lower courts encounter more difficulties in cases involving mailings by a third party, such as an insurance company or trustee, particularly when the purpose of the party making the mailing is—in whole or part—to determine whether a claim or application is valid or fraudulent. If the court characterizes the mailings as intended to further the processing of the defendant's claim, that leads to the conclusion that the mailing element is satisfied.[32] But another court may characterize a similar mailing as in furtherance of an investigation to defeat a fraudulent scheme, and hence not a sufficient jurisdictional basis for mail fraud.[33] In making this characterization, the lower courts have sometimes looked to the third party's intention at the time of the mailing, or to the timing of the mailing.[34]

F. LEGALLY REQUIRED MAILINGS AND WIRE TRANSMISSIONS

In *Parr v. United States*,[35] a decision from 1960, the Supreme Court wrote "we think it cannot be said that mailings made or caused to be made under the imperative command of duty imposed by state law are criminal under the mail fraud statute." *Parr* involved the allegation that school board members had misappropriated school revenues; the mail-

---

31. *See* Ellen S. Podgor, *Mail Fraud: Opening Letters*, 43 S.C.L.Rev. 223, 239–54 (1992) (reviewing pre-*Schmuck* authorities and concluding that *Schmuck* has left the lower courts "in a state of confusion").

32. For example, in United States v. Koen, 982 F.2d 1101, 1106–09 (7th Cir. 1992), the court held that the insurer's mailing of checks to retain fire investigators and attorneys could satisfy the mailing of the statute because they were intended to expedite processing of defendant's claim, though in fact they uncovered arson and a scheme to defraud the insurance company.

33. For example, in United States v. Merklinger, 16 F.3d 670, 678–79 (6th Cir. 1994), the court concluded that letters from government official for more information to aid in determination whether defendant qualified as surety were in furtherance of an investigation to thwart fraud, and not in furtherance of defendant's fraudulent scheme. The court gave no indication that the government official harbored any special doubts about the defendant's qualifica-

tions at the time she sent the letter, so it seems possible that another court would have treated this as part of the processing of his surety application, and hence sufficient to support a charge of mail fraud.

34. *Second Circuit:* United States v. Altman, 48 F.3d 96, 103 (2d Cir.1995) (holding, inter alia, that mailing of referee's report criticizing defendant's stewardship and recommending that he file additional accounting did not facilitate defendant's scheme, since he had already looted the estate in question).

Seventh Circuit: United States v. Koen, 982 F.2d 1101, 1106–09 (7th Cir.1992) (concluding that insurance company's mailing of checks to retain investigators and attorneys did facilitate defendant's scheme to defraud, where insurance company agent testified that these people were hired to expedite the processing of defendant's claim and such an investigation was a prerequisite to the payment of his claim).

35. 363 U.S. 370, 391, 80 S.Ct. 1171, 1183, 4 L.Ed.2d 1277 (1960).

ings were tax statements, tax payments, and receipts for tax payments. *Schmuck* distinguished *Parr* in a short footnote. Whereas the required mailings in Parr "would have been made regardless of the defendants' fraudulent scheme, the mailings in the present case, though in compliance with Wisconsin's car-registration procedure, were derivative of Schmuck's scheme to sell 'doctored' cars and would not have occurred but for that scheme."[36] The Court also noted that the tax notices themselves had not been increased as a result of Parr's fraud.

In the wake of these decisions, the lower courts are divided on the proper analysis of cases where the mailings were required by law. At least two circuits have held that legally required mailings can be prosecuted as mail fraud only if they (1) contain false statements and (2) are sent with the intention to defraud or conceal a fraudulent scheme.[37] Other courts that have not faced the issue head on have suggested that they would also adopt this approach.[38] There is precedent from the Ninth Circuit indicating that *Parr* does not preclude a mail fraud conviction for legally required mailings that are themselves false.[39] The Seventh Circuit has taken a different tack. One opinion held that a mail fraud prosecution may be based on legally-required mailings that are important to the success of the scheme to defraud, leaving open the question whether it is also necessary to show that legally required mailings were made with the specific intent to defraud the recipients of the mail.[40] Another Seventh Circuit opinion allowed a conviction to stand where legally required mailings were in furtherance of the fraudulent scheme, and the mailings would not have been made but for the fraudulent scheme.[41]

G. MANUFACTURED JURISDICTION

A few cases have raised the issue whether mail or wire fraud jurisdiction can be based upon a mailing or wire transmission that was prompted by the government itself. This issue traces its origins to the Second Circuit's decision in *United States v. Archer,*[42] a Travel Act case in which Judge Friendly held that the government could not manufac-

---

36. *Supreme Court:* Schmuck v. United States, 489 U.S. 705, 109 S.Ct. 1443, 103 L.Ed.2d 734 (1989).

37. *Fifth Circuit:* United States v. Curry, 681 F.2d 406, 412–13 (5th Cir.1982).

Sixth Circuit: United States v. Gray, 790 F.2d 1290, 1298 (6th Cir.1986), *rev'd on other grounds,* McNally v. United States, 483 U.S. 350, 107 S.Ct. 2875, 97 L.Ed.2d 292 (1987).

38. The Second Circuit's opinion upholding Leona Helmsley's mail fraud conviction is a variation on this theme. The prosecution was based upon the filing of false income tax returns, and for purposes of the appeal the Second Circuit assumed that she had been required by circumstances to mail her return. United States v.

Helmsley, 941 F.2d 71, 95 (2d Cir.1991). The court emphasized that Helmsley's mailings contained false representations that were part of the execution of her scheme to defraud; in contrast, *Parr* involved a scheme to steal funds that had been mailed, not a scheme to defraud. *Ibid. Accord* United States v. Kellogg, 955 F.2d 1244, 1247–48 (9th Cir.1992).

39. *Ninth Circuit:* United States v. Dadanian, 818 F.2d 1443, 1446 (9th Cir. 1987); United States v. Frega, 933 F.Supp. 1536, 1549 (S.D.Calif.1996).

40. *Seventh Circuit:* United States v. Green, 786 F.2d 247, 249–50 (7th Cir.1986).

41. *Seventh Circuit:* United States v. Ashman, 979 F.2d 469 (7th Cir.1992).

42. 486 F.2d 670 (2d Cir.1973).

ture jurisdiction by causing telephone calls to be made solely for the purpose of transforming a local crime into a federal offense. Judge Friendly noted that it was a matter of complete indifference to the defendant in the case before him where the agent was when he placed the call, and he observed that the agent's call to the defendant from Paris "served no purpose that would not have been served equally well" by a local call that would not trigger federal jurisdiction.

The lower courts have generally read *Archer* narrowly,[43] and to date the manufactured jurisdiction argument has not been successful in a mail or wire fraud prosecution. Several courts have held that convictions may be based upon mailings or wire transmissions induced by government agents.[44] It should be noted, however, that the facts in these cases were not as extreme as those in *Archer*. The Second Circuit—the court that decided *Archer*—later held that telephone calls prompted by federal agents could support a wire fraud conviction if the use of the wires was "reasonably foreseeable and not the result of the government's attempt to manufacture federal jurisdiction."[45] The court noted that this standard is a sufficient barrier to prevent any "government abuse" of the wire (or mail) fraud statute. Similarly, the Seventh Circuit upheld a conviction where an agent did prompt the use of the mails, but there was no "labored pretense" comparable to that in *Archer*, and the mailing was actually "an efficient means to accomplish the task."[46] Even a mailing or wire transmission performed by the government agent may be a sufficient basis for mail or wire fraud jurisdiction if the defendant prompted the mailing or transmission.[47]

Library References:

C.J.S. Postal Service and Offenses Against Postal Laws § 23; Telegraphs, Telephones, Radio, and Television § 116–123.

West's Key No. Digests, Postal Service ⚷35; Telecommunications ⚷362.

§ 17.29 Jurisdiction—The Intrastate Requirement In Wire Fraud Cases

Although the wire fraud statute was modeled on the mail fraud statute, there is one important difference between the two provisions. The wire fraud statute requires that the defendant transmit or cause the

---

43. *Seventh Circuit:* United States v. Kaye, 586 F.Supp. 1395, 1401–02 (N.D.Ill. 1984) (reviewing cases from Second and Seventh Circuits).

44. *Second Circuit*: United States v. Keats, 937 F.2d 58, 64 (2d Cir.1991) (collecting cases).

Seventh Circuit: United States v. Anderson, 809 F.2d 1281, 1288 (7th Cir. 1987); United States v. Kaye, 586 F.Supp. 1395, 1401–02 (N.D.Ill.1984).

45. *Second Circuit:* United States v. Keats, 937 F.2d 58, 64–65 (2d Cir.1991) (upholding jurisdiction in wire fraud case because the defendant "voluntarily chose to

involve in his scheme individuals residing in other states. His own actions formed the basis for federal jurisdiction.").

46. *Seventh Circuit*: United States v. Anderson, 809 F.2d 1281, 1288 (7th Cir. 1987).

47. *Seventh Circuit*: United States v. McClain, 1989 WL 68572 (N.D.Ill.1989), *aff'd in part, rev'd in part*, 934 F.2d 822 (7th Cir.1991). (The appeals court did not address the issue of manufactured jurisdiction, reversing the mail fraud conviction on other grounds).

transmission of writings, signals, or sounds "by means of wire, radio, or television communication, *in interstate or foreign* commerce."[1] No similar interstate requirement is found in the mail fraud statute. The courts have interpreted this reference to a transmission "in interstate or foreign commerce" to mean that the transmission must originate in one state and travel in or through another state,[2] or travel to or from a foreign country.[3]

The most litigated issue regarding the interstate aspect of wire fraud jurisdiction appears to be the mens rea requirement. Most circuits that have addressed this issue say that the defendant merely had to know he was making a phone call or other transmission, not that the transmission was interstate.[4] The only exception is an opinion that was subsequently withdrawn.[5]

The leading case is *United States v. Bryant,*[6] in which the defendants sent two telegrams from Kansas City, Missouri, to Bridgeton, Missouri, and Western Union routed both through Virginia. Although the defendants claimed that they had no idea their telegrams would be routed interstate, the court of appeals concluded that neither the text of the statute nor its purpose required knowledge of the interstate character of

§ 17.29

1. 18 U.S.C. § 1341 (1994) (emphasis added).

2. *See, e.g.,*

First Circuit: United States v. Cassiere, 4 F.3d 1006, 1011 (1st Cir.1993); United States v. Santagata, 924 F.2d 391, 393 (1st Cir.1991).

Fifth Circuit: United States v. Vaccaro, 115 F.3d 1211, 1221 (5th Cir.1997), *cert. denied,* ___ U.S. ___, 118 S.Ct. 689, 139 L.Ed.2d 635 (1998); United States v. Faulkner, 17 F.3d 745, 771 (5th Cir.1994).

Sixth Circuit: United States v. Smith, 39 F.3d 119, 122 (6th Cir.1994).

Seventh Circuit: United States v. Lindemann, 85 F.3d 1232, 1241 (7th Cir.), cert. denied, ___ U.S. ___, 117 S.Ct. 392, 136 L.Ed.2d 307 (1996); United States v. Briscoe, 65 F.3d 576, 583 (7th Cir.1995).

Eighth Circuit: United States v. Lefkowitz, 125 F.3d 608, 615–16 (8th Cir. 1997), *cert. denied,* ___ U.S. ___, 118 S.Ct. 1527, 140 L.Ed.2d 678 (1998).

Tenth Circuit: United States v. Cochran, 109 F.3d 660, 664 (10th Cir.1997); United States v. Galbraith, 20 F.3d 1054, 1056 (10th Cir.1994).

3. *Second Circuit:* United States v. Piervinanzi, 23 F.3d 670 (2d Cir.1994).

Third Circuit: United States v. Goldberg, 830 F.2d 459, 464 (3d Cir.1987).

4. *Second Circuit:* United States v. Blackmon, 839 F.2d 900, 907 (2d Cir.1988);

United States v. Blassingame, 427 F.2d 329 (2d Cir.1970).

Third Circuit: United States v. Pelullo, 964 F.2d 193, 213 (3d Cir.1992).

Fourth Circuit: United States v. Darby, 37 F.3d 1059, 1067 (4th Cir.1994).

Sixth Circuit: United States v. Griffith, 17 F.3d 865, 874 (6th Cir.1994).

Seventh Circuit: United States v. Lindemann, 85 F.3d 1232, 1241 (7th Cir.), *cert. denied,* ___ U.S. ___, 117 S.Ct. 392, 136 L.Ed.2d 307 (1996)

Eighth Circuit: United States v. Bryant, 766 F.2d 370, 375 (8th Cir.1985).

Ninth Circuit: Virden v. Graphics One, 623 F.Supp. 1417, 1422 (C.D.Cal.1985).

5. In *United States v. Brumley*, 59 F.3d 517, 520 (5th Cir.1995), the court stated that the government must show that the defendant knew or should have foreseen that the wire communication would be interstate. This opinion was withdrawn and rehearing en banc was granted, and the later opinions in the case do not discuss this issue. *See* United States v. Brumley, 79 F.3d 1430 (5th Cir.1996), *rev'd,* 116 F.3d 728 (5th Cir.1997) (en banc), *cert. denied,* ___ U.S. ___, 118 S.Ct. 625, 139 L.Ed.2d 606 (1997). Although the panel suggested that its statement was supported by prior Fifth Circuit precedents, the cases cited by the panel are not on point.

6. *Eighth Circuit:* United States v. Bryant, 766 F.2d 370 (8th Cir.1985).

the transmission. Read literally, the statute requires "only that the wire communication be interstate, not that defendants know that it is to be interstate."[7] The court concluded that the interstate transmission requirement serves a jurisdictional purpose, invoking the commerce power, and is unrelated to the gravamen of the offense. "The interstate nature of the communication does not make the fraud more culpable. Thus, whether or not a defendant knows or can foresee that a communication is interstate, the offense is still every bit as grave in the moral sense."[8] However, the court also suggested an exception to the above rule might be warranted on facts where the wire fraud statute is stretched to its limits. If the conduct giving rise to the scheme would not be a violation of state law and was not itself morally wrong, the court stated in dicta that there should be proof "that the accused knew or could have foreseen that a communication in furtherance of a fraudulent scheme was interstate."[9] None of the later wire fraud cases appears to make reference to this exception.

A few cases have raised the question whether knowledge or foreseeability should be necessary if the defendant caused an innocent third party to make a transmission, as opposed to making the transmission himself. The Second Circuit squarely addressed this question in *United States v. Blackmon*,[10] holding that it makes no difference whether the defendant made the transmission himself or caused a third party to do it. It appears that other circuits take the same view, treating transmissions made by the defendant no differently than those the defendant caused an innocent third party to make.[11]

Library References:
C.J.S. Telegraphs, Telephones, Radio, and Television § 116–123.
West's Key No. Digests, Telecommunications ⊘362.

§ 17.30   Jurisdiction—Mailings or Wire Transmissions Made By Third Parties

It is not necessary that the defendant himself actually mail anything or make a wire transmission in order to violate the mail and wire fraud

7. *Eighth Circuit:* United States v. Bryant, 766 F.2d 370, 375 (8th Cir.1985).

8. *Eighth Circuit:* United States v. Bryant, 766 F.2d 370, 375 (8th Cir.1985).

9. United States v. Bryant, 766 F.2d 370, 375 (8th Cir.1985), *citing* United States v. Feola, 420 U.S. 671, 684, 95 S.Ct. 1255, 1264, 43 L.Ed.2d 541 (1975).

10. 839 F.2d 900 (2d Cir.1988).

11. *See e.g.,*
First Circuit: United States v. Castillo, 829 F.2d 1194 (1st Cir.1987) (not requiring knowledge or foreseeability regarding the interstate aspect of a transmission made by an innocent third party).
Sixth Circuit: United States v. Griffith, 17 F.3d 865 (6th Cir.1994) (holding that "the defendant himself does not have to use

the mails or interstate telephone lines, provided it is foreseeable that the mails or wire services could be used to further his scheme").

Seventh Circuit: United States v. Lindemann, 85 F.3d 1232 (7th Cir.), *cert. denied*, ___ U.S. ___, 117 S.Ct. 392, 136 L.Ed.2d 307 (1996) (making blanket statement that in wire fraud cases, the government "need not prove that the interstate nature of the calls was foreseeable.").

Eighth Circuit: United States v. Bryant, 766 F.2d 370 (8th Cir.1985) (making blanket statement that "§ 1343 does not require knowledge or foresight of the interstate nature of communication.").

statutes. Both statutes expressly encompass the conduct that "causes" a third party to make a mailing or a wire transmission.[1] Thus the mail and wire fraud statutes can reach cases in which the victim[2] or some other innocent third party[3] used the mails or transmitted a communication by wire.

In *Pereira v. United States*[4] the Supreme Court explained that one "causes" a mailing when "one does an act with knowledge that the use of the mails will follow in the ordinary course of business, or where such use can reasonably be foreseen, even though not actually intended." Since the structure of the mail and wire fraud statutes is parallel, the lower courts recognize that the *Pereira* standard of reasonable foreseeability governs not only in mail fraud cases,[5] but also in wire fraud cases in which the government alleges that the defendant "caused" a third party to make a wire transmission.[6] It should be noted that this requirement of foreseeability is in addition to (not instead of) the requirement that the mailing or wire transmission further the fraud as a step in the plot or an incident to some essential element of the plan.[7]

Library References:
> C.J.S. Postal Service and Offenses Against Postal Laws § 23; Telegraphs, Telephones, Radio, and Television § 116–123.
> West's Key No. Digests, Postal Service ⟜35; Telecommunications ⟜362.

§ 17.31 Jurisdiction—Proof of the Requisite Mailing or Wire Transmission

In many cases the prosecution has no difficulty in establishing the required mailing or wire transmission. In the case of wire communica-

§ 17.30

1. The text of the mail and wire fraud statutes is reprinted in § 17.1.

2. *See, e.g.,*
Eighth Circuit: United States v. Nelson, 988 F.2d 798, 804–05 (8th Cir.1993) (mailing by victim); United States v. Alanis, 945 F.2d 1032, 1036 (8th Cir.1991) (same).

3. *First Circuit:* United States v. Boots, 80 F.3d 580, 585 (1st Cir.), *cert. denied,* ___ U.S. ___, 117 S.Ct. 263, 136 L.Ed.2d 188 (1996).
Second Circuit: United States v. Paccione, 949 F.2d 1183, 1195 (2d Cir.1991).

4. 347 U.S. 1, 8–9, 74 S.Ct. 358, 362–63, 98 L.Ed. 435 (1954)

5. *Second Circuit:* United States v. Paccione, 949 F.2d 1183, 1195 (2d Cir. 1991).
Fifth Circuit: United States v. Manges, 110 F.3d 1162, 1174 (5th Cir.1997).
Sixth Circuit: United States v. Griffith, 17 F.3d 865, 874 (6th Cir.1994); Hofstetter v. Fletcher, 905 F.2d 897, 902 (6th Cir. 1988).

Ninth Circuit: United States v. Lothian, 976 F.2d 1257, 1262 (9th Cir.1992).

6. *First Circuit:* United States v. Boots, 80 F.3d 580, 585 (1st Cir.), *cert. denied,* ___ U.S. ___, 117 S.Ct. 263, 136 L.Ed.2d 188 (1996).
Second Circuit: United States v. Muni, 668 F.2d 87, 89 (2d Cir.1981).
Third Circuit: United States v. Bentz, 21 F.3d 37, 40 (3d Cir.1994).
Sixth Circuit: United States v. Griffith, 17 F.3d 865, 874 (6th Cir.1994); Hofstetter v. Fletcher, 905 F.2d 897, 902 (6th Cir. 1988).
Ninth Circuit: United States v. Lothian, 976 F.2d 1257, 1262 (9th Cir.1992).
Tenth Circuit: United States v. Puckett, 692 F.2d 663, 668 & n. 6 (10th Cir. 1982).

7. For a discussion of this requirement, see § 17.28. For a case noting this distinction, see United States v. Bentz, 21 F.3d 37, 40 n. 3 (3d Cir.1994).

tions, records generally exist which document each transmission. The lower courts have held, however, that it is not necessary for the government to produce telephone bills or postmarked envelopes.[1] The prosecution may rely on more indirect proof, including circumstantial evidence, to demonstrate that certain communications were delivered by mail or interstate wire transmission. For example, the courts have held that testimony that the sender routinely used the U.S. mails for communications of this nature is sufficient to support an inference that a particular communication was mailed.[2] Testimony that an individual placed or received a telephone call from an individual in another state is also sufficient.[3]

Library References:

C.J.S. Postal Service and Offenses Against Postal Laws § 23; Telegraphs, Telephones, Radio, and Television § 116–123.
West's Key No. Digests, Postal Service ☞35; Telecommunications ☞362.

§ 17.32 Unit of Prosecution in Mail and Wire Fraud Cases

In *Badders v. United States*[1] the Supreme Court upheld the power of Congress to enact the mail fraud statute and observed that "there is no doubt that the law may make each putting of a letter into the post office a separate offense." The lower courts are in agreement that each mailing is a separate offense, even if they are intended to further a single scheme.[2] This conclusion flows from the structure of the mail statute, which characterize the use of the mails—not the fraud itself—as the punishable conduct. Since the structure of the wire fraud statute tracks that of the mail fraud statute, making the use of wire, radio, or television communications the gist of the offense, it follows that each such communication is also a separate offense.[3]

Since the maximum penalty for a single count of mail or wire fraud

---

§ 17.31

1. *Sixth Circuit:* United States v. Griffith, 17 F.3d 865, 874 (6th Cir.1994).

2. *E.g.,*

Eleventh Circuit: United States v. Waymer, 55 F.3d 564, 571 (11th Cir.1995), *cert. denied,* 517 U.S. 1119, 116 S.Ct. 1350, 134 L.Ed.2d 519 (1996).

3. *Sixth Circuit:* United States v. Griffith, 17 F.3d 865, 874 (6th Cir.1994).

§ 17.32

1. 240 U.S. 391, 394, 36 S.Ct. 367, 368, 60 L.Ed. 706 (1916).

2. *See, e.g.,*

Second Circuit: United States v. Upton, 856 F.Supp. 727, 741 (E.D.N.Y.1994) (referring to mail and wire fraud); United States v. Harris, 805 F.Supp. 166, 172 (S.D.N.Y. 1992) (same) (dicta).

Fifth Circuit: United States v. Krenning, 93 F.3d 1257, 1263 (5th Cir.1996) (referring to mail fraud); United States v. Pazos, 24 F.3d 660, 665 (5th Cir.1994) (same).

Seventh Circuit: United States v. Coonce, 961 F.2d 1268, 1283 (7th Cir.1992) (referring to mail fraud and noting that consecutive sentences arising from a single fraudulent scheme are not an abuse of discretion); United States v. Hartmann, 958 F.2d 774, 792 (7th Cir.1992) (referring to mail and wire fraud).

Eighth Circuit: United States v. Alanis, 945 F.2d 1032, 1036 (8th Cir.1991) (referring to mail fraud).

Tenth Circuit: United States v. Rogers, 960 F.2d 1501, 1514 (10th Cir.1992) (referring to mail fraud).

3. *See* the cases cited in note 2, *supra.*

is only five years absent special circumstances,[4] federal prosecutors frequently charge multiple counts of mail or wire fraud in order to increase the potential penalty. In some cases a large number of counts and a lengthy sentence are clearly justified by the size of the scheme and the number of victims involved. For example, in a case involving a scheme to sell distributorships in nonexistent businesses, where 629 victims were defrauded of a total of more than five million dollars, the prosecutors charged multiple counts of mail fraud and two defendants were sentenced to 60 and 75 years.[5] In other cases, however, there may be no relationship between the number of mailings and the size of the fraud or the number of victims involved. In the context of a fraudulent disability claim, for example, a separate count may be based upon the mailing of each monthly check to the claimant. In *United States v. Brown*[6] a defendant who obtained larger Veteran's benefits by fraudulently claiming total rather than partial disability was convicted of 41 counts of mail and wire fraud, permitting a maximum sentence of 205 years.[7] While the payments involved in *Brown* were substantial and they continued over a period of years, this analysis permits stacking of counts regardless of the size of the payments involved, the number of victims, or the complexity or duration of the scheme. Other cases demonstrate the same potential for multiple counts and a maximum sentence that is disproportionate to the defendant's culpability or the harm caused by the fraudulent scheme.[8]

The Sentencing Guideline decrease the importance of the prosecutor's ability to charge a large number of counts. Although the maximum penalty is still controlled by the number of counts, subject to that limitation the penalty actually imposed will be determined based upon a series of criteria that focus on nature of the offense (the amount of money involved in the scheme, the impact on the victims, etc.), and on the defendant's criminal history.[9]

4. Enhanced penalties are applicable in two situations. When the violation "affects a financial institution," the maximum penalty is increased to a fine of $1,000,000 and or 30 years imprisonment. 18 U.S.C. §§ 1341 (mail fraud), 1341 (wire fraud). When a violation occurs "in connection with the conduct of telemarketing" an additional term of five years is authorized, and an additional term of ten years is authorized if the defendant victimized or targeted persons over the age of 55. 18 U.S.C. § 2326 (1994).

5. *Fifth Circuit*: United States v. Helms, 897 F.2d 1293, 1299 (5th Cir.1990).

6. 948 F.2d 1076 (8th Cir.1991).

7. The defendant's actual sentence, based upon both the mail fraud convictions and one count of obstruction of justice, was 57 months and a three year term of supervised release. 948 F.2d at 1079.

8. *See, e.g.,*

Seventh Circuit: United States v. Draiman, 784 F.2d 248, 253 (7th Cir.1986) (upholding separate counts for mailing copies of same documents pursuant to single insurance fraud scheme).

Ninth Circuit: United States v. Vaughn, 797 F.2d 1485, 1493 (9th Cir.1986) (upholding separate counts for mailing petition for remission and three follow-up letters pursuant to single scheme to defraud government of airplane seized in connection with drug trafficking).

9. The sentence for a mail or wire fraud violation is calculated using the fraud guideline, U.S.S.S.G. § 2F1.1, which adjusts the base level of the offense based upon the amount of the loss, plus other offense characteristics. For a discussion of this provisions, see THOMAS W. HUTCHISON & DAVID YELLEN, FEDERAL SENTENCING LAW AND PRACTICE 263–77 (2nd ed. 1994).

§ 17.33 Bibliography

Bradley, Craig M., Foreword: *Mail Fraud After* McNally *and* Carpenter: *The Essence of Fraud*, 79 J. CRIM. L. & CRIMINOLOGY 573 (1988).

Brown, George D., *Should Federalism Shield Corruption?—Mail Fraud, State Law, and Post-*Lopez *Analysis*, 82 CORNELL L. REV. 225 (1997).

Bucy, Pamela H., *Fraud By Fright: White Collar Crime by Health Care Providers*, 67 N.C. L. REV. 855 (1989).

Coffee, John C., Jr., *Hush: The Criminal Status of Confidential Information After* McNally *and* Carpenter *and the Enduring Problem of Overcriminalization*, 26 AM. CRIM. L. REV. 121 (1988).

Coffee, John C., Jr., *The Metastasis of Mail Fraud: The Continuing Story of the Evolution of White–Collar Crime*, 21 AM. CRIM. L. REV. 1 (1983).

Ezwersky, Peter R., Note, *Intra-Corporate Mail and Wire Fraud: Criminal Liability for Fiduciary Breach*, 94 YALE L. J. 1427 (1985).

Gagliardi, John E., *Back to the Future: Federal Mail and Wire Fraud Under 18 U.S.C. § 1346*, 68 WASH. L. REV. 901 (1993).

Henning, Peter J., *Maybe It Should Just Be Called Federal Fraud: The Changing Nature of the Mail Fraud Statute*, 36 B.C. L. REV. 435 (1995).

Hurston, Daniel J., *Limiting the Federal Mail Fraud Statute—A Legislative Approach*, 20 AM. CRIM. L. REV. 423 (1980).

Maus, Donna M., Note, *License Procurement and the Federal Mail Fraud Statute*, 58 U. CHI. L. REV. 1125 (1991).

Motz, Todd E., Comment, *The Mail Fraud Statute: An Argument for Implied Repeal*, 64 U. CHI. L. REV. 983 (1997).

Moohr, Geraldine Szott, *Mail Fraud and the Intangible Rights Doctrine: Someone to Watch Over Us*, 31 HARV. J. LEGIS. 153 (1994).

Paley, Michael D., *Prosecuting Failed Attempts to Fix Prices as Violations of the Mail and Wire Fraud Statutes: Elliott Ness Is Back!*, 73 WASH. U. L. Q. 333 (1995).

Podgor, Ellen S., *Mail Fraud: Opening Letters*, 43 S.C. L. REV. 223 (1992).

Rakoff, Jed S., *The Federal Mail Fraud Statute (Part I)*, 18 DUQ. L. REV. 771 (1980).

Williams, Gregory H., *Good Government By Prosecutorial Decree: The Use and Abuse of the Mail Fraud Statute*, 32 ARIZ. L. REV. 137 (1990).

Whitaker, Charles N., Note, *Federal Prosecutions of State and Local Bribery: Inappropriate Tools and the Need for a Structured Approach*, 78 VA. L. REV. 1617 (1992).

*

CHAPTER 18

MONEY LAUNDERING AND CURRENCY REPORTING CRIMES

Table of Sections

WESTLAW Electronic Research

See WESTLAW Electronic Research Guide preceding the Summary of Contents.

---

§ 18.1 Introduction

Money laundering begins with money that is dirty because it was generated illegally or because it was generated legally but got dirty through tax evasion.[1] Once money is dirty it must be converted into an apparently legitimate form or "laundered" before it can be invested or spent.[2] " 'Money laundering' is the process by which one conceals the existence, illegal source, or illegal application of income, and then disguises that income to make it appear legitimate."[3] Money laundering is harmful because it does not absorb any portion of the tax burden and it

---

§ 18.1

1. Sarah N. Welling, *Smurfs, Money Laundering, and the Federal Criminal Law: The Crime of Structuring Transactions*, 41 Fla. L. Rev. 287, 290 n.11 (1989).

2. *Id.* at 290 n.16.

3. *Id.* at 290, *quoting* The President's Comm'n on Organized Crime, Interim Report to the President and Attorney General, The Cash Connection: Organized Crime, Financial Institutions, and Money Laundering, vii–viii (1984).

furthers the underlying criminal activity. Laundering is required only when large amounts of dirty cash are generated, since small amounts can be absorbed inconspicuously. The main impetus behind money laundering today is the huge amount of cash generated by the drug trade.[4]

Federal law criminalizes money laundering in two ways. The reporting laws take an indirect approach by requiring that certain transactions and accounts be reported to the government; failure to report accurately is a crime. Federal statutes also take a direct approach by defining the process of laundering as a substantive crime.

Money laundering prosecutions are increasing dramatically. From 1991 to 1993, the number of laundering prosecutions filed increased from 393 cases involving 743 defendants to 1164 cases involving 2371 defendants.[5] In 1995, laundering prosecutions filed based on the substantive crimes, §§ 1956 and 1957, involved 1870 defendants in 831 cases.[6]

Library References:

    C.J.S. United States § 125.
    West's Key No. Digests, United States ⬤—34.

§ 18.2   Reporting Laws—Introduction

In 1970 Congress first addressed money laundering by adopting the Bank Secrecy Act (BSA).[1] The BSA requires that certain large cash transactions and foreign bank accounts be reported to the government.[2] Congress explicitly concluded that these reports will help the government in the criminal, tax and regulatory areas.[3] Implicitly these laws reflect Congress' conclusion that large cash transactions and foreign bank accounts are suspicious.[4] Moreover, in 1996 the government imposed a duty on banks to report suspicious transactions. The four

---

    4. *Id.* at 292 n.23.

    5. Fiscal year 1991, 1992 and 1993 Caseload Statistics, Received, Pending, Terminated, Filed Counts, Department of Justice (document on file with authors). These numbers exclude prosecutions under I.R.C. § 6050I, which is counted as a tax crime rather than a laundering crime.

    6. Department of Justice statistics, document on file with the authors.

§ 18.2

    1. Pub.L.No. 91–508, 84 Stat. 1114 (1970) (codified at 31 U.S.C. § 5311 *et seq.*).

    2. These reporting requirements appeared in Title II of the BSA, which was separately titled the Currency and Foreign Transactions Reporting Act. This title is rarely used, however, and the laws are usually referred to as the BSA.

    3. *See* 31 U.S.C. § 5311. The Treasury Department has made the same findings, *see* 31 C.F.R. § 103.31; California

Bankers Assoc. v. Schultz, 416 U.S. 21, 31, 32, 94 S.Ct. 1494, 1502, 1503, 39 L.Ed.2d 812 (1974); United States v. Goldberg, 756 F.2d 949 (2d Cir.1985); H.R.Rep.No. 91–975, 2d Sess. 11–12 (1970), *reprinted in* 1970 U.S.C.C.A.N. 4394, 4396–97.

    4. *Supreme Court: California Banker's Assoc.*, 416 U.S. at 13, 94 S.Ct. at 1542.

    First Circuit: United States v. St. Michael's Credit Union, 880 F.2d 579, 582 (1st Cir.1989).

    Second Circuit: United States v. Goldberg, 756 F.2d at 949 (2d Cir.1985).

    See also H.R. Rep. No. 91–975, 2d Sess. 11–12 (1970), *reprinted in* 1970 U.S.C.C.A.N. 4394, 4396–97; Welling, *Smurfs, Money Laundering, and the Federal Criminal Law: The Crime of Structuring Transactions*, 41 Fla.L.Rev. 287 at 294 n.37.

reporting requirements of the BSA, together with another reporting requirement added later as part of the tax code,[5] are discussed below.

Library References:

C.J.S. United States § 125.
West's Key No. Digests, United States ⊕34.

§ 18.3 Reporting Laws—Currency Transactions at Financial Institutions: § 5313 CTR's

A. IN GENERAL

Section 5313 requires that financial institutions file a report with the government when they are involved in a currency transaction over $10,000.[1] Filing a false report or failing to file is a crime.

The duty to report cash transactions as imposed by the explicit language of the regulations runs only to financial institutions.[2] The usual defendants in these cases are individuals acting as financial institutions,[3] individuals acting for financial institutions,[4] and the financial institutions themselves.[5]

The conduct proscribed by this reporting law is not filing a currency transaction report (CTR) when one is due or filing a CTR with a false, fictitious or fraudulent statement or representation.[6]

B. FALSE FILING

No prosecutions for false filing of a CTR under this law have been reported. Two cases based on false statements in CTR's have been reported, but these were prosecuted under § 1001 rather than the CTR law,[7] presumably because the penalty under § 1001 was stiffer at the time.[8] In one case, the defendants got $200,000 in cash from undercover

---

5. I.R.C. § 6050I, discussed *infra* in § 18.5.

§ 18.3

1. 31 U.S.C. § 5313; 31 C.F.R. § 103.22(a)(1).

2. 31 C.F.R. § 103.22(a)(1) and *California Banker's Assoc.*, 416 U.S. at 24, 94 S.Ct. at 1500. *Cf.* one inexplicable variation, United States v. 1988 Oldsmobile, 983 F.2d 670, 674 (5th Cir.1993) ("business entities" must file under § 5313).

3. *Second Circuit:* United States v. Goldberg, 756 F.2d 949 (2d Cir.1985).

Fifth Circuit: United States v. Gollott, 939 F.2d 255 (5th Cir.1991).

Eighth Circuit: United States v. Hawley, 855 F.2d 595 (8th Cir.1988).

4. *Second Circuit:* United States v. Heyman, 794 F.2d 788 (2d Cir.1986).

Cf.

Ninth Circuit: United States v. Gebrayel, 788 F.2d 1567 (9th Cir.1986), *described in* Gebrayel v. United States, 990 F.2d 1257 (9th Cir.1993).

5. *First Circuit:* United States v. St. Michael's Credit Union, 880 F.2d 579 (1st Cir.1989); United States v. Bank of New England, 821 F.2d 844 (1st Cir.1987).

6. 31 C.F.R. §§ 103.22(a)(1) and 103.49(b)-(d).

7. *Ninth Circuit:* United States v. Gebrayel, 788 F.2d 1567 (9th Cir.1993), *described in* Gebrayel v. United States, 990 F.2d 1257 (9th Cir.1993); United States v. Murphy, 809 F.2d 1427 (9th Cir.1987).

8. A single false filing under § 5313 was a misdemeanor until February, 1987. *Murphy* was based on conduct occurring

IRS agents and deposited it into an account in the name of a front company they set up. On the CTR form, in the space that called for the "individual or organization for whom this transaction was completed,"[9] the defendants wrote the name of the company which *received* the money rather than the agents who were the *source* of the money. They were indicted for filing a false statement under § 1001 and conspiring to do so under § 371, but dismissal of the indictment was affirmed because the quoted CTR language did not clearly require depositors to identify the *source* of their funds, so a false filing conviction would be unconstitutional.[10] In another case, the defendant's use of a false name on a CTR was held sufficient for § 1001 liability.[11]

The statute setting out penalties for the BSA prohibits any *willful* violation.[12] The regulation on penalties prohibits *knowing* false, fictitious or fraudulent statements.[13] The existence of two different *mens rea* terms for false filing liability is curious. The drafters' intent is unclear, and the implications of the difference are unclear. As noted above, no prosecutions have been reported for false statements in a CTR, so no courts have construed the language.

C. FAILURE TO FILE

The offense of failure to file has three elements: (1) a duty to file, (2) failure to do so, and (3) a *mens rea* of willfulness.

i. Filing Duty

The duty to file is imposed on financial institutions when there is a transaction in currency over $10,000 by, through or to the institution.

Financial institutions have no duty to report transactions conducted by exempt entities.[14] Exemptions are described in the regulations.[15] The most important exemption is for companies with stock listed on national exchanges.[16]

a. *Financial Institution*

Financial institutions include:

— banks (except bank credit card systems)

— brokers or dealers in securities

— currency dealers or exchangers, including persons engaged in the business of cashing checks

before that date, so to obtain felony liability, § 1001 was used.

9. This was the version of the CTR form in effect before 1990. The current form has dropped this language and refers instead to the "person on whose behalf this transaction was conducted."

10. *Murphy*, 809 F.2d at 1427.

11. United States v. Gebrayel, 788 F.2d 1567 (9th Cir.1986), *described in* Ge-

brayel v. United States, 990 F.2d 1257 (9th Cir.1993).

12. 31 U.S.C. § 5322.

13. 31 C.F.R. § 103.49(d).

14. 31 C.F.R. § 103.22(h)(1).

15. *Id.* § 103.22(b)–(h).

16. *Id.* § 103.22(h)(2)(iv)–(v).

— funds transmitters

— telegraph companies

— casinos with annual revenue over $1,000,000, including tribal casinos and card clubs, and

— persons subject to supervision by any state or federal bank supervisory authority.[17]

The definition of financial institution includes not only these formal entities but also any person acting in one of the listed capacities "whether or not on a regular basis or as an organized business concern."[18] Based on this language, individuals may qualify as financial institutions and be prosecuted for failure to file.[19]

Generally, financial institutions are broadly defined.[20] Specifically, in the "currency dealer or exchanger"[21] category, a defendant will be

---

17. *See* 31 C.F.R. § 103.11(n).

The definition of financial institution is sometimes confusing because the definition of financial institution in the regulations is narrower than the definition of financial institution in the statute. *Compare* 31 C.F.R. § 103.11(n) *with* 31 U.S.C. § 5312(a)(2). For example, the statutory definition of financial institution includes pawnbrokers and car dealers, which are excluded from the regulatory definition. 31 C.F.R. § 103.11(n). The definition in the regulations is narrower because Congress listed in the statute all possible financial institutions but the Secretary of the Treasury chose only some to include in the regulatory definition of financial institution. The narrower definition in the regulations is the controlling definition because the statutory scheme is not self-executing; it is actuated only by the regulations. There can be no penalties except via the regulations. California Bankers' Assoc. v. Shultz, 416 U.S. 21, 26, 94 S.Ct. 1494, 1500, 39 L.Ed.2d 812 (1974).

Ninth Circuit: United States v. Murphy, 809 F.2d 1427 (9th Cir.1987).

18. 31 C.F.R. § 103.11(n).

19. *See*

Fifth Circuit: United States v. Gollott, 939 F.2d 255, 258 (5th Cir.1991).

Cf.

Ninth Circuit: United States v. Gebrayel, 788 F.2d 1567 (9th Cir.1986), *described in* Gebrayel v. United States, 990 F.2d 1257 (9th Cir.1993) (evidence sufficient to hold individual liable as a financial institution where he had considerable influence over but was not an officer of the bank).

The liability of individuals as financial institutions is clear under the current defi-

nition of financial institution. Under the definition of financial institution in effect before April 8, 1987, however, there was some ambiguity. Under that version, most courts held that individuals could be deemed financial institutions.

See

Second Circuit: United States v. Goldberg, 756 F.2d 949 (2d Cir.1985).

Eighth Circuit: United States v. Hawley, 855 F.2d 595 (8th Cir.1988).

Ninth Circuit: United States v. Dela–Espriella, 781 F.2d 1432 (9th Cir.1986).

Eleventh Circuit: United States v. Hernando–Cspina, 798 F.2d 1570 (11th Cir.1986).

But one circuit held that individuals could not be financial institutions.

See

Seventh Circuit: United States v. Bucey, 876 F.2d 1297 (7th Cir.1989). This holding is obsolete under the revised definition of financial institution which became effective April 8, 1987. As one court stated, "[The defendant's argument that he is not a financial institution] rests on a superseded and arguably less comprehensive definition of financial institution ... than the amended one under which he was convicted.... [*Bucey*] is inapposite both because it interpreted the superseded regulation and concededly espoused a minority position rejecting an individual's status as a financial institution." *Gollott,* 939 F.2d at 258 (5th Cir.1991) (citations and footnote omitted).

20. United States v. Clines, 958 F.2d 578, 582 (4th Cir.1992)(*citing Dela–Esprilla,* 781 F.2d at 1436).

21. 31 C.F.R. § 103.11(n)(3).

---

deemed a financial institution regardless of whether it exchanges cash for checks or vice versa, and the currency involved need not be foreign.[22]

b. Currency

Currency is simply defined as the coin and paper money of any country.[23] Currency includes legally generated and reported ("clean") cash as well as criminally generated or unreported ("dirty") cash, so it is no defense that the defendant did not file a report because he or she knew the cash was clean.[24]

c. Transaction

A *transaction in currency* is a transaction involving the physical transfer of currency from one person to another,[25] excluding the transfer of funds by bank check, bank draft, wire transfer or other written order.[26] Common transactions in currency include depositing cash to or withdrawing cash out of a bank account, exchanging denominations of cash, cashing a check, and buying a financial instrument with cash.

d. By, Through or To an Institution

A currency transaction is reportable only if it is *by, through or to* a financial institution. Moving cash into or out of a safety deposit box is not a reportable transaction because the cash was not transferred by, through or to the bank.[27]

e. Over $10,000

To define when the $10,000 threshold is crossed, the regulations state that certain multiple transactions must be combined and treated as one transaction. This "aggregation rule" is that multiple currency transactions are treated as a single transaction if the financial institution has knowledge that they are by or on behalf of one person and result in either cash in or cash out totalling more than $10,000 during any one business day.[28] This regulation requires that three conditions exist

---

22. United States v. Levy, 969 F.2d 136, 139–40 (5th Cir.1992).

23. 31 C.F.R. § 103.11(h).

24. United States v. Donovan, 984 F.2d 507, 510 (1st Cir.), *aff'd on reh. en banc sub nom.* United States v. Aversa, 984 F.2d 493, 494–95 (1st Cir.1993), *judgment vacated on other grounds,* 510 U.S. 1069, 114 S.Ct. 873, 127 L.Ed.2d 70 (1994).

25. 31 C.F.R. § 103.11(ii).

26. *Id.* These exclusions make sense in light of the purpose of the reporting laws, which is to create a paper trail for financial transactions where none would otherwise exist so they can be reconstructed. Thus if the transaction generates some traceable record, like a written order, the transaction does not need to be further memorialized in a CTR.

27. Treasury Private Ruling dated August 24, 1989, reported in Money Laundering Alert, Nov. 1989, at p. 4.

28. 31 C.F.R. § 103.22(a)(1).

This regulation was adopted in 1987. Before that time, the courts' response to the use of multiple transactions to avoid the reporting requirement was mixed. In some limited circumstances they were willing to collapse the transactions and aggregate the amounts to reach $10,000, so the defendant would be liable for failure to file. More often, the courts were reluctant to aggregate the transactions and they concluded that defendants' conduct was not criminal. *See* Welling, *Smurfs, Money Laundering and the Federal Criminal Law: The Crime of Structuring Transactions,* 41 FLA.L.REV. 287, 298 (1989). This aggregation regula-

before multiple transactions are treated as one. The transaction must be by or on behalf of any person, the transactions must amount to over $10,000 cash in or cash out in a single day, and the bank must have knowledge of both these conditions.

ii. Failure to File

Once there is a duty to file, the government must prove that the defendant failed to do so. The prescribed form for reporting cash transactions is a CTR, Treasury Form 4789. The CTR must be filed with the IRS within 15 days of the transaction.[29]

iii. *Mens Rea*

The CTR law includes no *mens rea* term; rather, the *mens rea* is defined in the statute and regulations on BSA sanctions. For failure to file, the statutes and regulations both define the *mens rea* as *willfully*.[30]

The defendant must intend to do the conduct (failure to file) and the defendant must be aware of the facts. Some courts describe this *mens rea* as a "specific intent to commit the crime."[31] When one defendant claimed that she was ignorant of the fact that CTR's were not being filed, the court treated this knowledge as necessary for a "willful" violation.[32] In other words, ignorance of the facts is a defense.

The defendant must also know the law; ignorance of the reporting requirements is a defense.[33] To prove knowledge of the law, the government may use a willful blindness theory.[34]

tion was written to close that loophole. *United States v. St. Michael's Credit Union*, 880 F.2d 579, 594 n. 5 (1st Cir.1989).

29. 31 C.F.R. § 103.27(a)(1).

30. 31 U.S.C. § 5322(a)-(b) ("A person willfully violating this subchapter ... shall be fined....""); 31 C.F.R. § 103.49 (b)-(c) ("Any person who willfully violates....").

31. *First Circuit:* Bank of New England, 821 F.2d at 854 (*quoting* United States v. Hernando Ospina, 798 F.2d 1570, 1580 (11th Cir.1986) and United States v. Eisenstein, 731 F.2d 1540, 1543 (11th Cir. 1984)).

32. *St. Michael's Credit Union*, 880 F.2d at 585–86. The court rejected the defendant's testimony and found the evidence sufficient to support the jury's determination of willful failure to file. The conviction was reversed on other grounds.

33. *Supreme Court:* Ratzlaf v. United States, 510 U.S. 135, 114 S.Ct. 655, 126 L.Ed.2d 615 (1994).

First Circuit: St. Michael's Credit Union, 880 F.2d at 586 (defendant claimed no knowledge of the "consequences" of not filing CTR's, Court treats knowledge of the law as required and finds the evidence sufficient to infer defendant's knowledge of the law, conv. rev'd on other grounds); *Bank of New England*, 821 F.2d at 854 (finding of willfulness must be supported by proof of the defendant's knowledge of the reporting requirements, evidence sufficient to support conviction).

Eighth Circuit: United States v. Shannon, 836 F.2d 1125, 1128 (8th Cir.1988)(evidence sufficient that the defendant, as chairman of the board of another bank, knew he should have caused a CTR to be filed and conviction was affirmed).

34. *See, e.g.,*

First Circuit: St. Michael's Credit Union, 880 F.2d at 584; *Bank of New England*, 821 F.2d at 855.

See also

Sixth Circuit: United States v. Sturman, 951 F.2d 1466 (6th Cir.1991)(willful blindness used under BSA to establish knowledge of the law).

D. INCHOATE LIABILITY

i. Solicitation

Solicitation is not covered in the CTR statute or the general BSA penalty provisions. Federal law includes no general solicitation statute, so there is no solicitation liability under the CTR law.

ii. Conspiracy

Conspiracy liability is available under the general conspiracy statute, § 371.[35]

iii. Attempt

Attempt liability is not included in the CTR law, but the anti-structuring statute[36] covers this conduct. That statute states that no person shall cause *or attempt to* cause a financial institution to fail to file or to file a report with a material omission or misstatement.[37]

E. ACCOMPLICE LIABILITY

Accomplice liability for CTR crimes is available under two possible provisions: the general accomplice liability statute, § 2,[38] or the specific accomplice liability provision in the anti-structuring statute.[39]

This specific accomplice liability provision in the anti-structuring statute was enacted when the question of whether customers were liable as accomplices to banks caused a split in the circuits. Some courts found that customers did have a duty to file a CTR and could therefore be held criminally liable for failure to file on the theory that the customers were accomplices of the financial institutions under § 2.[40] Other courts refused to hold customers liable for failure to file a report[41] on the basis that the regulations did not explicitly impose such a duty on customers and so criminal liability would be unconstitutional because the laws were too vague.[42] The government detoured this split in 1987 when Congress adopted the anti-structuring statute, which explicitly imposes liability on any person who causes a financial institution to fail to file or to file

35. *See, e.g.,*

Second Circuit: United States v. Heyman, 794 F.2d 788 (2d Cir.1986); United States v. Goldberg, 756 F.2d 949 (2d Cir. 1985).

Third Circuit: United States v. American Investors of Pittsburgh, Inc., 879 F.2d 1087, 1092 n. 8 (3d Cir.1989).

Eleventh Circuit: United States v. Puerto, 730 F.2d 627 (11th Cir.1984).

36. 31 U.S.C. § 5324.

37. 31 U.S.C. § 5324(a)(1); 31 C.F.R. § 103.53(a) (emphasis added). These anti-structuring attempt provisions are discussed *infra* in § 18.11(C).

38. 18 U.S.C. § 2; United States v. Martiarena, 955 F.2d 363 (5th Cir.1992).

39. 31 U.S.C. § 5324.

40. *See, e.g.,* United States v. American Investors of Pittsburgh, Inc., 879 F.2d 1087 (3d Cir.1989).

41. *See* Welling, *Smurfs, Money Laundering and the Federal Criminal Law: The Crime of Structuring Transactions,* 41 Fla. L.Rev. 287 at 296 n.46.

42. *Id.* at n.47.

falsely.[43]

F. CONSTITUTIONALITY

The constitutionality of the CTR law has been challenged but not seriously threatened.

i. Privilege Against Self-incrimination

When bank customers claimed that requiring the banks to report cash transactions over $10,000 to the government violated the customers' privilege against self-incrimination, the Supreme Court declined to rule on this issue.[44] The lower courts have all found no violation of the customers' privilege against self-incrimination.[45]

ii. Unreasonable Search and Seizure

A constitutional challenge was raised under the fourth amendment alleging that these reports constitute an unreasonable search. The Supreme Court held that the CTR law did not violate the banks' fourth amendment rights[46] and declined to rule on depositors' fourth amendment rights because the depositors lacked standing.[47] The lower courts have found no violation of customers' fourth amendment rights.[48]

iii. Other

Other constitutional challenges have also been rejected.[49]

---

43. *See* the anti-structuring statute, 31 U.S.C. § 5324, discussed *infra* in §§ 18.9–18.11.

44. California Bankers' Assoc. v. Shultz, 416 U.S. 21, 73–75, 94 S.Ct. 1494, 1523–24, 39 L.Ed.2d 812 (1974) (Court refused to rule on the merits, stating that the customers' claims were premature because the pleadings did not allege that the customers were engaging in cash transactions over $10,000).

45. *Second Circuit:* United States v. Mickens, 926 F.2d 1323, 1331 (2d Cir.1991) (no violation of 5th amendment because no compulsion of individuals and no information reported that would necessarily be criminal).

Fifth Circuit: United States v. Camarena, 973 F.2d 427 (5th Cir.1992).

Ninth Circuit: United States v. Kimball, 884 F.2d 1274 (9th Cir.1989).

Tenth Circuit: United States v. Kaatz, 705 F.2d 1237, 1242 (10th Cir.1983) (no compulsion because customers not forced to do cash transactions).

Eleventh Circuit: United States v. Giancola, 783 F.2d 1549 (11th Cir.1986).

46. The Court stated that incorporated associations had no unqualified right to conduct their affairs in secret and that the disclosure required by the regulations was reasonable. *California Banker's Assoc.*, 416 U.S at 66–68.

47. The Court found that the customers had not made a sufficient showing of injury because merely being a depositor did not mean that any of their transactions would be reportable cash transactions over $10,000. *Id.* at 67–69.

48. United States v. Kaatz, 705 F.2d 1237, 1242 (10th Cir.1983)(report is not a search under fourth amendment because customers have no reasonable expectation of privacy in bank records, *citing* United States v. Miller, 425 U.S. 435, 96 S.Ct. 1619, 48 L.Ed.2d 71 (1976)).

49. In *California Banker's Assoc.*, the ACLU argued that the reporting law violated the first amendment because it interfered with its associational interests. The Court refused to rule on this argument, calling it speculative and hypothetical. *California Banker's Assoc.*, 416 U.S. at 75–76, 94 S.Ct. at 1523. This argument has not been raised in any other reported cases.

G. ENHANCED PENALTY

If the violation of the cash transaction law occurs (1) while violating another federal law or (2) as part of a pattern of any illegal activity involving more than $100,000 in a 12–month period, the maximum penalty jumps to $500,000 and 10 years or both.[50]

Most prosecutions under this enhanced penalty provision are based on a pattern of illegal activity involving over $100,000 in 12 months.[51] In order to form a pattern, the transactions must be repeated and related.[52] However, relatedness among the underlying transactions is not required where the defendant files no reports at all; then the necessary connection can be shown by proving "that the financial institution chronically and consistently failed to file any CTR's."[53] In other words, the failure to file itself is the pattern.

The unit of prosecution of the enhanced penalty has been addressed twice. In its "maiden case"[54] under the enhancement provision, the government indicted on four enhanced counts based on four separate 12 month periods. This approach was endorsed on appeal, although the unit

---

50. 31 U.S.C. § 5322(b); 31 C.F.R. § 103.49(c)(1)-(2).

From its enactment in 1970 until 1987, this enhancement provision was important because it was the only way to impose felony liability under the BSA; simple violations were only misdemeanors. The enhancement provision in effect during that time used slightly different language from the one in effect today. This original version had some confusing language.

See

Second Circuit: United States v. Dickinson, 706 F.2d 88 (2d Cir.1983) ("transactions" means transactions as defined in the BSA).

Ninth Circuit: United States v. Beusch, 596 F.2d 871 (9th Cir.1979) (misdemeanor violations of BSA can be combined to activate enhancement provision; no other illegalities are required).

Eleventh Circuit: United States v. Valdes–Guerra, 758 F.2d 1411 (11th Cir. 1985).

In 1987 when the law was amended, simple violations were made felonies and the language was clarified.

51. *See, e.g.,*

First Circuit: United States v. St. Michael's Credit Union, 880 F.2d 579 (1st Cir.1989); United States v. Bank of New England, 821 F.2d 844 (1st Cir.1987).

Second Circuit: United States v. Dickinson, 706 F.2d at 88 (2d Cir.1983).

Third Circuit: United States v. American Investors of Pittsburgh, Inc., 879 F.2d 1087 (3d Cir.1989).

Fifth Circuit: United States v. Camarena, 973 F.2d 427 (5th Cir.1992).

Ninth Circuit: United States v. Gebrayel, 788 F.2d 1567 (9th Cir.1986), *described in* Gebrayel v. United States, 990 F.2d 1257 (9th Cir.1993); United States v. Beusch, 596 F.2d 871 (9th Cir.1979).

Eleventh Circuit: United States v. Kattan–Kassin, 696 F.2d 893 (11th Cir.1983).

52. *First Circuit:* St. Michael's Credit Union, 880 F.2d at 587 (transactions must be repeated and related); Bank of New England, 821 F.2d at 853 (defining pattern as repeated *and* related might have been more accurate, but instruction defining pattern only as repeated is "not even close" to plain error).

Second Circuit: Dickinson, 706 F.2d at 91 (transactions must be "related or connected").

53. St. Michael's Credit Union, 880 F.2d at 587. As the court explained, "It is incongruous to believe that Congress intended that a financial institution could insulate itself from [enhanced liability] by showing that it had not filed CTRs for any of its reportable transactions." Id. at 588.

54. Beusch, 596 F.2d at 873–74.

of prosecution was not specifically addressed.[55] In a later case, the government took a more aggressive approach and successfully prosecuted each violation within the pattern as a separate enhanced count rather than treating the pattern within 12 months as a single count.[56] Both these cases were decided before the 1987 changes in the law that make the unit of prosecution less significant.[57]

H. NOTE ON CORPORATE LIABILITY

Because the duty to report applies to financial institutions, the defendants are often corporations. Some important doctrines on corporate liability have developed in this context.

i. *Mens Rea* of Corporation

In a seminal prosecution for non-reporting, United States v. Bank of New England,[58] the First Circuit allowed expansive corporate liability. Noting that the defendant bank had to have knowledge of the reporting laws to be liable, the court allowed the government to prove the bank's knowledge using willful blindness.[59] More controversially, the court allowed the government to prove the bank's knowledge using collective knowledge. Under this doctrine, the knowledge of the corporation is the collected knowledge of all its agents.[60] Thus even though no one agent had knowledge of the facts and the law, the corporation might still be liable when the knowledge of all its agents was combined. The bank's conviction for 31 counts of non-reporting was affirmed.

ii. Successor Liability

The Fifth Circuit affirmed the conviction of a bank for non-reporting when the crimes were committed by a different entity years before the defendant merged with it.[61] In 1987, defendant Alamo Bank merged with Central National Bank. Central National became a branch of Alamo. Three or four years before the merger, officers of Central National Bank had committed numerous non-reporting crimes. Alamo Bank argued it should not be convicted for Central National Bank's pre-merger activities. The court, however, disagreed and affirmed Alamo's conviction, noting that Central National could not escape punishment by merging with another bank and adopting its corporate persona.[62]

Library References:

C.J.S. United States § 125.
West's Key No. Digests, United States ⊚34.

55. *Id.* at 878–79 (based on predecessor language). One judge dissents on this basis, *id.* at 879–81.

56. United States v. Kattan–Kassin, 696 F.2d 893 (11th Cir.1983).

57. Various changes in 1987 coincided to render the unit of prosecution less important: Simple violations now are felonies, the sentencing guidelines use grouping of counts, and the guidelines range rather than the statutory maximum generally defines the maximum sentence.

58. 821 F.2d 844 (1st Cir.1987).

59. *Id.* at 855.

60. *Id.* at 855–57.

61. United States v. Alamo Bank of Texas, 880 F.2d 828 (5th Cir.1989).

62. *Id.* at 830.

§ 18.4　Reporting　Laws—Import/Export　Reports:　§ 5316　CMIR's

A.　IN GENERAL

Section 5316 requires that a report be filed with the government when monetary instruments over $10,000 are transported into or out of the U.S.[1] The report is called a Currency or Monetary Instrument Report (CMIR). Filing a false report or failing to file is a crime. This reporting requirement was enacted along with the cash transaction reporting law in 1970.

The duty to report extends to all "persons" who import or export monetary instruments over $10,000.[2] As discussed *infra*, person is defined broadly so that any person or entity may be a defendant.

Two types of specific conduct are prohibited by the import/export reporting law: failing to file a report when due, and making a false, fictitious or fraudulent statement or representation in a report.[3]

B.　FALSE FILING

No prosecutions based on false filing have been reported.

The statute setting out penalties for the BSA prohibits any *willful* violation.[4] The regulation on penalties prohibits *knowing* false, fictitious or fraudulent statements.[5] The existence of two different *mens rea* terms for false filing liability is curious. The drafters' intent is unclear, and the implications of the difference are unclear. As noted above, no prosecutions have been reported for false statements in a CMIR (or in any kind of BSA report), so no courts have construed the language.

C.　FAILURE TO FILE

The offense of failure to file has three elements: a duty to file, a failure to do so, and a *mens rea* of willfulness.

i.　Filing Duty

A filing duty is imposed on all persons who (1) transport, mail, or ship into or out of the United States or who (2) receive from abroad in the United States, monetary instruments over $10,000.

a.　Who Must File; Person

Person includes all entities cognizable as "legal personalities."[6] Thus, an individual or an agent/bailee of a corporation, partnership,

§ 18.4
1.　31 U.S.C. § 5316.
2.　31 C.F.R. § 103.23(a).
3.　31　C.F.R.　§§ 103.23(a)-(b), 103.49(b)-(d).
4.　31 U.S.C. § 5322.
5.　31 C.F.R. § 103.49(d).
6.　*Id.* § 103.11(z).

trust or estate, joint stock company, association, syndicate, or joint venture may have to file a report.[7] Some entities are exempt from the reporting requirement, such as the Federal Reserve, banks or securities dealers in respect to monetary instruments sent through the postal service or by common carrier, and others.[8]

The duty to report falls on all persons transporting or receiving monetary instruments regardless of whether they are the true owners of the instruments or just temporary possessors. Thus it is no defense that the defendant was carrying monetary instruments which belonged to someone else;[9] mere possession triggers the duty to file.

b. Monetary Instrument

This law requires that monetary instruments over $10,000 be reported. *Monetary instruments* means all negotiable instruments, including:

— currency;

— traveler's checks (in any form);

— all negotiable instruments that are either in "bearer form, endorsed without restriction" or in any other form that passes title upon delivery, such as personal checks and cashier's checks;

— incomplete instruments such as personal checks that are signed but omit the payee's name; and

— bearer form stocks or securities.[10]

Warehouse receipts and bills of lading are not monetary instruments and so are not subject to the reporting requirement,[11] and no duty to report exists for non-negotiable instruments regardless of the amount.[12]

Travelers checks restrictively endorsed are monetary instruments and so must be reported.[13]

The Treasury Department has proposed regulations adding instruments drawn by foreign banks on accounts in the United States to the definition of monetary instruments under the import/export reporting law.[14] These regulations are not yet final.

7. *Id.*

See, e.g.,

Second Circuit: United States v. Dickinson, 706 F.2d 88 (2d Cir.1983) (individual convicted).

Ninth Circuit: United States v. Beusch, 596 F.2d 871 (9th Cir.1979) (corporation and individual corporate officer convicted for failure to file CMIR's).

8. *See* 31 C.F.R. § 103.23(c)(1)-(9).

9. United States v. Berisha, 925 F.2d 791 (5th Cir.1991). *See also* 31 U.S.C.

§ 5316(a) ("a person *or an agent or bailee of the person* shall file . . . .") (emphasis added).

10. 31 C.F.R. § 103.11(u)(1).

11. *Id.* § 103.11(u)(2).

12. United States v. $173,081.04 in U.S. Currency, 835 F.2d 1141, 1142 n. 3 (5th Cir.1988).

13. United States v. Larson, 110 F.3d 620, 625–26 (8th Cir.1997).

14. *See* 62 Fed.Reg. No. 14, pp. 3249–3252 (Jan. 22, 1997).

c. Transport, Ship, Receive

Persons have a duty to file if they (1) transport, (2) are about to transport, or (3) receive currency or monetary instruments to or from a place outside the U.S.

d. Over $10,000 and "At One Time"

Generally, a report must be filed only when the $10,000 threshold is crossed. This is easy enough to identify when the defendant is involved in one transportation or receipt; it is complicated when the defendant is involved in a series of events.

A report is due whenever a person transports, is about to transport, or receives monetary instruments exceeding $10,000 *at one time*.[15] A literal reading of the statutory language "at one time" would require the filing of a report only when the amount transported in one instance exceeds $10,000. Section 5316's regulations, however, impose a duty to file a report if a person transports over $10,000 in any time period, if the purpose is to evade the reporting requirements.[16] Hence, it is possible that a person may have a duty to file a report when the person did not exceed the $10,000 limit on one day, but transported an excess of $10,000 over multiple days, as long as the intent was to evade reporting. This is an odd result considering that the statute specifically states *at one time*.

Assuming that conduct is present, the question remains when the report is due. Reports are due to be filed:

— at the *time of departure* from the United States;

— at the *time of entry* into the United States;

— at the *time of the mailing or shipping* from the United States;[17] or

— *within 15 days of the time the person receives* the monetary instruments, unless the shipper previously filed a form.[18]

No definitions for the "time of mailing or shipping" or the "time the person receives" have been developed. But for traveling defendants, the "time of departure" and "time of entry" have been defined by the courts.

Logically, there must be a point in time at which the duty to file a report arises and a separate point in time at which it is too late to file, *i.e.*, the offense of failing to file has been completed. These two points cannot be the same, since that would render it impossible to comply with the duty. It is difficult to articulate a coherent standard based on the case law since, as discussed *infra*, some cases have described the arising of the duty and others have described the point at which the failure to

15. 31 U.S.C. § 5316(a)(1)-(2).

16. 31 C.F.R. § 103.11(b) ("if for the purpose of evading the reporting requirements, a person must file a report where the monetary instruments exceed $10,000 on one or more days.").

17. *Id.* § 103.27(b)(1) (emphasis added).

18. *Id.* § 103.23(b) (emphasis added).

file has been completed, but no case has distinguished the two points. In other words, the "time of departure" when the defendant incurs the duty to file is not distinguished from the "time of departure" when a defendant has committed a crime by not having already filed.

Courts define the "time of departure" as "when one is reasonably close, both spatially and temporally, to the physical point of departure itself, and manifests a definite commitment to leave."[19] Once the person reaches the time of departure, he or she must have submitted the form or attempted to submit the form.[20] Then failure to file is a violation, but only if the defendant is beyond the time of departure. For instance, in United States v. Jenkins, agents arrested the defendant ten hours prior to his flight while he was still in a Manhattan hotel.[21] The Southern District of New York dismissed the indictment after finding that Jenkins had not reached the time of departure by the time of his arrest, and, therefore, no duty to file had arisen.

The circuits agree that *time of departure* signifies the point at which the defendant is "reasonably close, both spatially and temporally, to the physical point of departure itself, and [has] manifested a definite commitment to leave."[22] Generally once the defendant has entered the jetport,[23] reached the last security checkpoint,[24] or entered the departure area with his boarding pass,[25] he has reached the point of departure and, therefore, has a duty to report.

Prior to these points in time, however, it seems unlikely that a defendant has sufficiently reached the time of departure. The *Jenkins* case is one example. Another example is United States v. Bareno–Burgos.[26] In *Bareno-Burgos*, agents arrested the defendant in New York City, while aboard a domestic flight bound for Miami that was later scheduled to leave for Columbia.[27] In finding the defendant not liable,

19. *Second Circuit:* Mercado v. United States Customs Service, 873 F.2d 641, 646 (2d Cir.1989); United States v. Bareno–Burgos, 739 F.Supp. 772, 781 (E.D.N.Y.1990).

Fifth Circuit: United States v. Rojas, 671 F.2d 159, 163 (5th Cir.1982).

See also

Fourth Circuit: United States v. Ozim, 779 F.2d 1017, 1018 (4th Cir.1985).

Ninth Circuit: United States v. $122,-043.00 in U.S. Currency, 792 F.2d 1476 (9th Cir.1986); United States v. $831,-160.45 in U.S. Currency, 607 F.Supp. 1407, 1413 (N.D.Cal.1985), *aff'd,* 785 F.2d 317 (9th Cir.1986).

20. Although § 5316 speaks of "about to transport," the duty to file depends on whether the defendant reached the point of departure. *See infra* § 18.4(D).

21. United States v. Jenkins, 689 F.Supp. 342, 343 (S.D.N.Y.1988), *aff'd,* 943 F.2d 167 (2d Cir.1991).

22. *Fourth Circuit:* United States v. Ozim, 779 F.2d at 1018.

See also

Second Circuit: Mercado, 873 F.2d at 646; United States v. Cutaia, 511 F.Supp. 619, 624 (E.D.N.Y.1981).

Fifth Circuit: Rojas, 671 F.2d at 163.

Ninth Circuit: $122,043.00 in U.S. Currency, 792 F.2d at 1476; *$831,160.45 in U.S. Currency,* 607 F.Supp. at 1412.

23. *Fifth Circuit:* United States v. Rojas, 671 F.2d at 163.

Ninth Circuit: United States v. $122,-043.00 in U.S. Currency, 792 F.2d at 1477.

24. United States v. $831,160.45 in U.S. Currency, 607 F.Supp. at 1413.

25. United States v. Ozim, 779 F.2d at 1018.

26. 739 F.Supp. 772 (E.D.N.Y.1990).

27. *Id.* at 774.

the court noted that although § 5316 states "about to transport," the defendant had yet to reach the time of departure. That is, the "defendant's ... international departure still required considerable affirmative action on his part."[28] Since no duty to report had arisen, the defendant was not liable, even in light of the "about to transport" language of § 5316.

The term "time of entry" signifies the point at which the person, or agent/bailee of the person, presents himself or herself for entry into the United States.[29] That person must report at least by the time of inspection by Customs.[30] Furthermore, the fact that Customs denied the person entry into the United States does not alleviate the person's duty to report.[31]

ii. Failure to File

a. Prescribed Form

The form prescribed by the Secretary of the Treasury for reporting the import/export of monetary instruments is Form 4790, a Currency and Monetary Instruments Report (CMIR).

b. Deadline

The Form 4790 must be filed by the time of departure or time of entry into the United States. The regulations permit filing by mail on or before the date of entry, departure, mailing or shipping, however, when the monetary instruments will not be physically accompanying a person entering or leaving the United States.[32]

iii. Mens Rea

The reporting statute applies only to persons who *knowingly* transport monetary instruments into or out of the United States.[33] On top of that *mens rea* term, criminal penalties apply only to persons who *willfully* fail to report.[34] The defendant must know the facts and intentionally breach the known duty to report.[35] The government must prove

28. *Id.* at 782.

29. United States v. $47,980.00 in Canadian Currency, 726 F.2d 532, 534 (9th Cir.1984).

30. *Id.*

31. *Id.*

32. 31 C.F.R. § 103.23.

33. 31 U.S.C. § 5316(a). The term knowingly appears in the statute, but the regulations are empty. On this point the regulations seem inconsistent with the statute, arguably defining a broader liability. For the BSA, it is clear that the regulations control. *See* California Bankers' Association v. Shultz, 416 U.S. 21, 26, 94 S.Ct. 1494,

1500, 39 L.Ed.2d 812 (1974). But they do so only to the extent they narrow liability; regulations cannot expand liability beyond that defined in the statute. Thus the statutory *mens rea* knowingly is an element even though the regulations are silent.

34. 31 U.S.C. § 5322(a)-(b); 31 C.F.R. § 103.49(b)-(d).

35. *Supreme Court:* Ratzlaf v. United States, 510 U.S. 135, 114 S.Ct. 655, 126 L.Ed.2d 615 (1994).

Fifth Circuit: United States v. O'Banion, 943 F.2d 1422, 1427 (5th Cir.1991).

Ninth Circuit: United States v. Ibarra–Alcarez, 830 F.2d 968, 974 (9th Cir.1987).

both these elements to convict a defendant,[36] but many courts allow the same evidence to satisfy both prongs.[37]

First, defendants must know the facts, *i.e.* that they are carrying monetary instruments worth over $10,000 into or out of the United States without filing a report.[38] Hence, a defense may exist where the defendant did not know the amount of money he was carrying exceeded $10,000,[39] or the defendant did not know that what he carried qualified as a monetary instrument.[40]

Although mistake of fact is a defense, one court has held it was not error to deny the defendant a specific instruction. In United States v. Gomez–Osorio,[41] the defendant argued that he mistakenly believed that what he carried was not a monetary instrument. The court stated that a jury instruction that described the elements of the offense as knowledge of the requirement to report transportation of monetary instruments and willful failure to report the transportation of the monetary instrument was be sufficient to encompass the theory of a good faith mistake, so no further instruction was necessary.[42]

Second, the defendant must know the reporting requirements. That is, he must know he has a duty to report[43] as a prerequisite to conviction.[44] Because knowledge is an element of the offense, ignorance of the

36. *Second Circuit:* United States v. Dichne, 612 F.2d 632, 635 (2d Cir.1979); United States v. San Juan, 545 F.2d 314, 318 (2d Cir.1976).

Fourth Circuit: United States v. Ozim, 779 F.2d 1017, 1018 (4th Cir.1985).

Fifth Circuit: United States v. Berisha, 925 F.2d 791, 795 (5th Cir.1991); United States v. Warren, 612 F.2d 887, 890 (5th Cir.1980).

Ninth Circuit: United States v. Ibarra–Alcarez, 830 F.2d at 973.

37. *See, e.g.,*

Fifth Circuit: United States v. O'Banion, 943 F.2d at 1429.

Ninth Circuit: United States v. Rodriguez, 592 F.2d 553, 557 (9th Cir.1979).

38. *Second Circuit:* United States v. Cutaia, 511 F.Supp. 619, 624 (E.D.N.Y. 1981).

Fourth Circuit: United States v. Ozim, 779 F.2d at 1018.

Fifth Circuit: United States v. Warren, 612 F.2d at 890.

Ninth Circuit: United States v. Ibarra–Alcarez, 830 F.2d at 974.

39. *Berisha,* 925 F.2d at 795 (defendant argued unsuccessfully that he was not required to report the $17,000 he carried because only $8,000 of it was his and $9,000 was a companion's).

40. United States v. Larson, 110 F.3d 620, 625 (8th Cir.1997) (defendant argued unsuccessfully he did not know travelers check restrictively endorsed was monetary instrument; evidence of defendant's knowledge sufficient).

41. 957 F.2d 636 (9th Cir.1992).

42. *Id.* at 642–43.

43. *See, e.g.,*

Second Circuit: United States v. Dichne, 612 F.2d at 635;

Fifth Circuit: United States v. O'Banion, 943 F.2d at 1426;

Ninth Circuit: United States v. Ibarra–Alcarez, 830 F.2d at 974.

44. *Supreme Court:* Ratzlaf v. United States, 510 U.S. 135, 114 S.Ct. 655, 126 L.Ed.2d 615 (1994).

Second Circuit: United States v. San Juan, 545 F.2d 314, 318 (2d Cir.1976).

Fourth Circuit: United States v. Ozim, 779 F.2d at 1018.

Fifth Circuit: United States v. Granda, 565 F.2d 922, 926 (5th Cir.1978); United States v. Schnaiderman, 568 F.2d 1208 (5th Cir.1978) (conviction based on § 1001), *overruled by* United States v. Rodriguez–Rios, 14 F.3d 1040 (5th Cir.1994).

Eighth Circuit: United States v. Larson, 110 F.3d 620, 624–25 (8th Cir.1997) (citing *Ratzlaf*).

law is a defense.[45] Moreover, courts have made it clear that sufficient proof of the defendant's knowledge of the requirements will not exist unless the government takes affirmative steps to make the requirements known to travelers.[46] For instance, in U.S. v. Granda, the court found the typewritten question whether the defendant was carrying more than $5,000 on the bottom of the customs form to be insufficient to establish the requisite level of knowledge.[47] Along the same lines, the defendant's acknowledged familiarity with "U.S. currency laws" is not sufficient to establish knowledge of the law.[48]

A court will infer knowledge of the reporting requirements, however, once the government includes language on the form to the effect of "if you are carrying over $10,000 in cash or monetary instruments you must file a report."[49] Likewise, oral notice[50] (either through announcements over the public address system[51] or individual advice from a government agent[52]) and posted signs[53] may be sufficient to put the traveler on notice. A jury may also infer knowledge of the requirements from a defendant's familiarity with the process of international travel and the number of previous international trips the defendant has made.[54]

All these cases were based on actual knowledge of the law, albeit sometimes actual knowledge that was inferred. No CMIR prosecutions have relied on willful blindness to prove knowledge of the law. But courts have used willful blindness to establish knowledge of the law in prosecutions under the CTR law.[55] These prosecutions were based on the

Ninth Circuit: United States v. Rodriquez, 592 F.2d at 557.

45. *Fifth Circuit:* United States v. Granda, 565 F.2d at 926; United States v. Schnaiderman, 568 F.2d 1208 (conviction based on § 1001 and overruled by *Rodriquez-Rios*).

See also Ratzlaf v. United States, 510 U.S. 135, 114 S.Ct. 655, 126 L.Ed.2d 615 (1994).

46. *See*

Second Circuit: United States v. San Juan, 545 F.2d at 319.

Fifth Circuit: United States v. Granda, 565 F.2d at 926; United States v. Schaiderman, 568 F.2d at 1208 (conviction based on § 1001 and overruled by *Rodriquez-Rios*).

See also

Fifth Circuit: United States v. Warren, 612 F.2d 887, 890 (5th Cir.1980) (reversing the convictions of two defendants who sailed across the international border without filing Form 4790 since the defendants were not advised of the reporting requirements, did not know of the requirements, and were not given the opportunity to file once informed).

47. *Granda,* 565 F.2d at 926.

48. United States v. Schnaiderman, 568 F.2d at 1212 (conviction based on § 1001 and overruled by *Rodriquez-Rios*).

49. United States v. Rodriguez, 592 F.2d 553, 557 (9th Cir.1979).

50. *See*

Second Circuit: United States v. Dichne, 612 F.2d 632, 637 (2d Cir.1979).

Fourth Circuit: United States v. Ozim, 779 F.2d 1017, 1018 (4th Cir.1985).

Fifth Circuit: United States v. Berisha, 925 F.2d 791, 796 (5th Cir.1991).

51. *See, e.g., Dichne,* 612 F.2d at 632.

52. *See, e.g.,* United States v. Berisha, 925 F.2d at 791.

53. *Second Circuit: Dichne,* 612 F.2d at 637.

Fifth Circuit: United States v. Salinas–Garza, 803 F.2d 834, 839 (5th Cir.1986) (posted signs in both Spanish and English).

54. *Second Circuit:* United States v. Dichne, 612 F.2d at 638.

Fourth Circuit: United States v. Ozim, 779 F.2d at 1018.

55. *First Circuit:* United States v. St. Michael's Credit Union, 880 F.2d 579 (1st

same BSA penalty provision which applies to the CMIR law, so it is likely that willful blindness is available as a basis for prosecution.

D. INCHOATE LIABILITY

i. Solicitation

Regulations under the import/export law criminalize the conduct itself (transporting, mailing, shipping, and receiving), and also criminalize *causing* the conduct, *attempting* the conduct and *attempting to cause* the conduct.[56] *Causing* is defined to include *requesting*. Thus a defendant who engaged in what is generally known as solicitation—attempting to cause the offense by requesting another to perform the conduct—is within the scope of the regulation and is liable.

ii. Conspiracy

The reporting laws include no particularized provision, but liability is available under the general conspiracy statute, § 371.[57]

iii. Attempt

The statute says *about to transport*.[58] The regulations cover "attempts to physically transport" and "attempts to cause to be physically transported...."[59] With all this language, it is ironic that attempt liability still does not exist. The explanation is that in an effort to include attempt liability, Congress in 1986 amended § 5316's "attempt to transport" language to read "about to transport."[60] However, the Secretary of the Treasury has failed to adopt regulations necessary to implement the statute.[61] As a result, the "about to transport" language fails to penalize a willful attempt on the part of an individual. Rather, the defendant must actually violate a duty to file, once such a duty has arisen, in order to be guilty of a § 5316 offense.[62]

E. ACCOMPLICE LIABILITY

The regulation implementing the import/export law extends liability to persons *causing* the conduct.[63] This is a particularized accomplice

---

Cir.1989); United States v. Bank of New England, 821 F.2d 844 (1st Cir.1987).

56. 31 C.F.R. § 103.23(a).

57. *See, e.g.,* United States v. Ozim, 779 F.2d at 1017.

58. 31 U.S.C § 5316(a)(1).

59. 31 C.F.R. § 103.23(a).

60. 31 U.S.C. § 5316(a)(1). Congress amended the language in an attempt to clarify the Secretary's authority to require the filing of reports prior to actual departure. United States v. Jenkins, 689 F.Supp. 342, 343 (S.D.N.Y.1988), *aff'd,* 943 F.2d 167 (2d Cir.1991). Considering the Secretary's continuing failure to enact regulations

which require reports before actual departure, the amendment has been ineffective.

61. Section 5316(b) states that the Secretary must prescribe, by issuing regulations, when and where a report must be filed. 31 U.S.C. § 5316(b).

62. United States v. Jenkins, 689 F.Supp. at 343. *See also* H.R.Rep.No. 99–855, 2d Sess., pt. 1 at 19 (1986) ("The offense of transporting currency or monetary instruments is only triggered once the duty to file the report has been created.").

63. 31 C.F.R. § 103.23(a).

liability provision. In addition, the general accomplice liability statute, § 2, may apply as well.[64]

F. CONSTITUTIONALITY

i. Privilege Against Self-incrimination

The guarantee against compelled self-incrimination is the primary constitutional challenge to the import/export reporting law. The defense argument is that the reporting law forces a person to provide the government with potentially self-incriminating information.[65] The Supreme Court declined to reach this question in *California Bankers Association*, finding it premature.[66] The few courts that have decided the issue have been unanimous in rejecting the argument.[67] For example, the Ninth Circuit, relying on Supreme Court cases,[68] balanced a number of criteria in an effort to determine whether the import/export reporting law so threatened self-incrimination that it should be declared unconstitutional.[69] After weighing the factors, the court concluded that the balance tipped in favor of a governmental interest in reporting. The court noted that the statute does not involve an area "permeated with criminal statutes" in comparison to other statutes declared to be invalid;[70] the disclosures do not provide a "direct link to any related criminal activity . . .", since they are only "tangentially related" to any criminal transaction;[71] and the purpose behind the statute is primarily tax-related rather than investigatory.[72]

ii. Unreasonable Search and Seizure

The Supreme Court has held that the reporting requirements do not violate the fourth amendment because they are analogous to tax reporting requirements held valid by the Court and because the reports require only "information as to a relatively limited group of financial transac-

64. *Second Circuit*: United States v. Goldberg, 756 F.2d 949 (2d Cir.1985)(construing FBAR reporting requirement).

Fifth Circuit: United States v. Martiarena, 955 F.2d 363 (5th Cir.1992).

65. *See, e.g.,* United States v. Dichne, 612 F.2d 632, 638 (2d Cir.1979).

66. California Bankers' Association v. Shultz, 416 U.S. 21, 73, 94 S.Ct. 1494, 1523, 39 L.Ed.2d 812 (1974).

67. *Second Circuit*: Dichne, 612 F.2d at 641; United States v. Cutaia, 511 F.Supp. 619, 623 (E.D.N.Y.1981).

Ninth Circuit: United States v. Des Jardins, 747 F.2d 499, 509 (9th Cir.1984), *vacated in nonpertinent part,* 772 F.2d 578 (9th Cir.1985).

68. Albertson v. Subversive Activities Control Bd., 382 U.S. 70, 86 S.Ct. 194, 15 L.Ed.2d 165 (1965); Marchetti v. United

States, 390 U.S. 39, 88 S.Ct. 697, 19 L.Ed.2d 889 (1968); California v. Byers, 402 U.S. 424, 91 S.Ct. 1535, 29 L.Ed.2d 9 (1971).

69. *United States v. Des Jardins,* 747 F.2d 499, 507 (9th Cir.1984), *vacated in nonpertinent part,* 772 F.2d 578 (9th Cir. 1985).

70. *Id.* at 508.

71. *Id.* at 509.

72. *Id. See also* United States v. Dichne, 612 F.2d 632 (2d Cir.1979) (using similar analysis in rejecting the defendant's 5th Amendment challenge). *But see* Jeremy Hugh Temkin, Comment, *Hollow Ritual[s]: The Fifth Amendment and Self-reporting Schemes,* 34 UCLA L.Rev. 467, 484 (1986) (criticizing the analysis used by the *Dichne* court and citing legislative history that supports an investigatory purpose as the primary purpose behind § 5316).

tions in foreign commerce, and are reasonably related to the statutory purpose of assisting in the enforcement of the laws of the United States."[73] Furthermore, the Court explained,

> The statutory authorization for the regulations was based upon a conclusion by Congress that international currency transactions and foreign financial institutions were being used by residents of the United States to circumvent the enforcement of the laws of the United States. The regulations are sufficiently tailored so as to single out transactions found to have the greatest potential for such circumvention and which involve substantial amounts of money. They are therefore reasonable in the light of that statutory purpose, and consistent with the Fourth Amendment.[74]

iii. Due Process

Defendants have also attempted to challenge the constitutionality of the import/export report law on due process grounds. In United States v. O'Banion,[75] the defendant was convicted of importing monetary instruments over $10,000 into the United States without reporting. The defendant appealed, claiming that the reporting law violated due process since it criminalizes importation of even legitimately-derived funds when a person fails to report[76] and that this result indicated that the government failed to use the least restrictive alternative. The court rejected the defendant's argument, noting only its reluctance to engage in a policy debate on the issue.[77]

G. ENHANCED PENALTY

If the defendant committed the crime while violating another federal law or committed a pattern of violations involving over $100,000 in a year, the defendant is subject to an enhanced penalty with a maximum fine of $500,000 or a maximum of ten years in prison, or both.[78] This is the same enhancement provision that applies to the CTR crime, and it is discussed in detail *supra* in that section.[79]

H. RELATIONSHIP BETWEEN THE REPORTING LAW AND § 1001

Section 1001[80] is often used in combination with the import/export reporting law in failure to file cases.[81] The import/export reporting law

---

73. California Bankers' Assoc. v. Shultz, 416 U.S. 21, 62, 94 S.Ct. 1494, 1517, 39 L.Ed.2d 812 (1974).

74. *Id.* at 63.

75. 943 F.2d 1422 (5th Cir.1991).

76. *Id.* at 1433.

77. *Id.*

78. 31 U.S.C. § 5322(b) and 31 C.F.R. § 103.49(c).

79. See § 18.3(G) *supra.*

80. 18 U.S.C. § 1001, discussed in §§ 12.7–12.10, *infra.*

81. *See, e.g.,*

Second Circuit: United States v. Cutaia, 511 F.Supp. 619 (E.D.N.Y.1981).

Fifth Circuit: United States v. Berisha, 925 F.2d 791 (5th Cir.1991).

and § 1001 are two distinct crimes and the defendant can be convicted of both.[82]

Library References:

C.J.S. United States § 125.
West's Key No. Digests, United States ⊱34.

§ 18.5 Reporting Laws—Section 6050I Trade or Business Transaction Reports: Form 8300's

A. IN GENERAL

Section 6050I requires persons who receive over $10,000 in cash in the course of their trade or business to report the transaction to the government. Filing a false report or failing to file is a crime.

This statute completes the scheme of transaction reporting laws. When these reports are combined with the other two reports discussed *supra*, the government is notified of all cash transactions over $10,000.

The reporting requirement is imposed on trades and businesses, so the defendants are generally employees of the trade or business[1] or the trade or business itself.[2] Customers of the trade or business have no duty to report under § 6050I(a) but may be liable for causing failure to file or structuring under § 6050I(f), discussed *infra* in §§ 18.10–18.11.

As with the other reporting laws, two kinds of conduct are criminal: failure to report or supply information, and filing a false report. Section 6050I is part of the tax code and violations are prosecuted thereunder. The crime of failing to file or supply information is prosecuted under I.R.C. § 7203[3] and false statements are prosecuted under I.R.C. § 7206.[4]

Ninth Circuit: United States v. Alzate–Restreppo, 890 F.2d 1061 (9th Cir.1989).

82. *Supreme Court:* United States v. Woodward, 469 U.S. 105, 105 S.Ct. 611, 83 L.Ed.2d 518 (1985).

See also

Ninth Circuit: United States v. Alzate–Restreppo, 890 F.2d at 1061.

Some courts initially concluded the two crimes did merge, *see, e.g.,* United States v. Des Jardins, 747 F.2d 499 (9th Cir.1984), *vacated in part,* 772 F.2d 578 (9th Cir. 1985). But the Supreme Court made clear in *Woodward* that they do not merge.

§ 18.5

1. *See, e.g.,*

D.C. Circuit: United States v. Geneva Enterprises, 1993 U.S.Dist.LEXIS 9381 (D.D.C.1993).

Second Circuit: United States v. Roges, 1991 WL 280721 (S.D.N.Y.1991).

2. *See, e.g.,* United States v. Geneva Enterprises, 1993 U.S.Dist. LEXIS 9381 (D.D.C.1993).

3. *See*

Sixth Circuit: United States v. Palazzolo, 73 F.3d 363 (6th Cir.1995) (unpublished disposition); United States v. Finch, 47 F.3d 1171 (6th Cir.1995) (unpublished disposition); United States v. Young, 985 F.2d 562 (6th Cir.1993) (unpublished disposition) (primarily an anti-structuring case under § 6050I(f) but relies on § 7203 for failure to file aspect).

Eighth Circuit: United States v. Jensen, 69 F.3d 906 (8th Cir.1995).

4. *See*

Second Circuit: United States v. Roges, 1991 WL 280721 (S.D.N.Y.1991) (pre-conviction decision; relies on § 7206).

Fifth Circuit: United States v. McGuire, 79 F.3d 1396 (5th Cir.1996) (conviction reversed on other grounds).

Section 7201, which prohibits tax evasion, is not applicable to § 6050I violations

B. FALSE FILING UNDER § 7206

The elements of I.R.C. § 7206 are: 1) the making or subscribing of a return; 2) which is false as to a material fact; 3) which the maker does not believe to be true and correct; 4) the return is signed under penalty of perjury; and 5) a *mens rea* of willfulness.[5] These elements are discussed in §§ 23.3–23.4 on tax crimes. In the one reported false filing case based on § 6050I, the Fifth Circuit reversed the defendant's conviction because the materiality of the false statement was not submitted to the jury.[6]

C. FAILURE TO FILE UNDER § 7203

The failure to file crime has three elements: a duty to file, a failure to do so and a *mens rea* of willfulness.[7]

i. Filing Duty

The filing duty is imposed on persons who receive over $10,000 in cash in one transaction or related transactions in the course of their trade or business. The terms of this formula are discussed below.

a. Cash

One might assume that *cash* means currency. But the definition of cash for this reporting law is broader and more complex. The surprisingly broad definition of cash makes this an area for caution.

Currency is always covered by the statute. Under certain circumstances, monetary instruments are also covered, depending on when the transaction occurred. If payment was received before February 3, 1992, then the term cash only includes U.S. and foreign coins and currency.[8] If the payment was received after February 3, 1992, the definition of cash is expanded to include "certain monetary instruments."[9] The "certain monetary instruments" are cashier's checks ("treasurer's checks" and "bank checks"), bank drafts, traveler's checks, or money orders where the face amount does not exceed $10,000.[10] The statute excludes checks drawn on the account of the writer in specified financial institutions from the definition of money instruments.[11] This provision excludes

---

because that section generates no tax liability.

5. Section 7206 is discussed with tax crimes in § ___.

6. United States v. McGuire, 79 F.3d 1396 (5th Cir.1996).

7. Section 7203 is discussed *infra* in § 23.6 with tax crimes.

8. 26 C.F.R. § 1.6050I–1(c)(1)(i). This date is a watershed because the regulations were amended on this date to expand the definition of cash, but the broader definition does not apply retroactively.

9. I.R.C. § 6050I(d); 26 C.F.R. § 1.6050I–1(c)(1)(ii). The definition of cash was expanded to include certain monetary instruments to make evasion of the reporting requirement more difficult.

10. 26 C.F.R. § 1.6050I–1(c)(1)(ii)(B).

11. 26 U.S.C. § 6050I(d)(2).

personal checks from the scope of § 6050I.[12]

The certain monetary instruments are only deemed cash if they were received during "designated reporting transactions"[13] or during a transaction where the recipient knows that the instrument is being used to avoid the reporting requirement.[14] There are also some exceptions where the monetary instruments will not be treated as cash.[15]

The designated reporting transactions include the retail sale of a consumer durable, a collectible or a travel or entertainment activity.[16] A consumer durable is an item of personal property that is suitable for ordinary consumption and has a sales price of more than $10,000.[17] For example, an automobile worth $15,000, whether purchased for personal or business purposes, is a consumer durable, but a factory machine or dump truck is not.[18] If Buyer purchases an automobile for her business from Seller for $15,000 and Buyer gives Seller (1) a cashier's check for $8,000 and (2) $7,000 in U.S. currency, then Seller will have to report the transaction. Because the automobile is a consumer durable, the sale is a designated reporting transaction and the cashier's check, which does not exceed $10,000, must be treated as cash. Seller will have to report the receipt of "cash" totalling $15,000.

A collectible includes any work of art, rug, antique, metal, gem, stamp, or coin.[19] For example, if a jeweler sells an emerald worth $12,000 and payment is made with a watch worth $5,000 and a traveler's checks totalling $7,000, the jeweler must report the transaction.

Finally, a sale of travel or entertainment activity is a designated transaction if (1) the amount received or the aggregate amount of several items received pertains to a single trip or event and (2) the total amount received exceeds $10,000.[20] For example, if an individual pays a travel agent for the costs of airfare, hotel and tickets to an event with several money orders with face amounts which collectively exceed $10,000, then the transaction is a designated transaction which the travel agent is required to report.[21]

As noted above, there are exceptions when monetary instruments received in a designated reporting transaction will not be considered cash.[22] First, if the monetary instrument constitutes proceeds from a bank loan, then the instrument is not considered cash.[23] Second, an instrument is not deemed cash if it is received in payment on a promissory note or installment sales contract.[24] This exception is subject

---

12. *See* 26 C.F.R. § 1.6050I (Example 3).

13. *Id.* § 1.6050I–1(c)(1)(ii)(B)(1).

14. *Id.* § 1.6050I–1(c)(1)(ii)(B)(2).

15. *See* 26 C.F.R. § 1.6050I–1(c)(iv)-(vi).

16. *Id.* § 1.6050I–1(c)(iii)(A)-(C).

17. *Id.* § 1.6050I–1(c)(2).

18. *Id.*

19. 26 C.F.R. § 1.6050I–1(c)(3) relies for this definition on I.R.C. § 408(m)(2)(A)-(D).

20. 26 C.F.R. § 1.6050I–1(c)(4).

21. *Id.* § 1.6050I–1(c)(vii) (Example 5).

22. *Id.* § 1.6050I–1(c)(iv)-(vi).

23. 26 C.F.R. § 1.6050I–1(c)(iv). *See also* § 1.6050I–1(c)(vii) (Example 2).

24. *Id.* § 1.6050I–1(c)(v).

to the limitations that the terms of the note or contract are used in the ordinary course of the particular trade or business and that the total amount of payments received within approximately two months of the sale date do not exceed 50% of the purchase price of the sale.[25] Third, there is an exception for certain down payment plans.[26]

Summarizing the definition of cash, the only occasion when a monetary instrument (such as a money order, traveler's check, or cashier's check) is considered cash for purposes of § 6050I is when the face amount of the instrument does not exceed $10,000,[27] and the amount of the transaction does exceed $10,000, and the transaction is either a designated reporting transaction or the recipient knows that the instrument is being used to avoid the reporting requirement. Therefore, if a trade or business sells a product or service for more than $10,000 and payment is made by specified monetary instruments, then the trade or business will still have a duty to report, even though the transaction is not a designated reporting transaction, if it knows that the instrument is being used to avoid the reporting requirement.

b. Trade or Business; in the Course of

Reports must be filed by persons who receive cash *in the course of* a *trade or business*.[28] To qualify as a trade or business, the primary purpose of the enterprise must be profit realization.[29] So if a businesswoman collects antiques for fun and sells one from her personal collection for $15,000 in cash, she has no duty to report the transaction.[30]

c. Transaction and Related Transactions

Cash payments over $10,000 must be reported if the payments are made "in 1 transaction (or 2 or more related transactions)."[31] A single transaction is the underlying event which causes the payment.[32] Related transactions are transactions conducted within a 24–hour period or transactions where the trade or business knows or has reason to know that each transaction is part of a series of transactions.[33] For example, an interior designer's renovation of a home is one underlying transaction, so cash payments received pursuant to monthly billings are combined for purposes of § 6050I. Several purchases at a one-day auction are related transactions, and an auction house would be required to report aggregate amounts exceeding $10,000 even though the buyer would be billed separately for each item.[34]

25. *Id.* § 1.6050I–1(c)(v)(A)-(B).

26. *Id.* § 1.6050I–1(c)(vi).

27. This is because monetary instruments exceeding $10,000 are already covered under different reporting requirements in Bank Secrecy Act.

28. I.R.C. § 6050I(a)(1); 26 C.F.R. § 1.6050I–1(a)(1).

29. 26 C.F.R. § 1.6050I–1(c)(7)(i) refers to I.R.C. § 162.

30. 26 C.F.R. § 1.6050I–1(c)(8)(iii) (Example 3).

31. I.R.C. § 6050I(a)(2); 26 C.F.R. § 1.6050I–1(a)(1).

32. 26 C.F.R. § 1.6050I–1(c)(7)(i).

33. *Id.* § 1.6050I–1(c)(7)(ii).

34. *Id. See also* § 1.6050I–1(c)(7)(iii) (Example 3).

d. Over $10,000; Aggregation

The duty to report the receipt of cash applies to a single transaction (or 2 or more related transactions) if the total amount received exceeds $10,000. If multiple transactions qualify as "related," the payments must be aggregated and reported every time the amount received by the trade or business exceeds $10,000.[35]

ii. Failure to File

The prescribed form for reporting under § 6050I is Treasury Form 8300.[36]

The Form 8300 must be filed within 15 days of receipt,[37] and multiple payments must be reported within 15 days of the date on which the $10,000 threshold is met either through a single payment or aggregate payments.[38]

iii. Mens Rea

Section 6050I(a) and its regulations include no *mens rea* term for criminal violations. Instead, the *mens rea* element is supplied by the statute under which § 6050I(a) violations are prosecuted, I.R.C. § 7203. This crime requires a *mens rea* of *willfulness*, interpreted as an intentional violation of a known legal duty.[39] This *mens rea* requires knowledge of the law.[40] The *mens rea* of § 7203 is discussed in detail in § 23.8 on tax crimes.

D. INCHOATE LIABILITY

Conspiracy liability is available under the general conspiracy statute, 18 U.S.C. § 371. Conspiracy to violate § 6050I(a) is deemed a conspiracy to defraud the IRS.[41] Prosecutions for conspiracy to violate the tax code are discussed in detail in § 23.7 on tax crimes.

35. 26 U.S.C. § 6050I(f)(1)(C). For example, if a trade or business receives an initial cash payment of $12,000 and three subsequent cash payments of $8,000, $3,000 and $11,000, then the trade or business will be required to file three reports: the first for the initial payment of $12,000, the second for $11,000 (the aggregate amounts of $8,000 and $3,000), and the third for the final payment of $11,000.

36. 26 C.F.R. § 1.6050I–1(e).

Second Circuit: Lefcourt v. United States, 125 F.3d 79, 81 (2d Cir.1997).

Sixth Circuit: United States v. Palazzolo, 73 F.3d 363 (6th Cir.1995).

37. 26 C.F.R. § 1.6050I–1(e).

38. *Id.* § 1.6050I–1(b)(1)-(3). For example, if a recipient gets an initial cash payment of $15,000 on January 1, 1994, and three subsequent cash payments of $4,000 on February 15, 1994, $6,000 on March 15, 1994, and $12,000, on May 15, 1994, then the recipient will be required to file two reports. The first, for the initial payment of $15,000, must be filed by January 15, 1994. The second, for $22,000 (the aggregate amounts of $4,000, $6,000, and $12,000), must be filed by May 30, 1994, which is 15 days from the date when the subsequent payments exceeded $10,000. *See* 26 C.F.R. § 1.6050I–1T(b)(4).

39. Cheek v. United States, 498 U.S. 192, 111 S.Ct. 604, 112 L.Ed.2d 617 (1991).

40. *Sixth Circuit:* United States v. Palazzolo, 73 F.3d 363 (6th Cir.1995) (*citing* United States v. Pomponio, 429 U.S. 10, 97 S.Ct. 22, 50 L.Ed.2d 12 (1976) and Cheek v. United States, 498 U.S. 192, 111 S.Ct. 604, 112 L.Ed.2d 617 (1991)); United States v. Finch, 47 F.3d 1171 (6th Cir.1995).

Eighth Circuit: United States v. Jensen, 69 F.3d 906, 912 (8th Cir.1995).

41. *See*

Fourth Circuit: United States v. Rogers, 18 F.3d 265 (4th Cir.1994) (defendant

E. ACCOMPLICE LIABILITY

Accomplice liability is imposed on persons causing false filing or failure to file Form 8300's by § 60501(f), the anti-structuring provision.[42]

F. CONSTITUTIONALITY

Constitutional attacks on this reporting law have been unsuccessful.

i. Privilege Against Self-incrimination

The reporting law is constitutional under the privilege against self-incrimination. First, the privilege is personal, so the buyer cannot object when the trade or business person is compelled to file Form 8300.[43] Assuming it is the seller who objects, the privilege will still not excuse reporting. As the Second Circuit briefly explained, the Form 8300 reporting laws "target transactions without regard to the purposes underlying them and do not require reporting of information that would necessarily be criminal."[44]

ii. Unreasonable Search and Seizure

The Second Circuit quickly dismissed an unreasonable search and seizure challenge to § 6050I by analogizing it to the reporting requirements under the BSA.[45] The BSA reporting requirements were upheld by the Supreme Court on the basis that incorporated associations had no unqualified right to conduct their affairs in secret and that the disclosures required were reasonable.[46]

iii. Other

Section 6050I is not void for vagueness, either facially or as ap-

indicted on one count of conspiracy under § 371 to evade the reporting requirements of § 6050I(a) (conviction vacated and remanded on other grounds)).

Section 371 is also available for violations of § 6050I(f), the anti-structuring provision, discussed *infra* at § 18.9.

See, e.g.,

Seventh Circuit: United States v. Wilson, 985 F.2d 348, 350 (7th Cir.1993) (facts indicating intent to structure an automobile purchase supported a conviction for conspiracy to impair the IRS in the computation of income taxes and the collection of information regarding cash transactions in excess of $10,000); United States v. Beverly, McNulty, Brown, & Griffin, 913 F.2d 337, 359 (7th Cir.1990) (conspiracy to structure a transaction to avoid the reporting requirement of § 6050I was a violation of 18 U.S.C. § 371), *aff'd sub nom.* Griffin v.

United States, 502 U.S. 46, 112 S.Ct. 466, 116 L.Ed.2d 371 (1991).

42. United States v. Palazzolo, 73 F.3d 363 (6th Cir.1995).

43. *See*

Second Circuit: United States v. Goldberger & Dubin P.C., 935 F.2d 501, 503 (2d Cir.1991)

Sixth Circuit: United States v. Ritchie, 15 F.3d 592, 602 (6th Cir.1994) (*citing* Couch v. United States, 409 U.S. 322, 328, 93 S.Ct. 611, 615, 34 L.Ed.2d 548 (1973)).

44. Goldberger & Dubin, 935 F.2d at 503.

45. *Id.*

46. California Bankers' Assoc. v. Shultz, 416 U.S. 21, 66–68, 94 S.Ct. 1494, 1519–20, 39 L.Ed.2d 812 (1974).

plied.[47]

Several constitutional challenges to § 6050I have been made because the law compels attorneys to report when clients pay over $10,000 in cash. These cases are discussed in the next section.

G. APPLICATION TO ATTORNEYS

The most controversial and complicated application of this reporting law is to criminal defense attorneys who receive cash fees in the course of their practice. It is clear that § 6050I applies to these payments,[48] and that the government has been pursuing attorneys to complete the forms.[49]

For example, the government recently won a $25,000 civil penalty against Gerald Lefcourt, a criminal defense attorney, for intentional disregard of § 6050I's filing requirements.[50] Lefcourt filed a Form 8300 omitting the payor's name, claiming that evidence of the client's unexplained wealth would incriminate the client in the same proceeding for which it had hired Lefcourt.[51] The court examined whether this rationale was objectively reasonable, and found it was not. The court noted that it had previously referred to "special circumstances" that might excuse nondisclosure,[52] but concluded here that possible or even likely client incrimination did not constitute a special circumstance justifying nondisclosure.[53]

Many § 6050I issues arise in the context of its application to attorneys, which is unique because it implicates additional constitutional provisions and lawyers' ethical rules.

i. Constitutional Objections

Constitutional challenges have been made on four grounds; all have been rejected.

47. United States v. Jensen, 69 F.3d 906, 912 (8th Cir.1995).

48. The regulations use an attorney as an example. *See* 26 C.F.R. § 1.6050I–1(c)(7)(iii) (Example 3) (retention of a criminal defense attorney).

See

Second Circuit: United States v. Goldberger & Dubin P.C., 935 F.2d 501 (2d Cir.1991).

See generally Ellen Podgor, *Form 8300: The Demise of Law as a Profession,* 5 Geo.J.L.Ethics 485, 491 (1992).

49. *See, e.g.,*

First Circuit: United States v. Gertner, 65 F.3d 963 (1st Cir.1995)(summons improperly issued so defendant not required to comply with summons and provide clients' names on 8300's).

Second Circuit: Lefcourt v. United States, 125 F.3d 79 (2d Cir.1997) (civil penalty); United States v. Goldberger & Dubin, P.C., 935 F.2d 501 (2d Cir.1991).

Fifth Circuit: United States v. McGuire, 99 F.3d 671 (5th Cir.1996) (en banc) (conviction for causing false filing affirmed where defendant listed only two of three payors on the Form 8300).

Eleventh Circuit: United States v. Leventhal, 961 F.2d 936 (11th Cir.1992).

50. Lefcourt v. United States, 125 F.3d 79 (2d Cir.1997).

51. *Id.* at 85.

52. *Id.*, citing *Goldberger & Dubin,* 935 F.2d at 505.

53. *Lefcourt,* 125 F.3d at 86.

a. Privilege Against Self-incrimination

Defense attorneys from whom the government seeks information have argued that compelling them to file Form 8300's revealing how much cash they received from clients violates the privilege against self-incrimination; the courts have uniformly rejected these arguments.[54]

b. Right to Counsel

The Sixth Amendment right to counsel has also been raised by attorneys opposing this reporting requirement. The claim is premised on three arguments: (1) the law interferes with the ability of clients to retain counsel; (2) the law discourages free and open communication between attorneys and clients; and (3) the law destroys the attorney-client relationship through the disqualification of counsel.[55] The majority of courts addressing this issue have followed *Goldberger & Dubin* and concluded that the reporting law only limits the client's payment options and does not interfere with a person's ability to retain counsel.[56] *Goldberger & Dubin* suggests that in order to avoid disclosure, payment need merely be made in a form other than cash.[57] Finally, *Goldberger & Dubin* states that there is no Sixth Amendment violation in regards to the attorney-client relationship or communications because a "meaningful relationship" is not guaranteed by the sixth amendment.[58]

c. Due Process

Another challenge raised by attorneys is based on due process.[59] Attorneys argue that § 6050I interferes with the adversarial process by forcing attorneys to provide information against their clients for use in criminal prosecution.[60] The courts have rejected this claim.[61]

---

54. *See*

Second Circuit: Goldberger & Dubin, 935 F.2d at 501.

Sixth Circuit: United States v. Ritchie, 15 F.3d 592, 602 (6th Cir.1994).

Tenth Circuit: United States v. Monnat, 853 F.Supp. 1301 (D.Kan.1994).

55. *Ritchie*, 15 F.3d at 601–602.

56. *See*

Second Circuit: United States v. Goldberger & Dubin, 935 F.2d at 504 (reasoning that the goal of the Sixth Amendment is to guarantee an advocate for every defendant and not necessarily guarantee that each defendant be represented by counsel of choice).

Sixth Circuit: United States v. Ritchie, 15 F.3d at 601–602.

Eleventh Circuit: United States v. Garland, 1992 WL 158444 (N.D.Ga.1992)

(§ 6050I does not preclude clients from obtaining effective counsel).

57. *Goldberger & Dubin*, 935 F.2d at 504.

58. *Id.*

59. "[N]or shall be deprived of life, liberty, or property, without due process of law...." U.S. Const. Amend. V.

60. *See* United States v. Ritchie, 15 F.3d 592, 602 (6th Cir.1994).

61. *See*

Second Circuit: United States v. Goldberger & Dubin P.C., 935 F.2d 501 (2d Cir.1991).

Sixth Circuit: United States v. Ritchie, 15 F.3d at 602.

Ninth Circuit: Tornay v. United States, 840 F.2d 1424 (9th Cir.1988).

d. First Amendment

The First Amendment has also been used to challenge § 6050I.[62] The attorneys argued that the first amendment protects the "flow of communication between the attorney and client"[63] and that communication will be stifled if the client knows that the attorney will be providing information to the government.[64] This argument was rejected without explanation by the court.[65]

ii. Ethical Objections

The ethical objections are based on the Model Rules of Professional Conduct and the Model Code of Professional Responsibility as adopted in each state. The § 6050I reporting requirement does not compromise lawyers' ethical duties,[66] although it does have troubling practical impacts.[67] At any rate, even if the crime did conflict with state ethical rules, the Supremacy Clause would have the federal law control.[68]

Library References:

C.J.S. United States § 125.
West's Key No. Digests, United States ⊂⇒34.

§ 18.6 Reporting Laws—Foreign Bank Account Reports: § 5314 FBAR's

A. IN GENERAL

Section 5314 requires every person subject to United States jurisdiction who has a financial interest in or authority over a financial account over $10,000 in a foreign country to report it to the U.S. government. Filing a false report or failing to file is a crime. This crime is infrequently prosecuted.

The duty to report runs to all persons subject to U.S. jurisdiction. The usual defendants in these cases are individuals in the U.S. who bank money in foreign countries and do not report it.

As with CTR's and CMIR's, the specific conduct proscribed is not

---

62. *See Goldberger & Dubin*, 935 F.2d at 501.

63. Ellen S. Podgor, *The Demise of Law as a Profession*, 5 GEO.J.LEGAL ETHICS 485, 510 (1992).

64. *Id.*

65. *Goldberger & Dubin*, 935 F.2d at 504 ("§ 6050I passes constitutional muster.").

66. *Second Circuit:* United States v. Goldberger & Dubin, P.C., 935 F.2d 501 (2d Cir.1991).

Eleventh Circuit: United States v. Leventhal, 961 F.2d 936, 939 (11th Cir.1992).

67. Eugene R. Gaetke & Sarah N. Welling, *Money Laundering and Lawyers*, 43 SYRACUSE L.REV. 1165 (1992).

68. *Second Circuit:* United States v. Goldberger & Dubin, P.C., 935 F.2d 501, 505 (2d Cir.1991); Lefcourt v. United States, 125 F.3d 79, 85 n. 3 (2d Cir.1997) (describing *Goldberger* language on this point as dicta and declining to resolve whether § 6050I overrides attorney-client privilege).

Eleventh Circuit: United States v. Leventhal, 961 F.2d 936, 940 (11th Cir.1992).

filing a report when due[1] or filing a report with a false, fictitious or fraudulent statement or representation.[2]

B. FALSE FILING

The regulations prohibit *false, fictitious or fraudulent* statements. No FBAR prosecutions based on this language have been reported. Actually, no prosecutions for false filing of any BSA reports (CTR's, CMIR's or FBAR's) have been reported, so the parameters of "false, fictitious or fraudulent" have not been explored.

The statute prohibits any *willful* violation,[3] and the regulation prohibits *knowing* false, fictitious or fraudulent statements.[4] The use of willful in the statute and knowing in the regulation is curious. The drafters' intent is unclear, and the implications of the difference are unclear. As discussed below under failure to file, the Supreme Court held in Ratzlaf v. United States that *willful* requires knowledge of illegality.[5]

C. FAILURE TO FILE

Failure-to-file liability has three elements: a duty on the defendant to file, failure to do so and a *mens rea* of willfulness.

i. Filing Duty

The duty to file is imposed on persons subject to U.S. jurisdiction (except foreign subsidiaries) having a financial interest in or other authority over a financial account over $10,000 in a foreign country.[6]

a. *Person Subject to U.S. Jurisdiction*

Foreign subsidiaries of U.S. companies are not required to file.[7]

b. *Financial Interest in or Other Authority Over*

In United States v. Clines,[8] a prosecution of a former senior CIA official growing out of the Iran–Contra deal, the court held the defendant's authority over a foreign account was sufficient to support his conviction where he had complete control over the account after his portion of the profits was allocated to him.[9] This control was evident because the defendant's requests for payments were honored in any form he directed, including wire transfers to his other account, currency transfers to him and currency transfers to other accounts he designated.[10]

§ 18.6

1. 31 U.S.C. § 5314(a); 31 C.F.R. § 103.24(a), 103.49(b)-(c).

2. 31 U.S.C. § 5314(a); 31 C.F.R. § 103.49(d).

3. 31 U.S.C. § 5322.

4. 31 C.F.R. § 103.49(d).

5. 510 U.S. 135, 114 S.Ct. 655, 126 L.Ed.2d 615 (1994).

6. 31 C.F.R. §§ 103.24, 103.27(c).

7. *Id.* § 103.24.

8. 958 F.2d 578 (4th Cir.1992).

9. *Id.* at 582–83.

10. *Id.*

c. Financial Account

In *Clines*[11] the court further defined financial account. The defendant controlled a capital account maintained on the ledger of a shell corporation set up by a Swiss financial services company, and he argued the capital account was a "mere bookkeeping entry" rather than a financial account.[12] The court rejected this argument, finding that the Swiss financial services company was a financial institution which accepted credits to and transmitted funds from the capital account, so the account qualified as a financial account.[13]

d. In Foreign Country

Foreign is simply defined as outside the U.S.[14]

e. Financial Institution

In *Clines*[15] the defendant also argued that the account he controlled was not "maintained with a financial institution" because the shell corporation was not a financial institution, but the court found that the Swiss financial services company which set up and operated the shell corporation was a financial institution, and since the Swiss company actually maintained the shell corporation's accounts and transmitted funds for the defendant at his direction, his account was maintained by a financial institution.[16]

ii. Failure to File

Once the defendant has a duty to file, the government must prove the defendant failed to do so. The single prescribed form for filing is Treasury Form 90–22.1, the Foreign Bank Account Report (FBAR).[17] The deadline to file is June 30 for accounts maintained during the previous calendar year.[18]

iii. Mens Rea

The FBAR law itself includes no *mens rea* term; rather, the statute and regulations defining the BSA penalties set out the *mens rea*.[19] For the crime of failure to file, both the statute and regulation use the term *willful*.[20] In Ratzlaf v. United States, the Supreme Court held this provision to require knowledge of illegality.[21] Defining this term in the

---

11. 958 F.2d 578 (4th Cir.1992).

12. United States v. Clines, 958 F.2d at 582–83.

13. *Id.*

14. 31 U.S.C. § 5312(b).

15. 958 F.2d 578 (4th Cir.1992).

16. *Id.* at 583.

17. 31 C.F.R. § 103.27(d) (persons must file on prescribed form). Filing is actually a "two step process." Form 1040 has a box asking about foreign accounts to be checked yes or no; if yes is checked, the

1040 directions refer the taxpayer to Form 90–22.1. *Clines,* 958 F.2d at 581–82.

18. 31 C.F.R. § 103.27(c).

19. This is like CTR's but unlike CMIR's. *Compare* 31 U.S.C. § 5313 *with* § 5316.

20. 31 U.S.C. § 5322(a)-(b); 31 C.F.R. § 103.49(b)-(c).

21. 510 U.S. 135, 114 S.Ct. 655, 126 L.Ed.2d 615 (1994). The *Ratzlaf* result as applied to § 5324 was overruled legislatively, but the opinion still indicates the Su-

FBAR context, the Sixth Circuit stated that "the test for statutory willfulness is 'voluntary, intentional violation of a known legal duty.' "[22] To meet this, the government must prove both that the defendant knew of the reporting law and that the defendant intentionally did not report.[23] The defendant's knowledge of the law can be inferred from (1) the defendant's efforts to conceal income and information and (2) his failure to pursue knowledge of the reporting law as suggested on Form 1040.[24] The court relied in part on willful blindness to establish the knowledge of the law element.[25]

This interpretation of the *mens rea* is consistent with the *mens rea* for failure to file under the other BSA reporting laws.[26]

A *mens rea* instruction referring to "knowingly and intentionally concealing information ... required by the law to be disclosed" was not erroneous because it did not cite the particular statutes violated.[27] The instructions considered as a whole had several references to "willfulness" and "knowing" and "intentional" participation, so the jury was correctly charged on the *mens rea*.[28]

D. INCHOATE LIABILITY

i. Solicitation

Solicitation is not covered in the FBAR statute or the general BSA penalty provisions. Federal law includes no general solicitation statute, so there is no solicitation liability associated with the FBAR law.

ii. Conspiracy

Conspiracy liability is available under § 371, the general conspiracy statute.[29] The Second Circuit has held that defendants who developed elaborate plans to help a supposed client hide money in foreign bank accounts could be indicted for conspiracy to violate the FBAR law even though the foreign accounts were never opened and the "client" was

---

preme Court's approach to defining willfulness under the BSA.

22. United States v. Sturman, 951 F.2d 1466, 1476 (6th Cir.1991) (*citing* Cheek v. United States, 498 U.S. 192, 111 S.Ct. 604, 112 L.Ed.2d 617 (1991)).

23. *Second Circuit:* United States v. DiTommaso, 817 F.2d 201, 217 (2d Cir. 1987) (citing United States v. Dichne, 612 F.2d 632, 636 (2d Cir.1979)).

See also

Sixth Circuit: United States v. Sturman, 951 F.2d at 1466 (6th Cir.1991).

24. United States v. Sturman, 951 F.2d at 1477.

25. *Id.* at 1476 (*citing* United States v. Bank of New England, 821 F.2d 844 (1st Cir.1987)).

26. The best analogue is 31 U.S.C. § 5313 (CTR's), where under identical language, courts have concluded that knowledge of the facts and law is required. *See, e.g., Bank of New England,* 821 F.2d at 844. Less perfectly analogous but still helpful is § 5316 (CMIR's); that section has different *mens rea* language but courts have still concluded that knowledge of the law and facts is required.

27. United States v. DiTommaso, 817 F.2d at 217 (2d Cir.1987).

28. *Id.*

29. United States v. DiTommaso, 817 F.2d at 201 (2d Cir.1987); United States v. Goldberg, 756 F.2d 949 (2d Cir.1985).

actually a government agent.[30] The court cited hornbook law in holding that the defendants could be liable for conspiracy even though the substantive crime never occurred.[31]

iii. Attempt

No language in the FBAR statute[32] or regulation[33] or the BSA penalty provisions[34] captures attempts. Federal law has no general attempt statute, so no liability for attempted FBAR crimes exists. This omission would not leave a hole in failure-to-file liability since it is impossible to attempt to fail to do something. For false filing liability, however, defendants who almost filed false FBAR's but did not actually do so would escape liability.

E. ACCOMPLICE LIABILITY

There is no specific provision in the FBAR laws or the BSA penalty provisions. Accomplice liability is available under the general accomplice liability statute, § 2.[35] The Second Circuit held that defendants who were working with an undercover agent to transfer money out of the country and hide it abroad without reporting it were indictable for conspiracy to aid and abet the violation of the FBAR law, and the indictment was sufficient even without a citation to § 2.[36]

F. CONSTITUTIONALITY

The FBAR crime has been challenged on two grounds, both unsuccessful.

i. Privilege Against Self-incrimination

The Supreme Court was presented with a privilege against self incrimination challenge to the FBAR law and declined to rule because the claims were premature.[37]

The lower courts have rejected this challenge. In United States v. Sturman, the court found a slew of reasons the FBAR law does not violate the privilege against self-incrimination.[38] The Supreme Court has established a three part test to define when a reporting statute violates

---

30. *United States v. Goldberg*, 756 F.2d 949 (2d Cir.1985).

31. *Id.* at 957–58.

32. 31 U.S.C. § 5314.

33. 31 C.F.R. § 103.24.

34. 31 U.S.C. § 5322; 31 C.F.R. § 103.49.

35. 18 U.S.C. § 2, discussed *supra* in §§ 4.1–4.7.

36. United States v. Goldberg, 756 F.2d 949 (2d Cir.1985). *See also* United

States v. DiTommaso, 817 F.2d 201, 218, n. 24 (2d Cir.1987) (sustaining conviction for conspiracy to violate or aid and abet the violation of § 5314 (the FBAR crime) where the defendant helped convert small denomination bills to big ones, smuggled money out of the country and prepared and hid incriminating documents).

37. California Bankers' Ass'n v. Shultz, 416 U.S. 21, 73, 94 S.Ct. 1494, 1523, 39 L.Ed.2d 812 (1974).

38. 951 F.2d 1466, 1486 (6th Cir. 1991).

the privilege.[39] Assuming the privilege was correctly raised,[40] the *Sturman* court found that the FBAR law did not meet any part of the test, much less all three parts.[41]

ii.   Unreasonable Search and Seizure

The Supreme Court has held that the FBAR reporting requirement does not violate the fourth amendment because it is analogous to tax reporting requirements held valid by the Court and because the reports require only "information as to a relatively limited group of financial transactions in foreign commerce, and are reasonably related to the statutory purpose of the assisting in the enforcement of the laws of the United States."[42] Furthermore, the Court explained,

> The statutory authorization for the regulations was based upon a conclusion by Congress that ... foreign financial institutions were being used by residents of the United States to circumvent the enforcement of the laws of the United States. The regulations are sufficiently tailored so as to single out transactions found to have the greatest potential for such circumvention and which involve substantial amounts of money. They are therefore reasonable in the light of that statutory purpose, and consistent with the Fourth Amendment.[43]

G.   ENHANCED PENALTY

If the violation of the FBAR law occurs (1) while violating another federal law or (2) as part of a pattern of any illegal activity involving more than $100,000 in a 12–month period, an enhanced maximum of $500,000 and 10 years or both is available.[44]

No prosecutions have been filed under this enhancement provision based specifically on FBAR's. But the same enhancement provision has been applied to CTR's. In that context, it is discussed *supra* in § 18.3(G).

Library References:

C.J.S. United States § 125.
West's Key No. Digests, United States ⊛34.

39. Marchetti v. United States, 390 U.S. 39, 47, 88 S.Ct. 697, 702, 19 L.Ed.2d 889 (1968), *cited in Sturman*, 951 F.2d at 1487.

40. The court stated that Sturman waived his self-incrimination objections under *United States v. Sullivan* by not raising them in a filed return. *Sturman*, 951 F.2d at 1486 (*citing* United States v. Sullivan, 274 U.S. 259, 47 S.Ct. 607, 71 L.Ed. 1037 (1927)). However, the court did not rely on waiver as the basis for its decision, but went on to explain that even assuming no

waiver, the FBAR law did not violate the privilege against self-incrimination.

41. United States v. Sturman, 951 F.2d at 1487 (6th Cir.1991).

42. California Bankers' Assoc. v. Shultz, 416 U.S. 21, 62, 94 S.Ct. 1494, 1517, 39 L.Ed.2d 812 (1974).

43. *Id.* at 63.

44. 31 U.S.C. § 5322(b); 31 C.F.R. § 103.49(c).

§ 18.7 Reporting Laws—Suspicious Activity Reports: § 5318(g) SAR's

Banks are required to file reports of suspicious activity with the government.[1] The report, called a Suspicious Activity Report (SAR), must be filed when a transaction is:

—conducted or attempted

—by, at or through a bank, and

—it involves or aggregates to over $5000, and

—the bank knows, suspects, or has reason to suspect that the transaction

    (i) involves money laundering, or

    (ii) is an effort to avoid a reporting requirement, or

    (iii) is unusual for that customer.[2]

The report must be filed on an SAR form with the Financial Crimes Enforcement Network (FinCEN), part of the Treasury Department, within 30 days of the date of initial detection by the bank.[3]

Failure to file and false filing of an SAR are subject to the civil and criminal sanctions of the BSA.[4] The criminal penalties are defined in § 5322, and are discussed above in connection with the other BSA reporting requirements.[5] In addition to these BSA penalties, failure to file or false filing could presumably also be prosecuted under § 1001.[6] Because this SAR reporting requirement only became effective on April 1, 1996, no prosecutions have been reported and it has not been discussed in the courts yet. It has been discussed in some law review writing.[7]

There are a couple interesting points to be made about this law. It imposes a duty to report crime, and possible crime, on banks at the risk of their own criminal liability. Turning a blind eye is no longer risk free. To that extent, banks have been deputized in the effort to eliminate money laundering and the underlying drug trade. Moreover, the duty to report arises if the bank even has *reason to suspect* that bad things are happening. This level of *mens rea* is low, and would theoretically allow banks to be prosecuted when they were negligent, *i.e.*, when they should have known something unusual was happening. Because the law is new and unusual, it is likely the government will be conservative in enforcing it; but if the government takes an aggressive approach, potential liability under this SAR reporting requirement is broad.

§ 18.7

1. 31 U.S.C. § 5318(g); 31 C.F.R. § 103.21.

2. *Id.* § 103.21(a).

3. *Id.* § 103.21(b).

4. *Id.* § 103.21(f).

5. *See* §§ 18.2–18.4 & 18.6 *supra*.

6. 18 U.S.C. § 1001, discussed *supra* in §§ 12.7–12.10.

7. Matthew Hall, An Emerging Duty to Report Criminal Conduct: Banks, Money Laundering and the Suspicious Activity Report, 84 Ky. L. J. 643 (1995–96).

Library References:

> C.J.S. United States § 125.
> West's Key No. Digests, United States ⊸34.

§ 18.8 Money Transmitting Businesses/Money Services Businesses

The BSA requires that money transmitting businesses register with the Treasury Department.[1] The filing of false or materially incomplete information is deemed a failure to comply with the BSA,[2] and so subjects the money transmitting business to the criminal and civil penalties of the BSA.[3] In addition, failure to register subjects the business to liability under § 1960, discussed below.[4] The Treasury Department has proposed regulations implementing this requirement, but they are not yet final.[5]

Library References:

> C.J.S. United States § 125.
> West's Key No. Digests, United States ⊸34.

§ 18.9 Anti-structuring Laws—In General

The three transaction reporting laws described above are all triggered by a $10,000 threshold. Launderers responded to these reporting laws in part by "structuring" their transactions—breaking them up so the amount involved in each transaction was under the $10,000 threshold. The government replied by making structuring transactions to evade the reporting requirements a separate crime.

There are three anti-structuring laws, one to back up each of the transaction reporting requirements.[1] Section 5324(a) prohibits structuring to evade filing CTR's; section 5324(b) applies to import/export reports (CMIR's); and section 6050I(f) applies to trade or business transaction reports (8300's). Like the reporting laws they bolster, these anti-structuring laws are codified partly in the Bank Secrecy Act and partly in the Internal Revenue Code, but the anti-structuring laws are basically identical, so they are discussed together below.

Each anti-structuring law includes three clauses and establishes generally three ways to commit the offense. The first two clauses cover causing another to fail to file a report or causing another to file a false

---

§ 18.8

1. 18 U.S.C. § 5330, Registration of money transmitting businesses.

2. *Id.* § 5330(a)(4).

3. These are set out in 31 U.S.C. § 5322, and discussed *supra* in §§ 18.2–18.4 & 18.6.

4. 18 U.S.C. § 1960, Illegal money transmitting businesses, discussed *infra* in § 18.17.

5. Three rules have been proposed, all dated May 21, 1997. *See* 62 Fed. Reg. No. 98 p. 27890 ("Definition and Registration of Money Services Businesses"); 62 Fed. Reg.

No. 98 p. 27900 ("Requirement of Money Transmitters and Money Order and Traveler's Check Issuers, Sellers, and Redeemers to Report Suspicious Transactions") and 62 Fed. Reg. No. 98 p. 27909 ("Special Currency Transaction Reporting Requirement for Money Transmitters").

§ 18.9

1. The other reporting requirement, which applies to foreign bank accounts, is not backed up by an anti-structuring statute.

report. The third clause makes it a crime to structure any transaction to evade the reporting requirement.

The first two clauses, which cover persons who cause a failure to file or the filing of a false report, are designed to cover customers of financial institutions and businesses. Customers have no direct duty to file under the reporting laws, and the courts were split on whether the general accomplice liability statute imposed a duty to file on customers.[2] These first two clauses in the anti-structuring statutes are particularized accomplice liability provisions Congress adopted to resolve the split in the courts and establish a sure basis for prosecuting customers. Note, however, that one court recently held that customers could still not be prosecuted for causing a bank to fail to file, even under the anti-structuring law, if the bank had no duty to file in the first place.[3] To prosecute customers when no duty to file had yet arisen, the government should have used the anti-structuring clause of the statute.

The third clause, which prohibits structuring transactions to evade the reporting requirements, applies to any person or entity involved in structuring the transactions, regardless of whether they have a duty to file reports.

The conduct proscribed by the first two clauses, causing failure to file and causing false filing, does not raise any new issues besides those already discussed under the reporting laws themselves and the general accomplice liability statute, so the discussion below focuses on the clause which prohibits structuring for the purpose of evading the reporting requirements.

Library References:
C.J.S. United States § 125.
West's Key No. Digests, United States ⊕34.

§ 18.10 Anti-structuring Laws—Elements

This crime prohibits structuring a transaction with the intent to evade the reporting requirements. These elements are discussed below.

As with the four reporting requirements, this crime does not require that the money be criminally derived.[1]

A. STRUCTURE A TRANSACTION

The verb *structure* means to conduct one or more transactions in currency in any amount, in any manner, for the purpose of evading the

---

2. *Compare* United States v. Tobon–Builes, 706 F.2d 1092 (11th Cir.1983)(customers do have duty to file) *with* United States v. Dela Espriella, 781 F.2d 1432 (9th Cir.1986)(customers do not have duty to file). See United States v. Phipps, 81 F.3d 1056, 1060 (11th Cir.1996)(listing cases in circuit split).

3. United States v. Phipps, 81 F.3d 1056, 1061–62 (11th Cir.1996).

§ 18.10

1. *See, e.g.,* United States v. Dollar Bank Money Market Account No. 1591768456, 980 F.2d 233, 242 (3d Cir.1992)(Greenberg, J., dissenting) (anti-structuring statute applies even when "dealing with legitimate money earned by hard working people rather than criminals stashing profits from an illegal enterprise.").

reporting requirements.[2] The regulations make it clear that the amount of money involved in the transaction does not have to exceed the $10,000 reporting threshold to constitute structuring. Therefore, structuring can occur even if no report was due to be filed.[3]

Structuring to avoid § 6050I typically occurs when automobiles are purchased through several forms of payment, including cash, personal checks, and trade-ins.[4]

In *United States v. Morales–Vasquez*,[5] before crossing the Mexican–United States border in a truck, the defendant divided $20,000 between his friends and himself to avoid the reporting requirement.[6] The Fifth Circuit determined that the defendant's act of dividing the funds qualified as structuring, although the case preceded the enactment of § 5324(b). In so doing, the court rejected the defendant's argument that structuring requires a series of multiple subtransactions occurring at different times or places. The single act of dividing the money between individuals in order to avoid the reporting requirement was sufficient to constitute structuring.[7]

B.   MENS REA

For the anti-structuring crimes in both § 5324 and § 6050I, the government must prove that the defendant acted with the purpose to evade the reporting requirements. However, the anti-structuring crimes under § 5324 do not require the government to prove knowledge of illegality, whereas under § 6050I the government does have to prove knowledge of illegality. This divergence is explained below.

i.   § 5324

The *mens rea* for the crime of structuring requires that defendants act *for the purpose of evading the reporting requirement*.[8] Thus defendants must know of the underlying reporting law and intend to evade it. Defendants do *not* have to know that structuring itself is a crime. Knowledge of illegality was eliminated as an element by Congress in September, 1994. Ignorance of the law is not a defense today.

Initially the Supreme Court held that defendants did have to know of the anti-structuring law to be liable. In Ratzlaf v. United States,[9] the Court held that the term *willfully*, which at the time applied to the crime of structuring, meant that the defendant had to know the conduct

---

2. 31 C.F.R. § 103.11(p).

3. United States v. Phipps, 81 F.3d 1056, 1061 (11th Cir.1996).

4. *Fourth Circuit:* United States v. McLamb, 985 F.2d 1284 (4th Cir.1993).

Sixth Circuit: United States v. Young, 985 F.2d 562 (6th Cir.1993).

Seventh Circuit: United States v. Wilson, 985 F.2d 348 (7th Cir.1993); United States v. Beverly, 913 F.2d 337 (7th Cir. 1990), *aff'd sub nom.* Griffin v. United

States, 502 U.S. 46, 112 S.Ct. 466, 116 L.Ed.2d 371 (1991).

5. 919 F.2d 258 (5th Cir.1990).

6. *Id.* at 260.

7. *Id.* at 263.

8. 31 U.S.C. § 5324(a) and (b).

9. 510 U.S. 135, 114 S.Ct. 655, 126 L.Ed.2d 615 (1994).

was illegal. Under this decision, ignorance of the law was a defense to structuring. But Congress disagreed, and within six months after *Ratzlaf* was decided amended the statute to delete the term *willfully* as it applied to the crime of structuring.[10]

Although *Ratzlaf* was nullified after Congress's amendment of the statute in September, 1994, the decision is still producing some interesting fallout. As an interpretation of the substantive law, *Ratzlaf* applies retroactively.[11] Thus many defendants convicted of structuring before the decision was rendered filed appeals and habeas corpus actions after the decision to set aside their convictions.[12] The circuits have disagreed on how to resolve these challenges. Some circuits have reversed or vacated the convictions.[13] Many circuits, on the other hand, have affirmed structuring convictions based on pre-*Ratzlaf* instructions.[14] These courts generally rely on two points: the scope of review is often limited to a plain error analysis,[15] which limits the defendant's chance of winning; and a footnote in *Ratzlaf* states that knowledge of the law can be inferred from conduct,[16] so courts examine the defendant's conduct and find that knowledge of illegality was proved.[17] So although *Ratzlaf*

10. The amendment is codified at 31 U.S.C. § 5324(c), which deletes *willfully* as applied to the structuring crime. *See*

Fifth Circuit: United States v. McGuire, 79 F.3d 1396, 1405 n. 9 (5th Cir. 1996) (citing H.R.Conf.Rep. 103–652, 103d Cong., 2d Sess. (1994), reprinted in 1994 U.S.C.C.A.N. 1977, 3034).

Eleventh Circuit: United States v. Phipps, 81 F.3d 1056, 1060–61 (11th Cir. 1996) (quoting Senate Report on the purpose of the amendment).

11. *See, e.g.,*

Second Circuit: Peck v. United States, 73 F.3d 1220, 1224–25 (2d Cir.1995).

Tenth Circuit: United States v. Dashney, 52 F.3d 298 (10th Cir.1995).

12. The Second Circuit describes the issue well: "[T]here has been considerable litigation in which, on direct appeal, structuring convictions have been challenged on the basis of pre-*Ratzlaf* instructions. Generally, no objection was taken at trial (pre-*Ratzlaf*) to the instruction that is challenged on appeal (post-*Ratzlaf*), so the plain error standard . . . governs." Peck v. United States, 73 F.3d 1220, 1226 (2d Cir.1995).

13. *D.C. Circuit:* United States v. Wynn, 61 F.3d 921 (D.C.Cir.1995).

Second Circuit: Peck v. United States, 73 F.3d 1220 (2d Cir.1995).

Third Circuit: United States v. Alston, 77 F.3d 713 (3d Cir.1996) (§ 371).

Fourth Circuit: United States v. Ismail, 97 F.3d 50 (4th Cir.1996).

Sixth Circuit: United States v. Palazzolo, 71 F.3d 1233 (6th Cir.1995) (§ 371); United States v. Rogers, 18 F.3d 265 (4th Cir. 1994).

Ninth Circuit: United States v. Kim, 65 F.3d 123 (9th Cir.1995).

Eleventh Circuit: United States v. High, 117 F.3d 464 (11th Cir.1997) (§ 371).

14. *First Circuit:* United States v. Hurley, 63 F.3d 1 (1st Cir.1995); United States v. Marder, 48 F.3d 564 (1st Cir. 1995).

Second Circuit: United States v. Simon, 85 F.3d 906 (2d Cir.1996).

Fourth Circuit: United States v. Beidler, 110 F.3d 1064 (4th Cir.1997).

Fifth Circuit: United States v. Palacios, 58 F.3d 635 (5th Cir.1995).

Sixth Circuit: United States v. Hudson, 52 F.3d 326 (6th Cir.1995).

Seventh Circuit: United States v. Griffin, 84 F.3d 912 (7th Cir.1996).

Ninth Circuit: United States v. Tipton, 56 F.3d 1009 (9th Cir.1995).

Eleventh Circuit: United States v. Vazquez, 53 F.3d 1216 (11th Cir.1995).

15. *See, e.g.,* Peck v. United States, 73 F.3d 1220, 1226 (2d Cir.1995).

16. Ratzlaf v. United States, 114 S.Ct. at 663 n.19.

17. *See, e.g.,*

Second Circuit: United States v. Simon, 85 F.3d 906, 909 (2d Cir.1996).

has no impact on future structuring prosecutions, it has divided the courts on the past prosecutions.

ii. § 6050I

United States v. Rogers[18] was the first case to define willfulness in the context of a § 6050I(f) violation. The Fourth Circuit held that in order for a defendant to be convicted of structuring under §§ 6050I(f) and 7203, the government must prove that the defendant knew his or her conduct was illegal[19] under Cheek v. United States.[20] More recently, the Fifth Circuit reached the same conclusion, holding that convictions under §§ 6050I(f) and 7206 are governed by tax law cases,[21] which hold that willfulness for § 7206 requires knowledge of illegality.[22]

Thus, structuring convictions under § 5324 do not require knowledge of illegality, whereas convictions under § 6050I(f) do require such knowledge.

Library References:

C.J.S. United States § 125.
West's Key No. Digests, United States ⚷34.

§ 18.11   Anti-structuring Laws—Inchoate Liability

A. SOLICITATION

Solicitation is not included in any of the anti-structuring statutes. Federal law includes no general solicitation statute, so there is no solicitation liability under the anti-structuring laws.

B. CONSPIRACY

Conspiracy is not included in any of the anti-structuring statutes, but conspiracy liability is available under the general conspiracy statute, § 371.[1]

C. ATTEMPT

All three anti-structuring provisions include specific language criminalizing attempt. The statutes prohibit attempts to cause failure to file,[2]

Fourth Circuit: United States v. Beidler, 110 F.3d 1064, 1068–70 (4th Cir.1997).

18. 18 F.3d 265 (4th Cir.1994) (conviction vacated and remanded on other grounds).

19. *Id.* at 267 n. 4.

20. 498 U.S. 192, 111 S.Ct. 604, 112 L.Ed.2d 617 (1991)(willfulness under § 7203 requires the "voluntary, intentional violation of a known legal duty").

21. United States v. McGuire, 79 F.3d 1396 (5th Cir.1996).

22. *Id.* at 1405, *citing* United States v. Pomponio, 429 U.S. 10, 97 S.Ct. 22, 50 L.Ed.2d 12 (1976).

§ 18.11

1. *See, e.g.,* United States v. Rogers, 18 F.3d 265 (4th Cir.1994). Section 371 is discussed *supra* in § 2.14.

2. 31 U.S.C. § 5324(a)(1), (b)(1); I.R.C. § 6050I(f)(1)(A). Although this conduct (attempted failure to file) is criminalized and the scheme of laws is complete, the

attempts to cause false filing,[3] and attempts to structure to evade reporting requirements.[4]

Library References:

C.J.S. United States § 125.
West's Key No. Digests, United States ☞34.

§ 18.12 Anti-structuring Laws—Accomplice Liability

The three anti-structuring provisions include accomplice liability because they all cover persons who *assist* or *attempt to assist* in structuring.[1]

Library References:

C.J.S. United States § 125.
West's Key No. Digests, United States ☞34.

§ 18.13 Substantive Money Laundering Crimes: §§ 1956, 1957—In General

In 1984, the President's Commission on Organized Crime released a report on the growth of money laundering and the absence of effective criminal sanctions in the area.[1] In response, Congress enacted the Money Laundering Control Act of 1986 to make money laundering a substantive crime. A House of Representatives Report observed:

> Money laundering is big business. Just how big nobody knows for sure, because drug rings and organized crime families do not prepare annual reports. The President's Commission on Organized Crime's interim report entitled The Cash Connection shows that Americans spend between $50 and $75 billion each year to buy illegal drugs; and there are estimates that this figure is increasing with no end in sight. This would make the illegal drug trade a bigger operation than all but one Fortune 500 companies, larger than even General Motors, and this is just from drug trafficking.[2]

Money laundering is a crime most often associated with drug trafficking.[3] However, it is a potential problem associated with any activity

idea of an attempted failure to file is not workable. United States v. $500,000, 62 F.3d 59 (2d Cir.1995) (reversing judgment of forfeiture under § 5317(c)).

3. 31 U.S.C. § 5324(a)(2), (b)(2); I.R.C. § 6050I(f)(1)(B).

4. 31 U.S.C. § 5324(a)(3), (b)(3); I.R.C. § 6050I(f)(1)(C).

§ 18.12

1. 31 U.S.C. § 5324(a)(3), (b)(3); I.R.C. § 6050I(f)(1)(C).

§ 18.13

1. The President's Comm'n on Organized Crime, Interim Report to the President and Attorney General, The Cash Connection: Organized Crime, Financial Institutions, and Money Laundering, vii–viii (1984). *See also* D. Randall Johnson, *The Criminally Derived Property Statute: Constitutional and Interpretive Issues Raised by 18 U.S.C. § 1957*, 34 WM. & MARY L.REV. 1292, 1298 nn. 2, 18–26 and accompanying text (1993).

2. H.R. Rep. No. 746, 99th Cong., 2d Sess. 16 (1986).

3. 132 Cong. Rec. S9986 (daily ed. July 31, 1986).

H.R. Rep. No. 99–855, pt. 1, at 13 (1986) states:

> The Subcommittee is aware that every person who does business with a drug trafficker, or any other criminal, does so

that generates large amounts of cash that must be concealed.[4]

Congress intended the money laundering crimes to apply to conduct occurring *after* the completion of the underlying criminal activity.[5] The overall theory of the laundering crimes was to create "a new Federal crime of money laundering which will punish transactions that are undertaken with the proceeds of crimes or are designed to launder the proceeds of crime."[6] As one court stated, "[t]he [1986] Act appears to be part of an effort to criminalize the conduct of those third persons— bankers, brokers, real estate agents, auto dealers and others—who have aided drug dealers by allowing them to dispose of the profits of drug activity, yet whose conduct has not been considered criminal...."[7]

The money laundering laws expanded liability two ways. For those who committed the underlying crime, laundering added a new layer of liability when they used the proceeds of the crime. For those who did not commit the underlying crime but nonetheless dealt with property they knew to be criminally derived, laundering imposed liability where none existed before.

At first, money laundering was charged, if at all, as a secondary offense; it is now charged as a primary offense.[8]

Library References:

    C.J.S. United States § 125.
    West's Key No. Digests, United States ⚭34.

§ 18.14 Substantive Money Laundering Crimes: §§ 1956, 1957—Money Laundering: § 1956

A. INTRODUCTION

The Money Laundering Control Act of 1986 created two money laundering offenses.[1] The first of these is § 1956.

at some substantial risk if the person knows that they are being paid with the proceeds of a crime and then use that money in a financial transaction.... "The only way we will get at this problem is to let the whole community, the whole population, know they are part of the problem and they could very well be convicted of it if they knowingly take these funds. If we can make the drug dealers' money worthless, then we have really struck a chord, and we have hit him where he bruises, and that is right in the pocketbook.... You have outstanding business people who are otherwise totally moral who are accepting these funds and profiting greatly from drug trafficking that is going on throughout this country, and this will put a stop to it." (quoting Mr. Shaw from the Markup by the Subcommittee on Crime of H.R. 5077, Money Laundering Control Act of 1986, Transcript, pp. 22–23.)

    4. The definition of underlying crimes ("specified unlawful activity") is broad and

includes many crimes beyond drug crimes. *See* § 18.14(B)(iii) *infra.*

    5. United States v. Johnson, 971 F.2d 562, 569 (10th Cir.1992) (finding this to be Congress' intention behind the money laundering provisions).

    6. Congressional report on the 1986 Act, cited in United States v. Lovett, 964 F.2d 1029, 1042 (10th Cir.1992).

    7. United States v. Johnson, 971 F.2d 562, 568 (10th Cir.1992).

    8. United States v. Termini, 992 F.2d 879, 881 n. 2 (8th Cir.1993) ("Money laundering has historically been an offense committed by financial managers or those with strong economic connections which allowed them to disguise criminal proceeds realized by others.... We note however, that this crime now seems to have been elevated from its previous status as an uncharged or subordinate offense to a primary offense.") (citations omitted).

§ 18.14

    1. 18 U.S.C. §§ 1956, 1957.

Section 1956 criminalizes certain dealings with money generated by a wide range of "specified unlawful activities" (SUA's). Generally the statute criminalizes two kinds of activity. First, it covers *financial transactions* in which the defendant knowingly uses dirty money to promote the illegal activity, evades taxes on the dirty money, or designs a transaction to conceal something about the dirty money or to avoid a currency reporting requirement. The second kind of activity covered by the statute is *international transportation* of money in order to promote specified unlawful activity or to hide something about it or to avoid a currency reporting requirement.

Subsection 1956(a) establishes the crime in three subsections. The first of these subsections, (a)(1), covers domestic money laundering using financial transactions.[2] The second, (a)(2), covers international transportation of monetary instruments and funds.[3] Finally, (a)(3) was added in 1988 to cover government sting operations; it basically parallels (a)(1).[4] Although there is considerable overlap of terminology, each of these subsections has distinct elements. Diagrams of the three subsections appear below.

   2.   18 U.S.C. § 1956(a)(1).
   3.   18 U.S.C. § 1956(a)(2).
   4.   18 U.S.C. § 1956(a)(3).

<u>**1956 (a)(1)**</u>

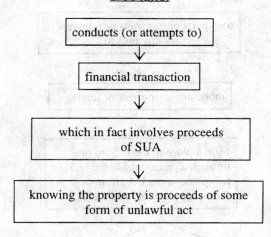

conducts (or attempts to)

↓

financial transaction

↓

which in fact involves proceeds
of SUA

↓

knowing the property is proceeds of some
form of unlawful act

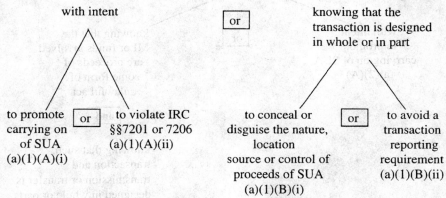

with intent   or   knowing that the
transaction is designed
in whole or in part

to promote   or   to violate IRC   to conceal or   or   to avoid a
carrying on   §§7201 or 7206   disguise the nature,   transaction
of SUA   (a)(1)(A)(ii)   location   reporting
(a)(1)(A)(i)   source or control of   requirement
                               proceeds of SUA   (a)(1)(B)(ii)
                               (a)(1)(B)(i)

1956 (a)(2)

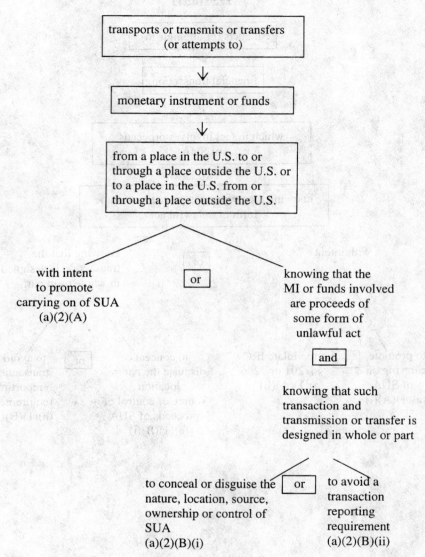

transports or transmits or transfers
(or attempts to)

↓

monetary instrument or funds

↓

from a place in the U.S. to or
through a place outside the U.S. or
to a place in the U.S. from or
through a place outside the U.S.

with intent
to promote
carrying on of SUA
(a)(2)(A)

or

knowing that the
MI or funds involved
are proceeds of
some form of
unlawful act

and

knowing that such
transaction and
transmission or transfer is
designed in whole or part

to conceal or disguise the
nature, location, source,
ownership or control of
SUA
(a)(2)(B)(i)

or

to avoid a
transaction
reporting
requirement
(a)(2)(B)(ii)

1956 (a)(3)

```
        ┌─────────────────────────────┐
        │  conducts  (or attempts to) │
        └─────────────────────────────┘
                      │
                      ▼
        ┌─────────────────────────────┐
        │    financial transaction    │
        └─────────────────────────────┘
                      │
                      ▼
  ┌───────────────────────────────────────┐
  │ involving property represented to      │
  │ be the proceeds of SUA or              │
  │ property used to conduct or            │
  │ facilitate SUA                         │
  └───────────────────────────────────────┘
                      │
                      ▼
             ┌─────────────┐
             │ with intent │
             └─────────────┘
```

| to promote carrying on of SUA (a)(3)(A) | or | to conceal or disguise the nature, location, source, ownership, or control of property believed to be the proceeds of SUA (a)(3)(B) | or | to avoid a transaction reporting requirement (a)(3)(C) |

B. DOMESTIC FINANCIAL TRANSACTIONS: § 1956(a)(1)

i. Financial Transaction

The first element of § 1956(a)(1) is that the defendant conduct a "financial transaction." The statutory definition provides that a financial transaction must fit into one of four categories.[5] It must be a transaction which affects commerce involving (1) the movement of funds by wire or other means; (2) one or more monetary instruments[6] (3) the

5. Subsection 1956(c)(4) defines a "financial transaction" as either:

(A) a transaction which in any way or degree affects interstate or foreign commerce (i) involving the movement of funds by wire or other means or (ii) involving one or more monetary instruments, or (iii) involving the transfer of title to any real property, vehicle, vessel or aircraft, or (B) a transaction involving the use of a financial institution which is

engaged in, or the activities of which affect, interstate or foreign commerce in any way or degree....

6. "Monetary instrument" is defined in subsection 1956(c)(5) as:

(i) coin or currency of the United States or of any other country, travelers' checks, personal checks, bank checks, and money orders, or (ii) investment securities or negotiable instruments, in bearer form or

transfer of title to any real property, vehicle, vessel or aircraft; or (4) a "financial institution" which is engaged in or affects commerce.[7]

Thus, a transaction does not necessarily have to involve a financial institution to satisfy the definition.[8] For example, if an individual merely transfers illegally derived money to another individual, the transferor has satisfied the transaction requirement if the transfer affects interstate or foreign commerce.[9]

The definition of "financial transaction" depends on the definition of "transaction." The statute defines "transaction" broadly.[10] Congress intended the definition to be broad.[11] It includes the purchase, sale or disposition of any kind of property.[12] It includes gifts,[13] and it includes use of a safe deposit box at a bank.[14]

Financial transactions have been held to include transferring title to

otherwise in such form that title thereto passes upon delivery. . . .

7. 18 U.S.C. § 1956(c)(4)(3). The term *financial institution* is defined in § 1956(c)(6) by referring to the definition in the Bank Secrecy Act, 31 U.S.C. § 5312(a)(2), discussed in § 18.3(C)(i)(a) *supra.*

8. *See* United States v. Conley, 833 F.Supp. 1121, 1138 (W.D.Pa.1993) ("A financial transaction can be shown one of two ways. First, there can be a disposition of property, the disposition affecting in any way or degree interstate or foreign commerce involving the movement of funds by wire or other means, involving one or more monetary instruments, or involving the transfer of title to real property, vehicle, vessel or aircraft. Second, there can be a transaction involving a financial institution engaged in, or the activities of which affect, interstate or foreign commerce in any way or degree."), *judgment vacated and remanded on other grounds*, United States v. Conley, 37 F.3d 970 (3d Cir. 1994).

9. *See*

First Circuit: United States v. Isabel, 945 F.2d 1193 (1st Cir.1991) (giving a check in exchange for cash is a financial transaction).

Fifth Circuit: United States v. Hamilton, 931 F.2d 1046 (5th Cir.1991) (sending cash through the mail is a financial transaction); United States v. Gallo, 927 F.2d 815 (5th Cir.1991) (transfer of box of currency from one individual to another is a financial transaction).

Eleventh Circuit: United States v. Castano–Martinez, 859 F.2d 925 (11th Cir. 1988) (a financial transaction includes various transfers of currency from the defendant's house to vehicles parked outside).

10. 18 U.S.C. § 1956(c)(4).

11. The Senate Report observed "that each transaction involving 'dirty' money is intended to be a separate offense. For example, a drug dealer who takes $1 million in cash from a drug sale and divides the money into smaller lots and deposits it in 10 different banks (or in different branches of the same bank) on the same day has committed 10 distinct violations of the new statute. If he then withdraws some of the money and uses it to purchase a boat or condominium, he will have committed two more violations, one for the withdrawal and one for the purchase." S. Rep. No. 433, 99th Cong. 2d Sess. 12–13 (1986) cited in United States v. Blackman, 904 F.2d 1250 (8th Cir.1990).

12. 18 U.S.C. § 1956(c)(3). See S.Rep. No. 433, 99th Cong. 2d Sess. 12–13 (1986) cited in United States v. Blackman, 904 F.2d 1250 (8th Cir.1990) and H.R. Rep. No. 855, 99th Cong., 2d Sess., Pt. 1, at 13 (1986) (listing "transactions").

In United States v. Blackman, 904 F.2d 1250, 1257 (8th Cir.1990), the court gave an example of a transaction: the deposit of money in a bank and the subsequent use of that money to purchase a house would constitute two separate transactions within the scope of § 1956.

13. United States v. Koller, 956 F.2d 1408 (7th Cir.1992).

14. The statute specifically lists "use of a safe deposit box" as a transaction in § 1956(c)(3). This was added to the statute in 1992 in response to cases holding that placing money in a safe deposit box within a bank did not constitute a transaction because the bank never exercised control over the money. *See, e.g.,* United States v. Bell, 936 F.2d 337, 341–42 (7th Cir.1991).

a vehicle;[15] the sale of automobiles;[16] writing a check to a vendor who provided services;[17] and gifts of bail money.[18] However, in United States v. Sanders[19] the Tenth Circuit cautions against turning the money laundering statute into a "money spending statute" by defining the term financial transaction too broadly.[20]

After some initial disagreement, the courts are settled that mere possession or transportation of dirty money is not a financial transaction; to qualify as a transaction, some disposition must be made.[21] As the Tenth Circuit explained the rationale, merely transporting concealed money is not laundering because, "The money laundering statute was designed to punish those drug dealers who [after transporting the money] take the additional step of attempting to legitimize their proceeds so that observers think their money is derived from legal enterprises. That extra step is missing ... with respect to the initial plan to transport the money...."[22] The Sixth Circuit *en banc* recently found the necessary disposition of the money was made (and so a transaction was established) when the defendant "arranged for the exchange of the proceeds, accepted them into her possession, exercised control over the proceeds for a period of time, and authorized the release of the proceeds to another individual. Under these facts, the defendant here would clearly have effected a disposition of the proceeds."[23]

ii. Conducts

The second element is that the defendant "conducts" a financial transaction.[24] The statute states that "[T]he term 'conducts' includes initiating, concluding, or participating in initiating or concluding a transaction...."[25] Thus, the statute applies to persons with the requi-

15. United States v. Blackman, 904 F.2d 1250, 1257 (8th Cir.1990), *called into doubt on other grounds by* United States v. ABC, Inc., 952 F.2d 155 (8th Cir.1991).

16. United States v. Werber, 787 F.Supp. 353, 356 (S.D.N.Y.1992).

17. United States v. Jackson, 935 F.2d 832 (7th Cir.1991).

18. United States v. Koller, 956 F.2d 1408, 1411 (7th Cir.1992).

19. 928 F.2d 940 (10th Cir.1991).

20. United States v. Sanders, 928 F.2d 940, 946 (10th Cir.1991).

21. *See*

Fifth Circuit: United States v. Puig–Infante, 19 F.3d 929, 938–939 (5th Cir. 1994)(mere transportation without disposition is not prohibited transaction under § 1956; conviction reversed); United States v. Ramirez, 954 F.2d 1035 (5th Cir. 1992)(mere possession is not within definition of financial transaction; conviction reversed).

Sixth Circuit: United States v. Reed, 77 F.3d 139 (6th Cir.1996)(en banc)(mere transportation is not financial transaction, some disposition is necessary; disposition met on facts, pre-trial dismissal of indictment reversed).

Tenth Circuit: United States v. Dimeck, 24 F.3d 1239, 1246 (10th Cir.1994)(term *transaction* includes delivery of drug proceeds, but conviction reversed because delivery was not designed to conceal or disguise anything about the proceeds).

See generally Jimmy Gurule, *The Money Laundering Control Act of 1986: Creating a New Federal Offense or Merely Affording Federal Prosecutors An Alternative Means of Punishing Specified Unlawful Activity?*, 32 Am. Crim. L. Rev. 823, 831 (1995).

22. United States v. Dimeck, 24 F.3d 1239, 1247 (10th Cir.1994).

23. United States v. Reed, 77 F.3d 139, 143 (6th Cir.1996)(en banc).

24. 18 U.S.C. § 1956(a)(1).

25. 18 U.S.C. § 1956(c)(2).

site mental state on both sides of any transaction.[26] Circumstantial evidence is sufficient to connect the defendant to the transaction.[27]

iii. Proceeds In Fact of Specified Unlawful Activity

a. *Specified Unlawful Activity*

The proceeds involved in the transaction must be "in fact the proceeds of a specified unlawful activity."[28] The statute includes an extensive list of SUA's, including but not limited to RICO predicate offenses, bribery, bank fraud, drug crimes, environmental crimes and Foreign Corrupt Practices Act violations.[29] Specifically excluded from the definition of SUA are the reporting requirements of the Bank Secrecy Act.[30] The most recent additions to the list of specified unlawful activities were made in 1996, and they include but are not limited to various assassination, terrorist acts, willful injury to government property and federal health care crimes.[31]

Most of the prosecutions are based on drug crimes, but other crimes have been the basis of laundering prosecutions as well.[32] The breadth of the concept of SUA is evident in a recent Seventh Circuit case: the defendant committed state prostitution crimes, which qualified as "unlawful activity" under the Travel Act which is a predicate for RICO, which qualified as SUA for money laundering.[33]

Conviction on the SUA is not required; the proceeds need only be generated by an act or activity that constitutes one of the offenses listed as SUA.[34]

The defendant's money laundering conviction does not have to be

---

26. The legislative history of the Act, S. Rep. No. 433, 99th Cong., 2d Sess. 12 (1986), states:

this ensures that section (a) applies not only to a person who deposits a cash in a bank knowing that the cash represents the proceeds of a crime, but also to a bank employee who accepts the cash if the employee knows that the money represents the proceeds of a crime.

27. United States v. Winfield, 997 F.2d 1076, 1080 (4th Cir.1993)(a rational jury could find that the defendant was the true purchaser of property although it had been put in others' names).

28. 18 U.S.C. § 1956(a)(1).

29. *Id.* § 1956(c)(7).

30. *Id.* These are excluded as specified unlawful activities but they still play a role in § 1956 because knowledge that a transaction is designed to avoid a reporting requirement can establish the § 1956 *mens rea*.

31. *See* P.L. 104–132, Title VII, Subtitle B, § 726, 110 Stat. 1301 (April 24,

1996); P.L. 104–191, Title II, Subtitle E, § 246, 110 Stat. 2018 (August 21, 1996).

32. *Third Circuit:* United States v. Paramo, 998 F.2d 1212 (3d Cir.1993)(embezzlement).

Sixth Circuit: United States v. Haun, 90 F.3d 1096 (6th Cir.1996)("[T]he legislative history reflects that although § 1956 was considered necessary to combat illegal narcotics conspiracies, it was also designed to reach financial transactions involving proceeds of a broad range of criminal activity.")(citations omitted).

Eighth Circuit: United States v. Hare, 49 F.3d 447 (8th Cir.1995)(wire fraud); United States v. Morris, 18 F.3d 562 (8th Cir.1994)(bank fraud).

Ninth Circuit: United States v. Montoya, 945 F.2d 1068 (9th Cir.1991) (bribery).

33. United States v. Griffith, 85 F.3d 284, 286–87 (7th Cir.1996).

34. United States v. Gurs, 83 F.3d 429 (9th Cir.1996) (unpublished).

reversed just because convictions on the SUA are reversed.[35] It depends on how the laundering counts allege the SUA. If the SUA is alleged to be the exact activity of the reversed counts, the laundering conviction may be reversed; if, however, the SUA is alleged more generally to be the type of crime of the reversed counts, the laundering conviction may be affirmed.[36]

The court is not required to instruct the jury on the elements of the underlying SUA.[37]

b. Proceeds

The statute does not define the term *proceeds*. Courts have concluded that *proceeds* are not confined to cash or money but include all that which results or accrues from some possession or transaction.[38]

The birth of proceeds. To qualify as proceeds, the underlying crime which generated them must be complete; the laundering transaction cannot be an integral part of the underlying crime.[39]

Directly tracing specific proceeds to specific SUA is not required.[40]

A particular problem arises when a defendant commingles the proceeds of specified unlawful activities with legally derived funds. In United States v. Jackson, the Seventh Circuit held that since Congress only required the transaction to "involve" the proceeds of SUA, it was sufficient to show that the financial transaction involved disbursements from commingled sources, otherwise, the defendant could avoid liability by commingling proceeds.[41] Other circuits agree.[42]

35. United States v. Tencer, 107 F.3d 1120, 1130–31 (5th Cir.1997).

36. *Id.* at 1130–31, *citing* United States v. O'Hagan, 92 F.3d 612, 628 (8th Cir.1996), *rev'd on other grounds*, 117 S.Ct. 2199 (1997); United States v. Brumley, 79 F.3d 1430, 1442 (5th Cir.1996), rehearing en banc granted on other grounds, 91 F.3d 676 (5th Cir.1996).

37. United States v. Golb, 69 F.3d 1417, 1429 (9th Cir.1995).

38. *Second Circuit:* United States v. Werber, 787 F.Supp. 353 (S.D.N.Y.1992)(*citing* Phelps v. Harris, 101 U.S. (11 Otto) 370, 25 L.Ed. 855 (1879) as the source of the common law definition of *proceeds*).

Eleventh Circuit: United States v. Ortiz, 738 F.Supp. 1394, 1400 (S.D.Fla.1990)(*citing Phelps* and holding that term *proceeds* is not limited to money).

39. *Fifth Circuit:* United States v. Allen, 76 F.3d 1348, 1360–62 (5th Cir.1996) (misapplication and fraud crimes complete at time of money laundering conduct; conviction affirmed); United States v. Gaytan, 74 F.3d 545 (5th Cir.1996)(money paid for drugs only becomes the proceeds of SUA upon the drug trafficker's receipt of it, so

the transaction of payment for the drugs is not money laundering, because the funds involved are not yet proceeds of an unlawful activity) (*citing* United States v. Puig–Infante, 19 F.3d 929, 939 (5th Cir.1994)).

40. *Sixth Circuit:* United States v. Bencs, 28 F.3d 555, 562 (6th Cir.1994)(Congress' choice of the term "involve" could not require direct tracing of funds, since otherwise defendants could escape conviction by commingling funds).

Eighth Circuit: United States v. Blackman, 904 F.2d 1250 (8th Cir.1990), *called into doubt on other grounds by* United States v. ABC, Inc., 952 F.2d 155 (8th Cir.1991).

Tenth Circuit: United States v. Hardwell, 80 F.3d 1471, 1483 (10th Cir. 1996)(§ 1956 "does not require the government to trace the money to a particular illegal drug transaction.") (*citing* United States v. Jackson, 983 F.2d 757, 766 (7th Cir.1993)).

41. 935 F.2d 832 (7th Cir.1991).

42. *Fifth Circuit:* United States v. Tencer, 107 F.3d 1120, 1130 (5th Cir.1997).

Sixth Circuit: United States v. Bencs, 28 F.3d 555, 562 (6th Cir.1994) (Congress'

In a case where the defendant has no legitimate source of funds, the government still must present sufficient proof that the money came from a specified unlawful activity.[43]

The death of proceeds. Another issue is how long property remains a proceed. Does the term cover only funds directly exchanged for drugs or does it go further and cover funds derived from such exchanges. There has been no judicial development of this issue.

iv. *Mens Rea*

Section 1956(a)(1) has a double tiered *mens rea.*[44] First, the defendant must act knowing the property represents proceeds of some form of unlawful act.[45] Second, the defendant must act with an additional level of culpability. This section of the statute is divided into four subsections based on this second level of culpability. Two use intent and two use knowledge. The government only has to prove one of these four, as they are listed in the statute in the disjunctive.[46] The four options are:

— § 1956(a)(1)(A)(i)—intent to promote the carrying on of specified unlawful activity;[47]

— § 1956(a)(1)(A)(ii)—intent to violate certain tax laws;

— § 1956(a)(1)(B)(i)—knowledge that the transaction was designed to conceal or disguise the source, ownership, control or location of the proceeds of specified unlawful activity;

— § 1956(a)(1)(B)(ii)—knowledge that the transaction was designed to avoid a transaction reporting requirement.

Each of these tiers of *mens rea* is discussed below.

a. First Tier: Knowing the Proceeds Come from Some Form of Unlawful Activity

To meet the first tier of the *mens rea,* the defendant must have *knowledge that the property represents proceeds of some form of unlawful*

---

choice of the term "involve" could not require direct tracing of funds, since otherwise defendants could escape conviction by commingling funds).

Eighth Circuit: United States v. Sutera, 933 F.2d 641 (8th Cir.1991) (commingling of funds suggests an intent to conceal or disguise the true nature of the funds).

Ninth Circuit: United States v. English, 92 F.3d 909, 916 (9th Cir.1996); United States v. Garcia, 37 F.3d 1359, 1365 (9th Cir.1994) ("[D]ue to the fungibility of money, it is sufficient to prove that the funds in question came from an account in which tainted proceeds were commingled with other funds.... [T]o rule otherwise would defeat the very purpose of the money laundering statutes.").

Eleventh Circuit: United States v. Cancelliere, 69 F.3d 1116 (11th Cir.1995) (*citing Jackson*).

43. *United States v. Blackman*, 904 F.2d 1250 (8th Cir.1990).

44. *See, e.g.,*

Second Circuit: United States v. Cota, 953 F.2d 753 (2d Cir.1992).

Fourth Circuit: United States v. Campbell, 977 F.2d 854, 857 (4th Cir.1992).

Ninth Circuit: United States v. Golb, 69 F.3d 1417 (9th Cir.1995).

45. § 1956(a)(1).

46. *See* United States v. Montoya, 945 F.2d 1068, 1076 (9th Cir.1991) (describing (a)(1)(A)(i) and (a)(1)(B)(i) as "set forth in the disjunctive" and *citing* United States v. Jackson, 935 F.2d 832, 842 (7th Cir.1991)).

47. United States v. Conley, 37 F.3d 970 979 (3d Cir.1994).

act. Somewhat unusually, Congress defined this *mens rea* in the statute.[48] The definition makes it clear that the defendant must know that the proceeds were from some unlawful activity, but the defendant need not know which specific form of unlawful activity the proceeds were derived from.[49]

The statute requires actual, subjective knowledge,[50] but this requirement is softened by the availability of willful blindness.[51] The Senate Report refers to the *Jewell* case[52] as a guide to using willful blindness for § 1956.[53] Courts have upheld willful blindness as a way to prove knowl-

---

48. Subsection (c)(1) contains a definition of the knowledge element:

the term "knowing that the property involved in a financial transaction represents the proceeds of some form of illegal activity" means that the person knew the property involved in the transaction represented proceeds from some form, though not necessarily which form, of activity that constitutes a felony under state, Federal, or foreign law, regardless of whether or not such activity is specified in paragraph (7).

49. *See*

Eighth Circuit: United States v. Blackman, 904 F.2d 1250, 1256 (8th Cir.1990)(circumstantial evidence such as proof that the defendant has no legitimate source of income and evidence of the defendant's involvement in drug trafficking was sufficient to support an inference that the money involved in a wire transfer represented proceeds of a SUA), *called into doubt on other grounds by* United States v. ABC, Inc., 952 F.2d 155 (8th Cir.1991).

Ninth Circuit: United States v. Stein, 37 F.3d 1407, 1410 (9th Cir.1994) (*citing* United States v. Montoya, 945 F.2d 1068, 1076 (9th Cir.1991) for the holding that the defendant must have known that the predicate activity was unlawful but holding that the defendant need not know that the secondary act of money laundering was itself illegal).

50. United States v. Heaps, 39 F.3d 479, 484 (4th Cir.1994) (conviction reversed on other grounds).

51. *See* United States v. Campbell, 977 F.2d 854, 857 (4th Cir.1992) (*cited* with approval in *Heaps,* 39 F.3d at 484):

In assessing [the defendant's] culpability, it must be noted that the statute requires actual subjective knowledge. [The defendant] cannot be convicted on what she objectively should have known. However, this requirement is softened somewhat by the doctrine of willful blindness. In this case, the jury was [correctly] instructed that:

'The element of knowledge may be satisfied by inferences drawn from proof that a defendant deliberately closed her eyes to what would otherwise have been obvious to her. A finding beyond a reasonable doubt of a conscious purpose to avoid enlightenment would permit an inference of knowledge.... A defendant's knowledge of a fact may be inferred upon willful blindness to the existence of a fact.

[T]he willful blindness charge does not authorize [a finding] that the defendant acted knowingly because she should have known what was occurring when the property ... was being sold, or that in the exercise of hindsight she should have known what was occurring or because she was negligent in failing to recognize what was occurring or even because she was foolish in failing to recognize what was occurring. Instead, the government must prove beyond a reasonable doubt that the defendant purposely and deliberately contrived to avoid learning all of the facts.'

See

Second Circuit: United States v. Lora, 895 F.2d 878, 880 (2d Cir.1990).

Seventh Circuit: United States v. Antzoulatos, 962 F.2d 720, 725 (7th Cir.1992).

52. 532 F.2d 697 (9th Cir.1976).

53. S. Rep. No. 433, 99th Cong., 2d Sess. 9–10 (1986). The Senate Judiciary Committee's Report states:

The "knowing" scienter requirements are intended to be construed, like existing "knowing" scienter requirements, to include instances of "willful blindness." See United States v. Jewell, 532 F.2d 697 (9th Cir.), cert. denied, 426 U.S. 951, 96 S.Ct. 3173, 49 L.Ed.2d 1188 (1976). Thus, a currency exchanger who participates in a transaction with a known drug dealer involving hundreds of thousands of dol-

edge for § 1956.[54]

Both direct and circumstantial evidence may be used to prove knowledge of the source of the proceeds.[55] One way the government can prove knowledge is to show that the defendant was the perpetrator of the predicate crime.[56] Where the defendant is accused of laundering proceeds of another's illegal activity, that knowledge may be inferred from the circumstances.[57] These circumstances include the relationship between the defendant and the perpetrator of the predicate act[58] or the way in which the transaction was conducted.[59] Sufficient evidence that the defendant knew the money was proceeds of crime can be inferred from factors such as lavish lifestyles with no visible source of income and

lars in cash and accepts a commission far above the market rate, could not escape conviction, from the first tier of the offense, simply by claiming that he did not know for sure that the currency involved in the transaction was derived from crime. On the other hand, a car dealer who sells a car at market rates to a person whom he merely suspects of involvement with crime, cannot be convicted of this offense in the absence of a showing that he knew something more about the transaction or the circumstances surrounding it. Similarly, the "intent to facilitate" language of this section is intended to encompass situations like those prosecuted under the aiding and abetting statute in which a defendant knowingly furnishes substantial assistance to a person whom he or she is aware will use that assistance to commit a crime. See e.g., Backun v. United States, 112 F.2d 635 (4th Cir.1940).

54. *See*

Second Circuit: United States v. Gleave, 786 F.Supp. 258, 267 (W.D.N.Y.1992)(criminal knowledge may include instances of willful blindness, but government must still prove that defendants were on notice of high probability of existence of fact), *reversed and remanded in part on other grounds,* United States v. Knoll, 16 F.3d 1313 (2d Cir.1994).

Fifth Circuit: United States v. Giraldi, 86 F.3d 1368 (5th Cir.1996).

Eighth Circuit: United States v. Jensen, 69 F.3d 906 (8th Cir.1995).

55. United States v. Heaps, 39 F.3d 479, 484 (4th Cir.1994) (circumstantial evidence sufficient).

56. *Sixth Circuit:* United States v. Haun, 90 F.3d 1096 (6th Cir.1996) ("Given defendant's leadership role in the [fraudulent] scheme, the jury could have rationally inferred that defendant knew that the

checks were proceeds of that fraudulent activity.").

Seventh Circuit: United States v. Jackson, 935 F.2d 832 (7th Cir.1991) (where defendant is a drug dealer with access to large amount of cash, and the cash is being deposited into the defendant's account, a jury may conclude that the defendant knew the cash was the proceeds of his drug trafficking activity).

57. Frequently this proof is a comparison between legitimate income and cash outflow. *See, e.g.,*

Fifth Circuit: United States v. Webster, 960 F.2d 1301, 1308 (5th Cir.1992) (such evidence sufficient to sustain conviction).

Seventh Circuit: United States v. Jackson, 935 F.2d 832, 839–41 (7th Cir.1991) (this comparison may be considered by the jury).

Eighth Circuit: United States v. Blackman, 904 F.2d 1250, 1257 (8th Cir.1990) (the jury may not rely exclusively on this factor), *called into doubt on other grounds by* United States v. ABC, Inc., 952 F.2d 155 (8th Cir.1991).

58. United States v. Atterson, 926 F.2d 649, 656 (7th Cir.1991) (defendant's status as the girlfriend of a drug dealer who asked her to transfer cash for him by wire when he travelled out of town permitted the jury to infer that the defendant knew that the cash she was transferring was the proceeds of some form of unlawful activity).

59. United States v. Brown, 944 F.2d 1377 (7th Cir.1991) (jury was able to draw inference that defendant knew proceeds involved some unlawful activity from defendant's elaborate, time-consuming efforts to keep all of his cash transactions under $10,-000 when such efforts would have made no sense if the defendant had not been aware that he was dealing with the proceeds of some form of unlawful activity).

$100,000 stored in a trash bag.[60] However, the circumstances must do more than merely raise suspicion.[61]

While the defendant must know that the underlying acts that generated the money were illegal, it is not necessary to prove the defendant knows that the money laundering activity itself is illegal.[62]

b. Second Tier: Intent or Knowledge—The Four Subsections

In addition to the above knowledge requirement, the defendant must also have one of the following four mental states. They are written in the disjunctive, so only one must be met.[63]

The presence of four options for proving *mens rea* under subsection (a)(1) has raised unanimity issues. As noted above, only one of the *mens reas* must be proved. But what if the government alleges two or three alternatives? The Third Circuit discussed this issue in United States v. Navarro.[64] The government alleged that the defendant committed laundering under subsection (a)(1) with three mental states: (A)(i) (intent to promote carrying on of SUA), (B)(i) (knowing the transaction is to conceal or disguise something about the proceeds of SUA), and (B)(ii) (knowing the transaction is designed to avoid a reporting requirement). No specific unanimity instruction was given. The defendant appealed,

60. United States v. Jenkins, 78 F.3d 1283, 1288 (8th Cir.1996).

61. United States v. Campbell, 977 F.2d 854 (4th Cir.1992)(knowledge that money was provided by a person with a flamboyant lifestyle does not equate with knowledge that the cash was the proceeds of some form of unlawful activity).

The knowledge standard received considerable attention in the House Judiciary Committee. It was agreed that "knowledge" did not include "should have known," "might have known," or "a reasonable person would have known." The Committee was concerned about merchants and businesspersons who willingly receive and invest drug money. H.R. Rep. No. 855, 99th Cong., 2d Sess. 13 (1986) states:

A person who engages in a financial transaction using the proceeds of a designated offense would violate this section if such person knew that the subject of the transaction were the proceeds of any crime. The subcommittee is aware that every person who does business with a drug trafficker, or any other criminal, does so at some substantial risk if that person knows that they are being paid with the proceeds of a crime and then use that money in a financial transaction, As argued by Mr. Shaw, "I am concerned about a broker who might take a quarter a million dollars of cash down to Fort Lauderdale taking that as payment. I am

concerned about the realtor who is going to make a $50,000 or $100,000 commission on a deal by knowingly doing it. I am sick and tired of watching people sit back and say, 'I am not part of the problem, I am not committing the crime, and, therefore, my hands are clean even though I know the money is dirty I am handling.' The only way we will get at this problem is to let the whole community, the whole population, know they are part of the problem and they could very well be convicted of it if they knowingly take these funds. If we can make the drug dealers' money worthless, then we have really struck a chord, and we have hit him where he bruises, and that is right in the pocketbook. You have outstanding business people who are otherwise totally moral who are accepting these funds and profiting greatly from drug trafficking that is going on throughout this country, and this will put a stop to it."

62. United States v. Golb, 69 F.3d 1417, 1428 (9th Cir.1995); United States v. Stein, 37 F.3d 1407, 1410 (9th Cir.1994) (conviction reversed because general instruction that defendant did not need to know his acts were unlawful conflicted with instruction requiring knowledge that predicate acts were unlawful).

63. *See, e.g.*, United States v. Montoya, 945 F.2d 1068, 1075 (9th Cir.1991).

64. 145 F.3d 580 (3d Cir.1998).

arguing the three mental states constituted three separate crimes, and with no unanimity instruction, the conviction might be based on a patchwork verdict.[65] The court did an exhaustive analysis of the issue, examining common law, legislative history and the possibility of jury confusion. It concluded that the three alternative *mens reas* were not three crimes but were three separate means of committing a single crime.[66] As the court reasoned, the fact that multiple purposes could satisfy the end of money laundering did not mean that Congress intended to create multiple offenses. Thus the absence of a specific unanimity instruction was not plain error.[67] The Eighth Circuit has reached the same conclusion, finding that subsections (A)(i) and (B)(i) were two *mens rea* options under the one crime stated in (a)(1), so using a general unanimity instruction rather than a specific one was not error.[68]

1. *Intent to Promote the Carrying on of Specified Unlawful Activity: (a)(1)(A)(i)*

This subsection deals with defendants who plow their profits back into a criminal money making activity, for example, a drug dealer who purchases a house where proceeds of future sales will be concealed[69] and cars to be driven to sites of drug sales.[70] This conduct promotes future specified unlawful activity so it is covered under this subsection.[71] Evidence of a defendant's intent to promote SUA may be inferred from the circumstances.[72] Several circuits have held that the fact that a criminal enterprise has been completed does not preclude the application of this section.[73] On the other hand, the Fourth Circuit has held that

65. *Id.* at 586.

66. *Id.* at 592, citing United States v. Holmes, 44 F.3d 1150, 1155–56 (2d Cir. 1995) ((B)(i) and (B)(ii) are alternative improper purposes for single crime under (a)(1)).

67. This holding was limited in two ways: although a specific unanimity instruction was not given, a general one was; and the court was reviewing only for plain error. Whether the court would decide the same way without these two conditions is unclear.

68. United States v. Nattier, 127 F.3d 655 (8th Cir.1997). The court said it was not error, much less plain error. *Id.* at 660.

69. United States v. Munoz–Romo, 947 F.2d 170 (5th Cir.1991), *vacated and remanded on other grounds by* Munoz–Romo v. United States, 506 U.S. 802, 113 S.Ct. 30, 121 L.Ed.2d 4 (1992). *See also* United States v. Jackson, 935 F.2d 832 (7th Cir.1991)(purchase of telephone pagers promoted future illegal drug trafficking).

70. United States v. Munoz–Romo, 947 F.2d 170 (5th Cir.1991), *vacated and remanded on other grounds by* Munoz–

Romo v. United States, 506 U.S. 802, 113 S.Ct. 30, 121 L.Ed.2d 4 (1992).

71. *Id.*; United States v. Jackson, 935 F.2d 832, 842 (7th Cir.1991).

72. United States v. Johnson, 971 F.2d 562, 566 (10th Cir.1992).

73. At least four circuits have held that conduct can be characterized as "promoting" an enterprise even though the enterprise has already been completed when the conduct is committed.

Third Circuit: United States v. Paramo, 998 F.2d 1212, 1216–18 (3d Cir.1993).

Fifth Circuit: United States v. Cavalier, 17 F.3d 90, 93 (5th Cir.1994).

Eighth Circuit: United States v. Nattier, 127 F.3d 655, 658–59 (8th Cir.1997) (although the underlying embezzlement may have been complete, overall criminal scheme continued, so intent to promote SUA sufficient).

Ninth Circuit: United States v. Montoya, 945 F.2d 1068, 1076 (9th Cir.1991).

But see Jimmy Gurulé, *The Money Laundering Control Act of 1986: Creating a New Federal Offense or Merely Affording*

evidence of defendant's intent to promote carrying on of SUA was insufficient where the laundering conduct merely completed the antecedent drug transaction, and there was no evidence of future transactions.[74]

2. Intent to Violate I.R.C. §§ 7201 or 7206: (a)(1)(A)(ii)

This section was added to the statute to allow the I.R.S., with its expertise in investigating financial transactions, to participate in developing cases under § 1956.[75]

3. Knowing the Transaction is Designed to

(a) Conceal or Disguise the Nature, Source, Ownership, or Control of Proceeds of SUA: (a)(1)(B)(i)

Proof that the defendant had knowledge that a transaction was designed in whole or in part to conceal or disguise may be based on circumstantial evidence, but it must be substantial.[76] Sufficient evidence includes the use of a third party to conduct a transaction,[77] statements by a defendant indicating an intent to conceal,[78] unusual secrecy surrounding transactions,[79] structuring transactions to avoid bank requirements,[80] unnecessarily complicated transactions[81] or commingling illegal

---

Federal Prosecutors an Alternative Means of Punishing Specified Unlawful Activity?, 32 Am. Crim. L. Rev. 823, 846–50 (1995) (criticizing these holdings as misconstruing the statute and sidestepping the statutory language).

74. United States v. Heaps, 39 F.3d 479, 484–86 (4th Cir.1994).

75. 134 Cong. Rec. S17367 (daily ed. November 10, 1988).

76. *See*

Fourth Circuit: United States v. Campbell, 977 F.2d 854, 857 (4th Cir.1992). In *Campbell*, the defendant was a real estate agent who took tainted cash from a drug trafficker who wanted to buy a house. At issue was the question of whether the defendant had knowledge of the potential buyer's purpose of laundering dirty money, not whether the real estate agent had the purpose of laundering dirty money. "The Government need not prove that the defendant had the purpose of concealing the proceeds of illegal activity. Instead, as the plain language of the statute suggests, the Government must only show that the defendant possessed the knowledge that the transaction was designed to conceal illegal proceeds. This distinction is critical in cases . . . in which the defendant is a person other than the individual who is the source of the tainted money."

Tenth Circuit: United States v. Garcia–Emanuel, 14 F.3d 1469, 1475 (10th Cir. 1994).

77. *See*

Seventh Circuit: United States v. Kaufmann, 985 F.2d 884, 894 (7th Cir.1993).

Eighth Circuit: United States v. Turner, 975 F.2d 490, 496–97 (8th Cir.1992); United States v. Martin, 933 F.2d 609 (8th Cir.1991) (use of drug proceeds to purchase stock in name of third party evidences intent to conceal or disguise).

Tenth Circuit: United States v. Edgmon, 952 F.2d 1206, 1210–11 (10th Cir. 1991). *But see* United States v. Garcia–Emanuel, 14 F.3d 1469 (10th Cir.1994) (construing *Sanders* as holding the use of a third party's name and large amounts of cash insufficient evidence of design to conceal and *Lovett* as holding that the defendant's other convictions on money laundering, use of a third party's name on the title, and statements regarding his lucrative business insufficient evidence of design to conceal).

78. *Sixth Circuit:* United States v. Beddow, 957 F.2d 1330, 1334–35 (6th Cir. 1992).

Eleventh Circuit: United States v. Saget, 991 F.2d 702, 712 (11th Cir.1993).

79. United States v. Cota, 953 F.2d 753, 760–61 (2d Cir.1992).

80. United States v. Massac, 867 F.2d 174, 178 (3d Cir.1989) (defendant's avoidance of formal banking procedures was sufficient to infer intent).

funds with legitimate business funds.[82] The defendant need not use a false identity to satisfy the concealment element.[83] It is sufficient if the defendant disguises drug proceeds as proceeds from some other source; he need not attempt to conceal his identity or ownership of the property.[84] The fact that the defendant merely spends dirty money for personal benefit or behaves in some suspicious manner, such as using large amounts of cash, is not enough to support an inference of a design to conceal.[85]

The defendant need not know which SUA generated the money being concealed.[86]

(b) Avoid a Transaction Reporting Requirement: (a)(1)(B)(ii)

The financial transaction must be designed in whole or in part to avoid any transaction reporting requirement under state or federal law.[87]

81. *See*

Fourth Circuit: United States v. Campbell, 977 F.2d 854, 858 & n. 4 (4th Cir. 1992).

Seventh Circuit: United States v. Jackson, 983 F.2d 757, 764, 766–67 & n. 4 (7th Cir.1993).

Eighth Circuit: United States v. Peery, 977 F.2d 1230, 1234 (8th Cir.1992).

Ninth Circuit: United States v. Manarite, 44 F.3d 1407, 1416 (9th Cir.1995) (cashing gambling chips in small quantities).

Tenth Circuit: United States v. Lovett, 964 F.2d 1029, 1036 (10th Cir.1992)(conflicting statements to bank employees about the source of funds used to purchase a house, together with convoluted series of transactions, held sufficient evidence for jury to find defendant intended to conceal the source of the money) (*citing* United States v. Beddow, 957 F.2d 1330, 1334 (6th Cir.1992)) (evidence of defendant's "convoluted financial dealing" with his banks and in his business "support a conclusion that he intended to disguise the illegal source of his money").

82. *See*

Seventh Circuit: United States v. Jackson, 935 F.2d 832, 842 (7th Cir.1991).

Eighth Circuit: United States v. Termini, 992 F.2d 879 (8th Cir.1993); United States v. Sutera, 933 F.2d 641, 648 (8th Cir.1991)(even though the illegal money "might have been better hidden if it had been mixed with [the legitimate business'] receipts, the money laundering statute does not require the jury to find that [the defendant] did a good job of laundering the proceeds. The jury simply has to find that [the defendant] intended to hide the [illegal] proceeds."); United States v. Martin, 933 F.2d 609 (8th Cir.1991) (deposit of gambling proceeds in account held by restaurant business, and paying personal expenses out of business account, evidences intent to conceal or disguise).

83. *Second Circuit:* United States v. Kinzler, 55 F.3d 70, 73 (2d Cir.1995).

Fifth Circuit: United States v. Tencer, 107 F.3d 1120, 1129–30 (5th Cir.1997).

Eighth Circuit: United States v. Nattier, 127 F.3d 655, 659 (8th Cir.1997).

84. United States v. Rounsavall, 115 F.3d 561, 566 (8th Cir.1997).

85. *Fourth Circuit:* United States v. Heaps, 39 F.3d 479, 486–87 (4th Cir.1994) (conviction reversed).

Eighth Circuit: United States v. Herron, 97 F.3d 234, 236–37 (8th Cir.1996) (conviction reversed because no evidence of concealment); United States v. Rockelman, 49 F.3d 418, 422 (8th Cir.1995) (conviction reversed because straightforward real estate transaction presented insufficient evidence of intent to conceal).

Tenth Circuit: United States v. Garcia–Emanuel, 14 F.3d 1469 (10th Cir.1994).

See also United States v. Dobbs, 63 F.3d 391, 397 (5th Cir.1995)(reversing conviction on money laundering because the evidence did not connect the fraud perpetrated by the defendant to the financial transactions for which he was charged and citing *Garcia-Emanuel* at 1474 for holding that "merely engaging in a transaction with money whose nature has been concealed through other means is not in itself a crime.").

86. United States v. Maher, 108 F.3d 1513, 1525–28 (2d Cir.1997).

87. 18 U.S.C. § 1956(a)(1)(B)(ii).

The language of this requirement parallels that of (a)(1)(B)(i) in that the defendant need only have knowledge of the design.

C. INTERNATIONAL TRANSPORTATION: § 1956(a)(2)

This subsection criminalizes three different categories of activity, distinguishing them on the basis of mental state.

Unlike (a)(1), there is no requirement in (a)(2) that the monetary instrument or funds involved be the proceeds of specified unlawful activity.[88] In other words, the money need not be dirty. This subsection criminalizes the movement of funds into or out of the United States with the intent to promote a criminal activity, without regard to whether the money is dirty.[89] Actually, subsection (a)(2)(A) criminalizes transportation of money with intent to promote certain crimes, not the "laundering" of money.

i. Transports, Transmits or Transfers

In 1988 this subsection of the statute was amended to replace the phrase "transports" with the phrase "transports, transmits, or transfers."[90] The purpose was to clarify that wire transfers were covered.[91]

ii. Monetary Instrument or Funds

The statute defines "monetary instruments" to include coin, currency, travelers' checks, personal checks, bank checks, money orders, and securities or negotiable instruments, in bearer form or otherwise if they are in a form that passes title at delivery.[92] The term *funds* indicates that wire transfers are covered.

88. United States v. Hamilton, 931 F.2d 1046 (5th Cir.1991)("For example, a foreign drug cartel might transfer proceeds from a legitimate business enterprise into a bank account in the United States. Such a transfer would not violate section 1956(a)(1), because the proceeds would not represent 'proceeds of unlawful activities.' Under section 1956(a)(2), however, the same transfer would be criminalized if the legitimate proceeds of that bank account were intended to provide the capital necessary for expanding a drug enterprise in the United States.").

89. *Second Circuit:* United States v. Piervinanzi, 23 F.3d 670, 679 (2d Cir. 1994)((a)(2) does not require that the funds be dirty).

Fifth Circuit: United States v. Hamilton, 931 F.2d 1046, 1052 (5th Cir. 1991)(clean foreign money deposited into bank account that was intended to promote illegal business in the United States would not violate (a)(1) because it would not be proceeds of a SUA, but it would violate

(a)(2) if shown to be intended to promote the carrying on of a SUA).

90. Subsection 6471(b) of the Anti–Drug Abuse Act of 1988.

91. See 134 Congressional Record, S17360 (daily ed., November 10, 1988).

Even under the old version of *transports,* however, some courts had concluded that wire transfers were covered. *See, e.g.,* United States v. Piervinanzi, 23 F.3d 670, 677–79 (2d Cir.1994); United States v. Monroe, 943 F.2d 1007, 1015 (9th Cir. 1991)("the contemporary meaning of 'transport' would have to include a wire transfer, since funds are increasingly 'conveyed' electronically" and citing cases interpreting the term "transport" in 18 U.S.C. § 2314 to include electronic transfers).

92. The term does not appear to include cashier's checks in non-bearer form. *See* United States v. Arditti, 955 F.2d 331, 337 (5th Cir.1992)(briefly discussing in dicta this question, which was unsuccessfully raised by the appellant).

Because the coverage of *funds* and the definition of monetary instrument in § 1956 is broader than the coverage of monetary instruments under the import/export reporting law,[93] it is possible to violate § 1956 by transporting funds internationally without violating the import/export reporting law.[94]

iii. Internationally

The defendant must transport, transmit or transfer the monetary instrument or funds from a point in the United States to or through a point outside the United States or to a place in the United States from or through a place outside the United States.[95]

iv. *Mens Rea*

Like subsection 1956(a)(1), subsection 1956(a)(2) requires a mental state of either intent or knowledge. Many of the terms used are repeated from the previous section, but a careful reading is necessary because the elements are, of course, different. There are two options: intent, or knowledge + knowledge. Subsection (a)(2)(A) requires the intent to promote the carrying on of a specified unlawful activity. An alternative provision, subsection (a)(2)(B), includes two knowledge requirements: first, the defendant must know that the property involved represents the proceeds of some unlawful act and second, the defendant must know that the transportation was designed either to conceal or disguise the proceeds ((a)(2)(B)(i)) or to avoid a reporting requirement ((a)(2)(B)(ii)). These two *mens rea* approaches are discussed below.

a. With the Intent to Promote the Carrying on of Specified Unlawful Activity: (a)(2)(A)

Under this subsection, there is no requirement that the defendant know that the monetary instrument or funds represent proceeds of unlawful activity.[96]

b. Knowing That the Monetary Instrument or Funds Involved Are Proceeds of Some Form of Unlawful Activity and Knowing That Such Transportation, Transmission or Transfer Is Designed To

Subsection (a)(2)(B) requires two types of knowledge. First, the defendant must know that the monetary instrument or funds represent

---

93. 31 U.S.C. §§ 5312(a)(3); 5316.

94. MONEY LAUNDERING: FEDERAL PROSECUTION MANUAL 281 n.716 (1993).

95. 18 U.S.C. § 1956(a)(2).

See

Eleventh Circuit: United States v. Kramer, 73 F.3d 1067, 1072–73 (11th Cir.1996)(defendant could not be convicted under subsection (a)(2) because he only was involved in a transaction outside the United States that was separate from the transaction originating in the United States.

"[M]oney laundering is not a continuous offense.").

But see

Second Circuit: United States v. Harris, 79 F.3d 223, 231 (2d Cir.1996) (defendant could be convicted under subsection (a)(2) because he was involved in a single transfer of funds that occurred in two stages—one inside the United States and one originating in the United States and ending outside the United States).

96. 18 U.S.C. § 1956(a)(2)(A).

proceeds of some form of unlawful activity.[97] Second, the defendant must also know that the transfer, transmission or transportation is designed in whole or in part to do one of two things. Transfers designed to conceal or disguise something about the proceeds of SUA are covered by subsection (a)(2)(B)(i). Transfers designed to avoid a transaction reporting requirement are covered by subsection (a)(2)(B)(ii).

1. Conceal or Disguise the Nature, Source, Ownership, or Control of Proceeds of SUA: (a)(2)(B)(i)

In addition to the knowledge requirement discussed above, this subsection requires proof parallel to that required by subsection (a)(1)(B)(i), except that there is no element of conduct requiring that the monetary instrument or funds in fact be the proceeds of SUA.[98] Arguably, then, a defendant could be convicted under this subsection if he had knowledge that the monetary instrument or funds represented the proceeds of some form of unlawful activity and had the required intent (i.e., to conceal or disguise the nature, location, etc.) regarding what he believed to be the proceeds of SUA (although it did not turn out to be proceeds in fact of SUA). However, there is no legislative history explaining this point and no case law developing it.[99]

2. Avoid a Transaction Reporting Requirement: (a)(2)(B)(ii)

Like subsection (a)(2)(B)(i), this subsection requires proof of the knowledge requirement discussed above. It also requires knowledge that the transfer was designed to avoid a reporting requirement.

D. STING OPERATIONS: § 1956(a)(3)

This subsection was added to allow prosecution of persons who believed the proceeds were from an unlawful activity when in fact they were not, such as the defendant in an undercover sting.[100] The sting

---

97. *First Circuit:* United States v. Lizotte, 856 F.2d 341 (1st Cir.1988).

Ninth Circuit: United States v. Savage, 67 F.3d 1435 (9th Cir.1995).

Tenth Circuit: United States v. Levine, 750 F.Supp. 1433 (D.Colo.1990).

Eleventh Circuit: United States v. Ortiz, 738 F.Supp. 1394 (S.D.Fla.1990).

Prior to the statutory amendment authorizing sting operations, when the proceeds involved in a violation were not "real" dirty money, but were represented to be real by the government, one court got around the knowledge requirement by equating the meaning of "know" with the everyday meaning of "believe." *See* United States v. Parramore, 720 F.Supp. 799, 802 (N.D.Cal.1989)("federal courts have consistently read 'know' to mean 'believe' where the results comport with congressional purpose and common sense").

98. 18 U.S.C. § 1956(a)(2)(B)(i).

99. *See generally* MONEY LAUNDERING: FEDERAL PROSECUTION MANUAL, 272 (1993).

100. 134 Cong. Rec. S17365 (daily ed. November 10, 1988). Senator Biden discussed the purpose in enacting subsection (a)(3):

This amendment to the money laundering statute, 18 U.S.C. § 1956, would permit undercover law enforcement officers to pose as drug traffickers in order to obtain evidence necessary to convict money launderers. The present statute does not provide for such operations because it permits a conviction only where the laundered money "in fact involves the proceeds of specified unlawful activity," 18 U.S.C. § 1956(a)(1). Since money provided by an undercover officer posing as a drug trafficker does not "in fact" involve

provision now permits convictions when the defendants believed the money was, in fact, the product of a specified unlawful activity, despite the fact that no illegal proceeds were used.[101] It thus accommodates sting operations.

i. "Represented"

Subsections (a)(1) and (a)(3) may be seen as parallel sections. One difference between (a)(1) and (a)(3) is the use of the term "represented" in this subsection. It is defined to mean any representation made by either a law enforcement officer or by another person at the direction of, or with the approval of, a federal officer.[102] The use of the term "represent" in the statute does not require an affirmative representation by the undercover officer.[103]

Generally, the government easily proves that the undercover officer made the required representation, even if it is implicit only. In United States v. Starke, the court noted that the agents' "appearance, actions, and words could convey to a reasonable person who is familiar with illicit activity that they were drug dealers and that the money they needed to launder was drug proceeds."[104] The agents kept a drug trafficker's hours, drove a car which indicated their status, a late model Jaguar trimmed in gold, wore expensive jewelry like a Rolex watch, asked for help in "cleaning up" some of their large amounts of money, and expressed fear of being caught by the police.[105]

Similarly, in United States v. Kauffman,[106] the informant and the agents sufficiently implied to the defendant that they were purchasing a Porsche with drug proceeds. The informant told the defendant that the car purchaser wanted to pay cash and wanted the car's title to be in someone else's name. The informant also told the defendant that the purchaser was a marijuana dealer. The informant gave the defendant a

drug money, the laundering of such money is not presently an offense under the statute.

101. United States v. Arditti, 955 F.2d 331, 339 (5th Cir.1992) (undercover agent's representation that he was in the cocaine business and that $15,000 was the proceeds of a collection satisfied the requirement for establishing the basis for money laundering sting operations that the government agent represented that the property involved in the transaction was the "proceeds of specified unlawful activity, or property used to conduct or facilitate specified unlawful activity.").

102. 18 U.S.C. § 1956(a)(3).

103. *Fifth Circuit:* United States v. Castaneda–Cantu, 20 F.3d 1325, 1331–32 (5th Cir.1994); United States v. Arditti, 955 F.2d 331, 339 (5th Cir.1992) ("To hold that a government agent must recite the alleged illegal source of each set of property at the

time he attempts to transfer it in a 'sting' operation would make enforcement of the statute extremely and unnecessarily difficult; 'legitimate criminals,' whom undercover agents must imitate, undoubtedly would not make such recitations before each transaction ... it is enough that ... the jury could have found beyond a reasonable doubt that [the agent] represented, and [the defendant] understood, that the funds they were laundering were the proceeds of the specified illegal activities.").

Eighth Circuit: United States v. Jensen, 69 F.3d 906 (8th Cir.1995).

Ninth Circuit: United States v. Nelson, 66 F.3d 1036, 1041 (9th Cir.1995).

104. 62 F.3d 1374, 1382–83 (11th Cir. 1995).

105. *Id.* at 1383.

106. United States v. Kaufmann, 985 F.2d 884 (7th Cir.1993).

letter from the "purchaser" which reiterated those requests and asked that the purchaser's name be kept secret. The court concluded that taken as a whole, this evidence would give any reasonable person in the defendant's position "a firm basis to believe that the money [was] derived from drug sales."[107]

ii. *Mens Rea* of Intent for All Conduct

A second difference between subsection (a)(1) and (a)(3) is that (a)(3) requires a mental state of intent for all three subsections, whereas (a)(1) allows a lesser knowing *mens rea* for (B)(i) and (ii).[108] Legislative history suggests that Congress intended this difference and "wanted to fine-tune" the sting provision.[109]

As with subsection (a)(1), the defendant need not know the nature of the underlying crime; as long as it is among those listed as SUA's, the precise nature is "inconsequential detail" the defendant need not know.[110]

E. INCHOATE LIABILITY

i. Solicitation

No language in the statute criminalizes solicitation of any § 1956 crimes. Because there is no general federal solicitation statute, solicitation of § 1956 laundering is not criminal.

ii. Conspiracy

Conspiracy to violate § 1956 may be charged under two provisions. First, § 1956 has its own conspiracy subsection, 1956(h).[111] Second, the general conspiracy statute, § 371, has been used with § 1956.[112]

iii. Attempt

Attempt is criminal under § 1956 because all three subsections expressly include the term *attempt* in their definition of the crime. The statute does not define *attempt*. Case law holds, consistent with the

107. *Id.* at 893.

108. United States v. Parramore, 720 F.Supp. 799, 804 (N.D.Cal.1989)((a)(3) has higher level of intent required).

109. 134 Cong. Rec. s. S17, 365 (daily ed. Nov. 10, 1988).

110. United States v. Stavroulakis, 952 F.2d 686, 691-92 (2d Cir.1992).

111. 18 U.S.C. § 1956(h).

See, e.g.,

Third Circuit: United States v. Navarro, 145 F.3d 580, 1998 WL 252491 (3d Cir. 1998).

Fifth Circuit: United States v. Knox, 112 F.3d 802 (5th Cir.1997)(reversing § 1956(h) conviction on other grounds).

112. *See, e.g.,*

Second Circuit: United States v. Piervinanzi, 23 F.3d 670 (2d Cir.1994).

Third Circuit: United States v. Carr, 25 F.3d 1194 (3d Cir.1994).

Fifth Circuit: United States v. Coscarelli, 105 F.3d 984 (5th Cir.1997)(vacated on other grounds).

Seventh Circuit: United States v. Griffith, 85 F.3d 284 (7th Cir.1996).

Eighth Circuit: United States v. Jenkins, 78 F.3d 1283 (8th Cir.1996).

federal treatment of attempt generally,[113] that the conduct must constitute a substantial step toward the commission of the offense.[114] Attempted § 1956 liability is discussed in more detail *supra* on § 2.7(D).

F. ACCOMPLICE LIABILITY

Section 1956 does not provide in its terms for accomplice liability, but aiding and abetting is criminalized by the general accomplice liability statute, § 2.[115] Under § 2 principles, to prove a defendant aided and abetted commission of § 1956, the Eighth Circuit explained in United States v. Termini that the government must show that the defendant "associated himself with the unlawful manipulations, that he participated in them as something he wished to bring about, and that he sought by his actions, to make the effort succeed."[116] In other words, "The government must prove 'some affirmative participation which at least encourages the perpetrator.' "[117] In *Termini*, the court reversed the conviction for aiding and abetting § 1956. The defendant collected money from gambling machines, some legal and some illegal. As he collected the money, he commingled it. The court held there was insufficient evidence of an intentional effort to hide the illegal source of some of the funds and that the defendant's mere knowledge of of others' laundering activities was legally insufficient to sustain his aiding and abetting conviction.[118]

G. CONSTITUTIONALITY

Section 1956 is constitutional.

i. Jurisdiction

Federal jurisdiction is conferred by the requirement that a transaction affect interstate or foreign commerce or be conducted by or through a financial institution which affects interstate or foreign commerce. This requirement appears explicitly in the definition of the term *transaction* which is in turn required under subsections (a)(1) (transactions) and (a)(3) (stings). For subsection (a)(2), no explicit jurisdictional language is included because (a)(2) by its terms only applies to transportations in foreign commerce. Congress was well within its power under the Commerce Clause in enacting § 1956.[119]

113. *See* § 2.7 *supra.*

114. *Eighth Circuit:* United States v. Wagner, 884 F.2d 1090 (8th Cir.1989).

Ninth Circuit: United States v. Candoli, 870 F.2d 496 (9th Cir.1989).

115. 18 U.S.C. § 2, discussed in §§ 4.1–4.7 *supra. See, e.g.,*

Second Circuit: United States v. Maher, 108 F.3d 1513 (2d Cir. 1997).

Fifth Circuit: United States v. Cavalier, 17 F.3d 90 (5th Cir.1994).

Ninth Circuit: United States v. Kimball, 975 F.2d 563 (9th Cir.1992).

116. United States v. Termini, 992 F.2d 879, 881 (8th Cir.1993)(*citing* United States v. Gaines, 969 F.2d 692, 698 (8th Cir.1992)).

117. United States v. Termini, 992 F.2d 879, 881 (8th Cir.1993)(*citing* United States v. Ivey, 915 F.2d 380, 384 (8th Cir. 1990)).

118. *Termini,* 992 F.2d at 881–82.

119. *Second Circuit*: United States v. Goodwin, 141 F.3d 394, 398 (2d Cir.1997) (unlike § 922(q), the crime construed in *Lopez*, "§ 1956 has everything to do with

Even showing a *de minimus* effect on interstate commerce establishes federal jurisdiction.[120]

There is some confusion as to whether the interstate commerce nexus is an essential element that must be proven beyond a reasonable doubt or merely a jurisdictional requirement.[121] It is possible to satisfy the interstate commerce requirement, according to one circuit, by showing that the underlying criminal activity affects interstate commerce.[122] A transaction which affects a federally insured bank affects interstate commerce.[123]

Subsection 1956(f) provides for extraterritorial jurisdiction if two conditions are met.[124] The conditions are that (1) the conduct is by a

commerce.... Money laundering is a quintessential economic activity. Indeed, it is difficult to imagine a more obviously commercial activity than engaging in financial transactions involving the profits of unlawful activity.").

Seventh Circuit: United States v. Griffith, 85 F.3d 284, 288 (7th Cir.1996).

120. United States v. Peay, 972 F.2d 71, 73 (4th Cir.1992)(*citing* United States v. Spagnolo, 546 F.2d 1117, 1119 (4th Cir. 1976)).

Tenth Circuit: United States v. Grey, 56 F.3d 1219, 1224–25 (10th Cir.1995)(*citing* United States v. Kelley, 929 F.2d 582, 586 (10th Cir.1991)).

121. *See*

Seventh Circuit: United States v. Koller, 956 F.2d 1408, 1412 (7th Cir. 1992)("since the purpose of the interstate commerce nexus is to provide a predicate for federal legislative jurisdiction ... the use of the financial institution involved in the transaction may be incidental ... and need not be shown to have been a part of, contributed to, or facilitated the design to conceal").

Tenth Circuit: United States v. Kelley, 929 F.2d 582, 586 (10th Cir.1991)(requirement that money laundering transaction affect interstate or foreign commerce is not an essential element of the offense, but must be met only to confer federal jurisdiction).

But see

Second Circuit: United States v. Goodwin, 141 F.3d 394, 398 (2d Cir.1997)(proof of a nexus with interstate or foreign commerce is an essential element).

Fourth Circuit: United States v. Bell, 1 F.3d 1234 (4th Cir.1993)(unpublished)(interstate commerce nexus requirement is an essential element of the offense and must be proven beyond a reasonable doubt).

122. *Fifth Circuit*: United States v. Gallo, 927 F.2d 815 (5th Cir.1991)(interstate commerce requirement of the statute satisfied by demonstrating that the property involved in the transaction was derived from narcotics trafficking, which Congress has determined affects interstate commerce).

See also

Third Circuit: United States v. Farley, 760 F.Supp. 461, 463 (E.D.Pa.1991)(drug money implicates interstate commerce).

Tenth Circuit: United States v. Kelley, 929 F.2d 582 (10th Cir.1991)(purchase of a car from a dealer who will use proceeds of sale to buy more inventory is in interstate commerce).

123. *Fourth Circuit*: United States v. Peay, 972 F.2d 71, 75 (4th Cir.1992)("Because Congress intended to reach all cases within its legislative power when it enacted § 1956, and because transactions involving financial institutions insured by the FDIC affect interstate commerce, we find no error in the district court's instructions to the jury that it could infer an effect on interstate commerce by the banks' status as FDIC-insured institutions.") and *Peay* at 73, citing cases holding that where Congress includes as an element that an activity "affects commerce," the court should infer a desire by Congress to take full advantage of its power to regulate commerce.

Seventh Circuit: United States v. Jackson, 935 F.2d 832 (7th Cir.1991) (drawing a check on a financial institution implicates interstate commerce).

124. Subsection 1956(f) states: "There is extraterritorial jurisdiction over the conduct prohibited by this section if— (1) the conduct is by a United States citizen or, in the case of a non-United States citizen, the conduct occurs in part in the United States; and (2) the transaction or series

United States citizen or, in the case of a non-United States citizen, the conduct occurs in part in the United States; and (2) the transaction or related transactions involve a value over $10,000.

ii. Vagueness

The statute has survived challenges to its constitutionality based on a vagueness argument.[125] The statute requires proof of specific intent[126] and the numerous and detailed definitions in the statute preclude discretionary enforcement.[127] Furthermore, an ordinary person would be able to understand what conduct is prohibited.[128]

iii. Double Jeopardy

The statute has survived challenges to its constitutionality based on a double jeopardy argument.[129]

Since Congressional intent in enacting § 1956 was to punish the act of laundering money and the elements of predicate SUA's were not disturbed by its enactment, prosecution under the statute is not multiplicious.[130] Prosecution of each financial transaction is likewise not multi-

---

of related transactions involves funds or monetary instruments of a value exceeding $10,000."

125. *Second Circuit:* United States v. Gleave, 786 F.Supp. 258, 268–70 (W.D.N.Y. 1992); United States v. Sierra–Garcia, 760 F.Supp. 252, 258–59 (E.D.N.Y.1991).

Fourth Circuit: United States v. Gilliam, 975 F.2d 1050, 1056–57 (4th Cir. 1992); United States v. McLamb, 985 F.2d 1284 (4th Cir.1993).

Fifth Circuit: United States v. Alford, 999 F.2d 818, 822–23 (5th Cir.1993).

Sixth Circuit: United States v. Haun, 90 F.3d 1096 (6th Cir.1996)(term proceeds is not unconstitutionally vague).

Seventh Circuit: United States v. Kaufmann, 985 F.2d 884 (7th Cir.1993)(subsections (a)(1) and (a)(3)(B) not unconstitutionally vague); United States v. Jackson, 983 F.2d 757 (7th Cir.1993); United States v. Antzoulatos, 962 F.2d 720 (7th Cir.1992); United States v. Jackson, 935 F.2d 832 (7th Cir.1991).

Eighth Circuit: United States v. Long, 977 F.2d 1264, 1273 (8th Cir.1992).

Ninth Circuit: United States v. Kimball, 711 F.Supp. 1031, 1034 (D.Nev.1989).

Eleventh Circuit: United States v. Awan, 966 F.2d 1415, 1424–25 (11th Cir.1992)(subsections (a)(1)(B) and (a)(2)(B) not unconstitutionally vague); United States v. Ortiz, 738 F.Supp. 1394, 1398 (S.D.Fla.1990)(knowledge requirement in (a)(1) not unconstitutionally vague and will-

ful blindness standard used to impute knowledge not unconstitutional).

126. *Second Circuit:* United States v. Stanton, 1992 WL 73408 (S.D.N.Y. 1992).

Fourth Circuit: United States v. Gilliam, 975 F.2d 1050 (4th Cir.1992).

127. *Fourth Circuit:* United States v. Gilliam, 975 F.2d 1050 (4th Cir.1992).

Seventh Circuit: United States v. Kaufmann, 985 F.2d 884 (7th Cir.1993).

128. United States v. Kaufmann, 985 F.2d 884, 895 (7th Cir.1993).

129. *Third Circuit:* United States v. Conley, 37 F.3d 970 (3d Cir.1994)(no violation of the double jeopardy clause where the SUA involves financial transactions because § 1956 requires a subsequent financial transaction, involving proceeds of the now completed SUA financial transactions, that promotes or furthers the SUA before money laundering can occur).

Sixth Circuit: United States v. Edgmon, 952 F.2d 1206 (10th Cir. 1991)(no violation of Double Jeopardy clause since Congress intended the SUA and the money laundering itself to be separate offenses).

Seventh Circuit: United States v. Jackson, 983 F.2d 757, 768–69 (7th Cir.1993).

Tenth Circuit: United States v. Hollis, 971 F.2d 1441, 50–51 (10th Cir.1992); United States v. Lovett, 964 F.2d 1029, 1041–42 (10th Cir.1992).

130. United States v. Skinner, 946 F.2d 176 (2d Cir.1991)(Congress intended

plicitous.[131]

iv. Overbreadth

Subsection 1956 (a)(3)(B) survived a challenge for overbreadth in United States v. Kaufmann.[132]

H. VENUE

The Supreme Court recently held that venue for § 1956 prosecutions lies only where the laundering transaction occurred, not where the underlying specified unlawful activity occurred.[133] However, the Court left open the possibility that venue could lie where the underlying crimes occurred if the money laundering charges alleged a continuing offense or included conspiracy or accomplice liability charges.[134]

I. DEPARTMENT OF JUSTICE GUIDELINES

The Department of Justice's United States Attorneys Manual includes one section on § 1956 prosecution standards. It provides that § 1956(a)(1)(A)(ii) (conducting a financial transaction with the intent to violate I.R.C. §§ 7201 or 7206) is

> intended to facilitate and enhance the prosecution of money launderers. It [is] not intended to provide a substitute for traditional Title 18 and Title 26 charges related to tax evasion, filing of false returns, including the aiding and abetting thereof, or tax fraud conspiracy. Consequently, appropriate tax-related Title 18 and Title 26 charges are to be utilized when the evidence warrants their use.[135]

The impact of this standard is uncertain because U.S.A.M. standards are not binding on the Department of Justice, and create no rights.[136]

multiple punishments for SUA's and § 1956).

131. United States v. Martin, 933 F.2d 609 (8th Cir.1991)(successive overt acts may be charged as separate criminal offenses under Blockburger v. United States, 284 U.S. 299, 52 S.Ct. 180, 76 L.Ed. 306 (1932), so two transactions involving the payment of cash for stock constituted separate financial transactions as that word is defined in § 1956(c)(4); the court pointed out that to call two different transactions on different dates, in different locations, and involving different amounts of money all one continuous course of action would mean that once a defendant started laundering money, he could keep going with impunity. That would frustrate intent of Congress, so not multiplicitous to prosecute for each transaction.)

132. 985 F.2d 884, 895 (7th Cir. 1993)("The statute does not impair an intimate human relationship, nor an association for the purpose of engaging in an activity protected by the first amendment.... Because § 1956 does not implicate constitutionally protected conduct, [the] overbreadth challenge fails.")

133. United States v. Cabrales, ___ U.S. ___, 118 S.Ct. 1772, 141 L.Ed.2d 1 (1998).

134. 118 S.Ct. at 1776.

135. U.S.A.M. § 9-105.750 (September 1997).

136. United States v. Piervinanzi, 23 F.3d 670, 682 (2d Cir.1994).

§ 18.15   Substantive Money Laundering Crimes: §§ 1956, 1957—Transactions in Criminally Derived Property: § 1957

A. IN GENERAL

Section 1957 essentially makes it a crime to knowingly put criminally derived money in amounts over $10,000 into the U.S. financial system. The crime is not the receipt or possession of dirty money, but engaging in a monetary transaction with it. Once money is generated by certain crimes, anyone along the route the money travels who knows it is criminally generated and puts amounts over $10,000 into a financial institution may be liable. As the Ninth Circuit observed, "It is a powerful tool because it makes any dealing with a bank potentially a trap for the drug dealer or any other defendant who has a hoard of criminal cash derived from the specified crimes. . . . This draconian law, so powerful by its elimination of criminal intent, freezes the proceeds of specific crimes out of the banking system."[1]

Defendants in § 1957 prosecutions tend to fall into two categories. The first includes persons who generated the money by committing the underlying crime. After the crime, if they do a monetary transaction with the proceeds (such as depositing it in a bank or with a broker), they face additional liability, beyond that for the underlying offense, under § 1957.

The second category of defendants includes persons who sell goods and services (including banking services) in exchange for criminally generated money. When these providers take over $10,000 in payment for goods or services knowing the money is criminally derived and deposit it in a financial institution, they become liable under § 1957. Congress specifically considered the category of defendants subject to prosecution under § 1957 and concluded it was unacceptable for merchants to knowingly engage in transactions with criminally generated money while justifying their conduct because they had not committed the underlying crime.[2]

This crime has seven elements. The conduct elements include two primary ones ((1) engage in (2) a monetary transaction), two elements which modify the property involved ((3) property of a value over $10,000 that is (4) derived from substantive unlawful activity), and two jurisdictional elements ((5) the transaction must affect interstate or foreign commerce and (6) the crime must either take place within the territorial jurisdiction of the U.S. or the defendant must be a United States person). The seventh element, the *mens rea*, is knowing.[3]

§ 18.15

1. United States v. Rutgard, 116 F.3d 1270, 1291 (9th Cir.1997).

2. *See* Emily J. Lawrence, *Let the Seller Beware: Money Laundering, Merchants and 18 U.S.C. §§ 1956 and 1957*, 33 B.C.L.Rev. 841, 862–63 (1992)(discussing Congress' intent on those targeted by the money laundering laws).

3. Courts agree on the elements but sometimes list them differently.

B. ELEMENTS

i. Engage

The main conduct element, *engage*, is not defined in the statute nor the case law. Courts will resort to the plain meaning of the term.[4]

ii. Monetary Transaction

A monetary transaction is defined as "the deposit, withdrawal, transfer, or exchange ... of funds or a monetary instrument ... by, through, or to a financial institution...."[5] The deposit of a check constitutes a monetary transaction.[6] One defendant argued that a mere deposit of funds was not sufficient, rather the government had to prove there was an exchange. This defendant had fraudulently procured a $180,000 certificate of deposit from his grandmother. Using the CD as collateral, he got a $150,000 loan from a bank and deposited the loan proceeds at a different bank. Convicted under § 1957, the defendant argued the government failed to prove that the loan was an exchange for the fraudulent CD. The court said this did not matter, the deposit of the criminally derived funds (the $150,000) into the bank was clearly within the language of the statute. The court saw "no basis for requiring the government to prove that each deposit was an 'exchange' of some sort when the conduct alleged ... relates to the deposits and not to the loan itself."[7]

To be a monetary transaction, the transaction must be by, through or to a *financial institution*. The definition of financial institution includes banks, securities brokers and dealers, currency dealers, funds transmitters and telegraph companies.[8] This definition means that § 1957 applies in many commercial settings.

Sixth Circuit: United States v. Leek, 78 F.3d 585 (6th Cir.1996) (identifying 6 elements).

Tenth Circuit: United States v. Lovett, 964 F.2d 1029, 1041 (10th Cir.1992) ("The elements of a § 1957 violation are that '(1) the defendant engage or attempt to engage (2) in a monetary transaction (3) in criminally derived property (4) knowing that the property is derived from unlawful activity, and (5) the property is, in fact, derived from specified unlawful activity.' ").

4. *See* United States v. Johnson, 971 F.2d 562, 568 (10th Cir.1992)(resorting to the plain meaning of the term "obtained" in § 1957 in the absence of a statutory definition for the term).

5. 18 U.S.C. § 1957(f)(1).

6. United States v. Ripinsky, 129 F.3d 518 (9th Cir.1997).

7. United States v. Lovett, 964 F.2d 1029, 1038 (10th Cir.1992).

8. This definition requires following a trail. To define financial institution, § 1957 refers to § 1956, which in turn refers to 31 U.S.C. § 5312 (the Bank Secrecy Act) "or the regulations promulgated thereunder." As noted above, see § 18.3(C), under the BSA the regulatory definition of financial institution is narrower than the statutory definition. For BSA purposes, the operative definition is the narrower, regulatory one. Presumably, the language of § 1956(c)(6) quoted above ("or the regulations promulgated thereunder") means the operative definition of financial institution for § 1957 would likewise be the narrower, regulatory one. However, the use of the disjunctive "or" leaves this uncertain. *Cf.* Rudnick, The U.S. Money Laundering Statutes: How Far Do They Extend Outside the U.S.?, 1997 White Collar Crime Institute, Vol. II, p. N13 n.1 (§ 1957 uses broader statutory definition of *financial institution* than regulatory definition).

The next two elements focus on the property involved in the transaction.

iii. Property of a Value Greater than $10,000

The property involved in the monetary transaction must have a value greater than $10,000.[9]

One question likely to arise is whether a person can avoid § 1957 liability by structuring the transaction to keep the amount involved under $10,000. No statute or regulation explicitly prohibits structuring under § 1957, and it is unlikely the courts would find structuring illegal without such language.[10] Section 1957 is one of two laundering laws based on a $10,000 threshold with no anti-structuring provision to back it up.[11]

iv. Derived from Specified Unlawful Activity

The property must also be "derived from specified unlawful activity."

a. Specified Unlawful Activity

Specified unlawful activity (SUA) includes numerous state and federal felonies.[12] It includes all RICO predicates (except the BSA reporting requirements), all federal drug felonies, all foreign drug felonies and a long list of miscellaneous bribery, white collar, fraud, environmental, export control and espionage crimes. Details about the SUA need not be alleged in the indictment.[13]

b. Derived From

The mere existence of specified unlawful activity and a later monetary transaction are not sufficient for a § 1957 conviction; there must also be proof that the funds involved in the transaction were *derived from* the specified unlawful activity.[14] For example, in United States v. Cavin,[15] the defendant formed an insurance company which lacked

---

9. Section 1957(a).

10. Courts were reluctant to find this structuring conduct criminal when a similar question arose under the reporting law before adoption of the anti-structuring statute. See Sarah N. Welling, *Smurfs, Money Laundering and the Federal Criminal Law: The Crime of Structuring Transactions*, 41 FLA.L.REV. 287 at 298 (1989); *see generally* Sarah N. Welling, *Money Laundering: The Anti–Structuring Laws,* 44 ALA.L.REV. 792, 798 (1993).

11. The other law is 31 U.S.C. § 5314, Foreign Bank Account Reports, discussed *supra* in § 18.6.

12. Section 1957(f)(3) refers to specified unlawful activity as it is defined in § 1956(c)(7), discussed in § 18.14(B)(iii)(a) *supra.*

Eighth Circuit: United States v. Hare, 49 F.3d 447 (8th Cir.1995)(Wire fraud under 18 U.S.C. § 1343 is specified unlawful activity).

13. United States v. Smith, 44 F.3d 1259, 1265 (4th Cir.1995).

14. *See*

Fourth Circuit: United States v. Moore, 27 F.3d 969 (4th Cir.1994).

Fifth Circuit: United States v. Cavin, 39 F.3d 1299 (5th Cir.1994).

15. United States v. Cavin, 39 F.3d 1299, 1307 (5th Cir.1994)(reversing § 1957 convictions because of insufficient evidence that the proceeds were derived from criminal activity).

enough capital to comply with state law.[16] He devised a complex scheme which artificially inflated the insurance company's assets, so the insurance company avoided state regulatory action and continued to write new policies.[17] The proceeds generated by the insurance company were later involved in a monetary transaction, but the court found there was no proof of this element and reversed the conviction, stating "The government presented no evidence that the . . . payments were proceeds of criminal activity, an essential element of the offense."[18] Although there was specified unlawful activity (false representations to a bank, mail fraud, wire fraud, and bank fraud), there was no proof that the funds used for the payments were *derived from* specified unlawful activity.[19]

This conclusion that there must be proof that the funds were derived from SUA is not surprising considering that the statute specifically includes the words "derived from." But *Cavin* also introduces the more complex question of whether the government has to trace criminally derived funds through commingled accounts to prove that funds in the transaction were derived from specified unlawful activity. The circuits disagree on what the government must prove.

The Tenth Circuit has concluded that the government does not have to prove that all the funds involved were criminally derived. In United States v. Johnson,[20] the defendant deposited $5.5 million into his account. Of this amount, $5.4 million was proved to be criminally derived in some way, but 1.2% of the money in the account had an unknown origin. Later the defendant withdrew $1.8 million. This withdrawal was the monetary transaction upon which the § 1957 conviction was based. The defendant argued it had to be reversed because the government had not proved that all of the $1.8 million was tainted. The court rejected this argument and found the proof sufficient. The court stated that while the government did have to show that the funds were derived from specified unlawful activity, this did not mean that it had to show that the funds "could not possibly have come from any source other than the unlawful activity."[21] Although there may have been some untainted funds commingled with the criminally derived funds, this did not invalidate the conviction.

The Third Circuit agrees with this conclusion.[22]

The Fourth Circuit also agrees and goes a step further. In United States v. Moore,[23] the court cited *Johnson* and reiterated that "the government is not required to prove that no 'untainted' funds were involved, or that the funds used in the transaction were exclusively derived from the specified unlawful activity."[24] The court explained:

16.   *Id.* at 1302–04.
17.   *Id.*
18.   *Id.* at 1307 (citation omitted).
19.   *Id.*
20.   971 F.2d 562 (10th Cir.1992).
21.   *Id.* at 570.

22.   United States v. Sokolow, 81 F.3d 397, 409–10 (3d Cir.1996), *vacated on den. of reh'g*, 91 F.3d 396 (3d Cir.1996).
23.   27 F.3d 969, 976 (4th Cir.1994).
24.   *Id.*

Money is fungible, and when funds obtained from unlawful activity have been combined with funds from lawful activity into a single asset, the illicitly-acquired funds and the legitimately-acquired funds ... cannot be distinguished from each other ...; that is, they cannot be traced to any particular source, absent resort to accepted, but arbitrary, accounting techniques....[25]

The Fourth Circuit declined to resort to arbitrary accounting fictions.[26] Instead, relying on § 1956 case law, the court held that, "It may be presumed, as the language of section 1957 permits, that the transacted funds, at least up to the full amount originally derived from crime, were the proceeds of the criminal activity or derived from that activity."[27] This presumption makes conviction more likely because the government is not required to trace the funds to the specified unlawful activity.

The Ninth Circuit disagrees and holds that the government does have to trace the criminally derived money through commingled accounts. In United States v. Rutgard,[28] the court stated that § 1956 case law was not persuasive in construing § 1957, declined to adopt the presumption that commingled funds were dirty up to the amount of dirty funds deposited, and held that the government had to prove the proceeds were criminally derived to get a conviction.[29] The defendant's conviction was reversed.

From a different angle, the Eleventh Circuit agreed with the majority of circuits that the government need not prove that all property in the transaction was proceeds of specified unlawful activity, but recommended that district courts "make it clear that although not all of the property at issue must be criminally derived, at least $10,000 worth of it must be derived from the criminal activity."[30]

c. Completion of Underlying Offense

Criminally derived property is defined as "any property constituting, or derived from, proceeds obtained from a criminal offense."[31] Section 1957 was "intended to separately punish a defendant for monetary transactions that follow in time the underlying specified unlawful activi-

25. *Id.*

26. These accounting techniques had been previously endorsed by the Second Circuit in civil forfeiture cases such as *United States v. Banco Cafetero Panama*, 797 F.2d 1154 (2d Cir.1986), involving the forfeiture of drug proceeds pursuant to 21 U.S.C. § 881. The Second Circuit suggested that drug proceeds mixed with legitimate proceeds could be traced using methods such as "first-in, first-out," "first-in, last-out," and "pro rata averaging." *Banco Cafetero Panama* is discussed *infra* in § 28.2(A) in connection with civil forfeiture.

The Fourth Circuit in *Moore* rejected the accounting techniques suggested in

Banco Cafetero Panama, referring to § 1956 cases which held that § 1956 does not require the government to prove the exact origin of the funds located in a commingled account.

27. 27 F.3d at 976, *citing* United States v. Johnson, 971 F.2d at 570.

28. United States v. Rutgard, 116 F.3d 1270 (9th Cir.1997).

29. *Id.* at *57–67.

30. United States v. Adams, 74 F.3d 1093, 1101 (11th Cir.1996).

31. 18 U.S.C. § 1957(f)(2).

ty that generated the criminally derived property in the first place."[32] Therefore, the cases addressing the issue of whether property is "criminally derived" have held that the underlying criminal activity must have been completed and the defendant must have obtained, controlled, or actually received the tainted money in order for this element of § 1957 to be proved.[33]

In United States v. Piervinanzi,[34] the defendant along with an employee of financial institution Morgan Guaranty Trust ("Morgan") conspired to steal funds from Morgan. The conspirators intended to transfer $24 million in stolen funds from Morgan to an overseas bank account in London.[35] However, a clerk at Morgan became suspicious of the transaction and the wire transfer was stopped and reversed before the funds reached the overseas account.[36] The *Piervinanzi* court adopted the reasoning of United States v. Johnson[37] and reversed the § 1957 conviction because the "funds never came into the possession or under the control of the conspirators."[38]

The *Johnson* court's reasoning that the defendant must control or be in possession of the proceeds before he or she can transfer those proceeds in violation of § 1957 is supported by a number of cases.[39] However, the defendant need not have actual possession of the dirty

---

32. United States v. Lovett, 964 F.2d 1029, 1042 (10th Cir.1992).

33. *See*

Second Circuit: United States v. Piervinanzi, 23 F.3d 670 (2d Cir.1994).

Fourth Circuit: United States v. Smith, 818 F.Supp. 132 (D.Md.1993), *aff'd*, 44 F.3d 1259 (4th Cir.1995).

Fifth Circuit: United States v. Leahy, 82 F.3d 624 (5th Cir.1996).

Sixth Circuit: United States v. Griffith, 17 F.3d 865 (6th Cir.1994); United States v. Wilson, 1993 WL 406798 (6th Cir.1993)(unpublished disposition).

Ninth Circuit: United States v. Savage, 67 F.3d 1435 (9th Cir.1995) (conviction affirmed; criminally derived funds were in defendant's control although not in his name).

Tenth Circuit: United States v. Massey, 48 F.3d 1560 (10th Cir.); United States v. Johnson, 971 F.2d 562 (10th Cir.1992).

34. 23 F.3d 670 (2d Cir.1994).

35. *Id.* at 675.

36. *Id.*

37. United States v. Johnson, 971 F.2d 562, 567–570 (10th Cir.1992)(use of the terms "proceeds" and "obtained" in the definition of "criminally derived property" indicates an intent to penalize only those monetary transactions that involve money which has been derived from a completed criminal activity and actually received by the defendant).

38. United States v. Piervinanzi, 23 F.3d 670 at 677.

39. *See*

Fourth Circuit: United States v. Smith, 818 F.Supp. 132 (D.Md.1993), *aff'd*, 44 F.3d 1259 (4th Cir.1995)(distinguishing *Johnson* because the defendant engaged in a monetary transaction after obtaining the proceeds from a completed wire transfer which was in itself a completed offense of wire fraud).

Sixth Circuit: United States v. Griffith, 17 F.3d 865, 878–879 (6th Cir.1994)(stating that *Johnson* holding should not be applied beyond its limited context and upholding defendant's § 1957 conviction because he was in control of the criminally derived property before he engaged in the illegal monetary transaction); United States v. Wilson, 1993 WL 406798 at *1 (6th Cir.1993)(unpublished disposition)(transaction did not involve "criminally derived property" because the defendants had not obtained possession of the illegal funds nor were the funds at the defendant's disposal when the transfer was made).

Tenth Circuit: United States v. Lovett, 964 F.2d 1029, 1042 (10th Cir.1992)(Congress intended to criminalize only those transactions occurring after proceeds have been obtained from the underlying crime).

money before transferring the proceeds. In United States v. Smith,[40] the Fourth Circuit held one defendant to be in "constructive control" of a scheme to defraud because he directed two other individuals to carry out the scheme; thus, the court reasoned that the defendant, by virtue of his control over others, was in "constructive possession" of the fraudulently obtained funds.[41]

The chronology must be as follows to violate § 1957:

1. *Completed offense:* An underlying crime generates tainted money.

2. *Possession:* The tainted money is then obtained by the defendant.

3. *§ 1957 Monetary Transaction:* The defendant then engages in a transaction with a financial institution. This could be as simple as depositing the tainted money into a bank account.

The problem illustrated by cases such as *Piervinanzi* occurs when the chronological events are not separate, distinguishable steps but rather happen at the same time. For example, in *Johnson*, the underlying criminal activity was wire fraud which began when the defendant defrauded investors of their money.[42] However, the wire fraud was not a completed offense until the investors wired their money into the defendant's bank account. At that time, the underlying crime was complete; the defendant had "obtained" possession of the criminally derived money; and a deposit to a financial institution had been made. Yet because the events occurred simultaneously, there was no § 1957 violation because "[t]he defendant . . . cannot be said to have obtained the proceeds of the wire fraud until the funds were credited to his account."[43] Section 1957 was intended to apply to the transactions occurring after the completion of the underlying offense rather than as an alternative means of punishing the underlying offense.[44]

The next two elements of § 1957 are relevant to jurisdiction.

v. Jurisdiction: The Defendant

The crime must either take place within the territorial jurisdiction of the United States or the defendant must be a United States person. A "United States person" includes U.S. nationals, permanent resident aliens, persons in the U.S. and corporations organized under U.S. law.[45]

vi. Jurisdiction: Affecting Commerce

The monetary transaction must affect interstate or foreign commerce.[46] The government need show only a "minimal effect" on com-

---

40. 44 F.3d 1259 (4th Cir.1995).

41. *Id.* at 1266.

42. United States v. Johnson, 971 F.2d 562, 569–570 (10th Cir.1992).

43. *Id.* at 570.

44. *Id.* at 569.

45. 18 U.S.C. § 1957(d)(1) & (2). The statute refers to the definition of U.S. person in 18 U.S.C. § 3077 (excluding subsection (2)(D)).

46. This element is found in the definition of monetary transaction, 18 U.S.C. § 1957(f)(1).

merce.[47] For example, the Tenth Circuit found an effect on commerce despite the defendant's contention that the transfer of funds between two Oklahoma bank accounts was wholly intrastate in nature.[48] Similarly, that circuit also found a sufficient effect on commerce established by (1) the defendant's deposit of checks into federally insured banks and (2) the defendant's use of the money to buy from out of state companies.[49]

One anomaly turns up in the case law. In United States v. Kelley,[50] the Tenth Circuit stated that "the requirement of section 1957 that the transaction be 'in or affecting interstate commerce' must be met in order to confer jurisdiction on federal courts. Such, however, is not an essential element of the crime charged."[51] This *Kelley* language is wrong and should be ignored. The Fourth Circuit recognized as much in United States v. Aramony,[52] the fraud prosecution of the chief executive officer of the United Way of America. The court vacated the § 1957 conviction for lack of any effect on commerce. The court held that although only a *de minimis* effect is required, an effect on commerce is an essential element of a § 1957 prosecution.[53] Other circuits agree.[54]

The Ninth Circuit, after concluding that an effect on commerce is an essential element, suggested that the jury must be instructed that the monetary transaction must be in or affecting commerce. Thus an instruction stating that the deposit of a check was a monetary transaction was inadequate but did not amount to plain error.[55]

vii. *Mens Rea*

The *mens rea* for § 1957 is *knowingly*.

a. *Elements to which the Mens Rea Applies*

It is clear that the knowingly *mens rea* modifies the main conduct element, "engages or attempts to engage" in a transaction.[56]

It is also clear that the defendant must know that the property involved in the transaction was criminally derived.[57]

47. *Tenth Circuit:* United States v. Lovett, 964 F.2d 1029, 1038 (10th Cir. 1992).

See also

Fourth Circuit: United States v. Aramony, 88 F.3d 1369 (4th Cir.1996) ("de minimis" effect required).

48. *Id.*

49. United States v. Kunzman, 54 F.3d 1522, 1527 (10th Cir.1995).

50. United States v. Kelley, 929 F.2d 582, 586 (10th Cir.1991).

51. *Id.* (citation omitted). *See also* United States v. Lowder, 5 F.3d 467, 472 (10th Cir.1993)(accord).

52. 88 F.3d 1369 (4th Cir.1996).

53. *Id.* at *54.

54. United States v. Ripinsky, 129 F.3d 518 (9th Cir.1997).

55. *Id.*

56. United States v. Lovett, 964 F.2d 1029 (10th Cir.1992).

57. *Fourth Circuit*: United States v. Campbell, 977 F.2d 854, 859–60 (4th Cir. 1992).

Fifth Circuit: United States v. Walker, 77 F.3d 1500, 1513 (5th Cir.1996)(conviction reversed).

Eleventh Circuit: United States v. Baker, 19 F.3d 605, 614 (11th Cir.1994).

The legislative history of § 1957 reflects Congress' intent that the defendant "know" that the monetary transaction involved criminally derived property. *See* D. Randall Johnson, *The Criminally Derived*

However, the defendant need not know that the property was derived from specified unlawful activity. The statute states: "[T]he Government is not required to prove the defendant knew that the offense from which the criminally derived property was derived was specified unlawful activity."[58] In other words, the prosecution must simply prove that the defendant knew the property was derived from crime in general; the prosecution does not have to prove that the defendant knew it was derived from particular crimes.

The next question is whether the government meets this burden of proof if the defendant believed the funds in the monetary transaction were derived from a misdemeanor. Although the language and legislative history of § 1956 indicate that the defendant must know that the funds are derived from some kind of *felony* in general, the language and legislative history of § 1957 are not as informative.[59] This question is open.

It is unclear whether the knowingly *mens rea* applies to more of the elements of § 1957. In United States v. Krenning,[60] the court concluded that the government must prove the defendant knew he engaged in a transaction involving criminally derived property in excess of $10,000.[61] The *Krenning* court based its conclusion on the finding that "the plain meaning of the statute does not restrict the application of the term 'knowingly' to 'monetary transaction' but rather applies it to all the elements except those specifically excluded by the statute."[62]

The government must prove that the value of the property exceeds $10,000,[63] but it is uncertain whether the government must prove the defendant knew this. One commentator has suggested that the government should not be required to prove knowledge of the value of the property.[64]

The knowledge element of § 1957 does not extend to tangential aspects of the offense. For example, the Fourth Circuit has rejected the defendant's argument that the government must prove the defendant knew that the recipient of the criminally derived property was a sham trust.[65] The court stated, "This argument ... fails to appreciate the essence of the money laundering offense. Section 1957 requires a showing that [the defendant] knowingly engage in a monetary transaction

Property Statute: Constitutional and Interpretive Issues Raised by 18 U.S.C. § 1957, 34 WM. & MARY L.REV. 1292, 1310 n.72 (1993) and accompanying text.

58. 18 U.S.C. § 1957(c).

59. *See* D. Randall Johnson, *The Criminally Derived Property Statute: Constitutional and Interpretive Issues Raised by 18 U.S.C. § 1957*, 34 WM. & MARY L.REV. 1292, 1311–12 (1993).

60. 1992 WL 178675 (E.D.La.) at *4.

61. It is unclear in *Krenning* whether the court believes that the defendant must know that the property exceeds $10,000 in value. Nevertheless, the case law and commentary on the topic suggest that the defendant does not have to know that the property is worth more than $10,000. *See infra* this section.

62. 1992 WL 178675 (E.D.La.) at *4.

63. 18 U.S.C. § 1957(a).

64. *See* D. Randall Johnson, *The Criminally Derived Property Statute: Constitutional and Interpretive Issues Raised by 18 U.S.C. § 1957*, 34 WM. & MARY L.REV. 1292, 1327 (1993).

65. United States v. Smith, 44 F.3d 1259 (4th Cir.1995).

involving criminally derived property with a value greater than $10,000, irrespective of the recipient in such a transaction."[66] In affirming the § 1957 conviction, the Fourth Circuit court concluded that a reasonable jury could have found beyond a reasonable doubt that the defendant knew the property was derived from crime; the court did not require proof that the defendant knew the trust to be a sham.[67]

Knowledge of illegality is not required for § 1957.[68]

b. Definition of Knowingly

As noted above, defendants must knowingly engage in a transaction or attempted transaction, and they must know that the property involved in the transaction was derived from crime. The Ninth Circuit has suggested that jury instructions defining "knowingly" as requiring only general intent may be erroneous if the jury relied on this more general definition rather than the more specific one given later.[69] However, the defendant had not objected at trial, so the Ninth Circuit was reviewing only for plain error, and concluded that that standard had not been met.[70] If the defendant had objected, however, the Ninth Circuit implies that it might have found error.

c. Establishing Knowledge Through Willful Blindness

As discussed above, the government must prove the defendant knowingly engaged or attempted to engage in a transaction, and that the defendant knew the property was criminally derived at the time of the monetary transaction. Traditionally, this means that the government must prove that the defendant had actual or positive subjective knowledge that the property involved in the monetary transaction was derived from crime. However, the legislative history of the 1986 Act shows that Congress was aware of the concept of willful blindness and endorsed it as an alternative to proving actual knowledge.[71]

The Fourth Circuit has allowed the use of willful blindness in a prosecution of §§ 1956 and 1957.[72] The issue was whether the defendant, a real estate agent, knew that the money used to purchase a home was derived from crime.[73] The defendant had arranged for a drug dealer to purchase a home.[74] The Fourth Circuit held that several factors, including evidence of the buyer's extravagant lifestyle, testimony that the defendant had once said that the money "might have been drug money," and the fraudulent nature of the real estate deal, presented a jury

---

66. Id. at 1270 (citation omitted).

67. Id.

68. United States v. Sokolow, 81 F.3d 397, 408–09 (3d Cir.1996), vacated on den. of reh'g, 91 F.3d 396 (3d Cir.1996).

See also

First Circuit: United States v. Gabriele, 63 F.3d 61, 65 (1st Cir.1995)(no willfulness requirement for § 1957).

69. United States v. Ripinsky, 129 F.3d 518 (9th Cir.1997).

70. Id.

71. S.Rep.No. 433, 99th Cong., Second Session., 11–12 (1986).

72. United States v. Campbell, 977 F.2d 854 (4th Cir.1992).

73. Id. at 859–60.

74. Id. at 855–56.

question regarding whether the defendant had actual knowledge of the criminal nature of the money involved.[75]

The Fourth Circuit noted that "the statute requires actual subjective knowledge. Campbell cannot be convicted on what she objectively should have known. However, this requirement is softened somewhat by the doctrine of willful blindness."[76] The court stated that negligence was not sufficient, but rather the government must prove beyond a reasonable doubt that the defendant "deliberately closed her eyes to what would otherwise have been obvious to her" or "purposely and deliberately contrived to avoid learning all of the facts."[77]

The First Circuit has also approved a willful blindness instruction.[78]

C. INCHOATE LIABILITY

i. Solicitation

There is no language in this crime on solicitation. Because no general solicitation statute exists in federal law, there is no liability for soliciting § 1957 crimes.

ii. Conspiracy

There is no reference to conspiracy in this statute, but the government may charge a conspiracy to violate § 1957 based on the general conspiracy statute.[79]

iii. Attempt

Section 1957 covers attempt liability as it extends to those who *attempt to* engage in monetary transactions.[80]

D. ACCOMPLICE LIABILITY

There is no reference to accomplice liability in § 1957, but accomplice liability is available under the general accomplice liability statute, § 2.[81]

---

75. *Id.* at 859–60. Thus the trial court's grant of a judgment of acquittal was reversed, but the Fourth Circuit let stand the trial court's conditional grant of a new trial.

76. *Id.* at 857.

77. *Id.*

78. United States v. Gabriele, 63 F.3d 61 (1st Cir.1995)(defendant consciously avoided import of conspicuous "red flags"— government surveillance, large stores of cash, use of coded language—so willful blindness instruction appropriate).

79. 18 U.S.C. § 371. *See, e.g.,* United States v. Montoya, 45 F.3d 1286 (9th Cir. 1995).

80. 18 U.S.C. § 1957(a).

81. 18 U.S.C. § 2, discussed *supra* in §§ 4.1–4.7.

See, e.g.,

Fourth Circuit: United States v. Smith, 44 F.3d 1259, 1264 n. 2 (4th Cir.1995).

Ninth Circuit: United States v. Montoya, 45 F.3d 1286 (9th Cir.1995); United States v. Saccoccia, 18 F.3d 795 (9th Cir. 1994).

Tenth Circuit: United States v. Smith, 1993 WL 144567 (D.Kan.1993).

E. CONSTITUTIONAL CHALLENGES

Constitutional challenges to § 1957 have all been unsuccessful.[82]

i. Due Process

In United States v. Krenning,[83] the defendant argued that the ambiguous language of § 1957 was void for vagueness because innocent commercial transactions could fall within its proscriptions.[84] As the *Krenning* court recited, the void for vagueness rule requires that, "A penal statute define the criminal offense with sufficient definiteness that ordinary people can understand what conduct is prohibited and in a manner that does not encourage arbitrary and discriminatory enforcement."[85] The court rejected the defendant's argument and concluded: "To the contrary, this statute sets forth with sufficient definiteness to an ordinary person what constitutes the prohibitive conduct; namely, the knowing engagement in a monetary transaction in 'criminally derived property' in excess of $10,000."[86]

Similarly, in United States v. Baker,[87] the defendant contended that § 1957 was unconstitutionally vague and overbroad. The court held that the defendant could not complain that the law was vague because the criminal conduct was "clearly proscribed" by § 1957.[88] Specifically, the defendant asserted that the prohibition on "engaging in monetary transactions in criminally derived property" was ambiguous, but the court held that the statute was not vague because it clearly requires the government to prove that the defendant knew the property was obtained from a criminal offense.[89]

The First Circuit has also concluded that § 1957 is not void for vagueness on its face or as applied.[90]

ii. Double Jeopardy

United States v. Lovett is the typical case for a double jeopardy

---

82. *See*

Fourth Circuit: United States v. Moore, 27 F.3d 969 (4th Cir.1994)(ex post facto clause).

Fifth Circuit: United States v. McCord, 33 F.3d 1434 (5th Cir.1994)(ex post facto); United States v. Krenning, 1992 WL 178675 (E.D.La.)(void for vagueness).

Sixth Circuit: United States v. Griffith, 17 F.3d 865 (6th Cir.1994)(double jeopardy); United States v. Kirkland, 34 F.3d 1068, 1994 WL 454864 (6th Cir.1994) (unpublished disposition)(double jeopardy).

Ninth Circuit: United States v. Saccoccia, 18 F.3d 795 (9th Cir.1994)(double jeopardy).

Tenth Circuit: United States v. Hilliard, 818 F.Supp. 309 (D.Colo.1993)(double jeopardy); United States v. Johnson, 971 F.2d 562 (10th Cir.1992)(double jeopardy); United States v. Lovett, 964 F.2d 1029 (10th Cir.1992)(double jeopardy).

Eleventh Circuit: United States v. Baker, 19 F.3d 605 (11th Cir.1994)(vagueness).

83. 1992 WL 178675 (E.D.La.).

84. *Id.* at *4.

85. *Id.* at *4.

86. *Id.* at *4.

87. 19 F.3d 605, 626–27 (11th Cir. 1994).

88. *Id.* at 27–28.

89. *Id.*

90. United States v. Gabriele, 63 F.3d 61 (1st Cir.1995).

challenge to § 1957.[91] In *Lovett*, the defendant was convicted of interstate transportation of fraudulently obtained funds in violation of 18 U.S.C. § 2314 and engaging in an illegal monetary transaction in violation of § 1957.[92] The defendant contended that his § 2314 conviction was a lesser included offense of § 1957 and not a distinct crime under the *Blockburger* test,[93] so his two convictions amounted to multiple punishments for the same offense in violation of the Double Jeopardy Clause.[94]

Although the court agreed with the defendant that the elements of the underlying unlawful activity under § 2314 were essential elements of § 1957 and that the two offenses did not each require proof of a fact which the other did not, the court still rejected the double jeopardy challenge.[95] The court conceded that the two offenses failed the *Blockburger* test yet held that there was a clearly expressed intent on the part of Congress to separately punish an individual for the underlying criminal activity and for the subsequent monetary transaction: " 'Insofar as the question is one of legislative intent, the Blockburger presumption must of course yield to a plainly expressed contrary view on the part of Congress.' "[96] Therefore, the Tenth Circuit held the two offenses to be separate and distinct crimes rather than an alternative means of punishing one offense.[97]

Whether the underlying crime is bank fraud,[98] interstate transportation of fraudulently obtained funds,[99] stealing from a program receiving federal funds,[100] or conspiracy to violate § 1957,[101] the courts have universally rejected double jeopardy challenges to § 1957.

iii. Right to Counsel

Section 1957 could apply to lawyers depositing fees they knew their clients had generated by crime. So two years after enacting it, Congress amended the statute to exclude some lawyers' fees. The amendment states that the definition of monetary transaction "does not include any transaction necessary to preserve a person's right to representation as guaranteed by the sixth amendment to the Constitution...."[102]

This is a strange amendment. Apparently it responds to concerns about the constitutionality of prosecuting criminal defense lawyers. Yet the fact that § 1957 is limited by the Constitution is certain even without Congress announcing it. If the statute intrudes on the sixth amendment, courts would dismiss prosecutions anyway. Congress's pur-

91. 964 F.2d 1029 (10th Cir.1992).

92. *Id*. at 1031.

93. *Id*. at 1041.

94. *Id*.

95. *Id*. at 1041–42.

96. *Id*. at 1042 (citation omitted).

97. *Id*.

98. United States v. Hilliard, 818 F.Supp. 309 (D.Colo.1993).

99. United States v. Griffith, 17 F.3d 865 (6th Cir.1994).

100. United States v. Kirkland, 34 F.3d 1068, 1994 WL 454864 (6th Cir.1994)(unpublished disposition).

101. United States v. Saccoccia, 18 F.3d 795 (9th Cir.1994).

102. Pub.L. 100–690, § 6182 (1988), codified at 18 U.S.C. § 1957(f)(1).

pose in adopting this amendment must have been not to work a substantive change in the law but to signal its concern about the constitutional implications of prosecuting criminal defense lawyers.

The reach of this statutory exception for lawyers should not be overstated. Because it is keyed to the sixth amendment, which does not attach until indictment,[103] the exception does not apply until then. A criminal defense lawyer depositing tainted fees from an unindicted client is not protected by the exception.

Any constitutional objections to § 1957 based on the client's right to counsel have presumably been obviated by this exception Congress added to the statute. No cases on this question have been reported.

F. VENUE

The Supreme Court recently held that venue in § 1957 prosecutions is not proper where the underlying crime occurred, but only where the laundering transaction occurred.[104] The Court left open the possibility that § 1957 charges could be triable in more than one place, for example, where the underlying crime occurred, if the laundering involved a continuing offense, or some conspiracy or accomplice liability charges.[105]

G. DEPARTMENT OF JUSTICE GUIDELINES

The Department of Justice has adopted two prosecution standards limiting the use of § 1957 against lawyers.[106] As a threshold, these guidelines require that the property transferred to the lawyer be a bona fide fee, not a sham designed to hide the property, and that the fee be paid for representing the client in a criminal, not civil matter. If these conditions are met, Justice will only prosecute lawyers who have actual knowledge that the fee was generated by crime, even if the lack of actual knowledge is due to the lawyer's willful blindness.[107] The lawyer's actual knowledge cannot come from confidential lawyer-client communications or the lawyer's own efforts in the course of representing the client. Practically, the lawyer's knowledge will need to have existed before the representation began. Furthermore, the Justice Department says it will not inform a lawyer that the fee may be criminally derived solely for the purpose of giving that lawyer the forbidden actual knowledge.[108]

These standards limit the factors Justices will rely on in deciding to prosecute lawyers, but their impact is uncertain. The standards are not

103. United States v. Gouveia, 467 U.S. 180, 191, 104 S.Ct. 2292, 2299, 81 L.Ed.2d 146 (1984).

104. United States v. Cabrales, ___ U.S. ___, 118 S.Ct. 1772, 141 L.Ed.2d 1 (1998).

105. *Id.* at 1776.

106. United States Attorneys Manual § 9–105.600 ("Prosecution Standards—Bona Fide Fees Paid to Attorneys for Representation in a Criminal Matter") and § 9–105.700 ("Prohibition on Giving Notice of the Criminal Derivation of Property").

107. U.S.A.M. § 9–105.600.

108. U.S.A.M. § 9–105.700.

binding on the Department.[109]

§ 18.16 Substantive Money Laundering Crimes: §§ 1956, 1957—Sections 1956 and 1957 Compared

Although both sections apply to funds or property generated by criminal activity, § 1957 has a threshold requirement that the value of the dirty property or funds exceed $10,000.[1] Also, § 1957 is broader than § 1956 in that it criminalizes conduct which does not necessarily involve furthering the unlawful activity or even disguising or concealing the proceeds of the unlawful activity.[2] The Ninth Circuit has identified five differences between §§ 1956 and 1957 and concluded that because the crimes are so different, § 1956 precedents are not relevant to § 1957.[3]

§ 18.17 Illegal Money Transmitting Businesses: § 1960

This crime, titled "Prohibition of illegal money transmitting businesses," was adopted in 1992 as part of the effort to control money laundering accomplished through money transmitting businesses.[1] It establishes liability for anyone who "conducts, controls, manages, supervises, directs or owns all or part of a business knowing the business is an illegal money transmitting business...."[2] "Illegal money transmitting businesses" are money transmitting businesses which affect interstate commerce and fail to register as required by state or federal law.[3] Federal law requiring registration is found in a statute in the BSA.[4] Regulations implementing this registration requirement were proposed in May, 1997, but are not yet final.[5] This crime has not been developed in the courts.[6]

109. *See e.g.*, United States v. Piervinanzi, 23 F.3d 670, 682 (2d Cir.1994).

§ 18.16

1. *See* D. Randall Johnson, *The Criminally Derived Property Statute: Constitutional and Interpretive Issues Raised by 18 U.S.C. § 1957*, 34 WM. & MARY L.REV. 1292, 1298–1301 (1993) (discussing the differences between §§ 1956 and 1957).

2. Id.

D.C.Circuit: United States v. Wynn, 61 F.3d 921, 926 (D.C.Cir.1995), *citing* Emily J. Lawrence, *Let the Seller Beware: Money Laundering, Merchants and 18 U.S.C. §§ 1956 and 1957*, 33 B.C.L.REV. 841 (1992).

See also D. Randall Johnson, *The Criminally Derived Property Statute: Constitutional and Interpretive Issues Raised by 18 U.S.C. § 1957*, 34 WM. & MARY L.REV. 1292, 1298–1301 (1993) (discussing the differences between §§ 1956 and 1957).

3. United States v. Rutgard, 116 F.3d 1270, 1291 (9th Cir.1997).

§ 18.17

1. P.L. 102–550, § 2, 106 Stat. 3681 (1992), *codified at* 18 U.S.C. § 1960.

2. 18 U.S.C. § 1960(a).

3. Id. § 1960(b).

4. 18 U.S.C. § 5330, "Registration of money transmitting businesses."

5. 62 Fed.Reg. No. 98, pp. 27890–27917 (May 21, 1997).

6. Some cases refer to § 1960 prosecutions but do not discuss them. *See* United States v. Khan, 129 F.3d 114 (2d Cir.), *cert. denied*, 118 S.Ct. 1085 (1997) (unpublished disposition) (defendant had pled guilty to § 1960); United States v. Cheng, 1995 WL 168905 (S.D.N.Y.)(defendant charged with conspiring under § 371 to violate § 1960; pretrial motions denied).

§ 18.18   Bibliography

BRICKEY, KATHLEEN F., CORPORATE CRIMINAL LIABILITY (2d ed. 1992)(three volume set includes coverage of money laundering crimes, *see* §§ 11:38 to 11:65).

VILLA, JOHN K., BANKING CRIMES (two volume set includes coverage of money laundering crimes, *see* Chapter 8).

Gaetke, Eugene R. and Sarah N. Welling, *Money Laundering and Lawyers,* 43 SYRACUSE L. REV. 1165 (1992).

Gonzalez, Rep. Henry B., *New and Continuing Challenges in the Fight Against Money Laundering,* 20 Fordham Int'l L.J. 1543 (1997).

Gurule, Jimmy, *The Money Laundering Control Act of 1986: Creating a New Federal Offense or Merely Affording Federal Prosecutors An Alternative Means of Punishing Specified Unlawful Activity?,* 32 AM. CRIM. L. REV. 823 (1995).

Strafer, G. Richard, *Money Laundering, The Crime of the Nineties,* 27 AM. CRIM. L. REV. 149 (1989).

Symposium: The Anti–Money Laundering Statutes: Where from Here? 44 ALA. L. REV. 657–861 (1993).

Welling, Sarah N., *Smurfs, Money Laundering, and the Federal Criminal Law: The Crime of Structuring Transactions,* 41 FLA. L. REV. 287 (1989).

Eighth Annual Survey of White Collar Crime: Money Laundering, 30 AM. CRIM. L. REV. 813 (1993).

Ninth Annual Survey of White Collar Crime: Money Laundering, 31 AM. CRIM. L. REV. 721 (1994).

Tenth Annual Survey of White Collar Crime: Money Laundering, 32 AM. CRIM. L. REV. 499 (1995).

Eleventh Annual Survey of White Collar Crime: Money Laundering, 33 AM. CRIM. L. REV. 881 (1996).

*

CHAPTER 19

OBSTRUCTION OF JUSTICE: THE VICTIM AND WITNESS PROTECTION ACT

Table of Sections

WESTLAW ELECTRONIC RESEARCH

See WESTLAW Electronic Research Guide preceding the Summary of Contents.

---

§ 19.1 Introduction

The Victim and Witness Protection Act (VWPA) was enacted in 1982 in response to concerns about widespread victim and witness intimi-

159

dation.[1] The Act's purpose is to expand the protection available to participants in the federal legal system.[2] The VWPA includes six crimes. They are:

— § 1503 Influencing or injuring officer or juror generally;
— § 1505 Obstruction of proceedings before departments, agencies and committees;
— § 1510 Obstruction of criminal investigations;
— § 1512 Tampering with a witness, victim or informant;
— § 1513 Retaliating against a witness, victim or informant;
— § 1518 Obstruction of criminal investigations of health care offenses.

The first three of these crimes, §§ 1503, 1505 and 1510, existed before the VWPA was enacted. These crimes were reformulated and adopted into the VWPA in 1982. The VWPA introduced two new crimes, §§ 1512 and 1513. In 1996, the health care obstruction crime was added.[3] The most familiar VWPA crime is § 1503, the original obstruction of justice statute. This crime contains the frequently prosecuted "Omnibus Clause," which is examined in detail in the next section.

Three of the VWPA crimes focus on *judicial* proceedings and participants: § 1503 protects participants in a judicial proceeding, § 1512 protects witnesses, victims and informants who will be communicating during a judicial proceeding from tampering, and § 1513 protects witnesses, victims and informants who did communicate during a judicial proceeding from retaliation. In contrast, § 1505 prohibits conduct which interferes with *administrative and legislative* proceedings, and §§ 1510 and 1518 prohibit conduct which interferes with *criminal investigations*.

Library References:

C.J.S. Obstructing Justice or Governmental Administration § 2–37.
West's Key No. Digests, Obstructing Justice ⬦1–21.

§ 19.2 Influencing or Injuring Officer or Juror: § 1503—In General

The basic obstruction of justice statute provides:

Whoever corruptly, or by threat or force, or by any threatening letter or communication, endeavors to influence, intimidate, or impede any grand or petit juror, or officer in or of any court of the United States, or officer who may be serving at any examination or other proceeding before any United States magistrate judge or other committing magistrate, in the discharge of his duty, or injures any such grand or petit juror in his person or property on account of any verdict or indictment assented to by him, or on account of his being or having been such juror, or injures any such officer, magistrate

§ 19.1

1. *See* S.Rep.No. 97–532, at 6 (1982), *reprinted in*, 1982 U.S.C.C.A.N. 2515.

2. *Id.* at Purpose.

3. P.L. 104–191, 110 Stat. 2017 (Aug. 21, 1996).

judge, or other committing magistrate in his person or property on account of the performance of his official duties, or corruptly or by threats or force, or by any threatening letter or communication, influences, obstructs, or impedes, or endeavors to influence, obstruct, or impede, the due administration of justice, shall be punished as provided in subsection (b).....[1]

Section 1503 is the original obstruction of justice statute, so it has a long history. It can be traced to the Judiciary Act of 1831.[2] That act covered obstructive conduct inside the courtroom and outside the courtroom in different ways. For conduct inside the courtroom, in the presence of the court, the judge penalized persons with a summary contempt power. In contrast, obstructive conduct outside the courtroom was deemed to be less immediately obstructive and less urgent, and so was penalized via the regular process of indictment and trial.[3] This latter provision on obstructive conduct outside the courtroom evolved into § 1503.[4] Today some remnants of § 1503's historical limit to conduct occurring outside the courtroom can still be found.[5]

Section 1503 can be divided into two parts. The first part prohibits influencing or injuring any grand or petit juror, or officer in the discharge of his or her duties. This clause has generated few prosecutions.[6]

The second clause, known as the Omnibus Clause,[7] penalizes conduct which influences, obstructs, or impedes the due administration of

§ 19.2

1. 18 U.S.C. § 1503. The statute goes on to list the possible punishments, but the part quoted in the text defines the crime.

2. The Judiciary Act of 1831 was Congress's response to a District Judge "imprisoning a lawyer for publishing a letter critical of one of his judicial decisions." United States v. Reed, 773 F.2d 477, 485 (2d Cir. 1985).

3. The first subsection of the Act governed contempt which took place in the presence of the court, and the second subsection governed contempt occurring outside the presence of the court.

Second Circuit: United States v. Reed, 773 F.2d 477 (2d Cir.1985).

Fourth Circuit: United States v. Cofield, 11 F.3d 413, 417–418 (4th Cir.1993).

Congress determined that contempt taking place outside the presence of the court did not need urgent attention justifying the "use of summary contempt power," United States v. Reed, 773 F.2d 477, 486 (2d Cir.1985) and therefore must be prosecuted by indictment and trial.

4. United States v. Brand, 775 F.2d 1460 (11th Cir.1985).

5. *Sixth Circuit:* United States v. Essex, 407 F.2d 214 (6th Cir.1969)("section 1503 prohibits contemptuous conduct away from court.").

Contra:

Fifth Circuit: United States v. Williams, 874 F.2d 968 (5th Cir. 1989)(§ 1503 is not limited to simply "filling the void presumably left by the limitation on the contempt power;" § 1503 may be violated by conduct punishable as contempt under the first section of the 1831 Act).

6. Only two prosecutions have been reported, and they both focused on defining a "court of the United States."

Third Circuit: United States v. George, 625 F.2d 1081 (3d Cir.1980)(Virgin Island District Court is not a court of the United States because it is a territorial court and not a federal court).

Fourth Circuit: United States v. Regina, 504 F.Supp. 629 (D.C.Md.1980)(the Superior Court of the District of Columbia is not a "court of the United States" under § 1503 because it is not an article III court).

7. *See, e.g.,* United States v. Aguilar, 515 U.S. 593, 598, 115 S.Ct. 2357, 2361, 132 L.Ed.2d 520 (1995).

justice.[8] Because the first part is so rarely prosecuted, the remaining discussion of § 1503 focuses on the Omnibus Clause.

A defendant need not be a party in the obstructed proceeding to violate § 1503.[9] Section 1503 defendants have included transporters of illegal aliens,[10] drug dealers,[11] DEA informants,[12] members of organized crime,[13] business managers,[14] and a pipe-bomber.[15] Defendants can also be corporations.[16] Many defendants are involved in the legal system, as legislators,[17] judges[18] or attorneys.[19]

Library References:

C.J.S. Obstructing Justice or Governmental Administration § 2–37.
West's Key No. Digests, Obstructing Justice ⚮1–21.

8. *Supreme Court:* United States v. Aguilar, 515 U.S. 593, 598, 115 S.Ct. 2357, 2361, 132 L.Ed.2d 520 (1995)("[T]he 'Omnibus Clause' serves as a catchall, prohibiting persons from endeavoring to influence, obstruct, or impede the due administration of justice.").

Fifth Circuit: United States v. Vesich, 724 F.2d 451 (5th Cir.1984).

Sixth Circuit: United States v. Bashaw, 982 F.2d 168 (6th Cir.1992).

Eleventh Circuit: United States v. Brand, 775 F.2d 1460 (11th Cir.1985); United States v. London, 714 F.2d 1558 (11th Cir.1983).

9. United States v. Barfield, 999 F.2d 1520, 1524 (11th Cir.1993).

10. *See* United States v. Plascencia–Orozco, 768 F.2d 1074 (9th Cir.1985); United States v. Gonzalez–Mares, 752 F.2d 1485 (9th Cir.1985).

11. *Third Circuit:* United States v. Rankin, 870 F.2d 109 (3d Cir.1989).

Seventh Circuit: United States v. Edwards, 36 F.3d 639 (7th Cir.1994); United States v. Williams, 858 F.2d 1218 (7th Cir.1988).

Eighth Circuit: United States v. Feldhacker, 849 F.2d 293 (8th Cir.1988).

Tenth Circuit: United States v. Allen, 24 F.3d 1180 (10th Cir.1994).

12. United States v. Barfield, 999 F.2d 1520 (11th Cir.1993).

13. *See*

Second Circuit: United States v. Langella, 776 F.2d 1078 (2d Cir.1985).

Seventh Circuit: United States v. Guzzino, 810 F.2d 687 (7th Cir.1987).

14. *See*

Fourth Circuit: United States v. Gravely, 840 F.2d 1156 (4th Cir.1988) (defendant was manager at a Pepsi bottling plant).

Ninth Circuit: United States v. Gordon, 844 F.2d 1397 (9th Cir.1988) (defendant was president of a manufacturing corporation); United States v. Lench, 806 F.2d 1443 (9th Cir.1986) (defendant was vice president of a firm).

15. United States v. Moody, 977 F.2d 1420 (11th Cir.1992).

16. *See, e.g.,* United States v. Washington Water Power Company, 793 F.2d 1079 (9th Cir.1986).

17. *Second Circuit:* United States v. Biaggi, 853 F.2d 89 (2d Cir.1988)(defendant was a Congressman).

Seventh Circuit: United States v. McComb, 744 F.2d 555 (7th Cir.1984) (defendant was an Indiana state legislator).

18. United States v. Aguilar, 515 U.S. 593, 115 S.Ct. 2357, 132 L.Ed.2d 520 (1995)(defendant was a United States District Judge).

19. *First Circuit:* United States v. Cintolo, 818 F.2d 980 (1st Cir.1987).

Second Circuit: United States v. Buffalano, 727 F.2d 50 (2d Cir.1984).

Fifth Circuit: United States v. Vesich, 724 F.2d 451 (5th Cir.1984).

Sixth Circuit: United States v. Schaffner, 771 F.2d 149 (6th Cir.1985).

Seventh Circuit: United States v. Lahey, 55 F.3d 1289 (7th Cir.1995); United States v. Machi, 811 F.2d 991 (7th Cir.1987).

Eleventh Circuit: United States v. Thomas, 916 F.2d 647 (11th Cir.1990); United States v. Silverman, 745 F.2d 1386 (11th Cir.1984).

§ 19.3 Influencing or Injuring Officer or Juror: § 1503—Elements

The Omnibus Clause has five elements: the defendant (1) knew or had notice of (2) a pending (3) judicial proceeding that he or she (4) corruptly or by threats (5) endeavored to influence, obstruct, or impede.[1]

A. DUE ADMINISTRATION OF JUSTICE/PENDING JUDICIAL PROCEEDING

Courts have interpreted the statutory phrase *due administration of justice* to require a pending judicial proceeding.[2] As the Sixth Circuit explained, the administration of justice is implicated only during a pending judicial proceeding.[3] Courts generally discuss *pending judicial proceeding* as one element, but defendants often raise the issue in two parts, arguing that the action is either not *pending*[4] or is not a *proceeding*[5] within the meaning of § 1503.

i. Pending

The first question is defining when a judicial proceeding begins and so qualifies as *pending*. Courts generally draw a line between law enforcement investigations and grand jury investigations, concluding that grand jury investigations are pending judicial proceedings but law enforcement investigations are not.[6] As one court put it, the issue is defining when "an investigation by law enforcement officials cross[es]

---

§ 19.3

1. The circuits vary somewhat in the way the elements are listed. The Second, Fourth and Fifth Circuits basically describe these core elements: (1) pending judicial proceeding (2) defendant knew of or had notice of the judicial proceeding and (3) the defendant acted corruptly, meaning intentionally, to influence, obstruct or impede the judicial proceeding.

Second Circuit: United States v. Biaggi, 853 F.2d 89 (2d Cir.1988); United States v. Capo, 791 F.2d 1054 (2d Cir.1986).

Fourth Circuit: United States v. Grubb, 11 F.3d 426 (4th Cir.1993).

Fifth Circuit: United States v. Neal, 951 F.2d 630 (5th Cir.1992); United States v. Williams, 874 F.2d 968 (5th Cir.1989).

The Eleventh Circuit describes the elements as that the defendant (1) corruptly or by threats (2) endeavored (3) to influence, obstruct or impede the due administration of justice.

Eleventh Circuit: United States v. Barfield, 999 F.2d 1520 (11th Cir.1993); United States v. Thomas, 916 F.2d 647 (11th Cir. 1990) United States v. Brand, 775 F.2d

1460 (11th Cir.1985); United States v. Silverman, 745 F.2d 1386 (11th Cir.1984).

2. *Supreme Court:* Pettibone v. United States, 148 U.S. 197, 205–07, 13 S.Ct. 542, 545–57, 37 L.Ed. 419 (1893).

Eleventh Circuit: United States v. Silverman, 745 F.2d 1386 (11th Cir.1984).

3. United States v. Bashaw, 982 F.2d 168 (6th Cir.1992).

4. *See, e.g.,*

Seventh Circuit: United States v. McComb, 744 F.2d 555 (7th Cir.1984).

Ninth Circuit: United States v. Washington Water Power Co., 793 F.2d 1079 (9th Cir.1986).

5. *See, e.g.,*

Second Circuit: United States v. Capo, 791 F.2d 1054 (2d Cir.1986).

Ninth Circuit: United States v. Ryan, 455 F.2d 728 (9th Cir.1971).

6. United States v. Tham, 960 F.2d 1391 (9th Cir.1991). Although law enforcement investigations are not covered under § 1503, they are covered by § 1510, discussed *infra* in §§ 19.12–19.16.

the threshold and become[s] a pending grand jury investigation."[7]

In defining this threshold, courts have held that the grand jury must be sitting when the subpoena is issued; otherwise, "the United States Attorney cannot be said to be acting as an agent for that body."[8] The grand jury need not have started to hear testimony; a proceeding can qualify as pending even before the grand jury has heard testimony.[9] Similarly, a proceeding can be pending even though the grand jury did not play an active role in the decision to issue a subpoena or was not aware one had been issued; courts have rejected defense arguments that nothing is pending unless the grand jury plays an active role in the decision to issue a subpoena, or unless the grand jury is aware of the subpoena at the time of the obstruction of justice.[10] The Fifth and Seventh Circuits explain that courts should do a case-by-case inquiry into "whether the subpoena is issued in furtherance of an actual grand jury investigation, i.e. to secure a presently contemplated presentation of evidence before the grand jury."[11] If the subpoena is so issued, then a proceeding is pending and § 1503 applies. The Ninth Circuit has not addressed the general question of when an investigation becomes a pending proceeding, but it has held that when a complaint is filed with a magistrate or an indictment has been issued, a proceeding is then pending.[12]

The next issue is defining when a judicial proceeding is no longer pending because it has ended. Generally, there must be a continuing judicial proceeding that the defendant obstructs to find a violation of § 1503.[13] The Second Circuit explained that § 1503 is not directed toward preventing efforts to frustrate an already rendered judgment.[14] However, the Eleventh Circuit has sustained a conviction for obstructing justice without a pending proceeding. In United States v. London,[15] the defendant-attorney lied to his clients and told them that a judgment had been rendered against them. The defendant wanted the clients to give him the money to pay to the other party. The court held that even though the scheme occurred after the resolution of the underlying lawsuit, the defendant could still be convicted under § 1503.[16]

---

7. United States v. McComb, 744 F.2d 555, 560 (7th Cir.1984).

See

Fifth Circuit: United States v. Vesich, 724 F.2d 451 (5th Cir.1984).

8. United States v. Nelson, 852 F.2d 706 (3d Cir.1988).

9. United States v. Vesich, 724 F.2d 451 (5th Cir.1984).

10. United States v. Nelson, 852 F.2d 706 (3d Cir.1988).

11. *Fifth Circuit:* United States v. Vesich, 724 F.2d 451 (5th Cir.1984).

Seventh Circuit: United States v. McComb, 744 F.2d 555 (7th Cir.1984).

12. United States v. Washington Water Power Co., 793 F.2d 1079 (9th Cir. 1986).

13. *See* United States v. Ardito, 782 F.2d 358 (2d Cir.1986) and United States v. Reed, 773 F.2d 477 (2d Cir.1985).

14. In re Grand Jury Subpoena Duces Tecum Dated September 15, 1983, Marc Rich and Co. A.G. v. United States, 731 F.2d 1032 (2d Cir.1984) (defendant sold his business and the government suggested that it was to thwart a judgment).

15. 714 F.2d 1558 (11th Cir.1983).

16. The Seventh Circuit described another instance when a defendant can violate § 1503 without an ongoing proceeding. The court discussed what it called obstructing

ii. Proceeding

The judicial proceeding must be federal.[17] It can be civil.[18] Examples of § 1503 judicial proceedings are magistrate proceedings,[19] probation officer presentence interviews,[20] and grand jury proceedings.[21] As noted above, a grand jury investigation also qualifies as a judicial proceeding.[22] Other law enforcement investigations are not proceedings within § 1503 unless they are associated with a "judicial or quasi-judicial" function.[23] Therefore, an investigation by the FBI or IRS does not constitute a judicial proceeding covered by § 1503.[24] However, obstructing investigations by agencies that have rule-making authority, such as the IRS, is a crime under § 1505 (obstruction of administrative proceedings)[25] and obstructing criminal investigations is a crime under § 1510 (obstruction of criminal investigations)[26] and § 1518 (obstruction of criminal investigations of health care offenses).[27]

B. INFLUENCE, OBSTRUCT OR IMPEDE

Courts have found many actions sufficient to influence, obstruct or impede, including giving a criminal defendant pills to induce vomiting during trial,[28] falsely promising to get a defendant's sentence reduced,[29] and obtaining transcripts of a grand jury investigation.[30]

justice in a "time-bomb" fashion: "A black-mailer who before even committing the crime instructs an accomplice to kill his victim and any other witnesses should the victim report the blackmail attempt." The court suggested that the defendant could still be convicted of a § 1503 violation. United States v. Van Engel, 15 F.3d 623, 627 (7th Cir.1993).

17. United States v. Ardito, 782 F.2d 358 (2d Cir.1986).

18. United States v. Reed, 773 F.2d 477 (2d Cir.1985).

19. *See, e.g.*, United States v. Plascencia–Orozco, 768 F.2d 1074 (9th Cir.1985).

20. *See, e.g.,* United States v. Gonzalez–Mares, 752 F.2d 1485 (9th Cir.1985).

21. United States v. Capo, 791 F.2d 1054 (2d Cir.1986).

22. *Second Circuit:* United States v. Jespersen, 65 F.3d 993 (2d Cir.1995).

Fifth Circuit: United States v. Vesich, 724 F.2d 451 (5th Cir.1984).

Sixth Circuit: United States v. Mullins, 22 F.3d 1365 (6th Cir.1994).

Seventh Circuit: United States v. Maloney, 71 F.3d 645, 656 (7th Cir.1995).

Tenth Circuit: United States v. Wood, 6 F.3d 692 (10th Cir.1993).

23. *See* United States v. Gonzalez–Mares, 752 F.2d 1485 (9th Cir.1985).

24. *Ninth Circuit:* United States v. Tham, 960 F.2d 1391, 1400 (9th Cir.1991); United States v. Ryan, 455 F.2d 728 (9th Cir.1971).

See also

Second Circuit: United States v. Reed, 773 F.2d 477 (2d Cir.1985).

25. United States v. McComb, 744 F.2d 555 (7th Cir.1984). *See* discussion in §§ 19.7–19.11, *infra*.

26. *See* discussion in §§ 19.12–19.16 *infra*.

27. *See* discussion in § 19.27 *infra*.

28. United States v. Ardito, 782 F.2d 358 (2d Cir.1986) (obstructionists were friends of a defendant in a trial for loan-sharking, and they provided him with pills to induce vomiting).

29. United States v. Machi, 811 F.2d 991 (7th Cir.1987). The defendants promised that in return for $50,000, they would get a person's sentence reduced. However, they only intended to defraud the person because they never intended to get the sentenced reduced. The court held that this was obstruction because the defendant would be induced to drop his appeal and pay $50,000 for a reduced sentence. *Id.* at 999.

30. United States v. Rosner, 485 F.2d 1213 (2d Cir.1973).

Courts have also found that some conduct is not obstruction. Two circuits hold that false testimony alone is not sufficient to find an obstruction,[31] and the Second Circuit has indicated that mere failure to submit subpoenaed documents is not an obstruction of justice.[32] Recently the Fourth Circuit reversed a conviction and stated that, "Obstruction of justice prosecutions cannot rest solely on the allegation or proof of perjury."[33]

The circuits disagree on whether witness tampering is covered under § 1503. It is clearly covered under § 1512; the only question is whether it is also covered under § 1503. The Second Circuit has concluded that witness tampering is covered only by § 1512.[34] On the other hand, several circuits have concluded that witness tampering is covered by § 1503 as well as § 1512.[35] The split arises because the courts disagree on the implications of two amendments to these statutes, one in 1982 and one in 1988.[36] The Second Circuit is alone in holding that § 1503 does not cover witness tampering. As the Sixth Circuit put it recently, that position is "still a minority one."[37]

Justice White advocated granting certiorari to settle whether witness tampering is still covered by § 1503, but the Court declined.[38]

C. MENS REA

The only *mens rea* term in the text of § 1503 requires the defendant to act *corruptly*.[39] The meaning of this term will be discussed below. In addition, courts have construed the statute to require that the defendant

31. *Fourth Circuit:* United States v. Littleton, 76 F.3d 614 (4th Cir.1996)(reversing conviction because false testimony at motion to suppress is insufficient).

Sixth Circuit: United States v. Essex 407 F.2d 214 (6th Cir.1969)(noting that § 1503 is a contempt statute requiring more than false testimony).

32. *Second Circuit:* United States v. Weiss, 491 F.2d 460, 466 (2d Cir.1974) (trial court held there must be some type of affirmative conduct, not just a "failure to produce," and the Second Circuit noted this ruling.)

See also

Supreme Court: United States v. Aguilar, 515 U.S. 593, 115 S.Ct. 2357, 132 L.Ed.2d 520 (1995)(making false statements to an investigating agent who might or might not testify before the grand jury was not obstruction of justice under § 1503). This conclusion was based on an insufficient mens rea; *Aguilar* is discussed in detail *infra* in § 19.3(c).

33. United States v. Littleton, 76 F.3d 614, 619 (4th Cir.1996).

34. United States v. Masterpol, 940 F.2d 760 (2d Cir.1991); United States v. Hernandez, 730 F.2d 895 (2d Cir.1984).

35. *Fourth Circuit:* United States v. Kenny, 973 F.2d 339 (4th Cir.1992).

Seventh Circuit: United States v. Maloney, 71 F.3d 645, 659 (7th Cir.1995).

Eleventh Circuit: United States v. Moody, 977 F.2d 1420 (11th Cir.1992).

36. United States v. Maloney, 71 F.3d 645 at 658 (7th Cir.1995).

37. United States v. Maloney, 71 F.3d 645 at 659 (7th Cir.1995).

38. *See* Risken v. United States, 479 U.S. 923, 107 S.Ct. 329, 93 L.Ed.2d 302 (1986)(denying cert.); Cooper v. United States, 471 U.S. 1130, 105 S.Ct. 2664, 86 L.Ed.2d 281 (1985)(denying cert.). The issue was briefed and argued in United States v. Aguilar, 515 U.S. 593, 115 S.Ct. 2357, 132 L.Ed.2d 520 (1995), but the Court decided that case on the *mens rea* instead.

39. 18 U.S.C. § 1503(a).

intend to obstruct the proceedings.[40] In order to intend to obstruct, the defendant must know of the pending proceeding[41] and know that his or her actions are likely to affect the proceeding.[42] The Supreme Court recently addressed this *mens rea* in United States v. Aguilar.[43]

In *Aguilar*, the issue was whether § 1503 covers a defendant who lies to potential grand jurors.[44] The court held that the obstruction statute did not apply to this conduct because the lies did not have the necessary relationship to judicial proceedings to constitute obstruction.[45] The lies must have the natural and probable effect of interfering with the administration of justice.[46] Phrased another way, in *mens rea* terms, the defendant must know that his actions are likely to affect a judicial proceeding or he lacks the requisite intent to obstruct.[47] The court concluded, "We do not believe that uttering false statements to an investigating agent—and that seems to be all that was proven here—who might or might not testify before a grand jury is sufficient to make out a violation of the catchall provision of § 1503."[48]

Similarly, the Fourth Circuit reversed the conviction of a mother who lied at her son's motion to suppress hearing.[49] The court found the evidence showed a motive to lie, but was insufficient to allow the jury to infer the required *mens rea* of intent to obstruct.

The defendant does not have to know that the proceeding is federal in nature.[50]

For the second level of *mens rea*, the defendant must act *corruptly, or by threats or force or by any threatening letter or communication*. This element can be established by some types of conduct (threats, force or

40. *Supreme Court:* United States v. Aguilar, 515 U.S. 593, 599, 115 S.Ct. 2357, 2362, 132 L.Ed.2d 520 (1995) (*citing* United States v. Brown, 688 F.2d 596, 598 (9th Cir.1982)).

Fourth Circuit: United States v. Littleton, 76 F.3d 614, 619 (4th Cir.1996).

41. *Supreme Court:* Pettibone v. United States, 148 U.S. 197, 13 S.Ct. 542, 37 L.Ed. 419 (1893); United States v. Aguilar, 515 U.S. 593, 115 S.Ct. 2357, 132 L.Ed.2d 520 (1995).

First Circuit: United States v. Frankhauser, 80 F.3d 641, 650 (1st Cir.1996), *citing* United States v. Aguilar, 515 U.S. 593, 115 S.Ct. 2357, 132 L.Ed.2d 520 (1995).

Fourth Circuit: United States v. Littleton, 76 F.3d 614 (4th Cir.1996).

Fifth Circuit: United States v. Vesich, 724 F.2d 451 (5th Cir.1984).

Sixth Circuit: United States v. Bashaw, 982 F.2d 168 (6th Cir.1992).

Seventh Circuit: United States v. Edwards, 36 F.3d 639 (7th Cir.1994); United

States v. Maloney, 71 F.3d 645 (7th Cir. 1995).

Ninth Circuit: United States v. Washington Water Power Co., 793 F.2d 1079 (9th Cir.1986).

42. *Supreme Court:* United States v. Aguilar, 515 U.S. 593, 599, 115 S.Ct. 2357, 2362, 132 L.Ed.2d 520 (1995).

Fourth Circuit: United States v. Littleton, 76 F.3d 614, 619 (4th Cir.1996).

43. 515 U.S. 593, 115 S.Ct. 2357, 132 L.Ed.2d 520 (1995).

44. 515 U.S. at 593, 115 S.Ct. at 2359.

45. *Id.* at 599.

46. *Id.*

47. *Id.*

48. *Id.* at 600.

49. United States v. Littleton, 76 F.3d 614, 619 (4th Cir.1996).

50. United States v. Ardito, 782 F.2d 358 (2d Cir.1986).

threatening communication[51]), but if none of these is present, the defendant must be acting *corruptly* to be convicted.

Generally, *corruptly* is defined as acting with the purpose of obstructing the administration of justice.[52] Several kinds of conduct have been deemed corrupt by the courts, including questioning grand jurors about secret information,[53] responding when a witness asks for help to avoid testifying,[54] and destroying or concealing documents.[55] One act that is not corrupt is refusing to testify based on reasonable and realistic fear for one's own safety or family safety.[56]

Library References:

C.J.S. Obstructing Justice or Governmental Administration § 2–4, 9, 16–17, 20–21.
West's Key No. Digests, Obstructing Justice ⊕1.

§ 19.4   Influencing or Injuring Officer or Juror: § 1503—Inchoate Liability

A. SOLICITATION

Solicitation is not mentioned in this statute but the term *endeavor* is. The Fourth and Eighth Circuits have described *endeavor* as being "some effort, although less than an attempt."[1] This definition of endeavor as covering conduct less than attempt suggests that the term may cover conduct usually referred to as solicitation, although no courts have discussed this.

B. ATTEMPT

Attempted obstruction of justice is covered under the term *endeavor*. The government does not have to show that a defendant actually obstructed justice under § 1503, because the statutory focus is on

---

51. *See* United States v. Neal, 951 F.2d 630 (5th Cir.1992)(defendant wrote a letter purporting to be from a juror in order to get a mistrial); United States v. Branch, 850 F.2d 1080 (5th Cir.1988)(defendant wrote threatening letters to witnesses before his trial).

52. *Fourth Circuit:* United States v. Grubb, 11 F.3d 426 (4th Cir.1993).

Sixth Circuit: United States v. Jeter, 775 F.2d 670 (6th Cir.1985).

Ninth Circuit: United States v. Plascencia–Orozco, 768 F.2d 1074 (9th Cir. 1985).

53. United States v. Saget, 991 F.2d 702 (11th Cir.1993).

54. United States v. Washington Water Power Co., 793 F.2d 1079 (9th Cir. 1986).

55. *Eleventh Circuit:* United States v. Banks, 942 F.2d 1576 (11th Cir.1991). *But*

see Second Circuit: United States v. Weiss, 491 F.2d 460 (2d Cir.1974) (suggesting that simply not producing documents is not a crime under § 1503. Rather, there must be some affirmative conduct on the defendant's part such as destruction, concealment or removal.)

Second Circuit: United States v. Weiss, 491 F.2d 460 (2d Cir.1974).

56. *See* United States v. Banks, 942 F.2d 1576 (11th Cir.1991).

§ 19.4

1. *See*

Fourth Circuit: United States v. Aragon, 983 F.2d 1306, 1315 (4th Cir.1993).

Eighth Circuit: United States v. Leisure, 844 F.2d 1347, 1366 (8th Cir.1988).

endeavor.[2] The Supreme Court has described the role of *endeavor*: "It makes conduct punishable where the defendant acts with an intent to obstruct justice, and in a manner that is likely to obstruct justice, but is foiled in some way."[3] The Supreme Court's discussion of the term endeavor shows that the term is limited to instances when a defendant intended to obstruct justice and when it was probable that the conduct would obstruct justice.[4] Therefore, attempt liability exists, but is limited by the *mens rea* requirement to instances where the attempt has the natural and probable effect of interfering with the due administration of justice.[5]

C. CONSPIRACY

Section 1503 makes no reference to conspiracy, but liability is available under the general conspiracy statute, § 371.[6]

Library References:

C.J.S. Obstructing Justice or Governmental Administration § 7, 10.
West's Key No. Digests, Obstructing Justice ⊄9.

§ 19.5 Influencing or Injuring Officer or Juror: § 1503—Accomplice Liability

The statute does not include liability for accomplices. The general accomplice liability statute, § 2, can be used to apply this crime to accomplices.[1]

Library References:

C.J.S. Obstructing Justice or Governmental Administration § 7, 10.
West's Key No. Digests, Obstructing Justice ⊄9.

2. *Supreme Court*: United States v. Aguilar, 515 U.S. 593, 599, 115 S.Ct. 2357, 2362, 132 L.Ed.2d 520 (1995), citing United States v. Russell, 255 U.S. 138, 41 S.Ct. 260, 65 L.Ed. 553 (1921).

3. United States v. Aguilar, 515 U.S. 593, 601, 115 S.Ct. 2357, 2362, 132 L.Ed.2d 520 (1995).

4. *Id.* at 602.

5. United States v. Aguilar, 515 U.S. 593, 599, 115 S.Ct. 2357, 2361, 132 L.Ed.2d 520 (1995).

6. *First Circuit:* United States v. Cintolo, 818 F.2d 980 (1st Cir.1987).

Fifth Circuit: United States v. Ed Moree, 897 F.2d 1329 (5th Cir.1990); United States v. Nelson, 852 F.2d 706 (3d Cir. 1988).

Sixth Circuit: United States v. Mullins, 22 F.3d 1365 (6th Cir.1994).

Seventh Circuit: United States v. Lahey, 55 F.3d 1289 (7th Cir.1995); United States v. Machi, 811 F.2d 991 (7th Cir. 1987).

Ninth Circuit: United States v. Lester, 749 F.2d 1288 (9th Cir.1984).

Eleventh Circuit: United States v. Perkins, 748 F.2d 1519 (11th Cir.1984).

§ 19.5

1. *Second Circuit:* United States v. Fayer, 573 F.2d 741 (2d Cir.1978); United States v. Rosner, 485 F.2d 1213 (2d Cir. 1973).

Third Circuit: United States v. Rankin, 870 F.2d 109 (3d Cir.1989).

Eighth Circuit: United States v. McKnight, 799 F.2d 443 (8th Cir.1986).

§ 19.6   Influencing or Injuring Officer or Juror: § 1503—Constitutionality

The Sixth Circuit rejected arguments that § 1503 is void for vagueness and overbroad.[1] The court held that the statute is not vague because the *mens rea corruptly* keeps the statute confined by requiring the defendant to act specifically to obstruct justice.[2] The court also held that the defendant's conduct, selling grand jury secrets, did not support an overbreadth argument because he never tried to sell to the public.[3] Therefore his conduct did not involve activity protected as free speech.

§ 19.7   Obstruction of Proceedings Before Departments, Agencies and Committees: § 1505—In General

Section 1505 prohibits conduct that could interfere with the integrity of administrative proceedings. The statute has two paragraphs. The first paragraph is narrow; it criminalizes withholding or tampering with any documents or oral testimony relating to any civil investigative demand made under the Antitrust Civil Process Act. This provision has generated no reported prosecutions and is not discussed further here.

The second and more important paragraph criminalizes influencing, obstructing, or impeding any pending proceeding before a government department or agency, or congressional committee. With this second paragraph Congress intended to capture any obstruction of the administrative process[1] as opposed to the judicial process covered by § 1503. The crime is drafted broadly "with an eye to 'the variety of corrupt methods by which the proper administration of justice may be impeded or thwarted, a variety limited only by the imagination of the criminally inclined.' "[2]

A corporation has been indicted for obstructing a proceeding, but its conviction was reversed;[3] the usual defendants are individuals.[4]

Library References:

C.J.S. Obstructing Justice or Governmental Administration § 4–9, 13–17, 20.
West's Key No. Digests, Obstructing Justice ⊶7.

§ 19.6

1. United States v. Jeter, 775 F.2d 670 (6th Cir.1985).

2. *Id.* at 679.

3. *Id.* at 678.

§ 19.7

1. *See*

Second Circuit: United States v. Persico, 520 F.Supp. 96, 101 (E.D.N.Y.1981), *order aff'd,* 774 F.2d 30 (2d Cir.1985).

Eighth Circuit: Rice v. United States, 356 F.2d 709, 712 (8th Cir.1966).

2. United States v. Mitchell, 877 F.2d 294, 299 (4th Cir.1989).

3. United States v. Browning, Inc., 572 F.2d 720 (10th Cir.1978).

4. *See*

Ninth Circuit: United States v. Laurins, 857 F.2d 529 (9th Cir.1988) (defendant was the managing director of a company under investigation by the IRS).

Tenth Circuit: United States v. Browning, 630 F.2d 694 (10th Cir.1980) (defendant was the president of Browning Arms Company); United States v. Sutton, 732 F.2d 1483 (10th Cir.1984).

§ 19.8 Obstruction of Proceedings Before Departments, Agencies and Committees: § 1505—Elements

This crime has five elements: a (1) pending (2) proceeding before a government department or agency or Congressional committee that (3) the defendant knew of, and (4) the defendant influenced, obstructed or impeded it with (5) a corrupt intent.[1] The courts disagree on whether the materiality of defendant's conduct is an element.[2]

A. PENDING PROCEEDING

Like § 1503, defendants have argued that the proceeding is not pending or the activity was not actually a proceeding.[3] Courts usually reject these defense arguments and define pending proceeding broadly to effectuate the statute's purpose of capturing any obstruction of administrative proceedings.[4]

i. Pending

One court concluded that there was nothing pending before the Immigration and Naturalization Service when the Service returned the defendant's application with directions to resubmit after he had included certain other documents.[5] The court defined pending as "being subject to awaiting some form of disposing action," and decided that since the "Immigration and Naturalization Service had no application in its hands ... and [did not engage in any] correspondence or taking of any action in relation to it," there was no proceeding pending.[6]

ii. Proceeding

An agency's activities qualify as proceedings during the investigative as well as the adjudicative stage,[7] so a variety of investigative proceed-

---

§ 19.8

1. *Cf.* United States v. Price, 951 F.2d 1028, 1031 (9th Cir.1991), in which the court characterizes § 1505 as having three elements: "First there must be a proceeding pending before a department or agency of the United States.... Second the defendant must be aware of the pending proceeding.... Third, the defendant must have intentionally endeavored corruptly to influence, obstruct or impede the pending proceeding."

2. *Compare*

Tenth Circuit: United States v. Browning, 630 F.2d 694, 698 (10th Cir.1980) (defendant's conduct must be material to the investigative proceeding; decision based on United States v. Ryan, 455 F.2d 728 (9th Cir.1971), a § 1503 case) *with*

Second Circuit: United States v. Sprecher, 783 F.Supp. 133 (S.D.N.Y.1992), *aff'd,* 50 F.3d 3 (2d Cir.1995)(expressly stat-

ing that materiality is not an element of obstructing proceedings).

3. *See*

Sixth Circuit: United States v. Fruchtman, 421 F.2d 1019, 1021 (6th Cir.1970).

Eighth Circuit: Rice v. United States, 356 F.2d 709, 712 (8th Cir.1966).

Ninth Circuit: United States v. Vixie, 532 F.2d 1277, 1278 (9th Cir.1976).

Tenth Circuit: United States v. Sutton, 732 F.2d 1483, 1490 (10th Cir.1984).

4. *See, e.g.,* United States v. Mitchell, 877 F.2d 294, 300 (4th Cir.1989).

5. Taran v. United States, 266 F.2d 561 (8th Cir.1959).

6. *Id.*

7. *Sixth Circuit:* United States v. Fruchtman, 421 F.2d 1019, 1021 (6th Cir. 1970).

Eighth Circuit: Rice v. United States, 356 F.2d 709, 712 (8th Cir.1966).

ings satisfy this element.[8] The Third Circuit has noted that "[t]he growth and expansion of agency activities have resulted in a meaning being given to 'proceeding' which is more inclusive and which no longer limits itself to formal activities in a court of law."[9] When the proceeding is a congressional inquiry, no formal authorization is required.[10] As the Fourth circuit explained, "[i]f it is apparent that the investigation is a legitimate exercise of the investigative authority by a congressional committee in an area within the committee's purview, it should be protected by section 1505."[11]

The agency involved in the proceeding must be one "with rule-making or adjudicative authority."[12] An investigation by a criminal investigatory agency is not a proceeding within the meaning of § 1505.[13] Without the authority to make rules or render judgments the agency's activity is merely an investigation rather than a proceeding. However, criminal investigations are picked up and covered by §§ 1510 and 1518.[14] This limit apparently is based on separation of powers concerns.[15]

The Third Circuit has construed this limit requiring rule making or adjudicative authority narrowly to hold a defendant liable. In United States v. Leo,[16] the defendant worked for a company which had a contract with the Army. In the course of his employment, the defendant submitted inflated sub-contractor prices, resulting in the Army paying

Ninth Circuit: United States v. Vixie, 532 F.2d 1277, 1278 (9th Cir.1976).

8. *See*

Sixth Circuit: United States v. Fruchtman, 421 F.2d 1019 (6th Cir.1970) (Federal Trade Commission's investigation of pricing practices is a proceeding).

Eighth Circuit: Rice v. United States, 356 F.2d 709 (8th Cir.1966) (investigation of the National Labor Relations Board is a pending proceeding notwithstanding the lack of a formal complaint).

Tenth Circuit: United States v. Browning, 630 F.2d 694 (10th Cir.1980) (Customs Service questioning a foreign corporation concerning the defendant's company was deemed a pending proceeding).

9. United States v. Leo, 941 F.2d 181 (3d Cir.1991).

10. United States v. Mitchell, 877 F.2d 294, 300 (4th Cir.1989).

11. *Id.*

12. *See* United States v. Wright, 704 F.Supp. 613 (D.Md.1989) (submitting false documents to the United States Attorney for District of Maryland did not violate § 1505 since the office does not have rulemaking or adjudicative authority.)

13. *See*

Sixth Circuit: United States v. Higgins, 511 F.Supp. 453 (W.D.Ky.1981) (investigation by the FBI which does not have rule making or adjudicative powers is not a proceeding).

See also

Second Circuit: United States v. Persico, 520 F.Supp. 96 (E.D.N.Y.1981), *order aff'd,* 774 F.2d 30 (2d Cir.1985) (criminal investigation by the IRS is an agency proceeding under § 1505 because the IRS has rule making powers).

Criminal investigation obstructions are covered by 18 U.S.C. § 1510 discussed *infra,* §§ 19.12–19.16.

14. *See infra* §§ 19.12–19.16 and § 19.27.

15. Courts rarely articulate the reason for distinguishing the types of agency proceedings. In United States v. Higgins, 511 F.Supp. 453 455 (W.D.Ky.1981), the court explained that "under our system of separation of powers, a criminal investigatory agency, in contradistinction to an administrative or regulatory agency, has no power to engage in rulemaking or adjudication. The Court is convinced ... that the meaning of proceeding in section 1505 must be limited to actions of an agency which relate to some matter within the scope of the rulemaking or adjudicative power vested in the agency by law."

16. 941 F.2d 181 (3d Cir.1991).

substantially more than was actually required. When the defendant came under investigation by the Defense Contract Audit Agency, he gave the agency purchase orders with altered dates. The defendant argued that he had not obstructed a proceeding within the meaning of § 1505 because the Defense Contract Audit Agency did not have rule-making or adjudicative authority. The court rejected the defendant's argument by reasoning that the "agency was acting under the direction of the Army's contracting officer, who had the authority to make adjudications on behalf of the Defense Department."[17] This broad interpretation of the Defense Contract Audit Agency's authority as adjudicative allowed the court to find that the defendant had obstructed agency proceedings under § 1505.

B. INFLUENCE, OBSTRUCT OR IMPEDE

Courts have found numerous actions sufficient to *influence, obstruct or impede*, including providing evasive answers to an administrative agency's questions,[18] advising an employee to destroy records sought by the Department of Energy,[19] altering dates on purchase orders,[20] and making conditional threats during an IRS investigation.[21] Courts construe the terms broadly to capture a wide range of conduct, consistent with the purpose of the statute to punish any obstruction of the administrative process.[22]

As noted above, the courts disagree on whether the defendant's conduct must be material to the proceeding.[23]

C. MENS REA

Section 1505 provides that the defendant must act "corruptly, or by threats or force, or by any threatening letter or communication...."[24] Additionally, courts have interpreted the statute to require that the defendant *know* of the pending proceeding[25] and *know* that his or her conduct would influence, impede or obstruct that proceeding.[26]

17. *Id.* at 198, 199.

18. United States v. Alo, 439 F.2d 751 (2d Cir.1971).

19. United States v. Sutton, 732 F.2d 1483 (10th Cir.1984).

20. United States v. Leo, 941 F.2d 181 (3d Cir.1991).

21. United States v. Price, 951 F.2d 1028 (9th Cir.1991).

22. United States v. Mitchell, 877 F.2d 294, 298 (4th Cir.1989)(noting the well-established rule that § 1505 and other omnibus clauses should be construed broadly).

23. *Compare*

Tenth Circuit: United States v. Browning, 630 F.2d 694, 698 (10th Cir.1980) (de-

fendant's conduct must be material to the investigative proceeding; decision based on United States v. Ryan, 455 F.2d 728 (9th Cir.1971), a § 1503 case) *with*

Second Circuit: United States v. Sprecher, 783 F.Supp. 133 (S.D.N.Y.1992), *aff'd,* 50 F.3d 3 (2d Cir.1995)(expressly stating that materiality is not an element of obstructing proceedings).

24. 18 U.S.C. § 1505.

25. *Ninth Circuit:* United States v. Price, 951 F.2d 1028, 1031 (9th Cir.1991).

Tenth Circuit: United States v. Sutton, 732 F.2d 1483, 1490 (10th Cir.1984).

26. As to whether a defendant must intend or merely know that her conduct would obstruct a proceeding is not clear.

The statutory *mens rea* quoted above can be satisfied by some types of conduct (*i.e.*, by threats, force or threatening communication), but if none of these is present, the defendant must be acting *corruptly* to face liability. The definition of corrupt generally becomes an issue when there is an absence of force or threats.[27] Like the other terms in § 1505, corrupt has been "given a broad and all inclusive meaning."[28] Courts have defined the term corruptly to mean that the "act must be done with the purpose of obstructing justice."[29] The Second Circuit held that corruptly simply means motivated by an improper purpose.[30] Acts which have been deemed corrupt include counseling a witness to give incomplete and misleading answers,[31] asking someone to back date a check,[32] ordering employees to box records sought by the IRS and concealing them in one's home,[33] and making conditional threats to the IRS.[34]

The importance of the term *corrupt* in defining the crime of obstruction of proceedings is illustrated by United States v. Mitchell.[35] The defendants used their close relationship with their uncle, who was on the House Committee for Small Business, to influence the committee's decision. They were convicted of obstructing a congressional proceeding. In deciding that the defendants' conduct was corrupt, the court stated: "The proper inquiry is whether a defendant had the requisite corrupt intent to improperly influence the investigation, not the means the defendant employed in bringing to bear this influence."[36] Thus the Fourth Circuit concluded that even talking with a relative is a crime if the intent is corrupt, *i.e.*, based on an improper purpose.

Knowledge of the law is not required. This issue has only been addressed once, and in that case the court held that "[a]ny reasonable man would realize that conduct which sought to mislead and did mislead the government ... was unlawful and therefore, it was not necessary for [the defendant] to be aware of the exact details of the statute."[37]

The Southern District of New York explains it this way: "While the statutory term 'corruptly endeavors' requires intent, such intent may be inferred from proof that the defendant knew that his corrupt actions would obstruct justice then actually being administered." United States v. Sprecher, 783 F.Supp. 133, 164 (S.D.N.Y.1992), *aff'd*, 50 F.3d 3 (2d Cir.1995) (citing United States v. Buffalano, 727 F.2d 50, 53 (2d Cir.1984)).

27. *See, e.g.*, United States v. Browning, 630 F.2d 694, 701 (10th Cir.1980).

28. *Id.*

29. United States v. Laurins, 857 F.2d 529, 536–37 (9th Cir.1988).

30. United States v. Fasolino, 586 F.2d 939, 941 (2d Cir.1978).

31. United States v. Browning, 630 F.2d 694, 701 (10th Cir.1980).

32. United States v. Lewis, 657 F.2d 44 (4th Cir.1981).

33. United States v. Laurins, 857 F.2d 529 (9th Cir.1988).

34. United States v. Price, 951 F.2d 1028 (9th Cir.1991).

35. 877 F.2d 294 (4th Cir.1989).

36. *Id.* at 299.

37. *Tenth Circuit:* United States v. Browning, 630 F.2d 694 (10th Cir.1980).

See also

D.C. Circuit: United States v. Poindexter, 951 F.2d 369 (D.C.Cir.1991) ("corrupt" found unconstitutionally vague because it does not "put the reasonable person on notice that the statute applies"). This ruling is discussed *infra* in § 19.11.

Third Circuit: United States v. Leo, 941 F.2d 181, 199 (3d Cir.1991) ("... we reject the contention that the statute did not give him fair notice that his conduct was prohibited.").

Library References:

C.J.S. Obstructing Justice or Governmental Administration § 2–4, 9, 16–17, 20–21.
West's Key No. Digests, Obstructing Justice ⊕1.

§ 19.9   Obstruction of Proceedings Before Departments, Agencies and Committees: § 1505—Inchoate Liability

A. SOLICITATION

Solicitation is not mentioned in this statute, but the statute does contain the term "endeavor" and it may cover conduct generally called solicitation. In discussing § 1503, the Fourth and Eighth Circuits defined *endeavor* as some effort, although less than an attempt.[1] Some effort, less than attempt, includes conduct usually referred to as solicitation.

B. ATTEMPT

Attempt liability is available under this statute, but under a different name. The statute expressly extends to defendants who *endeavor* to influence, obstruct or impede proceedings, as well as to those who actually do so. Courts' treatment of endeavor indicates that its meaning is the same as the more familiar term, attempt. Endeavor is used to capture unsuccessful efforts to obstruct proceedings.[2] "The criminality or legality of alleged obstructive conduct cannot turn on its success, as the effort to obstruct an inquiry is an evil the statute seeks to address."[3] This is the usual function of attempt liability.[4] Other courts have described synonyms for endeavor as "effort or assay."[5] Some courts use the terms endeavor and attempt interchangeably.[6]

---

§ 19.9

1. *Fourth Circuit:* United States v. Aragon, 983 F.2d 1306 (4th Cir.1993).

Eighth Circuit: United States v. Leisure, 844 F.2d 1347 (8th Cir.1988).

2. *See*

Second Circuit: United States v. Abrams, 427 F.2d 86 (2d Cir.1970) (defendant endeavored to influence a witness before the INS).

Fourth Circuit: United States v. Mitchell, 877 F.2d 294 (4th Cir.1989) (defendants corruptly endeavored to obstruct a congressional investigation).

Tenth Circuit: United States v. Browning, 630 F.2d 694 (10th Cir.1980) (defendant endeavored to obstruct the Customs duties laws by advising someone to give incomplete and misleading answers to questions by the Customs Service).

3. United States v. North, 716 F.Supp. 644, 649 (D.D.C.1989).

4. *See*

D.C. Circuit: United States v. North, 716 F.Supp. 644, 649 (D.D.C.1989).

Ninth Circuit: United States v. Vixie, 532 F.2d 1277, 1278 (9th Cir.1976).

5. United States v. Buffalano, 727 F.2d 50, 53 (2d Cir.1984).

6. In United States v. Browning, 630 F.2d 694, 696 (10th Cir.1980) the court describes the basis for defendant's conviction as he "*endeavored* to obstruct the due and proper administration of the Customs duties laws ...," and later in the same opinion the court refers to the defendant's charge as predicated on an "*attempted* corrupt obstructing or impeding...." *Id.* at 698 (emphasis added).

C. CONSPIRACY

Section 1505 makes no reference to conspiracy, but liability is available under the general conspiracy statute, § 371.[7]

Library References:

C.J.S. Obstructing Justice or Governmental Administration § 7, 10.
West's Key No. Digests, Obstructing Justice ⇒9.

§ 19.10 Obstruction of Proceedings Before Departments, Agencies and Committees: § 1505—Accomplice liability

This statute does not include liability for accomplices. The general accomplice liability statute can be used to apply this crime to accomplices.[1]

Library References:

C.J.S. Obstructing Justice or Governmental Administration § 7, 10.
West's Key No. Digests, Obstructing Justice ⇒9.

§ 19.11 Obstruction of Proceedings Before Departments, Agencies and Committees: § 1505—Constitutionality

A. FIRST AMENDMENT

The Fourth Circuit rejected defendants' arguments that using their close relationship with an uncle on the House Committee for Small Business to influence an investigation was merely an exercise of their first amendment right to lobby Congress.[1] The court distinguished between being paid for one's advocacy skills, which is legitimate lobbying, and being paid for the ability to thwart the investigation solely through familial relationships, which is obstructing proceedings.

B. VAGUENESS

The Fourth Circuit in *Mitchell* also rejected the argument that § 1505 is unconstitutionally vague when "corruptly" is given a broad

---

7. *Tenth Circuit:* United States v. Sutton, 732 F.2d 1483 (10th Cir.1984).

See

Sixth Circuit: United States v. Fruchtman, 421 F.2d 1019 (6th Cir.1970) (defendant is charged with conspiracy to violate § 1505, but the court does not mention § 371).

§ 19.10

1. *See*

D.C. Circuit: United States v. North, 716 F.Supp. 644, 646 (D.D.C.1989) (defendant was charged with a violation of § 1505 and § 2, relating to aiding and abetting an obstruction of Congress).

Third Circuit: United States v. Leo, 941 F.2d 181, 184 (3d Cir.1991).

Ninth Circuit: United States v. Laurins, 857 F.2d 529, 534 (9th Cir.1988).

§ 19.11

1. United States v. Mitchell, 877 F.2d 294, 300 (4th Cir.1989).

interpretation.[2] However, one court has found that § 1505 is unconstitutionally vague when corruptly is applied to the conduct of lying to Congress. In United States v. Poindexter,[3] the court concluded that neither the legislative history nor the prior judicial interpretations of § 1505 supplies the constitutionally required notice that the statute lacks on its face.[4] The court noted several cases which apparently held that lying is within § 1505, but concluded that the cases are not "sufficiently clear or consistent" in their reasoning.[5]

The holding of *Poindexter* is narrow. The court does not find "corruptly" unconstitutionally vague as applied to all conduct but only as applied to making false and misleading statements to the Congress.[6] Furthermore, there is a strong dissenting opinion by Chief Judge Mikva which reasons that the defendant "lied to Congress about the first Presidential finding and then later destroyed it. This is a clear violation of his oath of office, his oath to Congress, and his duty not to lie.... The allegations ... fall within the plain meaning of the term corruptly, and ... I cannot imagine that Congress meant to prohibit attempts to obstruct justice by influencing someone else to violate a legal duty, but did not mean to prohibit attempts to obstruct justice by violating one's own legal duty."[7]

§ 19.12　Obstruction of Criminal Investigations: § 1510—In General

Section 1510 contains three subsections which criminalize conduct. The most important is subsection 1510(a) which prohibits endeavors to obstruct, by means of bribery, the communication of information to criminal investigators. This is basically an inchoate crime. This section is "designed to close a loophole in former laws which protected witnesses only during the pending of the proceeding"[1] and not during the investigative stage.

---

2. United States v. Mitchell, 877 F.2d 294, 299 (4th Cir.1989).

3. 951 F.2d 369 (D.C.Cir.1991).

4. *Id.*

5. *Id.* The court distinguishes United States v. Alo, 439 F.2d 751 (2d Cir.1971), on the grounds that in *Alo* the defendant's conduct was giving evasive answers, while here the conduct is simply lying. Yet the court goes on to explain that it does not mean to support such distinctions, but that the discussion of *Alo* serves to demonstrate exactly how vague is the word "corrupt".

6. The court makes a point of stating that this holding does not limit § 1505 to the core behavior prohibited by the statute, which is defined by the court as all attempts to influence or obstruct a congressional inquiry by influencing another to violate his legal duty. United States v. Poindexter, 951 F.2d 369, 386 (D.C.Cir. 1991).

7. *Id.* at 391.

§ 19.12

1. *Fifth Circuit:* United States v. San Martin, 515 F.2d 317, 320 (5th Cir.1975). The "former laws" referred to are §§ 1503 and 1505.

Several other courts have voiced a similar understanding of the purpose of § 1510.

Ninth Circuit: "The Federal government should be able to provide the same protection and assurance to a witness ... at a later stage in the prosecution." United States v. Lester, 749 F.2d 1288 (9th Cir. 1984). *See also* United States v. Masterpol, 940 F.2d 760 (2d Cir.1991) (*Lester* has less force as precedent after 1988 amendment of § 1512).

Fourth Circuit: The purpose of section 1510 is "to keep unobstructed the 'communication of information ... to a criminal

The other subsections (1510(b) and 1510(d)) have generated no reported prosecutions. Subsection 1510(b)(1) prohibits officers of financial institutions from notifying anyone about subpoenas for financial records if the officer intends to obstruct a judicial proceeding. Subsection 1510(b)(2) also prohibits officers of financial institutions from notifying persons of subpoenas for financial records, but (b)(2) prohibits notification only of customers or persons named in the subpoena and does not require the mens rea of intent to obstruct a judicial proceeding. Subsection 1510(d) prohibits persons involved in insurance transactions from notifying anyone about subpoenas for financial records if they intend to obstruct a judicial proceeding. Because no prosecutions of subsections 1510(b) and 1510(d) have been reported, the following discussion of § 1510 focuses exclusively on subsection (a), dealing with communication of information to criminal investigators.

The defendants targeted by subsection 1510(a) are persons associated with organized crime who may try to influence witnesses during the investigative stage of a trial. The Fifth Circuit described the legislative rationale behind § 1510 this way:

> The real need for this legislation is in the difficulty encountered in the presentation of a case for trial in the field of organized crime. It is in these fields that witnesses consistently refuse to cooperate with the prosecution.... The ability of organized crime to impose silence on its members and thereby protect both the leaders and the membership of this criminal organization is the primary source of its power and affluence.... This frustration of criminal investigations should no longer be tolerated....[2]

Several defendants have been part of large gambling[3] and drug operations.[4] A number of defendants have also been attorneys.[5]

---

investigator.' Its primary subject of protection is the transmission of the words of a prospective informant or witness ... it is the giving of information for which security is sought." United States v. Fraley, 538 F.2d 626 (4th Cir.1976).

2. *Fifth Circuit:* United States v. Cameron, 460 F.2d 1394, 1400 (5th Cir. 1972), *overruled by* United States v. Howard, 483 F.2d 229 (5th Cir.1973)(quoting 1967 U.S.C.C.A.N. 1760, 1761–62).

See also

Second Circuit: United States v. Daly, 842 F.2d 1380 (2d.Cir.1988).

Eighth Circuit: United States v. Leisure, 844 F.2d 1347 (8th Cir.1988).

Ninth Circuit: United States v. Zemek, 634 F.2d 1159 (9th Cir.1980).

3. *Third Circuit:* United States v. Kozak, 438 F.2d 1062 (3d Cir.1971).

Tenth Circuit: United States v. Carleo, 576 F.2d 846 (10th Cir.1978).

4. *Second Circuit:* United States v. Coiro, 922 F.2d 1008 (2d Cir.1991).

Sixth Circuit: United States v. Lippman, 492 F.2d 314 (6th Cir.1974).

Eighth Circuit: United States v. Williams, 470 F.2d 1339 (8th Cir.1973).

Ninth Circuit: United States v. Lester 749 F.2d 1288 (9th Cir.1984).

5. *Second Circuit:* United States v. Coiro, 922 F.2d 1008 (2d Cir.1991).

Fifth Circuit: United States v. Cameron, 460 F.2d 1394 (5th Cir.1972).

Sixth Circuit: United States v. Qaoud, 777 F.2d 1105 (6th Cir.1985); United States v. Lippman, 492 F.2d 314 (6th Cir.1974).

Ninth Circuit: United States v. Lester 749 F.2d 1288 (9th Cir.1984).

Library References:

C.J.S. Obstructing Justice or Governmental Administration § 2–37.
West's Key No. Digests, Obstructing Justice ⚷1–21.

§ 19.13   Obstruction of Criminal Investigations: § 1510—Elements

This crime has four elements: the defendant must (1) willfully (2) endeavor by means of bribery to obstruct, delay or prevent the communication of information relating to a violation of any criminal statute by any person (3) to a criminal investigator (4) whom the defendant knows to be a criminal investigator.[1]

Before discussing these elements, note what is not an element. Although the statutory language specifically refers to obstructions of an *investigation*, § 1510 is not limited to the investigatory stage. Most courts hold that it does not matter that the obstruction took place during a judicial proceeding,[2] and this crime does not require that an investigation be in progress when the obstruction occurs.[3]

However, the Second Circuit has indicated that perhaps an investigation should be in progress before there can be any obstruction.[4] In United States v. Siegel[5] the court reversed the conviction, but limited its

---

§ 19.13

1. *Second Circuit:* United States v. Abrams, 543 F.Supp. 1184 (S.D.N.Y.1982) and

Fifth Circuit: United States v. San Martin, 515 F.2d 317 (5th Cir.1975).

Both these courts list three elements by grouping (2) and (3) together.

2. *See*

Seventh Circuit: United States v. Gorny 732 F.2d 597 (7th Cir.1984); United States v. Doe, 867 F.2d 986 (7th Cir.1989).

Ninth Circuit: United States v. Lester 749 F.2d 1288 (9th Cir.1984); United States v. Roberts, 638 F.2d 134 (9th Cir.1981).

Yet the Fifth Circuit has given mixed answers to the issue of whether § 1510 prohibits obstruction during a judicial proceeding.

Fifth Circuit: In United States v. San Martin, 515 F.2d 317, 319 (5th Cir.1975) and United States v. Cameron, 460 F.2d 1394, 1401 (5th Cir.1972), *overruled by* United States v. Howard 483 F.2d 229 (5th Cir.1973), the court's decision contained the language: "§ 1510 was designed to deter the coercion of potential witnesses by the subjects of federal criminal investigations prior to the initiation of judicial proceedings." However in United States v. Koehler, 544 F.2d 1326 (5th Cir.1977) the court clarified its opinion and held that "[t]he provisions of Section 1510 do not exclude its applicability merely because an indictment has been returned or judicial proceedings have been initiated."

3. *Ninth Circuit:* United States v. Zemek, 634 F.2d 1159, 1176–77 (9th Cir. 1980) held that § 1510 "does not require an investigation be taking place concurrently with the proscribed acts. Therefore it is not fatal that the IRS investigation terminated prior to the alleged acts and threats of violence."

See also

Second Circuit: United States v. Abrams, 543 F.Supp. 1184 (S.D.N.Y.1982) (government need not prove that a federal criminal investigation was actually taking place to prove a violation of § 1510.)

Sixth Circuit: United States v. Lippman, 492 F.2d 314 (6th Cir.1974) (statute does not require that an investigation be taking place, but prohibits the obstruction of any communication to an investigation).

4. The Second Circuit hinted that it is uncertain as to whether an investigation must be taking place in United States v. Siegel, 717 F.2d 9, 21 (2d Cir.1983). The court stated: "... we do not hold that § 1510 requires ... that an ongoing criminal investigation be in progress.... These questions we leave for another day."

5. 717 F.2d 9 (2d Cir.1983).

holding to the facts of the case.[6] It was important to the court was that the defendant was being blackmailed by the "informant"[7] and there was no federal investigation being conducted or contemplated, nor was there a criminal investigator about to receive information.[8] In a later case, the Second Circuit again decided not to resolve whether there needs to be an ongoing criminal investigation. In United States v. Daly[9] the court examined the legislative history of § 1510 and paid particular attention to the language of the House Report on § 1510 which states: "there is no statute which presently protects witnesses during the *investigative* stage."[10] However, the court did not resolve the issue because there was sufficient evidence to prove an ongoing investigation.[11]

A. ENDEAVOR BY MEANS OF BRIBERY TO OBSTRUCT, DELAY, OR PREVENT THE COMMUNICATION OF INFORMATION

The statute prohibits *endeavors to obstruct communication*.[12] The language " 'by means of bribery' restricts the form of the punishable endeavor to obstruct communications."[13] The bribery must be complete, not mere preparatory or inchoate bribery.[14]

Bribery is the only form of endeavor expressly prohibited by the statute. Yet several circuits have upheld convictions not involving bribery. The Ninth Circuit affirmed a conviction of subsection 1510(a) when the defendant threatened an informant that he would be "blown away" if he testified against the defendant.[15] The Seventh Circuit upheld a conviction for violating subsection 1510(a) when a defendant attempted to encourage the informer to lie.[16] These courts did not discuss the absence of the bribery element, and it is unclear whether the defendants raised it. These courts' interpretation seem curiously at odds with the statutory language on bribery, but perhaps consistent with Congress' intention. The Senate Report on the VWPA indicates that the Senate believed that § 1510 "requires bribery, misrepresentation, intimidation,

---

6. *Id.* at 21.

7. "We hesitate to interpret [§ 1510] in a manner that would encourage blackmailers." *Id.*

8. *Id.*

9. 842 F.2d 1380 (2d Cir.1988).

10. United States v. Daly, 842 F.2d 1380, 1390 (2d Cir.1988) (emphasis added) quoting H.R.Rep.No. 90–658, at 1761 (1982). This decision not to address the issue is the Second Circuit's most recent, direct statement on whether an investigation should be taking place. In later dicta the court seems to indicate that an ongoing investigation is not required for a violation of § 1510. *See* United States v. Romero, 54 F.3d 56 (2d Cir.1995).

11. *Daly*, 842 F.2d at 1391. The defendant also raised the issue of whether he

had to know there was an investigation, and the court also avoided answering this question.

12. United States v. Stafford, 831 F.2d 1479, 1483 (9th Cir.1987).

13. *Id.*

14. *Id.*

15. United States v. Murray, 751 F.2d 1528, 1534 (9th Cir.1985). The court described § 1510 as forbidding "threatening efforts designed to prevent a person from communicating information about a crime to a federal investigator."

16. United States v. Gorny, 732 F.2d 597 (7th Cir.1984); United States v. Doe, 867 F.2d 986 (7th Cir.1989).

force or threats."[17]

B. CRIMINAL INVESTIGATOR

Criminal investigator includes "any individual duly authorized by a department, agency, or armed force of the United States to conduct or engage in investigations of or prosecutions for violations of the criminal laws of the United States."[18] Employees of the SEC,[19] FBI agents,[20] and IRS agents[21] have all been held criminal investigators.

C. *MENS REA*

This crime requires basically two levels of *mens rea*. On the first level, the defendant must *know* that the "recipient or intended recipient of the information was a criminal investigator."[22] Once the defendant knows this, he or she does not have to know that the "obstructed party either conveyed information ... or was about to do so," but must only have a "reasonably founded belief that information had been or was about to be given."[23]

On the second level, the main *mens rea* is embodied in the requirement that the defendant act "willfully."[24] In spite of authority interpret-

---

17. S.REP.NO. 97–532, at 6 (1982), *reprinted in* 1982 U.S.C.C.A.N. 2515.

18. 18 U.S.C. § 1510(c).

19. *See* United States v. Abrams, 543 F.Supp. 1184 (S.D.N.Y.1982). The defendant argued as a matter of law SEC employees are not criminal investigators. The court disagreed because the Securities Act and Securities Exchange Act empower employees to investigate infractions of the securities laws with a view to criminal enforcement.

20. *See*

Fifth Circuit: United States v. San Martin, 515 F.2d 317 (5th Cir.1975).

Eighth Circuit: United States v. Segal, 649 F.2d 599 (8th Cir.1981).

Tenth Circuit: United States v. Carleo, 576 F.2d 846 (10th Cir.1978). Contrary to the limitation of § 1505, agencies do not have to have law-making or adjudicative authority. Therefore, FBI agents are criminal investigators within the meaning of § 1510.

21. United States v. Zemek, 634 F.2d 1159 (9th Cir.1980).

22. *Second Circuit:* United States v. Abrams, 543 F.Supp. 1184, 1187 (S.D.N.Y. 1982).

See also

Third Circuit: United States v. Kozak, 438 F.2d 1062 (3d Cir.1971).

Fifth Circuit: United States v. Nelson, 733 F.2d 364, 368–69 (5th Cir.1984); United States v. San Martin, 515 F.2d 317 (5th Cir.1975).

Eighth Circuit: United States v. Williams, 470 F.2d 1339 (8th Cir.1973).

23. *Second Circuit:* United States v. Abrams, 543 F.Supp. 1184, 1187 (S.D.N.Y. 1982).

See also

Third Circuit: United States v. Kozak, 438 F.2d 1062 (3d Cir.1971).

Fifth Circuit: United States v. San Martin, 515 F.2d 317 (5th Cir.1975).

Ninth Circuit: United States v. Zemek, 634 F.2d 1159 (9th Cir.1980).

24. 18 U.S.C. § 1510. A few cases have made statements as to what "willfully" means, *see e.g.,*

Third Circuit: United States v. Kozak, 438 F.2d 1062, 1062 (3d Cir.1971) (where the court held that the government need "only prove ... that defendants believed the [informer] would communicate such information, and that the force took place with an effort to obstruct, delay or prevent such communication.").

Fifth Circuit: United States v. San Martin, 515 F.2d 317, 320 (5th Cir.1975) (defendant had to threaten with the purpose of preventing a communication).

ing the word *willfully* in other statutes to require knowledge of the law,[25] under § 1510 a defendant does not have to know that his actions are criminal.[26]

Library References:

C.J.S. Obstructing Justice or Governmental Administration § 2–4, 9, 16–17, 20–21.

West's Key No. Digests, Obstructing Justice ⊜1.

§ 19.14   Obstruction of Criminal Investigations: § 1510—Inchoate Liability

A. SOLICITATION

Solicitation is not mentioned in this statute, but the statute does use the term "endeavor." The Ninth Circuit holds that endeavor should "be read broadly [to] encompass acts that are not sufficient to constitute an attempt."[1] This conclusion that endeavor covers conduct not yet amounting to attempt suggests that it may include the conduct usually called solicitation. This interpretation is consistent with those of §§ 1503 and 1505.[2]

B. ATTEMPT

The term "endeavor" does provide for attempt liability. Many courts hold that "it is not necessary to show that a defendant actually obstructed justice or prevented a person from communicating to law enforcement officers—the statutory focus is on endeavor."[3]

The Ninth Circuit has distinguished endeavors to bribe from endeavors to obstruct communication and held that the statute prohibits "endeavors to obstruct communication through the use of bribery."[4] The crime is not attempting to bribe an investigator; the crime is attempting to obstruct justice by using bribery. Hence, preparations for bribery are not sufficient for liability under § 1510; actual bribery is required.

---

25. *See, e.g.*, Ratzlaf v. United States, 510 U.S. 135, 114 S.Ct. 655, 126 L.Ed.2d 615 (1994) (construing § 5324); Cheek v. United States, 498 U.S. 192, 111 S.Ct. 604, 112 L.Ed.2d 617 (1991) (construing tax fraud laws). *See* §§ 23.8 *infra*.

26. United States v. Qaoud, 777 F.2d 1105, 1113 (6th Cir.1985) (defendant does not have to be aware of a violation of a federal criminal law before he can be convicted of obstruction).

§ 19.14

1. United States v. Stafford, 831 F.2d 1479 (9th Cir.1987).

2. *See* §§ 19.4 and 19.9 *supra*.

3. *Ninth Circuit:* United States v. Murray, 751 F.2d 1528, 1534 (9th Cir.1985).

See also

Third Circuit: United States v. Kozak, 438 F.2d 1062 (3d Cir.1971).

Ninth Circuit: United States v. Zemek, 634 F.2d 1159 (9th Cir.1980).

4. United States v. Stafford, 831 F.2d 1479, 1482 (9th Cir.1987).

C. CONSPIRACY

Section 1510 makes no reference to conspiracy, but liability is available under the general conspiracy statute, § 371.[5]

Library References:

C.J.S. Obstructing Justice or Governmental Administration § 7, 10.
West's Key No. Digests, Obstructing Justice ⊕9.

§ 19.15 Obstruction of Criminal Investigations: § 1510—Accomplice Liability

This statute does not provide liability for accomplices. The general accomplice liability statute, § 2, can be used to apply this crime to accomplices.[1]

There is an interesting wrinkle in § 1510's application to accomplices. Some courts hold that communications between accomplices are not subject to § 1510.[2] The Fifth Circuit ruled in United States v. Cameron that for a violation of § 1510 there must be at least three classes of people: the investigator, the third party who has information, and the party who endeavors to prevent the communication of that information. The defendants/accomplices had agreed that one of the defendants would not say anything to an investigator. The court held this was no crime under § 1510 because "the prosecution charged ... the somewhat startling proposition that Wright and Cameron imposed silence on Wright by misrepresentation.... Under logic nor law could Wright have been his own victim."[3] The Ninth Circuit reiterated the Cameron exception in a later case, stating that "section 1510 does not apply to communications between accomplices to a scheme to obstruct a criminal investigation."[4] However, the Ninth Circuit has limited Cameron by holding that accomplices involved in bribery schemes are outside the exception and so are liable under § 1510. The rationale for this exception to the exception is that "the victim of a scheme to use bribery to prevent communication with a federal investigator would always be an accomplice, because in return for the bribe ... the victim would voluntarily refrain from communicating with authorities."[5] They declined to adopt such a "stultifying interpretation."[6]

---

5. *See*

Second Circuit: United States v. Coiro, 922 F.2d 1008 (2d Cir.1991).

Fifth Circuit: United States v. Nelson, 733 F.2d 364 (5th Cir.1984).

Sixth Circuit: United States v. Lippman, 492 F.2d 314 (6th Cir.1974).

Ninth Circuit: United States v. Lester, 749 F.2d 1288 (9th Cir.1984).

§ 19.15

1. *See*

Fifth Circuit: United States v. Koehler, 544 F.2d 1326 (5th Cir.1977).

Ninth Circuit: United States v.Zemek, 634 F.2d 1159 (9th Cir.1980).

2. *Fifth Circuit:* United States v. Cameron, 460 F.2d 1394 (5th Cir.1972); United States v. Howard, 483 F.2d 229 (5th Cir.1973).

Ninth Circuit: United States v. Lester, 749 F.2d 1288 (9th Cir.1984).

Court of Military Appeals: United States v. Chasteen, 17 M.J. 800 (AFCMR 1983), *modified*, 24 M.J. 62 (CMA 1987).

3. United States v. Cameron, 460 F.2d 1394, 1402 (5th Cir.1972).

4. United States v. Lester, 749 F.2d 1288 (9th Cir.1984).

5. *Id.* at 1299.

6. *Id.*

Two other circuits have rejected the *Cameron* exception. The Seventh Circuit decided a case in which one accomplice encouraged the other to misrepresent their relationship to the investigators, similar to *Cameron*, and held that § 1510 can be applied to communication between accomplices.[7] And the Second Circuit rejected outright the conclusion that communications between accomplices are not subject to § 1510 because it disagreed with the *Cameron* court's reading of the legislative history of § 1510.[8]

Library References:

C.J.S. Obstructing Justice or Governmental Administration § 7, 10.
West's Key No. Digests, Obstructing Justice ⊜9.

§ 19.16   Obstruction of Criminal Investigations: § 1510—Constitutionality

A. VAGUENESS

The Sixth Circuit has rejected a vagueness challenge, holding that subsection 1510(a) meets the standard of giving "sufficiently definite warning as to the proscribed conduct when measured by common understanding and practices."[1]

B. OVERBREADTH

One defendant asserted that the statute was overly broad because it "does not require an actual investigation already have been commenced and that it attempts to include any information regarding any criminal violation."[2] The court responded that the statute as applied to the defendant was not unconstitutional, and did not analyze the question further.[3]

§ 19.17   Tampering with a Witness, Victim, or an Informant: § 1512—In General

Section 1512 generally prohibits tampering with victims, witnesses and informants. The statute reaches only "specifically enumerated" types of tampering.[1] The types of tampering are:

7. United States v. Gorny, 732 F.2d 597 (7th Cir.1984); United States v. Doe, 867 F.2d 986 (7th Cir.1989).

8. United States v. Coiro, 922 F.2d 1008, 1013–14 (2d Cir.1991).

§ 19.16

1. United States v. Lippman, 492 F.2d 314, 316 (6th Cir.1974).

2. *Id.* at 317.

3. *Id.* The conduct found sufficient by the court was that the defendant was an attorney who bribed a prisoner so that he would not inform on one of the attorney's clients.

§ 19.17

1. *Fifth Circuit:* United States v. Shively, 927 F.2d 804, 811 (5th Cir.1991).

See also

Second Circuit: United States v. King, 762 F.2d 232 (2d Cir.1985).

— killing or attempting to kill,[2]

— using intimidation, force or corrupt coercion,[3] and

— harassing[4]

to prevent a person from communicating with a law enforcement officer or to affect the integrity of evidence presented at a proceeding. Section 1512's role in the VWPA is to increase protection for victims and witnesses by providing a "lower threshold of criminal activity" than § 1503 because § 1512 prohibits tampering by intimidation and harassment as well as by force and threats.[5]

The range of defendants includes drug dealers,[6] police officers,[7] and a governor.[8] Corporations have also been convicted under § 1512.[9]

Library References:

C.J.S. Obstructing Justice or Governmental Administration § 9, 16–17.
West's Key No. Digests, Obstructing Justice ⚖4.

Ninth Circuit: United States v. Lester, 749 F.2d 1288 (9th Cir.1984).

2. Subsection 1512(a).

3. Subsection 1512(b).

4. Subsection 1512(c).

5. United States v. Risken, 788 F.2d 1361,1368 (8th Cir.1986). Section 1512 is also designed to "continue the general scope of the final paragraphs of 18 U.S.C. 1505." S.REP.NO. 97–532 at 19 (1982), *reprinted in* 1982 U.S.C.C.A.N. 2515.

6. *See, e.g.,*

First Circuit: United States v. Dawlett, 787 F.2d 771 (1st Cir.1986).

Second Circuit: United States v. Gonzalez, 922 F.2d 1044 (2d Cir.1991).

Fifth Circuit: United States v. Galvan, 949 F.2d 777 (5th Cir.1991).

Seventh Circuit: United States v. Edwards, 36 F.3d 639 (7th Cir.1994).

7. *See, e.g.,*

Fifth Circuit: United States v. Contreras, 950 F.2d 232 (5th Cir.1991).

Sixth Circuit: United States v. Mullins, 22 F.3d 1365 (6th Cir.1994).

8. *See* United States v. Bordallo, 857 F.2d 519 (9th Cir.1988) (Governor of Guam), *amended on reh'g*, 872 F.2d 334 (9th Cir.1989).

9. In United States v. Conneaut Indus., 852 F.Supp. 116 (D.R.I.1994), a corporation was found guilty of violating § 1512 when the office manager corruptly persuaded an employee to remove papers that would be used in official proceedings. The court found the corporation guilty be reasoning that, "[i]nstructions to an employee regarding the disposition of company papers is fully within the set of duties owed by an office manager to an employer. An employee is acting within the scope of his employment 'when he is doing something in furtherance of the duties he owes to his employer and where the employer is, or could be, exercising some control ... over the employee's activities.' " *Id.* at 124.

§ 19.18 Tampering with a Witness, Victim, or an Informant: § 1512—Elements

The three subsections of this statute include numerous elements. An overview is provided by the diagrams below, then the elements are discussed in detail.

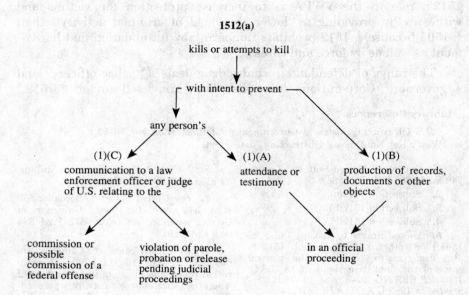

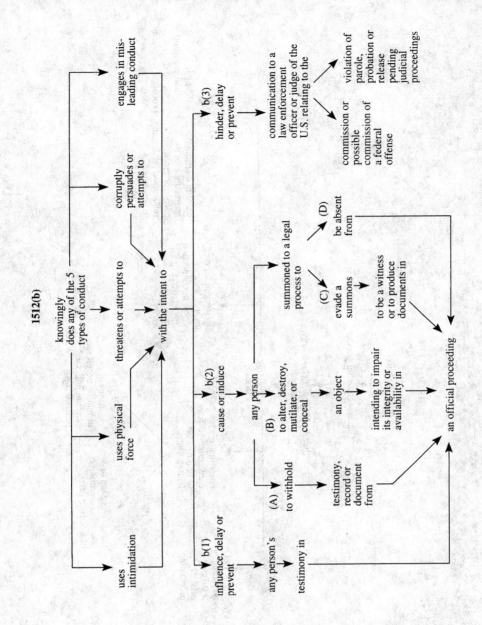

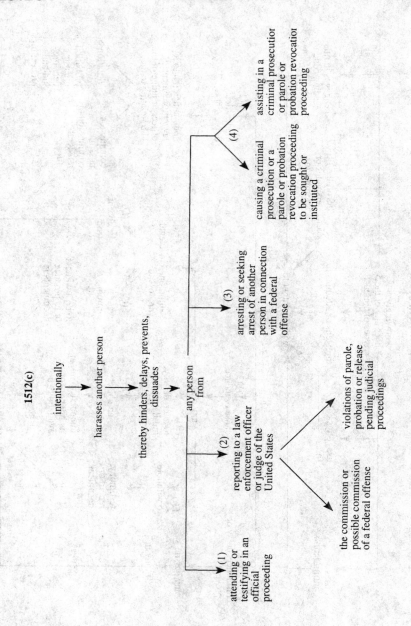

A. INTIMIDATION AND THREATS

This element appears in only one subsection, 1512(b). A threat is an "expression of an intention to do harm. It may be communicated by word or by gesture or by a combination of words and gestures."[1] The

§ 19.18   208, 211 (2d Cir.1992).
1. United States v. Johnson, 968 F.2d

government does not have to prove that the defendant intended to carry out the threat or that the target is actually frightened by the threats; rather, the government must prove only that the defendant's threats "created a reasonable likelihood that the person would be in fear of harm."[2]

B. OFFICIAL PROCEEDING

The term "official proceeding," which appears in parts of all three subsections, includes proceedings before United States courts and grand juries, Congress, and federal agencies.[3]

If a court is involved, the statute states it must be a "court of the United States,"[4] and one court has limited those to article III courts.[5] Thus a military court hearing did not qualify as an "official proceeding."[6] The rationale for this limit is that § 1503, the predecessor to § 1512, has been limited to article III courts.[7] Another rationale is that the statutory definition of official proceeding "include[s] proceedings other than proceedings before a 'court of the United States'" by listing magistrates and bankruptcy judges. This is "a strong indication that Congress was well aware of the traditional interpretation given to this term and intended the term 'court of the United States' to refer to a court established under article III of the Constitution."[8]

Federal grand jury proceedings,[9] Agency for International Development Office of the Inspector General investigations,[10] and DEA investigations[11] have all been considered official proceedings under § 1512. The Fifth Circuit has held that a state civil suit is not an official proceeding

2. *Id.* at 211.

3. The definition for proceeding in § 1512 is found in § 1515, which states: "As used in sections 1512 and 1513 of this title and in this section—(1) the term 'official proceeding' means—(A) a proceeding before a judge or court of the United States, a United States magistrate, a bankruptcy judge, or a Federal grand jury: (B) a proceeding before the Congress: or (C) a proceeding before a Federal Government agency which is authorized by law...."

4. Section 1512(1)(A).

5. *See*

Fourth Circuit: United States v. Ford, 641 F.Supp. 704 (D.S.C.1986) (military court hearing is not an official proceeding under § 1515(a)(A)(1) because the court was created under Article I and because of the "traditional separate existence of military ... courts and the fact that Congress has provided a uniform code of military justice to govern procedures before military courts...."). *Id.* at 706.

See also

D.C. Circuit: United States v. Allen, 729 F.Supp. 120, 121 (D.D.C.1989) (court refers to *Ford* in holding that a D.C. Superior Court hearing is not an official proceeding as defined in § 1515(a)(1)(A)).

6. United States v. Ford, 641 F.Supp. 704 (D.S.C.1986).

7. *Id.*

8. *Id.* at 705.

9. *See*

D.C. Circuit: United States v. Kelley, 36 F.3d 1118 (D.C.Cir.1994).

First Circuit: United States v. Conneaut Indus., 852 F.Supp. 116 (D.R.I.1994).

Eighth Circuit: United States v. Risken, 788 F.2d 1361 (8th Cir.1986).

10. United States v. Kelley, 36 F.3d 1118 (D.C.Cir.1994).

11. *Second Circuit:* United States v. Gonzalez, 922 F.2d 1044 (2d Cir.1991).

Seventh Circuit: United States v. Edwards, 36 F.3d 639 (7th Cir.1994).

under § 1512.[12]

Most of the subsections in § 1512 require an "official proceeding," but several subsections do not.[13] One subsection which does not expressly require an "official proceeding" is 1512(a)(1)(C), which prohibits killing or attempting to kill to prevent communication with a law enforcement officer. Even without this language, in United States v. Gonzalez,[14] the defendant argued that his conviction was wrong because a narcotics investigation does not meet the requirements of an "official proceeding." His theory was that although there is no mention of an official proceeding in subsection 1512(a)(1)(C), the term "official proceeding" appears in subsection 1512(h) which determines venue for the entire statute. Thus subsection 1512(a)(1)(C) is implicitly limited to official proceedings. The court apparently accepted the defendant's argument, but stated that "[i]n enacting section 1512(h), Congress surely did not aim to narrow the reach of the Victim and Witness Protection Act.... As a consequence, in construing section 1512(h) in conjunction with subsection 1512(a)(1)(C), we read the term 'official proceeding' broadly in order to effect Congress' purpose in passing it."[15] Thus, an official proceeding may be required for subsection 1512(a)(1)(C) through the venue provision, but the narcotics investigation satisfied the requirement. The *Gonzalez* approach of implying an official proceeding element may apply as well to the other subsections without the "official proceeding" term.

Although the obstructed information must have been intended for an official proceeding, the statute provides that no official proceeding needs to be pending or about to be instituted for a defendant to be convicted of violating § 1512.[16] Despite this express language, defendants often argue that a proceeding must be pending.[17] In general courts reject this argument.[18] For instance, the Seventh Circuit held that "the

---

12. United States v. Shively, 927 F.2d 804, 811 (5th Cir.1991) ("[A]n intent to influence testimony in a state civil suit is clearly not within the ambit of this statute.")

13. The ones that do not are 1512(a)(1)(C), (b)(3) and (c)(2)(3)(4).

14. United States v. Gonzalez, 922 F.2d 1044 (2d Cir.1991).

15. *Id.* at 1055.

16. 18 U.S.C. § 1512(e)(1). The Senate committee felt that this increased the scope of the section by expanding the "galaxy of witnesses and victims the protections of its language is meant to embrace." S.REP.NO. 97–532, at 9 (1982), *reprinted in* 1982 U.S.C.C.A.N. 2515.

17. *See*

First Circuit: United States v. Conneaut Indus., 852 F.Supp. 116 (D.R.I. 1994)(court reiterated the statute's provision that "an official proceeding need not be pending or about to be instituted at the time of the offense.").

Second Circuit: United States v. Romero, 54 F.3d 56 (2d Cir.1995) (court rejected defendant's argument that the government must demonstrate some form of investigation).

Sixth Circuit: United States v. Scaife, 749 F.2d 338 (6th Cir.1984)(court stated that defendant ignored the plain language of the statute).

18. *D.C. Circuit:* United States v. Kelley, 36 F.3d 1118 (D.C.Cir.1994) (§ 1512 does not require that a grand jury proceeding be pending or be about to be instituted).

See also

First Circuit: United States v. Conneaut Indus., 852 F.Supp. 116 (D.R.I.1994) (an official proceeding or investigation need not be pending or about to be instituted at the time of the offense).

Second Circuit: United States v. Romero, 54 F.3d 56 (2d Cir.1995) (for

presence of an investigation or judicial proceeding is immaterial as long as there is evidence that the defendant believed that a person might furnish information and that he killed that person in order to prevent such disclosure."[19] On the other hand, the Fifth Circuit has required at least that a proceeding be scheduled. The defendants tried to intimidate a witness during a civil suit for an insurance claim, and two and one-half years later they were indicted by a grand jury for insurance fraud.[20] The court reversed the defendants' convictions because it concluded it was not sufficient to demonstrate that a witness was prevented from testifying "honestly before any federal grand jury that *might* be convened."[21] The court stated that "[w]ithout at least a circumstantial showing of intent to affect testimony at some particular federal proceeding that is ongoing or is scheduled to be commenced in the future, this statute does not proscribe [the] conduct."[22] Thus, the Fifth Circuit did require a pending proceeding and reversed the conviction because there was no such proceeding.

C. ANY PERSON

The language of all three subsections prohibits tampering with the testimony or evidence of "any person."[23] This language means that the person tampered with need not have witness status.[24] If the person is a

§ 1512(a)(1)(A) and (C), there does not have to be some identifiable government investigative interest in possible federal wrong-doing by a defendant); United States v. Gonzalez, 922 F.2d 1044 (2d Cir.1991) (court noted that Congress explicitly overruled case law requiring that an official proceeding be pending).

Eighth Circuit: United States v. Risken, 788 F.2d 1361 (8th Cir.1986) (§ 1512 is not limited to "pending" official proceedings).

19. United States v. Edwards, 36 F.3d 639, 645 (7th Cir.1994).

20. United States v. Shively, 927 F.2d 804 (5th Cir.1991).

21. *Id.* at 812 (emphasis added).

22. *Id.* at 812–13. The court reached this conclusion after agreeing that the statute explicitly states that there does not have to be a pending proceeding or that one might be instituted. *Id.* at 812. Although the the court in United States v. Conneaut Indus., 852 F.Supp. 116, 125 (D.R.I.1994) agreed that the language of § 1512 and case law interpreting it mean that there does not have to be a pending proceeding, the court applied the Fifth Circuit's holding to a situation where the defendant did not know that a federal proceeding could be commenced in the future. The court explained

that, "The language of the statute does not require that an official proceeding be actually pending; it requires the preservation of the integrity of evidence or its availability for use in an official proceeding; this must encompass an investigation that the involved individual has reasonable cause to believe may be about to commence."

23. The legislative history explains Congress' intentional use of *any person* rather than *witness*: "[T]he term 'witness' is not directly mentioned. A useful consequence of dropping this term and talking in terms of threats to induce action by any person is that the scope of the offense extends to threats that are made, not against the witness himself, but against his family or anyone else of interest to him." S.REP. NO. 97–532, at 8 (1982), *reprinted in* U.S.C.C.A.N. 2515.

24. *Eighth Circuit:* United States v. Risken, 788 F.2d 1361, 1369 (8th Cir.1986).

See also

Third Circuit: United States v. DiSalvo, 631 F.Supp. 1398 (E.D.Pa.1986), *aff'd*, 826 F.2d 1057 (3d Cir.1987) (a person does not have to be the equivalent of a witness, *i.e.* know or be expected to know material facts and expected to testify to them before a pending judicial proceeding).

witness, the testimony does not have to be admissible at trial.[25]

The definition of "person" reached its broadest point when the Second Circuit held that since the statute covers potential witnesses, the "informant does not have to be willing to cooperate"[26] to be covered by § 1512. Therefore, a defendant who threatened a person who was not even going to testify is still guilty of witness tampering under § 1512. The court explained that this result was best because the statute is directed toward the defendant's intention to "frustrate *possible* cooperation."[27]

D. MISLEADING CONDUCT

The term "misleading conduct" appears only in subsection (b) and has been held to apply to conduct which is intended to mislead the witness, not to mislead the government.[28] If a witness knows that the defendant is encouraging him or her to tell a false story and knows the purpose of the story, there can be no misleading conduct.[29] Section 1512 does not criminalize "[u]rging and advising a witness to give false testimony."[30] It criminalizes "using misrepresentation to convince someone to lie."[31] For instance, in United States v. King,[32] the court held that the defendant's conduct was not misleading conduct under subsection 1512(b) because he " 'simply and flat-out tried to persuade [the person]

25. *Eighth Circuit:* United States v. Risken, 788 F.2d 1361, 1368 (8th Cir.1986).

The Seventh Circuit voiced similar reasoning when it held that the testimony of the informant does not have to be useful because the important aspect is that "the defendant believed that a person might furnish information to federal officials...".

Seventh Circuit: United States v. Edwards, 36 F.3d 639, 645 (7th Cir.1994).

26. United States v. Romero, 54 F.3d 56 at 62 (2d Cir.1995).

27. *Id.* (emphasis added).

See also

Fifth Circuit: United States v. Galvan, 949 F.2d 777 (5th Cir.1991)(although the informant was no longer an informant, the statute focuses on the defendant's intent: whether she thought she might be preventing the informant's future communication of information).

28. *See*

Second Circuit: United States v. Rodolitz, 786 F.2d 77 (2d Cir.1986); United States v. King, 762 F.2d 232 (2d Cir.1985).

Ninth Circuit: United States v. Kulczyk, 931 F.2d 542 (9th Cir.1991).

Note that the Ninth Circuit in United States v. Bordallo, 857 F.2d 519, 524 (9th

Cir.1988), *amended on reh'g*, 872 F.2d 334 (9th Cir.1989) characterized the Fifth Circuit decision in United States v. Wesley, 748 F.2d 962 (5th Cir.1984) as holding that a defendant is guilty of "misleading conduct" even though the defendant did *not* mislead the witness. However, Justice White in the Supreme Court's brief treatment of Wesley v. United States, 471 U.S. 1130, 105 S.Ct. 2664, 86 L.Ed.2d 281 (1985) (denying certiorari), stated that the Fifth Circuit "observed that section 1512 did not proscribe 'urging and advising' a witness to testify falsely...." A close reading of *Wesley* reveals that the Ninth Circuit was incorrect because the Fifth Circuit held that urging and advising a witness to give false testimony comes within § 1503, *not section 1512*, which is consistent with the general understanding of § 1512's "misleading conduct."

29. United States v. Rodolitz, 786 F.2d 77, 81 (2d Cir.1986); United States v. King, 762 F.2d 232 (2d Cir.1985).

30. United States v. Kulczyk, 931 F.2d 542, 542 (9th Cir.1991).

31. United States v. Rodolitz, 786 F.2d 77, 82 (2d Cir.1986).

32. United States v. King, 762 F.2d 232 (2d Cir.1985).

to lie' to mislead the government."[33] In essence, § 1512's "misleading conduct" prohibits lying to a witness or informant; it does not criminalize asking the witness or informant to lie.

Although asking a person to lie does not qualify as misleading conduct, asking a person to lie is covered by § 1512's "corruptly persuades" language. *Corruptly persuades* addresses nonmisleading and noncoercive behavior.[34] The Ninth Circuit decided a case in which the defendant argued that because the witnesses that he tampered with knew that the story he wanted them to tell was false, his conduct did not come under § 1512.[35] Although the defendant's conduct occurred before "corruptly persuades" was added to the statute so his conviction was reversed,[36] the court included a footnote stating that the addition of the term "corruptly persuades" means that § 1512 now encompasses cases where the defendant did not mislead the witness.[37] The Second Circuit has also held that "*corruptly persuades*" encompasses conduct that is nonmisleading and nonintimidating.[38]

E. MENS REA

Subsection 1512(a) requires that the defendant *intend* to prevent a person's cooperation with the government.

Subsection 1512(c) has a similar requirement in that the defendant must *intentionally* harass a person. But the language goes further and states that the defendant must intentionally harass the person and "thereby" interfere with the person's cooperation with the government.[39] It is unclear whether the defendant must intentionally harass *and* intend to interfere with cooperation, or whether the defendant must only intend to harass *with the result* of interfering. No reported cases have interpreted this language.

One *mens rea* requirement of subsection 1512(b) is *knowingly* acting

---

33. *Id.* at 237.

34. *See*

Second Circuit: United States v. Masterpol, 940 F.2d 760 (2d Cir.1991).

Ninth Circuit: United States v. Kulczyk, 931 F.2d 542, 545 (9th Cir.1991).

35. United States v. Kulczyk, 931 F.2d 542, 545 (9th Cir.1991).

36. Congress amended § 1512 in 1988 and added the term "corruptly persuades." *See* United States v. Kulczyk, 931 F.2d 542, 542 (9th Cir.1991).

37. *Ninth Circuit:* United States v. Kulczyk, 931 F.2d 542, 545 (9th Cir.1991).

Fourth Circuit: In a Fourth Circuit case, the defendant asserted that acts which do not mislead the witness are not covered by § 1512. The court quoted the statute as it was amended in 1988, but

accepted the defendant's interpretation of § 1512. United States v. Schmidt, 935 F.2d 1440 (4th Cir.1991). The court never addressed the issue of whether "corruptly persuades" encompasses nonmisleading conduct. In United States v. Kenny, 973 F.2d 339, 343 (4th Cir.1992), the Fourth Circuit quotes United States v. Masterpol, 940 F.2d 760 (2d Cir.1991) (discussed infra) which held that "corruptly persuades" addresses nonmisleading and noncoercive conduct, and therefore the Fourth Circuit appears to be agreeing that "corruptly persuades" encompasses nonmisleading conduct.

38. United States v. Masterpol, 940 F.2d 760 (2d Cir.1991). The court also held that "corruptly persuades" enables § 1512 to encompass nonthreatening and nonintimidating conduct as well.

39. 18 U.S.C. 1512(c).

with the *intent* to interfere with official proceedings in various ways.[40] The defendant's actions need not be "likely to affect" the witness' testimony before the grand jury; the Second Circuit recently refused to extend the *Aguilar* § 1503 nexus requirement to subsection 1512(b).[41] The defendant need not intend to carry out the threat; he or she must only intend to frustrate possible cooperation.[42] Although the defendant does not have to plan to carry out a threat, the defendant's conduct must be designed to "arouse fear that the defendant would do harm or cause harm to be done."[43] And whether the threat could influence a witness helps determine the defendant's state of mind.[44]

An alternative *mens rea* phrase in subsection 1512(b) prohibits the defendant from "corruptly persuading" someone to tamper with the system. The "corruptly persuades" language of subsection 1512(b) does not cover a defendant who makes a noncoercive attempt to persuade a co-conspirator to refrain, in accordance with his Fifth Amendment right, from volunteering information to federal investigators.[45]

Subsection 1512(f) provides that a defendant does not have to know of the "federal nature of the proceeding, the judge, the agency, or law enforcement officer."[46] Likewise, the defendant does not have to know that the proceedings were pending or about to be instituted.[47]

The Seventh Circuit has indicated that a defendant should know that a person is an informant.[48] In United States v. Johnson,[49] the defendant argued that the government failed to prove that he knew that the person was an informant. Without explicitly ruling on the validity of this defense, the court reviewed the evidence and decided that it was reasonable to conclude that the defendant did know the person was an informant.[50] Other courts have held that a defendant simply has to

---

40. *Second Circuit:* United States v. Kalevas, 622 F.Supp. 1523 (S.D.N.Y.1985).

Sixth Circuit: United States v. Mullins, 22 F.3d 1365 (6th Cir.1994).

Seventh Circuit: United States v. Johnson, 903 F.2d 1084 (7th Cir.1990); Joiner v. United States, 78 F.3d 586 (7th Cir.1996).

Ninth Circuit: United States v. Davison, 821 F.Supp. 1400 (E.D.Wa.1993), *affirmed*, 30 F.3d 140 (9th Cir.1994).

41. United States v, Gabriel, 125 F.3d 89, 104–05 (2d Cir.1997).

42. United States v. Johnson, 968 F.2d 208 (2d Cir.1992).

43. *Id.*

44. United States v. Maggitt, 784 F.2d 590 (5th Cir.1986) (defendant's state of mind must be proven circumstantially so the threat's ability to cause fear helps determine the defendant's intention).

45. United States v. Farrell, 126 F.3d 484 (3d Cir.1997) (reversing conviction).

46. *See also* United States v. Gonzalez, 922 F.2d 1044, 1054 (2d Cir.1991).

47. *D.C. Circuit:* United States v. Kelley, 36 F.3d 1118, 1128 (D.C.Cir.1994)(since § 1512 "does not require proof that a grand jury proceeding was actually pending or about to be instituted ... [i]t ... follows that § 1512 does not require explicit proof of knowledge ... that such proceedings were pending or about to be instituted.").

48. United States v. Joiner, 903 F.2d 1084, 1088 (7th Cir.1990); United States v. Johnson, 903 F.2d 1084 (7th Cir.1990).

49. 903 F.2d 1084 (7th Cir.1990).

50. United States v. Johnson, 903 F.2d 1084, 1088 (7th Cir.1990). The court noted that the informant's participation had received wide publicity and that the defense attorneys were fully informed of the informant's testimony.

Sixth Circuit: The Sixth Circuit also resolved a case in which the defendant argued that the government had not proven that he knew the victim was an informant.

believe that the person may testify or provide information to federal officials.[51]

F.   THE STATUTORY AFFIRMATIVE DEFENSE: CAUSING TRUTHFUL TESTIMONY

An affirmative defense is provided in subsection 1512(d)[52] because Congress wanted to "avoid the possibility that a judge or other officer of the court would violate this statute by threatening a witness or potential witness with a perjury or false statement prosecution if he testifies falsely."[53] To establish the defense, a defendant must prove "(a) that his conduct was entirely lawful, and (b) that his sole intent was to encourage, induce, or cause the other person to testify truthfully."[54] When the defendant claims that his conduct was entirely lawful, it is up to the government to articulate which federal or state crime the defendant arguably has violated, so that the defendant can better prepare.[55] Unlawful conduct includes felonies and misdemeanors.[56] This defense does not violate due process in shifting the burden of proof.[57]

Library References:

C.J.S. Obstructing Justice or Governmental Administration § 9, 16–17.
West's Key No. Digests, Obstructing Justice ⟜4.

§ 19.19   Tampering with a Witness, Victim, or an Informant: § 1512—Inchoate Liability

A.   SOLICITATION

Solicitation is not mentioned in this statute, and there is no general solicitation statute, so solicitation of § 1512 is not a crime.

There the court stated: "[the defendant] misconstrued the knowledge requirement . . . [it] requires the government to prove knowing use of, or a knowing attempt to use, intimidation or physical force . . . [the defendant's] armed presence at the rendezvous site . . . demonstrate[s] that [he] knowingly attempted to use intimidation or physical force against" the informant.

United States v. Scaife, 749 F.2d 338, 348 (6th Cir.1984).

51. *See*

Second Circuit: United States v. Romero, 54 F.3d 56 (2d Cir.1995).

Fifth Circuit: United States v. Galvan, 949 F.2d 777 (5th Cir.1991).

Seventh Circuit: United States v. Edwards, 36 F.3d 639 (7th Cir.1994).

52. 18 U.S.C. § 1512(d) provides that in a prosecution for an offense under that section, it is an affirmative defense, as to

which the defendant has the burden of proof by a preponderance of the evidence, that the conduct consisted solely of lawful conduct and that the defendant's sole intention was to encourage, induce, or cause the other person to testify truthfully.

53. United States v. Johnson, 968 F.2d 208, 213 (2d Cir.1992) (quoting S.REP. NO. 97–532 at 10 (1982), *reprinted in* 1982 U.S.C.C.A.N. 2515, which states "conceivably, it could also extend to the situation where a person threatens to institute legal action to recover a debt unless another person testifies truthfully.").

54. *Johnson*, 968 F.2d at 211. *See also* United States v. Kalevas, 622 F.Supp. 1523 (S.D.N.Y.1985).

55. United States v. Johnson, 968 F.2d 208, 212 (2d Cir.1992).

56. *Id.*

57. *Id.* at 214.

B. ATTEMPT

Attempt liability is expressly provided in subsections (b) and (c). Subsection (b) forbids actual or attempted witness tampering[1] and subsection (c) forbids attempting to harass someone into not testifying or attending an official proceeding. Under subsection (a), attempt liability also exists but is only implicit.[2] The Second Circuit explained that the crime of subsection (a) is "directed at the 'intent to prevent ... communication' with federal authorities."[3] Thus, although the defendant may not have prevented the communication, he or she still acted with the intention of preventing the communication and is therefore liable.

The Seventh Circuit expressed a similar understanding in a case where the informant was not assisting the government in any way and his cooperation was actually useless. The court held that the important point was that the defendant "believed that a person might furnish information to federal officials and that he killed or attempted to kill that person in order to prevent such disclosures."[4] The court implicitly held that attempt liability is provided for in subsection (a) because if the person tampered with was not really going to furnish information, there could be no actual witness tampering, only attempted witness tampering.

C. CONSPIRACY

Section 1512 makes no reference to conspiracy, but liability is available in conjunction with the general conspiracy statute, § 371.[5]

Library References:

C.J.S. Obstructing Justice or Governmental Administration § 9, 16–17.
West's Key No. Digests, Obstructing Justice ☞4.

§ 19.20   Tampering with a Witness, Victim, or an Informant: § 1512—Accomplice Liability

This statute does not include liability for accomplices. The general accomplice liability statute, § 2, can be used to apply to this crime to accomplices.[1]

§ 19.19

1. United States v. Shively, 927 F.2d 804, 811 (5th Cir.1991). The language of subsection (b) is "[w]hoever knowingly uses intimidation or physical force, ... or attempts to do so...."

2. "[T]he killing of an individual with the intent to frustrate the individual's possible cooperation with federal authorities is implicated by the statute." United States v. Romero, 54 F.3d 56, 62 (2d Cir.1995).

3. Id.

4. United States v. Edwards, 36 F.3d 639, 645 (7th Cir.1994).

5. See

   Fourth Circuit: United States v. Schmidt, 935 F.2d 1440 (4th Cir.1991).

   Fifth Circuit: United States v. Contreras, 950 F.2d 232 (5th Cir.1991).

   Sixth Circuit: United States v. Mullins, 22 F.3d 1365 (6th Cir.1994).

   Seventh Circuit: United States v. Johnson, 903 F.2d 1084 (7th Cir.1990); Joiner v. United States, 78 F.3d 586 (7th Cir.1996).

§ 19.20

1. See

Library References:

C.J.S. Obstructing Justice or Governmental Administration § 9, 16–17.
West's Key No. Digests, Obstructing Justice ⚷4.

§ 19.21   Tampering with a Witness, Victim, or an Informant: § 1512—Constitutionality

No serious challenge to § 1512's constitutionality has been raised. Recently, the Second Circuit concluded that § 1512 did not proscribe lawful or constitutionally protected speech and so was not overbroad under the first amendment; that § 1512 was not void for vagueness; and that the § 1512(d) affirmative defense did not violate due process by shifting the burden of proof.[1] District courts had earlier reached the same conclusions.[2]

Section 1512 also survived a vagueness challenge in United States v. Conneaut Industries.[3] The court held that "[o]n its face, [§ 1512] clearly proscribes specific conduct (corruptly persuading another to tamper with evidence . . .). An innocent destruction of documents is not within the purview of the act; it specifically requires an intentional corrupt act designed to impair the object's integrity or availability as evidence. . . ."[4] Therefore, when the defendant's employee had documents moved "in case anybody asked any questions about it," the statute was not unconstitutionally vague as applied to the defendant's conduct.[5]

§ 19.22   Retaliating Against a Witness, Victim, or an Informant: § 1513—In General

The Fifth Circuit explained § 1513's role in the VWPA by comparing it to § 1512: "[s]ection 1512 applies to offenses against witnesses, victims, or informants which occur *before* the witness testifies or the informant communicates with law enforcement officers; while section 1513 applies to offenses against witnesses or informants *after* they have testified or reported information about the crime to law enforcement officers."[1] Section 1512 is the front-end statute which makes it a crime for a defendant to *prevent* the communication of information, whereas § 1513 is the tail-end statute which makes it a crime for a defendant to *retaliate against* a witness or informant who has already communicated the information.

Second Circuit: United States v. Leris, 1985 WL 169 (S.D.N.Y.1985); United States v. Wilson, 565 F.Supp. 1416 (S.D.N.Y.1983).

Fourth Circuit: United States v. Schmidt, 935 F.2d 1440 (4th Cir.1991); United States v. Ford, 641 F.Supp. 704 (D.S.C.1986).

§ 19.21

1. United States v. Thompson, 76 F.3d 442, 452–53 (2d Cir.1996).

2. United States v. Wilson, 565 F.Supp. 1416, 1431 (S.D.N.Y.1983) (§ 1512 not overbroad in view of first amendment);

United States v. Kalevas, 622 F.Supp. 1523, 1527 (S.D.N.Y.1985) (shifting burden of proof in affirmative defense does not violate due process).

3. 852 F.Supp. 116 (D.R.I.1994).

4. 852 F.Supp. at 126.

5. *Id.* at 126.

§ 19.22

1. United States v. Maggitt, 784 F.2d 590, 600 (5th Cir.1986) (emphasis added).

Section 1513 contains two subsections which criminalize conduct. Subsection 1513(a) makes it a crime to kill or attempt to kill someone with the intent to retaliate against a person for cooperating with the federal government. Subsection 1513(b) makes it a crime to cause physical injury to person or property, or to threaten to cause such injury, with the intent to retaliate against a person for cooperating with the government. These provisions are diagrammed below.

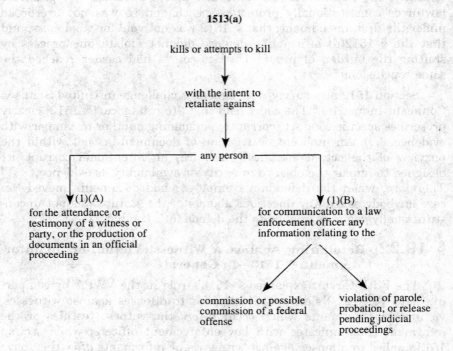

1513(a)

kills or attempts to kill

with the intent to
retaliate against

any person

(1)(A)
for the attendance or
testimony of a witness or
party, or the production of
documents in an official
proceeding

(1)(B)
for communication to a law
enforcement officer any
information relating to the

commission or possible
commission of a federal
offense

violation of parole,
probation, or release
pending judicial
proceedings

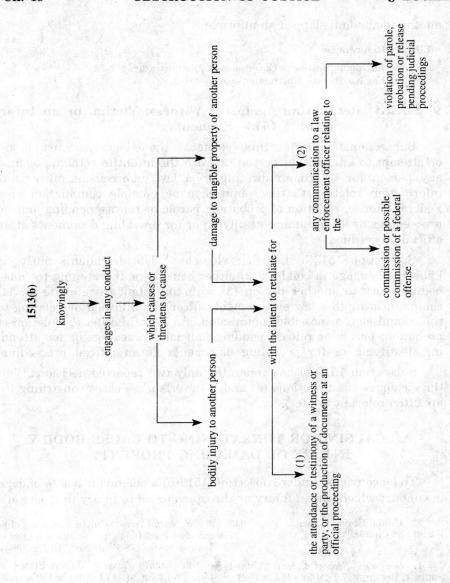

The defendants of § 1513 do not fall into any general patterns; they include motorcycle club members,[2] drug dealers,[3] the mafia[4] and the sister of a convicted criminal.[5] One defendant spit in a witness' face[6] and

2. *First Circuit:* United States v. Weston, 960 F.2d 212 (1st Cir.1992), *abrogated by* Stinson v. United States, 508 U.S. 36, 113 S.Ct. 1913, 123 L.Ed.2d 598 (1993).

3. *Fifth Circuit:* United States v. Galvan, 949 F.2d 777 (5th Cir.1991).

Seventh Circuit: United States v. Torres, 977 F.2d 321 (7th Cir.1992); United States v. Velasquez, 772 F.2d 1348 (7th Cir.1985).

4. United States v. McGuire, 45 F.3d 1177 (8th Cir.1995).

5. United States v. Maggitt, 784 F.2d 590 (5th Cir.1986).

6. United States v. Ferrugia, 604 F.Supp. 668, 671 (E.D.N.Y.1985), *aff'd,* 779 F.2d 36 (2d Cir.1985).

another defendant slapped an informant.[7]

Library References:

C.J.S. Obstructing Justice or Governmental Administration § 2–22.
West's Key No. Digests, Obstructing Justice ⚲1–9.

§ 19.23 Retaliating Against a Witness, Victim, or an Informant: § 1513—Elements

Subsection 1513(a) has three elements: the defendants must (1) kill or attempt to kill another person (2) with the intent to retaliate against any person for (3) communicating to a law enforcement officer any information relating to the commission or possible commission of a Federal offense, violation of probation, parole or release pending judicial proceedings or for attending, testifying or for providing documents at an official proceeding.

Subsection 1513(b) has four elements.[1] The defendants must (1) knowingly engage in conduct (2) either causing or threatening to cause bodily injury to another person (3) with the intent to retaliate for (4) communicating to a law enforcement officer any information relating to the commission or possible commission of a Federal offense, violation of probation, parole or release pending judicial proceedings or for attending, testifying or for providing documents at an official proceeding.

Subsection 1513(a) has generated only two reported decisions,[2] but the elements of subsections (a) and (b) overlap,[3] so cases construing (b) are often relevant to (a).

A. CAUSING OR THREATENING TO CAUSE BODILY INJURY OR DAMAGING PROPERTY

To be convicted under subsection 1513(b) a defendant has to engage in conduct which causes injury or threatens to cause injury to a person's

7. United States v. Garcia–Pupo, 845 F.2d 8 (1st Cir.1988).

§ 19.23

1. *See, e.g., Second Circuit:* United States v. Brown, 937 F.2d 32 (2d Cir.1991), characterizes § 1513 as having two elements: (1) engaging in conduct threatening bodily injury and (2) acting knowingly with the specific intent to retaliate.

Third Circuit: United States v. Cummiskey, 728 F.2d 200 (3d Cir.1984) ("(1) knowing engagement in conduct (2) either causing, or threatening to cause, bodily injury to another person (3) with the intent to retaliate for, inter alia, the attendance or testimony of a witness at an official proceeding.").

Fourth Circuit: United States v. Cofield, 11 F.3d 413 (4th Cir.1993).

Seventh Circuit: United States v. Johnson, 903 F.2d 1084 (7th Cir.1990); Joiner v. United States, 78 F.3d 586 (7th Cir.1996).

2. *Eighth Circuit:* United States v. McGuire, 45 F.3d 1177 (8th Cir.1995) (conviction affirmed for retaliating against an informant under § 1513(a); court provides no discussion of this section).

Eleventh Circuit: United States v. Tapia, 59 F.3d 1137 (11th Cir.1995) (evidence sufficient of intent to retaliate).

3. For example, both subsection 1513(a)(1) and (b)(2) require a law enforcement officer. Other overlapping elements required for (a)(1) and (b) are the commission of a Federal offense and official proceeding.

body or property.[4] The proscribed conduct includes verbal threats,[5] threatening gestures[6] and physically injuring the person[7] or the person's property.[8] The "bodily injury" a person suffers does not have to be severe. The Seventh Circuit has held that "[b]odily injury encompasses practically any adverse impact on the victim, including simple physical pain or an extremely transitory injury."[9] An example of an "extremely transitory injury" is when the defendant spit in a witness' face.[10]

B. COMMUNICATING TO A LAW ENFORCEMENT OFFICER OR TESTIFYING AT AN OFFICIAL PROCEEDING

i. Communicating

Despite the language in the statute which provides "[w]hoever knowingly engages in any conduct … with the intent to retaliate against *any person*," courts have hinted that the person must be an informant or witness.[11] For instance, in United States v. Maggitt[12] the court stated that the government "must establish that the victim had given testimony previously and that the defendant's acts were intended to be in retaliation for prior testimony."[13] The Seventh Circuit also decided a case in which the defendant argued that the government did

---

4. 18 U.S.C. § 1513(b).

5. *See*

First Circuit: United States v. Weston, 960 F.2d 212 (1st Cir.1992) (defendant threatened to grind the witness' face into the dirt).

Second Circuit: United States v. Amor, 24 F.3d 432 (2d Cir.1994) (defendant told co-workers that he would castrate the informant); United States v. Brown, 937 F.2d 32 (2d Cir.1991) (defendant called the informant and said that he would "erase her").

Eleventh Circuit: United States v. McLeod, 53 F.3d 322 (11th Cir.1995) (following the trial, the defendant told the witness that he was going to kill him when he got out of prison).

6. *See*

Third Circuit: United States v. Cummiskey, 728 F.2d 200 (3d Cir.1984)(defendant followed an informant's car and brandished a weapon in front of him).

Eighth Circuit: United States v. McGuire, 45 F.3d 1177 (8th Cir.1995)(defendant held a beer bottle behind a coat, resembling a gun).

7. *See*

Fifth Circuit: United States v. Galvan, 949 F.2d 777 (5th Cir.1991) (defendant shot the informant three times).

Seventh Circuit: United States v. Bolen, 45 F.3d 140 (7th Cir.1995) (defendant gave the victim a bloody nose).

8. *See*

Seventh Circuit: United States v. Torres, 977 F.2d 321 (7th Cir.1992) (defendant intentionally threatened the property and persons of the informants).

Eighth Circuit: United States v. Keller, 808 F.2d 34 (8th Cir.1986) (defendant vandalized the witness' home six times).

9. United States v. Cunningham, 54 F.3d 295, 298 (7th Cir.1995).

10. *See* United States v. Ferrugia, 604 F.Supp. 668 (E.D.N.Y.1985), *aff'd*, 779 F.2d 36 (2d Cir.1985). The court looked at § 1515(a)(5)(E)'s definition of "bodily injury" and explained that this action was "any injury to the body, no matter how temporary."

11. *Fifth Circuit:* United States v. Maggitt 784 F.2d 590, 599 (5th Cir.1986)(government must establish that the victim had given testimony previously and that the defendant's acts were intended to be in retaliation for the prior testimony).

Seventh Circuit: United States v. Cunningham 54 F.3d 295 (7th Cir.1995)(jury must find that each defendant knew of the witness' prior testimony).

12. 784 F.2d 590 (5th Cir.1986).

13. *Id.* at 599.

not prove that he "had a belief" that the person had given testimony.[14] In response to the defendant's claim, the court stated: "[b]y 'had a belief,' the instruction apparently meant to convey that to find guilt the jury must find that each defendant *knew* of [the witness'] prior testimony."[15]

This statement has several implications. A defendant must know that the witness testified, which means that the victim had to be a witness. Therefore, if a defendant mistakenly believes that a person was a witness, but that person was not a witness, then the defendant cannot be convicted under § 1513. To be convicted of retaliating against a witness or informant, the person must have actually been a witness or informant.[16]

ii. Official Proceeding

The language of subsection 1513(b)(1) refers to an official proceeding. The statutory definition of "official proceeding" is "a proceeding before a judge or court of the United States."[17] Courts have no trouble giving the language its plain meaning. The Eleventh Circuit stated that this language clearly indicates that it applies to any "proceeding before a judge or court."[18] Therefore, under § 1513, *official proceeding* includes both federal civil[19] and criminal actions. Section 1513 does not cover any state actions.[20]

iii. Law Enforcement Officer

The officials referred to in § 1513 must be officers or employees of the federal government.[21] An informant's contact with local authorities does not bring him or her within the protection of § 1513.[22]

C. MENS REA

The main *mens rea* for § 1513 is that the defendant *knowingly* engaged in conduct with the *intent to retaliate* against a witness or

---

14. United States v. Cunningham, 54 F.3d 295, 299 (7th Cir.1995).

15. *Id.* (emphasis added)

16. *Eighth Circuit*: United States v. Keller 808 F.2d 34 (8th Cir.1986)(witness who provides information on a non-prosecutable offense still comes within the protection of § 1513). This position has never been addressed directly and it is only the dicta of the opinions which leave this impression.

17. 18 U.S.C. § 1515(a).

18. United States v. McLeod, 53 F.3d 322, 324 (11th Cir.1995).

19. *Second Circuit*: United States v. Markiewicz, 978 F.2d 786, 796 (2d Cir. 1992).

Eleventh Circuit: United States v. McLeod, 53 F.3d 322 (11th Cir.1995).

20. 18 U.S.C. § 1515(a): "(1) the term official proceeding means—(A) a proceeding before a judge or court *of the United States....*" (emphasis added).

21. *See*

Second Circuit: United States v. Brown, 937 F.2d 32 (2d Cir.1991).

Fifth Circuit: United States v. Maggitt, 784 F.2d 590 (5th Cir.1986).

22. United States v. Brown, 937 F.2d 32 (2d Cir.1991).

informant.[23] Courts have not discussed the meaning of knowingly. To prove that the defendant intended to retaliate against a witness or informant, one court has stated that "a defendant must have known about the earlier testimony."[24] Other courts have not made such an explicit statement of the issue, but they have implied that the government must demonstrate the defendant knew about the witness' testimony or the informant's communication.[25] The courts reason that a jury cannot infer an intent to retaliate if the defendant did not know of the informant's or witness' status.[26]

Section 1513 prohibits retaliating against a witness or informant, and if the defendant's method of retaliation is to threaten the person, the government does not have to prove that the defendant intended to carry out the threat.[27] The Seventh Circuit has explained that "[w]hen making a threat one hopes not to have to carry it out; one hopes that the threat itself will be efficacious. Most threats, indeed, are bluffs. But if the bluff . . . is intended to succeed, it ought to be punished."[28]

Library References:

C.J.S. Obstructing Justice or Governmental Administration § 2–4, 9, 16–17, 20–21.
West's Key No. Digests, Obstructing Justice ☞1.

§ 19.24　Retaliating Against a Witness, Victim, or an Informant: § 1513—Inchoate Liability

A.　SOLICITATION

Solicitation is not mentioned in this statute, and there is no general solicitation statute. Therefore, solicitation of § 1513 conduct is not a crime.

B.　ATTEMPT

Liability for attempted retaliation is expressly provided for in subsection 1513(b).[1] Subsection 1513(a) mentions attempted killing with the

---

23.　18 U.S.C. 1513(b). *See Seventh Circuit:* United States v. Bolen, 45 F.3d 140 (7th Cir.1995).

　　Eleventh Circuit: United States v. Tapia, 59 F.3d 1137, 1140–41 (11th Cir.1995) (evidence sufficient of intent to retaliate).

24.　*See* United States v. Cunningham, 54 F.3d 295 (7th Cir.1995).

25.　*See* Joiner v. United States, 78 F.3d 586 (7th Cir.1996); United States v. Johnson, 903 F.2d 1084 (7th Cir.1990). In each of these cases the defendant raised the defense that the government did not prove his knowledge of the witness' or informant's status. The courts never directly addressed whether knowledge is required, but implied that it is by holding that the government can circumstantially prove that

a defendant knew that a person was a witness or informant.

26.　*Second Circuit:* United States v. Brown, 937 F.2d 32 (2d Cir.1991).

　　Seventh Circuit: United States v. Cunningham, 54 F.3d 295 (7th Cir.1995).

27.　United States v. Velasquez, 772 F.2d 1348 (7th Cir.1985).

28.　*Id.* at 1356–57.

§ 19.24

1.　The statute provides, "Whoever knowingly engages in any conduct . . . or attempts to do so. . . ."

　　See also

　　Second Circuit: United States v. Wilson, 565 F.Supp. 1416 (S.D.N.Y.1983).

intent to retaliate, but this is not the same as an attempted retaliation. Since there is no general attempt statute, attempted subsection 1513(a) conduct is not a crime.

C. CONSPIRACY

Section 1513 makes no reference to conspiracy, but liability is available under the general conspiracy statute, § 371.[2]

Library References:

> C.J.S. Obstructing Justice or Governmental Administration § 2–22.
> West's Key No. Digests, Obstructing Justice ⟜1–9.

§ 19.25   Retaliating Against a Witness, Victim, or an Informant: § 1513—Accomplice Liability

This statute does not provide liability for accomplices. The general accomplice liability statute, § 2, can be used to apply this crime to accomplices.[1]

Library References:

> C.J.S. Obstructing Justice or Governmental Administration § 2–22.
> West's Key No. Digests, Obstructing Justice ⟜1–9.

§ 19.26   Retaliating Against a Witness, Victim, or an Informant: § 1513—Constitutionality

Section 1513 has withstood several arguments claiming that the statute's prohibition of threats violates a defendant's right to freedom of speech. The Seventh Circuit rejected this argument by reasoning that "[t]he First Amendment is remotely if at all involved. A threat to break a person's knees or pulverize his automobile as punishment for his having given information to the government is a statement of intention rather than an idea or opinion and is not part of the marketplace of ideas."[1] Similarly, the Eastern District of New York rejected a defen-

---

Third Circuit: United States v. Cummiskey, 728 F.2d 200 (3d Cir.1984) (statute makes attempt to commit the acts an offense).

2. *See, e.g.,*

Second Circuit: United States v. Wardy, 777 F.2d 101 (2d Cir.1985); United States v. Wilson, 565 F.Supp. 1416 (S.D.N.Y.1983).

Third Circuit: United States v. Cummiskey, 728 F.2d 200 (3d Cir.1984).

Seventh Circuit: Joiner v. United States, 78 F.3d 586 (7th Cir.1996); United States v. Johnson, 903 F.2d 1084 (7th Cir. 1990); United States v. Velasquez, 772 F.2d 1348 (7th Cir.1985).

Eighth Circuit: United States v. McGuire, 45 F.3d 1177 (8th Cir.1995).

§ 19.25

1. *See, e.g.,*

Second Circuit: United States v. Wardy, 777 F.2d 101 (2d Cir.1985); United States v. Wilson, 565 F.Supp. 1416 (S.D.N.Y.1983).

Fourth Circuit: United States v. Cofield, 11 F.3d 413 (4th Cir.1993).

§ 19.26

1. *Seventh Circuit:* United States v. Velasquez, 772 F.2d 1348, 1357 (7th Cir. 1985).

Second Circuit: The Southern District Court of New York in United States v. Wilson, 565 F.Supp. 1416 (S.D.N.Y.1983), also dealt with this claim that § 1513 is overbroad and therefore violates First

dant's claim that the statute was facially invalid because his conduct, *i.e.*, spitting in the witness' face and threatening bodily injury at the close of a trial, was "emotional hyperbole."[2] The court ruled that § 1513 was facially valid and that it was for the jury to decide if the defendant's conduct fell within it.

§ 19.27 Obstruction of Criminal Investigations of Health Care Offenses: § 1518—In General

This crime was enacted in 1996, and no prosecutions have been reported yet.

§ 19.28 Bibliography

Adams, Cheryl Anne, *White-Collar Crime: Fourth Survey of Law Substantive Crimes*, 24 AM. CRIM. L. REV. 755 (1987).

Allen, Elizabeth A. and Teresa Klingensmith, *Tenth Survey of White Collar Crime: Obstruction of Justice*, 32 AM. CRIM. L. REV. 525 (1995).

Best, Judah and Virginia White–Mahaffey, *An Analysis of the Victim and Witness Protection Act of 1982*, in CONGRESSIONAL OVERSIGHT INVESTIGATIONS 1984 (PLI Litig. & Admin. Practice Course Handbook Series No. C4–4168, 1984).

DeMarco, Joseph V., Note, *A Funny Thing Happened on the Way to the Courthouse: Mens Rea, Document Destruction, and the Federal Obstruction of Justice Statute*, 67 N.Y.U. L.REV. 570 (1992).

Fitzpatrick, Tracey B. and Stacey L. Parker, *Ninth Survey of White Collar Crime: Obstruction of Justice*, 31 AM. CRIM. L. REV. 749 (1994).

Jeffress, William H., Jr., *The New Federal Witness Tampering Statute*, 22 AM. CRIM. L. REV. 1 (1984).

Pesce, Teresa Ann, Note, *Defining Witness Tampering Under 18 U.S.C. Section 1512*, 86 COLUM. L. REV. 1417 (1986).

Roush, Corey and Rishi Varma, *Eleventh Survey of White Collar Crime: Obstruction of Justice*, 33 AM. CRIM. L. REV. 903 (1996).

Schleck, Peter and Gregory S. Wright, *Eighth Survey of White Collar Crime Substantive Crimes: Interference with the Judicial Process*, 30 AM CRIM. L. REV. 789 (1993).

Varney, Joan E., Note, *The 1982 Victim and Witness Protection Act: The Conflict Between the Second and Fifth Circuits*, 37 SYRACUSE L. REV. 923 (1986).

Amendment because it prohibits "mere attempt at threats." See discussion of § 1512 constitutionality *supra* in § 19.21.

2. United States v. Ferrugia, 604 F.Supp. 668 (E.D.N.Y.1985), *aff'd*, 779 F.2d 36 (2d Cir.1985).

*

CHAPTER 20

PERJURY AND FALSE DECLARATIONS

The material in this chapter has been adapted from SARA SUN BEALE, WILLIAM C. BRYSON, JAMES E. FELMAN, AND MICHAEL ELSTON, GRAND JURY LAW AND PRACTICE (2nd ed. 1997).

Table of Sections

WESTLAW ELECTRONIC RESEARCH

See WESTLAW Electronic Research Guide preceding the Summary of Contents.

---

§ 20.1 Introduction

Federal law contains both a common-law-based perjury statute that traces its ancestry to the Judiciary Act of 1790 and a False Declarations Act of more modern origins. The False Declarations Act was enacted to supplement the perjury statute, not to supplant it.

The federal perjury statute, 18 U.S.C. § 1621 (1994), provides:

§ 1621. Perjury generally

Whoever—

(1) having taken an oath before a competent tribunal, officer, or person, in any case in which a law of the United States authorizes an oath to be administered, that he will testify, declare, depose, or certify truly, or that any written testimony, declaration, deposition, or certificate by him subscribed, is true, willfully and contrary to such oath states or subscribes any material matter which he does not believe to be true; or

(2) in any declaration, certificate, verification, or statement under penalty of perjury as permitted under section 1746 of title 28,

United States Code, willfully subscribes as true any material matter which he does not believe to be true;

is guilty of perjury and shall, except as otherwise expressly provided by law, be fined under this title or imprisoned not more than five years, or both. This section is applicable whether the statement or subscription is made within or without the United States.

The federal false declarations statute, 18 U.S.C. § 1623 (1994), provides:

§ 1623. False declarations before grand jury or court

(a) Whoever under oath (or in any declaration, certificate, verification, or statement under penalty of perjury as permitted under section 1746 of title 28, United States Code) in any proceeding before or ancillary to any court or grand jury of the United States knowingly makes any false material declaration or makes or uses any other information, including any book, paper, document, record, recording, or other material, knowing the same to contain any false material declaration, shall be fined under this title or imprisoned not more than five years, or both.

(b) This section is applicable whether the conduct occurred within or without the United States.

(c) An indictment or information for violation of this section alleging that, in any proceedings before or ancillary to any court or grand jury of the United States, the defendant under oath has knowingly made two or more declarations, which are inconsistent to the degree that one of them is necessarily false, need not specify which declaration is false if—

(1) each declaration was material to the point in question, and

(2) each declaration was made within the period of the statute of limitations for the offense charged under this section.

In any prosecution under this section, the falsity of a declaration set forth in the indictment or information shall be established sufficient for conviction by proof that the defendant while under oath made irreconcilably contradictory declarations material to the point in question in any proceeding before or ancillary to any court or grand jury. It shall be a defense to an indictment or information made pursuant to the first sentence of this subsection that the defendant at the time he made each declaration believed the declaration was true.

(d) Where, in the same continuous court or grand jury proceeding in which a declaration is made, the person making the declaration admits such declaration to be false, such admission shall bar prosecution under this section if, at the time the admission is made, the declaration has not substantially affected the proceeding, or it has not become manifest that such falsity has been or will be exposed.

(e) Proof beyond a reasonable doubt under this section is sufficient for conviction. It shall not be necessary that such proof be made by any particular number of witnesses or by documentary or other type of evidence.

Library References:

C.J.S. Perjury § 2–61.
West's Key No. Digests, Perjury ⊙1–41.

§ 20.2 Common Law Background and Legislative History of Perjury and False Declarations Statutes

Perjury is a notoriously difficult offense to prove.[1] The courts have traditionally required stronger proof in perjury cases than is required in other criminal cases,[2] scrutinized the charges and the evidence more closely on appeal, and been more willing to recognize "technical" defenses in the case of perjury than in the case of other crimes.

The justification commonly given for these restrictions on perjury prosecutions is to avoid making the law of perjury so expansive that it will discourage witnesses from appearing and testifying for fear that they will be exposed to an intolerably high risk of prosecution for perjury if their testimony does not please the prosecutor.[3] A less commonly stated theme, but one that has clearly affected the development of the law of perjury, is the courts' concern that perjury is an offense that is particularly subject to abuse by prosecutors, and one that therefore needs especially close scrutiny both by trial courts and on appeal.

This section explores the common law and statutory antecedents of the current federal perjury and false declarations statutes.

A. COMMON LAW ANTECEDENTS

At common law, perjury was limited to the act of giving a false oath in a judicial proceeding.[4] Under the common-law concept of perjury, the

---

§ 20.2

1. A 1969 Senate Report calculated that for the ten-year period 1956 through 1966, only 52.7% of all federal perjury trials resulted in guilty verdicts, while for federal criminal trials generally during the same period, approximately 78.7% ended in guilty verdicts. *See* S.Rep.No. 91–617, 91st Cong., 1st Sess. 57 (1969).

2. *See, e.g.,*

Third Circuit: *See also* United States v. Martino, 1988 WL 41468 at *3 n. 3 (E.D.Pa. 1988).

Eighth Circuit: Brown v. United States, 245 F.2d 549, 556 (8th Cir.1957) ("To sustain a conviction of perjury it must be shown by clear, convincing and direct evidence to a moral certainty and beyond a reasonable doubt that the defendant com-

mitted wilful and corrupt perjury, and the burden is on the government to prove the essential elements of the crime by substantive evidence excluding every other hypothesis than that of the defendant's guilt").

3. Study of Perjury, reprinted in Report of New York Law Revision Commission, Legis.Doc.No. 60, p. 249 (1935).

4. 4 William S. Blackstone, Commentaries on the Laws of England 137 (1769); 3 Edward Coke, Institutes of the Laws of England 163 (1797). The practice of punishing witnesses for the offense of perjury apparently originated in decisions by the Court of Star Chamber, although that court purported to be relying on legislation from the fifteenth century. See 3 James F. Stephen, History of the Criminal Law of England 241 (1883).

oath had to be willfully and corruptly false, and the testimony given under the oath had to be material to the proceeding in which it was given.[5] For the oath to be "willfully and corruptly" false meant that the testimony had to be given with the intent to deceive and with the belief that the testimony was false.[6] For the testimony to be material meant that it had to be capable of influencing the course of the proceeding in which it was given.[7] It was no defense at common law that the testimony was true; if the witness made the statement believing it to be false or not knowing whether it was true or false, his oath was false and the offense complete. Thus, the witness could be convicted of perjury even if the testimony turned out, contrary to the witness's belief at the time, to be factually accurate.[8] Moreover, because the common-law definition focused on the act of making a false oath, rather than on the act of making a false statement,[9] only a single charge of perjury could be brought as a result of the testimony given under a single oath, regardless of how many different false statements the witness made during his testimony.[10]

B. PRIOR FEDERAL STATUTES

The federal perjury statute[11] traces its origins to the First Congress. In 1790, the Congress included perjury among the relatively small number of offenses that comprised the first federal criminal "code."[12] As originally enacted, the perjury statute did not cover testimony before a grand jury, since it applied only to testimony in suits, matters, controversies, or causes "depending in any of the courts of the United States."[13]

The 1790 perjury statute was amended in 1825 and again in 1873. The 1825 revision broadened the perjury statute to reach all persons who "knowingly and willingly swear or affirm falsely" in any "case, matter, hearing, or other proceeding, when an oath or affirmation shall be required to be taken or administered under or by any law or laws of the United States."[14] This language still did not reach grand jury proceedings, since there was no provision of law that required an oath to be

---

5. 3 EDWARD COKE, INSTITUTES OF THE LAWS OF ENGLAND 167 (1797).

6. *Third Circuit.* United States v. Rose, 215 F.2d 617, 622–623 (3d Cir.1954).

Fifth Circuit: Beckanstin v. United States, 232 F.2d 1, 4 (5th Cir.1956).

7. 4 WILLIAM S. BLACKSTONE, COMMENTARIES ON THE LAWS OF ENGLAND 137 (1769).

8. 3 EDWARD COKE, INSTITUTES OF THE LAWS OF ENGLAND 166 (1797).

9. *See* ROLLIN M. PERKINS, CRIMINAL LAW 516–518 (1982).

10. AMERICAN LAW INSTITUTE, MODEL PENAL CODE AND COMMENTARIES § 241.1, at pp. 96–97.

11. 18 U.S.C. § 1621 (1994).

12. The 1790 code, in striking contrast to the current federal criminal code, contained only 21 substantive offenses. In addition to perjury, the federal code outlawed offenses such as treason, piracy, misprision of felony, counterfeiting, bribery, and murder and larceny on a federal reservation or on the high seas.

13. 1 Stat. 116 (1790). The 1790 statute prohibited the commission of perjury "on his or her oath or affirmation in any suit, controversy, matter or cause depending in any of the courts of the United States, or in any deposition taken pursuant to the laws of the United States."

14. Act of March 3, 1825, § 13, 4 Stat. 118 (1825).

taken by a witness before a grand jury. The offense of perjury was extended by implication to grand jury proceedings in the codification of the perjury statute that appeared in the Revised Statutes of 1873. In that codification, the language of the perjury statute was modified to reach any person who "having taken an oath before a competent tribunal, officer, or person, in any case in which a law of the United States authorizes an oath to be administered ... willfully and contrary to such oath states or subscribes any material matter which he does not believe to be true."[15] Because Congress had authorized the courts to appoint a foreman for each grand jury who would have the power to administer oaths and affirmations to witnesses before the grand jury,[16] the 1873 revision extended the reach of the perjury statute to witnesses before the grand jury.

§ 20.3 The Modern Federal Perjury and False Declarations Statutes

A. PERJURY

The current federal perjury statute[1] (reprinted *supra*, § 20.1) contains almost the same language as the 1873 version.[2] As in 1873, the application of the perjury statute to grand jury proceedings still turns on the statutory authority of the foreman of the grand jury to administer oaths.[3] Moreover, the statute still contains the express requirement, which was inserted for the first time in the 1873 version, that the false sworn statement must be in "a material matter."[4]

Because § 1621 grew from common law roots and has been left largely untouched for so long, the federal courts have continued to apply common-law doctrines in construing it, requiring a special form of corroboration in perjury cases, known as the "two-witness rule,"[5] and occasionally stating that direct evidence, rather than circumstantial evidence, must be offered to prove the falsity of the statement in question.

B. THE FALSE DECLARATIONS ACT

15. Rev.Stat. § 5392 (1873).

16. Act of March 3, 1865, § 1, 13 Stat. 500 (1865).

§ 20.3

1. 18 U.S.C. § 1621 (1994).

2. The only changes of substance are that the current statute expressly applies to statements made outside the United States, while the 1873 version provided that a person convicted of perjury would "thereafter be incapable of giving testimony in any court of the United States" until and unless his conviction for perjury was reversed. Rev.Stat. § 5392 (1873).

3. Fed.R.Crim.P. 6(c).

4. 18 U.S.C. § 1621 (1994).

5. *Supreme Court: See* Weiler v. United States, 323 U.S. 606, 65 S.Ct. 548, 89 L.Ed. 495 (1945).

Second Circuit: United States v. Maultasch, 596 F.2d 19 (2d Cir.1979).

Seventh Circuit: United States v. Chaplin, 25 F.3d 1373, 1377 (7th Cir.1994); United States v. Diggs, 560 F.2d 266 (7th Cir. 1977).

Eleventh Circuit: United States v. Forrest, 639 F.2d 1224, 1226 (5th Cir.1981).

In 1970, as part of the Organized Crime Control Act,[6] Congress enacted the False Declarations Act,[7] which was intended to reach false testimony before both courts and grand juries. The new statute (reprinted *supra*, § 20.1) was not intended to displace the federal perjury statute,[8] but rather to provide an alternative and less restrictive means for prosecuting false testimony.[9] The new statute provided that it was not necessary for the government to prove its case by "any particular number of witnesses or by documentary or other type of evidence."[10] That provision was designed to make clear that the "two-witness rule" and the "direct evidence rule" that were applied to the perjury statute would not be extended to the new Act.[11] In addition, Congress inserted two other features in the False Declarations Act that are commonly found in modern perjury and false statements statutes.

First, the False Declarations Act provided witnesses with a limited right of recantation, a right not traditionally available under the federal perjury statute.[12] Second, the statute provided that the prosecution could prove its case simply by proving that the witness made two inconsistent sworn statements, where the inconsistency in the statements is such that one of them must necessarily be false. Under the new provision, it was not necessary for the government to prove which of the two statements was false.[13]

C. COMPARISON OF THE PERJURY AND FALSE DECLARATIONS STATUTES

The federal perjury and false declarations statutes overlap substantially, but they are not identical. The Supreme Court has identified the three essential elements of the federal perjury under 18 U.S.C. § 1621 as follows: (1) an oath authorized by a law of the United States; (2) taken before a competent tribunal, officer or person, and (3) a false statement willfully made as to facts material to the hearing.[14] The elements of the federal False Declarations Act, 18 U.S.C. § 1623(a), are (1) an oath; (2) a knowing false material declaration; (3) in a proceeding before or ancillary to a court or a grand jury.

6. Organized Crime Control Act of 1970, Pub.L.No. 91–452, tit. IV, § 401(a), 84 Stat. 932. *See*

Second Circuit: United States v. Collins, 272 F.2d 650, 652 (2d Cir.1959).

Ninth Circuit: Radomsky v. United States, 180 F.2d 781 (9th Cir.1950).

7. 18 U.S.C. § 1623 (1994).

8. *Supreme Court:* Dunn v. United States, 442 U.S. 100, 107–111, 99 S.Ct. 2190, 2194–2196, 60 L.Ed.2d 743 (1979).

Second Circuit: United States v. Kahn, 472 F.2d 272, 283 (2d Cir.1973).

9. *See* S.Rep.No. 91–617, 91st Cong., 1st Sess. 57–59, 149 (1969).

10. 18 U.S.C. § 1623(e) (1994).

11. S.Rep.No. 91–617, 91st Cong., 1st Sess. 58–59, 148–149 (1969).

12. 18 U.S.C. § 1623(d). The Supreme Court had construed the federal perjury statute in accordance with the common-law rule, which held that the offense was complete at the time of the false testimony, and that recantation was not available as a defense. United States v. Norris, 300 U.S. 564, 57 S.Ct. 535, 81 L.Ed. 808 (1937).

13. 18 U.S.C. § 1623(c) (1994).

14. *Supreme Court*: United States v. Debrow, 346 U.S. 374, 74 S.Ct. 113, 98 L.Ed. 92 (1953).

Some of the elements of the two statutes are the same for all practical purposes. Both statutes require that the statement in question be sworn, and both require that the statement be material to the proceeding in which it is given. In addition, although the language of the perjury statute does not appear to require that the allegedly perjurious statement actually be false, the Supreme Court has read the statute to require proof of falsity. The False Declarations Act expressly requires proof that the statement is false. Both statutes require that the witness believe the statement is false at the time he makes it.

Despite the large degree of overlap, the differences between the elements of perjury and false declarations are significant. The limited recantation defense that is provided under the False Declarations Act[15] is not available under the perjury statute.[16] The provision of the False Declarations Act that permits proof of an offense by inconsistent sworn statements[17] is likewise not available under the perjury statute. And the False Declarations Act does not require special corroboration, while the perjury statute has been construed to incorporate the common-law "two-witness rule" and "direct evidence" rule. In addition, the perjury statute covers a wider variety of proceedings, while the False Declarations Act is somewhat broader with respect to those proceedings that it reaches.[18]

The perjury statute covers all false statements made after the witness has taken an oath before "a competent tribunal" in a case in which a federal law "authorizes an oath to be administered."[19] The False Declarations Act, however, applies only to sworn false statements "in any proceeding before or ancillary to any court or grand jury of the United States."[20] A proceeding "ancillary to any court or grand jury" has been construed to refer to a deposition, but to exclude sworn statements given in less formal settings.[21]

---

15. 18 U.S.C. § 1623(d) (1994).

16. *Supreme Court*: United States v. Norris, 300 U.S. 564, 57 S.Ct. 535, 81 L.Ed. 808 (1937). For purposes of Section 1621 the courts have uniformly held that recantation is not a defense, although they have recognized that recantation can be relevant to rebut the proof of intent.

Second Circuit: United States v. Kahn, 472 F.2d 272 (2d Cir.1973).

Fourth Circuit: United States v. De Vaughn, 414 F.Supp. 774 (D.Md.), *aff'd*, 556 F.2d 575 (4th Cir.1977).

Ninth Circuit: United States v. Lococo, 450 F.2d 1196 (9th Cir.1971).

17. 18 U.S.C. § 1623(c) (1994).

18. For example, the Eleventh Circuit has applied the False Declarations Act to a situation involving a person who has intentionally caused a witness to make a false statement under oath. The court held that

the responsible party can be convicted as a principal despite the fact that the defendant was neither under oath nor before the court and despite the fact that the third-party witness did not believe he was making a false statement. United States v. Walser, 3 F.3d 380, 387–89 (11th Cir.1993).

19. 18 U.S.C. § 1621(1) (1994).

20. 18 U.S.C. § 1623(a) (1994).

21. *Supreme Court*: Dunn v. United States, 442 U.S. 100, 111, 99 S.Ct. 2190, 2196, 60 L.Ed.2d 743 (1979).

Second Circuit: See also United States v. Kross, 14 F.3d 751, 754 (2d Cir.1994).

Fifth Circuit: United States v. McAfee, 8 F.3d 1010, 1013–14 (5th Cir.1993).

Sixth Circuit: United States v. Tibbs, 600 F.2d 19, 21 (6th Cir.1979).

Eighth Circuit: United States v. Scott, 682 F.2d 695, 698 (8th Cir.1982).

The two statutes also differ in the nature of the tribunal or officer who administers the oath. The perjury statute requires that the oath be taken "before a competent tribunal, officer, or person," while the False Declarations Act requires only that the statement be made "under oath."[22]

This distinction can be significant, since it provides a potential defense to a perjury prosecution that might not be available in a false statements prosecution. In cases involving prosecutions for perjury before legislative committees, for example, the courts have held that the prosecution fails if a quorum of the committee was not present at the time the defendant took the oath and made the false statement.[23] Likewise, on occasion courts have even held that a congressional committee that is questioning a witness for purposes other than to obtain information from him that it does not already possess is not a "competent tribunal" within the meaning of the perjury statute.[24] Although there have been no reported cases in which a grand jury has been held not to be a "competent tribunal" within the meaning of the perjury statute, the language of the statute, as applied in the congressional committee cases, suggests that a witness might have a defense to a perjury charge if there were some defect in the summoning or composition of the grand jury. That defense would be much harder to raise under the false statements statute, since that statute requires only that the witness be "under oath."[25]

One court has relied on the distinction between the two statutes with regard to the oath requirement to hold that the proof necessary to establish that a statement was made under oath is not as exacting under

---

22. *Compare* 18 U.S.C. § 1621(1) (1994) *with* 18 U.S.C. § 1623(a) (1994). A 1976 amendment to both statutes made them applicable to "any declaration, certificate, verification, or statement under penalty of perjury as permitted under section 1746 of title 28, United States Code." 18 U.S.C. § 1621(2); 18 U.S.C. § 1623(a). That amendment extended both statutes to written statements that are signed under a proviso stating that they are made "under penalty of perjury." *See* 28 U.S.C. § 1746 (1994). That amendment, however, had no effect on the application of the statutes to grand jury testimony.

23. *Supreme Court: See* Christoffel v. United States, 338 U.S. 84, 69 S.Ct. 1447, 93 L.Ed. 1826 (1949).

D.C. Circuit: United States v. Reinecke, 524 F.2d 435 (D.C.Cir.1975).

24. *D.C. Circuit: See* United States v. Icardi, 140 F.Supp. 383 (D.D.C.1956); United States v. Cross, 170 F.Supp. 303 (D.D.C. 1959).

The reasoning of these cases has not generally been applied to grand jury proceedings. Because of the grand jury's extremely broad investigative mandate, the courts have held that a grand jury can properly call witnesses even after it has obtained from other sources the information that it expects to obtain from the witnesses.

Second Circuit: United States v. Berardi, 629 F.2d 723, 728 (2d Cir.1980).

Eighth Circuit: United States v. Phillips, 540 F.2d 319, 328 (8th Cir.1976).

Second Circuit: United States v. Carson, 464 F.2d 424, 436 (2d Cir.1972).

25. In one reported case, a defendant argued that his indictment under the False Statements Act, 18 U.S.C. § 1623, could not stand because the grand jury before which he testified was subsequently found to have been unlawfully constituted. The district court rejected that contention. United States v. Caron, 551 F.Supp. 662 (E.D.Va. 1982). The court did not suggest whether the result would have been the same if the defendant had been charged under the perjury statute instead of the False Statements Act.

the False Declarations Act as it is under the perjury statute.[26] That decision, however, appears to make more of a distinction than the language suggests. The decision may be explained by the court's effort to distinguish an earlier perjury case in which a high standard of proof had been imposed for finding that the witness's testimony was given under oath.[27]

Finally, the two statutes differ formally in the level of intent required. The perjury statute requires that the offense be committed "willfully," while the False Declarations Act requires only that the false testimony be given "knowingly." This difference has been noted by the courts, and they have held that willfulness is not an element of a False Declarations Act offense.[28] The difference between the two levels of intent suggests that under the perjury statute, the government must prove that the witness intended to deceive the grand jury, while under the False Declarations Act, the government must prove only that the witness gave false testimony, knowing that it was false. In other words, the perjury statute requires "specific intent to deceive and to violate one's oath."[29]

Library References:

C.J.S. Perjury § 2–3, 5.
West's Key No. Digests, Perjury ⟲2.

§ 20.4 Intentional Falsehood

Both the perjury statute and False Declarations Act require a statement that was false and that the witness knew to be false at the time the statement was made. This requirement is explicit in the False Declarations Act, but not in the perjury statute. Although at common law a witness could be prosecuted for perjury if he believed that his sworn statement was false—even if it later turned out that the statement was actually true—the decisions construing the current federal perjury and false declaration statutes hold that a false statement is an essential element under both statutes.[1]

26. *Eleventh Circuit*: United States v. Molinares, 700 F.2d 647 (11th Cir.1983).

27. *Fifth Circuit*: Smith v. United States, 363 F.2d 143 (5th Cir.1966). The *Smith* case has been criticized as too restrictive.

Ninth Circuit: See also United States v. Arias, 575 F.2d 253, 254–255 (9th Cir.1978).

28. *First Circuit*: United States v. Goguen, 723 F.2d 1012, 1020 (1st Cir.1983).

Second Circuit: See United States v. Fornaro, 894 F.2d 508 (2d Cir.1990).

Third Circuit: United States v. Lardieri, 497 F.2d 317, 319–320 (3d Cir.1974).

Seventh Circuit: United States v. Watson, 623 F.2d 1198, 1207 (7th Cir.1980).

29. *First Circuit*: United States v. Goguen, 723 F.2d 1012, 1020 (1st Cir.1983).

§ 20.4

1. *Supreme Court*: Bronston v. United States, 409 U.S. 352, 360, 93 S.Ct. 595, 601, 34 L.Ed.2d 568 (1973) (18 U.S.C. § 1621); United States v. Debrow, 346 U.S. 374, 376, 74 S.Ct. 113, 114, 98 L.Ed. 92 (1953) (same).

D.C. Circuit: United States v. Dean, 55 F.3d 640, 662 (D.C.Cir.1995) (18 U.S.C. § 1621).

Fourth Circuit: United States v. Hairston, 46 F.3d 361, 375 (18 U.S.C. § 1623).

First Circuit: United States v. Reveron Martinez, 836 F.2d 684, 689 (1st Cir.1988) (18 U.S.C. § 1623).

The courts' insistence that perjury be based only on knowing false-hoods has given rise to a series of restrictive rules governing perjury prosecutions. Most importantly, the courts have required that the allegedly false testimony be shown to be unambiguously false; it is not enough that the testimony is unresponsive or misleading.[2] Even if the witness's testimony is wholly nonresponsive, it is not perjurious as long as it is literally true, even if the witness was purposefully evasive or was intent on misleading the grand jury with the answers he gave.[3]

As a corollary of this principle, the courts have insisted that the questioning that leads to the allegedly perjurious statements must be precise if the prosecution is to succeed. Ambiguity in the questioning is held against the government, and substantial ambiguity ordinarily vitiates the perjury charge.[4] The courts have also criticized the practice of bringing perjury charges based on a witness's responses to leading questions. A perjury charge based on a witness's "yes" or "no" answers to the prosecutor's leading questions poses the risk of manipulation by the prosecutor or lack of attention on the part of the witness.[5]

2. *Supreme Court*: Bronston v. United States, 409 U.S. 352, 93 S.Ct. 595, 34 L.Ed.2d 568 (1973);

First Circuit: United States v. Reveron Martinez, 836 F.2d 684, 689 (1st Cir.1988); United States v. Kehoe, 562 F.2d 65 (1st Cir.1977).

Third Circuit: United States v. Tonelli, 577 F.2d 194, 199–200 (3d Cir.1978).

Fourth Circuit: United States v. Hairston, 46 F.3d 361, 376–77 (4th Cir.1995) (evasive, misleading or confusing answers).

Seventh Circuit: United States v. Chaplin, 25 F.3d 1373, 1377 (7th Cir.1994); United States v. Williams, 536 F.2d 1202 (7th Cir.1976).

3. *D.C. Circuit*: United States v. Dean, 55 F.3d 640, 663 (D.C.Cir.1995).

First Circuit: United States v. Reveron Martinez, 836 F.2d 684, 691 (1st Cir.1988).

Third Circuit: United States v. Tonelli, 577 F.2d 194 (3d Cir.1978).

Fourth Circuit: United States v. Hairston, 46 F.3d 361, 375 (4th Cir.1995).

Fifth Circuit: United States v. Abrams, 568 F.2d 411 (5th Cir.1978).

4. *First Circuit: See also* United States v. Butt, 745 F.Supp. 34 (D.Mass. 1990).

Third Circuit: *See also* United States v. Tonelli, 577 F.2d 194, 197, 199–200 (3d Cir.1978).

Fourth Circuit: United States v. Hairston, 46 F.3d 361, 374 (4th Cir.1995).

Ninth Circuit: United States v. Tobias, 863 F.2d 685 (9th Cir.1988) (witness's understanding of the question is a factual issue for the jury);

Seventh Circuit: See also United States v. Martellano, 675 F.2d 940, 943–945 (7th Cir.1982).

Generally, if the questioning is "fundamentally ambiguous," the court must grant a judgment of acquittal to the defendant as a matter of law. *See* United States v. Bonacorsa, 528 F.2d 1218, 1221 (2d Cir.1976). If the question is merely subject to a possible claim of ambiguity, however, the witness's understanding of the question is considered to be a factual issue for the jury to resolve.

See

Second Circuit: United States v. Ford, 603 F.2d 1043, 1049 (2d Cir.1979); United States v. Alberti, 568 F.2d 617, 618 (2d Cir.1977); United States v. Bonacorsa, 528 F.2d 1218, 1221 (2d Cir.1976); United States v. Wolfson, 437 F.2d 862, 878 (2d Cir.1970); United States v. Diogo, 320 F.2d 898, 907 (2d Cir.1963)

Seventh Circuit: United States v. Martellano, 675 F.2d 940, 942 (7th Cir.1982).

Eighth Circuit: Seymour v. United States, 77 F.2d 577 (8th Cir.1935).

5. *Fifth Circuit:* United States v. Williams, 874 F.2d 968 (5th Cir.1989).

Eighth Circuit: United States v. Boberg, 565 F.2d 1059, 1062–1063 (8th Cir. 1977). *See also* United States v. Vesaas, 586 F.2d 101, 104–105 (8th Cir.1978).

Because of the strict proof requirement imposed on the issue of intentional falsehood, sophisticated witnesses can often minimize the risk of a perjury conviction simply by feigning lack of recollection on critical issues, by avoiding factual assertions in favor of statements of belief, or by answering questions in a very general or unresponsive fashion. Although a false assertion of lack of recollection is still perjurious,[6] it is extremely hard to prove that a witness in fact recalls something that he claims not to recall. Likewise, while a witness can be prosecuted for perjury even if he prefaces every statement by saying, "I believe," or "I am not certain, but I think," a prosecution in those circumstances is much more difficult than when the witness simply makes factual assertions in response to questioning.[7]

Library References:

C.J.S. Perjury § 2–3, 5–8, 21.
West's Key No. Digests, Perjury ⊕1.

§ 20.5 Requirement of Materiality

Both the federal perjury and false declarations statutes expressly require that the false sworn statements be material.[1] The requirement of materiality is not very demanding, particularly as applied to grand jury investigations.[2] All that is meant by the term is that the testimony at issue must be "capable of influencing the tribunal on the issue before it."[3] That is, the testimony is material if a false response could obstruct the investigation, or if a truthful response to the same inquiry could assist the investigation. It is not necessary that the prosecution prove that the investigation was actually impeded by the false testimony; the government need only show that the false testimony had the capacity to influence the course of the investigation.[4] Absent some suggestion of bad

6. *First Circuit:* United States v. Moreno Morales, 815 F.2d 725, 749 (1st Cir. 1987).

Seventh Circuit: United States v. Nicoletti, 310 F.2d 359 (7th Cir.1962).

Ninth Circuit: In re Battaglia, 653 F.2d 419, 421 (9th Cir.1981); United States v. Ponticelli, 622 F.2d 985, 988 (9th Cir.1980); Gebhard v. United States, 422 F.2d 281, 287–288 (9th Cir.1970).

7. *Ninth Circuit*: United States v. Ponticelli, 622 F.2d 985 (9th Cir.1980).

§ 20.5

1. *See* 18 U.S.C. §§ 1621(a), 1623(a) (1994).

2. *First Circuit:* United States v. Pandozzi, 878 F.2d 1526, 1534 (1st Cir.1989); United States v. Finucan, 708 F.2d 838, 848 (1st Cir.1983).

Second Circuit: United States v. Berardi, 629 F.2d 723, 728 (2d Cir.1980).

Third Circuit: United States v. Lardieri, 497 F.2d 317, 318 (3d Cir.1974).

Fourth Circuit: United States v. Paolicelli, 505 F.2d 971, 973 (4th Cir.1974).

Eighth Circuit: United States v. Phillips, 540 F.2d 319, 328 (8th Cir.1976).

3. *First Circuit*: United States v. Nazzaro, 889 F.2d 1158, 1165 (1st Cir.1989); United States v. Scivola, 766 F.2d 37, 44 (1st Cir.1985).

Fifth Circuit: Blackmon v. United States, 108 F.2d 572 (5th Cir.1940).

4. *First Circuit:* United States v. Finucan, 708 F.2d 838, 848 (1st Cir.1983).

Second Circuit: United States v. Regan, 103 F.3d 1072, 1081 (2d Cir.1997); United States v. Berardi, 629 F.2d 723 (2d Cir. 1980); United States v. Birrell, 470 F.2d 113 (2d Cir.1972).

Third Circuit: United States v. Lardieri, 497 F.2d 317 (3d Cir.1974).

*Fifth Circuit:*United States v. Thompson, 637 F.2d 267 (5th Cir.1981); United States v. Giarratano, 622 F.2d 153, 156 (5th

faith on the part of the prosecutors, the courts have almost never found false sworn testimony before a grand jury to fail the test of materiality, in part because of the very broad scope of the grand jury's investigative authority.[5] For that reason, false statements before a grand jury have been held to be material to the grand jury's inquiry even if the grand jury already had obtained the evidence in question from another source.[6] Likewise, the courts have held that the false testimony need not be material to the particular line of inquiry the grand jury was pursuing, but only to some subject that would be a proper line of inquiry if the grand jury sought to pursue it.[7] Moreover, testimony may be material even if it relates to events as to which the statute of limitations has run, since the grand jury may have legitimate reasons to inquire about such events aside from an expectation of returning an indictment charging those events as crimes. With a standard that broad, it is not surprising that the defense of lack of materiality has not often prevailed in perjury cases arising from grand jury testimony.

The courts have encountered more difficulty with questions about how materiality should be proved. In the grand jury context, the most common means of establishing the element of materiality is to call a member of the grand jury or the grand jury stenographer as a witness

Cir.1980); United States v. Makris, 483 F.2d 1082 (5th Cir.1973).

Sixth Circuit: United States v. Swift, 809 F.2d 320, 324 (6th Cir.1987).

Seventh Circuit: United States v. Waldemer, 50 F.3d 1379, 1382 (7th Cir.1995).

Eighth Circuit: United States v. Brown, 666 F.2d 1196 (8th Cir.1981); United States v. Masters, 484 F.2d 1251 (8th Cir.1973).

Ninth Circuit: United States v. Anfield, 539 F.2d 674 (9th Cir.1976); United States v. Lococo, 450 F.2d 1196 (9th Cir.1971).

5. *D.C. Circuit:* United States v. Paxson, 861 F.2d 730, 733 (D.C.Cir.1988); United States v. Moore, 613 F.2d 1029 (D.C.Cir. 1979) ("effect necessary to meet materiality test is relatively slight").

First Circuit: United States v. Nazzaro, 889 F.2d 1158, 1165 (1st Cir.1989); United States v. Moreno Morales, 815 F.2d 725, 747 (1st Cir.1987); United States v. Scivola, 766 F.2d 37, 44 (1st Cir.1985); United States v. Scivola, 766 F.2d 37, 44 (1st Cir. 1985).

Second Circuit: United States v. Stone, 429 F.2d 138, 140 (2d Cir.1970).

Other courts have held particular testimony to be material even if it related only to a subsidiary or collateral issue before the grand jury, rather than the principal subject of the grand jury's investigation. *See, e.g.,*

Fifth Circuit: United States v. Thompson, 637 F.2d 267, 268 n. 2 (5th Cir.1981); United States v. Gremillion, 464 F.2d 901 (5th Cir.1972).

Seventh Circuit: United States v. Wesson, 478 F.2d 1180 (7th Cir.1973).

Ninth Circuit: United States v. Anfield, 539 F.2d 674 (9th Cir.1976); United States v. Tyrone, 451 F.2d 16 (9th Cir.1971).

Eleventh Circuit: United States v. Molinares, 700 F.2d 647, 653 (11th Cir.1983).

6. *See*

Second Circuit: United States v. Carson, 464 F.2d 424, 436 (2d Cir.1972); United States v. Lee, 509 F.2d 645, 646 (2d Cir.1975).

Sixth Circuit: United States v. Richardson, 596 F.2d 157 (6th Cir.1979)

Eighth Circuit: United States v. Williams, 552 F.2d 226, 230 (8th Cir.1977); United States v. Phillips, 540 F.2d 319, 328 (8th Cir.1976).

7. *See*

First Circuit: United States v. Nazzaro, 889 F.2d 1158, 1165 (1st Cir.1989).

Fifth Circuit: United States v. Williams, 993 F.2d 451 (5th Cir.1993); United States v. Giarratano, 622 F.2d 153 (5th Cir.1980); United States v. Cuesta, 597 F.2d 903 (5th Cir.1979).

Seventh Circuit: United States v. Raineri, 670 F.2d 702, 708 (7th Cir.1982).

and to offer the grand jury transcript into evidence.[8] That method has uniformly been held adequate to prove materiality. Other methods have also been approved, including simply calling a member of the grand jury[9] or the prosecutor,[10] or by introducing an indictment that resulted from the proceeding at which the allegedly perjurious testimony was given.[11] The proof of materiality was considered inadequate, however, when the government simply called an investigating agent and a grand jury witness to describe the nature of the grand jury's investigation; the court reasoned in that case that neither person had sufficient knowledge of the course of the grand jury's investigation to provide an adequate basis for the court's ruling on materiality.[12]

At common law, and in most jurisdictions, the issue of materiality has been treated as a question of law to be decided by the court.[13] The Supreme Court held that the issue of materiality in a prosecution for contempt of Congress was a question of law for the court, and in dictum, the Court suggested that the same rule would apply to prosecutions for perjury.[14] Before 1995, the lower federal courts had followed that dictum and uniformly held that the issue of materiality in either a perjury or a false declarations prosecution is an issue of law.[15] These cases are no

8. *See*

D.C. Circuit: United States v. Bridges, 717 F.2d 1444, 1448 (D.C.Cir.1983).

First Circuit: United States v. Nazzaro, 889 F.2d 1158, 1165 (1st Cir.1989); United States v. Pandozzi, 878 F.2d 1526, 1533 (1st Cir.1989).

Second Circuit: United States v. Alu, 246 F.2d 29, 33–34 (2d Cir.1957).

Fifth Circuit: United States v. Damato, 554 F.2d 1371 (5th Cir.1977).

Seventh Circuit: United States v. Picketts, 655 F.2d 837, 840 (7th Cir.1981).

Eighth Circuit: United States v. Ostertag, 671 F.2d 262, 265 (8th Cir.1982).

9. *See*

Fifth Circuit: United States v. Damato, 554 F.2d 1371 (5th Cir.1977); United States v. Parr, 516 F.2d 458 (5th Cir.1975); United States v. Saenz, 511 F.2d 766 (5th Cir. 1975).

10. *See*

Fifth Circuit: United States v. Thompson, 637 F.2d 267, 269 (5th Cir.1981); United States v. Cuesta, 597 F.2d 903 (5th Cir. 1979).

11. *Fifth Circuit: See* United States v. Bell, 623 F.2d 1132, 1135 (5th Cir.1980); United States v. Thompson, 637 F.2d 267, 269 (5th Cir.1981).

12. *Fifth Circuit*: United States v. Cosby, 601 F.2d 754 (5th Cir.1979).

13. *See* STUDY OF PERJURY, *reprinted in* REPORT OF NEW YORK LAW REVISION COMMISSION, Legis Doc. No. 60 (1935).

14. *Supreme Court*: Sinclair v. United States, 279 U.S. 263, 298–299, 49 S.Ct. 268, 273–274, 73 L.Ed. 692 (1929).

15. *See First Circuit*: United States v. Scivola, 766 F.2d 37, 44 (1st Cir.1985); United States v. Kehoe, 562 F.2d 65 (1st Cir.1977).

Second Circuit: United States v. Mulligan, 573 F.2d 775, 779 (2d Cir.1978); United States v. Stone, 429 F.2d 138 (2d Cir. 1970).

Fourth Circuit: United States v. Paolicelli, 505 F.2d 971 (4th Cir.1974).

Fifth Circuit: United States v. Thompson, 637 F.2d 267, 268 (5th Cir.1981); United States v. Dudley, 581 F.2d 1193 (5th Cir.1978).

Seventh Circuit: United States v. Demopoulos, 506 F.2d 1171 (7th Cir.1974); United States v. Wesson, 478 F.2d 1180 (7th Cir.1973).

Eighth Circuit: United States v. Lasater, 535 F.2d 1041 (8th Cir.1976).

Ninth Circuit: United States v. Gordon, 844 F.2d 1397 (9th Cir.1988).

Tenth Circuit: United States v. Vap, 852 F.2d 1249, 1253 (10th Cir.1988).

Eleventh Circuit: United States v. Molinares, 700 F.2d 647, 653 (11th Cir.1983).

longer good law. In *United States v. Gaudin*,[16] the Supreme Court repudiated its earlier dicta. The Court held that for purposes of the federal false statement statute, 18 U.S.C. § 1001, materiality is an element of the offense presenting a mixed question of law and fact that must be submitted to the jury. In *Johnson v. United States*[17] the Supreme Court took the next step, holding that *Gaudin* compels the conclusion that materiality is a jury question in federal perjury cases. Most courts have held, however, that that the rule announced in *Gaudin* does not apply in cases that became final before the date of the Supreme Court's decision in that case.[18]

Absent a proper objection, Gaudin errors may be reviewed only for plain error under Federal Rule of Criminal Procedure 52(b).[19] In a 1997 decision, the Supreme Court rejected the argument that a Gaudin error is "structural," and, therefore, not subject to limited plain-error review.[20] The Court's decision, while limited to the facts of that case, strongly indicates that a Gaudin error will rarely "seriously affect the fairness, integrity or public reputation of judicial proceedings,"[21] which is a requirement that must be met for an appellate court to have the discretion to correct an unpreserved error, unless there is some argument that the statement in question was in fact not material.[22]

The *Gaudin* Court's determination that materiality is a question of fact will have an impact on the burden of proof as well. Although the burden of proof was not at issue in *Gaudin*, the Court noted the issue[23] and stated that the Fifth and Sixth Amendments "require criminal convictions to rest upon a jury determination that the defendant is guilty of every element of the crime with which he is charged, beyond a

---

16. 515 U.S. 506, 115 S.Ct. 2310, 132 L.Ed.2d 444 (1995).

17. 520 U.S. 461, 117 S.Ct. 1544, 1548, 137 L.Ed.2d 718 (1997).

18. Applying the Supreme Court's landmark decision in Teague v. Lane, 489 U.S. 288, 109 S.Ct. 1060, 103 L.Ed.2d 334 (1989), all of the federal courts to consider the issue have concluded that the *Gaudin* decision does not apply to convictions that had become final before the date of the Supreme Court's decision.

Fourth Circuit: United States v. Ismail, 97 F.3d 50, 60 (4th Cir.1996).

Fifth Circuit: United States v. McGuire, 79 F.3d 1396, 1401 (5th Cir.1996); United States v. Holland, 919 F.Supp. 431, 434 (N.D.Ga.1996).

Eighth Circuit: United States v. Baumgardner, 85 F.3d 1305 (8th Cir.1996).

Tenth Circuit: United States v. Wiles, 102 F.3d 1043, 1055 (10th Cir.1996).

Eleventh Circuit: United States v. Swindall, 107 F.3d 831, 836 (11th Cir.1997).

In Johnson v. United States, 520 U.S. 461, 117 S.Ct. 1544, 1549, 137 L.Ed.2d 718 (1997), the Court held that *Gaudin* applies to cases still pending on direct review at the time of the Supreme Court's decision.

19. *Supreme Court:* Johnson v. United States, 520 U.S. 461, 117 S.Ct. 1544, 137 L.Ed.2d 718 (1997).

20. *Supreme Court:* Johnson v. United States, 520 U.S. 461, 117 S.Ct. 1544, 137 L.Ed.2d 718 (1997).

21. *Supreme Court:* United States v. Olano, 507 U.S. 725, 736, 113 S.Ct. 1770, 1779, 123 L.Ed.2d 508 (1993) (quoting United States v. Atkinson, 297 U.S. 157, 160, 56 S.Ct. 391, 392, 80 L.Ed. 555 (1936)).

22. *Supreme Court:* Johnson v. United States, 520 U.S. 461, 117 S.Ct. 1544, 1550, 137 L.Ed.2d 718 (1997).

23. *Supreme Court*: United States v. Gaudin, 515 U.S. 506, 115 S.Ct. 2310, 2313 n. 1, 132 L.Ed.2d 444 (1995).

Seventh Circuit: United States v. Watson, 623 F.2d 1198 (7th Cir.1980).

reasonable doubt."[24]

Library References:

C.J.S. Perjury § 12–13.
West's Key No. Digests, Perjury ⊗—11.

§ 20.6   "Two Witness Rule"

The special requirement of corroboration in perjury cases, generally known as the "two-witness rule," derives from the common-law background; the Supreme Court has characterized the rule as being "deeply rooted in past centuries."[1] In 1926, the Supreme Court noted that the application of the "two-witness rule" in federal and state courts was "well nigh universal."[2] Because the rule was one of long standing and had not been repealed by legislation, the Court concluded that it had been deemed "sound and ... satisfactory in practice,"[3] and without examination of the policies underlying the rule, the Court embraced the rule as an element of all federal perjury prosecutions. In its modern application the "two-witness rule" has been substantially watered down, but the rule is still accepted by the great majority of jurisdictions, either by statute or court decision.[4]

The "two-witness rule" is more the product of history than policy. In attempting to justify the rule, courts have generally invoked the notion that a defendant should not be punished for perjury where the conviction rests entirely upon "an oath against an oath."[5] But that rationale would appear to apply with equal force to other, more serious crimes, yet the rule in other settings is generally that the uncorroborated testimony of a single witness is sufficient to support a conviction.

Although it has been argued that the "two-witness rule" is constitutionally required, that argument has been uniformly rejected.[6] Accordingly, the federal courts have upheld the constitutionality of the False Declarations Act, which expressly rejects the "two-witness rule" for prosecutions brought under that statute.[7]

24. *Supreme Court*: United States v. Gaudin, 515 U.S. 506, 115 S.Ct. 2310, 2313, 132 L.Ed.2d 444 (1995).

§ 20.6

1. *Supreme Court*: Weiler v. United States, 323 U.S. 606, 608–609, 65 S.Ct. 548, 549–550, 89 L.Ed. 495 (1945). See 7 WIGMORE, EVIDENCE § 2040 (1978).

2. *Supreme Court*: Hammer v. United States, 271 U.S. 620, 626, 46 S.Ct. 603, 604, 70 L.Ed. 1118 (1926).

3. *Supreme Court*: Hammer v. United States, 271 U.S. 620, 627, 46 S.Ct. 603, 605, 70 L.Ed. 1118 (1926).

4. The rule has been preserved for purposes of the federal perjury statute as a matter of court decision. Hammer v. United States, 271 U.S. 620, 46 S.Ct. 603, 70 L.Ed. 1118 (1926).

5. *See*

Supreme Court: Weiler v. United States, 323 U.S. 606, 608–609, 65 S.Ct. 548, 550, 89 L.Ed. 495 (1945).

Seventh Circuit: United States v. Diggs, 560 F.2d 266 (7th Cir.1977).

6. *Second Circuit*: United States v. Ruggiero, 472 F.2d 599 (2d Cir.1973).

Seventh Circuit: United States v. Diggs, 560 F.2d 266 (7th Cir.1977); United States v. Isaacs, 493 F.2d 1124 (7th Cir.1974); United States v. Killian, 246 F.2d 77, 82 (7th Cir.1957).

Eighth Circuit: United States v. Koonce, 485 F.2d 374, 376 (8th Cir.1973).

7. *D.C. Circuit*: United States v. Mitchell, 397 F.Supp. 166 (D.D.C.1974), *aff'd* 559 F.2d 31 (D.C.Cir.1976).

Second Circuit: United States v. Andrews, 370 F.Supp. 365 (D.Conn.1974).

In modern perjury prosecutions, the "two-witness rule" does not literally require the direct testimony of two witnesses to support the charge of perjury; it is enough if the prosecution can offer the direct testimony of one witness and independent evidence corroborating that witness's testimony.[8] It is not required that the corroborative evidence be so strong as to be sufficient, standing by itself, to support a conviction.[9] There is some disagreement, however, about how strong the corroborative evidence must be to withstand a directed verdict of acquittal. Some courts have held that the corroborative evidence must be inconsistent with the innocence of the defendant,[10] while others have held that it is enough that the corroborative evidence is substantial and that it tends to confirm the truth of the first witness's testimony in material respects.[11] The difference between these two statements of the standard is difficult to discern, and the difference may be, as several courts have commented, more a matter of semantics than a real distinction in the kind of proof required.[12]

The "two-witness rule" has been held not to apply at perjury prosecutions in which the falsity of the defendant's statements is proved by documentary evidence,[13] particularly when the documentary evidence originates from the defendant himself.[14]

Fifth Circuit: United States v. McGinnis, 344 F.Supp. 89 (S.D.Tex.1972).

Sixth Circuit: United States v. Morelli, 373 F.Supp. 458 (N.D.Ohio 1973).

Seventh Circuit: United States v. Isaacs, 493 F.2d 1124 (7th Cir.1974).

8. *Second Circuit*: United States v. Ford, 603 F.2d 1043 (2d Cir.1979).

Third Circuit: United States v. Gross, 511 F.2d 910 (3d Cir.1975).

Seventh Circuit: United States v. Chaplin, 25 F.3d 1373, 1377 (7th Cir.1994); United States v. Diggs, 560 F.2d 266 (7th Cir. 1977).

Ninth Circuit: United States v. Davis, 548 F.2d 840 (9th Cir.1977).

District of Columbia: Murphy v. United States, 670 A.2d 1361, 1365 (D.C.1996).

9. *See*

Second Circuit: United States v. Weiner, 479 F.2d 923 (2d Cir.1973).

Seventh Circuit: United States v. Diggs, 560 F.2d 266 (7th Cir.1977).

Ninth Circuit: United States v. Davis, 548 F.2d 840 (9th Cir.1977).

10. *Second Circuit:* United States v. Weiner, 479 F.2d 923 (2d Cir.1973).

Fifth Circuit: United States v. Forrest, 639 F.2d 1224 (5th Cir.1981).

Sixth Circuit: United States v. Erhardt, 381 F.2d 173 (6th Cir.1967).

Tenth Circuit: Cargill v. United States, 381 F.2d 849 (10th Cir.1967).

11. *First Circuit*: Brightman v. United States, 386 F.2d 695 (1st Cir.1967).

Ninth Circuit: United States v. Davis, 548 F.2d 840 (9th Cir.1977).

12. *Second Circuit:* United States v. Weiner, 479 F.2d 923, 926 (2d Cir.1973).

Seventh Circuit: United States v. Diggs, 560 F.2d 266 (7th Cir.1977).

13. *See*

Second Circuit: United States v. Brandyberry, 438 F.2d 226 (9th Cir.1971); United States v. Flores–Rodriguez, 237 F.2d 405 (2d Cir.1956).

Fifth Circuit: Stassi v. United States, 401 F.2d 259 (5th Cir.1968), *vacated on other grounds*, 394 U.S. 310, 89 S.Ct. 1163, 22 L.Ed.2d 297 (1969).

Sixth Circuit: United States v. Thompson, 379 F.2d 625 (6th Cir.1967).

Ninth Circuit: Vuckson v. United States, 354 F.2d 918 (9th Cir.1966).

14. *Second Circuit: See* United States v. Weiner, 479 F.2d 923 (2d Cir.1973).

Third Circuit: United States v. Rose, 215 F.2d 617 (3d Cir.1954).

§ 20.7   Inconsistent Sworn Statements

Traditionally, the courts have required the government in perjury cases to prove that a particular statement was false; it was not enough for the government to show that two statements were so irreconcilable that one of them had to be false.[1] That proof requirement caused difficulty in cases in which a witness made inconsistent sworn statements, but in which the state could not establish with certainty which of the two inconsistent statements was false. Thus, while it was clear that the witness had committed perjury (at least assuming that he was fully informed of the facts about which he testified on both occasions), the government could not prosecute him for perjury because of its inability to prove which statement was the false one.[2]

Because of frustration with the state's inability to prosecute for perjury in such cases, Congress adopted remedial legislation, section (c) of the False Declarations Act, 18 U.S.C. § 1623(c), which permits a defendant to be convicted for making inconsistent sworn statements without requiring the government to prove which statement was actually the false one.[3] Section 1623(c) provides that if a defendant has made two or more sworn declarations that are inconsistent "to the degree that one of them is necessarily false," the indictment need not specify which is false if (1) each declaration was material, and (2) each was made within the period of the statute of limitations for violations of Section 1623. The statute then provides that it shall be a defense "that the defendant at the time he made each declaration believed the declaration was true."[4]

Because the federal statute makes the defendant's belief as to the truth or falsehood of the two inconsistent statements an affirmative defense, Section 1623(c) relieves the government not only of the burden of showing which one of the statements is actually false, but also of the burden of proving that the defendant knew that one of them was false.

One special problem posed by Section 1623(c) arises when the witness has been granted immunity after having previously made sworn

---

§ 20.7

1. *Third Circuit: See* United States v. Nessanbaum, 205 F.2d 93 (3d Cir.1953).

2. *See*

Supreme Court: Dunn v. United States, 442 U.S. 100, 107–108, 99 S.Ct. 2190, 2195, 60 L.Ed.2d 743 (1979).

Second Circuit: United States v. Buckner, 118 F.2d 468, 470 (2d Cir.1941) ("it seems strange that in the federal courts an indictment for perjury may not yet be drawn in the alternative and that there may not be a conviction for deliberately making an oath to contradicting statements unless the prosecutor shows which of the statements was false").

3. *See* Dunn v. United States, 442 U.S. 100, 107–108, 99 S.Ct. 2190, 2195, 60 L.Ed.2d 743 (1979); S.Rep.No. 91–617, 91st Cong., 1st Sess., 57–59 (1969) (Senate Report on bill that added Section 1623 to the federal Criminal Code).

4. 18 U.S.C. § 1623(c). *See* United States v. Porter, 994 F.2d 470 (8th Cir. 1993) (conviction under 18 U.S.C. § 1623(c) reversed where statements were not "irreconcilably contradictory").

statements about the subject matter that he or she is to be questioned about. Witnesses in this situation have argued that they cannot constitutionally be compelled to testify, because even if they give truthful testimony under the grant of immunity, they can be prosecuted on the basis of the inconsistency between that testimony and their previous sworn statements.

The courts have uniformly rejected this argument. They have held that the immunity grant is sufficient to displace the witness's Fifth Amendment privilege, because the effect of the immunity grant is to ensure that testimony given under the grant of immunity will not be used in a prosecution against the witness for an offense previously committed.[5] Therefore, while the immunized witness can be prosecuted for perjury committed in the course of his immunized testimony, his immunized testimony cannot be used to prove that a previous sworn statement was false. Because the inconsistent declarations method of proof permits a conviction if the first statement is false and the second is true, the inconsistent declarations method of proof cannot constitutionally be used in the case of an immunized witness. In that setting, if the government seeks to prosecute the immunized witness for perjury, it must prove that the statement given under the grant of immunity is the false one.

Another problem that has arisen in the context of a prosecution under § 1623(c) involves whether the subsection applies only to statements made under oath. Prosecutions under § 1623(a) may be based on false statements made "in any declaration, certificate, verification, or statement under penalty of perjury," but subsection (c) refers only to declarations made under oath. At least one court has held that false-statement prosecutions based on inconsistent declarations must involve statements made under oath. The Ninth Circuit reversed a conviction under § 1623(c) because one of the two inconsistent statements was a witness statement signed by the defendant. Although the statement was signed "under penalty of perjury," there was no evidence that the statement was made "under oath."[6]

Library References:

C.J.S. Perjury § 40.
West's Key No. Digests, Perjury ⟲30.1.

§ 20.8 Recantation

At common law, the offense of perjury was complete as soon as the false sworn statement was made; later recantation of the statement was

5. *See, e.g.:*

Fifth Circuit: In re Grand Jury Proceedings, Greentree, 644 F.2d 348, 350 (5th Cir.1981).

Second Circuit: United States v. Papadakis, 802 F.2d 618, 621 (2d Cir.1986);

Eighth Circuit: United States v. McDougal (In re Grand Jury Subpoena), 97 F.3d 1090, 1094 (8th Cir.1996); In re Grand Jury Appearance of O'Brien, 728 F.2d 1172, 1174 (8th Cir.1984) (per curiam); In re Grand Jury Proceedings, Horak, 625 F.2d 767, 770 (8th Cir.1980).

See also

First Circuit: United States v. Parcels of Land, 903 F.2d 36, 44 (1st Cir.1990).

6. *Ninth Circuit*: United States v. Jaramillo, 69 F.3d 388, 391 (9th Cir.1995).

not a defense to a perjury prosecution in any circumstances.[1] A number of jurisdictions, however, have adopted a "recantation" or "retraction" defense to the offenses of perjury or making false declarations, although the scope of that defense varies from jurisdiction to jurisdiction.

The federal perjury statute, 18 U.S.C. § 1621 (1994), does not expressly incorporate a recantation defense, and the courts have not recognized recantation as a defense or a bar to prosecution for the crime of perjury.[2] The federal courts have recognized, however, that even under the federal perjury statute recantation is relevant to the question of whether the defendant intended to make a willfully false statement, and therefore evidence of recantation is admissible on the issue of intent.[3]

Unlike the federal perjury statute, the federal false declarations statute, 18 U.S.C. § 1623, expressly incorporates a "recantation defense."[4] The defense, however, is a narrow one. By its terms, it applies only when (1) the recantation is made "in the same continuous court or grand jury proceeding" in which the original false declaration was made; (2) the person making the recantation unambiguously admits that his prior statement was false; (3) the false statement has not "substantially affected the proceeding" at the time of the recantation; and (4) it has "not become manifest that the falsity of the original false statement; has been or will be exposed."[5]

Because Section 1623(d) states that recantation "shall bar prosecution" under § 1623 if all the elements of that subsection are satisfied, the courts have regarded the applicability of the recantation provision as a question for the court, not an affirmative defense that is for the jury.[6]

§ 20.8

1. *See*

Supreme Court: United States v. Norris, 300 U.S. 564, 57 S.Ct. 535, 81 L.Ed. 808 (1937).

Fifth Circuit: United States v. Denison, 663 F.2d 611 (5th Cir.1981).

2. *Supreme Court*: United States v. Norris, 300 U.S. 564, 57 S.Ct. 535, 81 L.Ed. 808 (1937).

Second Circuit: United States v. Diorio, 451 F.2d 21 (2d Cir.1971).

Fifth Circuit: United States v. McAfee, 8 F.3d 1010 (5th Cir.1993).

Ninth Circuit: United States v. Lococo, 450 F.2d 1196 (9th Cir.1971).

3. *See*:

Supreme Court: United States v. Norris, 300 U.S. 564, 57 S.Ct. 535, 81 L.Ed. 808 (1937).

Second Circuit: United States v. Kahn, 472 F.2d 272 (2d Cir.1973); United States v. Diorio, 451 F.2d 21 (2d Cir.1971); United States v. Hirsch, 136 F.2d 976 (2d Cir. 1943).

Fourth Circuit: United States v. De-Vaughn, 414 F.Supp. 774 (D.Md.1976), *aff'd* 556 F.2d 575 (4th Cir.1977).

Fifth Circuit: Beckanstin v. United States, 232 F.2d 1 (5th Cir.1956).

Sixth Circuit: United States v. Allen, 131 F.Supp. 323 (E.D.Mich.1955).

Eighth Circuit: Seymour v. United States, 77 F.2d 577 (8th Cir.1935).

Ninth Circuit:United States v. Lococo, 450 F.2d 1196 (9th Cir.1971).

4. 18 U.S.C. § 1623(d) (1994).

5. 18 U.S.C. § 1623(d) (1994).

6. 18 U.S.C. § 1623(d) (1994). *See*

First Circuit: United States v. Goguen, 723 F.2d 1012, 1017 (1st Cir.1983).

Second Circuit: United States v. Fornaro, 894 F.2d 508, 511 (2d Cir.1990); United States v. D'Auria, 672 F.2d 1085, 1091 (2d Cir.1982); United States v. Kahn, 472 F.2d 272, 283 n. 9 (2d Cir.1973); United States v. Tucker, 495 F.Supp. 607 (E.D.N.Y.1980).

The courts have therefore required the recantation issue to be raised in advance of trial and submitted to the court for resolution.[7]

There has not been much litigation over the question of what constitutes the "same continuous court or grand jury proceeding." However, it is clear that that clause does not restrict recantation to proceedings of the court or grand jury occurring on the same day that the false testimony was given. It is apparently enough that the grand jury or court be engaged in the same investigation or trial, and one court has held that the statute is satisfied as long as the same grand jury is still subject to being recalled for further sessions.[8]

The courts have rigorously enforced the statutory requirement that the recantation must constitute an unambiguous admission that the witness's prior testimony was false. For example, mere requests to return to the grand jury to "supplement" or "clarify" previous testimony are not enough to constitute recantation within the meaning of Section 1623(d).[9] Likewise, a defendant's statement to a federal agent that he "might have made a mistake about some of the answers to questions in the grand jury" was held to be too ambiguous to constitute a recantation within the meaning of the statute.[10]

Most of the litigation over the recantation provision in Section 1623 has arisen under the third and fourth elements, *i.e.*, the requirements that the false statement has not "substantially affected the proceeding" and that it "has not become manifest that such falsity has been or will be exposed." The courts have held that in order to invoke the recantation provision, the defendant must show that both of those requirements are satisfied.[11] Those requirements mean that when it becomes clear to

Fifth Circuit: United States v. Denison, 663 F.2d 611, 618 (5th Cir.1981), *aff'd* 508 F.Supp. 659 (M.D.La.1981); United States v. Parr, 516 F.2d 458, 472 (5th Cir.1975).

Sixth Circuit: United States v. Swainson, 548 F.2d 657 (6th Cir.1977).

Ninth Circuit: But see United States v. Tobias, 863 F.2d 685, 688 (9th Cir.1988) (treating recantation as affirmative defense and requiring government to prove inapplicability beyond a reasonable doubt).

7. *See*

Second Circuit: United States v. Tucker, 495 F.Supp. 607 (E.D.N.Y.1980).

Fifth Circuit: United States v. Denison, 663 F.2d 611, 618 (5th Cir.1981).

8. *Third Circuit*: United States v. Crandall, 363 F.Supp. 648 (W.D.Pa.1973), *aff'd*, 493 F.2d 1401 (3d Cir.1974).

9. *See*

First Circuit: United States v. Goguen, 723 F.2d 1012, 1017–18 (1st Cir.1983).

Second Circuit: United States v. D'Auria, 672 F.2d 1085, 1091–92 (2d Cir.1982).

Fifth Circuit: United States v. Vesich, 724 F.2d 451 (5th Cir.1984).

Ninth Circuit: United States v. Tobias, 863 F.2d 685 (9th Cir.1988); United States v. Anfield, 539 F.2d 674 (9th Cir.1976).

10. *First Circuit*: United States v. Goguen, 723 F.2d 1012, 1017–18 (1st Cir.1983).

11. *See*

D.C. Circuit: United States v. Moore, 613 F.2d 1029 (D.C.Cir.1979).

First Circuit: United States v. Scivola, 766 F.2d 37, 45 (1st Cir.1985).

Second Circuit: United States v. Kahn, 472 F.2d 272 (2d Cir.1973); United States v. Fornaro, 894 F.2d 508, 511 (2d Cir.1990).

Fifth Circuit: United States v. Denison, 663 F.2d 611 (5th Cir.1981), *aff'g* 508 F.Supp. 659 (M.D.La.1981); United States v. Scrimgeour, 636 F.2d 1019 (5th Cir.1981)

the witness that the falsity of his testimony has been or is likely to be discovered, the witness ordinarily loses his opportunity to recant.[12] Thus, it does not matter that the witness's false testimony could not affect the grand jury's deliberations because, for example, the prosecutor knew that the witness's testimony was false all along. In that case, there would still be no bar to prosecution for making the false declarations, as long as the witness did not recant before he recognized that his falsehood had been, or was about to be, discovered. Likewise, if the grand jury has acted in reliance on the false testimony, recantation is ineffective, even if the recantation comes before the falsehood of the witness's testimony has become clear.[13]

The courts uniformly have held that the prosecutor has no obligation to advise a witness of his statutory right to recant, even if the prosecutor has a good reason to believe that the witness's testimony is untrue.[14] Likewise, the prosecutor is not required to postpone charging the witness with making a false statement in order to give the witness an opportunity to consider whether to recant.[15] And finally, the courts have held that even if the prosecution is in possession of evidence that indicates that the witness's testimony is false, the prosecutor is not required to reveal that evidence to the witness in order to induce the witness to recant.[16]

The reasoning underlying a limited recantation defense is that the law should encourage the correction of false testimony whenever possible. For that reason, persons who have given false sworn testimony should not be discouraged by the threat of a perjury prosecution from correcting that testimony in good faith. On the other hand, making the recantation defense too broad can have the opposite effect of encouraging perjury. A broad recantation defense would encourage perjurers to give false testimony and then wait to see if the falsehood is discovered. They

---

Sixth Circuit: United States v. Swainson, 548 F.2d 657 (6th Cir.1977).

12. *See*

D.C. Circuit: United States v. Moore, 613 F.2d 1029 (D.C.Cir.1979).

First Circuit: United States v. Scivola, 766 F.2d 37, 45 (1st Cir.1985).

Second Circuit: United States v. Fornaro, 894 F.2d 508, 511 (2d Cir.1990).

Fifth Circuit: United States v. Denison, 663 F.2d 611 (5th Cir.1981).

Sixth Circuit: United States v. Swainson, 548 F.2d 657 (6th Cir.1977).

13. *D.C. Circuit: See* United States v. Krogh, 366 F.Supp. 1255 (D.D.C.1973).

14. *See*

Second Circuit: United States v. D'Auria, 672 F.2d 1085, 1092 (2d Cir.1982); United States v. Camporeale, 515 F.2d 184 (2d Cir.1975); United States v. Del. Toro, 513 F.2d 656, 666 (2d Cir.1975); United

States v. Cuevas, 510 F.2d 848, 851–852 (2d Cir.1975).

Third Circuit: United States v. Crocker, 568 F.2d 1049 (3d Cir.1977); United States v. Lardieri, 506 F.2d 319 (3d Cir.1974).

Fifth Circuit: United States v. Denison, 663 F.2d 611 (5th Cir.1981); United States v. Scrimgeour, 636 F.2d 1019 (5th Cir.1981); United States v. Parr, 516 F.2d 458 (5th Cir.1975).

Ninth Circuit: United States v. Anfield, 539 F.2d 674 (9th Cir.1976); United States v. Doulin, 538 F.2d 466 (2d Cir.1976).

15. *Fifth Circuit: See* United States v. Denison, 663 F.2d 611 (5th Cir.1981).

16. *Second Circuit: See* United States v. Jacobs, 531 F.2d 87, 89 (2d Cir.), *vacated*, 429 U.S. 909, 97 S.Ct. 299, 50 L.Ed.2d 277 (1976); United States v. Camporeale, 515 F.2d 184 (2d Cir.1975); United States v. Del Toro, 513 F.2d 656, 664–65 (2d Cir.1975).

could afford to do so, confident that the law would protect them if they recanted, even after they were confronted with the discovery of their falsehood. For this reason, the New York courts, which initially created a "recantation" defense as a matter of decisional law, have confined that defense to cases in which the defendant recants before it becomes manifest that the falsehood has been or will be discovered—essentially the same standard that is used in the federal false declarations statute and in most of the state statutes that recognize a recantation defense.[17]

Library References:

C.J.S. Perjury § 40.
West's Key No. Digests, Perjury ⊖30.1.

§ 20.9   "Perjury Trap"

Prosecutors are occasionally accused of calling a witness before the grand jury for the sole purpose of trying to set the witness up for a perjury prosecution. These charges are most often raised in one of the following three situations: (1) when a witness is summoned to testify about matters for which he could not be prosecuted because of the statute of limitations or some other legal impediment; (2) when an immunized witness is found to be far more culpable than the prosecutor thought at the time the immunity grant was arranged; and (3) when the prosecutor questions the witness about a meeting or conversation which, unbeknownst to the witness, has been tape-recorded by court-ordered surveillance or consensual monitoring.[1] When perjury prosecutions have been brought as a result of a witness's grand jury testimony in one of these three settings, the claim has been made that the prosecution is the improper product of a "perjury trap."[2] The "perjury trap" claim is not often successful, but there are a few cases, including several from New York, in which the claim has been sustained.[3] Perhaps the leading case in which a court has reversed a perjury conviction on what could be said to be "perjury trap" grounds is *United States v. Brown*,[4] a decision from the Eighth Circuit. In the *Brown* case, a grand jury sitting in Nebraska questioned the defendant about a matter that had occurred in a different district, several years earlier. The court of appeals found that the Nebraska grand jury had no valid basis for investigating that matter, and that the only purpose of calling the defendant as a witness was to

---

17. For a discussion of the state cases, see SARA SUN BEALE, WILLIAM C. BRYSON, MICHAEL ELSTON, AND JAMES FELMAN, GRAND JURY LAW & PRACTICE (2nd ed. 1997).

§ 20.9

1. *See, e.g.,* Brown v. United States, 245 F.2d 549 (8th Cir.1957). *See also* United States v. Williams, 874 F.2d 968, 973 (5th Cir.1989) (arguing that prosecutors brought defendants before grand jury to "trap" them into committing perjury, which could then serve as predicate act in a RICO prosecution).

2. The term was used in the decision of the New York Court of Appeals in People v. Tyler, 46 N.Y.2d 251, 258, 413 N.Y.S.2d 295, 299, 385 N.E.2d 1224, 1228 (1978). The concept of the "perjury trap" is discussed at length in Bennett L. Gershman, *The "Perjury Trap,"* 129 U.PA.L.REV. 624 (1981).

3. *See infra* n. 8.

4. *Eighth Circuit:* Brown v. United States, 245 F.2d 549 (8th Cir.1957).

extract from him testimony that was contrary to the testimony of several other witnesses, so that he could be indicted for perjury.[5] Because "extracting the testimony from defendant had no tendency to support any possible action of the grand jury within its competency,"[6] the court held the testimony immaterial. It therefore reversed the conviction and directed that the indictment be dismissed because of the insufficiency of the evidence.

While the *Brown* court used materiality as the device by which to reverse the conviction, there is little question that the driving force behind the decision was the court's firm conviction that the prosecutor had summoned Brown before the grand jury for the sole purpose of obtaining evidence for a perjury indictment. For that reason, the *Brown* decision has been cited not simply as a ruling on a narrow point of materiality, but as setting limits on the right of the prosecutor to summon witnesses for the sole or principal purpose of developing a basis for a perjury charge.[7]

The *Brown* decision was followed and expanded upon in two New York cases that struck down the use of "perjury traps" against grand jury witnesses. While these decisions sparked a flurry of litigation in the New York courts, the defense they recognized is a fairly narrow one.[8]

The later federal cases have likewise given the "perjury trap" doctrine a narrow construction. Although the courts have on occasion warned that questioning that is done for the purpose of "coaxing a witness into the commission of perjury or contempt" would be an abuse of the grand jury process,[9] the courts have held that if the government shows that the questioning was in some way material to the grand jury's investigation, that is sufficient to overcome "perjury trap" claims.[10] In

5. *Eighth Circuit:* Brown v. United States, 245 F.2d 549, 555 (8th Cir.1957).

6. *Eighth Circuit*: Brown v. United States, 245 F.2d 549, 555 (8th Cir.1957).

7. The analysis employed by the court in Brown v. United States, 245 F.2d 549, 555 (8th Cir.1957), was similar to that used in two contemporaneous federal district court cases involving charges of perjury before congressional committees. In both cases, United States v. Cross, 170 F.Supp. 303, 309 (D.D.C.1959), and United States v. Icardi, 140 F.Supp. 383, 388 (D.D.C.1956), the courts found that the purpose of calling the witnesses before the committees was not to obtain information pertinent to prospective legislation, but to create the foundation for a perjury prosecution. Questioning for that purpose was not material to the proceeding, the courts held, and false answers therefore could not support a prosecution for perjury. *See also* United States v. Chen, 933 F.2d 793, 796 (9th Cir.1991).

8. The leading New York cases are People v. Tyler, 46 N.Y.2d 251, 413 N.Y.S.2d 295, 385 N.E.2d 1224 (1978), and People v. Rao, 73 App.Div.2d 88, 425 N.Y.S.2d 122 (1980). These decisions and subsequent decisions from the New York courts are discussed in SARA SUN BEALE, ET AL. 2 GRAND JURY LAW AND PRACTICE, § 11.11 (2nd ed. 1997).

9. *Ninth Circuit*: Bursey v. United States, 466 F.2d 1059, 1080 n. 10 (9th Cir. 1972).

10. *See*

Second Circuit: United States v. Regan, 103 F.3d 1072, 1079 (2d Cir.1997); Wheel v. Robinson, 34 F.3d 60, 68 (2d Cir.1994).

Sixth Circuit: United States v. Brown, 49 F.3d 1162, 1167 (6th Cir.1995).

Seventh Circuit: United States v. Devitt, 499 F.2d 135, 140 (7th Cir.1974).

Eighth Circuit: LaRocca v. United States, 337 F.2d 39, 42–43 (8th Cir.1964); Masinia v. United States, 296 F.2d 871, 877 (8th Cir.1961).

light of the very broad construction given to the concept of materiality in the context of a grand jury investigation, it is unlikely that under this test many cases will be found in which the "perjury trap" defense will be upheld.[11] Even in a case in which the grand jury has questioned a witness about matters occurring outside the statute of limitations, one court rejected a "perjury trap" claim,[12] relying on the doctrine that questions about matters occurring outside the statute of limitations may be material, in that they may shed light on other matters that could give rise to current criminal liability.[13]

The fact that the prosecutor expects that the witness will perjure himself is not enough to make it improper to call the witness. As long as the questions put to the witness are material to the grand jury's investigation, the courts have held that the prosecutor is entitled to hope that upon taking the oath before the grand jury, the witness will decide to testify truthfully.[14] Most federal courts that have addressed the question have held that as long as the questioning relates to a subject that is material to the grand jury's investigation, it is not even appropriate to look into the matter of the prosecutor's motivation for asking the questions.[15] Using analysis borrowed from the doctrine of entrapment, the courts have held that absent a showing that the prosecutor "solicited or encouraged" the alleged perjury, the witness could not defend on the ground that the prosecutor had employed a "perjury trap."[16]

Federal cases have also rejected the suggestion that a witness must be confronted with evidence in the possession of the prosecutor that is contrary to the witness's testimony.[17] The rationale behind this rule is that otherwise the prosecutor would be forced to disclose his case to a potentially hostile witness, and the witness would be able to shape his testimony to be truthful only to the extent that the testimony is subject to independent verification.

11. *Sixth Circuit*: United States v. Lazaros, 480 F.2d 174, 178–179 (6th Cir.1973).

12. *Seventh Circuit*: United States v. Devitt, 499 F.2d 135, 140 (7th Cir.1974).

13. *First Circuit*: United States v. Nazzaro, 889 F.2d 1158, 1165 (1st Cir. 1989).

Second Circuit: United States v. Cohn, 452 F.2d 881, 883 (2d Cir.1971).

Seventh Circuit: United States v. Nickels, 502 F.2d 1173, 1176 (7th Cir.1974).

14. *First Circuit*: United States v. Chevoor, 526 F.2d 178, 185 (1st Cir.1975).

Fifth Circuit: United States v. Williams, 874 F.2d 968 (5th Cir.1989).

Seventh Circuit: United States v. Nickels, 502 F.2d 1173, 1176 (7th Cir.1974).

Eleventh Circuit: See also Gersten v. Rundle, 833 F.Supp. 906 (S.D.Fla.1993), *affirmed*, 56 F.3d 1389 (11th Cir.1995) (claim that State has indicated that it will prosecute for perjury if plaintiff testifies and State believes that testimony is untrue does not warrant injunctive relief; witness must raise claim after testimony when there is an imminent threat of prosecution).

15. *Sixth Circuit*: United States v. Lazaros, 480 F.2d 174, 177 (6th Cir.1973).

Seventh Circuit: United States v. Nickels, 502 F.2d 1173, 1176 (7th Cir.1974); United States v. Devitt, 499 F.2d 135, 140 (7th Cir.1974).

16. *Eighth Circuit*: United States v. Phillips, 540 F.2d 319, 322 n. 8 (8th Cir. 1976).

17. *Second Circuit*: United States v. Jacobs, 531 F.2d 87, 89 (2d Cir.), *vacated*, 429 U.S. 909, 97 S.Ct. 299, 50 L.Ed.2d 277 (1976); United States v. Camporeale, 515 F.2d 184 (2d Cir.1975); United States v. Del Toro, 513 F.2d 656, 664–665 (2d Cir.1975).

Likewise, the courts have not required the prosecutor to advise a witness that he is committing perjury, even if the prosecutor is convinced that the witness's testimony is false.[18] Nor is the prosecutor required to give repetitive instructions that the witness is required to tell the truth.[19] In sum, even if the prosecutor expects the witness to perjure himself, and even if the prosecutor does nothing to stop the witness from fulfilling that expectation, the witness's subsequent prosecution for perjury is not barred as the product of a "perjury trap" unless the witness can show that the sole reason that the prosecutor called him before the grand jury was to induce him to commit perjury.

Library References:

C.J.S. Perjury § 11, 29–33.
West's Key No. Digests, Perjury ☞15.

§ 20.10   Unit of Prosecution

A problem that arises regularly in the course of perjury prosecutions is how to define the proper unit of prosecution. At common law, because the offense of perjury was regarded as the act of making a false oath,[1] a witness would be guilty of only one offense even though he might make a number of false statements after taking the oath. Because the modern concept of perjury looks to the false statement (rather than the false oath) as the corpus delicti of the offense, a witness who swore only a single oath in a proceeding can make numerous false statements, and thus commit numerous offenses. Nonetheless, it is clear that it is not appropriate to charge and punish a defendant separately for each false statement he makes in the course of a grand jury proceeding. If that were the law, the prosecutor could multiply the available penalties simply by repeating the same question over and over, obtaining the same false answer again and again.[2]

The courts have reached a resolution of this issue that is sensible in theory but difficult to apply in practice. Both state and federal courts have held that a witness can be separately charged and punished for each "separate lie" that he tells. However, the witness cannot be separately punished for giving a false answer to the same question, even

---

18. *Second Circuit:* United States v. Sun Myung Moon, 532 F.Supp. 1360, 1371 (S.D.N.Y.1982).

19. *Second Circuit:* United States v. Winter, 348 F.2d 204, 210 (2d Cir.1965).

§ 20.10

1. *See* § 20.2(A).

2. *See:*

First Circuit: In re Poutre, 602 F.2d 1004, 1006 (1st Cir.1979).

Second Circuit: United States v. Doulin, 538 F.2d 466, 471 (2d Cir.1976).

Third Circuit: United States v. Stanfa, 685 F.2d 85, 88 (3d Cir.1982).

Fifth Circuit: United States v. De La Torre, 634 F.2d 792, 795 (5th Cir.1981).

Sixth Circuit: United States v. Lazaros, 480 F.2d 174, 179 (6th Cir.1973).

Eighth Circuit: United States v. Scott, 682 F.2d 695, 698 (8th Cir.1982); United States v. Feldhacker, 849 F.2d 293, 297 (8th Cir.1988); United States v. Williams, 552 F.2d 226, 228 (8th Cir.1977).

Ninth Circuit: United States v. Tyrone, 451 F.2d 16, 18 (9th Cir.1971); Gebhard v. United States, 422 F.2d 281, 289–290 (9th Cir.1970).

if that question is rephrased several times in slightly different language.[3] The usual formulation of this rule is that a witness can be separately punished for each falsehood that "requires separate factual proof of falsity."[4] While this rule protects defendants against the most transparent form of multiplying counts—simply repeating the same question over and over—it does not provide a very significant degree of protection from multiple charging. Under this test, the prosecution can charge a witness with multiple counts of perjury with respect to the witness's answers to a series of closely related questions. All the prosecution has to do is to add a single new fact to each question in order to provide the basis for charging a separate count of perjury for each question.[5] The witness can then be exposed to a substantial potential penalty, even though his offense, realistically viewed, may be the commission of a single falsehood, drawn out in a number of different stages.

§ 20.11   Bibliography

Aycock, George W., Note, *Nothing But the Truth: A Solution to the Current Inadequacies of the Federal Perjury Statutes*, 28 VAL. U. L. REV. 247 (1993).

Harris, Lisa C., Note, *Perjury Defeats Justice*, 42 WAYNE L. REV. 1755 (1996).

Saad, Angel, *Perjury*, 34 AM. CRIM. L. REV. 857 (1997).

Saks, Jeffrey, Note, *United States v. Gaudin: A Decision With Material Impact*, 64 FORDHAM L. REV. 1157 (1995).

Tiersma, Peter Miejes, *The Language of Perjury: "Literal Truth," Ambiguity, and the False Statement Requirement*, 63 S. CAL. L. REV. 373 (1990).

Underwood, Richard H., *False Witness: A Lawyer's History of the Law of Perjury*, 10 ARIZ. J. INT'L & COMP. L. 215 (1993).

Wydick, Richard C., *The Ethics of Witness Coaching*, 17 CARDOZO L. REV. 1 (1995).

3. *See, e.g.:*
First Circuit: United States v. Doherty, 867 F.2d 47, 69 (1st Cir.1989).
Third Circuit: United States v. Stanfa, 685 F.2d 85, 88 (3d Cir.1982).
Eighth Circuit: United States v. Scott, 682 F.2d 695, 698 (8th Cir.1982).
Ninth Circuit: Gebhard v. United States, 422 F.2d 281, 289–290 (9th Cir.1970).

4. *See, e.g.,*
D.C. Circuit: United States v. Clarridge, 811 F.Supp. 697, 703 (D.D.C.1992).

First Circuit: United States v. Doherty, 867 F.2d 47, 69 (1st Cir.1989).

Eighth Circuit: United States v. Graham, 60 F.3d 463, 467 (8th Cir.1995); United States v. Scott, 682 F.2d 695, 698 (8th Cir.1982).

Eleventh Circuit: London v. United States, 733 F.Supp. 1477, 1479 (S.D.Fla. 1990) *aff'd*, 937 F.2d 619 (11th Cir.1991).

5. *Third Circuit: See* United States v. Stanfa, 685 F.2d 85 (3d Cir.1982).

CHAPTER 21

RACKETEER INFLUENCED AND CORRUPT ORGANIZATIONS (RICO)*

Table of Sections

WESTLAW ELECTRONIC RESEARCH

See WESTLAW Electronic Research Guide preceding the Summary of Contents.

---

§ 21.1　Introduction[1]

Racketeer Influenced and Corrupt Organizations (RICO) is a prosecutor's powerhouse and a civil plaintiff's dream.[2] Passed in 1970 as part of a major crime fighting bill[3], RICO's stated goal is to protect the public from "parties who conduct organizations affecting interstate commerce through a pattern of racketeering activity."[4] According to legislative history a statute like RICO is needed because of the "insulation" crime

---

* The authors gratefully acknowledge the substantial work of V. Lynne Windham on this chapter.

§ 21.1

1.　18 U.S.C. § 1961–1968.

2.　Portions of the "Overview" are reprinted with permission from Bucy & Mar-

shall, *An Overview of RICO*, 51 ALA.LAW. 283–89 (1990).

3.　Organized Crime Control Act of 1970, Title IX, Pub.L.No. 91–452, 84 Stat. 941 (1970).

4.　115 CONG.REC. 9568 (1969), Remarks of Senator McClellan.

chieftains have developed:[5] "Their operating methods, carefully and cleverly evolved during decades of this century, generally are highly effective foils against diligent police efforts to obtain firm evidence that would lead to prosecution and conviction."[6]

One of the unique features of RICO is that it authorizes both criminal and civil claims for a violation of its provisions. Thus, the United States Department of Justice may seek a criminal indictment or file a civil complaint alleging RICO violations.[7] In addition, private parties may file a complaint alleging the same RICO violations. RICO has become renown, in part, because of the stiff sanctions it provides for violations: mandatory forfeiture of proceeds, imprisonment and fines for criminal convictions; treble damages and attorneys fees for civil judgments.

Today, RICO has been applied to a wide range of conduct. Private civil RICO actions have been successful in such areas as health care fraud, white collar crime, even sexual harassment and against abortion protesters.[8] Yet, Department of Justice policy explicitly rejects an "imaginative" approach to using RICO.[9] Prosecutors are directed to limit the use of RICO to the traditional organized crime context. All RICO prosecutions require centralized approval from the Organized Crime and Racketeering Section at the Department of Justice headquarters in Washington, D.C.[10]

With few exceptions, the United States Supreme Court has consistently rejected restrictive interpretations by lower courts to limit expan-

---

5. *Organized Crime and Illicit Traffic in Narcotics, Hearing Before the Permanent Subcommittee on Investigations of the Senate Committee on Government Operations, Organized Crime and Illicit Traffic in Narcotics*, 89th Cong., 1st Sess. 2 (1965).

6. *Organized Crime and Illicit Traffic in Narcotics: Hearing before the Permanent Subcommittee on Investigations of the Senate Committee on Government Operations*, 89th Cong., 1st Sess. 2 (1965).

7. *See* U.S. DEP'T OF JUSTICE, UNITED STATES ATTORNEYS' MANUAL, § 9–110.110 *et seq.*; U.S. DEP'T OF JUSTICE, RACKETEER INFLUENCED AND CORRUPT ORGANIZATIONS (RICO): A MANUAL FOR FEDERAL PROSECUTORS (1990); U.S. DEP'T OF JUSTICE, CIVIL RICO: A MANUAL FOR FEDERAL PROSECUTORS (1988).

8. *E.g.*:

Supreme Court: NOW v. Scheidler, 510 U.S. 249, 114 S.Ct. 798, 127 L.Ed.2d 99 (1994) (upheld standing for an abortion clinic to bring a civil RICO action against anti-abortion groups for participating in an alleged nationwide conspiracy to shut down abortion clinics through a pattern of extortion).

First Circuit: Sharpe v. Kelley, 835 F.Supp. 33 (D.Mass.1993) (denied dismissal of RICO claim by female carpenter apprentice against local union officials for pattern of sexual harassment extortion causing her lost wages).

Fifth Circuit: United States v. Jensen, 41 F.3d 946 (5th Cir.1994), *cert. denied*, 514 U.S. 1101, 115 S.Ct. 1835, 131 L.Ed.2d 754 (1995) (aff'd RICO conviction of chairman of failed savings and loan based on fraud).

Seventh Circuit: Rosario v. Livaditis, 963 F.2d 1013 (7th Cir.1992) (aff'd judgment for former students against sham cosmetology school).

Eleventh Circuit: Crestline Chiropractic Family Care v. Blue Cross Blue Shield of Ala. (N.D.Ala. 1996) (BC/BS recently obtained a jury verdict against a chiropractic clinic for fraudulent claims).

9. U.S. DEP'T OF JUSTICE, UNITED STATES ATTORNEYS' MANUAL, § 9–110.200 ("it is not the policy of the Criminal Division to approve "imaginative" prosecutions under RICO which are far afield from the congressional purpose of the RICO statute").

10. U.S. DEP'T OF JUSTICE, UNITED STATES ATTORNEYS' MANUAL, § 9–110.101.

sive uses of RICO.[11] In construing RICO, the Court relies on the expressed legislative intent that RICO "be liberally construed to effectuate its remedial purpose."[12] Recent Supreme Court cases during the past five years are typical. The Court has reaffirmed that the "interstate commerce" requirement is to be broadly construed;[13] that RICO violations do not require an "economic purpose,"[14] and that RICO forfeiture authority is expansive even in light of first amendment claims.[15]

Despite the Supreme Court's reluctance to interpret RICO restrictively, lower courts have shown consistent hostility to expansive RICO applications.[16] For example, a review of all Court of Appeals decisions over the past five years indicates that approximately one-third of civil RICO cases (112 out of 350) were dismissed before trial. As CHART 21A shows, most were dismissed for lack of standing; the next most common reason was for failure to allege sufficient "pattern of racketeering activity."

11. *See* NOW v. Scheidler, 510 U.S. 249, 114 S.Ct. 798, 127 L.Ed.2d 99 (1994) (rejecting a restrictive "economic purpose" requirement for standing); H. J. Inc. v. Northwestern Bell Telephone Co., 492 U.S. 229, 109 S.Ct. 2893, 106 L.Ed.2d 195 (1989) (rejecting a restrictive "multiple scheme" requirement for "pattern"); Sedima, S.P.R.L. v. Imrex Co., 473 U.S. 479, 105 S.Ct. 3275, 87 L.Ed.2d 346 (1985) (rejecting a judicially construed "racketeering injury" requirement for civil standing); United States v. Turkette, 452 U.S. 576, 101 S.Ct. 2524, 69 L.Ed.2d 246 (1981) (rejecting a restrictive "legitimate organization" requirement for "enterprise"). *Cf.* Reves v. Ernst & Young, 507 U.S. 170, 113 S.Ct. 1163, 122 L.Ed.2d 525 (1993) (imposing the most restrictive test for "participate" to section 1962(c) violations).

12. Pub.L.No. 91–452, § 904(a), 84 Stat. 947 (1970).

13. United States v. Robertson, 514 U.S. 669, 115 S.Ct. 1732, 131 L.Ed.2d 714 (1995).

14. NOW v. Scheidler, 510 U.S. 249, 114 S.Ct. 798, 127 L.Ed.2d 99 (1994).

15. Alexander v. United States, 509 U.S. 544, 113 S.Ct. 2766, 125 L.Ed.2d 441 (1993).

16. *See* Michael Goldsmith, *Judicial Immunity for White–Collar Crime*, 30 HARV. J.ON LEGIS. 1 (1993) (arguing against judicial activism by the lower courts, in the absence of Congressional reform. Goldsmith's research found that approximately 75% of RICO actions filed during six months in 1991 and six months in 1992 were dismissed prior to trial).

CHART 21A

REASONS FOR PRETRIAL DISMISSAL OF CIVIL RICO CASES

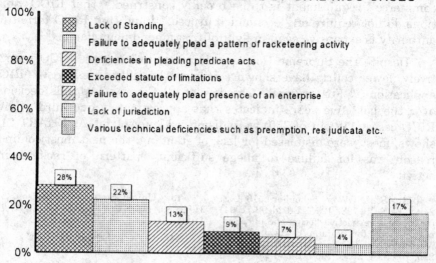

RICO is organized very logically. Section 1961 sets forth definitions. Section 1962 lists the four types of conduct that constitute a RICO violation. Section 1963 authorizes the criminal penalties; section 1964 authorizes the civil remedies. The remaining sections provide housekeeping details: section 1965 deals with venue and process; section 1966 provides for expedition of certain civil RICO actions by the government; section 1967 allows the court to close RICO proceedings to the public; and section 1968 authorizes the Attorney General to issue civil investigative demands for documents in certain circumstances.

There are four types of conduct prohibited by RICO. The gist of all four is using some form of business to commit crime. Whether the case is criminal or civil, the plaintiff must prove that the defendant committed at least one of these four types of conduct. There are three key definitions in RICO: a RICO offense can occur only when there is a "pattern" of "racketeering activity" affecting an "enterprise."

If, as one court has stated, RICO is "constructed on the model of a treasure hunt,"[17] sections 1963 and 1964 are the treasure. Section 1963 authorizes the criminal penalties for RICO violations, including a possible sentence of twenty years (or life in certain circumstances), fines of $250,000 or two times gross profits or losses caused, whichever is greater,[18] and mandatory forfeiture of all proceeds derived from any RICO activity. RICO contains many details pertaining to forfeiture,

17. Sutliff Inc. v. Donovan Companies, 727 F.2d 648, 652 (7th Cir.1984).

18. 18 U.S.C. § 3571.

including broad authority for the government "to preserve the availability of the property subject to forfeiture."[19] To do this, the government may obtain temporary restraining orders or performance bonds. In unusual cases such orders or bonds may be obtained before indictment, ex parte and without notice. RICO also sets forth the procedure for subsequent bona fide purchasers to establish their rights in otherwise forfeitable RICO property.

Section 1964 authorizes a civil cause of action for "any person injured in his business or property by reason of a violation of section 1962."[20] A prior criminal conviction is not required to bring a civil RICO action except for securities violations. Treble damages, court costs and attorneys fees are specified in RICO for victorious plaintiffs.

Despite the statute's organizational logic, RICO cases are complex. Each major RICO concept is subject to argument. Thus, there is an abundance of case law and commentary on RICO.[21] Pressures for statutory and judicial change are continual. This chapter attempts to highlight the current trends, but readers are advised to consult the precedential authority in their jurisdictions.

Library References:

C.J.S. RICO (Racketeer Influenced and Corrupt Organizations) § 2–11, 13–29.
West's Key No. Digests, Racketeer Influenced and Corrupt Organizations ⟢1–98.

§ 21.2   Definitions—In General

RICO provides ten definitions at 18 U.S.C. § 1961. The terms "racketeering activity," "enterprise" and "pattern of racketeering activity" have presented significant issues for the courts. Generally, the analysis of these concepts is the same whether the RICO action is criminal or civil.

Library References:

C.J.S. RICO (Racketeer Influenced and Corrupt Organizations) § 2, 4–11, 13.
West's Key No. Digests, Racketeer Influenced and Corrupt Organizations ⟢1–50.

§ 21.3   Definitions—"Racketeering Activity"

Section 1961(1) of title 18 defines "racketeering activity" as any crime specifically enumerated under this section. The following ten state crimes are "racketeering activity": acts or threats of murder, kidnaping,

---

19. 18 U.S.C. § 1963(d).

20. 18 U.S.C. § 1964(c).

21. Excellent sources on RICO include *see* PAUL A. BATISTA, CIVIL RICO PRACTICE MANUAL (2d ed.1997); KEVIN P. RODDY, RICO IN BUSINESS & COMMERCIAL LITIGATION. John J. Lulejian, Comment, *Making Sense of the Kaleidoscope of Patterns: A Practitioner's Guide to Understanding the Third Circuit's Interpretation of Civil RICO's "Pattern of Racketeering Activity"*, 69 TEMP. L.REV. 413 Spring (1996); Bryan T. Camp,

Dual Construction of RICO: The Road Not Taken in Reves, 51 WASH. & LEE L.REV. b1; Ira H. Raphaelson & Michelle D. Bernard, *RICO & The Operation or Management Test: The Potential Chilling Effect on Criminal Prosecutions*, 28 U.RICH.L.REV. 669 (1994); 2. Drew Sorrell, III, *Racketeering Influence Corrupt Organization Act—Forfeiture*, 64 GEO.WASH.L.REV. 1441 (1996); Melissa Harrison, *NEXUS: The Next of RICO's Text*, 70 DENV.U.L.REV. 69 (1992).

gambling, arson, robbery, bribery, extortion, dealing in obscene matter, dealing in a controlled substance or controlled chemical.[1] Many federal crimes indictable under titles 18 (Crimes), 29 (Labor), 11 (Bankruptcy) and 31 (Money and Finance), are racketeering activity, with some notable exceptions. Bankruptcy fraud is no longer included as a racketeering activity,[2] recent health care offenses created by Congress[3] are not included and, in civil RICO actions, securities fraud is not available as racketeering activity unless there has been a conviction on securities fraud offenses.[4]

A prior conviction of the predicate act is not required[5] unless, as noted, the action is a civil suit based on securities fraud. In 1995, Congress amended section 1964(c), precluding standing for such suits unless the defendant has already been criminally convicted for the underlying securities fraud.[6] An unsuccessful legislative proposal would have required a prior conviction for criminal RICO prosecutions based on predicate acts of securities fraud, as well.[7]

The underlying predicate act of "racketeering activity" must be adequately averred and proven. For example, in *Ideal Dairy Farms, Inc. v. John Labatt, Ltd.* the Third Circuit affirmed summary judgment in favor of defendants because the plaintiff failed to present adequate evidence of all elements of the underlying predicate acts, mail fraud and wire fraud. Similarly, in *Kenty v. Bank One*, the court affirmed the dismissal of a RICO class action suit by car buyers against their lender because fraud was not sufficiently alleged with particularity.[8] In *Kenty*, the car buyers had each contracted with the defendant bank for their automobile loans, which included the option of the bank to take out "loss or damage" insurance on the cars. The court held that the alleged misleading statement regarding the insurance obtained was ambiguous at best—not false: "A claim of fraud does not inevitably follow from every breach of contract."[9] *Smith v. Jackson*, provides another example. The Ninth Circuit affirmed the dismissal of a RICO claim by songwriters

§ 21.3

1. 18 U.S.C. § 1961(1). *See* U.S. DEP'T OF JUSTICE, UNITED STATES ATTORNEYS' MANUAL, § 9–110.200 (reemphasizing explicit Department of Justice policy to defer primary responsibility for enforcing state laws with the state concerned).

2. Pub.L.No. 103–394, 108 Stat. 4140 (1994).

3. The Health Insurance and Accountability Act of 1996 (HIPAA) created four new offenses in Title 18 pertaining to health care fraud: Pub.L. 104–91, §§ 217, 242–45. None of these are included as predicate acts under RICO, although each of these new offenses is a "specified unlawful activity" in the money laundering offense found at 18 U.S.C. § 1956. Money laundering is included as racketeering activity. Health care fraud charged as mail fraud or wire fraud is, of course, included as racketeering activity.

4. 18 U.S.C. § 1961(1).

5. Fort Wayne Books, Inc. v. Indiana, 489 U.S. 46, 61, 109 S.Ct. 916, 926, 103 L.Ed.2d 34 (1989); Sedima, S.P.R.L. v. Imrex Co., 473 U.S. 479, 488, ___ S.Ct. ___, ___ L.Ed.2d ___ (1986).

6. Pub.L.No. 104–67, 109 Stat. 758 (1995) amending 18 U.S.C. § 1964(c).

7. 141 CONG.REC. D791 (1995).

8. Kenty v. Bank One, Columbus, N.A., 92 F.3d 384 (6th Cir.1996).

9. *Id.* at 390.

against several musicians because copyright infringement is not a racketeering activity.[10]

Until 1994, lower courts dismissed RICO claims if the underlying predicate acts were not motivated by an "economic purpose." In *NOW v. Scheidler*, the Supreme Court unanimously rejected this restrictive requirement.[11] The Court reversed the Seventh Circuit's dismissal of various RICO claims by abortion clinics and their supporters. The plaintiffs had filed the action against anti-abortion groups for allegedly participating in a nationwide conspiracy to shut down abortion clinics through a pattern of extortion. The Court relied on the statute's text, finding no indication in the language of RICO that an economic motive is required.[12] The Court explicitly reaffirmed that RICO is to be read broadly: "[t]he occasion for Congress' action was the perceived need to combat organized crime. But Congress for cogent reasons chose to enact a more general statute, one which, although it had organized crime as its focus, was not limited in application to organized crime."[13] After the *NOW* opinion, Congress has considered, but not approved requiring a "profit-seeking purpose" for RICO actions.[14]

Congress is actively lobbied for changes in the racketeering activity requirement and has considered adding predicate acts such as gang-related activity, firearms trafficking, terrorism, computer-related crimes, use of minors to commit an offense and health care fraud.[15] Thus far, these efforts have been unsuccessful. Critics of such expansions argue that predicate acts should be restricted to violent crimes. Congress has also considered restrictions to the current predicate acts such as protecting conduct under the First Amendment, repealing the statute altogether, or making civil RICO applicable only after defendants have already been convicted for the underlying predicate acts.[16] With the exception of civil RICO brought on the ground that securities fraud has occurred, none of these proposals has won adequate support for passage.

§ 21.4　Definitions—"Enterprise"

Section 1961(4) of title 18 defines an "enterprise" as:

10.　Smith v. Jackson, 84 F.3d 1213 (9th Cir.1996).

11.　NOW v. Scheidler, 510 U.S. 249, 114 S.Ct. 798, 127 L.Ed.2d 99 (1994).

12.　*Id.* at 804.

13.　*Id.* at 805.

14.　140 Cong.Rec. H2236 (1994).

15.　*E.g.*, 143 Cong.Rec. S1661 (1997) (adding gang-related crimes); 143 Cong.Rec. S583 (1997) (adding firearms trafficking); 142 Cong.Rec. H9888 (1996) (adding terrorist-related crimes); 141 Cong.Rec. S9180 (1995) (adding computer-related crimes); 139 Cong.Rec. S15350 (1993) (adding the use of a minor in a crime); and 139 Cong. Rec. H10985 (1993) (adding health care fraud).

16.　*See* William Rehnquist, *Get RICO Cases Out of My Courtroom*, Wall St. J., May 19, 1989 (suggesting mail and wire fraud be removed from the list of predicate acts); Susan W. Brenner, *RICO, CCE and Other Complex Crimes: The Transformation of American Criminal Law?* 2 Wm. & Mary Bill Rts.J. 239 (Winter 1993) (suggesting "compound" crimes constitute cruel and unusual punishment). But see G. Robert Blakey & Thomas A. Perry, *Reforming RICO: If, Why and How?* 43 Vand.L.Rev. 851 (1990) (arguing reform efforts are misguided and that the list of RICO predicate acts should be expanded to include causing train wrecks and leaking hazardous waste).

any individual, partnership, corporation, association, or other legal entity, and any union or group of individuals associated in fact although not a legal entity....[1]

All RICO violations require the involvement of an "enterprise." In *United States v. Turkette*, the First Circuit reversed the defendant's RICO conviction because the association-in-fact drug enterprise operated solely for illegal purposes. The Supreme Court explicitly rejected this limiting construction.[2] The Court followed the expansive approach taken by most circuit courts and held that an enterprise included legitimate and illegitimate and formal and informal organizations as long as they were ongoing and functioned as a continuing unit.[3]

A number of cases provide descriptions of RICO enterprises. For example, in *United States v. Darden*, the United States Court of Appeals for the Eighth Circuit held that to prove the existence of an enterprise, the government must prove: (1) a common purpose; (2) a formal or informal organization of the participants in which they function as a unit; and, (3) an ascertainable structure.[4] The court affirmed RICO convictions against members of a religious cult engaged in a successful pattern of drug trafficking and murder,[5] finding that an "enterprise" was shown by the oversight and coordination over the members, sharing of information to protect their drug trade from competitors, and "post-shooting" reviews of technique "employed to snuff out rivals and informants."[6]

Davis v. MONY provides another helpful analysis of a RICO enterprise. In *MONY*, the United States Court of Appeals for the Sixth Circuit affirmed a RICO judgment against an insurance company after finding a fraudulent tax scheme by one of the company's agents.[7] The agent had marketed life insurance by emphasizing its tax advantages when insureds established a home-based business. The insureds filed suit against the agent and the insurer after the IRS rejected their deductions for the home-based business. The court held there was sufficient evidence of an enterprise comprised of the insurance agent, his associates and the insurance company because the agent's scam was firmly established and explicitly discussed prior to his association with MONY.[8] In addition, MONY retained the agent even after an internal report prepared by its own counsel warned of the agent's "fast-track hustle."[9]

Despite the broad statutory definition of "enterprise," many RICO actions are dismissed by lower courts for failure to allege or prove the

§ 21.4

1. 18 U.S.C. § 1961(4) (Supp.1997).

2. *Id.* at 587.

3. United States v. Turkette, 452 U.S. 576, 101 S.Ct. 2524, 69 L.Ed.2d 246 (1981).

4. *Id.* at 1520.

5. United States v. Darden, 70 F.3d 1507 (8th Cir.1995), *cert. denied*, 517 U.S.

1149, 116 S.Ct. 1449, 134 L.Ed.2d 569 (1996).

6. *Id.* at 1521.

7. Davis v. MONY, 6 F.3d 367 (6th Cir.1993), *cert. denied*, 510 U.S. 1193, 114 S.Ct. 1298, 127 L.Ed.2d 650 (1994).

8. *Id.* at 378.

9. *Id.* at 374.

presence of an enterprise.[10] These courts tend to focus on whether there is an ascertainable structure separate and apart from that inherent in the pattern of racketeering activity. The circuits are split on whether there must be an ascertainable structure separate from the pattern of racketeering activity, although the majority of jurisdictions require the enterprise to have a distinct structure.[11] Two circuits follow the broader approach of finding that an enterprise exists simply from the sum of the predicate racketeering acts.[12]

The courts requiring that the enterprise must have "an ascertainable structure distinct from that inherent in the conduct of a pattern of racketeering activity" reason that "an overly broad construction of the term 'enterprise' would render that element interchangeable with the 'pattern of racketeering element.'"[13] *Chang v. Chen* demonstrates the majority approach.[14] In *Chang*, victims of a fraudulent real estate scheme brought RICO claims against the real estate agent, broker and certain buyers. The court affirmed the dismissal of the RICO claims on the ground that plaintiffs failed to establish the existence of an enterprise.[15] The court reasoned that to do otherwise would render the "enterprise" element superfluous, strip RICO of its focus on "organized" crime, and create a danger of guilt-by-association,[16] whereby proof of a conspiracy would satisfy the enterprise element.

The Second and Eleventh Circuits, in rejecting the requirement of a distinct ascertainable structure, focus on statutory language (which contains no such requirement); the broad purpose of RICO; and the Supreme Court's interpretation of "enterprise" as an informal or formal organization[17] *United States v. Cagnina*,[18] provides an example of the minority approach. Cagnina was convicted on a variety of charges including RICO. All charges arose from drug, arson, murder, theft and securities activities. Cagnina argued that the government failed to prove

---

10. *See, e.g.*:

Sixth Circuit: Frank v. D'Ambrosi, 4 F.3d 1378, 1384 (6th Cir.1993).

Seventh Circuit: Richmond v. Nationwide Cassel, 52 F.3d 640 (7th Cir.1995).

Ninth Circuit: Chang v. Chen, 80 F.3d 1293, 1297 (9th Cir.1996).

11. *See*:

First Circuit: Libertad v. Welch, 53 F.3d 428, 441 (1st Cir.1995).

Third Circuit: United States v. Console, 13 F.3d 641, 650 (3d Cir.1993).

Fourth Circuit: United States v. Tillett, 763 F.3d 628, 632 (4th Cir.1985).

Fifth Circuit: Crowe v. Henry, 43 F.3d 198, 205 (5th Cir.1995).

Sixth Circuit: Frank v. D'Ambrosi, 4 F.3d 1378, 1386 (6th Cir.1993).

Seventh Circuit: Richmond v. Nationwide Cassel L.P., 52 F.3d 640, 646 (7th Cir.1995).

Eighth Circuit: Atlas Pile Driving v. DiCon Financial Co., 886 F.2d 986, 995 (8th Cir.1989).

Ninth Circuit: Chang v. Chen, 80 F.3d 1293, 1298 (9th Cir.1996).

Tenth Circuit: United States v. Sanders, 928 F.2d 940, 944 (10th Cir.1991).

12. *Second Circuit*: United States v. Bagaric, 706 F.2d 42, 55 (2d Cir.1983).

Eleventh Circuit: United States v. Cagnina, 697 F.2d 915, 921 (11th Cir.1983).

13. Chang v. Chen, 80 F.3d 1293, 1297 (9th Cir.1996).

14. *Id.* at 1293.

15. *Id.* at 1300.

16. *Id.* at 1298–99.

17. United States v. Cagnina, 697 F.2d 915, 921 (11th Cir.1983).

18. *Id.* at 921.

the existence of an enterprise. The Eleventh Circuit rejected the "distinct ascertainable structure" requirement and found the following evidence of enterprise sufficient: there was an informal association united in a common purpose of "making money from repeated criminal activity," the individuals functioned as a group under Cagnina's constant leadership, and there was substantial oversight of all group activities by Cagnina.[19]

Lower courts also dismiss RICO actions for failure to allege or prove an enterprise in instances involving corporate defendants by refusing to allow the corporation to be both the "enterprise" and the defendant in section 1962(c) cases.[20] All circuits, except the Third and Eleventh, hold that a corporation cannot be both the enterprise and the "person" charged with violating 1962(c).[21] The courts following this approach focus on the language of RICO. Whereas as 1962(a) and (b) specify that "any person" may engage in the conduct outlined in these sections, section 1962(c) specifies that only "a person employed by or associated with an enterprise" may violate 1962(c). These courts find this difference significant and conclude that it was intended to prevent an enterprise from being a defendant (i.e. logically, an enterprise cannot be "employed by or associated with" itself).[22] The courts following this approach acknowledge the injustice of this position when the corporation is the perpetrator of the RICO offense; however, they suggest that charging the RICO violation under section 1962(a), rather than section 1962(c), would alleviate the problem. The Seventh Circuit explained this view in *Haroco v. American Nat. B. & T. Co.*:[23]

> We are persuaded ... that section 1962(c) requires separate entities as the liable person and the enterprise which has its affairs conduct-

19. *Id.* at 921–22.

20. *See* Otto Immel, *Corporation-Employee Association-in-Fact Enterprises in Civil RICO*, 60 DEFENSE COUNSEL J. 88, 96 (1993) (supporting the "distinction" requirement as a way to foreclose RICO applications to ordinary commercial disputes).

21. *See*:

D.C. Circuit: Yellow Bus Lines, Inc. v. Drivers, Chauffeurs & Helpers Local Union 639, 839 F.2d 782, 791 (D.C.Cir.1988).

First Circuit: Doyle v. Hasbro, 103 F.3d 186, 190 (1st Cir.1996).

Second Circuit: Discon, Inc. v. NYNEX Corp., 93 F.3d 1055, 1063 (2d Cir.1996).

Fourth Circuit: Busby v. Crown Supply Inc., 896 F.2d 833, 840 (4th Cir.1990).

Fifth Circuit: Ashe v. Corley, 992 F.2d 540, 544 (5th Cir.1993).

Sixth Circuit: Davis v. Mutual Life Ins. Co., 6 F.3d 367, 377 (6th Cir.1993), cert. denied, 510 U.S. 1193, 114 S.Ct. 1298, 127 L.Ed.2d 650 (1994).

Seventh Circuit: Richmond v. Nationwide Cassel L.P., 52 F.3d 640, 646 (7th Cir.1995).

Eighth Circuit: United HealthCare Corp. v. American Trade Ins. Co., 88 F.3d 563, 570 (8th Cir.1996).

Ninth Circuit: Wilcox v. First Interstate Bank, 815 F.2d 522, 529 (9th Cir.1987).

Tenth Circuit: Bd. of County Commissioners v. Liberty Group, 965 F.2d 879, 885 (10th Cir.1992).

But See:

Third Circuit: Jaguar Cars v. Royal Oaks, 46 F.3d 258, 265 (3d Cir.1995) (overruling its prior "distinction" requirement).

Eleventh Circuit: United States v. Hartley, 678 F.2d 961, 988 (11th Cir.1982).

22. Securitron Magnalock Corp. v. Schnabolk, 65 F.3d 256 (2d Cir.1995), *cert. denied*, 516 U.S. 1114, 116 S.Ct. 916, 133 L.Ed.2d 846 (1996).

23. 747 F.2d 384 (7th Cir.1984).

ed through a pattern of racketeering activity.... [W]e focus our attention on the language in section 1962(c) requiring that the liable person be "employed by or associated with any enterprise" which affects interstate or foreign commerce. The use of the terms "employed by" and "associated with" appears to contemplate a person distinct from the enterprise....

At the policy level of the dispute, there are several significant competing arguments. The Eleventh Circuit [has] argued ... that where the defendant corporation is the central figure in a criminal scheme, as it was in that case, Congress could not have meant to let the central perpetrator escape RICO liability while subjecting only the sidekicks to RICO's severe penalties. Similarly, plaintiffs here argue that Congress intended to make a "deep pocket" (in the person of the corporation) liable where corporate agents engage in a pattern of racketeering activity redounding to the benefit of the corporation....

In our view, the RICO provisions have already taken into account these competing policies in different situations, and a careful parsing of section 1962 reveals a sensible balance among these policies....

In our view, the tensions between these policies may be resolved sensibly and in accord with the language of section 1962 by reading subsection (c) together with subsection (a). As we read subsection (c), the "enterprise" and the "person" must be distinct. However, a corporation-enterprise may be held liable under subsection (a) when the corporation is also a perpetrator. As we parse subsection (a), a "person" (such as a corporation-enterprise) acts unlawfully if it receives income derived directly or indirectly from a pattern or racketeering activity in which the person has participated as a principal within the meaning of 18 U.S.C. § 2, and if the person uses the income in the establishment or *operation* of an enterprise affecting commerce. Subsection (a) does not contain any of the language in subsection (c) which suggests that the liable person and the enterprise must be separate. Under subsection (a), therefore, the liable person may be a corporation using the proceeds of a pattern of racketeering activity in its operations. This approach to subsection (a) thus makes the corporation-enterprise liable under RICO when the corporation is actually the direct or indirect beneficiary of the pattern of racketeering activity, but not when it is merely the victim, prize, or passive instrument of racketeering. This result is in accord with the primary purpose of RICO, which, after all, is to reach those who ultimately profit from racketeering, not those who are victimized by it.[24]

Jaguar Cars, Inc. v. Royal Oak Motor Car Co., demonstrates the opposite view. In *Jaguar Cars*, the Third Circuit abandoned its adherence to the majority rule and held that RICO did not prevent charging

---

24. *Id.* at 400–02.

an enterprise as defendant.[25] A Jaguar car manufacturer obtained a judgment under section 1962(c) against Royal Oak Motors, a family-owned car dealership, for engaging in a systematic scheme of submitting fraudulent warranty claims to Jaguar Cars. Under the scheme, Royal Oak Motors submitted thousands of warranty claims for repairs that were either unnecessary or never actually performed. The court acknowledged that the dealership, as the RICO enterprise, was the "person" charged but rejected defendant's argument that this required dismissal. After analyzing recent Supreme Court cases, the Third Circuit rejected the "distinction" requirements on the ground that it could not survive Supreme Court precedent which made clear that in some circumstances the enterprise could be the "person" in 1962(c) actions.[26]

§ 21.5   Definitions—"Pattern of Racketeering Activity"

Section 1961(5) of title 18 defines "pattern of racketeering activity" as:

requir[ing] at least two acts of racketeering activity, one of which occurred after the effective date of this chapter and the last of which occurred within ten years (excluding any period of imprisonment) after the commission of a prior act of racketeering activity. . . .[1]

Each RICO violation under section 1962 requires not merely proof of multiple occurrences of a specifically enumerated racketeering activity, but also that a "relationship" exists among the occurrences. The Supreme Court discussed this requirement in *H. J. Inc. v. Northwestern Bell Telephone Co.*[2]

In *H. J. Inc.*, customers of Northwestern Bell telephone company filed a class action alleging that the company bribed members of the public utility commission in order to obtain excessive rates. The predicate acts included making outright cash payments to commissioners, promising the commissioner jobs in the future, providing commissioners tickets to sporting events, etc. The lower court dismissed the suit on the ground that the complaint alleged only a single scheme to improperly influence the commission, not "multiple illegal schemes" of fraudulent activity as is required for a "pattern."[3]

The Supreme Court rejected this restrictive approach and held that a "pattern of racketeering activity" required proof of "continuity plus relationship" among the predicate acts—not multiple schemes.[4] Accord-

---

25. Jaguar Cars v. Royal Oaks, 46 F.3d 258, 265 (3d Cir.1995).

26. *Id.* at 266 (referring to the Supreme Court's decisions in National Organization of Women v. Scheidler, 510 U.S. 249, 114 S.Ct. 798, 127 L.Ed.2d 99 (1994)); Reves v. Ernst & Young, 507 U.S. 170, 113 S.Ct. 1163, 122 L.Ed.2d 525 (1993).

§ 21.5

1. 18 U.S.C. § 1961(5) (Supp.1997).

2. H. J. Inc. v. Northwestern Bell Telephone Co., 492 U.S. 229, 109 S.Ct. 2893, 106 L.Ed.2d 195 (1989). On remand, H.J. Inc., 954 F.2d 485 (8th Cir.1992), was dismissed again pursuant to the filed rate doctrine. H. J. Inc. v. Northwestern Bell Telephone Co., 734 F.Supp. 879 (D.Minn. 1990).

3. *Id.* at 234.

4. *Id.* at 239.

ing to the Court: "Criminal conduct forms a pattern if it embraces criminal acts that have the same or similar purposes, results, participants, victims, or methods or commission, or otherwise are interrelated by distinguishing characteristics and are not isolated events."[5] The Court explained that "continuity" may be either a repeated conduct over a substantial period of time, or an open-ended specific threat of repetition.[6] Applying this test to the facts in *H. J. Inc.*, the Court found that the complaint adequately averred the necessary pattern among the predicate acts. The complaint alleged that various forms of bribery motivated by a common goal of influencing rates over a period of six years.[7]

Lower courts' application of the *H. J. Inc.* test reveals that the longer the scheme continues, the more complex it is and the more people and acts it involves, the greater the likelihood of plaintiffs meeting the *H. J. Inc.* test.

Uniroyal Goodrich Tire Co. v. Mutual Trading Corp., provides an apt example. Uniroyal Goodrich Tire Co. ("Uniroyal") obtained a RICO civil judgment against Mutual Trading Corp. ("Mutual") based on several different alleged schemes.[8] The major scheme arose from Mutual's exclusive right to sell a unique tire in Saudi Arabia. By bribing a single Uniroyal employee, Mutual was able to obtain reimbursement from Uniroyal for 5,000 tires; in actuality, Mutual had supplied no tires. On appeal, Mutual challenged the sufficiency of the pattern of racketeering activity arguing, "the evidence failed to establish anything more than an isolated and short-lived instance of fraud in an otherwise successful business relationship."[9] The Seventh Circuit considered several factors to determine whether there was a pattern: "the number and variety of predicate acts, the length of time over which they were committed, the number of victims, the presence of separate schemes, and the occurrence of distinct injuries."[10] The court reasoned, "neither the presence or absence of any one of these factors is determinative, and though these factors may be helpful, the touchstones of the inquiry remain the elements of relationship and continuity."[11] The court found that, "all but one factor weigh in Uniroyal's favor: the predicate acts were numerous and spread out over a period of years; there was proof of several different schemes, all intended to bleed money from Uniroyal; and each scheme caused a harm distinct from that caused by the others"—only the existence of a single victim favors the defendant and that by itself is not enough.[12]

Similarly, in *Allwaste v. Hecht*, the Ninth Circuit found the evidence of a pattern to be sufficient because the predicate acts pervaded the

5. *Id.* at 240.

6. *Id.* at 242.

7. *Id.* at 250.

8. Uniroyal Goodrich Tire Co. v. Mutual Trading Corp., 63 F.3d 516 (7th Cir. 1995), *cert. denied*, 516 U.S. 1115, 116 S.Ct. 916, 133 L.Ed.2d 846 (1996).

9. *Id.* at 523.

10. *Id.* at 524.

11. *Id.*

12. *Id.*

defendants' way of doing business. The Ninth Circuit reversed the district court's dismissal of a RICO suit brought by a recycling company against its corporate officers.[13] The district court had dismissed the complaint on the ground that the predicate acts were not alleged to have spanned at least one year.[14] The Ninth Circuit held there was no bright line rule that the predicate acts continue for a specific time. The court found further that the conduct alleged (kickbacks) constituted a pattern because it had become the corporate officers' "regular way of doing business."[15]

In *United States v. Aulicino*, the Second Circuit also affirmed RICO convictions on the ground that the predicate acts constituted a pattern because of their threatened continuity. The Second Circuit affirmed the convictions against drug traffickers based on predicate acts of kidnaping.[16] The defendants had appealed their convictions on the ground that a pattern was not shown since the kidnaping scheme alleged was in existence only three and one-half months. Moreover, argued that defendants, there was no continued threat because the ring broke up.[17] The court held the threat of a continuing pattern existed because of the nature of the criminal activity itself, even though the period spanned by the kidnaping scheme was short.[18]

The cases where courts find evidence of pattern to be inadequate generally involve few predicate acts by one or a few defendants over a short period of time.[19] *Word of Faith World Outreach Center Church v. Sawyer*, is an apt example. In this case, the Fifth Circuit affirmed the dismissal of a RICO claim against Diane Sawyer and PrimeTime Live brought by[20] plaintiffs who were the targets of critical news reports by the ABC program. The district court dismissed the suit after finding that the three broadcasts about the plaintiff over a span of six months did not establish sufficient continuity to form a pattern of racketeering activity.[21]

Similarly, in *GICC Capital Corp. v. Technology Finance Group*, the Second Circuit affirmed the dismissal of RICO claims against controlling shareholders on the ground that there was no continuity in the "single short-lived scheme" to form a pattern.[22] The plaintiff, a creditor of the corporation, claimed that the defendant shareholders systematically loot-

13. Allwaste v. Hecht, 65 F.3d 1523 (9th Cir.1995).

14. *Id.* at 1527.

15. *Id.* at 1528–29.

16. United States v. Aulicino, 44 F.3d 1102 (2d Cir.1995).

17. *Id.* at 1110.

18. *Id.* at 1111.

19. See William E. Marple, *"Pattern" Requirement Renders RICO Inapplicable to Ordinary Business Disputes*, 14 REV.LITIG. 343 (Spring 1995) (arguing this judicially created restriction is an appropriate way to limit suits for ordinary business disputes); G. Robert Blakey & Thomas A. Perry, *Re-forming RICO: If, Why and How?* 43 VAND. L.REV. 851 (1990) (arguing against statutory restrictions of RICO because "ordinary business disputes" should be dismissed based on an insufficient pattern).

20. Word of Faith World Outreach Center Church v. Sawyer, 90 F.3d 118 (5th Cir.1996).

21. *Id.* at 123.

22. GICC Capital Corp. v. Tech. Finance Group, 67 F.3d 463, 467 (2d Cir. 1995), *cert. denied*, 518 U.S. 1017, 116 S.Ct. 2547, 135 L.Ed.2d 1067 (1996).

ed the corporation in order to avoid repaying the $500,000 debt. The court held there was no continued threat of looting when the scheme was "inherently terminable," i.e., all available funds were gone within a year.[23]

In *Heller Financial Inc. v. Grammco Computer Sales Inc.*, the Fifth Circuit reversed a RICO judgment against a computer leasing company on the ground that there was an insufficient relationship among the predicate acts to establish a pattern.[24] The plaintiff had financed $2.65 million for the defendant's leases. The evidence at trial convinced the jury that the defendant committed underlying acts of fraud against the plaintiff and commercial bribery of a lessee's manager of information systems. Looking at the divergent purposes and different predicate acts used against the two victims—the first to induce a fraudulent loan by the plaintiff, the latter to maintain a usurious contract with a lessee—the court held the predicate acts were not sufficiently interrelated.[25]

§ 21.6   Definitions—Interstate Commerce

A RICO violation must involve an enterprise "engaged in" or "affect[ing] interstate or foreign commerce."[1] Although not expressly defined in RICO, courts have consistently construed the interstate commerce nexus requirement as slight.

This minimal nexus requirement was recently affirmed by the United States Supreme Court. In *United States v. Robertson*, the Court upheld the RICO conviction of a defendant who invested the proceeds of his California drug activity in an Alaskan gold mine.[2] The Court held that there was a sufficient nexus with interstate commerce when the goldmining operation used equipment purchased out-of-state, employed staff from out-of-state, and directly shipped 15% of retrieved gold out-of-state.[3]

Using this minimalist approach, courts have found interstate commerce present in instances where all activity occurred intrastate if a potential interstate affect is possible. For example, in *United States v. Doherty*, the First Circuit found a sufficient interstate nexus of an enterprise involved in stealing police exams because the defendants' activities prevented out-of-state applicants from getting jobs.[4] Similarly, in *United States v. Allen*, the Fourth Circuit held there was a sufficient

23. *Id.* at 466.

24. Heller Financial Inc. v. Grammco Computer Sales Inc., 71 F.3d 518 (5th Cir. 1996).

25. *Id.* at 524.

§ 21.6

1. 18 U.S.C. § 1962.

2. United States v. Robertson, 514 U.S. 669, 115 S.Ct. 1732, 131 L.Ed.2d 714 (1995).

3. *Id.* at 710. The lower court had reversed the defendant's conviction because the Alaskan gold mine had only an "incidental" effect on interstate commerce when its small operation was entirely local and its profits were not used to fund the illegal predicate acts. United States v. Robertson, 15 F.3d 862, 868 (9th Cir.1994), *rev'd* 514 U.S. 669, 115 S.Ct. 1732, 131 L.Ed.2d 714 (1995).

4. United States v. Doherty, 867 F.2d 47, 68 (1st Cir.1989).

interstate nexus when the strictly local bookmaking operation purchased supplies from out-of-state vendors.[5]

Despite the minimalist test, courts have found the interstate commerce nexus insufficient when the activity was purely intrastate. For example, in *Smith v. Ayres*, the Fifth Circuit held that a RICO claim based on predicate acts of wire fraud involving purely intrastate communication would be insufficient.[6] Similarly, in *Musick v. Burke*, the Ninth Circuit held that a RICO claim based on antitrust violations could not survive even though the strictly local enterprise had purchased out-of-state supplies, because the purchases had a mere "incidental" effect on interstate commerce.[7]

§ 21.7 Prohibited Activities—In General

RICO prohibits four types of conduct. Both civil and criminal plaintiffs must prove the same elements for RICO violations.[1] The difference lies in the burden of proof: the prosecutor bringing a criminal RICO action must prove all elements beyond a reasonable doubt; the plaintiff bringing a civil action must simply prove elements by a preponderance of evidence.

Library References:

C.J.S. RICO (Racketeer Influenced and Corrupt Organizations) § 2, 4–6, 13.
West's Key No. Digests, Racketeer Influenced and Corrupt Organizations ⊙4–23.

§ 21.8 Prohibited Activities—Investing RICO Proceeds: § 1962(a)

Section 1962(a) of title 18, United States Code, proscribes the following conduct:

It shall be unlawful for any person who has received any income derived, directly or indirectly, from a pattern of racketeering activity . . . to use or invest, directly or indirectly, any part of such income, or the proceeds of such income, in acquisition of any interest in, or the establishment or operation of, any enterprise which is engaged in, or the activities of which affect, interstate or foreign commerce. . . .[1]

Section 1962(a) makes unlawful the use or invest proceeds from racketeering activities in an enterprise which affects interstate or foreign commerce. This includes obvious conduct such as investing proceeds

5. United States v. Allen, 656 F.2d 964 (4th Cir.1981).

6. Smith v. Ayres, 845 F.2d 1360, 1366 (5th Cir.1988).

7. Musick v. Burke, 913 F.2d 1390, 1398 (9th Cir.1990).

§ 21.7

1. United States v. Baker, 63 F.3d 1478, 1493 (9th Cir.1995), *cert. denied*, 516

U.S. 1097, 116 S.Ct. 824, 133 L.Ed.2d 767 (1996).

§ 21.8

1. 18 U.S.C. § 1962(a).

from narcotics offenses in legitimate businesses although even in the most obvious case tracing the funds can become complex. For example, in *United States v. Vogt*, the court affirmed the RICO conviction of Vogt, a former U.S. customs agent.[2] Vogt received in excess of a half-million dollars for information which helped a drug smuggling operation in Florida. The section 1962(a) violation was based on Vogt's funneling illegally obtained money (with the help of his lawyer and the lawyer's firm) into foreign "dummy" corporations to be later invested in various legitimate enterprises after his retirement from the government. The court held the evidence sufficient to prove the following four elements: "(1) that Vogt derived income from a pattern of racketeering activity; (2) that he then used or invested, directly or indirectly, some part of that income in the establishment and operation, (3) of an enterprise, (4) which was engaged in or affected commerce by its activities."[3]

It helps in proving a section 1962(a) action that courts do not require rigorous proof "tracing" the exact course of ill-gotten gains into its ultimate use or investment.[4] For example, in *Vogt*, the government offered testimony by the drug smuggler of the amounts paid to Vogt; Vogt's income tax returns and his total net worth, which included a $280,000 motor home, a new Cadillac De Ville, two Mercedes, an expensive boat and airplane, and a $650,000 profit realized from a two year investment of an apartment complex. The court concluded, "[b]ecause Vogt's legitimately acquired net worth, as evidenced by his tax returns, would not have financed all these purchases, the jury could have found beyond a reasonable doubt that they were made at least in part with the money received as bribes or proceeds of that money."[5]

There is a split among the circuits as to whether a civil suit based on section 1962(a) requires an "investment injury" before the plaintiff has standing.[6] The majority view requires proof of an investment injury[7]

2. United States v. Vogt, 910 F.2d 1184 (4th Cir.1990).

3. *Id.* at 1194.

4. *Id.* at 1194.

5. *Id.* at 1195.

6. *See:*

D.C. Circuit: Danielsen v. Burnside–Ott Aviation Training Ctr., 941 F.2d 1220, 1229 (D.C.Cir.1991).

First Circuit: Rhone v. Energy North, Inc., 790 F.Supp. 353, 357 (D.Mass.1991).

Second Circuit: Ouaknine v. MacFarlane, 897 F.2d 75, 83 (2d Cir.1990).

Third Circuit: Glessner v. Kenny, 952 F.2d 702, 709 (3d Cir.1991).

Fifth Circuit: Crowe v. Henry, 43 F.3d 198, 205 (5th Cir.1995).

Sixth Circuit: Vemco v. Camardella, 23 F.3d 129, 132 (6th Cir.1994).

Seventh Circuit: Fujisawa Pharm. Co. v. Kapoor, 814 F.Supp. 720, 735 (N.D.Ill. 1993).

Eighth Circuit: Nagle v. Merrill Lynch, 790 F.Supp. 203, 209 (S.D.Iowa 1992).

Ninth Circuit: Nugget Hydroelec. L.P. v. Pacific Gas & Elec. Co., 981 F.2d 429, 437 (9th Cir.1992).

Tenth Circuit: Grider v. Texas Oil & Gas Corp., 868 F.2d 1147, 1150 (10th Cir. 1989).

Eleventh Circuit: Bowers v. Dairymen, Inc., 813 F.Supp. 1580, 1584 (S.D.Ga.1991).

7. *See*:

D.C. Circuit: Danielsen v. Burnside–Ott Aviation Training Ctr., 941 F.2d 1220, 1229 (D.C.Cir.1991).

First Circuit: Rhone v. Energy North, Inc., 790 F.Supp. 353, 357 (D.Mass.1991).

Second Circuit: Ouaknine v. MacFarlane, 897 F.2d 75, 83 (2d Cir.1990).

while the Fourth Circuit requires only proof that the injury suffered by the plaintiff be traceable to the predicate acts.[8]

Vemco v. Camardella demonstrates the majority view.[9] In *Vemco*, the plaintiff (Vemco) contracted with Camardella to build a $15 million paint finishing system for the automotive parts Vemco manufactured. Vemco never completed the system, allegedly because of breaches of contract and fraud by Camardella. The United States Court of Appeals for the Sixth Circuit affirmed dismissal of the section 1962(a) claim on the ground that the injuries incurred by Vemco were not a result of the underlying predicate acts of fraud—i.e., they did not result from Camardella's investment of the proceeds into the enterprise but simply from the alleged breach of contract and fraud.

Busby v. Crown Supply, Inc. demonstrates the Fourth Circuit's approach of not requiring proof of an investment injury in 1962(a) civil cases.[10] Busby was a sales representative for the defendant and was paid by commission. Busby alleged that Crown Supply fraudulently represented the true profit of goods sold, thus decreasing the amount of commissions Busby actually earned. The trial court dismissed the 1962(a) claim on the ground that the plaintiff's injury did not flow from the defendant's investment or use of the income, but from the harm suffered by the fraudulent predicate acts. The Fourth Circuit reversed the dismissal on the ground that the language of RICO does not require an "investment injury" and that requiring proof of such an injury "conflicts with the explicit policy that RICO be liberally construed."[11]

Library References:

C.J.S. RICO (Racketeer Influenced and Corrupt Organizations) § 8–10.
West's Key No. Digests, Racketeer Influenced and Corrupt Organizations ⬡33–48.

§ 21.9   Prohibited Activities—Acquiring or Controlling a RICO Enterprise: § 1962(b)

Section 1962(b) of title 18, United States Code, proscribes the following conduct:

> It shall be unlawful for any person through a pattern of racketeering activity or through collection of an unlawful debt to acquire or

Third Circuit: Glessner v. Kenny, 952 F.2d 702, 709 (3d Cir.1991).

Fifth Circuit: Crowe v. Henry, 43 F.3d 198, 205 (5th Cir.1995).

Sixth Circuit: Vemco v. Camardella, 23 F.3d 129, 132 (6th Cir.1994).

Seventh Circuit: Fujisawa Pharm. Co. v. Kapoor, 814 F.Supp. 720, 735 (N.D.Ill. 1993).

Eighth Circuit: Nagle v. Merrill Lynch, 790 F.Supp. 203, 209 (S.D.Iowa 1992).

Ninth Circuit: Nugget Hydroelec. L.P. v. Pacific Gas & Elec. Co., 981 F.2d 429, 437 (9th Cir.1992).

Tenth Circuit: Grider v. Texas Oil & Gas Corp., 868 F.2d 1147, 1150 (10th Cir. 1989).

Eleventh Circuit: Bowers v. Dairymen, Inc., 813 F.Supp. 1580, 1584 (S.D.Ga.1991).

8. Busby v. Crown Supply, Inc., 896 F.2d 833, 837 (4th Cir.1990).

9. Vemco v. Camardella, 23 F.3d 129 (6th Cir.1994).

10. Busby v. Crown Supply, Inc., 896 F.2d 833 (4th Cir.1990).

11. *Id.* at 838.

maintain, directly or indirectly, any interest in or control of any enterprise which is engaged in, or the activities of which affect, interstate or foreign commerce.[1]

Section 1962(b) makes unlawful the acquiring or controlling of an enterprise through a pattern of racketeering activity. This is the least used of the RICO violations.[2] Perhaps its most prevalent use is by the government in seeking to remove organized criminal influence from unions.[3] *United States v. Local 560, International Brotherhood of Teamsters* is a graphic example.[4] In *Local 560*, the court affirmed the removal of the entire governing board of a local Teamsters union for allowing organized crime to dominate union members. The government brought this civil RICO action against both an organized crime family—the "Provenzano Group"—and the Executive Board of the union, under accomplice liability theory. The government established a pattern of extortion and murder by the Provenzano Group to control union members' rights. An expert in labor law testified that the extreme fear apparently felt by union members prevented the members from exercising the normal rights of voting for union leaders and running for union offices. The Third Circuit affirmed the RICO judgment, finding the defendants' control over the union obvious: "[t]here seems to be no other plausible explanation for the silence of Local 560's membership in the face of repeated outrageous events."[5]

In a more recent 1962(b) case an employer was held vicariously liable for the racketeering acts of one of its top-level employees. In *Quick v. Peoples Bank*, the Eleventh Circuit affirmed a RICO judgment against a bank for the fraudulent loan activity by one of its top loan officers involving a small business.[6] The evidence showed that the loan officer had demanded a share of the profits from the business and personally pocketed repayments by the business on its revolving loan. The bank challenged the finding of vicarious liability. The Eleventh Circuit rejected the challenge, distinguishing vicarious liability for employers which benefit from the pattern of racketeering activity from that of employers which are victims of such activity. Noting that the bank knew of the employee's fraudulent conduct for at least one year and failed to take corrective action, while financially benefitting in the form of earned interest from the loan,[7] the court had little trouble affirming the conviction.

As the following two cases demonstrate, it can be difficult in a 1962(b) case to prove the link between the pattern of racketeering activity and acquisition of the enterprise. In *Protter v. Nathan's Famous*

§ 21.9

1. 18 U.S.C. § 1962(b).

2. U.S. DEP'T OF JUSTICE, RACKETEER INFLUENCED AND CORRUPT ORGANIZATIONS (RICO): A MANUAL FOR FEDERAL PROSECUTORS 76–77 (1990).

3. U.S. DEP'T OF JUSTICE, CIVIL RICO: A MANUAL FOR FEDERAL PROSECUTORS 3 (1988).

4. United States v. Local 560, Internat'l Brotherhood of Teamsters, 780 F.2d 267 (3d Cir.1985).

5. *Id.* at 278.

6. Quick v. Peoples Bank, 993 F.2d 793 (11th Cir.1993).

7. *Id.* at 798.

Systems, Inc., for example, a district court dismissed the RICO claim for failure to establish a nexus between the acquisition or control of the enterprise and the alleged racketeering activity.[8] Protter had purchased the franchise rights to three Nathan's Famous Hotdogs in New York City. He alleged various fraudulent representations regarding the value of the franchise and expected earnings for the three locations. After permitting Protter the chance to file a second amended complaint, the court found Protter still failed to establish any connection between the defendant's acquisition or control of Nathan's Famous Hotdogs and the alleged pattern of fraud.[9]

Similarly, in *Moffatt Enterprises, Inc. v. Borden, Inc.*, a district court dismissed the RICO claim on the ground that "control" was inadequately shown.[10] Moffatt Enterprises, Inc. (Moffatt) obtained the local distributor rights for a foam insulation product made by Borden. When Borden ceased production of the product, Moffatt went bankrupt. Moffatt alleged that Borden "controlled" Moffatt by inducing Moffatt to obtain the distributorship; by requiring approval of installation procedures; by specifying the geographic area of operation; by requiring development of a network of contractors satisfactory to the defendant; by specifying sales quotas; and, by specifying the training required. The court held the term "control" in section 1962(b) means the same as used in section 1962(a): "the 'control' contemplated is in the nature of the control one gains through the acquisition of sufficient stock to affect the composition of a board of directors."[11] The court found the controls asserted by the plaintiff were of the type incidental to a typical distributorship agreement—not even close to the nature of control over the board of directors.[12]

§ 21.10   Prohibited Activities—Participating In a RICO Enterprise: § 1962(c)

Section 1962(c) of title 18, United States Code, proscribes the following conduct:

> It shall be unlawful for any person employed by or associated with any enterprise engaged in, or the activities of which affect, interstate or foreign commerce, to conduct or participate, directly or indirectly, in the conduct of such enterprise's affairs through a pattern of racketeering activity or collection of unlawful debt.[1]

Section 1962(c) makes unlawful the participation in an enterprise's affairs through a pattern of racketeering activity by a person associated with an enterprise where the enterprise affects interstate or foreign commerce. Most RICO actions are filed under section 1962(c). Recently, the Supreme Court resolved a conflict among the circuits on the degree

8. Protter v. Nathan's Famous Systems, Inc., 925 F.Supp. 947 (E.D.N.Y.1996).

9. *Id.* at 955.

10. Moffatt Enterprises, Inc. v. Borden, Inc., 763 F.Supp. 143 (W.D.Pa.1990).

11. *Id.* at 147.

12. *Id.* at 148.

§ 21.10

1. 18 U.S.C. § 1962(c).

of participation required for section 1962(c) RICO liability.[2] Contrary to most of its prior holdings in RICO cases, which have been expansive, the Court favored a restrictive approach.[3]

In *Reves v. Ernst & Young*, a divided Court defined "participate" as "involved in the operation or management" of the enterprise and playing "*some* part in directing the enterprise's affairs."[4] *Reves* stopped short of limiting section 1962(c)'s reach to upper level management, noting that an enterprise may be operated "by lower-rung participants . . . under the direction of upper management."[5]

Reves involved the liability of outside accountants who allegedly prepared misleading audit reports for their client, a farmers' cooperative. The audit reports represented that the co-op was solvent by substantially overvaluing the co-op's assets. The audit reports were used by the co-op to perpetuate a securities fraud. Applying the "operation or management" test, the Court affirmed summary judgment for the defendants after finding that their participation—even though beyond mere auditing—failed to rise to the level of directing the "operation or management" of the co-op's securities fraud.[6] By following the "operation or management" test, the Court rejected broader tests which had been devised by the lower courts to find RICO liability for participants who played a minor role in the RICO enterprise.[7]

Since *Reves*, the Courts of Appeals have applied the "operation or management" test by examining the facts carefully to determine exactly what role a defendant played, whether the defendant was an insider in the enterprise and how vital the defendant was to the success of the enterprise. In *United States v. Gabriele*, for example, the First Circuit held that *Reves* applied only to "outsiders"—not to "insiders" of the enterprise.[8] The enterprise at issue in *Gabriele* involved an extensive money laundering operation for Columbian drug dealers. The defendant

2. Reves v. Ernst & Young, 507 U.S. 170, 113 S.Ct. 1163, 122 L.Ed.2d 525 (1993).

3. See J. N. Shapiro, Comment, *Attorney Liability Under RICO After Reves*, 61 U.Chi.L.Rev. 1153 (1994) (distinguishing lawyers from accountants to argue RICO claims against lawyers warrant a more refined standard than simply summarily dismissing case because defendant-attorney provided "traditional legal services" analogous to "traditional auditing functions"); I. H. Raphaelson, *RICO and the "Operation or Management" Test*, 28 U.Rich.L.Rev. 669 (1994) (disagreeing with Reves because of its chilling effect on criminal prosecutions, 98% of which indict under § 1962(c)); B.T. Camp, *Dual Construction of RICO*, 51 Wash. & Lee L.Rev. 61 (1994) (arguing for a broad construction of criminal RICO and a narrow construction for civil RICO); C. S. Howard, *RICO Claims Against Accountants After Reves*, 467 PLUSES/Lit 291 (1993)

(noting lower courts have been quick to dismiss claims against accountants performing traditional accounting or auditing services); D. R. Fischer, *Civil RICO After Reves: An Economic Commentary*, 1993 Sup. Ct.Rev. 157 (1993) (arguing expansive use of RICO is not efficient for our national economy, where the Court's limiting approach in Reves is second-best to Congressionally initiated restrictions).

4. *Id.*, 507 U.S. at 178, 113 S.Ct. at 1170 (emphasis in *Reves*).

5. *Id.*, 507 U.S. 184, 113 S.Ct. at 1173. Reves v. Ernst & Young, 507 U.S. 170, 184, 113 S.Ct. 1163, 1172, 122 L.Ed.2d 525 (1993).

6. *Id.* at 186.

7. *Id.* at 184.

8. United States v. Gabriele, 63 F.3d 61, 68 (1st Cir.1995).

was not the leader, but counted the money and kept records for one shop involved in the enterprise, a precious metal dealership. The court affirmed the defendant's conviction on the ground that "even employees not engaged in directing the operations of the RICO enterprise are criminally liable if they are plainly integral to carrying it out."[9]

Similarly, in *MCM Partners v. Andrews–Bartlett & Assoc.*, the Seventh Circuit held that "participate" under section 1962(c) includes "foot soldiers" under the direction of "generals."[10] In *MCM Partners*, two exhibition contractors who staged conventions and trade shows in Chicago were accused of violating various antitrust laws by refusing to rent materials and personnel from the plaintiff. The defendants won summary judgment before the District Court with their argument that they were outsiders and did not meet the *Reves* test of engaged in operation or management.[11] The Seventh Circuit disagreed, finding that the defendants were not outsiders but lower rung participants acting under the direction of the enterprise's upper management.[12] The court found it significant that the defendants in the case before it were part of the enterprise, whereas in *Reves* the accountants, who were found to be outsiders, were not. Moreover, the court found that "these defendants were vital to the achievement of the enterprise's primary goal; [t]hus even if [the defendants] may have been reluctant participants in a scheme devised by 'upper management,' they still knowingly implemented management's decisions, thereby enabling the enterprise to achieve its goals."[13]

United States v. Viola, provides another example. In this case, the Second Circuit reversed a section 1962(c) RICO conviction against a janitor.[14] The alleged enterprise involved a drug and stolen property importation and distribution ring at the Brooklyn, New York, waterfront. The janitor-defendant had performed odd jobs for the enterprise, such as light clean-up and maintenance work. The court viewed *Reves* as including lower-rung participants "who are under the direction of upper management" but precluding mere aiding and abetting liability.[15] Finding that the "taking of directions and performance of tasks necessary or helpful to the enterprise, without more, is insufficient" to meet *Reves*, the court reversed the defendant's conviction.[16]

The section 1962(c) cases involving "outside" professionals decided since *Reves* demonstrate a restrictive approach of *Reves*. For example, in *Baumer v. Pachl*, the Ninth Circuit affirmed the dismissal of a RICO action filed by investors in a real estate limited partnership against their lawyer.[17] The alleged enterprise involved transactions of fractional part-

---

9. *Id.*

10. MCM Partners v. Andrews–Bartlett & Assoc., 62 F.3d 967, 979 (7th Cir. 1995).

11. *Id.* at 977–78.

12. *Id.* at 979.

13. *Id.* at 979.

14. United States v. Viola, 35 F.3d 37, 41 (2d Cir.1994), *cert. denied*, 513 U.S. 1198, 115 S.Ct. 1270, 131 L.Ed.2d 148 (1995).

15. *Id.* at 41.

16. *Id.*

17. Baumer v. Pachl, 8 F.3d 1341 (9th Cir.1993).

nership interests, which were determined to be illegal sales of unregistered securities by the California Department of Corporations. The defendant participated by writing letters to the Department allegedly designed to forestall and cover-up the alleged fraud by mischaracterizing the improper activities. The court found that the defendant-attorney merely provided "legal services" analogous to the professional services rendered in *Reves* and thus was not involved in the "operation or management" of the partnership. The court noted that the defendant did not begin rendering legal services until well after the fraud commenced and thereafter his role was sporadic;[18] in addition, he held no formal role in the business nor directed any of the affairs of the business.[19]

Library References:

C.J.S. RICO (Racketeer Influenced and Corrupt Organizations) § 8–10.
West's Key No. Digests, Racketeer Influenced and Corrupt Organizations ⊕33–48.

§ 21.11 Prohibited Activities—Conspiracy: § 1962(d)

Section 1962(d) of title 18, United States Code, proscribes the following conduct:

It shall be unlawful for any person to conspire to violate any of the provisions of subsection (a), (b), or (c) of this section.[1]

Section 1962(d) makes unlawful agreements to commit any of the three other RICO substantive offenses.[2] Most RICO lawsuits, whether civil or criminal, include a conspiracy count along with one or more substantive counts. Sometimes the conspiracy count is crucial to the survival of the lawsuit. For example in *United States v. Antar*,[3] the Third Circuit held that a family member-shareholder was not liable under section 1962(c), but could, nevertheless, be liable for conspiracy to violate RICO. The defendant had been an active officer and director of Crazy Eddie's electronic stores in New York, but had resigned as an officer several years prior to the conduct in question because of a family feud. The statute of limitations had run on the substantive RICO counts (securities fraud) but not on the conspiracy count. The court affirmed the conspiracy conviction after finding that merely resigning from office was not a sufficient affirmative withdrawal from the conspiracy.[4]

There is a conflict among the circuits as to whether a defendant must agree to personally commit the predicate acts, or whether a defendant must merely agree that any member of the conspiracy commit

---

18. *Id.* at 1344; *See, e.g.,* University of Maryland at Baltimore v. Peat, Marwick, Main & Co., 996 F.2d 1534, 1539 (3d Cir. 1993).

19. *Id.* at 1344.

§ 21.11

1. 18 U.S.C. § 1962(d) (Supp.1997).

2. *Third Circuit:* United States v. Veksler, 62 F.3d 544 (3d Cir.1995), *cert.*

denied, 51 U.S. 1075, 116 S.Ct. 780, 133 L.Ed.2d 731 (1996).

Seventh Circuit: United States v. Stephens, 46 F.3d 587 (7th Cir.1995).

3. United States v. Antar, 53 F.3d 568 (3d Cir.1995).

4. *Id.* at 583.

the predicate acts. The majority of circuits have adopted the latter, broader rule.[5] *United States v. Neapolitan* is typical. In *Neapolitan*, the Seventh Circuit applied the majority rule and affirmed the RICO conspiracy conviction of a sheriff's investigator for his limited role in "fixing" titles for an auto "chop shop."[6] The defendant had become involved late in an ongoing conspiracy by soliciting one cash bribe and fixing one case. In adopting the majority rule, the court looked at the Supreme Court's consistent adherence "to a broad, literal reading of the statute," and held that § 1962(d) did not require that a defendant must agree to personally commit the underlying predicate acts.[7] The Seventh Circuit explained its view:

> * * * Section 1962(d) explicitly prohibits conspiracies to violate RICO. The natural reading of that phrase is the proscription of any agreement the object of which is the conducting of or participation in the affairs of an enterprise through a pattern of racketeering activity. In other words, rather than creating a new law of conspiracy, RICO created a new objective for traditional conspiracy law—a violation of sections 1962(a), (b), or (c). Requiring an agreement personally to commit two predicate acts would establish a new form of conspiring in contradistinction to section 1962(d) based in traditional conspiracy law. Under the defendants' theory section 1962(d) would require not only an agreement to join in the conspiracy's objective, a RICO violation, but also an agreement to personally commit the underlying offense through the commission of two predicate acts. This involves a degree of involvement in the affairs of the conspiracy that is not required in any other type of conspiracy, where agreeing to a prescribed objective is sufficient.
>
> Nothing on the face of the statute or its legislative history supports the imposition of a more stringent level of personal involvement in a conspiracy to violate RICO as opposed to a conspiracy to violate anything else. In fact, it seems more likely that Congress, in search of means to prosecute the leaders of organized crime, intended section 1962(d) to be broad enough to encompass those persons who, while intimately involved in the conspiracy, neither agreed to personally commit nor actually participated in the commission of the predicate crimes.[8]

5. *See*:

D.C. Circuit: Jones v. Meridian Towers Apts., 816 F.Supp. 762, 773 (D.C.1993).

Third Circuit: United States v. Traitz, 871 F.2d 368, 396 (3d Cir.1989).

Fourth Circuit: United States v. Pryba, 900 F.2d 748, 760 (4th Cir.1990).

Sixth Circuit: United States v. Joseph, 781 F.2d 549, 554 (6th Cir.1986).

Seventh Circuit: United States v. Korando, 29 F.3d 1114, 1117 (7th Cir.1994).

Eighth Circuit: United States v. Bennett, 44 F.3d 1364, 1374 (8th Cir.), *cert. denied*, 115 S.Ct. 2279 (1995).

Ninth Circuit: United States v. Blinder, 10 F.3d 1468, 1477 (9th Cir.1993).

Eleventh Circuit: United States v. Starrett, 55 F.3d 1525, 1543 (11th Cir.1995), *cert. denied*, 517 U.S. 1111, 116 S.Ct. 1335, 134 L.Ed.2d 485 (1996).

6. United States v. Neapolitan, 791 F.2d 489 (7th Cir.1986).

7. *Id.* at 495.

8. *Id.* at 497–98.

United States v. Elliott,[9] demonstrates the more restrictive minority approach. *Elliott* involved a large scale criminal enterprise which profited through arson, automobile and truck theft, dealing in counterfeit automobile titles, theft of interstate shipments of meat and dairy products, etc. The Fifth Circuit reversed the conspiracy conviction of one defendant, James Elliott, after finding that there was insufficient evidence that Elliott "agreed to participate, directly or indirectly, in the affairs of an enterprise through a pattern of racketeering activity."[10] The court emphasized that to be guilty of a 1962(d) conspiracy, a defendant "must have objectively manifested an agreement to participate, directly or indirectly, in the affairs of an enterprise *through the commission of two or more predicate crimes.*"[11] The court explained its reasoning:

> RICO * * * creat[es] a substantive offense which ties together these diverse parties and crimes. Thus, the object of a RICO conspiracy is to violate a substantive RICO provision—here, to conduct or participate in the affairs of an enterprise through a pattern of racketeering activity—and not merely to commit each of the predicate crimes necessary to demonstrate a pattern of racketeering activity. The gravamen of the conspiracy charge in this case is not that each defendant agreed to commit arson, to steal goods from interstate commerce, to obstruct justice, and to sell narcotics; rather, it is that each agreed to participate, directly and indirectly, in the affairs of the enterprise by committing two or more predicate crimes. Under the statute, it is irrelevant that each defendant participated in the enterprise's affairs through different, even unrelated crimes, so long as we may reasonably infer that each crime was intended to further the enterprise's affairs. To find a single conspiracy, we still must look for agreement on an overall objective. * * *

> We cannot say, * * * that [1962(d)] demands inferences that cannot reasonably be drawn from circumstantial evidence or that it otherwise offends the rule that guilt be individual and personal. The Act does not authorize that individuals "be tried *en masse* for the conglomeration of distinct and separate offenses committed by others." Nor does it punish mere association with conspirators or knowledge of illegal activity; its proscriptions are directed against conduct, not status.

There is also a conflict among the circuits as to whether standing for RICO conspiracy violations requires an injury by a predicate act of racketeering or by any overt act intended to further the enterprise.[12]

---

9. 571 F.2d 880 (5th Cir.1978).

10. *Id.* at 907.

11. *Id.* at 903 (emphasis in original).

12. *See*:

First Circuit: Miranda v. Ponce Fed. Bank, 948 F.2d 41, 48 (1st Cir.1991).

Second Circuit: Terminate Control Corp. v. Horowitz, 28 F.3d 1335, 1344 (2d Cir.1994).

Eighth Circuit: Bowman v. Western Auto Supply, 985 F.2d 383, 388 (8th Cir.1993).

Ninth Circuit: Reddy v. Litton Indus., Inc., 912 F.2d 291, 295 (9th Cir.1990).

But See:

Third Circuit: Shearin v. E.F. Hutton Group, Inc., 885 F.2d 1162, 1169 (3d Cir.1989).

Terminate Control Corp. v. Horowitz represents the majority view, which requires an injury caused by predicate acts.[13] Nu-Life, the plaintiff, had been awarded contracts by the City of New York's Board of Education to repair three school buildings. After the contract had been awarded, Nu-Life alleged, various Board of Education members demanded kickbacks and when Nu-Life failed to pay the kickbacks, withheld payments due Nu-Life. Nu-Life then brought a civil RICO action alleging violations of section 1962(c) and (d) and a pattern of racketeering activity of Hobbs Act violations (extortion).[14] The Second Circuit stated that "to maintain a private action for a RICO conspiracy, a plaintiff must prove injury caused by a predicate act of racketeering, and not merely by the agreement to commit such acts or by an overt, nonpredicate act in furtherance of such an agreement."[15] The court found that Nu-Life's damages (withholding of funds due, resulting in an inability to complete the project) were caused by the defendants' extortion[16] and thus, that a RICO conspiracy was shown.[17]

Gagan v. American Cablevision, demonstrates the minority rule. In *Gagan*, the Seventh Circuit affirmed judgment for former limited partners of a cable television (CATV) company[18] that had invested $2.5 million in the new venture started by the defendants. The new venture never materialized and investors lost most of their money because, they alleged, the defendants concealed and fraudulently dissipated invested funds.[19] The Seventh Circuit affirmed the finding on liability on the conspiracy charge. It noted that, "a plaintiff must allege that the defendant's overt act in furtherance of the RICO conspiracy injured the plaintiff's business or property ... however, ... that overt act need not be one of the predicate acts of racketeering under § 1961...."[20] The court explained its reasoning:

> Since § 1962(d) does not require that a predicate act actually be committed, it follows that the act causing claimant's injury does not need to be a predicate act of racketeering.... [A] 'person directly injured by an overt act in furtherance of a RICO conspiracy has been injured by reason of the conspiracy,' and thus should have standing to sue.[21]

Library References:

C.J.S. RICO (Racketeer Influenced and Corrupt Organizations) § 6.
West's Key No. Digests, Racketeer Influenced and Corrupt Organizations ⟜15.

Fourth Circuit: Flinders v. Datasec Corp., 742 F.Supp. 929, 934 (E.D.Va.1990).

Seventh Circuit: Gagan v. American Cablevision, 77 F.3d 951, 959 (7th Cir.1996).

13. Terminate Control Corp. v. Horowitz, 28 F.3d 1335 (2d Cir.1994).

14. *Id.* at 1338–39.

15. *Id.* at 1343–44. The Second Circuit held that the District Court's jury instructions did not convey this test but that the error was harmless. *Id.* at 1345–46.

16. *Id.* at 1346.

17. *Id.*

18. Gagan v. American Cablevision, 77 F.3d 951 (7th Cir.1996).

19. *Id.* at 957.

20. *Id.* at 959.

21. *Id.* at 959.

§ 21.12   Civil RICO—In General

This section addresses issues which dominate civil RICO litigation: standing, preemption, class actions, Rule 11 sanctions, and statute of limitations.

Section 1964 of Title 18 authorizes the following civil remedies:

> Any person injured in his business or property by reason of a violation of section 1962 of this chapter may sue therefor in any appropriate United States district court and shall recover threefold the damages he sustains and the cost of the suit, including a reasonable attorney's fee....[1]

By far, most RICO actions filed today are civil. Plaintiffs may recover treble damages plus court costs and attorneys' fees,[2] and seek injunctive and other equitable relief.[3]

Sedima, *S.P.R.L. v. Imrex Co.* is one of the most important Supreme Court case interpreting the RICO statute.[4] It involved a civil RICO action brought by private litigants. In *Sedima*, the Court reversed the dismissal of a RICO action by a foreign corporation which had entered into a joint business venture with a New York exporter of aviation parts. The thrust of the plaintiff's complaint was that the defendant had presented inflated bills for nonexistent expenses. This resulted in a smaller share of net profits going to the plaintiff per the parties' business contract to share net profits. The District Court's dismissal of the RICO complaint was affirmed by the Second Circuit. Both the District Court and the Second Circuit adopted restrictive interpretations of key RICO provisions. The Supreme Court reversed the dismissal and took the opportunity to elaborate on RICO's expansive scope. The Court held that a civil RICO action could proceed without prior criminal convictions for the underlying alleged predicate acts.[5] The Court also held that a RICO plaintiff need not have incurred a "racketeering injury" to obtain relief under RICO.[6] Finally, in dicta, the Court suggested that the burden of proof for civil RICO actions, including proof of the underlying predicate acts, was preponderance of the evidence.[7] The broad interpretation adopted by the Court in *Sedima* opened the door for the expansive uses for RICO today.

Library References:

C.J.S. RICO (Racketeer Influenced and Corrupt Organizations) § 3, 8–10, 13–23.
West's Key No. Digests, Racketeer Influenced and Corrupt Organizations ☜55–85.

§ 21.12

1. 18 U.S.C. § 1964(c).

2. 18 U.S.C. § 1964(b). See U.S. Dep't of Justice, Civil RICO: A Manual for Federal Prosecutors (1988).

3. 18 U.S.C. § 1964(a).

4. Sedima, S.P.R.L. v. Imrex Co., 473 U.S. 479 (1985).

5. *Id.* at 493. *But see* Pub.L. 104–67, 109 Stat. 943 (1995) (restricting § 1964(c) to require a prior conviction for predicate acts of Securities Fraud).

6. *Id.* at 500.

7. *Id.* at 491.

§ 21.13 Civil RICO—Standing

A significant number of civil RICO claims are dismissed for lack of standing. *Holmes v. Securities Investor Protection Corporation*, is the leading Supreme Court case on standing. In a unanimous decision, the Court affirmed dismissal of a civil RICO claim for lack of standing.[1] The plaintiff, Securities Investor Protection Corporation (SIPC), had filed suit for the $13 million losses it sustained because of the defendants' alleged securities fraud. The District Court entered summary judgment for Holmes on the RICO charges, ruling that SIPC "does not meet the 'purchaser-seller' requirements for standing to assert RICO claims which are predicated upon violation of Section 10(b) and Rule 10b–5."[2]

In determining whether SIPC had standing, the Court turned first to the language in section 1964(c), RICO's provision for civil actions. This section provides that "[a]ny person injured in his business or property by reason of a violation of section 1962 ... may sue therefor...." The Court considered whether this language allowed an expansive "but for" test of causation in determining whether a plaintiff is injured "by reason of" a RICO violation, or required a narrower causation test of proximate cause. Relying on statutory history, and noting the overwhelming view of the Courts of Appeals, the Court ruled that "proximate causation" must be shown between the plaintiff's injury and the RICO violation. The Court explained:

> Here we use 'proximate cause' to label generically the judicial tools used to limit a person's responsibility for the consequences of that person's own acts.... [There must be] some direct relation between the injury asserted and the injurious conduct alleged.

Since *Holmes*, lower courts have dismissed a number of RICO cases, finding that proximate cause is not shown between the plaintiff's damages and alleged RICO conduct. *McCarthy v. Recordex Service Inc.* is typical. In this case[3] the Third Circuit affirmed the dismissal of a RICO claim brought by clients of personal injury lawyers. The plaintiffs filed suit against hospitals and their exclusive copier service for charging different amounts to different groups who requested copies of hospital records. The hospitals charged lawyers $1 per page plus other administrative fees to copy medical records for their clients, but charged no fees to other requestors. Citing *Holmes*, the court held the plaintiffs had no standing because they were only "indirect victims" of the discriminatory pricing.

Similarly, in *Hirsch v. Arthur Andersen*, the Second Circuit affirmed the dismissal of a RICO claim brought by a bankruptcy trustee against the debtor's accountants and lawyers for their participation in a Ponzi scheme which led to the bankruptcy.[4] The defendants allegedly developed false forecasts and memoranda to help perpetuate the appearance

§ 21.13

1. Holmes v. Securities Investor Protection Corp., 503 U.S. 258, 112 S.Ct. 1311, 117 L.Ed.2d 532 (1992).

2. *Id.* at 263.

3. McCarthy v. Recordex Service Inc., 80 F.3d 842 (3d Cir.1996).

4. Hirsch v. Arthur Andersen, 72 F.3d 1085 (2d Cir.1995).

of profitability in various real estate ventures. The court held that only the defrauded investors had standing under state law—not the bankruptcy trustee.[5] The court explained:

> To have standing '[a] plaintiff must (1) allege personal injury (2) fairly traceable to the defendant's allegedly unlawful conduct, and (3) likely to be redressed by the requested relief.... Further, when creditors ... have a claim for injury that is particularized as to them, they are exclusively entitled to pursue that claim, and the bankruptcy trustee is precluded from doing so.[6]

When courts find standing, post-*Holmes*, they find a breach of some duty, or other damage, to the plaintiff. For example, in *Ceribelli v. Elghanayan*, the Second Circuit reversed the dismissal of a RICO claim brought by shareholders of a residential cooperative against the promoters of the cooperative for fraudulently concealing costly defects in the building.[7] The District Court had ruled that standing "would be appropriate only if the defendants had breached fiduciary duties owed to the plaintiffs." The Second Circuit, however, ruled that no fiduciary relationship was required. Citing *Holmes*, the court reversed the District Court, finding that standing was shown by any direct injury caused by the pattern of racketeering activity.[8]

Library References:

C.J.S. RICO (Racketeer Influenced and Corrupt Organizations) § 13–15.
West's Key No. Digests, Racketeer Influenced and Corrupt Organizations ⚷56–63.

§ 21.14   Civil RICO—Preemption

RICO actions may be preempted by various comprehensive administrative schemes. In *Kenty v. Bank One*, Columbus, N.A., for example, the Sixth Circuit held that an insurer was exempt from RICO liability pursuant to the McCarran–Ferguson Act.[1] Kenty alleged the insurer and Bank One, a finance company, had developed a scheme to provide excessive "forced place" insurance for car buyers. Dispositive of the preemption issue was whether RICO "invalidates, impairs or supersedes" the applicable state laws.[2] The court found that RICO, with its treble damages and a different burden of proof than applicable Ohio law, impaired the ability of Ohio to provide detailed regulation and remedies for unfair and deceptive trade acts. The court dismissed the suit against the insurer on the ground that RICO would subject insurance companies to a different standard of behavior than Ohio law.[3] RICO has also been found to be preempted by the National Labor Relations Act[4], the Railway

---

5. *Id.* at 1093.

6. *Id.* at 1091, 1093.

7. Ceribelli v. Elghanayan, 990 F.2d 62 (2d Cir.1993).

8. *Id.* at 64–65.

§ 21.14

1. Kenty v. Bank One, Columbus, N.A., 92 F.3d 384 (6th Cir.1996).

2. *Id.* at 392.

3. *Id.*

4. Brennan v. Chestnut, 973 F.2d 644 (8th Cir.1992). *Cf.* Hood v. Smith's Transfer Corp., 762 F.Supp. 1274 (W.D.Ky.1991).

Labor Act[5], the Labor–Management Relations Act[6] and the Federal Employees Health Benefits Act.[7]

§ 21.15   Civil RICO—Class Actions

Civil RICO claims may be brought as class actions. Certifications of class actions are governed by Rule 23 of the Federal Rules of Civil Procedure. The party seeking class certification bears the burden of establishing that the case is certifiable. There are four prerequisites to establish: (1) numerosity; (2) commonality; (3) typicality; and (4) fair and adequate representation.[1] Once these threshold issues are met, the potential class must also satisfy at least one provision of Rule 23(b).

Fogie v. Rent–A–Center, Inc. illustrates a successful certification of a RICO class action.[2] Plaintiff consumers filed suit against the defendant alleging its rent-to-own contracts were usurious. The defendant rented consumer goods through renewable leases which allowed the customer to become owner upon payment of a specified number of installments. However, the rent-to-contract only disclosed the fair market value of the goods, which was 55% of the total amount paid. Fogie entered into such a contract on September 19, 1990 for living room furniture valued at $815 and for which she ultimately paid $1500. Fogie moved to certify a class of "all persons who have entered into so-called 'rent-to-own' contracts in Minnesota with the Defendants, or any of their predecessors or successor in interest . . . ."[3]

The court granted certification, finding that the plaintiff had satisfied all four requirements: (1) the class potentially included thousands of plaintiffs, so it was too numerous to make joinder practicable; (2) there were common issues of law and fact when all class members signed the same contract; (3) the claims of the representative parties were typical of the class; and (4) the named plaintiff had vigorously prosecuted the action without conflict.[4] The court also found that the plaintiff had satisfied the requirements to seek injunctive relief under Rule 23(b)(2) as well as to obtain monetary relief under Rule 23(b)(3).

The defendants argued that issues of unconscionability, deceptive trade practices and fraudulent intent were questions of individual fact which predominated over the class issues. The court rejected this argument on the ground that the uniform practice of disclosing only the fair market value of the goods and not the purchase price could be dispositive for all the claims.[5] Moreover, the court reasoned, the differences in the individual amount of damages based on the goods purchased and pay-

5.   Mann v. Air Line Pilots Assoc'n, 848 F.Supp. 990 (S.D.Fl.1994).

6.   Chicago Dist. Council Carpenters Pension Fund v. Ceiling Wall Systems, Inc., 915 F.Supp. 939 (N.D.Ill.1996).

7.   Bridges v. Blue Cross and Blue Shield Assoc'n, 935 F.Supp. 37 (D.C.1996).

§ 21.15

1.   Fed.R.Civ.P. 23(a).

2.   Fogie v. Rent–A–Center, Inc., 867 F.Supp. 1398 (D.Minn.1993).

3.   *Id.* at 1401.

4.   *Id.* at 1402.

5.   *Id.* at 1403.

ments made was minor.[6] The individual claims were relatively small and the pursuit of individual litigation unlikely.[7] The court concluded: "A class action will provide a fair and efficient adjudication of the claims asserted by the plaintiffs and it is a superior method of adjudicating this controversy."

Predictably, in the instances where courts have found class certification to be inappropriate they have found that individual issues dominate common issues. In *Freedman v. Arista Records, Inc.*, for example, the District Court denied the plaintiffs' motion for class certification.[8] The plaintiffs tried to establish a class including "all persons in the United States, its territories and possessions who purchased Milli Vanilli recordings prior to November 15, 1990." In November 1990, it was revealed that Fabrice Morvan and Rob Pilatus, the two persons who won a Grammy Award for their song, "Girl You Know Its True," did not in fact sing the song on the album as represented. In this case, the court was persuaded that individual issues of fact predominated over the underlying fraud claims, thus precluding certification.[9] Through discovery, the defendants had been able to show that some purchasers, having listened to the music on the radio, bought the album without knowing anything about the musicians. Thus, individual testimony would have to be presented to determine if customers relied on any misrepresentation by the defendants.

In comparison is *Buford v. H & R Block, Inc.*, where the District Court denied certification because the class was too large.[10] The putative class of plaintiffs consisted of all those who received "Rapid Refund" loans for their income tax returns. The plaintiffs alleged various misrepresentations related to H & R Block's Rapid Refund program. The court found significant issues of individual fact regarding reliance, which when magnified by a potential class in the millions made a class action unmanageable and thus, inferior to other available means of adjudication.[11]

Library References:

C.J.S. RICO (Racketeer Influenced and Corrupt Organizations) § 13.
West's Key No. Digests, Racketeer Influenced and Corrupt Organizations ⊙56.

§ 21.16 Civil RICO—Rule 11 Sanctions

Federal Rule of Civil Procedure 11 provides that if a pleading, motion or other paper is presented for an improper purpose, is not warranted by existing law or by a nonfrivolous argument for extension or reversal of existing law, does not have evidentiary support or, in the instance of a denial, is not warranted on the evidence, the attorney so

6. *Id.* at 1404.
7. *Id.*
8. Freedman v. Arista Records, Inc., 137 F.R.D. 225 (E.D.Pa.1991).
9. *Id.* at 228.

10. Buford v. H & R Block, Inc., 168 F.R.D. 340 (S.D.Ga.1996).
11. *Id.* at 364.

certifying may be subject to "an appropriate sanction...."[1] Although lower courts tend to show hostility to RICO actions,[2] they also appear to order Rule 11 sanctions for inappropriate filing or pursuit of RICO actions only in egregious situations.

O'Ferral v. Trebol Motors Corp., demonstrates application of Rule 11 sanctions in a civil RICO action. In *O'Ferral*, the First Circuit affirmed Rule 11 sanctions against the plaintiff's attorneys.[3] The RICO class action alleged that a Volvo distributor in Puerto Rico advertised the availability of the more expensive 240 GLE model, when in fact, Volvo had stopped making it. Instead, the distributor modified a 240 DL with additional features and attached its own GLE label, which induced the plaintiffs to incur damages of $225 million. After more than two years, the complaint was dismissed as nothing more than "garden variety consumer deception," which failed to point to any affirmative misrepresentation constituting fraud.[4] The defendants moved for sanctions and the trial court awarded $8,000 in attorneys' fees and $4,000 as costs. The First Circuit affirmed the trial judge's judgment noting "we think it plain that the plaintiffs' suit was extremely thin."[5]

Similarly, in *Brandt v. Schal Associates, Inc.*, the Seventh Circuit affirmed a nearly half-million dollar award of attorneys' fees against plaintiff's counsel.[6] The litigation involved a contract dispute and continued for over seven years before being dismissed by plaintiff's counsel. The trial judge concluded that the plaintiff's counsel, David Campbell, had concocted the RICO fraud theory without any evidentiary basis. The Seventh Circuit was sympathetic to the trial judge's exasperation:

> We believe, however, that attorneys' fees are particularly justified in this case as both compensation for defendants' expenses and as a deterrent to any similar performance in the future. Not only does the award address the contents of the spurious complaint filed by Campbell, but it also addresses the bad-faith pursuit of the worthless complaint. Campbell inundated his opponent and the district court with lengthy (and insubstantial) briefs, mountains of discovery (affidavits hundreds of pages long), and measures designed simply to impede the rapid resolution of the case. Campbell's attempt to succeed on his RICO complaint by unnecessarily saddling his oppo-

---

§ 21.16

1. For sources discussing Rule 11 sanctions in RICO cases, see Kevin P. Roddy, RICO in Business and Commercial Litigation §§ 9.07–9.10 Jed Rakoff & Michael Goldstein, *Defending Civil RICO Actions, Civil RICO: A Guide to Practice and Strategy* 211 (1986); Michael Silberberg & Peter E. Scher, *Flawed RICO Complaint Draws Sanctions*, 216 N.Y.L.J. 3 (1996); Seth Kaberon, *Rule 11 Sanction Imposed for Frivolous RICO Claims*, 134 CHI.DAILY L.BULL. 1 (1988); Martin Flumenbaum and Brad S. Karp, *Attorney's Fees, Reach of RICO; Rule 11 Sanctions*, 216 N.Y.L.Y. 3 (1996).

2. *See, e.g., National Organization for Women v. Scheidler*, 510 U.S. 249, 114 S.Ct. 798, 127 L.Ed.2d 99 (1994); *H. J. Inc.*, 492 U.S. 299 (1989); *Sedima v. Imrex*, 473 U.S. 479, 105 S.Ct. 3275, 87 L.Ed.2d 346 (1985) (Supreme Court opinions rejecting restrictive approach of the lower courts).

3. O'Ferral v. Trebol Motors Corp., 45 F.3d 561 (1st Cir.1995).

4. *Id.* at 563.

5. *Id.*

6. Brandt v. Schal Associates, Inc., 960 F.2d 640 (7th Cir.1992).

nent with an exhausting and costly review of his submissions is an egregious and unjustified abuse of judicial process. Campbell's purposeful infliction of added waste—added to what would otherwise be required to dispense with his RICO claim—is a choice for which he must now pay a penalty.[7]

Avirgan v. Hull, provides another example of Rule 11 sanctions assessed in civil RICO actions. In this case, the Eleventh Circuit affirmed sanctions in excess of one million dollars against the plaintiffs, who were American journalists based in Costa Rica reporting on the Nicaraguan Contras.[8] While attending a press conference by the Contra leader, a bomb exploded, killing eight people and injuring the plaintiffs. The complaint alleged the formation of an enterprise involving CIA operatives, arm merchants, mercenaries and Columbian drug lords for the purpose of overthrowing the Nicaraguan government by means of explosives, murder, arms and drug trafficking, etc. After a two year discovery process, the trial court granted summary judgment for the defendants on the ground that the plaintiffs failed to establish evidence concerning the cause of their purported injuries. The Eleventh Circuit affirmed the sanctions against the plaintiffs and their lawyer for submitting twenty fabricated affidavits by unknown, nonexistent, deceased sources which they knew to be groundless prior to filing the lawsuit.[9]

In contrast is *McIntyre's Mini Computers v. Creative Synergy Corp.*, where the District Court refused to assess Rule 11 sanctions, even though the RICO complaint failed to allege an adequate pattern, distinct enterprise or the elements of conspiracy.[10] The action, lasting last than two months, involved the alleged theft of a customer list by a software consulting firm which had done work for the plaintiff. In denying sanctions, the judge emphasized, "we do not intend to stifle the enthusiasm or chill the creativity that is the very lifeblood of the law. Vital changes have been wrought by those members of the bar who have decided to challenge the received wisdom, and a rule that penalized such innovation and industry would run counter to our notions of the common law itself. Courts must strive to avoid the wisdom of hindsight in determining whether a pleading was valid when signed, and any and all doubts must be resolved in favor of the signer."[11]

§ 21.17 Civil RICO—Statute of Limitations

The statute of limitations for criminal RICO prosecutions is five years,[1] with the clock starting to run from the date of the last act of racketeering activity.[2] The returning of the indictment by the grand jury

7. *Id.* at 647.

8. Avirgan v. Hull, 932 F.2d 1572 (11th Cir.1991).

9. *Id.* at 1582.

10. McIntyre's Mini Computers v. Creative Synergy Corp., 644 F.Supp. 580 (E.D.Mich.1986).

11. *Id.* at 591 (quoting Eastway Constr. Corp. v. City of N.Y., 762 F.2d 243, 254 (2d Cir.1985)).

§ 21.17

1. 18 U.S.C. § 3282.

2. United States v. Starrett, 55 F.3d 1525, 1544 (11th Cir.1995), *cert. denied*, 517

tolls the statute of limitations, unless the indictment is sealed under Federal Rule of Criminal Procedure 6(e) and the defendant can show actual substantial prejudice.[3] Incarceration does not toll the statute of limitations.[4]

The statute of limitations for civil RICO is four years.[5] The Supreme Court has expressly left open the issue of when the RICO action accrues[6] and the circuits are divided. The First, Second, Fourth, Fifth, Seventh and Ninth Circuits follow the "injury discovery" rule, holding that the statute of limitations begins to accrue when the plaintiff discovered or should have discovered an injury.[7] *McCool v. Strata Oil Co.*, demonstrates application of this rule. Investors in an oil drilling project filed suit against Strata Oil Company (Strata) and Strata's founders, alleging securities fraud and RICO violation arising from misrepresentations allegedly made about the project.[8] Adopting and applying the "injury discovery" rule, the Seventh Circuit held that the RICO claims were not barred by the statute of limitations. The Seventh Circuit found the "injury discovery" rule to be the most consistent with the purpose of civil RICO (recovery for each injury). Applying it to the facts before it, the Seventh Circuit held that the plaintiffs should have discovered the alleged misrepresentations about the split of profits among investors and project founders when they signed agreements pertaining to certain wells. As such, the RICO action was not barred.[9]

The Sixth, Eighth, Tenth and Eleventh Circuits follow the "injury and pattern discovery" rule. Under this approach, the clock begins to run when the plaintiff discovered or should have discovered the pattern of racketeering activity, in addition to the existence of the injury.[10]

U.S. 1111, 116 S.Ct. 1335, 134 L.Ed.2d 485 (1996).

3. United States v. Srulowitz, 819 F.2d 37, 40 (2d Cir.1987).

4. Bontkowski v. First Nat'l Bank, 998 F.2d 459, 462 (7th Cir.1993).

5. Agency Holding Corp. v. Malley–Duff, 483 U.S. 143, 156, 107 S.Ct. 2759, 2766, 97 L.Ed.2d 121 (1987).

6. *Id.* at 156–57.

7. *See*:

First Circuit: Rodriguez v. Banco Cent., 917 F.2d 664, 666 (1st Cir.1990).

Second Circuit: Bankers Trust Co. v. Rhoades, 859 F.2d 1096, 1102 (2d Cir.1988).

Fourth Circuit: Pocahontas Supreme Coal Co. v. Bethlehem Steel Corp., 828 F.2d 211, 220 (4th Cir.1987).

Fifth Circuit: La Porte Constr. Co. v. Bayshore Nat. Bank, 805 F.2d 1254, 1256 (5th Cir.1986).

Seventh Circuit: McCool v. Strata Oil Co., 972 F.2d 1452, 1465 (7th Cir.1992).

Ninth Circuit: Grimmett v. Brown, 75 F.3d 506, 510 (9th Cir.1996), cert. denied, 519 U.S. 233, 117 S.Ct. 759, 136 L.Ed.2d 674 (1997).

8. *Id.* at 1454–55.

9. This conclusion also depended upon whether an agreement tolled the running of the statute of limitations. The court remanded for further findings of fact on this issue. *Id.* at 1466.

10. *See*:

Sixth Circuit: Caproni v. Prudential Securities, Inc., 15 F.3d 614, 620 (6th Cir. 1994).

Eighth Circuit: Granite Falls Bank v. Henrikson, 924 F.2d 150, 154 (8th Cir. 1991).

Tenth Circuit: Bath v. Bushkin, Gaims, Gaines & Jonas, 913 F.2d 817, 821 (10th Cir.1990).

Eleventh Circuit: Bivens Gardens Office Bldg. v. Barnett Bank, 906 F.2d 1546, 1554 (11th Cir.1990).

Granite Falls Bank v. Henrikson, demonstrates this approach. In *Henrikson,* the Eighth Circuit reversed the dismissal of a bank's RICO claim, finding that the District Court erred in holding that the statute of limitations had run.[11] After noting the Supreme Court's silence on this issue and reviewing the various tests adopted by different circuits, the Eighth Circuit adopted the "injury and pattern" test. The court reasoned that "[i]t seems fundamental ... that a civil RICO cause of action cannot accrue until all of its elements are present" and "[t]he primary source of RICO's unique character is its pattern requirement."[12] Thus, the court adopted the following rule:

> With respect to each independent injury to the plaintiff, a civil RICO cause of action begins to accrue as soon as the plaintiff discovers, or reasonably should have discovered, both the existence and source of his injury and that the injury is part of a pattern.[13]

Until overruled by the Supreme Court in 1997,[14] the Third Circuit follows the "last predicate act" rule, holding that the statute of limitations begins to run when the plaintiff discovered or should have discovered the last injury or the last predicate act of the pattern.[15] This is the rule followed by all circuits in criminal cases but, as the Supreme Court noted, "there are significant differences between civil and criminal RICO actions ..." Although disapproving of the "last predicate act" rule, the court did not find it necessary to choose between the other two leading approaches.

§ 21.18 RICO—Impact of *United States v. Lopez*

In *United States v. Lopez,* the United States Supreme Court held the Gun–Free School Zones Act, 18 U.S.C. § 922(q), unconstitutional.[1] The Court found that section 922 (q) had no reasonable connection to interstate commerce and thus was beyond the scope of Congress' Commerce Power.[2] The court gave two reasons for its decision. First, section 922(q) was a criminal statute that "by its terms ha[d] nothing to do with 'commerce' or any sort of economic enterprise, however broadly one might define those terms," and the statute did not regulate an activity which substantially affected interstate commerce.[3] Second, section 922(q) did not contain a "jurisdictional element which would ensure, through case-by-case inquiry, that the firearm possession in question affect[ed] interstate commerce."[4] For these reasons, the Court, for the first time in more than fifty years, invalidated a federal statute putatively based on Congress' Commerce Power.

11. Granite Falls Bank v. Henrikson, 924 F.2d 150 (8th Cir.1991).

12. *Id.* at 152–53.

13. *Id.* at 154 *quoting* Bivens Gardens Office Bldg. Inc. v. Barnett Bank of Florida, Inc., 906 F.2d 1546, 1554 (11th Cir.1990).

14. Klehr v. A.O. Smith Corp., 521 U.S. ___, 117 S.Ct. 1984, 138 L.Ed.2d 373 (1997).

15. Keystone Ins. Co. v. Houghton, 863 F.2d 1125, 1126 (3d Cir.1988).

§ 21.18

1. 514 U.S. 549, 552, 115 S.Ct. 1624, 1626, 131 L.Ed.2d 626 (1995).

2. *Id.* at 561.

3. *Id.*

4. *Id.*

After *Lopez*, criminal defendants have aggressively argued that various statutes underlying their convictions unconstitutionally exceeded Congress' power to regulate interstate commerce. However, most courts have refused to extend *Lopez* to other federal criminal statutes.[5] *Lopez* challenges have been brought by defendants in RICO prosecutions, but none have been successful.

One reason *Lopez* challenges to RICO have failed may be *United States v. Robertson*, which the Supreme Court decided only five days after *Lopez*.[6] In *Robertson*, the Court reversed the Ninth Circuit, which had reversed a RICO conviction.[7] The Ninth Circuit had found that the government failed to introduce sufficient evidence that an Alaskan gold mine, purchased by the defendant with proceeds from narcotics offenses, was "engaged in or affect[ed] interstate commerce," in violation of 18 U.S.C. § 1962(a).[8] The court issued a brief, per curiam opinion which noted that the government had proved that: (1) equipment and supplies for the gold mine were purchased in California and transported to Alaska for use in the mine, (2) Robertson had brought out-of-state workers to the mine, and (3) Robertson took $30,000 worth of gold from the mine out of Alaska.[9] The Court did not apply *Lopez*, but held:

> [w]hether or not these activities met (and whether or not, to ring the gold mine within the "affecting commerce" provision of RICO, they would have to meet) the requirement of substantially affecting interstate commerce, they assuredly brought the gold mine within § 1962(a)'s alternative criterion of "any enterprise ... engaged in ... interstate or foreign commerce."[10]

Thus, at least for the "enterprise engaged in interstate or foreign commerce" section 1962(a) is within the reach of Congress' Commerce Power.

Since *Robertson*, *Lopez* challenges to RICO have been denied by lower federal courts on the grounds that (1) RICO is aimed at activities which directly affect interstate commerce,[11] and (2) the RICO statute contains a satisfactory jurisdictional element.[12] Thus, the lower federal courts have upheld the RICO statute as a valid exercise of Congress' Commerce Power.

In *United States v. Three Juvenile Males*, the Ninth Circuit affirmed the defendants' conviction for conspiracy to participate in a racketeering enterprise for their participation with the "Rolling 30s" Crips gang, in

---

5. United States v. Wall, 92 F.3d 1444, 1448 (6th Cir.1996) (listing cases in which criminal defendants have brought *Lopez* challenges and the results of those challenges).

6. 514 U.S. 669, 115 S.Ct. 1732, 131 L.Ed.2d 714 (1995).

7. *Id.* at 672.

8. *Id.* at 670, quoting the opinion below, 15 F.3d 862, 868 (9th Cir.1994) (brackets in Supreme Court's opinion).

9. *Id.* at 671.

10. *Id.* at 671–72 (ellipses in original).

11. *See, e.g.*, United States v. Three Juvenile Males, 118 F.3d 1344 (9th Cir. 1997).

12. *See, e.g.*, United States v. Thomas, 114 F.3d 228, 253 (D.C.Cir.1997).

violation of 18 U.S.C. § 1962(d).[13] The defendants argued that under *Lopez*, the activities prohibited by RICO must substantially affect interstate commerce.[14] However, the Ninth circuit, relying on *Robertson* and analogizing RICO to the Hobbs Act, held that, "[b]ecause RICO is aimed at activities which directly affect interstate commerce, . . . all that is required to establish federal jurisdiction in a RICO prosecution is a showing that the individual predicate racketeering acts have a de minimus impact on interstate commerce."[15] Furthermore, the court noted that the RICO statute, like the Hobbs Act,[16] contains a jurisdictional requirement that limits its scope to "any enterprise engaged in, or the activities of which affect, interstate or foreign commerce."[17] For these reasons, the defendants' *Lopez* challenge to their RICO conspiracy convictions was unsuccessful, and their convictions were affirmed.

Similarly, in *United States v. Thomas*, the Court of Appeals for the District of Columbia affirmed a defendant's substantive RICO and RICO conspiracy convictions in the face of a *Lopez* challenge.[18] The court noted that the organization with which the defendant was involved had purchased nine to ten million dollars worth of cocaine from Colombian drug dealers in New York, 150 kilograms of cocaine from Los Angeles, and PCP from California.[19] The court then summarily dismissed the *Lopez* challenge, noting that RICO contains a jurisdictional element and finding that the RICO statute " 'contains a requirement that [the offense] be connected in any way to interstate commerce,' . . . and is 'directed specifically at a particular type of commercial activity.' "[20]

Finally, in two cases, defendants have cited *Lopez* to challenge the sufficiency of jury instructions for RICO offenses. The challenged jury instructions provided that the element of affecting interstate commerce could be satisfied by a finding of minimal effects on interstate commerce.[21] In *United States v. Miller*, the Second Circuit, quoting *Lopez*, noted that "where a general regulatory statute bears a substantial relation to commerce, the de minimus nature of individual instances arising under that statute is of no consequence."[22] The Second Circuit further noted that since the RICO enterprise's business was narcotics trafficking, a type of activity that Congress found to substantially affect interstate commerce, "that the enterprise must be viewed as substantially affecting interstate commerce, even if individual predicate acts occur[ed] solely within a state."[23] Thus, there was no error in the interstate commerce element of the jury instructions.[24]

13. 118 F.3d 1344.

14. *Id.* at *3.

15. *Id.* at *2.

16. *Id.* at *4.

17. *Id.* at *4, citing 18 U.S.C. § 1962.

18. 114 F.3d 228, 253 (D.C.Cir.1997).

19. *Id.*

20. *Id.*, quoting *Lopez*, 514 U.S. at 551, 115 S.Ct. at 1626 and United States v.

Hawkins, 104 F.3d 437, 439–90 (D.C.Cir. 1997).

21. *See* United States v. Miller, 116 F.3d 641 (2d Cir.1997); United States v. Maloney, 71 F.3d 645 (7th Cir.1995).

22. 116 F.3d at 674 (internal quotations and citations omitted).

23. *Id.*

24. *Id.*

Similarly, in *United States v. Maloney*, the Seventh Circuit found no error in the jury instruction given for a RICO conviction of a Cook County Circuit Court judge.[25] The district court instructed the jury, "that interstate commerce is affected if you find that the Circuit Court of Cook County has any impact, regardless of how small or indirect, on the movement of any money, goods, services, or persons from one state to another."[26] Under *Lopez*, the defendant contended that the jury instruction should have required a finding that the court "substantially affects" interstate commerce.[27] The Seventh Circuit noted that RICO contains a "jurisdictional element which would ensure, through case-by-case inquiry" that the enterprise in question affects interstate commerce, and that "[w]here a general regulatory statute bears a substantial relation to commerce, the de minimus character of individual instances arising under that statute is of no consequence."[28] The court further cited *Robertson* for the premise that "[i]t is by no means 'plain' that individual activities regulated by RICO must each 'substantially affect' interstate commerce."[29] Finally, the Seventh Circuit noted that even if the instruction was error, the defendant had not attempted to establish that the error was prejudicial, and the court therefore held that there was no basis for finding plain error.[30]

Thus, while the Supreme Court's *Robinson* decision appeared to have left open the issue of whether a RICO enterprise is required to "substantially affect" interstate commerce, lower federal courts have consistently denied *Lopez* challenges to RICO convictions on such grounds. Therefore, *Lopez*'s apparent limitation on federal criminal statutes under the Commerce Power does not appear to present a serious challenge to federal criminal prosecutions under RICO.

Library References:

C.J.S. RICO (Racketeer Influenced and Corrupt Organizations) § 16.
West's Key No. Digests, Racketeer Influenced and Corrupt Organizations ☞65.

§ 21.19 Current Trends

RICO continues to be a versatile tool—for both prosecutors and plaintiffs. It is increasingly employed in areas such as sexual harassment,[1] health care fraud,[2] environmental harms,[3] and employment.[4] For

25. 71 F.3d at 664.

26. *Id.* at 662.

27. *Id.*

28. *Id.* quoting *Lopez*, 514 U.S. at 674, 115 S.Ct. at 1736 (internal quotations and citations omitted).

29. *Id.*, citing 514 U.S. at 673, 115 S.Ct. at 1733.

30. *Id.* at 664.

§ 21.19

1. William H. Kaiser, Note, *Extortion in the Workplace: Using Civil RICO to Combat Sexual Harassment in Employment*, 61 Brook.L.Rev. 965 (1995). *See, e.g.*, Sharpe v. Kelley, 835 F.Supp. 33 (D.Mass.1993) (denied dismissal of claim by carpenter apprentice against local union officials for pattern of sexual harassment extortion causing her lost wages); Hunt v. Weatherbee, 626 F.Supp. 1097 (D.Mass.1986) (denied dismissal of claim by employee against her employer for pattern of quid pro quo sexual harassment over six months); *Compare* Fowler v. Burns Internat'l Security Services, 763 F.Supp. 862 (N.D.Miss.1991), aff'd by 979 F.2d 1534 (5th Cir.1992) (dismissed because quid pro quo sexual harassment was NOT extortion); McKinney v. Ill.,

two reasons, there likely will be increased use of civil RICO. Class actions under RICO are an especially appropriate device for "private attorney generals" to pursue complex business frauds such as large scale health care fraud. In addition, as more states limit punitive damages, the treble damages of civil RICO become more appealing. Use of RICO by prosecutors may continue to stagnate however. Many RICO offenses can also be prosecuted as money laundering offenses, which carry a higher guideline range under the federal Sentencing Guidelines. In addition, the substantial expansion of the forfeiture action, both criminally through 18 U.S.C. § 982 and civilly, through 18 U.S.C. § 981, make RICO, with its forfeiture provisions upon conviction, less essential. Certainly with § 982, civil forfeiture, and its lesser burden of proof make § 982 a more attractive option than RICO.

§ 21.20 Bibliography

BATISTA, PAUL A., CIVIL RICO PRACTICE MANUAL (2d ed. 1997).

Blakey, G. Robert & Brian Gettings, *Racketeer Influenced and Corrupt Organizations (RICO): Basic Concepts—Criminal and Civil Remedies*, 53 TEMP. L. Q. 1009 (1981).

Blakey, G. Robert & Thomas A. Perry, *Reforming RICO: If, Why and How?* 43 VAND. L. REV. 851 (1990).

720 F.Supp. 706 (N.D.Ill.1989) (dismissed RICO claim based on sexual harassment because failed to allege predicate acts listed under § 1961 as Racketeering Activity); Polsby v. Chase, 970 F.2d 1360 (4th Cir. 1992) (aff'd RICO dismissal because discrimination is not a racketeering activity, nor did pattern exist when only one victim).

2. PAMELA H. BUCY, HEALTH CARE FRAUD: CRIMINAL, CIVIL AND ADMINISTRATIVE LAW, § 4.02 (1996); D. Fitzpatrick, Comment, *Civil RICO and Antitrust Law: The Uneven Playing Field of the Worker's Compensation Fraud Game*, 25 PAC.L.J. 311 (1994) argues civil RICO is an appropriate remedy for California's Worker's Compensation insurers against pervasive fraud by employers (e.g. understating payroll or high risk jobs), employees (e.g. filing bogus "stress" claims or claims for nonjob-related injuries), medical clinics (e.g. double-billing employer's health insurer and Worker's Compensation insurer, or filing bogus claims for back injuries), lawyers (e.g. soliciting, or filing bogus claims), and physicians (e.g. conducting unnecessary medical evaluations, or filing bogus claims).

3. I. Lyngklip, Note, *RICO and Environmental Harms From Hazardous Substances*, 69 U.DET.MERCY L.REV. 255 (1992) argues hazardous waste RICO claims should not be preempted by CERCLA or RCRA, and offers creative ways to overcome common defenses (aff'd conviction for oper-

ating illegal landfill and illegally transporting medical waste); B. Rielly, Note, *Using RICO to Fight Environmental Crime*, 70 NOTRE DAME L.REV. 651 (1995) (arguing Congress should add RCRA as a predicate act to avoid the risks associated with using mail fraud for environmental hazardous waste violations). W.W. Cason, *Spiking the Spikers: The Use of Civil RICO Against Environmental Terrorists*, 32 HOUS.L.REV. 745 (Fall 1995). See, e.g., *United States v. Paccione*, 749 F.Supp. 478 (S.D.N.Y.1990), aff'd 949 F.2d 1183 (2d Cir.1991).

4. Raymond P. Green, In *The Application of RICO to Labor–Management and Employment Disputes*, 7 ST.THOMAS L.REV. 309 (1995); S.T. Ieronimo, Note, *RICO: Is It a Panacea or a Bitter Pill for Labor Unions, Union Democracy and Collective Bargaining?* 11 HOFSTRA LAB.L.J. 499 (1994); D.T. Fitzpatrick, Note, *Collective Institutional Guilt: The Emergence of International Unions' RICO Liability for Local Union Crimes*, 21 AM.J.CRIM.L. 291 (1994).

K. S. Marks, Note, *Wrongful Discharge and RICO Conspiracy Standing*, 16 W.NEW ENG.L.REV. 365 (1994); T.E. Loscalzo and S.J. Levitan, *RICO Conspiracy: Whistle blowers Coming in Through the Back Door*, 10 Lab.Law. 679 (1994); Schiffels v. Kemper Financial Services, 978 F.2d 344 (7th Cir. 1992); Bowman v. Western Auto Supply, 985 F.2d 383 (8th Cir.1993).

Brenner, Susan W., *RICO, CCE and Other Complex Crimes: The Transformation of American Criminal Law?* 2 WM. & MARY BILL RTS. J. 239 (Winter 1993)

BUCY, PAMELA H., WHITE COLLAR CRIME CASES AND MATERIALS (West 2d ed.1998).

BUCY, PAMELA H., HEALTH CARE FRAUD: CRIMINAL, CIVIL AND ADMINISTRATIVE LAW § 4.02 (1996).

Goldsmith, Michael, *Judicial Immunity for White–Collar Crime*, 30 HARV. J. ON LEGIS. 1 (1993).

Immel, Otto, *Corporation-Employee Association-in-Fact Enterprises in Civil RICO*, 60 DEFENSE COUNSEL J. 88 (1993).

Marple, William E., *"Pattern" Requirement Renders RICO Inapplicable to Ordinary Business Disputes*, 14 REV. LITIG. 343 (Spring 1995).

Rehnquist, William, *Get RICO Cases Out of My Courtroom*, WALL ST. J., May 19, 1989.

RODDY, KEVIN P., RICO IN BUSINESS & COMMERCIAL LITIGATION (Supp. Oct. 1995).

U.S. DEP'T OF JUSTICE, CIVIL RICO: A MANUAL FOR FEDERAL PROSECUTORS (1988).

U.S. DEP'T OF JUSTICE, RACKETEER INFLUENCED AND CORRUPT ORGANIZATIONS (RICO): A MANUAL FOR FEDERAL PROSECUTORS (1990).

U.S. DEP'T OF JUSTICE, UNITED STATES ATTORNEYS' MANUAL.

CHAPTER 22

SECURITIES FRAUD

Table of Sections

WESTLAW ELECTRONIC RESEARCH

See WESTLAW Electronic Research Guide preceding the Summary of Contents.

---

§ 22.1 Introduction

There are civil, administrative, and criminal avenues available to pursue the fraudulent securities trader. None should be studied in isolation because a securities trader often is subject to all sanctions for the same conduct. The government is the plaintiff in criminal actions. Most securities prosecutions are initiated by federal prosecutors with the United States Department of Justice although state attorneys general may also bring criminal charges in state courts using state criminal statutes and common law. Governmental entities may also institute civil causes of action, as may private parties. Most of the civil cases are filed in federal court, brought by the Securities and Exchange Commission

273

(SEC) and based on federal statutes and federal common law. The SEC or various specialized state agencies may initiate administrative actions seeking a consent decree or disbarment of a securities trader.

Library References:

C.J.S. Securities Regulation § 105–106, 164–165, 169–228.
West's Key No. Digests, Securities Regulation ☞60.10–60.70.

§ 22.2   What Is a Security?

The term "security" is defined by § 2(1) of the Securities Act of 1933,[1] § 3(a)(10) of the Securities Exchange Act of 1934,[2] § 2(a)(36) of the Investment Company Act of 1940,[3] as well as individual state "blue sky" laws.[4] Generally, securities include "notes," "stocks," "bonds," and "debentures." Additionally, an item which is not usually considered a traditional security may nevertheless fall under the jurisdiction of the federal securities laws if found to be an "investment contract," the catch-all for unique forms of investments. Regardless of the type, a security must exist in order for the federal securities laws to apply in a criminal action.[5] It is irrelevant whether a defendant knows that his or her conduct involved a "security."[6]

An instrument qualifies as an investment contract if it passes the "economic reality" test adopted in *SEC v. W.J. Howey Co.*[7] Under the *Howey* test, an item is a "security" if there is: (1) an investment of money;[8] (2) in a common enterprise;[9] (3) with an expectation of profit;[10]

---

§ 22.2

1. 15 U.S.C. § 77a et seq. The term "security" means any note, stock, treasury stock, bond, debenture, evidence of indebtedness, certificate of interest or participation in any profit-sharing agreement, collateral-trust certificate, preorganization certificate or subscription, transferable share, investment contract, voting-trust certificate, certificate of deposit for a security, factional undivided interest in oil, gas, or other mineral rights, any put call, straddle, option, or privilege on any security, certificate of deposit, or group or index of securities (including any interest therein or based on the value thereof), or any put, call, straddle, option, or privilege entered into on a national securities exchange relating to foreign currency, or, in general, any interest or instrument commonly known as a "security," or any certificate of interest or participation in, temporary or interim certificate for, receipt for, guarantee of, or warrant or right to subscribe to or purchase, any of the foregoing. 15 U.S.C. § 77(b)(1).

2. 15 U.S.C. § 78c(a)(10). (contains a substantially identical definition as 15 U.S.C. § 77a.)

3. 15 U.S.C. § 80a–2(36). (contains a substantially identical definition as 15 U.S.C. § 77a.)

4. Uniform Securities Act § 401(1). (contains a substantially identical definition as 15 U.S.C. § 77a.)

5. United States v. Morse, 785 F.2d 771, 775–76 (9th Cir.1986).

6. *Id.*

7. 328 U.S. 293, 298–299, 66 S.Ct. 1100, 1103, 90 L.Ed. 1244 (1946).

8. *See* Teamsters v. Daniel, 439 U.S. 551, 99 S.Ct. 790, 58 L.Ed.2d 808 (1979) (held an interest in a non-contributory pension plan not to be a security).

9. *See* Revak v. SEC Realty, 18 F.3d 81 (2d Cir.1994). (Courts are split on whether horizontal commonality (investors sharing in single pool of assets) or vertical commonality (profit-sharing agreement between a promoter and each individual investor) is required).

10. United Housing Foundation, Inc. v. Forman, 421 U.S. 837, 842–52, 95 S.Ct. 2051, 2055–2060, 44 L.Ed.2d 621 (1975).

(4) solely through the efforts of others.[11] However, the *Howey* test is not used to determine the existence of each and every security; it only applies to investment contracts. Courts have found the following investment contracts to be "securities" under the *Howey* test:[12] franchises,[13] real estate lots,[14] condominiums,[15] orange groves,[16] gold and silver bullion and coins,[17] diamonds and gems,[18] warehouse receipts,[19] various animal interests,[20] and merchandise marketing schemes.[21]

Stock, notes, and other instruments expressly listed within the 1933 and 1934 Acts' definitions are presumed to be securities, although the presumption may be rebutted. Historically, the Supreme Court has interpreted the term "security" very broadly in order to maximize investor protection through the federal securities laws. The Court generally focuses on whether a particular investment interest should require protection for the investor.[22] For example, in *Marine Bank v. Weaver*, the

---

11. This requirement has been applied in many ways. Franchises with the investor taking an active role in the business have been held not to be securities. *See* Wieboldt v. Metz, 355 F.Supp. 255 (S.D.N.Y.1973). "Solely" has been interpreted as efforts which affect the failure or success of the enterprise even where investors participated in order for securities laws to apply to fraudulent pyramid schemes. *See e.g.,*

Second Circuit: SEC v. Aqua–Sonic, 687 F.2d 577 (2d Cir.1982).

Fifth Circuit: SEC v. Koscot, 497 F.2d 473 (5th Cir.1974).

Ninth Circuit: SEC v. Glenn W. Turner, 474 F.2d 476 (9th Cir.1973).

12. *See generally* HAROLD S. BLOOMENTHAL AND HOLME ROBERTS & OWEN, SECURITIES LAW HANDBOOK 31 (1995 ed.); and LOUIS LOSS & JOEL SELIGMAN, 2 SECURITIES REGULATION 920–86, 1058–60 (3rd ed. 1989).

13. *See*

Second Circuit: SEC v. Aqua Sonic Prods. Corp., 687 F.2d 577 (2d Cir.1982).

Ninth Circuit: SEC v. Glenn W. Turner Enters., Inc., 474 F.2d 476, 482 (9th Cir. 1973).

Hawaii: State v. Hawaii Mkt. Center, Inc., 52 Haw. 642, 485 P.2d 105 (1971) (state law).

14. *See* SEC v. Great W. Land & Dev., Inc., [1964–1966 Transfer Binder] Fed.Sec. L.Rep. (CCH) ¶ 91,537 (D.Ariz.1965).

15. *See* Sec. Act Release No. 5347 (Jan. 4, 1973), [1972–1973 Transfer Binder] Fed.Sec.L.Rep. (CCH) ¶ 79,163, *reprinted in* 1 Fed. Sec. L. Rep. (CCH) ¶ 1049. *See also* Sec. Act Rel. 5382, 1 SEC Dock. No. 11 at 1 (1973); Cameron v. Outdoor Resorts of Am., Inc., 608 F.2d 187, 192–93 (5th Cir.1979)

modified on other grounds, 611 F.2d 105 (5th Cir.1980).

16. *See* SEC v. Howey Co., 328 U.S. 293, 66 S.Ct. 1100, 90 L.Ed. 1244 (1946).

17. *See*

D.C. Circuit: SEC v. American Inst. Counselors, Inc., [1975–1976 Transfer Binder] Fed.Sec.L.Rep. (CCH) ¶ 95,388 (D.D.C. 1975).

Second Circuit: SEC v. Brigadoon Scotch Distribs., Ltd., 388 F.Supp. 1288 (S.D.N.Y.1975).

Ninth Circuit: SEC v. Western Pac. Gold & Silver Exch. Corp., [1974–1975 Transfer Binder] Fed.Sec.L.Rep. (CCH) ¶ 95,064 (D.Nev.1975).

18. *See*

Alaska: American Gold & Diamond Corp. v. Kirkpatrick, 678 P.2d 1343 (Alaska 1984).

New York: Gardner v. Lefkowitz, 97 Misc.2d 806, 412 N.Y.S.2d 740 (N.Y.Sup.Ct. 1978).

19. *See* Sec. Act Rel. 5018 (1969), *reprinted in* 1 *Fed.Sec.L.Rep.* (CCH) ¶ 1047. Glen–Arden Commodities, Inc. v. Costantino, 493 F.2d 1027, 1034–1035 (2d Cir.1974).

20. *See*

Second Circuit: SEC v. Payne, 35 F.Supp. 873 (S.D.N.Y.1940) (foxes).

Eighth Circuit: Miller v. Central Chinchilla Group, Inc., 494 F.2d 414 (8th Cir. 1974) (chinchillas).

Tenth Circuit: Continental Mktg. Corp. v. SEC, 387 F.2d 466 (10th Cir.1967).

21. *See* SEC v. Koscot Interplanetary, Inc., 497 F.2d 473 (5th Cir.1974).

22. *See* Marine Bank v. Weaver, 455 U.S. 551, 102 S.Ct. 1220, 71 L.Ed.2d 409

court held that a Certificate of Deposit was not a security within the Securities Exchange Act of 1934 because certificates of deposit are protected as compared to other long-term debt obligations which have been deemed to be securities. A certificate of deposit is issued by a federally regulated bank subject to comprehensive regulation and is insured against loss. By comparison, the holder of an "ordinary long-term debt obligation assumes the risk of the borrower's insolvency."[23]

Names and titles are not always dispositive when determining whether an instrument will be classified as a security. Rejecting the "literal approach," the Supreme Court has held that shares in a cooperative housing corporation labeled "stock" were not securities for the purpose of the Acts' definitions because the investment was primarily a means of obtaining housing and was not made with an eye toward profit.[24] A "note," just as a "stock," may cause classification problems. The Supreme Court applies a "family resemblance" test for determining whether a note will be afforded the protection of a security.[25] Generally, there is a strong presumption that a note is a security if it has a term greater than nine months.[26] Other factors considered when determining whether a note is a "security" include: (1) the motivations and expectations of the parties participating in the transaction; (2) whether the instrument more closely resembles an investment or commercial undertaking; (3) the public's reasonable expectations; and (4) whether other regulatory schemes control the transaction and provide protection to the buyer.[27]

Commercial transactions not generally considered to be a "securities" may nevertheless be deemed to be for purposes of applying federal security laws. For instance, the Supreme Court has held that a sale of business through the transfer of all outstanding stock was a sale of a "security" within the intended coverage of the federal securities laws, regardless of the reason for the sale or percentage of the stock sold or acquired.[28] This decision was contrary to long settled decisions by lower courts which held that the "sale of business" is not a sale of securities because it merely facilitates a change in business control.

Various partnership interests also may qualify as securities if there is a lack of management power and reliance upon others for profit. Therefore, an interest in a limited partnership generally will be classified as a security due to lack of participation in the management while sharing in profits.[29] Conversely, general partnership interests are not

---

(1982) (federally insured certificate of deposit issued by a bank does not require protection by the federal securities laws).

23. *Id.* at 558.

24. SEC v. W. J. Howey Co., 328 U.S. 293, 298–99, 66 S.Ct. 1100, 1103, 90 L.Ed. 1244 (1946).

25. Reves v. Ernst & Young, 494 U.S. 56, 110 S.Ct. 945, 108 L.Ed.2d 47 (1990). (*See* Pollack v. Laidlaw Holdings, Inc., 27 F.3d 808 (2d Cir.1994), for application.)

26. *Id.* at 63–64.

27. *Id.* at 66–67.

28. Landreth Timber Co. v. Landreth, 471 U.S. 681, 105 S.Ct. 2297, 85 L.Ed.2d 692 (1985).

29. *See* Goodman v. Epstein, 582 F.2d 388 (7th Cir.1978).

usually classified as securities unless one member exerts so much control that the other general partners function more like passive investors. Limited liability companies may resemble either general partnerships or limited partnerships depending upon where management is located. A member-managed limited liability company more closely resembles a general partnership, but a manager-managed limited liability company more closely resembles a limited partnership. A careful examination of management determines whether the interest will be classified as a security.[30]

§ 22.3   Overview: Regulation of the Securities Industry—The Securities and Exchange Commission (SEC)

Created by the Securities Exchange Act of 1934, the SEC is an independent, nonpartisan, quasi-judicial regulatory agency composed of five members who are appointed by the President with the consent of the Senate.[1] The President designates one of the Commissioners to serve as chairperson. The SEC administers the following statutes:

— The Securities Act of 1933.[2]

— Securities Exchange Act of 1934.[3]

— Public Utility Holding Company Act of 1935.[4]

— Trust Indenture Act of 1939.[5]

— Investment Company Act of 1940.[6]

— Investment Advisers Act of 1940.[7]

— Securities Investor Protection Act of 1970.[8]

— The Securities Law Enforcement Remedies and Penny Stock Reform Act of 1990.[9]

The main office of the SEC is located in Washington, D.C. Regional offices are located in New York (Northeast regional office), Chicago (Midwest regional office), Denver (Central regional office), Miami (Southeast regional office), and Los Angeles (Pacific regional office). Additional district offices are located in Boston, Atlanta, Fort Worth, San Francisco, Philadelphia, and Salt Lake City. The Commission is assisted by a professional staff composed of accountants, lawyers, engineers, securities analysts and examiners. The SEC is a relatively small agency compared to other federal agencies.[10] The SEC staff is divided into divisions and offices. The major divisions are:

30. *See* Williamson v. Tucker, 645 F.2d 404 (5th Cir.1981); Koch v. Hankins, 928 F.2d 1471 (9th Cir.1991).

§ 22.3

1. SEC Home Page, http:// www.sec.gov.

2. 15 U.S.C. § 77a et seq.

3. 15 U.S.C. § 78a et seq.

4. 15 U.S.C. § 79 et seq.

5. 15 U.S.C. § 77aaa–77bbbb.

6. 15 U.S.C. § 80a–1–80a–52.

7. 15 U.S.C. §§§ 80b–1–80b–21.

8. 15 U.S.C. §§ 78aaa–78lll.

9. Pub.L. 101–429, 104 Stat. 931 (Oct. 15, 1990). (*Amending* 15 U.S.C. §§ § 77g, 78c, and 78o.)

10. S. SHAPIRO, WAYWARD CAPITALISTS 5 (1984).

1. **Division of Corporation Finance**. This Division establishes the standards for all documents filed with the SEC by publicly held companies registered with the Commission and reviews these filings (registration statements, and documents relating to tender offers, proxy solicitations, mergers and acquisitions) to see that they comply with these standards. The Chief Counsel of this Division provides legal advice to attorneys about the rules and regulations enforced by the SEC.

2. **Division of Markets Regulation**. This Division regulates the national stock exchanges and self-regulatory organizations, such as the National Association of Securities Dealers (NASD), brokers-dealers, clearing organizations, and transfer agents. Through statistical analysis, this Division looks for unusual trading practices. Market Regulation sets financial responsibility standards, regulates trading and sales practices, oversees policies affecting operation of the securities markets, and conducts industry surveillance.

3. **Division of Enforcement**. This Division is responsible for enforcing federal securities laws and regulations. It does so through administrative proceedings and by bringing civil injunctive actions against persons who are alleged to have violated these laws and regulations. This Division refers cases to the Department of Justice for criminal prosecution when it appears that a violation has been committed willfully.

4. **Division of Investment Management**. This Division regulates investment companies under the Investment Company Act of 1940 and the Investment Advisers Act of 1940 and the Public Utility Holding Company Act of 1935. Specifically, the division ensures compliance with registration, financial responsibilities, sales practices, and advertising by investment companies and advisors. Investment Management also reviews new products offered by these entities, and reviews and processes investment company registration statements, proxy statements, and periodic reports under the Security Act.

5. **Office of Compliance Inspections and Examinations.** The office inspects brokers, dealers, self-regulatory organizations, investment companies and advisers, clearing agencies, and transfer agents.

6. **Office of General Counsel.** The Office of General Counsel is the primary source of general legal advice for the Commission—particularly in special legal matters, litigations, and appellate matters.

The Commission is also comprised of offices of the Chief Accountant, International Affairs, Legislative Affairs, Economic Analysis, Administrative Law Judges, Secretary, and Inspector General. Furthermore, internal matters and administration are served by the offices of Executive Director, Comptroller, Filings and Information Services, Administrative and Personnel Management, Information Technology and Public Affairs, Policy Evaluation and Research.[11] Additionally, the Commission advises federal courts on matters concerning corporate reorganization under Chapter 11 of the Bankruptcy Act of 1978.

§ 22.4　Overview: Regulation of the Securities Industry—The National Securities Exchanges and Brokers–Dealers

The securities market has two parts: the primary or new-issue market, wherein companies generate new securities which are issued to the public through underwriters and dealers, and the secondary or trading markets, in which securities are bought and sold. The trading markets provide a quick and easy mechanism for investors to sell their securities. This liquidity is essential to a viable securities market. The trading markets include many stock exchanges and an over-the-counter market including Internet sales of securities.[1]

The over-the-counter (OTC) market is for all transactions that take place not on a stock exchange, but in other places, such as brokers' and dealers' offices. Brokers and dealers trading in the OTC market must register with the SEC. Most brokers-dealers serving the public are members of the National Association of Securities Dealers (NASD). A wide variety of securities is traded OTC, including government and corporate bonds, and some common stocks. When OTC trading involves securities traded on one or more stock exchanges, it is referred to as the "third market."

The Securities Exchange Act of 1934 regulates the behavior of the exchanges and brokers-dealers by requiring that certain records and reports be made and distributed; that stated net capital requirements be met; that customers' securities may be commingled only in carefully controlled circumstances; and, that brokers, dealers, and exchanges allow the SEC to inspect their records.

The securities exchanges and NASD are required to regulate themselves. They must adopt rules "designed to prevent fraudulent and manipulative acts and practices, to promote just and equitable principles of trade * * * to remove impediments to and perfect the mechanism of a free and open market and a national market system, and, in general, to protect investors and the public interest * * *."[2] Such rules must

---

11. SEC Home Page, http://www.sec.gov.

§ 22.4

1. Each stock exchange provides rules and procedures for selling and buying of stocks registered with that exchange. The exchanges sell "seats" or memberships on the exchange. Because only a member may buy or sell stock through an exchange, and because memberships in each exchange are limited, a "seat" on an exchange is viewed

as quite valuable. There is no limit as to how many exchanges on which a company may list its stock. As soon as a stock purchase is made, it is recorded and disseminated; this reporting influences the price of stocks. SECURITIES, EXCHANGES AND THE SEC 27–28 (Ed. Poyntz, ed.1965); MARSHALL BLUME, REVOLUTION ON WALL STREET: THE RISE AND FALL OF THE NEW YORK STOCK EXCHANGE 36 (1993).

2. 15 U.S.C. §§ 78f(b)(5).

provide for the disciplining of members, and persons associated with members, when they violate the exchange rules, the 1934 Exchange Act, or rules adopted thereunder.

§ 22.5 Overview: Regulation of the Securities Industry—Investment Advisors

The Investment Advisers Act of 1940[1] was enacted after testimony before the Senate Banking and Currency Committee[2]. Revised numerous times since 1940, the Investment Act imposes registration and disciplinary procedures on investment advisers similar to those imposed on broker-dealers.[3] The Investment Advisers Act defines "investment adviser" broadly to cover everyone who, for compensation, gives advice regarding securities. Depending on the extent of the advice rendered, professionals such as attorneys or accountants may be "investment advisers." Whether they are or not will depend upon whether the advice given is "incidental" to the practice of the attorney's or accountant's profession.[4] Difficult questions have arisen regarding authors and whether publishers of financial works are "investment advisers." A key consideration is the nature of the publication: publishing only "disinterested commentary and analysis" does not subject its author to the Investment Advisers Act but "promotional material disseminated by * * * hit and run tipsters" may.[5]

§ 22.6 Overview: Regulation of the Securities Industry— State Enforcement

In 1911, Kansas became the first state to adopt a comprehensive scheme of securities regulation, known as "blue sky" laws. The name originated because these laws were viewed as necessary to reach "speculative schemes which have no more basis than so many feet of blue

---

§ 22.5

1. 15 U.S.C. §§ 80b–1–b–21.

2. "Not only must the public be protected from the frauds and misrepresentations of unscrupulous tipsters and touts, but the *bona fide* investment counsel must be safeguarded against the stigma of the activities of these individuals. Virtually no limitations or restrictions exist with respect to the honesty and integrity of individuals who may solicit funds to be controlled, managed, and supervised. Persons who may have been convicted or enjoined by courts because of perpetration of securities fraud are able to assume the role of investment advisers. Individuals assuming to act as investment advisers at present can enter profit-sharing contracts which are nothing more than "heads I win, tails you lose" arrangements. Contracts with investment advisers which are of a personal nature may be assigned and the control of funds of investors may be transferred to others without the knowledge or consent of the client."

S.Rep.No. 1775, 76th Cong., 3d Sess. 21 (1940) reprinted in IV FEDERAL SECURITIES LAWS, LEGISLATIVE HISTORY at 3830, 3850–51 (1983).

3. [T]here are still differences, notably (1) provision for the filing of a registration application by "any person who presently contemplates becoming an investment adviser," (2) specification of the contents of the application for registration as an adviser, whereas the contents of the broker-dealer application are left entirely to the Commission, and (3) the absence of any prescribed qualifications or financial responsibility provisions for registration as an adviser. LOUIS LOSS, FUNDAMENTALS OF SECURITIES REGULATION 672 (1988).

4. 15 U.S.C. § 80b–2(a)(11).

5. Lowe v. SEC, 472 U.S. 181, 206, 105 S.Ct. 2557, 2571, 86 L.Ed.2d 130 (1985).

sky."[1] Securities laws are now in effect in 52 jurisdictions: the 50 states, the District of Columbia, and Puerto Rico. An administrative official, known as the Blue Sky Commissioner, administers each state's laws. Despite efforts to coordinate state and federal securities regulation, there is substantial overlapping and duplication of regulation.

Library References:

C.J.S. Securities Regulation § 2–3, 366–417, 429.
West's Key No. Digests, Securities Regulation ☞241–278.

§ 22.7   Overview: Regulation of the Securities Industry—Federal Enforcement

The SEC was created to enforce the federal securities laws. Investigations may arise from divisions of the SEC, and outside sources such as self-regulatory organizations and investor complaints. The SEC staff monitors unusual price movements on all securities markets, and routinely makes periodic inspections of broker-dealers. When its investigation uncovers potential securities violations, the violation is usually handled through administrative procedures set forth in the Administrative Procedure Act.[1] The Commission may issue subpoenas, formal orders of investigation, or other means necessary to enforce the federal securities laws or to investigate any form of non-compliance with the securities laws. A formal order of investigation is not required to be based upon probable cause. The SEC may investigate "to determine whether any person has violated, is violating, or is about to violate any provision of the federal securities laws or the rules of a self-regulatory organization of which the person is a member or participant."[2] An Administrative Law Judge renders the initial decision, which is subject to an independent review by the SEC. In this review, the SEC relies on the record developed before the Administrative Law Judge, and uses a preponderance of the evidence standard to determine if a violation has been proven.[3] SEC decisions are appealable to the Circuit Courts of Appeals. A variety of sanctions may be imposed at the administrative level including disgorgement of profits, suspension of trading, or injunctions against future violations.

Willful violations of the substantive provisions of the principal securities laws, including the registration and fraud provisions, are criminal offenses. Most cases ultimately prosecuted criminally begin with the SEC, which uses its broad subpoena powers to conduct the initial investigation. If upon conclusion of its investigation, the SEC determines that the violations were committed "willfully," it may refer the matter

§ 22.6

1. *Quoted in* Hall v. Geiger–Jones Co., 242 U.S. 539, 550, 37 S.Ct. 217, 220, 61 L.Ed. 480 (1917).

§ 22.7

1. 5 U.S.C. § 551 et seq.; 17 C.F.R. Part 201.

2. 17 C.F.R. § 202.5(a).

3. Steadman v. SEC, 450 U.S. 91, 101 S.Ct. 999, 67 L.Ed.2d 69 (1981).

to the Department of Justice (DOJ) with a recommendation that certain persons be indicted and prosecuted.[4] Factors weighing in favor of criminal prosecution include:

- The potential defendant is a chronic offender. This may be evidenced by prior convictions or agency injunctions. It may also be the result of investigative intelligence that has placed the defendant at the edge of schemes for years.

- The entity the potential defendant works for is a chronic offender.

- The criminal conduct is part of a larger criminal scheme in which the target's participation might not be provable beyond a reasonable doubt. The securities charges provide an alternative way to prosecute.

- The type of conduct has become pervasive in the industry, and a policy decision has been made to obtain compliance through criminal prosecutions.

- An attempt was made to conceal the substantive violation through perjury and obstruction of an SEC ... investigation.

- Books and records were falsified to conceal the violation.

- The seriousness and length of the illegal conduct. For example, the conduct caused a substantial financial risk to clients, shareholders or the firm and happened on more than one occasion.

- The violator's position in the firm. The more responsible and important the violator's job, the more likely he or she is to be prosecuted because of deterrence reasons.[5]

Factors weighing against prosecution include:

- The violator has no prior record or reputation as a chronic securities offender.

- The violation was not covered up through any scheme to conceal.

- There has been some action of a significant nature taken against the violator by the firm, an SRO or the SEC.

- The violation was voluntarily disclosed to the SRO, SEC or the U.S. Attorney's Office.

- The violator was a minor player in a much larger scheme, is fully cooperating with the authorities and will be sanctioned administratively.

- The violation was marginal and not at the core of activity the Rule or Statute prohibits.

4. 17 C.F.R. § 202.5.

5. Charles M. Carberry & Harold K. Gordon, *To Prosecute or Not to Prosecute*, 4 Bus.Crimes 3 (Feb.1997). Reprinted with permission of *Business Crimes Bulletin: Compliance and Litigation* ©1997, The New York Law Publishing Company.

- The experience level, age and position of the violator. If the offender is a young, inexperienced clerical employee, absent aggravating circumstances, like falsification of records, a criminal prosecution for a non-fraud violation is unlikely.

- The violation posed no potential risk to any firm, its clients or its shareholders.[6]

Once the matter has been referred to DOJ, further investigation is likely. If there is an indictment, the case generally will be prosecuted by a United States Attorney.[7]

Library References:

C.J.S. Securities Regulation § 2–7, 9–34, 103, 243–244.
West's Key No. Digests, Securities Regulation ⬯1–5.50.

§ 22.8 Overview: Civil Causes of Action—Express Causes of Action

A. THE SECURITIES ACT OF 1933

The Securities Act of 1933[1] was "designed to provide investors with full disclosure of material information concerning public offerings of securities in commerce, to protect investors against fraud, and ... to promote ethical standards of honesty and fair dealing."[2] The Act strives to do this by requiring publication of certain information about securities before they are offered for sale. A violation of the following provisions may also constitute a violation of antifraud regulations.

Section 11[3] of the Securities Act of 1933 expressly provides a remedy for persons who have been injured by material misstatements or omissions in a registration statement filed with the SEC, or in a prospectus distributed to potential purchasers. A registration statement provides comprehensive information about the corporation that is issuing shares to the public for purchase, including a description of the registrant's business, property, and financial condition; data regarding directors, officers and executive compensation; information on market price and dividends of the equity being offered.[4] The issuer's attorneys (both inside and outside counsel) and accountants, and the underwriter's attorneys and accountants prepare the registration statement. A "prospectus" is "any notice, circular, advertisement, letter or communication written or

---

6. *Id.*

7. *See* U.S. DEPT. OF JUSTICE, U.S. ATTORNEYS' MANUAL, § 9–3.400 B.

"The Fraud Section is charged with leading the federal law enforcement efforts against fraud and white collar crime. * * *

Organizationally, the work of the Section is divided by substantive subject matter into four major areas: ... 3. Government Regulatory Fraud—focused on criminal cases arising within the jurisdiction of various federal regulatory agencies, *e.g.*, the Securities and Exchange Commission...."

§ 22.8

1. 15 U.S.C. § 77a et seq.

2. Ernst & Ernst v. Hochfelder, 425 U.S. 185, 195, 96 S.Ct. 1375, 1382, 47 L.Ed.2d 668 (1976).

3. 15 U.S.C. § 77k.

4. 17 C.F.R. § 229 et seq. (1991).

transmitted by radio or television, which offers any security for sale or confirms the sale of any security."[5]

Section 11 imposes strict liability—a plaintiff, relying on Section 11, need only show that the registration statement or prospectus was materially false and misleading; it is not necessary to prove that the issuer had fraudulent intent.[6] This strict liability is imposed on five categories of defendants: (1) every person (including entities) who signs the registration statement, (2) every person who is a director (or performed similar functions) or partner of the issuer, (3) every person who is consensually named in the registration statement or is about to become a director or persons performing similar functions (4) various experts who prepare any part of the registration statement or any report or valuation used in preparing the registration statement, and (5) every underwriter regarding such security.[7]

Section 12(1)[8] of the Securities Act of 1933 also applies to registration statements but imposes civil liability for failure to file a registration statement rather than for filing a false registration statement. Section 12(1) also imposes strict liability—all a plaintiff must prove is that a security was purchased, the jurisdictional predicate exists (interstate commerce or the mails were used), a registration statement was required, and no registration statement was in effect.[9]

Whereas Section 12(1) applies to failure to file required registration statements, Section 12(2) of the Securities Act of 1933,[10] like Section 11, applies to misstatements. Unlike the misstatements in registration statements or prospectus which Section 11 addresses, however, Section 12(2) applies to any misrepresentations or omissions (made orally or in a prospectus) by a seller to an unaware purchaser in connection with an offer or sale of securities. Unlike Sections 11 and 12(1), Section 12(2) does not impose strict liability; rather, it requires proof of at least negligence, that is, "that the seller did not know and in the exercise of reasonable care could not have known, of such untruth or omission."[11] In a landmark decision, the Supreme Court announced in *Gustafson v. Alloyd Co.*, that liability under section 12(2) does not apply in private or secondary transactions. The decision limits the term "prospectus" as

5. 15 U.S.C. § 77b(10).

6. Fischman v. Raytheon Mfg. Co., 188 F.2d 783, 786–87 (2d Cir.1951).

7. 15 U.S.C. § 77k(a).

8. 15 U.S.C. § 77l(1).

9. *Second Circuit:* Byrnes v. Faulkner, Dawkins & Sullivan, 413 F.Supp. 453, 465–66 (S.D.N.Y.1976), *aff'd*, 550 F.2d 1303 (2d Cir.1977).

Fifth Circuit: Lynn v. Caraway, 252 F.Supp. 858, 862 (W.D.La.1966), *aff'd*, 379 F.2d 943 (5th Cir.1967); Swenson v. Engelstad, 626 F.2d 421, 424–25 (5th Cir.1980).

10. 15 U.S.C. § 77l(2).

11. *Id.; See e.g.,*

First Circuit: Murphy v. Cady, 30 F.Supp. 466, 468 (D.Me.1939), *aff'd*, 113 F.2d 988 (1st Cir.1940).

Fourth Circuit: John Hopkins Univ. v. Hutton, 297 F.Supp. 1165, 1219 (D.Md. 1968), *aff'd in part, rev'd in part on other grounds*, 422 F.2d 1124 (4th Cir.1970).

Compare:

Second Circuit: Jackson v. Oppenheim, 533 F.2d 826, 829, n. 7 (2d Cir.1976).

used in section 12(2) to initial public offerings by issuers or controlling shareholders.[12]

B. THE EXCHANGE ACT OF 1934

The Exchange Act of 1934[13] was passed to further protect investors from unduly speculative investments. The 1934 Act created the SEC and its powers, established requirements for corporate reporting, proxy solicitations, tender offer solicitations, insider trading prohibitions, margin trading, trading and sales practices, registration of exchanges, and broker-dealer registration.[14] To this end, the Securities Exchange Act of 1934 was designed to facilitate a national market system for trading securities and to safeguard the securities and funds traded in this market.[15]

Section 9[16] of the Securities Exchange Act of 1934 creates an express civil remedy against any person who engages in various specified "manipulative devices" such as entering a purchase order—or purchasing or selling stock—solely to create a misleading impression of trading activity, or representing information about a stock solely with the purpose of raising or depressing the prices of such securities. A high level of mens rea must be proven before a person is liable for a Section 9 violation: the defendant must be shown to have acted "willfully."[17]

Section 16(b)[18] of the Exchange Act of 1934 provides an express civil remedy, not for fraud, but for "short-swing" trading profits, that is, profits realized by certain insiders who purchase and sell, or sell and purchase, stock within a six month time period. According to the language of 16(b), an "insider" is a director, officer, or any person who is directly or indirectly the beneficial owner of not more than 10 per centum of any class of any equity security.[19] The damages awarded in a Section 16(b) action are limited to disgorgement of the short-swing profits realized. Although shareholders, as well as a company, may bring a Section 16(b) action, the damages collected (less attorneys fees for the plaintiff's counsel in some situations) must go to the company.[20] Section

12. 513 U.S. 561, 115 S.Ct. 1061, 131 L.Ed.2d 1 (1995).

13. 15 U.S.C. § 78a et seq.

14. In his message to Congress as it prepared to vote on this statute, President Roosevelt stated:

"This Congress has performed a useful service in regulating the investment business on the part of financial houses and in protecting the investing public in its acquisition of securities [referring to The Securities Act of 1933]. There remains the fact, however, that outside the field of legitimate investment naked speculation has been made far too alluring and far too easy for those who could not afford to gamble * * *. [I]t should be our national policy to restrict, as far as possible, the use of these exchanges for purely speculative operations."

78 Cong.Rec. 2264 (Feb. 9, 1934) (Letter to Congress from President Franklin D. Roosevelt).

15. 78 Cong.Rec. 2264–72 (Feb. 9, 1934) (Remarks by Senator Fletcher).

16. 15 U.S.C. § 78i.

17. 15 U.S.C. § 78i(e).

18. 15 U.S.C. § 78p(b).

19. 15 U.S.C. § 78p(a) and (b).

20. *Second Circuit:* Berkwich v. Mencher, 239 F.Supp. 792, 794 (S.D.N.Y. 1965); Magida v. Continental Can Co., 176 F.Supp. 781, 782–83 (S.D.N.Y.1956).

16(b) is a strict liability statute. It is irrelevant what the defendant knew or intended when conducting the short-swing transaction and it is specifically irrelevant whether inside information was used in either part of the transaction.[21]

Section 18[22] of the Exchange Act of 1934 creates a cause of action for false or misleading documents filed with the SEC, such as annual reports. To prevail on a Section 18 claim, a plaintiff must prove that (1) the statement in question was false and material, (2) the plaintiff relied upon the statement in a purchase or sale of stock, (3) the plaintiff did not know that the statement was false or misleading, and (4) the price at which the plaintiff bought or sold was affected by the statement.[23] Any person who prepared the document in question may be liable under Section 18. This is not a strict liability offense—any individual who can show that she acted in good faith and had no knowledge that such statement was false or misleading, will not be liable under Section 18.[24]

Library References:

C.J.S. Securities Regulation § 254–302, 304–307.
West's Key No. Digests, Securities Regulation ⟨⟩131–181.

§ 22.9 Overview: Civil Causes of Action—Implied Civil Causes of Action

In addition to the express civil remedies created by the 1933 and 1934 statutes discussed above, the courts have found implied civil remedies to exist under both statutes. The courts generally apply the four factor test in *Cort v. Ash*,[1] to determine whether an implied cause of action exists. Under this test the following conditions must be present before a cause of action will be implied: (1) the plaintiff belongs to the special class at which the legislation is aimed, (2) there is legislative intent to create an implied remedy, (3) an implied remedy is consistent with the overall thrust of the statute, and (4) the subject matter is not traditionally left to state law.

Although some implied causes of action are firmly entrenched, the Supreme Court has steadily narrowed the number of implied remedies available under federal statutes in general.[2] The Court has done so by focusing on legislative intent—unless the legislature's intent to create an implied cause of action is clear, the Court will not imply the existence of a cause of action.

Section 10(b)[3] of the Exchange Act of 1934, implemented by SEC

Seventh Circuit: Portnoy v. Standard–Pacific Corp., 666 F.Supp. 140, 142 (N.D.Ill. 1987).

21. T.L. HAZEN, THE LAW OF SECURITIES REGULATION 19–22 (1990).

22. 15 U.S.C. § 78r.

23. Ross v. A.H. Robins Co., Inc., 607 F.2d 545, 551–53 (2d Cir.1979).

24. *Id.*

§ 22.9

1. 422 U.S. 66, 80–84, 95 S.Ct. 2080, 2089–2091, 45 L.Ed.2d 26 (1975).

2. T.L. HAZEN, THE LAW OF SECURITIES REGULATION, 438–45 (1990).

3. 15 U.S.C. § 78j(b).

Rule 10b–5,[4] is the most important of the implied causes of action regarding securities violations.[5] To prevail on a claim of damages under Rule 10b–5, a plaintiff must prove that (1) the defendant (a) employed a scheme or artifice to defraud, or (b) misrepresented a material fact, or (c) failed to state a material fact, (2) the plaintiff's damage was caused by the act(s) of the defendant, (3) the defendant acted with the intent to deceive, manipulate or defraud, (4) the defendant's act was in connection with the purchase and sale of securities, and (5) the defendant's act was furthered by use of the United States mails or any facility of a national securities exchange.[6]

Unlike some of the express remedies, a Rule 10b–5 cause of action requires proof of scienter. However, the Supreme Court has not clarified exactly what mens rea must be proven except that there must be an intent to defraud.

Because the courts have developed this cause of action, they have established the statute of limitations. Historically, courts used two alternative statutes of limitation: that specified in the Securities statutes for some of the express remedies or, the statute of limitations in the forum state under state Blue Sky laws or common law fraud.[7] Adopting the forum state approach sometimes rendered the odd result that a cause of action was timely if filed in one federal court but barred if filed in another.

Then, in *Lampf v. Gilbertson*,[8] the Supreme Court resolved this issue, holding that the statute of limitations for 10b–5 actions should be the same as for most of the federal express causes of action. The standard is known as the "one year/three year" limitation.[9] The Court, in a 5–4 majority, opted for this rule because it could "imagine no clearer indication of how Congress would have balanced the policy considerations implicit in any limitations provision than the balance struck by the same Congress in limiting similar and related projections."[10] Con-

---

4. 17 C.F.R. § 240.10b–5 (1991).

5. Under Section 10(b) and Rule 10b–5, it is:

"unlawful in connection with the purchase or sale of any securities, for any person, directly or indirectly, to use the mails or interstate commerce to employ any device; scheme or artifice to defraud, make any untrue statement of material fact or omit to state a material fact, or engage in any act, practice or course of business which operates or would operate as a fraud or deceit upon any person."

6. *Supreme Court:* Blue Chip Stamps v. Manor Drug Stores, 421 U.S. 723, 730, 95 S.Ct. 1917, 1923, 44 L.Ed.2d 539 (1975).

Second Circuit: Lloyd v. Industrial Bio-Test Laboratories, Inc., 454 F.Supp. 807, 810 (S.D.N.Y.1978).

7. T.L. HAZEN, THE LAW OF SECURITIES REGULATION 476 (1990).

8. 501 U.S. 350, 111 S.Ct. 2773, 115 L.Ed.2d 321 (1991).

9. The limitation provides that:

"no action shall be maintained * * * unless brought within one year after the discovery of the untrue statement or omission, or after such discovery should have been made by the exercise of reasonable diligence, or * * * within one year after the violation upon which it is based. In no event shall any action be brought * * * more than three years after the security was offered to the public."

15 U.S.C. §§ 77m.

10. *Id.* at 2780.

gress affirmed the *Lampf* decision in the Private Securities Litigation Reform Act of 1995.

Also because this cause of action has been created by the courts, the courts have had to fix the measure of damages. There are few reported cases discussing the measure of damages, undoubtedly because most Rule 10b–5 cases settle. Nevertheless, authority exists for both "out-of-pocket"[11] and a "benefit-of-the-bargain"[12] measures of damages. In the Private Securities Litigation Act of 1995, Congress created section 21D(e) of the 1934 Act, a new section for calculating damages. Section 21D(e) provides a "look back" period which limits damages to those losses caused solely by the fraud and not by other market conditions which may have affected price during the time between the purchase of the security and when corrective information was available to the market. This is achieved by calculating a "mean trading price" for the security.[13]

In some circuits, Section 17(a)[14] of the Securities Act of 1933 has been held to create an implied cause of action,[15] making it unlawful to employ fraudulent or deceptive devices in connection with the sale of securities. However, fewer and fewer Circuits are recognizing this cause of action, with some Circuits overruling past decisions. The fate of Section 17(a) is uncertain.

Although Rule 10b–5 was modeled upon Section 17(a) of the Securities Act of 1933, there are the differences between the two causes of action. First, the federal courts have exclusive jurisdiction over 10b–5 actions while 17(a) actions may be brought in either state or federal court. If brought in state court there is no right of removal to federal court. Second, Section 17(a) does not contain the language "manipulative or deceptive device" that is found in Section 10(b) of the Exchange Act of 1934. It is this language that provides the basis for the fairly stringent scienter requirement imposed in 10b–5 actions. Thus, whereas the 10b–5 plaintiff must prove "willfulness," the Section 17(a) plaintiff must simply prove negligence. Third, 10b–5 actions apply to any "pur-

11. *Tenth Circuit:* Hackbart v. Holmes, 675 F.2d 1114, 1121 (10th Cir. 1982); Estate Counseling Serv. Inc. v. Merrill Lynch, Pierce, Fenner & Smith, Inc. 303 F.2d 527, 533 (10th Cir.1962).

Eleventh Circuit: Gaskins v. Gross, CCH Fed.Sec.L.Rep. ¶ 99, 105 (S.D.Ga. 1983).

12. *Second Circuit:* Osofsky v. Zipf, 645 F.2d 107, 111–114 (2d Cir.1981).

Third Circuit: Sharp v. Coopers & Lybrand, 649 F.2d 175 (3d Cir. 1981).

13. James Hamilton, *Private Securities Litigation Reform Act of 1995 in Derivatives 1996*: AVOIDING THE RISK AND MANAGING THE LITIGATION AT 34 (PLI Corp.L. & Prac. Course Handbook Series 1996).

14. 15 U.S.C. § 77q(a).

15. *Compare, e.g.*:

Second Circuit: Kirshner v. United States, 603 F.2d 234, 241 (2d Cir.1978) (cause of action does exists) with Simpson v. Southeastern Investment Trust, 697 F.2d 1257, 1258 (5th Cir.1983) (cause of action does not exist).

Ninth Circuit: *In re* Washington Publ. Power Supply Sys. Secs. Litg. Henry Puchall, et al. v. Houghton, Cluck, Coughlin & Riley, et al., 823 F.2d 1349 (9th Cir.1987) (overruling Mosher v. Kane, 784 F.2d 1385, 1391 (9th Cir.1986)).

See:

Tenth Circuit: Woods v. Homes and Structures, 489 F.Supp. 1270, 1284–85 (D.Kan.1980), for a thorough summary of the positions of various courts.

chase or sale" of a security while Section 17(a) actions are available for the "offer or sale of any security."[16]

Lastly, the Supreme Court has found an implied cause of action in Rule 14a–9.[17] This rule relates to Section 14[18] of the Exchange Act of 1934 which prohibits using the mails to solicit proxies in a manner that violates SEC regulations. Rule 14a–9 prohibits proxy solicitation by written or oral communication that contains any material misstatement or omission. The Supreme Court has implied a cause of action for violations of Rule 14a–9. The elements of this implied cause of action are (1) reliance by the plaintiff on the proxy or other communication (2) which contains a material misstatement or omission (3) causing damage to the plaintiff[19] (4) with at least negligence by the defendant.[20] Potential defendants include persons who solicited the proxies and who permitted their names to be used in such solicitation. Both damages and injunctive relief have been awarded in Rule 14a–9 actions.[21]

§ 22.10   Overview: Civil Causes of Action—The Private Securities Litigation Reform Act of 1995

Congress passed the Private Securities Litigation Reform Act of 1995[1] (1995 Act) in order to stop a perceived abuse of civil litigation for securities violations. However, the perceived abuses and goals of Congress were not universally shared. The law was passed only after Congress voted to overrule President Clinton's veto.[2] The law changes class actions requirements, encourages voluntary disclosures, provides sanctions for unsupported claims, limits liability in proportion to responsibility, and provides new auditing requirements designed to give greater protection against fraud.[3] A private securities litigant should consult the 1995 Act before any action is taken, particularly in the class action arena. Only relevant criminal and quasi-criminal issues resulting from the 1995 Act will be discussed throughout this chapter.

§ 22.11   Overview: Criminal Causes of Action

A violation of the Securities Act of 1933, the Securities Exchange Act of 1934, or any of the regulations promulgated thereunder, is a civil offense unless committed "willfully." If committed willfully, the violation becomes a criminal offense. Section 24 of the 1933 Statute[1] and

---

16. T.L. HAZEN, THE LAW OF SECURITIES REGULATION 507 (1990).

17. 17 C.F.R. § 240.14a–9 (1991); cf. J.I. Case Co. v. Borak, 377 U.S. 426, 430–34, 84 S.Ct. 1555, 1559–1561, 12 L.Ed.2d 423 (1964).

18. 15 U.S.C. § 78n(a).

19. Beatty v. Bright, 318 F.Supp. 169, 173 (D.C.Iowa 1970).

20. Gruss v. Curtis Publishing Co., 534 F.2d 1396, 1403 (2d Cir.1976).

21. See, e.g., Ronson Corp. v. Liquifin Aktiengesellschaft, 370 F.Supp. 597

(D.C.N.J.1974), aff'd, 497 F.2d 394 (3d Cir. 1974).

§ 22.10

1. Amending 15 U.S.C. §§ 77–78.

2. Pub.Law 104–67, 109 Stat. 737.

3. James Hamilton, Private Securities Litigation Reform Act of 1995 in DERIVATIVES 1996: AVOIDING THE RISK AND MANAGING THE LITIGATION, at 475 (PLI Corp.L. & Prac. Course Handbook Series, 1996).

§ 22.11

1. 15 U.S.C. § 77x.

Section 32(a) of the 1934 Statute[2] create this criminal liability. Innocent mistake, negligence or inadvertence are not enough to qualify for criminal liability.[3] The government need not show specific intent to violate the laws, just the intent to commit the act which is prohibited.[4] Although section 32(a) allows an individual to be convicted of willfully violating the 1934 Act even if unaware of the existence of an applicable section or rule, section 32(a) also provides, "no person shall be subject to imprisonment under this section for the violation of any rule or regulation if he proves that he had no knowledge of such rule or regulation."[5]

United States v. Weiner,[6] arises from one of the more notorious American securities frauds of the twentieth century and provides insight into the "willfulness" requirement for criminal securities cases. The defendants served as auditors and financial officers for Equity Funding, a company which sold insurance mutual funds known as "equity funding programs." With the defendants' approval, Equity Funding published inaccurate and false financial statements which overstated income and claimed nonexistent assets in order to increase the value of the stock. As a result, they were convicted of securities fraud.[7]

On appeal the defendants argued, among other things, that the trial court erred in instructing the jury on the intent element. Pursuant to 15 U.S.C. § 77x, the government had to prove that the defendants "willfully" committed the acts alleged. The jury was told that "an essential element of [the offenses with which the defendants are charged] is an evil or criminal intent." The jury was also told that it was:

> "entitled to consider in determining whether a defendant acted with such intent if he deliberately closed his eyes to the obvious or to the facts that certainly would be observed or ascertained in the course of his portion of the accounting works, or whether he recklessly states as facts matters of which he knew he was ignorant.

2. 15 U.S.C. § 78ff.

3. United States v. Dixon, 536 F.2d 1388, 1397 (2d Cir.1976).

4. *Second Circuit:* United States v. Schwartz, 464 F.2d 499, 509 (2d Cir.1972).

Eighth Circuit: United States v. Olson, 22 F.3d 783, 785 (8th Cir.1994).

5. 15 U.S.C. § 78ff.

6. 578 F.2d 757 (9th Cir.1978).

7. The defendants were convicted of the following provisions:

15 U.S.C. § 77x which provides:

"[a]ny person who willfully violates any of the provisions of [the Securities Act of 1933] or the rules and regulations promulgated by the Commission * * * shall upon conviction be fined not more than $10,000 or imprisoned not more than five years, or both."

15 U.S.C. § 77f (pertains to requirements for registering a security with the SEC).

15 U.S.C. § 77q(a) (makes it unlawful to use interstate commerce for purposes of fraud or deceit in the offer or sale of any securities).

15 U.S.C. § 78l (sets forth registration requirements for all securities transacted on the national exchanges).

15 U.S.C. § 78m (pertains to requirements for filing reports with the SEC).

15 U.S.C. § 78ff which provides:

"[a]ny person who willfully violats any provision of [the Exchange Act of 1934] or any rule or regulation thereunder * * * shall upon conviction be fined not more than $10,000 or imprisoned not more than five years, or both * * *."

Weiner, 578 F.2d at 763.

"If you find such reckless, deliberate indifference to or disregard for truth or falsity on the part of a given defendant when considered in the light of all other evidence relating to intent, you may, but you need not necessarily, infer therefrom that such defendant acted willfully and knowingly. Such an inference, of course, depends upon the weight and credibility extended to the evidence of reckless and indifferent conduct, if any."[8]

The Ninth Circuit rejected the defendants' argument, holding that "[t]he court properly instructed the jury on the need to find both deliberate avoidance and an awareness of impropriety. Defendants here, as auditors, had a duty carefully to investigate and review the information presented."[9]

In *Weiner*, the Ninth Circuit adopted the accepted view among the federal courts of appeal that proof of "reckless deliberate indifference" may constitute "willfulness" for purposes of determining criminal liability under the securities laws.[10] The Supreme Court has not yet ruled on this issue. In 1976, in *Ernst & Ernst v. Hochfelder*, when the Court held that proof of negligence was not sufficient to prove criminal scienter under the securities laws, it expressly reserved the question of whether proof of recklessness would suffice.[11]

One of the more widely adopted definitions of recklessness is that of the Seventh Circuit in *Sundstrand Corp. v. Sun Chemical Corp.*,[12] which adopted the following definition of reckless conduct:

> [R]eckless conduct may be defined as a highly unreasonable omission, involving not merely simple, or even inexcusable negligence, but an extreme departure from the standards of ordinary care, and which presents a danger of misleading buyers or sellers that is either known to the defendant or is so obvious that the actor must have been aware of it.[13]

A number of courts have adopted the *Sundstrand* definition of recklessness or defined recklessness in a substantially similar manner.[14]

---

8. *Id.* at 786.

9. *Id.* at 787.

10. *See, e.g.,* United States v. Natelli, 527 F.2d 311, 322–23 (2d Cir.1975).

11. Ernst & Ernst v. Hochfelder, 425 U.S. 185, 193, 96 S.Ct. 1375, 1381, 47 L.Ed.2d 668 (1976) ("In certain areas of the law recklessness is considered to be a form of intentional conduct for purposes of imposing liability from some act. We need not address here the question whether in some circumstances reckless behavior is sufficient for civil liability under [the Securities Statutes.]")

12. 553 F.2d 1033 (7th Cir.1977).

13. *Id.* at 1045 (*quoting* Franke v. Midwestern Okla. Dev. Auth., 428 F.Supp. 719, 725 (W.D.Okla.1976), *vacated sub nom. on other grounds*, Cronin v. Midwestern

Okla. Dev. Auth., 619 F.2d 856 (10th Cir. 1980)).

14. *See also*:

D.C. Circuit: SEC v. Steadman, 967 F.2d 636, 641–42 (D.C.Cir.1992).

First Circuit: Hoffman v. Estabrook & Co., 587 F.2d 509, 517 (1st Cir.1978).

Second Circuit: Rolf v. Blyth, Eastman Dillon & Co., 570 F.2d 38, 47 (2d Cir.1978).

Third Circuit: In re Phillips Petroleum Sec. Litig., 881 F.2d 1236, 1244 (3d Cir. 1989).

Fourth Circuit: Frankel v. Wyllie & Thornhill, Inc., 537 F.Supp. 730 (W.D.Va. 1982).

Fifth Circuit: Broad v. Rockwell Int'l Corp., 642 F.2d 929, 961–62 (5th Cir.1981).

Other courts have adopted a more stringent definition of recklessness. According to the Fifth and Eleventh Circuits, "severe" recklessness is needed to satisfy *Hochfelder's* scienter requirement. The Fifth Circuit has defined "severe recklessness" as:

> limited to those highly unreasonable omissions or misrepresentations that involve not merely simple or even inexcusable negligence but an *extreme departure from the standards of ordinary care*, and that present a danger of misleading buyers or sellers which is either known to the defendant or is so obvious that the defendant must have been aware of it.[15]

Defendants in criminal cases have argued that lowering the scienter requirement to "recklessness" in criminal 10b–5 prosecutions is improper. Numerous courts have rejected that claim. The Third Circuit's response in *United States v. Boyer*,[16] is typical:

> The standard of proof for civil liability in fraud is lower than the proof beyond a reasonable doubt required for a criminal conviction. But there is no reason to suppose that in enacting criminal statutes prohibiting mail fraud or securities fraud the congress intended that the substantive element of the offense—the scienter—should be different than for civil liability for fraud.[17]

In *Marksman Partners, L.P. v. Chantal Pharmaceutical Corporation*, the defendants argued that the Private Securities Litigation Reform Act of 1995 (PSLRA) abolished the reckless conduct standard for securities fraud liability. The District court disagreed, explaining that nowhere in the legislative history of the PSLRA did Congress indicate a desire to remove the recklessness standard: "The Conference Committee report, however, suggests that Congress did not intend to change the state of mind requirements of existing law, ... and this is confirmed by the absence of any express abrogation in the PSLRA of recklessness liability for the type of conduct at issues here."[18]

§ 22.12   Rule 10b–5: The "Catch All" Antifraud Provision

Section 10(b) of the Exchange Act of 1934 is generally referred to as

Sixth Circuit: Ohio Drill & Tool Co. v. Johnson, 625 F.2d 738, 741 (6th Cir.1980); Mansbach v. Prescott, Balls & Turben, 598 F.2d 1017 (6th Cir.1979); Ingram Industries, Inc. v. Nowicki, 502 F.Supp. 1060, 1064 (6th Cir.1980).

Seventh Circuit: Sanders v. John Nuveen & Co., 554 F.2d 790, 793 (7th Cir. 1977).

Eighth Circuit: Ligenfelter v. Title Ins. Co. of Minnesota, 442 F.Supp. 981 (D.Neb. 1977).

Ninth Circuit: Hollinger v. Titan Capital Corp., 914 F.2d 1564, 1569 (9th Cir. 1990).

Tenth Circuit: Hackbart v. Holmes, 675 F.2d 1114, 1118 (10th Cir.1982).

Eleventh Circuit: McDonald v. Alan Bush Brokerage Co., 863 F.2d 809, 814–15 (11th Cir.1989).

15. Warren v. Reserve Fund, Inc., 728 F.2d 741, 745 (5th Cir.1984) (*quoting* Broad v. Rockwell Int'l Corp., 642 F.2d 929, 961 (5th Cir.1981) (en banc) (emphasis in original)).

16. 694 F.2d 58 (3d Cir.1982).

17. *Id.* at 60.

18. 927 F.Supp. 1297, 1309, n. 9 (C.D.Calif.1996).

the "catch all" antifraud provision of the federal securities laws.[1] In 1942, the SEC adopted Rule 10b–5[2] to implement Section 10b. Since then it has been the source of extensive litigation: "Rule 10b–5 is perhaps the most well-known, or at least the most notorious, provisions of the federal securities laws."[3] Rule 10b–5 implements the overall goal of the 1934 Act, of "protect[ing] investors against manipulation of stock prices."[4] As Congress noted, when passing the 1934 Act, "There cannot be honest markets without honest publicity."[5] Rule 10b–5 declares that it is unlawful for any person "[t]o make any untrue statement of a material fact or to omit to state a material fact necessary in order to make the statements made . . . not misleading . . . in connection with the purchase or sale of a security." There are five elements in proving a 10b–5 violation: "(1) a misstatement or an omission (2) of a material fact (3) made with scienter (4) on which the plaintiff relied (5) that proximately caused the plaintiff's injury."[6]

In *Basic Inc. v. Levinson*,[7] the Supreme Court discussed the elements of materiality, reliance and causation in a 10b–5 action. The case was brought by sellers of stock in Basic Incorporated (Basic), a publicly traded company engaged primarily in the manufacturing of chemical refractories. Over a three year time period Basic engaged in merger negotiations with Combustion Engineering, Inc., a company producing mostly aluminum-based refractories. During this time, Basic made three public statements denying that any negotiations had occurred and denying knowledge of any developments which could explain the heavy trading of its stock.[8]

§ 22.12

1. Section 10(b) of the 1934 Act, 15 U.S.C. § 78j, prohibits the use "in connection with the purchase or sale of any security . . . [of] any manipulative or deceptive device or contrivance in contravention of such rules and regulations as the commission may prescribe."

2. In relevant part, Rule 10b–5 provides:

"It shall be unlawful for any person, directly or indirectly, by the use of any means or instrumentality of interstate commerce, or of the mails or of any facility of any national securities exchange,

* * *

"(b) To make any untrue statement of a material fact or to omit to state a material fact necessary in order to make the statements made, in the light of the circumstances under which they were made, not misleading. . . . ,

"in connection with the purchase or sale of any security."

3. John A. MacKerron, *The Price Integrity Cause of Action Under Rule 10b–5: Limiting and Expanding the Use of the*

Fraud on the Market Theory, 69 ORE.L.REV. 177 (1990).

4. *Id.* at 230.

5. H.R.Rep.No. 1383, 73rd Cong., 2d Sess., 11 (1934).

6. *Fifth Circuit:* Huddleston v. Herman MacLean, 640 F.2d 534, 543 (5th Cir. 1981) *aff'd in part, rev'd in part*, 459 U.S. 375, 103 S.Ct. 683, 74 L.Ed.2d 548 (1983).

See also:

Supreme Court: Dirks v. SEC, 463 U.S. 646, 657, 103 S.Ct. 3255, 3263, 77 L.Ed.2d 911 (1983) (duty to disclose); Santa Fe Industries, Inc. v. Green, 430 U.S. 462, 473–74, 97 S.Ct. 1292, 1301, 51 L.Ed.2d 480 (1977) ("manipulative or deceptive requirement"); Ernst & Ernst v. Hochfelder, 425 U.S. 185, 214, 96 S.Ct. 1375, 1391, 47 L.Ed.2d 668 (1976) (scienter); Blue Chip Stamps v. Manor Drug Stores, 421 U.S. 723, 749, 95 S.Ct. 1917, 1932, 44 L.Ed.2d 539 (1975) ("in connection with the purchase or sale" requirement).

7. 485 U.S. 224, 108 S.Ct. 978, 99 L.Ed.2d 194 (1988).

8. *Id.* at 226–27.

A class comprised of former Basic shareholders who sold their stock after the first public denial but before the merger announcement, filed an action against Basic and some of its directors. The class claimed that the denials by Basic were false or misleading, in violation of § 10(b) and Rule 10b–5 of the 1934 Act and resulted in class members' injury which occurred when they sold their interests in an artificially depressed market created by Basic.[9]

At issue were the materiality and reliance elements of 10b–5. The District Court certified the class but granted summary judgment for the defendants, holding that as a matter of law any misstatements made were not material.[10] The United States Court of Appeals for the Sixth Circuit affirmed the certification of the class but reversed and remanded on the issue of materiality, holding that the District Court applied the wrong test for materiality. In so ruling, the Sixth Circuit joined other circuits which recognized a "fraud on the market theory" in evaluating materiality for purposes of 10b–5.

In its ruling the Supreme Court disagreed with the standards for materiality adopted and applied by both of the lower courts, clarified the standard for judging materiality and remanded the case. The Court acknowledged that delineating a test of materiality in the context of preliminary merger discussions is problematic because when "the event is contingent or speculative in nature, it is difficult to ascertain whether the 'reasonable investor' would have considered the omitted information significant. . . ."[11] The Court began its analysis by considering the "agreement in principle" test for materiality urged by Basic and the other defendants and adopted by the District Court.[12] Under this test misstatements or omissions do not become material until the "would be merger parties" have reached an " 'agreement-in-principle' as to the price and structure of the transaction . . . ."[13] As the Court noted, "By definition, then, information concerning any negotiations not yet at the agreement-in-principle stage could be withheld or even misrepresented without a violation of Rule 10b–5." The Court noted the practical arguments in favor of this test: (1) investors need not be "overwhelmed by excessively detailed and trivial information"; (2) by limiting the scope of disclosure obligations, the "agreement-in-principle" test helps preserve the confidentiality of merger discussions where earlier disclosure might prejudice the negotiations, and (3) the test provides a bright line rule.[14]

The Court soundly rejected the first rationale noting that, "[d]isclosure, and not paternalistic withholding of accurate information, is the

9. *Id.* at 228.

10. *Id.* at 229.

11. *Id.* at 38.

12. The District Court in *Basic* applied the agreement-in-principle test. It focused on whether the statements at issue were made prior to the time that the negotiations were "destined, with reasonable

certainty, to become a merger agreement in principle." *Id.* at 229. Finding that they were so made, the District Court held that, as a matter of law, the statements were not material. *Id.*

13. *Id.* at 233.

14. *Id.* at 233–34.

policy chosen and expressed by Congress."[15] While acknowledging the need for secrecy (to avoid a " 'bidding war' "), the Court found that such a concern was irrelevant to the question of what information would be "significant to the reasonable investor's trading decision."[16] The timing of disclosures is more appropriately considered as part of the issuer's "duty to disclose," rather than as relevant to materiality.[17] The Court easily rejected the third rationale: ". . . ease of application alone is not an excuse for ignoring the purposes of the Securities Acts and Congress' policy decisions."[18]

Having rejected the agreement-in-principle standard of materiality, the Court also rejected the standard adopted by the Sixth Circuit that "once a statement is made denying the existence of any discussions, even discussions that might not have been material in absence of the denial are material because they make the statement made untrue." After finding the statements material,[19] the Sixth Circuit adopted the "fraud-on-the market theory 'to create a rebuttable presumption that respondents relied on petitioners' material misrepresentations . . .' ":

> This theory is based on the hypothesis that, in an open and developed securities market, the price of a company's stock is determined by the available material information regarding the company and its business. . . . Misleading statements will therefore defraud purchasers of stock even if the purchasers do not directly rely on the misstatements. . . . The causal connection between the defendants' fraud and the plaintiffs' purchase of stock in such a case is no less significant than in a case of direct reliance on misrepresentations.[20]

The Court found the Sixth Circuit's approach inadequate because it "fail[ed] to recognize that, in order to prevail on a Rule 10b–5 claim, a plaintiff must show that the statements were misleading as to a material fact. It is not enough that a statement is false or incomplete, if the misrepresented fact is otherwise insignificant."[21]

The Court then considered the merits of the standard enunciated in TSC Industries, Inc. v. Northway, Inc.[22] TSC involved allegations of facts omitted from proxy solicitations and arose under § 14(a), as amended, of the 1934 Act.[23] In TSC, the Court held that "[a]n omitted fact is material if there is a substantial likelihood that a reasonable shareholder would consider it important in deciding how to vote."[24] The Court found this test to be applicable to pre-merger suits brought under 10b–5. According to the Court, this test appropriately recognizes that some

---

15. *Id.* at 234.

16. *Id.* at 235.

17. *Id.*

18. *Id.* at 235.

19. *Id.* at 230 *quoting* 786 F.2d at 729.

20. 485 U.S. at 242, 108 S.Ct. 989 *quoting* Peil v. Speiser, 806 F.2d 1154, 1160–61 (3d Cir.1986).

21. *Id.* at 238.

22. 426 U.S. 438, 96 S.Ct. 2126, 48 L.Ed.2d 757 (1976).

23. 15 U.S.C. § 78n(a) and Rule 14a–9, 17 C.F.R. § 240.14a–9.

24. 426 U.S. 438, 448, 96 S.Ct. 2126, 2132, 48 L.Ed.2d 757 (1976).

information regarding corporate developments would be of "dubious significance" and thus is not set too low.[25] Yet, it also recognizes that because a merger is "the most important event that can occur in a small corporation's life, to wit, its death," information can "become material at an earlier stage than would be the case as regards lesser transactions...."[26] In short, the *TSC* standard, according to the Court, strikes an appropriate balance: "[t]he role of materiality requirement is not to 'attribute to investors a childlike simplicity, an inability to grasp the probabilistic significance of negotiations' but to filter out essentially useless information that a reasonable investor would not consider significant, even as part of a larger mix of factors to consider in making his investment decision."[27]

The Court noted the *TSC* standard was fact sensitive and that

a factfinder will need to look to indicia of interest in the transaction at the highest corporate levels. Without attempting to catalog all such possible factors, we note by way of example that board resolutions, instructions to investment bankers, and actual negotiations between principals or their intermediaries may serve as indicia of interest. To assess the magnitude of the transaction to the issuer of the securities allegedly manipulated, a factfinder will need to consider such facts as the size of the two corporate entities and of the potential premiums over market value. No particular event or factor short of closing the transaction need be either necessary or sufficient by itself to render merger discussions material.

Next, the Court turned to the reliance element and the fraud-on-the-market theory. Reliance by the plaintiff on the false statements or omissions allegedly made by the defendant is an element of a 10b–5 action.[28] Yet, class actions on 10b–5 grounds would be impossible if proof of individualized reliance from each class member was required, "since individual issues then would have overwhelmed the common ones."[29] The fraud on the market theory remedies this by taking into account the nature of the modern securities market where millions of shares are traded daily. This theory presumes that investors rely on the price of securities when making investment decisions, that the price of securities is affected by information available to the market, and thus finds reliance whenever the information at issue, or lack of it, is available to the public.[30] The Supreme Court approved use of the fraud-on-the-

25. *Id.*

26. *Id.* quoting Judge Friendly, SEC v. Geon Industries, Inc., 531 F.2d 39, 47–48 (2d Cir.1976).

27. *Id.* at 234.

28. Ernst & Ernst v. Hochfelder, 425 U.S. 185, 206, 96 S.Ct. 1375, 1387, 47 L.Ed.2d 668 (1976).

29. *Basic*, 485 U.S. at 242, 108 S.Ct. at 989.

30. "In face-to-face transactions, the inquiry into an investor's reliance upon information is into the subjective pricing of that information by that investor. With the presence of a market, the market is interposed between seller and buyer and, ideally, transmits information to the investor in the processed form of a market price. Thus the market is performing a substantial part of the valuation process performed by the investor in a face-to-face transaction. The

market theory, reasoning as follows: "Requiring a plaintiff to show a speculative state of facts, i.e., how he would have acted if omitted material information had been disclosed, or if the misrepresentation had not been made, would place an unnecessarily unrealistic evidentiary burden on the Rule 10b–5 plaintiff who has traded on an impersonal market."[31]

The Court noted that "[a]ny showing that severs the link between the alleged misrepresentation and either the price received (or paid) by the plaintiff, or his decision to trade at a fair market price, will be sufficient to rebut the presumption of reliance."[32] Such a showing could be made with evidence that the "market makers" were privy to the truth about the situation, or that the truth entered the market or that individual plaintiffs based their investment decisions on facts other than at issue.[33]

Thus, after *Basic*, the standard for judging materiality in 10b–5 actions is whether "there is a substantial likelihood that a reasonable shareholder would consider [the information] important in deciding how to vote." Additionally, the court approved of use of the fraud-on-the-market theory in proving reliance in 10b–5 actions.

§ 22.13　Insider Trading—In General

"Insider trading" is not statutorily defined but is a concept developed by the courts concerning the use of information about securities which is not available to the general public to make investment transactions.[1] Corporate insiders, even brokers-dealers must abstain from trading or disclose all material inside information before trading.[2] "The obligation to disclose or abstain derives from:

"[a]n affirmative duty to disclose material information[, which] has been traditionally imposed on corporate 'insiders,' particular officers, directors, or controlling stockholders. ... [T]he courts have consistently held that insiders must disclose material facts which are known to them by virtue of their position but

---

market is acting as the unpaid agent of the investor, informing him that given all the information available to it, the value of the stock is worth the market price." In re LTV Securities Litigation, 88 F.R.D. 134, 143 (N.D.Tex.1980).

Accord, e.g.,

Third Circuit: Peil v. Speiser, 806 F.2d 1154 (3d Cir.1986) 1161 ("In an open and developed market, the dissemination of material misrepresentations or withholding of material information typically affects the price of the stock, and purchasers generally rely on the price of the stock as a reflection of its value").

Ninth Circuit: Blackie v. Barrack, 524 F.2d 891, 908 (9th Cir.1975) ("[T]he same

causal nexus can be adequately established indirectly, by proof of materiality coupled with the common sense that a stock purchaser does not ordinarily seek to purchase a loss in the form of artificially inflated stock").

31. *Id.*

32. *Id.* at 248.

33. *Id.* at 249.

§ 22.13

1. United States v. Chiarella, 588 F.2d 1358, 1365–66 (2d Cir.1978).

2. Cady, Roberts & Co., 40 S.E.C. 907 (1961).

which are not known to persons with whom they deal and which, if known, would affect their investment judgment."[3]

This duty arises from "(i) the existence of a relationship affording access to inside information intended to be available only for a corporate purpose, and (ii) the unfairness of allowing a corporate insider to take advantage of that information by trading without disclosure."[4]

The courts have developed the law of insider trading from common law doctrines of fraud and fiduciary duty, and from statutory sources, including section 14(e) of the 1934 Exchange Act[5] and SEC Rule 14e–3[6] (false statements or material omissions in connection with a tender offer); Section 17(a) of the 1933 Securities Act[7] (employing a scheme to defraud); and, Section 10(b) of the 1934 Act[8] and SEC Rule 10b–5[9] (using any manipulative or deceptive device). Most criminal charges for insider trading are brought under Section 10b and Rule 10b–5.

Library References:

C.J.S. Securities Regulation § 179, 182.
West's Key No. Digests, Securities Regulation ⟋60.28.

§ 22.14   Insider Trading—Case Law Development

Who qualifies as an "insider" for purposes of the prohibition against insider trading is not yet settled. Initially, only directors and management officers were deemed to be "insiders." The Insider Trading and Securities Fraud Enforcement Act of 1988 (ITSFEA),[1] expanded the Insider Trading Sanctions Act of 1984 (ITSA).[2] ITSA allowed the Commission to impose civil penalties up to "three times the profit gained or loss avoid as a result of such unlawful purchase or sale" through insider trading in violation of Rule 10b–5 and/or Rule 14e–3.[3] In order to prevent future insider trading, ITSA requires registered broker-dealers and investment advisors to establish, maintain, and enforce written policies and procedures which are "reasonably designed to prevent the misuse of material nonpublic information."[4] Consequently, ITSA expanded the application of the civil penalty to persons who control the primary violator.[5] This civil remedy merely requires proof by a preponderance of the evidence. The Commission must bring such an action within five years of the date of the purchase or sale, but collection of the fine that may be collected is not limited.[6] Furthermore, ITSA allows the

---

3. *Id.* at 911.

4. *Id.* at 912, and n. 15.

5. 15 U.S.C. § 78n.

6. 17 C.F.R. 140.14e–3.

7. 15 U.S.C. § 77q.

8. 15 U.S.C. § 78j(b).

9. 17 C.F.R. § 240.10b–5.

§ 22.14

1. Pub.L.No. 100–704, § 3(a)(2), 102 Stat. 4677.

2. Pub.L.No. 98–376, 98 Stat. 1264.

3. Exchange Act § 21A(a); 15 U.S.C. § 78u–1(a); Insider Trading Sanctions Act of 1984, Pub.L.No. 98–737, 98 Stat. 1264.

4. Exchange Act § 21A(b)(1)(B); 15 U.S.C. § 78u1(b)(1)(B).

5. Exchange Act § 21A(b)(1); 15 U.S.C. § 78u1(b)(1).

6. Exchange Act § 21A(d)(5); 15 U.S.C. § 78u1(d)(5).

Commission to pay a "bounty" to whistle-blowers who give information about insider trading violations which ultimately lead to a civil penalty. The bounty may equal up to ten percent of the civil penalty or settlement.[7] ITSA also permits the Commission to investigate violations of foreign securities laws at the request of foreign authorities.[8] The Act expanded the maximum prison sentences and fines for criminal violations of the securities laws. Finally, ITSA created an express private remedy for investors who contemporaneously traded the same class of securities as the insider(s).[9] The concept of "insiders" includes persons outside the corporation, such as securities brokers.[10]

Chiarella v. United States,[11] a key Supreme Court case on insider trading demonstrates an unsuccessful effort to expand "insider" to third parties who hold no position with the companies involved. Chiarella was a printer who worked for a firm which was printing announcements of corporate takeover bids. Although the identities of the acquiring and target corporations were kept secret until the night of the final printing, Chiarella deduced the identity of the target of the corporate takeover bid after reading other materials provided for printing. Acting on this knowledge Chiarella purchased stock in the target companies, sold the shares immediately after the takeover attempts were made public and realized a gain of over $30,000. The SEC began an investigation which ended with a consent decree requiring that Chiarella return all profits to the sellers of the shares he bought. In addition, Chiarella was discharged by his employer, indicted on 17 counts of violating § 10(b) of the 1934 Exchange Act and, after a jury trial, convicted on all counts.[12]

Appealing his conviction to the United States Court of Appeals for the Second Circuit, Chiarella argued that he was not an "insider" for purposes of section 10b and Rule 10b–5 and thus had no duty to disclose the information he had before trading.[13] Conceding that Chiarella was not an insider,[14] the Second Circuit nevertheless affirmed his conviction by relying on the "misappropriation" theory. The misappropriation theory broadens the group of individuals who qualify as violators of § 10b and Rule 10b–5. Instead of requiring proof that a defendant had a duty to the sellers which the defendant breached in his trading, the misappropriation theory requires only proof that a defendant traded on the basis of wrongfully obtained, material, nonpublic information. As the Second Circuit explained:

> A major purpose of the anti-fraud provisions was to 'protect the integrity of the marketplace in which securities are traded.' *Anyone*—corporate insider or not—who regularly receives mate-

7. Exchange Act § 21A(e); 15 U.S.C. § 78u1(e).

8. Exchange Act § 21(a)(2); 15 U.S.C. § 78u(a)(2).

9. Exchange Act § 20A; 15 U.S.C. § 78t–1.

10. *In re Cady, Roberts & Co.*, 40 SEC 907, 912 (1961).

11. 445 U.S. 222, 100 S.Ct. 1108, 63 L.Ed.2d 348 (1980).

12. *Id.* at 224–25.

13. United States v. Chiarella, 588 F.2d 1358 (2d Cir.1978).

14. *Id.* at 1364.

rial nonpublic information may not use that information to trade in securities without incurring an affirmative duty to disclose. And if he cannot disclose [and Chiarella could not because of his duty to his employer not to reveal clients' confidences] he must abstain from buying or selling.

The Second Circuit also recognized that some proponents of the misappropriation theory required proof that the trader had obtained the information improperly.[15] Thus, it further held that Chiarella's conduct of obtaining facts through the secrecy entrusted to his employer was "sufficiently egregious to fit the most restrictive definition of quasi-insider who would be barred from trading by the general provisions of [the more restrictive misappropriation theory]."[16]

Without directly ruling on the efficacy of the misappropriation theory, the Supreme Court set aside Chiarella's conviction. It held that Chiarella had no duty to the sellers of stock to disclose the material information he had acquired about upcoming takeovers.[17] The Court relied on the settled common law principle that "one who fails to disclose material information prior to the consummation of a transaction commits fraud only when he is under a duty to do so."[18] Examining the evidence, the Court found that Chiarella had no duty to the sellers because he had no prior dealings with them. The Court acknowledged that Chiarella may have had a duty to the acquiring corporation which hired Chiarella's employer to do the printing but this company suffered no damages from Chiarella's purchases, making it questionable whether an actionable violation of Rule 10b–5 occurred.[19] Moreover, this theory was not presented to the jury.[20]

The Court did not address the merits of the misappropriation theory, finding that it was not submitted to the jury. The dissent, however, vigorously defended this theory, at least the more restrictive view of it which requires evidence that a trader obtain the material, nonpublic information *wrongfully*. Chief Justice Burger author of the dissent, offered the following rationale for the theory:

> [T]he way in which the buyer acquires the information which he conceals from the vendor should be a material circumstance. . . . Any time information is acquired by . . . an illegal act it would seem that there should be a duty to disclose that information.[21]

In *Dirks v. SEC.*,[22] the Supreme Court further clarified who could be an "insider" and, as in *Chiarella*, adopted a narrow definition of insider. Dirks was an officer at a broker-dealer firm who specialized in providing investment analysis of insurance company securities to institutional

---

15. *Id.* at 1365–66.

16. *Id.* at 1366.

17. *Id.* at 232.

18. 445 U.S. at 228, 100 S.Ct. at 1114.

19. *Id.* at 238 (Stevens, J., concurring).

20. *Id.* at 236.

21. 445 U.S. at 240, 100 S.Ct. at 1120 (Burger, C.J., dissenting), *quoting* W. Page Keeton, *Fraud—Concealment and Non-Disclosure*, 15 Texas L.Rev. 1, 25–26 (1936).

22. 463 U.S. 646, 103 S.Ct. 3255, 77 L.Ed.2d 911 (1983).

investors. Dirks received information from Ronald Secrist, a former officer of Equity Funding of America (Equity), that Equity had engaged in fraudulent practices and vastly overstated its assets. Secrist urged Dirks to investigate and verify the fraud, then disclose it publicly.[23] Dirks did so. He visited Equity's headquarters, interviewed Equity officers and employees and openly discussed Secrist's charges with clients and investors. Some of these clients and individuals sold their holdings in Equity, including five investment advisers who sold more than $16 million in Equity stocks.[24] During the two-week period when Dirks was openly investigating Equity, Equity's stock fell from $26 per share to less than $15 per share. Within three weeks of Secrist informing Dirks of Equity's difficulties, the New York Stock Exchange halted trading in Equity, the SEC filed a complaint against Equity and the Wall Street Journal published a story based on information gathered by Dirks.[25] The SEC then began investigating Dirks, concluding that he aided and abetted violations of Section 10(b) of the Securities and Exchange Act of 1934,[26] Rule 10b–5[27] and Section 17(a) of the Securities Act of 1933.[28] According to the SEC, Dirks aided in a "manipulative and deceptive device"[29] by "repeating the allegations of fraud to members of the investment community who later sold their Equity Funding Stock."[30] The SEC further found Dirks to be an insider within Section 10(b) by virtue of his status as a "tippee": one who "come[s] into possession of material corporate information that they know is confidential and know or should know came from a corporate insider. . . ."[31] As such the SEC concluded Dirks should not have assisted those clients and investors to whom he told of Equity's troubles, without disclosing his information to the public.[32] The Commission explained:

> In tipping potential traders, Dirks breached a duty which he had assumed as a result of knowingly receiving confidential information from [Equity Funding] insiders. Tippees such as Dirks who receive non-public, material information from insiders become subject to the same duty as [the] insiders. Such a tippee breaches the fiduciary duty which he assumes from the insider when the tippee knowingly transmits the information to someone who will probably trade on the basis thereof.[33]

The Court viewed the SEC's position as "rooted in the idea that the antifraud provisions require equal information among all traders."[34] Just as the Court rejected this view in *Chiarella*, it rejected it in *Dirks*.[35] The Court emphasized that one has a duty to disclose or refrain from trading only when "a party has legal obligations other than a mere duty to

---

23. *Id.* at 648–49.

24. *Id.* at 649.

25. *Id.* at 649–50.

26. 15 U.S.C. § 78j(b).

27. 17 C.F.R. § 240.10b–5.

28. 15 U.S.C. § 77q(a).

29. 15 U.S.C. § 78j(b).

30. 463 U.S. at 651, 103 S.Ct. at 3260.

31. *Id.* [internal quotation marks deleted].

32. *Id.* at 651, 653 n.10.

33. *Id.* at 656 *quoting* 21 SEC Docket, at 1410 n. 42.

34. *Id.* at 657.

35. *Id.* at 657.

comply with the general antifraud proscriptions in the federal securities laws."[36] If, however, the person giving the tippee the non-public, material information gives the tippee the information for "the improper purpose of exploiting the information for their personal gain," section 10(b) and rule 10b–5 are violated.[37] According to the Court:

> [A] tippee assumes a fiduciary duty to the shareholders of a corporation not to trade on material nonpublic information only when the insider has breached his fiduciary duty to the shareholders by disclosing the information to the tippee and the tippee knows or should know that there has been a breach. Whether disclosure is a breach of duty therefore depends in large part on the purpose of the disclosure. [The purpose is improper if] the insider personally will benefit, directly or indirectly, from his disclosure.[38]

Applying the above rule, the Court found that there was "no actionable violation by Dirks."[39] There was no evidence that Dirks had any preexisting relationship to Equity's shareholders or that Secrist stood to personally benefit from disclosing the information to Dirks. Instead, the facts simply showed a "desire to expose the fraud."[40]

In 1997, the Supreme Court squarely addressed and approved the misappropriation theory in affirming the conviction of an attorney, James Herman O'Hagan.[41] Whereas Dirks was given inside information by an insider and spread the information without personally profiting, O'Hagan was found to have stolen the information from insiders for the purpose of personally profiting.

O'Hagan was a partner in a Minnesota law firm, Dorsey & Whitney, which was retained for approximately two months in 1988 by Grand Metropolitan & PLC (Grand Met) regarding a potential tender offer for the common stock of Pillsbury Company, headquartered in Minneapolis. About one month before Grand Met publicly announced its tender offer, Dorsey & Whitney withdrew from representing Grand Met. At no time did O'Hagan work on the Grand Met matter.

Beginning during Dorsey & Whitney's representation of Grand Met, O'Hagan purchased 5,000 shares of Pillsbury common stock and 2,500 of unexpired call options for Pillsbury stock, ("apparently more than any other investor").[42] When Grand Met announced its tender offer, the price of Pillsbury stock shot up and O'Hagan made a profit of more than $4.3 million from his purchases of Pillsbury stock.[43]

The SEC began investigating O'Hagan's trades. Ultimately O'Hagan was indicted and convicted on 57 counts of fraud:

36. *Id.*
37. *Id.* at 659.
38. *Id.* at 660–62.
39. *Id.* at 665.
40. *Id.* at 666–67.

41. United States v. O'Hagan, __ U.S. __, 117 S.Ct. 2199, 138 L.Ed.2d 724 (1997).
42. *Id.* at 2205.
43. *Id.*

The indictment alleged that O'Hagan defrauded his law firm and its client, Grand Met, by using for his own trading purposes material, nonpublic information regarding Grand Met's planned tender offer. According to the indictment, O'Hagan used the profits he gained through this trading to conceal his previous embezzlement and conversion of unrelated client trust funds.[44]

The charges in the indictment included mail fraud (18 U.S.C. § 1341), money laundering (18 U.S.C. § 1956), securities fraud in violation of § 10(b) of the Securities Exchange Act of 1934 (15 U.S.C. § 78j(b) and SEC Rule 10b–5) and fraudulent trading in connection with a tender offer in violation of § 14(e) of the Exchange Act (115 U.S.C. § 78n (e), and SEC Rule 14e–3(a)).[45]

The Court of Appeals for the Eighth Circuit reversed all of O'Hagan's convictions, holding that the misappropriations theory, upon which all convictions were based, was invalid.[46]

The Supreme Court, acknowledging that it had yet to squarely address the validity of the misappropriations theory, upheld the theory as within § 10(b) of the 1934 Securities Exchange Act.[47] The Court noted that under the "classical theory" of insider trading, "§ 10(b) and Rule 10b–5 are violated when a corporate insider trades in the securities of his corporation on the basis of material, nonpublic information."[48] The "classical theory" has been applied "not only to officers, directors, and other permanent insiders of a corporation, but also to attorneys, accountants, consultants and others who temporarily become fiduciaries of a corporation."[49] The misappropriation theory, by comparison, "holds that a person commits fraud 'in connection with' a securities transaction * * * when he misappropriates confidential information for securities trading purposes, in breach of a duty owed to the source of the information."[50] The Court held that extending insider trading to those "outsiders" who obtain the information by misappropriation is consistent with the purpose of 10(b) and Rule 10b–5:

> The misappropriation theory is thus designed to protect the integrity of the securities markets against abuses by outsiders to a corporation who have access to confidential information that will affect the corporation's security price when revealed, but who owe no fiduciary or other duty to that corporation's shareholders.[51]

The Court discussed how the misappropriation theory met the elements of 10(b) and Rule 10b–5:

> [M]isappropriation * * * satisfies § 10(b)'s requirement that chargeable conduct involve a 'deceptive device or contrivance' * * *.

44. *Id.*

45. O'Hagan was also convicted of theft in state court, fined, and sentenced to 30 months imprisonment. He was disbarred from the practice of law in Minnesota.

46. 94 F.3d 612 (8th Cir.1996).

47. *Id.* at 2206.

48. *Id.*

49. *Id.*

50. *Id.*

51. *Id.* at 2207 (internal quotations omitted).

[M]isappropriators * * * deal in deception. A fiduciary who [pretends] loyalty to the principal while secretly converting the principal's information for personal gain dupes or defrauds the principal.

* * *

We * * * turn to the § 10(b) requirement that the misappropriator's deceptive use of information be 'in connection with the purchase or sale of [a] security.' This element is satisfied because the fiduciary's fraud is consummated, not when the fiduciary gains the confidential information, but when, without disclosure to his principal, he uses the information to purchase or sell securities. The securities transaction and the breach of duty thus coincide.[52]

Justice Thomas, joined by Chief Justice Rehnquist dissented, arguing that the misappropriation theory did not ensure that the deceptive device (misappropriating the information) was used or employed in connection with a securities transaction:[53]

It seems obvious that the undisclosed misappropriation of confidential information is not necessarily consummated by a securities transaction. In this case, for example, upon learning of Grand Met's confidential takeover plans, O'Hagan could have done any number of things with the information: He could have sold it to a newspaper for publication, he could have given or sold the information to Pillsbury itself, or he could even have kept the information and used it solely for his personal amusement, perhaps in a fantasy stock trading game. * * * If the relevant test under the 'in connection with' language is whether the fraudulent act is necessarily tied to a securities transaction, then the misappropriation of confidential information used to trade no more violates § 10(b) than does the misappropriation of funds used to trade.[54]

The majority agreed that this was a concern but argued that the misappropriation theory meets the "in connection with" requirement in some factual situations and thus, is properly confined to those situations:

The dissent's charge that the misappropriation theory is incoherent because information, like funds, can be put to multiple uses, misses the point. The Exchange Act was enacted in part 'to insure the maintenance of fair and honest markets,' and there is no question that fraudulent uses of confidential information fall within § 10(b)'s prohibition if the fraud is 'in connection with' a securities transaction. It is hardly remarkable that a rule suitably applied to the fraudulent uses of certain kinds of information would be stretched beyond reason were it applied to the fraudulent use of money.[55]

§ 22.15   Insider Trading—Rule 14e–3

In direct response to *Chiarella*, the SEC promulgated Rule 14e–3 pursuant to its authority under Section 14(e) of the Securities Exchange

52. *Id.* at 2208–09.   **54.** *Id.* at 2223.

53. *Id.* at 2222.   **55.** *Id.* at 2210.

Act of 1934 in order to prevent insider trading relating to tender offers.[1] Rule 14e–3 requires all persons who possess nonpublic information concerning tender offers to abstain from trading on the information if she knows or should know that the source of the information is the bidder or target of the tender offer.[2] Rule 14e–3 also makes it unlawful to provide or "tip" information relating to a tender offer,[3] regardless of any breach of fiduciary duty. Anyone who possesses and acts on nonpublic information violates the rule.[4]

§ 22.16   Aiding and Abetting and Conspiracy

No express right of action exists in the 1933, 1934, or 1995 Acts providing injured private investors with a cause of action against persons who aided and abetted securities violators. Nevertheless, private actions against aiding and abetting had been widely accepted by various federal Courts of Appeal. Following this view, the Private Securities Litigation Reform Act of 1995 expressly provides the SEC with authority to bring actions for injunctive relief or money damages against persons who aid and abet primary violators of the federal securities laws. However, no similar provision was bestowed upon private litigants. This Congressional approach reinforces the Supreme Court's decision in *Central Bank of Denver v. First Interstate Bank*, which held that there is no implied right of action for aiding and abetting in the anti-fraud provisions of Rule 10b–5.[1]

An ambiguous state of the law exists regarding private conspiracy actions.[2] There is no statutory conspiracy action specifically aimed at securities offenses.[3] Moreover, the Supreme Court has not addressed the issue. The lower courts appear to follow the lead of *Central Bank. In re GlenFed, Inc. Securities Litigation,* the Ninth Circuit held that "[t]he Court's rationale [in *Central Bank* under § 10(b)] precludes a private right of action for conspiracy liability."[4] A few courts have held that

§ 22.15

1. 17 C.F.R. § 240.14e–3 (1991).

2. *Id.*

3. 17 C.F.R. § 240.14e–3(a) (1991).

4. *See* SEC v. Wang, 944 F.2d 80 (2d Cir.1991) (Financial analyst disgorged profits of over $25 million obtained from using inside information received from employer).

§ 22.16

1. 511 U.S. 164, 114 S.Ct. 1439, 128 L.Ed.2d 119 (1994).

2. *See* Paul Vizcarrondo, Jr. & Andrew Houston, *Liability Under Sections 11, 12, 15 and 17 of the Securities Act of 1993 and Sections 10, 18 and 20 of the Securities Exchange Act of 1934* 63 UNDERSTANDING THE SECURITIES LAWS, (ed. Jeffry S. Hoffman and Larry D. Soderquist), (Practicing Law Institute 1995).

3. *See* S.E.C. v. U.S. Environmental, Inc., 897 F.Supp. 117, 119 (S.D.N.Y.1995) which cites the Act of March 4th, 1990, § 37, 35 Stat. 1096, as amended, 18 U.S.C. § 371 (criminal conspiracy statute); Packers and Stockyards Act, 1921, ch. 64 § 202, 42 Stat. 161, as amended, 7 U.S.C. § 192(f), (g) (civil conspiracy provision). There is no mention of conspiracy liability in § 10(b) and there is no provision in the statutes authorizing a private cause of action for conspiracy like other Congressional statutes which provide express provisions for that type of conduct.

4. McGann v. Ernst & Young, 95 F.3d 821, 823 (9th Cir.1996), *amended and superseded on den. of reh'g,* 102 F.3d 390 (9th Cir.1996); *See also* In re Syntex Corp. Securities Litigation, 855 F.Supp. 1086, 1098 (N.D.Cal.1994), *affirmed,* 95 F.3d 922 (9th Cir.1996) (Less than one month after Central Bank, the court held "the Court's ratio-

conspiracy is available for private securities litigation.[5]

Conspiracy is an important theory for plaintiffs in securities cases for it allows plaintiffs to include, as defendants, non-primary violators who are found to be co-conspirators in violating a securities law.[6] These non-primary violators, such as accountants and other professionals may be "deep pockets" and thus appealing as defendants.[7]

Conspiracy theories for securities violations are placed in doubt due to the Supreme Court's holding in *Central Bank* and the 1995 Act's[8] failure to address conspiracy. Congress's clear intention to eliminate private actions for aiding and abetting, as found in the 1995 Act, arguably strengthens the rationale for denying conspiracy to violate securities laws from being used in a private securities fraud action.

Library References:

C.J.S. Securities Regulation § 105–106, 164–165, 169–228.
West's Key No. Digests, Securities Regulation ⟳60.10–60.70.

§ 22.17 Use with Other Crimes

Securities fraud is usually charged with other crimes. In many cases mail or wire fraud will be charged instead of or along with specific securities violations. Generally, mail and wire fraud are less complicated to prove than securities offenses because they have, fewer elements and do not require the particularity needed in securities fraud pleadings.

The most significant change in the Private Securities Litigation Reform Act of 1995[1] concerns the Racketeer Influenced and Corrupt Organizations Act (RICO)[2]. When first created in 1970 as part of a major

nale ... also forecloses Plaintiff's conspiracy liability theory."); In re MTC Electronics Technologies Shareholders Litigation, 898 F.Supp. 974 (E.D.N.Y.1995), *vacated in part on reconsideration*, 993 F.Supp. 160 (D.N.Y. 1997). *See also* Securities Exchange Act of 1934, § 10(b); 15 U.S.C.A. § 78j(b); 17 C.F.R. § 240.10b–5.

5. Patricia O'Hara, *Erosion of the Privity Requirement in Section 12(2) of the Securities Act of 1933: The Expanded Meaning of Seller*, 31 UCLA L.Rev. 921 (1984). Daniel Fischel, *Secondary Liability under Section 10b–5 of the Securities Act of 1934*, 69 Calif.L.Rev. 80 (1981); David S. Ruder, *Multiple Defendants in Securities Law Fraud Cases: Aiding and Abetting, Conspiracy, In Pari Delicto, Indemnification, and Contribution*, 120 U.Pa.L.Rev. 597 (1972). Compare Robert A. Prentice, *Locating that "indistinct" and "Virtually nonexistent" Line Between Primary and Secondary Liability under Section 10b–5*, 75 N.C.L.Rev. 691 (1994).

6. *See* Dasho v. Susquehanna, 380 F.2d 262, 267 n. 2 (7th Cir.1967).

7. Walter G. Ricciardi *Auditor's Liability* 958 PLI/Corp 857, 862 (September–

October, 1996); Barbara Moses & David Sack, *Private Securities Litigation: A Shifting Landscape* CA14 ALI–ABA 115 (January 11, 1996); Donald C. Langevoort Symposium on the Private Securities Litigation Reform Act of 1995, *The Reform of Joint and Several Liability Under the Private Securities Litigation Reform Act of 1995: Proportionate Liability, Contribution Rights and Settlement Effects* 51 Bus.Law. 1157, 1159 (August, 1996) (noting that congress' choice to limit liability is controversial).

8. *See, e.g.,* Epstein v. MCA, Inc., 50 F.3d 644, 648–49 n. 7 (9th Cir.1995).

§ 22.17

1. James Hamilton, *Private Securities Litigation Reform Act of 1995 (Law & Explanation)*, CCH, at 35–36 (1996). *See* Act Sec. 107 at ¶ 208. *See* Committee Reports at ¶ 406, ¶ 404, ¶ 415, and ¶ 501. Amending 18 U.S.C. § 1964(c).

2. 18 U.S.C. §§ 1961–1968 (West 1996).

crime fighting bill,[3] RICO specifically included securities fraud as a "racketeering offense."[4] Over the years, many commentators and judges have voiced objections to the inclusion of securities fraud as a predicate act on the grounds that the federal securities laws already exist to protect against such violations[5] and that the complex system of regulating the securities industry is disrupted by the broad use of RICO. The 1995 Act satisfied these concerns by removing securities fraud as a racketeering activity for *civil* RICO actions unless the defendant has been convicted for the same conduct.[6] In addition, the legislative history expressly states that plaintiffs may not plead other specified offenses such as mail or wire fraud as predicate acts if these offenses could be based on conduct that would be actionable as securities fraud.[7] Congress believes that the securities laws which establish the liability provide sufficient protection for injured investors without the need for treble damages and forfeiture found in the civil RICO Act. The amendment does not apply to criminal actions brought by the government.

Library References:

C.J.S. Securities Regulation § 105–106, 164–165, 169–228.
West's Key No. Digests, Securities Regulation ⬚60.10–60.70.

3. Organized Crime Control Act of 1970, Title IX, Pub.L.No. 91–452, 83 Stat. 941 (1970).

4. 18 U.S.C. § 1961(1) (West 1996).

5. *See* Sedima, S.P.R.L. v. Imrex Company, Inc., 473 U.S. 479, 105 S.Ct. 3275, 87 L.Ed.2d 346 (1985). (Dissenting opinion by Justice Marshall, joined by Justice Brennan, Justice Blackmun, and Justice Powell, criticize the use of civil RICO rather than the Securities Act of 1933 or the Securities Exchange Act of 1934, in order to recover both treble damages and attorney's fees); Gary S. Abrams *The Civil RICO Controversy Reaches the Supreme Court* 13 HOFSTRA L.REV. 147, 180 (Fall, 1984) ("In addition, it seems logical that as the case law under RICO develops further, courts will look for guidance to legislative and judicial restrictions on claims of fraud brought under the securities laws in determining whether predicate acts have been adequately pleaded and proved."); Paul H. Dawes Dean A. Morehous, Jr., "Civil RICO Developments Affecting Securities Litigation: Strategies in Pleading and Proof, and Recent Developments" 313 PLI/LIT 761, 777 (1986) ("Justice Marshall pointed out in his dissent in *Sedima* that the inclusion of these three offenses, in particular, threatens to revolutionize securities litigation because of the ease with which these predicate acts serve as vehicles to bring RICO claims based on violations of the securities laws.")

Cf., Reform of the Private Civil Action Provision of RICO, ABA SECTION OF CORP., BANKING AND BUSINESS LAW, COMMITTEE ON FEDERAL LEGISLATION, 415 (1985) (Predicate acts based upon securities fraud account for at least 40% of all civil RICO claims); Louis C. Long, *Treble Damages For Violations of the Federal Securities Laws: A Suggested Analysis and Application of the Civil Cause of Action*, 85 DICK.L.REV. 201 (1981) (predicting many of Justice Marshall's concerns about the relationship between civil RICO and the securities laws). J. S. Rakoff, *Coda: Some Personal Reflections on the Sedima Case and on Reforming RICO*, 400–01, 155 PLI/CRIM. 59, 87–88 (1984). Walter F. McDonough *Does the Punishment Fit the Crime? How Federal and State Civil RICO Statutes Transfer Accountant Liability* 26 SUFFOLK U.L.REV. 1107, 1116 (1992). ("The inclusion of these three specific offenses (mail, wire and securities fraud) as predicate acts has given plaintiffs the opportunity to use civil RICO to litigate otherwise ordinary accounting malpractice claims.")

6. James Hamilton, *Private Securities Litigation Reform Act of 1995 (Law & Explanation)*, CCH, 35–36 (1996). *See* Act Sec. 107 at ¶ 208. *See* Committee Reports at ¶ 406, ¶ 404, ¶ 415, and ¶ 501. Amending 18 U.S.C. § 1964(c).

7. CCH ¶ 112, 208, 404.

§ 22.18   Investigation of Securities Fraud

The investigation of securities violations is conducted by either the SEC or the Department of Justice (DOJ). The two agencies are very different in their scope and power. Therefore, defense tactics should be adjusted accordingly. For instance, SEC administrative subpoenas issued during initial investigations may be limited in scope. However, if DOJ pursues the investigation it may use search warrants or grand jury subpoenas to obtain a greater range of evidence. Also an SEC investigation allows the presence of counsel during questioning, unlike a grand jury investigation, conducted by DOJ in which defense counsel is not allowed to be present. Finally, SEC investigations must allow the introduction of material exculpatory evidence by the defendant at administrative hearings conducted before the SEC. The government has no obligation to present exculpatory information to a grand jury.[1]

Library References:

C.J.S. Securities Regulation § 105–106, 164–165, 169–228.
West's Key No. Digests, Securities Regulation ⊕60.10–60.70.

§ 22.19   Defenses

Most criminal defenses focus upon lack of criminal intent or fraudulent purpose. This tactic is feasible because of the technical nature of securities statutes. A defendant may try to prove that she possessed a good faith belief in the truth of the allegedly false statements. This tactic would negate willful wrongdoing. However, such a defense may be rebutted if the defendant failed to properly conduct the requisite due diligence investigation of the alleged wrongful representation.

Reliance on counsel is another common defense used to argue lack of willful intent. Several elements must be satisfied in order to successfully use this defense: (1) the defendant must have sought legal advice of counsel pertaining to the legality of the suspect activity, (2) the defendant must have fully disclosed all relevant facts to counsel, (3) an uninterested counsel must have given her professional opinion that said action is legal, and (4) the defendant must have totally relied on this

§ 22.18

1. *Supreme Court:* United States v. Williams, 504 U.S. 36, 112 S.Ct. 1735, 118 L.Ed.2d 352 (1992) (Court held that district court may not dismiss otherwise valid indictment on ground that the gov't. failed to disclose to Grand jury "substantial exculpadge evidence.").

D.C. Circuit: Blinder, Robinson & Co., Inc. v. SEC, 837 F.2d 1099, 1112 (D.C.Cir. 1988) ("the Commission cannot adequately weigh the factors that it concedes should be considered without having before it the full set of facts necessary for reasoned consideration").

Jack F. Williams, *Process and Prediction: A Return to a Fuzzy Model of Pretrial* Detention, 79 MINN.L.REV. 325, 381, n. 379 (1994). ("Furthermore, the government does not even have the duty to disclose to the grand jury evidence of an exculpatory nature"); Richard J. Norvillo and Joseph I. Goldstein, *Securities Enforcement Prehearing Procedures Under the SEC's New Rules of Practice* 4, 6 (1995) (SEC revised its rules of practice on June 12, 1995. Release No. 34–35833; File No. S7–40–92. New Rule 230 requires that the Division of Enforcement not withhold materially exculpatory evidence in accordance w/*Brady v. MD*. Therefore, defendants are entitled to pretrial discovery of all exculpatory evidence as well as evidence which may lead to the discovery of such material.)

advice in good faith, without ignoring any information provided by counsel.[1]

A frequently used defense is that the allegedly injured party did not rely on the omission or misstatement. However, the government, unlike a private litigant, need not prove reliance to establish a violation of the securities laws.[2] Sometimes the reliance argument is based upon the "fraud on the market" theory, which views all traders in the public market as victims of fraud because the price of a security will reflect all information made available, including any misstatements or misrepresentations.[3] By relying on the market price to determine value, the victim establishes a presumption of reliance. This defense may be rebutted with evidence that accurate information was made available to the market by other sources. Thus, the "truth on the market" defense overcomes the reliance element found in a "fraud on the market" theory. The "truth on the market" defense has been adopted by the Second, Fourth, Fifth, Seventh, and Ninth Circuits.[4]

Library References:

C.J.S. Securities Regulation § 105–106, 164–165, 169–228.
West's Key No. Digests, Securities Regulation ⊯60.10–60.70.

§ 22.20 Sentencing—In General

Part F of the United States Sentencing Guidelines applies to securities fraud offenses.[1] Defendants convicted of violating the 1933 Act are

§ 22.19

1. C.E. Carlson, Inc. v. SEC, 859 F.2d 1429, 1436 (10th Cir.1988).

2. *Second Circuit:* United States v. Gleason, 616 F.2d 2, 28 (2d Cir.1979) (in criminal prosecution, district court correctly denied motion to dismiss 10b–5 counts for failure to prove reliance on the part of the victims; "the law is settled that the Government need only prove that the false representation is one that a reasonable stockholder would rely on in purchasing or selling the relevant corporate shares").

See also:

Second Circuit: North American Research and Development Corp., 424 F.2d 63, 84 (2d Cir.1970).

Sixth Circuit: SEC v. Blavin, 760 F.2d 706, 711 (6th Cir.1985).

Ninth Circuit: SEC v. Rana Research, Inc., 8 F.3d 1358, 1359 & 1363–64 (9th Cir.1993).

3. *Basic, Inc.*, 485 U.S. at 241–42.

4. *E.g.,*

Second Circuit: Seibert v. Sperry Rand Corp., 586 F.2d 949, 952 (2d Cir.1978) (summary judgment proper when material information was made available by third parties); Cooke v. Manufactured Homes,

Inc., 998 F.2d 1256, 1262–63 (4th Cir.1993) (market fully informed regardless of misrepresentation).

Fifth Circuit: Fine v. American Solar King Corp., 919 F.2d 290, 299 (5th Cir. 1990) (presumption of reliance was rebutted by proof that the market was unaffected by the misrepresentation).

Seventh Circuit: Wielgos v. Commonwealth Edison Co., 892 F.2d 509, 516 (7th Cir.1989) (market knowledge negates effects of misleading information).

Ninth Circuit: In re Apple Computer Securities Litigation, 886 F.2d 1109, 1115 (9th Cir.1989).

§ 22.20

1. The United States sentencing guidelines are promulgated by the United States Sentencing Commission, which was created under the Sentencing Reform Act of 1984, as amended, 28 U.S.C. §§ 991–998 (1994). This is an independent commission within the judicial branch whose members are selected by the President, with the advice and consent of the Senate. 28 U.S.C. § 991(a)(1994). The commission has established sentencing guidelines for federal courts. It reviews and revises the guidelines

sentenced in accordance with § 2F1.1 of the United States Sentencing Guidelines.[2] The background section found within the commentary to § 2F1.1 sets forth an explanation for the wide application of this section:

> This guideline is designed to apply to a wide variety of fraud cases. The statutory maximum term of imprisonment for most such offenses is five years. The guideline does not link offense characteristics to specific code sections. Because federal fraud statutes are so broadly written, a single pattern of offense conduct usually can be prosecuted under several code sections, as a result of which the offense of conviction may be somewhat arbitrary. Furthermore, most fraud statutes cover a broad range of conduct with extreme variation in severity.[3]

However, defendants convicted of insider trading under the 1934 Act are sentenced according to § 2F1.2 of the Guidelines.[4] The background section found within the commentary to § 2F1.2 explains the use of this particular section:

> This guideline applies to certain violations of Rule 10b–5 that are commonly referred to as 'insider trading.' Insider trading is treated essentially as a sophisticated fraud. Because the victims and their losses are difficult if not impossible to identify, the gain, *i.e.*, the total increase in value realized through trading in securities by the defendant and persons acting in concert with him or to whom he provided inside information, is employed instead of the victims' losses.[5]

§ 22.21 Sentencing—Collateral Consequences

Securities fraud epitomizes one of the differences between street crime and white collar crime, namely the existence of civil and administrative sanctions which track criminal sanctions. This means at least two things for the targets of criminal prosecution. First, with viable SEC administrative and civil sanctions available, it may be easier to convince a prosecutor not to pursue a case criminally. Prosecutors' resources are limited and pursuing one criminal case means others will not be charged. In these situations, it may be appropriate for a prosecutor to bypass the criminal prosecution of a defendant otherwise deserving in light of civil liability (makes victims whole) or administrative liability (forces the defendant to make changes in its business practices).

The fact that civil and administrative remedies track criminal offenses means that evidence obtained in civil or administrative proceedings may become available in the criminal prosecution. For example, whenever a suspect discusses a matter in the administrative, civil, or

as needed. 28 U.S.C. § 994(*o*) (1994); *See also* Mistretta v. United States, 488 U.S. 361, 368–69, 109 S.Ct. 647, 653, 102 L.Ed.2d 714 (1989).

2. United States Sentencing Guidelines, Guidelines Manual, App. A.

3. U.S.S.G. Ch. 2, Pt. F, background comment.

4. U.S.S.G. App. A.

5. U.S.S.G. Ch. 2, Pt. F, background comment.

simply investigative stage, statements made can be used later to prosecute the suspect. During these pre-criminal stages, there may be nothing to alert a suspect of this potential. Almost certainly there will be no advice of rights as required under *Miranda* since the suspect will not be in custody. Moreover, there may be nothing to alert a suspect that criminal charges are even a possibility when the SEC uses summonses to obtain records. Although a suspect is entitled to invoke her right not to incriminate herself during civil or administrative proceedings, the fact-finder in the administrative or civil proceeding is entitled to draw an adverse inference from the failure to testify.[1]

The outcome in the criminal proceeding may also affect the civil or administrative proceeding through collateral estoppel. Collateral estoppel bars relitigation of an issue previously decided if the party against whom the prior decision is asserted had a "full and fair opportunity" to litigate that issue in an earlier case.[2] In most jurisdictions the following four elements must exist for collateral estoppel to apply: (1) the issue was actually litigated in the first proceeding, (2) the first proceeding resulted in a valid and final judgment, (3) resolution of the issue was essential to the judgment rendered in the first proceeding, and (4) the issue in the second proceeding is identical to the issue in the first proceeding.[3]

§ 22.22   Venue

The Sixth Amendment to the United States Constitution provides that "an accused in a criminal prosecution has the right to be tried in the district wherein the crime shall have been committed."[1] "The test [for venue] is best described as a substantial contacts rule that take into account a number of factors—the site of the defendant's acts, the elements and nature of the crime, the locus of the effect of the criminal conduct, and the suitability of each district for accurate factfinding."[2] The government bears the burden of proving venue, but because venue is not an essential element of the offense, it need not be established beyond a reasonable doubt. Proof by a preponderance of the evidence is sufficient.[3] If lack of venue is apparent from the face of the indictment or information but is not raised by the defendant, it is waived.[4] If the venue defect is not apparent until the government presents its case, the

§ 22.21

1. Baxter v. Palmigiano, 425 U.S. 308, 318, 96 S.Ct. 1551, 1558, 47 L.Ed.2d 810 (1976).

2. *See* Allen v. McCurry, 449 U.S. 90, 94–95, 101 S.Ct. 411, 414–415, 66 L.Ed.2d 308 (1980); Ashe v. Swenson, 397 U.S. 436, 90 S.Ct. 1189, 25 L.Ed.2d 469 (1970).

3. *See Swenson*, 397 U.S. at 443, 90 S.Ct. at 1194.

§ 22.22

1. U.S. Const. (a)mend. VI; *See also* U.S. Const., art. III, § 2 Fed.R.Crim.P. 18.

2. United States v. Reed, 773 F.2d 477, 481 (2d Cir.1985).

3. *Second Circuit:* United States v. Maldonado–Rivera, 922 F.2d 934, 968 (2d Cir.1990).

Seventh Circuit: United States v. Griley, 814 F.2d 967, 973 (4th Cir.1987); United States v. Netz, 758 F.2d 1308, 1311 (8th Cir.1985).

4. United States v. Black Cloud, 590 F.2d 270, 272 (8th Cir.1979).

objection is waived if not raised by the defendant at the close of the government's case.[5]

Any offense, including securities offenses, may be prosecuted in any district where the offense began, continued or was completed. The Securities Act and Exchange Act provide for even broader venue. Prosecution may also be initiated in the district where the defendant resides, transacts business, or is simply found. Specifically, section § 22 of the Securities Act of 1933 allows actions to be initiated in any venue where the offer or sale took place if the defendant participated therein.[6] Section § 27 of the Securities Exchange Act of 1934 allows a prosecution to take place in any district in which any act or transaction involving the violation occurred.[7]

Process and personal jurisdiction may be obtained by serving the defendant in the district where she resides or any district in which she is found. These service provisions grant greater powers than the usual federal court process rules which require defendants to reside in the district where the action is brought or who are found and served in that district.[8]

§ 22.23   Statute of Limitations

For more than forty years, federal courts looked to state securities laws to determine the statute of limitations for securities violations. Then, in 1991, the Supreme Court held that all Rule 10b–5 actions must be commenced within one year after discovery of the violation, but not longer than three years after the violation occurred. The 1995 Act[1] retained this one year/three year statute of limitations for securities fraud litigation. However, actions for insider trading under either § 20A or § 21A may be brought up to 5 years after the violation occurred.[2]

§ 22.24   Bibliography

Armstrong, James J., Deidre Corkey, E. Michael Karol, Kevin Lombardi, and Paul Secunda, *Eleventh Survey of White Collar Crime: Securities Fraud*, 33 Am. Crim. L. Rev. 973 (1996).

Bloomenthal, Harold S. and Holme Roberts & Owen, Securities Law Handbook, (Clark Boardman Callgahan, 1995 edition).

Hazen, Thomas L., Federal Securities Law (Federal Judicial Center 1993).

Hazen, Thomas L., Treatise on the Law of Securities Regulation (West Publishing, Practitioner's Edition, 2d ed. 1996).

Hoffman, Jeffry & Larry D. Soderquist, Understanding the Securities Laws (Practicing Law Institute, 1996).

5.   *Id.*

6.   15 U.S.C. § 77v.

7.   15 U.S.C. § 78aa.

8.   Fed.R.Civ.Proc.4(f), 28 U.S.C. Rule 4(f).

§ 22.23

1.   Private Securities Litigation Reform Act of 1995, 15 U.S.C. §§ 77–78.

2.   15 U.S.C. § 78u–1(a)(5).

LOSS, LOUIS & JOEL SELIGMAN, SECURITIES REGULATION (Little Brown and Company, 3d ed., 1996).

SHIELDS, ROBERT E. & ROBERT H. STROUSE, SECURITIES PRACTICE HANDBOOK (American Law Institute–American Bar Institute, 5th ed., 1987).

The Securities and Exchange Commission Internet Home Page, http://www.sec.gov.

*

CHAPTER 23

TAX FRAUD*

Table of Sections

WESTLAW ELECTRONIC RESEARCH

See WESTLAW Electronic Research Guide preceding the Summary of Contents.

---

§ 23.1 Introduction

* Portions of this chapter were published at Pamela H. Bucy, *Criminal Tax Fraud:* *The Downfall of Murderers, Madams and Thieves*, 29 Az.St.L.J. 639 (1997).

Tax offenses are among the most versatile weapons in a prosecutor's arsenal. These offenses can be used to prosecute the garden-variety tax offender or the taxpayer who is failing to report all or some of his earned income. Tax offenses may also be useful in prosecuting the person who earns income illegally—through narcotics trafficking, extortion, bribery, etc.—and fails to report her ill-gotten gains. Often when an offender is able to distance himself from his criminal activity, it is easier to prosecute him for tax offenses than for the underlying criminal activity. Although many criminals are able to shield themselves from their illegal conduct, especially those higher up in the criminal organization, few are willing to forego the financial fruits of their illegal activity. Once an individual lives beyond his means of legally earned income, a tax case becomes possible. There are three basic factual patterns that lead to tax prosecutions: failure to file a return; falsifying the amount of one's income; and falsifying the amounts that reduce taxable income or taxes due (i.e., falsifying adjustments, deductions, exemptions, credits).

The preindictment stage of federal tax cases is handled differently within the Department of Justice (DOJ) than most federal crimes. With most federal crimes the ninety-four United States Attorneys make the decision whether to indict and for what offense, after reviewing the evidence gathered during an investigation.[1] There is no procedure or requirement that a charging decision be routed through a division within DOJ prior to filing the charges. With tax cases, however, investigation reports, prepared by agents with the Criminal Investigation Division (CID) of the Internal Revenue Service, are routed to the Tax Division of DOJ before the case is forwarded to the appropriate United States Attorney's office.

The IRS's Criminal Investigation Division has been operating as a unit for 77 years.[2] Currently this Division staffs 3,200 Special Agents who are trained in accounting and law enforcement, and 1500 support personnel.[3] The CID seeks to "identify and investigate cases which will generate the maximum deterrent effect and thus, have the most impact on voluntary compliance."[4] The current priorities of CID are Bankruptcy Fraud; Motor Fuel Exercise Tax Evasion; Health Care Fraud; Telemarketing Fraud; Questionable Refund Program; Illegal Tax Protestors; Computer Fraud; Public Corruption; Financial Institution Fraud; Illegal Narcotics and related Money Laundering Offenses.[5]

Once it receives a referral from CID, the Tax Division of DOJ decides whether further investigation, including a grand jury investigation, is needed, whether anyone should be indicted, and, if so, for what

---

§ 23.1

1. RICO and Money Laundering cases must receive prior approval from the Criminal Section of the Department of Justice before charges are filed. U.S. DEP'T OF JUSTICE, UNITED STATES ATTORNEY MANUAL, §§ 9–105.100, 9–110.100.

2. *Hearing Before the House Subcom. on Treasury Postal Service and General Government*, 104th Cong., 2nd Sess. at 587–88 (Mar. 12,1996).

3. *Id.* at 485.

4. *Id.*

5. *Id.* at 490–511.

offense. This oversight of tax offenses is designed to promote uniform enforcement of tax laws.[6] During the preindictment stage, the Tax Division affords the target of the investigation the opportunity to confer about the case. If prosecution is recommended, the Tax Division will determine which method of proof should be used to prove a tax offense and will attempt to ensure that the documentary evidence needed is included in the case file. Authorization from the Tax Division is also required in some cases not involving tax crimes; for example, when mail fraud is to be charged, either independently or as predicate acts for RICO,[7] and the only mailings are tax returns or other IRS documents, or the mailing is used to promote or facilitate what is "essentially only a tax fraud scheme. . . . "[8] When this review process is complete, the case is referred to the appropriate U.S. Attorney's office for prosecution. Some U.S. Attorney's offices will prosecute the case after referral; others decline to do so and trial attorneys from the Tax Division will travel to the jurisdiction to try the case.[9]

Library References:

C.J.S. Internal Revenue § 1273–1285.
West's Key No. Digests, Internal Revenue ☞5280–5319.

§ 23.2   Tax Offenses—Tax Evasion: 26 U.S.C. § 7201

Section 7201 provides:

> Any person who willfully attempts in any manner to evade or defeat any tax imposed by this title or the payment thereof shall . . . be guilty of a felony. . . .[1]

This section carries a maximum term of imprisonment of 5 years, a possible maximum fine of $250,000 (for individuals) or $500,000 (for organizations), plus costs of prosecution.[2]

Section 7201 covers attempts to evade the *assessment* of a tax as well as attempts to evade the *payment* of a tax.[3] This "evasion" offense can be used to prosecute any of the common factual patterns of tax fraud: failure to file a return, falsifying one's income or falsifying amounts that reduce taxable income or taxes due.

---

6. U.S. DEP'T OF JUSTICE, TAX DIV., CRIM. TAX MANUAL, § 6–4.127.

7. 18 U.S.C. § 1961 et seq.

8. *Id.* at § 6–4.211(1).

9. A helpful guide to the United States Department of Justice (DOJ) policies regarding tax offenses is the Criminal Tax Manual, prepared by DOJ, Tax Division, Criminal Section.

§ 23.2

1. 26 U.S.C. § 7201.

2. 26 U.S.C. § 7201; 18 U.S.C. § 3571.

3. *See:*

Supreme Court: Sansone v. United States, 380 U.S. 343, 354, 85 S.Ct. 1004, 1011, 13 L.Ed.2d 882 (1965).

First Circuit: United States v. Waldeck, 909 F.2d 555, 556–60 (1st Cir.1990).

A. ELEMENTS OF THE OFFENSE

Crucial to an evasion case is proof that the taxpayer owed taxes and willfully evaded paying these taxes. The elements of tax evasion are "(1) willfulness; (2) the existence of a tax deficiency; and (3) an affirmative act constituting an attempt to evade or defeat the payment of tax."[4]

The first element, willfulness, is discussed more thoroughly *infra* at § 23.8.

Determining whether the second element, the existence of a tax deficiency, is present may be straightforward, such as when a taxpayer simply hides her income. In other cases, proving a deficiency will require delving into the most arcane minutia of tax law.[5] *United States v. Benson*[6] provides an example of how complicated a simple evasion case can become. At issue was $264,856.82 Benson received from an insurance adjuster. The government claimed that this amount consisted of fees paid to Benson for work done. Benson claimed that the money was a nontaxable settlement for prior erroneous acts by the adjuster toward Benson.[7] To determine whether a tax deficiency existed, and thus whether Benson's tax evasion conviction should be affirmed, the United States Court of Appeals for the Seventh Circuit examined the Internal Revenue Code's definition of income, the Code's exceptions from taxable compensation, court interpretations of these sections, the adjuster's liability insurance policy, and the law of insurer's obligation to defend insureds against suits.[8]

The third element, the presence of an "affirmative act" constituting an attempt to evade or defeat the payment of the tax, requires proof of acts "done to mislead the government or conceal funds to avoid payment of an admitted and accurate deficiency." Affirmative acts associated with evasion of payment involve some type of concealment of the taxpayer's ability to pay his or her taxes or the removal of assets from the reach of the Internal Revenue Service.[9] Section 7201 includes two types of "affirmative behavior": evading the *assessment* by the IRS that taxes are due and evading *payment* due. Cases involving efforts to evade assessment are more common. Simply filing a false return is sufficient conduct to constitute "evasion of assessment." In evasion of payment cases, however, efforts to conceal are required before there is a finding of an affirmative act. Such efforts to conceal include placing assets beyond the government's reach *after* a tax liability has been assessed,[10] conducting

4. United States v. Benson, 67 F.3d 641, 644 (7th Cir.1995), *modified on den. of reh'g*, 74 F.3d 152 (7th Cir.1996).

See also:

Supreme Court: Sansone v. United States, 380 U.S. 343, 351, 85 S.Ct. 1004, 1010, ___, 13 L.Ed.2d 882 (1965).

First Circuit: United States v. Olbres, 61 F.3d 967, 971 (1st Cir.1995).

Fifth Circuit: United States v. Masat, 948 F.2d 923, 931 (5th Cir.1991).

5. *See* U.S. Dep't. of Justice, Tax Div., Crim. Tax Manual, § 8.05, 1994 ed.

6. 67 F.3d 641 (7th Cir.1995), *modified on den. of reh'g*, 74 F.3d 152 (7th Cir.1996).

7. *Id.* at 644.

8. *Id.* at 645–47.

9. United States v. McGill, 964 F.2d 222, 230 (3d Cir.1992). *See also* Spies v. United States, 317 U.S. 492, 499, 63 S.Ct. 364, 368, 87 L.Ed. 418 (1943).

10. *See:*

Third Circuit: United States v. McGill, 964 F.2d 222, 230 (3d Cir.1992).

financial affairs in the name of others[11] and dealing in currency.[12] Simply failing to pay taxes is not sufficient to constitute "evasion of payment."

United States v. McGill,[13] demonstrates the nuances of determining whether conduct is an "affirmative act" within the evasion statute. McGill, an attorney, was convicted by a jury on three counts of tax evasion, covering the years 1985 through 1987.[14] The United States Court of Appeals for the Third Circuit affirmed the conviction for 1985 but reversed the remaining two convictions after finding that there was insufficient evidence of affirmative acts of evasion by McGill in these two years.[15] McGill had filed accurate tax returns for each of the years in question, but failed to include, with his returns, payment of the tax which he admittedly owed. After McGill disregarded the IRS's directive to pay the taxes due, the IRS issued levies against his personal bank accounts.[16] After these levies were issued, McGill ceased using his personal bank accounts, which were closed by the banks. Thereafter McGill deposited and wrote checks on bank accounts held by his wife or by business associates.[17] The court found that banking through names of others sufficed as "an affirmative act."[18] Also, after his personal accounts were closed, McGill opened a new account in his own name. Although McGill apparently deposited funds subject to the IRS's levy into this account, the Court found that use of this account did not constitute an "affirmative act" of evasion under section 7201 because there was no evidence of concealment.[19] According to the court, "unless a taxpayer is in the situation of giving voluntary admissions during an investigation or a forced response to a subpoena, the failure of the taxpayer to report the opening of an account in his or her own name in his or her own locale cannot amount to an affirmative act of evasion. Omissions, including failures to report, do not satisfy the requirements of § 7201; the Government must prove a specific act to mislead or conceal."[20]

B.   TAX PROTESTORS

Tax protestors, i.e., those individuals who do not pay taxes they owe because, they allege, the Constitution forbids such taxation, are prose-

---

Ninth Circuit: United States v. Mal, 942 F.2d 682, 687 (9th Cir.1991).

11. *See*:

Sixth Circuit: United States v. Hook, 781 F.2d 1166, 1168 (6th Cir.1986), (defendant bought a house in his girlfriend's name).

Seventh Circuit: United States v. Conley, 826 F.2d 551, 557 (7th Cir.1987) (defendant placed assets in his son's name).

12. *See*:

Supreme Court: Spies v. United States, 317 U.S. 492, 500, 63 S.Ct. 364, 369, 87 L.Ed. 418 (1943) (defendant "insisted that certain income be paid to him in cash").

District of Columbia: United States v. Shorter, 809 F.2d 54, 57 (D.C.Cir.1987) (affirming an evasion conviction where the defendant carried on a "cash lifestyle").

13.   964 F.2d 222 (3d Cir.1992).

14.   *Id.* at 226.

15.   *Id.*

16.   *Id.* at 227.

17.   *Id.*

18.   *Id.* at 233.

19.   United States v. McGill, 964 F.2d 222, 235 (3d Cir.1992).

20.   *Id.* at 233.

cuted regularly under the evasion statute.[21] *United States v. Masat*,[22] is typical. Masat, an airline pilot who received a gross income which required that he file an income tax return,[23] failed to file returns. Masat submitted numerous W–4 forms to his employer to limit the income tax withheld from his wages. He also claimed that he was a minister and thus exempt from taxes. Masat used false social security numbers and false names to conceal assets.[24] Finding these actions sufficient affirmative acts of evasion, the United States Court of Appeals for the Fifth Circuit affirmed Masat's tax evasion convictions.

United States v. Huebner,[25] provides an example of a more intricate scheme by taxpayers to avoid their tax obligations. Huebner participated with other taxpayers in an effort to avoid levies executed on their property by the IRS for failure to pay taxes. Upon receiving the IRS's notice of levy on wages, the taxpayers filed petitions in bankruptcy. Although tax obligations are not dischargeable in bankruptcy, under 11 U.S.C. § 362(a) once an individual files in bankruptcy, an automatic stay requires the IRS to release the levies on wages. As long as the stay remains in effect, the taxpayers receive their wages in full.[26] As evidence of bankruptcy status, Huebner provided false information that the taxpayers had taken out loans which required monthly payments totaling thousands of dollars. The loans were shams, created solely to obtain status as bankrupt individuals entitled to the automatic stay of the IRS levy.[27] The United States Court of Appeals for the Ninth Circuit affirmed Huebner's convictions, finding that:

> Although the act of filing the petition was not an attempt to conceal income or otherwise escape liability for tax, it did put beyond the reach of the IRS a portion of the taxpayers' wages during the period the stay remained in effect.[28]

The court found evidence of Huebner's willfulness in the lies he told about the loans and the "trouble [he went to] to fabricate documentary support."[29]

C. SPECIAL PROBLEMS

Evasion cases are among the more difficult tax cases to prove because the government must establish that a defendant failed to pay a specific amount of tax which was due and owing. Information as to a defendant's income, adjustments to income, deductions, exemptions and credits must be available to prove that tax is due and owing. If adequate

21. *See* U.S. Dep't of Justice, Tax Div., Crim. Tax Manual, § 40.04, 1994 ed.

22. 948 F.2d 923 (5th Cir.1991).

23. "As reflected in records provided by [his employer], Continental [Airlines], Masat received the following salaries: $76,122.62 in 1979; $80,365.90 in 1980; and $85,821.47 in 1981. The evidence establishes that Masat's tax liability totaled $3,920.09 for 1979; $12,202.14 for 1980, and $12,689 for 1981." *Id.* at 925 n.1.

24. *Id.*

25. 48 F.3d 376 (9th Cir.1994).

26. *Id.* at 378.

27. *Id.*

28. *Id.* at 378.

29. *Id.* at 379.

records are not available as to these amounts, an evasion prosecution is not possible.

Library References:

C.J.S. Internal Revenue § 1280–1281.

West's Key No. Digests, Internal Revenue ☞5297–5306.

§ 23.3 Tax Offenses—False Statement on a Return or Related Documents: 26 U.S.C. § 7206(1)

Section 7206(1), known as the "tax perjury statute,"[1] provides:

Any person who ... willfully makes and subscribes any return, statement, or other document, which contains or is verified by a written declaration that it is made under the penalties of perjury, and which he does not believe to be true and correct as to every material matter; ... shall be guilty of a felony....[2]

Conviction of this offense carries a maximum term of imprisonment of three years, a maximum fine of $250,000 (for individuals) or $500,000 (for organizations), plus costs of prosecution.[3]

Although there are exceptions, proving a "false statement" case generally is easier and less complex for the government than proving an "evasion" case because in the false statement case the government must simply prove that one line item on the tax return is false.[4] There is no need to prove that any amount of taxes was due and was not paid. The elements of § 7206(1) are: (1) making and subscribing a return, statement, or other document under penalty of perjury; (2) that is not true and correct as to a material matter; and (3) the defendant acted willfully.[5]

Proving the first element is fairly simple. The government must prove that the taxpayer signed a tax return or other document. The "documents" covered by § 7206(1) are "any return, statement, or other document" signed under penalties of perjury.[6] Questions have arisen as to whether § 7206(1) applies only to documents which are required by statutes or regulations to be filed. The Fifth Circuit has followed a narrow approach, holding that § 7206(1) is restricted to statements or documents required by statute or regulation to be filed.[7] Other circuits

---

1. *See* United States v. Dale, 782 F.Supp. 615, 621 (D.D.C.1991).

2. 26 U.S.C. § 7206(1); *see also* 18 U.S.C. § 3571.

3. 26 U.S.C. § 7206(1); 18 U.S.C. § 3571.

4. *See* U.S. DEP'T OF JUSTICE, TAX DIV., CRIM. TAX MANUAL, § 12.08[2], 1994 ed.

5. United States v. Robinson, 974 F.2d 575, 579 (5th Cir.1992).

6. *See* 26 U.S.C. § 7206(1).

7. *See* United States v. Levy, 533 F.2d 969 (5th Cir.1976). More recently, the Fifth Circuit limited this interpretation, holding that § 7201 covers documents which are included by the taxpayer with his return and incorporated by reference in the return. *See* United States v. Damon, 676 F.2d 1060, 1064 (5th Cir.1982); United States v. Taylor, 574 F.2d 232, 237 (5th Cir.1978).

have rejected this narrow position holding that § 7206(1) applies to any verified return, statement or other document submitted to the IRS.[8]

Proving the second element, that the return is false as to a material matter, may be the most technically difficult element to prove in § 7206(1) cases. Care should be taken by the government prior to bringing a § 7206(1) case, to ensure that the statement actually is false. *United States v. Reynolds*,[9] demonstrates how this can become a problem. Reynolds accurately reported on his personal income tax form (an 1040EZ) as "total wages, salaries and tips" the amount shown on his W–2 as wages. He did not report additional amounts he received as reimbursement for expenses which were paid because of false invoices he submitted.[10] The United States Court of Appeals for the Seventh Circuit set aside Reynolds' § 7206(1) conviction, finding that the information Reynolds reported on his tax return was literally correct. The court noted approvingly the government's argument that "by filing form 1040EZ a taxpayer implicitly represents that he has no additional income." However, this implicit representation was not sufficient, in the court's view, to uphold the conviction since it was not the theory charged in the indictment.[11] The court noted that more appropriate charges for Reynolds' conduct were tax evasion (26 U.S.C. § 7201) or failure to supply information required by law (26 U.S.C. § 7203).[12]

The third element of a § 7206(1) case, willfulness, is discussed *infra* in § 23.8.[13]

Library References:

C.J.S. Internal Revenue § 1280.
West's Key No. Digests, Internal Revenue ☞5303.

§ 23.4   Tax Offenses—Aiding and Assisting in the Making or Subscribing of a False Return or Related Documents: 26 U.S.C. § 7206(2)

Section 7206(2) provides:

Any person who ... [w]illfully aids or assists in ... the preparation or presentation ... of a return, affidavit, claim, or other document,

8. *Second Circuit*: United States v. Holroyd, 732 F.2d 1122 (2d Cir.1984).

Tenth Circuit: United States v. Frank, 723 F.2d 1482, 1485–86 (10th Cir.1983).

9. 919 F.2d 435 (7th Cir.1990).

10. *Id.* at 436–37.

11. *Id.* at 437. According to the court, the indictment charged that a particular line of the return was false. *Id.*

12. *Id.* Similarly, in *United States v. Borman*, 992 F.2d 124, 126 (7th Cir.1993) the Seventh Circuit affirmed the district court's dismissal of an indictment where the government argued that the defendants' filing of a Form 1040A "implicitly represented that they received no income of a type or amount which would require the use of a different form."

In fact, the defendants had a legal obligation to file a Form 1040, but the court echoed the view of the *Reynolds* court, stating that "§ 7206(1) is not violated by filing the wrong form."

13. *See* U.S. Dep't of Justice, Tax Div., Crim. Tax Manual, § 12.09, 1994 ed.

which is fraudulent or is false as to any material matter . . . shall be guilty of a felony. . . .[1]

Conviction of § 7206(2) carries a maximum term of imprisonment of three years, a maximum fine of $250,000 (for individuals) or $500,000 (for corporations), plus costs of prosecution.[2]

The elements of violating § 7206(2) are: (1) the defendant aided or assisted in or advised the preparation or presentation of a document in connection with a matter arising under the internal revenue laws; (2) the document was false as to a material matter; and (3) the act of the defendant was willful.[3] The same issues as to which documents are covered discussed in § 23.3, *supra*, regarding § 7206(1) apply to § 7206(2) prosecutions.

The factual patterns of § 7206(2) cases fall into two groups. The first group involves those individual who, working in concert with the taxpayer, prepare false tax returns for the taxpayer.[4] The second group of cases involves those who cause taxpayers to file false tax returns unwittingly.[5]

An issue which arises in § 7206(2) cases is whether the defendant's conduct and intent were sufficient to constitute "aid and assistance" within this section. Mere knowledge that one's actions may result in a false tax return is not sufficient to convict; one must act with the "purpose and objective of violating internal revenue laws."[6]

§ 23.4

1. *See* 26 U.S.C. § 7206(2); *see also* 18 U.S.C. § 3571.

2. 26 U.S.C. § 7206(2); 18 U.S.C. § 3571.

3. *See*:

Sixth Circuit: United States v. Sassak, 881 F.2d 276, 278 (6th Cir.1989).

Ninth Circuit: United States v. Salerno, 902 F.2d 1429, 1432 (9th Cir.1990).

4. *See, e.g.*:

Eighth Circuit: United States v. Zimmerman, 832 F.2d 454, 456 (8th Cir.1987) (defendant "advised and assisted persons in sham transactions, check kiting and fund rotation schemes so they could avoid paying taxes.").

Ninth Circuit: United States v. Crum, 529 F.2d 1380, 1381–82 (9th Cir.1976) (defendant enticed taxpayers to invest in domesticated beavers as a tax shelter device and employed the fraudulent use of depreciation by backdating contracts with taxpayers' knowledge).

5. *See, e.g.*, United States v. Wolfson, 573 F.2d 216, 218 (5th Cir.1978) (defendant provided taxpayers with appraisals placing fair market value on yachts donated to university and taxpayers used appraisal to take a charitable deduction).

6. United States v. Foy, 794 F.Supp. 835 (M.D.Tenn.1992). Using falsified documents to conceal their scheme, Foy and others conspired to embezzle money from Service Merchandise Corporation. *Id.* at 836. Their activities resulted in Service Merchandise filing false tax returns. The defendants were charged with "willfully aid[ing] and assist[ing] in and procur[ing], counsel[ing] and advise[ing] in the preparation and presentation to the Internal Revenue Service an income tax return which was false and fraudulent as to a material matter." *Id.* Following similar rulings in the Courts of Appeals, the trial court acquitted the defendants, finding that "the purpose of the scheme was not related to taxes and . . . there was no intent to violate corporate tax law." *Id.* at 837.

See also:

Fifth Circuit: United States v. Enstam, 622 F.2d 857 (5th Cir.1980).

Ninth Circuit: United States v. Salerno, 902 F.2d 1429, 1432 (9th Cir.1990).

Eleventh Circuit: United States v. Pritchett, 908 F.2d 816 (11th Cir.1990).

Library References:

C.J.S. Internal Revenue § 1280.

West's Key No. Digests, Internal Revenue ⬦5303.

§ 23.5   Tax Offenses—Intimidating or Obstructing an IRS Officer, Employee, Function: 26 U.S.C. § 7212(a)

Section 7212(a) provides:

> Whoever corruptly or by force or threats of force ... endeavors to intimidate or impede any officer or employee of the United States acting in an official capacity under this title, or in any other way corruptly or by force or threat of force ... obstructs or impedes, or endeavors to obstruct or impede the due administration of this title, shall ... be guilty of a felony.

Conviction of this offense carries a maximum term of imprisonment of three years and a maximum fine of $250,000 (for individuals) or $500,-000 (for corporations), plus costs of prosecution.[1]

This statute has been used to prosecute a variety of schemes such as the filing of false 1099 forms,[2] transferring assets or purchasing assets in the names of third parties to avoid execution of liens or other efforts to collect back taxes,[3] and falsifying deductions on a return.[4]

There are two basic offenses contained in § 7212(a). The first focuses on actions against government officials.[5] It applies to one who (1) corruptly, or by force or threats of force, (2) endeavors to intimidate or impede any officer or employee of the United States who is acting in an official capacity under Title 26 of the United States Code. The second offense focuses on more general conduct. Its elements are: (1) corruptly, or by force or threats of force, (2) obstructs or impedes, or endeavors to obstruct or impede, the due administration of the Internal Revenue Code.[6] As can be seen, § 7212(a) includes attempts as well as completed conduct.

Courts have wrestled with the scope of the second, more general, offense. *United States v. Mitchell*,[7] demonstrates this struggle. Mitchell, a zoologist working for the United States Department of Interior, was charged with violating § 7212(a).[8] Mitchell's charges arose from the tax-exempt status he obtained from an organization he incorporated, American Ecological Union, Inc. (AEU). Allegedly, AEU promoted and facilitat-

§ 23.5

1. 26 U.S.C. § 7212(a) (1994); U.S.C. § 3571 (1994).

2. *See, e.g.*, United States v. Dykstra, 991 F.2d 450 (8th Cir.1993).

3. *See, e.g.*, United States v. Shriver, 967 F.2d 572 (11th Cir.1992).

4. *See, e.g.*, United States v. Krause, 786 F.Supp. 1151 (E.D.N.Y.), *aff'd*, 978 F.2d 706 (2d Cir.1992).

5. *See* United States v. Przybyla, 737 F.2d 828 (9th Cir.1984).

6. *See* United States v. Popkin, 943 F.2d 1535, 1539 (11th Cir.1991).

7. 985 F.2d 1275 (4th Cir.1993).

8. Mitchell was also charged with violations of 18 U.S.C. § 208, which prohibits violating federal conflict of interest laws, 26 U.S.C. § 7206(2), aiding in the preparation of false tax returns by others, 16 U.S.C. § 3372(a)(2), taking and transporting animals in violation of foreign law, and 18 U.S.C. § 545, smuggling. *Id.* at 1276.

ed scientific research in ecology.[9] In fact, Mitchell solicited "contributions" from big-game hunters for AEU in return for Mitchell's arranging hunting privileges and trips in Pakistan and China for contributors. Pursuant to Mitchell's direction, the hunters claimed their donations to AEU as tax-deductible contributions.[10] The District Court narrowly construed the reach of § 7212(a), found that Mitchell's activity did not fall within this section, and dismissed the § 7212(a) charge.[11] The United States Court of Appeals for the Fourth Circuit reversed, finding that the phrase, "in any other way corruptly ... obstructs or impedes, or endeavors to obstruct or impede the due administration of [the Internal Revenue Code]" includes efforts to gain an improper tax advantage by misrepresentation and fraud.[12] This is the position taken in the majority of courts.[13] As the Fourth Circuit explained, "[s]ection 7212(a) should be given the full scope its broad language commands" so as to reach "creative and multi-faceted scheme[s] to evade taxes."[14]

"Corruptly" is the key to § 7212(a)'s scope. This term has been applied broadly by the courts, which define it as "an effort to secure an unlawful advantage or benefit," usually a financial gain.[15] *United States v. Dykstra*,[16] demonstrates a typical application of "corruptly." Because of Dykstra's failure to pay taxes, the IRS seized his residence and began eviction proceedings. Dykstra retaliated by entering into a "redemption program," pursuant to which he filed false 1099 forms with the IRS, stating that he had paid nonemployee compensation to a variety of individuals including IRS officials, a United States Marshall, federal judges, bank employees and a former employer.[17] All of these individuals were involved in the seizure and eviction proceedings of Dykstra's residence. Dykstra also sought a reward from the IRS for informing the agency of individuals who had failed to pay their taxes.[18] For this activity, Dykstra was indicted under § 7212(a) for "corruptly endeavoring to obstruct or impede the due administration of the Internal Revenue

---

9. *Id.* at 1276–77.

10. *Id.*

11. *Id.*

12. *Id.* at 1277–78.

13. *See also*:

Eighth Circuit: United States v. Williams, 644 F.2d 696, 701 (8th Cir.1981) (holding that § 7212(a) was violated when defendant "physically assisted the willfully false filings of ... false w–4 forms").

Eleventh Circuit: United States v. Popkin, 943 F.2d 1535, 1540–41 (11th Cir.1991) (holding that § 7212(a) was violated by attorney's scheme of creating a corporation for the purpose of enabling a client to disguise the character of his income earned on drug deals).

In the following cases, a wide variety of conduct was charged under § 7212(a) but the scope of § 7212(a) was not an issue before the court:

Sixth Circuit: United States v. Hatchett, 918 F.2d 631, 634 (6th Cir.1990) (conversion of client checks to cash and purchase of goods in names of third parties to evade collection of back taxes).

Eighth Circuit: United States v. Yagow, 953 F.2d 423, 424 (8th Cir.1992) (filing false 1099 forms).

Eleventh Circuit: United States v. Shriver, 967 F.2d 572, 573 (11th Cir.1992) (transfer of property to avoid execution of IRS lien).

14. *Mitchell*, 985 F.2d at 1279.

15. United States v. Yagow, 953 F.2d 423, 427 (8th Cir.1992); *see also* U.S. DEP'T OF JUSTICE, TAX DIV., CRIM. TAX MANUAL, § 17.04, 1994 ed ..

16. 991 F.2d 450 (8th Cir.1993).

17. *Id.* at 451.

18. *Id.*

laws."[19] Dykstra argued that he did not act corruptly. The court found otherwise, reasoning:

> The evidence here adequately demonstrates that appellant acted with the intent to secure an unwarranted financial gain for himself. He admitted that he employed the "redemption program" in order to keep his house from being taken. In addition, he sent applications for monetary rewards to the IRS for reporting alleged tax law violations by each of his victims.[20]

Library References:

C.J.S. Internal Revenue § 1280.
West's Key No. Digests, Internal Revenue ☞5296.

§ 23.6 Tax Offenses—Failure to File (Misdemeanor): 26 U.S.C. § 7203

Section 7203 provides:

> Any person required under this title to pay any estimated tax or tax, or required by this title or by regulations made under authority thereof to make a return, keep any records, or supply any information, who willfully fails to pay such estimated tax or tax, make such return, keep such records or supply such information; at the time or times required by law or regulations, shall ... be guilty of a misdemeanor.

Conviction of § 72.03 is punishable by a possible maximum term of imprisonment of up to one year with a possible maximum fine of $100,000 (for an individual) and $200,000 (for an organization).[1] There is no felony offense for failure to file a tax return. To charge an individual who has failed to file a tax return with a felony offense the government must use § 7201 (evasion of taxes).[2]

The elements of § 7203 are (1) willfully (2) failing to file a required tax return.[3] The government is not required to show that federal income tax was due,[4] although lack of such liability may be relevant to a taxpayer's willfulness in failing to file.[5] The records for which one becomes liable under § 7203 for failing to file or the information for which one becomes liable for failing to supply is broad: *any* records or information which a taxpayer is required by the IRS Code or regulation to make, keep or supply.[6]

19. *Id.*
20. *Id.* at 453.

§ 23.6

1. *Id.*; *see also* 18 U.S.C. § 3571.

2. *See generally* U.S. Dep't of Justice, Tax Div., Crim. Tax Manual, § 10.01–08, 1994 ed., for a discussion of section 7203.

3. *Fifth Circuit*: United States v. Buckley, 586 F.2d 498, 503–04 (5th Cir. 1978).

Seventh Circuit: United States v. Matosky, 421 F.2d 410, 412–13 (7th Cir.1970).

4. *Fifth Circuit*: United States v. Wade, 585 F.2d 573, 574 (5th Cir.1978).

Tenth Circuit: United States v. Hairston, 819 F.2d 971, 974 (10th Cir.1987).

5. United States v. Schmitt, 794 F.2d 555, 560 (10th Cir.1986).

6. 26 U.S.C. § 7203.

Library References:

C.J.S. Internal Revenue § 1280.

West's Key No. Digests, Internal Revenue ☞5301.

§ 23.7   Tax Offenses—Conspiracy to Violate Tax Laws

There is no conspiracy charge in Title 26 so when more than one individual is involved in criminal tax fraud, the charge is conspiracy under 18 U.S.C. § 371. This section provides that:

> If two or more persons conspire either to commit any offense against the United States, or to defraud the United States, or any agency thereof in any manner or for any purpose, and one or more of such persons do any act to effect the object of the conspiracy each [shall be guilty of a crime].[1]

Section 371 contains two separate offenses: (1) conspiring "to commit any offense against the United States ...," that is, conspiring to engage in conduct prohibited by a substantive criminal statute,[2] and (2) conspiring "to defraud the United States ..." which includes not only cheating the government out of money or property but also, "interfer[ing] with or obstruct[ing] one of its lawful governmental functions by deceit, craft or trickery, or at least by means that are dishonest."[3] In tax cases the latter type of conspiracy is known as a "Klein" conspiracy.[4]

In *Klein*,[5] nine individuals used seventeen foreign corporations to sell whiskey in the United States in a way to avoid paying income taxes.[6] They were convicted under 18 U.S.C. § 371 with conspiring "to defraud the United States by impeding, impairing, obstructing and defeating the lawful functions of the Department of the Treasury in the collection of the revenue; to wit, income taxes."[7] The court reviewed the specific evidence against the defendants (multiple explanations for bank drafts; efforts to conceal the true nature of business activities and the source of income), and found it sufficient to support the jury verdict that the defendants conspired "to interfere with or obstruct ... lawful governmental functions by deceit, craft or trickery, or at least by means that are dishonest."[8]

In addition to not having to prove that the "fraud" was a crime in and of itself,[9] with a *Klein* conspiracy the government need not establish

§ 23.7

1. *See* 18 U.S.C. § 371 (1994); *see also* 18 U.S.C. § 3571.

2. Tax crimes most often are found in Title 26, United States Code, although they may also include money laundering statutes (18 U.S.C. §§ 1956, 1957) or typical white collar criminal statutes.

3. *Supreme Court*: Hammerschmidt v. United States, 265 U.S. 182, 188, 44 S.Ct. 511, 512, 68 L.Ed. 968 (1924).

Ninth Circuit: United States v. Helmsley, 941 F.2d 71, 90 (2d Cir.1991).

4. United States v. Klein, 247 F.2d 908, 915 (2d Cir.1957). U.S. DEPT. OF JUSTICE, TAX DIV., CRIM. TAX MANUAL § 23.02 (1995 Supp.)

5. 247 F.2d 908.

6. *Id.* at 910–11.

7. *Id.* at 915.

8. *Id.* at 916.

9. *First Circuit*: United States v. Hurley, 957 F.2d 1, 4–5 (1st Cir.1992).

Sixth Circuit: United States v. Jerkins, 871 F.2d 598, 603 (6th Cir.1989).

a monetary loss to the government,[10] that the government was actually harmed or that the scheme to defraud was a success.[11] Indeed, as in *Klein*, the government may be able to prove a conspiracy to impede and obstruct the Treasury Department even when the defendant is acquitted of the substantive offenses that were charged as the goal of the conspiracy.[12] With a *Klein* conspiracy the government must prove only that (1) there was an agreement to use deceit or trickery and that the target of the deceit or trickery was the United States or one of its agencies,[13] and (2) one or more conspirators committed an overt act in furtherance of the conspiracy. Some courts are hostile to *Klein* conspiracies, requiring the government to plead the indictment with greater than usual specificity[14] or include jury instructions informing jurors they must find "deceit, craft or trickery," not just obstructing the functions of the United States.[15]

Courts have struggled with the issue of exactly what mens rea must be proven in § 371 cases. Section 371 of title 18, U.S.C., requires proof that a defendant acted with the degree of criminal intent necessary for the substantive offense.[16] Every felony tax offense requires that the government prove that a defendant acted willfully. As discussed, *infra*,[17] this is a high burden, requiring proof that a person acted "voluntarily and intentionally and with the specific intent ... either to disobey or disregard the law."[18] The question is whether proof of such intent is required to convict one of conspiring to violate "willful" crimes.

In *United States v. Cyprian*,[19] the United States Court of Appeals for the Seventh Circuit addressed this issue, holding that proof of willfulness is not necessary to convict one of conspiring to violate felony tax offenses.[20] Rather, according to the Seventh Circuit, the government must simply prove that the defendant knew that he or his co-conspira-

---

10. *Ninth Circuit*: United States v. Tuohey, 867 F.2d 534, 537 (9th Cir.1989).

Eleventh Circuit: United States v. Puerto, 730 F.2d 627, 630 (11th Cir.1984).

11. *Second Circuit*: United States v. Rosengarten, 857 F.2d 76, 79 (2d Cir.1988).

Ninth Circuit: United States v. Everett, 692 F.2d 596, 599 (9th Cir.1982).

12. *Klein*, 247 F.2d at 910.

13. *Cf.*:

Supreme Court: United States v. Johnson, 383 U.S. 169, 170, 86 S.Ct. 749, 750, 15 L.Ed.2d 681 (1966).

Eighth Circuit: United States v. Pintar, 630 F.2d 1270, 1278 (8th Cir.1980).

See U.S. Dep't of Justice, Tax Div., Crim Tax Manual § 23.07[2][b] (1995 Supp.) for sample fact patterns in *Klein* conspiracies.

14. *Second Circuit*: United States v. Helmsley, 941 F.2d 71, 91 (2d Cir.1991).

Sixth Circuit: United States v. Mohney, 949 F.2d 899, 904 (6th Cir.1991).

15. United States v. Caldwell, 989 F.2d 1056, 1059 (9th Cir.1993). This approach has been criticized by the Department of Justice. U.S. Dept. of Justice, Tax Div., Tax Manual, § 23.07[2][c].

16. United States v. Feola, 420 U.S. 671, 687, 95 S.Ct. 1255, 1265, 43 L.Ed.2d 541 (1975).

17. See § 23.8.

18. Cheek v. United States, 498 U.S. 192, 200–01, 111 S.Ct. 604, 610, 112 L.Ed.2d 617 (1991).

19. 23 F.3d 1189 (7th Cir.).

20. *Cyprian*, 23 F.3d at 1201. *See* U.S. Dep't of Justice, Tax Div., Crim. Tax Manual, Inst. 103, 1994 ed ..

tors sought to avoid liability for federal taxes. It is not necessary to prove that the defendant knew that this conduct was criminal.[21]

At issue in *Cyprian* was an illegal bingo game. Although operated under the auspices of a church as a fundraiser for the church, the profits of the bingo game were distributed to the defendants. As such, the bingo game became an unlawful gambling business.[22] Williams, one of the defendants, hired security guards for the games, paying the guards, as well as himself, in cash. Williams never provided these guards with W–2 or 1099 forms.[23] Williams was not charged with a substantive tax offense, presumably 26 U.S.C. § 7201, which makes it a crime to willfully attempt to evade or defeat taxes. Rather, he was charged with conspiring to commit a substantive tax offense. According to the Seventh Circuit, "to convict Williams under the conspiracy to defraud clause of § 371, the government did not need to charge or prove that Williams agreed (or had the intent) to commit a substantive tax offense. Rather, the government was required to prove only that Williams 'agreed to interfere with or obstruct' the United States' ability to collect taxes by defrauding the IRS."[24]

Upon conviction of § 371, a defendant is subject to a maximum term of imprisonment of five years and a maximum fine of $250,000 (for an individual) and $500,000 (for an organization) if the object of the conspiracy was a felony. If, however, the object of the conspiracy was a misdemeanor, the maximum term of imprisonment is one year and the maximum possible fine is $100,000 (for an individual), and $200,000 (for an organization).[25]

Library References:

C.J.S. Internal Revenue § 1273–1285.
West's Key No. Digests, Internal Revenue ⬤5280–5319.

§ 23.8   Intent—Defining "Willfully"

"Willfully" has been defined as a "voluntary, intentional violation of a known legal duty."[1] After recent Supreme Court decisions, in *Cheek v. United States*[2] and *Ratzlaf v. United States*,[3] it is well settled at least in tax fraud prosecutions, that the government must prove that the defendant intentionally violated a known legal duty. In addition, in those instances where a defendant asserts that she had a good faith belief that

---

21. *Cyprian* 23 F.3d at 1201–02.

22. *Id.* at 1199.

23. *Id.* at 1192, 1201.

24. *Id.* at 1201–02 (quoting United States v. Bucey, 876 F.2d 1297, 1312 (7th Cir.1989)).

25. In tax fraud cases, this would pertain to conspiracies to violate 26 U.S.C. § 7203, failure to file required records or supply required information.

§ 23.8

1. United States v. Pomponio, 429 U.S. 10, 12, 97 S.Ct. 22, 24, 50 L.Ed.2d 12 (1976); U.S. Dept. of Justice, Tax Division, Criminal Tax Manual § 8.06 (1994 ed.).

2. Cheek v. United States, 498 U.S. 192, 111 S.Ct. 604, 112 L.Ed.2d 617 (1991).

3. Ratzlaf v. United States, 510 U.S. 135, 114 S.Ct. 655, 126 L.Ed.2d 615 (1994).

her conduct was proper, the defendant need not establish that her belief was objectively reasonable.[4]

Ratzlaf and *Cheek* are a departure from the past trend in American jurisprudence to abolish the notion of specific intent. Historically, the Supreme Court and many courts of appeal have condemned the concept of specific intent, holding that it "has been the source of a good deal of confusion."[5] Despite this trend, the Supreme Court resurrected the notion of specific intent in *Ratzlaf* and *Cheek*, apparently because these cases involved complex offenses and conduct not intuitively evil.

In *Ratzlaf v. United States*,[6] the Supreme Court reversed the "anti-structuring" conviction of Waldemar Ratzlaf because the government had not proven intent sufficiently. Ratzlaf repaid a $100,000 casino debt with cashier's checks, each check for less than $10,000 and from a different bank.[7] Ratzlaf personally traveled to Las Vegas banks in the casino's limousine to get these checks. By "structuring" his repayment with multiple checks, Ratzlaf avoided federal requirements that cash transactions of $10,000 and over be reported.[8] Whenever such structuring is done "willfully," it is a crime.[9]

The Court held that because structuring financial transactions is not "inevitably nefarious," the statutory requirement of "willfully" could be met only with proof of "specific intent to violate a *known* legal duty."[10] Because the government had not proven that the defendant knew that his conduct constituted a crime under this standard, the Court reversed the conviction and remanded the case for a new trial with proper intent instructions. The Court recognized that generally ignorance of the law is not a defense to criminal charges, but it found that "[i]n particular contexts," Congress may decree otherwise.[11]

In *Ratzlaf* the Supreme Court relied heavily on *Cheek v. United States*,[12] handed down three years earlier. In *Cheek*, the Court vacated and remanded the conviction of a taxpayer for evasion of income taxes

4. *Id.* at 203–04.

5. *Supreme Court*: United States v. Bailey, 444 U.S. 394, 403–406, 100 S.Ct. 624, 630–32, 62 L.Ed.2d 575 (1980).

Second Circuit: United States v. Golitschek, 808 F.2d 195, 201 n. 2 (2d Cir.1986).

Fourth Circuit: United States v. Moylan, 417 F.2d 1002, 1004 (4th Cir.1969).

Seventh Circuit: United States v. Arambasich, 597 F.2d 609, 612 (7th Cir.1979).

Eighth Circuit: United States v. Dougherty, 763 F.2d 970, 973 (8th Cir.1985).

Accord: Liparota v. United States, 471 U.S. 419, 433, n. 16, 105 S.Ct. 2084, 2092, 85 L.Ed.2d 434 (1985).

See, e.g., MANUAL OF MODEL CRIMINAL JURY INSTRUCTIONS FOR THE NINTH CIRCUIT, Instruction No. 5.04, Comment (1992); MANUAL ON MODEL CRIMINAL JURY INSTRUCTIONS FOR THE DISTRICT COURTS OF THE EIGHTH CIRCUIT, Instruction No. 7.01 (1992).

6. Ratzlaf v. United States, 510 U.S. 135, 114 S.Ct. 655, 126 L.Ed.2d 615 (1994).

7. *Id.,* 510 U.S. at 138, 114 S.Ct. at 657. Ratzlaf's actual debt to the casino was $160,000 for playing blackjack at the High Sierra Casino in Reno, Nevada on the evening of October 20, 1988.

8. 31 U.S.C. § 5313, 31 C.F.R. § 103.22(a).

9. 31 U.S.C. § 5324.

10. Ratzlaf v. United States, 510 U.S. 135, 114 S.Ct. 655, 126 L.Ed.2d 615 (1994).

11. *Id.,* 510 U.S. at 145, 149, 114 S.Ct. at 661, 663.

12. Cheek v. United States, 498 U.S. 192, 111 S.Ct. 604, 112 L.Ed.2d 617 (1991).

and failure to file tax returns.[13] The issue in *Cheek* was whether the government adequately proved intent. As in *Ratzlaf*, the statute for which Cheek was convicted required proof that a defendant act "willfully."[14] The Court held that at least in the tax area, "willfulness" required proof that the defendant knew what the law required and had the specific intent to violate the law.[15] As in *Ratzlaf*, the Court acknowledged that in most criminal cases ignorance of the law is not a defense. It found an exception, however, when the crime was complex, involving a "proliferation of statutes and regulations." The Court explained:

> Based on the notion that the law is definite and knowable, the common law presumed that every person knew the law. This common-law rule has been applied by the Court in numerous cases construing criminal statutes. The proliferation of statutes and regulations has sometimes made it difficult for the average citizen to know and comprehend the extent of the duties and obligations imposed by the tax laws. Congress has accordingly softened the impact of the common-law presumption by making specific intent to violate the law an element of certain federal criminal tax offenses.[16]

Library References:

C.J.S. Internal Revenue § 1280.
West's Key No. Digests, Internal Revenue ⊕5300.

§ 23.9   Intent—The "Good Faith" Defense

Often, in tax cases, a defendant will present a "good faith" defense—arguing that if there were an error in her tax matters, the error was not a willful effort to avoid her duties under the law but resulted from a good faith mistake about the law.[1] In *Cheek*,[2] the Supreme Court held that a claim of good faith belief need not be objectively reasonable

---

13.   *Id.* at 207.

14.   *Id. at 193.*

15.   *Id.* at 200–01.

16.   *Id.* Because the government must prove that the defendant had the specific intent to violate a *known* legal duty, the Court held that it was error for the trial court to give the "good faith" jury instruction requested by the defendant. The defendant sought an instruction informing the jury that if the defendant honestly and in good faith believed his conduct (of not filing personal income tax returns) was permissible, he could not have evaded the law willfully. The trial court rejected this instruction and gave instead an instruction informing the jury that only if the defendant's claimed belief or misunderstanding of his obligation to file tax returns and pay taxes was objectively reasonable, was willfulness negated. The Court explained why the trial court's decision was wrong: "[I]f the jury credited Cheek's assertion that he

truly believed that the [IRS] Code did not treat wages as income, the Government would not have carried its burden to prove willfulness, however unreasonable a court might deem such a belief." *Id.*, at 202.

§ 23.9

1.   *See, e.g.*:

Fourth Circuit: United States v. Schmidt, 935 F.2d 1440, 1448 (4th Cir. 1991) (regarding alleged tax shelters).

Fifth Circuit: United States v. Barnett, 945 F.2d 1296 (5th Cir.1991) (regarding belief that wages are not income under the tax laws and that filing a tax return is voluntary).

Ninth Circuit: United States v. Powell, 936 F.2d 1056, 1059 (9th Cir.1991) (regarding belief that filing tax returns is voluntary).

2.   498 U.S. 192, 111 S.Ct. 604, 112 L.Ed.2d 617 (1991).

as long as it is relevant to a "defendant's awareness of the legal duty at issue."[3] However, a jury may be instructed that it may consider "whether the defendant's belief about the tax statutes was actually reasonable as a factor in deciding whether he held that belief in good faith."[4]

One issue raised in cases where the defendant asserts a "good faith" defense is whether a defendant is entitled to a specific jury instruction explaining the defense.[5] Although it is well-settled that a defendant is entitled to present to the jury "any theory of the defense which is supported by law and which has some foundation in the evidence, however tenuous,"[6] a defendant is not entitled to a particular instruction on "good faith."[7] As the United States Court of Appeals for the Eleventh Circuit explained, "[a] refusal to give a requested theory of defense instruction is reversible error only if the requested instruction (1) was not correct, (2) was not substantially covered by the court's charge to the jury, and (3) dealt with some point in the trial so important that failure to give the requested instruction seriously impaired the defendant's ability to conduct his defense."[8] Generally, if the instructions, as given, adequately explain the government's burden to prove that a defendant acted "willfully," additional instructions on "good faith" are not given.[9]

It has also been held permissible for a court faced with a good faith defense to instruct the jury that a defendant's understanding of the law does not accurately reflect the state of the law.[10]

Library References:

C.J.S. Internal Revenue § 1280.
West's Key No. Digests, Internal Revenue ⊖5298.

§ 23.10 Intent—Reliance on Professional Advice

In some tax cases, the defendant argues that she did not violate the tax laws willfully because she relied on advice of a professional such as

3. 498 U.S. at 203, 111 S.Ct. at 611.

4. United States v. Becker, 965 F.2d 383, 388 (7th Cir.1992); *see also* United States v. Hilgeford, 7 F.3d 1340, 1344 (7th Cir.1993) (citing *Cheek*, 3 F.3d at 1063).

5. *See*:

Seventh Circuit: United States v. Cheek, 3 F.3d 1057 (7th Cir.1993).

Eleventh Circuit: United States v. Morris, 20 F.3d 1111 (11th Cir.1994).

6. *Cheek*, 3 F.3d at 1062.

7. *Id.*

8. *Morris*, 20 F.3d at 1116.

9. The following instruction which defines "willfully" has been held to adequately explain a good faith defense:

A defendant does not act willfully if he believes in good faith that he is acting within the law or that his actions comply with the law. Therefore, if defendant actually believed that what he was doing was in accord with the tax statutes, he cannot be said to have had the criminal intent to willfully evade or defeat taxes or to willfully fail to file tax returns. This is so even if defendant's belief was not objectively reasonable as long as he held the belief in good faith. Nevertheless, you may consider whether the defendant's stated belief about the tax statutes was reasonable as a factor in deciding whether he held that belief in good faith.

United States v. Cheek, 3 F.3d at 1063; United States v. Becker, 965 F.2d 383, 388 (7th Cir.1992), *cert. denied*, 507 U.S. 971, 113 S.Ct. 1411, 122 L.Ed.2d 783 (1993).

10. *See*:

Seventh Circuit: Cheek, 3 F.3d at 1063.

Ninth Circuit: United States v. Powell, 955 F.2d 1206, 1213 (9th Cir.1991).

an attorney or accountant.[1] The mere fact that a defendant sought and received advice from a professional is not by itself a defense.[2] The United States Court of Appeals for the Seventh Circuit, for example, has held that in order for a professional's advice to negate the element of willfulness, the professional's advice must "create (or perpetuate) an honest misunderstanding of one's legal duties."[3] If a person relies on an accountant or attorney and later finds that the advice was incorrect or has reason to believe that the advice was incorrect, then reliance cannot be used as a defense to tax fraud.[4]

Furthermore, blind reliance is not necessarily a defense where a taxpayer simply signed a return prepared by a professional. The United States Court of Appeals for the First Circuit has held that to sustain a conviction, a defendant does not have to order the professional to falsify the return.[5] Instead, the "critical datum is ... whether the defendants knew when they signed the return that it understated their income."[6] The First Circuit found that convictions could be upheld if the facts allowed a jury to infer that the defendants were aware of the contents of their return and knew that their income was substantially more than that reflected on the tax return.[7] The first element is fairly easy for the government to prove, because a jury may infer that a defendant who signed his return has knowledge of its contents.[8] The jury is not required to draw such an inference however,[9] and there is no presumption of knowledge, merely a permissible inference.[10]

The defense of reliance is not valid if the taxpayer withholds information or intentionally misleads the professional.[11] In fact, a defense of reliance sometimes may work against a taxpayer. Where a defendant does not make a full disclosure to the professional, the lack of disclosure may be used against the taxpayer.[12] In *United States v. Stone*,

---

§ 23.10

1. *See, e.g.*:

Fifth Circuit: United States v. Charroux, 3 F.3d 827, 831 (5th Cir.1993).

Tenth Circuit: United States v. Gonzales, 58 F.3d 506 (10th Cir.1995).

2. *Seventh Circuit*: United States v. Benson, 941 F.2d 598, 614 (7th Cir.1991), *mandate recalled, opinion amended by* 957 F.2d 301 (7th Cir.1992).

Eighth Circuit: United States v. Poludniak, 657 F.2d 948, 959 (8th Cir.1981).

3. *Id.*

4. *Id.*

5. United States v. Olbres, 61 F.3d 967, 970–71 (1st Cir.1995).

6. *Id.*

7. *Id.* at 971.

8. *Id.*; *First Circuit*: United States v. Drape, 668 F.2d 22, 26 (1st Cir.1982); Unit-

ed States v. Romanow, 505 F.2d 813, 814 (1st Cir.1974).

See:

Eleventh Circuit: United States v. Gaines, 690 F.2d 849, 853 (11th Cir.1982) (holding that a jury may infer that an apparently functionally illiterate defendant who signed his tax returns had knowledge of the contents of those returns).

9. *Gaines*, 690 F.2d at 852.

10. *Id.*

11. United States v. Scher, 476 F.2d 319, 321 (7th Cir.1973) (quoting Bender v. Comm'r of Internal Revenue, 256 F.2d 771, 774 (7th Cir.1958)) ("a taxpayer cannot shift the responsibility for admitted deficiencies to the accountants who prepared his returns if the taxpayer withholds vital information from his accountants, or takes positive action designed to mislead them.")

12. United States v. Stone, 431 F.2d 1286, 1289 (5th Cir.1970).

for example, a physician claimed reliance on his accountant as a defense to tax fraud.[13] The accountant in the case computed the doctor's income from financial records the physician kept as a part of his medical practice.[14] However, the physician failed to record substantial portions of income from his practice, and as a result, the accountant could not have accurately recorded Dr. Stone's income.[15] The Fifth Circuit held that the defense was invalid, quoting the district court which stated that the defense was "the worst one the Doctor could have asserted" since everything the accountants relied on had come from the Defendant, and everything the Defendant had furnished was "spectacularly wrong."[16] The Fifth Circuit has gone on to hold that criminal willfulness may be inferred where a taxpayer fails to supply the preparer with "evidence of substantial items of income."[17]

Library References:

C.J.S. Internal Revenue § 1280.
West's Key No. Digests, Internal Revenue ☞5298.

§ 23.11 Intent—Deliberate Disregard

Another intent issue which arises in tax cases is whether evidence of willfulness may be derived from efforts on the part of a defendant to avoid learning the requirements of the law. If the facts support such an argument, the government becomes entitled to a jury instruction informing the jury that it may infer willfulness from such facts. A typical instruction in regarding deliberate disregard is:

> The government may prove that the Defendant ... acted "knowingly" by proving, beyond a reasonable doubt, that this defendant deliberately closed [his] [her] eyes to what would otherwise have been obvious to [him] [her]. No one can avoid responsibility for a crime by deliberately ignoring what is obvious. A finding beyond reasonable doubt of an intent of the defendant to avoid knowledge or enlightenment would permit the jury to infer knowledge. Stated another way, a defendant's knowledge of a particular fact may be inferred from a deliberate or intentional ignorance or deliberate or intentional blindness to the existence of that fact.

> It is, of course, entirely up to you as to whether you find any deliberate ignorance or deliberate closing of the eyes and the inferences to be drawn from any such evidence.

> You may not infer that a defendant had knowledge, however, from proof of a mistake, negligence, carelessness, or a belief in an inaccurate proposition.[1]

13. *Id.*

14. *Id.* at 1287.

15. *Id.*

16. *Id.* at 1289.

17. *Fifth Circuit*: United States v. Stokes, 998 F.2d 279, 281 (5th Cir.1993).

Ninth Circuit: United States v. Frank, 437 F.2d 452, 453 (9th Cir.1971).

§ 23.11

1. 1 Devitt et al., Federal Jury Practice and Instructions: Civil and Criminal § 17.09 (1992); *see also* U.S. Dep't of Jus-

The "deliberate disregard" instruction requires proof that the defendant deliberately, not just recklessly, disregarded the law on tax requirements: "It is not enough that the defendant was mistaken, recklessly disregarded the truth or negligently failed to inquire."[2] Rather, the deliberate disregard instruction is designed for the situation where "a person suspects a fact, realizes its probability, but refrains from obtaining final confirmation in order to be able to deny knowledge if apprehended."[3] Facts which must be proven before the deliberate disregard instruction should be given are that the defendant "was aware of a high probability that his understanding of the tax laws was erroneous and consciously avoided obtaining actual knowledge of his obligations."[4] Even apparent efforts to educate oneself about tax laws can support this instruction where the efforts were selective.[5] It is inappropriate to give this instruction where the facts support actual knowledge or where the evidence justifies only two possible conclusions: knowledge or no knowledge. The deliberate disregard instruction is not routine and should be used "sparingly."[6]

As can be imagined, such a jury instruction is very helpful to the government. There is a split in the circuits as to whether the government is entitled to this instruction after the Supreme Court's decisions in *Cheek*[7] and *Ratzlaf*.[8] The Third Circuit has held that "actual knowledge" of the law's requirements is needed to prove willfulness and that this instruction is not appropriate in tax cases requiring proof of willfulness.[9] The United States Court of Appeals for the First Circuit disagrees, holding that the "reckless disregard" instruction remains proper after *Ratzlaf* even when the mens rea requirement is willfulness.[10]

Library References:

C.J.S. Internal Revenue § 1280.
West's Key No. Digests, Internal Revenue ☞5300.

§ 23.12   Methods of Proof In Tax Fraud Cases

There are two ways of proving tax offenses: direct (also known as a "specific items" method of proof) and indirect (which includes the "bank deposits," "net worth," and "cash expenditures" methods of proof).

Library References:

C.J.S. Internal Revenue § 1278.
West's Key No. Digests, Internal Revenue ☞5291.1.

TICE, TAX DIV., CRIM. TAX MANUAL, INSTR. 107–08, 1994 ed . .

2. United States v. Kelm, 827 F.2d 1319, 1324 (9th Cir.1987).

3. United States v. Mapelli, 971 F.2d 284, 286 (9th Cir.1992).

4. United States v. Fingado, 934 F.2d 1163, 1166 (10th Cir.1991).

5. *Id.* at 1167.

6. United States v. Sanchez–Robles, 927 F.2d 1070, 1073 (9th Cir.1991).

7. 498 U.S. 192, 111 S.Ct. 604, 112 L.Ed.2d 617 (1991).

8. 510 U.S. 135, 114 S.Ct. 655, 126 L.Ed.2d 615 (1994).

9. United States v. Retos, 25 F.3d 1220, 1229–30 (3d Cir.1994).

10. United States v. London, 66 F.3d 1227, 1242 (1st Cir.1995).

§ 23.13 Methods of Proof In Tax Fraud Cases—Direct Method of Proof

The direct method of proof is just that: a defendant's income is proven directly by showing specific amounts of income the defendant received but failed to report to the IRS.[1] Such evidence could come from W–2's, 1099s, or witnesses who paid the defendant for services. If a defendant willfully did not report all of his income, tax fraud may have been committed.[2] Proof by the specific items method is relatively simple, compared to the indirect methods of proof. The Department of Justice, Criminal Tax Manual lists the following four types of specific items cases:

1. Unreported income, where the evidence establishes that the total amount of income received is greater than the amount reported;

2. Unreported income, where the evidence establishes that identified items of income were not reported;

3. Failure to report a business or other sources of income;

4. Overstated deductions or expenses, including fictitious deductions and legitimate deductions that are inflated.[3]

Library References:

C.J.S. Internal Revenue § 1278.
West's Key No. Digests, Internal Revenue ⚷5291.1.

§ 23.14 Methods of Proof In Tax Fraud Cases—Indirect Methods of Proof

The indirect methods of proof are used when direct proof of a defendant's income is not available. With an indirect method of proof, the amount of income a defendant allegedly received is shown circumstantially by adding the amounts of money deposited by the defendant over a period of time ("bank deposits" method), calculating the increase in a defendant's visible wealth, such as new homes, automobiles, boats, etc. ("net worth" method), or simply documenting cash expenditures by a defendant ("cash expenditure" method). When these indirect methods of proof reveal an amount of income in excess of the defendant's income as reported to the IRS, a presumption arises that the defendant has not reported all of her income. The defendant bears the burden of rebutting this presumption. Government agents have a duty to investigate leads provided by a taxpayer regarding non-taxable sources of income.[1] Al-

§ 23.13

1. *See, e.g.,* United States v. Horton, 526 F.2d 884, 886 (5th Cir.1976).

2. *See generally* U.S. DEP'T OF JUSTICE, TAX DIV., CRIM. TAX MANUAL, § 30.01–10 for a discussion of the "specific items" method of proof.

3. U.S. DEP'T OF JUSTICE, TAX DIV., CRIMINAL TAX MANUAL, § 30.01.

§ 23.14

1. *Supreme Court*: Holland v. United States, 348 U.S. 121, 138, 75 S.Ct. 127, 136, 99 L.Ed. 150 (1954).

Second Circuit: United States v. Cramer, 447 F.2d 210, 218 (2d Cir.1971).

though a taxpayer is not required to come forth with leads, a defendant who fails to do so "remains quiet at his peril."[2] Such leads must be relevant and reasonably susceptible of being checked. Also, the "leads" must be furnished prior to trial.[3] At least one court has held that hearsay testimony is admissible, not for the truth of the matter but to demonstrate that the government, in fact, pursued leads.[4] In indirect method cases, the government is not required to disprove every possible source of nontaxable income,[5] or document the defendant's finances "to an absolute certainty."[6]

A. "BANK DEPOSITS" METHOD

The bank deposits method of proof proceeds on the theory that if a taxpayer is engaged in income-producing activity, and makes regular and periodic deposits of money into bank accounts in her own name or into bank accounts under her dominion or control, there is sufficient evidence for a jury to infer that the funds deposited represent income. An early case setting forth the requisites of this method is *Gleckman v. United States*.[7] The court noted that the Government cannot simply show that a person has received money or deposited it into a bank in order to draw the inference that those funds are income. But, as the court went on to say:

> On the other hand, if it be shown that a man has a business or calling of a lucrative nature and is constantly, day by day and month by month, receiving moneys and depositing them to his account and checking against them for his own uses, there is more potent testimony that he has income, and, if the amount exceeds exemptions and deductions, that the income is taxable.[8]

In order for the bank deposits method to be accurate, it is necessary for the Government to eliminate any non-income items.[9] Once the Government establishes that the defendant is engaged in income producing activity and eliminates those identifiable items which are not income, unidentified deposits may be presumed to be taxable income.[10]

B. "NET WORTH" METHOD

When using the "net worth" indirect method of proof, the government presents a *prima facie* case of tax fraud if it proves that a taxpayer's net worth at the end of a particular time period is greater than at the beginning of the time period, demonstrates the existence of a

---

Eighth Circuit: United States v. Caswell, 825 F.2d 1228, 1234 (8th Cir.1987).

2. United States v. Terrell, 754 F.2d 1139.

3. United States v. Vardine, 305 F.2d 60, 65 (2d Cir.1962).

4. United States v. Scott, 660 F.2d 1145, 1157 (7th Cir.1981).

5. *Holland*, 348 U.S. at 138, 75 S.Ct. at 137.

6. *Id.*

7. 80 F.2d 394 (8th Cir.1935).

8. *Id.* at 399.

9. *Id.* at 397.

10. *Id.*

likely source of taxable income and negates reasonable explanations by the defendant.[11] If the taxpayer's declared income is inadequate to explain an increase in net worth the fact-finder is instructed that it may presume that the unexplained amount is undeclared income. Because the net worth method of proof, like any indirect method is "fraught with danger for the innocent ..., courts closely scrutinize its use."[12] Common defenses in net worth cases include challenging the government's calculation of beginning or ending net worth,[13] and challenging the presumption that the increase in net worth is due to taxable income. In some net worth cases, the defense actively seeks to prove that the increase in net worth is due to nontaxable sources such as gifts or loans.[14]

C. "CASH EXPENDITURES" METHOD

With the cash expenditures method of indirect proof, the government "compares cash expenditures with known cash sources."[15] The United States Court of Appeals for the Seventh Circuit described this method as follows:

[T]he method first requires that all cash expenditures be determined and added together. Then, taxable and nontaxable cash sources are added together. These sources would include any cash accumulated and on hand at the beginning of the tax period in question that the taxpayer spends during the tax period (often called a 'cash hoard.') If cash expenditures exceed cash sources during the period in question, it is inferred that the excess amount is unreported income.[16]

Common defenses in cash expenditures cases include attacking the government's calculations of cash expenditures and presenting explanation of cash hoard or nontaxable explanations (gifts, loans) for the expenditures.[17]

Library References:

C.J.S. Internal Revenue § 1281.
West's Key No. Digests, Internal Revenue ☞5292.

§ 23.15 Use With Other Crimes

Tax offenses frequently are charged with other crimes. Although all charges in one indictment should be "of the same or similar character or [be] ... based on the same act or transaction or on two or more acts or transactions connected together or constituting parts of a common

11. Holland v. United States, 348 U.S. 121, 75 S.Ct. 127, 99 L.Ed. 150 (1954).

12. *Id.* at 125.

13. *Id.* at 127.

See, e.g.:

Sixth Circuit: United States v. Bencs, 28 F.3d 555, 563 (6th Cir.1994).

Cf.:

Fifth Circuit: United States v. Conaway, 11 F.3d 40, 43 (5th Cir.1993).

14. United States v. Bencs, 28 F.3d 555, 563 (6th Cir.1994).

15. United States v. Toushin, 899 F.2d 617, 619 (7th Cir.1990).

16. *Id.* at 619–20 (7th Cir.1990).

17. *Toushin*, 899 F.2d at 620.

scheme or plan,"[1] there is considerable leeway for grouping offenses. *United States v. Scott,*[2] demonstrates this. Scott was charged with intimidating a witness and submitting false tax returns. The United States Court of Appeals for the Fifth Circuit held that joinder of the offenses was proper because the defendant's intimidation of the witness was an attempt to escape liability for the fraudulent tax returns claims. Acknowledging that joinder created some prejudice, the court held that the prejudice was insufficient to warrant severance: "[t]he mere act of joining counts in an indictment ... results in some prejudice. Prejudice to this limited degree is anticipated by Rule 8."[3]

Charges commonly included with tax fraud include obstruction of justice for providing false testimony during an investigation[4] and perjury[5] for providing false information to a grand jury.[6] Whenever the income not reported or taxes evaded arise from fraudulent activity, the tax fraud charges may "piggy-back" other charges arising from the fraud such as RICO,[7] embezzlement, money laundering.[8]

Often, when an individual falsifies information about his or her financial status, the crimes escalate because the lie must be continued to avoid detection. *United States v. Mitan,*[9] demonstrates this. Mitan was a disbarred lawyer who continued to associate with his former firm and receive income from the firm.[10] Mitan filed for bankruptcy. In his petition for bankruptcy, he failed to report the income he was receiving from his firm.[11] Mitan's false petition gave rise to bankruptcy charges and his failure to report the $1,165,369 he received from the firm on his income tax return resulted in tax evasion charges.[12]

Library References:

C.J.S. Internal Revenue § 1273.
West's Key No. Digests, Internal Revenue ⚮5280.

§ 23.16 Investigations of Tax Fraud—Using Materials Obtained in Civil Audits for Criminal Investigations

Unique issues arise in the investigation of complex cases, especially where both civil and criminal prosecution of the case are possible. Tax investigations epitomize this.

§ 23.15

1. Fed.R.Crim.P. 8(a).
2. 659 F.2d 585, 589 (5th Cir.1981).
3. *Id.* at 589.
4. 18 U.S.C. § 1503.
5. 18 U.S.C. § 1623.
6. United States v. Barone, 913 F.2d 46 (2d Cir.1990).
7. *See, e.g.,* United States v. Long, 917 F.2d 691 (2d Cir.1990) (RICO, obstruction of justice, extortion, perjury, and filing false federal income tax returns charges brought against Teamsters officials for bribes and kickbacks they received in connection with decisions they made as to investment of union assets); United States v. Dyer, 922 F.2d 105 (2d Cir.1990) (RICO extortion, and filing false federal income tax returns charges brought against defendant in connection with sale of condominium.)

8. United States v. Holmes, 44 F.3d 1150, 1153 (2d Cir.1995).
9. 966 F.2d 1165 (7th Cir.1992).
10. *Id.* at 1167.
11. *Id.* at 1168.
12. *Id.* at 1167–68.

The Internal Revenue Service (IRS) investigates civil matters through audits. Although "[i]t is clear that the IRS may not develop a criminal investigation under the auspices of a civil audit,"[1] information obtained during a civil audit may be available to the government for use in any subsequent criminal prosecution. Recognizing that "[i]t would be a flagrant disregard of individuals' rights to deliberately deceive, or even lull, taxpayers into incriminating themselves during an audit when activities of an obviously criminal nature are under investigation," IRS auditors are required to turn a case over to the criminal investigation division (of the IRS) once they develop "firm indications of fraud."[2] When an auditor has a "firm indication of fraud," the "examination should be immediately suspended without disclosing to the taxpayer or representative the reason for the action."[3]

Once an individual has become a target[4] or subject[5] of any criminal investigation, internal Department of Justice guidelines require that the individual be supplied with a written warning of rights if documents are requested by grand jury subpoena as well as an oral warning of rights if the individual appears before the grand jury.[6] These warnings are attached to target or subject subpoenas in all circumstances except those in which notice "might jeopardize the investigation."[7] Even when this notice policy is violated, however, courts have been reluctant to take action against the government such as suppressing any evidence obtained or dismissing the charges. In so ruling, courts have noted the "very limited scope [of] supervisory powers" given to the courts regarding grand jury matters and the "[f]ew restraints [that] protect targets appearing before grand juries."[8] Courts will, however "consider referring internal policy violations to the Department's Office of Professional Responsibility for a report concerning the steps the Department proposes

§ 23.16

1. United States v. Grunewald, 987 F.2d 531, 534 (8th Cir.1993).

2. Audit Guidelines for Examiners, [1 Audit] Internal Revenue Manual (CCH) 7247–35 (Apr. 23, 1981); *see also* [2 Audit] *id.* at 8177–29 (May 24, 1983).

3. *Id.*

4. A "target," as defined by Department of Justice guidelines, is "a person as to whom the prosecutor or the grand jury has substantial evidence linking him/her to the commission of a crime and who, in the judgment of the prosecutor, is a putative defendant." U.S. DEP'T OF JUSTICE, UNITED STATES ATTORNEYS' MANUAL, § 9–11.150 at 10.

5. A "subject" of an investigation is an individual "whose conduct is within the scope of the grand jury's investigation" U.S. DEPT. OF JUSTICE, UNITED STATES ATTORNEYS' MANUAL, § 9–11.150 at 10.

6. The "Advice of Rights" form provides as follows:

A. The grand jury is conducting an investigation of possible violations of federal criminal laws involving: (State here the general subject matter of inquiry, *e.g.*, the conducting of an illegal gambling business in violation of 18 U.S.C. § 1955).

B. You may refuse to answer any question if a truthful answer to the question would tend to incriminate you.

C. Anything that you do say may be used against you by the grand jury or in a subsequent legal proceeding.

D. If you have retained counsel, the grand jury will permit you a reasonable opportunity to step outside the grand jury room to consult with counsel if you do so desire.

U.S. DEPT. OF JUSTICE, UNITED STATES ATTORNEYS' MANUAL, § 9–11.150 at 10.

7. *Id.* § 9–11.153 at 12.

8. United States v. Gillespie, 974 F.2d 796, 801 (7th Cir.1992).

to take to police its internal policy guidelines and to discipline those of its employees who choose not to follow them."[9]

§ 23.17   Investigations of Tax Fraud—Immunity

Immunity may be given pursuant to 18 U.S.C. § 6002 which provides that "no testimony or other information compelled ... may be used against the witness in any criminal case, except a prosecution for perjury, giving a false statement, or otherwise failing to comply with the order."[1] This "use" immunity prevents the government from using information it obtains from an immunized source to prosecute the source. "Use" immunity is narrower than "transactional" immunity which would confer immunity for the transaction at issue, regardless of where the government obtained the information about the offense.

To obtain immunity under 18 U.S.C. § 6002, precise steps and procedures must be followed. Because these steps are cumbersome and time-consuming to pursue, immunity pursuant to § 6002 often is not feasible when an individual approaches a prosecutor about the possibility of informing on herself or others in exchange for favorable treatment by the government. In these instances, the prosecutor gives informal use immunity, which is fully enforceable.[2] The government has a "heavy burden of proving that all of the evidence it proposes to use was derived from legitimate independent sources."[3]

United States v. Palumbo,[4] demonstrates how informal immunity works. Through his attorneys, Palumbo approached federal prosecutors who were investigating the importation and distribution of large marijuana shipments about cooperating with them. In making the initial inquiry about cooperation, Palumbo's attorneys did not reveal his identity.[5] The prosecutor told the attorneys that their client would "have to make a proffer—to demonstrate the truthfulness and relevance of his information—before he could engage in any plea negotiations."[6] The prosecutor offered "informal use and derivative use immunity for [the] proffer, tantamount to the protections provided by 18 U.S.C. section 6002."[7] After Palumbo appeared and made his proffer, he was indicted,

---

9. *Id.* at 802; *see also* Bank of Nova Scotia v. United States, 487 U.S. 250, 263, 108 S.Ct. 2369, 2378, 101 L.Ed.2d 228 (1988).

§ 23.17

1. 18 U.S.C. § 6002 (1994).

2. *See*:

Seventh Circuit: United States v. Palumbo, 897 F.2d 245, 248 (7th Cir.1990).

See also:

Fourth Circuit: United States v. Society of Indep. Gasoline Marketers of Am., 624 F.2d 461, 469–74 (4th Cir.1979), *cert. denied*, 449 U.S. 1078, 101 S.Ct. 859, 66 L.Ed.2d 801 (1981) (holding that defendant

acted reasonably in relying upon the Government's promise of immunity).

Fifth Circuit: United States v. Williams, 809 F.2d 1072, 1081–82 (5th Cir.), *on rehearing*, 828 F.2d 1 (5th Cir.1987) (holding that informal use immunity shielded defendant to the same extent as would a court order had it issued).

3. Kastigar v. United States, 406 U.S. 441, 461–62, 92 S.Ct. 1653, 1665, 32 L.Ed.2d 212 (1972).

4. 897 F.2d 245 (7th Cir.1990).

5. *Id.* at 246.

6. *Id.* at 247.

7. *Id.*

pled guilty to charges of tax evasion and conspiracy to distribute marijuana, and was sentenced to twelve years in prison. Palumbo pled guilty after reserving his right to appeal the district court's decision denying his motion to dismiss the indictment.[8] Palumbo argued in his motion and on appeal that the government breached its promise not to use information gained from the proffer against him.[9] The Seventh Circuit agreed, in part, with Palumbo. It found that the government had "ample evidence—apart from the proffer—demonstrating that Palumbo *was involved* in operations relating to the marijuana distribution scheme" but failed to demonstrate that it had sufficient evidence, apart from the proffer, to demonstrate that "Palumbo ... possessed the requisite *mens rea* to be guilty of conspiracy to distribute marijuana or tax evasion."[10] The court therefore ordered the indictment dismissed.[11]

§ 23.18   Discovery—In General

The same rules of discovery apply in criminal tax cases as apply in any federal criminal case. The government and the defendant are obliged to provide the information specified in Federal Rule of Criminal Procedure 16.[1] Upon request of the defendant, the Government must provide the defendant's statements; the defendant's prior criminal record; documents and tangible evidence "which are material to the preparation of the defendant's defense" or which belong to the defendant; reports of physical or mental examinations; and a written summary of expert testimony the Government intends to use. If the defendant requests disclosure and the Government complies, the defendant must produce documents and tangible evidence, reports of physical or mental tests, and a written summary of expert testimony the defendant intends to use.

Brady v. Maryland[2] also applies. *Brady* requires that the government produce, upon request, all evidence "material either to guilt or to punishment" which is "favorable to an accused."[3] Evidence is material under the *Brady* rule only if "there is a reasonable probability that, had [it] ... been disclosed to the defense, the result of the proceeding would have been different."[4]

When there has been a *Brady* or Rule 16 violation, the courts are empowered to "prescribe such terms and conditions as are just" to remedy a violation of a discovery order.[5] At least one court has held that assessing a monetary penalty, even as payment for additional costs or attorney's fees necessitated by the government's breach of Rule 16 and

---

8. *Id.* at 248.

9. *Id.* at 247.

10. United States v. Palumbo, 897 F.2d 245, 249 (7th Cir.1990) (emphasis in original).

11. *Id.* at 251.

§ 23.18

1. Fed.R.Crim.P. 16.

2. 373 U.S. 83, 83 S.Ct. 1194, 10 L.Ed.2d 215 (1963).

3. *Id.* at 87.

4. United States v. Bagley, 473 U.S. 667, 682, 105 S.Ct. 3375, 3383, 87 L.Ed.2d 481 (1985).

5. Fed.R.Crim.P. 16(d)(2).

Brady, is not a permissible sanction under Rule 16(d)(2) because this rule, unlike its counterparts in the Federal Civil Rules of Procedure, provides no independent authority for a monetary sanction.[6] As such, there has been no explicit waiver of sovereign immunity. Courts "may impose money awards against the United States only under an express waiver of sovereign immunity."[7]

The Jencks Act also applies.[8] Under this Act, no statement made by a Government witness or a prospective Government witness "shall be the subject of subpoena, discovery, or inspection until said witness has testified on direct examination in the trial of the case."[9] After a witness has testified, the court "shall, on motion of the defendant, order the United States to produce any statement . . . of the witness in the possession of the United States which relates to the subject matter as to which the witness has testified."[10] By custom or agreement, many courts require Jencks material to be provided at some point prior to the witness taking the stand.

The court will inspect the statement *in camera* if the United States claims that the statement contains matter unrelated to the subject matter of the witness' testimony[11] and will excise any unrelated portions of the statement.[12] Sanctions are statutorily provided if the United States does not comply with a court order to produce all or part of a statement: the court "shall strike from the record the testimony of the witness."[13]

Although government agents' reports generally are not available to defendants as discovery,[14] such reports may become available under the Jencks Act. *United States v. Cleveland*,[15] demonstrates this. Cleveland was convicted on three counts of tax evasion after a trial in which the government used the net worth method of proof. Finding that the Special Agent's report did "relate[] to the subject matter as to which witnesses ha[d] testified," the court ordered the government to turn over to the defendant the agent's report.[16] In reaching its conclusion, the court noted the special circumstances presented by the indirect method of proof:

> [T]hese reports disclose the manner in which the contents of those documents were employed by the agent to arrive at his conclusions regarding defendant's assets, liabilities and expenditures during each of the taxable years. The materials thus relate to the agent's direct testimony not only in their specific content, but also in what they disclose about the deductive process which led to the agent's

6. United States v. Woodley, 9 F.3d 774, 781 (9th Cir.1993).

7. *Id.* (citing Block v. North Dakota, 461 U.S. 273, 287, 103 S.Ct. 1811, 1820, 75 L.Ed.2d 840 (1983)).

8. 18 U.S.C. § 3500.

9. 18 U.S.C. § 3500(a) (1994).

10. *Id.* § 3500(b).

11. *Id.* § 3500(c).

12. *Id.*

13. *Id.* § 3500(d).

14. Federal Rule of Criminal Procedure 16(a)(2).

15. 507 F.2d 731 (7th Cir.1974).

16. *Id.* at 732.

conclusions. Indeed, where the agent's investigation comprises the very foundation of the government's case, as it invariably does in "net worth" prosecutions, such reports can be as important to the defense for what they do not say as for what they do; cross examination might well be structured to challenge not only the factual determinations made by the agent, but the very sufficiency of his investigation.[17]

§ **23.19** Discovery—Discovery Nuances in Criminal Tax Cases

A.   26 U.S.C. § 6103(h)(4)(d): OBTAINING TAX INFORMATION ABOUT WITNESSES

There are several discovery nuances in criminal tax cases. Unlike most cases, highly personal information such as that contained in personal or corporate income tax returns could be highly relevant if that individual is a government witness. In such instances, § 6103 of title 26, United States Code, provides a mechanism for the government or defendants to obtain these records.[1] Tax material obtained under § 6103 can be used by the government and the defendant both to cross-examine and to impeach the witness. It is also possible for both parties to obtain potential jurors' tax information under § 6103.

Section 6103(h)(4)(D) provides that "[r]eturns and return information shall be confidential," with certain exceptions. One of these exceptions is that "[a] return or return information may be disclosed in a Federal or State judicial or administrative proceeding pertaining to tax administration, under certain conditions, including a court order of disclosure under the Jencks Act (18 U.S.C. § 3500 (1994)) or Fed. R.Crim.P. 16."[2]

The party seeking disclosure pursuant to § 6103 bears the burden of demonstrating that disclosure would be "material to the preparation of his defense."[3] A requested item of discovery is material if it " 'bears some abstract logical relationship to the issues in the case.' "[4] This materiality standard normally " 'is not a heavy burden,' ... rather, evidence is material as long as there is a strong indication that it will 'play an important role in uncovering admissible evidence, aiding witness preparation, corroborating testimony, or assisting impeachment or rebuttal.' "[5]

---

17.   *Id.* at 736.

§ 23.19

1.   26 U.S.C. § 6103(a) (1994).

2.   *See* 26 U.S.C. § 6103(h)(4)(D).

3.   Fed.R.Crim.P. 16(a)(1)(C).

4.   United States v. Lloyd, 992 F.2d 348, 351 (D.C.Cir.1993) (citations omitted).

5.   *Id.* (citations omitted).

See also:

D.C. Circuit: United States v. Caicedo–Llanos, 960 F.2d 158, 164 n. 4 (D.C.Cir. 1992); United States v. George, 786 F.Supp. 56, 58 (D.D.C.1992); United States v. Felt, 491 F.Supp. 179, 186 (D.D.C.1979).

Fifth Circuit: United States v. Ross, 511 F.2d 757, 762–63 (5th Cir.1975).

United States v. Lloyd,[6] demonstrates how disclosure may be obtained under § 6103. Lloyd was accused of aiding and abetting the preparation of false federal income tax returns for three named taxpayers.[7] Prior to trial Lloyd sought copies of the tax returns, under Rule 16, for the named taxpayers for the three years prior to the tax years included in the indictment, arguing that they were material to the preparation of the defense.[8] The District Court denied his request, finding that the defendant had not met his "heavy burden" of showing that the requested records were material.[9] The Court of Appeals for the District of Columbia reversed and remanded for further findings on the issue of materiality, holding that the lower court imposed an inappropriately heavy burden on the defendant to show materiality.[10] The Court of Appeals noted that if the prior years' returns demonstrated "a similar treatment of a similar issue in a prior year, as to which the indicted tax preparer had played no role, [this] would tend to suggest that the falsity originated with the taxpayer rather than the preparer."[11]

B.   26 U.S.C. 6103(h)(5): OBTAINING TAX INFORMATION ABOUT JURORS

Pursuant to 26 U.S.C. § 6103(h)(5) both the government and the taxpayer in civil and criminal tax cases have the right to request from the Secretary of the Treasury confirmation of whether the potential juror has ever been audited or investigated by the IRS.[12] This section provides:

> In connection with any judicial proceeding [related to tax administration] . . . to which the United States is a party, the Secretary shall respond to a written inquiry from . . . any person (or his legal representative) who is a party to such proceeding as to whether an individual who is a prospective juror in such proceeding has or has not been the subject of any audit or other tax investigation by the Internal Revenue Service. The Secretary shall limit such response to an affirmative or negative reply to such inquiry.[13]

Section 6103(h)(5) was added to codify what had been a practice of the IRS of supplying tax information about potential jurors to the govern-

---

6.   992 F.2d 348 (D.C.Cir.1993).

7.   *Id.* at 349.

8.   *Id.* at 349–50.

9.   *Id.*

10.   *Id.* at 351–52.

11.   *Id.* at 351. The Court noted that although section 6103(h)(4)(D) provides for production of tax returns, upon court order, as required by rules of discovery in criminal cases, it goes on to require " 'such order to give due consideration to congressional policy favoring the confidentiality of returns and return information as set forth in this title.' " *Id.* at 352 (quoting 26 U.S.C. § 6103(h)(4)(D)). Whereas the lower court understood this language to impose a greater burden on the party seeking tax returns as discovery than applies in other types of discovery, the Court of Appeals held that this language does not, as the lower court interpreted, impose a "very heavy burden" on discovery sought, but simply requires that "confidentiality to be limited to such remedies as redacting portions that are plainly immaterial and especially sensitive." *Id.*

12.   *See id.*

13.   *Id.*

ment.[14] Two concerns led Congress to pass § 6103(h)(5): that jurors' privacy was being invaded when their tax information was obtained and that defendants were not getting the same access to the juror information as was the government.

Section 6103(h)(5) is silent about the procedure to follow in requesting juror information. One question with which the courts have dealt is the extent to which the IRS must go in providing juror tax information. The courts have had little trouble agreeing that § 6103(h)(5) does not require producing all tax information about prospective jurors. In *United States v. Spine*,[15] for example, the United States Court of Appeals for the Sixth Circuit held that the requirements of § 6103(h)(5) are met if the IRS cannot locate all of the jurors' tax histories from the time the jurors began paying taxes, if the district court obtains such information on voir dire. As the United States Court of Appeals for the Third Circuit noted: "[i]nterpreting § 6103(h)(5) to require tax investigations stretching back twenty or thirty years would transform § 6103(h)(5) into a significant practical bar to tax prosecutions."[16]

Another procedural issue the courts have had to resolve is at what stage the parties become entitled to juror information under § 6103(h)(5). Courts facing this issue have held that "the only way to carry out the intent of the statute as a useful voir dire tool is to allow early access to jury panel information."[17] However, most courts hold that failure to provide jury panel tax information when requested requires reversal only if the questioning of the panel during voir dire fails to elicit the same information.[18] This is true even if the IRS furnishes incomplete or inaccurate information.[19] In *United States v. Axmear*, for example, the United States Court of Appeals for the Eighth Circuit held that the district court did not commit reversible error when it denied the defendant a continuance to obtain additional juror information under § 6103(h)(5).[20] In this case, the IRS provided the defendant with infor-

14. *See* Treas. Reg. 301.6103(a)–1(h) (1973) (as amended by T.D. 7266, 1973–1 C.B. 593).

15. 945 F.2d 143, 148 (6th Cir.1991).

16. United States v. Copple, 24 F.3d 535, 542 (3d Cir.1994).

17. *Eleventh Circuit*: United States v. Schandl, 947 F.2d 462, 467 (11th Cir.1991).

See also:

Ninth Circuit: United States v. Hashimoto, 878 F.2d 1126, 1130 (9th Cir.1989).

Cf.:

First Circuit: United States v. Lussier, 929 F.2d 25, 30 (1st Cir.1991) (Although holding that the defendant has no right to early release of juror information, finds that early release may be appropriate in some circumstances.)

18. *See*:

Fifth Circuit: United States v. Masat, 896 F.2d 88, 95 (5th Cir.1990).

Eleventh Circuit: United States v. Schandl, 947 F.2d at 469.

Cf.:

Ninth Circuit: United States v. Hashimoto, 878 F.2d at 1134.

But see:

Ninth Circuit: United States v. Sinigaglio, 942 F.2d 581, 583 (9th Cir.1991), *overruled on other grounds by*, 108 F.3d 1031 (9th Cir.1997) (holding that the trial judge's questions during voir dire, which elicited the same information to which the parties would have had access under section 6103(h)(5), did not cure the prejudice created by the incomplete audit history given to the defendant).

19. *See Copple*, 24 F.3d at 544.

20. United States v. Axmear, 964 F.2d 792, 793 (8th Cir.1992).

mation about which prospective jurors had been audited or investigated during the past six years. The district court denied the defendant's request for a continuance to discover whether any juror had been audited during the past twenty-five years, stating that the defendant "could obtain the same information by questioning the jurors during voir dire."[21] Similarly, in *United States v. Droge*, the Second Circuit held that "appropriate voir dire" can render harmless the failure to comply with § 6103(h)(5).[22] In so holding, the court balanced the defendants' rights under § 6103(h)(5) with the "practical difficulties a district court faces in trying [to] manage its docket while awaiting the Treasury's response to a defendant's open ended request for jury tax audit information."[23] The court stated:

> [T]he responsibility of the district court is substantially met when the district court assists the defendant in obtaining § 6103(h)(5) information . . .; affords the defendant a reasonable period of time in which to receive the information . . .; and in the event that the information is not received within a reasonable period of time or is incomplete, (a) ascertains that the government is not in possession of any of the requested information that the defendant does not have and (b) inquires into the jurors' past audit history on *voir dire* so as to elicit comparable information.[24]

When these steps are taken, the defendant bears the burden of showing actual prejudice by the IRS's failure to provide complete juror audit information.[25]

§ 23.20 Evidentiary Issues In Tax Cases—Expert Witnesses

Expert witnesses are common in tax fraud prosecutions. They are used primarily to summarize testimony regarding the amount of alleged income, deductions and taxes due and owing.

Federal Rule of Evidence 702 provides that expert testimony is admissible if, by way of specialized knowledge, it assists the trier of fact in understanding the evidence.[1] According to the Advisory Committee on

---

21. *Id.* at 793. During voir dire, several jurors admitted they had been audited, the defendant did not object to the voir dire, and he remained silent when given the opportunity to ask additional questions about the jurors' audit histories.

22. United States v. Droge, 961 F.2d 1030, 1034 (2d Cir.1992). In *United States v. Hardy*, 941 F.2d 893 (9th Cir.1991) the Ninth Circuit went even further than the Second Circuit in *Droge*, by holding that complete failure to comply with § 6103(h)(5) was cured by the district court's questions to the jurors on voir dire as to whether they had been audited or investigated. *Id.* at 895. In *Hardy*, the government responded to the defendant's § 6103(h)(5) request "in a timely fashion," but due to an administrative error by the

clerk, a panel different from the one as to which the defendant had been given information was brought into court. *Id.* at 895–96. The court on voir dire asked each juror chosen from the panel whether the juror had been audited by the IRS. *Id.* at 895.

23. *Id.*

24. *Id.* at 1036.

25. *Id.* at 1037.

§ 23.20

1. FRE 702 provides:

If scientific, technical, or other specialized knowledge will assist the trier of fact to understand the evidence or to determine a fact in issue, a witness qualified as an expert . . . may testify thereto in the form of an opinion or otherwise.

the Federal Rules of Evidence, " 'There is no more certain test for determining when experts may be used than the common sense inquiry whether the untrained layman would be qualified to determine intelligently and to the best possible degree the particular issue without enlightenment from those having a specialized understanding of the subject involved in the dispute.' "[2]

Federal Rule of Evidence 703 sets forth the evidence on which an expert may base an opinion.[3] Like Rule 702, it provides broad discretion to the witness and the court. The expert need not have personally observed any facts or event; instead, Rule 703 provides that the expert may base "an opinion or inference ... [on facts or data] perceived by or made known to the expert at or before the hearing."[4] The basis for the opinion need not even be admissible. Rule 703 provides, "[i]f of a type reasonably relied on by experts in the particular field in forming opinions or inferences upon the subject, the facts or data need not be admissible in evidence."[5]

Because of the wide latitude provided by Rule 703, it is possible for an expert who has not been present during the entire trial to testify, even if some or all of the expert's opinion is based upon the evidence admitted. Rule 703 provides that the opinion may be based upon facts or data "perceived by *or made known to*" the expert.[6] Thus, it is possible for those present at trial to "brief" the expert on what has transpired in the trial.

Rule 1006 provides the authority for using a summary expert witness. This Rule provides that "voluminous writings, recordings, or photographs which cannot conveniently be examined in court may be presented in the form of a chart, summary, or calculation."[7]

The government, almost always, and defendants, sometimes, offer at the conclusion of their cases an expert witness who has been present in the courtroom during the entire trial and is prepared to summarize the evidence in the case concluding with how the evidence supports the income, deductions, adjustments or tax due and owing alleged as existing by the parties.[8] The parties generally are given wide latitude in presenting experts who summarize their evidence.[9] The level of expertise this summary expert witness should possess is a college, or higher, degree in

Fed.R.Evid. 702.

2. Fed.R.Evid. 702 Advisory Committee's Note (*citing* Mason Ladd, *Expert Testimony*, 5 VAND.L.REV. 414, 418 (1952)); *see also* 3 JACK B. WEINSTEIN & MARGARET A. BERGER, WEINSTEIN'S EVIDENCE § 702–2 (1985).

3. *See* Fed.R.Evid. 703.

4. *Id.*

5. *Id.*

6. *Id.* (emphasis added).

7. Fed.R.Evid. 1006. Rule 1006 further provides that "[t]he originals, or dupli-

cates, shall be made available for examination or copying, or both, by other parties at [a] reasonable time or place. The Court may order that they be produced in Court."

8. *See, e.g.*:

Seventh Circuit: United States v. Beall, 970 F.2d 343, 347–48 (7th Cir.1992).

See also:

Fifth Circuit: United States v. West, 58 F.3d 133 (5th Cir.1995); United States v. Charroux, 3 F.3d 827, 833–35 (5th Cir. 1993); United States v. Moore, 997 F.2d 55 (5th Cir.1993).

9. *See, e.g.*, *Moore*, 997 F.2d at 57–58

accounting or other comparable financial training. Government experts typically are IRS agents with additional experience as an IRS agent, including IRS income tax courses.[10]

The parties must offer their experts for the proper reasons, that is, to summarize or interpret evidence on which they have expertise. *United States v. Benson*[11] demonstrates this. In this case, Benson was convicted of willfully failing to file income tax returns and tax evasion. One issue was whether Benson was entitled to both the Social Security benefits he received and the income he received for alleged services rendered since if he was able to work, he was not disabled within Social Security guidelines. The defendant claimed that the money he received was not payment for services rendered but was settlement of a dispute.[12] The government's expert witness not only summarized the evidence that had been introduced and explained how the government arrived at its figures of alleged failure to file tax returns and tax evasion. This witness also opined that the funds in question were received for services rendered rather than as the settlement of a dispute, thus making the defendant ineligible for the Social Security disability benefits.[13] The United States Court of Appeals for the Seventh Circuit reversed the conviction, holding that the matters testified to by the expert were not within the IRS agent's area of expertise because they involved "no tax law concept" and there was no "accounting principle to explain."[14]

The reported cases reveal that defendants have had more difficulty in presenting expert testimony than has the government. Problems encountered by the defense experts have included the proffered expert's unfamiliarity with the evidence, inappropriate scope of the proffered expert testimony, and lack of relevance of the proffered testimony.

Although FRE 703 permits an expert to give an opinion based on facts or data "perceived by *or made known* to" the expert (emphasis added), reported cases show that using an expert who has not been present in the courtroom for the entire trial risks disqualification of the expert or serious assaults on the expert's credibility. *United States v. Price*[15] demonstrates one defense effort at calling an expert witness which failed, in part, because the expert was unfamiliar with the evidence admitted. Price and Brinson were principal shareholders and officers of Vegetarian Health Society (VHS). Both were convicted of conspiracy and tax evasion charges for failing to report all sales made by VHS.[16] They were allowed to call a certified public accountant, Ira Edelson, as their expert witness. On appeal, the defendants argued that the trial court erred by excluding portions of this witness's testimony as "irrelevant, too general, and likely to confuse the jury."[17] The United States Court of Appeals for the Seventh Circuit affirmed the trial court's

10. *See, e.g.*, United States v. DeClue, 899 F.2d 1465, 1473 (6th Cir.1990).

11. 941 F.2d 598 (7th Cir.1991).

12. *Id.* at 601.

13. *Id.* at 603–04.

14. *Id.* at 605.

15. 995 F.2d 729 (7th Cir.1993).

16. *Id.* at 730.

17. *Id.* at 731.

decision to exclude Edelson's testimony, noting the following difficulties with his testimony.

> [T]he statistics utilized by Edelson related to manufacturers, not a mail order business [VHS was a mail order business]; ... Edelson found no evidence that specific expenditures by Brinson or VHS went to particular VHS purposes; Edelson was not aware that certain payments were allegedly supported by fraudulent invoices and check notations; and Edelson did not know VHS's correct cost of sales figures. The government additionally elicited on cross-examination in front of the jury that Edelson did not know VHS's gross receipts; Edelson did not review all of VHS's checks.[18]

A well-settled rule regarding expert testimony is that experts should not encroach upon the role of the court by offering statements of law.[19] *United States v. Rice*[20] provides an extreme example of an expert attempting to do this. Rice, a CPA, was convicted of subscribing a false income tax return and making a false claim for an income tax refund.[21] At trial, he sought to call an attorney, formerly employed in the Tax Division of the Department of Justice and the Internal Revenue Service, who would testify that:

> [A]s a former prosecutor, he would not have filed a case against Mr. Rice based on the evidence the government had in its possession. Additionally, ... 'in his experience [this case] seems to be replete with error, mistake, confusion and certainly not enough evidence for a jury to convict a man beyond a reasonable doubt.'[22]

The United States Court of Appeals for the Tenth Circuit affirmed the District Court's decision to prevent such testimony, finding that the expert "was ... not called upon to supply specialized knowledge but to speculate and hypothesize."[23] Further, the court noted, "whether [this witness] thought the evidence justified the filing of charges is irrelevant. Guided by proper instructions, the sufficiency of the evidence is for the jury to decide from the facts established at trial."[24]

Although *Rice* is an extreme example, the rule that experts should not encroach on the role of the court in tax cases is easier to state than to apply. In criminal tax fraud cases the legality, or perceived legality, of complex transactions becomes relevant in assessing whether the defendant acted willfully in participating in the tax transaction at issue where the defendant wished to submit expert testimony on the legality of the transactions at issue. As such, expert testimony on the state of the law, or the confusion regarding the law, becomes relevant where the defendant submits such testimony on the issue "of willfulness."[25]

18. *Id.* at 731–32.

19. *See, e.g.,* United States v. Bilzerian, 926 F.2d 1285, 1294 (2d Cir.1991).

20. 52 F.3d 843 (10th Cir.1995).

21. *Id.* at 844.

22. *Id.* at 847.

23. *Id.*

24. *Id.*

25. *See, e.g.,* United States v. Bryan, 896 F.2d 68, 72–73 (5th Cir.1990).

United States v. Klaphake[26] provides an apt example of a court's struggle with this issue. Klaphake, a farmer, entered into a "business trust," allegedly to save on his taxes.[27] According to the government, the business trust "lacked any economic substance and was part of a series of transactions designed to evade income taxes."[28] The defendant proffered an expert who would testify as to the alleged legality of the business trust. The United States Court of Appeals for the Eighth Circuit upheld the district court's decision excluding the expert because "[a]s a general rule, 'questions of law are the subject of the court's instructions and not the subject of expert testimony.' "[29] Even so, the appellate court acknowledged that the expert should be allowed to testify as to matters within his personal knowledge regarding his transactions with the defendants and to introduce a letter from him to the defendants stating that the trusts were legitimate. This way, "the jury was made aware of [this expert's] opinion."[30]

United States v. Bryan,[31] demonstrates another unsuccessful effort by the defense in presenting expert testimony that confusion existed in the tax laws regarding commodities transactions. Through such testimony, the defense hoped to "challenge the willfulness element" required to prove that the defendants aided and assisted in the preparation or presentation of fraudulent tax returns.[32] The United States Court of Appeals for the Fifth Circuit acknowledged that in a closer case such expert testimony may be admissible: "In certain cases uncertainty in the application of the law relative to legitimate commodities straddles might be relevant to the willfulness element of the substantive offenses."[33] In this case, however, the evidence against the defendants overwhelmingly showed that the transactions created by the defendants were "sham transactions lacking a valid business purpose," and thus, held the appellate court, the trial court properly disallowed the testimony.[34]

Library References:

C.J.S. Internal Revenue § 1279–1281.
West's Key No. Digests, Internal Revenue ⇒5294–5306.

§ 23.21   Evidentiary Issues In Tax Cases—Proof of Similar Acts

Federal Rule of Evidence 404(b) provides that courts may admit evidence of bad acts a party (or witness) may have committed other than those alleged in the immediate charges. FRE 404(b) forbids use of evidence of "other crimes, wrongs, or acts . . . to prove the character of a person in order to show action in conformity therewith."[1] Such evidence

26. 64 F.3d 435 (8th Cir.1995).
27. *Id.* at 436.
28. *Id.* at 437.
29. *Id.* at 438 (*citing* United States v. Vreeken, 803 F.2d 1085, 1091 (10th Cir. 1986)).
30. *Id.* at 439.
31. 896 F.2d 68 (5th Cir.1990).

32. *Id.* at 72.
33. *Id.* at 73.
34. *Id.* at 72–73.

§ 23.21

1. Fed.R.Evid. 404(b).

is admissible, however, to show "motive, opportunity, intent, preparation, plan, knowledge, identity, or absence of mistake or accident."[2] All fifty states have adopted a rule of evidence similar to FRE 404(b).[3] Under FRE 404(b) the prosecution may not use such evidence if, upon request by the defendant, it failed to provide "reasonable notice ... of the general nature of any such evidence...."[4]

Because of the type of defense often used in tax fraud cases, namely, that the defendant did not have criminal intent when she committed the act at issue, tax fraud prosecutions are prime candidates for use of extrinsic act evidence. In addition, extrinsic act evidence is widely available in many tax fraud cases because of the many opportunities most taxpayers have for reporting income—these are also opportunities for a taxpayer to make inconsistent statements about income, expenses and other financial information which contradict a tax return.[5]

The Supreme Court has provided guidance for admitting Rule 404(b) evidence. In *Huddleston v. United States*,[6] the Court held that similar act evidence is admissible if the evidence is offered for a proper purpose; the evidence is relevant; the probative value of the similar acts evidence is substantially outweighed by its potential for unfair prejudice; and the trial court, upon request, instructs the jury that the similar acts evidence is to be considered only for the limited purpose for which it was admitted.[7]

The reported cases reveal a large variety in the type of similar act evidence admitted in tax fraud prosecutions. Most common is admission of additional examples of the same type of conduct charged. For example, in *United States v. Ayers*, the Ninth Circuit held that evidence that the defendant concealed large amounts of cash was admissible because it was "highly probative of an intent to defraud the United States in the collection of income taxes," and the defendant had been charged with conspiracy to defraud the United States in the collection of income taxes in violation of 18 U.S.C. § 371.[8] *United States v. Kallin*[9] demonstrates another approach aside from reliance on 404(b), which also permits introduction of other "bad acts." During Kallin's trial, the government was allowed to introduce evidence regarding falsity in corporate tax returns which had not been included in the indictment because the statute of limitations had run. These returns were, however, alleged to be false in the same manner as the returns charged in the case.[10] The United States Court of Appeals for the Ninth Circuit held that the evidence was admissible, not as proof of similar acts, but as proof of the

2. *Id.*

3. See 2 Jack B. Weinstein & Margaret A. Berger, Weinstein's Evidence § 404[21] (1985), for a detailed discussion of the rules in the various states compared to FRE 404(b).

4. FRE 404(b).

5. *See, e.g.,* United States v. Alker, 260 F.2d 135, 144 (3d Cir.1958).

6. 485 U.S. 681, 691–92, 108 S.Ct. 1496, 1502, 99 L.Ed.2d 771 (1988).

7. *Id.*

8. *See* United States v. Ayers, 924 F.2d 1468, 1471–73 (9th Cir.1991).

9. 50 F.3d 689 (9th Cir.1995).

10. *Id.* at 695.

full scheme for which the defendant had been charged: "Because the challenged returns are inextricably intertwined in the larger scheme, they are not 404(b) evidence and the district court did not err in admitting them."[11]

More unusual is admission of "bad" acts by third parties which may show knowledge on the part of the defendant. In *United States v. Owen*,[12] for example, evidence of conduct by individuals other than the defendant was admitted to demonstrate the defendant's knowledge that political contributions were falsely reported as business expenses on corporate tax returns. Political contributions made by the defendant's wife and employees, as well as an additional corporate tax return which had not been included in the indictment, were admitted as similar act evidence.[13] Despite the defendant's argument that this evidence was highly prejudicial and irrelevant, the appellate court held that the evidence had been properly admitted, agreeing with the District Court that the " 'fact that [the defendant] had structured similar transactions in the past, in conjunction with the totality of evidence in the case, is probative of defendant's plan and/or knowledge in taking the alleged action.' "[14]

Library References:

C.J.S. Internal Revenue § 1279.
West's Key No. Digests, Internal Revenue ⟜5294.

§ 23.22   Evidentiary Issues In Tax Cases—Use of Original Tax Returns

In tax cases a point of contention may well involve a filed tax return: what was included on the return, what was paid as taxes, when payments were made. Unless the parties agree to the contrary, the original tax returns, or certified copies of the original tax returns, should be introduced for the years in question. Federal Rule of Evidence 1002 requires that the original document must be introduced "[t]o provide the content of a writing."[1] For years besides those charged, however, an IRS transcript may be introduced. This transcript, usually a brief (one or a few pages) summary purporting to describe all transactions concerning the taxpayer's liability for the year in question, is available. Some of the notations on this transcript are in code and an IRS code book (a "6209" code book) is necessary to interpret the transcript.[2] Because this code book "contain[s] sensitive and confidential information concerning the IRS's policies and procedures," the government, when introducing a transcript, is not required to turn over copies of the entire code books,

---

11. *Id.* at 696.

12. 15 F.3d 1528 (10th Cir.1994).

13. *Id.* at 1535.

14. *Id.* at 1536.

§ 23.22

1. Fed.R.Evid. 1002; *see also* Charles J. Alexander, *Trial of a Criminal Tax Case,*

U.S. DEP'T OF JUSTICE, TAX DIV., CRIM.TAX MANUAL, 60–16 through–17.

2. *See, e.g.,* United States v. Ryan, 969 F.2d 238, 239 (7th Cir.1992).

only a "redacted version ... containing only those pages necessary to decode the disputed documents."[3]

United States v. Jones,[4] demonstrates use of an IRS transcript. Jones was convicted for failing to file federal income tax returns for the calendar years 1984 through 1986. An IRS transcript was introduced for the year 1982. The United States Court of Appeals for the Second Circuit rejected the defendant's argument that the original 1982 return, instead of the transcript, should have been introduced.[5] At trial the defendant argued "that she did not file her tax returns from 1984 through 1987 because she believed that a taxpayer could not file a return without paying taxes due."[6] In 1982, however, as shown by the 1982 IRS transcript, the defendant had done exactly that—she filed her return without paying taxes and later made payments on her tax liability.[7] Finding that the transcript was not introduced to prove the content of the 1982 return, the court affirmed the use of the transcript.[8]

The Second Circuit's opinion regarding the foundation that must be laid to introduce an IRS transcript is helpful. The Court held that it was not necessary for the witness testifying about the transcript to verify its accuracy or be the original compiler of the information. Citing Federal Rule of Evidence 803(8), the court noted that public records and reports are deemed admissible without verification as to their accuracy unless the report appears untrustworthy.[9]

Library References:

C.J.S. Internal Revenue § 1279.
West's Key No. Digests, Internal Revenue ⊕5294.

§ 23.23 Evidentiary Issues In Tax Cases—Introduction of Official Records by the Defense

Especially in tax protestor cases, the defendant may seek to introduce court opinions, portions of the Congressional record, and other official records, such as copies of the United States Constitution.[1] In

3. *Id.* at 239 n.5.

4. 958 F.2d 520 (2d Cir.1992).

5. *Id.*

6. *Id.* at 521.

7. *Id.*

8. *Id.* The court noted that the defendant contested the scenario reflected on the transcript, arguing that the payments shown were not a payment on taxes but were to remedy a miscalculation on her 1982 return. Recognizing that the defendant's argument "put the content of the return in issue," the court nevertheless held that this did not require production of the original return.

This reasoning seems problematic. When a substantial question is raised about whether a prior tax history which is accu-

rately or completely portrayed on the transcript and the inaccuracy is relevant to an issue in the case, such as the defendant's explanation for her alleged criminal conduct, it appears that admission of the transcript is inappropriate. This is especially true since the courts do not require that the witness testifying about the transcript verify its accuracy.

9. *Id.; see also* Charles J. Alexander, *Trial of a Criminal Tax Case,* U.S. DEP'T OF JUSTICE, TAX DIV., CRIM.TAX MANUAL, 60–62, 1994 ed.

§ 23.23

1. *See, e.g.:*

First Circuit: United States v. Lussier, 929 F.2d 25, 31 (1st Cir.1991).

See also:

these instances, the defendant generally argues that he made a good faith mistake and that such evidence is "relevant to show the sincerity of his good faith belief that he need not file a tax return."[2] These defendants almost always rely on *United States v. Cheek*[3] as requiring admission of such records for this purpose. In *Cheek*, the Supreme Court held that the trial court erred when it instructed the jury to disregard evidence that the defendant had a good faith misunderstanding of the tax laws.[4]

Some courts appear willing to admit such evidence: "Since the critical element in a tax case is often the defendant's mental state, many courts have given the accused 'wide latitude' in the introduction of evidence which may tend to show a lack of willfulness or specific intent."[5] *United States v. Gaumer*[6] is typical of this view. The United States Court of Appeals for the Sixth Circuit reversed the convictions of Gaumer for failing to file federal income tax returns for 1983, 1984 and 1985 because the trial court refused to permit Gaumer to introduce three court opinions. At trial Gaumer explained why he wished to introduce the records: " 'since ... one of the issues in the crime is willfulness, it's important that the jury be able to know that I relied upon this information.' "[7] Citing *Cheek*, the Sixth Circuit held that although the trial court was not required to permit the physical introduction of hundreds of pages of exhibits, "[a]t a minimum, however, defendant Gaumer should have been allowed to read relevant excerpts to the jury."[8] Noting that "[a]s a legal matter, the exhibits do not validate Mr. Gaumer's views," the court nevertheless found that "[a]s a factual matter ... we think a jury might have discerned a nexus between these materials and Mr. Gaumer's stated belief that he was not required to file income tax returns."[9]

Other courts have been unsympathetic to defendants' arguments that such evidence was improperly excluded from trial, finding, variously, that the evidence would be "unduly confusing" to the jury, that failure to admit such evidence was harmless error,[10] and that there was insufficient foundation laid for the records to show that the defendant actually reviewed and relied upon such records at the time he decided not to file tax returns.[11]

Library References:

C.J.S. Internal Revenue § 1279.
West's Key No. Digests, Internal Revenue ⟡5294.

Sixth Circuit: United States v. Gaumer, 972 F.2d 723, 724–25 (6th Cir.1992).

Tenth Circuit: United States v. Willie, 941 F.2d 1384, 1391 (10th Cir.1991).

2. *Willie*, 941 F.2d at 1391.

3. 498 U.S. 192, 111 S.Ct. 604, 112 L.Ed.2d 617 (1991).

4. 498 U.S. at 203, 111 S.Ct. 611. See § 20.03 *supra*.

5. *Lussier*, 929 F.2d at 31 (*citing* United States v. Sternstein, 596 F.2d 528, 530 (2d Cir.1979)).

6. 972 F.2d 723 (6th Cir.1992).

7. *Id.* at 724.

8. *Id.* at 725.

9. *Id.*

10. *See, e.g., Willie*, 941 F.2d at 1398.

11. *See, e.g., Lussier*, 929 F.2d at 31.

§ 23.24   Evidentiary Issues In Tax Cases—Charts

Charts summarizing evidence are almost a necessity in a criminal tax case for both sides. From the government's perspective, if a jury cannot understand the evidence, they cannot and should not convict. Charts summarizing complex or tedious evidence can help make the government's case clearer. From the defense perspective, especially when the defense challenges specific allegations of proof made by the government, charts are essential if the defense hopes to persuade the jury that its version of the facts, rather than the government's, should be accepted.

Federal Rule of Evidence 1006 provides broad support for using charts during trials. It states that:

> The contents of voluminous writings ... which cannot conveniently be examined in court may be presented in the form of a chart, summary, or calculation. The originals, or duplicates, shall be made available for examination or copying, or both, by other parties at a reasonable time and place. The court may order that they be produced in court.[1]

Charts introduced into evidence must accurately summarize the evidence in the case[2] and contain no "partisan" headings or designations.[3] *United States v. Lawhon*[4] demonstrates this. Lawhon was charged with tax evasion for commingling monies received from his children's orange groves with his own funds. Although Lawhon occasionally purchased certificates of deposits for his children and wrote checks to cover their personal expenses from the monies received from their groves, only a fraction of these payments were reported by the children on their respective income tax returns.[5] The Government presented a chart at trial listing all amounts which the Government recognized as allowable reductions from the defendant's fruit receipts.[6] The Fifth Circuit held that the use of the summary chart was proper:

> [T]he primary evidence on which the chart was based was available for testing the accuracy of the summary; the agent who prepared the chart was available for cross-examination; and the jury was properly instructed that the chart was merely to aid in understanding the underlying documents and records.[7]

---

§ 23.24

1. Fed.R.Evid. 1006; *see also* Charles J. Alexander, *Trial of a Criminal Tax Case*, U.S. Dep't' of Justice, Tax Div., Crim.Tax Manual, 60–92 through–98, 1994 ed. (discussing use of summaries and schedules).

2. *See, e.g.*, United States v. Lawhon, 499 F.2d 352, 356 (5th Cir.1974), *cert. denied*, 419 U.S. 1121, 95 S.Ct. 804, 42 L.Ed.2d 820 (1975).

3. An example of a "partisan" heading is titling a chart *Defendant's Illegal Income*. A more appropriate title would be *Defendant's Income*.

4. *Fifth Circuit*: 499 F.2d 352 (5th Cir.1974).

See also:

Second Circuit: United States v. Conlin, 551 F.2d 534, 538–39 (2d Cir.1977).

Eighth Circuit: United States v. Orlowski, 808 F.2d 1283, 1289 (8th Cir.1986).

5. *Id.* at 354.

6. *Id.* at 354–55.

7. *Id.* at 357. The Court did note, however, that a "more neutral term" than "Computation of Fruit Income" as a cap-

Library References:

C.J.S. Internal Revenue § 1279.

West's Key No. Digests, Internal Revenue ⊙⇒5294.

§ 23.25   Sentencing—Costs of Prosecution

Defendants convicted of tax fraud are required by statute to pay the "costs of prosecution."[1] This is a mandatory portion of a sentence upon conviction.[2] Assessment of costs of prosecution against the losing party is discretionary after judgment in a civil tax action.[3]

None of the tax offenses specify which costs are to be included so courts regularly turn to 28 U.S.C. § 1920 for guidance.[4] Section 1920 applies to "any court of the United States" and includes the following list of costs to be assessed:

    (1)   Fees of the clerk and marshal;

    (2)   Fees of the court reporter for all or any part of the stenographic transcript necessarily obtained for use in the case;

    (3)   Fees and disbursements for printing and witnesses;

    (4)   Fees for exemplification and copies of papers necessarily obtained for use in the case;

    (5)   Docket fees under section 1923 of this title;

    (6)   Compensation of court appointed experts; compensation of interpreters, and salaries, fees, expenses, and costs of special interpretation services under section 1828 of this title.[5]

Courts have held that even though government witnesses, including agents who may have worked on the case, may not be paid a witness fee, their expenses may be assessed against a convicted defendant under this section.[6]

The Circuits disagree as to whether assessment of costs upon conviction of tax offenses is mandatory for a defendant who has been

tion for the chart would have been preferable.

§ 23.25

1. *See* 26 U.S.C. § 7201 (tax evasion); 26 U.S.C. § 7202 (failure to pay tax); 26 U.S.C. § 7203 (failure to file); 26 U.S.C. § 7206(1) (fraud and false statement); 26 U.S.C. § 7206(2) (aid or assist); 26 U.S.C. § 7206(4) (removal or concealment with intent to defraud).

2. *Eighth Circuit:* United States v. Wyman, 724 F.2d 684, 688 (8th Cir.1984).

See also:

Ninth Circuit: United States v. Chavez, 627 F.2d 953 (9th Cir.1980).

3. *Seventh Circuit:* United States v. Dunkel, 900 F.2d 105, 108 (7th Cir.1990),

vacated on other grounds, 498 U.S. 1043, 111 S.Ct. 747, 112 L.Ed.2d 768 (1991).

Eighth Circuit: United States v. May, 67 F.3d 706 (8th Cir.1995); United States v. Hiland, 909 F.2d 1114, 1141–42 (8th Cir. 1990).

4. *See United States v. Dunkel,* 900 F.2d 105 (7th Cir.1990), *on remand,* 927 F.2d 955 (1991).

5. 28 U.S.C. § 1920.

6. *Dunkel,* 900 F.2d at 108. Fees paid to government experts may not be taxed under 28 U.S.C. § 1920, but fees paid to court appointed experts may be assessed under 28 U.S.C. § 1920. *May,* 67 F.3d at 708.

declared indigent for purposes of appointment of counsel. Citing the statutory language, the United States Court of Appeals for the Seventh Circuit has held that the assessment is mandatory.[7] This court found the following language significant: "Any person [convicted of a crime under this section] *shall* be fined not more than $100,000 ($500,000 in the case of a corporation), imprisoned not more than five years, or both, *together with the costs of prosecution.*"[8] The Seventh Circuit noted the difference in this language and in other statutory provisions in which the assessment of costs is clearly discretionary. Section 1918(b) of title 28, U.S.C., for example, provides: "[w]henever any conviction for any offense not capital is obtained in a district court, the court *may* order that the defendant pay the costs of prosecution."[9]

Other circuits disagree, reasoning that assessment of costs is analogous to assessment of a fine, which is not assessed against an indigent person.[10]

Library References:

C.J.S. Internal Revenue § 1285.
West's Key No. Digests, Internal Revenue ⏝5319.

§ 23.26 Sentencing—Restitution

The Sentencing Guidelines require that restitution shall be ordered in accordance with 18 U.S.C. § 3663.[1] Section 3663 provides that the "court ... may order that the defendant make restitution to any victim" and "may also order restitution ... to the extent agreed to by the parties in a plea agreement."[2] Under § 3663(d), however, "the court may decline to make such an order" if the court "determines that the complication and prolongation of the sentencing process resulting from the fashioning of an order of restitution ... outweighs the need to provide restitution to any victims."[3] Restitution may not be ordered for any amount beyond what was at issue in the criminal case. The Supreme Court's decision in *Hughey v. United States,*[4] indicates that restitution should be limited to the loss actually suffered as a result of the criminal acts.[5] In *Hughey,* the Court held that the "loss caused by the conduct underlying the offense of conviction establishes the outer limit of a restitution order."[6] According to the United States Court of Appeals for the Sixth Circuit, restitution under the Sentencing Guidelines is appropriate as to any amount of tax liability for which the defendant was

---

7. United States v. Jungels, 910 F.2d 1501, 1503–04 (7th Cir.1990).

8. *Id.* at 1503–04 (emphasis in original).

9. *Id.* at 1504 (emphasis in original).

10. *See May,* 67 F.3d at 708; United States v. Bauer, 19 F.3d 409, 412–13 (8th Cir.1994).

§ 23.26

1. *See* U.S.S.G. § 5E1.1.

2. 18 U.S.C. 3663(a) (1994).

3. *Id.* § 3663(d).

4. 495 U.S. 411, 110 S.Ct. 1979, 109 L.Ed.2d 408 (1990).

5. *Id.* at 418 (construing the restitution provisions of the Victim and Witness Protection Act of 1982 (VWPA), 18 U.S.C. §§ 3579, 3580 (1982 ed.), recodified and currently appearing as 18 U.S.C. §§ 3663, 3664 (1994)).

6. 495 U.S. at 420, 110 S.Ct. 1984.

convicted.[7] Thus, according to the Sixth Circuit, restitution under the Sentencing Guidelines for back taxes should be assessed as the amount determined as due in the criminal matter and not for additional "civil liabilities."[8]

Library References:
> C.J.S. Internal Revenue § 1285.
> West's Key No. Digests, Internal Revenue ⊕5319.

§ 23.27   Sentencing—Collateral Consequences

Tax fraud epitomizes one of the differences between street crime and white collar crime, namely, the existence of civil and administrative sanctions which track criminal sanctions. This means at least two things for the taxpayers targeted for criminal prosecution. First, with viable administrative and civil sanctions available, it may be easier to convince prosecutors not to pursue a case criminally. Prosecutors' resources are limited and pursuing one criminal case means others will not be pursued because of the lack of resources. When a defendant is subject to civil liability, which makes victims whole, or is subject to administrative liability, which forces the defendant to make changes in its business practices, it may be possible to convince a prosecutor to forego criminal prosecution.

In addition, the existence of civil and administrative remedies which track criminal offenses means that evidence obtained in civil or administrative proceedings may become available in the criminal prosecution. For example, whenever a taxpayer discusses a matter in the administrative, civil, or simply audit stage, the statements made can be used later to prosecute the taxpayer. During these pre-criminal stages, there may be nothing to alert a taxpayer of this potential use in any subsequent criminal action. Almost certainly there will be no advice of rights as required under *Miranda* since the taxpayer will not be in custody. Moreover, there may be nothing to alert a taxpayer that criminal charges are even a possibility when the IRS uses summonses to obtain records.[1] Although a taxpayer may, at a civil or administrative proceeding, invoke her right not to incriminate herself and thus seek to protect herself from subsequent criminal prosecution, the fact finder in the administrative or civil proceeding will be entitled to draw an adverse inference from the failure to testify.[2]

The outcome in the criminal proceeding may also affect the civil or administrative proceeding in the form of collateral estoppel. Collateral

---

7. United States v. Daniel, 956 F.2d 540, 543–44 (6th Cir.1992).

8. *Id.* at 544.

§ 23.27

1. *See:*

Supreme Court: United States v. Powell, 379 U.S. 48, 57–58, 85 S.Ct. 248, 255, 13 L.Ed.2d 112 (1964).

Seventh Circuit: United States v. Jungels, 910 F.2d 1501, 1503 (7th Cir.1990); United States v. Gimbel, 782 F.2d 89, 93 (7th Cir.1986).

2. Baxter v. Palmigiano, 425 U.S. 308, 318, 96 S.Ct. 1551, 1558, 47 L.Ed.2d 810 (1976).

estoppel bars relitigation of an issue previously decided if the party against whom the prior decision is asserted had a "full and fair opportunity" to litigate that issue in an earlier case.[3] In most jurisdictions the following four elements must exist for collateral estoppel to apply: (1) the issue was actually litigated in the first proceeding, (2) the first proceeding resulted in a valid and final judgment, (3) resolution of the issue was essential to the judgment rendered in the first proceeding, and (4) the issue in the second proceeding must be identical to the issue in the first proceeding.[4]

Thus, if a taxpayer is convicted of criminal charges, the conviction almost certainly will prevent the taxpayer from contesting civil liability for taxes due on the same facts or from contesting assessment of tax fraud penalties.[5] The civil fraud penalty is particularly steep (currently equal to 50% of the underpayment attributable to fraud).[6] *Blohm v. CIR*,[7] demonstrates this. Blohm entered an *Alford* plea to tax evasion charges.[8] Shortly thereafter the Commissioner issued the Blohms a notice of deficiency of $133,749 plus another $119,725 as a fraud penalty under 26 U.S.C. § 6653(b).[9] The Tax Court upheld the assessments, holding that Blohm was estopped from denying liability because of his *Alford* plea.[10] The United States Court of Appeals for the Eleventh Circuit affirmed, dismissing Blohm's argument that an *Alford* plea is analogous to a plea of *nolo contendere* and thus has no collateral estoppel effect in a subsequent civil proceeding.[11] The court found it irrelevant whether a guilty plea is accompanied by a plea of innocence: "A guilty plea's basic chemistry is not transformed by a concurrent claim of innocence. The collateral consequences stemming from a guilty plea

3. *See* Allen v. McCurry, 449 U.S. 90, 94–95, 101 S.Ct. 411, 415, 66 L.Ed.2d 308 (1980); Ashe v. Swenson, 397 U.S. 436, 90 S.Ct. 1189, 25 L.Ed.2d 469 (1970).

4. *See*

Supreme Court: *Swenson*, 397 U.S. at 443.

See also:

Eleventh Circuit: In re Raiford, 695 F.2d 521, 523 (11th Cir.1983).

5. *See, e.g.*:

First Circuit: Manzoli v. CIR, 904 F.2d 101, 105 (1st Cir.1990).

Eleventh Circuit: Blohm v. C.I.R., 994 F.2d 1542, 1554 (11th Cir.1993).

6. 26 U.S.C. § 6653.

7. 994 F.2d 1542 (11th Cir.1993).

8. *Id.* at 1546. "In *Alford* the Supreme Court addressed the question of whether an express admission of guilt is required before a court may impose sentence upon a defendant who pleads guilty but nonetheless maintains his or her innocence. The defendant in *Alford* pled guilty

to murder, but maintained his innocence. During his arraignment, Alford denied committing the crime, but elected to plead guilty to avoid the death penalty should he be convicted at trial. The Supreme Court affirmed the conviction and the imposition of the sentence, holding that

[w]hile most pleas of guilty consist of both a waiver of trial and an express admission of guilt, the latter element is not a constitutional prerequisite to the imposition of a criminal penalty. An individual accused of crime may voluntarily, knowingly, and understandably consent to the imposition of a prison sentence if he is unwilling or unable to admit his participation in the acts constituting the crime."

Id. at 1546 n.6 (11th Cir.1993) (*citing* North Carolina v. Alford, 400 U.S. 25, 37, 91 S.Ct. 160, 167, 27 L.Ed.2d 162 (1970)).

9. *Id.* at 1547.

10. *Id.* at 1548.

11. *Id.* at 1553–54.

remain the same whether or not accompanied by an assertion of innocence."[12]

§ 23.28 Venue

The Sixth Amendment to the United States Constitution provides
that "an accused in a criminal prosecution has the right to be tried in
the district wherein the crime shall have been committed."[1] "The test
[for venue] is best described as a substantial contacts rule that takes into
account a number of factors—the site of the defendant's acts, the
elements and nature of the crime, the locus of the effect of the criminal
conduct, and the suitability of each district for accurate factfinding."[2]
The government bears the burden of proving venue, but because venue
is not an essential element of the offense, it need not be established
beyond a reasonable doubt. Proof by a preponderance of the evidence is
sufficient.[3] If lack of venue is apparent from the face of the indictment or
information but is not raised by the defendant, it is waived.[4] If the venue
defect is not apparent until the government presents its case, the
objection is waived if not raised by the defendant at the close of the
government's case.[5]

Any offense, including tax fraud offenses, may be prosecuted in any
district in which the offense began, continued or was completed.[6] Section
3237 of title 18, United States Code, provides:

> [A]ny offense against the United States begun in one district and
> completed in another, or committed in more than one district, may
> be inquired of and prosecuted in any district in which such offense
> was begun, continued, or completed.[7]

---

12. *Id.* at 1555.

§ 23.28

1. U.S. Const. amend. VI; *see also*
U.S. Const., art. III, § 2; Fed.R.Crim.P. 18.

2. United States v. Reed, 773 F.2d
477, 481 (2d Cir.1985).

3. *Second Circuit*: United States v.
Maldonado–Rivera, 922 F.2d 934, 968 (2d
Cir.1990).

Fourth Circuit: United States v. Griley,
814 F.2d 967, 973 (4th Cir.1987).

Seventh Circuit: United States v. Netz,
758 F.2d 1308, 1311 (8th Cir.1985).

4. United States v. Black Cloud, 590
F.2d 270, 272 (8th Cir.1979).

5. *Id.*

6. *See, e.g.*:

Second Circuit: United States v. Slutsky, 487 832, 839 (2d Cir.1973).

Eighth Circuit: United States v. Mar-
chant, 774 F.2d 888, 891 (8th Cir.1985).

See generally U.S. Dep't of Justice, Tax
Div., Crim.Tax Manual, § 6.01–6.04, 1994
ed., for discussion of venue in criminal tax
cases.

7. 18 U.S.C. § 3237(a) (1994). There
is, however, a special provision for venue in
tax prosecutions when venue is based solely
on a mailing:

> [W]here venue for prosecution of an of-
> fense described in section 7201 ... is
> based solely on a mailing to the Internal
> Revenue Service, and prosecution is be-
> gun in a judicial district other than the
> judicial district in which the defendant
> resides, he may upon motion filed in the
> district in which the prosecution is be-
> gun, elect to be tried in the district in
> which he was residing at the time the
> alleged offense was committed. *Id.*

It is required that the motion for a change
in venue be filed within twenty days after
arraignment of the defendant upon indictment or information. *Id.*

Taxpayers have no right to be tried in any particular district for which there is venue,[8] however, the Department of Justice policy is "to generally attempt to establish venue for a criminal tax prosecution in the judicial district of the taxpayer's residence or principal place of business. . . ."[9]

Applying these rules, when a taxpayer is being prosecuted for filing false tax returns, she may be prosecuted in any venue where she prepared, signed, mailed or filed a false tax return,[10] or where her preparer, at the taxpayer's instruction, received information from the taxpayer or worked on the false tax return.[11]

In tax evasion cases, a taxpayer may be prosecuted "in any district where an affirmative act constituting an 'attempt to evade' was begun, continued or completed."[12] As noted in section 23.2 *supra*, the Supreme Court has held that the affirmative act requirement should be read broadly. Thus, in *United States v. Strawberry*,[13] where the professional baseball player, Darryl Strawberry, was convicted of income tax evasion, the court held that Strawberry's receipt of cash in a district gave venue over prosecution for the offense in that district even though Strawberry neither resided nor had a principal place of business in the district.[14] Other affirmative acts sufficient to establish venue include filing of the tax return;[15] preparing or signing of the tax return;[16] filing, preparing or signing a false W–4 form;[17] making a false statement to an IRS agent;[18] concealing assets.[19]

Section 3237(b) ameliorates, somewhat, the broad authority given to the government to choose venue in tax evasion prosecutions brought under 26 U.S.C. § 7201. It provides that where prosecution is based solely on a mailing to the IRS, a defendant charged under this offense has the right to remove his or her case to the district where the defendant resides.[20]

8. *In re Chesson*, 897 F.2d 156, 158 (5th Cir.1990).

9. U.S. Dept. Of Justice, U.S. Attorney's Manual, § 6.01[2].

10. *Second Circuit*: United States v. Slutsky, 487 F.2d 832, 839 (2d Cir.1973).

Seventh Circuit: United States v. Marrinson, 832 F.2d 1465, 1475 (7th Cir.1987).

11. *Second Circuit*: United States v.Rooney, 866 F.2d 28, 31 (2d Cir.1989).

Eighth Circuit: United States v. Humphreys, 982 F.2d 254, 260 (8th Cir.1992).

12. United States v. Strawberry, 892 F.Supp. 519 (S.D.N.Y.1995) (citing United States v. Slutsky, 487 F.2d 832, 839 (2d Cir.1973)).

13. 892 F.Supp. 519 (S.D.N.Y.1995).

14. 892 F.Supp. at 522–24.

15. *Second Circuit*: United States v. King, 563 F.2d 559, 562 (2d Cir.1977).

Fifth Circuit: Holbrook v. United States, 216 F.2d 238 (5th Cir.1954).

16. *King*, 563 F.2d at 562; United States v. Marrinson, 832 F.2d 1465, 1475 (7th Cir.1987).

17. United States v. Felak, 831 F.2d 794, 798–99 (8th Cir.1987).

18. United States v. Goodyear, 649 F.2d 226, 228 (4th Cir.1981).

19. *Fourth Circuit*: Beaty v. United States, 213 F.2d 712, 715 (4th Cir.1954), *vacated and remanded*, 348 U.S. 905, 75 S.Ct. 312, 99 L.Ed. 710, *reaff'd*, 220 F.2d 681 (4th Cir.1955).

Fifth Circuit: Reynolds v. United States, 225 F.2d 123, 128 (5th Cir.1955).

20. 18 U.S.C. § 3237(b).

In failure to file cases, venue lies in any jurisdiction in which a taxpayer is required to file.[21] Title 26 U.S.C., Section 6091(b) provides that individual tax returns should be filed where the taxpayer resides or has his principal place of business, or at the IRS Service Center serving these locations.[22]

Library References:

C.J.S. Internal Revenue § 1273.
West's Key No. Digests, Internal Revenue ☞5280.

§ 23.29 Statute of Limitations

The statute of limitations for the following criminal tax offenses is six years: 26 U.S.C. §§ 7201, 7202,[1] 7203, 7206(1) and (2), 7207. The statute of limitations for the following criminal tax offenses is three years: 26 U.S.C. §§ 7203, 7205.[2]

The statute of limitations does not begin to run until the underlying crime has been committed.[3] In prosecutions for filing false tax returns,

21. United States v. Rice, 659 F.2d 524, 526 (5th Cir.1981); United States v. Quimby, 636 F.2d 86, 89 (5th Cir.1981).

22. Treas. Reg. § 1.6091–2 (26 C.F.R.). There are some exceptions for individuals residing outside the United States, and for those who are present in the United States but have no legal residence or place of business. Treas. Reg. § 1.6091–2(a)(1) (26 C.F.R.), § 1.6091–3(b) (26 C.F.R.).

§ 23.29

1. The Courts of Appeals disagree about the statute of limitations for § 7202 offenses. The Second and Tenth Circuits hold that a six-year statute of limitations period applies. United States v. Musacchia, 900 F.2d 493, 500 (2d Cir.1990). United States v. Porth, 426 F.2d 519, 521–22 (10th Cir.1970). At least one district court has held that a three-year limitations period applies. United States v. Block, 497 F.Supp. 629, 630–32 (N.D.Ga.), aff'd, 660 F.2d 1086 (5th Cir.1981). The Tax Division takes the position that the Second and Tenth Circuits are correct, and that the six-year limitations period under 26 U.S.C. § 6531(4) applies to section 7202.

2. See 26 U.S.C. § 6531 (1994); see also U.S. DEP'T OF JUSTICE, TAX DIV., CRIM.TAX MANUAL, § 7.01–7.05, 1994 ed., for a discussion of the statute of limitations in criminal tax cases. Section 6531 provides:

No person shall be prosecuted, tried, or punished for any of the various offenses arising under the internal revenue laws unless the indictment is found or the information instituted within 3 years next after the commission of the offense,

except that the period of limitation shall be 6 years—

(1) for offenses involving the defrauding or attempting to defraud the United States or any agency thereof, whether by conspiracy or not, and in any manner;

(2) for the offense of willfully attempting in any manner to evade or defeat any tax or the payment thereof;

(3) for the offense of willfully aiding or assisting in ... the preparation or presentation ... of a false or fraudulent return;

(4) for the offense of willfully failing to pay any tax, or make any return ... at the time or times required by law or regulations;

(5) for offenses described in sections 7206(1) and 7207 (relating to false statements and fraudulent documents);

(6) for the offense described in section 7212(a) (relating to intimidation of officers and employees of the United States);

. . .

(8) for offenses arising under section 371 of Title 18 of the United States Code, where the object of the conspiracy is to attempt in any manner to evade or defeat any tax or the payment thereof.

26 U.S.C. § 6531.

3. See United States v. Habig, 390 U.S. 222, 225, 88 S.Ct. 926, 928, 19 L.Ed.2d 1055 (1968).

the statute of limitations begins to run on the date the false tax return is filed even if the return is filed late. If the tax return is filed early, the statute of limitations begins running on the day the return was due.[4] In prosecutions for failure to file required tax returns, the statute of limitations begins to run when the return is due.[5] If an extension is sought and granted, the statute of limitations begins to run on the extension date.[6] In prosecutions for tax evasion the statute of limitations begins to run on the date the last affirmative act took place, or the date on which the return was due, whichever is later.[7] In prosecutions under 18 U.S.C. § 371 for conspiracy to evade taxes, pursuant to 26 U.S.C. § 6531(8),[8] the statute of limitations begins to run from the last overt act proven.[9]

Library References:

> C.J.S. Internal Revenue § 1274.
> West's Key No. Digests, Internal Revenue ☞5281.

§ 23.30 Bibliography

Alexander, Charles J., *Trial of a Criminal Tax Case*, U.S. DEP'T OF JUSTICE, TAX DIV., CRIM. TAX MANUAL, 1994.

AUDIT GUIDELINES FOR EXAMINERS, [1 AUDIT] INTERNAL REVENUE MANUAL (CCH) 7247–35 (Apr. 23, 1981).

DEVITT, EDWARD, ET AL., FEDERAL JURY PRACTICE AND INSTRUCTIONS: CIVIL AND CRIMINAL (1992).

Goldstein, Abraham, *Conspiracy to Defraud the United States*, 68 YALE L.J. 405 (1959).

Knight, Ray A., and Knight, Lee G., *Criminal Tax Fraud: An Analytical Review*, 50 MO.L.REV. 175 (1992).

Kuhns, Richard B., *The Propensity to Misunderstand the Character of Specific Acts Evidence*, 66 IOWA L.REV. 777 (1981).

Ladd, Mason, *Expert Testimony*, 5 VAND.L.REV. 414 (1952).

MANUAL ON MODEL CRIMINAL JURY INSTRUCTIONS FOR THE DISTRICT COURTS OF THE EIGHTH CIRCUIT (1992).

MANUAL OF MODEL CRIMINAL JURY INSTRUCTIONS FOR THE NINTH CIRCUIT (1992).

---

4. United States v. Habig, 390 U.S. 222, 223–25, 88 S.Ct. 926, 927–928, 19 L.Ed.2d 1055 (1968).

5. United States v. Phillips, 843 F.2d 438, 443 (11th Cir.1988).

6. *Id.* at 442–43.

7. *Supreme Court*: United States v. Beacon Brass Co., 344 U.S. 43, 46, 73 S.Ct. 77, 79, 97 L.Ed. 61 (1952).

Second Circuit: United States v. DiPetto, 936 F.2d 96, 97 (2d Cir.1991).

8. *Second Circuit*: United States v. Aracri, 968 F.2d 1512, 1517 (2d Cir.1992).

Eighth Circuit: United States v. White, 671 F.2d 1126, 1133–34 (8th Cir.1982).

Tenth Circuit: United States v. Brunetti, 615 F.2d 899, 901 (10th Cir.1980).

9. Grunewald v. United States, 353 U.S. 391, 397, 77 S.Ct. 963, 970, 1 L.Ed.2d 931 (1957).

MARCUS, PAUL, PROSECUTION AND DEFENSE OF CRIMINAL CONSPIRACY CASES (1979).

MCCOWEN, DARRELL, CRIMINAL AND CIVIL TAX FRAUD (2d ed.1994).

Reitz, Kevin R., *Sentencing Facts: Travesties of Real Offense Sentencing*, 45 STAN.L.REV. 523 (1993).

Ritholz, Jules, and Kohane, David M., *Supreme Court Finds Subjective Ignorance of the Law a Defense to Criminal Tax Fraud*, 74 J. TAX'N 254 (1991).

Slough, M. C. & Knightly, J. William, *Other Vices, Other Crimes*, 41 IOWA L.REV. 325 (1956).

UNITED STATES DEPARTMENT OF JUSTICE, TAX DIV., CRIM. TAX MANUAL, 1994.

UNITED STATES DEPARTMENT OF JUSTICE, UNITED STATES ATTORNEY MANUAL.

Uviller, H. Richard, *Evidence of Character to Prove Conduct: Illusion, Illogic an Injustice in the Courtroom*, 130 U.PA.L.REV. 845 (1982).

WEINSTEIN, JACK B. & BERGER, MARGARET A., WEINSTEIN'S EVIDENCE (1985).

Weissenberger, Glenn, *Making Sense of Extrinsic Act Evidence: Federal Rule of Evidence* 404(b), 70 IOWA L.REV. 579 (1985).

Wilkins, William W. Jr. & Steer, John R., *Relevant Conduct: The Cornerstone of the Federal Sentencing Guidelines*, 41 S.C.L.Rev. 495 (1990).

Yellen, David, *Illusion, Illogic and Injustice: Real–Offense Sentencing and the Federal Sentencing Guidelines*, 78 MINN.L. REV. 403 (1993).

*

PART III

DEFENSES

CHAPTER 24

ENTRAPMENT AND OUTRAGEOUS GOVERNMENT CONDUCT

Table of Sections

WESTLAW ELECTRONIC RESEARCH

See WESTLAW Electronic Research Guide preceding the Summary of Contents.

---

§ 24.1 Introduction

Entrapment is an affirmative defense based on the idea that the defendant was induced to commit the crime by a government agent. The defense was not recognized by English law nor by early American law.[1] In this century, however, American courts began to accept the defense in a variety of criminal prosecutions.[2] The defense received media attention when it was raised in the "Abscam" cases[3] and in the prosecution of

---

§ 24.1

1. Board of Commissioners v. Backus, 29 How.Pr. 33, 42 (N.Y.Sup.Ct.1864)(Bacon, J.) quoted in Yale Kamisar, et. al., *Modern Criminal Procedure* 399 (8th ed.1994)("Even if inducements to commit crime could be assumed to exist in this case, the allegation of the defendant would be but the repetition of the plea as ancient as the world, and first interposed in Paradise: 'The serpent beguiled me and I did eat.' That defense was overruled by the great Lawgiver, and whatever estimate we may form, or whatever judgment pass upon the character or conduct of the tempter, this plea has never since availed to shield crime

or give indemnity to the culprit, and it is safe to say that under any code of civilized, not to say christian ethics, it never will.").

2. The first federal court recognition of the defense was in Woo Wai v. United States, 223 F. 412 (9th Cir.1915). *See* S.Rep. 97–307 at 118 (1981) for a comprehensive history of the defense in federal courts.

3. In the early 1980's, an FBI investigation involving, among other things, a fictitious Arab corporation interested in offering bribes to United States congressmen, brought widespread public attention to the defense of entrapment offered by the defen-

millionaire John DeLorean.[4] Entrapment remains a common law defense in federal law.[5] The defense is often raised in drug-related offenses,[6] and it has recently been raised in prosecutions for other "victimless" crimes such as receiving child pornography through the mail,[7] bribery,[8] money laundering,[9] and trafficking in food stamps.[10]

The difficulty with the entrapment defense is that government encouragement to commit a crime is not *per se* impermissible; merely setting a trap to ensnare a criminal is not entrapment.[11] As Justice Warren's often repeated test describes it, "To determine whether entrapment has been established, a line must be drawn between the trap for the unwary innocent and the trap for the unwary criminal."[12] The court must evaluate where that line is to be drawn based on the facts of each case by focusing on the individual defendant's predisposition.[13]

dants. *See, e.g.*, United States v. Kelly, 707 F.2d 1460 (D.C.Cir.1983). For analysis of the Abscam cases and a complete list of Abscam case cites, see Maura F.J. Whelan, *Lead Us Not Into (Unwarranted) Temptation: A Proposal to Replace the Entrapment Defense with a Reasonable Suspicion Requirement*, 133 U.Pa.L.Rev. 1193, at n.6 and 1200–03 (1985). *See also* Bennett L. Gersham, *Abscam, The Judiciary, and the Ethics of Entrapment*, 91 Yale L.J. 1565 (1982).

4. John DeLorean was prosecuted in federal court and was acquitted based on the defense of entrapment. The jury was instructed to apply the subjective test for entrapment (discussed more fully below). Apparently, the jurors instead applied an objective test and acquitted him because of their distaste for the government's methods. For a description of that case, see Maura F.J. Whelan, *Lead Us Not Into (Unwarranted) Temptation: A Proposal to Replace the Entrapment Defense with a Reasonable Suspicion Requirement*, 133 U.Pa.L.Rev. 1193, 1197–1200 (1985).

5. *See* S. Rep. 97–307, at 118 (1981). *See also* Michael A. DeFeo, *Entrapment as a Defense to Criminal Responsibility: Its History, Theory, and Application*, 1 U.S.F.L.Rev. 243, 244–52 (1967) and Warren Bennett, *From Sorrells to Jacobson: Reflections on Six Decades of Entrapment Law and Related Defenses in Federal Court*, 27 Wake Forest L.Rev. 829 (1992).

6. *See, e.g.*, United States v. Gonzalez, 19 F.3d 1169, 1172–73 (7th Cir.1994).

7. *See, e.g.*,

Supreme Court: Jacobson v. United States, 503 U.S. 540, 542, 112 S.Ct. 1535, 1537, 118 L.Ed.2d 174 (1992).

First Circuit: United States v. Gendron, 18 F.3d 955, 960 (1st Cir.1994).

8. *See, e.g.*,

Supreme Court: Mathews v. United States, 485 U.S. 58, 59–62, 108 S.Ct. 883, 885–886, 99 L.Ed.2d 54 (1988).

Fifth Circuit: United States v. Sandoval, 20 F.3d 134, 136–39 (5th Cir.1994).

9. *See, e.g.*, United States v. Hollingsworth, 9 F.3d 593, 595–96 (7th Cir.1993), *vacated en banc*, 27 F.3d 1196 (7th Cir.1994).

10. *See, e.g.*, United States v. Eldeeb 20 F.3d 841, 842–43 (8th Cir.1994).

11. United States v. Gendron, 18 F.3d 955, 960 (1st Cir.1994).

12. Sherman v. United States, 356 U.S. 369, 372, 78 S.Ct. 819, 821, 2 L.Ed.2d 848 (1958).

13. Since the focus of the defense is on the defendant's predisposition, not the conduct of the government, merely setting a trap or providing an opportunity to commit a crime is not entrapment. In United States v. Russell, 411 U.S. 423, 93 S.Ct. 1637, 36 L.Ed.2d 366 (1973), the Supreme Court reiterated its holdings in Sorrells v. United States, 287 U.S. 435, 441, 53 S.Ct. 210, 212, 77 L.Ed. 413 (1932) and Sherman v. United States, 356 U.S. 369, 372, 78 S.Ct. 819, 821, 2 L.Ed.2d 848 (1958). " '[Those cases] both recognize that the fact that officers or employees of the Government merely afford opportunities or facilities for the commission of the offense does not defeat the prosecution.... ' Nor will the mere fact of deceit defeat a prosecution, for there are circumstances when the use of deceit is the only practicable law enforcement technique available. It is only when the Government's deception actually implants the criminal design in the mind of the defendant that the defense of entrapment comes into play." 411 U.S. at 435–36, 93 S.Ct. 1644–45 (quoting Sherman v. United States, 356 U.S. 369,

The defense is supported by two rationales. One is that persons should not be held liable for acts they would not have committed without encouragement from a government agent.[14] Another is that the government ought to spend its resources stopping crime rather than encouraging people to commit it.[15] These somewhat conflicting rationales have translated into two definitions of the entrapment defense: the current Federal law and a persistent dissenting view.

A. CURRENT FEDERAL LAW: THE SUBJECTIVE APPROACH

The Supreme Court has always adopted a subjective definition of the entrapment defense.[16] The government must show that the particular defendant was predisposed to commit the offense before and independent of the government's action. The thrust is to avoid conviction when the defendant's original criminal intent was implanted by the government.[17]

78 S.Ct. 819, 2 L.Ed.2d 848 (1958)) (citations omitted).

14. This statement represents the current federal law, discussed *infra*, otherwise referred to as the subjective approach. The most recent Supreme Court ruling on the defense was in 1992 in Jacobson v. United States, 503 U.S. 540, 112 S.Ct. 1535, 118 L.Ed.2d 174 (1992). The majority stated its rationale for the defense: "When the Government's quest for convictions leads to the apprehension of an otherwise law-abiding citizen who, if left to his own devices, likely would have never run afoul of the law, the courts should intervene." Jacobson v. United States, 503 U.S. 540, 553–54, 112 S.Ct. 1535, 1543, 118 L.Ed.2d 174 (1992).

Second Circuit: In United States v. Becker, 62 F.2d 1007, 1009 (2d Cir.1933), Judge Learned Hand described the rationale as: "a spontaneous moral revulsion against using the powers of government to beguile innocent, though ductile, persons into lapses which they might otherwise resist."

15. This statement summarizes the view taken by a minority of the Supreme Court (*see* Mathews v. United States, 485 U.S. 58, 108 S.Ct. 883, 99 L.Ed.2d 54 (1988); United States v. Russell, 411 U.S. 423, 93 S.Ct. 1637, 36 L.Ed.2d 366 (1973); Sherman v. United States, 356 U.S. 369, 78 S.Ct. 819, 2 L.Ed.2d 848 (1958)); by the drafters of the Model Penal Code (*see* § 2.13) and by many states. *See generally* Paul Marcus, *The Entrapment Defense* (2d ed.1995). As described below, it is sometimes called the objective approach. It also encompasses the defense of Outrageous Government Conduct, discussed *infra* in § 24.5. The defense of entrapment is not

envisioned by the Supreme Court as a control on government conduct. United States v. Russell, 411 U.S. 423, 433–34, 93 S.Ct. 1637, 1643–44, 36 L.Ed.2d 366 (1973).

16. Jacobson v. United States, 503 U.S. 540, 548–49, 112 S.Ct. 1535, 1540, 118 L.Ed.2d 174 (1992)(reaffirming the view of the defense first enunciated in *Sorrells,* 298 U.S. at 441, 56 S.Ct. at 768); Mathews v. United States 485 U.S. 58, 62, 108 S.Ct. 883, 99 L.Ed.2d 54 (1988)(reaffirming the view of the defense first enunciated in *Sorrells*); Hampton v. United States, 425 U.S. 484, 488–91, 96 S.Ct. 1646, 1649–50, 48 L.Ed.2d 113 (1976)(plurality opinion)(entrapment is not established where a government agent supplied contraband to a predisposed defendant); United States v. Russell, 411 U.S. 423, 429, 93 S.Ct. 1637, 1641, 36 L.Ed.2d 366 (1973)(rejecting the defense when the defendant was predisposed to commit the crime); Sherman v. United States, 356 U.S. 369, 376, 78 S.Ct. 819, 822–23, 2 L.Ed.2d 848 (1958)(finding entrapment as a matter of law where "[T]he Government plays on the weaknesses of an innocent party and beguiles him into committing crimes which he otherwise would not have attempted")(footnote omitted); and Sorrells v. United States, 287 U.S. 435, 451–52, 53 S.Ct. 210, 216, 77 L.Ed. 413 (1932) (predisposition and criminal design of the defendant are relevant to the "controlling question whether the defendant is a person otherwise innocent whom the government is seeking to punish for an alleged offense which is the product of the creative activity of its own officials").

17. *See, e.g.,* Hampton v. United States, 425 U.S. 484, 488, 96 S.Ct. 1646,

To support this theory, courts have found an implied congressional intent in criminal statutes to avoid conviction of the defendant when the effect of government conduct has been the manufacture of crime.[18] The Supreme Court has consistently insisted that the defense of entrapment does not exist to "give the federal judiciary a 'chancellor's foot veto' over law enforcement practices of which it did not approve."[19] The subjective approach has both supporters and critics.[20]

B. A DISSENTING VIEW: THE OBJECTIVE APPROACH

Early in the development of the defense, a minority of the Supreme Court concluded that the focus of the defense should not be the individual defendant's subjective predisposition to commit the crime, but rather the intrusiveness of the government's conduct. This approach has come to be known as the objective test for entrapment.[21] Under this view, entrapment occurs when an ordinary person would have been enticed to commit the offense by the conduct of the government agent.[22] The main distinction between the dissenters' objective approach and the majority's subjective approach is that predisposition of the defendant is irrelevant under the objective approach while under the subjective approach, it is the key element.[23] The current federal law is that the focus should rest

1649, 48 L.Ed.2d 113 (1976)("In Russell, [w]e reaffirmed the principle of Sorrells v. United States ... and Sherman v. United States ..., that the entrapment defense 'focuses on the intent or predisposition of the defendant to commit the crime,' ... rather than upon the conduct of the Government's agents. We ruled out the possibility that the defense ... could ever be based upon governmental misconduct in a case, such as this one, where the predisposition of the defendant to commit the crime was established.")(citations omitted).

18. The Supreme Court has based its subjective approach on this implied legislative intent. *See, e.g.,* United States v. Russell, 411 U.S. 423, 435, 93 S.Ct. 1637, 1644, 36 L.Ed.2d 366 (1973)("... entrapment is a relatively limited defense. It is rooted, not in any authority of the Judicial Branch to dismiss prosecutions for what it feels to have been 'over zealous law enforcement,' but instead in the notion that Congress could not have intended criminal punishment for a defendant who has committed all the elements of a proscribed offense but was induced to commit them by the government.").

19. *Russell,* 411 U.S. at 435, 93 S.Ct. 1644.

20. For criticism and support of the subjective approach as it has developed in the federal courts, see Paul Marcus, *The Entrapment Defense,* § 2 (2d ed.1995); Louis M. Seidman, *The Supreme Court, En-*

trapment, and Our Criminal Justice Dilemma, 1981 SUP.CT.REV. 111 (1981); and Leslie W. Abramson & Lisa L. Lindeman, *Entrapment and Due Process in the Federal Courts,* 8 AM.J.CRIM.L. 139 (1980).

21. Justice Roberts described an objective test for entrapment in his dissenting opinion in Sorrells v. United States, 287 U.S. 435, 454-55, 53 S.Ct. 210, 217, 77 L.Ed. 413 (1932); Justice Frankfurter labeled the test "as objective a test as the subject matter permits" in his concurrence, joined by Justices Douglas, Harlan, and Brennan, in Sherman v. United States, 356 U.S. 369, 384, 78 S.Ct. 819, 826, 2 L.Ed.2d 848 (1958).

22. *Id.*

23. S.Rep.No. 97-307 at 118 (1981)(footnotes omitted) compares and contrasts the two approaches:

A comparison of the competing views of the entrapment defense as they have emerged ... reveals a considerable area of common ground.... Under either theory, for example, entrapment may result only from governmental inducement; inducement ... by a private person does not establish the defense. Similarly both [approaches] recognize that undercover activity, artifice, stratagem, as well as the mere furnishing of an opportunity or facility to commit an offense, do not constitute unlawful entrapment. Where the two

on the subjective predisposition of the defendant, but opposition to that view remains.[24]

§ 24.2 Elements

The defense has two elements. These elements are 1) the government induced the defendant to commit the offense, and 2) the defendant was not predisposed to commit it.[1] Once the defendant shows govern-

theories differ almost exclusively is on the question whether predisposition of the defendant is an element of the defense. While this difference may result in divergent conclusions being reached as to the availability of the defense in certain factual settings, it is relatively rare for Federal agents to engage in active inducement beyond the level that would cause a normally law-abiding person to be unable to resist commission of an offense.[]

Since, under the [subjective approach] the entrapment defense is not constitutionally rooted but reflects a judicial determination of Congress' implicit intent in enacting penal statutes not to entrap individuals, it follows that Congress may ... construe certain statutes ... as not allowing the defense.

24. For example, Model Penal Code § 2.13 adopted the objective approach to the entrapment defense. Subsection (1) provides that the defense is available when a law enforcement official or person acting in cooperation with such an official induces or encourages another person to engage in conduct constituting an offense by either "(a) making knowingly false representations designed to induce the belief that such conduct is not prohibited; or (b) employing methods of persuasion or inducement that create a substantial risk that such an offense will be committed by persons other than those who are ready to commit it." Subsection (2) states that "The defendant shall be acquitted if he proves by a preponderance of evidence that his conduct occurred in response to an entrapment. The issue of entrapment shall be tried by the Court in the absence of the jury." Subsection (3) disallows the defense where "causing or threatening bodily injury is an element of the offense charged ..." and the defendant causes or threatens bodily injury to someone other than the official who perpetrates the entrapment. For rationale, historical analysis, and procedural implica-

tions of this section, see Comment, Model Penal Code, § 2.13.

For support and criticism of the objective approach and a comparison to the subjective approach, see Warren Bennett, *From Sorrells to Jacobson: Reflections on Six Decades of Entrapment Law, and Related Defenses, in Federal Court,* 27 WAKE FOREST L. REV. 829, 833–38 (1992) and Scott C. Paton, *"The Government Made Me Do It": A Proposed Approach to Entrapment Under Jacobson v. United States,* 79 CORNELL L.REV. 995 (1994).

§ 24.2

1. As discussed more fully below, the defense is initially raised by the defendant by showing there is some evidence government inducement. Once the defense is raised by the defendant, the burden of proof shifts to the government to prove that the defendant was predisposed. If the defendant was predisposed to commit the offense, the defense will fail regardless of the government's actions to induce the commission of the offense. Hampton v. United States, 425 U.S. 484, 488–89, 96 S.Ct. 1646, 1649, 48 L.Ed.2d 113 (1976).

Supreme Court: The defense was defined as consisting of two elements in Mathews v. United States, 485 U.S. 58, 62–63, 108 S.Ct. 883, 886–87, 99 L.Ed.2d 54 (1988).

See also

First Circuit: United States v. Rodriguez 858 F.2d 809, 812 (1st Cir.1988)(citing United States v. Polito, 856 F.2d 414, 416 (1st Cir.1988) (stating that the two elements of the defense are "inducement and unreadiness")).

Seventh Circuit: United States v. Higham, 98 F.3d 285 (7th Cir.1996).

Eighth Circuit: United States v. Jensen, 69 F.3d 906 (8th Cir.1995), *cert. de-*

ment inducement, the burden of proof shifts to the government to prove he was predisposed. These elements are examined below.

A. GOVERNMENT INDUCEMENT

Inducement to commit an offense may be proper or improper.[2] Proper inducement occurs when a government agent merely provides an opportunity to commit an offense, makes commission of the offense easier, or participates in the conduct that the offense requires.[3] Improper inducement, on the other hand, occurs when government conduct exceeds the mere provision of an opportunity to commit the offense and includes a further step to encourage the commission of the offense.[4] If the defendant was predisposed to commit the offense, however, the defense is unavailable regardless of the inducement offered by the agent.[5]

B. LACK OF PREDISPOSITION

To overcome a showing of improper inducement, the government must show that the defendant was willing to commit the offense independent of and prior to any action taken by the government.[6] If the defendant was predisposed to commit the offense before a government agent induced its commission, the defense is unavailable.[7]

The Supreme Court clarified this element in *Jacobson v. United States*.[8] *Jacobson* was a child pornography case wherein the defendant received repeated invitations and inquiries from several fictitious organi-

---

nied, 517 U.S. 1169, 116 S.Ct. 1571, 134 L.Ed.2d 669 (1996).

2. *D.C. Circuit:* United States v. McKinley, 70 F.3d 1307, 1312–13 (D.C.Cir. 1995).

First Circuit: United States v. Montanez, 105 F.3d 36 (1st Cir.1997); United States v. Gendron, 18 F.3d 955, 961 (1st Cir.1994); United States v. Coady, 809 F.2d 119, 122 (1st Cir.1987); United States v. Espinal, 757 F.2d 423, 425 (1st Cir.1985).

Ninth Circuit: United States v. Lorenzo, 43 F.3d 1303, 1305 (9th Cir.1995).

Eleventh Circuit: United States v. Brown, 43 F.3d 618, 623 (11th Cir.1995).

3. *See, e.g.,* United States v. Singh, 54 F.3d 1182, 1190–91 (4th Cir.1995)(solicitation not improper inducement).

See also S.Rep. 97–307, at n. 177 (1981) ("This does not mean that every time a person is entrapped by a government official the defense is available. The public servant must be acting in an official capacity, offering inducements for a legitimate law enforcement purpose rather than in aid of a criminal frolic of his own such as a bribe.")

4. United States v. Gendron, 18 F.3d 955, 961–62 (1st Cir.1994)(collecting 7 examples of improper inducement from case law).

5. Hampton v. United States, 425 U.S. 484, 488–89, 96 S.Ct. 1646, 1649, 48 L.Ed.2d 113 (1976).

6. *See* United States v. Miller, 71 F.3d 813 (11th Cir.1996)(examining methods of proving subjective predisposition).

7. Hampton v. United States, 425 U.S. 484, 488–89, 96 S.Ct. 1646, 1649, 48 L.Ed.2d 113 (1976).

8. 503 U.S. 540, 112 S.Ct. 1535, 118 L.Ed.2d 174 (1992). The *Jacobson* decision did not invent the requirement that the government must prove predisposition independent of government action. See 503 U.S. 540, 548–49 n. 2, 112 S.Ct. 1535, 1540, 118 L.Ed.2d 174. For a discussion of this holding in the context of prior Supreme Court decisions describing the predisposition element, see Scott C. Paton, *"The Government Made Me Do It": A Proposed Approach to Entrapment Under Jacobson v. United States,* 79 Cornell L.Rev. 995, 1007–12 n.2 (1994).

zations.[9] He was also invited to place orders with several businesses.[10] Many of the communications from the bogus organizations referred to freedom of speech and censorship. The Court held that Jacobson's conviction for receiving child pornography could not be upheld as a matter of law because the government had not shown that "Jacobson was predisposed, independent of the Government's acts and beyond a reasonable doubt, to violate the law by receiving child pornography through the mails."[11] By the time he committed the offense, in other words, Jacobson had already been exposed to so much inducement by the government that he had become predisposed to commit it, but only because of the government's inducement.[12] Thus the government must prove that a defendant was predisposed to commit the offense, and so predisposed before any government action to induce the commission of the offense.[13]

The Seventh and Ninth Circuits have identified five criteria relevant to predisposition.[14] These criteria are (1) the defendant's character and

9. The Court paid particular attention to the spirit of the communications sent to Jacobson by the government. The bogus organizations were: "the American Hedonist Society" (an organization with the doctrine that "members had the right to 'read what we desire, the right to discuss similar interests with those who share our philosophy, and ... the right to seek pleasure without restrictions being placed on us by outdated puritan morality'"); *Jacobson,* 503 U.S. at 544, 112 S.Ct. 1538; "Midlands Data Research" (which sought information from people who "believe in the joys of sex and the complete awareness of those lusty and youthful lads and lasses of the neophyte age"), *id.*; "Heartland Institute for a New Tomorrow" (a lobbying organization with the goal of "repealing statutes related to regulation of sexual activities"), *id.*; "Produit Outouais" (a "Canadian" mail order company), *id.* at 546; and "Far Eastern Trading Company, Ltd." (offering to avoid the "prying eyes of U.S. Customs" by sending materials through the mail via "American solicitors"), *id.* at 546–47.

The Court stated, "... the strong arguable inference is that, by waving the banner of individual rights and disparaging the legitimacy and constitutionality of efforts to restrict the availability of sexually explicit materials, the Government not only excited petitioner's interest in sexually explicit materials banned by law but also exerted substantial pressure on petitioner to obtain and read such material as part of a fight against censorship and the infringement of individual rights." *Id.* at 552.

10. Jacobson had been targeted for investigation because, at a time when such materials were legal, he had ordered porno-

graphic materials from a bookstore. His name appeared on a postal inspector's list because it had been on that bookstore's mailing list.

11. 503 U.S. at 554, 112 S.Ct. 1543.

12. *Id.*

13. *D.C. Circuit:* United States v. Vaughn, 80 F.3d 549 (D.C.Cir.1996).

First Circuit: United States v. Acosta, 67 F.3d 334 (1st Cir.1995); United States v. Gendron, 18 F.3d 955, 961–2 (1st Cir.1994)(comparing another child pornography case to *Jacobson* on the predisposition element).

Fifth Circuit: United States v. Hernandez, 92 F.3d 309 (5th Cir.1996).

Seventh Circuit: Eaglin v. Welborn, 57 F.3d 496, 503 (7th Cir.1995)(interpreting *Hollingsworth*); United States v. Hollingsworth, 27 F.3d 1196 (7th Cir.1994) (en banc).

Ninth Circuit: United States v. Lorenzo, 43 F.3d 1303, 1306–07 (9th Cir.1995) (jury instruction stating defense is denied if defendant had a previous intent or disposition accurately reflects *Jacobson*).

Tenth Circuit: United States v. Cecil, 96 F.3d 1344 (10th Cir.1996).

Louis M. Seidman, *The Supreme Court, Entrapment, and Our Criminal Justice Dilemma,* 1981 Sup.Ct.Rev. 111, 118–20 (1981); Paul Marcus, *Presenting, Back from the [Almost] Dead, the Entrapment Defense,* 47 Fla.L.Rev. 205 (1995).

14. *Seventh Circuit:* United States v. Hollingsworth, 27 F.3d 1196, 1205 n. 1 (7th

reputation; (2) whether the criminal activity was initially suggested by the government; (3) whether the criminal activity was for profit; (4) whether the defendant showed any reluctance; and (5) the nature of the government inducement.[15] The most important of these factors is whether the defendant was reluctant.[16]

A split of authority has developed in the circuits on the meaning of *Jacobson*. The Seventh Circuit, en banc, has concluded that although *Jacobson* did not add a new element to the entrapment defense, it did clarify predisposition in such a way as to mean that the defendant must be ready or in a position to commit the crime.[17] The court stated "The defendant must be so situated by reason of previous training or experience or occupation or acquaintances that it is likely that if the government had not induced him to commit the crime some criminal would have done so; only then does a sting or other arranged crime take a dangerous person out of circulation."[18] The court reversed the defendant's conviction with directions to acquit him.[19] The decision was close (6–to–5), and the dissents are spirited.[20] In the wake of *Hollingsworth*, the Ninth Circuit has explicitly rejected the "positional" requirement,[21] while the Fifth Circuit has agreed with and adopted the requirement.[22]

The Eleventh Circuit has clarified that *Jacobson* does not mean that the government must have evidence of the defendant's disposition prior to the investigation but rather the government must prove that the defendant's predisposition existed before the government got involved.[23] Thus it doesn't matter when the evidence of predisposition is developed, before or during the investigation, as long as the evidence shows the defendant's predisposition predated the government involvement.[24]

The Eleventh Circuit also concluded that *Jacobson* does not require any change in jury instructions on the burdens of proof of the entrap-

Cir.1994)(Coffey, J., dissenting), *quoting* United States v. Cervante, 958 F.2d 175, 179 (7th Cir.1992).

Ninth Circuit: United States v. Thomas, 134 F.3d 975, 978 (9th Cir.1998); United States v. Thickstun, 110 F.3d 1394, 1396 (9th Cir.1997), *citing* United States v. McClelland, 72 F.3d 717, 722 (9th Cir. 1995).

15. *Seventh Circuit: Hollingsworth,* 27 F.3d at 1205 n.1 (7th Cir.1994)(Coffey, J., dissenting), *quoting* United States v. Cervante, 958 F.2d 175, 179 (7th Cir.1992).

Ninth Circuit: United States v. Thomas, 134 F.3d 975, 978 (9th Cir.1998); *Thickstun,* 110 F.3d at 1396 (9th Cir. 1997), *citing* United States v. McClelland, 72 F.3d 717, 722 (9th Cir.1995).

16. *Seventh Circuit:* United States v. Hollingsworth, 27 F.3d 1196, 1205 n. 1 (7th Cir.1994)(Coffey, J., dissenting), *quoting* United States v. Cervante, 958 F.2d 175,

179 (7th Cir.1992); United States v. Kaminski, 703 F.2d 1004, 1008 (7th Cir.1983).

Ninth Circuit: United States v. Thickstun, 110 F.3d 1394, 1397 (9th Cir.1997), *citing* United States v. McClelland, 72 F.3d 717, 722 (9th Cir.1995).

17. United States v. Hollingsworth, 27 F.3d 1196, 1199–1200 (7th Cir.1994)(en banc).

18. *Id.* at 1200.

19. *Id.* at 1205.

20. *Id.* at 1205 (Coffey, J., dissenting) and 1212 (Easterbrook, J., dissenting).

21. United States v. Thickstun, 110 F.3d 1394, 1397–98 (9th Cir.1997).

22. United States v. Knox, 112 F.3d 802, 808 (5th Cir.1997).

23. United States v. King, 73 F.3d 1564, 1568 (11th Cir.1996).

24. *Id.*

ment defense.[25]

Library References:

C.J.S. Constitutional Law § 993–995; Criminal Law § 55, 57–58, 92.
West's Key No. Digests, Constitutional Law ☞257.5; Criminal Law ☞36.5–37.

§ 24.3   Related Defenses—In General

Several other defenses have evolved from or with the defense of entrapment. The Supreme Court has not addressed them directly and they have received varying degrees of acceptance in the Courts of Appeal. They include entrapment by estoppel, outrageous government conduct and third party entrapment.

§ 24.4   Related Defenses—Entrapment by Estoppel

Reliance on official misstatement of law, or entrapment by estoppel, is an affirmative defense related to entrapment.[1] The Second Circuit recently defined the defense:

> Entrapment by estoppel applies when an authorized government official tells the defendant that certain conduct is legal and the defendant believes the official. To invoke the entrapment by estoppel defense, the defendant must show that he relied on the official's statement and that his reliance was reasonable in that a person sincerely desirous of obeying the law would have accepted the information as true and would not have been put on notice to make further inquiries.[2]

The defense requires not only actual communication between the defendant and the government,[3] but active misleading of a defendant as to the state of the law that implicates the defendant's due process rights.[4] The reliance must be "reasonable in light of the identity of the agent, the point of law misrepresented, and the substance of the misrepresentation."[5] The courts are reluctant to apply this theory[6] and will use it only

25. *Id*. at 1570–71.

§ 24.4

1. *See, e.g.,*

Eighth Circuit: United States v. French 46 F.3d 710 (8th Cir.1995).

Ninth Circuit: United States v. Collins, 61 F.3d 1379, 1385 (9th Cir.1995)(defining the defense).

2. United States v. Corso, 20 F.3d 521, 528 (2d Cir.1994) (citing United States v. Weitzenhoff, 1 F.3d 1523, 1534 (9th Cir.1993)(citations omitted)).

See

Fifth Circuit: United States v. Trevino–Martinez, 86 F.3d 65 (5th Cir.1996).

Seventh Circuit: United States v. Sanchez, 82 F.3d 750 (7th Cir.1996).

3. United States v. Corso, 20 F.3d 521 (2d Cir.1994).

4. *Tenth Circuit:* United States v. Nichols, 21 F.3d 1016 (10th Cir.1994)(defendant based his entrapment by estoppel defense on his erroneous belief that he could lawfully own a firearm after his probation because his probation officer said that he could not own one during his probation)(citations omitted).

But see

Eighth Circuit: United States v. Achter, 52 F.3d 753, 755 (8th Cir.1995)(defense includes unintended misleading).

5. United States v. Tallmadge, 829 F.2d 767, 773–75 (9th Cir.1987).

Tenth Circuit: United States v. Nichols, 21 F.3d 1016 (10th Cir.1994), citing United

when it "does not interfere with underlying government policies or unduly undermine the correct enforcement of a particular law or regulation."[7] The defendant's reasonable reliance is an element of the defense, so the very low mental capacity of an individual defendant could be relevant to a successful defense.[8]

Library References:

C.J.S. Constitutional Law § 993–995; Criminal Law § 55, 57–58, 92.
West's Key No. Digests, Constitutional Law ⊱257.5; Criminal Law ⊱36.5–37.

§ 24.5   Related   Defenses—Outrageous   Government   Conduct/Due Process

The theory behind the outrageous government conduct/due process defense is that conduct by the government could be so unreasonable and unfair that it violates the defendant's due process right.[1] This defense was first suggested in some Supreme Court dicta.[2] It has been recognized by two circuits[3] and rejected outright by two circuits.[4] In the circuits that allow the defense, it is rarely successful.[5] This defense may be supported by showing either that the defendant's right to due process has been violated or by appealing to the court's general supervisory powers to curtail the overreaching of law enforcement officials that it finds shocking.[6]

States v. Clark, 986 F.2d 65, 69 (4th Cir. 1993).

But see

Second Circuit: United States v. Abcasis, 45 F.3d 39, 44 (2d Cir.1995)(actual authority not required).

6. United States v. Browning, 630 F.2d 694, 702 (10th Cir.1980)(allowing an entrapment by estoppel defense, but stating that it will be allowed only with "great reluctance").

7. United States v. Corso, 20 F.3d 521, 528 (2d Cir.1994), citing United States v. Browning, 630 F.2d 694, 702 (10th Cir. 1980).

8. In United States v. Nichols, 21 F.3d 1016 (10th Cir.1994) the defendant had a very low mental capacity. The court described the elements of the entrapment by estoppel defense as including reasonable reliance, but also stated, "We do not foreclose the possibility that a serious deficiency in a defendant's mental capacity might in some future case be relevant to formulating an entrapment by estoppel defense. . . . " 21 F.3d at 1018. Presumably, this statement was intended to leave the door open for this defense when such a defendant relied unreasonably. In *Nichols*, the court found no "active misleading," so the defense failed.

§ 24.5

1. *See* Louis M. Seidman, *The Supreme Court, Entrapment, and Our Crimi-*

nal Justice Dilemma, 1981 Sup.Ct.Rev. 111 (1981).

2. United States v. Russell, 411 U.S. 423, 431–32, 93 S.Ct. 1637, 1643, 36 L.Ed.2d 366 (1973).

3. *Second Circuit:* United States v. Archer, 486 F.2d 670 (2d Cir.1973).

Third Circuit: United States v. Twigg, 588 F.2d 373 (3d Cir.1978).

4. *Sixth Circuit:* United States v. Tucker, 28 F.3d 1420 (6th Cir.1994), discussed in detail *infra*.

Seventh Circuit: United States v. Boyd, 55 F.3d 239, 241 (7th Cir.1995).

5. *See, e.g.,* United States v. Archer, 486 F.2d 670 (2d Cir.1973)(recognizing defense but reversing conviction on a different, more limited ground).

6. *Supreme Court:* Hampton v. United States, 425 U.S. 484, 496, 96 S.Ct. 1646, 1653, 48 L.Ed.2d 113 (1976)(Brennan, J., dissenting)(plurality opinion); United States v. Russell, 411 U.S. 423, 431–32, 93 S.Ct. 1637, 1643, 36 L.Ed.2d 366 (1973) (Rehnquist, J., concurring).

Ninth Circuit: United States v. Simpson, 813 F.2d 1462, 1465 n. 2 (9th Cir.1987).

A. EXISTENCE OF THE DEFENSE

In 1973, the Supreme Court suggested there might be a defense based on due process violations by law enforcement officers.[7] In United States v. Russell,[8] an undercover government agent assigned to locate a suspected methamphetamine lab approached the defendant. The agent supplied an essential and hard to find chemical used in the production of the drug. Russell was convicted after asserting an entrapment defense and on appeal argued that even though a reasonable jury could have found him predisposed to commit the offense, there was entrapment as a matter of law. The Court of Appeals focused on the government agent's level of participation in the offense in reversing the conviction.[9]

In the Supreme Court, Russell urged the adoption of an exclusionary rule based on a revised constitutional defense of entrapment, since "the same factors that led this Court to apply the exclusionary rule to illegal searches and seizures ... and confessions ... should be considered here."[10] The Court was unpersuaded, however, since the government's conduct in this case "violated no independent constitutional right of the respondent. Nor did [the agent] violate any federal statute or rule or commit any crime in infiltrating the respondent's drug enterprise."[11] Russell also urged a *per se* rule to "preclude any prosecution when it is shown that the criminal conduct would not have been possible had not an undercover agent 'supplied an indispensable means to the commission of the crime that could not have been obtained otherwise, through legal or illegal channels.' "[12] The Court declined to adopt this suggested rule, as well, and stated:

> Even if we were to surmount the difficulties attending the notion that due process of law can be embodied in fixed rules, and those attending respondent's particular formulation, the rule he proposes would not appear to be of significant benefit to him [, because, on the facts of the record he is not within the terms of the] rule he proposes ... [since the chemical the agent supplied is not impossible to obtain and the defendant had in his possession two bottles of it that were not supplied by the agent.] ... *While we may some day be presented with a situation in which the conduct of law enforcement agents is so outrageous that due process principles would absolutely bar the government from invoking judicial processes to obtain a conviction* ... the instant case is distinctly not of that breed.[13]

Although the *Russell* Court had left open the possibility of a due process defense, that possibility was significantly limited three years

---

7. *See* United States v. Russell, 411 U.S. 423, 431–32, 93 S.Ct. 1637, 1643, 36 L.Ed.2d 366 (1973).

8. 411 U.S. 423, 93 S.Ct. 1637, 36 L.Ed.2d 366 (1973).

9. 411 U.S. at 427, 93 S.Ct. at 1640.

10. 411 U.S. at 430, 93 S.Ct. 1642 (citations omitted).

11. 411 U.S. at 430, 93 S.Ct. 1642.

12. 411 U.S. at 431, 93 S.Ct. 1642 (citation omitted).

13. 411 U.S. at 431–32, 93 S.Ct. 1642 (emphasis added).

later in Hampton v. United States.[14] In that case, the defendant conceded predisposition to distribute heroin.[15] The three member plurality of the court found that predisposition renders both the entrapment defense and a due process defense unavailable under United States v. Russell.[16] The two concurring members found that *Russell* did not preclude a due process defense when defendants were predisposed, but that the facts of this case did not require reversal.[17] Three members dissented because they would prefer an entrapment defense focused on the conduct of the government rather than a subjective approach, and under the former, the conviction would be reversed.[18] Thus a total of five members of the Court held that a defense based on the Due Process Clause, though not supported here, had not been precluded by the holding in *Russell* and did not exclude predisposed defendants.[19]

The Supreme Court has left the door open for the defense, but has never been presented with facts that support it.

The circuit courts disagree whether the defense exists. Two circuits recognize the defense,[20] and two circuits expressly reject any possibility of the defense.[21]

The Sixth Circuit recently held that no outrageous government conduct defense exists. In United States v. Tucker,[22] the defendants were indicted for purchasing, and aiding and abetting the purchase of, food stamps.[23] The defendants were targeted in a reverse sting operation by an "operative" working for the government whose compensation was that she kept half of the money she collected from the illegal sale of food stamps. The operative, Hancock, had been a friend of the defendant, Tucker, for more than ten years. Hancock contacted Tucker and attempted to induce Tucker to buy food stamps from her by describing her poor health and her financial distress. Hancock told her friend how she hoped to provide a "proper Christmas" for her children.[24] Tucker resisted at first, but then agreed to the purchase after Hancock appeared at Tucker's business dressed as if she were in dire financial straits. Tucker then encouraged Hancock to contact McDonald, Tucker's employee; after

---

14. 425 U.S. 484, 96 S.Ct. 1646, 48 L.Ed.2d 113 (1976)(plurality opinion).

15. 425 U.S. 484, 96 S.Ct. 1646, 48 L.Ed.2d 113.

16. *Id.* at 485 (opinion of Rehnquist, J., with Burger, C. J. & White, J.).

17. *Id.* at 493–94 (Powell & Blackmun, JJ, concurring).

18. *Id.* at 495–500 (Brennan, Stewart, & Marshall, JJ., dissenting).

19. Paul Marcus, *Presenting, Back from the [Almost] Dead, the Entrapment Defense,* 47 Fla.L.R. 205, 277–78 (1995).

20. *See*

Second Circuit: United States v. Archer, 486 F.2d 670, 678 (2d Cir.1973)("[W]e

are not prepared to say that, absent Congressional limitation, a federal court may never dismiss a prosecution as an abuse of federal power.... ")(reversing conviction on other grounds).

Third Circuit: United States v. Twigg, 588 F.2d 373 (3d Cir.1978).

21. *Sixth Circuit:* United States v. Tucker, 28 F.3d 1420 (6th Cir.1994).

Seventh Circuit: United States v. Boyd, 55 F.3d 239, 241 (7th Cir.1995).

22. 28 F.3d 1420 (6th Cir.1994).

23. 28 F.3d at 1421.

24. *Id.*

listening to Hancock's story, McDonald also agreed to purchase Hancock's food stamps.

The district court dismissed the indictment because the offense of trafficking in food stamps did not justify the ploys used in the investigation.[25] The court held that there would be no problem with such individual tactics as using undercover agents, targeting of an agent's friends, paying an agent, or using deceptive ploys. However, it held that "when they are employed in totality with people who are not otherwise suspected of engaging in crime ... the conduct ... crosses [the constitutional] boundary."[26]

The Sixth Circuit reviewed the dismissal *de novo*. The court began by examining the entrapment defense and noted that the objective approach to entrapment was clearly rejected by the United States Supreme Court in *Russell*. It also stated that the language so often cited in support of the proposition that the door has been left open for a due process defense was plainly dicta.[27]

The court noted that the Sixth Circuit has been presented with more than two dozen cases in which the defense has been raised but that "on the facts" the defense has been rejected every time.[28] Thus, according to the majority,

> there is no authority in this circuit which holds that the government's conduct in inducing the commission of a crime, if "outrageous" enough, can bar prosecution of an otherwise predisposed defendant under the Due Process Clause of the Fifth Amendment ... [the cases cited] do nothing more that "assume" the existence of such a defense while "holding" that it would not apply under the present facts.... [T]he legal existence of ... [the] due process defense is an open question in this circuit which we are free to address in the first instance.[29]

The court next examined authority in other circuits and concluded that only one other appellate court has barred a prosecution under *Russell*, and that holding improperly relied on an earlier Third Circuit case that had been limited by other Third Circuit holdings.[30] Otherwise, the other

---

25. *Id.*

26. *Id.* (alteration in *Tucker*)(citation omitted).

27. *Id.* at 1423.

28. *Id.* at 1424 (citing cases as examples of the Sixth Circuit's previous holdings in which the defense was offered by defendants but rejected "on the facts").

29. *Id.* at 1424–25 (citations omitted).

But see Circuit Judge Martin's concurrence, in which he concurs in the result because he found the government's conduct was not outrageous in this case, but stated that prior Sixth Circuit opinions recognizing the existence of an "outrageous government conduct" defense are binding authority. The concurrence cites United States v. Payne, 962 F.2d 1228, 1231–33 (6th Cir. 1992) as analyzing at length four factors weighed by the Sixth Circuit in determining whether government conduct was outrageous, and rejecting the majority's notion that such treatment by the Sixth Circuit itself is dicta. *Id.* at 1428 (Martin, J., concurring).

30. 28 F.3d at 1425 (citing United States v. Twigg, 588 F.2d 373 (3d Cir.1978), which had relied on United States v. West, 511 F.2d 1083 (3d Cir.1975), which had been limited by *Hampton* and other decisions (citations omitted)).

circuits, according to the *Tucker* court, had proceeded just as the Sixth in applying the dicta and finding on every occasion that the facts did not bar prosecution.[31]

After concluding that there is no binding authority from the Supreme Court or the Sixth Circuit, the *Tucker* court held that the due process defense "simply does not exist" in that circuit.[32] The court concluded that a defendant who raises a defense based on inducement to commit the offense "... is, by congressional intent and Supreme Court precedent, limited to the defense of entrapment and its key element of predisposition."[33]

The *Tucker* holding has three bases. First, inducement does not itself violate due process even if it is "outrageous."[34] Second, the trial court lacks authority to dismiss an indictment because of governmental misconduct unless an independent constitutional right has been violated.[35] Finally, the fact that this defense continues to exist "stands as an invitation to violate the constitutional separation of powers, intruding not only on the province of the Executive Branch but the Legislative Branch as well."[36]

The Seventh Circuit, without citing *Tucker*, similarly rejected the existence of any outrageous government conduct defense.[37] The court, in refusing to find that prosecutorial misconduct warranted a new trial, stated:

> In great tension with [the principle that appellate courts should not reverse convictions to punish prosecutors], there are intimations that "outrageous governmental misconduct" is an independent ground for ordering a new trial in a federal criminal case; but we agree with the First Circuit that "the doctrine [of outrageous governmental misconduct] is moribund." "Stillborn" might be a better term, for it never had any life; and it has no support in the decisions of this court, which go out of their way to criticize the doctrine. Today we let the other shoe drop, and hold that the doctrine does not exist in this circuit.[38]

Thus two circuits have accepted the defense, and two circuits have recently and expressly rejected it.[39]

31. 28 F.3d at 1425.

32. *Id.* at 1426–27.

33. *Id.* at 1428.

34. *Id.*

35. *Id.*

36. *Id.*

37. United States v. Boyd, 55 F.3d 239, 241 (7th Cir.1995), *citing* United States v. Okey, 47 F.3d 238, 240 n. 2 (7th Cir.1995); United States v. Nava–Salazar, 30 F.3d 788, 800 (7th Cir.1994); United States v. Cyprian, 23 F.3d 1189, 1197 (7th Cir.1994); United States v. Van Engel, 15 F.3d 623, 631–32 (7th Cir.1993); United States v. Olson, 978 F.2d 1472, 1481–82 (7th Cir.1992); United States v. Miller, 891 F.2d 1265, 1271–73 (7th Cir.1989) (concurring opinion).

38. United States v. Boyd, 55 F.3d 239, 241 (7th Cir.1995)(citations omitted).

39. *See generally* Stephen A. Miller, *The Case for Preserving the Outrageous Government Conduct Defense*, 91 Nw. U.L.Rev. 305 (1996); Jason R. Schultz, *United States v. Tucker: Can the Sixth Circuit Really Abolish the Outrageous Government Conduct Defense?*, 45 DePaul L.Rev. 943 (1996).

B. COMPARISON OF ENTRAPMENT AND OUTRAGEOUS GOVERNMENT CONDUCT

The outrageous government conduct and entrapment defenses could easily arise from the same facts[40] but are two distinct defenses.[41] Entrapment is an affirmative defense focused primarily on the predisposition of the defendant as decided by a jury. The defendant who asserts a due process claim, on the other hand, asks the court to overturn a conviction or dismiss an indictment because of what the government has done, notwithstanding the defendant's predisposition.[42] In fact, the due process claim is often not even a defense, technically, since it is generally raised in a preliminary motion to dismiss the indictment.[43] Whether the defendant's due process right has been violated is a question of constitutional law decided by the court.[44]

C. WHEN THE DEFENSE IS RAISED

Among the law enforcement strategies that defendants argue violate their due process right, but which courts uphold, are: initiating contact with a target to offer opportunities to commit a crime;[45] full circle stings;[46] using a relative, sexual partner, or close friend as a government

40. For example, the principal case from which the defense is derived, United States v. Russell, 411 U.S. 423, 93 S.Ct. 1637, 36 L.Ed.2d 366 (1973), was one in which the defendant raised both the defense of entrapment and the claim of due process violation. Both claims were also raised in United States v. Jenrette, 744 F.2d 817 (D.C.Cir.1984).

41. *See* United States v. Sneed, 34 F.3d 1570, 1576 (10th Cir.1994)("The outrageous governmental conduct defense is distinct from the entrapment defense because [the latter] considers the predisposition of the defendant to commit the crime.... In contrast, [the former] looks only at the government's conduct"(citations omitted)); and Paul Marcus, *The Due Process Defense in Entrapment Cases: The Journey Back*, 27 Am.Crim.L.Rev. 456, 457 (1991); John David Buretta, *Reconfiguring the Entrapment and Outrageous Government Conduct Doctrines*, 84 Geo. L.J. 1945 (1996).

The due process defense is also distinct from the objective approach favored by a minority of the Supreme Court. While both defenses focus on the behavior of government officials, the due process defense is based on constitutional protections but the objective entrapment defense relies on the general supervisory powers of the court.

42. United States v. Matta–Ballesteros, 71 F.3d 754, 763–64 (9th Cir.1995); United States v. Luttrell, 923 F.2d 764 (9th Cir.1991)(en banc).

43. United States v. Montoya, 45 F.3d 1286, 1300 (9th Cir.1995); United States v. Bogart, 783 F.2d 1428, 1432 n. 2 (9th Cir. 1986), *vacated on other grounds by*, 790 F.2d 802 (9th Cir.1986).

44. United States v. McClelland, 72 F.3d 717, 721 (9th Cir.1995) (whether governmental conduct is outrageous is a question of law); Paul Marcus, *The Due Process Defense in Entrapment Cases: The Journey Back*, 27 Am.Crim.L.Rev. 456, 458–59 (1991) (citing United States v. Graves, 556 F.2d 1319, 1322 (5th Cir.1977) (due process claim is question of law for the judge)).

45. United States v. Goodwin, 854 F.2d 33 (4th Cir.1988).

46. Willis v. United States, 530 F.2d 308 (8th Cir.1976).

But see United States v. West, 511 F.2d 1083 (3d Cir.1975)(full circle sting violates due process).

A "full circle sting" is one in which a government agent supplies contraband to the target, who then re-sells it to another agent. These are typically used in drug cases but are not so limited.

agent to convince the target of the sting to commit an offense;[47] promises of legitimate and profitable business deals;[48] indicting an informant to encourage cooperation;[49] instigating a conspiracy;[50] facilitating or encouraging a conspiracy and actually committing the offense;[51] giving contraband to a defendant so that it can be exchanged for other contraband;[52] threatening a defendant or his friends;[53] sentencing entrapment;[54] and deciding to refer a case for prosecution to federal rather than state authorities in the absence of a policy to do so.[55]

D. WHEN THE DEFENSE SUCCEEDS

Defendants have prevailed on the outrageous government conduct/due process defense in few cases.[56] Some courts look to factors like whether the defendant instigated the criminal enterprise or was drawn in by a government agent and whether the defendant was responsible for directing the enterprise as relevant to a finding of a due process violation.[57] However, these factors are not universally accepted by the circuits and no factors have been endorsed by the Supreme Court.

47. *Ninth Circuit:* United States v. Smith, 802 F.2d 1119 (9th Cir.1986).

See also

Third Circuit: United States v. Voigt, 89 F.3d 1050 (3d Cir.1996)(alleged attorney-client relationship with government informant).

Fifth Circuit: United States v. Johnson, 68 F.3d 899 (5th Cir.1995)(attorney-client privilege allegedly breached but due process not violated).

48. United States v. Rivera, 778 F.2d 591 (10th Cir.1985).

49. United States v. Dudden, 65 F.3d 1461 (9th Cir.1995).

50. United States v. Rodriguez–Ramos, 704 F.2d 17 (1st Cir.1983).

51. *Fifth Circuit:* United States v. Arias–Diaz, 497 F.2d 165 (5th Cir.1974).

Ninth Circuit: United States v. Duque, 62 F.3d 1146, 1151 (9th Cir.1995).

52. United States v. Davis, 809 F.2d 1194 (6th Cir.1987).

53. United States v. Johnson, 565 F.2d 179 (1st Cir.1977).

54. *Fifth Circuit:* United States v. Tremelling, 43 F.3d 148, 151–52 (5th Cir. 1995).

Eighth Circuit: United States v. Doyle, 60 F.3d 396, 398 (8th Cir.1995).

55. *Eighth Circuit:* Bell v. United States, 48 F.3d 1042, 1043 (8th Cir.1995).

Tenth Circuit: United States v. Langston, 970 F.2d 692 (10th Cir.1992).

56. *See Third Circuit:* United States v. Twigg, 588 F.2d 373 (3d Cir.1978)(holding due process was violated where government agents suggested setting up the operation, supplied equipment, expertise, a location and raw materials to the defendant at no cost and with very little participation by the defendant); United States v. West, 511 F.2d 1083 (3d Cir.1975)(holding a "full circle" narcotics sting was intolerable and reversing the defendant's conviction, but failing to label the rationale as one based on due process); United States v. Gardner, 658 F.Supp. 1573 (W.D.Pa.1987)(dismissing an indictment on Due Process grounds where an undercover agent persuaded a non-predisposed fellow postal worker to obtain cocaine by using their friendship and repeatedly asking for the favor. The court noted that the defendant made no profit on the sales and had no other customers.).

Ninth Circuit: Greene v. United States, 454 F.2d 783, 787 (9th Cir.1971)(reversing conviction because of government "enmeshment" in the criminal enterprise the court found "repugnant to American criminal justice"); United States v. Batres–Santolino, 521 F.Supp. 744 (N.D.Cal.1981)(dismissing an indictment because of the conduct of an undercover agent who set up a cocaine importation operation and promised defendants that profits from drug sales would only be used in legitimate business deals. The court focused on the complete inability of the defendants to carry out the offense absent the agent who organized them.).

57. *See,* Paul Marcus, *The Entrapment Defense,* § 7 (2d ed.1995) (identifying

E. TARGETING OF DEFENDANTS

One question frequently raised is whether a defendant may be targeted for investigation in the absence of a particular level of suspicion. The Supreme Court has never directly addressed the question of whether due process requires that the government demonstrate some level of suspicion before targeting a defendant in a sting. The Court declined to examine this question when it accepted for review its most recent entrapment case, *Jacobson*.[58] The original Eighth Circuit panel in that case reversed the conviction because the government agents had not targeted the defendant based on reasonable suspicion.[59] On rehearing, the panel held that the conviction was valid since the mere lack of a reasonable basis to target the defendant did not violate due process and since the defendant was not entrapped.[60] The opinion issued by the Supreme Court addressed only the question of whether Jacobson had been entrapped as a matter of law.[61]

None of the circuit courts that has addressed this issue has held that a demonstrable level of suspicion is required by due process.[62] In other words, the fact that the defendant was chosen as a target for a sting

factors such as instigation by the defendant, active vs. passive participation, control over the criminal enterprise and noting which circuits have used these factors).

58. Jacobson v. United States, 503 U.S. 540, 112 S.Ct. 1535, 118 L.Ed.2d 174 (1992).

59. United States v. Jacobson, 893 F.2d 999 (8th Cir.1990), *vacated*, 899 F.2d 1549 (8th Cir.1990).

60. United States v. Jacobson, 916 F.2d 467 (8th Cir.1990) *cert. granted in part, rev'd*, 503 U.S. 540, 112 S.Ct. 1535, 118 L.Ed.2d 174 (1992).

61. Jacobson v. United States, 503 U.S. 540, 112 S.Ct. 1535, 118 L.Ed.2d 174 (1992).

62. *D.C. Circuit:* United States v. Jenrette, 744 F.2d 817, 824 (D.C.Cir.1984)(failure to demonstrate reasonable suspicion of defendant before targeting in sting did not constitute a violation of due process).

First Circuit: Kadis v. United States, 373 F.2d 370 (1st Cir.1967)(declining to rule that entrapment exists where inducement was offered without a showing of predisposition).

Second Circuit: United States v. Myers, 635 F.2d 932 (2d Cir.1980)(sting operations are not prohibited by the Constitution).

Third Circuit: United States v. Jannotti, 673 F.2d 578, 609 (3d Cir.1982)("Where the conduct of the investigation itself does not offend due process, the mere fact that the investigation may have been com-

menced without probable cause does not bar the conviction of those who rise to its bait.").

Fourth Circuit: United States v. Blevins, 960 F.2d 1252 (4th Cir.1992)(rejecting a reasonable suspicion requirement before a defendant may be targeted in a sting operation, although court based this holding on the fact that the focus of the entrapment defense is on the defendant's subjective predisposition, making the government's knowledge of such predisposition irrelevant); United States v. Osborne, 935 F.2d 32 (4th Cir.1991)("In this circuit the contrary principle has been fixed in the law for almost 70 years ... that the government need not have reasonable grounds to suspect illegal conduct before offering the opportunity to commit a crime.")(citations omitted).

Fifth Circuit: United States v. Allibhai, 939 F.2d 244, 249 (5th Cir.1991)("We also join our sibling circuits in rejecting the suggestion ... that the government should have reasonable suspicion that an individual is involved in some illegality before targeting him in a sting operation.").

Ninth Circuit: United States v. Luttrell, 923 F.2d 764 (9th Cir.1991)(en banc)(rejecting a "reasoned grounds" requirement for investigation of an individual under the due process clause).

Tenth Circuit: United States v. Gamble, 737 F.2d 853, 860 (10th Cir.1984)("We have held that the government need not have a

prior to any suspicion of wrong-doing does not constitute outrageous conduct.

In 1989, the Ninth Circuit held that the government could not target a defendant in a sting operation without a showing of reasonable suspicion.[63] That opinion, however, was vacated on rehearing *en banc*.[64] In the panel opinion, the court imposed a pre-targeting reasonable suspicion requirement and criticized "suspicionless investigations" as being "inefficient" and "arbitrary."[65] The panel opinion was vacated *en banc* without explanation except that the Ninth Circuit would, by rejecting a "reasoned grounds" requirement, "follow four of our sister circuits."[66] In dissent, Judge Pregerson stated that purposeful criminal investigation is required by the Bill of Rights, that targeting a defendant without reasonable suspicion is itself outrageous government conduct, and that informants should not be allowed to "go out on fishing expeditions to find targets for undercover sting operations."[67]

F. CONTINGENT FEE ARRANGEMENTS WITH INFORMANTS

Another topic of litigation is the use of paid informants as government agents in sting operations. The concern is that a conviction based on evidence supplied by a paid informant who is eager to earn "consideration" may violate the due process rights of the target of investigation when that consideration is based on the informant's performance in the operation.[68]

The Ninth Circuit issued an interesting series of decisions on this question. In the *Luttrell* panel opinion which was subsequently vacated,[69] the court spent some time expressing its concern on the role of confidential informants who "have a strong incentive to find targets for police

reasonable suspicion of wrongdoing in order to conduct an undercover investigation of a particular defendant.")(citations omitted).

Eleventh Circuit: United States v. King, 73 F.3d 1564, 1568 (11th Cir.1996) (government need not have evidence of predisposition prior to investigation).

63. United States v. Luttrell, 889 F.2d 806 (9th Cir.1989), *vacated*, 923 F.2d 764 (9th Cir.1991)(en banc).

64. 923 F.2d 764 (9th Cir.1991)(en banc).

65. United States v. Luttrell, 889 F.2d 806 (9th Cir.1989).

66. 923 F.2d 764 (9th Cir.1991).

67. 923 F.2d at 764–65 (Pregerson, J., dissenting).

68. *Ninth Circuit:* United States v. Solorio, 37 F.3d 454 (9th Cir.1994) (recognizing the defense where the informer was

paid by the number of persons convicted, the quantity of drugs involved, and the value of assets seized).

Eleventh Circuit: United States v. Williams, 59 F.3d 1180, 1184 (11th Cir. 1995) (contingent fee arrangement not per se violative of due process).

For a discussion of the traditional view of informants with contingent fee arrangements, see Paul Marcus, *The Entrapment Defense*, § 7.08 (2d ed.1995)(noting that the claim is generally raised with regard to drug offenses and citing United States v. Porter, 764 F.2d 1 (1st Cir.1985) as typical in that the court focused on society's legitimate interest in stopping drug trafficking). *See also* Roger Park, *The Entrapment Controversy*, 60 Minn.L.Rev. 163, 197 (1976).

69. 889 F.2d 806 (9th Cir.1989), *vacated*, 923 F.2d 764 (9th Cir.1991)(en banc).

investigations."[70] The court described the dangers of using paid informants:

> ... [i]n this case, the investigation utilized the services of an informant, a member of a group that in its eagerness to gain rewards does not always obey the niceties of police protocol. Many informants play their roles because of completed or prospective plea bargaining arrangements. They have a strong incentive to find targets for police investigation, regardless of the reasonableness or the accuracy of their information. Their tips to the police may be based either on legitimate information about the criminal underworld or they may be wholly fabricated. The origin of the information may be direct observation or it may be innuendo, conjecture or even just plain animus. While in some cases informant activities may be conducted in a fair and decent manner, in others there appears to be little regard for fundamental concepts of honesty and fair play. We see substantial reason to scrutinize these operations for governmental overreaching and to do so with the greatest care.[71]

In United States v. Solorio,[72] the Ninth Circuit went further in condemning contingent fee informers. The court was initially under the impression that the agent was paid based on the number of persons convicted, the quantity of drugs involved, and the value of assets seized.[73] The court held that the government's conduct was a violation of the defendant's due process right because the evidence on which the conviction was based was so likely to be unreliable.[74] However, the court withdrew this opinion based on a motion by the United States.[75] The Ninth Circuit subsequently re-issued the opinion, but failed to find the outrageous governmental conduct discussed in its original decision because a review of the record convinced the court that the agent had not been paid a contingent fee based on convictions, but rather a contingent fee based on "successful" investigations.[76] The Ninth Circuit stated: "Because the record does not establish that the informant's fee arrangement was contingent upon obtaining convictions, we cannot say that, under the totality of the circumstances, [the defendant] was subjected to outrageous government conduct."[77] From this language it is logical to infer that the Ninth Circuit would consider the reverse to be proof of outrageous governmental conduct. The value of this re-issued decision is uncertain, however, because the court chose not to publish it.[78] Under

---

70. 889 F.2d at 813. In this case, the informant was paid by the government and was "instructed by the government to solicit prospective clients for illegal credit card draft deals. [The informant] was awaiting sentencing for a credit card fraud conviction." *Id.* at 808.

71. 889 F.2d at 813–14.

72. 37 F.3d 454 (9th Cir.1994).

73. *Id.*

74. *Id.*

75. United States v. Solorio, 43 F.3d 1334 (9th Cir.1995).

76. United States v. Solorio, 53 F.3d 341, 1995 WL 242324, at *3 (9th Cir.1995)(unpublished).

77. *Id.* at *4.

78. United States v. Solorio, 53 F.3d 341, 1995 WL 242324, at *3 (9th Cir.1995)(unpublished).

Ninth Circuit rules, unpublished opinions are not precedential and should not be cited.[79]

Most recently, however, the Ninth Circuit upheld contingent fees for informers without objection. In United States v. Cuellar,[80] the court found that paying an informant based on a percentage of money laundered for a criminal organization did not warrant dismissal of the indictment, even though the informant "got paid a ton of money."[81] The *Cuellar* court reasoned that an informant's motive to lie does not preclude his use by the government.[82]

Library References:

C.J.S. Constitutional Law § 993–995; Criminal Law § 55, 57–58, 92.
West's Key No. Digests, Constitutional Law ⟐257.5; Criminal Law ⟐36.5–37.

§ 24.6   Related Defenses—Third Party Entrapment

Generally, a defendant cannot use the defense of entrapment when a private agent induces commission of the offense.[1] However, a defense of entrapment without direct contact with a government agent[2] has been recognized in some circuits.[3]

A good example is United States v. Manzella.[4] The Seventh Circuit found that on the facts of that case, no defense of vicarious entrapment was available to the defendant, but described the possibility that such a defense existed:

> There is no defense of private entrapment. Private entrapment is just another term for criminal solicitation, and outside the narrow

79. Ninth Cir.R. 36–3.

80. 96 F.3d 1179 (9th Cir.1996), *supplemented*, 97 F.3d 1461 (9th Cir.1996).

81. 96 F.3d at 1182.

82. 96 F.3d at 1183.

§ 24.6

1. *Fifth Circuit:* United States v. Manarite, 44 F.3d 1407, 1408 (9th Cir.1995) (inducement by private party does not give rise to entrapment).

Seventh Circuit: United States v. Neville, 82 F.3d 750, 760 (7th Cir.1996); United States v. Hollingsworth, 27 F.3d 1196, 1203 (7th Cir.1994) (en banc). United States v. Manzella, 791 F.2d 1263, 1269 (7th Cir.1986).

Ninth Circuit: Sanchez v. United States, 50 F.3d 1448, 1452 (9th Cir.1995) (distinguishing an informant from an agent).

2. Courts have not settled on a label for such a defense. It has been referred to as vicarious entrapment, third party entrapment, derivative entrapment, entrapment by an unwitting agent, and indirect entrapment. The Second Circuit has recognized "indirect inducement," see United States v. Salerno, 66 F.3d 544 (2d Cir.1995).

3. *First Circuit:* In United States v. Bradley, 820 F.2d 3 (1st Cir.1987), the court held that one defendant's sympathy for his co-defendant upon being informed of threats of violence did not establish a defense of entrapment for the sympathetic friend. However, the court stated that a defense of entrapment would be recognized if the threatened co-defendant had pressured the sympathetic friend at the instruction of the government. The court noted that such a defense would not truly be a third party entrapment case because the threatened intermediary would be acting as a government subagent.

Seventh Circuit: In United States v. Manzella, 791 F.2d 1263, 1269–70 (7th Cir. 1986), the court found that on the facts of that case, no defense of vicarious entrapment was available to the defendant, but described the possibility that such a defense existed.

4. 791 F.2d 1263, 1269–70 (7th Cir. 1986).

haven created by the defense of necessity or compulsion, the person who yields to the solicitation and commits the solicited crime is guilty of that crime. All crime is a yielding to temptation, the temptation to obtain whatever gains, pecuniary or nonpecuniary, the crime offers. The temptation is a cause of the crime but not a cause that exonerates the tempted from criminal liability if he yields, just as poverty is not a defense to larceny. Cause and responsibility are not synonyms.[5]

However, the court goes on to describe a scenario in which the government agent offers overwhelming inducement to one non-predisposed defendant (calling him "A"), and that person immediately offers similarly overwhelming inducement to another non-predisposed person (calling her "B").

Would only [A] have a defense of entrapment? Could the government be allowed to do indirectly, through [A] as an unwitting agent, what it would not have been allowed to do in face-to-face dealings between [A] and [B]—namely, induce [B] to commit a crime to which he was not predisposed and then prosecute him for the crime? Or should the government's lack of control over persons who are not its agents be a complete defense to any effort to use the conduct of such a person as the basis for a defense of entrapment by someone with whom the government has not dealt directly?

In *Hollingsworth,* the en banc Seventh Circuit concluded that although "vicarious entrapment" was not a defense, "derivative entrapment" was a defense based on the principle that the entrapment defense lies whether the government uses its own employee or an informant.[6] Other circuits have agreed[7] and disagreed,[8] so there is a split in the circuits.[9]

Library References:

C.J.S. Constitutional Law § 993–995; Criminal Law § 55, 57–58, 92.
West's Key No. Digests, Constitutional Law ⏣257.5; Criminal Law ⏣36.5–37.

§ 24.7 Procedural Issues

A. BURDENS OF PRODUCTION AND PROOF

Entrapment is an affirmative defense and as such must be raised initially by the defendant.[1] To get a jury instruction on the defense, the defendant must meet an "entry level burden" of raising government

5. United States v. Manzella, 791 F.2d 1263, 1269–70 (7th Cir.1986).

6. United States v. Hollingsworth, 27 F.3d 1196, 1204 (7th Cir.1994).

7. United States v. Knox, 112 F.3d 802, 808 (5th Cir.1997).

8. United States v. Thickstun, 110 F.3d 1394, 1399 (9th Cir.1997).

9. *See* United States v. Thickstun, 110 F.3d at 1399-1400 (collecting cases).

§ 24.7

1. *See, e.g.,* United States v. Rodriguez, 858 F.2d 809 (1st Cir.1988); Paul Marcus, *The Entrapment Defense,* § 2 (2d ed.1995).

inducement and producing some evidence of it.[2] The burden of proving predisposition beyond a reasonable doubt then falls on the government.[3] The jury instruction on entrapment need not detail the shifting burdens of production and proof.[4]

B. EVIDENTIARY ISSUES REGARDING PREDISPOSITION

To defeat the defense, the government is required to disprove one or both of the elements of it. Direct evidence is not required to show the defendant's predisposition; this may be properly inferred by the jury.[5] Once the defendant raises the issue of predisposition, character evidence becomes admissible.[6] The Ninth Circuit recently concluded that this includes "good character" evidence offered by the defendant.[7]

C. USE OF MULTIPLE DEFENSES

Entrapment is generally considered an affirmative defense. A defendant is entitled to an instruction provided the initial "entry level" burden has been met.[8] Even if the defendant denies one or more element[s] of the substantive offense, he is entitled to the instruction as long as there has been some evidence of entrapment presented.[9]

2. *D.C. Circuit:* United States v. Layeni, 90 F.3d 514 (D.C.Cir.1996).

First Circuit: Mathews v. United States, 485 U.S. 58, 63–65, 108 S.Ct. 883, 887–88, 99 L.Ed.2d 54 (1988); United States v. Rogers, 102 F.3d 641 (1st Cir.1996); United States v. Joost, 92 F.3d 7 (1st Cir.1996).

Fifth Circuit: United States v. Bradfield, 113 F.3d 515 (5th Cir.1997).

3. *See*

Second Circuit: United States v. Hurtado, 47 F.3d 577, 585 (2d Cir.1995)(burden shifts to government).

Seventh Circuit: United States v. Theodosopoulos, 48 F.3d 1438, 1442 (7th Cir. 1995) (burden shifts to government); United States v. Gonzalez, 19 F.3d 1169, 1172 (7th Cir.1994) (listing factors relevant to determining the absence of entrapment).

Ninth Circuit: United States v. LaRizza, 72 F.3d 775, 778–79 (9th Cir.1995)(describing government's burden of proof on element of predisposition).

4. United States v. Davis, 799 F.2d 1490 (11th Cir.1986) (11th Cir. pattern instruction on entrapment is adequate).

5. United States v. Sandoval, 20 F.3d 134 (5th Cir.1994).

6. Not all evidence of prior acts, however, is proof of predisposition. Such evidence must not be too remote. Sherman v. United States, 356 U.S. 369, 375–76, 78 S.Ct. 819, 822, 2 L.Ed.2d 848 (1958).

7. United States v. Thomas, 134 F.3d 975 (9th Cir.1998) (evidence of defendant's good character admissable under FRE's 404(b) and 405(b); conviction reversed and new trial granted) (one judge dissenting)).

See also

D.C. Circuit: United States v. Tyson, 470 F.2d 381, 384–85 (D.C.Cir.1972).

Fifth Circuit: United States v. Privett, 68 F.3d 101, 105–06 (5th Cir.1995).

For a discussion of the impact of an entrapment defense on the admissibility of evidence, see Wayne R. LaFave & Jerold H. Israel, *Criminal Procedure*, § 5.3(d) (2d ed.1992) and Jack B. Weinstein & Margaret A. Berger, *Weinstein's Evidence*, § 303 (Joseph M. McLaughlin ed., 2d ed.1997).

8. Mathews v. United States, 485 U.S. 58, 108 S.Ct. 883, 99 L.Ed.2d 54 (1988).

9. *See* Mathews v. United States, 485 U.S. 58, 108 S.Ct. 883, 99 L.Ed.2d 54 (1988); S.Rep.No. 97–307, at 118 (1981), for a discussion of whether admission of guilt has traditionally been required. *See also* Thomas J. Rauchbach, *Denial of the Crime and the Availability of the Entrapment Defense in the Federal Courts*, 22 B.C.L.Rev. 911 (1987).

D. QUESTIONS OF LAW AND FACT

Whether the entry level burden of production of evidence has been met by the defendant, and thus whether the defendant will receive a jury instruction on the defense, is a question for the trial judge.[10] However, where there is conflicting evidence as to the elements of the defense, the factfinder must resolve the question.[11] The trier of fact also decides whether the government has met its burden of proof as to one or both of the elements of the defense.[12]

Library References:

C.J.S. Constitutional Law § 993–995; Criminal Law § 55, 57–58, 92.
West's Key No. Digests, Constitutional Law ⚖=257.5; Criminal Law ⚖=36.5–37.

§ 24.8 Bibliography

A.L.I. Model Penal Code § 2.13, Comment.

Marcus, Paul, *The Entrapment Defense* (2d ed.1995).

S. Rep. No. 97–307, at 118 (1981).

Abramson, Leslie W. & Lisa L. Lindeman, *Entrapment and Due Process in the Federal Courts,* 8 Am.J.Crim.L. 139 (1980).

10. *Sixth Circuit:* United States v. Nelson, 922 F.2d 311, 317 (6th Cir.1990); United States v. Meyer, 803 F.2d 246, 249 (6th Cir.1986).

Eighth Circuit: United States v. Felix, 867 F.2d 1068, 1074 n. 11 (8th Cir.1989).

Ninth Circuit: United States v. Marbella, 73 F.3d 1508 (9th Cir.1996).

Where there is no contention that the defendant was not entrapped, the court may find entrapment as a matter of law. Sherman v. United States, 356 U.S. 369, 78 S.Ct. 819, 2 L.Ed.2d 848 (1958).

See also

Supreme Court: Sorrells v. United States, 287 U.S. 435, 53 S.Ct. 210, 77 L.Ed. 413 (1932).

Eighth Circuit: United States v. Hulett 22 F.3d 779(8th Cir.1994).

Tenth Circuit: United States v. Beal 961 F.2d 1512 (10th Cir.1992).

See S.Rep.No. 97–307, at 128–29 (1981)(citing examples of conduct determined as a matter of law to be entrapment: "(1) sale of liquor to government agent disguised to deceive defendant into thinking he was not an Indian to whom liquor could not be sold, Voves v. United States, 249 F. 191 (7th Cir.1918); United States v. Healy, 202 F. 349 (D.Mont.1913); (2) repeated solicitations of narcotics by addict informer claiming to be suffering from withdrawal,

Sherman v. United States, 356 U.S. 369, 78 S.Ct. 819, 2 L.Ed.2d 848 (1958); (3)informer's supplying of contraband (heroin) to defendant to sell to undercover agent, United States v. Bueno, 447 F.2d 903 (5th Cir. 1971); United States v. Chisum, 312 F.Supp. 1307 (C.D.Cal.1970). The rationale of these cases has, however, been effectively vitiated by the holding in Hampton v. United States, 425 U.S. 484, 96 S.Ct. 1646, 48 L.Ed.2d 113 (1976).").

11. *Second Circuit:* United States v. Henry, 417 F.2d 267 (2d Cir.1969)("Only slight evidence of entrapment is necessary for submission of the issue to the jury.").

Ninth Circuit: United States v. Shapiro, 669 F.2d 593 (9th Cir.1982); United States v. Brandon 633 F.2d 773 (9th Cir.1980)(finding no error in refusal of an instruction where no evidence of the elements was presented); United States v. Ratcliffe, 550 F.2d 431 (9th Cir.1976); Shaw v. United States, 374 F.2d 888 (9th Cir.1967)(failure to instruct sua sponte is not error when there was no request for the instruction and a different defense was offered by the defendant). *See also* Manual of Model Criminal Jury Instructions for the Ninth Circuit § 6.02 & cmt. (Comm. on Model Jury Instructions, Ninth Circuit ed., 1992).

12. *See, e.g.,* United States v. Jones, 575 F.2d 81, 83–84 (6th Cir.1978).

Bennett, Warren, *From Sorrells to Jacobson: Reflections on Six Decades of Entrapment Law, and Related Defenses In Federal Court,* 27 Wake Forest L. Rev. 829 (1992).

DeFeo, Michael A., *Entrapment as a Defense to Criminal Responsibility: Its History, Theory and Application,* 1 U.S.F.L. Rev. 243 (1967).

Hanson, Jarrod S., *Entrapment in Cyberspace: A Renewed Call for Reasonable Suspicion,* 1996 U. Chi. Legal F. 535 (1996).

Lord, Kenneth M., *Entrapment and Due Process: Moving Toward a Dual System of Defenses,* 25 Fla.St.L.Rev. 463 (1998).

Marcus, Paul, *Presenting, Back from the [Almost] Dead, the Entrapment Defense,* 47 Fla. L. R. 205 (1995).

Park, Roger, *The Entrapment Controversy,* 60 Minn. L. Rev. 163 (1976).

Paton, Scott C., *"The Government Made Me Do It": A Proposed Approach To Entrapment Under Jacobson v. United States,* 79 Cornell L. Rev. 995 (1994).

Seidman, Louis M., *The Supreme Court, Entrapment, and Our Criminal Justice Dilemma,* 1981 Sup. Ct. Rev. 111 (1981).

Underhill, Robert Eldridge, *Sentence Entrapment: A Casualty of the War on Crime,* 94 Ann. Surv. Am. L. 165 (1994).

Whelan, Maura F.J., *Lead Us Not Into (Unwarranted) Temptation: A Proposal To Replace The Entrapment Defense With A Reasonable Suspicion Requirement* 133 U. Pa. L. Rev. 1193 (1985).

CHAPTER 25

MISTAKE OF FACT AND IGNORANCE OF LAW

Table of Sections

WESTLAW ELECTRONIC RESEARCH

See WESTLAW Electronic Research Guide preceding the Summary of Contents.

---

§ 25.1 Introduction

The availability and scope of the defenses of mistake of fact and ignorance of law generally depend upon the mens rea requirements of the offense in question. With the exception noted in § 25.12, *supra*, the defenses of mistake and ignorance operate to negate mens rea, rather than to establish an independent excuse or justification (such as self defense). Why then are ignorance and mistake traditionally characterized as "defenses," rather than simply evidence that disproves mens rea? The answer is largely historical. At common law these defenses developed independently from mens rea,[1] and it took many hundreds of years for their kinship to become apparent. If the federal code were rewritten today, it would probably follow the lead of the Model Penal Code and the modern state codes that treat ignorance and mistake as mens rea issues.[2]

§ 25.1

1. Mens rea is of course a central part of the prosecution's case in chief. In contrast, evidence of ignorance and mistake are typically introduced by the defense, and the judicial rulings developing these doctrines were generally responses to claims that certain evidence established a "defense."

2. *See* MODEL PENAL CODE § 2.04(1)(a) (1962) (ignorance or mistake of fact or law is a defense if it "negatives the purpose, knowledge, belief, recklessness or negli-

The chief obstacle to be overcome when the defenses of ignorance and mistake are raised in federal prosecutions is the determination of the mens rea level of the offense. As the Supreme Court recognized in *United States v. Bailey*,[3] "[f]ew areas of criminal law pose more difficulty than the proper definition of the mens rea required for any particular crime." Although the federal courts have praised the clarity of the Model Penal Code's mens rea terminology and analysis, Congress has not adopted a Model Penal Code-based statutory revision. The current federal code is a hodgepodge of mens rea terms that have accumulated over two centuries. A blue ribbon study commission concluded in 1970 that the federal code already employed a "staggering array" of some 78 different combinations of words to describe mens rea.[4] The commission also found that "there is no discernible pattern or consistent rationale which explains why one crime is defined or understood to require one mental state and another crime another mental state or indeed no mental state at all."[5] Since conditions have not improved since 1970, the federal courts have relatively little guidance in determining the mens rea requirements for particular offenses, which in turn will determine the scope of any "defense" that might be available for a mistake of fact or law. This uncertainty greatly complicates the task of both the courts and counsel.

Although some commentators employ the general and specific intent terminology to analyze mistake/mens rea issues, these terms do not play a prominent role in the federal ignorance and mistake cases. Instead, the federal courts tend to turn directly to the question what mens rea is required by the statutes in question, and how any claim of ignorance or mistake might bear on the presence or absence of the required mental state.[6]

There is, however, one form of mistake that calls for a different kind of analysis. Some defenses that might be characterized as mistakes of law are based upon the Due Process clause. We discuss the Due Process analysis in §§ 25.10–25.12.

gence required to establish a material element of the offense"). Many states have adopted revised codes including provisions based upon § 2.04. MODEL PENAL CODE AND COMMENTARIES § 2.04 commentary at 271–72 nn.6–7 (1985). A national commission empaneled to draft a revision of the federal criminal code included the following provision, which adopts the Model Penal Code approach:

§ 304. Ignorance or Mistake Negativing Culpability.

A person does not commit an offense if when he engages in conduct he is ignorant or mistaken about a matter of fact or law and the ignorance or mistake negates the kind of culpability required for the commission of the offense.

NATIONAL COMMISSION ON REFORM OF FEDERAL CRIMINAL LAWS, STUDY DRAFT OF A NEW CRIMINAL CODE, § 304 (1970).

3. 444 U.S. 394, 403, 100 S.Ct. 624, 631, 62 L.Ed.2d 575 (1980).

4. 1 NATIONAL COMMISSION ON REFORM OF FEDERAL CRIMINAL LAWS, WORKING PAPERS 119–20 (1970).

5. *Id.* at 120.

6. *See, e.g.*, Liparota v. United States, 471 U.S. 419, 433 n. 16, 105 S.Ct. 2084, 2092, 85 L.Ed.2d 434 (1985) ("A more useful instruction might relate specifically to the mental state required under [the statute in question] and eschew use of difficult legal concepts like 'specific intent' and 'general intent.'").

Library References:

C.J.S. Criminal Law § 46–49, 56, 87–88, 93–94, 122, 136.
West's Key No. Digests, Criminal Law ⟜31–33.

§ 25.2 Ignorance or Mistake of Fact—In General

The federal courts generally follow the common law rule that an honest[1] mistake of fact is a defense if (1) it negatives the required mens rea, and (2) the defendant's acts would have been lawful if the facts had been as he supposed them to be.[2] The first step in the analysis of a mistake of fact claim is to determine the mens rea of the offense with which the defendant has been charged. A mistake that disproves mens rea is a defense, but a mistake that does not negate mens rea ordinarily has no bearing on criminal liability. For example, in *United States v. Cook*[3] a defendant charged with theft of an interstate shipment claimed that he had been mistaken about the contents of some of the boxes. The court rejected this argument with the comment that:

> [t]he obvious flaw in this argument is that [the defendant's] actions would not have been lawful had the facts been as he supposed them to be. . . . The fact that [the defendant] intended to take different merchandise than he eventually stole simply cannot operate as an excuse for his crime. Mistake of fact only affects criminal guilt if the mistake demonstrates that the defendant did not have the state of mind required for the crime.[4]

In contrast, if the offense had required knowledge or intent to steal property of a certain nature, then the defendant's misunderstanding could have negated the required mens rea.

Library References:

C.J.S. Criminal Law § 93.
West's Key No. Digests, Criminal Law ⟜33.

§ 25.2

1. The requirement that the mistake be "honest" means that it must be honestly entertained, or sincere, and is sometimes associated with the requirement that the mistake be reasonable. For a discussion of the reasonableness requirement, see § 26.3.

2. Some federal cases state the general rule.

D.C. Circuit: United States v. Barker, 546 F.2d 940, 946 (D.C.Cir.1976) (Wilkey, J.); *Id.* at 961–62 (Leventhal, J., dissenting).

Ninth Circuit: United States v. Vasarajs, 908 F.2d 443, 447–48 n. 7 (9th Cir. 1990); United States v. Brooks, 841 F.2d 268, 269–70 (9th Cir.1988).

Many more cases are resolved in a manner that is consistent with this general rule without any express reference to it.

For a general discussion of the common law doctrine, see Edwin R. Keedy, *Ignorance and Mistake in the Criminal Law*, 22 HARV.L.REV. 75 (1908); WAYNE R. LAFAVE & AUSTIN W. SCOTT, JR., CRIMINAL LAW § 5.1 (2d ed. 1986); Rollin M. Perkin, *Ignorance and Mistake in Criminal Law*, 88 U.PA.L.REV. 54–58 (1939).

3. 967 F.2d 431 (10th Cir.1992).

4. 967 F.2d at 433 (citations omitted). The court also observed that a mistaken belief that the boxes belonged to the defendant would have negated the state of mind required for the crime of larceny. *Id.*

§ 25.3   Ignorance or Mistake of Fact—Reasonableness of a Mistake

Some general authorities state that only a reasonable mistake will constitute a defense, but that statement is overbroad. As noted above, the mens rea required for each offense determines the scope of any defense that can arise from either ignorance or mistake. If an offense requires "knowledge" in the sense of subjective awareness, even an unreasonable mistake can disprove the existence of the requisite mental state.[1] This is simply a matter of defining the required mens rea. In some cases "knowledge" has been statutorily defined to include "reckless disregard," which has the effect of narrowing the scope of the mistakes that will constitute a defense.[2] Certainly the reasonableness of a mistake is a relevant consideration in the case of any federal offense that requires only recklessness or negligence.

Library References:

    C.J.S. Criminal Law § 93.
    West's Key No. Digests, Criminal Law ⚍33.

§ 25.4   Ignorance or Mistake of Fact—Deliberate Ignorance

Sometimes the question of deliberate ignorance—often referred to as "willful blindness"—may be couched as a claim of mistake or ignorance. The federal courts follow the common law rule: when a statute requires knowledge, an actor cannot avoid liability by deliberately closing his eyes to what otherwise would have been obvious to him.[1] The leading case on this issue is the Ninth Circuit's en banc decision in *United States v. Jewell*,[2] which explains the rationale for the willful blindness doctrine:

> The substantive justification for the rule is that deliberate ignorance and positive knowledge are equally culpable. The textual justification is that in common understanding one "knows" facts of which

---

§ 25.3

    1. *See*

    Supreme Court: United States v. International Minerals & Chem. Corp., 402 U.S. 558, 563–64, 91 S.Ct. 1697, 1701, 29 L.Ed.2d 178 (1971) (person who believed "in good faith that he was shipping distilled water when in fact he was shipping some dangerous acid would not be covered" by statute that required "knowing" shipment of dangerous chemicals).

    First Circuit: United States v. Currier, 621 F.2d 7, 10 (1st Cir.1980) (to establish "knowing" failure to maintain proper firearms records government must prove that defendant knew he did not complete the required forms).

    Eleventh Circuit: United States v. Hayes Int'l Corp., 786 F.2d 1499, 1505–06 (11th Cir.1986) (belief that hazardous waste recycler had permit and would recycle haz-

ardous waste would be a defense, but evidence did not support this claim).

    2. *See* United States *ex rel.* Hagood v. Sonoma County Water Agency, 929 F.2d 1416, 1421 (9th Cir.1991) (discussing scope of mistake defense in qui tam action brought under 31 U.S.C. § 3729, which defines knowledge to include "actual knowledge," "deliberate ignorance" of truth or falsity, and "reckless disregard" of truth or falsity).

§ 25.4

    1. *See*

    Second Circuit: United States v. Squires, 440 F.2d 859, 864 (2d Cir.1971).

    Ninth Circuit: United States v. Sanchez–Robles, 927 F.2d 1070, 1073 (9th Cir. 1991).

    2. 532 F.2d 697 (9th Cir.1976) (en banc).

he is less than absolutely certain. To act "knowingly," therefore, is not necessarily to act only with positive knowledge, but also to act with an awareness of the high probability of the existence of the fact in question. When such awareness is present, "positive" knowledge is not required.[3]

Whether a willful blindness or deliberate ignorance instruction is proper turns on the question whether the statute in question requires positive knowledge, or merely knowledge that a certain fact is highly probable or virtually certain.[4]

Library References:

C.J.S. Criminal Law § 93.
West's Key No. Digests, Criminal Law ⚎33.

§ 25.5 Ignorance or Mistake of Fact—Strict Liability Offenses

A mistake of fact defense "is possible only if there is some 'mental state required to establish a material element of the crime' that the mistake can negate."[1] Since strict liability offenses require no criminal state of mind, mistake of fact is no defense.

It should be noted, however, that the absence of a mens rea term is no guarantee that a federal statute will be interpreted as a strict liability offense. Generally federal criminal liability requires an "evil-meaning mind,"[2] and "mere omission [from the statute] of any mention of intent will not be construed as eliminating that element from the crimes denounced."[3] In the case of federal statutes based on common law crimes, the Supreme Court has recognized "an interpretative presumption that mens rea is required."[4] Absent a contrary legislative intent, federal criminal statutes are deemed to carry forward the common law

3. 532 F.2d at 700.

4. As the *Jewell* court noted:

It begs the question to assert that a "deliberate ignorance" instruction permits the jury to convict without finding that the accused possessed the knowledge required by the statute. Such an assertion assumes that the statute requires positive knowledge. But the question is the meaning of the term "knowingly" in the statute. If it means positive knowledge, then, of course, nothing less will do. But if "knowingly" includes a mental state in which the defendant is aware that the fact in question is highly probable but consciously avoids enlightenment, the statute is satisfied by such proof.

32 F.2d at 703. Although most federal criminal statutes do not define terms such as knowledge, there are exceptions. In the absence of any statutory definition, the federal courts have adopted many different definitions of knowledge. For a discussion of

knowledge as a continuum from positive or actual knowledge to constructive knowledge, and varying points along that range, see *supra* § 4.2(v).

§ 25.5

1. *Seventh Circuit:* United States v. Anton, 683 F.2d 1011, 1013 (7th Cir.1982) (quoting WAYNE R. LaFAVE & AUSTIN W. SCOTT, JR., CRIMINAL LAW § 47 at 356 (1972)).

Accord,

Tenth Circuit: United States v. Miranda–Enriquez, 842 F.2d 1211, 1213 (10th Cir.1988).

2. Morissette v. United States, 342 U.S. 246, 251, 72 S.Ct. 240, 244, 96 L.Ed. 288 (1952).

3. *Id.* at 263.

4. United States v. United States Gypsum Co., 438 U.S. 422, 437, 98 S.Ct. 2864, 2873, 57 L.Ed.2d 854 (1978).

mens rea requirement.[5] Because of the "disfavored status"[6] of offenses that contain no mens rea, the federal courts also presume that criminal statutes that are not based on common law crimes require mens rea, though that presumption can be overcome.[7]

Library References:

C.J.S. Criminal Law § 93.
West's Key No. Digests, Criminal Law ⊨33.

§ 25.6   Ignorance or Mistake of Fact—Jurisdictional Facts

Because generally no mens rea is required regarding jurisdictional facts,[1] ignorance or mistake regarding those facts will seldom—if ever— be a defense. As the Supreme Court explained in *United States v. Feola*,[2] "[t]he concept of criminal intent does not extend so far as to require that the actor understand not only the nature of his act but also its consequence for the choice of a judicial forum."[3] In the view of the federal courts, a defendant who has chosen to engage in wrongful conduct "may not complain that facts out of his knowledge brought into play federal penalties or enhanced punishment."[4]

Library References:

C.J.S. Criminal Law § 93.
West's Key No. Digests, Criminal Law ⊨33.

§ 25.7   Ignorance or Mistake of Law—In General

The Supreme Court has repeatedly endorsed the common law rule that ignorance or mistake of law is no defense.[1] The traditional rule

5. *See* Morissette v. United States, 342 U.S. 246, 262, 72 S.Ct. 240, 249, 96 L.Ed. 288 (1952) ("Congressional silence as to mental elements in an Act merely adopting into federal statutory law a concept of crime already so well defined in common law and statutory interpretation by the states may warrant quite contrary inferences than the same silence in creating an offense new to general law").

6. United States v. United States Gypsum Co., 438 U.S. 422, 437–38, 98 S.Ct. 2864, 2873–74, 57 L.Ed.2d 854 (1978).

7. In Holdridge v. United States, 282 F.2d 302, 310 (8th Cir.1960), Judge (later Justice) Blackman set out five main factors that can overcome the presumption against strict liability: (1) the crime is not derived from the common law; (2) legislative policy would be undermined by requiring mens rea; (3) the standard imposed by the statute is "reasonable and adherence thereto properly expected of a person"; (4) the penalty is small; and (5) the "conviction does not gravely besmirch" the actor. *See generally* GEORGE FLETCHER, RETHINKING CRIMINAL LAW § .932 716–36 (1978); WAYNE R. LaFAVE &

AUSTIN W. SCOTT, JR., CRIMINAL LAW § 3.8(a)-(c) (2d ed. 1986).

§ 25.6

1. For a discussion of jurisdiction, see Chapter 1.

2. United States v. Feola, 420 U.S. 671, 95 S.Ct. 1255, 43 L.Ed.2d 541 (1975).

3. 420 U.S. at 685, 95 S.Ct. 1264.

4. United States v. Bolin, 423 F.2d 834, 837 (9th Cir.1970).

§ 25.7

1. *Supreme Court:* Ratzlaf v. United States, 510 U.S. 135, 148, 114 S.Ct. 655, 663, 126 L.Ed.2d 615 (1994); Cheek v. United States, 498 U.S. 192, 199, 111 S.Ct. 604, 609, 112 L.Ed.2d 617 (1991); United States v. International Minerals & Chem. Corp., 402 U.S. 558, 563, 91 S.Ct. 1697, 1701, 29 L.Ed.2d 178 (1971); Lambert v. California, 355 U.S. 225, 228, 78 S.Ct. 240, 243, 2 L.Ed.2d 228 (1957) (quoting Shevlin–Carpenter Corp. v. Minnesota, 218 U.S. 57, 68, 30 S.Ct. 663, 666, 54 L.Ed. 930 (1910)).

For a discussion of the policies and application of the general rule, see MODEL

relieves the prosecution of the difficult task of proving what each defendant knew about the law, and it provides an incentive for knowledge rather than ignorance. It also ensures that the same legal standards are applicable to everyone. It is important to understand the scope of this general principle, which is often "greatly overstated."[2] It means only that generally speaking "knowledge of the existence, meaning or application of the law determining the elements an offense is not an element of that offense."[3] In other words, the government is not ordinarily required to prove that the defendant understood or was even aware of the criminal law under which he is prosecuted.[4] On the other hand, the general principle that ignorance of the law is no defense has no application to collateral legal issues that are made material by the elements of the offense.[5]

Library References:

C.J.S. Criminal Law § 56, 94.
West's Key No. Digests, Criminal Law ☞32.

§ 25.8 Ignorance or Mistake of Law—Mistake or Ignorance that Negates Mens Rea

The general rule that ignorance of law is no defense does not alter the mens rea requirements of particular statutes, and ignorance or

PENAL CODE AND COMMENTARIES § 2.02 comment 11 at 250–52 & § 2.04 comment 3 at 274–77 (1985); JEROME HALL, GENERAL PRINCIPALS OF CRIMINAL LAW 376–401 (2d ed.1960); WAYNE R. LaFAVE & AUSTIN W. SCOTT, JR., CRIMINAL LAW § 5.1(d) (2d ed. 1986); GLANVILLE WILLIAMS, CRIMINAL LAW: THE GENERAL PART 287–93 (2d ed. 1961). *See also* 1 J.AUSTIN, JURISPRUDENCE 497 (4th ed. 1879) (the law is "definite and knowable"); 4 WILLIAM BLACKSTONE, COMMENTARIES ON THE LAWS OF ENGLAND 27 (1769) ("[e]very person of discretion ... is bound and presumed to know [the law]") (the legal system need objectivity in order to sustain judicial process).

2. MODEL PENAL CODE AND COMMENTARIES § 2.02 comment 11 at 250 (1985).

3. *Id.*

4. *See* United States v. Baker, 807 F.2d 427, 429 (5th Cir.1986) (footnote omitted):

It is not surprising that Congress would allow conviction of one who knows that he is selling bogus "Rolex" watches even though he does not know his conduct is punishable as a crime. While it is true that "the general principle that ignorance or mistake of law is no excuse is usually greatly overstated" (American Law Institute, MODEL PENAL CODE § 2.02 comment 131 (Tent.Draft no. 4 1955)), the principle continues to be valid to the extent that ordinarily "the criminal law

does not require knowledge that an act is illegal, wrong, or blameworthy." United States v. Freed, 401 U.S. 601, 612, 91 S.Ct. 1112, 1120, 28 L.Ed.2d 356 (1971) (Brennan, J., concurring). Baker's claim is merely that, even though he had the mental states required by the face of the statute, he should not be convicted because he did not know that Congress had passed a statute criminalizing his conduct. This clearly is not the law. A defendant cannot "avoid prosecution by simply claiming that he had not brushed up on the law." Hamling v. United States, 418 U.S. 87, 123, 94 S.Ct. 2887, 2910, 41 L.Ed.2d 590 (1974).

Similarly in United States v. de Cruz, 82 F.3d 856, 867 (9th Cir.1996), the court characterized the defendant's claim that she "did not know that her conduct violated federal law" as "a classic mistake or ignorance of law argument," which "is not a valid defense."

5. *See generally* WAYNE R. LaFAVE & AUSTIN W. SCOTT, JR., CRIMINAL LAW § 5.1(a) (2d ed. 1986). *But see* United States v. Aguilar, 883 F.2d 662, 672–76 (9th Cir.1989) (defendants would not be entitled to introduce evidence of their erroneous belief that aliens were entitled to enter United States as refugees as a defense in a prosecution for violation of the immigration laws).

mistake of law *does* operate as a defense if it negates the required mens rea under a particular statute. For example, the Supreme Court has held that a "willful" tax violation requires "an act done with a bad purpose" and that "an evil motive is a constituent element of the crime."[1] In light of the tax code's complexity, the Court concluded that Congress did not intend to treat a bona fide misunderstanding of the tax laws as a crime.[2] In 1991 the Supreme Court reaffirmed this analysis, holding that a defendant charged with income tax evasion is entitled to introduce evidence of any belief—however unreasonable—to show that he was ignorant of his legal obligations under the tax code.[3] For the purposes of criminal tax laws, the mens rea term willfulness "requires the Government to prove that the law imposed a duty on the defendant, that the defendant knew of this duty, and that he voluntarily and intentionally violated that duty."[4] In effect, the statutory requirement of willfulness created a defense of mistake of law:

> [I]f the Government proves actual knowledge of the pertinent legal duty, the prosecution, without more, has satisfied the knowledge component of the willfulness requirement. But carrying this burden requires negating a defendant's claim of ignorance of the law or a claim that because of a misunderstanding of the law, he had a good-faith belief that he was not violating any of the provisions of the tax laws. This is so because one cannot be aware that the law imposes a duty upon him and yet be ignorant of it, misunderstand the law, or believe that the duty does not exist. In the end, the issue is whether, based on all the evidence, the Government has proved that the defendant was aware of the duty at issue, which cannot be true if the jury credits a good-faith misunderstanding and belief submission, whether or not the claimed belief or misunderstanding is objectively reasonable.[5]

The Supreme Court focused again on statutory language in *Liparota v. United States*[6] and *Ratzlaf v. United States*,[7] concluding in both cases that the required mental state was one that could be negated by a mistake of law. The statute at issue in *Liparota* proscribed the "knowing" use, transfer, or possession of food stamps in a manner not authorized by law, and the question was whether the requirement of knowledge applied only to the conduct, or also to the fact that the conduct was in violation of the law. The Supreme Court held that the statute required proof that Liparota knew that his possession or acquisition was unlawful. The Court emphasized that it was merely giving effect to an element of the statute, not endorsing a general ignorance of

§ 25.8

1. United States v. Murdock, 290 U.S. 389, 394–95, 54 S.Ct. 223, 225, 78 L.Ed. 381 (1933).

2. 290 U.S. at 396, 54 S.Ct. at 225.

3. Cheek v. United States, 498 U.S. 192, 203–04, 111 S.Ct. 604, 611–12, 112 L.Ed.2d 617 (1991).

4. 498 U.S. at 201, 111 S.Ct. at 610.

5. 498 U.S. at 202, 111 S.Ct. 611.

6. 471 U.S. 419, 105 S.Ct. 2084, 85 L.Ed.2d 434 (1985).

7. 510 U.S. 135, 114 S.Ct. 655, 126 L.Ed.2d 615 (1994).

law defense.[8] *Ratzlaf v. United States*[9] involved a prosecution under the anti-structuring statute, 31 U.S.C. § 5324, which prohibits willfully breaking up a financial transaction to avoid the currency reporting laws. A closely divided Court ruled that willfulness required not only that the defendant knew of the bank's duty to report cash transactions in excess of $10,000, but also "of his duty not to avoid triggering such a report." Accordingly, the defendants were entitled to an instruction that the government was required to prove they knew structuring was unlawful. Congress subsequently amended the anti-structuring law to overrule the *Ratzlaf* decision.[10]

These decisions were founded on the language of the statutes in question as well as the Court's understanding of the intent of Congress. The cases indicate a degree of judicial receptivity to mistake/mens rea arguments in the context of regulatory offenses. Indeed, one commentator has argued that they have set the stage for the general recognition of a mistake of law defense to mala prohibita offenses.[11] The lower court decisions focus on the type of conduct being regulated as well as the statutory language and structure, rejecting the defense where the statutes in question concern health and safety[12] or conduct that is malum in se,[13] but showing greater receptivity where the offense in question is perceived as merely regulatory in nature.[14] This said, it should be noted

8.   471 U.S. at 425 n.9, 105 S.Ct. at 2088.

9.   510 U.S. 135, 114 S.Ct. 655, 126 L.Ed.2d 615 (1994).

10.   For a discussion of the current anti-structuring law, see *supra* § 18.7 et seq.

11.   Michael L. Travers, *Mistake of Law in* Mala Prohibita *Crimes*, 62 U.CHI. L.REV. 1301 (1995).

12.   *Fifth Circuit*: United States v. Baytank (Houston), Inc., 934 F.2d 599, 609–12 (5th Cir.1991) (distinguishing *Liparota* in prosecution for violating statute requiring knowing storage of hazardous wastes without a permit, since *Liparota* Court acknowledged that case did not involve " 'a type of conduct that a reasonable person should know is subject to stringent public regulation, and may seriously threaten the community's health and safety.")

Ninth Circuit: United States v. Weitzenhoff, 35 F.3d 1275, 1280 (9th Cir.1993) (suggesting in prosecution for violation of Clean Water Act that *Ratzlaf* does not apply to public health and welfare offenses).

13.   *Ninth Circuit*: United States v. English, 92 F.3d 909, 914–16 (9th Cir.1996) (rejecting defense in securities fraud prosecution; characterizing fraudulent schemes as "inherently nefarious;" and suggesting *Ratzlaf* has no application to malum in se offenses); United States v. Baker, 63 F.3d

1478 (9th Cir.1995), *cert. denied*, 516 U.S. 1097, 116 S.Ct. 824, 133 L.Ed.2d 767 (1996), and *cert. denied*, 516 U.S. 1117, 116 S.Ct. 921, 133 L.Ed.2d 850 (1996) (concluding that statute making it an offense knowingly to ship, receive or possess contraband cigarettes, unlike statute in *Ratzlaf*, is not trap for the unwary).

14.   *Third Circuit*: United States v. Curran, 20 F.3d 560, 567–69 (3d Cir.1994) (following *Ratzlaf* in prosecution charging defendant with causing election campaign treasurers to file false statements; noting the underlying conduct was not obviously evil, but was made illegal by regulatory statute; and concluding that prosecution must prove defendant knew of the treasurers' reporting obligations, attempted to frustrate those obligations, and knew his conduct was illegal).

Seventh Circuit: United States v. Obiechie, 38 F.3d 309 (7th Cir.1994) (construing 18 U.S.C. §§ 922(a)(1)(a) & 924(a)(1)(D), which proscribe willful dealing in firearms without a license, to require knowledge of the law, since statute distinguishes between willfulness and mere knowledge).

Eleventh Circuit: United States v. Sanchez–Corcino, 85 F.3d 549, 552–54 (11th Cir.1996) (concluding that conviction for dealing in firearms without a license in violation of 18 U.S.C. § 924(a)(1)(D) requires knowledge of existence of licensing requirement).

that, with only a few exceptions,[15] to date most lower courts have rejected claims based upon *Liparota* and *Ratzlaf*.[16]

The highly publicized prosecution of Col. Oliver North illustrates the continuing difficulty of determining whether the mens rea of a federal statute using a term such as "corrupt" or "willful" can be negated by proof of a mistake of law. A panel of the D.C. Circuit split three ways on North's contention that his reliance on the authorization of his superiors, including President Reagan, negated any criminal intent. A per curiam opinion concluded that his reliance on his superiors' authorization could negate the intent required for count 9 ("willful" and unlawful concealment or destruction of federal records),[17] but not the

---

15. *Third Circuit:* United States v. Curran, 20 F.3d 560, 567–69 (3d Cir.1994) (following *Ratzlaf* in prosecution charging defendant with causing election campaign treasurers to file false statements; noting the underlying conduct was not obviously evil, but was made illegal by regulatory statute; and concluding that prosecution must prove defendant knew of the treasurers' reporting obligations, attempted to frustrate those obligations, and knew his conduct was illegal).

Seventh Circuit: United States v. Obie-chie, 38 F.3d 309 (7th Cir.1994) (construing 18 U.S.C. §§ 922(a)(1)(a) & 924(a)(1)(D), which proscribe willful dealing in firearms without a license, to require knowledge of the law, since statute distinguishes between willfulness and mere knowledge).

Eleventh Circuit: United States v. Sanchez-Corcino, 85 F.3d 549, 552–54 (11th Cir.1996) (concluding that conviction for dealing in firearms without a license in violation of 18 U.S.C. § 924(a)(1)(D) requires knowledge of existence of licensing requirement).

16. *Third Circuit*: United States v. Sokolow, 91 F.3d 396, 407–09 (3d Cir.1996) (suggesting in money laundering prosecution that *Ratzlaf* and its progeny are limited to offenses requiring willfulness).

Fifth Circuit: United States v. Baytank (Houston), Inc., 934 F.2d 599, 609–12 (5th Cir.1991) (distinguishing *Liparota* in prosecution for violating statute requiring knowing storage of hazardous wastes without a permit, since *Liparota* Court acknowledged that case did not involve " 'a type of conduct that a reasonable person should know is subject to stringent public regulation, and may seriously threaten the community's health and safety.'")

Ninth Circuit: United States v. English, 92 F.3d 909, 914–16 (9th Cir.1996) (rejecting defense in securities fraud prosecution; characterizing fraudulent schemes as "inherently nefarious;" and suggesting *Ratzlaf*

has no application to malum in se offenses); United States v. Baker, 63 F.3d 1478 (9th Cir.1995), *cert. denied*, 516 U.S. 1097, 116 S.Ct. 824, 133 L.Ed.2d 767 (1996), and *cert. denied*, 516 U.S. 1117, 116 S.Ct. 921, 133 L.Ed.2d 850 (1996) (concluding that statute making it an offense knowingly to ship, receive or possess contraband cigarettes, unlike statute in *Ratzlaf*, is not trap for the unwary); United States v. Weitzenhoff, 35 F.3d 1275, 1280 (9th Cir.1993) (suggesting in prosecution for violation of Clean Water Act that *Ratzlaf* does not apply to public health and welfare offenses).

Eighth Circuit: United States v. Jain, 93 F.3d 436 (8th Cir.1996) (structure of Medicare kickback statute indicates that defendant need only know that his conduct is wrongful, not that it is illegal).

Tenth Circuit: United States v. Blair, 54 F.3d 639, 643 (10th Cir.1995) (distinguishing *Ratzlaf* in prosecution for conspiracy to conduct illegal gambling business on ground that 18 U.S.C. § 371 does not evince clear intent of Congress to require that defendant have knowledge that his conduct was prohibited by law).

17. United States v. North, 910 F.2d 843, 884–888 (D.C.Cir.) (per curiam), *opinion withdrawn in part and superceded in part*, 920 F.2d 940 (D.C.Cir.1990). The per curiam opinion determined that "it was error to preclude the jury from considering whatever evidence of authorization exists in the record as it bears on the jury's determination whether North had subjective knowledge of unlawfulness." *Id.* at 885 (footnote omitted). The court commented that the the unlawful "authorization" of one's superiors "cannot convert illegal activity into legal, yet it surely can affect a defendant's *belief* that his conduct was lawful—particularly when we are dealing in an area of international security concerns, and when the authorization is thought to come from the President himself." *Id.*

intent required for count 6 ("corrupt" obstruction of a congressional investigation).[18] Judge Silberman dissented on the ground that the defense should have been applicable to both counts.[19] Chief Judge Wald, in contrast, dissented on the ground that the district court had properly restricted the scope of the defense under count 9.[20] After the original panel decision the Independent Counsel sought rehearing on the court's conclusion under count 6, noting that 26 federal statutes included language similar to the wording of the statute on which that count 6 was based.[21] The court modified another portion of its decision but denied review on this issue, concluding that the Independent Counsel had conceded the issue in his original brief and oral argument.[22] Although the court achieved little agreement, the individual opinions include a variety of interesting arguments.[23]

Library References:

> C.J.S. Criminal Law § 56, 94.
> West's Key No. Digests, Criminal Law ⊕32.

§ 25.9   Ignorance or Mistake of Law—Willful Blindness

Where ignorance or mistake of law is recognized is a defense, there is authority holding that the defense is limited by the willful blindness doctrine.[1] In other words, one may not claim a defense of mistake of law if he has conducted himself to be deliberately ignorant of a specific regulation that would otherwise be obvious. However, as noted above, this is really a question of how the mens rea for the statute in question is defined.[2]

Library References:

> C.J.S. Criminal Law § 93.
> West's Key No. Digests, Criminal Law ⊕33.

18. 910 F.2d at 881 (concluding that the statute used the term corrupt in its usual sense of depraved, evil, moral weakness or "debased political morality," and did not require knowledge of illegality); *id.* at 882 (behavior that is not inadvertent, negligent, or even recklessly nonpurposeful reflects a corrupt attempt to interfere with the administration of justice).

19. 910 F.2d at 937–46 (Silberman, J., dissenting).

20. 910 F.2d at 926–32 (Wald, C. J., dissenting).

21. *See* 920 F.2d at 958 (Wald, C.J., dissenting).

22. 920 F.2d at 949–50.

23. *See, e.g.,* 910 F.2d at 885 (authorization from one's superiors is particularly likely to affect an individual's belief that his conduct is lawful "when we are dealing in

an area of international security concerns, and when the authorization is thought to come from the President himself"); *id.* at 926 (Wald, C.J., dissenting) (comparing North's arguments to the Nuremberg defense of "following orders"); id. at 930–31 (Wald, C.J., dissenting) (lack of reasonable belief that one's beliefs are lawful is the same thing as knowledge that they are unlawful).

§ 25.9

1. *See* United States v. Squires, 440 F.2d 859, 864 (2d Cir.1971) ("[w]henever a defense of ignorance of the law or ignorance of fact is claimed, one may not deliberately close his eyes to what otherwise would have been obvious to him"). This issue is also implicated in the *North* case, see *supra,* text accompanying nn. 17–23.

2. See § 25.4.

§ 25.10 Ignorance of the Law and Due Process—*Lambert v. California*

Some claims of ignorance or mistake rest on a constitutional foundation. The Due Process Clause requires that the law give fair notice of what is prohibited, and some claims of ignorance or mistake of law raise Due Process issues.

In *Lambert v. California*[1] the Supreme Court recognized a Due Process defense based upon ignorance of the law. The Court observed that lawmakers have "wide latitude" to dispense with mens rea, but it held that a Los Angeles ordinance exceeded that latitude and violated Due Process. The ordinance required all convicted felons to register with the police if they stayed in Los Angeles longer than five days.[2] Observing that the "conduct" in question here was "wholly passive—mere failure to register,"[3] the majority concluded:

> We believe that actual knowledge of the duty to register or proof of the probability of such knowledge and subsequent failure to comply are necessary before a conviction under the ordinance can stand. As Holmes wrote in *The Common Law*, "A law which punished conduct which would not be blameworthy in the average member of the community would be too severe for that community to bear." *Id.*, at 50. Its severity lies in the absence of an opportunity either to avoid the consequences of the law or to defend any prosecution brought under it. Where a person did not know of the duty to register and where there was no proof of the probability of such knowledge, he may not be convicted consistently with due process. Were it otherwise, the evil would be as great as it is when the law is written in print too fine to read or in a language foreign to the community.[4]

The impact of the *Lambert* "fair notice" rule has been limited. Although *Lambert* has been cited in more than 170 federal cases, it has been directly followed by the federal courts only a handful of times to invalidate convictions.[5] Indeed, in 1985 the Supreme Court noted that the application of *Lambert* has been so limited that it "lend[s] some credence to Justice Frankfurter's colorful prediction in dissent that the case would stand as 'an isolated deviation from the strong current of

§ 25.10

1. 355 U.S. 225, 228, 78 S.Ct. 240, 242–43, 2 L.Ed.2d 228 (1957).

2. 355 U.S. at 228–29, 78 S.Ct. at 243.

3. 355 U.S. at 228, 78 S.Ct. at 243.

4. 355 U.S. at 229–230, 78 S.Ct. at 243–44 (quoting OLIVER WENDELL HOLMES, JR., THE COMMON LAW 50 (1881)).

5. *D.C. Circuit:* United States v. Nofziger, 878 F.2d 442 (D.C.Cir.1989); United States v. Holland, 810 F.2d 1215 (D.C.Cir. 1987).

Second Circuit: United States v. Mancuso, 420 F.2d 556 (2d Cir.1970); United States v. Toomey, 404 F.Supp. 1377 (S.D.N.Y.1975).

Fifth Circuit: United States v. Anderson, 853 F.2d 313, 318 (5th Cir.1988) (stating that "[a]lthough *Lambert* raises more questions than it answers," it could apply to a situation where a person bought a rifle without any good reason to know that it had been converted to an illegal mode of operation) (dicta).

Tenth Circuit: United States v. Brown, 376 F.Supp. 451 (W.D.Mo.1974).

Federal Circuit: Sisson v. United States, 630 F.Supp. 1026 (D.Ariz.1986), *reversed*, 814 F.2d 634 (Fed.Cir.1987).

precedents—a derelict on the waters of the law.' "[6] *Lambert* is most likely to be followed where the statute reaches a failure to act and the conduct (or inaction) in question is everyday behavior, rather than a highly regulated or ultrahazardous undertaking.[7] For example, the Supreme Court distinguished *Lambert* in *United States v. Freed*,[8] in which it held that the government was not required to prove that the recipient of unregistered hand grenades knew that they were unregistered. The Court commented that "one would hardly be surprised to learn that possession of hand grenades is not an innocent act."[9]

It should be noted, however, that the scope of the Due Process/fair warning doctrine is a good deal more sweeping when the case involves an exercise of the First Amendment or other constitutionally protected conduct.[10]

Library References:

C.J.S. Criminal Law § 56, 94.
West's Key No. Digests, Criminal Law ☞32.

§ 25.11 Due Process, Fair Warning, and Reliance on Official Statements of the Law

A second line of Due Process cases also deals with claims that could be characterized as mistake or ignorance of the law. In these cases the principal problem is not, as in *Lambert*, the lack of a clear statutory standard, but rather the affirmative conduct of government officials who mislead the defendant about the law. The Supreme Court dealt with this issue in three cases during the 1950s and 1960s. In *Raley v. Ohio*,[1] the Court held that defendants could not be convicted for refusing to answer incriminating questions before a state un-American activities commission. The defendants had been informed by the commission that they had a right under the Ohio Constitution to protect themselves from self-incrimination, but the Ohio Supreme Court ruled that they were nonetheless presumed to have been aware of an Ohio immunity statute which stripped them of that privilege.[2] In reversing the convictions, the Su-

---

6. Texaco Inc. v. Short, 454 U.S. 516, 537–38 n. 33, 102 S.Ct. 781, 796, 70 L.Ed.2d 738 (1982).

7. The outcome in *Lambert* may also have been affected by the whiff of improper governmental conduct that hung over the case, as exemplified by two points noted in the majority opinion: (1) the defendant was originally arrested on "suspicion" of other charges which were not pursued, and (2) she was not permitted to register after she was made aware of the registration law. 355 U.S. at 226 & 229, 78 S.Ct. at 242 & 243. These points suggest that the city's real motive may not have been to enforce the ordinance (which the Court characterized as merely a "convenience" for law enforcement agencies). Perhaps it served the city's purpose to have no publicity and no compli-

ance, so that prosecutors had a ready-made charge to bring against any previously convicted felon whom they suspected of other crimes.

8. 401 U.S. 601, 91 S.Ct. 1112, 28 L.Ed.2d 356 (1971).

9. 401 U.S. at 609, 91 S.Ct. at 1118.

10. For a discussion of the void-for-vagueness doctrine, see WAYNE R. LaFAVE & AUSTIN W. SCOTT, JR., CRIMINAL LAW § 2.3 (2d ed. 1986); LAWRENCE TRIBE, AMERICAN CONSTITUTIONAL LAW § 12–31 (1988).

§ 25.11

1. 360 U.S. 423, 79 S.Ct. 1257, 3 L.Ed.2d 1344 (1959).

2. 360 U.S. at 425, 79 S.Ct. at 1259.

preme Court stated that "[a]fter the Commission, speaking for the State, acted as it did, to sustain the Ohio Supreme Court's judgment would be to sanction an indefensible sort of entrapment by the State—convicting a citizen for exercising a privilege which the State had clearly told him was available to him."[3] In *Cox v. Louisiana*[4] the Supreme Court followed *Raley* to reverse the conviction of a civil rights leader who had acted in reliance on the town's highest police official, who erroneously advised demonstrators that they could legally protest 101 feet from the courthouse steps. Finally, in *United States v. Laub*[5] the Supreme Court held that reliance on the assurance of State Department officials concerning passport regulations was a defense to criminal prosecution. Recalling *Raley* the Court held:

> Crimes are not to be created by inference. They may not be constructed *nunc pro tunc*. Ordinarily, citizens may not be punished for actions undertaken in good faith reliance upon authoritative assurances that punishment will not attach.[6]

Some lower court decisions *Raley*, *Cox*, and *Laub* have fleshed out to some degree the due process analysis applicable to reliance on erroneous official statements of the law. A pair of Ninth Circuit cases split on the question whether a defendant may rely on a lower court decision unless and until it is overruled, sending conflicting signals on the scope of the protection provided by the Due Process clause. In *United States v. Albertini*[7] the Ninth Circuit held that Due Process required the reversal of a demonstrator's conviction because he had acted in reliance on the Ninth Circuit's earlier ruling—not yet reversed by the Supreme Court—that his previous conduct was protected by the First Amendment. The court reasoned that if the Due Process clause is to mean anything, it should mean that—

> a person who holds the latest controlling court opinion declaring his activities to be constitutionally protected should be able to depend on that ruling to protect like activities from criminal conviction until that opinion is reversed, or at least until the Supreme Court has granted certiorari.[8]

In contrast, however, in *Ostrosky v. Alaska*,[9] the Ninth Circuit held that the defendant was not entitled to rely on the decision of a lower state court in his own case while it was pending on appeal. Emphasizing that Alaska law permits the state to enforce a statute while a decision holding it unconstitutional is on appeal, and also that under Alaska law the decision of one superior court does not bind other superior courts,[10] the court distinguished *Albertini* on several grounds. First, Ostrosky knew that the decision in his favor would be reviewed by a higher court, since

3. 360 U.S. at 425–26, 79 S.Ct. at 1259.

4. 379 U.S. 559, 85 S.Ct. 476, 13 L.Ed.2d 487 (1965).

5. 385 U.S. 475, 87 S.Ct. 574, 17 L.Ed.2d 526 (1967).

6. 385 U.S. at 487, 87 S.Ct. at 581.

7. 830 F.2d 985 (9th Cir.1987).

8. 830 F.2d at 989.

9. 913 F.2d 590 (9th Cir.1990).

10. 913 F.2d at 596.

it was on appeal, whereas Albertini knew only that there was a small chance that certiorari would be granted.[11] Second, Albertini relied upon an appellate decision from the Ninth Circuit, while Ostrosky relied upon the decision of a trial court.[12]

Raley, *Cox*, and *Laub* have also given rise to a series of lower court decisions that treat reliance on misleading or incorrect legal pronouncements as "entrapment by estoppel." The development of this defense is discussed below.

Library References:

C.J.S. Criminal Law § 56, 94.
West's Key No. Digests, Criminal Law ⊙⇒32.

§ 25.12   Entrapment by Estoppel and the Defense of Reliance on an Official (Mis)statement of the Law

Although *Raley*, *Cox*, and *Laub* were clearly identified as Due Process decisions, many of the more recent cases appear to be common law decisions that are influenced by—but do not rest directly on—the Due Process clause. Although this development is especially noticeable in the lower courts, at least one Supreme Court decision seems to conform to this pattern. In *United States v. Pennsylvania Indust. Chem. Corp.*[1] the Supreme Court held that "traditional notions of fairness inherent in our system of criminal justice prevent the Government from proceeding with the prosecution" where the defendant had relied upon administrative regulations promulgated by the responsible administrative agency, the Corps of Engineers. Accordingly the Court concluded that it was error for the district court to refuse to permit the defendant to present evidence in support of the claim "that it had been affirmatively misled into believing that the discharges in question were not a violation of the statute."[2] The Supreme Court did not refer to Due Process, or to *Raley*, *Cox*, or *Laub*. It did, however, refer to two law review articles on the principles of estoppel.[3]

Most of the lower courts in the past two decades have adopted the estoppel terminology and treated claims of reliance on misleading official statements as raising the defense of "entrapment by estoppel."[4] Some

11. 913 F.2d at 597–98.

12. 913 F.2d at 598.

§ 25.12

1. 411 U.S. 655, 674, 93 S.Ct. 1804, 1816, 36 L.Ed.2d 567 (1973).

2. 411 U.S. at 674, 93 S.Ct. at 1816.

3. *Id.* at 1817, citing Frank C. Newman, *Should Official Advice Be Reliable?— Proposals as to Estoppel and Related Doctrines in Administrative Law*, 53 Colum.L.Rev. 374 (1953), and Note, *Applying Estoppel Principles in Criminal Cases*, 78 Yale L.J. 1046 (1969).

4. Ten circuits have recognized the defense of entrapment by estoppel—though not necessarily holding it applicable in the case at bar.

First Circuit: United States v. Troncoso, 23 F.3d 612, 615 (1st Cir.1994); United States v. Smith, 940 F.2d 710, 714 (1st Cir.1991).

Second Circuit: United States v. Abcasis, 45 F.3d 39, 42–45 (2d Cir.1995); United States v. Corso, 20 F.3d 521, 528–29 (2d Cir.1994).

Third Circuit: United States v. Palmieri, 21 F.3d 1265, 1288 (3d Cir.1994), *cert. granted, judgment vacated,* 513 U.S. 957,

decisions recognize that entrapment by estoppel is a Due Process defense, or that the defense is grounded on the fundamental fairness concerns of the Due Process clause,[5] but others reflect no recognition that constitutional principles are involved.

Although the formulations of the defense of entrapment by estoppel vary slightly, most of the lower courts would agree with the following statement:

> The defense of entrapment by estoppel is applicable when a government official or agent actively assures a defendant that certain conduct is legal and the defendant reasonably relies on that advice and continues or initiates the conduct.[6]

This defense has several elements. The lower court decisions generally require (1) that the one misleading the defendant be a federal official, (2)

115 S.Ct. 413, 130 L.Ed.2d 329 (1994) (Cowen, J., dissenting); United States v. Conley, 859 F.Supp. 909, 926 (W.D.Pa. 1994).

Fourth Circuit: United States v. Clark, 986 F.2d 65, 69–70 (4th Cir.1993).

Fifth Circuit: United States v. Spires, 79 F.3d 464, 466 (5th Cir.1996).

Sixth Circuit: United States v. Levin, 973 F.2d 463, 468 (6th Cir.1992); United States v. Neufeld, 908 F.Supp. 491, 499 (S.D.Ohio 1995).

Seventh Circuit: United States v. Howell, 37 F.3d 1197, 1203 (7th Cir.1994).

Eighth Circuit: United States v. Bazargan, 992 F.2d 844, 849 (8th Cir.1993); United States v. LaChapelle, 969 F.2d 632, 637 (8th Cir.1992); United States v. Austin, 915 F.2d 363, 366 (8th Cir.1990).

Ninth Circuit: United States v. Weitzenhoff, 35 F.3d 1275, 1290–91 (9th Cir. 1993); United States v. Clegg, 846 F.2d 1221, 1223–24 (9th Cir.1988). *See also* United States v. Tallmadge, 829 F.2d 767, 773–74 (9th Cir.1987) (not using term estoppel by entrapment).

Tenth Circuit: United States v. Nichols, 21 F.3d 1016, 1018 (10th Cir.1994).

Eleventh Circuit: United States v. Baptista–Rodriguez, 17 F.3d 1354, 1368 n. 18 (11th Cir.1994); United States v. Thompson, 25 F.3d 1558, 1563 (11th Cir.1994); United States v. Hedges, 912 F.2d 1397, 1404–05 (11th Cir.1990).

The D.C. Circuit has not recognized the defense in a published opinion, though there is a passing reference in an unpublished opinion. United States v. Campbell, 1995 WL 555618 *1 (D.C.Cir.1995).

5. *First Circuit:* United States v. Smith, 940 F.2d 710, 714 (1st Cir.1991)(en-

trapment by estoppel is a "due process concept[]").

Third Circuit: United States v. Conley, 859 F.Supp. 909, 926 (W.D.Pa.1994) (in lower federal courts "the Due Process reliance on misleading government conduct defense has come to be known as the 'entrapment by estoppel' defense").

Fifth Circuit: United States v. Spires, 79 F.3d 464, 466 (5th Cir.1996) (defense "is based on fundamental fairness concerns of the Due Process Clause").

Seventh Circuit: United States v. Howell, 37 F.3d 1197, 1204 (7th Cir.1994) (defense is "grounded in the Due Process Clause of the Fifth Amendment").

Ninth Circuit: United States v. Brebner, 951 F.2d 1017, 1025 (9th Cir.1991) (defense "rests on a due process theory which focuses on the conduct of the government officials rather than on a defendant's state of mind").

Tenth Circuit: United States v. Nichols, 21 F.3d 1016, 1018 (10th Cir.1994) (defense "implicates due process concerns under the Fifth and Fourteenth amendments"); In United States v. Brady, 710 F.Supp. 290, 295 (D.Colo.1989), the court rejected the estoppel characterization, arguing that it obscures the constitutional nature of the defense:

> Though the defense recognized by *Raley* and *Cox* has been called "entrapment by estoppel," it is not an estoppel at all in any meaningful sense. Neither *Cox* nor *Raley* use the word "estoppel" even once. The doctrine stems from the due process clause, not from the common law of contract, equity or agency.

6. United States v. Spires, 79 F.3d 464, 466 (5th Cir.1996).

that the official actively mislead the defendant, (3) and that the defendant's reliance be reasonable.[7] Since the defense focuses on the unfairness of permitting the government to bring a prosecution when it has assured the defendant that certain conduct is lawful, the courts have generally concluded that the defense is available for strict liability offenses as well as those for which mens rea is required.[8]

A. CONDUCT BY AN AGENT OF THE STATE

The premise of entrapment by estoppel is that assurances by government agents that certain conduct is legal should bind the government in its dealings with the parties to whom that assurance was given. This rationale is not applicable in a federal prosecution unless the defendant can show that he did in fact rely upon the statement of a federal agent. Accordingly, the lower federal courts have generally rejected estoppel claims when the person upon whom the defendant relied was a private person rather than a government agent, or an agent of the state rather than the federal government.

i. Assurances by State or Local Officials

Generally the federal courts have treated assurances given by state or local officials as insufficient to estop the federal government.[9] For example, in *United States v. Etheridge*[10] the Fourth Circuit rejected the claim that a federal firearms prosecution was estopped in the case of a defendant who claimed that he relied on a state judge's advice that he could own guns for hunting purposes despite his conviction. The court reasoned that applying the estoppel defense under those circumstances " 'would penalize the wrong government—the government that prosecuted appellant rather than the government that mistakenly and misleadingly interpreted the law.' "[11] If the entrapment doctrine is intended to create an incentive for federal authorities to better know and articulate the law, this rationale does not apply to erroneous assurances made

---

7. *Seventh Circuit*: United States v. Howell, 37 F.3d 1197, 1204 (7th Cir.1994).

Some courts add a final criterion, which is a showing that given the defendant's reliance the prosecution would be unfair.

Sixth Circuit: United States v. Levin, 973 F.2d 463, 468 (6th Cir.1992).

8. *First Circuit:* United States v. Smith, 940 F.2d 710, 714 (1st Cir.1991).

Eleventh Circuit: United States v. Thompson, 25 F.3d 1558, 1564 (11th Cir. 1994); United States v. Hedges, 912 F.2d 1397, 1405 (11th Cir.1990).

9. *First Circuit:* United States v. Caron, 64 F.3d 713, 715–17 (1st Cir.1995) (refusing to apply entrapment by estoppel to actions of state authorities who issued firearm identification card, but refusing to hold

that action of state official could never give rise to defense), *vacated and remanded on other grounds*, 77 F.3d 1 (1st Cir.1996) (en banc).

Fourth Circuit: United States v. Etheridge, 932 F.2d 318, 320–21 (4th Cir.1991) (state judge).

Ninth Circuit: United States v. Brebner, 951 F.2d 1017, 1026 (9th Cir.1991) (state and local law enforcement officials lacked authority to bind federal government).

Eleventh Circuit: United States v. Bruscantini, 761 F.2d 640, 641–42 (11th Cir. 1985) (state judge).

10. 932 F.2d 318 (4th Cir.1991).

11. 932 F.2d at 321, quoting United States v. Bruscantini, 761 F.2d 640, 641 (11th Cir.1985).

by agents of the state.[12] In considering the issue raised by a defendant who claimed that a federal firearms prosecution was estopped because of state authorities' issuance of a firearm identification card, the First Circuit commented:

> We live under a federal system, with national and state governments coexisting with a dual legal structure. We are expected generally to know what each government requires. There are inevitably many areas where state and federal laws overlap. Appellant would in essence have us proclaim that the more permissive criminal law trumps the more severe one unless, somehow, either the permissive government or the stricter government makes sure that the individual actor is informed of both sets of requirements. While a state licensing authority, under a more permissive law, may very well try to disseminate information about federal law, we see no constitutional requirement that it do so. And in cases where only a law and not a license is involved, we see no practical way in which actual notice of disparate requirements could be given. Moreover, disparity in the criminal law field can run in the opposite direction. If the federal law were more lenient, we could not contemplate a constitutional requirement that the federal government must alert an individual concerning the differing standards of all the states.[13]

One district court has expressed strong disagreement with the analysis in *Etheridge* and similar cases. In *United States v. Brady*[14] the district court held that it would violate due process to convict a defendant whose conduct conformed to a state judge's statement of the law. The court observed that in light of the "unique role of the judiciary in interpreting the law," the case for allowing a defense is particularly compelling when the defendant relied upon the advice of a judge.[15] The court reasoned that the defense recognized by the Supreme Court in *Raley* and *Cox* was based upon concerns of Due Process and fundamental fairness, not principles of agency and estoppel, and it rested its decision on the "fundamental unfairness of punishing a defendant for conforming his conduct to an erroneous interpretation of the law by a judge having the power to confine him."[16]

One way of viewing this disagreement is to see it as a variant of the dual sovereignty issue. Although at one time the Supreme Court treated the federal and state governments as two entirely separate sovereigns for

---

12. *First Circuit:* United States v. Caron, 64 F.3d 713, 715–17 (1st Cir.1995), *vacated and remanded on other grounds*, 77 F.3d 1 (1st Cir.1996) (en banc).

Fourth Circuit: United States v. Etheridge, 932 F.2d 318, 321 (4th Cir.1991).

Eleventh Circuit: United States v. Bruscantini, 761 F.2d 640, 641–42 (11th Cir. 1985).

13. United States v. Caron, 64 F.3d 713, 717, *vacated and remanded on other grounds*, 77 F.3d 1 (1st Cir.1996) (en banc).

14. 710 F.Supp. 290 (D.Colo.1989).

15. 710 F.Supp. at 295. *See also* United States v. Mancuso, 139 F.2d 90, 92 (3d Cir.1943) (footnote omitted):

While it is true that men are, in general, held responsible for violations of the law, whether they know it or not, we do not think the layman participating in a lawsuit is required to know more than the judge.

16. 710 F.Supp. at 296.

constitutional purposes, it has swept the dual sovereignty doctrine away in cases dealing with the privilege against self incrimination and unreasonable searches and seizures,[17] while maintaining it in the analysis of double jeopardy claims.[18] In essence, the district court in *Brady* rejects any dual sovereignty limitation on the fundamental fairness analysis. The other courts tend to analyze the cases without much reflection on the Due Process foundation of the defense, and to assume that the the federal and state governments are distinct sovereigns.

ii. Assurances by Private Persons

Although assurances by federal agents can estop a federal prosecution, similar assurances by private parties ordinarily have no effect.[19] This distinction has led to a sharp debate over the question whether federal firearm dealers are agents of the government for purposes of the defense of entrapment by estoppel. In *United States v. Tallmadge*[20] a divided panel of the Ninth Circuit treated a dealer as a federal official for that purpose. Judge Kozinski dissented at length, arguing that the majority set a dangerous precedent by allowing "individuals with only the most tenuous relationship to the government to bind it with respect to the interpretation and enforcement of the criminal laws."[21] Judge Kozinski argued that the estoppel defense is applicable only when the official relied upon " 'is the appropriate official—the one authorized to render the particular advice or opinion later found to be erroneous.' "[22] Judge Kozinski also argued that allowing private gun dealers to bind the government would "create an administrative nightmare" in the enforcement of the gun laws and have the "explosive potential" to apply as well to the "countless" holders of other government licenses.[23] He accused the majority of allowing private parties to "suspend or alter the law"

17. *See* Murphy v. Waterfront Comm'n, 378 U.S. 52, 78–80, 84 S.Ct. 1594, 1609–10, 12 L.Ed.2d 678 (1964) (rejecting the separate sovereign doctrine for purposes of Fifth Amendment privilege against self incrimination); Elkins v. United States, 364 U.S. 206, 213–14, 80 S.Ct. 1437, 1442–43, 4 L.Ed.2d 1669 (1960) (rejecting the "silver platter" doctrine that had permitted evidence obtained illegally by state officials to be admitted in federal prosecutions).

18. For a general discussion of the dual sovereignty doctrine in double jeopardy analysis, see 3 WAYNE R. LaFAVE & JEROLD H. ISRAEL, CRIMINAL PROCEDURE § 24.5 (1984). For more recent scholarship on the application of the dual sovereignty doctrine to double jeopardy issues, see Akhil Reed Amar & Jonathan L. Marcus, *Double Jeopardy Law After Rodney King*, 95 COLUM.L.REV. 1 (1995); Sandra Guerra, *The Myth of Dual Sovereignty: Multijurisdictional Drug Law Enforcement and Double Jeopardy*, 73 N.C.L.REV. 1159 (1995); Kevin J. Hellman,

Note & Comment, *The Fallacy of Dueling Sovereignties: Why the Supreme Court Refuses to Eliminate the Dual Sovereignty Doctrine*, 2 J.L. & POL'Y 149 (1994).

19. *Fourth Circuit:* United States v. Clark, 986 F.2d 65, 69–70 (4th Cir.1993) (private taxidermist).

Seventh Circuit: United States v. Howell, 37 F.3d 1197, 1204–06 (7th Cir.1994) (firearms dealer).

Eighth Circuit: United States v. Austin, 915 F.2d 363, 366–67 (8th Cir.1990) (federally licensed firearms dealer).

20. 829 F.2d 767 (9th Cir.1987).

21. 829 F.2d at 776.

22. 820 F.2d at 777, quoting Note, *United States v. Barker: Misapplication of the Reliance on an Official Interpretation of the Law Defense*, 66 CAL.L.REV. 809, 825–26 (1978).

23. 829 F.2d at 779–80.

and issue " 'Get Out of Jail Free' cards."[24] Judge Kozinski's dissent appears to have carried the day outside of his own circuit, and other circuits have declined to follow *Tallmadge* on this point.[25]

iii. Apparent Authority

Although the idea that apparent authority should be sufficient to give rise to the defense has been advanced,[26] it has generally been rejected.[27] It should be noted, however, that reliance on apparent authority *is* sufficient to negate certain forms of mens rea, such as the knowledge of the illegality of one's conduct.[28]

B. ACTIVELY MISLEADING STATEMENTS OR CONDUCT

There is general agreement that the defense of estoppel by entrapment requires government conduct that is actively misleading,[29] or

24. 829 F.2d at 780.

25. *Seventh Circuit:* United States v. Howell, 37 F.3d 1197, 1205–06 (7th Cir. 1994).

Eighth Circuit: United States v. Austin, 915 F.2d 363, 365–67 (8th Cir.1990).

Eleventh Circuit: United States v. Billue, 994 F.2d 1562, 1568–69 (11th Cir. 1993).

26. In United States v. Barker, 546 F.2d 940, 949 (D.C.Cir.1976), Judge Wilkens concurred in the per curiam disposition of the case and indicated that he would recognize a defense based upon the apparent authority of Howard Hunt if the defendants could establish *"both* (1) *facts* justifying their reasonable reliance on Hunt's apparent authority and (2) a *legal theory* on which to base a reasonable belief that Hunt possessed such authority." *See generally* Thomas W. White, Note, *Reliance on Apparent Authority as a Defense to Criminal Prosecution,* 77 COLUM.L.REV. 775 (1977).

27. *First Circuit:* United States v. Holmquist, 36 F.3d 154, 161 n. 6, 162 (1st Cir.1994) ("defense" of apparent public authority "is not a defense at all").

Second Circuit: United States v. Schwartz, 924 F.2d 410, 422 (2d Cir.1991) (defendants may not claim reliance on persons who had no authority to authorize the criminal behavior in question); United States v. Duggan, 743 F.2d 59, 84 (2d Cir. 1984) (declining "to adopt Judge Wilkey's view that a defendant may be exonerated on the basis of his reliance on an authority that is only apparent and not real").

Fourth Circuit: United States v. Sparks, 67 F.3d 1145, 1153 n. 4 (4th Cir. 1995) (noting district court's instruction

that "defense of good faith reliance on a government official 'is limited to objectively reasonable reliance only on those with actual authority, and may not be based on reliance on someone whom defendant subjectively believes has authority' ").

Ninth Circuit: See also United States v. Clegg, 846 F.2d 1221, 1225 n. 1 (9th Cir. 1988) (Skopil, J., dissenting) (noting that majority did not consider this issue).

Eleventh Circuit: United States v. Anderson, 872 F.2d 1508, 1515–16 (11th Cir.1989); United States v. Rosenthal, 793 F.2d 1214, 1235 (11th Cir.1986) (endorsing "better view ... that a defendant may only be exonerated on the basis of his reliance on real and not merely apparent authority"); United States v. Lopez–Lima, 738 F.Supp. 1404, 1408 (S.D.Fla.1990).

28. The relationship between mistakes of law and the requirement that one know one's conduct to be illegal is discussed in § 25.8. Similarly, a mistaken belief that CIA agents had authorized the release of secret information can demonstrate that the defendant had no intent to injure the interests of the United States. United States v. Smith, 592 F.Supp. 424, 430–34 (E.D.Va.1984), *vacated and remanded on other grounds,* 780 F.2d 1102 (4th Cir. 1985). As the district court pointed out, such a mistake of fact is treated no differently than a mistake of law—it is a defense if it negatives mens rea. *Id.* at 431.

29. *Fifth Circuit:* United States v. Trevino–Martinez, 86 F.3d 65, 69–70 (5th Cir.1996).

Ninth Circuit: United States v. Brebner, 951 F.2d 1017, 1025 (9th Cir.1991) (Ninth Circuit cases that have sustained

constitutes an affirmative assurance that the conduct in question is lawful.[30] It is not sufficient merely to show that a government official or agency was aware of the defendant's conduct but remained silent or failed to take action.[31]

C. REASONABLE RELIANCE BY THE DEFENDANT

A defendant must demonstrate that he actually relied upon the government's assurances that his conduct was lawful, and that this reliance was reasonable.[32] The standard articulated by some courts is whether a person who sincerely desired to obey the law would have accepted the information as true, and thus would not have been put on notice to make further inquiries.[33] Courts assess the reasonableness of the defendant's reliance in light of "the identity of the agent, the point of law misrepresented, and the substance of the misrepresentation."[34]

the defense involved affirmative misleading which was not present in case at bar).

Tenth Circuit: United States v. Nichols, 21 F.3d 1016, 1018 (10th Cir.1994).

30. *Second Circuit:* United States v. Corso, 20 F.3d 521, 528 (2d Cir.1994) (requiring "communication from an authorized government official to the defendant to the effect that his acquisition of the receivers was lawful").

Seventh Circuit: United States v. Howell, 37 F.3d 1197, 1205 (7th Cir.1994) (no basis for defense where defendants received no affirmative advice or specific misleading statement; firearm dealer's signature on part B of ATF form after defendant completed part A did not constitute active misleading).

31. *See also*

Fourth Circuit: United States v. Wilson, 721 F.2d 967, 974–75 (4th Cir.1983) (rejecting defense where defendant occasionally met with government officials and sent them unsolicited information, and then claimed that his conduct was authorized as intelligence gathering).

Fifth Circuit: United States v. Lichenstein, 610 F.2d 1272, 1280 (5th Cir.1980); United States v. Mann, 517 F.2d 259, 270 (5th Cir.1975).

Ninth Circuit: United States v. Brebner, 951 F.2d 1017, 1025–26 (9th Cir.1991) (failure of firearms dealer to follow up after defendant told him of conviction which had been expunged did not constitute affirmative misleading and was not sufficient to give rise to defense); United States v. Tallmadge, 829 F.2d 767, 777–78 (9th Cir.1987) (Kozinski, J., dissenting).

32. *First Circuit:* United States v. Smith, 940 F.2d 710, 714–15 (1st Cir.1991).

Second Circuit: United States v. Abcasis, 45 F.3d 39, 43–44 (2d Cir.1995).

Third Circuit: United States v. Frezzo Brothers, Inc., 491 F.Supp. 1339, 1342–43 (E.D.Pa.1980).

Fourth Circuit: United States v. Clark, 986 F.2d 65, 69–70 (4th Cir.1993).

Fifth Circuit: United States v. Trevino–Martinez, 86 F.3d 65, 69–70 (5th Cir.1996).

Ninth Circuit: United States v. Weitzenhoff, 35 F.3d 1275, 1290–91 (9th Cir. 1993).

Tenth Circuit: United States v. Meraz–Valeta, 26 F.3d 992, 996 (10th Cir.1994).

33. *Cf.*

D.C. Circuit: McCord v. Bailey, 636 F.2d 606, 611–12 (D.C.Cir.1980) (requiring objective basis for believing government agent's assurances that conduct was legal).

Second Circuit: United States v. Abcasis, 45 F.3d 39, 44 (2d Cir.1995).

Third Circuit: United States v. Kline, 354 F.Supp. 931, 935 (M.D.Pa.1972).

Eighth Circuit: United States v. Burton, 472 F.2d 757, 758–60 (8th Cir.1973).

Ninth Circuit: United States v. Weitzenhoff, 35 F.3d 1275, 1290–91 (9th Cir. 1993); United States v. Lansing, 424 F.2d 225, 226–27 (9th Cir.1970).

34. United States v. Nichols, 21 F.3d 1016, 1018 (10th Cir.1994).

For cases in other circuits, see:

Second Circuit: United States v. Corso, 20 F.3d 521, 528–29 (2d Cir.1994) (since advertisement upon which defendant relied stated categories of persons whose possession would be legal and he fell into none of

D. COMPARISON WITH OTHER DEFENSES

Estoppel by entrapment is a close cousin to several other defenses, and the parties and the courts sometimes have difficulty keeping them separated.[35] As noted above, ignorance or mistake of law negates some forms of mens rea, and lack of mens rea poses a separate defense from a Due Process claim of reliance on an official statement of law (or estoppel by entrapment). These defenses have different requirements and limitations. A no-mens-rea defense is not available for strict liability offenses, and is available for other defenses if and only if it negates the requisite mens rea. Depending upon the mens rea required by a given statute, even an unreasonable mistake of law may be sufficient. A no-mens-rea defense is available even if the information upon which the defendant relied came from a private citizen or a state official, rather than a federal agent. Estoppel by entrapment is also closely related to the defense of public authority, which exonerates a defendant who relied upon the authority of a public official to engage in otherwise illegal activity.[36] The validity of this defense depends upon the authority of the government official to empower the defendant to perform the conduct in question.

In some cases the line between the various defenses is blurred where the defendant alleges that government agents solicited him to act as a confidential informant or cooperating witness, and assured him that he was authorized to participate in otherwise illegal conduct in this capacity. For example, in *United States v. Abcasis*[37] defendants who had worked for six years as drug informants testified that they believed they were authorized by DEA agents to act as informants in connection with the transactions for which they were prosecuted. DEA agents testified that they had been terminated as informants a year before the events in question, and that their renewed contacts at roughly the time of the offense did not constitute a reauthorization. The district court instructed the jury to convict if they found that the defendants were in fact authorized, but it refused to instruct the jury to acquit if they found that the defendants' belief was mistaken. The court of appeals reversed with the following comment:

the categories, defendant was on notice that he must at least make further inquiries).

Seventh Circuit: United States v. Howell, 37 F.3d 1197, 1204 (7th Cir.1994) (collecting cases).

Ninth Circuit: United States v. Clegg, 846 F.2d 1221, 1224 (9th Cir.1988) (defendant entitled to rely on "officials of the highest rank" when he was "operating far from the territory of the United States, in a place not obviously covered by American law"); United States v. Tallmadge, 829 F.2d 767, 778 (9th Cir.1987) (Kozinski, J., dissenting) (reliance on federally licensed firearms dealer's advice should be deemed "inherently unreasonable" in light of dealer's economic interest in consummating transaction).

35. *See* United States v. Baptista–Rodriguez, 17 F.3d 1354, 1368 n. 18 (11th Cir.1994) (contrasting no-mens-rea, public authority, and entrapment by estoppel defenses and admonishing counsel to "state with precision the theory (or theories) they are advancing").

36. For an example of a case raising the public authority defense, see United States v. Burrows, 36 F.3d 875, 880–83 (9th Cir.1994) (claim that defendant was working as undercover agent when he received methamphetamine).

37. 45 F.3d 39 (2d Cir.1995).

We conclude that the defense of entrapment by estoppel can arise in the circumstances testified to by the defendants. If a drug enforcement agent solicits a defendant to engage in otherwise criminal conduct as a cooperating informant, or effectively communicates an assurance that the defendant is acting under authorization, and the defendant, relying thereon, commits forbidden acts in the mistaken but reasonable, good faith belief that he has in fact been authorized to do so as an aid to law enforcement, then estoppel bars conviction. Needless to say, the defendant's conduct must remain within the general scope of the solicitation or assurance of authorization; this defense will not support a claim of an open-ended license to commit crimes in the expectation of receiving subsequent authorization. Furthermore, for a defendant's reliance to be reasonable, the jury must conclude that " 'a person sincerely desirous of obeying the law would have accepted the information as true and would not have been put on notice to make further inquiries.' "[38]

In *Abcasis* the defense testimony could have supported the defense of public authority if the jury believed that the agents did authorize the defendants to act as informants, or the defense of entrapment by estoppel if the agents did not so authorize the defendants but nonetheless gave them assurances that their conduct was legal. In cases where the court concludes that the defense fails because the government agents lacked the authority to empower the defendants to act contrary to general law, it is important to consider whether the defendant is raising—or the court is considering—the defense of entrapment by estoppel or public authority.[39]

E. APPLICATION TO ERRONEOUS ADVICE ABOUT SENTENCING

In a series of cases defendants received erroneous advice about the maximum punishment applicable to certain conduct. The cases raising this issue arose from an immigration form containing an erroneous statement that a deported person who returned to the United States within five years would be subject to a maximum penalty of 2 years; this form took no account of a statutory amendment increasing the maxi-

---

38. 45 F.3d at 43–44 (citations omitted).

39. The Eleventh Circuit has had a particularly difficult time separating these defenses in cases dealing with the so-called "CIA defense." In United States v. Thompson, 25 F.3d 1558, 1564 n. 7 (11th Cir. 1994), the court analyzed such a claim using the language of entrapment by estoppel. It distinguished the claim that federal officials had authorized conduct in violation of firearm statutes from the CIA defense on the ground that the CIA "never has the authority to authorize narcotics violations,"

and hence any reliance on the conduct of such an official is a mistake of law that does not exculpate. *Id.* In contrast, earlier cases in the same circuit seem to treat this more as a mens rea issue or public authority defense. *See* United States v. Anderson, 872 F.2d 1508, 1515–17 & n. 11 (11th Cir.1989) (mens rea and " 'apparent authority defense' "); United States v. Rosenthal, 793 F.2d 1214, 1235 (11th Cir.1986) ("C.I.A. defense [of] 'reliance of apparent authority' "); United States v. Lopez–Lima, 738 F.Supp. 1404, 1411 (S.D.Fl.1990) ("public authority defense").

mum sentence.[40] The lower federal courts have uniformly concluded that the erroneous form did not give rise to an entrapment by estoppel or due process defense, because the defendants were never given erroneous advice suggesting that their conduct would be legal.[41] Accordingly, the government has not been estopped from prosecuting these defendants, nor was it error to impose a sentence in excess of 2 years in conformity with the amended statute.

§ 25.13 Bibliography

Alexander, Larry, *Inculpatory and Exculpatory Mistakes and the Fact/Law Distinction: An Essay in Memory of Myke Balyes*, 12 LAW & PHIL. 33 (1993).

Borrks, A.F. II, Note, *When Ignorance of the Law Became an Excuse: Lambert and Its Progeny*, 19 AM.J.CRIM.L. 279 (1992).

Grace, Bruce R., Note, *Ignorance of the Law as an Excuse*, 86 COLUM.L.REV. 1392 (1986).

Hall, Jerome, GENERAL PRINCIPALS OF CRIMINAL LAW, 376–401 (2d ed.1960).

Levinson, Laurie L., *Good Faith Defenses: Reshaping Strict Liability Crimes*, 78 CORNELL L.REV. 401 (1993).

Hall, Livingston, & Seligman, Selig J., *Mistake of Law and Mens Rea*, 8 U.CHI.L.REV. 641 (1941).

Kristovich, Stephen M., Comment, *United States v. Barker: Misapplication of the Reliance on an Official Interpretation of the Law Defense*, 66 CAL.L.REV. 809 (1978).

LaFAVE, WAYNE, & SCOTT, AUSTIN, CRIMINAL LAW § 5.1 (2d ed. 1986).

Low, Peter W., *The Model Penal Code, the Common Law, and Mistakes of Fact: Reckless, Negligence, or Strict Liability?*, 19 RUTGERS L.J. 539 (1988).

Northey, Rebecca, Comment, *Expanding the Mistake of Law Doctrine: United States v. Barker*, 57 B.U.L.REV. 882 (1977).

PERKINS, ROLLIN M., & BOYCE, RONALD N., CRIMINAL LAW, 1028–54 (3d ed.1982).

Tigar, Michael E., *"Willfulness" and "Ignorance" in Federal Criminal Law*, 37 CLEV.ST.L.REV. 525 (1989).

---

40. *See* United States v. Cruz–Flores, 56 F.3d 461, 462 (2d Cir.1995).

41. *See also*
First Circuit: United States v. Troncoso, 23 F.3d 612, 615 (1st Cir.1994) (advice about maximum sentence did not assure defendant that his conduct was legal, and was correct when information was provided).
Second Circuit: United States v. Cruz–Flores, 56 F.3d 461, 463–64 (2d Cir.1995).

Fifth Circuit: United States v. Perez–Torres, 15 F.3d 403, 405–06 (5th Cir.1994).

Ninth Circuit: United States v. Ullyses–Salazar, 28 F.3d 932, 936 (9th Cir.1994), *overruled on other grounds by*, 96 F.3d 1262 (9th Cir.1996).

Tenth Circuit: United States v. Meraz–Valeta, 26 F.3d 992, 996 (10th Cir.1994).

Travers, Michael L., Comment, *Mistake of Law in Mala Prohibita Crimes*, 62 U.CHI.L.REV. 1301 (1995).

WILLIAMS, GLANVILLE, CRIMINAL LAW: THE GENERAL PART (2d ed.1961).

White, Thomas N., Note, *Reliance on Apparent Authority as a Defense to Criminal Prosecution*, 77 COLUM.L.REV. 775 (1977).

Ghent, Jeffrey, Annotation, *Criminal Law: "Official Statement" Mistake of Law Defense*, 89 A.L.R. 4th 1026 (1991).

*

CHAPTER 26

INSANITY

Table of Sections

WESTLAW ELECTRONIC RESEARCH

See WESTLAW Electronic Research Guide preceding the Summary of Contents.

---

§ 26.1 Introduction

The insanity defense is an anomaly. In general, Congress has not codified the traditional criminal defenses, such as self defense, intoxication, duress and necessity.[1] Insanity also developed as a federal common law defense, but in 1984 Congress overhauled the federal insanity defense by passing the Insanity Defense Reform Act of 1984 (IDRA).[2] IDRA defines the insanity defense as follows:

18 U.S.C. § 17. Insanity defense

(a) **Affirmative Defense.**—It is an affirmative defense to a prosecution under any Federal statute that, at the time of the commission of the acts constituting the offense, the defendant, as a result of a severe mental disease or defect, was unable to appreciate the nature and quality or the wrongfulness of his acts. Mental disease or defect does not otherwise constitute a defense.

(b) **Burden of proof.**—The defendant has the burden of proving the defense of insanity by clear and convincing evidence.

IDRA also adopted new procedures for the determination of competency to stand trial and the hospitalization of defendants with mental illness-

---

§ 26.1

1. *See* United States v. Bailey, 444 U.S. 394, 100 S.Ct. 624, 62 L.Ed.2d 575 (1980) (applying common law notions of duress and necessity in prosecution for escape from federal custody, 18 U.S.C. § 751(a)).

2. For IDRA's legislative history, *see* S.Rep.No. 98–225, 2d Sess. at 222–29

(1983), *reprinted in* 1984 U.S.C.C.A.N. 3182, 3404–13.

The changes IDRA made in federal law are summarized in United States v. Cameron, 907 F.2d 1051, 1061–62 (11th Cir.1990), and Henry T. Miller, Comment, *Recent Changes in Criminal Law: The Federal Insanity Defense*, 46 LA.L.REV. 337 (1985).

es,[3] and it amended the Federal Rules of Evidence to prohibit expert testimony concerning the ultimate issue of a defendant's legal sanity.[4]

The Senate Report accompanying the Act states that "The difficulties experienced under the current Federal insanity defense center on three major areas: (1) the definition of the defense; (2) the burden of proof; and (3) the scope of expert testimony."[5] IDRA addresses all three of these problems. As the Senate Report explains:

> The legislation includes a definition of the insanity defense that will substantially narrow the definition, which has evolved from case law, presently applied in the Federal system. [IDRA] also provides that the defendant shall have the burden of proving the insanity defense by clear and convincing evidence and prohibits expert opinion testimony on the ultimate legal issue of whether the defendant was insane.[6]

IDRA also made other procedural changes. In contrast to prior federal law, IDRA authorizes a jury to enter a verdict of "not guilty only by reason of insanity"[7] ("NGI verdict"). The Act also establishes civil commitment procedures for defendants acquitted by an NGI verdict.[8] If such a verdict is reached, the Act requires that the defendant be committed to a suitable treatment facility[9] and to undergo a psychiatric evaluation.[10] Within forty days, a hearing is required,[11] at which time the defendant must prove by clear and convincing evidence that he no longer poses a substantial risk of danger to other persons or to property.[12] Only if such a showing is made will the defendant be released from custody.

Library References:

C.J.S. Criminal Law § 96–108, 113.
West's Key No. Digests, Criminal Law ☞46–51.

§ 26.2 Shifting the Burden of Proof to the Defendant

One of the most significant changes made by IDRA is its reallocation of the burden of proof. Under 18 U.S.C. § 17(b), the Act shifts the

---

3. These provisions are codified as 18 U.S.C. §§ 4241–4247 (1994 & Supp.II 1996).

4. *See* § 26.7(B).

5. S.Rep.No. 98–225, 2d Sess. at 222 (1983), *reprinted in* 1984 U.S.C.C.A.N. 3182, 3404.

6. S.Rep.No. 98–225, 2d Sess. at 222 (1983), *reprinted in* 1984 U.S.C.C.A.N. 3182, 3404.

7. 18 U.S.C. § 4242(b) (1994). That section reads in its entirety:

(b) Special Verdict.—If the issue of insanity is raised by notice as provided in Rule 12.2 of the Federal Rules of Criminal Procedure on motion of the defendant or of the attorney for the Government, or on the court's own motion, the jury shall be instructed to find, or, in the event of a nonjury trial, the court shall find the defendant—

(1) guilty;

(2) not guilty; or

(3) not guilty only by reason of insanity.

8. 18 U.S.C. §§ 4243–4247 (1994 & Supp.II 1996).

9. 18 U.S.C. § 4243(a) (1994).

10. 18 U.S.C. § 4243(b) (1994).

11. 18 U.S.C. § 4243(c) (1994).

12. 18 U.S.C. § 4243(d) (1994).

burden of persuasion to criminal defendants, requiring them to prove the elements outlined in § 17(a) by clear and convincing evidence.[1]

The Senate Report contains an extensive discussion of the rationale for the shift in the burden of proof. Prior to IDRA the government had the burden of disproving the defense beyond a reasonable doubt—i.e., to prove beyond a reasonable doubt that the defendant was able to distinguish right from wrong and that he had the capacity to control his criminal behavior.[2] The Report quotes with approval from a statement on behalf of the National District Attorney's Association:

> The most widely criticized aspect of the insanity law in some jurisdictions is the impossible burden sometimes placed on the Government of proving someone's sanity beyond a reasonable doubt. . . .
>
> [T]he overwhelming majority of American jurisdictions recognize that the evidence of the *defense* of insanity should be produced by the defendant. . . . It is an affirmative defense to legal and moral responsibility. It says, "even if I did it, I'm not responsible." As such, it is entirely proper that the defendant have the burden of establishing non-responsibility. A defendant is required to present the evidence in all other affirmative defenses and this is particularly fitting in the case of insanity. Such evidence is peculiarly available, if at all, to the defendant. On the other hand, evidence to establish sanity—beyond any reasonable doubt—is frequently unavailable to the prosecution.
>
> I have heard judges, prosecutors and defense counsel roundly denounce the Herculean task of requiring the Government to prove anyone is not insane beyond a reasonable doubt. The single most attractive provision of this Act is to fairly require the accused to prove his sanity by the lesser standard of clear and convincing evidence.[3]

The Senate Report concludes that "a more rigorous requirement than proof by a preponderance of the evidence is necessary to assure that only

---

§ 26.2

1. 18 U.S.C. § 17(b) (1994). Clear and convincing evidence means:

that weight of proof which "produces in the mind of the trier of fact a firm belief or conviction as to the truth of the allegations sought to be established, evidence so clear, direct and weighty and convincing as to enable the fact finder to come to a clear conviction, without hesitancy, of the truth of the precise facts" of the case.

United States v. Barton, 992 F.2d 66, 69 n. 6 (5th Cir.1993) (*quoting* Cruzan v. Director, Mo. Dep't of Health, 497 U.S. 261, 285, 110 S.Ct. 2841, 2855, 111 L.Ed.2d 224 (1990)).

See also

Eleventh Circuit: United States v. Owens, 854 F.2d 432, 436 n. 8 (11th Cir.1988) (defining clear and convincing evidence).

2. *See, e.g.*, Davis v. United States, 160 U.S. 469, 16 S.Ct. 353, 40 L.Ed. 499 (1895). This allocation of the burden of proof was one of the most roundly criticized components of the pre-IDRA insanity defense. S.Rep.No. 98–225, 2d Sess., at 225, 229–30 (1983), *reprinted in* 1984 U.S.C.C.A.N. 3182, 3406, 3411–12.

3. S.Rep.No. 98–225, 2d Sess. at 229–30 (1983), *reprinted in* 1984 U.S.C.C.A.N. 3182, 3411–12 (ellipses and emphasis in original).

those defendants who plainly satisfy the requirements of the defense are exonerated from what is otherwise culpable criminal behavior."[4]

Thus, Congress' rationale in requiring the defendant to prove insanity by clear and convincing evidence appears to be three-fold: (1) to make the burden of proof in the insanity defense congruent with the burden of proof in other affirmative defenses; (2) to ensure greater fairness by requiring the defendant to prove insanity—something that is peculiarly available to him/her; and (3) to make certain that the law excuses from criminal sanction only those defendants who clearly are not responsible for their criminal conduct.

Relying primarily on the Supreme Court's decision in *Leland v. Oregon*[5] the lower federal courts have rejected the argument that this shift in the burden of proof violates due process,[6] In *Leland*, the Court upheld an Oregon statute that required criminal defendants asserting that state's insanity defense to prove their insanity beyond a reasonable doubt.[7] The Court reasoned that the previous rule—that the prosecution must prove the defendant's sanity beyond a reasonable doubt[8]—was not a constitutional requirement but was merely an exercise of the Supreme Court's authority to supervise prosecutions in federal courts.[9] Thus, given *Leland's* holding that the Due Process Clause of the Fourteenth Amendment does not prohibit a state from imposing on the defendant a higher burden of proof than IDRA requires, the Fifth Amendment's Due Process Clause likewise does not appear to prohibit Congress from requiring a federal defendant to prove insanity by clear and convincing evidence.[10] The lower courts view *Leland* as settling the issue of the constitutionality of IDRA's shift in the burden of proof.[11]

4. *Id.*

5. 343 U.S. 790, 72 S.Ct. 1002, 96 L.Ed. 1302 (1952).

6. *See*

First Circuit: United States v. Pryor, 960 F.2d 1, 3 (1st Cir.1992).

Eighth Circuit: United States v. Byrd, 834 F.2d 145, 146–47 (8th Cir.1987); United States v. Amos, 803 F.2d 419, 420–22 (8th Cir.1986).

Eleventh Circuit: United States v. Freeman, 804 F.2d 1574, 1575–76 (11th Cir. 1986).

7. 343 U.S. at 799, 72 S.Ct. at 1008.

8. *See* Davis v. United States, 160 U.S. 469, 485, 16 S.Ct. 353, 357, 40 L.Ed. 499 (1895).

9. Leland v. Oregon, 343 U.S. 790, 799, 72 S.Ct. 1002, 1008, 96 L.Ed. 1302 (1952). See also United States v. Freeman, 804 F.2d 1574, 1575 (11th Cir.1986). Thus, the rule in *Davis* appears only to have represented the default rule in federal

courts, applicable only absent some legislative pronouncement such as IDRA.

10. *See* United States v. Freeman, 804 F.2d 1574, 1576 (11th Cir.1986) ("No logical basis exists to distinguish between a state legislature's constitutional power to require a defendant to prove insanity and the United States Congress' power to require a defendant to prove insanity."); United States v. Amos, 803 F.2d 419, 422 (8th Cir.1986) ("We find no authority to support [the proposition that a state may allocate the burden of proof in this way while Congress may not] and therefore find this argument to be without merit."); S.Rep.No. 98–225, *supra* note 2, at 224–25, *reprinted in* 1984 U.S.C.C.A.N. 3182, 3407 ("[I]t is clear that the question of which party ... should be the burden of proof on the insanity defense, as well as the appropriate standard, are not of constitutional dimensions beyond the power of Congress to legislate.").

11. United States v. Pryor, 960 F.2d 1, 3 (1st Cir.1992).

§ 26.3 The Elements of the Insanity Defense

A. APPLICABILITY TO PROSECUTIONS UNDER ANY FEDERAL STATUTE

Section 17(a) provides that the insanity defense applies to "a prosecution under any Federal statute."[1] The legislative history of the Act does not address the meaning or scope of this provision,[2] and the cases do not generally discuss it. One circuit has concluded, however, that a probation revocation proceeding is not a "prosecution" within the meaning of IDRA, and therefore a defendant in such a proceeding could not raise the insanity defense.[3]

B. SEVERE MENTAL DISEASE OR DEFECT

The first fact that § 17 requires a defendant to prove by clear and convincing evidence is that, "at the time of the commission of the acts constituting the offense," the defendant was suffering from a "severe mental disease or defect."[4] The Act's legislative history states:

> The concept of severity was added to emphasize that non-psychotic behavior disorders or neuroses such as an "inadequate personality," "immature personality," or a pattern of "antisocial tendencies" do not constitute the defense. The Committee also intends that, as has been held under present case law interpretation, the voluntary use of alcohol or drugs, even if they render the defendant unable to appreciate the nature and quality of his acts, does not constitute insanity or any other species of legally valid affirmative defense.[5]

In light of Congress' intent that the insanity defense should not apply to certain types of maladies, courts have concluded that various mental conditions fall outside IDRA's reach. Among these *excluded* conditions are the following: "abnormalit[ies] manifested only by repeated criminal or anti-social conduct,"[6] drug addiction (at least without some showing that the addiction either was evidence of another underlying condition or caused actual physical damage resulting in some other

---

§ 26.3

1. 18 U.S.C. § 17(a) (1994).

2. *See* S.Rep.No. 98–225, 2d Sess. at 225–31 (1983), *reprinted in* 1984 U.S.C.C.A.N. 3182, 3407–13.

3. United States v. Brown, 899 F.2d 189 (2d Cir.1990). The first decision interpreting this language held that the defense applies to a prosecution for possession of a firearm, because the offense in question contains no statement that insanity is not a defense. United States v. Owens, 854 F.2d

432 (11th Cir.1988). This analysis suggests the possibility that Congress might exempt some federal crimes from the insanity defense, but no such offenses have yet been identified.

4. 18 U.S.C. § 17(a) (1994).

5. S.Rep.No. 98–225, 2d Sess. at 229 (1983), *reprinted in* 1984 U.S.C.C.A.N. 3182, 3411 (footnotes omitted).

6. United States v. Birdsell, 775 F.2d 645, 655 (5th Cir.1985).

mental defect),[7] memory loss due to stress,[8] intense fear of being raped,[9] and compulsive or obsessive behavior combined with exposure to the brainwashing techniques of a religious cult.[10] All of these ailments, with the possible exception of involuntary intoxication,[11] seem clearly to fall within the IDRA Committee's statement concerning the type of conditions that should not legally constitute a severe mental disease or defect.[12]

The district courts have concluded that the following conditions may qualify as a "severe mental disease or defect" and thus may be submitted to the jury in an appropriate case: multiple personality disorder,[13] paranoid disorders,[14] delusional conditions,[15] various forms of schizophrenia,[16] assorted types of psychoses,[17] post-traumatic stress disorder,[18]

7. *Fifth Circuit:* United States v. Lyons, 731 F.2d 243, 244–47 (5th Cir.1984). While *Lyons* was decided prior to IDRA's passage, the opinion seems to accord with IDRA's legislative history quoted above.

See also

Seventh Circuit: United States v. Hillsberg, 812 F.2d 328, 331 (7th Cir.1987) (stating that the defendant voluntarily abandoned his insanity defense after the examining psychiatrist found that the defendant had a substance abuse disorder but not a "mental disease or defect").

Cf.

Eighth Circuit: United States v. F.D.L., 836 F.2d 1113, 1116–17 (8th Cir.1988) (stating, in dicta, that involuntary intoxication which renders a defendant unable to appreciate the nature and quality or wrongfulness of his acts may be a sufficiently severe mental disease or defect to invoke the insanity defense).

8. United States v. Holsey, 995 F.2d 960, 961–62 (10th Cir.1993).

9. United States v. Roy, 830 F.2d 628, 637–38 (7th Cir.1987). In *Roy*, the defendant was convicted of escaping from federal custody. He proffered evidence that he had been raped as a young child, that he had an uncontrollable fear of being raped again, that a fellow prisoner was threatening to sexually assault him, and that he escaped to avoid the assault. *Id.* at 638. The trial judge ruled, and the Seventh Circuit agreed, that this was insufficient evidence to support an insanity defense. *Id.*

10. United States v. Fishman, 743 F.Supp. 713, 715–21 (N.D.Cal.1990) (excluding expert testimony on the "coercive persuasion" tactics of religious cults on the ground that the experts' theories were not generally accepted within their scientific field).

11. *See* United States v. F.D.L., 836 F.2d 1113, 1116–17 (8th Cir.1988).

12. *See* S.Rep.No. 98–225, 2d Sess. at 229 (1983), *reprinted in* 1984 U.S.C.C.A.N. 3182, 3411. The Committee report only explicitly addresses voluntary intoxication. *Id.* at 229, *reprinted in* 1984 U.S.C.C.A.N. at 3411.

13. *See, e.g.,*

Tenth Circuit: United States v. Denny–Shaffer, 2 F.3d 999, 1013–14 (10th Cir. 1993).

Eleventh Circuit: United States v. Davis, 835 F.2d 274, 276 (11th Cir.1988).

14. *See, e.g.,*

Seventh Circuit: United States v. Salava, 978 F.2d 320, 323 (7th Cir.1992) ("paranoid personality disorder" with "psychotic appearing behavior").

Eighth Circuit: United States v. Amos, 803 F.2d 419, 420 (8th Cir.1986) ("paranoid disorder with 'erotomania' and delusional thinking").

15. *Sixth Circuit:* United States v. Medved, 905 F.2d 935, 940 (6th Cir.1990) ("delusionary disorder, persecutory type").

Eighth Circuit: United States v. Blumberg, 961 F.2d 787, 790 (8th Cir.1992).

16. *See, e.g.,*

Seventh Circuit: United States v. Reed, 997 F.2d 332, 334 (7th Cir.1993); United States v. Reno, 992 F.2d 739, 741 (7th Cir. 1993).

Eighth Circuit: United States v. Neavill, 868 F.2d 1000, 1001–02 (8th Cir.), *vacated and reh'g en banc granted*, 877 F.2d 1394 (8th Cir.), *appeal voluntarily dismissed*, 886 F.2d 220 (8th Cir.1989).

Ninth Circuit: United States v. Knott, 894 F.2d 1119, 1121 (9th Cir.1990).

Eleventh Circuit: United States v. Thigpen, 4 F.3d 1573, 1575–76 (11th Cir.1993);

bipolar disorder,[19] schizoaffective disorder,[20] and organic personality syndrome.[21] Although all of these conditions appear to be in harmony with Congressional intent,[22] this list is by no means exhaustive.[23]

Although the severity of the psychiatric impairment suffered by a particular defendant is a question of fact for the jury, the IDRA also requires a determination whether a given psychiatric condition meets the statutory criteria of a "severe mental disease or defect." The legal issue may be raised, for example, when the defendant seeks to introduce psychiatric evidence[24] or requests that the court instruct the jury on the insanity defense.[25]

United States v. Cameron, 907 F.2d 1051, 1055, 1068 (11th Cir.1990).

17. *See, e.g.,*

Fifth Circuit: United States v. Barton, 992 F.2d 66, 68 (5th Cir.1993) (brief reactive psychosis).

Eighth Circuit: United States v. Dubray, 854 F.2d 1099, 1101 (8th Cir.1988) (transient psychotic disorder).

Tenth Circuit: United States v. Austin, 981 F.2d 1163, 1164–65 (10th Cir.1992) (simple psychosis).

Eleventh Circuit: United States v. Owens, 854 F.2d 432, 433–34 (11th Cir.1988) (simple psychosis).

18. *See, e.g.,*

D.C. Circuit: United States v. Rezaq, 918 F.Supp. 463, 467–68 (D.D.C.1996).

Ninth Circuit: United States v. Whitehead, 896 F.2d 432, 433–34 (9th Cir.1990).

Eleventh Circuit: United States v. Thigpen, 4 F.3d 1573, 1575 (11th Cir.1993).

19. *See, e.g.,*

Tenth Circuit: United States v. Eagan, 965 F.2d 887, 889 (10th Cir.1992).

Eleventh Circuit: United States v. Manley, 893 F.2d 1221, 1222 (11th Cir.1990); United States v. Freeman, 804 F.2d 1574, 1577 (11th Cir.1986).

20. *See, e.g.,* United States v. West, 962 F.2d 1243, 1245 (7th Cir.1992).

21. *See, e.g.,* United States v. Fisher, 10 F.3d 115, 117 (3d Cir.1993).

22. *See* S.Rep.No. 98–225, 2d Sess. at 229 (1983), *reprinted in* 1984 U.S.C.C.A.N. at 3411; United States v. Denny–Shaffer, 2 F.3d 999, 1013 n. 14 (10th Cir.1993).

23. Because the pre-IDRA insanity defense contained a mental disease or defect requirement, see S.Rep.No. 98–225, 2d Sess. at 224 (1983), *reprinted in* 1984 U.S.C.C.A.N. 3182, 3406, many of the mental conditions alleged in pre-IDRA cases would also probably constitute severe mental diseases or defects under IDRA.

24. In both United States v. Shlater, 85 F.3d 1251 (7th Cir.1996), and United States v. Cartagena–Carrasquillo, 70 F.3d 706 (1st Cir.1995), the appellate courts upheld the exclusion of expert testimony that did not establish a "severe" mental disease. In *Shlater* the excluded testimony characterized the defendant as having a mild to moderate delusional disorder and some paranoid personality traits that did not prevent him from understanding that what he was doing was wrong. In *Cartagena-Carrasquillo* the excluded testimony concerned post traumatic stress disorder (PTSD). The appellate court noted that the expert's singularly unfocused report did not address whether at the time of the offense the defendant was unable to appreciate the nature and quality of his act because of the PTSD. 70 F.3d at 712. The court also noted that the report never stated that defendant suffered from a "severe" mental disease; at most it characterized his condition as "significant." *Id.*

25. IDRA's heightened burden of proof has affected the quantum of evidence necessary to justify an instruction on the insanity defense. In federal proceedings a defendant is not entitled to an instruction on the issue of insanity unless the evidence would allow a reasonable jury to find that insanity has been shown with convincing clarity.

Eighth Circuit: United States v. Long Crow, 37 F.3d 1319, 1323 (8th Cir.1994).

Ninth Circuit: United States v. Whitehead, 896 F.2d 432, 435 (9th Cir.1990).

Tenth Circuit: United States v. Denny–Shaffer, 2 F.3d 999, 1015–16 (10th Cir. 1993).

Eleventh Circuit: United States v. Owens, 854 F.2d 432, 435 (11th Cir.1988).

This standard requires consideration not only of the strength of the evidence, but

C. INABILITY TO APPRECIATE THE NATURE AND QUALITY OR WRONGFULNESS OF ACTS

In addition to proving that s/he suffered from a severe mental disease or defect, a federal criminal defendant asserting the insanity defense must also demonstrate that, as a result of that condition, s/he "was unable to appreciate the nature and quality or the wrongfulness of his acts" (the "inability to appreciate" requirement).[26] IDRA's legislative history surprisingly lacks any affirmative reference to what Congress intended by requiring that the defendant be "unable to appreciate the nature and quality or the wrongfulness of his acts."[27] The only indication the report gives as to what Congress had in mind is to quote the *M'Naghten* test. The report states:

> The foundation of the [insanity] defense was established in *M'Naghten's* case, in which the "right-wrong" test was introduced:

>> To establish a defense on the ground of insanity, it must be clearly proved that, at the time of the committing of the act, the party accused was labouring under such a defect of reason, from disease of the mind, as not to know the nature and quality of the act he was doing; or, if he did know it, that he did not know he was doing what was wrong.[28]

Like the "severe mental disease or defect" requirement, the "inability to appreciate" requirement is a question for the trier of fact.[29] Appellate courts will not reverse the trier of fact's conclusions unless the finding is

also whether it is probative of a condition that falls within the statutory definition of "a severe mental disease or defect."

26. 18 U.S.C. § 17(a) (1994). Prior federal law defining this requirement stated that "[a] person is not responsible for criminal conduct if . . . he lacks substantial capacity to appreciate the criminality of his conduct. . . ." Model Penal Code § 4.01; S.Rep.No. 98–225, 2d Sess. at 224 (1983), *reprinted in* 1984 U.S.C.C.A.N. 3182, 3406. IDRA thus changed prior law by requiring the defendant to show that he was completely unable (as opposed to lacking substantial capacity) to appreciate the nature and quality or wrongfulness of his acts (as opposed to the criminality of his conduct).

27. 18 U.S.C. § 17(a) (1994).

28. S.Rep.No. 98–225, 2d Sess. at 223 (1983), *reprinted in* 1984 U.S.C.C.A.N. 3182, 3405 (footnote omitted).

29. *See, e.g.*, United States v. Reed, 997 F.2d 332, 334 (7th Cir.1993). Indeed, in contrast to the "severe mental disease or defect" requirement, in insanity cases it is the "ultimate issue" and is to be left to the trier of fact alone. *See* Fed.R.Evid. 704(b);

United States v. West, 962 F.2d 1243, 1246 (7th Cir.1992) (stating that, in insanity cases, the " 'ultimate issues' are whether . . . the defendant 'appreciated the nature and quality or wrongfulness of his acts.' "); S.Rep.No. 98–225, 2d Sess. at 230–31 (1983), reprinted in 1984 U.S.C.C.A.N. 3182, 3413 ("Determining whether a criminal defendant was legally insane is a matter for fact-finders, not experts.").

On the other hand, as with the criterion of severe mental disease or defect, the question whether proffered testimony meets the inability to appreciate criteria presents a legal issue.

See

First Circuit: United States v. Cartagena–Carrasquillo, 70 F.3d 706, 712 (1st Cir. 1995).

Second Circuit: United States v. Griffin, 1996 WL 140073 * 9 (S.D.N.Y.1996).

But cf. United States v. Meader, 914 F.Supp. 656, 657–59 (D.Me.1996) (expert testimony that defendant suffered from transient psychosis admissible despite witness's further conclusion that this condition

clearly erroneous.[30] Thus, all of the problems associated with determining what legally constitutes a severe mental disease or defect also apply, with perhaps even greater force, to defining the legal content of the "inability to appreciate" requirement.[31] As such, appellate cases discussing the substantive meaning of this requirement are quite scarce.[32]

Three post-IDRA cases analyzing the "inability to appreciate" requirement have raised rather interesting legal issues. First, in *United States v. Knott*[33] the Ninth Circuit addressed whether the defendant's inability to appreciate the nature and quality or wrongfulness of his acts must arise *solely* as a result of a severe mental disease or defect or whether voluntary intoxication could be considered in combination with the mental condition. The defendant in *Knott* had been diagnosed as a schizophrenic,[34] but his mental condition alone did not render him unable to appreciate the nature and quality or wrongfulness of his acts.[35] The defendant requested an instruction which would permit the jury to consider his voluntary intoxication in combination with his schizophrenia.[36] The district judge refused the defendant's proffered instruction, and the Ninth Circuit affirmed, reasoning that because IDRA was intended both to narrow the insanity defense and to preclude voluntary intoxication as an excuse from criminal liability, substance abuse could

did not prevent defendant from appreciating wrongfulness of act).

30. *See, e.g.,*

Fifth Circuit: United States v. Barton, 992 F.2d 66, 68–69 (5th Cir.1993).

Eleventh Circuit: United States v. Freeman, 804 F.2d 1574, 1577 (11th Cir.1986).

31. These problems may apply with even greater force to the "inability to appreciate" requirement because both IDRA's legislative history and its statutory language place fewer purely legal constraints on the jury's discretion. *See* S.Rep.No. 98–225, 2d Sess. at 225–28 (1983), *reprinted in* 1984 U.S.C.C.A.N. 3182, 3407–10.

32. One opinion that treats this issue is United States v. Hiebert, 30 F.3d 1005, 1007–08 (8th Cir.1994), where the appellate court reviewed the conclusions of the district court after a bench trial, finding that the record supported the district court's conclusion that the defendant failed to establish that he was not aware of the wrongfulness of his acts. The appellate court concluded that awareness of the wrongfulness of one crime was evidence that the defendant could understand the wrongfulness of another offense, and that defendant's incredible beliefs (*e.g.*, that the United States had been invaded since Pearl Harbor) did not establish that he could not understand the wrongfulness of his conduct. *Id.*

33. 894 F.2d 1119 (9th Cir.1990).

34. *Id.* at 1121. Schizophrenia satisfies the "severe mental disease or defect" requirement. *See, e.g.,*

Seventh Circuit: United States v. Reed, 997 F.2d 332, 334 (7th Cir.1993); United States v. Reno, 992 F.2d 739, 741 (7th Cir. 1993).

Eighth Circuit: United States v. Neavill, 868 F.2d 1000, 1001–02 (8th Cir.), *vacated and reh'g en banc granted*, 877 F.2d 1394 (8th Cir.), *appeal voluntarily dismissed*, 886 F.2d 220 (8th Cir.1989).

Ninth Circuit: United States v. Knott, 894 F.2d 1119, 1121 (9th Cir.1990).

Eleventh Circuit: United States v. Thigpen, 4 F.3d 1573, 1575–76 (11th Cir.1993); United States v. Cameron, 907 F.2d 1051, 1055, 1068 (11th Cir.1990).

35. 894 F.2d at 1121.

36. *Id.* Knott's proposed instruction read in part:

You may consider the defendant's voluntary substance abuse in combination with defendant's mental disease in determining whether or not the defendant was unable to appreciate the nature and quality of his acts or was unable to appreciate the wrongfulness of his acts.... You may find that the defendant was insane at the time of the alleged conduct as a result of his severe mental disease in combination with his substance abuse or voluntary intoxication.

not be considered in combination with a severe mental disease as a means of satisfying the "inability to appreciate" requirement.[37] Thus, it seems clear that, at least in the Ninth Circuit, voluntary intoxication will not be used to broaden the insanity defense. It remains to be seen whether other types of behavior may be considered in combination with a severe mental defect in order to satisfy the "inability to appreciate" requirement.

Second, in *United States v. Dubray*[38] the Eighth Circuit analyzed the distinction between "legal" and "moral" definitions of wrongfulness. The defendant had requested an instruction that " 'wrongfulness' implies moral, rather than criminal, wrongdoing."[39] Although the Eighth Circuit concluded that the evidence in the case would not support such an instruction,[40] it hinted that in a proper case an instruction distinguishing between legal and moral wrongfulness might be appropriate.[41] Thus, the current insanity defense, like its predecessor, seems to leave open the question of whether "wrongfulness" is a legal or a moral concept, providing the possibility of future litigation.[42]

Third, in *United States v. Denny–Shaffer*[43] the Tenth Circuit addressed the "inability to appreciate" requirement in the context of multiple personality disorder (MPD). Here the defendant, an MPD victim, requested an insanity instruction. The evidence at trial seemed to indicate that while the defendant's dominant personality may have been legally insane (in other words, "unable to appreciate the nature and quality or wrongfulness of her acts"), the alter personality in control of the defendant at the time of the offense was not.[44] Reasoning that the defendant had not satisfied the "inability to appreciate" requirement regarding the alter personality in control at the time of the offense, the district judge refused to instruct the jury on insanity.[45] The Tenth Circuit reversed, holding that there was a genuine factual issue as to whether the dominant personality might have been legally insane.[46] The

---

Id. at 1121 n.2.

37. *Id.* at 1121–23.

38. 854 F.2d 1099 (8th Cir.1988).

39. *Id.* at 1101. The proposed instruction was derived from United States v. Segna, 555 F.2d 226, 232 (9th Cir.1977), and would have defined wrongfulness as meaning.

moral wrongfulness rather than criminal wrongfulness. In other words, if you find that the defendant, because of a [severe] mental disease or defect [was unable] to appreciate the moral wrongfulness of his conduct even if he knows his conduct to be criminal but commits it because of a delusion that he was morally justified then your verdict must be not guilty [by reason of insanity] . . .

40. 854 F.2d at 1101.

41. 854 F.2d at 1101.

42. To the extent that pre-IDRA definitions of insanity employed the term "wrongfulness" rather than "criminality," future litigation on this issue will probably turn on how the circuits have construed the pre-IDRA insanity defense. At this point, only the Eighth and Ninth Circuits appear to have adopted some form of the distinction between legal and moral wrongfulness.

See,

Eighth Circuit: United States v. Dubray, 854 F.2d 1099, 1101 (8th Cir.1988); United States v. Ming Sen Shiue, 650 F.2d 919, 922 n. 7 (8th Cir.1981).

Ninth Circuit: United States v. Segna, 555 F.2d 226, 232–33 (9th Cir.1977).

43. 2 F.3d 999 (10th Cir.1993).

44. 2 F.3d at 1008.

45. 2 F.3d at 1011.

46. 2 F.3d at 1021.

court remanded the case with instructions to entertain evidence on the legal sanity of the dominant personality and to instruct the jury that the defendant could be found not guilty by reason of insanity if the defendant's dominant personality was unable to appreciate the nature and quality or wrongfulness of her conduct at the time of the offense.[47] One scholar has gone further, suggesting that it might be appropriate to presume that MPD victims are not criminally responsible.[48]

D. INABILITY TO CONTROL CONDUCT (THE "VOLITIONAL" PRONG)

One of the principal ways in which IDRA narrowed the insanity defense was by eliminating the "volitional" prong of prior federal insanity law.[49] Prior to the enactment of IDRA the federal courts followed the Model Penal Code rule that " '[a] person is not responsible for criminal conduct if at the time of such conduct as a result of mental disease or defect he lacks substantial capacity to appreciate the criminality of his conduct or *to conform to the requirements of law.*' "[50] The principal reason for the elimination of the volitional prong was a concern that it is ultimately impossible to prove with any degree of certainty whether the defendant could not, or simply did not, control himself. This concern was expressed in the American Psychiatric Association's statement concerning the insanity defense:

> Many psychiatrists . . . believe that psychiatric information relevant to determining whether a defendant understood the nature of his act, and whether he appreciated its wrongfulness, is more reliable and has a stronger scientific basis than, for example, does psychiatric information relevant to whether a defendant was able to control his behavior. The line between an irresistible impulse and an impulse not resisted is probably no sharper than that between twilight and dusk.[51]

Whatever the merits of the theoretical claim that a defendant should not be held criminally responsible if serious mental illness substantially eroded his capacity to control his behavior, Congress decided that juries in criminal cases should not be asked to make a determination as subtle as the distinction between twilight and dusk when there is no reliable scientific basis for this determination. Perhaps the day will come when the scientific community will be able to determine with greater certainty

---

47. 2 F.3d at 1020–21.

48. Elyn R. Saks, *Multiple Personality Disorder and Criminal Responsibility*, 25 U.C.DAVIS L.REV. 383 (1992).

49. S.Rep.No. 98–225, 2d Sess. at 224 (1983), *reprinted in* 1984 U.S.C.C.A.N. 3182, 3406 (*quoting* MODEL PENAL CODE § 4.01; emphasis added). The italicized portion of this test constituted the so-called "volitional" prong.

50. MODEL PENAL CODE § 4.02(1).

51. S.Rep.No. 98–225, 2d Sess. at 228 (1983), *reprinted in* 1984 U.S.C.C.A.N. 3182, 3410. For the report's complete statement of reasons for eliminating the volitional prong, *see id.* at 225–28, *reprinted in* 1984 U.S.C.C.A.N. at 3407–3411. For criticism of IDRA's elimination of the volitional prong, see Jodie English, *Light Between Twilight and Dusk: Federal Criminal Law and the Volitional Insanity Defense*, 40 HASTINGS L.J. 1 (1988).

the degree to which a defendant's control was impaired by his mental illness, and at that time Congress may reopen the issue of the volitional prong of the insanity defense.

Library References:

C.J.S. Criminal Law § 99–108.
West's Key No. Digests, Criminal Law ⊕47–51.

§ 26.4 Relation to Other Defenses—In General

A fair amount of litigation has arisen concerning the relationship between the insanity defense and other criminal defenses. Section 17(a)'s final sentence provides: "Mental disease or defect does not otherwise constitute a defense."[1] The legislative history states that this language was included—

> to insure that the insanity defense is not improperly resurrected in the guise of showing some other affirmative defense, such as that the defendant had a "diminished responsibility" or some similarly asserted state of mind which would serve to excuse the offense and open the door, once again, to needlessly confusing psychiatric testimony.[2]

The meaning of this provision has been litigated in relation to lack of mens rea, the "diminished capacity" defense, and the defense of entrapment.

Library References:

C.J.S. Criminal Law § 99–108.
West's Key No. Digests, Criminal Law ⊕47–51.

§ 26.5 Relation to Other Defenses—Relation to Defense of Lack of Mens Rea or "Diminished Capacity"

The government has repeatedly argued that the final sentence of § 17(a) prohibits any proffer of psychiatric evidence that is not used in conjunction with the insanity defense. Although this issue has not reached the Supreme Court, the courts of appeals have consistently ruled against the government.[1] Relying on IDRA's legislative history and the

---

§ 26.4

1. 18 U.S.C. § 17(a) (1994).

2. S.Rep.No. 98–225, 2d Sess. at 229 (1983), *reprinted in* 1984 U.S.C.C.A.N. 3182, 3411.

§ 26.5

1. *See, e.g.,*

D.C. Circuit: United States v. Hardy, 730 F.Supp. 1141, 1142–44 (D.D.C.1990); United States v. Gold, 661 F.Supp. 1127, 1129–31 (D.D.C.1987).

Third Circuit: United States v. Pohlot, 827 F.2d 889 (3d Cir.1987).

Fifth Circuit: United States v. Hill, 750 F.Supp. 524 (N.D.Ga.1990) (holding that § 17(a) does not prohibit psychiatric evidence offered to negate specific intent).

Sixth Circuit: United States v. Newman, 889 F.2d 88, 91 n. 1 (6th Cir.1989).

Seventh Circuit: United States v. Fazzini, 871 F.2d 635, 641 (7th Cir.1989)(panel of the Seventh Circuit assumed this conclusion to be true without authoritatively deciding the issue).

Eighth Circuit: United States v. Bartlett, 856 F.2d 1071, 1077–83 (8th Cir.1988).

Ninth Circuit: United States v. Brown, 880 F.2d 1012, 1017 (9th Cir.1989); United

language of its statutory provisions, the lower courts have generally held that § 17(a) only prohibits psychiatric evidence which would serve to establish an affirmative defense, justification, or excuse; it does not prohibit psychiatric evidence offered to negate the mens rea element of the offense.[2] Passages in both the Senate and House reports support this distinction.[3]

States v. Twine, 853 F.2d 676, 678–79 (9th Cir.1988).

Eleventh Circuit: United States v. Cameron, 907 F.2d 1051, 1060–68 (11th Cir. 1990).

The Second and Tenth Circuits have not addressed the issue.

The positions of the Fourth and First Circuits are not clear. In an unpublished opinion, the Fourth Circuit adopted the position that § 17(a) prohibits all psychiatric testimony not used to establish the insanity defense, United States v. Hood, 857 F.2d 1469, 1988 WL 96130 (4th Cir.1988), but then later qualified that holding in another unpublished case, United States v. Moran, 937 F.2d 604, 1991 WL 125461, **2–3 (4th Cir.1991). *See also* United States v. Robinson, 804 F.Supp. 830 (W.D.Va.1992) (holding that § 17(a) prohibits psychiatric evidence offered to disprove premeditation). The First Circuit has stated in dicta that it believes § 17(a) precludes all non-insanity psychiatric evidence, United States v. White, 766 F.2d 22, 24 (1st Cir.1985), but has indicated that it might reconsider its position if a future case presents the appropriate facts, United States v. Lopez–Pena, 912 F.2d 1536, 1541 (1st Cir.1989). Some courts have hinted that the position urged by the government and adopted by the First Circuit in *White* and the Fourth Circuit in *Hood* might violate due process by eliminating the government's burden of proving mens rea.

See, e.g.,

Third Circuit: United States v. Pohlot, 827 F.2d 889, 900–01 (3d Cir.1987).

Eleventh Circuit: United States v. Cameron, 907 F.2d 1051, 1065–66 (11th Cir. 1990).

2. *See, e.g.,*

First Circuit: United States v. Skodnek, 896 F.Supp. 60 (D.Mass.1995); United States v. Marenghi, 893 F.Supp. 85 (D.Me. 1995).

Third Circuit: United States v. Pohlot, 827 F.2d 889, 894–907 (3d Cir.1987).

Eighth Circuit: United States v. Bartlett, 856 F.2d 1071, 1077–83 (8th Cir.1988).

Eleventh Circuit: United States v. Westcott, 83 F.3d 1354, 1358 (11th Cir.

1996); United States v. Cameron, 907 F.2d 1051, 1060–68 (11th Cir.1990).

These courts also rely on two of IDRA's statutory provisions for additional support. First, they say, Fed.R.Crim.P. 12.2(a) requires notice of an intent to rely on the insanity defense, while Fed.R.Crim.P. 12.2(b) requires notice of an intent to introduce expert testimony bearing on the issue of guilt. If § 17(a) prohibited all non-insanity psychiatric evidence, these courts reason, Rule 12.2(b) would be meaningless.

See, e.g.,

Third Circuit: Pohlot, 827 F.2d at 899 n.8.

Eighth Circuit: Bartlett, 856 F.2d at 1081.

Eleventh Circuit: Cameron, 907 F.2d at 1057 n.8, 1065 n.27.

Second, Fed.R.Evid. 704(b) prohibits experts from testifying on the "ultimate issue" both as to "whether the defendant did or did not have the mental state or condition *constituting the element of the crime charged* or of a *defense* thereto" (emphasis added). Thus, they conclude, Rule 704(b) also distinguishes between affirmative defense psychiatric evidence and psychiatric evidence employed to disprove mens rea.

See, e.g.,

Third Circuit: Pohlot, 827 F.2d at 899.

Eighth Circuit: Bartlett, 856 F.2d at 1081.

Eleventh Circuit: Cameron, 907 F.2d at 1065 n.27.

3. The House report states that IDRA:

provides that [§ 17(a)] constitutes the only affirmative defense based on mental disorder that will be applicable in Federal courts. Mental disorders will remain relevant [sic], of course, to the issue of the existence of a mental state required for the offense, such as the specific intent required for certain crimes. This accords with current practice.

H.R.Rep.No. 98–577, 1st Sess., 14–15 (1983). The Senate report states that the

Many of the cases in which this issue is raised use the terms "diminished capacity" and "diminished responsibility." There appears to be a great deal of confusion about the meaning of these terms.[4] Some courts employ both terms to mean the use of psychiatric evidence to disprove the mens rea element of specific intent.[5] Others use both terms to refer to the use of psychiatric evidence to excuse or mitigate a defendant's criminal responsibility because of his/her mental condition.[6] Still others evidently hold that "diminished capacity" refers to the former while "diminished responsibility" refers to the latter.[7]

In an attempt to dispel this confusion, the Eleventh Circuit has taken a slightly different approach. In *United States v. Cameron*,[8] that circuit discarded the terms "diminished capacity" and "diminished responsibility" and replaced them with a distinction between " 'affirmative defense' evidence of mental impairment"[9] and evidence of mental impairment which serves to negate specific intent or a subjective state of mind.[10] While one court has criticized the *Cameron* approach,[11] the distinction it draws is conceptually accurate and appears to be a crucial

---

last sentence of § 17(a) was "intended to insure that the insanity defense is not improperly resurrected in the guise of showing some other *affirmative* defense . . . ." S.Rep. No. 98–225, 2d Sess. at 229 (1983), *reprinted in* 1984 U.S.C.C.A.N. 3182, 3411 (emphasis added). The report later states that while voluntary intoxication does not constitute a severe mental disease or defect under § 17(a), "intoxication may negate a state of mind required for the commission of the offense charged." *Id.* at 229 n.30, *reprinted in* 1984 U.S.C.C.A.N. at 3411 n.30. For judicial opinions citing these portions of the legislative history, *see, e.g.,*

Third Circuit: United States v. Pohlot, 827 F.2d 889, 898 (3d Cir.1987).

Eighth Circuit: United States v. Bartlett, 856 F.2d 1071, 1079–81 (8th Cir.1988).

Eleventh Circuit: United States v. Cameron, 907 F.2d 1051, 1065 n. 26 (11th Cir. 1990).

4. *See, e.g.,* United States v. Cameron, 907 F.2d 1051, 1062–63 (11th Cir.1990); Stephen J. Morse, *Undiminished Confusion in Diminished Capacity*, 75 J.CRIM.L. & CRIMINOLOGY 1 (1984).

5. *See, e.g.,*

Third Circuit: United States v. Pohlot, 827 F.2d 889, 897 (3d Cir.1987).

Ninth Circuit: United States v. Twine, 853 F.2d 676, 678 (9th Cir.1988).

Eleventh Circuit: United States v. Cameron, 907 F.2d 1051, 1062 (11th Cir.1990).

Some courts have held that this meaning of "diminished capacity" only applies to crimes requiring the mens rea of specific

intent and not to those requiring general intent.

See, e.g.,

D.C. Circuit: United States v. Hardy, 730 F.Supp. 1141, 1143–44 (D.D.C.1990).

Ninth Circuit: United States v. Twine, 853 F.2d 676, 679 (9th Cir.1988).

Eleventh Circuit: United States v. Cameron, 907 F.2d 1051, 1063 n.20 (11th Cir. 1990).

6. *See, e.g.,*

Third Circuit: United States v. Pohlot, 827 F.2d 889, 890 (3d Cir.1987).

Eleventh Circuit: United States v. Cameron, 907 F.2d 1051, 1062 (11th Cir.1990).

7. *Eighth Circuit:* United States v. Bartlett, 856 F.2d 1071, 1077 n. 6 (8th Cir.1988).

Eleventh Circuit: United States v. Cameron, 907 F.2d 1051, 1062–63 (11th Cir. 1990).

Ninth Circuit: United States v. Frisbee, 623 F.Supp. 1217, 1221 n. 2 (N.D.Cal.1985).

8. 907 F.2d at 1062–63.

9. *Id.* at 1063.

10. *Id.* (specific intent); United States v. Westcott, 83 F.3d 1354, 1358 (11th Cir. 1996) ("subjective state of mind").

11. United States v. Hill, 750 F.Supp. 524, 525 n. 3 (N.D.Ga.1990) (finding the *Cameron* court's " 'new' nomenclature . . . cumbersome and not particularly helpful").

one in thinking about the problems posed by the final sentence of § 17(a).

Although the lower federal courts admit psychiatric evidence when it is offered to negate mens rea, the line between disproving specific intent and excusing a guilty defendant from criminal responsibility is often blurry, and the courts are wary of the potential for abuse of psychiatric evidence by the defense.[12] Appellate courts have stated that "[d]istrict courts should admit evidence of mental abnormality on the issue of mens rea only when, if believed, it would support a legally acceptable theory of mens rea."[13] The district courts have the difficult chore of determining whether the defendant is attempting to disprove mens rea through a legally acceptable theory or really attempting to establish a justification or excuse other than insanity.[14] IDRA permits the former but prohibits the latter.

A 1996 case posed the question whether the admission of psychiatric evidence on the issue of mens rea allows the defense to have its cake and eat it too, effectively presenting the insanity defense while avoiding the difficult burden of proof imposed by 18 U.S.C. § 17(b). In *United States v. Westcott*[15] the defendant wanted to introduce evidence of a psychiatric condition to negate specific intent, but he did not claim the insanity defense, and he objected to any instruction on the insanity defense. The proffered psychiatric testimony fulfilled all of the elements of the insanity defense under 18 U.S.C. § 17(a). The court of appeals held that the district court had properly refused to allow the admit the evidence in the absence of an instruction on the insanity defense. Under these circumstances the court concluded that allowing the defendant to present psychiatric testimony *only* on the issue of mens rea would, in effect, "allow defendant to present insanity defense evidence while avoiding the burden of proof mandated by the Insanity Defense Reform Act."[16] This case is rather troubling, since it suggests that a less severely impaired defendant—who clearly could not make out the insanity defense—would be permitted to introduce psychiatric evidence on the issue of mens rea alone, while a more severely impaired defendant would have to choose between foregoing the expert testimony or allowing the jury to be instructed on the insanity defense, a defense on which the defendant bears the burden of proof. If the court was concerned that some of the

---

12. The *Cameron* court has opined that:

psychiatric evidence (1) will only rarely negate specific intent, (2) presents an inherent danger that it will distract the jury from focusing on the actual presence or absence of mens rea, and (3) "may easily slide into wider usage that opens up the jury to theories of defense more akin to justification ..."

907 F.2d at 1067 (*quoting* United States v. Pohlot, 827 F.2d 889, 905 (3d Cir.1987)).

13. *Third Circuit:* United States v. Pohlot, 827 F.2d 889, 905–06 (3d Cir.1987).

Eleventh Circuit: United States v. Cameron, 907 F.2d 1051, 1067 (11th Cir.1990).

14. For one attempt to distinguish between disproving specific intent and establishing an affirmative defense of "diminished capacity," see United States v. Pohlot, 827 F.2d 889, 903–06 (3d Cir.1987). For an analysis of the *Pohlot* decision, see John S. Anooshian, Comment, *Insanity Defense Reform Act Does Not Bar Defendant From Offering Psychiatric Evidence of Mental Abnormality on Issue of Mens Rea*, 20 Rutgers L.J. 271 (1988).

15. 83 F.3d 1354 (11th Cir.1996).

16. 83 F. 3d at 1359.

expert's testimony was relevant solely to the insanity defense, and not to mens rea,[17] the preferable course would have been to admit only the portion of the expert's testimony that would be clearly germane to mens rea, without requiring an instruction on the insanity defense, since the defendant might rightly fear that such an instruction would prejudice his chances of an outright acquittal.

Library References:

C.J.S. Criminal Law § 96–108, 113.
West's Key No. Digests, Criminal Law ☜46–51.

§ 26.6 Relation to Other Defenses—Relation to Entrapment

There is also some potential for overlap between the insanity defense and the entrapment defense, since a defendant may be able to establish that his mental condition makes him peculiarly susceptible to government inducement.[1] Only one circuit appears to have addressed this issue. In *United States v. Newman*,[2] the Fifth Circuit rejected the government's contention that § 17(a) precluded psychiatric evidence of the defendant's particular susceptibility to inducement due to a mental condition.[3] The *Newman* court stated that "nothing in [IDRA] or its legislative history suggest a Congressional intent to preclude psychiatric testimony relevant to the entrapment defense."[4]

This statement not only appears to have been dicta,[5] but it also seems to be inconsistent with the "diminished capacity" decisions. To the extent that the defendant in *Newman* was relying on entrapment as a *defense*,[6] and to the extent that this defense hinged on his mental condition, it appears that this is precisely the type of evidence Congress intended to exclude.[7] Case law on the relation between insanity and "diminished capacity" also appears to support this conclusion.[8]

On the other hand, there is an hint in IDRA's legislative history supporting the position that Congress intended for certain types of

---

17. *See* 83 F.3d at 1358–59 (noting repeatedly that Dr. Miller's testimony did not relate solely to mens rea, but went also to the issue whether the defendant could appreciate the wrongfulness of his conduct).

§ 26.6

1. The test for establishing entrapment is (1) that government conduct induced the crime; and (2) that the defendant was not predisposed to engage in criminal conduct. *See* Mathews v. United States, 485 U.S. 58, 62–63, 108 S.Ct. 883, 886, 99 L.Ed.2d 54 (1988) (citing cases).

2. 849 F.2d 156 (5th Cir.1988).

3. *Id.* at 165.

4. *Id.*

5. The Fifth Circuit affirmed the trial court's decision to exclude the proffered testimony on the ground that the district court did not abuse its discretion by con-

cluding that the testimony would needlessly confuse the jury. *Id.*

6. As *Mathews* attests, lack of mens rea and entrapment are two very different arguments. Indeed, except for Justice Scalia, 485 U.S. at 67–68, 108 S.Ct. at 888–89 (Scalia, J., concurring), the *Mathews* majority views the two arguments as inconsistent. 485 U.S. at 62–66, 108 S.Ct. at 886–88. Thus, it is inaccurate to treat the entrapment defense as another form of the argument that the defendant lacked the required mens rea.

7. S.Rep.No. 98–225, 2d Sess. at 229 (1983), *reprinted in* 1984 U.S.C.C.A.N. 3182, 3411.

8. *See, e.g.,*

Third Circuit: United States v. Pohlot, 827 F.2d 889, 905 (3d Cir.1987) ("[T]he strict use of psychiatric evidence to negate mens rea may easily slide into wider usage

psychiatric testimony relating to entrapment to be admitted. In discussing Rule 704(b), the Senate Committee report states, "The Committee has fashioned its Rule 704 provision to reach all such 'ultimate' issues, e.g., premeditation in a homicide case, or *lack of predisposition in entrapment*."[9] One way to read this sentence would be to argue that it expresses Congress' intent that psychiatric testimony concerning a defendant's predisposition is indeed admissible to prove entrapment, so long as that testimony does not include the expert's opinion about the "ultimate" issue. Thus, there appears to be a certain tension on this issue between Rule 704's legislative history and the "diminished capacity" decisions. The tension will remain until other circuits more squarely address the question.

Another facet of the overlap between the insanity and entrapment defenses appears to be of historical interest only. In *United States v. Prickett*[10] the Sixth Circuit held that arguing the insanity defense precludes reliance on entrapment.[11] Prior to the U.S. Supreme Court's 1988 decision in *Mathews v. United States*,[12] the circuits were split on the issue of whether a defendant could concurrently argue both that s/he lacked the requisite mens rea and that s/he was entrapped.[13] *Prickett* extended the prohibition on arguing entrapment while denying mens rea to the insanity context, reasoning that insanity is a "mens rea-related defense."[14] *Mathews* holds that a federal criminal defendant may argue both entrapment and lack of mens rea even though these arguments may be inconsistent with one another.[15] In the same vein, it would appear that after *Mathews* a defendant should also be permitted to argue both insanity and entrapment as defenses, even if insanity is construed as a mens rea-related defense.

Library References:

C.J.S. Criminal Law § 96–108, 113.
West's Key No. Digests, Criminal Law ⊙46–51.

§ 26.7   Procedural Issues

IDRA also raises procedural issues that have played, and will continue to play, an important role in the development of the federal insanity

that opens up the jury to theories of defense more akin to justification.").

Eleventh Circuit: United States v. Cameron, 907 F.2d 1051, 1067 (11th Cir.1990) (quoting *Pohlot*, 827 F.2d at 905).

9. S.Rep.No. 98–225, *supra* note 7, at 231, *reprinted in* 1984 U.S.C.C.A.N. 3413 (emphasis added).

10. 790 F.2d 35 (6th Cir.1986).

11. *Id.* at 36.

12. 485 U.S. 58, 108 S.Ct. 883, 99 L.Ed.2d 54 (1988).

13. For an analysis of the various approaches to this problem prior to the *Mathews* decision, see Karis A. Hastings, Note, *Entrapment and Denial of the Crime: A*

Defense of the Inconsistency Rule, 1986 Duke L.J. 866.

The Sixth Circuit was one of the circuits that precluded reliance on entrapment if the defendant failed to admit the mens rea element. *See* United States v. Prickett, 790 F.2d 35, 36 (6th Cir.1986) (citing cases).

14. 790 F.2d at 36. This conclusion seems dubious. In light of the federal courts' treatment of the "diminished capacity" issue, *see* § 27.5, the term "mens rea-related defense" appears to be an oxymoron.

15. 485 U.S. at 62, 108 S.Ct. at 886.

defense. Although procedural issues fall outside the focus of this work, three procedural matters will be noted briefly here: (1) instructions to the jury about the consequences of returning a verdict of not guilty by reason of insanity, (2) the prohibition on expert testimony about the trial's "ultimate issues," and (3) judicial imposition of the defense on an unwilling defendant.

A. JURY INSTRUCTION ABOUT THE CONSEQUENCES OF A "NOT GUILTY BY REASON OF INSANITY" VERDICT

In *Shannon v. United States*[1] the Supreme Court considered the question whether a defendant who has raised the insanity defense is entitled to have his jury instructed regarding the consequences of an NGI verdict. The Court began its analysis with the settled proposition that a jury which possesses no sentencing function should reach its verdict without regard to the verdict's potential consequences.[2] The Court concluded that IDRA's text provides no support for altering this settled rule to require an instruction about the consequences of the NGI verdict. The Act only provides that the jury return a verdict of guilty, not guilty, or NGI.[3] It says nothing about instructing juries about the consequences of its verdict. The legislative history does include a statement endorsing the practice of instructing juries about the consequences of the NGI verdict,[4] but the Court declined to give this statement authoritative weight because it was not "anchored to the text of the statute."[5]

The Court also refused to employ its supervisory authority over federal criminal practice to require the instruction in question. The Court rejected the argument that such an instruction is needed to counter the erroneous assumption that a defendant will be released if he is found not guilty by reason of insanity. The Court questioned whether jurors are really unfamiliar with the consequences of an NGI verdict[6] and expressed doubt in any event that a correct instruction could allay any such fears.[7] More important, since the jury is instructed not to

---

§ 26.7

1. 512 U.S. 573, 114 S.Ct. 2419, 129 L.Ed.2d 459 (1994). *See generally* Randi Ellias, Note, *Should Courts Instruct Juries as to the Consequences to a Defendant of a "Not Guilty By Reason of Insanity" Verdict?*, 85 J.Crim.L. & Criminology 1062 (1995); and Masha Bach, Note, *The Not Guilty By Reason of Insanity Verdict: Should Juries Be Informed of Its Consequences?*, 16 Whittier L.Rev. 645 (1995).

2. 512 U.S. at 579, 114 S.Ct. at 2424.

3. 512 U.S. at 579–80, 114 S.Ct. at 2424–2425. *See* 18 U.S.C. § 4242(b) (1994).

4. The Senate Report states:

The Committee endorses the procedure used in the District of Columbia whereby the jury, in a case in which the insanity defense has been raised, may be instructed on the effect of a verdict of not guilty by reason of insanity. If the defendant requests that the instruction not be given, it is within the discretion of the court whether to give it or not.

S.Rep.No. 98–225, 2d Sess., at 222, 240 (1980), *reprinted in* 1984 U.S.C.C.A.N. 3182, 3422 (footnotes omitted).

5. 512 U.S. at 582, 114 S.Ct. at 2426.

6. 512 U.S. at 584, 114 S.Ct. at 2427 & n.10.

7. 512 U.S. at 584, 114 S.Ct. at 2427 (noting that a correct instruction would state that a defendant is entitled to a post-verdict hearing within 40 days to determine if s/he is entitled to immediate release).

consider any potential punishment in reaching its verdict, the Court declined to depart from the assumption that the jurors would follow the court's instruction.[8] Finally, the Court noted that IDRA is a comprehensive reformulation of the federal insanity defense; if Congress had intended to require an instruction on the consequences of an insanity verdict, it would have provided for such an instruction.[9]

The Court did not, however, preclude the possibility that an instruction on the consequences of an NGI verdict might be necessary in certain limited circumstances.[10] For example, such an instruction might be required if a prosecutor or witness stated in the jury's hearing that a defendant would go free if he or she were found not guilty by reason of insanity.

The lower courts have begun to implement *Shannon*, denying an instruction on the consequences of an insanity verdict in the absence of special circumstances,[11] and seeking to determine when such special circumstances exist.[12]

B. EXPERT TESTIMONY ON "ULTIMATE ISSUES" UNDER RULE 704(B)

IDRA substantially altered how expert testimony could be employed in insanity defense cases. The Act amended Rule 704 of the Federal Rules of Evidence, which previously permitted expert witnesses to render opinions on all ultimate issues to be decided by the trier of fact. The Act added the following language to Rule 704:

> (b) No expert witness testifying with respect to the mental state or condition of a defendant in a criminal case may state an opinion or inference as to whether the defendant did or did not have the mental state or condition constituting an element of the crime charged or of a defense thereto. Such ultimate issues are matters for the trier of fact alone.

Thus, in cases raising the insanity defense, Rule 704(b) now prohibits experts from expressing an opinion as to whether a defendant possessed the mental state necessary to satisfy the defense.

Congress' stated purpose in amending Rule 704 was:

> to eliminate the confusing spectacle of competing expert witnesses testifying to directly contradictory conclusions as to the ultimate legal issue to be found by the trier of fact. Under this proposal, expert psychiatric testimony would be limited to presenting and

---

8. 512 U.S. at 585, 114 S.Ct. at 2427.

9. 512 U.S. at 586, 114 S.Ct. at 2428.

10. 512 U.S. at 586, 114 S.Ct. at 2428.

11. United States v. Tracy, 36 F.3d 187, 196 (1st Cir.1994).

12. Reeves v. Hopkins, 871 F.Supp. 1182, 1209–10 (D.Neb.1994) (in light of brevity and ambiguity of prosecutor's statement that if state didn't win defendant "should walk out of this courtroom a free man," defendant had not established that he was prejudiced by failure to give instruction), *rev'd in part on other grnds*, 76 F.3d 1424 (8th Cir.1996).

explaining their diagnoses, such as whether the defendant had a severe mental disease or defect and what the characteristics of such a disease or defect, if any, may have been.

. . .

Moreover the rationale for precluding ultimate opinion psychiatric testimony extends beyond the insanity defense to any ultimate mental state of the defendant that is relevant to the legal conclusion sought to be proven. The Committee has fashioned its Rule 704 provision to reach all such "ultimate" issues, *e.g.*, premeditation in a homicide case, or lack of predisposition in entrapment.[13]

The question of what types of expert testimony fall within Rule 704(b)'s parameters has been one of the most heavily litigated issues arising out of IDRA's passage,[14] and it has been discussed at length by evidence scholars.

---

13. S.Rep.No. 98–225, 2d Sess., at 230 (1983), *reprinted in* 1984 U.S.C.C.A.N. 3182, 3412–13. The basis for this limitation on expert testimony in insanity cases is ably stated by the American Psychiatric Association:

[I]t is clear that psychiatrists are experts in medicine, not the law. As such, it is clear that the psychiatrist's first obligation and expertise in the courtroom is to "do psychiatry," i.e., to present medical information and opinion about the defendant's mental state and motivation and to explain in detail the reason for his medical-psychiatric conclusions. When, however, "ultimate issue" questions are formulated by the law and put to the expert witness who must then say "yea" or "nay," then the expert witness is required to make a leap in logic. He no longer addresses himself to medical concepts but instead must infer or intuit what is in fact unspeakable, namely, the probable relationship between medical concepts and legal or moral constructs such as free will. These impermissible leaps in logic made by expert witnesses confuse the jury. Juries thus find themselves listening to conclusory and seemingly contradictory psychiatric testimony that defendants are either "sane" or "insane" or that they do or do not meet the relevant legal test for insanity. This state of affairs does considerable injustice to psychiatry and, we believe, possibly to criminal defendants. In fact, in many criminal insanity trials both prosecution and defense psychiatrists do agree about the nature and even the extent of mental

disorder exhibited by the defendant at the time of the act.

Psychiatrists, of course, must be permitted to testify fully about the defendant's diagnosis, mental state and motivation (in clinical and commonsense terms) at the time of the alleged act so as to permit the jury or judge to reach the ultimate conclusions about which they and only they are expert. Determining whether a criminal defendant was legally insane is a matter for legal fact-finders, not for experts.

Ibid.

14. *See, e.g.,*

Sixth Circuit: United States v. Cox, 826 F.2d 1518, 1523–26 (6th Cir.1987).

Seventh Circuit: United States v. Reno, 992 F.2d 739, 741–44 (7th Cir.1993); United States v. West, 962 F.2d 1243, 1244–50 (7th Cir.1992); United States v. Salava, 978 F.2d 320, 322–23 (7th Cir.1992); United States v. Hillsberg, 812 F.2d 328, 331–33 (7th Cir. 1987).

Eighth Circuit: United States v. Blumberg, 961 F.2d 787, 789–90 (8th Cir.1992); United States v. Dubray, 854 F.2d 1099, 1102 (8th Cir.1988).

Tenth Circuit: United States v. Austin, 981 F.2d 1163 (10th Cir.1992).

Eleventh Circuit: United States v. Manley, 893 F.2d 1221 (11th Cir.1990); United States v. Davis, 835 F.2d 274 (11th Cir. 1988); United States v. Edwards, 819 F.2d 262 (11th Cir.1987).

C. JUDICIAL IMPOSITION OF THE INSANITY DEFENSE

IDRA seems to alter significantly the law governing when a trial judge may impose the insanity defense on an unwilling criminal defendant. Prior law rested on the policy judgment that " 'insanity' is not strictly an affirmative defense and [it] can be raised by either the court or the prosecution" and that " 'imprisonment was wrong in the case of a mentally ill person.' "[15] IDRA's requirement that the defendant carry the burden of proof by clear and convincing evidence has recharacterized insanity as an affirmative defense, and thereby undermined the rationale courts relied upon in imposing the insanity defense on unwilling defendants.[16]

Given the profound changes IDRA made in insanity defense policy, the current approach seems to require that the trial judge respect a competent defendant's wishes concerning how his/her defense will proceed, including whether or not ιο raise the insanity defense.[17] One court has suggested, however, that "[w]hen a defendant can make no clear choice for or against the defense, and the evidence suggests that the defense is viable, it might then be appropriate for the court to exercise its discretion to instruct the jury [on insanity] sua sponte."[18] In any event, IDRA appears to have substantially narrowed the trial judge's discretion to impose the insanity defense on a defendant who is mentally competent when she or he makes the decision to forego the insanity defense. How this issue will play out regarding incompetent defendants remains to be seen.

§ 26.8 Bibliography

Anooshian, John S., Comment, *Insanity Defense Reform Act Does Not Bar Defendant From Offering Psychiatric Evidence of Mental Abnormality on Issue of Mens Rea*, 20 RUTGERS L.J. 271 (1988).

Bach, Masha, Note, *The Not Guilty By Reason of Insanity Verdict: Should Juries Be Informed of Its Consequences?*, 16 WHITTIER L.REV. 645 (1995).

Caplan, Lincoln, THE INSANITY DEFENSE AND THE TRIAL OF JOHN W. HINKLEY (1987).

Ellias, Randi, Note, *Should Courts Instruct Juries as to the Consequences to a Defendant of a "Not Guilty By Reason of Insanity" Verdict?*, 85 J.CRIM.L. & CRIMINOLOGY 1062 (1995).

English, Jodie, *Light Between Twilight and Dusk: Federal Criminal Law and the Volitional Insanity Defense*, 40 HASTINGS L.J. 1 (1988).

Goldstein, Abraham, THE INSANITY DEFENSE (1967).

15. United States v. Marble, 940 F.2d 1543, 1547 (D.C.Cir.1991) (*quoting* Overholser v. Lynch, 288 F.2d 388, 392, 393 (D.C.Cir.1961)).

16. United States v. Marble, 940 F.2d 1543, 1547 (D.C.Cir.1991).

17. *Id.* at 1547; United States v. Moody, 763 F.Supp. 589, 602–06 (M.D.Ga. 1991), *affirmed*, 977 F.2d 1420 (11th Cir. 1992).

18. United States v. Marble, 940 F.2d 1543, 1547–48 (D.C.Cir.1991).

Miller, Henry T., Comment, *Recent Changes in Criminal Law: The Federal Insanity Defense*, 46 La.L.Rev. 337 (1985).

Saks, Elyn R., *Multiple Personality Disorder and Criminal Responsibility*, 25 U.C.Davis L.Rev. 383 (1992).

PART IV

RELATED CIVIL CAUSES OF ACTION.

CHAPTER 27

FRAUD AGAINST THE GOVERNMENT: THE CIVIL FALSE CLAIMS ACT*

Table of Sections

WESTLAW ELECTRONIC RESEARCH

See WESTLAW Electronic Research Guide preceding the Summary of Contents.

---

§ 27.1 Introduction

The False Claims Act ("FCA") is aimed at the "world's second oldest profession ... stealing"[1] and provides "the primary vehicle by

* Portions of this chapter are based on materials appearing in PAMELA H. BUCY, HEALTH CARE FRAUD: CRIMINAL, CIVIL AND ADMINISTRATIVE LAW. To the extent there is reproduction of these materials, it is included with the permission of the publisher and copyright holder, Law Journal Seminars Press, 345 Park Avenue South, New York, New York 10010. All rights reserved as to reproduction.

§ 27.1

1. 132 Cong.Rec. H6483 (daily ed. Sept. 9, 1986) (statement of Rep. Bedell).

which the government prosecutes civil fraud."[2] The FCA gives the federal government as well as "any person" a cause of action against those who submit false claims to the government.[3] The statutorily set damages and penalties are formidable: treble damages plus a mandatory penalty of $5,000–10,000 per false claim.[4] This mounts up. Between 1986, when the FCA was substantially amended, and 1996, total fraud recoveries by the federal government have exceeded $3 billion. Of this amount $1.13 billion has been recovered as a result of FCA actions filed by private persons.[5] Although a civil statute, the False Claims Act, like RICO[6] and the civil asset forfeiture statutes,[7] requires proof of criminal conduct to establish civil liability.

Applying the FCA is complicated by three features of the act. First, both the hybrid civil/criminal nature of the Act (establishing civil liability by proving the commission of a crime) and the dual plaintiff system (either the government or a private party can bring the case) complicate the procedural aspects of these cases. At various points the statute directs deviations from the Federal Rules of Civil Procedure.[8] Second, much of the law on the FCA, historically and currently, is judge-made, a fact further complicated by the 1986 amendments which dramatically changed the FCA and rendered much of the judicial precedent on the FCA out of date, inapplicable, or of questionable guidance. Third, there are significant issues left unresolved by the statute. For example, it is not clear when FCA actions are jurisdictionally barred,[9] how to calculate

2. 132 Cong.Rec. H6479 (daily ed. Sept. 9, 1986) (statement of Rep. Glickman). *See,* JOHN T. BOESE, CIVIL FALSE CLAIMS AND QUI TAM ACTIONS (1994). Boese's treatise is an excellent source on the False Claims Act.

3. 31 U.S.C. § 3730(a)-(b).

4. 31 U.S.C. § 3729(a).

5. TAXPAYERS AGAINST FRAUD, THE 1986 FALSE CLAIMS ACT AMENDMENTS, 1986–1996, 15 (1996).

6. 18 U.S.C. § 1961–68; Like civil RICO, the FCA provides that *either* the government *or* private individuals may bring a FCA action 31 U.S.C. § 3730(a)-(b). The private plaintiff provisions of the FCA differ from those in RICO in two major ways, however. First, whereas RICO requires that a private party demonstrate that he/she has been harmed "in his business or property" by the defendant's conduct, the FCA permits "any person" to bring a FCA suit. See, 18 U.S.C. § 1964(c); 31 U.S.C. § 3730(b)(1). Second, whereas RICO allows a private party plaintiff to litigate the action without any interference from the government, the FCA permits the federal government to intervene in a FCA lawsuit initiated by a private party and if the government chooses, to take over the

action with minimal involvement by the private party plaintiff. See 18 U.S.C. § 1964(c); 31 U.S.C. § 3730(b)-(c).

7. Money Laundering Control Act, 18 U.S.C. § 981. *See, e.g.,* Comprehensive Forfeiture Act, 21 U.S.C. § 853.

8. For example, when the qui tam relator files an FCA action, the relator does not serve the complaint on the defendant. Instead the plaintiff serves the complaint plus a written report of "substantially all material evidence and information the person possesses." The government has at least 60 days to review the material before the defendant is served with the complaint. 31 U.S.C. § 3730(b)(2). In addition, rules of discovery are altered in FCA actions. The defendant may be entitled to the written report the qui tam plaintiff provided to the government upon filing the lawsuit. United States *ex rel.* Hindo v. University of Health Sciences, 1992 WL 300996 at *2 (N.D.Ill. 1992) (holding that the defendant is entitled to the report). The government also gets expanded discovery under the FCA. It is able to use civil investigation demands (CIDs) prior to filing or joining a FCA suit. 31 U.S.C. § 3733.

9. *See* § 27.10.

damages[10] or the statute of limitations,[11] or to what extent the Federal Rules of Procedure regarding pleading apply to FCA complaints.[12] Because of these unusual aspects, an understanding of the history and evolution of the FCA is especially helpful in determining its applicability and litigating strategies.

Library References:

C.J.S. United States § 168–172, 174.
West's Key No. Digests, United States ☞120–122.

§ 27.2 History

Sawdust and diseased mules led to the passage of the False Claims Act in 1863. Union soldiers discovered that crates of arms purchased by the Union Army were full of sawdust, not muskets.[1] Allegedly fit mules purchased by the Army were delivered diseased, blind, overpriced or, had already been purchased (several times).[2] There was no federal law enforcement machinery to stop corrupt war profiteers: no Federal Bureau of Investigation or Inspectors General; a very small Department of Justice; a War Department with no investigators to monitor contractors.[3] Federal lawmakers turned to an available resource—private citizens. With the passage of the FCA, private citizens were guaranteed half of

10. *See* § 27.18.

11. *See* § 27.17.

12. *See* § 27.16.

§ 27.2

1. 132 Cong.Rec. H6482 (daily ed. Sept. 9, 1986) (statement of Rep. Berman.)

2. *False Claim Act Amendments: Hearings on H. R. 3334 Before the Subcomm. on Admin. Law & Gov't Relations of the House Comm. on the Judiciary*, 99th Cong., 2d Sess. 1 (1986)[hereinafter *Hearings: False Claims Act Amendments*] (Opening Statement of Rep. Glickman, Feb. 5, 1986) (also, 132 Cong.Rec. H6482, Sept. 9, 1986). The following report from this 1863 investigation concerns sweetheart deals arranged by Major Justus McKinstry, Quarter–Master for the U.S. Army at St. Louis.

Major Justus McKinstry, on or about the twentieth day of August, 1861, having need to purchase a large number of artillery horses and calvary horses for his department, did not and would not purchase the same in the market nor for the market value; but without any advertisement for proposals, authorized one Benjamin P. Fox ... to furnish the same to him at one hundred and nineteen dollars each for cavalry horses, and one hundred and fifty dollars each for artillery horses ... the market value of which was about ninety dollars each and ... one hundred each [respectively].

Major McKinstry did on the first day of July 1861, and on divers days between that day and the sixth October ... purchase for his department a large number of mules ... altogether about one thousand mules ... which were unfit for the service, and almost worthless, for being too old or too young, blind, weak-eyed, damaged, worn out or diseased ... Major McKinstry, acting in that behalf in gross carelessness and disregard of the interest of the service, to the waste and squandering of the public funds.

McKinstry, on or about the 27th September, 1861, at St. Louis, having need to purchase overcoats for his department, did not and would not purchase the same in the market nor for the market price; but, without any advertisement for proposals, authorized Child, Pratt & Fox to furnish the same to him; and when they had then and there from Martin & Brothers 802 overcoats for the price of seven dollars and fifty cents each, he, said McKinstry, then and there purchased the same 802 overcoats from Child, Pratt & Fox for $10.50 each ... He, said McKinstry, thereby then and there intending to secure to Child, Pratt & Fox, and others in collusion with them, large gains, to the waste of the public funds.

3. *Cf. Hearings: False Claims Act Amendments, supra* note 2 at 399–400 (Statement of John Phillips); Inspector General Act of 1978, 5 U.S.C. Appendix 3.

any recovery collected under the Act.[4] The 1863 statute also provided for criminal liability.[5] Nine years after its passage, the criminal provisions were codified separately from the civil provisions.[6]

The idea of using private citizens to rout out frauds upon the government has a long tradition in English and American law. Known as "qui tam" actions, these lawsuits derive their name from the Latin phrase, "qui tam pro domino rege quam pro si ipso in hac parte sequitur" which means he who sues on behalf of the King as well as for himself.[7]

The 1863 statute remained intact until 1943 when it was amended to reduce the incentives for private persons to bring qui tam actions under the Act. While Congress emasculated the qui tam provisions of the FCA, the courts were restricting the reach of the FCA overall by imposing a heavy burden of proof on the plaintiff (whether the government or private party) especially as to intent.

Not surprisingly, after the 1943 amendments and restrictive court opinions, the FCA was not widely used. By 1986, however, Congress was ready to invigorate the FCA as a major fraud-fighting tool. High profile frauds had convinced many in Congress that new and innovative tools were needed to combat fraud. As one legislator explained:

> Fraud in federal programs is pervasive, affecting benefit and assistance programs, as well as programs for mortgage insurance, crop subsidies, disaster relief and the like. Procurement fraud, in particular, has seemingly flourished in the past few years with the plethora of reports on mischarging, cross-charging and egregious overcharging. . . .
>
> The consequence . . . is that the federal government loses tens, if not hundreds, of millions of dollars to fraud each year. Beyond the actual monetary loss, fraud in federal programs also erodes public confidence in the administration of these programs by allowing ineligible persons to benefit from them.[8]

In 1986 Congress responded to the rising concerns about fraud by substantially amending and strengthening the FCA. These amendments

---

4. "*And be it further enacted*, That . . . persons liable to such suit . . . [shall] be proceeded against . . . for the recovery of . . . for forfeiture and damages . . . not exceeding the . . . sum of two thousand dollars, and twice the amount of the damages. . . .

"*And be it further enacted,* that the person bringing said suit and prosecuting it to final judgment shall be entitled to receive one half the amount of such forfeiture, as well as one half the amount of the damages he shall recover and collect; and the other half thereof shall belong to and be paid over to the United States. . . ."

Act of March 2, 1863, at c. 67, 12 Stat. 696–98. *Hearings: False Claim Act Amendments*, *supra*, note 2 at 295. (Remarks of Representative Fortney H. (Pete Stark)).

5. "[A]ny person . . . who shall make or cause to be made . . . any claim upon or against the Government of the United States . . . knowing such claim to be false, fictitious, or fraudulent . . . shall be deemed guilty of a criminal offence." *Id.*

6. Rev.Stat. §§ 3490–94 and 5438.

7. BLACK'S LAW DICTIONARY 1251 (6th ed. 1990).

8. (Statement of Senator William S. Cohen) *Hearings: False Claims Act Amendments*, *supra* note 2 at 296–98.

(1) provided more effective investigative tools to detect civil fraud, (2) defined the mens rea requirement to make clear that specific intent was not required proof, (3) established "preponderance of the evidence" as the applicable burden of proof (4) increased the penalties and damages, (5) broadened the venue and jurisdiction provisions so as to cover multi-defendant and multi-district frauds, and (6) broadened the definition of "claim." The 1986 amendments also made it more attractive and feasible to serve as a qui tam plaintiff (termed a "relator") by (1) making it easier to qualify as a qui tam relator, (2) enlarging the role of the qui tam relator even if the government was also a plaintiff, (3) guaranteeing minimum recoveries to successful qui tam relators, (4) providing whistle-blower protection to any employee (whether a qui tam relator or not) who "assisted in the FCA case." In combination they invigorated the FCA, converting it into a formidable weapon against fraud upon the government.

Originally most FCA cases filed concerned fraud by defense contractors. This remained true immediately after the 1986 amendments revitalized the FCA. In recent years, however, the majority of FCA cases concern fraud by health care providers. In 1996, for example, 40% of pending qui tam cases concerned health care fraud, while 38% concerned defense fraud.[9]

Library References:

C.J.S. United States § 168–172, 174.
West's Key No. Digests, United States ⊙120–122.

§ 27.3 Elements of the False Claims Act—*Mens rea*

Since 1863 the FCA has required that the defendant commit the prohibited conduct "knowingly" but until the 1986 amendments the statute did not define "knowingly." Prior to 1986 a number of courts interpreted "knowingly" as "specific intent to defraud".[1] Disapproving of this interpretation, Congress defined "knowingly" in the 1986 amendments as follows:

(1) [A]ctual knowledge of the information;

(2) act[ing] in deliberate ignorance of the truth or falsity of the information; or

(3) act[ing] in reckless disregard of the truth or falsity of the information.[2]

The drafters of the 1986 amendments gave a two-fold explanation for this amendment: they wanted to make it easier to prove liability under the FCA and they intended to standardize the mens rea requirement in

9. Taxpayers Against Fraud, The 1986 False Claims Act Amendments, 1986–1996, 19 (1996).

§ 27.3

1. United States v. Mead, 426 F.2d 118, 122 (9th Cir.1970). Other courts inter-

preted knowingly as stringently but in different terms: "guilty knowledge of a purpose on the part of [the defendant] to cheat the Government,. . . ." United States v. Priola, 272 F.2d 589, 594 (5th Cir.1959).

2. 31 U.S.C. § 3729(b).

the statute.[3] The drafters were especially concerned about "corporate officers who insulate themselves from knowledge of false claims submitted by lower-level subordinates" and as such, drafted the new mens rea requirements to make it more difficult for these officers to avoid liability.[4] Innocent mistake and mere negligence, however, remain defenses to FCA liability.[5]

Taking advantage of a disputed legal issue is not enough to show scienter under the FCA. The Ninth Circuit so ruled in *Hagood v. Sonoma County Water Agency*,[6] when it affirmed summary judgment in favor of defendants in a qui tam action. The court explained what evidence is needed to show mens rea under the FCA:

> The False Claims Act ... requires a showing of knowing fraud. 'The requisite intent is the knowing presentation of what is known to be false,' as opposed to innocent mistake or mere negligence. 'Bad math is no fraud,' proof of mistakes 'is not evidence that one is a cheat,' and 'the common failings of engineers and other scientists are not culpable under the Act.' The statutory phrase 'known to be false' ... does not mean scientifically untrue; it means a lie.[7]

Library References:

C.J.S. United States § 168–172, 174.
West's Key No. Digests, United States ⊂⇒120–122.

§ 27.4 Elements of the False Claims Act—Claim

The FCA does not define "claim" but the courts have defined it, for purposes of the FCA, as "a demand for money or for some transfer of public property."[1] "Claims" include progress payment vouchers.[2]

One type of claim that has caused some controversy in FCA cases is the "reverse false claim." In a "reverse false claim," the claimant makes

---

3. "The Committee's interest is not only to adopt a more uniform standard, but a more appropriate standard for remedial actions." S.Rep.No. 345, 99th Cong., 2d Sess. 7 (1986), reprinted in 1986 U.S.C.C.A.N. 5266, 5272 [hereinafter S.Rep. No. 345].

4. S.Rep.No. 345, *supra* note 3, at 7, reprinted in 1986 U.S.C.C.A.N. at 5272.

5. *See, e.g.*, Wang v. FMC Corp., 975 F.2d 1412 (9th Cir.1992). In *Wang*, FMC was sued under the FCA for allegedly submitting false claims regarding four separate defense projects. *Id.* at 1415. The court, in dicta, affirmed summary judgment in favor of FMC holding that the qui tam plaintiff had proven, at most, "innocent mistake" on the part of FMC engineers. *Id.* at 1420. According to the court, "[b]ad math is no fraud" "[p]roof of one's mistakes or inabilities is not evidence that one is a cheat." *Id.* at 1420–21. The court chastised the qui tam relator for misconstruing the intent requirement in the FCA:

Wang's case betrays a serious misunderstanding of the Act's purpose. ... The phrase "known to be false" ... does not mean "scientifically untrue;" it means "a lie." The Act is concerned with ferreting out "wrongdoing," not scientific errors. *Id.* at 1421.

6. 81 F.3d 1465, 1478 (9th Cir.1996).

7. *Id.* at 1478 quoting United States *ex rel.* Anderson v. Northern Telecom, Inc. 52 F.3d 810, 815–16 (9th Cir.1995).

§ 27.4

1. United States v. McNinch, 356 U.S. 595, 599, 78 S.Ct. 950, 952–53, 2 L.Ed.2d 1001 (1958) (*quoting* United States v. Tieger, 234 F.2d 589, 591 (3d Cir.1956)).

2. AB–Tech Const. Inc. v. United States, 31 Fed.Cl. 429, 433 (1994), *aff'd*, 57 F.3d 1084 (1995).

a material misrepresentation to avoid paying money owed to the Government. The classic example is the individual who is obliged to pay to the government a percentage of profits and falsely understates income and/or overstates expenses in calculating the government's share of profits.[3] Prior to the 1986 amendments courts routinely held that"reverse false claims" did not fall within the FCA.[4] In the 1986 amendments, however, Congress amended the FCA to make clear that "claim" covered reverse claims.[5]

Another type of claim that has caused some confusion is a loan application. The Supreme Court addressed this situation in *United States v. Neifert–White Co.*,[6] and held that when the false statement is made "with the purpose and effect of inducing the Government immediately to part with money," the loan application is a "claim" within the scope of the FCA.[7] Thus, for example, a false application to a federal agency for a loan from that agency is a claim within the FCA[8] but a false application to a private bank that is insured by the government is not a claim within the FCA.[9] In the latter instance, a false claim within the FCA occurs only if there is a demand for payment on the guarantee.[10]

Library References:

C.J.S. United States § 168–172, 174.
West's Key No. Digests, United States ⬤120–122.

§ 27.5 Elements of the False Claims Act—The Prohibited Conduct

The FCA prohibits seven types of conduct, all revolving around submission of false claims to the government.

---

3. "For instance, the manager of HUD-owned property may falsely understate income and/or overstate expenses in order to reduce the rental receipts which must be paid to HUD at the end of each month." 132 Cong.Rec. H6480 (daily ed. Sept. 9, 1986) (remarks of Rep. Fish).

4. *See, also:*

Second Circuit: United States *ex rel.* Kessler v. Mercur Corp. 83 F.2d 178, 179 181–82 (2d Cir.), *cert. denied* 299 U.S. 576, 57 S.Ct. 40, 81 L.Ed. 424 (1936).

Ninth Circuit: United States v. Howell, 318 F.2d 162 (9th Cir.1963). In *Howell*, the Ninth Circuit held that the defendants' act of understating total receipts to the Government pursuant to an agreement that the defendants and the Government would split receipts was not a false claims. *Id.* at 164. The court noted the Government's argument that there is no difference, in terms of the effect on the government, "between a situation where the claimant is fraudulently demanding money and one where he is fraudulently seeking a reduction in the amount of money to be paid by him...."

Id. at 165. Acknowledging that such "reasoning would be valid ... with a general fraud statute," the Court held that the FCA specifically required presentation of a claims. *Id.* at 166.

But see:

Fifth Circuit: Smith v. United States 287 F.2d 299, 304 (5th Cir.1961).

5. 31 U.S.C. § 3729(a)(7). *See, e.g.,* United States v. American Heart Research Foundation, Inc., 996 F.2d 7 (1st Cir.1993).

6. 390 U.S. 228, 88 S.Ct. 959, 19 L.Ed.2d 1061 (1968).

7. *Id.* at 390 U.S. 232, 88 S.Ct. 961.

8. *Id.* at 229–33.

9. United States v. McNinch, 356 U.S. 595, 597–99, 78 S.Ct. 950, 951–52, 2 L.Ed.2d 1001 (1958).

10. *See also:*

Third Circuit: United States v. Veneziale, 268 F.2d 504, 505 (3d Cir.1959).

Fifth Circuit: United States v. Miller, 645 F.2d 473 (5th Cir.1981).

A. SECTION 3729(A)(1)

The conduct prohibited in § 3729(a)(1) is "present[ing] or caus[ing] to be presented, . . . a false or fraudulent claim for payment or approval" . . . to an officer or employee of the U.S. Government or a member of the Armed Forces of the United States.[1] The elements of a § 3729(a) action are:

a. That the defendant "knowingly presents or causes to be presented, to an officer or employee of the government a false or fraudulent claims for payment or approval";

b. That the claim was false or fraudulent;

c. The defendant knew the claim was false or fraudulent;

d. That the United States suffered damages as a result of the false or fraudulent claims.[2]

This is the most common type of conduct prohibited by the FCA.[3] Seeking reimbursement for goods or services never provided or falsely describing the goods or services that were provided is a § 3729(a) action.[4] "Causing" a false claim to be presented often occurs in a subcontractor situation where the subcontractor submits false claims to the contractor who in turn, incorporates the falsity into the claim it submits to the government.[5] *Murray & Sorenson, Inc. v. United States*[6] exemplifies this. Contractors hired by the government to build a naval base employed a purchasing agent who inflated the cost of parts.[7] Unaware of the falsification, the contractors submitted the inflated cost to the government and were reimbursed at the inflated amount.[8] The court held that the purchasing agent was liable under the FCA for causing the submission of false claims.[9]

B. SECTION 3729(A)(2)

Section 3729(a)(2) prohibits making, using or causing to be made or used "a false record or statement to get a false or fraudulent claim paid

§ 27.5

1. 31 U.S.C. § 3729(a)(1).

2. United States v. Truong, 860 F.Supp. 1137, 1140 (E.D.La.1994).

3. S.Rep.No. 345, *supra*, § 27.3, note 3, at 9, *reprinted in* 1986 U.S.C.C.A.N. at 5274.

4. *Supreme Court*: United States v. McNinch, 356 U.S. 595, 599, 78 S.Ct. 950, 952, 2 L.Ed.2d 1001 (1958).

First Circuit: United States v. Collyer Insulated Wire Co., 94 F.Supp. 493, 495 (D.R.I.1950).

5. *See*:

Supreme Court: United States v. Bornstein, 423 U.S. 303, 96 S.Ct. 523, 46 L.Ed.2d 514 (1976).

First Circuit: Murray & Sorenson, Inc. v. United States, 207 F.2d 119, 123 (1st Cir.1953).

Eleventh Circuit: United States ex rel. Luther v. Consolidated Indus., Inc., 720 F.Supp. 919, 922 (N.D.Ala.1989).

6. 207 F.2d 119 (1st Cir.1953).

7. *Murray & Sorenson*, 207 F.2d at 121.

8. *Id.* at 121–22, 123.

9. *Id.* at 123.

or approved by the Government."[10] This section is aimed at those who supply false documentation in support of a false claim.[11] Such documentation may include invoices, a schedule for completion of projects, results of inspections, safety or performance tests, evidence of eligibility to contract, etc.[12]

Both § 3729(a)(1) and § (a)(2) may apply to a given situation. However, the number of claims may vary, depending on which section is charged.[13] For example, assume that a subcontractor submits 50 false invoices to a contractor who, unaware of the falsity, includes the invoices when submitting a claim to the government for reimbursement. Assuming other elements of the FCA are met, the subcontractor could be charged with 50 counts of violating § 3729(a)(2) for causing submission of 50 false statements to get a claim paid, or with one count of violating § 3729(a)(1) for causing submission of a false claim.

C. SECTION 3729(A)(3)

Section 3729(a)(3) prohibits conspiring to defraud the Government to get a false or fraudulent claim allowed or paid.[14] The elements of this offense are (1) the defendant conspired with one or more persons to get a false or fraudulent claims allowed or paid by the United States, and (2) one or more conspirators performed an act to effectuate the object of the conspiracy.[15] It is not necessary to show that a false claim was actually presented to or paid by the government as a result of the conspiracy.[16]

---

10. 31 U.S.C. § 3729(a)(2).

11. The leading FCA expert, John T. Boese, has suggested that although "the explicit language of [§ 3729(a)(2)] appears to require actual payment or approval by the Government," the language of this section does not require actual payment or approval—it prohibits knowingly making, using or causing to be made or used a false statement *to get* a false or fraudulent claim paid or approved by the Government. JOHN T. BOESE, CIVIL FALSE CLAIMS AND QUI TAM ACTIONS, § 2–11 n.14. The key to liability would seem to the defendant's intent: did the defendant make or use the false record with the goal of getting a false or fraudulent claim filed? A focus on intent would seem to be more consistent with both the FCA's goals and Congress's admonition to construe the Act's provisions broadly. Surely Congress would not have intended that a person who submitted false invoices to get a false claim paid escape liability simply because her fraud was detected prior to payment or approval of the claim by the Government.

12. *See, e.g.,* United States *ex rel.* Butler v. Hughes Helicopter Co., 1993 WL 841192, at *2 (C.D.Calif. 1993), *aff'd* 71 F.3d 321 (9th Cir.1995).

13. *See* United States v. Bornstein, 423 U.S. 303, 96 S.Ct. 523, 46 L.Ed.2d 514 (1976). Here the Supreme Court held that a subcontractor caused a false claim to be submitted to the government when the subcontractor causes the primate contractor to submit a false claim. The subcontractor, United National Labs (United) supplied electron tubes to the prime contractor, Model Engineering & Manufacturing Corp., Inc. (Model) which included the tubes in radio kits Model supplied to the government. United provided Model with electron tubes of inferior quality and falsely marked invoices to conceal the defects. *Id.* at 307–08.

14. 31 U.S.C. § 3729(a)(3).

15. *D.C. Circuit:* United States v. Bouchey, 860 F.Supp. 890 (D.D.C.1994).

Second Circuit: Blusal Meats, Inc. v. United States, 638 F.Supp. 824, 828 (S.D.N.Y.1986), aff'd, 817 F.2d 1007 (2d Cir.1987).

16. *Second Circuit:* Blusal Meats, Inc. v. United States, 638 F.Supp. 824, 828 (S.D.N.Y.1986), aff'd, 817 F.2d 1007 (2d Cir.1987).

Eleventh Circuit: Stinson v. Provident Life, 721

Each co-conspirator is jointly and severally liable for the damages and penalties resulting from this violation.[17]

D. SECTION 3729(A)(4)

Section 3729(a)(4) essentially prohibits embezzlement of government property by delivery contractors. It provides liability for any person who

> has possession, custody, or control of property or money used, or to be used, by the Government and, intending to defraud the Government or willfully to conceal the property, delivers, or causes to be delivered, less property than the amount for which the person receives a certificate or receipt. . . .

Note that this section and § 3729(a)(5) require proof of a higher mens rea than is required in any other section of § 3729. Before one violates § 3729(a)(4), it must be shown that he or she acted "*intending* to defraud the Government or *willfully* to conceal the property."

The elements of § 3729(a)(4) are:

(1) the defendant had possession, custody, or control of money or property used or to be used by the government;

(2) the defendant delivered or caused to be delivered less property than the amount for which he received a certificate or receipt;

(3) with intent to defraud or to willfully concealed [sic] the property; and

(4) the United States suffered damages as a result.[18]

United States ex rel. Stinson et al. v. Provident Life demonstrates a § 3729(a)(4) cause. In its complaint, Stinson, a law firm, alleged that Provident Life paid as secondary insurer on health care claims when it should have paid as primary insurer. The result was fraud upon Medicare which, because of Provident's concealment, paid as primary insurer instead of as secondary.

E. SECTION 3729(A)(5)

Section 3729(a)(5) encourages those who receive or make deliveries to the Government to verify that the delivery is complete. It provides liability for any person who is

> authorized to make or deliver a document certifying receipt of property used, or to be used, by the Government and, intending to defraud the Government, makes or delivers the receipt without completely knowing that the information on the receipt is true. . . .

17. United States v. Bd. of Educ., 697 F.Supp. 167, 176 (D.N.J.1988).

18. United States *ex rel.* Stinson, et al. v. Provident Life, 721 F.Supp. 1247, 1257 (S.D.Fla.1989).

Section 3729(a)(5), like § 3729(a)(4) requires proof of a higher mens rea than is required in other sections of § 3729. Before one is found to have violated § 3729(a)(5), it must be shown that he or she acted "intending to defraud the Government."

F. SECTION 3729(A)(6)

Section 3729(a)(6) reaches those who buy property on the "black market" from Government officers, employees or from a member of the Armed Forces. It provides liability for any person who:

> knowingly buys, or receives as a pledge of an obligation or debt, public property from an officer or employee of the Government, or a member of the Armed Forces, who lawfully may not sell or pledge the property. . . .

Like all sections except § 3729(a)(4) and (5), this section requires only proof that the defendant acted "knowingly."

G. SECTION 3729(A)(7)

Section 3729(a)(7), added in 1986, prohibits knowingly making, using, or causing to be made or used, "a false record or statement to conceal, avoid, or decrease an obligation to pay or transmit money or property to the Government." This section was added to make clear that "reverse false claims" were covered by the statute. In a reverse false claims, the claimant makes a material misrepresentation to avoid paying money otherwise due the Government. Because of reimbursement rules under Medicare and Medicaid, § 3729(a)(7) also applies to "cost reporting" fraud. Medicare and Medicaid restrict the reimbursement due certain providers when those providers obtain goods or services from a "related organization." A "related organization" for such purposes occurs when the provider "to a significant extent is associated with or affiliated with, or has control of, or is controlled by, the organization furnishing the services, facilities or supplies."[19] *United States v. Oakwood Downriver Medical Center*[20] demonstrates this application of § 3729(a)(7). Two hospitals and various individuals associated with the hospitals[21] were sued under § 3729(a)(1)-(3) and (7) for failing to reveal their related party status.[22] The government alleged that annual cost reports submitted by Oakwood to Medicare "falsely declared that none of Medicare reimbursement costs sought by Oakwood involved related parties."[23] In fact, according to the government, West Outer Drive Medical Center (WODMC) which provided various medical services to

---

19. *Id.* at 304 *citing* HCFA Publication 15, Part 1.

20. 687 F.Supp. 302, 305 (E.D.Mich. 1988) (*quoting* 31 U.S.C. § 3729(a)(7)).

21. United States v. Oakwood Downriver Medical Center, 687 F.Supp. 302, 303 (E.D.Mich.1988). The individuals sued included the Chief Executive Officer and part-

ner at one of the hospitals, a member of the Board of Trustees and part-owner of one of the hospitals, a CPA who worked on the hospitals' accounts and the CPA's firm. *Id.*

22. *Id.*

23. *Id.* at 304.

Oakwood was a related party. One defendant served as Oakwood's CEO and was a partner in WODMC. Another defendant was on Oakwood's Board of Trustees and was a part owner of WODMC. A Third defendant was the C.P.A. for both Oakwood and WODMC.[24]

Library References:

C.J.S. United States § 168–172, 174.
West's Key No. Digests, United States ⚷120–122.

§ 27.6 Elements of the False Claims Act—Falsity of Claim

For FCA liability to attach, the claim must be "false or fraudulent."[1] While the typical FCA case involves overcharging the government under a government contract,[2] FCA cases have also been found to exist on the theory that substandard products or services were supplied.[3]

One question concerning falsity that has arisen is whether a claim is false if it accurately lists the goods or services provided and their costs but the goods or services were rendered pursuant to a contract obtained improperly, for example, through collusion or kickbacks.[4] The Supreme Court addressed the collusion situation in *United States ex rel. Marcus v. Hess*[5] and held that such claims were "false" within the FCA.[6] Finding that the government never would have entered into the contracts at issue had it known of the collusion, the Court found that the taint from such collusion "entered into every swollen estimate which was the basic cause for payment of every dollar paid by the [government], ... "and thus was false within the FCA.[7]

Two courts have addressed this issue in the context of health care fraud. In *United States ex rel. Pogue v. American Healthcorp, Inc.*,[8] the District Court for the Middle District of Tennessee held that allegations

---

24. *Id.* at 303.

§ 27.6

1. 31 U.S.C. § 3729. Given the complexity and ambiguity of billing regulations, this may not be straightforward to determine in health care fraud cases. *See, e.g.*, United States *ex rel.* Glass v. Medtronic, Inc., 957 F.2d 605 (8th Cir.1992). Glass, a patient who received a second pacemaker after experiencing complications with his first pacemaker brought a FCA action against the pacemaker manufacturer. *Id.* at 607. Glass alleged that the manufacturer violated the FCA by improperly directing him to seek reimbursement from Medicare when the manufacturer should have paid the health care costs associated with the replacement surgery. *Id.* at 606. According to Glass, the manufacturer "caused a false claim to be filed when it told him to submit his claim to Medicare for reimbursement, when [the manufacturer] knew it was responsible for any costs." *Id.* at 608. The court dismissed Glass' complaint finding that there was no falsity. *Id.* Citing regula-

tions from the Health Care Financing Agency, the court found that the manufacturer properly instructed Glass to seek reimbursement from Medicare. *Id.*

2. United States *ex rel.* Hopper v. Anton, 91 F.3d 1261, 1266 (9th Cir.1996).

3. United States v. Aerodex, 469 F.2d 1003 (5th Cir.1972).

4. Clearly, when the claims include costs inflated to cover the kickbacks paid, the claims are false.

Second Circuit: United States v. General Dynamics Corp., 19 F.3d 770, 772 (2d Cir.1994).

Eleventh Circuit: United States v. Killough, 848 F.2d 1523, 1525 (11th Cir.1988).

5. 317 U.S. 537, 63 S.Ct. 379, 87 L.Ed. 443 (1943).

6. *Id.* at 543.

7. *Id.*

8. 914 F.Supp. 1507 (M.D.Tenn.1996).

that claims for services rendered to Medicare patients were false within the FCA even though they were for services actually rendered because, in submitting the claims, the defendants implicitly represented that they had complied with all statutes, rules, and regulations governing the Medicare program. The FCA complaint alleged that defendants violated Medicaid law prohibiting certain kickback and self-referrals between providers.[9] The District Court agreed with the relator that such representations, if false, constituted claims within the FCA even though the relator could show no actual loss to the government.[10] Recognizing, however, that the FCA "was not intended to operate as a stalking horse for enforcement of every statute, rule, or regulation," the court held that the relator must "show that defendants engaged in the fraudulent conduct with the purpose of inducing payment from the government."[11]

In *United States ex rel. Thompson v. Columbia/Healthcare Corporation* the Fifth Circuit agreed that FCA liability may exist if the underlying contract was obtained in violation of applicable laws, even if all services were provided and accurately described in claims.[12] Thompson, the relator, was a medical doctor engaged in private practice in Corpus Christi, Texas. Thompson alleged that Columbia/Healthcare Corporation (Columbia) engaged in investment arrangements with physicians which violate Medicare antikickback and self referral laws. Like Pogue's FCA action, Thompson's complaint alleged that the defendant submitted false claims when it implicitly represented that it had complied with all Medicare laws and regulations.[13] Like Pogue, Thompson did not allege that such false certification, if it occurred, caused a loss to the government.[14] The Court held that "where the government has conditioned payment of a claim on a claimant's certification of compliance with . . . a statute or regulation, a claimant submits a false or fraudulent claim when he or she falsely certifies compliance with that statute or regulation."[15]

In 1997, the Supreme Court had the opportunity to rule on whether proof of harm or potential harm to the public fisc is necessary to prevail in a FCA action.[16] Such a ruling would have shed light on, if not resolved, the question whether violations of the antikickback statute constitute a false claim within the FCA since financial harm usually is too speculative to prove in a kickback case. The Supreme Court bypassed the issue, however, resolving the case before it on other grounds.[17]

Another question concerning falsity is under what circumstances a certification of compliance constitutes a false claim within the FCA. This

9. *Id.* at 1509.

10. *Id.* at 1512.

11. *Id.* at 1513.

12. 125 F.3d 899 (5th Cir.1997).

13. 938 F.Supp. 399, 403 (S.D.Tx. 1996), *order aff'd in part, vacated in part by*, 125 F.3d 899 (5th Cir.1997).

14. *Id.* at 404.

15. 125 F.3d at 902.

16. Hughes Aircraft Co. v. United States ex rel. Schumer, 520 U.S. 939, 117 S.Ct. 1871, 138 L.Ed.2d 135 (1997).

17. The Court ruled that the 1986 amendments did not apply retroactively in *Hughes*, and that pre–1986 law required dismissal of the action. *Id.* at 1875.

situation arose in *United States ex rel. Hopper v. Anton*.[18] Hopper was a Special Education teacher in the Los Angeles school system. She filed a qui tam action alleging that the school system submitted false claims when it submitted forms to the California State Department of Education (CDOE) indicating the number of special education students in the district. Hopper argued that because the district failed to comply with regulations regarding placement of students in the special education program, these forms were false. Because the CDOE received some federal funds for special education Hopper argued, the alleged falsity was a false claim upon the federal government.[19] The Ninth Circuit affirmed the District Court's summary judgment in favor of the school district on the ground that the forms were not "false claims" within the FCA.[20]

The Ninth Circuit acknowledged that false certification cases differ from the typical false claims case. Quoting FCA expert, John T. Boese, the court reasoned that two questions must be resolved in such cases: "(1) whether the false statement is the cause of the Government's providing the benefit; and (2) whether any relation exists between the subject matter of the false statement and the event triggering Government's loss." Answering both questions in the negative, the court found that there was no false claim in the case before it. The court concluded:

> Hopper misinterprets the breadth of the Act. Violations of laws, rules, or regulations alone do not create a cause of action under the FCA. It is the false certification for compliance which creates liability when certification is a prerequisite to obtaining a government benefit.[21]

Another issue concerning falsity is whether promises can constitute false claims under the FCA. In rare circumstances promises may be actionable under the FCA, but only if evidence shows that a specific promise was knowingly false when made.[22]

Library References:

C.J.S. United States § 168–172, 174.
West's Key No. Digests, United States ⚯120–122.

§ 27.7   Elements of the False Claims Act—"Submitted to the Government"

Before the FCA applies, the claims must be submitted "to an officer or employee of the United States Government or a member of the Armed Forces of the United States....."[1] Because the federal government often contracts with private parties to perform various functions on behalf of the government, questions have arisen whether claims submitted to these "contractors" are within the FCA. For example, in *Peterson v.*

---

18. 91 F.3d 1261 (9th Cir.1996).

19. *Id.* at 1265.

20. *Id.*

21. *Id.* at 1266.

22. United States *ex rel.* Hopper v. Anton, 91 F.3d 1261, 1267 (9th Cir.1996).

§ 27.7

1. 31 U.S.C. § 3729(a)(1).

Weinberger,[2] the government brought suit under the FCA against a physician and an owner of a nursing home for billing Medicare for physical therapy never provided.[3] Although the claims were actually submitted to a private insurer, the court found the federal government to be the real party in interest.[4] The court noted that the insurers were Medicare fiscal intermediaries who act as agents at the sole discretion of the Secretary of Health, Education and Welfare (currently Health and Human Services).[5]

Although it is not necessary for a claim to be made, presented, or submitted directly to the government, it is necessary to demonstrate that the ultimate financial victim would be the federal treasury.[6] In instances where claims are submitted to an entity under contract with the federal government, the complaint must "contain allegations showing the relationship between the United States Treasury and the defendants sufficient to establish that claims were actually made against the United States Government ... [covering issues such as] the legal relationship between the agency disbursing the funds, the defendants and the United States as well as the mechanisms involved in paying any such claims and the manner in which the relevant United States agency did or did not directly oversee the funds."[7]

A variation of this issue occurs where a program is jointly funded with federal and state resources, such as Medicaid. In these cases the key to FCA coverage appears to be in the amount of control retained by the federal government. *United States ex rel. Davis v. Long's Drugs Inc.*,[8] demonstrates this. Davis, a pharmacist working at Long's Drugs, filed a FCA lawsuit alleging that his employer submitted numerous false claims to the California Medicaid program. The defendants argued that "the mere fact that federal funds are advanced for a state program is insufficient to warrant a characterization of fraudulent claims under that program as claims against the United States government within the meaning of the [FCA]."[9] The court rejected this argument finding that there were "substantial contacts"[10] between the State medicaid programs and the federal government, including required compliance with a "myriad of federal regulations,"[11] and joint funding.[12]

---

2. 508 F.2d 45 (5th Cir.1975).

3. *Id.* at 47–48.

4. *Id.* at 51–52, n.7 (citing 20 CFR § 405.670 (1973): "In the performance of their contractual undertakings, the carriers act on behalf of the Secretary, carrying on for him the administrative responsibilities imposed by the law. The Secretary, however, is the real party in interest in the administration of the program....")

5. *Id.* at 51.

6. United States *ex rel.* Simmons v. Smith, 629 F.Supp. 124, 127 (S.D.Ala.1985).

7. *Simmons*, 629 F.Supp. at 127.

8. 411 F.Supp. 1144 (S.D.Cal.1976).

9. *Id.* at 1146.

10. *Id.*

11. *Id.* at 1146–47.

12. *Ninth Circuit*: *Long's Drugs*, 411 F.Supp. at 1147.

See also:

Seventh Circuit: United States v. Azzarelli Constr. Co., 647 F.2d 757, 759 (7th Cir.1981); United States *ex rel.* Fahner v. Alaska, 591 F.Supp. 794, 798 (N.D.Ill.1984).

The 1986 amendments resolved any doubt about this issue by including § 3729(c):

> For purposes of this section, 'claim' includes any request or demand, whether under a contract or otherwise, for money or property which is made to a contractor, grantee, or other recipient if the United States government provides any portion of the money or property which is requested or demanded, or if the Government will reimburse such contractor, grantee, or other recipient for any portion of the money or property which is requested or demanded.

Library References:

C.J.S. United States § 168–172, 174.
West's Key No. Digests, United States ⊙120–122.

§ 27.8 *Qui Tam* **Provisions—Background**

The FCA provides that the federal government or any "person" may bring an action under the Act.[1] In this way, the FCA empowers "private attorneys general" to supplement the government's efforts against fraud upon the government. One legislator summed up the rationale for this dual prosecuting authority during the 1986 revision of the FCA: "[i]n the face of sophisticated and widespread fraud, the Committee believes only a coordinated effort of both the Government and the citizenry will decrease this wave of defrauding public funds."[2] When an FCA case is brought by a person or entity other than the Attorney General it is known as a "qui tam"[3] action and the party bringing the action is known as the "relator."

§ 27.8

1. 31 U.S.C. 3730(a)-(b); "Former or present members of the armed forces" are disqualified from serving as "persons" for purposes of the FCA. In recent litigation a corporation urged that its former in-house counsel was ineligible to serve as a qui tam relator. United States *ex rel.* Doe v. X Corp., 862 F.Supp. 1502, 1507 (E.D.Va.1994). Although it acknowledged that ethical and policy problems potentially existed where counsel sues client in an FCA action, the court found that Congress had not precluded attorneys who sue their clients from serving as relators in FCA actions. *Id.* at 1508–09. However, in the case before it, Doe could not serve as relator because in making written disclosure to the government as required in § 3730(b)(2) Doe would violate an injunction prohibiting him from revealing confidences of his client. *Id.* at 1510. The court noted, however, that in other circumstances, it may be possible for an attorney to sue his client under the FCA without breaching ethical requirements. *Id.* at 1510 n.20.

2. S.Rep.No. 345, 99th Cong., 2d Sess. 2 (1986) *reprinted in* 1986 U.S.C.C.A.N. at 5267.

3. "Qui tam" comes from the Latin phrase "qui tam pro domino rege quam pro si ipso in hac parte sequitur" which means "[w]ho sues on behalf of the King as well as for himself." Black's Law Dictionary 1251 (6th ed. 1990).

Qui tam actions are similar to citizen lawsuits familiar in the environmental field. See, e.g., Federal Water Pollution Control Act Amendments of 1972 (The Clean Water Act of 1972) § 505, 33 U.S.C. § 1365; Saboe v. Oregon, 819 F.Supp. 914 (D.Or.1993). Both attempt to mobilize private citizens to supplement law enforcement resources. Citizens lawsuits confer standing on "any citizen," *See, e.g.,* 33 U.S.C. § 1365(a)(1), whereas the False Claims Act confers standing or "any person." 31 U.S.C. § 3730(a). The relief available through the two avenues is different, however. Unlike the qui tam provisions, which confer a monetary award on a successful litigant, most citizen lawsuits only compel the wrongdoer to comply with statutory directives or compel the

Qui tam FCA actions have become renown in recent years for the large recoveries they bring to relators. In 1997 alone, notable qui tam recoveries by relators included: $2.4 million (on a $10 million recovery); $2.34 million (on a $12.65 million recovery); $2.16 million (on an $12 million recovery); $1.56 million (on a $15.5 million recovery).[4]

Elaborate procedures exist to protect the federal government's role in qui tam FCA suits. Upon filing a qui tam action, the relator must provide the government with a copy of the complaint and "substantially all material evidence and information the person possesses."[5] The complaint is sealed for at least 60 days to allow the government time to determine whether it will join as a plaintiff in the suit.[6] Even if the government chooses not to join at the time the complaint is filed, it may join later for "good cause" shown,[7] and is entitled to copies of pleadings filed throughout the case even if it does not join the relator as plaintiff.[8]

Library References:
C.J.S. United States § 168–172, 174.
West's Key No. Digests, United States ⚷120–122.

§ 27.9 *Qui Tam* Provisions—Constitutionality

Defendants challenging the constitutionality of the FCA's qui tam provisions have focused on issues of standing, separation of powers, the appointments clause and due process. Thus far, these challenges have not been successful.[1]

Unlike other private attorney general provisions, such as RICO,[2] the FCA does not require the private plaintiff to show any injury to the plaintiff from the defendant's conduct.[3] Defendants have seized upon this, arguing that failure to require injury on the part of the plaintiff violates Article III's requirement of "cases and controversies."[4] The

Executive branch to enforce public law obligations. *See, e.g.,* 33 U.S.C. § 1365(a) (compelling the wrongdoer to comply with the Clean Water Act and compelling agency action in situations where the agency has failed to fulfill a mandatory duty under the Clean Water Act). *See also,* 33 U.S.C. § 1365(d) (authorizing the award of litigation costs) (i.e., reasonable attorney fees) to any party in the discretion of the court.

4. TAXPAYERS AGAINST FRAUD, FALSE CLAIMS ACT AND *QUI TAM* QUARTERLY REVIEW, 40 (1998).

5. 31 U.S.C. § 3730(b)(2).

6. *Id.*

7. *Id.* at § 3730(b)(3).

8. *Id.* at § 3730(c)(3).

§ 27.9

1. On October 21, 1997 the District Court for the Southern District of Texas held the qui tam provisions of the False

Claim constitutionally defective for lack of standing. United States ex rel. Riley v. St. Luke's Episcopal Hospital, 982 F.Supp. 1261 (S.D.Tx.1997). This case is on appeal to the Fifth Circuit Court of Appeals. Ct. of Appeals Doc. #97–20948 Telephone Conversation Sept. 16, 1998, Clerk's Office, S.D.Tx.

2. Racketeer Influenced and Corrupt Organizations Act, 18 U.S.C. § 1961–68.

3. Section 1964(c) of RICO states that "[a]ny person injured in his business or property by reason of a violation of [RICO] may sue therefor in any appropriate United States district court and shall recover threefold the damages he sustains and the cost of the suit, including a reasonable attorney's fee." 18 U.S.C. § 1964(c).

4. Article III of the Constitution provides: that the judicial power "shall extend to all cases, in Law and Equity, arising under this constitution, the Laws of the United States . . . to Controversies between

courts have pursued two rationales in rejecting this standing argument.[5] Some courts find that the qui tam plaintiff's standing derives from that of the federal government as victim of the fraud in that "the FCA effectively assigns the government's claims to qui tam plaintiffs ... who then may sue based upon an injury to the federal treasury."[6]

Other courts focus on the time and expense of the qui tam plaintiff in investigating and litigating the false claim action. "Because the qui tam relator: (1) funds the prosecution of the FCA suit, (2) will receive a private share in the government's recovery only upon prevailing and (3) may be liable for costs if the suit is frivolous, the relator's personal stake in the case is sufficiently ensured."[7] These courts find the investment by the qui tam plaintiff in the suit is adequate to insure effective advocacy.[8]

Constitutional challenges to the qui tam provisions also have focused on the separation of powers doctrine. Litigants have argued that Congress usurped the prosecuting role of the Executive Branch in two ways when it passed the qui tam provisions of the FCA (1) by giving private persons the authority to prosecute injuries to the public,[9] and (2) by giving the federal courts the power to determine the Executive branch's ability to enter the qui tam lawsuit if it chooses to do so after the complaint is unsealed.[10] Courts have rejected both arguments. They have found that because the Department of Justice retains sufficient control over a qui tam action if it chooses to join the action, the Executive branch's prosecuting authority is not infringed on by the qui tam plaintiff.[11] Additionally, courts have held that the judiciary's supervision of the government's belated right to intervene in a qui tam action is a proper exercise of the Judicial branch's supervisory role, rather than a usurpation of the Executive branch's authority.[12]

two or more States; between a State and Citizens of another State, between Citizens of different States...." See e.g., United States ex rel. Kreindler v. United Technologies Corp., 985 F.2d 1148, 1153 (2d Cir. 1993).

5. *Third Circuit:* United States ex rel. Givler v. Smith, 775 F.Supp. 172, 180–81 (E.D.Pa.1991) (holding that the "FCA complies with constitutional standing requirements.").

Ninth Circuit: United States ex rel. Truong v. Northrop Corp., 728 F.Supp. 615, 618 (C.D.Cal.1989) ("Where there is evidence of ... injury to the entity ... it is superfluous to require that the relator be ... aggrieved"); United States ex rel. Stillwell v. Hughes Helicopters, Inc., 714 F.Supp. 1084, 1098–99 (C.D.Cal.1989) ("There is no constitutional prohibition ... under a statutory grant of standing...."); United States ex rel. Kelly v. Boeing Co., 9 F.3d 743, 749 (9th Cir.1993) (holding that the "FCA's qui tam provisions do not run foul of Article III.").

Tenth Circuit: United States ex rel. Woodard v. Country View Care Center, Inc., 797 F.2d 888, 893 (10th Cir.1986).

6. *See also:*

Fourth Circuit: United States ex rel. Milam v. M.D. Anderson Cancer Center, 961 F.2d 46, 49 (4th Cir.1992).

Ninth Circuit: United States ex rel. Kelly v. Boeing 9 F.3d 743, 748 (9th Cir.1993) (1994).

7. *Kreindler,* 985 F.2d at 1154 (citing *Givler,* 775 F.Supp. at 181).

8. *Id.*

9. *Kelly,* 9 F.3d at 751–52.

10. *Id.*

11. *Id.* at 749–55; United States ex rel. Taxpayers Against Fraud v. General Electric, 41 F.3d 1032, 1041 (6th Cir.1994).

12. *Boeing,* 9 F.3d at 756. The Attorney General has sole power to decide whether to enter a qui tam lawsuit in its initial stages but if the Attorney General declines to do so then the Department of Justice must demonstrate to the court

The third constitutional challenge to the FCA is that the qui tam provisions violate the Appointments Clause, which states that "The President ... shall nominate ... Officers of the United States."[13] Litigants argue that qui tam relators wield so much governmental power that they must be appointed in conformity with the Appointments Clause.[14] In support of their argument, these litigants point to Supreme Court precedent that persons who discharge "significant authority pursuant to the laws of the United States" are "Officers" who must be appointed under the Appointments Clause.[15] Thus far, courts have rejected this argument, finding that qui tam relators do not exercise "significant authority" under the FCA or retain "primary responsibility" for enforcing the Act.[16]

The last constitutional argument advanced against the FCA's qui tam provision is that it violates the due process clause of the fifth amendment by vesting power to vindicate public rights in a private prosecutor whose goal is to reap pecuniary gain rather than seek a just and fair result.[17] The courts have summarily dismissed this argument.[18]

"good cause" in order to intervene at a later date. *Id.*

13. U.S.CONST.ART II, § 2, cl.2. See, e.g., *Kelly,* 9 F.3d at 757. Article II, § 2, cl. 2 of the U.S. Constitution provides:

"The President ... shall nominate, and by and with the Advice and Consent of the Senate, shall appoint Ambassadors, other public Ministers and Consuls, Judges of the Supreme Court, and all other Officers of the United States, whose Appointments are not herein otherwise provided for, and which shall be established by Law: but the Congress may by Law vest the Appointment of such inferior Officers, as they think proper, in the President alone, in the Courts of Law, or in the Heads of Departments."

14. *Kelly,* 9 F.3d at 757.

15. Buckley v. Valeo, 424 U.S. 1, 126 96 S.Ct. 612, 685 46 L.Ed.2d 659, 732 (1976). In *Buckley,* the Supreme Court held that provisions vesting the Federal Election Commission with "primary responsibility for conducting civil litigation in the courts of the United States for vindicating public rights" violated the Appointments clause because only officers may perform such functions. *Id.* at 140.

16. *Kelly,* 9 F.3d at 758. The court pointed out that simply suing in the name of the federal government does not give qui tam relators the resources of the federal government. The relators conduct FCA cases with private resources. Also, qui tam relators have no greater power than does the Attorney General to enforce the FCA. Lastly, when the federal government does intervene, it has primary responsibility for

conducting the litigation. Acknowledging that when the government chooses not to intervene "close question" may be presented under Buckley, the court nevertheless found no problem since the relator's involvement is limited to a single case and the relator's actions are subject to government control should the government, upon a showing of good cause, choose to intervene later. *Id.* See also United States *ex rel.* Taxpayers Against Fraud v. General Electric, 41 F.3d 1032, 1041–42 (6th Cir.1994).

17. *Kelly,* 9 F.3d at 759.

18. *See, e.g., Kelly,* 9 F.3d at 759–60. The Ninth Circuit not only held that "[p]rosecutors need not be entirely 'neutral and detached'", ... but also that the FCA has created congruent, non conflicting interests for the qui tam plaintiff and the public. *Id.* at 759–60 (quoting Marshall v. Jerrico, Inc., 446 U.S. 238, 248, 100 S.Ct. 1610, 1616, 64 L.Ed.2d 182 (1980)).

But in the FCA context, Congress has created a scheme in which the interests of the private prosecutor (that is, the relator) coincide with the public interest in remedying harm to the federal treasury. Under the explicit terms of the Act, a qui tam action is taken on behalf of *both* the government and the relator, indicating that the two share a single interest in successful litigation. Indeed, the only private interest at stake in a qui tam action is the interest which Congress has created in a reward for successful prosecution; thus the public's interest in successfully enforcing the FCA and the relator's private interest are intertwined rather than conflicting.

Library References:

C.J.S. United States § 168–172, 174.
West's Key No. Digests, United States ⋑120–122.

§ 27.10   *Qui Tam* Provisions—Jurisdictional Bar

The part of the FCA that has generated the most litigation is the "jurisdictional bar" provision which applies when the suit is brought by a qui tam relator.[1] This provision states: "No court shall have jurisdiction over an action . . . based upon the public disclosure of allegations or transactions in a criminal, civil, or administrative hearing, in a congressional, administrative, or Government Accounting Office report, hearing, audit or investigation, or from the news media, unless the action is brought by the Attorney General or the person bringing the action is an original source of the information."[2] The relator bears the burden of proving that a court has jurisdiction over the case.[3]

There are two questions to resolve in applying the jurisdictional bar provision: (1) whether the allegations in the FCA action have previously been disclosed publicly, and (2) if so, whether the qui tam plaintiff is an "original source" of the information.[4] Even if the allegations in the lawsuit have been publicly disclosed, the relator is not jurisdictionally barred from bringing the law suit if the plaintiff was an "original source" of the information. If the relator does not qualify as an original source for publicly disclosed allegations, the FCA lawsuit can continue but not as a qui tam action; only the Attorney General may bring the action.[5]

A. BACKGROUND

In 1863, the FCA did not contain a "jurisdictional bar" provision. It was added in 1943 and substantially revised in 1986. The impetus for adding it in 1943 was the Supreme Court's decision in *United States ex rel. Marcus v. Hess.*[6] Prior to the filling of the qui tam action in *Hess*, the defendants, all electrical engineers, had been convicted of defrauding the government by conspiring to rig the bidding on federal public works projects in the Pittsburgh area.[7] Apparently, the qui tam relator simply took the information publicly available in the indictment and filed it as a qui tam action.[8] The Supreme Court held that the FCA allowed such parasitical suits.[9] The Court noted that whatever "strong arguments of

---

Kelly, 9 F.3d at 760 (citation omitted).

§ 27.10

1. 31 U.S.C. § 3730(e)(4)(A).

2. 31 U.S.C. § 3730(e)(4)(A).

3. *D.C. Circuit:* United States *ex rel.* Herbert v. National Academy of Sciences, 1992 WL 247587, at *4 (D.D.C., 1992).

Seventh Circuit: United States *ex rel.* Kalish v. Desnick, 1992 WL 32185, at *2 (N.D.Ill. 1992).

4. *Id.*; United States *ex rel.* Precision Co. v. Koch Indus., 971 F.2d 548, 552 (10th Cir.1992).

5. 31 U.S.C. 3730(a); S.Rep.No. 345, *supra* § 27.8 note 2, at 12–13, *reprinted in* 1986 U.S.C.C.A.N. at 5277–78.

6. 317 U.S. 537, 63 S.Ct. 379, 87 L.Ed. 443 (1943).

7. *Id.* at 540 n.1.

8. *Id.* at 545.

9. *Id.* at 546.

policy [militate] against the statutory plan," such arguments should be addressed to Congress because the statute, as passed by Congress, allowed qui tam relators to use public information to file a qui tam suit.[10]

After the *Hess* decision, the House of Representatives moved to repeal the FCA, at the Attorney General's urging.[11] The Senate sought to save the statute but agreed to reduce the powers of the qui tam relator. The Senate prevailed and the FCA was amended to include a "jurisdictional bar" provision barring parasitical FCA qui tam suits. This provision declared that no court had jurisdiction over a qui tam lawsuit if the government had *any* knowledge of the fraud at the time the lawsuit was filed.[12] The 1943 amendments also restricted the rights of the relator to participate in the lawsuit. Prior to the amendment the relator directed the lawsuit even if the government intervened. After the 1943 amendment, DOJ directed the case and the qui tam relator had no role in the lawsuit.[13] Lastly, the 1943 amendments reduced the amount of recovery available to the relator. Instead of a guaranteed one-half of the recovery, the relator was eligible to receive no more than 10% of the recovered amount (if the government entered the case) and no more than 25% (if the government did not enter the case). Either way, the court had discretion to award any amount below these percentages, or none at all.[14]

A 1984 Seventh Circuit opinion highlighted a major inequity in this jurisdictional bar provision and prompted its revision in 1986. The case, *United States ex rel. Wisconsin v. Dean*[15] was brought by the State of Wisconsin. Wisconsin successfully prosecuted Alice R. Dean, M.D., under state criminal statutes for submitting fraudulent Medicaid claims. Dean was fined and sentenced to probation. As required by the Medicaid program, Wisconsin reported Dean's state conviction to the federal government.[16] Thereafter Wisconsin, as a qui tam relator under the FCA, sued Dean for damages resulting from many of the false claims at issue in the criminal case. The Seventh Circuit ordered the complaint dismissed since, as all parties agreed, the FCA suit was "based upon evidence or information in the possession of the United States . . . at the time [the] complaint was filed."[17] Acknowledging the inequity of dismissing Wisconsin's complaint since it was the party which originally provided the federal government with information about the case, the court

---

10. *Id.* The damages sustained by the government because of the defendant's collusive bidding were $101,500. This amount was doubled according to the FCA. Added to the doubled damages was $112,000: $2,000 for each of the fifty-six false claims submitted. The FCA in effect allocated one half of the total award to the qui tam plaintiff. 12 Stat. 696, c.67, § 5438.

11. S.Rep.No. 345, *supra* § 27.8 note 2, at 10–11, *reprinted in* 1986 U.S.C.C.A.N. at 5275–76.

12. Act of Dec. 23, 1943, ch. 377, 57 Stat. 608 (*codified at* 31 U.S.C. § 232).

13. *Id.*

14. *Id.*

15. 729 F.2d 1100 (7th Cir.1984).

16. United States *ex rel.* Wisconsin v. Dean, 729 F.2d 1100, 1102 (7th Cir.1984).

17. *Id.* at 1103 (*quoting* 31 U.S.C. § 232(c)). This provision was designed to prevent "parasitical suits" whereby private litigants took public information or information otherwise known to the government, and simply filed a qui tam FCA suit based upon such information. *Id.* at 1104.

held that it was bound by the statute to dismiss the action.[18] The court noted that if the parties wanted relief from such a result they should direct their efforts to Congress.[19]

In 1986, Congress responded by enacting jurisdictional bar provision:

> No court shall have jurisdiction over an action ... *based upon* the public disclosure of *allegations or transactions* in a criminal, civil, or administrative *hearing*, in a congressional, administrative, or Government Accounting Office report, hearing, audit, or investigation, or from the news media, unless the action is brought by the Attorney General or the person bringing the action is *an original source* of the *information*.[20]

Although remedying the inequity highlighted in *Dean*, this jurisdictional bar provision, which remains in effect today, has created interpretative difficulties for courts and litigants. The major difficulties center on the above italicized language.

B. "BASED UPON THE PUBLIC DISCLOSURE OF ALLEGATIONS OR TRANSACTIONS"

If the information in the FCA suit has been publicly disclosed and the qui tam relator is not the original source of the information, the suit is barred. The FCA lists a number of sources which constitute public disclosure: criminal, civil or administrative hearing; congressional, administrative or Government Accounting Office reports, hearings, audits or investigations; the news media. Questions have arisen when the disclosure occurs during discovery in a case other than the FCA action. The courts have consistently held that disclosure during such discovery constitutes "public disclosure" within the FCA even if the discovery is not actually made public. As the Third Circuit held, "[w]e do not think that it is significant, for purposes of interpreting the 'public disclosure' provision of the FCA, whether the discovery has in fact been filed [and thus made public]."[21] Rather "we look ... [to] whether there is a recognition that [the discovery] can be filed and hence available for public access."[22] The only exception to this view is when a protective order is in place for discovery.[23]

18. *Id.* at 1105–06.

19. "If the State of Wisconsin desires a special exemption to the False Claims Act because of its requirement to report Medicaid fraud to the federal government, then it should ask Congress to provide the exemption." *Id.* at 1106.

20. 31 U.S.C. § 3730(e)(4) (emphasis added).

21. United States *ex rel.* Stinson v. Prudential Ins., 944 F.2d 1149, 1158 (3d Cir.1991).

22. *Id.* at 1159. *See also:*

D.C. Circuit: United States *ex rel.* Springfield Terminal Ry. Co. v. Quinn, 14 F.3d 645 (D.C.Cir.1994).

Cf.:

Fourth Circuit: United States *ex rel.* Siller v. Becton Dickinson & Co., 21 F.3d 1339 (4th Cir.1994).

23. *See, Stinson*, 944 F.2d at 1159.

The harder question is whether the qui tam lawsuit is *based upon* the public disclosure. Courts of Appeals agree that this requirement is fulfilled if the qui tam action is based, in any part, upon publicly disclosed allegations or transactions.[24] Problems with this requirement have arisen when some or all of the information in the relator's FCA lawsuit was publicly available prior to filing the lawsuit but the relator claims to have obtained the information independently and not to have based the qui tam lawsuit upon the publicly disclosed information.[25]

There is no clear-cut answer in this situation. As one court noted, there is no "mathematical formulae ... [for] quantum or centrality of non public information that must be in the hands of the *qui tam* relator in order for suits to proceed."[26] The courts have handled this situation in several ways. The District of Columbia and the First, Fourth, Eighth and Eleventh Circuits have adopted approaches favorable to the qui tam relator.[27]

The District of Columbia Circuit strictly construes the statutory language, "based upon the public disclosure of *allegations or transactions*" holding that only if a qui tam lawsuit is based upon publicly disclosed "allegations or transactions," not just publicly disclosed "information," will it fit within the first prong of the jurisdictional bar provision.[28] This court's analysis in *U.S. ex rel. Springfield Terminal Railway Co v. Quinn* demonstrates this approach.[29] Quinn was appointed by the National Mediation Board to arbitrate a labor dispute between Springfield, a rail carrier, and its employees. Springfield initiated litigation contesting the arbitration process.[30] During discovery in this litigation, Springfield obtained access to vouchers for reimbursement Quinn submitted to the government. Springfield claimed to have conducted investigation on its own into the accuracy of these vouchers[31] determining that some vouchers were fraudulent.[32] Springfield filed a qui tam action under the FCA asserting that Quinn violated the FCA by submitting these false vouchers for reimbursement. The district court dismissed the action finding that Springfield's qui tam action was based upon information uncovered during discovery and thus fit within the first

24. U.S. *ex rel.* Precision Co. v. Koch Indus., 971 F.2d 548 (10th Cir.1992).

25. *See, e.g.,* Springfield Terminal v. Quinn, 14 F.3d 645 (C.A.D.C. 1994); Siller v. Becton, 21 F.3d 1339 (4th Cir.1994).

26. *Springfield Terminal,* 14 F.3d at 653.

27. *D.C. Circuit*: United States *ex rel.* Springfield Terminal Ry. Co. v. Quinn, 14 F.3d 645 (D.C.Cir.1994).

First Circuit: United States *ex rel.* S. Prawer & Co. v. Fleet Bank, 24 F.3d 320 (1st Cir.1994).

Fourth Circuit: United States *ex rel.* Siller v. Becton Dickinson & Co., 21 F.3d 1339 (4th Cir.1994).

Eighth Circuit: United States *ex rel.* Rabushka v. Crane, 40 F.3d 1509 (8th Cir. 1994).

Eleventh Circuit: Cooper v. Blue Cross & Blue Shield, 19 F.3d 562 (11th Cir.1994).

28. *Springfield Terminal,* 14 F.3d at 652–53 (*quoting* 31 U.S.C. § 3730(e)(4)(A)) (emphasis added).

29. *Id.*

30. *Id.* at 647.

31. *Id.* at 648.

32. *Id.* at 648–49.

prong of the jurisdictional bar provision.[33] The D.C. Circuit reversed holding that the first prong of the jurisdictional bar provision is met only if the qui tam lawsuit is "based upon [publicly disclosed] *allegations or transactions*."[34] It found that "the information put in the public domain by the discovery[35] . . . did not present so clear or substantial an indication of foul play as to qualify as either an allegation of fraud or a fraudulent transaction upon which a *qui tam* suit could be based."[36]

The Eighth Circuit has followed this approach.[37] The First Circuit indicates that it will look to the underlying purpose of the FCA in applying the "based upon" language to determine whether the qui tam action "seeks recovery from alleged defrauders of the government for fraud that has not yet been the subject of a claim by the government" and whether it "has the potential to restore money to the public fisc that would not and could not have been restored in [a related] case."[38] Finding that both interests would be served in the case before it, the court held that the qui tam action was not based upon allegations or transactions in a related pending civil case.[39]

The Fourth Circuit has adopted another approach, also favorable to the qui tam relator. The Fourth Circuit does not delve into the distinction between "allegations or transaction" and "information" but focuses instead on whether the relator actually derived knowledge from the public disclosure of the facts underlying the action.[40] *United States ex rel. Siller v. Becton*,[41] exemplifies this approach. The Fourth Circuit found that the relator was not jurisdictionally barred from bringing the qui tam lawsuit even though many of the facts alleged in the lawsuit had been publicly disclosed during discovery and settlement of related litigation.[42] Finding it "certainly possible that, as Siller contends, Siller actually learned of [the defendant's] alleged fraud entirely independently of the [prior lawsuit], and derived his allegations from that independent knowledge,"[43] the Fourth Circuit remanded the case for further findings by the lower court on the issue.[44]

In *Cooper v. Blue Cross & Blue Shield (BCBS)*,[45] the Eleventh Circuit employed an approach similar to the Fourth Circuit's focus on whether the relator *actually* based his lawsuit on the public disclosure, but the Eleventh Circuit analyzed the issue as whether the relator could qualify as an "original source" of the information that had been dis-

---

33. *Springfield Terminal*, 14 F.3d at 648–49. The district court also found that Springfield was not an original source of this information. *Id.*

34. *Id.* at 655 (emphasis added).

35. The court was referring to telephone records and vouchers submitted by Quinn for reimbursement. *Id.* at 655.

36. *Id.* at 656.

37. United States *ex rel.* Rabushka v. Crane Co., 40 F.3d 1509, 1512 (8th Cir. 1994).

38. United States *ex rel.* S. Prawer & Co. v. Fleet Bank, 24 F.3d 320, 329 (1st Cir.1994).

39. *Id.*

40. United States *ex rel.* Siller v. Becton Dickinson & Co., 21 F.3d 1339 (4th Cir.1994).

41. *Id.*

42. *Id.*

43. *Id.*

44. *Id.*

45. 19 F.3d 562 (11th Cir.1994).

closed. While receiving medical treatment Herbert Cooper learned that BCBS was engaged in "secondary payer" fraud and had filed false claims with Medicare resulting from this fraud.[46] Secondary payer fraud occurs when Medicare is billed as the primary insurer when another insurer is responsible for primary coverage and Medicare is only responsible as secondary payer.[47] Cooper conducted his own investigation and made repeated complaints to the BCBS and government agencies prior to filing a FCA suit. By the time Cooper filed his suit, this particular fraud had received extensive publicity in GAO reports, Congressional hearings, OIG reports and newspaper articles.[48] Finding that Cooper's lawsuit was based upon publicly disclosed allegations or transactions, the court addressed the question whether Cooper qualified as an "original source" of the information.[49] Finding that Cooper obtained his information "directly and independently" of the public information,[50] the court found that Cooper qualified as an "original source." The Court rejected the defendant's argument that "Cooper's knowledge is not 'substantive' information that 'seriously contributes to the disclosure of fraud.' "[51] It found that Cooper's "information is more than background information which enables him to understand the significance of a more general public disclosure."[52]

Unlike the above courts, the Second, Third and Tenth Circuits have adopted views less favorable to the relator.[53] According to the Second Circuit, the relator is jurisdictionally barred from bringing the FCA when the qui tam relator's allegations are "the same as those that ha[ve] been publicly disclosed ... regardless of where the relator obtained his information."[54] In *United States ex rel. Doe v. John Doe Corp.*,[55] the Second Circuit was faced with a qui tam action instituted by an attorney privy to fraud, discovered during the course of representation.[56] The attorney's client had been subject to investigation concerning a defense contract scam allegedly undertaken by his employer.[57] In exchange for use immunity, negotiated by the attorney, the client provided sworn testimony implicating the corporation.[58] Subsequently, the attorney obtained a waiver of the attorney-client privilege from the client and

46. *Cooper*, 19 F.3d at 564.

47. *Id.* at 564–65.

48. *Id.* at 565 n. 5 (referring to Office of Inspector General and Government Accounting Office Reports).

49. *Id.* at 568.

50. *Id.*

51. *Cooper*, 19 F.3d at 568 n.12. Ironically, Cooper's recovery under the FCA apparently has been preempted by settlement in another FCA action to which Mr. Cooper is not a party. United States *ex rel.* Burr v. Blue Cross & Blue Shield, 153 F.R.D. 172, 176 (M.D.Fla.1994).

52. *Id.*

53. *Second Circuit:* United States *ex rel.* Doe v. John Doe Corp., 960 F.2d 318 (2d Cir.1992).

Third Circuit: United States *ex rel.* Stinson, Lyons, Gerlin & Bustamante v. Prudential Ins. Co., 944 F.2d 1149 (3d Cir. 1991).

Tenth Circuit: United States *ex rel.* Fine v. MK–Ferguson Company, 99 F.3d 1538 (10th Cir.1996).

54. United States *ex rel.* Doe v. John Doe Corp., 960 F.2d 318, 324 (2d Cir.1992).

55. *Id.*

56. *Id.* at 319.

57. *Id.*

58. *Id.* at 320.

brought a qui tam action under the FCA.[59] In barring the attorney/relator's claim, the court adopted the broad interpretation of the jurisdictional bar provision.[60]

The Third Circuit's approach is similar for it holds that qui tam suits are jurisdictionally barred if based upon information that would have been available to others if they had looked for it.[61] Similarly, the Tenth Circuit holds that the relator's suit is barred if it is " 'substantially identical' to the allegations contained in the public disclosure, regardless of whether the relator actually got the allegations in her suit from the public disclosure."[62]

Another issue which has arisen is whether public disclosure for purposes of the FCA occurs only when the allegations or transactions are *actually* disclosed to the public or also occurs when the allegations or transactions are *potentially* accessible to the public. In *United States ex rel. Ramseyer v. Century Healthcare Corp.*,[63] the Tenth Circuit addressed this issue and concluded "that in order to be publicly disclosed, the allegations or transactions upon which a qui tam suit is based must have been made known to the public through some affirmation act of disclosure."[64]

In *Ramseyer*,[65] the District Court dismissed the qui tam action brought by Ramseyer, a consultant and then clinical director of a mental health facility operated by Century Healthcare Corp. (Century). During her eight months of employment with Century, Ramseyer observed widespread noncompliance with Medicaid requirements. Although Ramseyer communicated this noncompliance to the defendants, the defendants did nothing to correct the problems and continued to send noncomplying claims to Medicaid. Defendants terminated Ramseyer's employment after eight months of service.[66]

During this time period and completely independent of Ramseyer's efforts to alert defendants of the problems, a routine audit and inspection by the Oklahoma Department of Human Services (DHS) uncovered the same problems. A DHS Program Supervisor, Roy Hughes, prepared a

59. *Id.*

60. *Id.* at 324. There is a split of authority on this issue among the circuits. In dicta, the District Court for the District of Massachusetts recognized this split, analyzed the relevant Circuit Court decisions and adopted the reasoning of the Fourth Circuit in *Becton Dickinson*, thus rejecting the analysis in *Doe*. United States *ex rel.* LeBlanc v. Raytheon Co., 874 F.Supp. 35, 39–41 (D.Mass.1995), *aff'd*, 62 F.3d 1411 (1st Cir.1995).

See also:

Seventh Circuit: Houck on behalf of the United States v. Folding Carton Admin. Comm., 881 F.2d 494, 504 (7th Cir.1989).

Ninth Circuit: Wang v. FMC Corp., 975 F.2d 1412, 1419 (9th Cir.1992).

Cf.:

Tenth Circuit: United States *ex rel.* Precision Co. v. Koch Indus., 971 F.2d 548, 552 (10th Cir.1992).

61. *Stinson, Lyons,* 944 F.2d at 1155–56.

62. *Fine,* 99 F.3d at 1546.

63. 90 F.3d 1514 (10th Cir.1996).

64. United States *ex rel.* Ramseyer v. Century Healthcare Corp., 90 F.3d 1514, 1519 (10th Cir.1996): United States *ex rel.* Fine v. MK–Ferguson Company, 99 F.3d 1538 (10th Cir.1996).

65. *Id.*

66. *Id.* at 1516–17.

report summarizing these findings. Three copies of the report were made: one copy was given to the defendants; one remained in DHS files; and, one was given to a DHS Administrator. The only way a member of the public could obtain a copy of this report was to specifically request it in writing and obtain approval for its release from DHS legal counsel.[67] This was not done.[68]

The Tenth Circuit viewed the issue as "whether theoretical or potential accessibility—as opposed to actual disclosure—of allegations or transactions is sufficient to bar a qui tam suit that is based upon such information."[69] Following the approach adopted by the Ninth[70] and District of Columbia Circuits[71] and rejecting the view of the Third Circuit[72] the Court held that actual disclosure to the public was necessary to find "public disclosure" under the FCA.[73] The court reasoned that the common usage and understanding of the term "public disclosure" implies actual disclosure. The court also found that finding public disclosure to exist merely upon the possibility that the public could gain access to the information would frustrate the goal of the FCA of "encourag[ing] private citizens with first-hand knowledge to expose fraud."[74] Applying its reasoning to the case before it, the court found that "DHS did not affirmatively 'disclose' either the existence of the contents of the Hughes Report; instead DHS simply placed the report in its investigative file and restricted access to those persons clairvoyant enough to specifically ask for it."[75] As such, the allegations and transactions in Ramseyer's FCA qui tam suit had not been publicly disclosed. The Tenth Circuit reversed the District Court's dismissal of Ramseyer's suit.[76]

C. "ORIGINAL SOURCE"

Even if the first prong of the jurisdictional bar provision is met and the qui tam lawsuit is "based upon" publicly disclosed allegations or transactions, the relator may go forward if the relator is "an original source" of the publicly disclosed information.[77] The FCA defines "original source" as "an individual who has direct and independent knowledge of the information on which the allegations are based and has voluntarily provided the information to the Government before filing an action under this section which is based on the information."[78] The major controversies concerning the "original source" language are the inter-

---

67. *Id.* at 1517.

68. *Id.* at 1518.

69. *Id.* at 1519.

70. Schumer v. Hughes Aircraft Co., 63 F.3d 1512, 1519–20 (9th Cir.1995) rev'd on other grounds 520 U.S. 939, 117 S.Ct. 1871, 138 L.Ed.2d 135 (1997).

71. United States *ex rel.* Springfield Terminal Ry. v. Quinn, 14 F.3d 645, 652–53 (D.C.Cir.1994).

72. United States *ex rel.* Stinson, Lyons, Gerlin & Bustamante, P.A. v. Prudential Ins. Co., 944 F.2d 1149, 1158 (3d Cir.1991).

73. *Ramseyer*, 90 F.3d at 1519.

74. *Id.*

75. *Id.* at 1521.

76. *Id.* at 1521–22.

77. 31 U.S.C. § 3730(e)(4)(A).

78. 31 U.S.C. § 3730(e)(4)(B).

pretation of "direct and independent" and whether the qui tam relator must disclose information to the source which publicly disclosed the information in order to qualify as an "original source."

i. "Direct and Independent"

The specificity and uniqueness of the information and the manner and timing in which the qui tam relator obtained the information appear to be the key factors in determining whether the relator obtained the information "directly and independently" so as to qualify as an original source. In *United States ex rel. Precision v. Koch*,[79] for example, the Court found that the relator's information was not obtained directly and independently but was "weak, informal and strikingly redundant" of allegations previously disclosed in civil lawsuits, a congressional hearing and news releases.[80] Thus, the court ruled, the plaintiff did not qualify as an original source.[81]

In contrast is *Cooper v. Blue Cross, Blue Shield.*[82] As in *Precision*, there was substantial prior publicity of the allegations contained in the qui tam relator's FCA action prior to the filing of the FCA complaint. The Eleventh Circuit, however, held that the relator's information qualified the relator as an "original source." The court noted that the relator had conducted a thorough investigation on his own prior to the publicity, and that his information was "potentially specific" and was "more than background information which enables him to understand the significance of a more general public disclosure."[83]

The courts have provided some guidance on this issue. A relator's knowledge is deemed to be "direct" if the relator's knowledge was gained by the relator's own efforts rather than from the labors of others. The relator's knowledge is independent unless it derived from others, even if the others are original sources.[84] As the Ninth Circuit explained, relators must "see the fraud with their own eyes or obtain their knowledge of it through their own labor unmediated by anything else...."[85]

ii. Disclosure

There is a disagreement among the Circuit Courts as to what is needed to find adequate disclosure by an "original source." The Second

79. 971 F.2d 548 (10th Cir.1992).

80. *Precision*, 971 F.2d at 554.

Third Circuit: See also United States *ex rel.* Stinson v. Prudential Ins. 944 F.2d 1149, 1160 (3d Cir.1991).

Seventh Circuit: Houck on Behalf of the United States v. Folding Carton Admin. Comm., 881 F.2d 494, 505 (7th Cir.1989).

81. *Precision*, 971 F.2d at 554.

82. Cooper v. Blue Cross & Blue Shield, 19 F.3d 562 (11th Cir.1994).

83. *Id.* at 568 n.11. *See also:*

Ninth Circuit: United States *ex rel.* Fine v. Chevron, U.S.A., Inc., 39 F.3d 957, 961–62 (9th Cir.1994).

84. United States *ex rel.* Fine v. Advanced Sciences, 99 F.3d 1000, 1006–07 (10th Cir.1996).

85. United States *ex rel.* Devlin v. State of California, 84 F.3d 358, 361 (9th Cir.1996).

and Ninth Circuits have adopted restrictive interpretations.[86] The Fourth and Eleventh Circuits have adopted a more expansive interpretation.[87]

In *United States ex rel. Dick v. Long Island Lighting, Co.*,[88] the Second Circuit held that the relator "must have directly or indirectly been a source to the entity that publicly disclosed the allegations on which a suit is based."[89] The Second Circuit focused on statutory language in reaching this conclusion.[90]

The Ninth Circuit reached a similar result but with different reasoning. In *Wang v. FMC*[91] the Ninth Circuit found the statutory language to be ambiguous, but focused on the legislative history: "qui tam jurisdiction was meant to extend only to those who had played a part in publicly disclosing the allegations and information on which their suits were based."[92] The Ninth Circuit also considered policy arguments, reasoning that the "conscientious or enterprising person" brave enough to bring the fraud to the public's attention should be rewarded with the bounty provided in the FCA rather than the person who "sat quietly in the shadows and breathed not a word" of the fraud.[93]

The Fourth and Eleventh Circuits disagree.[94] They also focus on the statutory language. The Fourth Circuit characterized the Second Circuit's approach as "wholly indefensible" and constituting "misreading of the legislative history . . . to create an ambiguity in the statute where none exists. . . ."[95] These courts hold that

> In addition to having direct and independent knowledge of the information on which the allegations in the public disclosure is based, he need only provide his information to the government before instituting his *qui tam* action. . . . [96]

The latter view seems preferable. Holding that a qui tam relator qualifies as an original source only if the relator disclosed the information in the FCA lawsuit to the entity that publicly disclosed the same allegations or transactions, would seem to turn on fortuities that have nothing to do with a relator's eligibility to bring a lawsuit. Such a holding would also seem to discourage individuals from fully investigating the facts surrounding the false claims for fear that they may lose the "race to publicize."

---

86. *Second Circuit:* United States *ex rel.* Dick v. Long Lighting Co., 912 F.2d 13, 16–17 (2d Cir.1990).

Ninth Circuit: Wang v. FMC, 975 F.2d 1412, 1418 (9th Cir.1992).

87. *Fourth Circuit:* United States *ex rel.* Siller v. Becton Dickinson & Co., 21 F.3d 1339, 1353–54 (4th Cir.1994).

Eleventh Circuit: Cooper v. BCBS, 19 F.3d 562, 567 (11th Cir.1994).

88. 912 F.2d 13 (2d Cir.1990).

89. *Long Island Lighting*, 912 F.2d at 16.

90. *Id.* at 16–17.

91. 975 F.2d 1412, 1418 (9th Cir. 1992).

92. *Wang*, 975 F.2d at 1418.

93. *Id.* at 1419–20.

94. *Becton Dickinson*, 21 F.3d at 1353–54; *Cooper*, 19 F.3d at 568, n.13.

95. *Becton Dickinson*, 21 F.3d at 1352. *Accord*, *Cooper*, 19 F.3d at 568 n.13.

96. *Becton Dickinson*, 21 F.3d at 1355.

Library References:

C.J.S. United States § 168–172, 174.
West's Key No. Digests, United States ☞120–122.

§ 27.11 *Qui Tam* Provisions—Reconciling Sections 3730(e)(4) and 3730(d)(1)

At first glance the jurisdictional bar provision of § 3730(e)(4) appears to conflict with § 3730(d)(1) which sets a limit of 10% on the award available to relators if the lawsuit is based upon public disclosure.[1] Section 3730(e)(4) prohibits FCA suits brought by a relator based upon publicly disclosed allegations or transactions unless the relator is an "original source" of the information, yet § 3730(d)(1) appears to recognize and reward such suits.

As interpreted by the courts, these sections are not inconsistent. As previously noted,[2] a qui tam lawsuit may be based upon publicly held information yet the suit is allowed to proceed because the relator qualifies as an original source. In a § 3730(d)(1) situation, the information supplied by the qui tam plaintiff is a small part of the allegations in the FCA suit. The 10% limit on the relator's award applies when the action is "based primarily on disclosures of specific information (other than information provided by the [relators]....[3] As one court explained:

> "... 3730(d) addresses the situation where the relator was an original source of the information, and therefore had a right of action to bring the case, even though the bulk of the information used to prove the case did not originate with the relator."[4]

Library References:

C.J.S. United States § 168–172, 174.
West's Key No. Digests, United States ☞120–122.

§ 27.12 *Qui Tam* Provisions—Government Employees as *Qui Tam* Relators

The courts addressing the issue of whether government employees

---

§ 27.11

1. Section 3730(d)(1) provides in part: "Where the action is one which the court finds to be based primarily on disclosures of specific information (other than information provided by the person bringing the action) relating to allegations or transactions in a criminal, civil, or administrative hearing, in a congressional, administrative, or Government Accounting Office report, hearing, audit, or investigation, or from the news media, the court may award such sums as it considers appropriate, but in no case more than 10 percent of the proceeds, taking into account the significance of the information and the role of the person bringing the action in advancing the case to litigation." 31 U.S.C. § 3730(d)(1).

2. See § 23.04(C)(2) *supra*.

3. United States v. CAC–Ramsay, Inc., 744 F.Supp. 1158, 1161 (S.D.Fla.1990), *aff'd* 963 F.2d 384 (11th Cir.1992).

4. United States v. Crescent City EMS, Inc., 1994 WL 518171, (E.D.La.1994), *aff'd*, 72 F.3d 447 (5th Cir.1995). *See e.g.*, United States v. Stern, 818 F.Supp. 1521, 1522 (M.D.Fla.1993). (Original sources who rely on publicly disclosed allegations or transactions are limited to 10% of the recovery unless the contributed "substantially and independently to the government's recovery.")

qualify as qui tam relators have held that they do, in principle.[1] These courts reason that the FCA explicitly excludes four classes of persons as eligible to serve as qui tam relators, none of which are government employees. While some of these courts acknowledge the public policy difficulties created when government employees are eligible to serve as qui tam relators,[2] other courts reason that allowing government employees to serve as qui tam relators furthers one of the goals of the 1986 amendments reviving the FCA: motivating individuals to serve "as a check that the Government does not neglect evidence, cause unduly [sic] delay, or drop the false claims case without legitimate reason."[3]

While the courts concede that in principle the FCA does not prohibit government employees from serving as qui tam relators, some of the courts nevertheless dismiss the government employee's qui tam suit. In *United States ex rel. LeBlanc v. Raytheon Company, Inc.*[4] for example, the First Circuit held that LeBlanc, a government employee, failed to qualify as an independent source because the allegations in his compliant had been publicly disclosed; thus he was jurisdictionally barred from bringing his suit.[5] Similarly, in *United States ex rel. Fine v. MK–Ferguson Company,*[6] the Tenth Circuit found that Fine, a government employee, did not have direct and independent knowledge, also requiring dismissal of Fine's suit.[7]

There are public policy problems in allowing government employees to serve as qui tam relators: government investigations may be prematurely disclosed or otherwise compromised; races to the courthouse may be encouraged as the government employee strives to beat the Attorney General in filing the lawsuit; a government employee's duty, as an employee, includes reporting fraud to the government, not profiting personally from such fraud through private litigation;[8] to qualify as an original source, one must also "voluntarily disclose" one's information to the government. Because a government employee's job requires such disclosure, it cannot be "voluntary." There are also potentially "serious ethical conflicts" that may arise if government employees are allowed to

§ 27.12

1. *First Circuit:* United States *ex rel.* LeBlanc v. Raytheon, 913 F.2d 17, 20 (1st Cir.1990), *cert. denied,* 499 U.S. 921, 111 S.Ct. 1312, 113 L.Ed.2d 246 (1991).

Fourth Circuit: Erickson v. Am. Inst. of Bio. Sciences, 716 F.Supp. 908, 912–18 (E.D.Va.1989).

Tenth Circuit: United States *ex rel.* Fine v. MK–Ferguson Co., 99 F.3d 1538, 1548–49 (10th Cir.1996); United States *ex rel.* Fine v. Advanced Sciences, 99 F.3d 1000 (10th Cir.1996).

2. *Williams,* 931 F.2d at 1503.

3. United States v. CAC—Ramsay, Inc., 744 F.Supp. 1158, 1160 (S.D.Fla.1990) (citing S. Rep. 347 at 5290–91).

4. 913 F.2d 17 (1st Cir.1990).

5. *Id.* at 20.

6. 99 F.3d 1538 (10th Cir.1996).

7. *Id.* at 1548; See also United States *ex rel.* Fine v. Advanced Sciences, Inc., 99 F.3d 1000, 100b–07 (10th Cir.1996).

8. Although the Eleventh Circuit held that government employees were eligible to serve as qui tam plaintiffs, the court noted public policy problems created by such a ruling. The Eleventh Circuit stated that it based its ruling on the statutory language which it found permitted government employees to serve as qui tam plaintiffs. The Eleventh Circuit opined that if the Congress wanted to prohibit government employees from serving as qui tam plaintiffs, it should amend the statute. *Williams,* 931 F.2d at 1502.

reap "huge bounties" simply by "fulfilling their employment responsibilities."[9] Such bounties could have the unfortunate effect of encouraging government fraud investigators *not* to report fraud they discover so they can use it themselves to file a qui tam lawsuit.[10] Mindful of these problems, the courts have directed litigants to address their concerns to Congress.[11]

Library References:

C.J.S. United States § 168–172, 174.
West's Key No. Digests, United States ☞120–122.

§ 27.13   *Qui Tam* Provisions—Rights of the Parties in *Qui Tam* Lawsuits

The dynamics of qui tam FCA suits are complex, creating strange bedfellows. Often the government, after intervening as a plaintiff, aggressively seeks disqualification of the relator without whom the case would not have been brought. There are reasons for this tension. By filing the FCA action the qui tam relator may have preempted or interfered with ongoing civil or criminal government investigations or cases. Also, because the relator is allowed to remain active in the case within limits after the government has intervened, there is potential for conflicts over strategy. Lastly, if the suit is victorious, the relator pockets proceeds that would otherwise go to the government. Thus, although the qui tam provisions were designed to aid government efforts to fight fraud, the relator may be viewed as a thorn in the side of the government.[1]

Sometimes the relator and defendant team up against the government. In *United States ex rel. Killingsworth v. Northrop*,[2] for example, the government accused the relator and the defendant of structuring a settlement so as to deprive the government of funds it would otherwise receive under the FCA.[3]

A. RIGHTS OF THE GOVERNMENT

The FCA gives the government considerable power in a qui tam action. Upon filing a complaint, the relator must provide the government a copy of the complaint and "written disclosure of substantially all material evidence and information the person possesses...."[4] The complaint remains sealed for 60 days to allow the government time to decide

---

9. *Fine*, 821 F.Supp. at 1361.

10. *Fine*, 821 F.Supp. at 1361. *Id.*

11. *See, e.g.*, United States *ex rel.* Fine v. MK–Ferguson Co., 861 F.Supp. 1544, 1549 (D.N.M.1994) *aff'd* 99 F.3d 1538 (10th Cir.1996).

§ 27.13

1. *See*, JOHN T. BOESE, CIVIL FALSE CLAIMS AND QUI TAM ACTIONS § 4–76–77.

2. 25 F.3d 715 (9th Cir.1994).

3. *Killingsworth*, 25 F.3d at 718. The qui tam plaintiff and defendant teamed up to argue that by not intervening in the action, the government forfeited its right to oppose the settlement. *Id.* at 719. The court remanded the case for a hearing as to whether the settlement agreement was fair and reasonable. *Id.* at 725.

4. *Id.* at § 3730(b)(2).

whether it will intervene in the case as a co-plaintiff.[5] The Government is entitled to extensions of this 60 day time period "for good cause shown."[6]

If the government intervenes as a co-plaintiff, it has "primary responsibility for prosecuting the action...."[7] The government may obtain restrictions on the relator's involvement in the case such as limiting the number of witnesses the relator may call, the length of testimony of such witnesses, the cross-examination of witnesses by the relator, "or otherwise limiting the participation by the person in the litigation."[8] To obtain such limitations, the government must show that "unrestricted participation during the course of the litigation by the [relator] would interfere with or unduly delay the Government's prosecution of the case, or would be repetitious, irrelevant, or for purposes of harassment...."[9]

The government may dismiss the action, or settle the action notwithstanding the objections of the relator as long as the court provides the relator with a hearing and in the case of settlement, "determines ... that the proposed settlement is fair, adequate and reasonable under all the circumstances."[10] Relators have been able to prevent settlements. For example in one case the government was not allowed to settle because the qui tam relator objected to the settlement of $234,000. On the eve of trial, the case was settled, with the qui tam party's consent, for $3.5 million. The relator received $770,000, 22% of the government's recovery.[11]

If the government opts not intervene in the case initially, it retains the right, upon request, to be served with copies of all pleadings filed in the action and copies of all depositions (at the government's expense).[12] Upon a showing of good cause, the government may intervene in the action "at a later date."[13] Additionally, even if the government does not intervene in the case, it may obtain a stay of discovery in the FCA action upon a showing that "certain actions of discovery by the [relator] would interfere with the Government's investigation or prosecution of a criminal or civil matter arising out of the same facts."[14]

After the qui tam action is filed, the government may elect to seek civil monetary penalties against the defendant through administrative proceedings rather than recovery through the FCA. If the Government

---

5. *Id.* at § 3730(b)(2).

6. *Id.* at § 3730(b)(3).

7. 31 U.S.C. § 3730(c).

8. *Id.* at § 3730(c)(2)(C)(iv).

9. *Id.* at § 3730(c)(2)(C).

10. 31 U.S.C. § 3730(c)(2)(A)(B).

11. Steve France, *The Private War on Pentagon Fraud*, 76 ABA JOURNAL 46, 47 (1990).

12. 31 U.S.C. § 3730(c)(3).

13. *Id. See, e.g.,* United States v. Texas Instruments Corp., 25 F.3d 725, 727–28 (9th Cir.1994) citing United States *ex rel.* Killingsworth v. Northrop Corp., 25 F.3d 715 (9th Cir.1994).

14. 31 U.S.C. § 3630(c)(4).

elects to pursue an administrative penalty, the relator retains the same rights it would have if the claim proceeded as a qui tam action.[15]

One issue that has arisen is whether the government may object to a settlement reached between the relator and the defendant when the government has not intervened. The Ninth Circuit confronted this situation in *United States ex rel. Gibeault v. Texas Instruments*,[16] and *United States ex rel. Killingsworth v. Northrop*.[17] In both cases the government, which had not intervened, sought to prevent the settlement reached by the parties. The government argued that the structure of the settlement diverted funds otherwise due to the government under the FCA.[18] In both cases the government pointed to § 3730(b)(1) which provides, "the Action may be dismissed only if the court and the Attorney General give written consent to the dismissal...."[19] The government argued that this section conferred absolute power on the government to block the settlements, regardless of whether or not the government had intervened. The Ninth Circuit disagreed, holding that the government had power to block a settlement only if the government intervened or if the settlement came about during the time period statutorily allotted for the government to decide whether to intervene.[20] The court went on to hold, however, that even if the government did not have the power to block a settlement when it was not party to the suit, it retained the right, upon a showing of good faith, to object to a proposed settlement where it has not intervened.[21]

B. RIGHTS OF THE RELATOR

The relator has responsibilities under the FCA such as providing the government with a copy of the complaint and "written disclosure of substantially all material evidence and information the [qui tam relator] possesses [regarding the lawsuit]."[22] The relator's rights as a litigant may be circumscribed upon motion of the government[23] or in an unusual case, upon motion of the defendant.[24]

In spite of this possible restriction, the relator enjoys unusual rights as a litigant. First and foremost, the relator has the right to bring an

---

15. *Id.* at § 3630(c)(5).

16. 25 F.3d 725 (9th Cir.1994).

17. Killingsworth v. Northrop, 25 F.3d 715 (9th Cir.1994).

18. *Killingsworth*, 25 F.3d at 718–19; *Gibeault*, 25 F.3d at 728.

19. *Killingsworth*, 25 F.3d at 721; *Gibeault*, 25 F.3d at 726.

20. *Killingsworth*, 25 F.3d at 722. Realistically, such a settlement is unlikely since the complaint is still sealed. if the government declines to intervene the person bringing the qui tam action has the right to conduct the action. The government may intervene at any later time, upon

a showing of good cause. 31 U.S.C. § 3630 (c)(3).

21. *Killingsworth*, 25 F.3d at 723. The Ninth Circuit also held that a settlement allocating a major portion of the proceeds to a personal claim, of which the government would get no share, instead of to the FCA claim, of which the government is guaranteed a share, when the personal claim appeared to fall outside the statute of limitations, constituted good cause. *Id.* at 724.

22. 31 U.S.C. § 3730(b)(2).

23. *Id.* at § 3730(c)(2)(C).

24. *Id.* at § 3730(c)(2)(D).

FCA action with an unusually minimal showing of standing.[25] If the government chooses not to intervene, the relator enjoys all rights of any litigant. Even if the government intervenes, the relator retains some ability to participate as co-plaintiff,[26] including the potential ability to block a settlement or dismissal.[27]

One of the major difficulties relators encounter in investigating and preparing qui tam actions is gathering information. Unlike the government which can use civil investigative demands,[28] the relator has no official mechanism for investigating. Even if relators are current employees of the offender and thus possess inside information about the fraud,[29] these employees may be barred by employment contracts from revealing the information or removing copies of documents, even regarding acts of fraud.[30] Attorneys wishing to serve as relators in suits based upon information obtained through clients will have to overcome the jurisdictional bar hurdle[31] as well as the additional hurdle posed by the Code of Ethics preventing disclosure of confidential information about a client obtained during representation of the client.[32] This ethical duty does not apply if "a reasonable attorney in the same circumstances would find convincing evidence of alleged fraudulent activities." The attorney seeking to make the disclosure bears the "heavy burden" of proving this test.[33]

Some relators seek to obtain information from related lawsuits. Gaining access to information in these lawsuits may be difficult. While the public has access to judicial records,[34] material generated though discovery may not be publicly available, especially if protective orders have been obtained.[35] Even if the qui tam relator gains such access, the jurisdictional bar provision may disqualify the qui tam relator.[36]

25. See, § 53.04(B) supra.

26. 31 U.S.C. § 3730(c)(1) provides: "If the Government proceeds with the action, it shall have the primary responsibility for prosecuting the action.... Such person shall have the right to continue as a party to the action, subject to the limitations set forth in paragraph (2) [regarding settlement, dismissal and conducting the litigation.]"

27. BOESE, FALSE CLAIMS, supra note 1, at § 4–80.

28. See, § 27.15.

29. Current employees are the most common type of qui tam plaintiffs. See BOESE, FALSE CLAIMS supra note 1, at 4–9.

30. X Corp. v. Doe, 805 F.Supp. 1298 (E.D.Va.1992) [hereinafter X Corp. I], aff'd sub nom., Under Seal v. Under Seal, 17 F.3d 1435 (4th Cir.1994).

31. See, § 53.04(C) supra.

32. Model Rules of Professional Conduct Rule 1.6(a) (1983); Model Code of Pro-

fessional Responsibility DR 401(B)-(C) (1980).

33. X Corp. v. John Doe, 816 F.Supp. 1086, 1091 (E.D.Va.1993) (citing X Corp. I, 805 F.Supp. at 1091).

34. Supreme Court: Nixon v. Warner Communications Inc., 435 U.S. 589, 597, 98 S.Ct. 1306, 1311, 55 L.Ed.2d 570, 575 (1978).

Third Circuit: Republic of the Philippines v. Westinghouse Elec. Corp. 949 F.2d 653 (3d Cir.1991).

35. First Circuit: Anderson v. Cryovac Inc., 805 F.2d 1, 12 (1st Cir.1986).

Third Circuit: Leucadia v. Applied Extrusion Technologies, Inc., 998 F.2d 157, 163 (3d Cir.1993).

Contra:

D.C. Circuit: Mokhiber v. Davis, 537 A.2d 1100 (D.C. Cir.1988).

36. See, § 23.04(C).

If the FCA action is successful, the qui tam relator is entitled to the following awards: If the government does *not* intervene, the qui tam relator is entitled to 25–30% of the proceeds of the recovery or settlement[37] with the court determining the ultimate amount. If the government intervenes, the relator is entitled to 15–25% of the proceeds of the recovery or settlement, where the final award depends upon "the extent to which the person substantially contributed to the prosecution of the action."[38] If the FCA lawsuit is based primarily on publicly disclosed allegations or transactions *other* than information from the relator but the relator qualified as an original source, the relator is entitled to no more than 10% of the award.[39] In setting the award in this situation the court is to consider "the significance of the information and the role of the person bringing the action in advancing the case to litigation."[40]

In every successful FCA suit the qui tam relator is entitled to receive an amount for reasonable expenses which the court finds to have been necessarily incurred, plus reasonable attorneys' fees and costs, all of which shall be awarded against the defendant.[41]

C. RIGHTS OF THE DEFENDANT

The defendant retains the same rights it has under the Federal Rule of Civil Procedure with several exceptions. The FCA alters discovery otherwise available in civil cases. It enhances a defendant's discovery rights by according the defendant the right to examine the "written disclosure of substantially all material evidence and information" the [qui tam relator] provided to the government pursuant to 3730(b)(2).[42] However, the FCA also gives the government a powerful discovery tool not available in most civil cases, the Civil Investigative Demand (CID), which allows the government to obtain discovery *prior* to filing a lawsuit.[43]

Under the FCA the defendant may apply to the court for restrictions on the qui tam relator's involvement in the case. Section 3730(c)(2)(D) provides that "Upon a showing by the defendant that unrestricted participation during the course of the litigation [by the qui tam relator] would be for purposes of harassment or would cause the defendant undue burden or unnecessary expense," the court may limit the participation of the qui tam relator.[44]

Especially after the Seventh Circuit's scathing opinion in *United*

---

37. 31 U.S.C. § 3730(d)(2).

38. *Id.* at § 3730(d)(1).

39. *Id.* at § 3730(d)(1).

40. *Id.* at § 3730(d)(1).

41. 31 U.S.C. § 3730(d).

42. 31 U.S.C. § 3730(b)(2).

Sixth Circuit: United States *ex rel.* Grand v. Northrop Corp., 811 F.Supp. 333, 337 (S.D.Ohio 1992).

Seventh Circuit: United States *ex rel.* Robinson v. Northrop Corp., 824 F.Supp. 830, 838–39 (N.D.Ill.1993).

Tenth Circuit: United States *ex rel.* Stone v. Rockwell Int'l Corp., 144 F.R.D. 396, 401 (D.Colo.1992).

43. *See* § 24.15.

44. 31 U.S.C. § 3730(c)(2)(D).

States ex rel. Fallon v. Accudyne,[45] it is clear that defendants do not have the right to relitigate issues after settlement. Accudyne Corporation attempted to do this when the District Court ordered Accudyne to pay the relators $1.5 million in attorney's fees and costs. Accudyne argued that the award was excessive since the relators would have lost if the case had not settled. Describing Accudyne's behavior of continuing litigation of matters resolved by settlement as "outrageous,"[46] the court was not sympathetic to Accudyne's claim that the relators' counsel charged too much:

> This was a big-stakes case with potentially difficult legal and factual issues. Accudyne hired a large and expensive law firm in Chicago; it can't grouse that the relators also engaged out-of-town commercial litigators whose hourly rates are normal for commercial cases.[47]

The FCA, like Federal Rule of Civil Procedure 11, provides relief for defendants who prevail on the merits.[48] If the defendant prevails in an action brought by a qui tam relator, the court may award to the defendant "its reasonable attorneys' fees and expenses ... if the court finds that the claim ... was clearly frivolous, clearly vexatious, or brought primarily for purposes of harassment."[49] If the defendant prevails in an FCA action brought by the government or in which the government intervened, the defendant may collect attorneys fees under the Equal Access to Justice Act if the defendant proves that the government's position was not "substantially justified."[50]

Library References:

C.J.S. United States § 168–172, 174.
West's Key No. Digests, United States ⊜120–122.

§ 27.14 Whistleblower Provisions

Dramatic testimony before Congress in 1986 demonstrated the need for protecting employees who disclose fraud by their employers. As one attorney familiar with such cases explained:

> After filing a [qui tam FCA suit], such person might be immediately fired by his employer, threatened or harassed by supervisors or co-workers, and blackballed from the industry in which he works. Thus, most individuals would be very reluctant to risk their jobs, their livelihood, and their personal security to expose either through

---

45. 97 F.3d 937 (7th Cir.1996).

46. *Id.* at 939.

47. *Id.* at 941.

48. But, Rule 11 limits the possibility of awards to the defendant. First, sanctions are limited to an amount sufficient to deter vexatious conduct. Second, the prevailing party's gain is limited to fees derived from the sanctions motion. Third, sanctions may be brought by motion or by the court's initiative. Fed.R.Civ.P. 11.

49. *Id.* at § 3730(d)(4).

50. 28 U.S.C. § 2412(d)(1)(A). In determining whether the action was substantially justified courts use a standard a little more stringent than "reasonably justified." Spencer v. NLRB, 712 F.2d 539, 558 (D.C.Cir.1983).

filing a lawsuit or providing testimony the fraudulent practices of their employer or former employer in a False Claims Act suit.[1]

To protect employees and encourage them to come forward, Congress included § 3730(h) in the 1986 Amendments to the FCA. This section provides a cause of action for

> [a]ny employee who is discharged, demoted, suspended, threatened, harassed or in any other manner discriminated against in the terms and conditions of employment by his or her employer because of lawful acts done by the employee ... in furtherance of an action under this section.... [The Employee] is entitled to reinstatement with the same seniority status such employee would have had but for the discrimination, 2 times the amount of back pay, interest on the back pay, and compensation for any special damages sustained as a result of the discrimination, including litigation costs and reasonable attorneys' fees.[2]

To prevail on a whistleblower retaliation claim, an employee must demonstrate a causal link between whistleblower activities and the discriminatory employment action. *X Corp. v. Doe*,[3] demonstrates this requirement. Former in-house counsel (Doe) counterclaimed under § 3730(h) in a suit brought by X Corp. against Doe for breach of confidentiality agreement. In his counterclaim Doe alleged that he had been fired as in-house counsel in retaliation for Doe's filing of a qui tam action against X Corp.[4] The court dismissed the counterclaim finding that Doe failed to demonstrate a causal connection between his firing and the filing of the qui tam action.[5] The court explained that in order to prevail, "Doe must prove (i) he took acts in furtherance of a qui tam suit; (ii) X Corp. knew of these acts; and (iii) X Corp. discharged him because of these acts."[6] In this instance all but one of the acts Doe identified as taken in furtherance of a qui tam suit were, in fact, an exercise of his responsibilities as in-house counsel. Doe was unable to prove that the Management Committee of X Corp. was aware of the one

---

§ 27.14

1. *False Claims Act Amendment: Hearings Before the Subcomm. on Admin. Law and Govt'l Relations of the House Comm. on the Judiciary*, 99th Cong., 2d Sess. 405 (1986) (statement of John Phillips, Exec. Dir., Center for Law in the Public Interest). *Id.* at 340–41. John Michael Gravitt, a tool room machinist foreman testified before Congress about his experience at a General Electric, Aircraft Engine Business Group in Ohio from 1980–83:

> [I] was instructed, along with at least one other foreman and probably others, to alter my hourly employees' time vouchers. The changed vouchers were supposed to reflect that all time spent by employees under my supervision on their 8–hour shifts was time spent on specific Government jobs, regardless of whether the machinist had been idle because he was waiting for an engineer, waiting for parts, or did not have work to be done.

Gravitt spoke to his supervisors and refused to falsify and change vouchers. He learned that when he did not change the vouchers, his supervisors did. Gravitt was "laid-off" from G.E. allegedly for lack of work (however G.E. received a major defense contract at the same time Gravitt was laid off).

2. 31 U.S.C. § 3730(h).

3. 816 F.Supp. 1086 (E.D.Va.1993); *See also* United States *ex rel.* Ramseyer v. Century Healthcare Corp. 90 F.3d 1514 (10th Cir.1996).

4. 816 F.Supp. 1086.

5. *Id.* at 1095.

6. *Id.* at 1095.

act that he took in furtherance of the qui tam action, secretly copying and removing documents.[7]

Employees and former employees may not be able to bring retaliatory action suits under the FCA if they previously litigated the same issues in other lawsuits or jurisdictions.[8]

Thus far, courts have interpreted the whistleblower provisions in favor of the employee on a number of issues. Courts have ruled in the worker's favor when addressing the initial issue of whether the worker is an employee, who is covered by the FCA's whistleblower protection, or an independent contractor, who is not covered. In *Godwin v. Visiting Nurse Ass'n*[9] the court noted that it would look to what the relationship " 'really was under the facts and applicable rules of law' and not in the way in which the parties regarded this relationship."[10] Focusing on factors such as how much the worker controlled the results of the work and the right to direct how the work would be done, the court found Godwin, a bookkeeper-accountant, was an employee of a Visiting Nurse Association.[11]

Similarly, the only courts ruling on another preliminary issue have held that it is not necessary for an employee to bring a qui tam action under the FCA to qualify as a plaintiff in a retaliatory action suit under § 3730(h). Both the Seventh and Eleventh Circuits have ruled in the employees' favor on this issue.[12]

In *Neal v. Honeywell, Inc.*[13] the Seventh Circuit held that an employee who had not and could not bring an action under the FCA was eligible to sue her employer for harassment under the FCA[14] The employee, Judith Neal, reported her suspicions of fraud on the part of

7. *Id.*

8. *See, e.g.,* United States *ex rel.* Paul v. PBQ & D, 860 F.Supp. 370, 372–75 (S.D.Tex.1994) (holding that suit brought by former employee was barred by res judicata).

9. 831 F.Supp. 449 (E.D.Pa.1993), *aff'd* 39 F.3d 1173 (3d Cir.1994) (*citing* Jones v. Century Oil U.S.A., Inc., 957 F.2d 84, 86 (3d Cir.1992)).

10. *Id.* at 453. Other factors to consider are "the skill required, the source of the instrumentalities and tools; the location of the work; the duration of the relationship between the parties; whether the hiring party has the right to assign additional projects to the hired party; the extent of the hired party's discretion over when and how long, to work; the method of payment; the hired party's role in hiring and paying assistants; whether the work is part of the regular business of the hiring party; whether the hiring party is in business; the provision of employee benefits; and the tax treatment of the hired party." Shapiro v. Sutherland, 835 F.Supp. 836, 837–38 (E.D.Pa.1993) (*citing* Nationwide Mutual

Insurance Co. v. Darden, 503 U.S. 318, 112 S.Ct. 1344, 117 L.Ed.2d 581 (1992)). In *Shapiro*, the court applied the above test in finding that there was a "material issue of fact as to whether whistleblower was an 'employee' covered by the FCA." *Id.* at 838.

11. *Id.* at 453.

12. *Eleventh Circuit*: Childree v. UAP/GA AG CHEM., Inc., 92 F.3d 1140 (11th Cir.1996).

Seventh Circuit: Neal v. Honeywell Inc., 33 F.3d 860 (7th Cir.1994).

Contra:

Fifth Circuit: Robertson v. Bell Helicopter Textron, Inc., 32 F.3d 948 (5th Cir. 1994). The Fifth Circuit held that an employee did not qualify as a plaintiff under the FCA's whistleblower provisions but the facts were unique in that the employee had taken few steps to alert anyone of the overcharging problem. *See* discussion *infra* § 53.5.

13. 33 F.3d 860 (7th Cir.1994).

14. *Id.* at 861–64.

her employer, Honeywell. Her report resulted in an investigation, criminal charges and guilty pleas by Honeywell employees and a settlement of civil liability with the government.[15] In light of the settlement, Neal could not bring a FCA suit. When Neal was harassed by her employer for her whistleblowing efforts, she quit and filed suit under § 3730(h). Noting that it was the first appellate court to interpret § 3730(h), the Seventh Circuit examined the requirement in § 3730(h) that the harassment condemned must be because of lawful acts by an employee "in furtherance" of a FCA action. Holding that Neal could bring a suit under § 3730(h) the court reasoned that Congress would not have "wanted to protect employees in doubtful cases (the kind that breed litigation) but leave them unprotected when the fraud is so clear that the employer capitulates, averting litigation."[16]

Similarly, in *Childree v. UAP/GA AG CHEM. Inc.*,[17] the Eleventh Circuit found that Childree, a former employee of the defendants, was able to bring suit under the FCA whistleblower provisions even though she had not filed a FCA action.[18] Acknowledging that the employee must "at a minimum ... show some nexus between her conduct and the furtherance of a potential False Claims Act action," the court found such a nexus to exist.[19] Following the Seventh Circuit's approach, the Eleventh Circuit held that

> § 3730(h) protection is available not only where a false claims action is actually filed, but also where the filing of such an action, by either the employee or the government, was a "distinct possibility" at the time the assistance was rendered.

Turning to the facts before it, the Eleventh Circuit noted that Childree who had reluctantly testified at a Department of Agriculture hearing about a suspected fraudulent billing scheme at her employer's, never contemplated filing a qui tam FCA action.[20] However, the court found that it was a distinct possibility that the government might file an FCA action at the time Childree rendered her assistance.[21]

In contrast is *Robertson v. Bell Helicopter Textron, Inc.* decided by the Fifth Circuit.[22] Robertson had voiced concerns to his superiors about overcharging but had never referred to the overcharging as illegal, never indicated an intention to file a qui tam action, and never spoken to government officials about the alleged overcharging. Unlike the employees in *Neal* and *Childree*, Robertson had never publicly communicated his suspicions whatsoever. The Fifth Circuit ruled that Robertson did not qualify to bring a whistleblower action under the FCA "because there was insufficient evidence that he furthered or assisted in any

15. *Id.* at 861.
16. *Id.* at 864.
17. 92 F.3d 1140 (11th Cir.1996).
18. *Id.* at 1144.
19. *Id.*
20. *Id.* at 1146.
21. *Id.* at 1146.
22. 32 F.3d 948 (5th Cir.1994).

'action,' and because there was insufficient evidence that his employer was aware that the plaintiff was investigating the overcharging."[23]

Additionally, courts have held that a whistleblower action may be alleged against persons who were employees of a predecessor employer at the time of the discriminatory act. In *United States ex rel. Kent v. Aiello* the court held that the FCA's whistleblower protection extended to employers who "caused" the current employer to engage in such discrimination.[24] In *Kent*, the court denied defendants' motion to dismiss on a variety of grounds including defendants' argument that a § 3730(h) whistleblower claim could not be made against them since they were not plaintiffs employer at the time of her termination.[25] Plaintiff was hired by defendants 2½ years before defendants turned over their business to CBM Group, Inc. (CBM). CBM assumed the employment contract entered into by plaintiff and defendants.[26] In her § 3730(h) action, plaintiff alleged that the defendants "so influenced and controlled CBM so as to cause them to terminate plaintiff's employment in retaliation for lawful acts done in furtherance of the qui tam action."[27] The court found that prior employers were eligible defendants under § 3730(h). In so concluding, the court focused on the fact that the FCA is a remedial statute and thus should be construed broadly. The court also looked at Title VII litigation where courts have held that former employers were eligible defendants.[28]

One issue on which courts have not ruled in employees' favor is whether federal employees suing the federal government qualify as whistleblowers. Courts have relied on two rationales in holding that federal employees cannot invoke the whistleblower provisions of the FCA. The first is sovereign immunity[29] which provides that the federal government is immune from suits "if judgment sought would expend itself on the public treasury or domain...."[30] Suits against the United States are permitted only where the federal government has unequivocally waived sovereign immunity.[31] Courts have reasoned that because

---

23. *Id.*

24. 836 F.Supp. 720, 724–25 (E.D.Ca. 1993). *Cf.* Gomez v. Alexian Brothers Hospital of San Jose, 698 F.2d 1019, 1021 (9th Cir.1983) (previous employer who interfered with subsequent employment opportunities may be liable under Title VII).

25. *Id.* at 723.

26. *Id.* at 720.

27. *Id.* at 722.

28. *Id.* at 725–26.

29. Daly v. Dept. of Energy, 741 F.Supp. 202 (D.Colo.1990).

30. U.S. Const. amend. XI; Dugan et al. v. Rank et al., 372 U.S. 609, 620, 83 S.Ct. 999, 1006, 10 L.Ed.2d 15 (1963) (citing Land v. Dollar, 330 U.S. 731, 738, 67 S.Ct. 1009, 1012, 91 L.Ed. 1209 (1947)).

Eleventh amendment claims by states, named as defendants in qui tam actions have not been successful. The courts have held that the United States is the real party in interest even if it does not intervene in the qui tam action. This resolves any Eleventh Amendment claim since "the United States may sue states in federal courts notwithstanding the Eleventh Amendment."

See, e.g.:

Fourth Circuit: United States *ex rel.* Milam v. University of Texas M.D. Anderson Cancer Center, 961 F.2d 46, 48 (4th Cir.1992).

Tenth Circuit: United States v. Rockwell Int'l Corp., 730 F.Supp. 1031, 1035 (D.Colo.1990).

31. United States v. Testan, 424 U.S. 392, 399, 96 S.Ct. 948, 953, 47 L.Ed.2d 114 (1976).

§ 3130(h) does not address the sovereign immunity issue, much less unequivocally waive it, the FCA does not waive this immunity.[32] The second rationale is that Congress intended the Civil Service Reform Act[33] to provide the exclusive remedy for federal employees who suffer retaliation for whistleblowing.[34]

Whistleblowers who "planned and initiated" the false claim conduct but sue as qui tam relators may see their share of any proceeds reduced by the court. The FCA provides that when the relator has "planned and initiated" the fraudulent activity, "the court may, to the extent the court considers appropriate, reduce the share of the proceeds of the action which the person would otherwise receive...."[35] The court is to take into account "the role of that person in advancing the case to litigation and any relevant circumstances pertaining to the violation."[36] Further, if the qui tam relator is convicted of a crime arising from his or her role in the violation she "shall be dismissed from the civil action and shall not receive any share of the proceeds of the action."[37] The Department of Justice has attempted to reduce a qui tam relator's share of the recovery by utilizing a version of this provision. In *United States v. General Electric*,[38] the government argued that had the qui tam relator acted quicker, the relator could have reduced the amount of the loss from the fraud. The court rejected the argument, finding that the government's position was unreasonable. The "should have" argument, according to the court, was tantamount to a hindsight analysis at odds with the purposes behind whistleblower provisions.[39]

Another issue in which courts have ruled against whistleblowers is whether the Eleventh Amendment's[40] immunity for states from suit by citizens applies to whistleblower suits under the FCA. Citing the absence of language in § 3730(h) abrogating such immunity, the only court to consider the issue thus far ruled that states were immune.[41]

Library References:

C.J.S. United States § 168–172, 174.
West's Key No. Digests, United States ☞120–122.

32. *Daly*, 741 F.Supp. at 205–06.

33. Pub.L. 95–454 (codified as amended in scattered sections of 5 U.S.C.)

34. *Daly*, 741 F.Supp. at 204–05.

35. 31 U.S.C. § 3730(d)(3).

36. *Id.*

37. *Id.*

38. 808 F.Supp. 580, 583 (S.D.Ohio 1992).

39. *Id.* at 583.

40. The Eleventh Amendment provides:

The judicial power of the United States shall not be construed to extend to any suite in law or equity commenced or prosecuted against one of the United States by Citizens of another State, or by Citizens or Subjects of any Foreign State. U.S. CONST. amend. XI.

The Supreme Court has extended this bar to suits against a State by its own citizens. Hans v. Louisiana, 134 U.S. 1, 11, 10 S.Ct. 504, 505–06, 33 L.Ed. 842 843–44 (1890). Congress may abrogate States' constitutional immunity but it must do so with unequivocal statutory language. Atascadero State Hospital v. Scanlon, 473 U.S. 234, 105 S.Ct. 3142, 87 L.Ed.2d 171 (1985).

41. United States *ex rel.* Moore v. University of Michigan, 860 F.Supp. 400, 405 (E.D.Mich.1994).

§ 27.15   FCA Procedure—Discovery

Because FCA actions are federal civil cases, the Federal Rules of Civil Procedure (FRCP) apply, unless preempted by the FCA. There are some procedural variances from the FRCP in FCA cases because of the FCA's qui tam provisions.

One way FCA actions differ in procedure from other federal civil actions is in discovery. Prior to bringing an FCA action or intervening in it, the government may use a Civil Investigative Demand (CID)[1] which provides for extraordinary pretrial discovery: "Whenever the Attorney General has reason to believe that any person may be in possession, custody, or control of any documentary material or information relevant to a false claims law investigation, the Attorney General may ... issue a civil investigative demand requiring such person to produce such documentary material, ... to answer ... written interrogatories, ... to give oral testimony...."[2] The major difference between a CID and discovery otherwise available in the FRCP is that CIDs may be used prior to the filing of a lawsuit.

The purpose of the CID is to "enable the Government to determine whether enough evidence exist[s] to warrant the expense of filing [a civil] suit, as well as to prevent the potential defendant from being dragged into court unnecessarily."[3] In passing the 1986 amendments, Congress found that government attorneys and investigators lacked adequate tools for investigating civil allegations of fraud against the government. Often they had to rely on possible disclosure of grand jury material, which was not always available, given the secrecy that surrounds the grand jury.[4] Relying on traditional methods of discovery in the FRCP meant the government could gather information only after a

§ 27.15

1. *Id.* at § 3733.

2. *Id.* at § 3733(a)(1)(A)-(C).

3. H.R.Rep.No. 660, 99th Cong. 2d Sess. 26 (1986).

4. In United States v. Sells Engineering Inc., the issue before the Court was whether Department of Justice lawyers could obtain "(A)(i) disclosure of grand jury materials for use in a civil suit, or whether they [had to] seek a (C)(i) court order for access." 463 U.S. 418, 427, 103 S.Ct. 3133, 3139, 77 L.Ed.2d 743 (1983). The Court held that restricted access to grand jury materials was the proper course in light of policy concerns and legislative intent. *Id.* at 442. Further, the Court ruled that courts are to use a "particularized need" standard in reviewing a (c)(i) disclosure request. *Id.* at 443. In a similar vein, the Court ruled that (c)(i) "contemplates only uses related fairly directly to some identifiable litigation, pending or anticipated," thus reflecting "a judgment that not every beneficial purpose, or even every valid governmental purpose,

is an appropriate reason for breaching grand jury secrecy." United States v. Baggot, 463 U.S. 476, 480, 103 S.Ct. 3164, 3167, 77 L.Ed.2d 785, 789 (1983). FRCRP 6(e) provides that matters occurring before a grand jury shall not be disclosed except voluntarily by the grand jury witness (e)(2) or "when so directed by a court preliminary to or in connection with a judicial proceeding." Fed.R.Crim.P. 6(e)(3)(C)(i). There is some flexibility in the way "matters occurring before the grand jury" is interpreted. For example, some courts hold that documents presented to the grand jury albeit pursuant to a grand jury subpoena are not "matters occurring before the grand jury" unless "their disclosure would convey otherwise unavailable information about the nature of the grand jury proceedings." United States v. Stanford, 589 F.2d 285, 291 (7th Cir.1978), *cert. denied* 440 U.S. 983, 99 S.Ct. 1794, 60 L.Ed.2d 244 (1979); United States v. Interstate Dress Carriers, Inc., 280 F.2d 52, 54 (2d Cir.1960).

case has been filed and often had to engage in protracted court proceedings to get discovery.[5]

Section 3733(a)(1) provides that "the Attorney General may ... issue ... a civil investigative demand...." The Attorney General may not delegate this authority. This was demonstrated in *Moog Inc. v. United States*,[6] where the court granted the petitioners' motion to set aside CIDs issued under the FCA because the sitting Attorney General designated a Deputy Attorney General as "Acting Attorney General" for purposes of authorizing CIDS.[7]

Because CIDS are designed for investigative purposes, they may be used only *prior* to the government commencing or intervening in a civil proceeding brought under the FCA.[8] Information gathered with CIDs may not be disclosed to anyone other than the false claims investigator designated by the Attorney General, or under limited circumstances, to an attorney of the Department of Justice.[9]

The FCA specifies the procedure for serving, enforcing and complying with CIDs. Upon receipt of a CID, the recipient has 20 days to comply.[10] If the recipient fails to comply, the Attorney General may file a petition in district court for a court order enforcing the CID.[11] Likewise, the recipient of a CID may file a petition in district court to modify or set aside the CID.[12] CID proceedings in district court are "summary" proceedings and the parties do not have right to conduct full discovery under the FRCP with regard to such proceedings.[13] As one court reasoned:

> CIDs are a form of administrative subpoena. As a general rule, proceedings to enforce administrative subpoenas are summary. In such summary proceedings, a subpoena recipient does not have a right to discovery in the normal course of events. Rather, a subpoena recipient is entitled to limited discovery only after making a substantial and supported showing that enforcement of the subpoena would work an abuse of the Court's process.[14]

Because the transactions at issue in a FCA investigation may also give rise to criminal liability, discovery in the civil matter may create

5. S.Rep.No. 345, 99th Cong., 2d Sess. at 7–8 (1986), *reprinted in* 1986 U.S.C.C.A.N. at 5272–73.

6. Moog, Inc. v. United States, 1991 WL 46518, at *1 (N.D.N.Y. 1991).

7. Because the investigation concerned a corporation in which the Attorney General held stock, the Attorney General determined that such designation was required. The count questioned whether refusal or divestiture was the better alternative. *Moog v. United States*, 1991 WL 46518, at *2 (1991).

8. 31 U.S.C. § 3733(a)(1).

9. Section 3733(a)(1) bestows non-delegable authority upon the Attorney General

to issue CIDs and as such, the CIDs ordered were ineffectual.

10. 31 U.S.C. § 3733(a)(2)(E).

11. 31 U.S.C. § 3733(j)(1).

12. *Id.* at § 3733(j)(2)

13. United States v. Witmer, 835 F.Supp. 201, 204, 206, *vacated in part, on other grounds*, 835 F.Supp. 208 (M.D.Pa. 1993), *aff'd* 30 F.3d 1489 (3d Cir.1994) (distinguishing cases holding that "reasonable discovery is available as a matter of right to petitioners in proceedings to set aside or limit CIDs" on the ground that the actual holdings of such cases was narrower than their language).

14. *Id.* at 205 (citations omitted).

difficult choices for the individual targeted. The individual may have to choose between responding to the CID and risking incrimination in a possible criminal prosecution and not responding to the CID by invoking his or her privilege against self incrimination which permits adverse inferences in the civil case.[15] The major relief available in such a circumstance is a stay of the civil proceedings: "[A] court may decide in its discretion to stay civil proceedings, postpone civil discovery, or impose protective orders and conditions 'when the interest of justice seem [] to require such action . . . .' "[16]

Library References:

C.J.S. United States § 168–172, 174.
West's Key No. Digests, United States ☞120–122.

§ 27.16 FCA Procedure—Pleading

Federal Rules of Civil Procedure (FRCP) 9(b) supplies the pleading requirements for an FCA complaint. For example, in *United States v. Crescent City, EMS, Inc.*,[1] the Fifth Circuit dismissed an FCA complaint because it did not comply with FRCP 9(b)'s requirement that allegations of fraud be pleaded with particularity.[2] Here, the government filed the FCA action against an ambulance service that allegedly falsified patients' eligibility for services under Medicare. The court opined that to comply with FRCP 9(b), the complaint must allege "the exact dates the alleged false claims were made, the identity of the person making the representation, . . . the place where the alleged fraud took place,[3] . . . the contents of the [alleged false] statement[s] and identity of the party who made the alleged mispresentation[s] or . . . the factual basis supporting its belief that fraud occurred."[4]

In contrast is the complaint in *United States v. Nazon*,[5] which the court found sufficient to comply with FRCP 9(b). The complaint against

15. Baxter v. Palmigiano, 425 U.S. 308, 318, 96 S.Ct. 1551, 1558, 47 L.Ed.2d 810 (1976). "In a civil case, a party's invocation of the privilege against self incrimination givers rise to a legitimate inference that the witness was engaged in criminal activity." *Id.* The other choice is foregoing their privilege and risking incriminating themselves in subsequent criminal proceedings. *See, e.g.*, *Witmer*, 835 F.Supp. at 208 (holding that even limited discovery will not be allowed).

16. SEC v. Dresser Indus. Inc., 628 F.2d 1368, 1375 (D.C.Cir.), *cert. denied*, 449 U.S. 993, 101 S.Ct. 529, 66 L.Ed.2d 289 (1980) (*quoting* United States v. Kordel, 397 U.S. 1, 12, 90 S.Ct. 763, 770, 25 L.Ed.2d 1 (1970)).

§ 27.16

1. 151 F.R.D. 288 (E.D.La.1993), *aff'd*, 72 F.3d 447 (5th Cir.1995). *See also* United States *ex rel.* Mikes v. Straus, 853 F.Supp. 115, 117–19 (S.D.N.Y.1994) (FCA suit brought by employee against physicians dismissed for failure to comply with FRCP 9(b).)

2. Fed.R.Civ.P. 9(b) requires:

In all averments of fraud or mistake, the circumstances constituting fraud or mistake shall be stated with particularity. Malice, intent, knowledge, and other condition of mind of a person may be averred generally. Fed.R.Civ.P. 9(b).

To comply with 9(b), a complaint must set forth the "who, what, when, where, and how" of the fraud. DiLeo v. Ernst & Young, 901 F.2d 624, 627 (7th Cir.1990).

3. *Id.* at 290.

4. *Id.* at 291.

5. No. 93–C–5456, 1993 WL 410150, at *1 (N.D.Ill.1993).

Nazon, an obstetrician/gynecologist, alleged that he filed 61 claims against Medicare that were false or fraudulent because he had been excluded from Medicare. Although the complaint was worded in general terms, it included the number of claims submitted, the time period which they were submitted, the explanation of why the claims were false and an allegation of defendant's knowledge when submitting them.[6] The government also attached, as an exhibit to the complaint, a list of Nazon's Medicare billings during the time in question. This list included "the patient's name, date of service, amount billed, amount paid and date of payment."[7] The court found that this exhibit provided the particularity required by Rule 9(b).[8]

Library References:

C.J.S. United States § 168–172, 174.
West's Key No. Digests, United States ⟐120–122.

§ 27.17 FCA Procedure—Statute of Limitations

Section 3731(b) of the FCA provides that actions must be brought within 6 years after the date of the violation, or within 3 years "after the date when facts material to the right of action are known or reasonably should have been known by the official of the United States charged with responsibility to act in the circumstances...."[1] In no case may an action be brought more than 10 years after the violation has been committed.[2] By incorporating a "tolling" period until the facts are known or reasonably should be known, the FCA codifies the common law equitable principle followed by courts. The Ninth Circuit explained the history and rationale of this principle and the FCA's adoption of it:

> Prior to the 1986 amendments, an action under the FCA had to be brought within six years of the alleged violation. Although the pre–1986 statute did not contain a tolling provision, several courts applied equitable tolling principles to FCA suits to hold that the limitations period begins to run from the time the government discovers or should have discovered the fraud, rather from the date of the violation itself. Equitable tolling, as the name suggests, is an equitable doctrine grounded in the venerable notion that it would be unfair to bar a fraud action as untimely where the defendant successfully concealed the fraud from the plaintiff during the limitations period. Fraud by its very nature is concealed and difficult to discover. The most successful fraud may be the one least likely discovered within the limitations period. Courts have barred such inequitable reliance on statutes of limitations, applying the maxim

---

6. *Id.* at 1.

7. *Id.* at 2.

8. *Id.*

§ 27.17

1. 31 U.S.C. § 3731(b)(2).

2. *Id.* This section "include[s] an explicit tolling provision on the statute of

limitations under the [FCA]. The statute of limitations does not begin to run until the material facts are known by an official within the Department of Justice...." S.Rep.No. 345, *supra* note 5, at 30, reprinted in 1986 U.S.C.C.A.N. at 5295.

"no man may take advantage of his own wrong." *Glus v. Brooklyn E. Dist. Terminal*, 359 U.S. 231, 232, 79 S.Ct. 760, 762, 3 L.Ed.2d 770 (1959). Under equitable tolling, courts toll the running of the statute of limitations until the plaintiff knew or reasonably should have known of the facts underlying his cause of action. As a general rule, equitable tolling is read into every federal statute of limitations.

The 1986 FCA amendments codified this equitable tolling principle in 31 U.S.C. § 3731(b)(2), which tolls the statute of limitations until the facts underlying the fraud are or should have been discovered by "the official of the United States charged with responsibility to act in the circumstances," up to a maximum of ten years.[3]

The major question that has arisen regarding the 6 and the 10 year time periods is how to determine when the violation occurred. Although a few courts have held that the presentation of the claim activates the statute of limitations,[4] the majority view is that the limitations period "begins to run on the date the claim is made or, if the claim is paid, on the date of the payment."[5]

Several questions remain unresolved regarding the 3 year time period. One question is which official of the United States must know of the violation before the statute of limitations begins to run. Several courts have held that "[t]he 'official of the United States charged with responsibility' could only have been the appropriate official of the Civil Division of the Department of Justice, which alone has the authority to initiate litigation under the Act."[6] Other courts disagree, holding that the responsible government official should be the agent charged with investigating such fraud.[7] The latter view seems preferable. As John Boese, the leading expert on the FCA argues, a rule requiring presentation to an official in the Civil Division is easily manipulated simply by controlling when the case is referred to the Civil Division.[8] In addition such a rule would necessitate intrusive discovery into internal communications and procedures of the Department of Justice and the Civil Division to track the chronology of a referral.

3. United States *ex rel.* Hyatt v. Northrop Corp. 91 F.3d 1211, 1216 (9th Cir. 1996).

4. *First Circuit:* United States *ex rel.* LaValley v. First Nat. Bank of Boston, 707 F.Supp. 1351 (D.Mass.1988).

Eighth Circuit: United States v. Cherokee Implement Co., 216 F.Supp. 374, 375 (N.D.Iowa 1963).

Eleventh Circuit: United States v. Entin, 750 F.Supp. 512, 517 (S.D.Fla.1990).

5. *D.C. Circuit:* United States v. Uzzell, 648 F.Supp. 1362, 1366–68 (D.D.C. 1986).

Second Circuit: Blusal Meats, Inc. v. United States, 638 F.Supp. 824, 829 (S.D.N.Y.1986), *aff'd*, 817 F.2d 1007 (2d Cir.1987); United States *ex rel.* Duvall v. Scott Aviation, 733 F.Supp. 159 (W.D.N.Y. 1990).

6. United States v. Macomb Contracting Corp., 763 F.Supp. 272, 274 (M.D.Tenn. 1990).

7. United States v. Kensington Hospital, 1993 WL 21446 at *11 (E.D.Pa.1993); ¶ 41,053 Medicare & Medicaid Guide.

8. JOHN T. BOESE, CIVIL FALSE CLAIMS AND QUI TAM ACTIONS § 5–17.

A second question is how to judge whether the responsible government official "should have known" of the violation. Few courts have addressed this issue.[9]

A third question is whether the three year time period applies at all when the government is not a party to the case. In *Hyatt v. Northrop Corp.*,[10] the court dismissed the qui tam suit as barred by the statute of limitations. The suit, brought at least 7 years after the qui tam relator learned of the alleged false claims, could survive the statute of limitations only if the provision tolling the statute of limitations to three years after the material facts became known or reasonably should have been known to the responsible government official, applied. The court held that the tolling provision did not apply to suits where the government was not a party. The court recognized that the FCA states that the three year tolling provision applies to "[a] civil action under section 3730," which would appear to include all qui tam actions, not just those where the government joins as plaintiff. The court held, however, that following the "plain meaning" would lead to "an absurd result."[11] In *Hyatt*, for example, noted the court, the qui tam relator was an employee of the defendant, Northrop, and was aware of the material facts giving rise to the FCA suit three years before bringing the action.[12] As the District Court noted, delay by the relator in bringing the suit harms the government by "prevent[ing] the government from knowing about (and hence taking prompt action on) an otherwise discoverable False Claims Act violation.... Such a delay is also harmful to the defendant, because it increases unnecessarily the difficulty in discovering the facts necessary to respond to the charges of fraud."[13]

Library References:

C.J.S. United States § 168–172, 174.
West's Key No. Digests, United States ⊕120–122.

§ 27.18 Damages and Penalties—In General

The FCA awards treble the damages sustained by the Government because of the false claim[1] or double damages if the defendant qualifies under the voluntary disclosure provisions of the FCA. Additionally, the FCA provides for penalties of $5,000–10,000 per false claim submitted.[2]

Library References:

C.J.S. United States § 168–172, 174.
West's Key No. Digests, United States ⊕120–122.

9. *See* United States v. Village of Island Park, 791 F.Supp. 354, 363 (E.D.N.Y. 1992) (holding that the Department of Justice should have known about matters at the time other government agencies knew).

10. 91 F.3d 1211 (9th Cir.1996).

11. *Id.* at 1215.

12. *Id.* at 1218.

13. 883 F.Supp. 484, 487 and n. 5 (C.D.Cal.1995), *aff'd*, 91 F.3d 1211 (9th Cir. 1996).

§ 27.18

1. 31 U.S.C. § 3729(a)(7).

2. *Id.* at § 3729(a).

§ 27.19 Damages and Penalties—Damages

A. CAUSATION

Although the FCA does not directly address materiality in the context of damages, it refers to the "damages which the Government sustains *because* of the act of the defendants."[1] [emphasis supplied] The courts have held that this requires proof of some relationship between the defendant's false statement and [the government's] damages.[2]

B. CALCULATING DAMAGES SUSTAINED

The manner of calculating the amount of damages sustained by the government varies greatly with the type of falsity at issue.[3] The general rule is that "the Government should recover, as *single* damages, the amount of money it actually paid *minus* the amount it would have paid had the claim not been false."[4] Damages are most easily calculated in cases where the defendant submitted claims for services never rendered. In these instances the full amount actually paid by the government is the amount of damage sustained.

In cases where the defendants actually supplied services of goods complying with the contract but overcharged the government for them, the amount of damages sustained is the amount overpaid by the government. For example, in *United States v. Halper*,[5] the defendant, a manager of a medical laboratory, was found to have submitted 65 claims, falsely claiming $12 per claim when the actual service rendered entitled the laboratory to only $3 per claim. The amount of damage per claim ($9) was multiplied by the number of claims (65) for a total of $585 in single damages.[6]

Calculating damages becomes more difficult in cases where the falsity is due to the improper way in which the defendant obtained the contract (i.e., bidrigging, defective pricing, kickbacks, etc.). In these instances the government received goods or services at a price it agreed to pay. Determining whether the government would have paid less without the impermissible conduct and if so, what amount, can be highly speculative. Similarly, in false certification cases, where the defendant falsified its qualifications to receive benefits or provide goods or services,

§ 27.19

1. *Id.* at § 3729(a)(7).

2. *See, e.g.:*

Third Circuit: United States v. Hibbs, 568 F.2d 347 (3d Cir.1977).

Fifth Circuit: United States v. Miller, 645 F.2d 473 (5th Cir.1981); United States v. Thomas, 709 F.2d 968 (5th Cir.1983).

Contra:

Seventh Circuit: United States v. First Nat'l Bank of Cicero, 957 F.2d 1362 (7th Cir.1992) (holding that "a demonstration that the government would not have guaranteed the loan 'but for' the false statements is sufficient to establish the causal relationship between the false claim and the government's damages....").

3. *See* JOHN T. BOESE, CIVIL FALSE CLAIMS AND QUI TAM ACTIONS Chapter 3.

4. *Id.*

5. 490 U.S. 435, 109 S.Ct. 1892, 104 L.Ed.2d 487 (1989).

6. *Id.*

it can be very difficult to determine causation and the actual loss sustained.

The difficulty in calculating damages in substandard product cases—where the defendants misrepresented the quality of the goods or services delivered—lies in determining the value of the goods or services that were actually provided. There are three tests used by courts to calculate damages in these cases. With the "benefit of the bargain" test, damages are the difference between the market value of the product the government actually received and the market value of the product the government contracted and paid for.[7] With the "out of pocket" test, damages are the difference between the contract price and the value of the product or service received. Because it relies upon an uncontestable amount, the contract price, this test is useful when the actual loss to the Government cannot be established. The problem, of course, is that this test leaves unresolved any calculation of the value of goods or services the Government actually received. A third test, which focuses on the "total value" of goods or services may be appropriate if the items supplied have no real value to the government. With this test the amount of damages is the amount paid for the goods.[8]

C.   THE MULTIPLIER: WHETHER TO DOUBLE OR TRIPLE THE SINGLE DAMAGES

Once the amount of "single" damages sustained by the government has been calculated, the court must decide whether to double or triple the amount. Defendants qualify for double damages only if they voluntarily disclose their wrongdoing to the government within "30 days after the date on which the defendant first obtained the information" and cooperate with any Government investigation of such violation.[9] The "voluntary" disclosure cannot be made in anticipation of an investigation: "at the time such person furnished the United States with the information about the violation, no criminal prosecution, civil action, or administrative action had commenced under this title with respect to such violation, and the person did not have actual knowledge of the existence of an investigation into such violation."[10]

There are risks to voluntarily disclosing wrongdoing: ferreting out the information to disclose and "turning in" individual wrongdoers can be disruptive to business and morale; voluntary disclosure may waive attorney client and work product privilege as to all the world, not just to the government; the disclosure may notify private parties of other civil

---

7.   United States v. Bornstein, 423 U.S. 303, 316 n. 13, 96 S.Ct. 523, 531, 46 L.Ed.2d 514.

8.   *See, e.g.:*

Fifth Circuit: Faulk v. United States 198 F.2d 169 (5th Cir.1952); United States v. Aerodex, Inc. 469 F.2d 1003 (5th Cir. 1972).

9.   31 U.S.C. § 3729(a)(7)(A). There are no reported cases of defendants qualifying for the double damages, probably because most cases settle where the defendant has been cooperative to such an extent.

10.   31 U.S.C. § 3729(7)(a)(c).

actions, such as medical malpractice, they may have against the disclosing entity. Plus, after incurring these risks, a court may decide that the defendant's efforts do not qualify under the FCA.

D. CREDITS

In some cases the defendant, or a third party, will have reimbursed the government in whole or part, prior to calculation of damages. Whether these credits are applied before or after damages are multiplied is significant. Supposedly, the Supreme Court resolved this issue in *United States v. Bornstein*[11] when it held that credits should have been applied after damages were multiplied.[12] The court gave several reasons for its holding: (1) The statutory language: "The statute speaks of doubling 'damages' and not doubling 'net damages' or 'uncompensated damages.' "[13] (2) Fairness: "[multiplied] damages are necessary to compensate the Government completely for the costs, delays, and inconveniences occasioned by fraudulent claims."[14] (3) Policy: It undercuts deterrence to permit the defrauder to benefit simply because other persons may compensate the government.[15]

Library References:
> C.J.S. United States § 168–172, 174.
> West's Key No. Digests, United States ⬤120–122.

§ 27.20 Damages and Penalties—Penalties

The FCA provides that persons found to have violated the Act are liable for a "civil penalty of not less than $5,000 and not more than $10,000" for each false or fraudulent claim submitted.[1] Assessing this penalty per claim is mandatory,[2] with one caveat. Courts may reduce the amount of the total award if it finds that the award violates the Constitution's prohibition against excessive fines or double jeopardy.[3]

A. ASSESSING THE PENALTY AMOUNT WITHIN THE $5,000–10,000 RANGE

11. 423 U.S. 303, 96 S.Ct. 523, 46 L.Ed.2d 514 (1976).

12. *Id.* 423 U.S. at 316–17, 96 S.Ct. at 531. One expert has suggested, however, that applying credits *after* multiplying the damages may not always be appropriate. Boese, False Claims *supra* note 5, at 3–37. Boese points out that in *Bornstein* the credits at issue were paid by a party other than the defendant in a related, but separate lawsuit. In such an instance, the harsher option of applying the credits after the multiplier makes sense. However, rewarding the defendant who voluntarily makes restitution would distinguish between cooperative and uncooperative defendants while still achieving deterrence though the double damages. *Id.*

13. *Bornstein*, 423 U.S. at 314 n. 10 (2), 96 S.Ct. at 530.

14. *Id.* at 315.

15. *Id.* at 315–17.

§ 27.20

1. 31 U.S.C. § 3729(a).

2. *Seventh Circuit:* United States v. Hughes, 585 F.2d 284, 286 (7th Cir.1978).

Eleventh Circuit: United States v. Killough, 848 F.2d 1523, 1533 (11th Cir.1988).

3. "Excessive bail shall not be required, nor excessive fines imposed, nor cruel and unusual punishments inflicted." U.S. Const., amend. VIII.

The FCA does not include guidance for courts in setting the penalty within the $5,000 to $10,000 range. Factors fashioned by the courts to set the penalty include the defendant's prior involvement in fraudulent conduct,[4] the expenses of investigation and prosecutions,[5] and the egregiousness and extent of the fraud.[6] The government bears the burden of proving that a penalty higher than $5000 is appropriate.[7]

B.   CONSTITUTIONAL CONSIDERATIONS

Beginning in 1989 with the Supreme Court's decision in *United States v. Halper*[8] and continuing until 1997 when the Court overruled *Halper*[9] there was considerable discussion as to whether penalties imposed under the False Claim Act which preceded or followed a criminal conviction constituted double jeopardy under the Fifth Amendment.

In *Halper*, the Court held: "We therefore hold that under the Double Jeopardy Clause a defendant who already has been punished in a criminal prosecution may not be subjected to an additional civil sanction to the extent that the second sanction may not fairly be characterized as remedial, but only as a deterrent or retribution."[10] The Court found that if the total award against Halper in the FCA suit was disproportionate to the actual damages caused by Halper's submission of false claims, such an award would be punitive.[11] Since the defendant had already been convicted for crimes arising from the same transaction, the punitive civil award would violate the double jeopardy clause.[12] Although the Court held that the rule announced in *Halper* would apply only in the "rare" case where the civil sanction assessed is "overwhelmingly disproportionate to the damages ... caused,"[13] *Halper* defense arguments became routine, although usually unsuccessful.

In *Hudson v. United States*,[14] the Supreme Court "in large part disavow[ed] the method of analysis used in [*Halper*]."[15] Hudson and his colleagues were bank officials and shareholders of two banks in Oklahoma. An investigation by the Office of the Comptroller of the Currency (OCC) concluded that they "had used their bank positions to arranged a series of loans to third parties, in violation of various federal banking

---

4. United States v. Murphy, 937 F.2d 1032, 1035–36 (6th Cir.1991).

5. *Second Circuit:* United States v. Pani, 717 F.Supp. 1013, 1017–19 (S.D.N.Y. 1989).

Seventh Circuit: United States v. Stocker, 798 F.Supp. 531, 536 (E.D.Wis.1992).

6. Pena v. United States Dept. of Agriculture, 811 F.Supp. 419, 425–26 (E.D.Ark.1992).

7. *See, e.g.,* United States v. Fliegler, 756 F.Supp. 688, 694 (E.D.N.Y.1990).

8. 490 U.S. 435, 109 S.Ct. 1892, 104 L.Ed.2d 487 (1989).

9. Hudson v. United States, ___ U.S. ___, 118 S.Ct. 488, 139 L.Ed.2d 450 (1997).

10. *Id.* at 448–49.

11. *Id.* at 452. The Court remanded the case "to permit the Government to demonstrate that the District Court's assessment of the injuries was erroneous." *Id.,* 490 U.S. at 452, 109 S.Ct. at 1903.

12. *Halper,* 490 U.S. at 449.

13. *Id.*

14. ___ U.S. ___, 118 S.Ct. 488, 139 L.Ed.2d 450 (1997).

15. *Id.* at 491.

statutes and regulations."[16] The OCC issued an assessment of penalties and barred them from further participation "in the conduct of any insured depository institution."[17] Thereafter, all were charged in a 22–count indictment alleging conspiracy, misapplication of bank funds and making false bank entries. The defendants' motion to dismiss the charges on grounds of double jeopardy was denied. The Supreme Court affirmed the denial.

Describing the *Halper* decision as "ill-considered,"[18] the Court noted that the *Halper* Court "deviated from traditional double jeopardy doctrine."[19] To determine whether the double jeopardy protection was applicable the *Halper* Court focused on whether the sanction at issue appeared excessive in relation to its nonpunitive purposes. Instead, according to the Court in *Hudson*, the *Halper* Court should have focused on the traditional double jeopardy question: whether the punishment at issue is "criminal." The Court noted that:

> Whether a particular punishment is criminal or civil, is at least initially, a matter of statutory construction. A court must first ask whether the legislature, in establishing the penalizing mechanism, indicated either expressly or impliedly a preference for one label or the other.[20]

Holding that *Halper's* test for determining whether a particular sanction is punitive "has proved unworkable,"[21] the Court emphasized the importance of looking to Congress' intent. In the case before it, the Court held that "[i]t is evident that Congress intended the OCC money penalties and debarment sanctions ... to be civil in nature."[22] Moreover, the Court found "little evidence, much less the clearest proof we require, suggesting that the OCC money penalties or debarment sanctions are so punitive in form and effect as to render them criminal despite Congress' intent to the contrary."[23] While recognizing that the OCC sanctions would deter others from conduct similar to that of the defendants and that deterrence is a traditional goal of criminal punishments, the Court nevertheless held that "the mere presence of this purpose is insufficient to render a sanction criminal."[24]

The Court concluded by noting that "some of the ills at which *Halper* was directed are addressed by other constitutional provisions[,]" including the Due Process and Equal Protection clauses and the protection against excessive fines contained in the Eighth Amendment.[25]

In *Austin v. United States*[26] the Supreme Court relied upon the excessive fines clause of the Eighth Amendment of the Constitution[27] to

16. *Id.* at 492.

17. *Id.*

18. *Id.* at 494.

19. *Id.*

20. *Id.* at 493 (internal quotation marks and citations deleted).

21. *Id.* at 494.

22. *Id.* at 495.

23. *Id.*

24. *Id.* at 496.

25. *Id.* at 495.

26. 509 U.S. 602, 113 S.Ct. 2801, 125 L.Ed.2d 488 (1993).

27. "Excessive bail shall not be required, nor excessive fines imposed, nor cruel and unusual punishments inflicted." U.S. Const. amend. VIII.

set aside the civil forfeiture of residential and business property[28] where a drug transaction had taken place. Recognizing the punitive and deterrent purposes of civil forfeiture, the Court held that the Eight Amendment's Excessive Fines provision applied to civil sanctions as well as criminal sanctions and remanded the case to determine whether the forfeiture of Austin's property was excessive as prohibited by the Eighth Amendment. *United States ex rel. Smith v. Gilbert Realty Co., Inc.*[29] demonstrates the *Austin* analysis in an FCA case. Gilbert Realty Co., a landlord of inexpensive residential apartments, was found to have violated the FCA 58 times "by making 7 false statements to a local housing authority and by endorsing 51 rental checks."[30] The actual damages were $1,630. Tripled, the damages were $4,890. Penalties of $5,000 for 58 false claims totaled $290,000.[31] The court acknowledged that the $5,000–10,000 penalty per claims was mandatory under the FCA but, citing *Austin*, the court found application of the mandatory penalty provision excessive. It set aside the penalties for the rental checks, leaving intact total penalties of $35,000.[32]

Although investigative costs are not included when calculating the damages incurred by the government, investigative costs may be relevant in determining whether the total award violates the constitutional prohibition of excessive fines. For example in *United States v. Pani*,[33] the government sued Pani, a neurosurgeon, and Pani's medical clinic under the FCA for filing 157 claims with Medicare for surgeries never performed. Pani had already been convicted on federal felony charges arising from many of these false claims.[34] Pani argued that pursuant to *Halper*, the civil judgment constituted double jeopardy because the civil award bore "no rational relation to the goal of compensating the Government for its loss. . . ."[35] If true the civil penalty would be punitive under *Halper*. In rejecting Pani's argument the court looked to "expenses of investigation and prosecution as well as the actual damages to find that the civil remedy bore 'a rational relationship to the goal of compensating the Government for its loss.' "[36]

28. The property included a mobile home and auto body shop. *Austin* 509 U.S. at 604, 113 S.Ct. at 2802.

29. 840 F.Supp. 71 (E.D.Mich.1993).

30. *Gilbert Realty*, 840 F.Supp. at 72.

31. *Id.* at 74. "[E]ach governed by a contract that stated an endorsement constitutes certification of nonreceipt of additional rent beyond the amount allowed." 840 F.Supp. at 72.

32. *Id.* at 15. Each act is a violation leading to . . . $5,000 for each false certification to the housing authority. *Id.* at 75. *See* United States v. Killough, 848 F.2d 1523, 1534 (11th Cir.1988) (finding amount of damages to be remedial, not punitive, and thus not within Halper double jeopardy problem).

33. 717 F.Supp. 1013 (S.D.N.Y.1989).

34. *Id.* at 1014.

35. *Id.* at 1019 (quoting *Halper*, 490 U.S. at 447, 109 S.Ct. at 1901).

36. *Id.* quoting *Halper*, 490 U.S. at 447, 109 S.Ct. at 1901. *Cf.* United States v. Ridglea State Bank, 357 F.2d 495, 497 (5th Cir.1966), In *Ridglea* the court rejected defendant's argument that no cause of action is stated under the FCA if the Government has not paid money on the false claims. The court noted: "The investigation necessary to detect a false claim costs the Government money even if no money is paid on the claims." *Id.* at 497.

§ 27.20 Bibliography

132 Cong. Rec. H6483 (daily ed. Sept. 9, 1986).

BOESE, JOHN T., CIVIL FALSE CLAIMS AND QUI TAM ACTIONS.

BUCY, PAMELA H., HEALTH CARE FRAUD: CRIMINAL, CIVIL AND ADMINISTRATIVE LAW § 4.01 (1996).

Callahan, Uleta Sangrey, & Dworkin, Terry Monehe, *Do Good and Get Rich: Financial Incentives for Whistleblowing and The False Claims Act*, 37 VILL.L.REV. 273 (1992).

DeWitt, Anthony L., *Badges? We Don't Need No Stinking Badges! Citizen Attorney Generals and The False Claims Act*, 65 UMKC L. REV. 30 (1996).

False Claims Act Amendments: Hearings on H.R. 334 Before the Subcomm. on Admin. Law & Gov't Relations of the House Comm. on the Judiciary.

France, Steve, *The Private War on Pentagon Fraud*, 76 ABA JOURNAL 46, 47 (Mar. 1990).

Helmer, James B., Jr., & Neff, Robert Clark, Jr., *War Stories: A History of the Qui Tam Provision's of the False Claims Act*, 18 OHIO N.U.L.REV. 35 (1991).

MEDICARE & MEDICAID GUIDE (CCH).

Note, *Research and Relators: The False Claims Act and Scientific Misconduct*. 70 WASH U.L.Q.

*

PART V

FORFEITURE

CHAPTER 28

CIVIL FORFEITURE

Table of Sections

WESTLAW Electronic Research Guide

See WESTLAW Electronic Research Guide preceding the Summary of Contents.

Library References:

C.J.S. Forfeitures § 1–10; RICO (Racketeer Influenced and Corrupt Organizations)
§ 30–34.
West's Key No. Digests, Forfeitures ⚖1–11.

§ 28.1 Introduction

Civil forfeiture is one of two types of forfeiture. The other type, criminal forfeiture, is discussed in §§ 29.1–29.23, *infra*.

Civil forfeiture does not depend on a criminal conviction but is a free-standing civil action. The government is the plaintiff, and the defendant is the property that the government is trying to seize. Civil forfeitures are actions *in rem* rather than actions *in personam* because they are actions against a thing or *res* rather than against a person. Because civil forfeiture is an action against a thing, jurisdiction is established by seizing it. Once the government files a civil forfeiture action, all persons having an interest in the property must appear in the lawsuit and establish their claim or forfeit their property.

The history of forfeiture indicates it is an ancient concept traceable to the earliest notions of law and justice in the Judeo–Christian tradition.[1] The concept existed in English common law in the form of deodand, forfeiture of estate, and statutory forfeiture.[2] Deodand was the confiscation of any "inanimate object" which caused the accidental death of a King's subject.[3] Forfeiture of estate was essentially a criminal sanction levied against convicted felons and traitors. This doctrine did not rest on the "guilty property" fiction but rather was grounded in the belief that property ownership was "a right derived from society which one lost by violating society's laws."[4] Finally, statutory forfeiture allowed forfeiture of illegal goods and the ships (conveyances) that transported them. Statutory forfeiture has been described as a "product of the confluence and merger of the deodand tradition and the belief that the right to own property could be denied the wrongdoer."[5]

Of the three English common law doctrines of forfeiture (deodand, forfeiture of estate, and statutory forfeiture), only statutory forfeiture survived in America.[6] The common law courts of the colonies, and subsequently the Confederation of States, adopted statutory forfeiture to enforce customs laws. The doctrine was codified by the First Congress, which promulgated statutes providing for the forfeiture of ships and cargoes involved in customs violations. While subsequent legislation

§ 28.1

1. *See*

Supreme Court: Calero–Toledo v. Pearson Yacht Leasing Co., 416 U.S. 663, 681, 94 S.Ct. 2080, 2090, 40 L.Ed.2d 452 (1974).

Second Circuit: United States v. All Right, Title and Interest in Real Property and Appurtenances thereto Known as 785 St. Nicholas Ave., 983 F.2d 396 (2d Cir.1993)(tracing forfeiture to ancient Roman law).

2. *See* Calero–Toledo v. Pearson Yacht Leasing, 416 U.S. 663, 681–83, 94 S.Ct. 2080, 2090–91, 40 L.Ed.2d 452 (1974); Austin v. United States, 509 U.S. 602, 113 S.Ct. 2801, 125 L.Ed.2d 488 (1993).

3. *Calero-Toledo*, 416 U.S. at 681.

4. *Austin,* 509 U.S. at 612, 113 S.Ct. at 2806, *citing* 1.W. Blackstone, Commentaries.

5. Calero–Toledo v. Pearson Yacht Leasing Co., 416 U.S. 663, 682, 94 S.Ct. 2080, 2091, 40 L.Ed.2d 452 (1974); Austin v. United States, 509 U.S. at 612, 113 S.Ct. at 2806.

6. Calero–Toledo v. Pearson Yacht Leasing Co., 416 U.S. at 682, 94 S.Ct. at 2091; *Austin v. United States,* 509 U.S. 602, 613, 113 S.Ct. 2801, 2807, 125 L.Ed.2d 488.

expanded the reach of forfeiture (to include ships engaged in piracy, for example), the scope of forfeitable property remained rooted in tradition, and thus limited to contraband and property which had been "misused," *i.e.*, used in criminal activity.[7]

Forfeiture was largely ignored until 1970 when Congress enacted the drug forfeiture statute, § 881. Since 1970 Congress has consistently expanded not only the transactions which support forfeiture, but the scope of forfeitable property as well. Modern statutory definitions of forfeitable property include not only contraband and instruments of crime but the proceeds of crime and property facilitating crime as well.

Today there are over 100 civil forfeiture statutes.[8] The most frequently used ones are § 881,[9] which covers forfeiture based on drug transactions, and § 981,[10] which covers forfeiture based on a collection of federal crimes. Another civil forfeiture statute, § 5317,[11] covers forfeiture for one of the money laundering crimes—reports on the import and export of monetary instruments. These three main forfeiture statutes are discussed in detail. The numerous other civil forfeiture provisions are noted briefly *infra.*[12]

§ 28.2   Forfeiture Based on Drugs: 21 U.S.C. § 881—Property Which is Subject to Forfeiture

Defining property as forfeitable under § 881 requires that the statute list the property as subject to forfeiture and that the common law nexus test be met.

A.   PROPERTY DESCRIBED IN THE STATUTE

Section 881 authorizes forfeiture of various kinds of property when it is connected in various ways with drugs. The statute has eleven subsections which describe the property subject to forfeiture.

— Subsection (a)(1) allows forfeiture of the drugs themselves, when they were manufactured, distributed, dispensed or acquired in violation of Title 21.

— Subsection (a)(2) covers raw materials, products, and equipment used or intended for use in drug manufacture, compounding,

---

7. For a detailed history of forfeiture, *see generally*

Supreme Court: Austin v. United States, 509 U.S. 602, 113 S.Ct. 2801, 125 L.Ed.2d 488 (1993); United States v. A Parcel of Land, Buildings, Appurtenances and Improvements, Known as 92 Buena Vista Ave., Rumson, N.J., 507 U.S. 111, 113 S.Ct. 1126, 122 L.Ed.2d 469 (1993); Calero–Toledo v. Pearson Yacht Leasing Co., 416 U.S. 663, 94 S.Ct. 2080, 40 L.Ed.2d 452 (1974).

Second Circuit: United States v. All Right, Title and Interest in Real Property and Appurtenances thereto Known as 789 St. Nicholas Ave., 983 F.2d 396 (2d Cir. 1993).

8. *See* United States v. Marolf, 973 F.Supp. 1139, (C.D.Cal.1997)("over 100" civil forfeiture statutes exist), *citing* Judith Secher, Asset Forfeiture: Practice and Procedure (1995).

9. 21 U.S.C. § 881.

10. 18 U.S.C. § 981.

11. 31 U.S.C. § 5317.

12. *See* § 28.15.

processing, delivery, import or export.[1]

— Subsection (a)(3) authorizes forfeiture of containers for drugs and drug equipment.

— Subsection (a)(4) allows forfeiture of conveyances used or intended for use to transport or in any manner to facilitate the transportation, sale, receipt, possession, or concealment of drugs, with exceptions for common carriers and innocent owners.

— Subsection (a)(5) covers books, records, and research used or intended for use in violation of drug laws.

— Subsection (a)(6) covers things of value furnished or intended to be furnished in exchange for drugs; all proceeds traceable to such an exchange; and all moneys, negotiable instruments, and securities used or intended to be used to facilitate drug crimes. This section has an exception for innocent owners.

— Subsection (a)(7) allows forfeiture of real property and interests in real property when it is used or intended to be used in any manner or part to commit or facilitate commission of a drug felony, with an exception for innocent owners.

— Subsection (a)(8) covers drugs that are possessed.

— Subsection (a)(9) covers chemicals and equipment used to violate the drug laws.

— Subsection (a)(10) covers drug paraphernalia.

— Subsection (a)(11) authorizes forfeiture of firearms used or intended to be used to facilitate transportation, sale, receipt, possession or concealment of drugs or drug equipment.

The three subsections under which the government usually seeks forfeiture are § 881(a)(4)(conveyances), § 881(a)(6)(monies and proceeds), and § 881(a)(7)(real property).

Before examining these sections individually, some common issues can be described. The term *facilitate* appears in all three of the subsections. Courts have interpreted facilitate broadly as making an activity "more or less free from obstruction or hindrance"[2] and making it "easy or less difficult."[3] All three of the subsections also include property that is not only used with drug activity but is *intended to be used* with drug activity. Courts have had no trouble reading this to mean that the

§ 28.2

1. Other "equipment" besides that used to manufacture the drugs can also be within the scope of this subsection.

See, e.g.,

Fourth Circuit: United States v. Real Property Known as 5528 Belle Pond Drive, 783 F.Supp. 253 (E.D.Va.1991), *aff'd,* 979 F.2d 849 (4th Cir.1992)(computer used to store data about marijuana growing operation subject to forfeiture under § 881(a)(2)).

Ninth Circuit: United States v. Kim, 803 F.Supp. 352 (D.Haw.1992), *aff'd,* 25 F.3d 1426 (9th Cir.1994)(cellular phone subject to forfeiture under § 881(a)(2) because it was used to arrange drug transactions).

2. United States v. Premises Known as 3639–2nd St., Minneapolis, 869 F.2d 1093 (8th Cir.1989).

3. United States v. One 1971 Chevy Corvette, 496 F.2d 210, 212 (5th Cir.1974).

property needn't actually be used with drugs as long as it was intended to be used that way.[4] The courts often conclude that intent is determinative.[5]

i. Conveyances: § 881(a)(4)

Subsection (a)(4) allows forfeiture of "conveyances, including aircraft, vehicles, or vessels, which are used or intended for use, to transport, or in any manner to facilitate the transportation, sale, receipt, possession, or concealment, of" drugs or drug equipment.[6]

Under the theory of facilitating drug trafficking, a vehicle may be forfeited when it is used to get to the scene of a drug transaction,[7] as an escort vehicle,[8] or to get to a meeting of co-conspirators to arrange for a drug transaction.[9]

As noted above, the vehicle need not be actually used with drugs;

4. *See, e.g.,*

Second Circuit: United States v. One 1974 Eldorado Sedan, 548 F.2d 421 (2d Cir.1977).

Fifth Circuit: United States v. One 1977 Cadillac Coupe DeVille, 644 F.2d 500 (5th Cir.1981).

Sixth Circuit: United States v. One 1980 Cadillac Eldorado and $43,000, 705 F.2d 862 (6th Cir.1983).

Eighth Circuit: United States v. $88,-500, 671 F.2d 293 (8th Cir.1982)(intent, not the actual presence of a controlled substance, is the determining factor).

Eleventh Circuit: United States v. One 1980 Bertram 58' Motor Yacht, 876 F.2d 884 (11th Cir.1989).

5. *See*

Third Circuit: United States v. RD. 1, Box 1, Thompsontown, Delaware, 952 F.2d 53 (3d Cir.1991)(§ 881(a)(7)).

Sixth Circuit: United States v. Lots 12, 13, 14, 15, 869 F.2d 942 (6th Cir.1989) (§ 881(a)(7)); United States v. One 1980 Cadillac Eldorado, 705 F.2d 862 (6th Cir. 1983) (§ 881(a)(4)).

6. 21 U.S.C. § 881(a)(4).

7. *See*

Second Circuit: United States v. One 1974 Cadillac Eldorado Sedan, 548 F.2d 421 (2d Cir.1977).

Fourth Circuit: United States v. 1966 Beechcraft Aircraft Model King Air A90, 777 F.2d 947 (4th Cir.1985).

Fifth Circuit: United States v. One 1979 Mercury Cougar, 666 F.2d 228 (5th Cir.1982).

Sixth Circuit: United States v. One 1984 Cadillac, 888 F.2d 1133 (6th

Cir.1989)(*citing* United States v. One 1977 Cadillac Coupe Deville, 644 F.2d 500 (5th Cir.Unit B 1981) for its holding that transporting a dealer to a drug drop would meet the substantial connection test).

Eleventh Circuit: United States v. One 1979 Porsche Coupe, 709 F.2d 1424, 1427 (11th Cir.1983).

However, at least two circuits have required an "antecedent connection" between the vehicle used to transport the co-conspirators to the scene and the transaction itself before such facts will support forfeiture of the vehicle under a facilitation theory.

See

First Circuit: United States v. One 1972 Chevrolet Corvette, 625 F.2d 1026, 1029 (1st Cir.1980)("We find no decision upholding forfeiture on the basis of the facilitation clause in which there was not an antecedent relationship between the vehicle and the sale of narcotics.")(*citing, inter alia,* United States v. One 1970 Pontiac GTO, 529 F.2d 65 (9th Cir.1976)).

Furthermore, the First, Ninth and Tenth Circuits have held that the mere transportation of conspirators to the scene of a transaction does not meet the required substantial connection.

See

First Circuit: United States v. One 1972 Chevrolet Corvette, 625 F.2d 1026 (1st Cir.1980).

Ninth Circuit: Howard v. United States, 423 F.2d 1102 (9th Cir.1970).

Tenth Circuit: Platt v. United States, 163 F.2d 165 (10th Cir.1947).

8. United States v. 1980 BMW 3201, 559 F.Supp. 382, 384 (E.D.N.Y.1983).

9. United States v. 1990 Toyota 4Runner, 9 F.3d 651, 653–54 (7th Cir.1993).

intent to use is enough.[10] Thus a vehicle purchased and modified for future use in the transportation of drugs, even if it is never so used, is subject to forfeiture.[11]

Items that are affixed to the conveyance are forfeited along with it if they are considered permanent parts of it.[12]

However, not every vehicle involved with a drug transaction is subject to forfeiture; it must have a sufficiently close connection to the drug transaction.[13] This limit is discussed *infra* in the nexus section.

While the amount of drugs for which the conveyance was used is not controlling, a mere trace of a controlled substance is insufficient.[14]

ii.　Moneys and Proceeds: § 881(a)(6)

Subsection (a)(6) allows forfeiture of three kinds of property: (1) things of value furnished or intended to be furnished in exchange for drugs, (2) proceeds of such exchanges, and (3) moneys used or intended to be used to facilitate a drug crime.

As to things exchanged for drugs, it is usually money, and is sometimes called "buy money."[15] But the statute is not limited to money; it covers all *things of value* exchanged for drugs. As the Second Circuit stated, "The statute covers any asset exchanged directly for narcotics, such as a bar of gold or a car."[16]

The statute also covers proceeds traceable to drug exchanges. Assets purchased with drug proceeds,[17] interest on proceeds, or rents or dividends on property purchased with proceeds are all forfeitable under this

10. United States v. One 1980 Cadillac Eldorado, 705 F.2d 862 (6th Cir. 1983)(§ 881(a)(4)).

11. *See*

Second Circuit: United States v. One 1974 Eldorado Sedan, 548 F.2d 421 (2d Cir.1977).

Sixth Circuit: United States v. One 1980 Cadillac Eldorado and $43,000, 705 F.2d 862 (6th Cir.1983), *citing* United States v. One 1977 Cadillac Coupe DeVille, 644 F.2d 500 (5th Cir.1981).

Eighth Circuit: United States v. $88,-500, 671 F.2d 293 (8th Cir.1982)(intent, and not the actual presence of a controlled substance, is the determining factor).

Eleventh Circuit: United States v. One 1980 Bertram 58' Motor Yacht, 876 F.2d 884 (11th Cir.1989)(yacht fitted with hidden storage bins was "intended for use" within the statute even though the vessel was seized before any controlled substances were transported).

12. United States v. One 1978 Mercedes Benz, 711 F.2d 1297 (5th Cir.

1983)(car telephone not forfeited along with car based on analogy to law of fixtures).

13. *See* United States v. $39,000 in Canadian Currency, 801 F.2d 1210, 1221 n. 10 (10th Cir.1986)(collecting cases in which the nexus between the vehicle and the underlying drug transaction was insufficient).

14. *See* United States v. One Gates Learjet, 861 F.2d 868, 872 (5th Cir.1988)(denying forfeiture because "The amount in question [3–4 milligrams] was too small to be possessed, used, exchanged, or enhanced.").

15. *See, e.g.,* The Forfeiture (Confiscation) of the Proceeds of Drug Trafficking by the United States Government, Office of Chief Counsel, Drug Enforcement Administration, United States Department of Justice, Nov., 1994, page 6.

16. United States v. Banco Cafetero Panama, 797 F.2d 1154, 1158 (2d Cir.1986).

17. United States v. A Parcel of Land, Buildings, Appurtenances and Improvements Known as 92 Buena Vista Ave., Rumson, N.J., 507 U.S. 111, 129, 113 S.Ct. 1126, 1137, 122 L.Ed.2d 469 (1993).

subsection.[18]

One question under this language is how long proceeds remain proceeds, and therefore subject to forfeiture. Do proceeds ever lose their taint from drug activity? The Second Circuit has said, "Congress has also make it clear that 'traceable proceeds' includes an asset indirectly exchanged for narcotics in one or more 'intervening legitimate transactions, or otherwise changed in form. . . .' . . . If the seller of drugs uses the cash he received to buy a bar of gold or a car, that asset is 'traceable proceeds,'. . . ."[19] No court has set a limit on how long the characterization of the property as proceeds continues.

Another question raised by forfeiting proceeds is whether cumulative forfeiture is allowed. The Second Circuit stated that it may be generally available, but not in the context of bank accounts. As the court explained:

> There is a plausible argument . . . for cumulative forfeiture of all assets exchanged for drugs or drug proceeds. For example, if $100 from the sale of drugs is exchanged for a watch, both the $100 in the hands of the watch seller and the watch in the hands of the drug seller are vulnerable to forfeiture as traceable proceeds, and the Government may well be entitled to forfeit both. However, cumulative forfeiture is not permissible simply because available accounting rules afford the Government more than one route in tracing forfeitable proceeds. For example, if $100 from the sale of drugs is deposited in an account funded with untainted money, $100 in the account and each $100 withdrawal are all vulnerable to forfeiture, but the Government can obtain only a single forfeiture of $100.[20]

Another issue in defining proceeds of drug transactions is deciding whether a credit balance in a bank account is proceeds traceable to drug exchanges. If the account is used only for drug money, the solution is clear: it's all traceable to drug transactions, and it's all forfeitable.[21] But when legitimate money is commingled in the account with the drug proceeds, the question is what part of that account is forfeitable as proceeds traceable to drug dealing? In United States v. Banco Cafetero Panama,[22] the Second Circuit answered this question by adopting the "lowest intermediate balance" approach.[23] It described this approach this way: "If $100 from a drug sale is deposited into an active account, one approach is to consider the account to be 'traceable proceeds' to the extent of $100 as long as the account balance never falls below that sum. This might be called a 'drugs-in, last-out' rule."[24] This was the approach

18. United States v. One Parcel of Real Estate Located at 116 Villa Rella Dr., 675 F.Supp. 645, 646 (S.D.Fla.1987).

19. United States v. Banco Cafetero Panama, 797 F.2d 1154, 1158 (2d Cir.1986).

20. United States v. Banco Cafetero Panama, 797 F.2d 1154, 1161 n. 9 (2d Cir. 1986).

21. United States v. Banco Cafetero Panama, 797 F.2d 1154, 1158 (2d Cir.1986).

22. 797 F.2d 1154 (2d Cir.1986).

23. *Id.* at 1159.

24. *Id.* (footnote omitted).

the court adopted. *Banco Cafetero* is the leading case on defining proceeds of drug transactions in a bank account.

The drawback of this approach is that an account holder can insulate money from forfeiture by periodically emptying out the account so the balance is zero for a time. Thereafter, untainted money added to the account is immune from forfeiture.[25] When this practice of "zeroing out" accounts to defeat forfeiture arose under the money laundering forfeiture provisions in § 981, Congress passed a statute closing this loophole under § 981.[26] The problem remains, however, under § 881.

The final property forfeitable under § 881(a)(6) is moneys used or intended to be used to facilitate a drug crime. As noted above, facilitate is defined as making an activity more or less free from obstruction or hindrance, or making it easy or less difficult.[27]

iii. Real Property: § 881(a)(7)

Subsection (a)(7) allows forfeiture of real property interests (in a whole lot or a tract of land and appurtenances and improvements) when the property is "used or intended to be used, in any manner or part, to commit, or to facilitate the commission of" a drug felony.[28] The statute expressly includes the real property itself and "any right, title, and interest (including any leasehold interests)"[29] in the property.

The typical cases under this section involve real property where a drug deal is made[30] or drugs are stored.[31]

Under a facilitation theory, the property does not have to be an essential part of the commission of the underlying conduct.[32] The subsection allows forfeiture of the entire parcel of land when any part of it is used *in any manner or part* in the proscribed fashion.[33] Thus a defendant

25. *Id.* n.5.

26. 18 U.S.C. § 984, discussed in § 28.9(A)(i)(b) *infra.*

27. *See* § 28.2(A) *supra.*

28. 21 U.S.C. § 881(a)(7).

29. *Id.*

30. *See, e.g.,*

Second Circuit: United States v. All Right, Title and Interest in Real Property and Appurtenances Thereto Known as 785 St. Nicholas Ave., 983 F.2d 396 (2d Cir. 1993).

Fourth Circuit: United States v. Nelson, 62 F.3d 1415 (4th Cir.1995); United States v. Santoro, 866 F.2d 1538 (4th Cir. 1989).

31. *See* United States v. Schifferli, 895 F.2d 987 (4th Cir.1990)("the typical factual setting for § 881(a)(7) forfeitures" is where a "drug dealer uses real property, often a home, to store or sell illegal drugs."). *See, e.g.,* United States v. Nelson, 62 F.3d 1415 (4th Cir.1995).

32. *See*

Fourth Circuit: United States v. Schifferli, 895 F.2d 987 (4th Cir.1990)("It is ... irrelevant whether the property's role in the crime is integral, essential or indispensable. The term 'facilitate' implies that the property need only make the prohibited conduct 'less difficult' or 'more or less free from obstruction or hindrance.' ").

Eighth Circuit: United States v. Premises Known as 3639–2nd St., 869 F.2d 1093 (8th Cir.1989).

Eleventh Circuit: United States v. Approximately 50 Acres of Real Property Located at 42450 Highway 441 North Fort Drum, 920 F.2d 900 (11th Cir.1991)(citing various examples of language used to define "facilitate").

33. *See*

First Circuit: United States v. A Parcel of Land with a Building Located Thereon at 40 Moon Hill Road, 884 F.2d 41, 45 (1st Cir.1989).

who conducts a drug sale on his driveway subjects the lot and the house on it to forfeiture,[34] and a defendant who writes illegal prescriptions at her dental office forfeits the office.[35] Another example of real property forfeited under this subsection is growing fields.[36] Also, land pledged as security to finance a drug deal is forfeitable as facilitating real property.[37]

iv. Relation Back

The statute states that all right, title, and interest in forfeitable property vests in the United States upon the commission of the act that gives rise to forfeiture.[38] Thus the government's title relates back to the time of the act that gives rise to forfeiture, and a claimant cannot defeat the forfeiture by transferring the property after the act. Transferees by sale, gift or devise[39] as well as "finders"[40] are all defeated since, under the legal fiction of relation back, title is in the government at the time of the transfer. However, the innocent owner defense, discussed *infra* in § 28.6(A), protects the interests of some transferees.

B. NEXUS REQUIREMENT

Once the property is described in the statute, to be forfeitable it must also have a sufficient connection to the drug activity. This is called the nexus requirement.[41] The nexus requirement is not based on any

Second Circuit: United States v. 141st St. Corp., 911 F.2d 870, 880 (2d Cir.1990).

Third Circuit: United States v. One 107.9 Acre Parcel of Land Located in Warren Township, Bradford County, 898 F.2d 396, 400 (3d Cir.1990).

Fourth Circuit: United States v. Santoro, 866 F.2d 1538 (4th Cir.1989).

Ninth Circuit: United States v. Tax Lot 1500, Township 38 South, Further Identified as 300 Cove Road, 861 F.2d 232, 235 (9th Cir.1988).

34. *Fourth Circuit:* United States v. Santoro, 866 F.2d 1538 (4th Cir.1989); *Eleventh Circuit:* United States v. 3097 S.W. 111th Ave., 921 F.2d 1551, 1557 (11th Cir.1991).

35. *See* United States v. Schifferli, 895 F.2d 987, 991 (4th Cir.1990). However, the court limited its holding, stating, "Cognizant of the severity of forfeiture, however, we do not hold that any writing of an illegal prescription on a given property automatically renders the property forfeitable. Instead, we believe that the facts of each case will determine whether forfeiture is appropriate. In this case, the direct and continuing relationship between the property and the crimes easily supports a finding of forfeiture under § 881(a)(7)."

36. *See*

Second Circuit: United States v. Premises and Real Property at 250 Kreag Road, 739 F.Supp. 120 (W.D.N.Y.1990).

Sixth Circuit: United States v. Miller, 870 F.2d 1067 (6th Cir.1989).

Eighth Circuit: United States v. Klein, 850 F.2d 404 (8th Cir.1988).

Ninth Circuit: United States v. Roberts, 747 F.2d 537 (9th Cir.1984).

37. United States v. RD. 1, Box 1, Thompsontown, Delaware, 952 F.2d 53 (3d Cir.1991).

38. 21 U.S.C. § 881(h).

39. *In re* One 1985 Nissan, 300ZX, 889 F.2d 1317, 1319 (4th Cir.1989).

40. Sanchez v. United States, 781 F.Supp. 835, 840 (D.P.R.1991), *aff'd*, 976 F.2d 724 (1st Cir.1992)(claimants alleged they found $43 million in buried barrels).

41. *See, e.g.,*

Fifth Circuit: United States v. One 1978 Mercedes Benz Four–Door Sedan, 711 F.2d 1297, 1303 (5th Cir.1983).

Eighth Circuit: United States v. Premises known as 3639–2nd St., Minneapolis, 869 F.2d 1093, 1096 (8th Cir.1989) (describing the "so-called nexus test").

specific language in the statute; courts infer it based on the words of the statute generally.

Two nexus tests have developed,[42] resulting in a fairly even split in the circuits. One approach, the "substantial connection" approach, requires that the property to be forfeited have a substantial connection to the prohibited drug transaction.[43] This approach is used in the First,[44] Fourth[45] and Sixth[46] Circuits. This approach is more rigorous for the government; it has to prove a closer connection between the drugs and the property. The other approach is to impose no requirement of a substantial connection.[47] This is sometimes called the "sufficient nexus" approach,[48] and theoretically allows forfeiture based on a looser connection between the drugs and property. This approach is taken by the Second,[49] Third,[50] Seventh,[51] Ninth[52] and Tenth[53] Circuits. The Eleventh Circuit has discussed the two standards but has not adopted one or the other.[54]

42. *See* United States v. RD. 1, Box 1, Thompsontown, Delaware, 952 F.2d 53, 56–57 (3d Cir.1991) (identifying two tests).

43. *See*

First Circuit: United States v. Parcel of Land and Residence at 28 Emery Street, Merrimac, 914 F.2d 1 (1st Cir.1990).

Third Circuit: United States v. RD. 1, Box 1, Thompsontown, Delaware, 952 F.2d 53 (3d Cir.1991).

Fourth Circuit: United States v. Nelson, 1995 WL 470851 *1 (4th Cir.)(unpublished opinion).

44. United States v. Parcel of Land and Residence at 28 Emery Street, Merrimac, 914 F.2d 1 (1st Cir.1990).

45. United States v. Nelson, 62 F.3d 1415, 1995 WL 470851 *1 (4th Cir.1995); United States v. Borromeo, 995 F.2d 23, 26 (4th Cir.) *vacated in part on other grounds,* 1 F.3d 219 (4th Cir.1993); United States v. Schifferli, 895 F.2d 987 (4th Cir.1990); United States v. Santoro, 866 F.2d 1538 (4th Cir.1989)(substantial connection test used).

46. United States v. One 1984 Cadillac, 888 F.2d 1133 (6th Cir.1989).

47. *See, e.g.,* United States v. One Parcel of Real Estate Commonly Known as 916 Douglas Ave., Elgin, 903 F.2d 490 (7th Cir.1990).

48. *See*

Second Circuit: United States v. Premises and Real Property at 4492 S. Livonia Road, 889 F.2d 1258, 1264 (2d Cir.1989).

Third Circuit: United States v. RD. 1, Box 1, Thompsontown, Delaware, 952 F.2d 53 at 56 (3d Cir.1991), *citing 4492 S. Livonia Road,* 889 F.2d at 1264 (2d Cir.1989).

Tenth Circuit: United States v. 9844 S. Titan Court, Unit 9, Littleton, Colo., 75 F.3d 1470 (10th Cir.1996).

49. *See*

Second Circuit: United States v. All Right, Title and Interest in Real Property and Appurtenances Thereto Known as 785 St. Nicholas Ave., 983 F.2d 396 (2d Cir.1993).

Ninth Circuit: United States v. Daccarett, 6 F.3d 37, 51 (2d Cir.1993).

50. United States v. RD. 1, Box 1, Thompsontown, Delaware, 952 F.2d 53 (3d Cir.1991).

51. United States v. One Parcel of Real Estate Commonly Known as 916 Douglas Ave., Elgin, 903 F.2d 490 (7th Cir.1990)(plain language is clearly broad in scope so no need to superimpose substantial connection requirement; nexus must only be more than incidental or fortuitous).

52. United States v. 1 Parcel of Real Property, 904 F.2d 487 (9th Cir.1990)(rejecting the substantial connection requirement); United States v. $5,644,540, 799 F.2d 1357 (9th Cir.1986).

53. *See* United States v. 9844 S. Titan Court, Unit 9, Littleton, Colo., 75 F.3d 1470 (10th Cir.1996).

54. *See* United States v. Real Property and Residence at 3097 S.W. 111th Ave., 921 F.2d 1551 (11th Cir.1991)(court does not adopt a test, but explains the difference and cites numerous courts adopting one or the other); United States v. Approximately 50 Acres of Real Property Located at 42450 Highway 441 North Fort Drum, 920 F.2d 900 (11th Cir.1991)(again discussing the two standards but declining to adopt one).

In adopting or declining the substantial connection test, some courts distinguish among the three statutory subsections governing forfeiture.[55] These distinctions are based on language in the statute[56] and a piece of legislative history.[57]

How meaningful these tests and disagreements are is uncertain. Courts have called the distinction "blurry at best"[58] and "semantic rather than practical."[59] Often courts decline to choose one approach or the other, concluding that either test would be met on the facts before it.[60] Even courts adopting the more rigorous substantial connection test recognize that it is easy to meet.[61] Under either test, courts rarely deny forfeiture based on the nexus requirement.[62]

§ 28.3 Forfeiture Based on Drugs: 21 U.S.C. § 881—Defenses—In General

To file any sort of claim to the property, claimants must first satisfy standing requirements. Thereafter claimants can either rebut the gov-

55. *See, e.g.,* United States v. 1964 Beechcraft Baron Aircraft, 691 F.2d 725 (5th Cir.1982).

56. *See*

Fifth Circuit: United States v. One 1978 Mercedes Benz Four–Door Sedan, 711 F.2d 1297, 1303 n. 49 (5th Cir.1983), *quoting* United States v. 1964 Beechcraft Baron Aircraft, 691 F.2d 725, 727 (5th Cir. 1982)(no substantial connection required under § 881(a)(4) because of "in any manner" language).

Seventh Circuit: United States v. One Parcel of Real Estate Commonly Known as 916 Douglas Ave., Elgin, 903 F.2d 490 (7th Cir.1990)(substantial connection not required for § 881(a)(7) due to "in any manner or part" language).

57. *See* United States v. 1964 Beechcraft Baron Aircraft, 691 F.2d 725, 727 (5th Cir.1982)(legislative history shows "substantial connection" test may apply to § 881(a)(6) but no such showing for § 881(a)(4)).

58. United States v. One Parcel of Real Estate Commonly Known as 916 Douglas Ave., Elgin, 903 F.2d 490, 494 (7th Cir.1990), *quoted in* United States v. Parcel of Land and Residence at 28 Emery St., Merrimac, 914 F.2d 1, 4 n. 8 (1st Cir.1990).

59. *Seventh Circuit:* United States v. One Parcel of Real Estate Commonly Known as 916 Douglas Ave., Elgin, 903 F.2d 490 (7th Cir.1990).

Eleventh Circuit: United States v. Approximately 50 Acres of Real Property Located at 42450 Highway 441 N. Fort Drum, 920 F.2d 900, 902 (11th Cir.1991)(*quoting 916 Douglas Avenue*).

60. *See*

Sixth Circuit: United States v. One 1984 Cadillac, 888 F.2d 1133 (6th Cir.1989).

Eleventh Circuit: United States v. Real Property and Residence at 3097 S.W. 111th Ave., Miami, 921 F.2d 1551 (11th Cir.1991); United States v. Approximately 50 Acres of Real Property Located at 42450 Highway 441 N. Fort Drum, 920 F.2d 900 (11th Cir.1991).

61. *Fourth Circuit:* United States v. Borromeo, 995 F.2d 23 (4th Cir.), *vacated in part on other grounds*, 1 F.3d 219 (4th Cir.1993)("The hurdle posed by the 'substantial connection' requirement is not . . . a particularly high one.") *quoted in* United States v. Nelson, 1995 WL 470851 (4th Cir.) at *2 (unpublished). *See also* United States v. Schifferli, 895 F.2d 987, 990 (4th Cir. 1990) (adopting substantial connection requirement but stating that at minimum, property must have more than incidental or fortuitous connection to criminal act).

62. In none of the cases cited in this nexus section was forfeiture denied because of an insufficient nexus. On the rare occasions when courts do deny forfeiture for too remote a connection between the property and the criminal activity, they usually do so on the basis that the use does not fall within the definition of "facilitation."

See, e.g.,

First Circuit: United States v. One 1972 Chevrolet Corvette, 625 F.2d 1026 (1st Cir.1980).

Eighth Circuit: United States v. One 1976 Ford F–150 Pick–Up, 769 F.2d 525 (8th Cir.1985).

ernment's showing or establish an affirmative defense.[1] Affirmative defenses include the statutory innocent owner defense and two constitutional defenses.

§ 28.4 Forfeiture Based on Drugs: 21 U.S.C. § 881—Defenses—Standing

There are two standing requirements.[1] The first, based on Article III of the Constitution,[2] requires a case or controversy capable of adjudication in federal court; without this, there is no jurisdiction.[3] There is no Article III standing if the claimant contracted in a guilty plea to forfeit the property in an earlier criminal action.[4]

The other standing requirement is based on Admiralty Rule C(6), a procedural rule which governs civil forfeiture actions. This rule provides that a claim "shall be verified on oath ... and shall state the interest in the property by virtue of which the claimant demands its restitution and the right to defend the action."[5] Courts have interpreted this to mean that the claim of ownership must be timely filed or the claimant lacks standing.[6] Also, the claimant must be authorized to act for the corpora-

§ 28.3

1. *See*

Eleventh Circuit: United States v. A Single Family Residence and Real Property Located at 900 Rio Vista Blvd., 803 F.2d 625, 629 (11th Cir.1986)(claimant can defend by rebutting government's showing that property was proceeds or by showing it was innocent owner).

See also

Ninth Circuit: United States v. $5,644,-540 in U.S. Currency, 799 F.2d 1357, 1362 (9th Cir.1986)(claimant can defend by refuting government's two showings).

The innocent owner exception is often referred to as a defense, although in the posture of civil forfeiture cases, the property is the defendant and people asserting interests in it are claimants.

§ 28.4

1. *See* United States v. 47 West 644 Route 38, Maple Park, IL, 962 F.Supp. 1081 (N.D.Ill.1997).

2. *See*

Second Circuit: United States v. The New Silver Palace Restaurant, Inc., 810 F.Supp. 440 (E.D.N.Y.1992); United States v. One 1982 Porsche 928, 732 F.Supp. 447 (S.D.N.Y.1990).

Fifth Circuit: United States v. $38,570 U.S. Currency, 950 F.2d 1108 (5th Cir. 1992).

Eleventh Circuit: United States v. $38,-000, 816 F.2d 1538 (11th Cir.1987).

This constitutional standing requirement is not unique to civil forfeiture but applies to all civil actions in federal court.

3. United States v. 47 West 644 Route 38, Maple Park, IL, 962 F.Supp. 1081 (N.D.Ill.1997).

4. *See* United States v. Real Property Described in Deeds, 962 F.Supp. 734 (W.D.N.C.1997).

5. Rule C(6), Supplemental Rules for Certain Admiralty and Maritime Claims.

See

Fifth Circuit: United States v. $38,570 U.S. Currency, 950 F.2d 1108, 1111 (5th Cir.1992).

Eleventh Circuit: United States v. $38,-000, 816 F.2d 1538 (11th Cir.1987).

6. *See*

First Circuit: United States v. One Urban Lot, 978 F.2d 776 (1st Cir.1992).

Fourth Circuit: United States v. Ragin, 215 Peyton Road S.W. Atlanta, 1997 WL 268576 (4th Cir.1997).

Fifth Circuit: United States v. $38,570 U.S. Currency, 950 F.2d 1108 (5th Cir. 1992).

Seventh Circuit: United States v. Currency in the Amount of $2,857.00, 754 F.2d 208 (7th Cir.1985).

Eleventh Circuit: United States v. Properties Described in Complaints, 612 F.Supp. 465 (N.D.Ga.1984), aff'd, 779 F.2d 58 (11th Cir.1985).

tion to file a claim on behalf of the corporation.[7]

Bare legal title not enough to satisfy these standing requirements.[8] The reason is that relying on bare legal title would foster manipulation of nominal ownership to frustrate Congress's intent.[9]

The term *standing* is often used as another way of characterizing the requirement that the claimant have an interest in the forfeited property, without reference to Article III or Rule C(6).[10]

§ 28.5   Forfeiture Based on Drugs: 21 U.S.C. § 881—Defenses—Failure of Proof Defenses

The government must prove that the property is subject to forfeiture at a level of probable cause.[1] If the government fails to prove this or the claimant rebuts the showing with a preponderance of evidence, forfeiture is denied.[2]

§ 28.6   Forfeiture Based on Drugs: 21 U.S.C. § 881—Defenses—Affirmative Defenses

There are three affirmative defenses. These are the statutory innocent owner defense and constitutional defenses based on the excessive fines clause and the due process clause.

Laches is not a defense to civil forfeiture.[1]

---

7. *See* United States v. One Dassault Falcon 50, XA–RXZ, 1996 WL 359922 (9th Cir.1996).

8. *Third Circuit:* United States v. One 1973 Rolls Royce, 43 F.3d 794, 806 (3d Cir.1994) (describing the "nominal ownership rule").

Sixth Circuit: United States v. 37.29 Pounds of Semi-Precious Stones, 7 F.3d 480, 483 (6th Cir.1993). *But see* United States v. Certain Real Property Located at 16510 Ashton, Detroit, 47 F.3d 1465, 1470–72 (6th Cir.1995) (forfeiture reversed for hearing; *Semi-Precious Stones* superseded on facts by *James Daniel Good* hearing requirement).

Eighth Circuit: United States v. One 1990 Chevrolet Corvette, 37 F.3d 421 (8th Cir.1994).

Ninth Circuit: United States v. Star Route, Box 63, Oroville, Washington, 1996 WL 393990 (9th Cir.1996); United States v. One Parcel of Land Known as Lot 111–B, 902 F.2d 1443 (9th Cir.1990).

Eleventh Circuit: United States v. A Single Family Residence and Real Property Located at 900 Rio Vista Blvd., 803 F.2d 625 (11th Cir.1986).

9. *See*

Sixth Circuit: United States v. Premises Known as 526 Liscum, 866 F.2d 213, 217

(6th Cir.1989), *citing* United States v. A Single Family Residence, 803 F.2d 625, 630 (11th Cir.1986). *But see* United States v. Certain Real Property Located at 16510 Ashton, Detroit, 47 F.3d 1465 (6th Cir. 1995).

Eighth Circuit: United States v. One 1945 Douglas C–54 Aircraft, 604 F.2d 27 (8th Cir.1979).

See also

Eleventh Circuit: United States v. One 1977 36′ Cigarette Ocean Racer, 624 F.Supp. 290 (S.D.Fla.1985).

10. *See, e.g.,* United States v. Schifferli, 895 F.2d 987, 989 n. * (4th Cir.1990)(claimant's wife had no standing because she had no property interest under state law).

§ 28.5

1. *See* § 28.23 *infra.*

2. *See, e.g.,* United States v. $49,576, 116 F.3d 425 (9th Cir.1997)(forfeiture dismissed because government failed to prove probable cause).

§ 28.6

1. *See*

Sixth Circuit: United States v. Residence, 705 Caden Lane, Lexington, Fayette

A. INNOCENT OWNER DEFENSE

If claimants establish that they are innocent owners, they are entitled to recover the full amount of their interest in the property, including the principal amount and any costs, fees or interest.[2]

Section 881 includes three innocent owner exceptions, one for each of the main categories of forfeitable property.[3] The defenses are similar and the issues common, so they are discussed together. The one variation in the innocent owner provisions is in the use of willful blindness as a *mens rea*, and that variation is examined under that heading below.[4]

The basic § 881 innocent owner exception provides that "No property shall be forfeited ... by reason of any act ... established by the owner to have been committed without the knowledge or consent [or willful blindness] of that owner."[5] The innocent owner defense raises five issues: how to define the term *owner*, how to define the mental state of the innocent owner, how to define *consent*, whether to construe the phrase *without knowledge or consent* conjunctively or disjunctively, and whether to treat post-illegal act transferees differently.

i. Owner

The words of the forfeiture statute refer to an exception for innocent *owners*,[6] and the courts sometimes say that only "owners"[7] or those with "an ownership interest"[8] can raise the innocent owner defense. These

County, Kentucky, 1996 WL 490377 (6th Cir.1996).

Ninth Circuit: United States v. Marolf, 973 F.Supp. 1139, (C.D.Cal.1997); United States v. Property Entitled in the Names of Alexander Morio Toki, 779 F.Supp. 1272, 1278 (D.Haw.1991).

2. United States v. 1980 Lear Jet, 38 F.3d 398 (9th Cir.1994)(claimant entitled to recover principal amount of $55,736.53 and costs, fees and interest on that amount).

3. Subsection (a)(4) (conveyances) includes a three-part exception for innocent owners. Subsection (a)(4)(A) exempts common carriers except when the owner or other person in charge consented or was privy to the drug violation. Subsection (a)(4)(B) exempts the interest of an owner when that owner establishes that the use of his property that would subject it to forfeiture was committed by someone else while it was unlawfully in another's possession. Subsection (a)(4)(C) exempts an owner if such use was committed without his knowledge, consent, or willful blindness.

Subsection (a)(6)(moneys and proceeds) includes an exemption for innocent owners when the owner proves the thing of value was used without his knowledge or consent.

Subsection (a)(7)(real property) exempts from forfeiture of an owner who proves that the underlying conduct giving rise to forfeiture was conducted without his knowledge or consent.

4. *See* § 28.6(A)(ii)(b) *infra.*

5. Sections 881(a)(6) and (a)(7). The bracketed language on willful blindness is included in § 881(a)(4) only. This difference is discussed in § 28.6(A)(ii)(b) *infra.*

6. 21 U.S.C. §§ 881(a)(4)(C), (a)(6), (a)(7).

7. *See*

Second Circuit: United States v. The New Silver Palace Restaurant, Inc., 810 F.Supp. 440, 442 (E.D.N.Y.1992).

Fifth Circuit: United States v. $38,570 U.S. Currency, 950 F.2d 1108, 1111 (5th Cir.1992), *citing* United States v. One Parcel of Real Property, 831 F.2d 566, 567–68 (5th Cir.1987).

8. *See*

Fifth Circuit: United States v. $38,570 U.S. Currency, 950 F.2d 1108, 1112 (5th Cir.1992)(describing United States v. $321,-470 in U.S. Currency, 874 F.2d 298 (5th Cir.1989)).

statements are somewhat misleading, though, because the term *owner* is construed broadly to include those with property interests other than ownership. For example, courts have allowed bailees (a possessory interest),[9] lienholders[10] and leaseholders[11] to assert the innocent owner defense. Sometimes courts explain this by equating these interests with ownership.[12] Other courts simply characterize the interest that claimants need to assert this defense as a property interest.[13] Several courts note that Congress specifically endorsed a broad interpretation, stating, "The term owner should be broadly interpreted to include any person with a recognizable legal or equitable interest in the property seized."[14]

Although the property interests that allow a claimant to count as an owner are interpreted broadly, not all property interests qualify. For example, mere legal title without more is not enough.[15] The reason is that if all a claimant has is mere legal title, it may be part of a scheme to shield assets from forfeiture.[16] Other claimants whose interests have

Ninth Circuit: United States v. $69,292 in U.S. Currency, 62 F.3d 1161 (9th Cir. 1995) (construing § 5317).

9. *See*

Ninth Circuit: United States v. Real Property Described as Lot 18, 1996 WL 405048 (9th Cir.1996)(bailee may assert claim if bailee is authorized to make claim and bailee names owner); United States v. $69,292 in U.S. Currency, 62 F.3d 1161 (9th Cir.1995)(construing § 5317), *citing* United States v. $5,644,540.00, 799 F.2d 1357, 1365 (9th Cir.1986)(construing § 881(a)(6)).

10. *See*

First Circuit: United States v. One Urban Lot, 865 F.2d 427 (1st Cir.1989); Town of Sanford v. United States, 961 F.Supp. 16 (D.Me. 1997).

Fourth Circuit: United States v. Federal National Mortgage Association, 946 F.2d 264 (4th Cir.1991).

11. United States v. 121 Nostrand Ave., 760 F.Supp. 1015 (E.D.N.Y.1991)(construing § 881(a)(7))(explaining that in 1988, Congress amended the forfeiture statute to add leasehold interests to the list of forfeitable real property, and although the terms of the innocent owner defense in subsection (a)(7) were not likewise changed to add leaseholders, and the subsection (a)(7) defense continues to refer only to *owners*, if the interest being forfeited is a leasehold, courts use an innocent *leaseholder* defense).

12. *See, e.g.,* United States v. $38,570 U.S. Currency, 950 F.2d 1108, 1112 (5th Cir.1992) ("We recognize that ownership can be evidenced in a variety of ways. Courts generally look to indicia of dominion and control such as possession, title, and financial stake.")

13. *See, e.g.,*

Second Circuit: United States v. 121 Nostrand, 760 F.Supp. 1015, 1019 (E.D.N.Y.1991).

Ninth Circuit: United States v. One Parcel of Land Known as Lot 111–B, 902 F.2d 1443, 1444 (9th Cir.1990) ("The claimant has the burden of showing he owns or has an interest in the forfeited property.").

14. Joint Explanatory Statement of Titles II and III, 95th Cong. 2d Sess. (1978), *reprinted* in 1978 U.S.C.C.A.N. 9518, 9522, *quoted in* United States v. $38,570 U.S. Currency, 950 F.2d 1108, 1112 n. 4 (5th Cir.1992) and United States v. The New Silver Palace Restaurant, Inc., 810 F.Supp. 440, 443 (E.D.N.Y.1992).

15. *See*

Third Circuit: United States v. One 1973 Rolls Royce, 43 F.3d 794, 806 (3d Cir.1994) (describing the "nominal ownership rule").

Eighth Circuit: United States v. One 1990 Chevrolet Corvette, 37 F.3d 421 (8th Cir.1994).

Ninth Circuit: United States v. Star Route, Box 63, Oroville, Washington, 1996 WL 393990 (9th Cir.1996); United States v. One Parcel of Land Known as Lot 111–B, 902 F.2d 1443 (9th Cir.1990).

Eleventh Circuit: United States v. A Single Family Residence and Real Property Located at 900 Rio Vista Blvd., 803 F.2d 625 (11th Cir.1986).

16. *See*

Second Circuit: United States v. One 1982 Porsche 928, 732 F.Supp. 447, 451 (S.D.N.Y.1990)(owner must be more than

been held inadequate to assert the defense include lenders,[17] shareholders,[18] and general (unsecured) creditors.[19]

Ownership is determined by state law.[20] Legal and equitable owners
may both have a sufficient interest to raise the defense.[21]

The term "owner" refers to the person who owns the property at
the time of the forfeiture proceeding, not at the time the property is used
to commit the act giving rise to forfeiture.[22]

Whatever property interest the claimant relies on, a bare assertion
of that interest by the claimant is not sufficient to establish it.[23] More
evidence is required. The reason is to reduce the danger of false or

mere "strawman" set up to avoid forfeiture).

Third Circuit: United States v. One
1973 Rolls Royce, 43 F.3d 794, 806 (3d
Cir.1994).

Ninth Circuit: United States v. Star
Route, Box 63, Oroville, Washington, 1996
WL 393990 (9th Cir.1996)(requirement is
effort to avoid sham transactions designed
to evade forfeiture).

17. United States v. $47,875 in Unit-
ed States Currency, 746 F.2d 291, 293 (5th
Cir.1984)(lenders who were not engaged in
joint venture with person from whom property was seized have no standing), *quoted in*
United States v. $38,570 U.S. Currency, 950
F.2d 1108, 1111 (5th Cir.1992).

18. United States v. The New Silver
Palace Restaurant, Inc., 810 F.Supp. 440
(E.D.N.Y.1992). The court considered the
innocent owner claim of the shareholders of
a corporation. The government sought the
forfeiture of the corporation's assets, the
main one being a restaurant. The court
denied the shareholders' claim based upon
the fact that, as shareholders, they were not
owners of the property in question. "Shareholders do not hold legal title to any of the
corporation's assets. Instead, the corporation—the entity itself—is vested with title."
Id. at 441.

19. *See*

Second Circuit: United State v. Coluc-
cio, 51 F.3d 337, 339 (2d Cir.1995).

Ninth Circuit: United States v. 1975
GMC House Car, 1996 WL 481620 (9th
Cir.)(unpublished); United States v. $20,-
193, 16 F.3d 344, 346 (9th Cir.1994) (rejecting the innocent owner claim of unsecured
creditors, stating "Federal courts have consistently held that unsecured creditors do
not have standing."). Although secured
creditors can identify the item in which
they have an interest, "general creditors
cannot claim an interest in any particular

asset that makes up the debtor's estate."
Id. Since general creditors cannot show an
interest in a particular piece of property,
they do not have dominion and control, nor
a sufficient interest to allege ownership.

$20,193 construed § 981 rather than
§ 881, but the difference in statutes is not
important. If general creditors' interests
are insufficient under the language of
§ 981, which refers to "owners or lienholders," they are necessarily insufficient under
the narrower language of § 881, which refers only to "owners."

20. *See*

Third Circuit: United States v. One
1973 Rolls Royce, 43 F.3d 794, 806 (3d
Cir.1994).

Fifth Circuit: United States v. 1977
Porsche Carrera, 946 F.2d 30, 34 (5th Cir.
1991); United States v. Lot 9, Block 2 of
Donnybrook Place, 919 F.2d 994, 1000 (5th
Cir.1990).

Ninth Circuit: United States v. Ranch
Located in Young, Arizona, 50 F.3d 630,
632 (9th Cir.1995)(transfer voidable under
Arizona fraudulent conveyance law so
claimant is not "owner").

Tenth Circuit: United States v. 9844 S.
Titan Court, Unit 9, Littleton, Colorado, 75
F.3d 1470 (10th Cir.1996)(applying Colora-
do marital property law).

21. United States v. The New Silver
Palace Restaurant, Inc., 810 F.Supp. 440
(E.D.N.Y.1992).

22. *See* United States v. Land in the
Name of Mikell, 33 F.3d 11 (5th Cir.1994).

23. *See*

Second Circuit: Mercado v. U. S. Customs Service, 873 F.2d 641 (2d Cir.1989)
(possession).

Fifth Circuit: United States v. $38,570
U.S. Currency, 950 F.2d 1108, 1112 (5th
Cir.1992) (ownership).

frivolous claims to property.[24]

Courts sometimes refer to the requirement that the claimant have an adequate property interest to qualify for the innocent owner defense as a "standing" requirement.[25] This is a loose use of the term "standing" and should not be confused with two other standing requirements claimants must satisfy to file claims in civil forfeiture actions.[26]

This discussion has so far assumed a single person claiming the property interest at all relevant times. But sometimes the property interest has been transferred among several people, either by purchase or by gift. Although there was some disagreement originally,[27] it is now clear that transferees of the property may raise the innocent owner defense.[28] Transferees (or, more specifically, post-illegal act transferees) are persons whose interest in the property resulted from a transfer, either gift or sale, after the property was illegally used. The conclusion that transferees may qualify as owners reflects a change in the law brought about by the Supreme Court in 1993 in *92 Buena Vista Avenue*.[29]

Prior to 1993, many claimants who were transferees were denied the opportunity to raise the innocent owner defense despite the fact that they had exercised dominion and control over the property based on the government's interpretation of the relation back clause.[30] This clause provides that all right, title and interest in the property vests in the United States at the time of the illegal use.[31] The government argued, and many courts agreed, that this meant that as soon as the illegal act was committed, title vested in the United States and could not thereafter be passed to a transferee.[32] Thus transferees who acquired the property after the illegal activity giving rise to the forfeiture could never qualify as the "owner" of that property for the innocent owner defense.

In *92 Buena Vista Avenue*, the Supreme Court held that the relation back clause does not make the government the owner of the property

---

24. *See*

Second Circuit: Mercado v. U. S. Customs Service, 873 F.2d 641 (2d Cir.1989) (possession).

Fifth Circuit: United States v. $38,570 U.S. Currency, 950 F.2d 1108, 1112 (5th Cir.1992).

25. *See, e.g.,*

Fifth Circuit: United States v.$38,570 U.S. Currency, 950 F.2d 1108 (5th Cir. 1992); United States v. $47,875 in United States Currency, 746 F.2d 291, 294 (5th Cir.1984).

Ninth Circuit: United States v. Ranch Located in Young, Arizona, 50 F.3d 630, 632 (9th Cir.1995); United States v. $69,292 in U.S. Currency, 62 F.3d 1161 (9th Cir. 1995); United States v. One Parcel of Land Known as Lot 111–B, 902 F.2d 1443 (9th Cir.1990).

26. *See* discussion *supra* in § 28.4.

27. *Compare In re* 1985 Nissan, 300ZX, 889 F.2d 1317, 1320 (4th Cir. 1989)(en banc)("no third party can acquire a legally valid interest in the property ... after the illegal act takes place.") *with* Eggleston v. Colorado, 873 F.2d 242, 247 (10th Cir.1989)(the relation back provision is subject to the innocent owner exception).

28. United States v. A Parcel of Land, Buildings, Appurtenances and Improvements, Known as 92 Buena Vista Avenue, Rumson, New Jersey, 507 U.S. 111, 113 S.Ct. 1126, 122 L.Ed.2d 469 (1993).

29. *Id.*

30. *See, e.g., In re* 1985 Nissan 300ZX, 889 F.2d 1317 (4th Cir.1989).

31. 21 U.S.C. § 881(h).

32. *Buena Vista*, 507 U.S. at 123.

instantaneously at the time of the illegal act.[33] Rather, the government's interest is retroactive to the time of the illegal act, but only once forfeiture is decreed.[34] Thus before forfeiture is decreed, transferees can qualify as "owners" for purposes of asserting the innocent owner defense.[35] To succeed with the defense, of course, they must meet all the elements. But transferees are not automatically disqualified for not being "owners."

ii. Mental State

The main question, which has splintered the circuits, is how to define the mental state that defeats the innocent owner defense. A subsidiary issue is whether an individual's knowledge is imputed to a corporation.

    a. Actual Knowledge. Two of the innocent owner provisions, §§ 881(a)(6) and (a)(7), state that the innocent owner defense is disallowed if the claimant has *knowledge* the property was used illegally. Many courts hold that knowledge means *actual* knowledge, including the Eleventh,[36] Second,[37] Fourth,[38] and Seventh Circuits.[39] Under this standard, a claimant who was negligent or reckless or willfully blind about whether the property was involved with crime but did not actually know that it was could still qualify as an innocent owner. This approach gives claimants a comparatively broad innocent owner defense. Courts choosing the actual knowledge standard find support in the plain language of the statute[40] and the legislative history.[41]

---

33. *Id.* at 127–29.

34. *Id.*

35. Three dissenters would distinguish between transferees who are donees and those who are purchasers. Bona fide purchasers could become owners, but donees never could. *See* United States v. A Parcel of Land, Buildings, Appurtenances and Improvements, Known as 92 Buena Vista Avenue, Rumson, New Jersey, 507 U.S. 111, 139–40, 113 S.Ct. 1126, 1142–43, 122 L.Ed.2d 469 (1993)(Kennedy, Rehnquist and White, JJ., dissenting).

36. United States v. One Single Family Residence Located at 6960 Miraflores Avenue, 995 F.2d 1558, 1561 (11th Cir.1993) (construing §§ 881(a)(6) and (a)(7)), *rev'd on other grounds sub nom.* Republic National Bank v. United States, 506 U.S. 80, 113 S.Ct. 554, 121 L.Ed.2d 474 (1992), *citing* United States v. Real Property at 5000 Palmetto Drive, 928 F.2d 373, 375 (11th Cir. 1991); United States v. One Single Family Residence Located at 15603 85th Avenue North, 933 F.2d 976, 982 (11th Cir.1991)(construing § 881(a)(6)); United States v. $4,255,000, 762 F.2d 895 (11th Cir.1985)(construing § 881(a)(6)).

37. *See* United State v. 141st Street Corp., 911 F.2d 870, 877 (2d Cir.1990)(con-

struing § 881(a)(7))(affirming lower court's instruction requiring actual knowledge); *but see* United States v. Milbrand, 58 F.3d 841 (2d Cir.1995).

38. *See* United States v. $10,694 in U.S. Currency, 828 F.2d 233, 234–35 (4th Cir.1987), *overruled on other grounds by*, 889 F.2d 1317 (4th Cir.1989)(§ 881(a)(6) "envisions an actual knowledge inquiry.").

39. *See* United States v. One Parcel of Land Located at 7326 Highway 45 North, 965 F.2d 311, 315 (7th Cir. 1992)(§ 881(a)(7) "focuses on the claimant's actual knowledge.").

40. *See, e.g.,* United States v. $10,694, 828 F.2d 233, 234–235 (4th Cir.1987), *overruled on other grounds by*, 889 F.2d 1317 (4th Cir.1989) (construing § 881(a)(6)). The government argued that "the proper inquiry focuses on whether the claimant knew or should have known that the money was derived from drug proceeds." *Id.* In dismissing this argument and adopting an actual knowledge standard, the court stated: "There is nothing in the plain language ... requiring courts to look to the objective rather than subjective knowledge of the owner when determining whether forfeiture is proper...." *Id.*

b. Willful Blindness. A second mental state that may defeat the innocent owner defense is willful blindness. One of the innocent owner provisions, § 881(a)(4), explicitly states that willful blindness defeats the innocent owner defense. The other two innocent owner provisions, (a)(6) and (a)(7), do not mention willful blindness explicitly, but courts nonetheless sometimes incorporate it under the *mens rea* of knowledge.[42] The type of knowledge established by proof of willful blindness is called *constructive* knowledge or *implied* knowledge as opposed to *actual* knowledge. In this way willful blindness may play a role under all three of the innocent owner defenses.

Defining willful blindness has led to some confusion,[43] but two standards seem to be evolving.[44] The "mainstream" definition of willful blindness is a subjective one, focusing on whether the claimants deliberately closed their eyes to what otherwise would have been obvious.[45] This standard involves "much greater culpability than simple negligence or recklessness, and [is] more akin to knowledge."[46] On the other hand, some courts appear to adopt a more objective, due care definition of willful blindness.[47]

Whatever definition is adopted for willful blindness, using it under § (a)(4) is not controversial because the statute expressly authorizes it, but using willful blindness under §§ (a)(6) and (a)(7) has caused controversy. Under these two subsections, some courts refuse to use willful blindness and limit the definition of knowledge to actual knowledge,[48]

41. *See, e.g.,* United States v. 6960 Miraflores Ave., 995 F.2d 1558, 1564 (11th Cir.1993), *rev'd on other grounds sub nom.* Republic National Bank v. United States, 506 U.S. 80, 113 S.Ct. 554, 121 L.Ed.2d 474 (1992) ("There is nothing in the legislative history of the statute that requires a standard of 'should have known.' ").

42. United States v. 1973 Rolls Royce, 43 F.3d 794, 809 & n. 14 (3d Cir. 1994)(many courts incorporate willful blindness under (a)(6) and (a)(7) despite its textual absence).

See

Second Circuit: United States v. 755 Forest Road, 985 F.2d 70, 72 (2d Cir.1993) (willful blindness fulfills the knowledge element under § 881(a)(7)).

Ninth Circuit: United States v. 1980 Red Ferrari, 827 F.2d 477, 480 (9th Cir. 1987).

43. United States v. One 1973 Rolls Royce, 43 F.3d 794, 808 n. 12 (3d Cir.1994)("Willful blindness has proven to be an elusive concept and much disagreement still exist over the appropriate definition of the term.")(collecting sources of confusion). *See also* Robin Charlow, *Wilful Ignorance and Criminal Culpability*, 70 Tex.L.Rev. 1351 (1992); Douglas N. Husak

& Craig A. Callender, *Wilful Ignorance, Knowledge, and the "Equal Culpability" Thesis: A Study of the Deeper Significance of the Principle of Legality*, 1994 Wis.L.Rev. 29, 35 (1994) ("Commentators and courts differ not only in the names they give to this state [willful blindness], but also in the details of the descriptions they provide—if, indeed, they provide any details at all.").

44. *See One 1973 Rolls Royce*, 43 F.3d at 807 (circuit split appears to be developing between two approaches).

45. *See Third Circuit:* United States v. One 1973 Rolls Royce, 43 F.3d 794, 808 n. 12 (3d Cir.1994).

Eighth Circuit: United States v. One 1989 Jeep Wagoneer, 976 F.2d 1172 (8th Cir.1992).

46. *One 1973 Rolls Royce*, 43 F.3d at 808.

47. *See, e.g.,* One 1980 Bertram 58' Motor Yacht, 876 F.2d 884, 888 (11th Cir. 1989), *cited in One 1973 Rolls Royce*, 43 F.3d at 807.

48. *See*

Second Circuit: United States v. 141st Street Corp., 911 F.2d 870, 877 (2d Cir.1990)(construing § 881(a)(7))(affirming

while other courts allow the use of willful blindness as a surrogate of knowledge.[49] In criminal law generally, willful blindness is recognized as a way to establish the *mens rea* of knowledge.[50] But for §§ 881(a)(6) and (a)(7), this conclusion is called into question by the absence of any reference to willful blindness, an absence rendered conspicuous by the proximity of the reference to willful blindness just paragraphs earlier in § (a)(4).

On the question of whether willful blindness should be used under subsections (a)(6) and (a)(7), the better position is to treat willful blindness as part of knowledge, and read it into the innocent owner defense even if it is not expressly mentioned in the statute. Some courts have reached this conclusion.[51] This is the better approach because it will keep civil forfeiture law in line with the traditional criminal law understanding of the *mens rea* of knowledge. Also, incorporating willful blindness under subsections (a)(6) and (a)(7) is wise because it keeps the innocent owner defenses under those sections consistent with the innocent owner defense under subsection (a)(4). There is no reason based on the type of property being forfeited under the three sections to treat the innocent owner exceptions differently. Finally, reading willful blindness in is probably in line with Congress's intent.[52] The better position is to interpret the three innocent owner provisions the same notwithstanding the absence of an explicit reference to willful blindness in two of the three provisions.

    c. Negligence. Finally, the Ninth Circuit appears to interpret knowledge to include an objective negligence standard.[53] Under this analysis, claimants who fail to exercise due care or should have known of

---

lower court's instruction requiring actual knowledge); *but see* United States v. Milbrand, 58 F.3d 841 (2d Cir.1995)

    Fourth Circuit: United States v. $10,-694, 828 F.2d 233 (4th Cir.1987), *overruled on other grounds by*, 889 F.2d 1317 (4th Cir.1989) (construing § 881(a)(6))

    *Seventh Circuit:*United States v. One Parcel of Land Located at 7326 Highway 45 North, 965 F.2d 311, 315 (7th Cir. 1992)(§ 881(a)(7) "focuses on the claimant's actual knowledge.")

    Eleventh Circuit: United States v. One Single Family Residence Located at 6960 Miraflores Avenue, 995 F.2d 1558, 1561 (11th Cir.1993) (construing §§ 881(a)(6) and (a)(7)), *rev'd on other grounds sub nom.* Republic National Bank v. United States, 506 U.S. 80, 113 S.Ct. 554, 121 L.Ed.2d 474 (1992).

    49. *See* United States v. Milbrand, 58 F.3d 841 (2d Cir.1995), *quoting* United States v. One Parcel of Property Located at 755 Forest Road, 985 F.2d 70, 72 (2d Cir. 1993).

    50. *See* Model Penal Code § 2.02(7).

    51. *See*

    Second Circuit: United States v. Milbrand, 58 F.3d 841, (2d Cir.1995), *quoting* United States v. One Parcel of Property Located at 755 Forest Road, 985 F.2d 70, 72 (2d Cir.1993).

    Third Circuit: One 1973 Rolls Royce, 43 F.3d 794, 809 n. 14. (3d Cir.1994).

    52. *See* United States v. 890 Noyac Road, 739 F.Supp. 111, 115 (E.D.N.Y.1990)(although "willful blindness" is absent in (a)(6) and (a)(7), court suggests that the legislative history indicates that Congress intended for it to apply anyway).

    53. *See* United States v. Real Property Located at 10936 Oak Run Circle, 9 F.3d 74, 76 (9th Cir.1993)(construing § 881(a)(6)); United States v. $215,300 United States Currency, 882 F.2d 417, 420 (9th Cir.1989)(construing § 881(a)(6)); United States v. 1980 Red Ferrari, 827 F.2d 477, 480 (9th Cir.1987)(construing § 881(a)(6))(denying innocent owner defense where claimant was "at least on notice of" the vehicle's connection to crime).

the illegal use of the property are considered to have knowledge and lose the protection of the innocent owner defense. The Ninth Circuit reaches this result not by applying an objective willful blindness approach, but rather by directly employing a negligence theory. This approach provides the narrowest defense for claimants.

A good example of this approach is United States v. $215,300.[54] A traveler was stopped carrying drug-tainted currency strapped to his body. When the government forfeited the money, a claimant filed for it under the innocent owner exception. He alleged he was the owner of the money, that the traveler was carrying it for him to buy gold and jewelry, and that he had no knowledge that the traveler would use the cash illegitimately. The court denied the owner's claim, explaining that the owner "took no precautions to guard against illegal use. He argues, essentially, that believing [the traveler] to be 'trustworthy' constituted an honest mistake in judgment. This is merely another way of pleading negligence. Failure to exercise due care precludes reliance upon the innocent owner defense."[55]

d. Corporations. A question arises in defining the knowledge of a corporate claimant. A corporation can "know" only through its agents.[56] When a corporate officer commits an act which gives rise to forfeiture, should the actor's knowledge be attributed to the corporation to defeat it's claim of innocent ownership? Two circuits have held that it depends on whether the agent obtained knowledge of the property's prohibited use within the scope of employment.[57]

The Seventh Circuit addressed the issue of imputing knowledge to a corporation.[58] Three individuals, two parents and their son, owned the stock in a company which in turn owned the forfeited property. The son managed the day-to-day running of the resort property and also sold drugs. The latter activity resulted in the forfeiture of the resort property. The question was whether the son's knowledge of his own criminal conduct should be imputed to the corporation to defeat the corporation's

---

54.   882 F.2d 417 (9th Cir.1989).

55.   *Id.* at 420.

Another good example is United States v. 10936 Oak Run Circle, 9 F.3d 74 (9th Cir.1993). A drug dealer transferred his home, worth around $88,000, to his girlfriend's parents who in return forgave an $11,000 debt. When the parents asserted they were innocent owners because they did not know the home was purchased with drug money, the court stated:

We hold ... that innocence is incompatible with knowledge that puts the owner on notice that he should inquire further. In the instant case the [parents] were offered what appears to have been a remarkable bargain. Should they have asked why? Did they ask why? What answers were they given? These and any

other factual questions must be resolved in the district court, whose task it will be to determine the credibility of the evidence and explanations tendered by the [parents].

Id. at 76.

56.   United States v. 7326 Highway 45, 965 F.2d 311, 316 (7th Cir.1992), *citing* United States v. Bank of New England, N.A., 821 F.2d 844, 856 (1st Cir.1987).

57.   *See*

Seventh Circuit: United States v. 7326 Highway 45, 965 F.2d 311 (7th Cir.1992).

Eleventh Circuit: United States v. Route 2, Box 472, 60 F.3d 1523 (11th Cir. 1995).

58.   United States v. 7326 Highway 45, 965 F.2d 311 (7th Cir.1992).

innocent owner defense.[59] The court defined which knowledge could legitimately be imputed from the agent to the corporation and which could not:

> Where a corporate agent obtains knowledge while acting in the scope of his agency, he presumably reports that knowledge to his corporate principal so the court imputes such knowledge to the corporation. However, where an agent obtains knowledge while acting outside the scope of his agency, the standard presumption is unfounded, and the court will not impute the agent's knowledge to the corporation.... Only knowledge obtained by corporate employees acting within the scope of their employment is imputed to the corporation.... [A]cting within the scope of employment means "with intent to benefit the employer".... Therefore, the agent is outside the scope of his employment when he is not acting at least in part for the benefit of the corporation, and any knowledge the agent obtains is not imputed to the corporation.[60]

The court determined that because the son's actions were not to benefit the corporation at all, his knowledge was not imputed to the corporation and the corporation qualified as an innocent owner.[61]

Quoting heavily from this decision, the Eleventh Circuit reached a similar conclusion.[62]

Both the Seventh and Eleventh Circuits distinguished a Second Circuit decision which held that a president's knowledge was attributable to the corporation.[63] In that case, the claimant corporation argued that the knowledge of the individual officer who acted illegally could not be attributed to the corporation because the officer was acting adversely to the corporation. The court rejected this argument and held that the officer's knowledge was attributable to the corporation because the claimant corporation, which bore the burden of proof, offered no evidence to show it did not benefit from the illegal dealings.[64] The court stated that it had to reject the corporation's argument because, "followed to its logical extreme, it would mean that corporation's property would never be subject to forfeiture because the very actions of the agent that cause an imputation of knowledge are 'adverse' to the principal."[65]

Finally, the Ninth Circuit held that an employee's knowledge was attributable to the corporate employer based on respondeat superior.[66]

59. *Id.* at 314.

60. *Id.* at 316.

61. *Id.* at 320. Judge Posner filed a blistering dissent, stating, "The court is critical of fictions but says without blushing that '[the corporation] has no *actual* knowledge of proscribed activities taking place on its land.' A corporation is not a living being. It has no mind. When we say a corporation 'knows' something, ... we mean that a *responsible* agent of the corporation knows the thing. There is no more responsible agent of [this corporation] than Harry, its manager [and one-third owner]." (citations omitted). *Id.* at 321.

62. United States v. Route 2, Box 472, 60 F.3d 1523 (11th Cir.1995).

63. United States v. 141st St. Corp., 911 F.2d 870, 876–77 (2d Cir.1990).

64. *Id.* at 876.

65. *Id.*

66. United States v. Nissan Van 1987, 1994 WL 711941 (9th Cir.1994)(unpublished).

The court distinguished the Seventh Circuit's decision refusing to attribute knowledge because in that case the son dealt drugs to benefit only himself, not the corporation.[67] The Ninth Circuit said its case was "readily distinguishable."[68]

In summary, the courts agree that when the claimant/corporate agent acts to benefit the corporation, the individual's knowledge is imputed to the corporation to defeat the innocent owner defense. Conversely, if the agent is acting just to benefit himself and not the corporation, courts do not attribute the knowledge to the corporation. As such, there is basic agreement but this line of cases reveals some differences in the courts' willingness to characterize the agent's actions as benefitting just the agent, or the corporation as well.

iii. Consent

All three of the § 881 innocent owner provisions mention consent to the prohibited use of the property.[69] The question in the courts is whether proving lack of consent requires claimants to prove they did "all that could reasonably be expected to prevent the proscribed use of the property." The circuits are split.

Three circuits define consent to include the requirement that the claimant have done all that could reasonably be expected to prevent the illegal use of the property.[70] Courts find authority for this interpretation in the Supreme Court's dictum in Calero–Toledo v. Pearson Yacht Leasing.[71] In *Calero-Toledo*, the Supreme Court stated that a constitutional defense to forfeiture might be implied if the owner could prove "not only that he was uninvolved in and unaware of the wrongful activity, but also that he had done all that reasonably could be expected to prevent the proscribed use of his property."[72] Some courts have

---

67. *Id.* at *2 n.2.

68. *Id.* at *3.

69. *See* §§ 881(a)(4)(C), (a)(6) and (a)(7). All three use the term consent, but whether a claimant in a particular case is required to show lack of consent will be depend in part on resolution of the conjunctive or disjunctive interpretation, discussed *infra* in § 28.6(A)(v)(a).

The use of the term consent is one of the differences between the innocent owner exceptions in the two main civil forfeiture statutes, §§ 881 and 981. In § 981, the term does not appear. See *infra* . . . .

70. *See*

Second Circuit: United States v. One Parcel of Property Located at 121 Allen Place, 75 F.3d 118 (2d Cir.1996); United States v. 141st Street Corporation, 911 F.2d 870 (2d Cir.1990).

Fourth Circuit: United States v. 31 Endless Street, 8 F.3d 821 (4th Cir.1993).

Eleventh Circuit: United States v. One Single Family Residence Located at 15603 85th Avenue North, 933 F.2d 976 (11th Cir.1991).

71. 416 U.S. 663, 94 S.Ct. 2080, 40 L.Ed.2d 452 (1974).

See

Second Circuit: United States v. One Parcel of Property Located at 121 Allen Place, 75 F.3d 118 (2d Cir.1996); United States v. 141st Street Corporation, 911 F.2d 870 (2d Cir.1990).

Fourth Circuit: United States v. 31 Endless Street, 8 F.3d 821 (4th Cir.1993).

Eleventh Circuit: United States v. One Single Family Residence Located at 15603 85th Avenue North, 933 F.2d 976 (11th Cir.1991).

72. 416 U.S. 663, 689, 94 S.Ct. 2080, 2094, 40 L.Ed.2d 452 (1974). The Court stated,

This is not to say, however, that the 'broad sweep' of forfeiture statutes re-

engrafted this requirement onto the definition of consent. Imposing this requirement makes it more difficult for claimants to prove consent and qualify as innocent owners.

The Second Circuit is one of the courts which has expressly incorporated the *Calero-Toledo* standard into the definition of consent.[73] In doing so, the court acknowledged that the legislative history makes no reference to the standard.[74] However, the court concluded that the government-oriented *Calero-Toledo* standard was "appropriate" for forfeiture cases because, when combined with the court's claimant-oriented interpretation of other language,[75] it strikes "a balance between the two congressional purposes of making drug trafficking prohibitively expensive for the property owner and preserving the property of an innocent owner."[76]

Two other circuits deciding the issue have taken the same stance. The Fourth Circuit cited the Second Circuit and expressly incorporated the *Calero-Toledo* standard into their consent definition.[77] The Eleventh Circuit also found the *Calero-Toledo* standard applicable, stating that "a claimant who has actual knowledge . . . may be spared forfeiture as an innocent owner if the claimant can prove that everything reasonably possible was done" to prevent the illegal use of the property.[78]

On the other hand, three circuits have rejected the *Calero-Toledo* standard for defining consent.[79] These courts note that § 881 itself contains no language supporting this gloss on the definition of consent.[80]

marked in Coin & Currency could not, in other circumstances, give rise to serious constitutional questions. . . . It . . . has been implied that it would be difficult to reject the constitutional claim of an owner whose property subjected to forfeiture had been taken from him without his privity or consent. Similarly, the same might be said of an owner who proved not only that he was uninvolved in and unaware of the wrongful activity, but also that he had done all that reasonably could be expected to prevent the proscribed use of his property; for, in that circumstance, it would be difficult to conclude that forfeiture served legitimate purposes and was not unduly oppressive. *Id.* at 688–89 (citations omitted).

73. United States v. Millar Elevator Service Co., 77 F.3d 648, 657 (2d Cir.1996); United States v. 141st St. Corp., 911 F.2d 870, 879 (2d Cir.1990).

74. *141st St. Corp.*, 911 F.2d at 879.

75. The Second Circuit takes the disjunctive approach, *see* United States v. One Parcel of Property Located at 121 Allen Place, 75 F.3d 118 (2d Cir.1996) and United States v. 141st St. Corp., 911 F.2d 870, 879 (2d Cir.1990), which provides a wider innocent owner defense than the conjunctive approach.

76. *141st St. Corp.*, 911 F.2d at 879.

77. United States v. 31 Endless St., 8 F.3d 821 (4th Cir.1993), *citing United States v. 141st St. Corp.*, 911 F.2d 870, 879 (2d Cir.1990).

78. United States v. 15603 85th Ave. N., 933 F.2d 976, 982 (11th Cir.1991). This case dealt specifically with § 881(a)(6), but the Eleventh Circuit later extended the ruling to cover § 881(a)(7), noting the two provisions contain an "identically worded innocent ownership exception." United States v. 1012 Germantown Road, 963 F.2d 1496, 1505 (11th Cir.1992).

79. *See*

First Circuit: United States v. One Urban Lot Located at 1 St., A–1, 865 F.2d 427 (1st Cir.1989).

Sixth Circuit: United States v. Certain Real Property at 14307 Four Lakes Drive, 1993 WL 264687 (6th Cir.1993); United States v. Lots 12, 13, 14, 15, 869 F.2d 942 (6th Cir.1989).

Eighth Circuit: United States v. One 1989 Jeep Wagoneer, 976 F.2d 1172 (8th Cir.1992).

80. *See*

First Circuit: United States v. One Urban Lot Located at 1 St., A–1, 865 F.2d 427, 430 (1st Cir.1989).

They also distinguish *Calero-Toledo* because it did not involve the federal forfeiture statute, § 881, but rather a state forfeiture statute that included no innocent owner defense at all.[81] They also note the incongruity of using Supreme Court *dicta* on a constitutional minimum in a way that *limits* a statutory defense.[82]

For example, in United States v. Lots 12, 13, 14, and 15,[83] the Sixth Circuit rejected the use of the *Calero-Toledo* standard in determining whether the owner had given "consent." The wife claimed property forfeited as a result of her husband's illegal drug activities.[84] She asserted, in her defense, that she was "not involved in or aware of the illegal behavior and had done all that [she] could be reasonably expected to do to prevent the offensive use of her property."[85] In reversing the district court's grant of summary judgment for the government, the court responded that the *Calero-Toledo* standard was an inappropriate consideration. "[T]he statute with which we are concerned imposes no [such] requirement.... It is enough, under the statute, that the owner establish that the proscribed act was committed 'without the knowledge or consent of that owner.' "[86]

Similarly, the First Circuit rejected incorporation of the *Calero-Toledo* standard:[87]

> The reference to Calero–Toledo seems inapposite. The case involved a Puerto Rico forfeiture statute as applied to the lessor of a yacht. The Court upheld the statute even as applied to the lessor who had no knowledge of the illegal activity. It is in considering the constitutionality of the Puerto Rico statute that the court sets out the limits of the forfeiture powers of the state. Here, however, we have a statute that provides for an exception for innocent owners.... This statute does not in any way limit innocent owners to those who have done "all that reasonably could be expected to prevent the proscribed use of the property".... In fact, the statute specifically

Sixth Circuit: United States v. Certain Real Property at 14307 Four Lakes Drive, 1993 WL 264687 at *4 (6th Cir.1993); United States v. Lots 12, 13, 14, 15, 869 F.2d 942, 946–47 (6th Cir.1989).

Eighth Circuit: United States v. One 1989 Jeep Wagoneer, 976 F.2d 1172, 1175–76 (8th Cir.1992).

81. *See*

First Circuit: United States v. One Urban Lot Located at 1 St., A–1, 865 F.2d 427, 430 (1st Cir.1989).

Sixth Circuit: United States v. Certain Real Property at 14307 Four Lakes Drive, 1993 WL 264687 at *4 (6th Cir.1993); United States v. Lots 12, 13, 14, 15, 869 F.2d 942, 946–47 (6th Cir.1989).

Eighth Circuit: United States v. One 1989 Jeep Wagoneer, 976 F.2d 1172, 1175–76 (8th Cir.1992).

82. *First Circuit:* United States v. One Urban Lot Located at 1 St., A–1, 865 F.2d 427, 430 (1st Cir.1989).

Sixth Circuit: United States v. Certain Real Property at 14307 Four Lakes Drive, 1993 WL 264687 at *4 (6th Cir.1993); United States v. Lots 12, 13, 14, 15, 869 F.2d 942, 946–47 (6th Cir.1989).

Eighth Circuit: United States v. One 1989 Jeep Wagoneer, 976 F.2d 1172, 1175–76 (8th Cir.1992).

83. 869 F.2d 942 (6th Cir.1989).

84. *Id.* at 942.

85. *Id.* at 946.

86. *Id.* at 947.

87. United States v. 1 St. A–1, 865 F.2d 427 (1st Cir.1989).

refers to the knowledge and consent of the owner as the appropriate considerations in determining who is excepted.[88]

Finally, the Eighth Circuit has also rejected the *Calero-Toledo* definition of consent, but not so clearly.[89]

The practical effect of adopting the *Calero-Toledo* language into the definition of consent under § 881 is to limit the innocent owner defense, and the results can be harsh for claimants. In another case which demonstrates the government-oriented effect of adopting the *Calero-Toledo* consent standard, the claimant was the owner of a grocery store located in a drug-infested neighborhood. The claimant was aware of drug activity in his parking lot and around his property, and he took steps to halt it. He called the police on numerous occasions. He personally chased people out of his parking lot. He placed large yellow "No Loitering" signs in his front window. He installed cameras and mirrors inside his store. He removed telephones from the outside of his building so they could not be used to arrange drug deals. He erected fences, installed an alarm system, and used watchdogs. Despite these measures, a jury found that the claimant had not done everything that he could reasonably have been expected to do to prevent his property from being used to violate the drug laws. The government had argued that the claimant had not kept logs of his telephone calls to police, that he only chased the drug dealers away when the police were able to observe him doing so, and that he should have released his dogs to drive away the dealers.

The better position is to reject the *Calero-Toledo* definition of consent and develop a definition of consent tailored for § 881. The *Calero-Toledo* decision states the minimum protection required for a forfeiture statute to be constitutional. Congress can always provide more protection if it chooses. In construing consent in § 881, the courts should recognize this and define consent in a way that is less harsh on claimants than the constitutional minimum of *Calero-Toledo*.

While there are criticisms of incorporating the *Calero-Toledo* language into the statutory innocent owner defense, courts which follow this approach do have the benefit of a definition of consent. The courts which reject *Calero-Toledo* and find it irrelevant for § 881 have not articulated an interpretation of consent.

iv. Conjunctive or Disjunctive Approach

Apart from debates over what the individual terms *knowledge* and *consent* mean, the relationship between the two is uncertain. The innocent owner provisions state that the prohibited use of the property must occur *"without the knowledge or consent* of the claimant."[90] The question

---

88. *Id.* at 430.

89. United States v. One 1989 Jeep Wagoneer, 976 F.2d 1172, 1174 (8th Cir. 1992)(court states that only question is willful blindness, an approach which presupposes absence of consent).

90. 21 U.S.C. §§ 881(a)(6) and (a)(7). Section 881(a)(4) has the additional willful blindness reference discussed in § 28.6(A)(ii)(b) *supra.*

is whether the claimant must disprove both knowledge and consent of the prohibited use or merely one of the two. In other words, is the phrase *without knowledge or consent* interpreted conjunctively or disjunctively? Courts taking a conjunctive view hold that claimants must prove *both* lack of knowledge of the prohibited use *and* lack of consent to it. Courts taking the disjunctive view hold that claimants may prove *either* lack of knowledge of the use *or* lack of consent to it.

The practical difference between the two is that under the conjunctive interpretation, for which the claimant must disprove both, a claimant who knew of the illegal use can never establish the innocent owner defense. If the claimant knew of the use, that precludes the defense, regardless of whether the claimant consented to the use. This interpretation could cause harsh results where the claimant knew of the illegal use and wanted to prevent it but was unable to do so. In this situation, the disjunctive approach would allow claimants to show that even though they knew of the illegal use, they still did not consent to it and so qualified as innocent owners. The disjunctive approach provides a broader innocent owner defense, while the conjunctive interpretation narrows the defense and makes forfeiture easier for the government.

The circuits are divided on which approach is better. The disjunctive approach clearly prevails in the First,[91] Second,[92] Third,[93] Fourth[94] and Sixth Circuits.[95] The Ninth Circuit disagrees, adopting the conjunctive interpretation.[96] The Eleventh Circuit is confused, with cases following both the conjunctive and disjunctive approaches,[97] but probably the prevailing law is the disjunctive view.[98] The Seventh[99] and Eighth Circuits[100] have specifically declined to choose an approach.

Supporters of both the conjunctive and disjunctive interpretations rely on principles of statutory construction for authority. Disjunctive courts conclude that the word "or" in the statute clearly indicates Congress's intent to give claimants the option of proving either no knowledge or no consent.[101] These courts add that Congress would have

---

91. United States v. One Parcel of Real Property Located at 77 Walnut Street, 923 F.2d 840 (1st Cir.1990).

92. United States v. One Parcel of Property Located at 121 Allen Place, 75 F.3d 118 (2d Cir.1996); United States v. 141st St. Corp., 911 F.2d 870 (2d Cir.1990).

93. United States v. 6109 Grubb Road, 886 F.2d 618 (3d Cir.1989).

94. United States v. 31 Endless Street, 8 F.3d 821 (4th Cir.1993).

95. United States v. 14307 Four Lakes Drive, 1993 WL 264687 (6th Cir. 1993).

96. United States v. Lot 111–B, 902 F.2d 1443 (9th Cir.1990).

97. *Compare* United States v. 1012 Germantown Road, 963 F.2d 1496, 1503 (11th Cir.1992) (disjunctive) *with* United

States v. 15603 85th Avenue, 933 F.2d 976 (11th Cir.1991).

98. The cases taking the disjunctive view are more recent, *see* United States v. 1012 Germantown Road, 963 F.2d 1496 (11th Cir.1992); United States v. 15603 85th Avenue, 933 F.2d 976 (11th Cir.1991). *See also* Jimmy Gurule, Symposium, *Federal Asset Forfeiture Reform*, 21 J.Legis. 155, 169 (1995)(characterizing the Eleventh Circuit as taking the disjunctive view while noting conflicting cases).

99. United States v. 7326 Highway 45, 965 F.2d 311, 315 (7th Cir.1992).

100. United States v. One 1989 Jeep Wagoneer, 976 F.2d 1172, 1174 n. 1 (8th Cir.1992).

101. 886 F.2d at 625–26, *citing* Reiter v. Sonotone, 442 U.S. 330, 339, 99 S.Ct. 2326, 2331, 60 L.Ed.2d 931 (1979).

chosen "and" if it had intended a conjunctive rule.[102] Conjunctive courts respond by pointing out cases in which courts have recognized that the word "or" does not mean "or" at all.[103] In fact, the Supreme Court has specifically held that courts should not conclude that a statute must be read in the disjunctive just because it contains the word "or."[104]

Conjunctive courts also rely on a principle of logic called De Morgan's theorem.[105] De Morgan's theorem states that, "The negation of a disjunction of two statements is logically equivalent to the conjunction of their negations."[106] This means that although "knowledge or consent" is ordinarily a disjunction, the addition of the word "without" to make it "without knowledge or consent" negates the disjunction and actually makes the meaning of the entire phrase the equivalent of "without knowledge and without consent."[107] Therefore, according to conjunctive courts, claimants must prove both a lack of knowledge and a lack of consent.[108]

Continuing with statutory construction principles, disjunctive courts note that a statute should not be construed to render any words superfluous. The conjunctive approach makes the word "consent" irrelevant because if the claimant has knowledge, the defense is denied and consent is not implicated.[109]

A good example of the disjunctive approach is United States v. 141st St. Corp.[110] The Second Circuit stated that "the ordinary meaning of the word 'consent' dictates the construction we adopt."[111] The court considered that "consent" means " 'compliance or approval esp[ecially] of what

102. *See, e.g.,* United States v. 6109 Grubb Road, 886 F.2d 618, 626 (3d Cir.1989)(basing decision on the use of the traditionally disjunctive meaning of the word "or"); United States v. One 1973 Rolls Royce, 43 F.3d 794, 813 (3d Cir.1994) (reaffirming the *Grubb Road* analysis, at least as it pertains to persons owning subject property at the time of the illegal act).

103. *See, e.g.,* United States v. Lot 111–B, 902 F.2d 1443 (9th Cir.1990); United States v. 1980 Red Ferrari, 827 F.2d 477 (9th Cir.1987).

104. De Sylva v. Ballentine, 351 U.S. 570, 76 S.Ct. 974, 100 L.Ed. 1415 (1956).

105. *See, e.g.,* United States v. One 1973 Rolls Royce, 43 F.3d 794, 815 n. 19 (3d Cir.1994) (explaining De Morgan's theorem).

106. Irving M. Copi, Symbolic Logic 29 (5th ed. 1979); *see also One 1973 Rolls Royce,* 43 F.3d at 815.

107. Another example is if you say, "You can play outside if it is not raining or sleeting," you mean that it can be neither raining nor sleeting. *See* Robert E. Blacher, *Clearing the Smoke of the Battlefield: Understanding Congressional Intent Regarding the Innocent Owner Provision of 21*

U.S.C. § 881(a)(7), 85 J.Crim.L. & Criminology 502, 531 n.86 (1994).

108. Commentators provide additional support for the conjunctive interpretation, noting that "[m]ost decisions holding that lack of consent is a defense ignore the fact that the phrase 'without the knowledge or consent' is cast in the negative." 1 David B. Smith, Prosecution and Defense of Forfeiture Cases ¶ 4.02, at 4–36.4.

109. *See*

First Circuit: United States v. 77 Walnut Street, 923 F.2d 840 (1st Cir.1990).

Second Circuit: United States v. 121 Allen Place, 75 F.3d 118 (2d Cir.1996); United States v. 141st Street Corp., 911 F.2d 870 (2d Cir.1990).

Third Circuit: United States v. 6109 Grubb Road, 886 F.2d 618 (3d Cir.1989).

Fourth Circuit: United States v. 31 Endless Street, 8 F.3d 821 (4th Cir.1993).

Sixth Circuit: United States v. 14307 Four Lakes Dr., 1993 WL 264687 (6th Cir. 1993).

110. 911 F.2d 870 (2d Cir.1990).

111. United States v. 141st St. Corp., 911 F.2d 870, 878 (2d Cir.1990).

is done or proposed by another.' "[112] The court reasoned that without knowledge of an activity it would be impossible to approve of or comply with the activity:

> If we were to construe ["knowledge or consent"] to mean that a claimant's knowledge alone precludes the innocent owner defense (i.e., that a claimant must disprove both knowledge and consent), then "consent" as used in the statute would be totally unnecessary. In other words, the factfinder would never reach the issue of consent once it concluded that the claimant had knowledge. Similarly, under this construction it would be necessary to determine whether the claimant consented only if the factfinder first concluded that the claimant did not have knowledge of the drug activity, a result that cannot be squared with the ordinary meaning of the word "consent."[113]

The court, therefore, refused to require the claimant to shoulder the additional burden of disproving both elements as such a burden would "ignore[] Congress' desire to preserve the property of innocent owners and ... render[] the phrase 'or consent' superfluous, a result that should be avoided."[114]

Conjunctive and disjunctive courts both find some legislative history to support their views. A Congressional report, which purports to explain the "knowledge or consent" language, states that "property would not be subject to forfeiture unless the owner of such property knew or consented to the [illegal conduct]."[115] Although this report does little more than parrot the statutory language, the Ninth Circuit reads this report to mean that Congress intended the innocent owner defense to be the narrower, conjunctive version.[116] On the other hand, parts of the same report indicate confusion regarding the operation of the forfeiture statute, and disjunctive courts have questioned whether the report should be given any weight.[117]

Finally, on a policy level, the Ninth Circuit expressed concern that, were the disjunctive approach taken, the "policy [of seizing all property with a 'substantial connection' to illegal drug activity] would be substantially undercut if persons who were fully aware of the illegal connection or source of their property were permitted to reclaim the property as 'innocent' owners."[118]

112. *Id.* at 878, *citing* Webster's Third New International Dictionary 482 (1971).

113. *Id.* at 878.

114. *Id.* at 878, *citing* United States v. Menasche, 348 U.S. 528, 538–39, 75 S.Ct. 513, 519–20, 99 L.Ed. 615 (1955) and United States v. Berrios, 869 F.2d 25, 28–29 (2d Cir.1989).

115. Joint Explanatory Statement of Titles II and III, 95th Cong., 2nd Sess., *reprinted in* 1978 U.S.Code Cong.Admin. News 9510, 9522–23.

116. *Lot 111–B,* 902 F.2d at 1445.

117. *See*

Second Circuit: United States v. 141st Street Corp., 911 F.2d 870, 878–80 (2d Cir. 1990).

Third Circuit: United States v. 6109 Grubb Road, 886 F.2d 618, 625–26 (3d Cir. 1989).

118. *Lot 111–B,* 902 F.2d at 1445.

v. Post–Illegal–Act Transferees

Post-illegal-act transferees are persons who were not owners of the property at the time of the prohibited use but became owners after the use and before the forfeiture action was filed. They can become owners either by sale or gift.[119]

The widely used term "post-illegal-act transferees" is somewhat misleading because it suggests a distinction from *pre*-illegal-act transferees. Actually, *pre*-illegal-act transfers of the property are irrelevant; obviously, the history of the property before it was used in a forfeitable way does not matter. The only property transfers that matter are *post*-illegal-act transfers, those accomplished after the government has some interest in the property. Thus we sometimes use the plain term *transferees* and omit the modifier *post-illegal-act* because that quality is implicit.

Issues on how the innocent owner defense applies to transferees began to arise in 1993 after the Supreme Court held in *Buena Vista* that transferees could raise the defense.[120] When a transferee files an innocent owner claim, two questions arise: whether the disjunctive interpretation of the innocent owner defense should be modified, and how to define the time for measuring knowledge and/or consent.

a. Conjunctive or Disjunctive. As described above, the Supreme Court held in *Buena Vista* that transferees may invoke the innocent owner defense.[121] Combining this holding with the disjunctive interpretation of the defense leads to questionable results. Applying the disjunctive interpretation to transferees, a person who knew that the property in question had been used in connection with illegal narcotics activities could take ownership of the property, and as a result, the property would be shielded from forfeiture. The reason for this is that it is impossible for someone to consent to a prohibited use of property that they do not yet own. Therefore, in disjunctive jurisdictions (where claimants need only prove lack of knowledge *or* lack of consent), transferees will always qualify as innocent owners and escape forfeiture by showing lack of consent.[122] This could lead to intentional shielding of assets through transfers by drug dealers to "innocent" third parties, a result which civil forfeiture is meant to prevent.

Two jurisdictions faced this question and reached different conclusions. Both cases involved attorneys claiming they were innocent owners of their fees. The Eleventh Circuit decided that when the claimant is a transferee, the consent prong of the innocent owner defense is inapplicable.[123] Thus the claimant must prove lack of knowledge. If the claimant cannot prove lack of knowledge, *i.e.*, if the claimant had knowledge of the illegal activity, that claimant is not an innocent owner and forfeiture is

---

119. *United States v. 92 Buena Vista Ave.*, 507 U.S. 111, 140, 113 S.Ct. 1126, 1143, 122 L.Ed.2d 469 (1993)(Kennedy, J., dissenting).

120. *See* § 28.6(A)(i) *supra.*

121. *See supra* § 28.6(A)(i).

122. United States v. 6640 S.W. 48th St., 41 F.3d 1448 (11th Cir.1995).

123. 41 F.3d 1448, 1453 (11th Cir. 1995).

ordered.[124] In contrast, the Third Circuit decided that the disjunctive interpretation applies regardless of whether the claimant is a transferee, so if a transferee claimant proves lack of consent, forfeiture is denied.[125]

The Eleventh Circuit modified the disjunctive approach. In support of its decision modifying the usual disjunctive approach in the context of transferees, the Eleventh Circuit pointed to two policy goals of § 881, to punish criminals and ensure that innocent parties were not punished for their "unwitting association with wrongdoers."[126] The court concluded that allowing a "lack of consent" defense for transferees would be inconsistent with the purposes of the forfeiture statute and would lead to absurd results.[127] Owners like the claimant in this case, reasoned the court, are not innocent persons who have "unwittingly" associated with wrongdoers.[128] In closing, the court pointed to the fact that a large loophole would be created if the "lack of consent defense" were permitted in cases involving post-illegal act transferees.[129] So the attorney did not qualify as an innocent owner and his claim to the property was denied.[130]

The Third Circuit reached the opposite conclusion in a case involving an attorney whose fee was paid with a Rolls Royce that the government claimed had been used to shuttle people to and from meetings on drug trafficking.[131] The court held that the attorney would qualify as an innocent owner if he could "show that he did not know that the Rolls Royce was being used or going to be used ... in the ... meetings at the time they took place."[132] Thus the court decided that the disjunctive interpretation applied, even to post-illegal act transferees. The court's rationale was that having previously held the disjunctive interpretation to be the correct one, it refused to treat post-illegal-act transferees differently and thus condone "a schizophrenic reading of the text."[133] The court also reasoned that "it is not unreasonable to think that post-illegal act transferees of property interests would not be subject to forfeiture."[134] The principal goal of § 881, according to the court, is "to give owners of property an incentive to prevent use of that property in the drug trade," and "[p]eople who are not owners at the time the act is committed are simply in no position to prevent the improper use."[135] On remand, the attorney presumably qualified as an innocent owner and got to keep the Rolls Royce.[136]

b. Time of Measuring Knowledge. Another problem unique to transferees, which can affect both disjunctive and conjunctive jurisdic-

---

124. Id.

125. United States v. One 1973 Rolls Royce, 43 F.3d 794, 799–800 (3d Cir.1994).

126. 41 F.3d at 1452.

127. Id. at 1453.

128. Id. at 1454.

129. Id.

130. Id. at 1453.

131. United States v. One 1973 Rolls Royce, 43 F.3d 794, 799–800 (3d Cir.1994).

132. Id. at 819.

133. Id. at 820.

134. Id. at 819.

135. Id.

136. Id.

tions,[137] is the question of the time for measuring knowledge and/or consent. When transferees are not involved, one court has decided that the time to measure knowledge is the time of the forfeiture proceeding rather than the time of the prohibited use.[138] But when transferees are involved, the existence of the transfer date raises the question whether the claimant's knowledge should be measured at the time of the prohibited use or at the time the property was transferred?[139] Again, the courts disagree.

The Eleventh Circuit holds that the relevant time for judging knowledge is when the property is transferred rather than when the prohibited use occurred.[140] The Third Circuit, on the other hand, holds that the relevant time for determining knowledge is when the prohibited act occurred. The Third Circuit said the claimant would qualify as an innocent owner if he could "show that he did not know that the Rolls Royce was being used or going to be used … in the … meetings at the time they took place."[141] Thus the court decided that the relevant time for judging knowledge [for transferees] was the point when the illegal acts took place rather than at the time of transfer of the car. As support for its position, the court pointed to Justice Scalia's concurrence in *Buena Vista*.[142] Anticipating the questions that *Buena Vista* would raise, Justice Scalia wrote:

> I do not find inconceivable the possibility that post-illegal-act transferees with post-illegal-act knowledge of the earlier illegality are provided a defense against forfeiture. The Government would still be entitled to the property held by the drug dealers and by close friends and relatives who are unable to meet their burden of proof as to ignorance of the illegal act when it occurred.[143]

137. Even in conjunctive jurisdictions, the point in time when knowledge is measured can effect the outcome of an innocent owner determination. For example, if the claimant had knowledge at the time of the transfer but not at the time of the prohibited use, conjunctive jurisdictions would reach different conclusions on whether the claimant had knowledge for purposes of the defense.

The *Buena Vista* decision also may affect courts following the conjunctive interpretation of "knowledge or consent." The important decision for these courts will be what is the appropriate time for determining knowledge—the time of the illegal act or the time of transfer. No courts following the conjunctive interpretation have addressed this question.

138. *See* United States v. Land in Name of Mikell, 33 F.3d 11, 13 (5th Cir. 1994).

139. This is often a critical question for attorneys attempting to keep fees paid to them by defendants accused of drug crimes. At the time of transfer of the property to an attorney, the attorney usually knows that his or her client is accused of a drug crime and that any payment may arise from profits from that crime. Thus, if knowledge at the time of transfer is the correct standard these attorneys will lose. However, they may keep the payment if the relevant time period is the time of the illegal act, presuming of course, that the attorney had no knowledge of the illegal act at that time.

140. *6640 S.W. 48th St.,* 41 F.3d at 1451–52.

141. *One 1973 Rolls Royce,* 43 F.3d at 819.

142. *Id.* at 820.

143. *United States v. 92 Buena Vista Ave.,* 507 U.S. 111, 139, 113 S.Ct. 1126, 1142, 122 L.Ed.2d 469 (1993) (Scalia, J., concurring).

Based on these factors, the Third Circuit concluded that allowing post-illegal-act transferees with post-illegal-act knowledge to avoid forfeiture as innocent owners was defensible.[144]

B. CONSTITUTIONAL DEFENSES: EXCESSIVE FINES CLAUSE AND DUE PROCESS

Two constitutional defenses exist, based on the excessive fines clause and the due process clause. These are discussed *infra* in § 28.17 and § 28.19, respectively, on constitutional issues.

§ 28.7   Forfeiture Based on Drugs: 21 U.S.C. § 881—Reform Proposals

With civil forfeiture expanding and these numerous disagreements in the courts, legislative revisions have been proposed. As of Fall, 1997, Congress has two bills pending before it which would make sweeping revisions to civil forfeiture.[1] Representative Hyde (Chairman of the House Judiciary Committee) and a coalition of others have introduced H.R. 1835. This bill would, *inter alia,* change the burden of proof for forfeiture and establish an uniform innocent owner defense. A second bill, drafted by the Department of Justice, has been introduced by Representative Schumer. Some legislative revision to the forfeiture laws is possible.

§ 28.8   Forfeiture Based on General Federal Crimes: 18 U.S.C. § 981—In General

The general civil forfeiture statute, § 981, was adopted in 1986.[1] It has much less common law than § 881, which was adopted in 1970.[2] Wherever § 881 is analogous, it provides a helpful source of common law which the courts gladly use.[3] Similarities and differences are described below.

§ 28.9   Forfeiture Based on General Federal Crimes: 18 U.S.C. § 981—Property Subject to Forfeiture

Defining property as forfeitable under § 981 requires that the statute list the property as subject to forfeiture and that the common law nexus test be met.

144. *One 1973 Rolls Royce*, 43 F.3d at 820.

§ 28.7

1. Federal Forfeiture Guide, Vol. 2, No. 1 at page 1 (James Publishing Company, August 1997).

§ 28.8

1. P.L. 99–570, 100 Stat. 3207–35 (October 27, 1986).

2. *See* United States v. Certain Accounts Together with all Monies on Deposit Therein, 795 F.Supp. 391 (S.D.Fla.1992) at 395 (noting "wealth" of caselaw for § 881 and "relative paucity" of caselaw for § 981). This is still true today.

3. *See, e.g.,* United States v. All Assets of G.P.S. Automotive Corp., 66 F.3d 483, 487 (2d Cir.1995) (analogizing nexus requirement of § 981 to that of § 881), and at 487–88 (analogizing innocent owner defense of § 981 to that of § 881).

A. PROPERTY DESCRIBED IN THE STATUTE

Civil forfeiture under § 981 covers five categories of property.

i. Property Involved in or Traceable to Property Involved in Money Laundering

The first category is property associated with money laundering transactions.[1] The statute includes an exception for one kind of money laundering committed by one kind of defendant. The statute states, "However, no property shall be seized or forfeited in the case of a violation of [the CTR law] by a domestic financial institution examined by a Federal bank supervisory agency or a financial institution regulated by the [SEC] or a partner, director, or employee thereof."[2] This exception means that many financial institutions and their employees will not be liable for forfeiture for violating the CTR laws. However, they remain liable for forfeiture under any of the other laundering laws.

Beyond this limited exception, the statute allows forfeiture of any property, real or personal, *involved in* or *traceable to property involved in* transactions or attempted transactions illegal under certain money laundering crimes.[3]

a. Involved in Money Laundering. Courts define *involved in* as synonymous with *facilitating* under § 881.[4] This conclusion is based on the legislative history of § 981, wherein Congress stated, "The term 'property involved' is intended to include the money or other property being laundered (the corpus), and any commissions or fees paid to the launderer, and any property used to facilitate the laundering offense."[5] Courts also rely on subsequent amendments to § 981 to support Congressional intent for this interpretation of *involved in*.[6]

A particular issue that troubles courts is whether this facilitation theory reaches clean money that is commingled with dirty money in a

---

§ 28.9

1. The money laundering transactions are failing to file accurate CTR's under 31 U.S.C. § 5313(a), structuring transactions to evade CTR's under 31 U.S.C. § 5324, laundering of monetary instruments under 18 U.S.C. § 1956, and engaging in monetary transaction in property derived from specified unlawful activity under 18 U.S.C. § 1957.

2. 18 U.S.C. § 981(a)(1)(A).

3. 18 U.S.C. § 981(a)(1)(A).

4. *See*

Second Circuit: United States v. Contents of Account Numbers 208–06070 and 208–06068–1–2, 847 F.Supp. 329, 335 (S.D.N.Y.1994); United States v. Certain Funds on Deposit in Account No. 01–0–71417, 769 F.Supp. 80, 84 (E.D.N.Y.1991).

Ninth Circuit: United States v. All Monies ($477,048.62) in Account No. 90–3617–

3, 754 F.Supp. 1467, 1472–73 (D.Haw. 1991).

Eleventh Circuit: United States v. Certain Accounts, 795 F.Supp. 391 (S.D.Fla. 1992).

But see

Second Circuit: United States v. All Funds Presently on Deposit or Attempted to Be Deposited, 832 F.Supp. 542, 562 (E.D.N.Y.1993)(rejecting "facilitation theory" as basis for forfeiture under § 981 in that case).

5. United States v. All Monies ($477,048.62) in Account No. 90–3617–3, 754 F.Supp. 1467, 1473 (D.Haw.1991), *quoting* 134 Cong.Rec. S17365 (daily ed. Nov. 10, 1988).

6. United States v. Certain Accounts Together with all Monies on Deposit Therein, 795 F.Supp. 391, 396 (S.D.Fla.1992).

bank account. Since forfeiture in this context is based on money launder-ing, the usual property the government seeks to forfeit is money in a bank account. The dirty money in the account or money traceable to dirty money is forfeitable, either under the theory that it is involved in laundering or is the proceeds of laundering. A different question is whether the legitimately derived or clean money in the account is also forfeitable, based on the theory that it is *involved in* laundering. No courts of appeal have decided this question,[7] but some district courts have. The district courts disagree.

Several district courts have held that clean money in an account is forfeitable as involved with laundering.[8] The first court to reach this conclusion was the District of Hawaii.[9] The claimant owned a bank account under the name Ontivero in New York. The Ontivero account received several deposits traced to a laundering organization.[10] The government argued that the account was used to "facilitate" the money laundering and that *all* of the money in the Ontivero account—both that traced to the drug transactions and the legitimate funds—was forfeitable because the money from legitimate sources helped to conceal the tainted money.[11] The court concluded that "[e]ven though 981 does not express-ly include the words 'facilitate' or 'facilitating,' the statute covers prop-erty 'involved in' illegal money laundering transactions.... The legisla-tive history makes it clear that 'property involved in' includes property used to facilitate money laundering offenses."[12] The court then held:

> There is probable cause to believe that the Ontivero account was being used to help launder drug proceeds. As such, both the legiti-mate and tainted money in the account aided that end. The account provided a repository for the drug proceeds in which the legitimate could provide a "cover" for those proceeds, thus making it more difficult to trace the proceeds. There is, therefore, probable cause to believe that all of the money in the Ontivero account facilitated the illegal activities of the Melendez and Dirimex organizations, making the entire account forfeitable....[13]

The same reasoning has been adopted by the district court for the Eastern District of New York.[14]

7. *Cf.* United States v. Tencer, 107 F.3d 1120 (5th Cir.1997) (clean funds com-mingled in an account with dirty funds are forfeitable as "involved in" laundering un-der the criminal forfeiture statute, § 982).

8. *See*

Second Circuit: United States v. Con-tents of Account Numbers 208–06070 and 208–06068–1–2, 847 F.Supp. 329, 335 (S.D.N.Y.1994); United States v. Certain Funds on Deposit in Account No. 01–0–71417, 769 F.Supp. 80 (E.D.N.Y.1991).

Ninth Circuit: United States v. All Mo-nies in Account No. 90–3617–3, 754 F.Supp. 1467 (D.Haw.1991).

Eleventh Circuit: United States v. Cer-tain Accounts Together with all Monies on

Deposit Therein, 795 F.Supp. 391, 396 (S.D.Fla.1992)(approving forfeiture of direct recipient accounts but dismissing forfeiture as to indirect recipient accounts).

9. United States v. All Monies ($477,-048.62) in Account No. 90–3617–3, 754 F.Supp. 1467 (D.Haw.1991).

10. *Id.* at 1470.

11. *Id.* at 1472.

12. *Id.* at 1473.

13. *Id.* at 1475–76.

14. United States v. Certain Funds on Deposit in Account No. 01–0–71417, 769 F.Supp. 80 (E.D.N.Y.1991).

Another district court has also concluded that clean money in the account is forfeitable as being involved in laundering, but refused to extend this holding any further.[15] This forfeiture involved two kinds of bank accounts—direct recipient accounts and indirect recipient accounts. The direct recipient accounts received deposits of dirty money, and also held some clean money. The indirect recipient accounts received deposits from the direct recipient accounts. The government argued for forfeiture of all the money in both kinds of accounts based on a facilitation theory. The court allowed forfeiture of the direct recipient accounts, including the clean money therein, but rejected forfeiture of money in the indirect recipient accounts, stating, "Like a contagious disease, each direct account could contaminate any account that had dealings with it. The indirect accounts could then conceivably pass on the infection to other accounts, and so forth ad infinitum. The outer limits of this theory would be bounded only by Plaintiff's [the government's] imagination. The court rejects such a theory."[16]

In contrast, two district courts have held that clean money commingled in an account with dirty money is not covered by the facilitation theory. One district court's holding is not reported, but is described by the Second Circuit in Marine Midland Bank, N.A. v. United States.[17] The account in question contained $7.7 million, $1.7 of which was dirty. The government sought forfeiture of not only the $1.7 million but the other $6 million as well. The district court for the Southern District of New York denied forfeiture of the $6 million on a facilitation theory.[18] The government did not appeal this ruling, so it was not before the Second Circuit, which only described it as part of the background of the case.[19]

The other district court holding that clean money commingled with dirty money cannot be reached as involved in laundering reached this result because such a forfeiture would be inconsistent with the implications of § 984.[20]

Thus there is disagreement in the district courts. No courts of appeal have reached the issue. The district courts are about evenly split, with a margin of authority holding that clean money commingled with dirty money in a single account is forfeitable as involved in the laundering.

b. Traceable to Property Involved—§ 984. Although the statute does not use the word, the courts generally refer to property forfeitable under this "traceable to" theory as *proceeds*.[21]

---

15. United States v. Certain Accounts Together with all Monies on Deposit Therein, 795 F.Supp. 391 (S.D.Fla.1992).

16. *Id.* at 397–98.

17. 11 F.3d 1119 (2d Cir.1993).

18. *Id.* at 1122, describing the district court's "May order."

19. *Id.* at 1123.

20. United States v. All Funds Presently on Deposit or Attempted to be Deposited in any Account Maintained at American Express Bank, 832 F.Supp. 542, 562 (E.D.N.Y.1993). The court held that allowing a facilitation theory to reach clean money would erode the limitations period in § 984. Section 984 is discussed further *infra* in this section.

21. *See, e.g.,*

Second Circuit: United States v. All Funds Presently on Deposit or Attempted to Be Deposited in Any Accounts at Ameri-

Again, because the underlying prohibited transaction is laundering, the property the government seeks to forfeit is often money in bank accounts. Initially when § 981 was enacted, the government had to prove that the funds it was seeking to forfeit as proceeds were traceable to dirty funds, and courts denied forfeiture otherwise.[22] Money in bank accounts is difficult to trace because it is fungible. Tracing rules were developed for the same problem under § 881 in United States v. Banco Cafetero Panama.[23] As described above, *Banco Cafetero* held that a traceable connection existed between a drug sale and money on deposit in a bank account if the "lowest intermediate balance" analysis was satisfied.[24] In effect, the theory was "drugs in-last out."[25] When those tracing rules were applied under § 981, launderers began to periodically "zero out" accounts to beat the tracing rules.[26] So in 1992, Congress adopted a statute, § 984, to overrule the *Banco Cafetero* tracing rules for forfeiture under § 981.[27]

Section 984 "permits the forfeiture of money in a bank account even when the money seized is not directly traceable to the laundered funds so long as the account previously contained the funds involved in or traceable to the illegal activity."[28] This statute prohibits "zeroing out" an account so that the money in it is not traceable to dirty money and is immune from forfeiture.[29] It means the "lowest intermediate balance defense" from *Banco Cafetero* is not effective in forfeitures for money laundering.[30]

In *Marine Midland*, the Second Circuit did not rule on whether the money in the account not directly traceable to dirty money was forfeitable on a "traceable proceeds" theory because it ruled the government had waived that theory. However, the court discussed § 984, again with no ruling, but the court's description is useful:

> The enactment of § 984 was intended to lessen the government's burden of proof in forfeiture proceedings against fungible property.

can Express Bank, 832 F.Supp. 542, 551 (E.D.N.Y.1993) ("traceable proceeds").

Third Circuit: United States v. Eleven Vehicles, 836 F.Supp. 1147 (E.D.Pa.1993).

Seventh Circuit: United States v. $448,-342.85, 969 F.2d 474 (7th Cir.1992).

22. *See, e.g.,*

Second Circuit: United States v. Eleven Vehicles, 836 F.Supp. 1147 (E.D.Pa.1993).

Seventh Circuit: United States v. $448,-342.85, 969 F.2d 474 (7th Cir.1992)(allowing forfeiture because the proceeds vastly exceeded the sums on deposit at the time of the seizure, but stating that "proceeds" theory of forfeiture does not extend to clean money in account).

Eleventh Circuit: United States v.Certain Accounts, Together with all Monies on Deposit Therein, 795 F.Supp. 391 (S.D.Fla. 1992).

23. 797 F.2d 1154 (2d Cir.1986).

24. *Id.* at 1159. *Banco Cafetero* and § 881 are discussed *supra* in § 28.2(A)(ii).

25. *Id.* at 1159 n.5.

26. *See* United States v. All Funds Presently on Deposit or Attempted to be Deposited in any Account Maintained at American Express Bank, 832 F.Supp. 542, 549 (E.D.N.Y.1993).

27. 18 U.S.C. § 984. P.L. 102–550, 106 Stat. 4063 (October 28, 1992).

28. United States v. $814,254 U.S. Currency, 51 F.3d 207, 209 (9th Cir.1995).

29. United States v. All Funds Presently on Deposit or Attempted to Be Deposited, 832 F.Supp. 542, 557 (E.D.N.Y.1993).

30. *Id.* at 551–52.

Prior to its enactment, illegal proceeds deposited in a bank account were subject to forfeiture only to the extent that the account balance fell below the amount of the tainted deposit.... In a forfeiture proceeding under § 984, however, the government no longer is required to show that money in a bank account is the specific money involved in the underlying offense.... Moreover, it is no longer a defense that money involved in the underlying offense has been removed from the account and replaced with legally obtained money.[31]

Section 984 allows broad substitute seizures but limits the government power in two ways. First, the statute has a specific exemption for interbank accounts.[32] The Second Circuit acknowledged the possible application of this exemption in *Marine Midland*, but because the district court had not considered it, the court just remanded that issue to the district court.[33] Second, § 984 is limited because it only applies for one year.[34] As one court described it, the statute gives the government broad new powers but "simultaneously tempers the additional power given the government by means of a statute of limitations...."[35] The legislative history of § 984 explains:

Section 984 provides that in cases involving fungible property, property is subject to forfeiture if it is identical to otherwise forfeitable property, is located or maintained in the same way as the original forfeitable property, and not more than one year has passed between the time the original property subject to forfeiture was so located or maintained and the time the forfeiture action was initiated by seizing the property or filing the complaint.... (The time limitation is considered necessary to ensure that the property forfeited has a reasonable nexus to the offense giving rise to the original action for forfeiture.)[36]

This statute became effective on October 28, 1992; it does not apply retrospectively.[37]

ii. Foreign Drug Felonies

The statute allows forfeiture of any property within the jurisdiction of the U.S. constituting, derived from, or traceable to proceeds obtained

31. Marine Midland Bank, N.A. v. United States, 11 F.3d 1119, 1126–27 (2d Cir.1993).

32. 18 U.S.C. § 984(d)(1).

33. *Marine Midland Bank*, 11 F.3d at 1127.

34. 18 U.S.C. § 984(c).

35. United States v. All Funds Presently on Deposit or Attempted to Be Deposited in Any Accounts Maintained at American Express Bank, 832 F.Supp. 542, 558–59 (E.D.N.Y.1993).

36. H.R.Rep.No. 102–28, 102d Cong., 1st Sess. (1991), *quoted in* United States v. All Funds Presently on Deposit or Attempted to Be Deposited in Any Accounts Maintained at American Express Bank, 832 F.Supp. 542, 558 (E.D.N.Y.1993).

37. *See*

Second Circuit: United States v. Contents of Accounts Numbered 208–06070, 847 F.Supp. 329 (S.D.N.Y.1994).

Ninth Circuit: United States v. $814,-254 in United States Currency, 51 F.3d 207, 212 (9th Cir.1995).

directly or indirectly from foreign drug felonies.[38]

iii. Proceeds of Crimes Affecting Financial Institutions

The statute allows forfeiture of any property, real or personal, which constitutes or is derived from proceeds traceable to certain crimes affecting financial institutions.[39] Forfeitures under this section are infrequent but some have been reported.[40]

iv. Gross Receipts from Crimes Involving Assets Held by Conservators for Financial Institutions

The statute allows forfeiture of any property, real or personal, which represents or is traceable to the gross receipts obtained, directly or indirectly, from crimes involving assets held by conservators for financial institutions.[41] This section has a special definition of "gross receipts" if the crime is mail fraud—gross receipts are defined as "all property, real or personal, tangible or intangible, [obtained by fraud] directly or indirectly."[42]

v. Proceeds of Certain Motor Vehicle Crimes

The statute allows forfeiture of any property, real or personal, which represents or is traceable to the gross proceeds obtained, directly or indirectly, from certain motor vehicle crimes.[43]

vi. Relation Back

As with the main forfeiture statutes, § 981 includes the relation back doctrine, so title to the property vests in the U.S. at the time of the prohibited transaction.[44]

38. 18 U.S.C. § 981(a)(1)(B).

39. 18 U.S.C. § 981(a)(1)(C) allows forfeiture when real or personal property constitutes or is derived from proceeds traceable to a violation of 18 U.S.C. §§ 215, 471, 473, 474, 476, 477, 478, 479, 480, 481, 485, 486, 487, 488, 501, 502, 510, 542, 545, 656, 657, 842, 844, 1005, 1006, 1007, 1014, 1028, 1029, 1030, 1032, 1344, and mail and wire fraud if they relate to financial institutions.

40. *See*

Second Circuit: United States v. Certain Funds on Deposit in Account No. 01-0-71417, 769 F.Supp. 80 (E.D.N.Y.1991)(forfeiture based, *inter alia,* on violations of §§ 657, 1006, 1014 and 1344).

Third Circuit: United States v. Various Computers and Computer Equipment, 82 F.3d 582 (3d Cir.1996) (forfeiture based on violation of § 1029); United States v. Eleven Vehicles, 836 F.Supp. 1147 (E.D.Pa.1993)(forfeiture based on violation of § 1343).

Ninth Circuit: United States v. Real Property 874 Gartel Dr., Walnut, Cal., 79 F.3d 918 (9th Cir.1996)(forfeiture based on violation of § 1014)(Judge Aldisert concurred but noted that forfeiture based on this theory is unusual, so he was "on guard.").

Cf.

Second Circuit: In Re The Seizure of All Funds in Accounts in the Names Registry Publishing Inc., 68 F.3d 577 (2d Cir.1995)(forfeiture based on mail fraud under § 981, but not specifying which subsection of § 981).

41. 18 U.S.C. § 981(a)(1)(D).

42. 18 U.S.C. § 981(a)(1)(E).

43. 18 U.S.C. § 981(a)(1)(F).

44. 18 U.S.C. § 981(f) ("All right, title and interest in property [subject ot forfeiture] shall vest in the United states upon commission of the act giving rise to forfeiture. . . .").

B. NEXUS REQUIREMENT

Generally, for property to be subject to forfeiture under § 981, there must be a nexus between the property and the prohibited conduct.[45] Courts interpreting the nexus analogize to § 881, the drug civil forfeiture statute.[46] There are too few cases interpreting § 981 to determine if the nexus requirement there will divide the circuits, as it did under § 881, between a sufficient connection and a substantial connection.[47] The Second Circuit has discussed § 981 using the plain term "nexus."[48]

§ 28.10 Forfeiture Based on General Federal Crimes: 18 U.S.C. § 981—Defenses—In General

The defenses to § 981 forfeitures are generally the same as defenses to § 881 forfeitures with one exception. That exception is the innocent owner defense; the variation in that defense is described in detail below.[1] Otherwise, the defenses are the same: To file any sort of claim to the property, claimants must first satisfy standing requirements.[2] Thereafter claimants can either rebut the government's showing or establish an affirmative defense.[3] Affirmative defenses include the statutory innocent owner defense and two constitutional defenses.

§ 28.11 Forfeiture Based on General Federal Crimes: 18 U.S.C. § 981—Defenses—Standing

The standing requirements for § 981 are the same as those under § 881 because standing is based on the Constitution and Admiralty Rule C(6), both of which apply to § 981 as well as § 881.[1] One district court stated that the claimant "must demonstrate a possessory or ownership interest in the contents of the accounts, which may be proven by actual possession, dominion, control, title or financial stake."[2] This conclusion mirrors the law under § 881, and the court cited cases from other forfeiture statutes, including § 881, as authority.[3] Another court held

---

45. United States v. All Assets of G.P.S. Automotive Corp., 66 F.3d 483 (2d Cir.1995); Marine Midland Bank, N.A. v. United States, 11 F.3d 1119, 1126 (2d Cir. 1993).

46. See, e.g., Marine Midland Bank, N.A. v. United States, 11 F.3d 1119 (2d Cir.1993).

47. See § 28.2(B) supra.

48. United States v. All Assets of G.P.S. Automotive Corp., 66 F.3d 483 (2d Cir.1995); Marine Midland Bank, N.A. v. United States, 11 F.3d 1119, 1126 (2d Cir. 1993).

§ 28.10

1. See infra § 28.13(A).

2. United States v. Various Computers and Computer Equipment, 82 F.3d 582 (3d Cir.1996).

3. United States v. Real Property 874 Gartel Dr., Walnut, California, 79 F.3d 918, 923 (9th Cir.1996).

The innocent owner exception is often referred to as a defense, although in the posture of civil forfeiture cases, the property is the defendant and people asserting interests in it are claimants.

§ 28.11

1. Standing under § 881 is discussed supra in § 28.4.

2. United States v. Contents of Account Numbers 208–06070 and 208–06068–1–2, 847 F.Supp. 329, 332 (S.D.N.Y.1994).

3. Id. The court denied summary judgment to the government in a § 981 action because although the accounts were in the husband's name alone, allegations

that where the claim was not verified, standing cannot be denied under Rule C(6) because the court and government both knew of the basis for the claim and verification would not have added anything.[4]

§ 28.12   Forfeiture Based on General Federal Crimes: 18 U.S.C. § 981—Defenses—Failure of Proof

The same proof requirements apply to § 981 as to § 881.[1] The government must prove that the property is subject to forfeiture by probable cause;[2] then the burden of proof shifts to the claimant.[3]

§ 28.13   Forfeiture Based on General Federal Crimes: 18 U.S.C. § 981—Defenses—Affirmative Defenses

As with § 881, there is one statutory affirmative defense, the innocent owner defense, and two constitutional defenses, based on the due process and excessive fines clauses. The constitutional defenses are described in the constitutional section, *infra*.[1] Laches is not a defense to civil forfeiture.[2]

A. INNOCENT OWNER

Like § 881, § 981 includes an innocent owner defense in the statute.[3] Comparing the language reveals three differences in the two innocent owner defenses: § 981 refers to innocent owners *or lienholders* whereas § 881 mentions only *owners*; § 981 does not mention *consent* whereas § 881 does; and § 981 does not mention *willful blindness* whereas one clause of § 881 does. As these provisions of the two statutes have been interpreted by the courts, however, only two differences are

that the wife had access created a genuine issue of material fact. *Id.* at 333.

4. United States v. Various Computers and Computer Equipment, 82 F.3d 582, 584 (3d Cir.1996).

§ 28.12

1. *See*

Fifth Circuit: United States v. 1988 Oldsmobile Cutlass Supreme, 983 F.2d 670, 675 (5th Cir.1993)(applying the same proof standard in § 981 forfeiture).

Ninth Circuit: United States v. $814,-254.76 in U.S. Currency, 51 F.3d 207, 212 n. 5 (9th Cir.1995).

2. Marine Midland Bank v. United States, 11 F.3d 1119, 1125–26 (2d Cir.1993), *citing* § 981(d) and 19 U.S.C. § 1615. *See* § 28.23 *infra* for discussion of the standard of proof.

3. United States v. $814,254.76 in U.S. Currency, 51 F.3d 207, 212 n. 5 (9th Cir.1995). *See* § 28.23 *infra* for discussion of the standard of proof.

§ 28.13

1. *See* §§ 28.17 (excessive fines clause) and 28.19 (due process clause) *infra*.

2. *See*

Sixth Circuit: United States v. Residence, 705 Caden Lane, Lexington, Fayette County, Kentucky, 1996 WL 490377 (6th Cir.1996).

Ninth Circuit: United States v. Marolf, 973 F.Supp. 1139, (C.D.Cal.1997); United States v. Property Entitled in the Names of Alexander Morio Toki, 779 F.Supp. 1272, 1278 (D.Haw.1991).

3. 18 U.S.C. § 981(a)(2).

See also Second Circuit: United States v. All Assets of G.P.S. Automotive Corp., 66 F.3d 483 (2d Cir.1995).

Sixth Circuit: United States v. One Parcel of Real Property Located at 4560 Kingsbury, 1994 WL 28772 (6th Cir.1994).

Ninth Circuit: United States v. Real Property 874 Gartel Dr., Walnut, Cal., 79 F.3d 918 (9th Cir.1996).

important.[4] Those differences are the absence of any reference to consent in § 981, and the consistent absence throughout § 981 of any reference to willful blindness. These differences are highlighted below. Otherwise, interpretations of the § 881 innocent owner defense are useful in the context of § 981.

i. Owner or Lienholder

The claimant must have some ownership or possessory interest in the property at issue, and courts look to state law for the definition of property interests.[5] The term *lienholder* excludes general (unsecured) creditors.[6]

ii. Mental State

The innocent owner defense is available if the prohibited use of the property was without the knowledge of the owner or lienholder.[7] Knowledge includes willful blindness even though it is not mentioned in the text of the statute.[8] This is one of the differences between the § 881 and § 981 innocent owner defenses. One of the § 881 subsections mentions willful blindness specifically, causing some courts to refuse to use willful blindness as part of knowledge when it is not specifically mentioned. Under § 981, courts have no similar problem and unanimously find willful blindness to be included by the reference to knowledge.

To use the innocent owner defense, the claimant must lack knowledge of the transactions, not merely lack knowledge of their illegality.[9]

iii. Consent

Section 981, unlike § 881, does not include a reference to the claimant's consent. Section 981 states "[n]o property shall be forfeited . . . by reason of any act or omission . . . committed or omitted without the knowledge of that owner. . . ."[10] Several courts have rejected incorporation of the *Calero-Toledo* consent standard into § 981 forfeitures.[11]

---

4. The difference between owners under § 881 and owners or lienholders under § 981 is insignificant because courts have interpreted owner under § 881 to include lienholders, *see* § 28.6(A)(i) *supra*.

5. *See* United States v. $79,000 in Account No. 2168050/6749900, 1996 WL 648934 (S.D.N.Y.1996)(court analyzes New York law on bank accounts and concludes the claimant does have not "title, dominion or control" over the seized accounts so claim is stricken).

6. United States v. $20,193.39 U.S. Currency, 16 F.3d 344 (9th Cir.1994).

7. 18 U.S.C. § 981(a)(2).

8. *See*

Ninth Circuit: United States v. Real Property 874 Gartel Dr., Walnut California, 79 F.3d 918 (9th Cir.1996); United States v.

3814 N.W. Thurman St., Portland, 946 F.Supp. 843 (D.Ore.1996)(rejecting innocent owner defense based on willful blindness, *citing 874 Gartel*).

9. United States v. Real Property 874 Gartel Dr., Walnut California, 79 F.3d 918, 924 (9th Cir.1996).

10. 18 U.S.C. § 981(a)(2).

11. *See*

Second Circuit: United States v. All Assets of G.P.S. Automotive Corp., 66 F.3d 483 (2d Cir.1995).

Sixth Circuit: United States v. 4560 Kingsbury Rd., 1994 WL 28772 at *2 (6th Cir.1994).

Ninth Circuit: United States v. Real Property 874 Gartel Dr., Walnut, California, 79 F.3d 918, 924 (9th Cir.1996).

This is good news because, as noted under § 881, it is anomalous to use a constitutional minimum standard to dilute the level of protection provided for claimants expressly by statute. Moreover, considering that § 981 does not even use the word *consent*, it is surprising that the *Calero-Toledo* standard should be raised as an issue at all.

Most recently, the Ninth Circuit rejected any consent element in the § 981 innocent owner defense based on the plain language of the statute.[12] The Second Circuit has reached the same conclusion,[13] as has the Sixth Circuit.[14]

In the Sixth Circuit case, the government sought forfeiture of the claimant's home due to her husband's use of it for running an illegal gambling operation.[15] Despite the claimant's assertion that she was unaware of her husband's gambling business, the district court granted the government's motion for summary judgment because she "did not allege that she made an affirmative attempt to stop the illegal use of her property."[16] The Sixth Circuit rejected that formulation of the claimant's burden, stating "[t]his minimal innocent owner protection applies only where Congress has not provided for a more expansive defense."[17] The court continued, "Congress does not leave the innocent owner defense at a constitutional minimum, but instead provides an innocent owner defense for persons who merely lack knowledge of the illegal act causing the forfeiture proceeding."[18]

Later, the Southern District of Florida similarly rejected the application of *Calero-Toledo* to § 981. The government alleged that the money constituted personal property involved in a transaction for which no Currency Transaction Report ("CTR") was filed and so was forfeitable under § 981.[19] Relying on the interpretation of § 881(a)(6) & (7), the government argued that, under § 981, a claimant must demonstrate that he made all reasonable efforts to prevent the illegal use of his property. The court concluded that the "all reasonable efforts" language applied in analyzing "consent" for purposes of § 881, but stated that "Because

12. United States v. Real Property 874 Gartel Dr., Walnut, California, 79 F.3d 918, 924 (9th Cir.1996).

13. United States v. All Assets of G.P.S. Automotive Corp., 66 F.3d 483 (2d Cir.1995).

14. United States v. 4560 Kingsbury Rd., 1994 WL 28772 (6th Cir.1994) at *2. *4560 Kingsbury Rd.* was an action brought under 18 U.S.C. § 1955(d) which provides "any property, including money, used in violation of the provisions of this section may be seized and forfeited to the United States." Section 1955 does not contain an innocent owner defense, but incorporates "all provisions of law relating to the seizure, summary, and judicial forfeiture procedures." In response to that, the Sixth Circuit, citing § 981(a)(2), stated that "For civil forfeitures, Congress does not leave the

innocent owner defense at a constitutional minimum, but instead provides an innocent owner defense for persons who merely lack knowledge of the illegal act causing the forfeiture proceeding. Consequently, that defense is a legal provision incorporated by [section] 1955." *Id.* at *2.

15. *Id.* at *1.

16. *Id.* at *1.

17. *Id.* at n.2.

18. *Id.* at *2.

19. United States v. $705,270.00, 820 F.Supp. 1398 (S.D.Fla.1993), *aff'd without opinion*, 29 F.3d 640 (11th Cir.1994). In addition to the § 981 action, the government also asserted that the currency was proceeds of drug activity and so was also forfeitable under 21 U.S.C. § 881(a)(6).

[§ 981(a)(2)] does not include a consent element in its innocent owner provision, a claimant is not required to show he took all reasonable efforts to prevent the illegal use of his property."[20]

B.　CONSTITUTIONAL DEFENSES: EXCESSIVE FINES AND DUE PROCESS

Two constitutional defenses exist, based on the due process clause and the excessive fines clause. Austin v. United States, discussed in § 28.17(A) *infra,* held that the excessive fines clause applied to § 881, and the courts agree that based on the *Austin* analysis, the excessive fines clause applies to § 981 as well. These defenses are discussed in detail *infra* in §§ 28.17 and 28.19 on constitutional issues.

§ 28.14　Import/Export Reporting of Monetary Instruments: § 5317

Section 5317[1] applies when property is associated with either of two money laundering crimes: the import/export reporting requirement[2] or structuring to evade that reporting requirement.[3] For the import/export reporting requirement, § 5317 allows forfeiture of the monetary instruments associated with the report,[4] and "any interest in property, including a deposit in a financial institution, traceable to such instrument...."[5] Thus forfeitable property includes the instruments and proceeds of the instruments. For structuring under the import/export reporting requirement, this statute allows forfeiture of "[a]ny property, real or personal, involved in a transaction or attempted transaction in violation of [the structuring provision], or any property traceable to such property...."[6] Under this language, forfeitable property includes property involved in structured transactions and proceeds of structured transactions.

The procedure for § 5317 forfeitures is the same as for forfeitures under §§ 881 and 981.[7]

To establish its case, the government has to prove to a level of probable cause that a prohibited transaction occurred under § 5316 or § 5324(b), and that the property has the required relationship to the violation. This means that courts have to determine if the time of departure was met so a report was required. As discussed under the crime of § 5316, defining the time of departure has given the courts a

20. Id. at 1402.

§ 28.14

1. 31 U.S.C. § 5317.

2. *Id.* § 5316, discussed in § 18.4 *supra.*

3. *Id.* § 5324(b), discussed in § 18.10 *supra.*

4. This includes instruments for which a report is not filed or for which a report is filed containing a material omission or misstatement. *Id.* § 5317(c).

5. *Id.*

6. *Id.*

7. United States v. $94,000, 2 F.3d 778, 782 (7th Cir.1993), *citing* 19 U.S.C. § 1600, adopted in 1984, as explicitly making the Admiralty rules applicable.

hard time.[8] The courts have had a similarly hard time defining that time in the forfeiture context.[9]

Another issue that has divided the courts is whether the government must prove knowledge of illegality for a § 5317 forfeiture. It is clear that for a criminal conviction of § 5316, the import/export reporting requirement, the government has to prove knowledge of illegality—it has to prove that the defendant knew the law required a report.[10] On the question of whether the same must be proved for a forfeiture under § 5317, the courts disagree. Most courts have concluded that knowledge of illegality is not an element of the forfeiture.[11] This conclusion is based on comparing the language applicable to criminal convictions ("willful") with the language applicable to forfeitures ("knowingly").[12] On the other hand, the Eleventh Circuit has clearly held that the government must prove knowledge of illegality in forfeiture actions as well.[13] The court's rationale was that the terms of § 5316 could not have one meaning in a criminal prosecution and another meaning in a civil forfeiture.[14]

Once the government has established probable cause, as with the other forfeiture statutes, to assert any sort of defense the claimant must establish standing.[15] The cases on § 5317 standing refer to holdings under the other forfeiture statutes and reach the same conclusions.[16]

---

8. *See* § 18.4(C)(ii) *supra.*

9. *See*

Second Circuit: United States v. $500,000 in United States Currency, 62 F.3d 59 (2d Cir.1995); United States v. U.S. Currency in the Amount of $170,000, 903 F.Supp. 373 (E.D.N.Y.1995).

Ninth Circuit: United States v. $122,043 in United States Currency, 792 F.2d 1470 (9th Cir.1986)(time of departure met, one judge dissenting; regulation on time of departure not unconstitutionally vague).

10. *See* § 18.4(C)(iii) *supra.*

11. *See*

Second Circuit: United States v. United States Currency in the Amount of $145,139, 18 F.3d 73 (2d Cir.1994); United States v. $359,500 in United States Currency, 828 F.2d 930 (2d Cir.1987).

Seventh Circuit: United States v. $94,000 in United States Currency, 2 F.3d 778 (7th Cir.1993).

Eighth Circuit: United States v. $20,757.83 Canadian Currency, 769 F.2d 479 (8th Cir.1985).

Ninth Circuit: United States v. $47,980 in Canadian Currency, 804 F.2d 1085, 1090 (9th Cir.1986); United States v. $122,043 in United States Currency, 792 F.2d 1470, 1474 (9th Cir.1986).

12. *See*

Second Circuit: United States v. $359,500 in United States Currency, 828 F.2d 930, 933 (2d Cir.1987).

Seventh Circuit: United States v. $94,000 in United States Currency, 2 F.3d 778, 787 (7th Cir.1993).

13. United States v. $24,900, 770 F.2d 1530 (11th Cir.1985).

14. *Id.* at 1533.

15. *See*

Second Circuit: United States v. $83,132 in United States Currency, 1996 WL 599725 (E.D.N.Y.1996).

Ninth Circuit: United States v. $122,043 in United States Currency, 792 F.2d 1470 (9th Cir.1986).

16. *See*

Second Circuit: Mercado v. The U.S. Customs Service, 873 F.2d 641, 644 (2d Cir.1989)(citing § 881 cases, conclusory ownership allegations of claimant's attorney not sufficient due to danger of false claims); United States v. $83,132 in United States Currency, 1996 WL 599725 (E.D.N.Y.1996)(citing § 881 cases, bare assertion of property interest not sufficient for standing).

Ninth Circuit: United States v. $122,043 in United States Currency, 792 F.2d 1470 (9th Cir.1986)(citing a § 881 case, possessory interest sufficient for standing).

For defenses to § 5317 forfeitures, the claimants can rebut the government's probable cause showing under the same procedural rules that govern the other forfeiture statutes. Affirmative defenses to § 5317 forfeitures, however, have distinct characteristics, and it is not advisable to rely on cases from the other forfeiture statutes.

Section 5317 has no innocent owner defense in the statute. The Ninth Circuit has decided to read an innocent owner defense into § 5317 forfeitures based on dicta from *Calero-Toledo* describing due process requirements.[17] The defense has three elements for the claimant to establish: (1) an ownership interest, (2) that the illegal use of the property was done without the claimant's knowledge or consent, and (3) that the claimant took all reasonable steps to prevent the proscribed use of the property.[18]

The constitutional requirement of an innocent owner defense, and the continuing vitality of the *Calero-Toledo* dicta hinting at one, was called into question in 1995 by Michigan v. Bennis.[19] In the wake of *Bennis*, the Eastern District of New York district court has concluded that no constitutional innocent owner defense exists, and so § 5317 has no innocent owner defense.[20] The Ninth Circuit, in contrast, has made clear in a case decided after *Bennis* that the innocent owner defense to § 5317 forfeitures continues to exist in the Ninth Circuit.[21]

Whether the Excessive Fines Clause applies to § 5317 forfeitures (and so establishes an affirmative defense) has also led to disagreement in the courts. The Ninth Circuit has held that the Excessive Fines Clause applies to § 5317 forfeitures,[22] and the Eleventh Circuit has agreed.[23] In contrast, the Eastern District of New York court has held that § 5317 does not serve a punitive purpose, so under *Austin* the Excessive Fines Clause does not apply to it.[24]

§ 28.15 Other Forfeiture Statutes

The consensus description of how many civil forfeiture statutes exist is "over 100."[1] Before the 1997 revision of the United States Attorneys

17. United States v. $69,292 in United States Currency, 62 F.3d 1161 (9th Cir. 1995).

18. *Id.* at 1165.

19. *See* § 28.22 *infra.*

20. United States v. $83,132 in United States Currency, 1996 WL 599725 (E.D.N.Y.1996).

21. United States v. $1,102,720 U.S. Currency, 1995 WL 746172 (9th Cir.1995).

22. United States v. $69,292 United States Currency, 62 F.3d 1161 (9th Cir. 1995).

23. United States v. Dean, 87 F.3d 1212 (11th Cir.1996).

24. United States v. $83,132 in United States Currency, 1996 WL 599725 (E.D.N.Y.1996). The court states that the Second Circuit has reached this conclusion and cites United States v. United States Currency $145,139, 18 F.3d 73 (2d Cir. 1994). *See $83,132* at *3. This Second Circuit decision does conclude that forfeiture of the entire monetary instrument in that case was not excessive, but it does so based on Congress's intent and does not mention *Austin* or do an independent excessiveness review. It is dubious authority for the conclusion that § 5317 forfeitures are not covered by the Excessive Fines Clause.

§ 28.15

1. *See* United States v. Marolf, 973 F.Supp. 1139, (C.D.Cal.1997)("over 100" civil forfeiture statutes exist, *citing* Judith

Manual, it listed and surveyed "approximately 140."[2]

§ 28.16   Constitutional Issues—In General

The constitutional provisions implicated most directly by civil forfeiture[1] are the Eight Amendment's Excessive Fines Clause and the Fifth Amendment's Due Process Clause. The Double Jeopardy Clause was the subject of confusion and litigation until the Supreme Court held that it does not apply to civil forfeiture. The Supreme Court has also held that the Due Process Clause does not mandate an innocent owner defense. The Fourth Amendment's exclusionary rule applies in civil forfeitures.

§ 28.17   Constitutional Issues—8th Amendment Excessive Fines Clause

A.   THE DECISION IN AUSTIN v. UNITED STATES

In Austin v. United States,[1] the Supreme Court held unanimously that courts could overturn civil forfeitures based on the Excessive Fines Clause.

The Court first pointed out that nothing in the history or the text of the Eighth Amendment or the Excessive Fines Clause confined it to criminal cases.[2] Rather the history of the amendment suggests that the drafters intended it to limit "the government's power to extract payments, whether in cash or in kind, 'as punishment for some offense.' "[3] The definition of punishment does not depend on the classification of an action as criminal or civil, and any punishment falls within the limits of the Excessive Fines Clause. If the Court found that a civil forfeiture served in part to punish, rather than having a purely remedial purpose, then the Eighth Amendment would apply. Thus the threshold question of applicability rests not on the distinction between civil and criminal actions by the government, but on the punitive or remedial nature of the fine.

To decide if the forfeiture was punitive or remedial, the Court reviewed the historical development of civil forfeiture in England, and then in the United States. It stated that the understanding of forfeiture found in early cases and the early writings of Congress equated forfeitures with fines and viewed both as punishment.[4] Nothing in the history of the modern statutes in question, §§ 881(a)(4) & (7), contradicted this

Secher, Asset Forfeiture: Practice and Procedure (1995)).

2. United States Attorneys Manual, Vol. 11, Title B, § B–3100 page B–975 (1996). *See also id.* at page B–996 (statutory index listing forfeiture statutes). These were deleted in the 1997 revision.

§ 28.16

1. Many of the constitutional protections applied in criminal forfeiture do not apply to civil forfeiture, *see* United States v.

Premises Known as 281 Syosset Woodbury Road, 71 F.3d 1067 (2d Cir.1995)(recounting constitutional provisions applicable to criminal forfeiture but not civil forfeiture).

§ 28.17

1. 509 U.S. 602 (1993).

2. *Id.* at 608.

3. *Id.* at 608–09.

4. *Id.* at 612.

historical understanding of forfeiture as punishment.[5] Therefore, these sections serve at least in part to punish the owner of the property, and so the Excessive Fines Clause applies.

B. THE SCOPE OF *AUSTIN*—TO WHAT FORFEITURES DOES THE EXCESSIVE FINES CLAUSE APPLY?

After *Austin*, the difference between punitive and non-punitive, rather than civil and criminal, forfeitures, appears to define the scope of the excessiveness inquiry. *Austin* almost certainly has implications for a broad range of civil actions, and its relevance to a given claim will depend on the punitive or remedial nature of the statute in issue.

i. Facilitating Property

Austin expressly applied the Excessive Fines Clause to §§ 881(a)(4) and (7), which authorize the forfeiture of vehicles and real property used to facilitate a drug offense. The Supreme Court decided that these sections of § 881 served at least in part to punish and deter the underlying criminal behavior. Therefore, all actions brought under these two sections must undergo Excessive Fines scrutiny.

Furthermore, it seems that the same analysis would apply to any forfeiture statute with similar provisions and legislative purpose. Thus, courts have held that the excessiveness test applicable to § 881 applies as well to those sections of § 981 which deal with facilitating property.[6] Likewise the Excessive Fines Clause applies to § 5317 forfeitures, although there is some disagreement.[7] At least one court has stated that *Austin* will apply to all punitive forfeitures, without regard to the specific nature of the underlying crime, or the methods used to accomplish the forfeiture.[8] Therefore, the courts agree that the Constitution requires forfeitures of facilitating property be limited to the amount necessary to achieve legitimate punitive and remedial goals.

---

5. *Id.* at 619.

6. *See*

Second Circuit: United States v. GPS Automotive, 66 F.3d 483, 501 n. 19 (2d Cir.1995).

Fourth Circuit: United States v. Taylor, 13 F.3d 786, 789–90 (4th Cir.1994)(*Austin* applies to forfeiture under § 981 and to forfeiture under § 1955).

Eighth Circuit: United States v. $21,-282., 47 F.3d 972, 973 (8th Cir.1995).

7. *See*

Ninth Circuit: United States v. $69,-292, 62 F.3d 1161 (9th Cir.1995).

But see

Second Circuit: United States v. $83,-132 United States Currency, 1996 WL 599725 (E.D.N.Y.1996)(Excessive Fines

Clause does not apply to § 5317 forfeitures).

8. *See* Quinones–Ruiz v. United States, 873 F.Supp. 359, 363 (S.D.Cal.1995) (applying *Austin* to an administrative forfeiture of currency and stating that *Austin* "held that punitive forfeitures are subject to the Excessive Fines Clause."). State forfeiture statutes modeled after their federal counterparts and in court on § 1983 claims must also pass muster under the Excessive Fines Clause, because the state's seizure of property used to facilitate the commission of a crime, in all probability, also serves to punish and deter. *See* Hill v. Tennessee, 868 F.Supp. 221 (M.D.Tenn.1994) (applying *Austin* to a state statute modeled after § 881).

ii. Contraband

The lower courts have adopted a similarly uniform approach to the seizure of contraband, and consistently decline to apply the Excessive Fines Clause to such forfeitures because the goal of removing the offending material from circulation fully explains the forfeiture and provides the statute with a purely remedial purpose.[9] This logic applies as well to a forfeiture of "derivative contraband" or property essential to the commission of the underlying offense.[10] When the government removes, for example, the scales used to measure drugs or the lab equipment used to manufacture them, it does so because such property creates a danger to society. No matter what the value of this property, its seizure serves a purely remedial purpose because it prevents future violations. Therefore, *Austin* does not apply.

iii. Proceeds

Austin's applicability to a third type of property, the proceeds of prohibited transactions, presents a more difficult question. The fact that § 881(a)(6), which provides for the forfeiture of drug proceeds, also reaches two other types of property ((1) things exchanged for or intended to be exchanged for drugs and (2) moneys facilitating or intended to facilitate drug crimes), has complicated the courts' approach to the problem. With three different theories of forfeiture combined in one statutory subsection, it is difficult to treat the whole subsection the same.

a. Courts Which Refuse to Apply Austin to Proceeds

The law developing in the appellate courts is that forfeiture of proceeds can never be excessive. The Tenth Circuit first stated clearly, but without elaboration, that "Austin's excessive fines analysis does not apply to proceeds."[11] It later explained in more detail why forfeiture of proceeds can never by constitutionally excessive.[12]

The rationale for this holding is based on the rationale courts developed under the double jeopardy clause. The Fifth Circuit first adopted the position that proceeds under § 881(a)(6) presented a ques-

---

9. *See*

Second Circuit: United States v. Two A–37 Cessna Jets, 1994 WL 167998 (W.D.N.Y.1994).

Eleventh Circuit: United States v. The Proceeds from Approx. 15,538 (sic) Lobster Tails, 834 F.Supp. 385 (S.D.Fla.1993).

See also

Supreme Court: Austin v. United States, 509 U.S. 602, 621, 113 S.Ct. 2801, 2811, 125 L.Ed.2d 488 (1993).

10. In an unpublished opinion, the Ninth Circuit distinguished the FCC's seizure of illegal broadcasting equipment because "unlike the assets seized in Austin,

the equipment was the instrumentality of the misbehavior, and its seizure prevented future violations." United States v. Reveille, 1994 WL 118068 at *2 (9th Cir.1994). *See also* Cooper v. Greenwood, 904 F.2d 302, 304–05 (5th Cir.1990) (explaining the definition of derivative contraband).

11. United States v. Various Tracts of Land in Muskogee and Cherokee Counties, 1996 WL 563847 (10th Cir.1996), *citing* United States v. Salinas, 65 F.3d 551 (6th Cir.1995).

12. United States v. One Parcel of Real Property Described as Lot 41, Berryhill Farm Estates, 128 F.3d 1386 (10th Cir. 1997).

tion different than that posed by the other sections in a case dealing with a double jeopardy claim.[13] Relying on the Supreme Court case United States v. Halper,[14] the circuit court felt bound to classify the forfeiture, whether civil or criminal, as punishment only if the forfeiture proved so great that it "bore no rational relationship to the costs incurred by the government and society resulting from the defendant's criminal conduct."[15] By comparing the value of the proceeds of the illegal drug sales forfeited in the case to the costs of "detection, investigation, and prosecution of drug traffickers and reimbursing society for the costs of combatting the allure of illegal drugs, caring for the victims of the criminal trade when preventive efforts prove unsuccessful, lost productivity, etc.,"[16] the court concluded that forfeitures of proceeds under § 881(a)(6) serve the wholly remedial purpose of reimbursing the government. The court went on to contrast this section with the other sections of 881: "Unlike the real estate forfeiture statute that can result in the confiscation of the most modest mobile home or the stateliest mansion, the forfeiture of drug proceeds will always be directly proportional to the amount of drugs sold. The more drugs sold, the more proceeds that will be forfeited. As we have held, these proceeds are roughly proportional to the harm inflicted upon the government and society by the drug sale. Thus the logic of *Austin* is inapplicable to § 881(a)(6)—the forfeiture of drug proceeds."[17]

Even without the *Halper* rational relation test, the court felt that the confiscation of proceeds could not require *Austin* analysis. Since the forfeiture in this case takes away property derived from unlawful activities, "the forfeiting party loses nothing to which the law ever entitled him."[18] The court compared the seizure of the drug proceeds to the repossession of money stolen from a federal bank. Since the claimant had not invested "honest labor" in producing the proceeds, she had no reasonable expectation that the law would protect her continued possession. Therefore, "instead of punishing the forfeiting party, the forfeiture of illegal proceeds, much like the confiscation of stolen money from a bank robber, merely places that party in the lawfully protected financial status quo that he enjoyed prior to launching his illegal scheme."[19] Since this does not constitute punishment, the case did not implicate the Double Jeopardy Clause, and by analogy, the Excessive Fines Clause does not apply. The Fifth Circuit clearly only addressed proceeds in its decision, and the opinion does not indicate how it would treat the other types of property which § 881(a)(6) covers.

The Sixth Circuit has reached the same conclusion, calling drug proceeds under § 881(a)(6) "inherently proportional to the damages caused by the illegal activity"[20] and explicitly adopting the Fifth Circuit's

---

13. United States v. Tilley, 18 F.3d 295, 300 (5th Cir.1994).

14. 490 U.S. 435, 448–49, 109 S.Ct. 1892, 1901–02, 104 L.Ed.2d 487 (1989).

15. *Tilley*, 18 F.3d at 298.

16. *Id.* at 299.

17. *Id.* at 300.

18. *Id.*

19. *Id.*

20. United States v. Salinas, 65 F.3d 551, 554 (6th Cir.1995).

conclusion in *Tilley* that "the forfeiture of drug proceeds is not punishment, but is remedial in nature."[21]

These cases from the Fifth and Sixth Circuits were decided in the context of double jeopardy challenges (made before the Supreme Court effectively ended those in *Ursery*[22]) as opposed to excessive fines challenges. Both courts took account of the *Austin* decision,[23] and the courts' conclusions are not necessarily called into doubt by the subsequently-decided *Ursery* case. Reinforcing their analogous value is the fact that the Tenth Circuit, in reaching its conclusion that proceeds are never excessive, cited the Sixth Circuit case on the double jeopardy clause. On the other hand, *Ursery* did establish that the characterization of civil forfeiture as punishment is different under the double jeopardy clause and the excessive fines clause. This calls into question whether the cases from the Fifth and Sixth Circuits have any meaning in excessive fines inquiries. The Tenth Circuit has rendered the only unambiguous decision that forfeiture of proceeds can never be excessive.

b. Courts which Apply Austin to Proceeds

Other courts have rejected these arguments and concluded that the Excessive Fines Clause does apply to all types of property forfeitable under § 881(a)(6). The Northern District of Illinois felt that "the critical question is whether forfeitures under § 881(a)(6) can be defined as solely remedial."[24] Because it read forfeitures under § 881(a)(6) as stretching beyond merely the proceeds of illegal activity, the Court felt that the section did not serve a purely remedial purpose. A forfeiture of money the owner intends to use to purchase drugs or to purchase property to facilitate a drug offense will, in the court's view, serve in part to punish the owner. Such a forfeiture falls under the protection of *Austin* and the Excessive Fines Clause. However, after examining the forfeiture in question, the court concluded that it did not violate the Eighth Amendment as it was not grossly disproportionate.[25]

Thus the courts all seem to acknowledge that the application of *Austin* depends on the punitive nature of the statute, but while some turn to the purpose of the statute or the section as a whole to make their evaluation, others focus on the specific character of the property involved.

C. TESTS FOR EXCESSIVENESS

In *Austin,* the Supreme Court declined to establish a "multi-factor test for determining whether a forfeiture is constitutionally 'exces-

---

21. *Id.*

22. United States v. Ursery, 518 U.S. 267, 116 S.Ct. 2135, 135 L.Ed.2d 549 (1996), discussed in § 28.18 *infra.*

23. The Fifth Circuit stated that *Austin* did not change its conclusion, *see Tilley,* 18 F.3d at 299–300, and the Sixth Circuit's decision is based on the rationale developed in *Austin, see Salinas,* 65 F.3d 551 at 553.

24. United States v. 4204 Thorndale Ave., 1994 WL 687628, at *9 (N.D.Ill.).

25. Additionally, different panels of the Fourth Circuit have disagreed over whether the Clause applies to proceeds, so that the law in that circuit remains unsettled. *See* United States v. Shifflett, 1995 WL 125506 *9 n. 2 (4th Cir.)(unpublished).

sive'.''[26] Five years later, in United States v. Bajakajian,[27] the Court did establish a test. In *Bajakajian,* the Court stated, "Until today ..., we have not articulated a standard for determining whether a punitive forfeiture is constitutionally excessive. We now hold that punitive forfeiture violates the Excessive Fines Clause if it is grossly disproportional to the gravity of a defendant's offense.''[28]

The Court went on to explain how it arrived at the "grossly disproportional" standard. Because the text and history of the Excessive Fines Clause provided little guidance, the Court turned to two other considerations it found particularly relevant. These were deference to the judgment of the legislature on the severity of the punishment for crime, and recognition that judicial determinations on the gravity of a particular crime will be imprecise. Thus the Court adopted the standard of gross disproportionality from the Cruel and Unusual Punishments Clause cases.[29]

Applying this grossly disproportional standard to the facts in *Bajakajian,*the Court affirmed the Ninth Circuit's reduction of a potential forfeiture of $357,144 to $15,000. The defendant pled guilty to failure to report export of currency under § 5316 of the cash reporting laws. Under the criminal forfeiture laws, the government sought forfeiture of the entire $357,144. The Ninth Circuit held this would be excessive and reduced the forfeiture to $15,000. This was the decision the Supreme Court affirmed.

In deciding that forfeiture of the entire amount would be grossly disproportional, the Court focused on two factors. The first was the seriousness of the crime, as indicated by the potential sentence under the sentencing guidelines.[30] Then the Court looked to the harm caused by the crime. It found the harm to be minimal, stating that there was no inherent correlation between the amount of money not reported and the harm the government suffered from being deprived of that information.[31]

One possible limit on the application of *Bajakajian* to civil forfeiture laws is that the decision was based on a criminal forfeiture statute. However, the language throughout the decision is broad enough to suggest that the Court was announcing the standard for the Excessive Fines Clause as applied to all punitive forfeitures, not just criminal forfeitures.[32]

26. Austin v. United States, 509 U.S. 602, 622, 113 S.Ct. 2801, 2812, 125 L.Ed.2d 488 (1993).

27. ___ U.S. ___, 118 S.Ct. 2028, 141 L.Ed.2d 314, (1998).

28. 118 S.Ct. 2028, 2036.

29. *Id.* at 2037, citing Solem v. Helm, 463 U.S. 277, 288, 103 S.Ct. 3001, 3008, 77 L.Ed.2d 637 (1983) and Rummel v. Estelle, 445 U.S. 263, 271, 100 S.Ct. 1133, 1137, 63 L.Ed.2d 382 (1980).

30. *Id.* at 2038.

31. *Id.* at 2039.

This conclusion has implications for forfeiture based on all the cash reporting crimes.

32. *See Bajakajian* at 2036 ("We now hold that a punitive forfeiture violates the Excessive Fines Clause if it is grossly disproportional to the gravity of a defendant's offense.").

D. THE REMEDY FOR EXCESSIVENESS—SHOULD THE COURT MITIGATE THE FORFEITURE?

If the forfeiture as sought by the government is determined to be excessive, should the court deny the forfeiture altogether or mitigate it by ordering a forfeiture of only a portion of the property? Until *Bajakajian* was decided, the answer was unclear and courts reached different results. After *Bajakajian*, though, it seems that courts should mitigate the forfeiture rather than deny it altogether. As noted above, the decision in *Bajakajian* affirmed the Ninth Circuit's decision reducing a possible forfeiture of $357,144 to $15,000. The only qualification to the conclusion that the Court endorsed mitigation is that the Court wrote a footnote seeking to limit the implications of its holding.[33] The Court said the question it decided was only that full forfeiture of the $357,144 would be excessive. Because the defendant did not cross-appeal the reduction to $15,000, the Court said that the propriety of the $15,000 judgment was not before it. The dissent by four members of the Court challenges this statement as artificially narrowing the issues before it.[34] As the dissent points out, the majority in effect approved the $15,000 forfeiture.[35] In terms of impact rather than words, it seems the Court endorses, or at least does not disapprove of, mitigation of otherwise excessive forfeitures.

§ 28.18   Constitutional Issues—5th Amendment Double Jeopardy

The double jeopardy clause generally does not apply to civil forfeitures because they do not constitute punishment under that clause.[1] Thus the government does not violate an individual's right against double jeopardy by subjecting the defendant to a civil forfeiture action and a criminal prosecution arising from the same conduct. But the Supreme Court cautioned that it did not hold "that in rem civil forfeiture is per se exempt from the scope of the Double Jeopardy Clause."[2] Rather, the Court establishes a presumption that civil forfeiture is not subject to double jeopardy, but where the "clearest proof" indicates that the forfeiture is "so punitive either in purpose or effect" as to be equivalent to a criminal case, forfeiture my be subject to double jeopardy.[3]

---

33. 118 S.Ct. at 2038.

34. *Id.* at 2043 ("This narrow holding is artificial in constricting the question presented for this Court's review.")(Kennedy, Rehnquist, O'Connor & Scalia, JJ., dissenting).

35. *Id.*

§ 28.18

1. United States v. Ursery, 518 U.S. 267, 116 S.Ct. 2135, 135 L.Ed.2d 549 (1996).

2. *United States v. Ursery*, 518 U.S. 267, 116 S.Ct. 2135 at n.3, 135 L.Ed.2d 549 (1996).

3. *Id., citing* United States v. One Assortment of 89 Firearms, 465 U.S. 354, 363, 104 S.Ct. 1099, 1105, 79 L.Ed.2d 361 (1984).

§ 28.19   Constitutional Issues—5th Amendment Due Process

A. PRESEIZURE NOTICE AND HEARING—
JAMES DANIEL GOOD

The Supreme Court held in United States v. James Daniel Good Real Property[1] that in civil forfeitures, due process requires the government to provide both pre-seizure notice and an opportunity to be heard unless the government establishes exigent circumstances. When the property being seized is real property, the court noted that because real property is immobile, it generally does not present exigent circumstances. The Court stated that to establish exigent circumstances for real property, "the government must show that less restrictive measures— i.e., a *lis pendens,* restraining order or bond—would not suffice to protect the government's interests in preventing the sale, destruction or continued unlawful use of the real property."[2]

The Eleventh Circuit has interpreted "seizure" to extend beyond the physical assertion of control by the government to include actions that deprive claimants of significant property interests.[3] Thus where the government did not exercise physical control over premises (*i.e.*, did not change the locks, evict the residents or post warning signs) but only executed the arrest warrant, *Good* still applies to require a due process analysis. After analyzing due process under Mathews v. Eldridge, the court held that claimants must be given notice and a hearing before the warrant can be executed.[4]

The circuit courts disagree over the remedy for an unconstitutional seizure under the *Good* due process analysis.[5] The Second Circuit allows the claimant to suppress evidence obtained through the invalid seizure at the forfeiture trial.[6] The Eighth and Eleventh Circuits have ruled that the forfeiture should be dismissed altogether.[7] The rationale is that the usual remedy for an unconstitutional seizure of suppressing evidence is not adequate in forfeitures when the purpose of the seizure is not to acquire evidence but to assert a possessory interest.[8] Other circuits do not go so far as to require dismissal of the forfeiture, but require instead

---

§ 28.19

[1] 510 U.S. 43, 114 S.Ct. 492, 126 L.Ed.2d 490 (1993).

[2] *James Daniel Good,* 510 U.S. at 62.

[3] United States v. 408 Peyton Road, S.W., Atlanta, 112 F.3d 1106 (11th Cir. 1997).

[4] 112 F.3d at 1109 (11th Cir.1997), discussing Mathews v. Eldridge, 424 U.S. 319, 96 S.Ct. 893, 47 L.Ed.2d 18 (1976).

[5] *See* United States v. All Assets and Equipment of West Side Building Corp., 58 F.3d 1181, 1193 (7th Cir.1995).

[6] *See* United States v. Premises and Real Property at 4492 South Livonia Road, 889 F.2d 1258, 1265–66 (2d Cir.1989).

[7] *See*

Eighth Circuit: United States v. One Parcel of Real Property, Located at 9638 Chicago Heights, 27 F.3d 327, 330 (8th Cir. 1994).

Eleventh Circuit: United States v. 2751 Peyton Woods Trail, 66 F.3d 1164 (11th Cir.1995).

[8] *See United States v. 9638 Chicago Heights,* 27 F.3d 327, 330 (8th Cir.1994).

that the government pay rent to the claimant for the time the seizure was illegal.[9]

B. NOTICE FOR ADMINISTRATIVE FORFEITURES

As described in the process section, civil forfeiture may proceed in three ways. With one approach, administrative forfeiture, if the government gives adequate notice, and no claim is filed within 20 days of publication, the government can declare forfeiture administratively. This administrative approach is easier for the government than judicial forfeiture because no claimant appears. With this approach, an important issue is defining what constitutes adequate notice.

Notice requirements are established by the due process clause and by the procedural statute, § 1607.[10] The statute describes two types of notice required—actual notice and notice by publication. Notice by publication is not usually an issue. The actual notice requirement, however, has resulted in some administrative forfeitures being reversed.[11]

For example, the Tenth Circuit held that where the claimant had three residences that the DEA had notice of or should reasonably have become aware of from local authorities' seizure records, notice was insufficient when letters were sent to only two of the three addresses.[12] The court listed six factors relevant to deciding the sufficiency of mailed notice:

> Factors to consider include: (1) whether there is physical evidence linking the claimant to the address, such as the storage of the claimants' personalty; (2) whether there are other indicia of residency, such as the receipt of mail, the listing of a phone number, or the payment of utilities; (3) whether the claimant has a real property interest in the property represented by the address, whether a leasehold or ownership interest; (4) whether there is any direct evidence linking the claimant to the address, such as informant testimony or eyewitness observation; (5) whether there is evidence suggesting that a notice letter mailed to the address will be forwarded to the claimant; and (6) whether there are alternative methods of providing actual notice that may be available to the government.

9. *See*

Fourth Circuit: United States v. Marsh, 105 F.3d 927 (4th Cir.1997).

Seventh Circuit: United States v. All Assets and Equipment of West Side Building Corp., 58 F.3d 1181, 1193 (7th Cir. 1995).

Tenth Circuit: United States v. 51 Pieces of Real Property, Roswell, New Mexico, 17 F.3d 1306, 1316 (10th Cir.1994)(requiring accounting for rent collected where

forfeiture judgment followed default judgment for government).

10. 19 U.S.C. § 1607.

11. *See, e.g.,*

Seventh Circuit: United States v. Williams, 1997 WL 137205 (7th Cir.1997).

Tenth Circuit: United States v. Rodgers, 108 F.3d 1247 (10th Cir.1997).

12. United States v. Rodgers, 108 F.3d 1247 (10th Cir.1997).

These factors are neither exhaustive nor mandatory; however, they serve as guideposts in a murky terrain.[13]

It is unclear whether the court's conclusion that the notice was insufficient is based on the constitution or the statute or both; the court quotes both cases on due process and § 1607.[14]

Other courts have found the government's actual notice insufficient based on constitutional due process. In United States v. Williams,[15] the court held that the government's notice efforts were inadequate when its certified letter to the claimant's old address was returned as undeliverable, the government did nothing further, and the claimant's correct address and his lawyer's address were readily available from court records in a related criminal action.[16] The court relied on Mullane v. Central Hanover Bank & Trust Company[17] and two decisions from other circuits applying *Mullane* in this context.[18] Similarly, the Second Circuit found notice unconstitutional when letters were sent to a federal prison where the claimant was sent initially, but the claimant had been transferred to a state facility, the letters to the federal prison were returned marked undeliverable, and the government made no further efforts.[19]

The second issue on the notice required in administrative forfeiture is the remedy if notice is insufficient. Should the forfeiture simply be denied? Should the government be allowed to recommence the administrative forfeiture with adequate notice? What if the statute of limitations has expired? Should the claimant be entitled to have the claim heard on the merits in a judicial forfeiture? These questions have led the circuits to disagree.

These remedy questions were most recently reviewed by the Second Circuit.[20] After finding notice insufficient, the district court had limited the claimant on remand to an administrative hearing, but the appellate court reversed this and ordered that the claimant's right to seek a hearing in the district court be restored. The court reviewed its precedents and stated, "These cases support the view that, when the government is responsible for a known claimant's inability to present a claim, through the government's disregard of its statutory obligation to give notice (or otherwise), a hearing on the merits is available in the district court."[21] The court described how district courts in the Second Circuit had "taken various approaches to remedying a due process violation in an administrative forfeiture proceeding."[22] The court also reviewed the disagreement among the circuit courts, summarizing it this way:

13. *Id.* at 1252.

14. *Id.* at 1250.

15. 1997 WL 137205 (7th Cir.1997).

16. *Id.* at *1.

17. *Id.* at *2, *citing* Mullane v. Central Hanover Trust, 339 U.S. 306, 70 S.Ct. 652, 94 L.Ed. 865 (1950).

18. *See*

First Circuit: Sarit v. U.S. Drug Enforcement Administration, 987 F.2d 10, 14 (1st Cir.1993).

Eighth Circuit: United States v. Woodall, 12 F.3d 791 (8th Cir.1993).

19. Boero v. Drug Enforcement Administration, 111 F.3d 301 (2d Cir.1997).

20. Boero v. Drug Enforcement Administration, 111 F.3d 301 (2d Cir.1997).

21. 111 F.3d at 306.

22. *Id.* at 307 (citing two district court cases).

The First and Eight Circuits have ruled that when notice of administrative forfeiture is inadequate, the district court must set aside the forfeiture and either order return of the seized property or direct the government to commence judicial forfeiture in district court. *See, e.g.,* United States v. Volanty, 79 F.3d 86, 88 (8th Cir.1996); United States v. Giraldo, 45 F.3d 509, 512 (1st Cir.1995); United States v. Woodall, 12 F.3d 791, 795 (8th Cir.1993). The Federal Circuit has held that a district court can excuse a property owner's failure to comply with the statutory requirements when notice in an administrative forfeiture proceeding is inadequate. Litzenberger v. United States, 89 F.3d 818, 822 (Fed.Cir.1996). The Ninth Circuit, upon ruling that a district court has jurisdiction over due process challenges to administrative forfeiture proceedings under 28 U.S.C. § 1331, remanded the case for an adjudication on the merits. Marshall Leasing, 893 F.2d at 1103. The Fifth Circuit, in Armendariz–Mata v. DEA, 82 F.3d 679, 683 (5th Cir.1996), *cert. denied,* ___ U.S. ___, 117 S.Ct. 317, 136 L.Ed.2d 232 (1996), having found notice in an administrative forfeiture proceeding to be insufficient, directed the district court to vacate the DEA's administrative forfeiture without providing further instructions or comment.[23]

Recently, the Central District of California court relied on this Second Circuit decision to hold that the remedy for inadequate notice is not to deny the forfeiture altogether but to have the district court consider the claims on the merits.[24]

C. THE BURDEN OF PROOF—STANDARD AND ALLOCATION

Some circuits have recently expressed doubts about the constitutionality of the standards and allocation of the burden of proof in civil forfeiture actions. The procedure of civil forfeiture requires the government to show initially that the property is subject to forfeiture by a standard of probable cause.[25] The burden then shifts to the claimant to prove that the elements of forfeiture are not met or to establish an affirmative defense; the proof standard for claimants is a preponderance of evidence.[26] Thus the burden of proof not only shifts to claimants, but increases to require claimants to show more to defeat the action than the government showed to get it started.

Historically this procedure was sustained against due process challenges,[27] but recently two circuits have indicated that the procedure may be vulnerable on due process grounds.

The Second Circuit first questioned the constitutionality of the

23. *Id.* 307 n.6.

24. United States v. Marolf, 973 F.Supp. 1139 (C.D.Cal.1997).

25. *See* § 28.23 *infra.*

26. *See* § 28.23 *infra.*

27. *See, e.g.,* One 1970 Pontiac GTO 2 Door Hardtop, 529 F.2d 65 (9th Cir.1976).

process in 1993.[28] It noted that the constitutionality of congress's allocation of the burdens of proof had been upheld, but went on to say, "We
therefore stress the need for courts to ensure that what little due process
is provided for in the statutory scheme is preserved in practice."[29] When
the Second Circuit revisited the issue in 1996, it went further. It held
that due process is not violated by putting the burden of proof for the
innocent owner defense on claimants,[30] but stated that two questions
remained open: Whether due process was violated by limiting the government's burden for obtaining a warrant *in rem* allowing seizure to
probable cause, and whether due process requires the government to
sustain a burden higher than probable cause before a seizure is made
and a claimant is put to proof of the innocent owner defense.[31] On the
facts before it, the court held the claimant waived these issues, so it did
not rule on them, but characterized them as open questions.[32]

The Ninth Circuit echoed these concerns in a 1997 case. The court
reversed a forfeiture under § 881(a)(6) on the basis that the government
had failed to establish probable cause.[33] Because the court reversed on
this basis, it did not rule on the constitutionality of forfeiture's "burden-
shifting" mechanism. However, it did discuss the issue, stating that it
felt constrained to do so to answer the government's assertion that the
challenge was foreclosed by Ninth Circuit case law.[34] The court then
concluded that the question of whether the government's burden of
probable cause was sufficient was reopened in the wake of recent
Supreme Court rulings.[35] The court agreed with the Second Circuit that
the question was open, and concluded, "We leave the ultimate resolution
of this question for another day."[36]

Thus the Second and Ninth Circuits have in dictum questioned the
constitutionality of the government's burden of proof in civil forfeitures.

§ 28.20 Constitutional Issues—Fifth Amendment Privilege Against Self–Incrimination

A difficult situation arises frequently in civil forfeiture actions when
the government files the action and pursues it under the civil discovery
rules. In due course, the government asks the claimant something
incriminating. The claimant declines to answer, citing the privilege
against self-incrimination. The claimant then loses in the civil forfeiture
action because the claimant does not sustain his or her burden of proof.

28. United States v. Daccarett, 6 F.3d 37 (2d Cir.1993).

29. 6 F.3d at 56 (citations omitted).

30. United States v. One Parcel of Property Located at 194 Quaker Farms Road, 85 F.3d 985 (2d Cir.1996).

31. *Id.* at 990–91.

32. *Id.* at 991.

33. United States v. $49,576, 116 F.3d 425 (9th Cir.1997).

34. *Id.* at 428.

35. *Id.*, *citing* Mathews v. Eldridge, 424 U.S. 319, 96 S.Ct. 893, 47 L.Ed.2d 18 (1976); United States v. James Daniel Good Real Property, 510 U.S. 43, 114 S.Ct. 492, 126 L.Ed.2d 490 (1993) and Austin v. United States, 509 U.S. 602, 113 S.Ct. 2801, 125 L.Ed.2d 488 (1993).

36. 116 F.3d at 429. Judge Hall concurred in the decision but objected to Judge Koziniski's "disquisition ... on the constitutionality of burden-shifting in forfeiture proceedings" as "entirely dictum." *Id.*

This anomalous interaction of civil and criminal liability has led courts to make special efforts to accommodate both the privilege against self-incrimination and legislative intent for forfeiture.[1] If the claimant asserts the privilege and then seeks to withdraw the assertion and testify, courts examine the situation carefully but may preclude the claimant from testifying if the facts show an improper use of the privilege.[2]

§ 28.21   Constitutional Issues—Fourth Amendment Search and Seizure

Evidence collected in violation of the Fourth Amendment is excluded in civil forfeitures.[1]

§ 28.22   Constitutional Issues—No Constitutional Innocent Owner Defense

There is no due process requirement of an "innocent owner" defense for civil forfeiture, according to Bennis v. Michigan.[1] In Bennis, Michigan brought an in personam forfeiture action against Tina Bennis and her husband in order to abate their car, held in joint tenancy, as a public nuisance. Bennis' husband was arrested with a prostitute in his car and was convicted of a misdemeanor. Though Bennis had no knowledge of her husband's activity, and surely did not consent to it, the Michigan Supreme Court allowed forfeiture of her half of the car since the state abatement statute had no innocent owner defense.[2]

The Supreme Court held that this was constitutional under the due process clause and was not an impermissible taking of property. Rather than finding a constitutionally mandated "innocent owner" defense, the court concluded that one was not necessary.[3] Bennis's application to federal civil forfeiture is somewhat clouded because the Michigan state forfeiture action at issue in the case was a hybrid of civil and criminal forfeiture characteristics. The action was classified as a civil action under the Michigan forfeiture scheme, which suggests it was like federal civil forfeiture, but it was also an in personam forfeiture in an abatement action under a state public nuisance statute, which suggests it was analogous to a federal criminal forfeiture action. Application or not of Bennis does not affect §§ 881 and 981, which include statutory innocent owner defenses. But for forfeitures under § 5317, which includes no statutory innocent owner defense, Bennis has caused some disagreement.

§ 28.20

1. United States v. Certain Real Property and Premises Known as 4003–4005 5th Ave., Brooklyn, 55 F.3d 78, 82–83 (2d Cir. 1995).

2. Id. at 85–86.

§ 28.21

1. One 1958 Plymouth Sedan v. Pennsylvania, 380 U.S. 693, 696–702, 85 S.Ct. 1246, 1248–51, 14 L.Ed.2d 170 (1965).

§ 28.22

1. 516 U.S. 442, 116 S.Ct. 994, 134 L.Ed.2d 68 (1996).

2. Id.

3. Id.

As noted above, the Ninth Circuit has decided to read an innocent owner defense into § 5317 forfeitures based on dicta from *Calero-Toledo* describing due process requirements.[4] But in the wake of *Bennis*, the Eastern District of New York court has concluded that no constitutional innocent owner defense exists, and so § 5317 has no innocent owner defense.[5] The Ninth Circuit, in contrast, has made clear in a case decided after *Bennis* that the innocent owner defense to § 5317 forfeitures continues to exist in the Ninth Circuit.[6]

§ 28.23   The Process

Because civil forfeitures are actions *in rem*, jurisdiction is based on seizing the thing (the *res*) to be forfeited. The government must have control over the res to seek civil forfeiture.[1]

The government may pursue civil forfeiture by three methods. *Summary forfeiture* is available against all schedule I and II controlled substances, dangerous raw materials, and certain equipment, containers, and plants.[2] Property subject to summary forfeiture is characterized as contraband or derivative contraband, cannot be legally possessed, and thus does not enjoy the procedural safeguards afforded other property.

Administrative forfeiture is designed to keep seizures which are unlikely to be contested out of the court system.[3] Administrative forfeiture applies to cash and conveyances of any value, and personal property worth $500,000 or less.[4] Real property is not subject to administrative

---

4. United States v. $69,292 in United States Currency, 62 F.3d 1161 (9th Cir. 1995).

5. United States v. $83,132 in United States Currency, 1996 WL 599725 (E.D.N.Y.1996).

6. United States v. $1,102,720 U.S. Currency, 1995 WL 746172 (9th Cir.1995).

§ 28.23

1. *See*

Supreme Court: Republic National Bank of Miami v. United States, 506 U.S. 80, 84, 113 S.Ct. 554, 557, 121 L.Ed.2d 474 (1992).

See also

Second Circuit: United States v. All Funds On Deposit in Any Accounts Maintained in the Names of Heriberto Castro Meza, 63 F.3d 148 (2d Cir.1995)(in rem jurisdiction established by constructive control over res).

Ninth Circuit: United States v. $46,-588.00 in US Currency and $20 in Canadian Currency, 103 F.3d 902, 905 (9th Cir.1996)(jurisdiction over res established where cashier's check is substituted for cash because check was "an appropriate,

fungible surrogate for the seized currency").

Tenth Circuit: United States v. 51 Pieces of Property, Roswell, New Mexico, 17 F.3d 1306 (10th Cir.1994)(error to enter judgment of forfeiture because government had no in rem jurisdiction over property).

2. 21 U.S.C. § 881(f), (g).

3. The following cases summarize and explain administrative forfeiture procedures:

Second Circuit: Boero v. DEA, 111 F.3d 301 (2d Cir.1997).

Third Circuit: United States v. Terry, 1997 WL 430975 (E.D.Pa.1997).

Fourth Circuit: Ibarra v. United States, 120 F.3d 472 (4th Cir.1997).

Ninth Circuit: United States v. Marolf, 973 F.Supp. 1139, (C.D.Cal.1997).

4. 19 U.S.C. §§ 1607–09; 21 C.F.R. §§ 1316.75–77.

See

Eighth Circuit: Muhammed v. DEA, 92 F.3d 648 (8th Cir.1996).

Ninth Circuit: United States v. $46,-588.00 in US Currency and $20 in Canadian Currency, 103 F.3d 902 (9th Cir.1996).

forfeiture.[5] The government must give post-seizure notice of its intention to forfeit the property.[6] Interested parties may seek administrative relief from the seizing agency, or contest the forfeiture and demand a judicial forfeiture proceeding. If the intended forfeiture is not validly contested within 20 days of the date of first publication, the property is deemed administratively forfeited. Completed administrative forfeitures are not subject to challenge.[7]

Contested administrative forfeiture actions, actions against personal property worth more than $500,000, and actions against real property must proceed by *judicial forfeiture*.[8] These actions are governed by the a set of procedural rules called the customs rules.[9] Under these rules, the forfeiture procedures are well established.[10] To seize property the government must have probable cause to believe that the property is subject to forfeiture.[11] Probable cause requires reasonable grounds, more than mere suspicion.[12] The circuit courts are evenly split over whether evi-

---

5. *United States v. James Daniel Good*, 510 U.S. 43, 114 S.Ct. 492, 126 L.Ed.2d 490 (1993).

6. These cases are discussed under constitutionality in § 28.19(A), *supra*.

7. *Seventh Circuit:* Linarez v. Department of Justice, 2 F.3d 208 (7th Cir.1993).

Eighth Circuit: Muhammed v. DEA, 92 F.3d 648, 651 (8th Cir.1996) (if there is no opposition and the property is administratively forfeited, courts may review the administrative procedure but not the forfeiture itself). In *Muhammed*, the Eighth Circuit is critical of administrative forfeiture, stating, "We realize that the war on drugs has brought us to the point where the government may seize up to $500,000 of a citizen's property, without any initial showing of cause, and put the onus on the citizen to perfectly navigate the bureaucratic labyrinth in order to liberate what is presumptively his or hers in the first place.... Should the citizen prove inept, the government may keep the property, without ever having to justify or explain its actions." *Id.* at 654 (citations omitted). Judge Arnold concurred and dissented, *id.* at 655.

8. Muhammed v. DEA, 92 F.3d 648 (8th Cir.1996), *citing* 19 U.S.C. §§ 1608, 1615.

9. The Supplemental Rules for Certain Admiralty and Maritime Claims, 19 U.S.C. § 1615, are incorporated into the forfeiture statutes by 21 U.S.C. § 881(d) and 18 U.S.C. 981(d). These rules govern forfeiture under § 5317 as well. *See* Mercado v. The United States Customs Service, 873 F.2d 641, 645 (2d Cir.1989)(parties agreed and court accepted that customs rules governed § 5317 forfeiture). For deci-

sions explaining the applicability of the customs procedures, *see*

First Circuit: United States v. One Lot of Currency ($36,634), 103 F.3d 1048, 1053 (1st Cir.1997); United States v. One Urban Lot Located at Road 143, 1994 WL 9790 (1st Cir.1994).

Fifth Circuit: United States v. 1988 Oldsmobile Supreme, 983 F.2d 670, 675 (5th Cir.1993)(applying standards in § 981 forfeiture).

10. United States v. $87,118 United States Currency, 95 F.3d 511 (7th Cir. 1996).

11. *See, e.g.,*

First Circuit: United States v. One Lot of U.S. Currency ($36,634), 103 F.3d 1048, 1053 (1st Cir.1997); United States v. One Urban Lot Located at Road 143, 1994 WL 9790 (1st Cir.1994).

Second Circuit: United States v. Banco Cafetero Panama, 797 F.2d 1154, 1160 (2d Cir.1986).

Seventh Circuit: United States v. $87,118 U.S. Currency, 95 F.3d 511 (7th Cir. 1996).

Ninth Circuit: United States v. $49,576 United States Currency, 116 F.3d 425 (9th Cir.1997)(forfeiture denied because government did not establish probable cause).

12. *See*

Second Circuit: United States v. All Right Title and Interest in Real Property and Appurtenances Thereto Known as 785 St. Nicholas Ave., 983 F.2d 396, 403 (2d Cir.1993) (government must establish reasonable grounds, more than mere suspicion).

dence gathered after the forfeiture procedure is instituted can be used to establish probable cause, or whether only evidence gathered before the suit is instituted can be considered.[13] Seizure and forfeiture are separate events, both requiring probable cause, but the government is not required to demonstrate probable cause until trial unless the claimant objects; then the government must show probable cause at seizure.[14]

The next part of the forfeiture process is described well by the Second Circuit:

> Once the government has demonstrated probable cause, the second step in the forfeiture proceeding shifts the burden of proof to the claimant to demonstrate by a preponderance of the evidence that the factual predicates necessary to show probable have not been met or to show claimants lack knowledge or consent to the drug-related activities.... Once probable cause has been shown, the ultimate burden of proof on whether factual predicates have been met or whether there is a lack of knowledge or consent is shouldered by the claimant.[15]

Thus the claimant can either rebut the government's proof or establish an affirmative defense. If the claimant is successful, they recover their entire interest in the property, including costs, fees and interest.[16]

§ 28.24   Bibliography

Cheh, Mary M., *Constitutional Limits on Using Civil Remedies to Achieve Criminal Law Objectives: Understanding and Transcending the Criminal–Civil Law Distinction,* 42 HASTINGS L.J. 1325 (1991).

Seventh Circuit: United States v. $87,-118 U.S. Currency, 95 F.3d 511, 518 (7th Cir.1996).

Ninth Circuit: United States v. 1 Parcel of Real Property, Lot 4, Block 5, 904 F.2d 487, 490–91 (9th Cir.1990).

Eleventh Circuit: United States v. One 1979 Porsche, 709 F.2d 1424, 1426 (11th Cir.1983) (probable cause is "reasonable ground for a belief of guilt, supported by less than prima facie proof but more than mere suspicion").

13. United States v. $87,118.00 in United States Currency, 95 F.3d 511, 515 (7th Cir.1996)(chronicling and explaining the split in the circuits).

14. Marine Midland Bank, N.A. v. United States, 11 F.3d 1119, 1124–25 (2d Cir.1993); United States v. Daccarett, 6 F.3d 37, 47–49 (2d Cir.1993).

15. United States v. All Right, Title and Interest in Real Property and Appurtenances Thereto Known as 785 St. Nicholas Ave., 983 F.2d 396, 403 (2d Cir.1993)(citations omitted).

See also

First Circuit: United States v. One Urban Lot Located at Road 143, 1994 WL 9790 (1st Cir.1994). In *One Urban Lot,* the First Circuit is critical of this burden shifting, noting that "The statutory burden shifting procedures stack the deck heavily in favor of the government." 1994 WL 9790 at *5 n. 4.

Second Circuit: United States v. Banco Cafetero Panama, 797 F.2d 1154, 1160 (2d Cir.1986)

Ninth Circuit: United States v. One 1985 Mercedes, 917 F.2d 415, 419 (9th Cir. 1990).

Eleventh Circuit: United States v. Two Parcels of Real Property Located in Lee Co., Alabama, 92 F.3d 1123, 1126 (11th Cir. 1996).

16. *See* United States v. 1980 Lear Jet, 38 F.3d 398 (9th Cir.1994), discussed *supra* in § 28.6(A).

Cheh, Mary M., *Can Something This Easy, Quick and Profitable Also Be Fair? Runaway Civil Forfeiture Stumbles on the Constitution*, 39 N.Y.L. SCH. L. REV. 1 (1994).

Dery, George M., *Adding Injury to Insult: The Supreme Court's Extension of Civil Forfeiture to Its Illogical Extreme in Bennis v. Michigan*, 48 S.C. L. REV. 359 (1997).

Guerra, Sandra, *Family Values?: The Family as an Innocent Victim of Civil Drug Asset Forfeiture*, 81 CORNELL L. REV. 343 (1996).

Gurule, Jimmy & Sandra Guerra, THE LAW OF ASSET FORFEITURE (1998) (one volume treatise).

Klein, Susan, *Civil In Rem Forfeiture and Double Jeopardy*, 82 Iowa L. Rev. 183 (1996).

Levy, Leonard W., LICENSE TO STEAL: THE FORFEITURE OF PROPERTY (1996)(historical treatment of forfeiture law in the United States).

Mack, Barbara, *Double Jeopardy—Civil Forfeitures and Criminal Punishment: Who Determines What Punishments Fit the Crime*, 19 SEATTLE U. L. REV. 217 (1996).

Pappas, George T., *Civil Forfeiture and Drug Proceeds: The Need to Balance Societal Interests with the Rights of Innocent Owners*, 77 MARQ. L. REV. 856 (1995).

Schwarcz, Stephen L. and Alan E. Rothman, *Civil Forfeiture: A Higher Form of Commercial Law?* 62 FORDHAM L. REV. 287 (1993).

Scheinfeld, Myron M., Teresa L. Maines and Mark W. Wege, *Civil Forfeiture and Bankruptcy: The Conflicting Interests of the Debtor, Its Creditors and the Government*, 69 AM. BANKR. L. J. 87 (1995).

Smith, David B., PROSECUTION AND DEFENSE OF FORFEITURE CASES (1996)(two-volume, regularly updated treatise on the substantive and procedural law of civil and criminal forfeiture).

Subin, Andrew L., *The Double Jeopardy Implications of in rem Forfeiture of Crime Related Property: The Gradual Realization of a Constitutional Violation*, 19 SEATTLE U. L. REV 253 (1996).

Symposium, *Federal Asset Forfeiture Reform*, 21 Notre Dame J. of Leg. 155–254 (1995).

Symposium, *What Price Civil Forfeiture? Constitutional Implications and Reform Initiatives*, 39 N.Y.L.School L.Rev. 1–371 (1994).

*

CHAPTER 29

CRIMINAL FORFEITURE

Table of Sections

WESTLAW Electronic Research

See WESTLAW Electronic Research Guide preceding the Summary of Contents.

Library References:

C.J.S. Constitutional Law § 1399–1401; Drugs and Narcotics § 138–155; Forfeitures § 1–10; RICO (Racketeer Influenced and Corrupt Organizations) § 30–34; Searches and Seizures § 220.

West's Key No. Digests, Constitutional Law ⟐303; Drugs and Narcotics ⟐190–198; Forfeitures ⟐1–11.

§ 29.1 Introduction

Criminal forfeiture is one of two types of asset forfeiture used by the federal government. The other type, civil forfeiture, is discussed in Chapter 28, *supra*.

Criminal forfeiture allows the government to take property from defendants when they are convicted for particular substantive crimes. It is "an aspect of punishment imposed following conviction of a substantive criminal offense."[1] The law is set up in three main statutes:[2] the drug criminal forfeiture statute,[3] the RICO forfeiture statute,[4] and the general criminal forfeiture statute.[5]

These three forfeiture statutes are very similar.[6] The drug criminal forfeiture statute and the RICO forfeiture statute were adopted together in 1970 and are identical in many ways. Courts often find authority under one persuasive for the other.[7] The general criminal forfeiture statute, enacted later, adopts by reference most of the drug criminal forfeiture statute.[8] These three statutes are discussed together below.

§ 29.1

1. Libretti v. United States, 516 U.S. 29, 38, 116 S.Ct. 356, 363, 133 L.Ed.2d 271 (1995).

2. Other criminal forfeiture statutes exist, see 18 U.S.C. § 2253 (criminal forfeiture authorized for crimes of sexual exploitation and other abuse of children involving visual depictions under 18 U.S.C. §§ 2251 *et seq.*); 18 U.S.C. § 1467 (criminal forfeiture authorized for violations of 18 U.S.C. §§ 1460 *et seq.* involving obscene materials). These forfeiture provisions are not widely used and are not discussed in this treatise.

3. 21 U.S.C. § 853; *see also* 21 U.S.C. § 970.

4. 18 U.S.C. § 1963. RICO does not authorize civil forfeiture, so any RICO forfeiture is necessarily criminal.

5. 18 U.S.C. § 982.

6. Of course, the crimes authorizing forfeiture vary among the statutes, as do the definitions of forfeitable property. Otherwise, the statutes are the same, with the following three exceptions. First, the drug forfeiture statute, § 853, sets up a rebuttable presumption in § 853(d) that property is forfeitable if acquired during the drug crime and there is no other likely source of income. This provision is discussed in § 29.18 *infra.* The other two statutes do not use any like presumption. Second, the general criminal forfeiture statute, § 982, includes a limit on the government's ability to seize substitute assets when the underlying crime is money laundering; no comparable limit exists for RICO forfeiture when the underlying RICO crime is based on racketeering acts of money laundering. This distinction is discussed in § 29.5(A)(i) *infra.* Finally, the drug forfeiture statute, § 853, allows the government to get a seizure warrant before trial under § 853(f). No comparable authorization exists under the RICO

forfeiture statute and parts of the general forfeiture statute. *See* 18 U.S.C. § 982(b)(1)(B) (not adopting § 853(f) for forfeitures under § 982(a)(2) but adopting it for forfeitures under § 982(a)(1) and (a)(6)).

7. *See*

First Circuit: United States v. White, 116 F.3d 948, 950 (1st Cir.1997)(drug and RICO forfeiture statutes should be interpreted "in pari passu").

Fourth Circuit: United States v. McHan, 101 F.3d 1027, 1042 (4th Cir.1996), *cert. den.,* ___ U.S. ___, 117 S.Ct. 2468, 138 L.Ed.2d 223 (1997); United States v. Shiflett, 1995 WL 125506 at **3 (4th Cir.1995) (legislative history shows Congress intended RICO and drug forfeiture statutes to be relevant to each other).

Ninth Circuit: United States v. Bennett, 147 F.3d 912 (9th Cir.1998); United States v. Ripinsky, 20 F.3d 359, 362 n. 3 (9th Cir.1994)(referring to cases and legislative history discussing RICO and drug forfeiture statutes interchangeably).

Tenth Circuit: United States v. Libretti, 38 F.3d 523, 528 n. 6 (10th Cir.1994), *aff'd,* 516 U.S. 29, 116 S.Ct. 356, 133 L.Ed.2d 271 (1995).

Eleventh Circuit: United States v. Bissell, 866 F.2d 1343, 1348 n. 3 (11th Cir. 1989).

But cf.

Third Circuit: United States v. Voigt, 89 F.3d 1050, 1083 (3d Cir.1996)(prior decisions of that circuit interpreting different criminal forfeiture provisions do not constitute binding precedent, although they may be persuasive).

8. 18 U.S.C. § 982(b)(1) provides:

Property subject to forfeiture under this section, any seizure and disposition there-

First we describe the property forfeitable under each statute, then we consider the defenses, constitutional issues and process for the three statutes generally.

Criminal forfeiture is a sanction that can be imposed on defendants only after they are convicted of an authorizing substantive crime. Thus criminal forfeiture is basically another sentencing option for particular crimes. It is clearly a part of the sentence rather than a charge in itself.[9] Yet some aspects of criminal forfeiture have charge-like characteristics.[10] For example, criminal forfeiture is defined as an *in personam* action against a defendant as opposed to a civil *in rem* action.[11] The government's demand for forfeiture is filed as a count in the indictment with the underlying substantive crimes.[12] And forfeiture is a jury decision: if the defendant is convicted on the underlying crimes, the forfeiture count is then submitted to the jury.[13] The jury must make predicate factual findings on the forfeiture.[14] If the jury decides to impose forfeiture, the

of, and any administrative or judicial proceeding in relation thereto, shall be governed—

  (A) in the case of a forfeiture under subsection (a)(1) or (a)(6) of this section, by subsections (c) and (e) through (p) of section 413 of the Comprehensive Drug Abuse Prevention and Control Act of 1979 (21 U.S.C.A. 853); and

  (B) in the case of a forfeiture under subsection (a)(2) of this section, by subsections (b), (c), (e), and (g) through (p) of section 413 of such Act.

Also, § 982(a)(7)(B) adopts parts of § 853.

9. *See* Libretti v. United States, 516 U.S. 29, 116 S.Ct. 356, 133 L.Ed.2d 271 (1995).

10. United States v. Hurley, 63 F.3d 1, 23 (1st Cir.1995) (criminal forfeiture orders are "something of a mongrel"); United States v. Bornfield, 145 F.3d 1123, 1134 (10th Cir.1998) (same, quoting *Hurley*); United States v. Saccoccia, 58 F.3d 754, 784 (1st Cir.1995) (describing "mixed heritage" of criminal forfeiture and resulting "hybrid").

11. *See*

First Circuit: United States v. Saccoccia, 58 F.3d 754 (1st Cir.1995), *cert. den.*, 517 U.S. 1105, 116 S.Ct. 1322, 134 L.Ed.2d 474 (1996).

Third Circuit: United States v. Voigt, 89 F.3d 1050 (3d Cir.1996), *cert. den.* ___ U.S. ___, 117 S.Ct. 623, 136 L.Ed.2d 546 (1996).

Eleventh Circuit: United States v. Bissell, 866 F.2d 1343 (11th Cir.1989).

United States v. Huber, 603 F.2d 387, 396 (2d Cir.1979) is often cited in this regard:

[W]hat is innovative about RICO is not that it imposes forfeiture as a consequence of criminal activity, but rather that it imposes it directly on an individual as part of a criminal prosecution rather than in a separate proceeding in rem against the property subject to forfeiture. Statutes providing for in rem forfeiture of property related to criminal activity are relatively common.

See generally Arthur W. Leach & John G. Malcolm, *Criminal Forfeiture: An Appropriate Solution to the Civil Forfeiture Debate*, 10 Ga.St.U.L.Rev. 241, 295 n.164 (1994).

12. *See* Fed.R.Crim.P. 7(c)(2) ("No judgment of forfeiture may be entered in a criminal proceeding unless the indictment of the information shall allege the extent of the forfeiture.").

13. *See* Fed.R.Crim.P. 31(e) ("If the indictment or the information alleges that an interest or property is subject to criminal forfeiture, a special verdict shall be returned as to the extent of the interest or property subject to forfeiture, if any.").

14. This is usually in the form of a series of questions on whether the property was used in the manner claimed by the government. The jury may or may not be asked to make an actual finding that forfeiture is appropriate. For example, the jury form may simply ask the jurors to find whether property was used in the commission of the underlying crime rather than whether forfeiture is appropriate. If the jury is only asked the preliminary question, the trial judge will simply declare that there is a forfeiture based on the other findings. *See* United States v. Sokolow, 91 F.3d 396, 414 (3d Cir.1996)(example of special verdict form held proper).

judge has no discretion to overrule the jury.[15]

Criminal forfeiture has a short history. Between 1790 and 1970 it was used only once.[16] In 1970, Congress revived criminal forfeiture for the most serious drug crime, the Continuing Criminal Enterprise (CCE), and RICO.[17] The rationale was that crime kingpins were less likely to continue their criminal activity after prison if their economic base was destroyed.[18] In 1984, forfeiture was expanded to apply to all drug felonies,[19] and in 1986, Congress passed a third criminal forfeiture statute that applied to money laundering crimes.[20] During the last ten years, Congress has added so many other crimes to this forfeiture statute that it is now more of a general criminal forfeiture statute.[21]

The government uses criminal forfeiture less frequently than civil forfeiture because civil forfeiture is easier for the government. In civil forfeiture actions, among other advantages, the government's burden of proof is lower, the burden shifts off the government to claimants, and claimants have no privilege against self-incrimination or right to counsel.[22] Because civil forfeiture is usually an option whenever criminal forfeiture is available,[23] the government usually chooses civil forfeiture. Thus reported decisions on civil forfeiture are numerous while reported decisions on criminal forfeiture are fewer. However, this may change in the future as the 1997 United States Attorneys Manual encourages prosecutors to include forfeiture counts in all drug indictments.[24]

For criminal forfeiture to apply, (1) the defendant must be convicted of an authorizing substantive crime, (2) the defendant must own or possess property defined by the forfeiture statute, and (3) the defined property must be used in or connected with the crime (the "nexus" requirement).

15. See § 29.19 infra.

16. United States v. Nichols, 841 F.2d 1485, 1487 (10th Cir.1988)(between 1790 and 1970, criminal forfeiture used only once, to recover life estates of Confederate soldiers).

17. 21 U.S.C. § 848; 18 U.S.C. §§ 1961–64. See generally United States v. Bajakajian, ___ U.S. ___ at ___ and n. 7, 118 S.Ct. 2028, at 2035 and n. 7, 141 L.Ed.2d 314 (1998) (describing history of criminal forfeiture as beginning in 1970).

18. See

First Circuit: United States v. Rogers, 102 F.3d 641 (1st Cir.1996) ("Although section 853 is a criminal penalty, it is apparent that Congress was endeavoring not only to increase punishment of drug offenses but also to discourage them by making them highly unprofitable.")

Seventh Circuit: United States v. Ben–Hur, 20 F.3d 313 (7th Cir.1994) ("[T]he purpose behind criminal forfeiture under

section 853 is not just to sanction illegal conduct, but also to strip drug dealers of their economic power.")

19. See 21 U.S.C. § 853(a).

20. 18 U.S.C. § 982.

21. See § 29.5 for a chart outlining the expansion of the general criminal forfeiture statute.

22. See, e.g., United States v. Bajakajian, ___ U.S. ___, ___, 118 S.Ct. 2028, 2046, 141 L.Ed.2d 314 (U.S.Cal.1998) (in rem forfeitures avoid mens rea as a predicate and give owners fewer procedural protections) (Kennedy, O'Connor and Scalia, JJ., dissenting).

23. Civil forfeiture covers all the crimes criminal forfeiture does, with the exception of the recent additions in § 982(a)(6) and (a)(7) of health care crimes and immigration and naturalization offenses.

24. U.S.A.M. § 9–100.040.

§ 29.2   Forfeiture Based on Drug Crimes: 21 U.S.C. § 853— Drug Crimes Which Authorize Forfeiture

All drug felonies in title 21 support forfeiture.[1] If the defendant's drug conviction is reversed, the "resulting criminal forfeiture orders also must fall."[2]

§ 29.3   Forfeiture Based on Drug Crimes: 21 U.S.C. § 853— Property Subject to Forfeiture

To be forfeitable, the subject property must fall within the statutory definition for forfeitable property, and it must have some connection to the underlying crime—the "nexus" requirement.

A.   SCOPE AND DEFINITION OF PROPERTY

The term "property" is defined as "(1) real property, including things growing on, affixed to, and found in land; and (2) tangible and intangible personal property, including rights, privileges, interests, claims and securities."[1] Any type of property is forfeitable, as long as it falls within one of the three theories of forfeiture in § 853(a).[2]

For real property, regardless of the theory under which it is found to be forfeitable (proceeds, facilitating property or CCE property), the entire tract of the real property with all of the fixtures thereon is forfeitable.[3] This includes any houses, outbuildings, crops, and any other permanent fixture on the property.[4] Real property interests are defined by the instruments and documents that created the defendant's interest.[5]

---

§ 29.2

1. 21 U.S.C. §§ 853(a) & 970. Drug crimes are dealt with in detail in § 9.1–9.42 *supra.*

Forfeiture was first allowed in 1970 for the CCE drug crime, and in 1984 expanded to cover all drug felonies under title 21.

2. United States v. Messino, 122 F.3d 427, 430 (7th Cir.1997).

§ 29.3

1. 21 U.S.C. § 853(b)(1).

2. One limit to the broad definition of forfeitable property is 21 U.S.C. § 861, which exempts from forfeiture an array of government subsistence benefits. This statute was used by one district court to deny a forfeiture of a defendant's government-subsidized lease for a first-time cocaine conviction. United States v. Robinson, 721 F.Supp. 1541 (D.R.I.1989).

3. *See, e.g.,*

Eighth Circuit: United States v. Bieri, 21 F.3d 819 (8th Cir.1994)(all four contiguous tracts of a farm were forfeitable even though the drug operation was located only on the fourth tract).

Ninth Circuit: United States v. Littlefield, 821 F.2d 1365 (9th Cir.1987).

But see

Second Circuit: United States v. McKeithen, 822 F.2d 310 (2d Cir.1987) (holding that only 43% of defendant's business was forfeitable in a CCE forfeiture).

See generally Sean D. Smith, Comment, *The Scope of Real Property Forfeiture for Drug Related Crime Under the Comprehensive Forfeiture Act,* 137 U.Pa.L.Rev. 303 (1988).

4. *See, e.g.,* United States v. Smith, 966 F.2d 1045 (6th Cir.1992) (forfeiting a working farm which included crops and outbuildings).

5. *See*

Sixth Circuit: United States v. Smith, 966 F.2d 1045, 1053 (6th Cir.1992).

Eighth Circuit: United States v. Bieri, 21 F.3d 819 (8th Cir.1994).

The property being forfeited must be owned or possessed by the defendant, but it is not required that the defendant personally use the property.[6]

Courts look to state law to define the defendant's property interests.[7] Thus some forfeiture cases focus on state property law, especially where the dispute is over the extent of the forfeiture rather than whether the property is subject to forfeiture.[8]

Each defendant in the crime allowing forfeiture is liable for the entire amount of forfeitable property regardless of whether the individual defendant had actual possession of the property; the courts reach this conclusion using either a conspiracy or a joint and several liability rationale.[9] Sometimes the calculations to determine the amount of forfeitable property are complex.[10]

B. THEORIES OF FORFEITURE

The statute defines forfeitable property in § 853(a) in three categories: proceeds, facilitating property, and property involved in a CCE (Continuing Criminal Enterprise). If the government alleges one theory of forfeiture in the indictment, forfeiture based on another theory is not error if either theory justifies the forfeiture.[11]

i. Proceeds

Property forfeitable as proceeds is described in the statute as "any property constituting, or derived from, any proceeds the person obtained,

6. *See* United States v. White, 116 F.3d 948 (1st Cir.1997).

7. *See*

Sixth Circuit: United States v. Smith, 966 F.2d 1045 (6th Cir.1992).

Ninth Circuit: United States v. Weaver, 1996 WL 528412 at *1 (9th Cir.1996) (unpublished opinion); United States v. Littlefield, 821 F.2d 1365 (9th Cir.1987).

But cf.

Second Circuit: United States v. McKeithen, 822 F.2d 310, 313 (2d Cir.1987)(property interest should not be at the whim of the "nuances and niceties of local real property law.").

8. *See, e.g.,*

Sixth Circuit: United States v. Smith, 966 F.2d 1045 (6th Cir.1992).

Seventh Circuit: United States v. Ben–Hur, 20 F.3d 313 (7th Cir.1994).

Ninth Circuit: United States v. Lester, 85 F.3d 1409 (9th Cir.1996); United States v. Weaver, 1996 WL 528412 (9th Cir.1996) (unpublished opinion).

9. *See*

First Circuit: United States v. Hurley, 63 F.3d 1 (1st Cir.1995).

Second Circuit: United States v. Benevento, 836 F.2d 129 (2d Cir.1988) (joint and several liability rationale).

Fourth Circuit: United States v. McHan, 101 F.3d 1027 (4th Cir.1996)(conspiracy rationale).

Seventh Circuit: United States v. Jarrett, 133 F.3d 519, 529–31 (7th Cir.1998) (affirming joint-and-several liability forfeiture order).

D.C. Circuit: United States v. Gaviria, 116 F.3d 1498, 1530 (D.C.Cir.1997)(declining to decide but noting that every circuit to decide has allowed joint and several liability).

10. United States v. Jarrett, 133 F.3d 519, 530 (7th Cir.1998) (calculating amount of unrecovered drug proceeds for forfeiture).

11. United States v. Holmes, 1998 WL 13538 at *3 (4th Cir.1998) (unpublished per curiam).

directly or indirectly, as the result of [the] violation."[12] Proceeds do not exist before the crime because the defendant's interest in the property is generated by the crime. An important but unresolved question is how long proceeds retain the character of proceeds *after* the crime. No decisions are reported on this question. An argument can be made from the statutory language that proceeds remain proceeds regardless of how many times the property is converted into other forms. For example, property directly derived from a drug deal remains proceeds even if drug money is used to purchase real property. The parcel of land is then the proceed. There is no time limit in the statute on how long defined property is a proceed. Presumably, the property will thereafter be a proceed, and a conversion of that proceed into another type of property will simply mean that that property is now the proceed.

Proceeds can take many forms. One common form is money from the sale of drugs.[13] Proceeds can also take the form of anything purchased with the drug profits, such as automobiles or real property.[14]

Proceeds is interpreted as the gross proceeds, not net profits.[15]

One situation in which it is difficult to define proceeds is when the proceeds are in the form of money, and it has been commingled in an account with legitimate money. The question of how to identify which part of the account is proceeds is academic when the defendant still has enough property of any type to cover the forfeiture order, because the government can take it as substitute assets.[16] If money has been transferred out of the account to third parties, the government can take it from the hands of third parties.[17] However, if the government is taking money from third parties, it has to trace the money and cannot merely take substitute assets from the third party.[18]

ii. Facilitating Property

Facilitating property is defined in the statute as "any of [the defendant's] property used, or intended to be used, in any manner or part, to commit, or to facilitate the commission of, such violation."[19] Facilitation occurs when the property "makes the prohibited conduct 'less difficult or more or less free from obstruction or hindrance.' "[20] The

12. 21 U.S.C. § 853(a)(1).

13. *See, e.g.,* United States v. McHan, 101 F.3d 1027 (4th Cir.1996) (forfeiting cash as proceeds).

14. *See, e.g.,* United States v. Elgersma, 929 F.2d 1538 (11th Cir.1991) (forfeiting several parcels of real property, a cashier's check, and a coin collection as proceeds of drug sales).

15. United States v. McHan, 101 F.3d 1027, 1041–1043 (4th Cir.1996).

16. United States v. Voigt, 89 F.3d 1050 (3d Cir.1996) (government has burden of tracing proceeds through a commingled account, but burden is not so great since

the government can just forfeit the account as substitute assets). *See also* § 29.3(E), which discusses substitute assets. This option of taking substitute assets is not available in civil forfeiture for drug crimes, and in that context, commingling remains a difficult issue. *See* § 28.2(A) *supra.*

17. *See* § 29.3(F) *infra.*

18. United States v. Moffitt, Zwerling, & Kemler, P.C., 83 F.3d 660 (4th Cir.1996).

19. 21 U.S.C. § 853(a)(2).

20. United States v. Tencer, 107 F.3d 1120, 1137 (5th Cir.1997), *cert. denied* ___ U.S. ___, 118 S.Ct. 390, 139 L.Ed.2d 305 (1997)(construing § 982), *citing* United

statutory language "in any manner or part" means that the whole category of property is forfeitable even when only a part was used to facilitate the crime.[21]

Property the courts have found to be facilitating includes land, a cellular phone, a veterinary hospital, horses and cash.[22] Land has been held forfeitable as facilitating property when it was used not to grow marijuana but it actually physically concealed the land on which the marijuana was grown.[23]

Unlike proceeds, the defendant does have title to facilitating property before the commission of the crime. Facilitating property has a legitimate genesis unconnected to the underlying criminal activity.

Also forfeitable under this subsection is property "intended to be used" in drug crimes. In United States v. Rogers,[24] the First Circuit upheld the forfeiture of a defendant's diamond, gold coins and motor home on the theory that they were "intended to be used" in a drug conspiracy when these items were discussed by the conspirators as possible collateral for the drug deal. The conspirators reached no final agreement on these items, and the defendant argued that the crime, conspiracy, was therefore committed without any direct use of the property. The court rejected this argument and held that the property was forfeitable, stating that the statute defines the property to be forfeited broadly and that "Congress was endeavoring not only to increase punishment of drug offenses but also to discourage them by making them highly unprofitable."[25]

iii. CCE Property

CCE property is defined as the "enterprise" through which the defendants conducted their criminal activity.[26] The other categories of

States v. Schifferli, 895 F.2d 987, 990 (4th Cir.1990).

21. United States v. Harris, 903 F.2d 770, 777–78 (10th Cir.1990)(upholding forfeiture of all currency found in a truck without proof all of it was used to facilitate crime).

22. *See*

Fourth Circuit: United States v. McHan, 101 F.3d 1027, 1042–1043 (4th Cir. 1996) (upholding forfeiture of cash as facilitating property).

Seventh Circuit: United States v. Ben–Hur, 20 F.3d 313 (7th Cir.1994)(upholding forfeiture of veterinary hospital).

Eighth Circuit: United States v. Bieri, 21 F.3d 819, 821 (8th Cir.1994) (upholding forfeiture of 4 tract farm); United States v. Lewis, 987 F.2d 1349, 1356–1357 (8th Cir. 1993) (upholding a forfeiture of a cellular phone the defendant used to conduct a drug transaction).

Tenth Circuit: United States v. Harris, 903 F.2d 770, 777–78 (10th Cir.1990)(upholding forfeiture of cash as facilitating property).

Eleventh Circuit: United States v. Rivera, 884 F.2d 544 (11th Cir.1989)(upholding forfeiture of horses on a horse farm).

23. United States v. Smith, 966 F.2d 1045, 1055 (6th Cir.1992).

24. 102 F.3d 641 (1st Cir.1996).

25. 102 F.3d 641, 648.

26. 21 U.S.C. § 853(a)(3)("in the case of a person convicted of engaging in a continuing criminal enterprise in violation of section 408 of this title (21 U.S.C. 848), the person shall forfeit, in addition to any property described in paragraph (1) or (2), any of his interest in, claims against, and property or contractual rights affording a source of control over, the continuing criminal enterprise."). *See also* United States v. McKeithen, 822 F.2d 310, 315 (2d Cir.1987)

forfeitable property can be reached indirectly through CCE property since a CCE conviction is a compound one, relying on underlying drug crimes.[27] If the property does not directly fall within the CCE definition, the government can forfeit it on the basis of the underlying drug crimes.[28]

C. THE NEXUS REQUIREMENT: THE RELATIONSHIP BETWEEN THE CRIME AND THE PROPERTY

The nexus requirement does not appear explicitly in the statutes; courts infer it from the statutory definitions of what property is forfeitable. Under this requirement, a piece of property cannot be forfeited unless it has some connection to the crime beyond merely falling within the statutory definitions of what is forfeitable.[29] Presumably the nexus requirement applies to property forfeited under all three theories.[30]

i. Proceeds

The nexus requirement applies here[31] but is not important for proceeds because by definition, proceeds are solidly connected to the underlying criminal activity. Proceeds only exist as a result of the underlying crime.[32]

ii. Facilitating Property

The nexus requirement serves its most important function when applied to facilitating property because in contrast to proceeds, facilitating property may have only a slight connection to the drug crime. The nexus requirement is not well developed in the courts.[33] Generally,

---

(construing language in CCE crime, § 848, to authorize forfeiture only of that portion of realty that provided a source of influence, here determined to be 43%).

27. The CCE crime, 21 U.S.C. § 848, is discussed in §§ 9.21–9.23 *supra*.

28. *See* United States v. Moya–Gomez, 860 F.2d 706, 715 (7th Cir.1988) (forfeiting all property obtained with drug proceeds in a CCE prosecution).

29. *See, e.g.*,

First Circuit: United States v. White, 116 F.3d 948, 950 (1st Cir.1997) (nexus met because defendant owned property co-conspirators used to facilitate drug crime and the defendant knew of the use).

Eighth Circuit: United States v. Lewis, 987 F.2d 1349 (8th Cir.1993).

Eleventh Circuit: United States v. Rivera, 884 F.2d 544 (11th Cir.1989).

30. *See* United States v. White, 116 F.3d 948, 952 (1st Cir.1997) (nexus requirement applies to both "property obtained" [*i.e.*, proceeds] and "property used" [*i.e.*,

facilitating property]; no mention of CCE property because not involved in case).

31. United States v. White, 116 F.3d 948, 952 (1st Cir.1997) (nexus requirement applies to "property obtained" [*i.e.*, proceeds]).

32. This is one reason why it is in the government's interest to try to forfeit certain property as proceeds rather then facilitating property, if it has an option. In addition to largely falling outside of the nexus requirement, a definition as proceeds would exclude the third-party defense under § 853(n)(6)(A) of having title superior to the defendant at the commission of the crime (*see infra* § 29.9(B)) and it makes it even more difficult for a defendant successfully to assert an excessive fines claim (*see infra* § 29.14).

33. *See*

First Circuit: United States v. White, 116 F.3d 948, 950 (1st Cir.1997) ("exact dimensions of nexus requirement are largely uncharted").

courts require only a slim connection to the underlying crime.[34] This slim connection can be as tenuous as one phone call on a cellular phone to cement a drug sale.[35] The forfeiture statute expressly requires liberal construction,[36] and courts rely on this language to find that property is forfeitable when the language of the statute does not necessarily compel this result.[37]

iii. CCE Property

The nexus requirement presumably applies as well to CCE property, but no cases are reported discussing the nexus requirement in this context.

D. RELATION BACK

The drug forfeiture statute includes a subsection which creates a legal fiction through which the title to forfeitable property vests in the federal government at the time the crime is committed.[38] Since title vests in the government at the time of the crime, anything that is done to the property after that by the defendant or a third party does not change its character from that of the government's property.

The relation back provision has a different effect based on the type of forfeitable property. For proceeds, the relation back doctrine means that proceeds are never the property of the criminal defendant, because at their "creation," *i.e.*, when the defendant generates them through the crime, title vests in the government. The defendant never has any claim of title. For facilitating property, on the other hand, relation back means that title *shifts*. Facilitating property legitimately belonged to the defendant at the time of the crime, and the relation back doctrine shifts the title from the defendant to the government when the property is used to facilitate crime, *i.e.*, when the crime is committed.

The statute includes two defenses for third parties that can over-

---

Tenth Circuit: United States v. Harris, 903 F.2d 770, 777–78 (10th Cir.1990)(finding sufficient nexus without explanation).

34. *See*

Sixth Circuit: United States v. Smith, 966 F.2d 1045, 1055 (6th Cir.1992)("When defendant uses real property to actually physically conceal the commission of the offense on adjacent property, the 'nexus' is sufficient to support a finding that the property 'facilitated' commission of the offense....").

Eleventh Circuit: United States v. Rivera, 884 F.2d 544, 546 (11th Cir.1989)(forfeiture of horses on a farm used to distribute drugs was appropriate even though the horses were never directly used to facilitate the drug transaction; the horses made the farm look more legitimate, thus facilitating the drug dealer's cover).

35. *See* United States v. Lewis, 987 F.2d 1349, 1356–1357 (8th Cir.1993)(defendant's Blazer and cellular phone had a sufficient nexus to the crime after only one telephone call on the phone from the Blazer).

36. 21 U.S.C. § 853(*o*).

37. *See, e.g.,*

Eighth Circuit: United States v. Lewis, 987 F.2d 1349, 1356–57 (8th Cir.1993).

Eleventh Circuit: United States v. Rivera, 884 F.2d 544, 546 (11th Cir.1989).

38. 21 U.S.C. § 853(c)("All right, title, and interest in property described in subsection (a) vests in the United States upon the commission of the act giving rise to forfeiture under this section....").

come the government's title under the relation back clause.[39]

E. SUBSTITUTE ASSETS

The substitute assets provision allows the government to take property from the defendant beyond that defined as forfeitable if the government has a forfeiture order for property which is missing or diminished in value.[40] The government can take other property from the defendant as a substitute up to the amount that was due to the government under the forfeiture order.

One court has explained that an asset cannot logically be both forfeitable and a substitute asset.[41] These characterizations are mutually exclusive, or the substitute assets provision would be rendered meaningless.[42]

The government cannot use the substitute assets provision to seize an innocent spouse's interest in community property to satisfy the forfeiture obligations of the guilty spouse.[43]

The provision allowing seizure of substitute assets applies only to the defendant's property and not to third parties' property.[44] The government can take the transferred assets out of the hands of the third party, but if that party has since, for example, spent the money and it is untraceable, the government cannot seize substitute assets under the forfeiture laws but must resort to state common law actions of conversion and detinue to recover the money.[45]

39. *See* § 29.9(B) *infra.*

40. 21 U.S.C. § 853(p) provides:

(p) Missing property or property diminished in value: If any of the property described in subsection (a) [the types of forfeitable property], as a result of any act or omission of the defendant—

(1) cannot be located upon the exercise of due diligence;

(2) has been transferred or sold to, or deposited with, a third party;

(3) has been placed beyond the jurisdiction of the court;

(4) has been substantially diminished in value; or

(5) has been commingled with other property which cannot be divided without difficulty;

the court shall order the forfeiture of any other property of the defendant up to the value of the property described in paragraphs (1) through (5).

41. United States v. Bornfield, 145 F.3d 1123, 1139 (10th Cir.1998).

42. *Id.*

43. *See*

Ninth Circuit: United States v. Lester, 85 F.3d 1409 (9th Cir.1996).

See also

Eleventh Circuit: United States v. Jimerson, 5 F.3d 1453, 1454 (11th Cir.1993) (disallowing seizure of innocent spouse's interest in marital property).

44. United States v. Moffitt, Zwerling & Kemler, 83 F.3d 660 at 668 (4th Cir. 1996).

45. United States v. Moffitt, Zwerling & Kemler, P.C., 83 F.3d 660 (4th Cir.1996), in which the attorneys for a large scale drug dealer took drug proceeds as fees and the government pursued the law firm when it was unable to obtain a sufficient return from the convicted defendants. By the time the government tried to obtain a forfeiture order against the firm, it had allegedly already spent the money out of its general fund, and the government could only pursue the firm through state common law tort actions.

F. PROPERTY IN THE HANDS OF THIRD PARTIES

The government can take forfeitable property out of the hands of third parties.[46] Combined with the relation back doctrine, this means that the defendant cannot hide property from the government by giving it or selling it to others. There are two defenses for third parties in the statute,[47] which are discussed *infra* in § 29.9(B).

Substitute assets cannot be seized from third parties.[48] If the third party cannot establish either of the two statutory defenses for third parties,[49] then the court must determine exactly how much of the truly forfeitable property is left in the third parties' hands. If the forfeitable money is commingled with other funds, and there has been an outflow of funds from the commingled account, the court must determine if the outflow came from the clean funds or the forfeitable money, much as is done under the civil forfeiture or money laundering laws where the courts have developed tracing rules for commingled accounts.[50] If there is not enough truly forfeitable money left to satisfy the forfeiture judgment, the government cannot seize substitute assets under the forfeiture laws but it can resort to state common law actions of conversion and detinue to recover the money.[51]

§ 29.4 General Criminal Forfeiture: 18 U.S.C. § 982—Crimes which Authorize Forfeiture

The general criminal forfeiture statute was adopted after the drug and RICO forfeiture statutes. It adopts most of the drug forfeiture statute.[1]

The general criminal forfeiture statute authorizes forfeiture for:

46. *See* 21 U.S.C. § 853(c)("Any such property that is subsequently transferred to a person other than the defendant may be the subject of a special verdict of forfeiture and thereafter shall be ordered forfeited to the United States . . . .").

47. *See* 21 U.S.C. § 853(n).

48. United States v. Moffitt, Zwerling & Kemler, P.C., 83 F.3d at 668 (4th Cir. 1996).

49. *See* § 29.9(B), which details third party claims.

50. *See* § 29.5(A) *supra* (tracing under money laundering laws) and § 28.2(A) *infra* (tracing under civil forfeiture laws).

51. United States v. Moffitt, Zwerling & Kemler, P.C., 83 F.3d 660 (4th Cir.1996), in which the attorneys for a large scale drug dealer took drug proceeds as fees and the government pursued the law firm when it was unable to obtain a sufficient return from the convicted defendants. By the time the government tried to obtain a forfeiture order against the firm, it had allegedly already spent the money out of its general fund, and the government could only pursue the firm through state common law tort actions.

§ 29.4

1. 18 U.S.C. § 982(b)(1) provides:

Property subject to forfeiture under this section, any seizure and disposition thereof, and any administrative or judicial proceeding in relation thereto, shall be governed—

(A) in the case of a forfeiture under subsection (a)(1) of this section, by subsections (c) and (e) through (p) of section 413 of the Comprehensive Drug Abuse Prevention and Control Act of 1979 (21 U.S.C.A. 853); and

(B) in the case of a forfeiture under subsection (a)(2) of this section, by subsections (b), (c), (e), and (g) through (p) of section 413 of such Act.

18 U.S.C. § 982(b)(1). Also, § 982(a)(7)(B) adopts parts of § 853.

(1) money laundering;[2]

(2) crimes involving financial institutions;[3]

(3) some general crimes such as false statements to federal authorities, mail fraud, and wire fraud as they apply to conservators for financial institutions;[4]

(4) crimes involving motor vehicles in interstate commerce;[5]

(5) health care crimes;[6] and

(6) immigration and naturalization crimes.[7]

When this statute was first enacted in 1986, it only applied to money laundering crimes, but Congress amended the statute several times and the list of crimes grew to include many others. The evolution of the statute is charted below.

General Criminal Forfeiture—18 U.S.C. § 982

date	provision adopted	forfeiture authorized for
1986–88	§ 982(a)(1)	money laundering
1989	§ 982(a)(2)	financial institution crimes
1990	§ 982(a)(3)	crimes involving assets held by conservators
1992	§ 982(a)(5)	motor vehicle crimes
1996	§ 982(a)(6)	health care crimes
1996	§ 982(a)(7)	immigration and naturalization crimes

§ 29.5   General Criminal Forfeiture: 18 U.S.C. § 982—Property Subject to Forfeiture

Each general type of underlying crime that supports forfeiture has its own definition of what property is subject to forfeiture. In addition, all are subject to the nexus requirement.

A.   PROPERTY IDENTIFIED IN THE STATUTE

i.   Money Laundering Crimes—§ 982(a)(1)

Property subject to forfeiture under this subsection includes "any property, real or personal, *involved in* such offense, or any property *traceable to* such property."[1] The statutory words are different, but as the courts interpret this language, it is another way of articulating the concepts of facilitating property and proceeds as used in the drug forfeiture statute.[2]

---

2. 18 U.S.C. § 892(a)(1) (authorizing forfeiture for 31 U.S.C. §§ 5313, 5316, & 5324; 18 U.S.C. §§ 1956–57, 1960)

3. 18 U.S.C. § 982(a)(2)-(3).

4. *Id.* § 982(a)(3).

5. *Id.* § 982(a)(5).

6. *Id.* § 982(a)(6).

7. *Id.* § 982(a)(7).

§ 29.5

1. 18 U.S.C. § 982(a)(1)(emphasis added).

2. *See* § 29.3(B) *supra* for a discussion of facilitating property and proceeds as

Property "involved in" money laundering includes the dirty money being laundered (the corpus), any commissions or fees paid the launderer, and any property facilitating the laundering.[3] Facilitating property is defined the same here as it is for drug forfeiture: facilitating property is any property making the crime less difficult or more or less free from obstruction or hindrance.[4] Although it is preferable that the jury be instructed on the meaning of "involved in," it is not plain error for the court to omit a definition.[5]

Under the "traceable to" language, the government must prove that money commingled in a bank account is indeed traceable or "has some nexus" to property involved in the money laundering crime.[6] Property is traceable to other property if its acquisition is attributable to money laundering rather than to property from untainted sources.[7] However, this burden is not significant because the government can rely on substitute assets.[8]

Under the "traceable to" prong, the forfeiture must be reduced to the extent the defendant returns property before the forfeiture order is entered, but no reduction is required for value the defendant adds to forfeitable property. The Eighth Circuit reached this conclusion in United States v. Hawkey.[9] In that case, a sheriff was convicted under § 1957 for engaging in monetary transactions in money derived from mail fraud. He misappropriated funds from a charitable account, and used some of the money to buy a motor home. He also made deposits back to the charitable account to partially replace the depleted funds. The district court ordered forfeiture of $140,450.08, the entire corpus of his criminally derived money. The defendant argued the forfeiture should be reduced to the extent he replaced money he'd taken from the account. The court agreed, and remanded the forfeiture for a hearing on how much money was returned. On the other hand, when the defendant argued the forfeiture of the motor home should be reduced to the extent he increased the value of it, the court refused, stating, "Irrespective of whether the increased value to the converted property is the result of wise investment, personal effort by Hawkey, or by adding Hawkey's personal untainted funds, because the converted property is traceable to

forfeitable under the drug criminal forfeiture statute.

3. *Fifth Circuit*: United States v. Tencer, 107 F.3d 1120, 1134 (5th Cir.1997), *cert. den.*, ___ U.S. ___, 118 S.Ct. 390, 139 L.Ed.2d 305 (1997).

Eighth Circuit: United States v. Hawkey, 1998 WL 331182 at *6 (8th Cir.1998).

Tenth Circuit: United States v. Bornfield, 145 F.3d 1123, 1134 (10th Cir.1998).

4. *Fifth Circuit*: United States v. Tencer, 107 F.3d 1120, 1134 (5th Cir.1997), *cert. den.*, ___ U.S. ___, 118 S.Ct. 390, 139 L.Ed.2d 305 (1997).

Eighth Circuit: United States v. Hawkey, 1998 WL 331182 at *6 (8th Cir.1998).

Tenth Circuit: United States v. Bornfield, 145 F.3d 1123, 1134 (10th Cir.1998)(forfeiture reversed on other grounds).

5. United States v. Bornfield, 145 F.3d 1123, 1136 (10th Cir.1998).

6. United States v. Voigt, 89 F.3d 1050, 1087 (3d Cir.1996).

7. *Eighth Circuit*: United States v. Hawkey, 1998 WL 331182 at *6 (8th Cir. 1998).

Tenth Circuit: United States v. Bornfield, 145 F.3d 1123, 1136 (10th Cir.1998).

8. *Voigt*, 89 F.3d at 1088.

9. 1998 WL 331182 (8th Cir.1998).

the unlawful monetary transaction, we conclude that the property is subject to forfeiture under the statute."[10]

One particular question is whether clean money commingled in an account with dirty money is forfeitable on the theory that it facilitates the laundering of the dirty money. The Fifth Circuit has recently said yes. In United States v. Tencer,[11] the government sought forfeiture of $1,050,000 in a bank account. Some of the money was dirty, and was being laundered, but some was legitimate. The court reviewed authority from the civil forfeiture context, which included district court cases allowing forfeiture of commingled clean money as facilitating and a Seventh Circuit decision disallowing such forfeiture.[12] The court held that mere pooling without more does not render the clean money in the account forfeitable, but that clean money was forfeitable if the defendant pooled the funds to disguise the nature and source of the scheme. Here, the court held, the jury was entitled to infer that all the funds were involved in the laundering, so they were all forfeitable.[13]

This decision was a big win for the government. It allows the government to forfeit an entire account if any part of the money is dirty, as long as the money was commingled for a laundering purpose. It will be unusual to find a case where funds were commingled for other purposes. Recently, the Tenth Circuit endorsed the Fifth Circuit's decision in *Tencer* that clean money commingled with dirty money is forfeitable under the "involved in" standard if it was pooled for a laundering purpose, *i.e.*, to disguise the nature and source of the funds.[14]

Two statutory limits apply to property forfeited based on money laundering. First, the statute has an exemption for financial institutions. They are not subject to forfeiture for one kind of money laundering crime, reporting violations under the cash transaction law.[15] This exception applies only to violations of the cash transaction law; if a bank is subject to forfeiture under any of the other underlying crimes, including the substantive laundering crimes of §§ 1956–57, the exception provides no protection.

The second limit disallows forfeiture of substitute assets for an intermediary in a money laundering operation who did nothing but handle the property.[16] The statute provides that the substitute assets

---

10. United States v. Hawkey, 1998 WL 331182 at *7 (8th Cir.1998).

11. 107 F.3d 1120 (5th Cir.1997), *cert. den.*, ___ U.S. ___, 118 S.Ct. 390, 139 L.Ed.2d 305 (1997).

12. United States v. Tencer, 107 F.3d 1120, 1135. The Seventh Circuit case disallowing such forfeitures, United States v. $448,342.85, 969 F.2d 474 (7th Cir.1992) was overruled legislatively by 18 U.S.C. § 984. *See* § 28.9(A)(i)(b) *supra.*

13. *Tencer,* 107 F.3d at 1135.

14. United States v. Bornfield, 145 F.3d 1123, 1134 (10th Cir.1998)(forfeiture

reversed on other grounds). *See also* United States v. Hawkey, 1998 WL 331182 at *7 n. 13 (8th Cir.1998)(endorsing in dicta the idea that clean money may be forfeitable as if it is commingled with dirty money).

15. 18 U.S.C. § 982(a)(1) ("However, no property shall be seized or forfeited in the case of a violation of section 5313(a) of title 31 by a domestic financial institution regulated by the Securities and Exchange Commission or a partner, director, or employee thereof.").

16. The statute states:

provision shall not be used "to order a defendant to forfeit assets in place of the actual property laundered where such defendant acted merely as an intermediary who handled but did not retain the property in the course of the money laundering offense.... "[17] The point of this limit is best illustrated by example. If a defendant launders $80,000 in exchange for a 5% fee ($4000), the government cannot seek forfeiture of substitute assets from the defendant for the entire $80,000 but only for the $4000 the defendant retained as his or her own.

This exception disallowing forfeiture of substitute assets operates to allow a "passing on" defense when the crime is money laundering.[18] The government can only seize property involved with money laundering that the defendant still holds or substitute assets for money the defendant retained. The government cannot seize substitute assets from the defendant for the amount of all the money that ever passed through his or her hands in the laundering process. In United States v. Bornfield, the Tenth Circuit discussed this limit, which it called the "intermediary exception."[19] The court reversed the forfeiture in that case on other grounds, but along the way noted that the defendant fell within the intermediary exception, so he would not have been subject to forfeiture of substitute assets anyway.[20]

This limit has a limit. The government cannot use the substitute assets provision against defendants involved in relatively small money laundering transactions, but it can seize substitute assets if the defendant conducts three or more separate transactions involving a total of $100,000 or more in any twelve month period.[21] The point is to put relatively big launderers at increased risk. As the Tenth Circuit explained, "[O]nly intermediaries ... who are financially capable of laundering large amounts of property are required to forfeit substitute assets.... "[22]

Although substitute assets cannot be seized from launderers under § 982, the general forfeiture statute, they can be seized from launderers under the RICO forfeiture statute; it contains no such limit on forfeiture of substitute assets.[23]

The substitution of assets provision of subsection 413(p) [21 U.S.C. § 853(p)] shall not be used to order a defendant to forfeit assets in place of the actual property laundered where such defendant acted merely as an intermediary who handled but did not retain the property in the course of the money laundering offense unless the defendant, in committing the offense or offenses giving rise to the forfeiture, conducted three or more separate transactions involving a total of $100,000 or more in any twelve month period.
18 U.S.C. § 982(b)(2).

17. 18 U.S.C. § 982(b)(2).

18. United States v. Hurley, 63 F.3d 1, 21–22 (1st Cir.1995).

19. United States v. Bornfield, 145 F.3d 1123, 1134 (10th Cir.1998)(forfeiture reversed on other grounds).

20. Id.

21. 18 U.S.C. § 982(b)(2).

22. United States v. Bornfield, 145 F.3d 1123, 1139 (10th Cir.1998)(citing United States v. Hendrickson, 22 F.3d 170, 175 (7th Cir.1994)).

23. United States v. Hurley, 63 F.3d 1, 21–22 (1st Cir.1995).

The amount of property forfeitable based on a particular kind of money laundering, import/export reports of $10,000 under § 5316,[24] is uncertain these days in the wake of Bajakajian v. United States. That decision is discussed in detail *infra* in § 29.14 on the excessive fines clause.

ii. Crimes Affecting Financial Institutions—§ 982(a)(2)

Forfeitable property under this section includes "[a]ny property constituting, or derived from, proceeds the person obtained directly or indirectly, as the result of such violation."[25] Forfeiture here is limited to proceeds and does not extend to facilitating property. What Congress had in mind with the "indirectly" modifier is unclear. It may imply that Congress intended to give proceeds a broad definition.

iii. Crimes Involving Assets Held by Conservators for Financial Institutions—§ 982(a)(3)

Property forfeitable under this section is "any property, real or personal, which represents or is traceable to the gross receipts obtained, directly or indirectly, as a result of such violation."[26] "Gross receipts" is defined as "any property, real or personal, tangible or intangible, which is obtained, directly or indirectly, as a result of such violation."[27] Under this subsection, forfeiture is authorized only for proceeds and not for facilitating property. The statutory definition of gross receipts makes clear that forfeiture of proceeds is not limited to profits.[28]

iv. Motor Vehicle Crimes—§ 982(a)(5)

Under this section, the government may forfeit "any property, real or personal, which represents or is traceable to the gross receipts obtained, directly or indirectly, as a result of such violation."[29] This is the same definition of forfeitable property as in the preceding section, § 982(a)(3) covering crimes involving assets held by conservators for financial institutions. The statutory definition of gross receipts quoted *supra* does not apply to this section (§ 982(a)(5)), but only to the previous one (§ 982(a)(3)). Probably this was not deliberate by Congress but was a result of the way the statute grew historically. The gross receipts definition was adopted at the same time as subsection (a)(3) to apply to it, and subsection (a)(5) was not adopted until two years later. At that time, Congress likely intended the definition to apply to this subsection as well but neglected to state that. The courts will likely resort to the same definition of gross receipts for (a)(5) as the statute requires under the identical language in (a)(3).

---

24. 31 U.S.C. § 5316, discussed *supra* in § 18.4.

25. 18 U.S.C. § 982(a)(2).

26. *Id.* § 982(a)(3).

27. *Id.* § 982(a)(4).

28. Forfeiture is generally held to extend to the gross amount under the word "proceeds." *See* United States v. McHan, 101 F.3d 1027 (4th Cir.1996) (error to limit forfeiture to net profits under drug forfeiture) and cases cited in § 29.8(B) (RICO forfeiture). Here, the statutory definition of gross receipts makes this result all the more certain.

29. 18 U.S.C. § 982(a)(5).

v. Health Care Crimes—§ 982(a)(6)

Under this subsection, the government may forfeit "property, real or personal, that constitutes or is derived, directly or indirectly, from gross proceeds traceable to" the crime.[30] This subsection was added in 1996 and has not generated any reported cases.

vi. Immigration and Naturalization Crimes—§ 982(a)(7)

Under this subsection, the government can forfeit proceeds and facilitating property under a list of immigration and naturalization crimes.[31] This section was added in 1996 and has generated no reported cases.

B. THE NEXUS REQUIREMENT: THE RELATIONSHIP BETWEEN THE UNDERLYING CRIME AND THE PROPERTY

No reported cases have discussed the nexus requirement in the context of the general criminal forfeiture statute. Presumably the nexus requirement is treated the same as under the drug forfeiture statute.

C. RELATION BACK

This forfeiture statute incorporates the the drug forfeiture statute provisions on relation back,[32] so the case law interpreting relation back under the drug forfeiture statute also applies here.[33]

D. SUBSTITUTE ASSETS

As with relation back, the general forfeiture statute adopts the substitute assets provision of the drug forfeiture statute by reference,[34] so the law is the same with the exception noted below. See § 29.3(E) for a fuller discussion of the substitute assets provision.

The general forfeiture statute includes an exception on forfeiting substitute assets when the crime is money laundering.[35] As described

30. *Id.* § 982(a)(6).

31. *Id.* § 982(a)(7)(i) and (ii).

32. 18 U.S.C. § 982 has a provision that adopts most of 21 U.S.C. § 853:

Property subject to forfeiture under this section, any seizure and disposition thereof, and any administrative or judicial proceeding in relation thereto, shall be governed—

(A) in the case of a forfeiture under subsection (a)(1) of this section, by subsections (c) and (e) through (p) of section 413 of the Comprehensive Drug Abuse Prevention and Control Act of 1979 (21 U.S.C.A. 853); and

(B) in the case of a forfeiture under subsection (a)(2) of this section, by subsections (b), (c), (e), and (g) through (p) of section 413 of such Act.

18 U.S.C. § 982(b)(1).

33. *See* § 29.3(D) for a discussion of relation back under § 853.

34. 18 U.S.C. § 982(b)(1).

35. The statute states:

The substitution of assets provision of subsection 413(p) [21 U.S.C. § 853(p)] shall not be used to order a defendant to forfeit assets in place of the actual property laundered where such defendant acted merely as an intermediary who han-

above, if the money is already gone and irretrievable, then the intermediary, or launderer, cannot be held liable for the entire sum under the substitute assets provision. This allows a kind of "passing on" defense— someone who handles $1,000,000 to launder it but keeps only a 5% commission is liable to pay substitute assets not for the full $1,000,000 but only for the 5% retained.[36] This exception does not apply if the defendant was a conduit for more than $100,000 through three or more separate transactions in a twelve month period.[37] This intermediary exception is discussed in more detail *supra*.[38]

E.   PROPERTY IN THE HANDS OF THIRD PARTIES

As with relation back and substitute assets, on this issue the general criminal forfeiture statute adopts the drug criminal forfeiture statute,[39] so assets can be seized from third parties.[40] The statute also incorporates both third party defenses of the drug statute.[41]

§ 29.6   RICO Forfeiture: 18 U.S.C. § 1963—In General

This statute was adopted simultaneously with the drug forfeiture statute; they are basically the same with two differences. One difference is that RICO has no presumption like the drug forfeiture statute that money generated during the time of the crime for which there is no likely other source is forfeitable.[1] The second difference is that RICO does not authorize seizure warrants as the drug forfeiture statute does.[2] Outside of these distinctive provisions, courts often rely on authority from one criminal forfeiture statute in interpreting the other.[3]

RICO forfeiture is not as frequently used today as the other two criminal forfeiture statutes because the substantive crime of RICO is harder for the government to prove than are the substantive crimes for the other forfeiture statutes. Under the drug forfeiture statute, any drug felony will allow forfeiture, and under the general criminal forfeiture statute, the list of authorizing crimes keeps getting longer.

To prove a RICO forfeiture, the government must convict the defendant of a substantive violation of RICO, establish that the property to be forfeited is listed in the statute and that there is a relationship between the property and the crime.

---

dled but did not retain the property in the course of the money laundering offense unless the defendant, in committing the offense or offenses giving rise to the forfeiture, conducted three or more separate transactions involving a total of $100,000 or more in any twelve month period.
18 U.S.C. § 982(b)(2).

36. United States v. Hurley, 63 F.3d 1, 21–22 (1st Cir.1995).

37. 18 U.S.C. § 982(b)(2).

38. *See* § 29.5(A)(i) *supra*.

39. It adopts §§ 853(c) and (n).

40. *See* discussion in § 29.3(F) *supra*.

41. *See* discussion in § 29.9(B) *infra*.

§ 29.6

1. *See* 21 U.S.C. § 853(d). *See, e.g.*, United States v. DeFries, 129 F.3d 1293, 1312 (D.C.Cir.1997) (forfeiture must be reversed because RICO convictions were reversed).

2. *See* 21 U.S.C. § 853(f).

3. *See* § 29.1 *supra*.

§ 29.7   RICO Forfeiture: 18 U.S.C. § 1963—RICO Conviction

Before RICO forfeiture may be imposed, the government must convict the defendant of a substantive violation of RICO.[1] Elements of the RICO crimes are discussed in §§ 21.1–21.20 *supra*.

§ 29.8   RICO Forfeiture: 18 U.S.C. § 1963—Property Subject to Forfeiture

In the statute, Congress wrote a definition of property and then listed three basic categories of property which may be forfeited.[1]

A.   SCOPE AND DEFINITION OF PROPERTY

The term "property" is defined as "(1) real property, including things growing on, affixed to, and found in land; and (2) tangible and intangible personal property, including rights, privileges, interests, claims and securities."[2] This is identical to the definition of forfeitable property in the drug forfeiture statute.[3] Given that the language is identical and courts acknowledge that the drug and RICO forfeiture statutes are generally persuasive in interpreting each other,[4] the case law from the drug statute, § 853, is relevant here. The following paragraphs summarize the principles defining property in the drug forfeiture context.

Courts look to state law to define the defendant's property interests.[5] Thus some forfeiture cases focus on state property law, especially where the dispute is over the extent of the forfeiture rather than whether the property is subject to forfeiture.[6] Real property interests are defined by the instruments and documents that created the defendant's interest.[7]

§ 29.7

1. Section 1963(a) provides that "[w]hoever violates any provision of section 1962 of this chapter" shall forfeit property. *See* United States v. Pelullo, 14 F.3d at 901 (3d Cir.1994)(RICO forfeiture requires a violation of § 1962).

§ 29.8

1. 18 U.S.C. § 1963(a) and (b).

2. 18 U.S.C. § 1963(b)(1) and (2).

3. 21 U.S.C. § 853(b), discussed *supra* in § 29.3(A).

4. *See* § 29.1 *supra* (courts find RICO and § 853 forfeiture authority persuasive in construing each other).

5. *See*

Sixth Circuit: United States v. Smith, 966 F.2d 1045 (6th Cir.1992).

Ninth Circuit: United States v. Weaver, 1996 WL 217927 at *1 (9th Cir.1996) (un-

published opinion); United States v. Littlefield, 821 F.2d 1365 (9th Cir.1987).

But cf.

Second Circuit: United States v. McKeithen, 822 F.2d 310, 313 (2d Cir.1987)(property interest should not be at the whim of the "nuances and niceties of local real property law.").

6. *See, e.g.,*

Sixth Circuit: United States v. Smith, 966 F.2d 1045 (6th Cir.1992).

Seventh Circuit: United States v. Ben–Hur, 20 F.3d 313 (7th Cir.1994).

Ninth Circuit: United States v. Lester, 85 F.3d 1409 (9th Cir.1996); United States v. Weaver, 1996 WL 217927 at *1 (9th Cir.1996)(unpublished opinion).

7. *See*

Sixth Circuit: United States v. Smith, 966 F.2d 1045, 1053 (6th Cir.1992).

Eighth Circuit: United States v. Bieri, 21 F.3d 819 (8th Cir.1994).

Each defendant in the crime allowing forfeiture is liable for the entire amount of forfeitable property regardless of whether the individual defendant had actual possession of the property; the courts reach this conclusion using either a conspiracy or a joint and several liability rationale.[8]

B. THEORIES OF FORFEITURE

The RICO statute authorizes forfeiture of three categories of property: (a)(1), (a)(2), and (a)(3). Subsection (a)(1) covers interests acquired and maintained in violation of RICO; (a)(2) covers interests in the RICO enterprise; and (a)(3) covers proceeds. One court has characterized (a)(1) and (a)(3) as "fruits of crime" forfeitures and noted that the "broad sweep" of forfeiture available under (a)(2) has made it more controversial.[9]

The statute is phrased in the conjunctive, so the government can use multiple subsections together,[10] but the government cannot use multiple subsections to "double" a verdict.[11]

i. Interests Acquired or Maintained in Violation of RICO— § 1963(a)(1)

Subsection 1963(a)(1) provides that a defendant may forfeit "any interest the person has acquired or maintained in violation of" RICO.[12]

The word *interest* is not defined in the statute. In Russello v. United States,[13] the Supreme Court said that courts should assume Congress intended it to have its ordinary meaning.[14] The Court then held that an

---

8. *See*

First Circuit: United States v. Hurley, 63 F.3d 1 (1st Cir.1995), *cert. den. sub nom.* Saccoccia v. United States, 517 U.S. 1105, 116 S.Ct. 1322, 134 L.Ed.2d 474 (1996).

Second Circuit: United States v. Benevento, 836 F.2d 129 (2d Cir.1988) (joint and several liability rationale).

Fourth Circuit: United States v. McHan, 101 F.3d 1027 (4th Cir.1996), *cert. den.*, ___ U.S. ___, 117 S.Ct. 2468, 138 L.Ed.2d 223 (1997)(conspiracy rationale).

Seventh Circuit: United States v. Jarrett, 133 F.3d 519, 529–31 (7th Cir.1998) (upholding joint-and-several liability forfeiture under § 853).

D.C. Circuit: United States v. Gaviria, 116 F.3d 1498 (C.A.D.C.1997)(declining to decide but noting at 1530 that every circuit to decide has allowed joint and several liability).

9. United States v. Sarbello, 985 F.2d 716, 723 n. 13 (3d Cir.1993).

10. *See, e.g.*, Alexander v. United States, 509 U.S. 544, 548, 113 S.Ct. 2766, 2770, 125 L.Ed.2d 441 (1993) (government

sought forfeiture under §§ 1963(a)(1), (a)(2), and (a)(3); judgment vacated and remanded on other grounds).

11. United States v. Ofchinick, 883 F.2d 1172, 1182 & n. 9 (3d Cir.1989)(structure of § 1963(a) indicates that Congress did not intend "forfeiture verdicts to double if property forfeitable under section 1963(a)(1) also happened to be forfeitable under section 1963(a)(2).").

12. 18 U.S.C. § 1963(a)(1). Property is not forfeitable if the defendant's interest was legitimately acquired prior to the commencement of the RICO enterprise. *See* United States v. Kramer, 73 F.3d 1067, 1075–76 (11th Cir.1996) (nightclub and casino could not be forfeited because defendant legitimately acquired his interest prior to the start of the RICO enterprise).

13. 464 U.S. 16, 104 S.Ct. 296, 78 L.Ed.2d 17 (1983).

14. 464 U.S. 16, 21, 104 S.Ct. 296, 299, 78 L.Ed.2d 17 (1983).

interest is not restricted to a criminal defendant's interest in a RICO enterprise but can include as well profits and proceeds received as a result of racketeering activity.[15] Congress subsequently wrote this holding into the statute explicitly.[16]

Courts have generally construed the term *interest* broadly.[17] Courts have held that a defendant's job,[18] pension plan,[19] and "ill-gotten gains" or "booty"[20] are forfeitable interests under this subsection. Additionally, when a defendant uses tainted profits to buy new property, he or she acquires interests that are also forfeitable.[21]

Courts allow forfeiture of the gross amount the defendant obtained, and do not allow defendants to deduct taxes.[22]

15. 464 U.S. 16, 22, 104 S.Ct. 296, 300, 78 L.Ed.2d 17 (1983).

16. The 1984 amendments added § 1963(a)(3), which was intended to incorporate the Court's holding in *Russello*. As noted in the legislative history,

Paragraph (3) is new, and specifically provides for the forfeiture of proceeds derived from prohibited racketeering activity or unlawful debt collection. Both direct and derivative proceeds are forfeitable. As noted above, several courts have held that racketeering proceeds are not encompassed within current RICO forfeiture provisions and Supreme Court review of this issue is now pending [the *Russello* case]. This limiting interpretation has significantly diminished the utility of the RICO criminal forfeiture sanction and is at odds with the overall purpose of this statute.

S.REP. NO. 98–225, 98th Cong., 2d Sess., at 199 (1984), *reprinted in* 1984 U.S.C.C.A.N. 3182, 3382.

17. *See*

First Circuit: United States v. Hurley, 63 F.3d 1 (1st Cir.1995) (defendants had acquired a forfeitable property interest even though they acted solely as intermediaries in a money laundering scheme and kept none of the profits and had only temporary custody of the money).

Second Circuit: United States v. Lizza Indus., 775 F.2d 492, 498 (2d Cir.1985) (reading the term "any interest" expansively to include forfeiture of gross profits, rather than net profits, and noting that the purpose of the RICO forfeiture provisions is to prevent racketeering, not to make the economic risk worth the potential gain).

Liberal construction of the RICO forfeiture provisions led one trial court to order that the defendants pay interest to the government on particular real estate that was found to be forfeitable. Final judgment was not issued for three years after the jury's original finding of forfeitability, at which time the trial court ordered the defendant to pay interest of 8.6% per year, and the Court of Appeals for the First Circuit affirmed. United States v. Angiulo, 897 F.2d 1169, 1215–16 (1st Cir.1990).

18. *See*

Third Circuit: United States v. Kravitz, 738 F.2d 102, 103–04, 107 (3d Cir.1984).

Fifth Circuit: United States v. Rubin, 559 F.2d 975, 991 (5th Cir.1977), *vacated on other grounds*, 439 U.S. 810, 99 S.Ct. 67, 58 L.Ed.2d 102 (1978).

Seventh Circuit: United States v. Horak, 833 F.2d 1235, 1242 (7th Cir.1987).

19. United States v. Horak, 833 F.2d 1235, 1242 (7th Cir.1987) (suggesting that the defendant's profit-sharing and pension plans may be forfeitable), *but see* United States v. Infelise, 938 F.Supp. 1352 (N.D.Ill. 1996) (holding that defendant's IRA was not forfeitable because the language of 26 U.S.C. § 408 specifically precludes this).

20. United States v. Horak, 833 F.2d 1235, 1242 (7th Cir.1987).

21. United States v. Porcelli, 865 F.2d 1352,1365 (2d Cir.1989). However, these properties are not necessarily forfeitable in their entirety. *Id.; see also infra* this section (discussing what portion of the interest is forfeitable). The *Porcelli* opinion was based upon the pre-amendment statute, which did not expressly provide for the forfeiture of property derived from proceeds of racketeering.

22. *D.C.Circuit:* United States v. De-Fries, 129 F.3d 1293, 1313–15 (D.C.Cir. 1997) (reversing forfeiture because RICO conviction reversed, but addressing forfeiture issue for remand, and concluding that taxes paid on illegitimate severance pay which union officers awarded themselves could not be deducted from the amount to be forfeited).

The circuits disagree on whether subsection (a)(1) interests (interests which are acquired or maintained in violation of RICO) are forfeitable in their entirety or only insofar as they are "tainted" by the violation. For example, the First Circuit distinguished between interests in a RICO enterprise and interests outside of the enterprise, holding that only interests in the enterprise are subject to forfeiture in their entirety.[23] The court stated that § 1963(a)(1) interests are considered to be outside the enterprise and, therefore, are not necessarily 100% forfeitable.[24] Other courts have held, however, that the defendant's entire interest is forfeitable, regardless of whether it is tainted by the racketeering activity.[25]

The majority conclusion is that interests forfeitable under subsection (a)(1) are subject to a rule of proportionality. In other words, there must be a causal relationship: the defendant only forfeits interests that would not have been acquired or maintained "but for" the racketeering activities.[26] Under this test, forfeiture is limited to property acquired by

Second Circuit: United States v. Lizza Indus., Inc., 775 F.2d 492, 498 (2d Cir. 1985).

23. United States v. Angiulo, 897 F.2d 1169 (1st Cir.1990).

24. *Id.* at 1211. Because these assets are "outside" the RICO enterprise, they are "subject to a rule of proportionality." *Id.* "Such outside interests include proceeds or profits forfeitable under § 1963(a)(1). . . ." *Id.*

25. *See*

Seventh Circuit: United States v. Ginsburg, 773 F.2d 798, 801 (7th Cir.1985) (stating that RICO forfeiture deprives a defendant of profits and proceeds of racketeering activity "regardless of whether those assets are themselves 'tainted' by use in connection with the illicit activity"). The Seventh Circuit seems to have implicitly overruled *Ginsburg* on this issue in United States v. Horak, 833 F.2d 1235 (7th Cir. 1987), wherein the court held that interests under this section were subject to a "but for" proportionality test. *Id.* at 1243. Under this test, forfeiture is limited to interests that would not have been maintained or acquired "but for" the defendant's racketeering activities. *Id.* In so holding, the *Horak* court did not cite *Ginsburg*.

Ninth Circuit: United States v. Busher, 817 F.2d 1409, 1413–16 (9th Cir.1987) (holding that the entire interest is forfeitable, except to the extent that the Eighth Amendment forbids a disproportionate punishment).

Despite a finding that a particular interest is forfeitable in its entirety, Eighth Amendment issues must still be considered. *See infra* § 29.14 (discussing Eighth Amendment excessive fines clause in criminal forfeiture).

26. *See*

D.C.Circuit: United States v. DeFries, 129 F.3d 1293, 1312–13 (D.C.Cir.1997) ("Because the but-for test usefully articulates the requirement of a nexus between the targeted property and the racketeering activity, we adopt it.") (forfeiture reversed on other grounds).

First Circuit: United States v. Angiulo, 897 F.2d 1169, 1213 (1st Cir.1990) ("To put it another way, defendants' racketeering activities must be shown to be 'a cause in fact of the acquisition or maintenance of these interests or some portion of them.' ").

Second Circuit: United States v. Porcelli, 865 F.2d 1352, 1365 (2d Cir.1989) (stating that interests under this section are "forfeitable . . . to the extent of the contribution from the offending company, but not necessarily in their entirety").

Third Circuit: United States v. Ofchinick, 883 F.2d 1172, 1183–84 (3d Cir.1989) ("In the instant case, the government has failed to meet its burden of proving that [the defendant's] racketeering activities were a cause in fact of his acquisition of or maintenance of an ownership interest in the Norsub stock.").

Seventh Circuit: United States v. Horak, 833 F.2d 1235, 1243 (7th Cir.1987) (advocating use of the "but for" test in this situation). In describing the difference between interests that fall under § 1963(a)(1) and those under § 1963(a)(2), the Seventh Circuit in *Horak* stated that under subsection (1), the focus is on the racketeering

a criminal defendant after he or she joined the RICO enterprise. "If property were acquired before the defendants joined the enterprise, it could not be said that the property would not have been acquired but for the defendants' racketeering activities."[27]

ii. Interests in the RICO Enterprise—§ 1963(a)(2)

Subsection 1963(a)(2) provides that:

"(2) any

(A) interest in;

(B) security of;

(C) claim against; or

(D) property or contractual right of any kind affording a source of influence over;

any enterprise which the person has established, operated, controlled, conducted, or participated in the conduct of in violation of section 1962,"[28] is forfeitable. Under this subsection, the focus is on the enterprise itself rather than the racketeering activity.[29]

Most courts agree that a criminal defendant's interest in a RICO enterprise is forfeitable in its entirety under the first three parts of the subsection, subsections (a)(2)(A)–(C).[30] This is true even if portions of

activity, without attention to whether the interests were part of the enterprise or not. Under subsection (2), the inquiry focuses on the enterprise itself rather than the racketeering activity. *Horak*, 833 F.2d at 1243.

Cf.

Second Circuit: United States v. Walsh, 700 F.2d 846, 857 (2d Cir.1983) (allowing, without discussion, the trial court's use of the proportionality test in this situation).

27. United States v. Angiulo, 897 F.2d 1169, 1213 (1st Cir.1990).

28. 18 U.S.C. § 1963(a)(2).

29. United States v. Horak, 833 F.2d 1235, 1243 (7th Cir.1987).

30. *See, e.g.,*

First Circuit: United States v. Angiulo, 897 F.2d 1169, 1211 (1st Cir.1990) (any interest in an enterprise is 100% forfeitable).

Second Circuit: United States v. Regan, 726 F.Supp. 447, 457 (S.D.N.Y.1989) ("a defendant is required to forfeit 100 percent of his interest in the illegal enterprise, even though some parts of the activities of the enterprise might be legitimate"), *rev'd on other grounds*, 937 F.2d 823 (2d Cir.), *and amended*, 946 F.2d 188 (2d Cir.1991); United States v. Porcelli, 865 F.2d 1352, 1364 (2d Cir.1989) (defendant's interest in a RICO enterprise is forfeitable in its entire-

ty); United States v. Walsh, 700 F.2d 846, 857 (2d Cir.1983) (noting that where the enterprise is "substantially engaged in legitimate business," the Eighth Amendment may require a limit on the forfeiture).

Third Circuit: United States v. Sarbello, 985 F.2d 716, 724 (3d Cir.1993) (establishing rebuttable presumption of 100% forfeiture under subsection (a)(2)).

Ninth Circuit: United States v. Busher, 817 F.2d 1409, 1414 (9th Cir.1987) (stating that the defendant's entire interest in the RICO enterprise is forfeitable).

Cf.

Third Circuit: United States v. Ofchinick, 883 F.2d 1172, 1179 n. 4 (3d Cir.1989) ("There would appear to be a circuit split as to how section 1963(a)(2) should be interpreted in a section 1962(a) case," but not deciding the issue under § 1963(a)(2)).

Seventh Circuit: United States v. Horak, 833 F.2d 1235, 1243–44 (7th Cir.1987) (discussing proportionality in a § 1963(a)(1) context; the court did not decide this issue under subsection (a)(2)).

The Third Circuit in *Ofchinick* stated that there is a circuit split on the treatment of § 1963(a)(2) property in § 1962(a) cases and cited *Porcelli* and *Horak* as contrary holdings, suggesting that the court's deci-

the enterprise are engaged in legitimate business activities.[31] The Third Circuit, in United States v. Sarbello,[32] went so far as to "recognize a presumption of 100% forfeiture under § 1963(a)(2), which may be rebutted by a *prima facie* showing of gross disproportionality."[33] Under this approach the only limit on forfeiture of the entire interest is the Excessive Fines Clause.[34]

Under the fourth subsection, (a)(2)(D), which covers "source of influence" property, some courts have held that a proportionality rule is required by the statute.[35] For example, in United States v. Angiulo,[36] the First Circuit held that "source of influence" property is subject to a rule of proportionality because it is considered an interest outside the enter-

sions turned on the underlying violation. *Ofchinick*, 883 F.2d at 1179 n.4. However, *Porcelli* and *Horak* are not necessarily conflicting. The *Porcelli* court held that only property under § 1963(a)(2)(D) is limited by the proportionality rule. *Porcelli*, 865 F.2d at 1365. The *Horak* court, on the other hand, stated that under § 1963(a)(2), the focus is on the enterprise rather than the racketeering activity, but did not decide the case under § 1963(a)(2). The *Horak* court held that a proportionality test was required under § 1963(a)(1). *Horak*, 833 F.2d at 1243. Therefore, the *Horak* and *Porcelli* holdings are not in direct conflict with one another, as the *Ofchinick* opinion suggests.

There is further confusion in the case law regarding which position the Ninth Circuit has taken regarding § 1962(a)(2) property in United States v. Busher, 817 F.2d 1409 (9th Cir.1987). For example, in United States v. Horak, 833 F.2d 1235 (7th Cir. 1987), the Seventh Circuit stated that "[t]he *Busher* case would seem to construe section (a)(2) to require forfeiture of a defendant's entire interest in the enterprise except where the Eighth Amendment prohibits it." *Id.* at 1251 (*citing Busher*, 817 F.2d at 1415); *see also* United States v. Regan, 726 F.Supp. 447, 455 (S.D.N.Y.1989) (*citing Busher* for the proposition that a defendant's entire interest is forfeitable), *rev'd on other grounds*, 937 F.2d 823 (2d Cir.), *and amended*, 946 F.2d 188 (2d Cir. 1991). On the other hand, the Third Circuit in United States v. Sarbello, 985 F.2d 716 (3d Cir.1993), stated that "some courts of appeals have applied a rule of proportionality to § 1963(a)(2) forfeitures" and then cited to *Busher* in support of this statement. *Id.* at 722 (*citing Busher*, 817 F.2d at 1414–15).

Perhaps this confusion stems from the fact that the Ninth Circuit did not expressly state in the *Busher* opinion whether the focus was on subsection (a)(1) property or subsection (a)(2) property. The court did, however, hint in a footnote and in subse-

quent language in the opinion that only subsection (a)(1) property was involved. *Busher*, 817 F.2d at 1413 n.5, 1414. In conclusion, it seems that the *Busher* court held that "[o]nce the jury determines that property was acquired, maintained or operated in violation of section 1962, it must find forfeitable the defendant's entire interest in that property." *Id.* at 1414. The forfeiture sentence is, however, also subject to Eighth Amendment limitations. *Id.* at 1414–16.

All these cases were decided before *Alexander* made it clear that the Excessive Fines Clause applies to and limits criminal forfeitures. *Alexander* and the Excessive Fines Clause analysis is discussed in § 29.14 *infra*. Courts may be less concerned with finding a statutory proportionality requirement now that it is certain a constitutional one applies.

31. United States v. Regan, 726 F.Supp. 447, 457 (S.D.N.Y.1989) ("a defendant is required to forfeit 100 percent of his interest in the illegal enterprise, even though some parts of the activities of the enterprise might be legitimate"), *rev'd on other grounds*, 937 F.2d 823 (2d Cir.), *and amended*, 946 F.2d 188 (2d Cir.1991).

32. 985 F.2d 716 (3d Cir.1993).

33. *Id.* at 724. The Third Circuit apparently held that a proportionality analysis was required only by the Eighth Amendment, and not by the statute itself.

34. *See infra* § 29.14 (discussing application of the Eighth Amendment Excessive Fines Clause analysis).

35. United States v. Porcelli, 865 F.2d 1352, 1365 (2d Cir.1989); United States v. McKeithen, 822 F.2d 310, 315 (2d Cir.1987)(construing similar language in CCE crime, § 848, to authorize forfeiture only of that portion of realty that provided a source of influence, here determined to be 43%).

36. 897 F.2d 1169 (1st Cir.1990).

prise.[37] At the same time, the court held that any interest in an enterprise is 100% forfeitable.[38] Likewise, the Second Circuit in United States v. Porcelli[39] distinguished between subsection (a)(2)(D) property and other subsection (a)(2) property, holding that forfeiture of the former is limited by a "but for" proportionality test.[40]

Of course, an Excessive Fines Clause analysis is required regardless of whether a statutory proportionality rule is also required.[41]

iii. Proceeds—§ 1963(a)(3)

Under this subsection, "any property constituting, or derived from, any proceeds which the person obtained, directly or indirectly, from racketeering activity or unlawful debt collection in violation of section 1962"[42] is forfeitable. This subsection was added in 1984 to reflect the Supreme Court's holding in Russello v. United States[43] that RICO forfeiture is not limited to a defendant's interest in an enterprise but includes proceeds and profits of a RICO enterprise as well.[44]

In determining what proceeds a defendant has obtained by racketeering activity, a court may consider proceeds obtained both "directly and indirectly."[45] Therefore, a defendant may "obtain" proceeds even though he or she never had physical possession of them. This joint and several liability is based on conspiracy theory.[46]

Moreover, all proceeds that "pass through the hands" of a RICO defendant are automatically considered to have been *obtained* by him or her; the defendant need not have any interest in the proceeds greater than temporary custody.[47]

---

37. *Id.* at 1210–12. The court's holding hinged on an "inside/outside" distinction. The court did not base its application of the proportionality test on which subsection of § 1963(a) was applicable.

38. *Id.* at 1211.

39. 865 F.2d 1352 (2d Cir.1989).

40. *Id.* at 1365. Prior to the 1984 amendments, there was some ambiguity in the statute "as to whether the 'source of influence' qualification pertained to all of the categories of forfeitable property listed in [subsection (a)(2)], or whether it modified only the last category (property or contractual right of any kind)." United States v. Sarbello, 985 F.2d 716, 721–22 (3d Cir. 1993). Therefore, cases discussing the proportionality rule in relation to "source of influence" properties that were decided under the pre-amendment statute provide little guidance.

41. *See infra* § 29.14 (discussing application of the Eighth Amendment Excessive Fines Clause to criminal forfeitures).

42. 18 U.S.C. § 1963(a)(3).

43. 464 U.S. 16, 104 S.Ct. 296, 78 L.Ed.2d 17 (1983). *See* United States v.

Hurley, 63 F.3d 1, 21 (1st Cir.1995) (§ 1963(a)(3) added in 1984 to reflect Supreme Court's and Congress's command to interpret RICO forfeiture broadly).

44. According to *Russello*, these interests were forfeitable under § 1963(a)(1). 464 U.S. at 22, 104 S.Ct. at 300. The precise question in *Russello* was whether insurance proceeds that the defendant received as a result of his arson activities constituted an "interest" within the meaning of section 1963(a)(1). *Id.* at 20; *see also supra* § 29.8(B)(i) (discussing the legislative history of the 1984 amendments).

45. 18 U.S.C. § 1963(a)(3).

46. United States v. Hurley, 63 F.3d 1, 22–23 (1st Cir.1995).

47. *Hurley*, 63 F.3d at 21. So if the RICO predicate crimes are money laundering crimes, the government can forfeit substitute assets for the entire amount of the money that passed through the launderer's hands. This is true for RICO forfeiture but not forfeiture under § 982. That statute has an exception, *see* § 29.5(A)(i).

While it is now clear that profits are forfeitable under RICO, there is some disagreement on the application of § 1963(a)(3) to profits of a racketeering enterprise. The Seventh Circuit has held that the RICO statute's reference to "proceeds" is to "net, not gross, revenues—profits, not sales, for only the former are gains."[48] The court based its holding on the language of the statute, reasoning that the forfeiture provision intended to divest the defendants, rather than their enterprises, of ill-gotten gains.[49] Other courts have come to the opposite conclusion, holding that forfeiture should be based on gross proceeds rather than net profits, as this is the money acquired through illegal activity.[50]

C. THE NEXUS REQUIREMENT: THE RELATIONSHIP BETWEEN THE UNDERLYING CRIME AND THE PROPERTY

Finally, the government must prove a relationship between the RICO crime and the property alleged to be forfeitable. This element is based on the general language of § 1963(a) that authorizes forfeiture of the property only if it is associated with a RICO violation.[51]

The RICO nexus requirement is not well developed in the courts for several reasons. RICO forfeiture is not as frequently used now since the government can get criminal forfeiture based on lesser crimes under the other two statutes. Also, the RICO statute has a description of forfeitable property that is more specific than the descriptions in the other forfeiture statutes. The RICO statute does not provide for forfeiture of "facilitating property," which is the well spring for cases discussing the nexus requirement. Finally, the concerns that led courts to develop the nexus requirement are often characterized and resolved in RICO forfeiture cases as statutory proportionality requirements.[52]

D. RELATION BACK

Here the statute is identical to the drug forfeiture statute, so the

---

48. United States v. Masters, 924 F.2d 1362, 1369–70 (7th Cir.1991).

49. *Id.* at 1370.

50. *See*

First Circuit: United States v. Hurley, 63 F.3d 1, 21 (1st Cir.1995) ("Given the legislative history and Russello, the broader definition of 'proceeds' seems to us a rather easy call.")(citing the legislative history of the 1984 amendment, which shows that Congress intended forfeitable 'proceeds' to encompass more than the net gain realized by a defendant).

Second Circuit: United States v. Lizza Indus., 775 F.2d 492, 497–98 (2d Cir.1985) (construing pre-amendment § 1963(a)(1)).

Fourth Circuit: United States v. McHan, 101 F.3d 1027 at 1042 (4th Cir. 1996) (RICO forfeiture of "proceeds" covers gross proceeds, not just net profits). *See also* S.Rep. No. 98–225, 98th Cong., 2d Sess., at 199 (1984), *reprinted in* 1984 U.S.C.C.A.N. 3182, 3382 ("In paragraph (3), the term 'proceeds' has been used in lieu of the term 'profits' in order to alleviate the unreasonable burden on the government of proving net profits. It should not be necessary for the prosecutor to prove what the defendant's overhead expenses were.").

See also United States v. DeFries, 129 F.3d 1293, 1313 (D.C.Cir.1997) (criticizing Seventh Circuit language in *Masters*).

51. 18 U.S.C. § 1963(a)(1)–(3).

52. *See* discussion in § 29.8(B) *supra* (statutory proportionality rules).

discussion from § 29.3(D) should be consulted.

E. SUBSTITUTE ASSETS

Here the statute is identical to the drug forfeiture statute, so the discussion from § 29.3(E) should be consulted.

Note that RICO authorizes broader forfeiture of substitute assets when the underlying crime is money laundering than does the general criminal forfeiture statute, § 982.[53]

F. PROPERTY IN THE HANDS OF THIRD PARTIES

Here the statute is identical to the drug forfeiture statute, so the discussion from § 29.3(F) should be consulted.

§ 29.9 Defenses

The defenses are similar under the three criminal forfeiture statutes[1] and they are analyzed in this section together.

A. FOR THE DEFENDANT

The defendant can oppose a criminal forfeiture count with failure of proof defenses by either (1) defeating the underlying conviction or (2) demonstrating that the property does not fall into the statutory definition of forfeitable property or does not have the required nexus. The drug forfeiture statute makes this second type of failure of proof defense more difficult than the other two statutes because it includes a rebuttable presumption that property generated during the time of the crime for which there is no other likely source is forfeitable.[2]

In addition, defendants can defeat forfeiture by arguing that they have no property interest in the property the government is trying to forfeit.[3] The defendant's interest in property is defined by state law, but courts are willing to look behind transactions to find a defendant the de facto owner.[4]

Defendants cannot fail to appeal their conviction and then assert a third party interest in property being forfeited because they have no

---

53. *See* United States v. Hurley, 63 F.3d 1, 21–22 (1st Cir.1995) discussed in § 29.5(A)(i) *supra.*

§ 29.9

1. The differences are (1) the rebuttable presumption in the drug statute, § 853(d), discussed *infra* in § 29.18, which makes failure-of-proof defenses more difficult under the drug statute than under the other two statutes; and (2) the specific exclusions in the general statute, § 982, which limit forfeitures under that statute based on money laundering in two ways.

These limits are discussed *supra* in §§ 29.5(A)(i) and 29.5(D).

2. 21 U.S.C. § 853(d).

3. *See* United States v. Ben–Hur, 20 F.3d 313, 316 (7th Cir.1994).

4. *See*

First Circuit: United States v. Houlihan, 92 F.3d 1271, 1299 (1st Cir.1996) (finding defendant the de facto owner of house although his uncle held title).

Seventh Circuit: United States v. Ben–Hur, 20 F.3d 313, 316 (7th Cir.1994).

stake in that property, and so no standing.[5]

Some affirmative defenses exist. They are not statutory but constitutional. They include a limited defense based on the Fifth Amendment due process clause; and a defense based on the Eight Amendment Excessive Fines Clause. These are discussed in detail *infra* in §§ 29.11 and 29.14.

Defendants cannot appeal to the trial judge for leniency in forfeiture because once the jury returns a verdict of forfeiture, it is mandatory; the judge has no discretion to change the forfeiture.[6]

The government is not required to get a restraining order to stop mortgage holders from foreclosing on the defendant when he quits making payments because of his arrest; the defendant is not entitled to have the government preserve his property this way.[7]

B.   FOR THIRD PARTIES

The forfeiture statutes provide two defenses for third parties.[8] These are the only defenses for third parties,[9] aside from the constitutional ones.[10] These defenses divide third parties into two broad classes: those with an interest in the property developed *before* the government's title vests (*i.e.*, the time of the crime) and those with an interest developed *after* the government's title vests (again, the time of the crime). To assert either of these defenses, the third party must have an interest in the property.

i.   An Interest in the Property/Standing

The third party must have an interest in the property before he or she may object to forfeiture of it.[11] The third party's interest is deter-

---

5.   United States v. Brunson, 1996 WL 306438 at *2 (10th Cir.1996)(unpublished opinion).

6.   *See* § 29.19(A) *infra*. Although the trial judge has no discretion to change the forfeiture generally, the judge does review the forfeiture for excessiveness under the Eighth Amendment and may reduce the forfeiture on that basis. *See* § 29.14 *infra*.

7.   United States v. McCullough, 1998 WL 196667 (9th Cir.1998) (unpublished).

8.   *See* 21 U.S.C. § 853(c) and (n)(6); 18 U.S.C. § 1963(c) and (*l*)(6); 18 U.S.C. § 982(b)(1).

9.   *See*

Fourth Circuit: United States v. Holmes, 1998 WL 13538, *3 (4th Cir.1998) (unpublished disposition) (only two classes of third party claimants are protected).

Ninth Circuit: United States v. Alcaraz–Garcia, 79 F.3d 769 at 773 n. 7 (9th Cir.1996).

Eleventh Circuit: United States v. Smith, 844 F.Supp. 734, 735 (M.D.Fla. 1994).

See also

Eleventh Circuit: United States v. Jimerson, 5 F.3d 1453, 1455 (11th Cir.1993)(no innocent owner defense in criminal forfeiture).

10.   Constitutional defenses are discussed *infra* in §§ 29.10–29.16.

11.   *See*

Second Circuit: United States v. Ribadeneira, 105 F.3d 833, 835 (2d Cir.1997); United States v. Schwimmer, 968 F.2d 1570, 1579–81 (2d Cir.1992).

Third Circuit: United States v. Lavin, 942 F.2d 177, 187 (3d Cir.1991).

Ninth Circuit: United States v. Bennett, 147 F.3d 912, 1998 WL 309269, *2 (9th Cir.1998) (father has no standing to assert claim on behalf of the third party

mined by state law.[12] Bailors have a sufficient property interest to assert the third party defenses.[13] Most courts hold that general creditors do not have a sufficient interest to establish standing,[14] but some courts disagree and allow general creditors to assert the third party defenses.[15] Although the statute requires third parties to have a "legal" interest in property, this does not exclude equitable interests; it merely means legal in the sense of being "under the law."[16] The circuits disagree whether interests arising under constructive trusts are sufficient to allow the third party to raise a defense.[17]

ii.   Third Parties with a Prior Interest

If a third party has a legal interest that vested[18] prior to the government's interest (taking into account the action of relation-back) or is superior to the defendant's at the time of the crime, then the third party may assert a claim to the property and avoid forfeiture.[19] Proceeds

daughter); United States v. Ken Int'l Co. Ltd., 1997 WL 229114 (9th Cir.1997) (third party petition denied due to no standing becuase no interest in the property)(unpublished opinion); United States v. Weaver, 1996 WL 217927 (9th Cir.1996)(unpublished opinion)(petition of third party wife dismissed because no property interest under state law).

D.C. Circuit: United States v. BCCI Holdings, 961 F.Supp. 287 (D.D.C.1997)(American Express had standing to file third party claim based on state law statutory right of set off).

12. See

Seventh Circuit: United States v. Ben–Hur, 20 F.3d 313, 317 (7th Cir.1994).

Ninth Circuit: United States v. Alcaraz–Garcia, 79 F.3d 769, 774 (9th Cir.1996).

13. United States v. Alcaraz–Garcia, 79 F.3d 769, 774 (9th Cir.1996).

14. See

Second Circuit: United States v. Ribadeneira, 105 F.3d 833, 835 (2d Cir.1997); United States v. Schwimmer, 968 F.2d 1570, 1579–81 (2d Cir.1992).

Sixth Circuit: United States v. Campos, 859 F.2d 1233, 1239 (6th Cir.1988).

D.C. Circuit: United States v. BCCI Holdings, 46 F.3d 1185, 1192–92 (D.C.Cir. 1995) (bank depositors are general creditors with no interest under RICO).

15. See

Fourth Circuit: United States v. Reckmeyer, 836 F.2d 200 (4th Cir.1987).

Ninth Circuit: United States v. Mageean, 649 F.Supp. 820 (D.Nev.1986), aff'd without opinion, 822 F.2d 62 (9th Cir.1987).

16.   See

Second Circuit: United States v. Schwimmer, 968 F.2d 1570, 1582 (2d Cir. 1992).

D.C. Circuit: United States v. BCCI Holdings, 46 F.3d 1185, 1190 (D.C.Cir. 1995).

17.   Compare Schwimmer, 968 F.2d at 1582–83 (constructive trust is enough property interest) with BCCI, 46 F.3d at 1190–91 (constructive trust not enough property interest since trust is not real but fictional and didn't exist at time of the crime).

18.   The statute uses the term "vested," so a strict reading of the statutory language would preclude a party with a nonvested interests (such as a contingent remainder in real property law) in the property at issue from protection under this provision. The third party may still have a superior interest in terms of property law, but it is not protected under the statute. See United States v. Campos, 859 F.2d 1233, 1238–39 (6th Cir.1988)(claims for debt as trade creditor not "vested" so third party defense denied).

19.   Section 853(n)(6)(A) states:

(6) If after, the hearing, the court determines that the petitioner has established by a preponderance of the evidence that—

(A) the petitioner has a legal right, title, or interest in the property, and such right, title, or interest renders the order of forfeiture invalid in whole or part because the right, title, or interest was vested in the petitioner rather than the defendant or was superior to any right, title, or interest of the defendant at the time of the commission of

can never fall into this category since they do not exist before the commission of the crime; they are generated by it. This defense is therefore limited to facilitating or CCE property.[20]

This defense has five elements.[21] The basic theory of the defense is that this property is exempt from forfeiture because it is not really "property of the defendant."[22]

In cases where a party made a transfer prior to the crime in order to subvert the criminal forfeiture, courts have been willing to set aside the prior transfers.[23] The third party's uncorroborated testimony may not be enough in these cases to successfully assert the third party's interest. Sometimes, a court will require more evidence that the third party does indeed have the claim that is asserted.[24]

iii. Transferees Who Get the Property after the Crime—Bona Fide Purchasers

Subsequent transferees can make claims against property forfeited under any of the forfeiture theories, since this defense is not dependent on the defendant or third party having title before the time of the underlying crime. However, this defense is harder to establish since it involves a *mens rea* element in addition to some property law characteristics.

To assert this defense, the transferee must (1) be a bona fide purchaser for value and (2) have no reasonable cause to believe that the property was subject to forfeiture at the time of the transfer.[25]

the acts which gave rise to the forfeiture under this section . . .

the court shall amend the order of forfeiture in accordance with its determination.

20. This is one reason why the government likes to define the forfeiture as one of proceeds: the third party defenses are limited.

21. United States v. Schwimmer, 968 F.2d 1570, 1580 (2d Cir.1992).

22. *Schwimmer*, 968 F.2d at 1581 (2d Cir.1992), *citing* S.Rep. No. 98–225, 98th Cong., 2nd Sess., *reprinted in* 1984 U.S.C.C.A.N. 3182, 3391.

23. *See*

Fourth Circuit: United States v. Shifflett, 1995 WL 125506 at *3 (4th Cir.1995) (unpublished opinion)(denying third party defense because title to truck in third party was sham; defendant was the de facto owner).

Sixth Circuit: United States v. Henry, 1995 WL 418635 (6th Cir.1995)(per curiam) (third party wife's interest in house forfeit-

ed because court concluded she had only nominal title which court looked behind to deny both third party defenses).

Seventh Circuit: United States v. Ben-Hur, 20 F.3d 313 (7th Cir.1994)(court set aside the transfer of a veterinary hospital to a third party; defendant transferred title to the third party and took a lease back before he started his drug dealing operation out of the hospital; court decided that the transfer was made only to avoid forfeiture of the property and that the defendant was the equitable titleholder).

24. *See* United States v. Rockwell, 677 F.Supp. 836 (W.D.Pa.1988).

25. Section 853(n)(6)(B) states:

(6) If, after the hearing the court determines the petitioner has established by a preponderance of the evidence that— . . .

(B) the petitioner is a bona fide purchaser for value of the right, title, or interest in the property and was at the time of purchase reasonably without cause to believe that the property was subject to forfeiture under this section;

a. Bona Fide Purchaser

To win on this defense, the claimant must be an actual purchaser for value.[26] General, or unsecured, creditors are not bona fide purchasers.[27] This purchaser requirement would exclude anyone who received the property as a gift. The purpose of this provision is presumably to prevent the defendant from giving or simply transferring the property to a friend or relative (with no knowledge of an impending forfeiture) in order to avoid the government's forfeiture order against the defendant. This is consistent with the property laws and commercial laws governing subsequent bona fide purchasers who received title from one who only had voidable title.[28]

b. Mental State

To establish this defense, the bona fide purchaser must be "reasonably without cause to believe that the property was subject to forfeiture at the time of the transfer."[29] This mental state sounds like a recklessness or negligence standard. It relies on *cause* to believe rather than actual belief, and the lack of cause to believe must be *reasonable*, again suggesting objective standards.[30] Willful blindness will likely be a sufficient mental state to disqualify a third party from the defense because a person who is willfully blind could not have been "reasonably without cause to believe" the property was subject to forfeiture.

The Fourth Circuit has discussed this *mens rea* twice.[31] In one case, the court found that a third party qualified as "reasonably without cause to believe" the property was subject to forfeiture. The third party was the defendant's father, and although he knew that his two sons were under investigation and that some of a second son's property was forfeited, the court held that this did not put the father on notice to defeat his claim to the first son's property.[32] In contrast, in United States v. Moffitt, Zwerling & Kemler, the court rejected the third party/lawyers' argument that they were "reasonably without cause to believe" the property was forfeitable.[33] The facts of *Moffitt, Zwerling* are

---

the court shall amend the order of forfeiture in accordance with its determination.

26. *See*

Third Circuit: United States v. Lavin, 942 F.2d 177 (3d Cir.1991)(tort claimant is not a purchaser).

D.C Circuit: United States v. BCCI Holdings, 961 F.Supp. 287 (D.D.C.1997)(denying American Express's third party petition because there simply was no purchase).

27. *See*

Sixth Circuit: United States v. Campos, 859 F.2d 1233, 1237 (6th Cir.1988)(unsecured creditors are not bona fide purchasers).

D.C. Circuit: United States v. BCCI Holdings, 46 F.3d 1185, 1191–92 (D.C.Cir.

1995) (bank depositors, as general creditors, are not bona fide purchasers).

28. *See* Uniform Commercial Code §§ 2–403 (sales of goods), discussed in United States v. Lavin, 942 F.2d 177 (3d Cir. 1991).

29. 21 U.S.C. § 853(c).

30. Eugene R. Gaetke & Sarah N. Welling, *Money Laundering and Lawyers*, 43 Syracuse L.Rev. 1165, 1186 (1992).

31. United States v. Moffitt, Zwerling & Kemler, 83 F.3d 660 (4th Cir.1996); United States v. Reckmeyer, 836 F.2d 200 (4th Cir.1987).

32. United States v. Reckmeyer, 836 F.2d 200 (4th Cir.1987).

33. United States v. Moffitt, Zwerling & Kemler, 83 F.3d 660, 666 (4th Cir.1996).

discussed in detail in § 29.15 on the sixth amendment implications of attorney fee forfeiture.

In summary, the appellate courts have once found a third party to have the qualifying *mens rea*, and have once found a third party not to. In *Moffitt, Zwerling*, it was likely an important factor in the court's decision to deny the third party defense that the third parties were lawyers.[34] Regular lay third parties may as a practical matter have an easier time proving they are "reasonably without cause to believe" the property is subject to forfeiture.

Timing is important under this requirement, because the mental state is to be judged at the time of the transfer.[35] Any later knowledge of the underlying crime is irrelevant. For example, assume the defendant sells his home used for drug dealing at fair market value to his son, who has no knowledge of his father's activities and no reason to have any knowledge. The next day, the son learns that his father sold drugs from the house. The son can claim the protections of this section regardless of the later knowledge since he fulfilled the requirements of the statute at the time of the transfer.[36]

§ 29.10   Constitutional Limits—In General

The criminal forfeiture statutes have raised some constitutional issues. The statutes do not provide for hearings on post-indictment, pretrial restraining orders, but some courts have held that due process requires notice and a hearing. No innocent owner defense is required by the due process clause, and failure to provide such a defense does not violate the fifth amendment takings clause. Generally criminal forfeiture does not implicate the double jeopardy clause. The forfeiture statutes may, however, violate the eighth amendment excessive fines clause. Finally, RICO forfeiture based on obscenity predicates can pose some first amendment issues.

§ 29.11   Constitutional Limits—Fifth Amendment Due Process

A. CLAIMS BY THE DEFENDANT

When a defendant's assets are restrained *before* indictment, the forfeiture statutes require notice to persons appearing to have an interest.[1] In contrast, when the defendant's assets are restrained *after* indict-

34. *See* United States v. Moffitt, Zwerling & Kemler, P.C., 83 F.3d 660, 671 (4th Cir.1996) ("This conduct disappoints.").

35. *See* 21 U.S.C. § 853(n)(6)(B). The statute states: "the petitioner ... *was at the time of purchase* reasonably without cause to believe the property was subject to forfeiture under this section." *Id.* (emphasis supplied).

36. *See generally* Eugene R. Gaetke & Sarah N. Welling, *Money Laundering and Lawyers*, 43 Syracuse L.Rev. 1165, 1189 (1992).

§ 29.11

1. 21 U.S.C. § 853(e)(1)(B).

ment but before trial, the forfeiture statutes do not require that the defendant be given notice or an opportunity to be heard.[2] The theory is that the indictment establishes probable cause and constitutes a sufficient basis to allow a restraining order without a hearing. Some defendants have argued that this deprived them of due process, because notwithstanding the indictment, restraint of their property was ex parte, and they would get no opportunity to challenge the restraint until trial.[3] If they needed the assets to hire a lawyer to defend them, waiting until trial to challenge the restraint would be too late.

Several courts have agreed with defendants that due process requires notice and a hearing on restraining their assets even after an indictment has been handed down. The leading case is United States v. Monsanto,[4] in which the Second Circuit held that due process does require an adversary hearing, after the restraining order is entered, in order to continue to restrain assets needed to retain counsel of choice.[5] Other courts have reached this conclusion as well,[6] although all the holdings other than *Monsanto* were decided before the Supreme Court held that pretrial restraint of assets needed to hire counsel of choice did not violate the sixth amendment right to counsel.[7] It may be that the Supreme Court's rejection of any sixth amendment violation casts some doubt on these earlier cases. However, the Second Circuit's decision in *Monsanto* and another recent reference from the First Circuit[8] indicate that post-indictment, pretrial restraints without a hearing before trial may still be held to violate due process.[9]

2. *Id.* § 853(e)(1)(A).

3. *See, e.g.,*

Second Circuit: United States v. Monsanto, 924 F.2d 1186 (2d Cir.1991)(en banc).

Fourth Circuit: United States v. Harvey, 814 F.2d 905 (4th Cir.1987).

Seventh Circuit: United States v. Moya–Gomez, 860 F.2d 706 (7th Cir.1988).

Ninth Circuit: United States v. Crozier, 777 F.2d 1376 (9th Cir.1985).

Eleventh Circuit: United States v. Bissell, 866 F.2d 1343 (11th Cir.1989).

4. 924 F.2d 1186 (2d Cir.1991)(en banc).

5. *Monsanto*, 924 F.2d at 1188.

6. *See*

Fourth Circuit: United States v. Harvey, 814 F.2d 905, 929 (4th Cir.1987).

Seventh Circuit: United States v. Moya–Gomez, 860 F.2d 706 (7th Cir.1988).

Ninth Circuit: United States v. Crozier, 777 F.2d 1376, 1382 (9th Cir.1985).

But cf.

Eleventh Circuit: United States v. Bissell, 866 F.2d 1343 (11th Cir.1989)(delay of post-restraint hearing until trial on these facts did not violate due process).

7. *See* United States v. Caplin & Drysdale, 491 U.S. 617, 109 S.Ct. 2646, 105 L.Ed.2d 528 (1989) and United States v. Monsanto, 491 U.S. 600, 109 S.Ct. 2657, 105 L.Ed.2d 512 (1989). These cases are discussed in § 29.15 *infra* (sixth amendment right to counsel).

8. United States v. DeCato, 64 F.3d 752, 757 (1st Cir.1995)(identifying issue as one court is specifically not deciding).

9. In United States v. Monsanto, 491 U.S. 600, 615 n. 10, 109 S.Ct. 2657, 2666 n. 10, 105 L.Ed.2d 512 (1989), the Court declined to resolve a related but distinct question. The Court declined to decide whether due process requires a hearing *before the assets are restrained*. In contrast, the issue the courts of appeal considered is whether a hearing is required, after the restraining order has been entered but sometime earlier than the trial itself.

B. CLAIMS BY THIRD PARTIES

The procedure set up in the statutes for third parties to file a claim is constitutional.[10]

There is apparently no due process requirement of an "innocent owner" defense for third parties in criminal forfeiture. In Bennis v. Michigan,[11] the Supreme Court held that such a defense is not constitutionally compelled in the context of an *in personam* forfeiture in an abatement action under a public nuisance statute. Though the abatement action was classified as a civil action under the Michigan forfeiture scheme, its *in personam* nature suggests that the ruling is relevant to federal criminal forfeiture as well.

In *Bennis*, Michigan brought an in personam forfeiture action against both Tina Bennis and her husband in order to abate their car, held in joint tenancy, as a public nuisance. Bennis' husband was caught with a prostitute in his car and was convicted of a misdemeanor. Though Bennis had no knowledge of her husband's activity, and surely did not sanction it, the Michigan Supreme Court took her property interest in the car since the state abatement statute had no third party defenses.

The Supreme Court held that this was permissible under the due process clause and was not an impermissible taking of property. Rather than finding a constitutionally mandated "innocent owner" defense, the court concluded that one was not necessary.[12] Thus the Due Process Clause does not require any defense for third parties based on their ignorance of the property being subject to forfeiture.

The three federal criminal forfeiture statutes expressly provide two defenses for third parties in the statute. As long as the defenses are provided in the statute, *Bennis* has no impact on federal criminal forfeiture defenses.

§ 29.12 Constitutional Limits—Fifth Amendment Double Jeopardy

There is no double jeopardy conflict between criminal forfeiture and a criminal conviction based on the same underlying conduct since forfeiture is viewed as a punishment carrying out the conviction.[1] They are a single action consisting of a substantive charge and its authorized punishment. Furthermore, the Supreme Court has held that civil forfei-

---

10. United States v. Holmes, 1998 WL 13538 (4th Cir.1998) (unpublished per curiam) (*citing* Libretti v. United States, 516 U.S. 29, 116 S.Ct. 356, 133 L.Ed.2d 271 (1995)). *But cf.* United States v. Messino, 122 F.3d 427, 430 (7th Cir.1997) (whether Seventh Amendment requires jury for third party hearings is "challenging question").

11. 516 U.S. 442, 116 S.Ct. 994, 134 L.Ed.2d 68 (1996).

12. *Id.*

§ 29.12

1. *See*

Sixth Circuit: Westine v. United States, 1996 WL 456031 (6th Cir. 1996) (unpublished opinion) (stating the general principle).

Ninth Circuit: United States v. Hollingsworth, 1996 WL 138583 (9th Cir.1996) (unpublished opinion) (holding that a 2 day delay between the written judgment and the entry of forfeiture is still not enough to constitute double jeopardy).

ture or an administrative forfeiture coupled with a criminal prosecution does not constitute double jeopardy either.[2]

§ 29.13 Constitutional Limits—Fifth Amendment Takings

Another issue is whether forfeiture violates the takings clause of the Fifth Amendment.[1] In Bennis v. Michigan,[2] the Supreme Court reviewed the third party claimant's argument that the forfeiture without providing an innocent owner defense was a taking for which just compensation was required. The Court rejected the argument easily, explaining, "The government may not be required to compensate an owner for property which it has already lawfully acquired under the exercise of governmental authority other than the power of eminent domain."[3] One case decided before *Bennis* did hold that forfeiture violated the takings clause,[4] but that holding is not the law after *Bennis*.

§ 29.14 Constitutional Limits—Eighth Amendment Excessive Fines Clause

In Alexander v. United States, the Supreme Court held that the Eighth Amendment prohibition against excessive fines applies to criminal forfeitures under RICO.[1] In United States v. Bajakajian,[2] the Supreme Court held that excessive fines clause applies to criminal forfeitures under the general statute, § 982.[3] The lower courts have since concluded that the excessive fines clause applies to criminal forfeitures under the drug statute as well.[4] Many defendants have brought claims

2. *See*

Supreme Court: United States v. Ursery, 518 U.S. 267, 116 S.Ct. 2135, 135 L.Ed.2d 549 (1996).

Sixth Circuit: United States v. Branham, 97 F.3d 835 (6th Cir.1996)(jeopardy never attached to an administrative forfeiture since it was never contested).

Eighth Circuit: United States v. Field, 62 F.3d 246 (8th Cir.1995) (prior civil settlement with an insurer coupled with a criminal prosecution did not implicate double jeopardy).

§ 29.13

1. "[N]or shall private property be taken for public use, without just compensation." U.S. Const. amend. V.

2. 516 U.S. 442, 116 S.Ct. 994, 134 L.Ed.2d 68 (1996).

3. Bennis v. Michigan, 516 U.S. 442, 116 S.Ct. 994, 134 L.Ed.2d 68 (1996).

4. The Federal Circuit ruled that RICO forfeiture can amount to a compensable taking. In Shelden v. United States, 7 F.3d 1022 (Fed.Cir.1993), a piece of mortgaged property was seized following defendant's RICO conviction. The mortgagee still held a valid lien on the property, and

sought to exercise the right of redemption because the mortgage was unpaid for several months. The Court of Claims found no taking because there was no interference with a compensable property interest. On appeal, the Federal Circuit held, "In accordance with the principles of the Fifth Amendment, the Sheldens must be compensated."

Id. at 1026. The court remanded the case to the Court of Claims for a determination of just compensation.

§ 29.14

1. 509 U.S. 544, 113 S.Ct. 2766, 125 L.Ed.2d 441 (1993). The Supreme Court also held that the cruel and unusual punishments clause does not apply to forfeitures. *Id.*

2. ___ U.S. ___, 118 S.Ct. 2028, 141 L.Ed.2d 314 (1998).

3. 118 S.Ct. at 2033.

4. *See*

Fourth Circuit: United States v. Locklear, 1997 WL 526020 (4th Cir.1997) (unpublished per curiam); United States v. Garcia, 1996 WL 55992 (4th Cir. 1996) (unpublished opinion); United States v. Tan-

under the excessive fines clause, but courts rarely find the forfeiture excessive.[5]

After holding that the excessive fines clause applies to criminal forfeitures in *Alexander*, the Supreme Court did not provide any test for determining whether a forfeiture was excessive. Five years later, in *Bajakajian*, the Court did provide a test. The Court stated: "We now hold that a punitive forfeiture violates the Excessive Fines Clause if it is grossly disproportional to the gravity of a defendant's offense."[6]

Elaborating on the meaning of "grossly disproportional," the Court stated that since the text and history of the Excessive Fines Clause were not helpful, the Court looked to two other considerations in deriving a constitutional excessiveness standard.[7] Those considerations were deference to the legislature and recognition that judicial conclusions on proportionality will be inherently imprecise. These factors led the Court to adopt the standard of gross disproportionality from the Cruel and Unusual Punishment Clause cases.[8]

The Court then concluded that under this gross disproportionality standard, forfeiture of the entire $357,144 would violate the Excessive Fines Clause.[9] Specifically the Court reached this conclusion by comparing the amount of the forfeiture to the gravity of the crime. It found that the money was clean—unrelated to other crime—and that only a failure to report was involved. The sentencing guidelines for mere failure to report indicate a minimum level of culpability. Finally, the Court said the harm caused by the crime was minimal: there was no fraud, no loss of money to the government. It suffered only a loss of information, and that loss was not inherently proportional to the amount of money involved.[10] The defendant did not argue that his wealth or income was relevant and the Court did not consider that issue.[11]

This decision evoked a hearty dissent from four justices.[12] They stated first that *in personam* customs fines have long been upheld as

ner, 61 F.3d 231 (4th Cir.1995); United States v. Wild, 47 F.3d 669 (4th Cir.1995).

Sixth Circuit: United States v. Galloway, 1996 WL 479120 (6th Cir. 1996)(unpublished opinion).

Eighth Circuit: United States v. Bieri, 68 F.3d 232 (8th Cir.1995).

5. *See, e.g.,*

Fourth Circuit: United States v. Locklear, 1997 WL 526020 (4th Cir.1997) (unpublished per curiam); United States v. Alcaraz–Garcia, 79 F.3d 769 (9th Cir. 1996)(per curiam) (forfeiture of defendant's house and business not excessive).

Sixth Circuit: United States v. Galloway, 1996 WL 479120 (6th Cir. 1996)(unpublished opinion); United States v. Freshour, 1995 WL 496662 (6th Cir. 1995)(unpublished opinion).

Eighth Circuit: United States v. Bieri, 21 F.3d 819 (8th Cir.1994).

But see

Ninth Circuit: United States v. Bajakajian, 84 F.3d 334 (9th Cir.1996)(forfeiture of any funds for mere failure to report under § 5316 is excessive), *aff'd,* ___ U.S. ___, 118 S.Ct. 2028, 141 L.Ed.2d 314 (1998).

6. ___ U.S. ___ at ___, 118 S.Ct. 2028, 2036, 141 L.Ed.2d 314 at ___.

7. 118 S.Ct. at 2037–2039.

8. *Id.* at 2037, *citing* Solem v. Helm, 463 U.S. 277, 103 S.Ct. 3001, 77 L.Ed.2d 637 (1983) and Rummel v. Estelle, 445 U.S. 263, 100 S.Ct. 1133, 63 L.Ed.2d 382 (1980).

9. *Id.* at 2038.

10. *Id.*

11. *Id.* at 2039 n.15.

12. *Id.* at 2041 (Kennedy, Rehnquist, O'Connor & Scalia, JJ. dissenting). The dissent called the majority opinion "disturb-

constitutional.[13] At any rate, even assuming the grossly disproportional standard is appropriate, it was misapplied to the facts.[14] Because the violation was willful, the defendant lied several times, and Congress defined failure to report as serious, the forfeiture of $357,144 would not be grossly disproportional.[15] Finally, the dissent stated that the decision undermines Excessive Fines Clause law by according fines more scrutiny than mandatory prison terms and by creating tension with *Austin's* approach to excessiveness.[16]

All the implications of *Bajakajian* won't be clear for a while, but it raises many questions. First, the procedural posture of the case was strange. The District Court held that forfeiture of $357,144 would be excessive and reduced the forfeiture to $15,000.[17] The Ninth Circuit affirmed this decision, but on slightly different grounds. It found that unreported cash would never be an instrumentality of the crime, so any forfeiture under § 5316 would be excessive.[18] However, because the defendant did not appeal the $15,000 forfeiture, the Ninth Circuit concluded it had no jurisdiction to change it, and affirmed it. The Supreme Court also affirmed the $15,000 forfeiture, but again on slightly different grounds. Under the grossly disproportional standard, the Court said, whether the cash is an instrumentality is irrelevant.[19] But because forfeiture of the entire $357,144 would be grossly disproportional, the Ninth Circuit judgment forfeiting $15,000 was affirmed.[20]

The result of the judgment being affirmed but on slightly shifting theories with no appeal by the defendant is uncertainty on the breadth of the decision. The majority characterizes the holding as narrow, holding only that forfeiture of $357,144 would be unconstitutional.[21] Questions the majority said it specifically did not decide include the validity of the district court's reduction and the amount of the reduction (to $15,000). In contrast, the dissent claimed the characterization of the holding as narrow is artificial.[22] The result is that only a couple things are certain: The standard for excessiveness is "grossly disproportional," and forfeiture of $357,144 would meet that standard. Although the Court affirmed the $15,000 forfeiture, it did so while disclaiming any meaning in it.[23]

The Court's discussion of the cash's role as an instrumentality is also difficult to read. The Ninth Circuit said cash would never be an instrumentality of the failure-to-report crime.[24] The Supreme Court said that whether the cash was an instrumentality of the crime was irrele-

ing" and noted the "broader upheaval it foreshadows." *Id.*

13. *Id.* at 2042.
14. *Id.* at 2043.
15. *Id.* at 2043–46.
16. *Id.* at 2046–47.
17. *Id.* at 2029.
18. *Id.* at 2030; *see* United States v. Bajakajian, 84 F.3d 334 (9th Cir.1996).

19. United States v. Bajakajian, ___ U.S. ___, ___, 118 S.Ct. 2028, 2035, 141 L.Ed.2d 314 (1998).
20. *Id.* at 2031.
21. *Id.* at 2038 n.11.
22. *Id.* at 2043.
23. *Id.* at 2038 n.11.
24. *Id.* at 2032–33; *see* United States v. Bajakajian, 84 F.3d 334 (9th Cir.1996).

vant,[25] but also dropped in a footnote saying that it agreed with the Ninth Circuit that the cash was not an instrumentality of the crime.[26] The point of this footnote is uncertain. The Court is clear enough in its text that the currency's characterization as an instrumentality or not is irrelevant under the new grossly disproportional standard. But the characterization of cash as an instrumentality or not is the crux of the excessiveness inquiry many circuits have developed under *Austin.*[27] The Court's points that (1) instrumentalitiness is irrelevant, and (2) cash is not an instrumentality of failure to report, may have a confusing impact in the civil forfeiture context.

Along the same lines, one of the most serious questions raised by *Bajakajian* is its effect on *Austin* and the Excessive Fines Clause jurisprudence developing in the civil forfeiture context.[28] The majority did not cite *Alexander,* which held RICO criminal forfeitures subject to the Excessive Fines Clause, but cited instead *Austin,* introducing the cite with a "cf." And the minority noted that the majority decision is in tension with *Austin* and that it makes conflicting points on that topic.[29]

Finally, the Court's discussion of the gravity of the crime of failure to report the import/export of currency is curious. The Court relied exclusively on the sentencing guidelines to show that the sanction for the crime was low (six months incarceration and a fine of $5000), so the crime is not considered serious. But the dissent identified several problems with this reliance on the guidelines. For one, it ignores Congress's statutory maximum of five years incarceration and fine of $250,000.[30] Moreover, the majority's overall conclusion that one of the currency reporting crimes is not considered grave is questionable.[31]

Bajakajian provides a few answers and raises lots of questions for the lower courts to deal with under the Excessive Fines Clause. At any rate, the Supreme Court has indicated that this clause imposes some constitutional limits on criminal forfeiture.

Two questions beyond the definition of the excessiveness test will likely surface in the courts. One issue is whether the forfeiture of proceeds can ever be excessive. In one of the earliest excessiveness cases, when *Alexander* was remanded from the Supreme Court, the Eighth Circuit stated, "Forfeiture of proceeds cannot be considered punishment, and thus, subject to the excessive fines clause, as it simply parts the owner from the fruits of the criminal activity."[32] Likewise, the Fourth Circuit reached the same conclusion, stating that a "forfeiture of proper-

---

25. United States v. Bajakajian, ___ U.S. ___ at ___, 118 S.Ct. 2028, 2035, 141 L.Ed.2d 314 (U.S.Cal.1998).

26. *Id.* at 2036 n.9.

27. *See* § 28.17(C)(i) *infra.*

28. *See* § 28.17 *infra.*

29. United States v. Bajakajian, ___ U.S. ___ at ___, 118 S.Ct. 2028, 2046, 141 L.Ed.2d 314 (1998) (Kennedy, Rehnquist, O'Connor & Scalia, JJ., dissenting)(using the signal "but see" to refer to two of the majority's points).

30. *Id.* at 2044.

31. *Id.* at 2044–47.

32. United States v. Alexander, 32 F.3d 1231, 1236 (8th Cir.1994), *citing Austin,* 509 U.S. at 622 n. 14, 113 S.Ct. at 2812 n. 14.

ty constituting, or derived from, proceeds of an illegal activity can never be 'excessive' in a constitutional sense."[33] However, three weeks later a different panel of the Fourth Circuit concluded that forfeiture of proceeds could be excessive and criticized the earlier case.[34] The law is currently unclear on whether proceeds are necessarily proportional to the crime, and this will be a developing area.

The second issue is, if a court finds the forfeiture to excessive, what is the remedy? The court could either vacate the entire forfeiture or it could reduce the forfeiture until it is not constitutionally excessive. The Eighth Circuit has endorsed mitigating or reducing the forfeiture in the criminal context rather than vacating it altogether,[35] as has the Third Circuit.[36] This is as far as the law has come on this issue, probably because courts so rarely find forfeitures to be excessive. The possibility that a court could reduce a forfeiture to comport with the Excessive Fines Clause is the only power the court has over the amount of the forfeiture found by the jury.[37]

§ 29.15   Constitutional Limits—Sixth Amendment Right to Counsel and Forfeiture of Fees in the Hands of a Third Party Lawyer

The Supreme Court has held that the criminal forfeiture laws authorize forfeiture of fees paid by a defendant in the hands of a third party lawyer. The first step to this conclusion was taken in United States v. Monsanto,[1] in which the Court construed the criminal forfeiture statutes to apply to fees transferred by defendants to their lawyers. The next step was taken in Caplin & Drysdale, Chartered v. United States,[2] in which the Court held that forfeiture of attorney's fees is constitutional.[3]

In *Caplin & Drysdale*, the petitioner law firm argued that allowing forfeiture of fees paid to criminal defense attorneys was unconstitutional under the sixth amendment right to counsel and the fifth amendment due process clause. The Court rejected both of these arguments. It held that the sixth amendment right to counsel did not include the right to use other persons' money (in this case, it was the United States' money under the relation back clause) to pay a lawyer, even if using that money would be the only way a defendant could pay the lawyer of his or her

---

33. United States v. Wild, 47 F.3d 669, 676 (4th Cir.1995), *cited with approval* in United States v. Locklear, 1997 WL 526020 at *2 n. 12 (4th Cir.1997). In addition, the court said that a forfeiture of facilitating or CCE property will rarely be disproportionate (this was a forfeiture of proceeds). *Id.*

34. United States v. Shifflett, 1995 WL 125506, at *2–3, n. 2 (4th Cir.1995) (unpublished).

35. United States v. Bieri, 21 F.3d 819, 824 (8th Cir.1994).

36. United States v. Sarbello, 985 F.2d 716, 717–18 (3d Cir.1993).

37. *See* § 29.19, describing how forfeiture is mandatory if the jury orders it.

§ 29.15

1. 491 U.S. 600, 109 S.Ct. 2657, 105 L.Ed.2d 512 (1989).

2. 491 U.S. at 617, 109 S.Ct. at 2666.

3. *Id.* at 619–20.

choice.[4] A defendant has a right to adequate counsel, and to counsel of choice if he or she can afford it, but no more. If a defendant's money is unavailable due to forfeiture, the defendant has no constitutional right to use it to hire the lawyer the defendant wants.[5] Moreover, criminal forfeiture of attorneys fees does not violate the fifth amendment due process clause by generally upsetting the balance of power between the government and the defense.[6] If prosecutorial over-reaching occurs, the Court held, cases can be dealt with individually.[7]

The Court took the right to counsel analysis one step further in *Monsanto*.[8] In that case the government got a pretrial restraining order that froze all the defendant's assets. Since he had no access to money, the defendant could not hire an attorney. Instead, he was represented by a lawyer appointed under the Criminal Justice Act. The defendant argued that this violated his sixth amendment right to counsel.[9] The Supreme Court disagreed, stating there is no exception for pre-trial restraint of assets that would be used to pay an attorney.[10] A restraining order does not preclude the defendant from obtaining counsel because after the restraint, he is entitled to a public defender. Finally, the court found no constitutional problem with restraining assets pre-trial based only on probable cause.[11] One constitutional question the Court did not resolve was "whether the due process clause requires a hearing before a pretrial restraint order can be imposed."[12]

Lawyers will have a difficult time qualifying under either of the third party defenses in the statute.[13] The attorney must argue he or she is a bona fide purchaser as opposed to a party with a prior interest since he or she did not receive the money until after the criminal act. It is difficult for any defense attorney to establish that he or she is a bona fide purchaser reasonably without knowledge that the property is subject to forfeiture because this *mens rea* requires some investigation of the fee source by the lawyer, and most lawyers are reluctant to do the investigation. At any rate, all lawyers are on notice that some property, and maybe the fee, will be subject to forfeiture once the indictment comes down. Thus lawyers are exposed to the risk of forfeiture since they may not qualify under a defense and there is no constitutional exception for attorneys fees.[14]

The Department of Justice has acknowledged the impact this risk of fee forfeiture may have on defense lawyers. The United States Attorneys

---

4. *Id.*

5. *Id.*

6. *Id.* at 633–34.

7. *Id.* at 635.

8. 491 U.S. 600, 109 S.Ct. 2657, 105 L.Ed.2d 512 (1989).

9. *Id.* at 612–14.

10. *Id.* at 614.

11. *Id.* at 615.

12. *Id.* at 615 n.10.

13. See § 29.9(B), which discusses the third party claims. *See also* United States v. Schwimmer, 968 F.2d 1570, 1573 (2d Cir.1992)(defense attorneys feel particularly vulnerable to criminal forfeiture).

14. *See, e.g.,* United States v. Moffitt, Zwerling & Kemler, P.C., 83 F.3d 660 (4th Cir.1996) (lawyers did not qualify under the bona fide purchaser defense and fees ordered forfeited to the extent still held by firm).

Manual includes a series of guidelines on attorney fee forfeiture.[15] Fee forfeitures require approval from main Justice.[16] One guideline lists factors Justice will consider in exempting fees from forfeiture.[17] These U.S.A.M. guidelines are not binding on Justice.

The Department of Justice has not frequently pursued forfeiture of attorneys fees, but it did pursue them, doggedly, in one recent case. In United States v. Moffitt, Zwerling & Kemler, P.C.,[18] the law firm of Moffitt, Zwerling was hired by defendant Covington to represent him in a drug trafficking investigation. He paid the firm $103,800 to secure the representation. The payment was made in two deliveries, and much of it was in $100 bills which the defendant delivered in a cracker box or shoe box.[19] Several months later, Covington was indicted, and the indictment contained a forfeiture count seeking proceeds and facilitating property including cash of $168,000. The defendant eventually pled guilty and agreed to forfeit property including the $103,800 fee paid to Moffitt, Zwerling.

The firm objected to forfeiture and asserted the third party defense that it was a bona fide purchaser. The court rejected that defense, holding that the firm was not "reasonably without cause to believe" that the fee was subject to forfeiture. The court was critical of the law firm's conduct, stating,

> [D]uring the supposedly extensive interviews with Covington, the firm's partners tiptoed around the most pertinent questions. They did not even ask Covington what legitimate sources of income he had. And, conspicuously, they avoided asking Covington exactly where he had obtained the $103,800 in cash to pay his legal fee.... The meetings ... create the impression that the participants were engaging in some sort of wink and nod ritual whereby they agreed not to ask—or tell—too much.

When the government tried to collect the money from the firm, the firm claimed that almost all of the fee had been spent. When the government made various arguments to collect it all, the court denied them. Finally, the government filed common law actions of detinue and conversion to recover the fee, and those actions are presumably proceeding today.[20]

This case provides some guidance on how attorneys can minimize the risk of the government forfeiting their fees.[21] Criminal defense attorneys should try to determine the source for the money being used to pay their fees. If necessary, they should ask clients directly where they

---

15. U.S.A.M. §§ 119.104, 119.200, 119.202, 119.203.

16. U.S.A.M. §§ 119.104, 119.202.

17. U.S.A.M. § 9–119.203

18. 83 F.3d 660 (4th Cir.1996) (the government sought forfeiture of the fees of the attorneys for a large-scale drug dealer).

19. *Moffitt, Zwerling*, 83 F.3d at 663.

20. *Id.* at 670 (federal forfeiture law does not preempt state conversion actions; government stated conversion claim).

21. The best source of advice on fee forfeiture for criminal defense attorneys is RICO CASES COMMITTEE, AMERICAN BAR ASS'N, PROTECTING YOURSELF AND YOUR FEE: A DEFENSE LAWYER'S PRACTICE GUIDE IN A NEW AGE OF FEDERAL LAW (1991).

got the money for the fee. If lawyers investigate and otherwise make an effort to take fees paid only from non-forfeitable sources, they will maximize their chances of proving that they are "reasonably without cause to believe the property is subject to forfeiture."[22]

§ 29.16   Constitutional Limits—RICO and the First Amendment

RICO forfeiture based on obscenity predicate offenses may implicate First Amendment rights. Defendants have argued that their First Amendment rights were being unconstitutionally chilled or restrained because the government seized either non-obscene material or material not yet adjudged to be obscene in addition to obscene material.[1] The need for additional procedural safeguards depends upon the time at which the government seeks seizure of the property.[2]

If the government seeks a temporary restraining order before indictment, more than just a probable cause hearing may be required.[3] "[W]hile the general rule [as to seizures] is that any and all contraband, instrumentalities, and evidence of crimes may be seized on probable cause ..., it is otherwise when materials presumptively protected by the First Amendment are involved."[4] Because expressive materials associated with an obscenity predicate offense are presumptively protected, there must be an adversary proceeding before the materials may be seized.[5]

---

22. *See generally* Eugene Gaetke and Sarah Welling, *Money Laundering and Lawyers*, 43 SYRACUSE L.REV. 1165, 1182–89 (1992).

§ 29.16

1. *See, e.g.,* Alexander v. United States, 509 U.S. 544, 113 S.Ct. 2766, 125 L.Ed.2d 441 (1993); Fort Wayne Books, Inc. v. Indiana, 489 U.S. 46, 109 S.Ct. 916, 103 L.Ed.2d 34 (1989).

In *Fort Wayne Books*, the Supreme Court held the Constitution does not forbid the use of obscenity violations as predicates for a RICO conviction. *Fort Wayne Books*, 489 U.S. at 57–60, 109 S.Ct. 924–25. The Court did not, however, decide whether the pretrial seizure of "nonexpressive property" was proper. *Id.* at 67 n.12. This question was later addressed by the Court in Alexander v. United States, 509 U.S. 544, 113 S.Ct. 2766, 125 L.Ed.2d 441 (1993).

2. Alexander v. United States, 509 U.S. 545, 549–553, 113 S.Ct. 2766, 2770–72, 125 L.Ed.2d 441 (1993).

3. 18 U.S.C. § 1963(d)(2) allows the government to seek an ex parte restraining order upon a showing of probable cause that the property will be subject to forfeiture and that notice to the interest parties would imperil the availability of the property for forfeiture. *Id.*

4. Fort Wayne Books, Inc. v. Indiana, 489 U.S. 46, 63, 109 S.Ct. 916, 927, 103 L.Ed.2d 34 (1989). *Fort Wayne Books* involved interpretation of Indiana's RICO provision. It appears from the Court's opinion that the state RICO provision for pretrial forfeiture upon probable cause was slightly different than the federal RICO statute in that: 1) it only required the state to show "probable cause to believe that a violation of [the State's RICO law] involving the property in question had occurred," *id.* at 51; and 2) forfeiture for a state RICO violation could be pursued civilly, which was the case in *Fort Wayne Books. Id.* at 50–53.

5. *Id.* at 67. The Court did not express an opinion on the pretrial seizure of nonexpressive property. *Id.* at 67 n.12.

While *Fort Wayne Books* was based on a state RICO claim, it would appear to apply to pre-trial seizures under federal RICO as well. While the Court considered related issues in the federal RICO context in Alexander v. United States, 509 U.S. 544, 113 S.Ct. 2766, 125 L.Ed.2d 441 (1993), that case dealt with the post-trial seizure of obscenity-related materials after the defendant had been found guilty of a RICO violation based on obscenity predicates. *Fort Wayne Books*, on the other hand, dealt with the pre-trial seizure of forfeitable materials.

Seizure resulting from a RICO conviction, on the other hand, does not require additional procedural safeguards.[6] This is true regardless of the nature of the material.[7] In Alexander v. United States,[8] the Court reasoned that "[i]n this case ... the assets in question were not ordered forfeited because they were believed to be obscene, but because they were directly related to petitioner's past racketeering violations."[9] As a practical matter, the opinion in *Alexander* allows forfeiture of material in the absence of an adjudication that it is obscene or otherwise of an unprotected character if the defendant has been convicted of a RICO violation based on obscenity predicates. In other words, RICO is oblivious to the nature of the materials; as long as they play a financial role in the operation of the racketeering enterprise, they are forfeitable.

It is settled that RICO obscenity provisions do not unconstitutionally chill protected speech or constitute a prior restraint on speech, and that, as applied to obscenity, RICO is not overbroad.[10]

Therefore, it appears that the First Amendment requires a determination of obscenity in an adversary hearing prior to the seizure of property presumed to be protected under the First Amendment, whether dealing with state or federal RICO.

   See

   Ninth Circuit: Adult Video Ass'n v. Barr, 960 F.2d 781, 788 (9th Cir.1992) (stating that the holding in *Fort Wayne Books* "translates readily to the federal RICO context" and holding "that the portion of section 1963(d) [authorizing] pretrial seizures is unconstitutional on its face"); *vacated and remanded,* 509 U.S. 917, 113 S.Ct. 3028, 125 L.Ed.2d 716; *on remand,* the Ninth Circuit decided its original assessment of unconstitutionality was correct *sub nom.* Adult Video Ass'n v. Reno, 41 F.3d 503 (9th Cir.1994)(pre-trial seizure violates the First Amendment).

   6. Alexander v. United States, 509 U.S. 544, 113 S.Ct. 2766, 125 L.Ed.2d 441 (1993).

   7. *Id.* at 549–53.

   8. 509 U.S. 544, 113 S.Ct. 2766, 125 L.Ed.2d 441 (1993).

   9. *Id.* at 551. Therefore, forfeiture after a RICO conviction does not require any determination of obscenity in an adversary hearing.

   It is difficult to completely reconcile this language with the Court's discussion in Fort Wayne Books, Inc. v. Indiana, 489 U.S. 46, 109 S.Ct. 916, 103 L.Ed.2d 34 (1989). In that case, the district court held that the pre-trial seizure of certain materials did not require a pre-seizure adversary hearing as to their obscenity because "the pretrial sei-

zures ... were not based on the nature or suspected obscenity of the contents of the items seized, but upon the neutral ground that the sequestered property represented assets used and acquired in the course of racketeering activity." *Id.* at 64. Nonetheless, the Court stated that it was "quite sure that the special rules applicable to removing First Amendment materials from circulation [were] relevant here." *Id.* at 65. It is not clear why such concerns were not present in *Alexander,* but the distinction seems to turn on the timing of the government's seizure. In attempting to distinguish *Fort Wayne Books,* the Court stated the following:

   Here, by contrast, the seizure was not premature, because the Government established beyond a reasonable doubt the basis for the forfeiture. Petitioner had a full criminal trial on the merits of the obscenity and RICO charges during which the Government proved that four magazines and three videotapes were obscene and that the other forfeited assets were directly linked to petitioner's commission of racketeering offenses.

Alexander, 509 U.S. at 552, 113 S.Ct. at 2772. Four justices dissented on this issue. *See id.* at 559 (Souter, J., concurring in part and dissenting in part) ("the First Amendment forbids the forfeiture of petitioner's expressive material in the absence of an adjudication that it is obscene or otherwise of unprotected character").

   10. Alexander v. United States, 509 U.S. 544, 549–53, 113 S.Ct. 2766, 125 L.Ed.2d 441 (1993).

§ 29.17 The Process—Standard of Proof

The consensus is that a preponderance is the burden of proof for forfeiture.[1] The rationale is that criminal forfeiture is part of the sentence, and the preponderance standard is sufficient in the sentencing phase.[2] This consensus developed before the Supreme Court decided Libretti v. United States,[3] and that decision corroborated the lower courts' conclusion that criminal forfeiture is a punishment rather than a crime.

One court has held that the beyond a reasonable doubt standard is the burden of proof.[4] However, this decision predates *Libretti,* so its continued vitality is unclear.

§ 29.18 The Process—Evidentiary Presumption in the Drug Statute

The drug criminal forfeiture statute sets up an evidentiary presumption that property is forfeitable if the government shows by a preponderance that (1) the property was acquired at the time of the commission of the underlying crime or immediately thereafter; and (2) that there is no likely source for the property other than the crime.[1] Though evidentiary presumptions in criminal cases cannot be mandatory,[2] it is not clear if that rule extends to matters in the sentencing phase, like forfeiture. The RICO and general criminal forfeiture statutes, § 982, do not have

§ 29.17

1. *See*

D.C. Circuit: United States v. DeFries, 129 F.3d 1293, 1312 (D.C.Cir.1997) (RICO forfeiture burden is preponderance).

First Circuit: United States v. Rogers, 102 F.3d 641 (1st Cir.1996).

Third Circuit: United States v. Voigt, 89 F.3d 1050 (3d Cir.1996) (§ 982 burden is preponderance); United States v. Sandini, 816 F.2d 869 (3d Cir.1987)(§ 853 burden of preponderance is not violation of due process).

Fourth Circuit: United States v. Tanner, 61 F.3d 231 (4th Cir.1995) (§ 853 burden is preponderance).

Sixth Circuit: United States v. Smith, 966 F.2d 1045 (6th Cir.1992)(§ 853 burden is preponderance).

Seventh Circuit: United States v. Ben-Hur, 20 F.3d 313 (7th Cir.1994)(§ 853 burden is preponderance); United States v. Herrero, 893 F.2d 1512 (7th Cir.1990).

Eighth Circuit: United States v. Myers, 21 F.3d 826, 829 (8th Cir.1994)(§ 982 burden is preponderance); United States v. Bieri, 21 F.3d 819 (8th Cir.1994).

Ninth Circuit: United States v. Waldron, 1996 WL 219616 (9th Cir. 1996) (§ 982 burden is preponderance)(unpublished opinion); United States v. Hernandez–Escarsega, 886 F.2d 1560 (9th Cir. 1989)(§ 853 burden is preponderance).

Eleventh Circuit: United States v. Elgersma, 971 F.2d 690 (11th Cir.1992)(en banc)(§ 853 burden is preponderance).

Cf.

First Circuit: United States v. Houlihan, 92 F.3d 1271, 1299 n. 33 (1st Cir.1996) (leaving question of burden of proof for RICO forfeiture open).

2. United States v. Rogers, 102 F.3d 641, 647 (1st Cir.1996).

3. 516 U.S. 29, 116 S.Ct. 356, 133 L.Ed.2d 271 (1995).

4. United States v. McKeithen, 822 F.2d 310, 312 (2d Cir.1987)(§ 853 burden is beyond a reasonable doubt).

§ 29.18

1. 21 U.S.C. § 853(d).

2. *See* Sandstrom v. Montana, 442 U.S. 510, 99 S.Ct. 2450, 61 L.Ed.2d 39 (1979); County Court of Ulster Co. v. Allen, 442 U.S. 140, 99 S.Ct. 2213, 60 L.Ed.2d 777 (1979).

comparable presumptions.[3]

§ 29.19　The Process—Trial

A.　FOR THE DEFENDANT

The criminal forfeiture process starts with a count in the indictment alleging that certain property owned or possessed by the defendant[1] falls into the statutory definition of forfeitable property for the substantive crimes included in the indictment.[2] The government need not list all forfeitable interests in the indictment as long as it gives the defendants notice that it will seek to forfeit all property subject to forfeiture.[3]

The court may bifurcate the trial, withholding proof on the forfeiture count unless and until the jury convicts on the substantive charges,[4] or the proof on the substantive crimes and the forfeiture counts may be heard at the same time and decided by the jury at the same time.

If the jury decides in favor of forfeiture, it is mandatory; the judge has no discretion to change the forfeiture[5] except under the Excessive

---

3. The RICO statute simply has no such provision; and the general criminal forfeiture statute specifically declines to adopt this section of the drug statute. See § 982(b) (not incorporating § 853(d) of the drug statute). *See* United States v. Voigt, 89 F.3d 1050, 1083 (3d Cir.1996) (§ 982 does not use the rebuttable presumption of § 853(d)).

§ 29.19

1. The property must be owned by or be in the possession of the defendant since criminal forfeiture is an in personam action and, at this point, there is no one else before the court in the immediate action.

2. *See* FED.R.CRIM.P. 7(c)(2) ("No judgment of forfeiture may be entered in a criminal proceeding unless the indictment of the information shall allege the extent of the interest or property subject to forfeiture.").

3. United States v. DeFries, 129 F.3d 1293, 1315 n. 17 (D.C.Cir.1997).

4. *See, e.g.,*

First Circuit: United States v. Saccoccia, 58 F.3d 754, 782 (1st Cir.1995) (bifurcating crimes and forfeiture count).

Third Circuit: United States v. Sandini, 816 F.2d 869, 874 (3d Cir.1987)(invoking supervisory powers to require bifurcated trials in all criminal forfeitures).

Sixth Circuit: United States v. Christunas, 126 F.3d 765 (6th Cir.1997) (bifurcating guilt and forfeiture issues).

Many courts favor this approach for its simplicity. It is also favored in jurisdictions that apply a preponderance standard for the forfeiture to keep the jury from confusing the two standards of proof.

5. 21 U.S.C. § 853(a) ("Any person convicted of a violation of this title . . . *shall* forfeit. . . ."); 18 U.S.C. § 982(a)(1) ("The court . . . *shall* order that person forfeit. . . ."); 18 U.S.C. § 1963(a)(the defendant *"shall* forfeit") (all emphasis added); 18 U.S.C. § 3554 (court "shall" order forfeiture).

See

Third Circuit: United States v. Kravitz, 738 F.2d 102, 105 (3d Cir.1984).

Fourth Circuit: United States v. Hess, 691 F.2d 188, 191 (4th Cir.1982).

Fifth Circuit: United States v. L'Hoste, 609 F.2d 796, 809–13 (5th Cir.1980).

Eighth Circuit: United States v. Bieri, 68 F.3d 232, 235 (8th Cir.1995).

Ninth Circuit: United States v. Busher, 817 F.2d 1409, 1414 (9th Cir.1987); United States v. Godoy, 678 F.2d 84, 88 (9th Cir. 1982).

See also S.REP. No. 98–225, 98th Cong., 2d Sess., at 200 (1984), *reprinted* in 1984 U.S.C.C.A.N. 3182, 3383 ("[T]he final sentence of section 1963(a) emphasizes the mandatory nature of criminal forfeitures, requiring the court to order forfeiture in addition to any other penalty imposed. This is in accord with case law holding the forfei-

Fines Clause.[6]

To find in favor of forfeiture, the jury must make factual findings that the property was involved in the substantive crime in the way necessary for a forfeiture under the applicable statute.[7] The judge then must enter a preliminary order of forfeiture.[8] This preliminary finding allows the government to invoke its seizure powers[9] and investigate to see if it needs to move for substitute assets. At the final hearing, the judge will rule on the exact extent of the forfeiture and whether the government has a right to substitute assets.[10] At sentencing, the forfeiture order must be announced orally by the court; if it is not announced, it cannot be added later.[11]

Forfeiture is part of the sentence and so does not require the same procedural protections as a criminal charge. The Supreme Court reached this conclusion in Libretti v. United States.[12] Defendant Libretti pled guilty and agreed to forfeit certain of his assets. He later complained that the trial judge had not found a factual basis for the plea to the forfeiture count nor advised him of his right to a jury trial on the forfeiture count specifically. The Court rejected both these arguments. It concluded that the trial judge in this case did not have to find a factual basis for the guilty plea to the forfeiture count under Rule 11(f),[13] and

ture provision of the present RICO statute to be mandatory on the trial court.").

6. Under the Excessive Fines Clause, the judge may reduce forfeitures deemed to be excessive. *See, e.g.,* United States v. Bajakajian, ___ U.S. ___, 118 S.Ct. 2028, 141 L.Ed.2d 314 (1998) (adjusting forfeiture from $357,144 to $15,000); United States v. Sarbello, 985 F.2d 716, 718 (3d Cir. 1993)(court may reduce statutory penalty to conform to Excessive Fines Clause) and *see* § 29.14 on the judges' power to mitigate under the Excessive Fines Clause.

7. *See* FED.R.CRIM.P. 31(e) ("If the indictment or information alleges that an interest or property is subject to criminal forfeiture, a special verdict shall be returned as to the extent of the interest or property subject to forfeiture, if any."); United States v. Sokolow, 91 F.3d 396 (3d Cir.1996)(special verdict forms held proper).

8. *See* FED.R.CRIM.P. 32(d)(2). The rule states:

If a verdict contains a finding that property is subject to a criminal forfeiture, or if a defendant enters a guilty plea subjecting property to such forfeiture, the court may enter a preliminary order of forfeiture after providing notice to the defendant and a reasonable opportunity to be heard on the timing and form of the order. The order of forfeiture shall authorize the Attorney General to seize the property subject to forfeiture....

Id.

9. *See* 21 U.S.C. § 853(g); 18 U.S.C. 1963(e). *See also* § 29.20 on post-conviction restraint of assets.

10. *See* FED.R.CRIM.P. 32(d)(2) ("At sentencing, a final order of forfeiture shall be made part of the sentence and included in the judgment. The court may include in the final order such condition as may be reasonably necessary to preserve the value of the property pending any appeal.") The judge must orally state that he or she is entering a forfeiture order during the sentencing, however, or the order may be invalid. *See* United States v. Shannon, 1996 WL 341352 (9th Cir.1996)(unpublished opinion).

11. United States v. Shannon, 1996 WL 341352 (9th Cir.1996) (unpublished opinion) (forfeiture order must be verbally announced at sentencing; forfeiture order added later vacated).

12. 516 U.S. 29, 116 S.Ct. 356, 133 L.Ed.2d 271 (1995). One of the co-authors of this treatise, Sara Sun Beale, was counsel for Libretti before the Supreme Court.

13. This holding is somewhat ambiguous because of the Court's conclusion that the district judge in this case, having listened to four days of testimony before the defendant pled guilty, could have concluded that there was a factual basis for the forfeiture. *Libretti,* 516 U.S. at 40, 116 S.Ct. at

that the defendant's right to jury trial on the forfeiture count under Rule 31(e) was statutory only, not constitutional, so the defendant's waiver did not have to meet constitutional standards and was adequate.[14] Justice Stevens dissented, noting the risk that unless the district judge is required to find a factual basis for the guilty plea to the forfeiture count, a wealthy defendant might bargain for a light sentence by voluntarily forfeiting property to which the government was not entitled under the law.[15]

In 1997, the United States Attorneys Manual included a series of guidelines on plea bargains involving criminal forfeiture.[16] These guidelines provide that the government should not use forfeiture to gain advantage in a criminal case, that the settlement documents must show sufficient facts to establish the basis for forfeiture, and that the government does not permit defendants to submit property otherwise not subject to forfeiture to lighten the potential incarceration component.

B. FOR THIRD PARTY CLAIMANTS

The best description of the third party claim process is from the Seventh Circuit:

If a jury finds that property is forfeitable as drug proceeds under 21 U.S.C. § 853(a), the court will enter a preliminary order of forfeiture. Third parties who have claims to property which the government seeks to have criminally forfeited cannot intervene in the criminal action against the defendant. *21 U.S.C. § 853(k).* Instead, they must wait until the court has entered a forfeiture order based on a criminal conviction, and then petition the court under *21 U.S.C. § 853(n)* for a hearing to adjudicate their interest in the property. To succeed, third parties must prove by a preponderance of the evidence either that they had superior title to the property at the time of the crime or that they are bona fide purchasers of the property. *21 U.S.C. § 853(n)(6).* If third parties make such proof, the court will amend the preliminary order of forfeiture it entered following the jury finding of forfeitability. Id. Once the third-party hearings have been held, or the time for filing third-party claims has passed, the government has clear title to the property forfeited. *21 U.S.C. § 853(n)(7).*[17]

The statute expressly bars intervention by third party claimants in the criminal action or civil suits by a third party during the pendency of

364. The Court explained, "We do not mean to suggest that a district court must simply accept a defendant's agreement to forfeit property, particularly when that agreement is not accompanied by a stipulation of facts supporting forfeiture, or when the trial judge for other reasons finds the agreement problematic.... In this case, however, we need not determine the precise scope of a district court's independent obligation, if any, to inquire into the propriety of a stipu-

lated asset forfeiture embodied in a plea agreement." *Id.* at 365.

14. *Libretti,* 516 U.S. at 47–49, 116 S.Ct. at 367–68.

15. *Libretti,* 516 U.S. at 53, 116 S.Ct. at 370.

16. U.S.A.M. §§ 9–113.100, 9–113.101, 9–113.106 and 9–113.420.

17. United States v. Messino, 122 F.3d 427, 428 (7th Cir.1997).

the criminal action.[18] However, intervention by third parties is allowed in motions for pre-trial restraining orders.[19]

All third party claims must be made in a motion to the court between the preliminary order[20] and the final order of forfeiture. Third parties cannot file a claim until the preliminary order of forfeiture is entered.[21] Once notice of a claim is entered, the court will hold a hearing to determine the validity of the claims. If the claims are valid, the court will make the required adjustments in the final order. This procedure for third party claims is constitutional.[22]

Though it is heard in the context of a criminal case, a third party claim is a civil action. Therefore, a third party who was unfairly treated within the terms of the Equal Access to Justice Act (EAJA) may bring an action under those provisions and recover attorney's fees for the action.[23]

§ 29.20   The Process—Restraining Orders and Preliminary Injunctions

The government can get restraining orders and preliminary injunctions in narrow situations.[1] In this way the government protects its interest in the property should there be some reason to believe that the defendant will transfer or dissipate the value of the property. The timing of the request for the restraining order determines what the government must show in order to get the restraining order. This is discussed below. A restraining order is immediately appealable under the same rationale applied to injunctions.[2]

---

18. The statute states:

Bar on intervention. Except as provided in subsection (n), no party claiming an interest in property subject to forfeiture may—

(1) intervene in a trial or appeal of a criminal case involving the forfeiture of such property under this section; or

(2) commence an action at law or equity against the United States concerning the validity of his alleged interest in the property subsequent to the filing of an indictment or information alleging that the property is subject to forfeiture under this section.

21 U.S.C. § 853(k); 18 U.S.C. § 1963(i). *See* Roberts v. United States, 141 F.3d 1468, 1470 (11th Cir.1998) (per curiam) (civil action by third party with claimed interest in property being forfeited "clearly barred" by plain meaning of § 853(k)(2)). *See also* United States v. DeCato, 64 F.3d 752 (1st Cir.1995)(third-party claimants could not receive a restraining order to fight an indictment under § 853).

19. *See* United States v. DeCato, 64 F.3d 752, 755–56 (1st Cir.1995).

20. After the preliminary order, the property will be seized by the government, and the third party will have to obtain any portion of the property from the government. *See* § 29.20 on restraining orders and preliminary injunctions.

21. United States v. Messino, 122 F.3d 427, 430–31 (7th Cir.1997).

22. United States v. Holmes, 1998 WL 13538 (4th Cir.1998) (unpublished per curiam) (*citing* Libretti v. United States, 516 U.S. 29, 116 S.Ct. 356, 133 L.Ed.2d 271 (1995)). *But cf.* United States v. Messino, 122 F.3d 427, 430 (7th Cir.1997) (whether Seventh Amendment requires jury for third party hearings is "challenging question").

23. United States v. Douglas, 55 F.3d 584, 585 (11th Cir.1995).

§ 29.20

1. *See* 21 U.S.C. § 853(e); 18 U.S.C. § 1963(d).

2. United States v. Ripinsky, 20 F.3d 359, 362 (9th Cir.1994).

According to the United States Attorneys Manual, if the government seizes real property, occupants should be permitted to remain in the property under an occupancy agreement pending forfeiture.[3]

A. PRE-INDICTMENT

For the government to get a restraining order before indictment, the government must satisfy a two-part test. First, the government must show that "there is a substantial probability" that the property is forfeitable[4] and that a failure to enter the order will mean that the defendant will defeat the forfeiture by removing, destroying, or dissipating the value of the property.[5] Second is a balancing prong where the government must show that the need for the restraining order outweighs the burden on the defendant.[6] A pre-indictment restraining order of this type cannot be entered without notice to the defendant,[7] and it may only remain in effect for 90 days unless there is an indictment in that 90 days. Then the government can move for a restraining order based on the indictment.

The statute provides for a temporary restraining order that may be entered without notice to the defendant.[8] The government may obtain this with a showing of probable cause that the defendant will remove, destroy, or dissipate the value of the property and that notice to the defendant will defeat the purpose behind the injunction. It can only be in effect for 10 days from entry unless the government shows good cause or the defendant consents to an extension.[9] For an extension, the defendant must be given notice and an opportunity to be heard.

Pre-trial restraining orders are immediately appealable.[10]

B. POST-INDICTMENT

Post-indictment restraining orders are easier to obtain since the government has the force of the grand jury's indictment behind it. The language of the statute[11] provides that the court can grant a motion for a

---

3. U.S.A.M. § 9–115.203.

4. *See* 21 U.S.C. § 853(e)(1)(B)(i); 18 U.S.C. § 1963(d)(1)(B)(i). This would mean that the government must show that there is a substantial probability that the defendant will be convicted on the underlying substantive charge and that the property will then be forfeitable under the statute.

5. *Id.*

6. 21 U.S.C. 853(e)(1)(B)(ii); 18 U.S.C. § 1963(d)(1)(B)(ii).

7. 21 U.S.C. § 853(e)(1)(B); 18 U.S.C. § 1963(d)(1)(B).

8. 21 U.S.C. § 853(e)(2); 18 U.S.C. § 1963(d)(2).

9. *Id.*

10. *See* United States v. Floyd, 992 F.2d 498 (5th Cir.1993).

11. The statute reads:

(1) Upon application of the United States, the court may enter a restraining order or injunction, require the execution of a satisfactory performance bond, or take any other action to preserve the availability of property described in subsection (a) for forfeiture under this section

(A) upon the filing of an indictment or information charging a violation of this title or title III for which forfeiture may be ordered under this section and alleging that the property with respect to which the order is sought would, in

restraining order based purely on the indictment; there are no other statutory requirements except a showing that the property would be subject to forfeiture in case of a conviction. Some courts have held that due process requires an adversary hearing on the restraining order to be held after it is entered but before trial, especially where the assets may be needed to hire a lawyer for trial.[12]

If the government feels that an injunction may not be enough, the drug forfeiture statute authorizes the court to allow the government to seize the assets before the trial.[13] In order to succeed on this motion, the government must show (1) that there is probable cause that the government will ultimately succeed in obtaining a forfeiture and (2) that a restraining order will not be sufficient to protect the government's interest.[14]

C. POST-CONVICTION

After conviction, the court will enter a warrant of seizure that allows the government, through the Attorney General, to take possession of the property.[15] This is done after the court enters the preliminary forfeiture order, but before third party interests are adjudicated.[16]

D. SUBSTITUTE ASSETS

An issue that has divided the circuits is whether the forfeiture statutes authorize pre-trial restraint of substitute assets. A slight majority of circuits holds that pre-trial restraint of substitute assets is not allowed.[17] This conclusion is based on the plain language of the statute[18] and some legislative history.[19] These courts are concerned that such measures are too burdensome on a defendant not yet convicted.[20] Other

---

the event of conviction, be subject to forfeiture under this section. . . .

21 U.S.C. § 853(e)(1)(A); 18 U.S.C. § 1963(d)(1)(A).

12. See § 29.11(A) supra.

13. 21 U.S.C. § 853(f).

14. Id.

15. 21 U.S.C. § 853(g); 18 U.S.C. 1963(e).

16. 21 U.S.C. § 853(g); 18 U.S.C. 1963(e).

17. See

Third Circuit: In re Assets of Martin, 1 F.3d 1351, 1357–61 (3d Cir.1993)(pretrial restraint not permitted under RICO).

Fifth Circuit: United States v. Floyd, 992 F.2d 498, 502 (5th Cir.1993)(pretrial restraint not permitted under § 853).

Eighth Circuit: United States v. Riley, 78 F.3d 367 (8th Cir.1996)(pretrial restraint not permitted under RICO); United States

v. Field, 62 F.3d 246 (8th Cir.1995)(pretrial restraint not permitted under § 982).

Ninth Circuit: United States v. Ripinsky, 20 F.3d 359, 362–63 (9th Cir.1994)(pretrial restraint not permitted under § 982).

18. See, e.g.,

Eighth Circuit: United States v. Field, 62 F.3d 246, 248–49 (8th Cir.1995).

Ninth Circuit: United States v. Ripinsky, 20 F.3d 359, 363 (9th Cir.1994).

19. See, e.g., Ripinsky, 20 F.3d at 363–64.

20. See, e.g., Ripinsky, 20 F.3d at 365 ("In asking us to authorize the pretrial restraint of substitute assets, the government asks us to grant them an even more powerful weapon, a weapon available against the accused, indeed, the presumed innocent. . . . Such restraints can cripple a business and destroy an individual's livelihood.")

circuits have concluded that pre-trial restraint of substitute assets is authorized.[21] These courts cite the purpose of forfeiture law as a whole to prevent dissipation of assets[22] and some legislative history.[23] This is a close question; recent and well-reasoned district court decisions have gone both ways.[24]

According to the United States Attorneys Manual, when orders are entered restraining substitute assets, prosecutors should allow an exemption for legitimate assets needed for attorneys fees, living expenses and the cost of maintaining the restrained assets.[25]

E. THIRD-PARTY TRANSFERS

A related issue is whether pre-trial restraining orders can be entered against third parties holding forfeitable property. Pre-trial restraint of assets in the hands of third parties is not expressly precluded by the statute. Some courts have allowed pretrial restraint of assets in third parties' hands. The leading case is United States v. Regan,[26] in which the Second Circuit held that pretrial restraint of traceable assets in the hands of a third party was authorized under RICO.[27] The Fourth Circuit has also allowed pretrial restraint of assets in the hands of third parties.[28] Actually, the Fourth Circuit went further and allowed pretrial

---

21. *See*

Second Circuit: United States v. Regan, 858 F.2d 115 (2d Cir.1988)(pretrial restraint of defendant's substitute assets proper when restraint of tainted property in hands of third party would be burden to third party).

Fourth Circuit: United States v. McGill, 1996 WL 149366 (4th Cir.1996)(unpublished opinion); In re Billman, 915 F.2d 916 (4th Cir.1990).

Seventh Circuit: United States v. Schmitz, 153 F.R.D. 136 (E.D.Wis.1994).

22. *See*

Second Circuit: United States v. Regan, 858 F.2d 115, 119–20 (2d Cir.1988).

Seventh Circuit: United States v. Schmitz, 153 F.R.D. 136, 140 (E.D.Wis.1994)(looking to design of statute as a whole).

23. *See*

Second Circuit: United States v. Regan, 858 F.2d 115, 119–20 (2d Cir.1988).

Seventh Circuit: United States v. Schmitz, 153 F.R.D. 136, 140 (E.D.Wis. 1994) (disagreeing with Third Circuit's interpretation of legislative history in Assets of Martin, 1 F.3d 1351 (3d Cir.1993)).

24. *Compare* United States v. Schmitz, 153 F.R.D. 136 (E.D.Wis.1994)(pretrial restraint of substitute assets under § 853 allowed) *with* Unit-

ed States v. Bellomo, 954 F.Supp. 630 (S.D.N.Y.1997)(pre-conviction restraints too burdensome even if proper notice is given in the pleadings) and United States v. Gigante, 948 F.Supp. 279 (S.D.N.Y.1996). The *Gigante* court explored rulings subsequent to United States v. Regan, 858 F.2d 115, 121 (2d Cir.1988)(allowing pretrial restraint of substitute assets under RICO if restraining fruits of crime would be burden to third parties), noting that four of the five circuits it examined found pre-conviction restraints too burdensome. The court went on to hold that such restraints would be acceptable only in the unlikely event that both prosecutors and the accused agreed to them. *Gigante*, 948 F.Supp. at 282. *See also* United States v. Gotti, 996 F.Supp. 321 (S.D.N.Y.1998) (pretrial restraint of substitute assets under §§ 982 and 1963 not authorized by statute; restraining order vacated; good discussion of split in circuits).

25. U.S.A.M. § 9–112.230.

26. 858 F.2d 115 (2d Cir.1988).

27. 858 F.2d 115, 119–20 (2d Cir. 1988), *citing* United States v. Long, 654 F.2d 911 (3d Cir.1981)(pretrial restraint of traceable assets in hands of third party attorney proper under drug criminal forfeiture statute).

28. In re Billman, 915 F.2d 916 (4th Cir.1990).

---

restraint of *substitute* assets in the hands of third parties.[29]

On the other hand, the Fourth Circuit has more recently held that if a third party transfers forfeitable property so it cannot be traced, the government cannot collect substitute assets from the third party.[30] The government can pursue other assets in the hands of third parties, but through state actions for conversion and detinue rather than the criminal forfeiture laws.[31]

Third parties can participate in restraining order hearings, both pre-indictment and post-indictment, if they claim an interest in potentially restrainable property.[32]

§ 29.21   The Process—Plea Agreements

A defendant subject to forfeiture can agree to forfeiture as part of a plea agreement.[1] In the hearing on the plea agreement, the requirement of Rule 11(f) that the court find a factual basis for the plea does not apply to the forfeiture count.[2] Forfeiture is to be treated no differently than the rest of the sentence even though the defendant must, in effect, enter a plea to the forfeiture count.[3]

§ 29.22   The Process—Appeal

As to the defendant, the preliminary order of forfeiture entered after the verdict or plea agreement is a final, appealable judgment.[1] Thus the defendant must file the notice of appeal within ten days of that order or waive the appeal.[2] Although this preliminary order is not final as to third parties' claims, it is final as to the defendant.[3]

When reviewing forfeiture verdicts, the Courts of Appeal apply the "substantial evidence" standard. In other words, the verdict of a jury must be sustained if there is substantial evidence, taking the view most favorable to the government, to support it.[4]

---

29. *Id.* at 921.

30. *See* United States v. Moffitt, Zwerling & Kemler, P.C., 83 F.3d 660 (4th Cir.1996).

31. *Id.*

32. United States v. Decato, 64 F.3d 752, 755–56 (1st Cir.1995).

§ 29.21

1. *See* Libretti v. United States, 516 U.S. 29, 116 S.Ct. 356, 133 L.Ed.2d 271 (1995).

2. *Id.*

3. *See Libretti,* 516 U.S. at 29; FED. R.CRIM.P. 32(d)(2) (addressing entry of judgment in case of a plea).

§ 29.22

1. *Sixth Circuit:* United States v. Christunas, 126 F.3d 765 (6th Cir.1997).

Ninth Circuit: United States v. Bennett, 147 F.3d 912, 1998 WL 309269 at *2 (9th Cir.1998).

2. Christunas, 126 F.3d at 767–68.

3. *Sixth Circuit:* Christunas, 126 F.3d at 767–68.

Ninth Circuit: United States v. Bennett, 147 F.3d 912, 1998 WL 309269 at *1–2, *citing* United States v. Libretti, 38 F.3d 523 (10th Cir.1994), *aff'd* 516 U.S. 29, 116 S.Ct. 356, 133 L.Ed.2d 271 (1995).

4. *Third Circuit:* United States v. Aguilar, 843 F.2d 155, 157 (3d Cir.1988). The Third Circuit held that this standard was required because it "is the standard of review that has traditionally been used when reviewing jury verdicts in a criminal case on issues on which the government has the burden of proving the facts beyond a reasonable doubt." United States v. Ofchinick, 883 F.2d 1172, 1177 (3d Cir.1989).

§ 29.23   Bibliography

Barnet, Todd and Ivan Fox, *Trampling on the Sixth Amendment: The Continued Threat of Attorney Fee Forfeiture*, 22 OHIO N.U.L.REV. 1 (1995).

Boudreaux, Donald J. and A.C. Pritchard, *Innocence Lost: Bennis v. Michigan and the Forfeiture Tradition*, 61 MO.L.REV. 593 (1996).

Cassella, Stefan D., *Third-Party Rights in Criminal Forfeiture Cases*, 32 CRIM.L.BULL. 499 (1996).

Cassella, Stefan D., *Symposium: Federal Asset Forfeiture Reform: Forfeiture Reform: a View from the Justice Department*, 21 J. Legis. 211 (1995).

Cheh, Mary M., *Constitutional Limits on Using Civil Remedies to Achieve Criminal Law Objectives: Understanding and Transcending the Criminal–Civil Law Distinction*, 42 HASTINGS L.J. 1325 (1991).

Gurule, Jimmy and Sandra Guerra, THE LAW OF ASSET FORFEITURE (1998) (one volume treatise).

King, Michael Todd, Note, *Expanding the Courts' Power to Preserve Forfeitable Assets: The Pretrial Restraint of Substitute Assets Under RICO and CCE*, 29 GA.L.REV. 245 (1994).

Leach, Arthur W. and John M. Malcolm, *Criminal Forfeiture: An Appropriate Solution to the Civil Forfeiture Debate*, 10 GA.ST.U.L.REV. 241 (1994).

Levy, Leonard W., LICENSE TO STEAL: THE FORFEITURE OF PROPERTY (1996) (a historical treatment of forfeiture law in the United States).

Palm, Craig, RICO Forfeiture and the Eighth Amendment: When is Everything Too Much?, 53 U.Pitt.L.Rev. 1 (1991).

Schimmelbusch, Erik S., Comment, *Pretrial Restraint of Substitute Assets Under RICO and the Comprehensive Drug Abuse Prevention and Control Act of 1970*, 26 PAC.L.J. 165 (1995).

Smith, David B., PROSECUTION AND DEFENSE OF FORFEITURE CASES (1996) (two-volume, regularly updated treatise on the substantive and procedural law of civil and criminal forfeiture).

Smith, Sean D., Comment, *The Scope of Real Property Forfeiture for Drug Related Crime Under the Comprehensive Forfeiture Act*, 137 U.PA. L.REV. 303 (1988).

Stahl, Mark B., Asset Forfeiture, Burdens of Proof and the War on Drugs, 83 J. Crim. L & Criminology 274 (1992).

Zeldin, Michael F. & Roger G. Weiner, Innocent Third Parties and Their Rights in Forfeiture Proceedings, 28 Am.Crim.L.Rev. 843 (1991).

See also

First Circuit: United States v. Angiulo, 897 F.2d 1169, 1214 (1st Cir.1990) ("[W]e must sustain the jury's forfeiture verdict if, viewing the evidence in the light most favorable to the government, there is substantial evidence to support it.").

PART VI

COLLATERAL CONSEQUENCES OF FEDERAL CRIMINAL LIABILITY

Introduction

Sometimes the collateral consequences which flow from a criminal conviction are as devastating, or more devastating, to a defendant than is the conviction. Certain professionals, for example, lose their professional licenses upon conviction. Individuals or businesses which contract with the federal government may be prevented from completing ongoing contracts or entering into new contracts. For those whose livelihood depends upon such contracts, this action equals financial ruin.

In addition, especially in the area of white collar crime where defendants tend to have assets, those damaged by the defendant's action often are sued civilly. The plaintiff in the civil suit may be a private party or, when the federal or a state government has been defrauded, a governmental entity. In any of these situations, the doctrine of collateral estoppel may alleviate the plaintiff's burden of proof in the civil case by permitting the plaintiff to prove elements in the civil case simply by introducing evidence of conviction in the criminal matter. Complications can arise in parallel actions; for example, if the same governmental entity prosecutes a defendant criminally then sues civilly for damages or forfeiture, constitutional issues of double jeopardy and excessive fines arise. The next three chapters discuss these issues.

*

CHAPTER 30

COLLATERAL ESTOPPEL

Table of Sections

WESTLAW Electronic Research Guide

See WESTLAW Electronic Research Guide preceding the Summary of Contents.

Library References:

C.J.S. Criminal Law § 208.
West's Key No. Digests, Double Jeopardy ⊷3.

§ 30.1 Introduction

Collateral estoppel is a doctrine developed by the courts to promote judicial efficiency. First established in civil cases, this doctrine provides that a party is estopped from relitigating an issue of fact which has already been litigated and resolved in a prior judicial proceeding. Thus the name: the second proceeding is deemed to be "collateral" to the first. Until 1970, collateral estoppel had been only used "defensively": a party was able to defend against liability or damages by demonstrating that certain issues of fact had been resolved in its favor in a prior judicial proceeding. In 1970, however, the Supreme Court dramatically loosened the requirements for collateral estoppel; one result of this change was to permit "offensive" use of collateral estoppel. When used offensively, collateral estoppel absolves a plaintiff from proving a fact essential in obtaining a verdict against a defendant if the plaintiff can demonstrate that the fact has already been found against the defendant in another proceeding, even if the former proceeding was brought by *another* plaintiff.

Use of collateral estoppel when one of the proceedings is a criminal prosecution has been permitted. Several things are clear about such use of collateral estoppel. First, a defendant may use collateral estoppel defensively as long as she was a defendant in both the first and second proceedings and both proceedings were criminal prosecutions. Second, because of the different burdens of proof: preponderance in civil matters and beyond a reasonable doubt in criminal matters, it is not permissible for the government to use collateral estoppel offensively when the first proceeding is civil and the collateral proceeding is criminal. Questions remain however, about other uses of collateral estoppel when criminal liability is at stake, primarily whether such use denies a defendant her constitutional rights to confront witnesses against her and to trial by jury.

§ 30.2 The Elements

The doctrine of collateral estoppel is a court created doctrine which originally provided that "[w]here a question of fact essential to the judgment is actually litigated and determined by a valid and final judgment, the determination is conclusive between the parties."[1] Collateral estoppel is to be distinguished from res judicata which provides that "a judgment on the merits in a prior suit bars a second suit involving the same parties or their privies based on the same cause of action."[2] Thus, while res judicata requires that the cause of action in both proceedings be identical, collateral estoppel requires only that an issue of fact be identical.[3]

In most jurisdictions, the following requirements must be met for collateral estoppel to apply: (1) the issue of fact was actually litigated in the first proceeding, (2) the first proceeding resulted in a valid and final judgment, (3) resolution of the issue of fact was essential to the judgment rendered in the first proceeding, and (4) the issue of fact in both proceedings was identical. Until 1970 a fifth requirement existed—the parties to both proceedings had to be identical. In *Parklane Hosiery Company, Inc. v. Shore*,[4] however, the Supreme Court considered this requirement and held that in some situations where collateral estoppel was invoked, it was not necessary that the parties to both proceedings be identical, it was only necessary that the party *against* whom the prior judgment was being used be a party in both proceedings.[5] Thus, after the Supreme Court's ruling in *Parklane*, "mutuality of parties" was no longer required in federal courts. A number of state courts have followed the Supreme Court's lead, although many still require mutuality of parties.[6]

§ 30.2

1. RESTATEMENT OF JUDGMENTS § 68(1) (1942); CHARLES ALAN WRIGHT, ARTHUR R. MILLER, EDWARD H. COOPER, FEDERAL PRACTICE AND PROCEDURE, §§ 4301–4478 (1981, Supp. 1996).

2. Parklane Hosiery Company, Inc. v. Shore, 439 U.S. 322, 326 n. 5, 99 S.Ct. 645, 649 n. 5, 58 L.Ed.2d 552 (1979).

3. *Id.*

4. 439 U.S. 322, 99 S.Ct. 645, 58 L.Ed.2d 552 (1979).

5. *Id.* at 331.

6. 18 CHARLES ALAN WRIGHT, ET AL, FEDERAL PRACTICE & PROCEDURE, § 4463, n.4,

§ 4464 nn.24–27 (1982). States abandoning mutuality requirement:

Arkansas: J. D. Fisher v. Jones, 311 Ark. 450, 844 S.W.2d 954 (Ark.Sup.Ct. 1993).

Delaware: Messick v. Star Enterprise, 655 A.2d 1209 (Del.Sup.Ct.1995).

Hawaii: Morneau v. Stark Enterprises, Ltd., 56 Haw. 420, 539 P.2d 472 (1975).

Illinois: Herzog v. Lexington Township, 167 Ill.2d 288, 212 Ill.Dec. 581, 657 N.E.2d 926 (Ill.Sup.Ct.1995).

Indiana: Wilcox v. State, 664 N.E.2d 379 (Ind.Ct.App.1996); Sullivan v. Ameri-

§ 30.3 The Demise of the "Mutuality of Parties" Element

In 1976 the Securities and Exchange Commission (SEC) filed suit against Parklane Hosiery Co., Inc. (Parklane) and 13 of its officers, directors and stockholders, alleging that Parklane had issued a materially false and misleading proxy statement.[1] After a trial, the District Court found the proxy statement to be materially false and misleading as

can Casualty Company of Reading, Pennsylvania, 605 N.E.2d 134 (Ind.Sup.Ct.1992).

Iowa: Hall v. Barrett, 412 N.W.2d 648 (Iowa Ct.App.1987).

Maine: Hossler v. Barry, 403 A.2d 762 (Me.1979).

Maryland: Prande v. Bell, 105 Md.App. 636, 660 A.2d 1055 (1995).

Massachusetts: Miles v. Aetna Casualty and Surety Company, 412 Mass. 424, 589 N.E.2d 314 (1992).

Missouri: Arthur v. Evangelical Deaconess Society, 615 S.W.2d 438 (Mo.Ct.App. 1981); MFA Mutual Insurance Company v. Howard Construction Company, 608 S.W.2d 535 (Mo.Ct.App.1980).

Nebraska: State v. Secret, Jr., 246 Neb. 1002, 524 N.W.2d 551 (Neb.Sup.Ct.1994), *overruled on other grounds by*, 255 Neb. 190, 583 N.W.2d 31 (1998).

New Hampshire: Cutter v. Town of Durham, 120 N.H. 110, 411 A.2d 1120 (1980).

New Jersey: Busch v. Biggs, 264 N.J.Super. 385, 624 A.2d 1017 (1993); Perry v. Tuzzio, 288 N.J.Super. 223, 672 A.2d 213 (N.J.Super.Ct.1996).

New York: Koch v. Consolidated Edison Company of New York, Inc., 62 N.Y.2d 548, 479 N.Y.S.2d 163, 468 N.E.2d 1 (N.Y.Ct. App.1984); Davidoff v. Air Surface Coordinators, Inc. and CF, 94 Misc.2d 196, 403 N.Y.S.2d 969 (N.Y.Sup.Ct.1978).

North Carolina: Gardner v. Davis, 123 N.C.App. 527, 473 S.E.2d 640 (N.C.Ct.App. 1996).

Ohio: Balboa Insurance Company v. S.S.D. Distribution System, Inc., 109 Ohio App.3d 523, 672 N.E.2d 718 (Ohio Ct.App. 1996).

Oregon: J.D. Hanson v. Oregon Department of Revenue, 294 Or. 23, 653 P.2d 964 (Or.Sup.Ct.1982) (en banc).

Pennsylvania: Commonwealth v. Martinelli, 128 Pa.Cmwlth. 448, 563 A.2d 973 (1989); Gulentz v. Schanno Transportation, Inc., 355 Pa.Super. 302, 513 A.2d 440 (1986).

South Carolina: South Carolina Property and Casualty Insurance Guaranty Association v. Wal–Mart Stores, Inc., 304 S.C. 210, 403 S.E.2d 625 (1991).

Texas: Robbins v. HNG Oil Company, 878 S.W.2d 351 (Tex.App.1994).

Vermont: Trepanier v. Getting Organized, Inc., 155 Vt. 259, 583 A.2d 583 (1990).

Washington: State v. Dupard, 93 Wash.2d 268, 609 P.2d 961 (Wash.Sup.Ct. 1980) (en banc).

West Virginia: Walden v. Hoke, 189 W.Va. 222, 429 S.E.2d 504 (1993); Galanos v. National Steel Corp., 178 W.Va. 193, 358 S.E.2d 452 (1987).

Wisconsin: Crowall v. Heritage Mutual Insurance Company, 118 Wis.2d 120, 346 N.W.2d 327 (Wis.Ct.App.1984).

States which maintain Mutuality requirement:

Alabama: Jones v. Blanton, 644 So.2d 882 (Ala.Sup.Ct.1994).

Connecticut: Labbe v. Hartford Pension Commission, 239 Conn. 168, 682 A.2d 490 (Conn.Sup.Ct.1996).

Florida: Khan v. Simkins Industries, Inc., 687 So.2d 16 (Fla.Dist.Ct.App.1996).

Kansas: Patrons Mutual Insurance Association v. Harmon, 240 Kan. 707, 732 P.2d 741 (Kan.Sup.Ct.1987).

Kentucky: Montgomery v. Taylor–Green Gas Co., 306 Ky. 256, 206 S.W.2d 919 (1947).

Michigan: Alterman v. Provizer, Eisenberg, Lichtenstein & Pearlman, P.C., 195 Mich.App. 422, 491 N.W.2d 868 (Mich.Ct. App.1992).

Minnesota: Howe v. Nelson, 271 Minn. 296, 135 N.W.2d 687 (Minn.Sup.Ct.1965).

New Mexico: Reeves v. Wimberly, 107 N.M. 231, 755 P.2d 75 (N.M.Ct.App.1988).

Virginia: Race Fork Coal Co. v. Turner, 5 Va.App. 350, 363 S.E.2d 423 (Va.Ct.App. 1987), *rev'd on other grounds*, 237 Va. 639, 379 S.E.2d 341 (1989).

§ 30.3

1. Shore v. Parklane Hosiery Co., Inc., 565 F.2d 815, 816 (2d Cir.1977), *aff'd* 439 U.S. 322, 99 S.Ct. 645, 58 L.Ed.2d 552 (1979).

alleged. It ordered the defendants to amend Parklane's prior filings with the SEC and file all necessary forms with the SEC.[2]

Thereafter, Parklane stockholders filed a class action suit against the same defendants, also alleging that the proxy statement was materially false and misleading, in the same manner as alleged and proven by the SEC in the prior suit. The plaintiffs moved for summary judgment, "asserting that the [defendants] were collaterally estopped from relitigating the issues that had been resolved against them in [the SEC action]."[3] The District Court denied the motion, on the ground that permitting this use of collateral estoppel would deny the defendants their right to a jury trial under the Seventh Amendment.[4] The Court of Appeals for the Second Circuit reversed, finding that the defendants had no right to a jury trial as to issues of fact which they had already had the opportunity to fully and fairly litigate previously, even if the prior opportunity was in a non-jury trial.[5]

The Supreme Court affirmed the holding of the Second Circuit. The Court recognized that the plaintiffs in the second suit (the shareholders) were different than the plaintiff in the first suit since the SEC brought the first suit as an enforcement action,[6] however, the Court noted that the mutuality requirement had been "criticized almost from its inception."[7] The Court reasoned that in some instances, the mutuality of parties requirement served no useful purpose as, for example, when the parties in the prior lawsuit had incentive to fully litigate the issues. The Court found that the defendants in the current case before the Court, as defendants in the prior SEC action, had "every incentive to litigate the SEC lawsuit fully and vigorously."[8] Not only were the allegations in the SEC complaint serious, it was foreseeable that subsequent private suits would "typically follow a successful Government judgment."[9] Thus, they had to allow collateral estoppel. As the Court explained: "Since the petitioners received a 'full and fair' opportunity to litigate their claims in the SEC action, the contemporary law of collateral estoppel leads inescapably to the conclusion that the petitioners are collaterally estopped from relitigating the question [at issue in the SEC action.]"[10]

By not requiring identity of parties in prior and subsequent law suits, the Supreme Court opened the door for "offensive" use of collateral estoppel, whereby "the plaintiff seeks to foreclose the defendant from litigating an issue the defendant has previously litigated unsuccessfully in an action with another party."[11]

---

2. 565 F.2d at 818.

3. 565 F.2d at 818.

4. 439 U.S. at 325, 99 S.Ct. at 648.

5. *Id.*

6. *Id.*

7. *Id.* at 327.

8. *Id.* at 332.

9. *Id.*

10. *Id.* at 332–33.

11. *Id.* at 326 n.4. By comparison, "[d]efensive use occurs when a defendant seeks to prevent a plaintiff from asserting a claim the plaintiff has previously litigated and lost against another defendant." *Id.* For discussion of the mutuality of parties requirement see Laura Gaston Dooley, *The Cult of Finality: Rethinking Collateral Estoppel in the Postmodern Age,* 31 VAL. U.L.REV. 43, 60–62 (1996).

The Court acknowledged that there were disadvantages in permitting offensive use of collateral estoppel. Such use would promote inefficiency in the judicial system since plaintiffs would resist joining together in a single suit against a single defendant, opting instead to "wait and see." If the first plaintiff fails, the next plaintiff—armed with observations from the first trial—would sue the defendant on the same issues. In this sense "potential plaintiffs will have everything to gain and nothing to lose by not intervening in the first action."[12] In addition, the Court noted that offensive use of collateral could be unfair to defendants who would be forced to aggressively defend or lawsuit for the smallest amount of damages so as to protect themselves against more substantial suits which could be brought subsequently by additional plaintiffs. The Supreme Court's holding in *Parklane* attempts to overcome these problems by declining to adopt a per se rule permitting offensive use of collateral estoppel in favor of giving the lower courts discretion as to when they would or would not permit offensive use of collateral estoppel:

> We have concluded that the preferable approach for dealing with these problems in the federal courts is not to preclude the use of offensive collateral estoppel, but to grant trial courts broad discretion to determine when it should be applied. The general rule should be that in cases where a plaintiff could easily have joined in the earlier action or where, either for the reasons discussed above or for other reasons, the application of offensive estoppel would be unfair to a defendant, a trial judge should not allow the use of offensive collateral estoppel.[13]

§ 30.4 Offensive Use of Collateral Estoppel by the Government When All Relevant Proceedings Are Criminal Prosecutions

Bob Fred Ashe and three others were charged with robbing Don Knight during a poker game in which Knight was participating. The government's evidence at trial was that three or four men, armed with pistols and a shotgun, broke into the home of John Gladson while a poker game was in progress and robbed each of the players of money and personal effects.[1] At trial, the government's evidence that Ashe was one of the robbers was weak; none of the witnesses offered strong evidence identifying Ashe as one of the robbers. Ashe was acquitted.

Following the acquittal of Ashe on the charges of robbing Don Knight, Ashe was tried again, this time on charges of robbing another player at the same game. Ashe sought dismissal of these charges on the ground "that the second prosecution ... violated his right not to be

---

12. *Id.* at 330.   (1970).
13. *Id.* at 331.

§ 30.4
1. Ashe v. Swenson, 397 U.S. 436, 437, 90 S.Ct. 1189, 1191, 25 L.Ed.2d 469

twice put in jeopardy."[2] Ashe lost this argument before the trial court, the Missouri Supreme Court and, on collateral appeal, before the United States District Court and United States Court of Appeals for the Eighth Circuit. At the Supreme Court, however, Ashe was victorious. In *Ashe v.Swenson* the Court held that collateral estoppel "is embodied in the Fifth Amendment guarantee against double jeopardy"[3] and protects "a man who has been acquitted from having to 'run the gauntlet' a second time."[4] Examining the trial testimony and jury instructions, the Court had little difficulty finding that the jury in the first trial found the evidence insufficient to prove that Ashe was one of the robbers.[5] Because the same factual issue was at the heart of the second prosecution, the second prosecution was barred: "the State could not present the same or different identification evidence in a second prosecution for the robbery of Knight in the hope that a different jury might find that evidence more convincing."[6]

Ashe v. Swenson has been heavily criticized. One criticism is that any right to collateral estoppel is more properly found in the Fifth Amendment's protection of due process, rather than in the Fifth Amendment's protection against double jeopardy.[7] As one commentator explained, blending collateral estoppel into double jeopardy confuses the two similar, but distinct doctrines:

> [T]he *Ashe* opinion did not persuasively provide a source for collateral estoppel in double jeopardy. The two doctrines share similar policy concerns, but collateral estoppel, as the Seventh Circuit recently noted, 'is applicable in criminal cases only when the double jeopardy is not.' The Double Jeopardy Clause bars reprosecution entirely when a defendant has already been in jeopardy for the same offense; if these conditions do not apply, collateral estoppel is a more precise tool that bars relitigation of specific facts, whether or not jeopardy attached for the offense in question in the previous or subsequent trials.[8]

Critics assert that the practical significance of this "doctrinal confusion" is the "erosion" of collateral estoppel as a defense and point to the Supreme Court's decision in *Dowling v. United States*,[9] as evidence of such erosion.

Reuben Dowling was charged with bank robbery and armed robbery for robbing a bank and a bank customer in St. Croix, Virgin Islands, of cash and personal travelers' checks.[10] He was convicted and sentenced to 70 years imprisonment. The key issue was identity. At trial, the government was permitted to introduce evidence from a woman, Ms. Vena

---

2. *Id.* at 440.

3. *Id.* at 445.

4. *Id.* at 446.

5. *Id.* at 444–46.

6. *Id.* at 446.

7. Note, *The Due Process Roots of Criminal Collateral Estoppel*, 109 HARV. L.REV. 1729 (1996).

8. *Id.* at 1735.

9. 493 U.S. 342, 110 S.Ct. 668, 107 L.Ed.2d 708 (1990).

10. *Id.* at 344.

Henry, that two men, one of whom she identified as Dowling, had robbed her at gun point, in her home, approximately two weeks after the bank robbery. Despite the fact that Dowling had previously been acquitted of committing the home robbery of Ms. Henry, the government sought introduction of Ms. Henry's testimony at Dowling's bank robbery trial on two grounds: first, that her description of Dowling and the modus operandi of her home robbery matched the description and modus operandi of the bank robbers, second, the second man identified by Ms. Henry was the same individual suspected of driving the planned getaway car after the bank robbery.[11]

Dowling argued that his acquittal on charges of robbing Ms. Henry collaterally estopped the government from using the evidence in any manner at his bank robbery trial.[12] The Court disagreed, finding that Dowling's prior acquittal "did not determine the *ultimate issue* in the bank robbery case."[13] The Court noted that it "decline[d] to use the Due Process Clause as a device for extending the double jeopardy protection to cases where it otherwise would not extend."[14]

This reasoning, according to the *Ashe v. Swenson* critics, shows the problem in anchoring collateral estoppel in the double jeopardy protection rather than in due process. Arguably, if the Court had tied the defendants' protective use of collateral estoppel to the due process clause, it could more easily weigh the fundamental fairness issues inherent in allowing admission of acts for which a defendant has been acquitted.

Whatever the doctrinal wisdom of the Supreme Court's reasoning in *Ashe*, the Court's holdings in *Ashe* and *Dowling* have opened the door to use of collateral estoppel in criminal actions. The issue now winding its way through the courts—and being resolved inconsistently—is how aggressively the government may use collateral estoppel offensively against defendants. The Eighth and Ninth Circuits have approved the government's use of collateral estoppel against defendants. The Third and Eleventh Circuits have disapproved such use.

The Ninth Circuit's opinion in *United States v. Colacurcio*,[15] demonstrates the view that offensive use of collateral estoppel by the government against a defendant in a criminal prosecution is permissible, assuming of course, that all elements of collateral estoppel are met. Frank F. Colacurcio was convicted of income tax evasion for the years 1967–1969. Previously, he had been convicted of conspiring with others to promote bingo games in violation of the laws of the State of Washing-

---

11. *Id.* at 344–45. The government sought introduction of this evidence under Federal Rule of Evidence 404(b) which provides that evidence of other crimes, wrongs, or acts may be admissible against a defendant for purposes such as proving motive, opportunity, intent, etc., and other than as character evidence. *Cf.* Cynthia L. Randall, Comment: *Acquittals in Jeopardy: Criminal*

Collateral Estoppel and the Use of Acquitted Act Evidence 141 U.PaL.Rev. 283 (1992).

12. *Id.* at 346.

13. *Id.* at 342.

14. *Id.* at 354.

15. 514 F.2d 1 (9th Cir.1975).

ton.[16] At Colacurcio's income tax evasion trial, the government introduced evidence from the bingo conspiracy case as to sums of money received by the defendant from the bingo games. This evidence was used by the government to calculate the defendant's true taxable income for years in question. The jury was instructed to accept these figures in its deliberations on the tax evasion charges.[17]

The defendant argued, in part, that permitting use of collateral estoppel against him deprived him of his Sixth Amendment rights of trial by jury and confrontation of witnesses. The Ninth Circuit rejected these arguments. It found that when the facts regarding his bingo payments were litigated during his conspiracy trial, Colacurcio had the opportunity to cross examine all witnesses against him and to trial by jury.[18] Thus, while recognizing that most reported cases dealing with use of collateral estoppel in criminal cases concerned instances in which the doctrine is invoked by a defendant for the defendant's benefit, the court held that the government's offensive use of collateral estoppel against a defendant was permissible when all elements of collateral estoppel were met. Having approved of offensive use of collateral estoppel by the government in a criminal prosecution in principle, the court turned to the facts before it. It found that not all elements were met: although the fact that bingo payments were made to the defendant had been decided and was essential to a judgment in the prior case, the *amount* of the payments had not been decided. According to the court, "Since the amount of the [bingo] payments was not a necessary element of the conviction in the prior case and was not 'distinctly put in issue and directly determined,' it was not subject to collateral estoppel."[19]

The Third Circuit's opinion in *United States v. Pelullo*,[20] demonstrates the view that the government should not be able to use collateral estoppel offensively against a defendant in a criminal case. Leonard A. Pelullo was charged with wire fraud and RICO arising from alleged diversion of corporate funds. The jury hung in Pelullo's first trial; Pelullo was convicted in his second trial. However, all counts, with one exception (Count 54), were reversed because of evidentiary errors committed by the trial court. In Pelullo's third trial, the government introduced the judgment of conviction obtained on Count 54 from the second trial. Count 54 charged a violation of wire fraud arising from the diversion of particular corporate funds and constituted one predicate act listed in the RICO count. The court instructed the jury that "as a matter of law, the defendant has committed the wire fraud offense described in Racketeering Act 60. That means you don't have to consider whether the government has proved this offense."[21]

16. *Id.* at 2–3.
17. *Id.* at 3.
18. *Id.* at 6.
19. *Id.* at 6. *See also* Hernandez–Uribe v. United States, 515 F.2d 20 (8th Cir. 1975) (Government permitted to use defendant's prior convictions for unlawfully entering the United States as an alien in a current prosecution for the same offense.)

20. 14 F.3d 881 (3d Cir.1994).
21. *Id.* at 887.

Acknowledging that courts have accepted the position that prior convictions are admissible to show predicate acts in a RICO prosecution, Pellullo argued that permitting the government to "present evidence of the actual judgment of conviction from a previous jury trial on the same indictment[22] deprived him of his right to a jury trial."[23] The Third Circuit agreed. It found that the only argument in favor of applying collateral estoppel (of which, the court conceded, all elements were met) was "efficient judicial administration and judicial perceptions of expeditious public policy."[24] In the court's view, this benefit was outweighed by the defendant's constitutionally guaranteed right to a jury trial.[25] The Court noted that collateral estoppel originated in the context of civil litigation, where, in the United States, the Seventh Amendment governs the right to a jury trial. The Seventh Amendment's right to a jury is not absolute (the right to trial is "preserved to the extent it existed at common law when the Amendment was ratified in 1791.")[26] By comparison, the Sixth Amendment's right to a jury trial, which controls in criminal cases, is absolute ("In all criminal prosecutions, the accused shall enjoy the right to a speedy and public trial, by an impartial jury.") Based on this distinction, the Third Circuit held, "[T]he right to a jury trial ... in every and all criminal prosecutions ... necessitates that every jury empaneled for a prosecution considers evidence of guilt afresh and without the judicial direction attending collateral estoppel."[27]

In summary, while offensive use of collateral estoppel is recognized in the federal courts as appropriate in civil cases, even when there are different plaintiffs in the two proceedings, offensive use of collateral estoppel in criminal matters is controversial and recognized only in some courts. Defensive use of collateral estoppel, however, is well recognized in the civil and criminal arenas with the caveat that it is permissible in a criminal matter only if the prior proceeding was also a criminal case.

§ 30.5 Use of Collateral Estoppel When a Civil Proceeding Follows a Criminal Prosecution

Collateral estoppel has been asserted, and found applicable, when the government successfully convicts a defendant, then seeks to obtain summary judgment in a subsequent civil suit, on the ground that some

---

22. *Id.* at 888.

23. *Id.* at 889.

24. *Id.* at 891.

25. *Id.*

26. The Seventh Amendment states:

In suits a common law, where the value in controversy shall exceed twenty dollars, the right to trial by jury shall be preserved, and no fact tried by jury, shall be otherwise re-examined in any Court of the United States, than according to the rules of the common law.

27. *Id.* at 896. *See also* United States v. Harnage, 976 F.2d 633 (11th Cir.1992)

(Held that the government could not prevent the defendant, charged with conspiracy to distribute marijuana, from litigating whether communications with his attorney were privileged even though this issue had been decided against the defendant in another criminal case. Applying collateral estoppel against a defendant, the Court held,

"would create more problems than it was designed to solve. We are not convinced that allowing the government to bar a defendant from relitigating an unfavorable determination of facts in a prior proceeding would serve the original goal of collateral estoppel—judicial economy.") *Id.* at 635.

or all of the facts at issue in the civil action were litigated and resolved against the defendant in the criminal action. Moreover, because of the lesser burden of proof in the subsequent civil proceeding, the government is not collaterally estopped when the prior criminal prosecution concludes with acquittal or dismissal.[1]

Most recently, use of collateral estoppel in a civil action after a related criminal action has arisen in the context of civil forfeitures where the government obtains summary judgment in an in rem forfeiture action based upon a defendant's conviction on criminal charges arising from the same facts.[2] The elements which must be proven in a civil forfeiture action are (1) the property was involved in (2) specific criminal activity such as drug crimes or money laundering. The elements which must be proven in a related criminal action are (1) the defendant (2) intentionally (3) engaged in certain criminal conduct such as illegal drug dealing or money laundering. Sometimes evidence linking the property to crime will be presented, fully litigated and necessary to the criminal conviction, but not always. When it is not, only a partial summary, if any at all, will be possible.[3]

Although *Parklane* did away with the mutuality of parties requirement for plaintiffs seeking to use offensive collateral estoppel, it is still necessary that the defendant be the same in both proceedings. Although the defendant in the criminal action and the property, as defendant in the forfeiture action, will not be the same, courts tend to overlook this discrepancy as long as the claimant to the property was the defendant in the prior criminal action.[4]

§ 30.5

1. United States v. One Assortment of 89 Firearms, 465 U.S. 354, 360, 104 S.Ct. 1099, 1103, 79 L.Ed.2d 361 (1984).

2. DAVID B. SMITH, PROSECUTION AND DEFENSE OF FORFEITURE CASES, § 10.06[2] (1996);

See, e.g.:

Supreme Court: United States v. Ursery, 518 U.S. 267, 116 S.Ct. 2135, 135 L.Ed.2d 549 (1996) (Government's motion for summary judgment was granted in forfeiture action brought under 18 U.S.C. § 981(a)(1)(A) alleging money laundering and under 21 U.S.C. § 881(a)(6) as the proceeds of a felonious drug transaction, after the defendants were convicted on drug and money laundering charges under 21 U.S.C. § 846 and 18 U.S.C. §§ 371 and 1956. *Id.* at 2137).

Eleventh Circuit: United States v. One Single Family Residence Located at 18755 North Bay Road Miami, 13 F.3d 1493 (11th Cir.1994) (Government's motion for summary judgment was granted in forfeiture action brought under 18 U.S.C. § 1955(d) alleging gambling violations after defendants had been convicted of gambling in violation of 18 U.S.C. § 1955(a).)

3. *See, e.g.:*

Sixth Circuit: United States v. Smith, 730 F.2d 1052, 1057 (6th Cir.1984) (reversed granting of summary judgment in forfeiture action because issue of use of property to facilitate drug offense not actually litigated nor necessary in the criminal trial).

Ninth Circuit: United States v. Real Property Located at Section 18, 976 F.2d 515, 518–19 (9th Cir.1992) (reversed granting of summary judgment in forfeiture action because guilty plea did not resolve issues concerning use of property in drug offense).

4. *See, e.g.:*

Second Circuit: United States v. $228,-536 in U.S. Currency, 895 F.2d 908, 915–16 (2d Cir.1990); United States v. $26,660 in U.S. Currency, 777 F.2d 111, 112 (2d Cir. 1985).

Fifth Circuit: United States v. Monkey, 725 F.2d 1007, 1010 (5th Cir.1984); United States v. One 1976 Mercedes 450 SLC, 667 F.2d 1171, 1176 (5th Cir.1982).

Cf. DAVID B. SMITH, PROSECUTION AND DEFENSE OF FORFEITURE CASES § 12.09[6] (1996).

An interesting question arises when the defendant is acquitted in the criminal case yet the government seeks to obtain forfeiture in a subsequent civil in rem action against the property involved in the transaction at issue in the criminal case. Initially, the Supreme Court held that the defendant could use collateral estoppel defensively to prevent the civil forfeiture. In *Coffey v. United States*,[5] the government sought forfeiture against 10 barrels of apple brandy, various equipment used to distill the brandy and land belonging to A.G. Coffey, which had been used for the distilling activity.[6] Previously, Coffey had been acquitted on various tax and fraud charges arising from the same facts set forth as grounds for the forfeiture (failure to pay tax on distilled spirits). The Court ruled that the judgment in the criminal action was conclusive in the civil action, despite the difference in burdens of proof in the criminal action (beyond a reasonable doubt) and the civil forfeiture action (preponderance of proof). The Court reasoned: "[T]he fact or act has been put in issue and determined against the United States; and all that is imposed by the statute, as a consequence of guilt, is a punishment therefor. There could be no new trial of the criminal prosecution after the acquittal in it; and a subsequent trial of the civil suit amounts of substantially the same thing, with a difference only in the consequences following a judgment adverse to the claimant."[7]

Almost one century later, *Coffey* was reversed by the Supreme Court. In *United States v. One Assortment of 89 Firearms*,[8] the Court was faced with almost identical facts. The government sought forfeiture of property (a cache of firearms) after the owner of the property had been acquitted of firearm offenses (knowingly engaging in the business of dealing in firearms without a license, in violation of 18 U.S.C. § 922(a)(1)). After overruling *Coffey*,[9] the court noted that "an acquittal on criminal charges does not prove that the defendant is innocent; it merely proves the existence of a reasonable doubt as to his guilt. ... [T]he jury verdict in the criminal action did not negate the possibility that a preponderance of the evidence could show that [the defendant] was engaged in an unlicensed firearms business."[10]

In summary, it is well recognized that collateral estoppel may be used offensively by the government when the civil proceeding follows the criminal proceeding.

5. 116 U.S. 436, 6 S.Ct. 437, 29 L.Ed. 684 (1886).

6. *Id.* at 436.

7. *Id.* at 443.

8. 465 U.S. 354, 104 S.Ct. 1099, 79 L.Ed.2d 361 (1984).

9. "The time has come to clarify that neither collateral estoppel nor double jeopardy bars a civil, remedial forfeiture proceeding initiated following an acquittal on related criminal charges. To the extent that Coffey v. United States suggests otherwise, it is hereby disapproved." *Id.* at 361.

10. *Id.* at 361 citing Helvering v. Mitchell, 303 U.S. 391, 397, 58 S.Ct. 630, 632, 82 L.Ed. 917 (1938) (Court held that collateral estoppel did not bar action by Commissioner of IRS to recover a substantial monetary penalty for fraudulent avoidance of income tax after acquittal in prior criminal action against defendant taxpayer.)

§ 30.6 Bibliography

Dooley, Laura Gaston, *The Cult of Finality: Rethinking Collateral Estoppel in the Postmodern Age*, 31 VAL. U.L. REV. 43, 60–62 (1996).

Note, *The Due Process Roots of Criminal Collateral Estoppel*, 109 HARV. L.REV. 1729 (1996).

Randall, Cynthia L., Comment: *Acquittals in Jeopardy: Criminal Collateral Estoppel and the Use of Acquitted Act Evidence* 141 U.PA.L.REV. 283 (1992).

RESTATEMENT OF JUDGMENTS § 68(1) (1942).

UNITED STATES DEPARTMENT OF JUSTICE, U.S. ATTORNEYS MANUAL.

WRIGHT, CHARLES ALAN, MILLER, ARTHUR R., COOPER, EDWARD H., FEDERAL PRACTICE AND PROCEDURE, § 468 (1981, Supp. 1996).

CHAPTER 31

CONSTITUTIONAL ISSUES IN PARALLEL PROCEEDINGS.

Table of Sections

WESTLAW Electronic Research Guide

See WESTLAW Electronic Research Guide preceding the Summary of Contents.

---

§ 31.1   *United States v. Halper*

For almost a decade (1989–1997), the paramount constitutional concern in parallel proceedings was double jeopardy. This concern began with the Supreme Court's decision in *United States v. Halper*.[1]

Decided in 1989, *Halper* transformed double jeopardy from a little-used, theoretical issue to a gangbuster defense.[2] Irwin Halper was the manager of New City Medical Laboratories, Inc., which provided medical laboratory services for patients covered by Medicare. In 1985, Halper was convicted on 81 felony counts of mail fraud and submitting false claims to the federal Medicare program. The government's evidence showed that in 65 claims for reimbursement, Halper misrepresented the laboratory service performed on patients, thereby collecting $12 per claim, instead of $3. Upon conviction Halper was sentenced to two years imprisonment and fined $5,000.

Thereafter, the federal government sued Halper for damages under the civil False Claims Act.[3] The claims at issue in this civil suit were the same claims for which Halper had been convicted. Halper argued that the civil suit was barred by the Fifth Amendment's prohibition against

---

§ 31.1

1.   490 U.S. 435, 109 S.Ct. 1892, 104 L.Ed.2d 487 (1989).

2.   For sources discussing the significance of *Halper*, see Stanley E. Cox, *Halper's Continuing Double Jeopardy Implications: A Thorn By Any Other Name Would Prick As Deep*, 39 St.L.U.L.J., 1235, 1236–37 (1995); George C. Thomas, III, *A Blame-worthy Act Approach to the Double Jeopardy Same Offense Problem*, 83 Cal.L.Rev. 1027, 1058–60 (1995); Linda S. Eads, *Separating Crime From Punishment: The Constitutional Implications of United States v. Halper*, 68 Wash.U.L.Q. 929, 929–31 (1990).

3.   31 U.S.C. § 3729 et seq. (1994).

double jeopardy. The Supreme Court held that in "the rare case," double jeopardy may bar parallel civil actions.

Until *Halper*, it was assumed that only criminal prosecutions activated the double jeopardy prohibition. In *Halper*, however, the Supreme Court held that civil liability—when brought by the same sovereign which had prosecuted the defendant—"may constitute punishment for the purpose of the Double Jeopardy Clause."[4] Noting that "the labels 'criminal' and 'civil' are not of paramount importance,"[5] the Supreme Court stated:

> [U]nder the Double Jeopardy Clause a defendant who already has been punished in a criminal prosecution may not be subjected to an additional civil sanction to the extent that the second sanction may not fairly be characterized as remedial, but only as a deterrent or retribution.[6]

The key in determining whether double jeopardy bars a civil suit based on the same transaction as a preceding criminal prosecution against the same defendant is whether the civil action is "punitive." To assess the punitiveness of a civil action, one is to examine the damages sustained by the government. If the "penalty sought in the [civil] proceeding bears no rational relation to the goal of compensating the government for its loss," the civil penalty may constitute a second punishment.[7] After setting forth this guidance, the Supreme Court remanded Halper's case to the District Court for a calculation of the government's actual cost arising from Halper's fraud and an assessment of whether the penalty assessed against Halper under the False Claims Act "is sufficiently disproportionate" to this actual cost "that the sanction constitutes a second punishment in violation of double jeopardy."[8]

Not surprisingly, after the Court's decision in *Halper*, defendants sued civilly by the government routinely asserted a *"Halper"* defense if they have been prosecuted previously for the same offense.[9] Similarly, defendants prosecuted criminally after being found liable civilly in a related civil action, argued that the criminal action constituted double jeopardy.[10] The courts rarely held that double jeopardy existed, however, finding in most cases that the civil remedy was not "punitive" under the *Halper* test and thus did not activate double jeopardy.[11]

4. 490 U.S. at 449, 109 S.Ct. at 1902.

5. *Id.* at 447.

6. *Id.* at 448–49.

7. *Id.* at 449.

8. 490 U.S. at 452, 109 S.Ct. at 1903.

9. *See, e.g.:*

First Circuit: United States v. Emerson, 107 F.3d 77, 82–83 (1st Cir.1997).

Sixth Circuit: United States v. Alt, 83 F.3d 779, 781–83 (6th Cir.1996).

10. *See, e.g.:*

Seventh Circuit: United States v. Furlett, 781 F.Supp. 536, 538–47 (N.D.Ill.1991).

Tenth Circuit: United States v. Bizzell, 921 F.2d 263, 266–67 (10th Cir.1990).

11. *See, e.g.:*

First Circuit: Emerson, 107 F.3d at 82–83.

Fifth Circuit: United States v. Boutte, 907 F.Supp. 239, 242–43 (E.D.Tx.1995).

Sixth Circuit: Alt, 83 F.3d at 781–83.

Seventh Circuit: Furlett, 781 F.Supp. at 538–47.

Eighth Circuit: United States v. Peters, 927 F.Supp. 363, 369–70 (D.Neb.1996), aff'd, 110 F.3d 616 (8th Cir.1997).

After *Halper*, defendants also attempted a "reverse" *Halper* argument, advocating that a prior civil sanction was punitive under the *Halper* test and precluded criminal prosecution of the same defendant for the same transaction. Most courts facing this issue held that the preceding civil action is remedial not punitive[12] and thus that there was no double jeopardy problem. However, in resolving these cases the courts have seemed willing to accept that *Halper* applied in the "reverse" situation whenever the civil sanction is deemed punitive. The reasoning of the United States Court of Appeals for the Eleventh Circuit was typical:

> "[W]e recognize that in *Halper* the civil penalty followed a criminal conviction, while in the instant case, the civil penalty precedes the criminal proceeding. We believe that the order of proceedings matters not to the analysis; the *Halper* principle that a civil penalty can be factored into the double jeopardy matrix should apply whether the civil penalty precedes or follows the criminal proceeding."[13]

Halper's influence ended in 1997 with the Supreme Court's decision in Hudson v. United States,[14] where the Supreme Court "in large part disavow[ed] the method of analysis used in [*Halper*]."[15] Hudson and his colleagues were bank officials and shareholders of two banks in Oklahoma. An investigation by the Office of the Comptroller of the Currency (OCC) concluded that they "had used their bank positions to arrange a series of loans to third parties, in violation of various federal banking statutes and regulations."[16] The OCC issued an assessment of penalties and barred them from further participation "in the conduct of any

Tenth Circuit: Bernstein v. Sullivan, 914 F.2d 1395, 1403 (10th Cir.1990); *Bizzell*, 921 F.2d at 266–67.

But see:

Seventh Circuit: Healy Co. v. OSHA, 96 F.3d 906, 911 (7th Cir.1996), *cert. granted, judgment vacated*, 118 S.Ct. 623, 139 L.Ed.2d 604 (1997).

12. *See, e.g.*:

First Circuit: United States v. Stoller, 78 F.3d 710, 715–23 (1st Cir.1996) (Although either criminal or civil proceedings instituted by the same sovereign may result in punishment sufficient to violate the double jeopardy protection; civil remedy here (FDIC debarment of former CEO of bank) was remedial and did not bar subsequent prosecution).

Fifth Circuit: United States v. Gonzalez, 76 F.3d 1339, 1343–47 (5th Cir.1996) (remanded to determine whether civil forfeiture was punitive, preventing subsequent criminal prosecution.) Although the Supreme Court resolved that civil forfeiture is not punishment in United States v. Ursery, 518 U.S. 267, 116 S.Ct. 2135, 135 L.Ed.2d 549 (1996) the point of this case remains: courts will invalidate a subsequent criminal prosecution if prior civil action is punitive. United States v. Perez, 70 F.3d 345, 347 (5th Cir.1995), *cert. granted, judgment vacated*, 117 S.Ct. 478, 136 L.Ed.2d 373 (1996) (holding that civil forfeiture was punitive and barred subsequent criminal prosecution); United States v. Sanchez–Escareno, 950 F.2d 193, 198–201 (5th Cir.1991) (drug importation fines were not punishment, preventing subsequent criminal prosecution).

Tenth Circuit: United States v. Hudson, 14 F.3d 536, 539–41 (10th Cir.1994) (Order of Office of Comptroller of Currency to defendants to refrain from participating in further banking activities was remedial and did not bar subsequent prosecution for banking crimes).

13. *Id.* at 1127.

14. __ U.S. __, 118 S.Ct. 488, 139 L.Ed.2d 450 (1997).

15. *Id.* at 491.

16. *Id.* at 492.

insured depository institution."[17] Thereafter, all were charged in a 22–count indictment alleging conspiracy, misapplication of bank funds and making false bank entries. The defendants' motion to dismiss the charges on grounds of double jeopardy was denied. The Supreme Court affirmed the denial.

Describing the *Halper* decision as "ill-considered,"[18] the Court noted that the *Halper* Court "deviated from traditional double jeopardy doctrine."[19] To determine whether the double jeopardy protection was applicable, the *Halper* Court focused on whether the sanction at issue appeared excessive in relation to its nonpunitive purposes. Instead, according to the Court in *Hudson,* the *Halper* Court should have focused on the traditional double jeopardy question: whether the punishment at issue is "criminal." The Court noted that:

> Whether a particular punishment is criminal or civil, is at least initially, a matter of statutory construction. A court must first ask whether the legislature, in establishing the penalizing mechanism, indicated either expressly or impliedly a preference for one label or the other.[20]

Holding that *Halper's* test for determining whether a particular sanction is punitive "has proved unworkable,"[21] the Court emphasized the importance of Congress' intent. In the case before it, the Court held that "[i]t is evident that Congress intended the OCC money penalties and debarment sanctions ... to be civil in nature."[22] Moreover, the Court found "little evidence, much less the clearest proof we require, suggesting that the OCC money penalties or debarment sanctions are 'so punitive in form and effect as to render them criminal despite Congress' intent to the contrary.' "[23] While recognizing that the OCC sanctions would deter others from conduct similar to that of the defendants and that deterrence is a traditional goal of criminal punishments, the Court nevertheless held that "the mere presence of this purpose is insufficient to render a sanction criminal."[24]

The Court concluded by noting that "some of the ills at which *Halper* was directed are addressed by other constitutional provisions[,]" including the Due Process and Equal Protection clauses and the protection against excessive fines contained in the Eighth Amendment.[25]

§ 31.2 *Austin v. United States*

In 1993, the Supreme Court held that a constitutional protection previously assumed to apply only in criminal cases also applied in civil cases. At issue was the Excessive Fines Clause of Eighth Amendment. In

17. *Id.*
18. *Id.* at 494.
19. *Id.*
20. *Id.* at 493 (internal quotation marks and citations deleted).
21. *Id.* at 494.

22. *Id.* at 495.
23. *Id.*
24. *Id.* at 496.
25. *Id.* at 495.

Austin v. United States,[1] the Court held that at least one type of civil liability—*in rem* civil forfeiture—was subject to this Eighth Amendment protection.

In 1990, Richard Lyle Austin pled guilty to one count of possession of cocaine with intent to distribute, in violation of South Dakota's drug laws. Soon thereafter the United States filed an in rem civil forfeiture action under 21 U.S.C. § 881(a)(4), (7). The government sought forfeiture of Austin's automobile body shop and nearby mobile home. It presented evidence that Austin met an individual at the body shop, agreed to sell him cocaine, went to his [Austin's] mobile home and returned to the body shop with 2 grams of cocaine, which he sold to the individual. Upon execution of a search warrant on the body shop and mobile home police found marijuana, cocaine, a weapon and ammunition, drug paraphernalia and approximately $4700 in cash. The District Court rejected Austin's argument that forfeiture violated the Eighth Amendment and entered summary judgment for the Government.[2]

The Supreme Court reversed. Emphasizing once again that "[t]he notion of punishment ...cuts across the division between the civil and the criminal law," the Court examined the history of civil forfeiture to determine whether it should be viewed as punishment. Finding that civil forfeiture was designed to serve some punitive and some remedial goals, the Court held that if the civil forfeiture served *only* a remedial purpose, it was not subject to the Eighth Amendment's protection. However, if the civil forfeiture served a retributive or deterrent purpose *in addition to a* remedial purpose, the civil forfeiture was subject to the Eighth Amendment's protection.[3] After so ruling, the Court remanded *Austin* to determine whether the forfeiture of the mobile home and auto body shop, was excessive in light of the distribution offense committed on the property.[4] The Supreme Court expressly declined the opportunity to identify factors relevant in assessing whether a fine was excessive under the Eighth Amendment in favor of allowing the lower courts to do so. Factors used by lower courts include the seriousness of the defendant's conduct including its "moral gravity" and the "magnitude and nature of its harmful reach;" the benefit reaped by the defendant; the defendant's motive and culpability; the extent to which, in cases of forfeiture, the property is tainted by criminal conduct.[5]

§ 31.3 *Department of Revenue v. Kurth Ranch*

In 1994, the Supreme Court decided *Department of Revenue v. Kurth Ranch*.[1] For the third time in five years, the Court held that a civil

---

§ 31.2

1. 509 U.S. 602, 113 S.Ct. 2801, 125 L.Ed.2d 488 (1993).

2. *Id.* at 604.

3. *Id.* at 605.

4. *Id.* at 606.

5. *First Circuit*: United States v. Emerson, 107 F.3d 77, 80–81 (1st Cir.1997);

United States v. Pilgrim Market Corporation, 944 F.2d 14, 21–22 (1st Cir.1991).

Third Circuit: United States v. Sarbello, 985 F.2d 716, 724 (3d Cir.1993).

§ 31.3

1. 511 U.S. 767, 114 S.Ct. 1937, 128 L.Ed.2d 767 (1994).

sanction was subject to a constitutional protection previously assumed as applicable only to criminal sanctions. At issue was a tax levied on persons who had been convicted of various drug offenses. The Court held that the drug tax constituted a second punishment and thus violated the prohibition against double jeopardy.[2]

The tax had been levied by the Montana Revenue Department, in an administrative proceeding, on the possession and storage of the marijuana which the Kurth ranch owners and family had been convicted of growing on the ranch.[3] Although citing *Halper* for the proposition that the tax "has punitive characteristics that subject it to the constraints of the Double Jeopardy Clause,"[4] the Court found, however, that *Halper's* method of determining whether a sanction is remedial or punitive (comparing the sanction to the damage suffered by the government) "simply does not work in the case of a tax statute." Instead, according to the Court, other characteristics of the tax statute were relevant: (1) the amount of tax imposed, (2) the purpose of the tax, (3) whether the tax required a conviction, and (4) whether the tax was assessed on property of the taxpayer. Although the Montana tax was high (8 times the marijuana's value) and had an "obvious deterrent purpose," the Supreme Court found that these two characteristics did not "automatically mark[] this tax a form of punishment."[5] Two other characteristics of the tax, however, led the Court to conclude that the tax was punitive: first, the tax was conditioned on the commission of a crime and second, it was levied on property (drugs) the taxpayer no longer had.[6] As contraband, the property (illegal drugs) had been destroyed at the time the tax was levied. According to the Court: "A tax on 'possession' of goods that no longer exist and that the taxpayer never lawfully possessed has an unmistakable punitive character."[7] The Court concluded that the latter two characteristics of the Montana tax made it "depart[] so far from normal revenue laws as to become a form of punishment."[8]

§ 31.4   *United States v. Ursery*

In 1996, the Supreme Court clarified its prior decisions of *Austin* and *Kurth Ranch* in *United States v. Ursery*.[1] The Court reaffirmed its position in *Halper* and *Kurth Ranch* that civil sanctions activate the double jeopardy protection of the Fifth Amendment if those sanctions are punitive. The Court also reaffirmed its position in *Austin* that forfeitures are subject to the Excessive Fines clause. However, the Court

---

2. *Id.* at 784.

3. MONT. CODE ANN. § 15–25–111 (1987).

4. 510 U.S. at 210, 114 S.Ct. at 778.

5. *Id.* at 779.

6. Montana's tax was not conditioned on a conviction, only the arrest, Mont.Admin.Rule 42.–34.102 (1) (1988). *But see Kurth Ranch*, 114 S.Ct. at 1950–51 (Rehnquist, J., dissenting) (suggesting that this administrative rule did not require the commission of a crime but simply acknowledged

the reality that taxes on illegal activity likely will be imposed only after the taxpayer is arrested for such activity.)

7. 511 U.S. 767, 114 S.Ct. 1937, 128 L.Ed.2d 767.

8. *Id.*

§ 31.4

1. 518 U.S. 267, 116 S.Ct. 2135, 135 L.Ed.2d 549 (1996).

demonstrated, once again, its difficulty with *Halper*. Cutting back on *Halper's* reach, the Court distinguished among civil sanctions for purposes of the Fifth Amendment, drawing a bright line between civil *forfeiture* and civil *penalties*. Whereas criminal penalties were at issue in *Halper* and a drug tax was at issue in *Kurth Ranch*, civil forfeitures were before the Court in *Ursery*. Focusing on the history and purpose of the civil forfeiture sanction, the Court held that the civil forfeiture is not punishment and thus does not activate the double jeopardy provision.

Two cases were consolidated in this 1996 decision: *United States v. Ursery* and *United States v. $405,089.23 in United States Currency*.[2] In *Ursery*, the United States filed civil forfeiture proceedings against a house owned by Guy Ursery on the ground that the house had been used to process and distribute marijuana.[3] Next, a grand jury indicted Ursery on federal charges of manufacturing marijuana, in violation of 21 U.S.C. § 841(A)(1). Ursery settled the forfeiture action prior to his conviction on the criminal charges. On appeal, Ursery argued that his criminal conviction constituted double jeopardy. The United States Court of Appeals for the Sixth Circuit agreed and reversed Ursery's criminal conviction, holding that his conviction violated the Double Jeopardy Clause of the Fifth Amendment.[4] To reach its conclusion the Sixth Circuit quickly resolved the issue of whether civil forfeiture is punishment for purposes of double jeopardy by citing to the Supreme Court's description in *Austin* of civil forfeiture as punishment.[5] Noting that the double jeopardy clause protects the accused from multiple punishments in multiple proceedings only for *the same offense*, the Sixth Circuit spent most of its analysis on the issue of whether a criminal conviction and civil forfeiture were the same offense. The court held that the two sanctions were the same offense even though forfeiture requires proof that *property* has been involved in a criminal violation and prosecution requires proof that a *person* has been involved in a criminal offense.[6] The court reasoned, "The criminal offense is in essence subsumed by the forfeiture statute and thus does not require an element of proof that is not required by the forfeiture action."[7]

In *U.S. Currency*, consolidated with *Ursery*, Charles Wesley Arlt and James Wren had been indicted on various drug and money laundering offenses. Before their criminal trial began, the United States filed a civil forfeiture complaint against various property seized from or titled to the defendants or their corporations. More than a year after Arlt and Wren were convicted, the government obtained summary judgment on its civil forfeiture complaint. On appeal Arlt and Wren argued that the forfeiture constituted double jeopardy. The Ninth Circuit agreed.

The Ninth Circuit began its analysis by noting that the Double Jeopardy Clause protects "against efforts to impose punishment for the

2. *Id.*
3. *Id.*
4. United States v. Ursery, 59 F.3d 568, 569 (6th Cir.1995).

5. *Id.* at 573.
6. *Id.* at 573–75.
7. *Id.* at 574.

same offense in two or more separate proceedings." Like the Sixth Circuit, the Ninth Circuit found the Supreme Court's ruling in *Austin*— that forfeiture constitutes punishment—to be determinative on the issue of whether civil forfeiture is punishment: "We believe that the only fair reading of the Court's decision in *Austin* is that it resolves the 'punishment' issue with respect to forfeiture cases for purposes of the Double Jeopardy Clause as well as the Excessive Fines Clause. In short, if a forfeiture constitutes punishment under the *Halper* criteria, it constitutes 'punishment' for purposes of *both* clauses."[8] The Ninth Circuit did not address the "same offense" requirement focused upon by the Sixth Circuit. Instead, the Ninth Circuit dealt primarily with the issue of whether the civil forfeiture and criminal prosecution constituted separate "proceedings"[9] since double jeopardy protects only against separate proceedings. The court held that the criminal and civil actions were separate proceedings because they were instituted at different times, tried at different times before different fact finders, presided over by different judges, and resolved by separate judgments.[10]

The Supreme Court reversed both the Sixth and Ninth Circuits, finding no double jeopardy problem and, at least implicitly, noting its difficulty with *Halper* analysis. The Court began by reviewing judicial precedents in forfeiture cases, noting that courts had consistently viewed civil forfeiture as a sanction additional to criminal prosecution.[11] The Court then looked to Congress's intent when passing various civil forfeiture statutes and concluded that Congress intended civil forfeiture to be a remedial sanction. Lastly, the Court looked to the purposes of civil forfeiture finding that it has a remedial purpose: "to require disgorgement of the fruits of illegal conduct,"[12] and a preventative purpose (to "prevent[] illegal uses . . . by imposing an economic penalty, thereby rendering illegal behavior unprofitable.")[13] As such, the Court concluded, "civil forfeiture does not constitute punishment for the purpose of the Double Jeopardy Clause."[14]

Furthermore, the Court noted, the method set forth in *Halper* for determining whether a civil penalty is punitive (looking to the value of the penalty and comparing it to the harm suffered by the Government) is "virtually impossible" in a civil forfeiture action and thus inapplicable.[15] Rather than being statutorily set, as are the penalties under the False Claims Act, the value of property subject to forfeiture is determined by the conduct involved, where the conduct occurred, and the property used to commit the conduct.

8. *Id.*

9. *Id.* at 1216.

10. *Id.* at 1216.

11. United States v. One Assortment of 89 Firearms, 465 U.S. 354, 104 S.Ct. 1099, 79 L.Ed.2d 361 (1984); Various Items of Personal Property v. United States, 282 U.S. 577, 51 S.Ct. 282, 75 L.Ed. 558 (1931); One Lot Emerald Cut Stones v. United States, 409 U.S. 232, 93 S.Ct. 489, 34 L.Ed.2d 438 (1972).

12. *Id.* at 2145.

13. *Id.* at 2148 quoting Bennis v. Michigan, 516 U.S. 442, 451, 116 S.Ct. 994, 1000, 134 L.Ed.2d 68 (1996).

14. *Id,* at 2147.

15. *Id.* at 2145.

Upon concluding its double jeopardy analysis, the Court turned to the question of whether civil forfeiture violated the Eighth Amendment's prohibition of excessive fines. The Court reaffirmed its ruling in *Austin* that excessive forfeitures may violate the Excessive Fines Clause of the Eighth Amendment and remanded the case for consideration of this issue.

§ 31.5 Conclusion

From these cases, several points are clear. Civil penalties assessed in a civil lawsuit and drug taxes levied on contraband will not constitute punishment for purposes of double jeopardy unless it is clear that Congress intended the remedy, albeit labeled civil or administrative, to serve as a criminal action. Civil forfeiture may be excessive and thus violative of the Eighth Amendment's protection against excessive fines. The Supreme Court has not yet ruled on the issue of whether awards in civil cases and drug taxes may run afoul of the Excessive Fines Clause.

§ 31.6 Bibliography

Cox, Stanley E., *Halper's Continuing Double Jeopardy Implications: A Thorn By Any Other Name Would Prick As Deep*, 39 St.L.U.L.J., 1235 (1995).

Eads, Linda S., *Separating Crime From Punishment: The Constitutional Implications of United States v. Halper*, 68 WASH.U.L.Q. 929 (1990).

Hall, Lynn C., *Note, Crossing the Line Between Rough Remedial Justice and Prohibited Punishment: Civil Penalty Violates the Double Jeopardy Clause–United States v. Halper*, 65 WASH.L.REV. 437 (1990).

LaSala, Todd A., Comment, *The Decisive Blow to Double Jeopardy Defense in Kansas Drunk Driving Prosecutions: State v. Mertz*, 44 U. KAN.L.REV. 1009 (1996).

SMITH, DAVID B., PROSECUTION AND DEFENSE OF FORFEITURE CASES (1996).

Thomas, George C. III, *A Blameworthy Act Approach to the Double Jeopardy Same Offense Problem*, 83 CAL.L.REV. 1027 (1995).

UNITED STATES DEPARTMENT OF JUSTICE, U.S. ATTORNEYS MANUAL.

WRIGHT, CHARLES ALAN, MILLER, ARTHUR R., COOPER, EDWARD H., FEDERAL PRACTICE AND PROCEDURE, (1981, Supp.1996).

*

CHAPTER 32

DUAL SOVEREIGNTY

Table of Sections

WESTLAW Electronic Research Guide

See WESTLAW Electronic Research Guide preceding the Summary of Contents.

---

§ 32.1 Dual Prosecutions by Separate Sovereignties

The courts have long recognized that both the federal government and a state government may prosecute a defendant for the same conduct[1] and similarly, that two states may prosecute the same defendant for the same conduct.[2] The rationale for dual prosecutions is both "pragmatic": each sovereignty has its own interest to protect and "formalistic": even if the statutes proscribing such conduct are identical, they were passed by separate independent legislative bodies and thus, are not the same offense.[3] Interestingly, a number of states have statutorily proscribed a state trial when another sovereign has already prosecuted the same defendant for the same conduct.[4]

§ 32.2 The United States Department of Justice Petite Policy

A lawyer indicted for subornation of perjury, a Greek seaman and a false birth certificate led to the Department of Justice's (DOJ) policy on dual prosecutions which, like the approach adopted in the majority of states, proscribes dual prosecutions. The DOJ's policy, however, is flexible, permitting dual prosecution under some circumstances.

Georgios Modestou Kostatos was a Greek citizen who arrived in Baltimore on October 12, 1951, as a crewman on a Greek ship. Kostatos was not on his ship when it departed the next day and soon thereafter,

---

§ 32.1

1. Houston v. Moore, 18 U.S. (5 Wheat) 1, 16, 5 L.Ed. 19 (1820).

2. Heath v. Alabama, 474 U.S. 82, 92–94, 106 S.Ct. 433, 439–40, 88 L.Ed.2d 387 (1985); United States v. Wheeler, 435 U.S. 313, 330–32, 98 S.Ct. 1079, 1089–90, 55 L.Ed.2d 303 (1978).

3. For a fuller discussion, see George C. Thomas III, *A Blameworthy Act Approach to the Double Jeopardy Same Of-*

fense Problem, 83 Cal.L.Rev. 1027, 1055–58 (1995).

4. *Id.* at 1057 n.137.

See, e.g.:

California: Cal. Penal Code § 656; Ind. Code § 35–41–4–5 (1986).

New Jersey: N.J. Stat. Ann. § 2C:1–11.

Washington: Wash. Rev. Code § 10.43.040.

was arrested and scheduled for deportation. George Petite represented Kostatos at his deportation hearings. Testimony was taken before a Deportation Examiner on February 14, 1952 in Baltimore, on April 24, 1952 in Philadelphia and again, on June 16, 1952, in Baltimore. At these hearings, Kostatos claimed that he was John George Sitaras; he was born in Chester, Pennsylvania; he was baptized in Philadelphia; he was sent to Greece to live with a grandfather when he was 4 or 5 years old, and he was attempting to return home by serving as a crewman on the ship. Kostatos explained that he used the false name of Georgios Modestou Kostatos to get employment on the ship.[1] Apparently, a Greek male was not acceptable for employment unless he could demonstrate military service and discharge in the Greek armed forces. Kostatos explained that he adopted the identity of a Greek citizen ("Kostatos") to falsify such service.

None of what Kostatos testified to was the truth. His attorney, George Petite, allegedly told Kostatos what to say; gave Kostatos a false name to use (knowing that the real John George Sitaras, had died); located witnesses who would falsely testify in support of Kostatos' claim; and made efforts to locate documents, such as a false baptismal certificate, to corroborate Kostatos' story.[2]

Because the deportation hearings had taken place in both Philadelphia and Baltimore, Petite was subject to prosecution in both places for the alleged subornation of perjury. He was indicted in Pennsylvania on federal charges of conspiring to defraud the United States government and the Immigration and Naturalization Services. He pled *nolo contendere* to this charge. Thereafter Petite was indicted in Maryland on federal charges of subornation of perjury. Petite argued, unsuccessfully, that the Baltimore charges constituted double jeopardy and should be dismissed.[3] Certiorari was granted.[4] The Supreme Court's grant of certiorari in *United States v. Petite* followed "repeated expressions of concern" about dual prosecutions. For example, as early as 1847, the Court had noted:

> It is almost certain, that, in the benignant spirit in which the institutions both of the state and federal systems are administered, an offender who should have suffered the penalties denounced by the one would not be subjected a second time to punishment by the other for acts essentially the same, unless indeed this might occur in instances of peculiar enormity, or where the public safety demanded extraordinary rigor.[5]

§ 32.2

1. Petite v. United States, 262 F.2d 788, 790 (4th Cir.1959).

2. *Id.* at 790; United States v. Petite, 147 F.Supp. 791, 792 (D.Md.1957).

3. United States v. Petite, 147 F.Supp. 791 (1957), *affirmed*, 262 F.2d 788 (4th Cir.1959).

4. Petite v. United States, 360 U.S. 908, 79 S.Ct. 1293, 3 L.Ed.2d 1259 (1959).

5. Fox v. Ohio, 46 U.S. (5 How.) 410, 435, 12 L.Ed. 213 (1847) *quoted by* Chief Justice Taft in United States v. Lanza, 260 U.S. 377, 383, 43 S.Ct. 141, 143, 67 L.Ed. 314 (1922); *See also* Bartkus v. Illinois, 359 U.S. 121, 79 S.Ct. 676, 3 L.Ed.2d 684 (1959); Abbate v. United States, 359 U.S. 187, 79 S.Ct. 666, 3 L.Ed.2d 729 (1959).

Before judgment was rendered by the Supreme Court in *Petite*, the Department of Justice (DOJ) filed a motion to vacate the judgment below "on the ground that it is the general policy of the Federal Government that several offenses arising out of a single transaction should be alleged and tried together and should not be made the basis of multiple prosecutions, a policy dictated by considerations both of fairness to defendants and of efficient and orderly law enforcement."[6] The Court had little trouble, given this motion, in remanding Petite's appeal to the District Court with instructions to dismiss the indictment.[7]

After its motion in *Petite* and dismissal of the case, the United States DOJ developed what is known as the "Petite Policy." This policy "precludes the initiation or continuation of a federal prosecution, following a prior state or federal prosecution based on substantially the same act(s) or transaction(s)" unless the matter involves a "substantial federal interest," which was left "demonstrably unvindicated" by the prior prosecution.[8] A full copy of the "Petite Policy" is attached as an appendix to this chapter.

An issue which has arisen in dual prosecution cases is what happens when the DOJ violates its Petite Policy. When the DOJ agrees that it has violated the Petite Policy and joins in seeking dismissal or vacation of charges, such relief has been granted.[9] When the DOJ is alleged to have violated its Petite Policy, but contests that conclusion, or acknowledges such a violation but opposes dismissal of the charges, the weight of authority is that the courts have no authority to dismiss or vacate the charges.[10] There are two reasons supporting this view. First, the Petite Policy is not constitutionally required.[11] Second, "according the internal policy such binding effect would discourage the Department from adopting other such laudable policies."[12]

§ 32.3 Bibliography

Thomas, George C., III, *A Blameworthy Act Approach to the Double Jeopardy Same Offense Problem*, 83 CAL.L.REV. 1027 (1995).

UNITED STATES DEPARTMENT OF JUSTICE, U.S. ATTORNEY'S MANUAL § 9–2.142 et seq.

6. Petite v. United States, 361 U.S. 529, 530–31, 80 S.Ct. 450, 451, 4 L.Ed.2d 490 (1960).

7. *Id.* at 492.

8. U.S. DEPT. OF JUSTICE, U.S. ATTORNEYS MANUAL, § 9–2.142 (1988).

9. *Rinaldi*, 434 U.S. at 30, 98 S.Ct. at 85.

10. *Fourth Circuit*: United States v. Howard, 590 F.2d 564, 567–68 (4th Cir. 1979).

Fifth Circuit: United States v. Martin, 574 F.2d 1359, 1361 (5th Cir.1978).

Seventh Circuit: United States v. Hutul, 416 F.2d 607, 626 (7th Cir.1969).

Eighth Circuit: United States v. Wallace, 578 F.2d 735, 740 n. 4 (8th Cir.1978).

Ninth Circuit: United States v. Snell, 592 F.2d 1083, 1087–88 (9th Cir.1979).

Tenth Circuit: United States v. Fritz, 580 F.2d 370–375 (10th Cir.1978); United States v. Thompson, 579 F.2d 1184, 1188 (10th Cir.1978).

11. *Rinaldi*, 434 U.S. at 29, 98 S.Ct. at 85.

12. *Snell*, 592 F.2d at 1088.

WRIGHT, CHARLES ALAN, MILLER, ARTHUR R., COOPER, EDWARD H., FEDERAL PRACTICE AND PROCEDURE, (1981, Supp. 1996).

Appendix

Dual and Successive Prosecution Policy ("Petite Policy")
U.S. DEPT. OF JUSTICE, U.S. ATTY'S MANUAL, § 9–2.142

I. STATEMENT OF POLICY

A. This policy establishes guidelines for the exercise of discretion by appropriate officers of the Department of Justice in determining whether to bring a federal prosecution based on substantially the same act(s) or transaction(s) involved in a prior state or federal proceeding.[1]

B. The purpose of this policy is to vindicate substantial federal interests through appropriate federal prosecutions; to protect persons charged with criminal conduct from the burdens associated with multiple prosecutions and punishments for substantially the same act(s) or transaction(s); to promote efficient utilization of Department resources; and to promote coordination and cooperation between federal and state prosecutors.

C. This policy precludes the initiation or continuation of a federal prosecution, following a prior state or federal prosecution based on substantially the same act(s) or transaction(s), unless:

    1. The following three substantive prerequisites are satisfied:

        a. the matter must involve a substantial federal interest;

        b. the prior prosecution must have left that interest demonstrably unvindicated; and

        c. applying the same test applicable to all federal prosecutions, the government must believe that the defendant(s) conduct constitutes a federal offense, and that the admissible evidence probably will be sufficient to obtain and sustain a conviction by an unbiased trier of fact; and

    2. The following procedural prerequisite is satisfied: the prosecution must be approved by the appropriate Assistant Attorney General.

D. Satisfaction of the substantive prerequisites in ¶ I.C.1 does not mean that a proposed prosecution must be approved or brought. The traditional elements of federal prosecutorial discretion con-

---

Appendix

1. *See Rinaldi v. United States*, 434 U.S. 22, 27, 98 S.Ct. 81, 84, 54 L.Ed.2d 207 (1977); *Petite v. United States*, 361 U.S. 529, 80 S.Ct. 450, 4 L.Ed.2d 490 (1960). Although there is no general statutory bar to a federal prosecution where the defendant's conduct already has formed the basis for a state prosecution, Congress expressly has provided that, as to certain specific offenses, a state judgment of conviction or acquittal on the merits shall be a bar to any subsequent federal prosecution for the same act or acts. *See* 18 U.S.C. 659, 660, 1992, 2101, 2117; 15 U.S.C. 80a–36, 1282.

tinue to apply. *See Principles of Federal Prosecution*, [DOJ Manual 9–27.110], *et seq.*

E. In order to ensure the most efficient use of law enforcement resources, whenever a matter involves overlapping federal and state jurisdiction, federal prosecutors should at the earliest possible time coordinate with their state counterparts to determine the most appropriate single forum in which to proceed to satisfy the substantial federal and state interests involved, and to resolve all criminal liability for the acts in question if possible.

II. *TYPES OF PROSECUTIONS AS TO WHICH THIS POLICY APPLIES*[2]

A. This policy applies whenever the contemplated federal prosecution is based on substantially the same act(s) or transaction(s) involved in a prior state or federal prosecution.

B. This policy constitutes an exercise of the Department's prosecutorial discretion, and applies even where:

1. a prior state prosecution would not legally bar a subsequent federal prosecution under the Double Jeopardy Clause, due to the doctrine of dual sovereignty, *see Abbate v. United States*, 359 U.S. 187, 79 S.Ct. 666, 3 L.Ed.2d 729 (1959); or

2. a prior prosecution would not legally bar a subsequent state or federal prosecution under the Double Jeopardy Clause, because each offense requires proof of an element not contained in the other, *see United States v. Dixon*, 509 U.S. 688, 113 S.Ct. 2849, 125 L.Ed.2d 556 (1993); *Blockburger v. United States*, 284 U.S. 299, 52 S.Ct. 180, 76 L.Ed. 306 (1932).

C. This policy does not apply (and prior approval therefore is not required pursuant to it[3]) where the prior prosecution involved only a minor part of the contemplated federal charges. For example, a federal conspiracy or RICO prosecution may allege overt acts or predicate offenses previously prosecuted, as long as those acts or offenses do not represent substantially the whole of the contemplated federal charge, and (in a RICO prosecution) as long as there are a sufficient number of predicate offenses to sustain the RICO charge if the previously prosecuted offenses were excluded.

2. This policy applies only to charging decisions, and does not apply to (and prior approval therefore is not required with respect to) pre-charge investigations. However, where a prior prosecution has been brought based on substantially the same act(s) or transaction(s), generally a subsequent federal investigation should focus initially on evidence relevant to determining whether a subsequent federal prosecution would be warranted in light of the prerequisites listed in ¶ I.C.1 *supra*.

3. Other prior approval requirements remain in force, however, even if approval is not required under the provisions of the Dual and Successive Prosecution Policy *See, e.g.*, [*DOJ Manual* 9–110.101] (Criminal Division approval required for all RICO indictments).

D. This policy does not apply (and prior approval therefore is not required pursuant to it) where the contemplated federal prosecution could not have been brought in the initial federal prosecution, for example, because of venue restrictions or joinder or proof problems.

E. Notwithstanding anything contained within this policy, no prosecution may be brought where it would be barred by the Double Jeopardy Clause.

III. *STAGES OF PROSECUTION AT WHICH POLICY APPLIES*

A. This policy applies whenever there has been a prior state or federal prosecution resulting in an acquittal, a conviction (including one resulting from a plea agreement), or a dismissal or other termination of the case on the merits after jeopardy has attached.

B. Once a prior prosecution reaches one of the above-listed stages, this policy applies (and approval therefore is required) before a federal prosecution can be initiated or continued, even if an indictment or information has already been filed in the federal prosecution at issue.

C. Exception: This policy does not apply if a prior prosecution reaches one of the above-listed stages after trial commences on the federal prosecution at issue; however, it does apply when a federal trial results in a mistrial, dismissal or reversal on appeal, and when, in the interim, a prior prosecution has reached one of the above-listed stages.

IV. *SUBSTANTIVE PREREQUISITES FOR APPROVAL OF A PROSECUTION AS TO WHICH THIS POLICY APPLIES*

The following three substantive prerequisites must be satisfied before approval may be granted for initiation or continuation of a prosecution as to which this policy applies.

A. The Matter Must Involve a Substantial Federal Interest

1. This determination will be made on a case-by-case basis, applying the considerations applicable to all federal prosecutions. *See Principles of Federal Prosecution*, [*DOJ Manual 9–27.230*]

2. Matters that come within the national investigative or prosecutorial priorities established by the Department are more likely than others to satisfy this requirement.

B. The Prior Prosecution Must Have Left That Substantial Federal Interest Demonstrably Unvindicated

In general, the Department will presume that a prior prosecution, regardless of result, has vindicated the relevant federal interest. There may be an unvindicated federal interest. however, in the following circumstances:

1. When a conviction was not achieved in the prior prosecution because of factors of the following kinds:

    a. incompetence, corruption, intimidation, or undue influence:

    b. court or jury nullification, in clear disregard of the evidence or the law;

    c. the unavailability of significant evidence, either because it was not timely discovered or known by the prosecution, or because it was kept from the trier of fact's consideration on an erroneous view of the law;

    d. the failure in a prior state prosecution to prove an element of a state offense which is not an element of the contemplated federal offense; or

    e. the exclusion of charges in a prior federal prosecution out of concern for fairness to other defendants or for significant resource considerations that favored separate federal prosecutions.

2. When a conviction was achieved in the prosecution, if:

    a. the prior sentence was manifestly inadequate in light of the federal interest involved, and a substantially enhanced sentence (which may include elements such as forfeiture and restitution, as well as imprisonment and fines) is available through the contemplated federal prosecution; or

    b. the choice of charges, or the determination of (guilt or severity of sentence in the prior prosecution), was affected by a factor of the kind listed in ¶ IV.B.1 above.[4]

3. Irrespective of the result in a prior state prosecution, in the rare case where (a) the alleged violation involves a compelling federal interest, particularly one implicating an enduring national priority; (b) the alleged violation involves egregious conduct, including that which threatens or causes loss of life, severe economic or physical harm, or the impairment of the functioning of an agency of the federal government or the due administration of justice; and (c) the result in the prior prosecution was manifestly inadequate in light of the federal interest involved.

C. Applying the same test applicable to all federal prosecutions, the government must believe that the defendant(s)' conduct constitutes a federal offense and that the admissible evidence probably will be sufficient to obtain and sustain a conviction by an unbiased trier of fact.

---

4. An example might be a case in which the charges in the initial prosecution trivialized the seriousness of the contemplated federal offense: e.g., a state prosecution for assault and battery in a case involving the murder of a federal official.

1. This is the same test applied to all federal prosecutions, *see Principles of Federal Prosecution*, [*DOJ Manual 9–27.220*], *et seq.*

2. This requirement turns on an evaluation of the admissible evidence that will be available at the time of trial. The potential that—despite the law and the facts—the fact-finder may acquit the defendant because of the unpopularity of some factor involved in the prosecution, or because of the overwhelming popularity of the defendant or his or her cause, is not a factor inhibiting prosecution.

3. When (in the case of a prior conviction), the unvindicated federal interest in the matter arises because of the availability of a substantially enhanced sentence, the government also must believe that the admissible evidence meets the legal requirements for such sentence.

V. *PROCEDURAL PREREQUISITE TO BRINGING A PROSECUTION AS TO WHICH THIS POLICY APPLIES*

A. Whenever a substantial question exists as to whether this policy applies to a prosecution, the matter should be submitted to the appropriate Assistant Attorney General for resolution.

B. Prior approval from the appropriate Assistant Attorney General must be obtained before bringing a prosecution as to which this policy applies.

C. The United States will move to dismiss any prosecution as to which this policy applies, and as to which prior approval was not obtained, unless the Assistant Attorney General retroactively approves it on the grounds that: (1) there are unusual or overriding circumstances justifying retroactive approval, and (2) the prosecution would have been approved had approval been sought in a timely fashion. Appropriate administrative action may be initiated against prosecutors who violate this policy.

VI. *RESERVATION AND SUPERSEDING EFFECT*

A. This policy is set forth solely for the purpose of internal Department of Justice guidance. It is not intended to, does not, and may not be relied upon to create any rights, substantive or procedural, that are enforceable at law by any party in any matter, civil or criminal, nor does it place any limitations on otherwise lawful litigative prerogatives of the Department of Justice.[5]

---

5. All of the Courts of Appeals that have considered the question have held that a criminal defendant cannot invoke the Department's policy as a bar to federal prosecution. *See, e.g.*, United States v. Snell, 592 F.2d 1083 (9th Cir.1979); United States v. Howard, 590 F.2d 564 (4th Cir.1979); United States v. Frederick, 583 F.2d 273 (6th Cir.1978); United States v. Thompson, 579 F.2d 1184 (10th Cir.1978) (en banc); United States v. Wallace, 578 F.2d 735 (8th Cir. 1978); United States v. Nelligan, 573 F.2d 251 (5th Cir.1978); United States v. Hutul, 416 F.2d 607 (7th Cir.1969). The Supreme Court, in analogous contexts, has concluded that Department policies governing its in-

B. This policy statement supersedes all prior Department guidelines and policy statements on the subject.

9–2.143 Juvenile Prosecutions

Prior approval from the Criminal Division is required before the U.S. Attorney may file a Motion to Transfer, *i.e.*, a Motion to Proceed Against a Juvenile as an Adult under 18 U.S.C. § 5032.

9–2.144 Interstate Agreement on Detainers

A. General Overview

By virtue of the Interstate Agreement on Detainers Act Pub. L. No. 91–538, 84 Stat. 1397 to 1403 (1970), the United States (and the District of Columbia) entered into the Interstate Agreement on Detainers, 18 U.S.C.

ternal operations do not create rights which may be enforced by defendants against the Department. *See* United States v. Caceres, 440 U.S. 741, 99 S.Ct. 1465, 59 L.Ed.2d 733 (1979); Sullivan v. United States, 348 U.S. 170, 75 S.Ct. 182, 99 L.Ed. 210 (1954).

*

CHAPTER 33*

LOSS OF CREDENTIALS: DEBARMENT, EXCLUSION AND SUSPENSION

Table of Sections

WESTLAW Electronic Research Guide

See WESTLAW Electronic Research Guide preceding the Summary of Contents.

---

§ 33.1 Introduction

One of the more serious possible consequences of being convicted of a crime is debarment, exclusion or suspension from future participation in government contracts for a specified period of time, usually 3 to 5 years. Debarment, exclusion and suspension are administrative remedies handed out by the agency with which an individual or entity was doing business upon commission of certain acts, such as failure to meet performance or delivery schedules. Most federal agencies have the authority to terminate existing contracts between an entity, or individual, and the federal government and declare the contractor ineligible to enter into future contracts with the government for a specified period of time. For those contractors whose livelihood depends upon securing contracts with the government, debarment, exclusion or suspension may have devastating consequences, effectively putting them out of business.[1]

* Portions of this chapter are based on materials appearing in Pamela H. Bucy, Health Care Fraud: Criminal, Civil and Administrative Law. To the extent there is reproduction of these materials, it is included with the permission of the publisher and copyright holder, Law Journal Seminars Press, 345 Park Avenue South, New York, New York, 10010. All rights reserved as to production.

§ 33.1

1. AMERICAN BAR ASS'N (ABA) COMM. ON DEBARMENT AND SUSPENSION, SECTION OF PUBLIC CONTRACT LAW, THE PRACTITIONER'S GUIDE TO SUSPENSION AND DEBARMENT, 1–2 (2d ed.1996) [hereinafter ABA, PRACTITIONER'S GUIDE].

The stated purpose of debarment, exclusion and suspension is to protect the government from dealing with irresponsible contractors.[2] The grounds and procedures for debarring, excluding or suspending have been somewhat standardized among the agencies although each agency is free to supplement the "Common Rule" agreed to by multiple agencies.

Suspension is available to all federal agencies which have debarment or exclusion authority. Prior to being debarred or excluded, which is for a set period of years, a contractor may be "suspended" from participating in government programs for an indefinite period of time, presumably just long enough to allow the agency to investigate whether the contractor should be debarred or excluded for a definite term of years.[3] Suspension is a discretionary option available to the affected agency. A contractor may be suspended from further dealings with an agency if the agency has "adequate evidence" that the contractor has committed certain acts. By comparison, an entity or individual is debarred and/or excluded if the agency proves, by a "preponderance of the evidence," that the contractor committed certain acts. Because of the temporary nature of suspension, fewer procedural steps exist before a contractor is suspended. Thus, a contractor may be suspended from dealing with the government upon a mere suspicion of wrongdoing and before an opportunity to be heard.

A large number of contractors are potentially subject to debarment, exclusion or suspension. In fiscal year 1995, for example, approximately 84,000 firms contracted with the federal government, doing $203 billion in business.[4] The number of parties in debarred, excluded or suspended status has increased substantially in recent years.

2. *D.C. Circuit*: Caiola v. Carroll, 851 F.2d 395, 398 (D.C.Cir.1988).

Sixth Circuit: Transco Sec., Inc. v. Freeman, 639 F.2d 318, 321 (6th Cir.1981).

3. *Hearings: Debarment and Reinstatement of Federal Contractors: An Interim Report*, 102nd Cong., 2d Sess. 2 (1992); *Reform of Government-wide Debarment and Suspension Procedures: Report by the Subcomm. on Oversight of Gov't Management*, Senate Comm.of Gov't.Affairs, 97th Cong., 1st Sess. 3 (1981).

4. Telephone Interview with Federal Procurement Data Center, Unique Government Contractor Establishments (Nov. 27, 1996); E-mail from United States Postal Service, Encompass Database (Nov. 28, 1996); DEPARTMENT OF COMMERCE, ECONOMICS AND STATISTICS ADMINISTRATION; BUREAU OF THE CENSUS FOR THE OFFICE OF MANAGEMENT AND BUDGET, CONSOLIDATED FEDERAL FUNDS REPORT: FISCAL YEAR 1995.

CHART 33A: PARTIES IN EXCLUDED STATUS FROM
FEDERAL PROCUREMENT OR NONPROCUREMENT
PROGRAMS IN THE YEARS 1988-1995

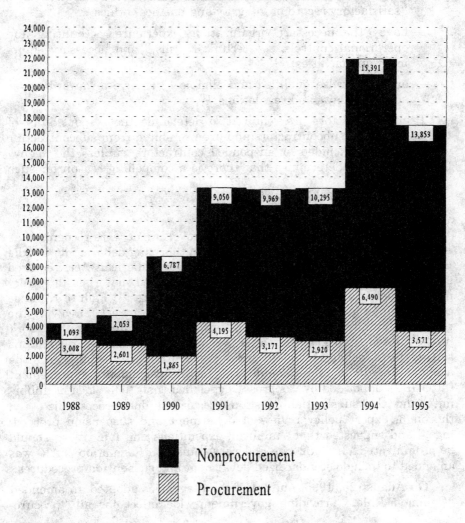

Nonprocurement

Procurement

An entity or individual may be debarred, excluded or suspended if it behaves "irresponsibly."[5] Government contracts are to be awarded only to "responsible" contractors.[6] "Responsible" contractors are those which:

— have "adequate financial resources to perform the contract;"

5. *Debarment and Reinstatement of Federal Contractors: An Interim Report, 37th Report by the House Comm. on Gov't Operations*, 102nd Cong. 2d Sess. (1992).

6. Federal Acquisition Regulation (FAR), 48 C.F.R. § 9.103(a) (1995).

— are able to perform the work, meeting all performance and delivery schedules;

— demonstrate a "satisfactory performance record" as well as a "satisfactory record of integrity and business ethics;"

— have "the necessary organization, experience, accounting and operational controls, ... technical skills," and necessary equipment and facilities;

— are "otherwise qualified and eligible to receive an award under applicable laws and regulations."[7]

Prime contractors are required to determine the responsibility of their prospective subcontractors and are prohibited from subcontracting with debarred, excluded or suspended contractors "unless the agency head or designee determines that there is a compelling reason for such action...."[8]

§ 33.2 History

Although debarments by the federal government were recognized as early as 1928[1] the first statute expressly authorizing debarment was the Buy American Act, passed in 1933.[2] The Buy American Act, required government contractors to use American-produced materials in "every public building or public work in the United States."[3] Failure to do so could result in a three year debarment from any contract "involving the construction, alteration, or repair of any public building or public work in the United States."[4] Thereafter, various agencies passed regulations setting forth debarment procedures for contractors dealing with the agency. In 1972, the Commission on Government Procurement ("COGP"), appointed by Congress,[5] concluded that "[t]he lack of uniformity and the substantial questions regarding due process dictate a thorough, expert policy review of debarment and suspension proceedings," and suggested that "uniform, expeditious and fair rules" should be promulgated.[6] In 1982, the Federal Acquisition Regulation (FAR) was amended to include standardized debarment and suspension procedures.[7]

On August 25, 1995, multiple federal agencies adopted an amended "Common Rule," providing government-wide effect for all "procure-

7. FAR § 9.104–2.
8. FAR §§ 9–104, 9–405.

§ 33.2

1. *Reform of Government-wide Debarment and Suspension Procedures: A Report Prepared by the Subcomm. on Oversight of Gov't Management of the Senate Comm. on Gov't Affairs*, 3 (1981).
2. 41 U.S.C. § 10a-d.
3. 41 U.S.C. § 10b(a).
4. 41 U.S.C. § 10b(b).
5. Act of Nov. 26, 1969, Pub.L.No. 91–129, §§ 1–9, 83 Stat. 269, as amended,

Act of July 9, 1971, Pub.L.No. 92–47, 85 Stat. 102.

6. *Report of the Commission on Government Procurement 161.4, Pt. G., Ch. 5, p. 68 (1972)* [hereinafter *COGP Report*].

7. 47 Fed.Reg. 28,854 (July 1, 1982). *See* Brian D. Shannon, *The Government–Wide Debarment and Suspension Regulations After a Decade—A Constitutional Framework—Yet, Some Issues Remain in Transition*, 21 Pub.Cont.L.J. 370, 372–75 (1992).

ment" and "nonprocurement" debarments, exclusions and suspensions.[8] "Procurement programs" are those where a federal agency acquires goods, services and construction by contract.[9] "Nonprocurement programs" are those whereby individuals or businesses receive federal assistance through "grants, cooperative agreements, scholarships, fellowships, assistance contracts, loans, loan guarantees, subsidies, insurance, and similar assistance transactions."[10] Thus, a contractor debarred, excluded or suspended from one program becomes ineligible to participate in all procurement programs and non-procurement programs. In addition, a debarred, excluded or suspended contractor becomes ineligible to participate in privately funded contracts that require Federal approvals or licenses.[11]

It is interesting to note the differences in agency debarment or exclusion activity, which presumably is based, at least in part, on the volume of contractors with which the agency deals. The Departments of Health and Human Resources (HHS), Defense (DOD), and Justice (DOJ) had the most contractors in debarred, excluded or suspended status during the years examined while the Departments of Housing and Urban Development (HUD), Commerce (DOC) and Energy (DOE) had the least.

§ 33.3   Constitutional Issues

Exactly which procedural and substantive rights should be accorded a contractor facing debarment, exclusion or suspension has not been definitively resolved. While it is clear that "procedural due process safeguards apply only when a person is deprived 'of life, liberty, or property,' "[1] it is not clear whether government contractors have a property or liberty interest in serving as government contractors, or if they do, which procedural protections are constitutionally required.

One has a property interest when, according to "state law rules or understandings that secure certain benefits,"[2] one has a "legitimate claim of entitlement."[3] Acknowledging that "[m]uch of the existing wealth in this country takes the form of rights that do not fall within the traditional common-law concepts of property,"[4] courts have struggled with the question of what rights government contractors possess.

The Supreme Court has not ruled on this issue. *Perkins v. Lukens Steel Co.,*[5] a 1940 Supreme Court decision, is often cited as authority for

8. 60 Fed.Reg. 33,037–33066 (June 27, 1995).

9. AMERICAN BAR ASSOCIATION (ABA) COMM. ON DEBARMENT AND SUSPENSION, SECTION OF PUBLIC CONTRACT LAW, THE PRACTITIONER'S GUIDE TO SUSPENSION AND DEBARMENT, iv (2d ed.1996) [hereinafter ABA, PRACTITIONER'S GUIDE].

10. *Id.* at iii.

11. *Id.* at 97–98.

§ 33.3

1. Cervoni v. Secretary of Health, Education & Welfare, 581 F.2d 1010, 1017 (1st Cir.1978).

2. Board of Regents v. Roth, 408 U.S. 564, 577, 92 S.Ct. 2701, 2709, 33 L.Ed.2d 548 (1972).

3. *Id.*

4. *Id.*

5. 310 U.S. 113, 60 S.Ct. 869, 84 L.Ed. 1108 (1940).

the proposition that government contractors are not entitled to any procedural protections before they are debarred because contracting with the government is a privilege, not a right. However, the issue before the Court in *Perkins* did not involve the authority to debar, exclude or suspend but whether iron and steel manufacturers had standing to challenge a determination by Secretary of Labor as to the amount of minimum wage manufacturers were required to pay their employees under the Public Contracts Act.[6] Noting that the manufacturers, along with other businesses subject to the Act, had already fully litigated this issue within the Department of Labor, the Court held that the manufacturers were obligated to comply with the administrative ruling. In passing, the Court noted that the manufacturers "claim standing by asserting that they have particular rights under and even apart from the statute [Public Contracts Act] to bid and negotiate for Government contracts free from compliance with the determination [regarding the amount of the minimum wage] made by the Secretary of Labor...." The Court rejected this standing argument, noting that the Public Contracts Act "was not intended to be a bestowal of litigable rights upon those desirous of selling to the Government...."[7] Thus, beyond this general reference in the context of standing to challenge what had already been administratively decided, the Supreme Court has not discussed what procedural protections, if any, are required prior to debarring, excluding or suspending a contractor from doing business with the federal government.

In cases involving debarment by the Commodity Credit Corporation (CCC)[8] and the Air Force,[9] the United States Court of Appeals for the District of Columbia has ruled that certain procedural protections are required. In these cases, the D.C. Circuit acknowledged the inherent power of agencies to debar contractors which behave irresponsibly, but held that minimum procedural protections must be accorded, such as notice of specific charges, an opportunity to present evidence and cross-examine witnesses, and issuance of findings and conclusions based on the record.[10] In *Horne Brothers, Inc. v. Laird*[11] involving the Navy's authority to suspend contractors, the D.C. Circuit reached a similar conclusion. The court held that while emergency situations may require immediate suspension of a governmental contractor, the contractor must be given an opportunity to rebut the government's evidence before the suspension extends beyond a "short period, not to exceed one month. . . ."[12] The court reasoned:

> [W]e think an action that suspends a contractor and contemplates that he may dangle in suspension for a period of one year or more, is such as to require the Government to insure fundamental fairness

6.   *Id.* at 116, 132.

7.   *Id.* at 127.

8.   Gonzalez v. Freeman, 334 F.2d 570 (D.C.Cir.1964).

9.   Old Dominion Dairy v. Secretary of Defense, 631 F.2d 953 (D.C.Cir.1980).

10.   *Gonzalez*, 334 F.2d at 577–78; *Old Dominion Dairy*, 631 F.2d at 963.

11.   463 F.2d 1268 (C.A.D.C.1972).

12.   *Id.* at 1270.

to the contractor whose economic life may depend on his ability to bid on government contracts.[13]

As in the debarment cases, the court held that "notice of specific charges, opportunity to present evidence and to cross-examine adverse witnesses, were required prior to extending suspension beyond a brief, emergency time period."[14]

The rationale for the decisions conferring these rights is unclear. In *Gonzalez v. Freeman*,[15] concerning the CCC's authority to debar, the Court of Appeals for the District of Columbia declined to find a "right" to Government contracts but found that "[c]onsiderations of basic fairness require administrative regulations establishing standards for debarment."[16] Similarly, in *Horne Brothers v. Laird*,[17] this court found that the "serious economic impact" on a person facing suspension necessitated procedural protections.[18] Most recently the D.C. Circuit found that a contractor's liberty interest required certain procedural protections prior to denial of a contract on the ground that the contractor "lacked integrity."[19] (The court defined "liberty interest" in this context as "a right to be free from stigmatizing governmental defamation having an immediate and tangible effect on its ability to do business.")[20]

The courts addressing the nature of the interest held by Medicare or Medicaid providers facing exclusion are more muddled. Three courts of appeals: the First,[21] the Ninth[22] and the Tenth,[23] have held that a Medicare provider does not have a property interest in continued participation in Medicare or Medicaid. On the additional question of whether a Medicare or Medicaid provider has a liberty interest in serving as a provider, the First Circuit did not rule,[24] the Tenth Circuit found that the provider's "allegations of deprivations of liberty [were] sufficiently colorable to obtain the jurisdiction of the federal court,"[25] and the Ninth Circuit clearly ruled that a provider has a protectable liberty interest in being excluded.[26] The Fourth Circuit stands alone in holding that a health care provider's "expectation of continued participation in the Medicare program is a property interest protected by the due process clause of the fifth amendment."[27]

Even after finding that property or liberty interests exists, these courts have held that fairly minimal procedural protections are required

---

13. *Id.* at 1271.

14. *Id.*

15. 334 F.2d 570 (D.C.Cir.1964).

16. *Id.* at 577.

17. 463 F.2d 1268 (D.C.Cir.1972).

18. *Id.* at 1271.

19. *Id.* at 955.

20. Old Dominion Dairy Products v. Secretary of Defense, 631 F.2d 953, 961 (D.C.Cir.1980).

21. Cervoni v. Secretary of Health, Education & Welfare, 581 F.2d 1010, 1017–19 (1st Cir.1978).

22. Erickson v. United States, 67 F.3d 858, 862 (9th Cir.1995).

23. Koerpel v. Heckler, 797 F.2d 858, 863–65 (10th Cir.1986).

24. *Cervoni*, 581 F.2d at 1010.

25. *Koerpel*, 797 F.2d at 866.

26. *Erickson*, 67 F.3d at 862–63.

27. Ram v. Heckler, 792 F.2d 444, 447 (4th Cir.1986).

to protect these rights. Key to these courts' conclusion that only minimal protections are required before debarment, exclusion or suspension is the fact that in many instances the action is based upon a conviction, where substantial procedural protections have already been accorded.[28]

§ 33.4   Procedure for Imposing Suspension and Debarment

Because two agencies, the Department of Defense and the Department of Health and Human Services, dominate in debarring, excluding and suspending contractors, the following two sections focus on these two agencies in discussing, generally, the procedural steps involving in imposing debarment, exclusion or suspension.

§ 33.5   Suspension and Debarment Procedures by the Department of Defense (DOD)

A.   CERTIFICATION

Procedures designed to implement debarment and suspension begin as soon as a contractor enters into an agreement with the DOD. Each entity or individual seeking to enter into a contract or nonprocurement arrangement with the federal government must certify that the entity or individual:

"(A) . . . is not currently debarred, suspended, proposed for debarment or declared ineligible for the award of contracts by any Federal agency;

(B) . . . has not, within a three year period preceding this offer, been convicted of or had a civil judgement rendered against them the entity or individual for: committing fraud or a criminal offense in connection with obtaining, attempting to obtain, or performing a public (Federal, state, or local) contract or subcontract; violating Federal or state antitrust statutes relating to the submission of offers; or, committing embezzlement, theft, forgery, bribery, falsification or destruction of records, making false statements, tax evasion or receiving stolen property;

(C) . . . is not currently indicted for, or otherwise criminally or civilly charged by a governmental entity with committing any of the offenses enumerated in . . . of this provision; and

(D) . . . has not, within a three-year period preceding this offer, had one or more contracts terminated for default by any Federal agency."[1]

---

28. *See, e.g., Ram,* 792 F.2d at 446; *Erickson,* 67 F.3d at 863.

§ 33.5
1. Federal Acquisition Regulation (FAR) § 52.209–5; Common Rule Appendix

The certification for nonprocurement agreements is similar.[2] Certification that any of the above conditions exist will not necessarily prevent the offeror from receiving an award but will be taken into account in determining the offeror's suitability for the award.

B. INVESTIGATIONS

Most suspension and debarments are initiated when the agency receives a copy of an indictment or conviction. This information could come from U.S. attorneys' offices, Inspector General offices, newspaper articles, trade publications, competitors and qui tam relators. Fewer suspensions and debarments are initiated from an agency's own investigation of facts indicating cause exist for suspension or debarment.

There is no "debarment investigation." Rather, allegations of wrongdoing are investigated with debarment as one possible outcome.[3] Each agency is required to designate a "debarring official" and a "suspending official."[4] All contracting personnel within an agency are required to review the General Services Administration (GSA) List to ensure that the agency is not soliciting or awarding contracts to contractors listed. They are also required to report wrongdoing or suspicion of "cause" for debarment or suspension to the GSA.[5]

C. NOTICE OF PROPOSAL TO DEBAR

Under the Federal Acquisition Regulation (FAR), the government must issue notice of proposed debarment, informing the recipient that debarment is being considered, the reasons for the proposed debarment, the effect of the proposal and the recipient's rights.[6] In instances of suspension, the notice is similar but should inform the recipient that it has been suspended. In both instances, within thirty days after receiving the notice, the recipient may submit (in writing, in person or through a representative) "information and argument" in opposition to the debarment or suspension.[7]

As soon as a contractor is proposed for debarment, it is placed on the General Services Administration (GSA) List of "Parties Excluded from

---

A.

2. The only difference is that nonprocurement contractors must certify that they "[h]ave not within a three-year period preceding this application/proposal had one or more public transactions (Federal State or local) terminated for cause or default." Common Rule 610(a).

3. *Debarment and Reinstatement of Federal Contractors: An Interim Report,* 102nd Cong., 2d Sess. 9 (1992).

4. FAR § 9.403; *See, e.g.,* 48 C.F.R. § 1509.403 (1995) (Environmental Protection Agency.)

5. *See, e.g.,* 48 C.F.R. § 1509.406–3 (1995) (Environmental Protection Agency (EPA)); 48 C.F.R. § 609.4 (1995) (State Department); 48 C.F.R. § 209.403 (1995) (Department of Defense); 48 C.F.R. § 1809.403 (1995) (National Aeronautics and Space Administration); 48 C.F.R. § 1909.403 (1995) (United States Information Industry); 48 C.F.R. § 3509.403 (1995) (Panama Canal Commission).

6. FAR § 9.406–3(c).

7. FAR §§ 9.406–3(c), 9.407–3(c); Common Rule .312, .411.

Federal Procurement and Nonprocurement Programs."[8] This List consists of "all contractors debarred, suspended, proposed for debarment or declared ineligible by agencies or by the General Accounting Office."[9] It also includes the names and addresses of all eligible contractors; the agency taking the action, the reason for the action; the effect of the action; and, the termination date.[10] Once placed on the List a contractor is prohibited from soliciting contracts with federal agencies, entering into such contracts or subcontracts with others who have contracted with the federal government and conducting business with the government as an agent for other contractors.

The impact of being placed on the GSA List differs in the procurement[11] and nonprocurement areas.[12] Procurement contractors are disqualified from contracting, soliciting a contract or representing others in contract matters as soon as the proposed suspension or disbarment has been issued. In the nonprocurement area, however, this disqualification becomes applicable only upon suspension or debarment.[13]

D. GROUNDS

The grounds for suspension include:

— Committing fraud or a criminal offense in connection with . . . obtaining, . . . attempting to obtain . . . or performing a public contract or subcontract;

— Violating federal or statute antitrust laws "relating to the submission of offers;"

— Committing embezzlement, theft, forgery, bribery, falsification or destruction of records, making false statements, or receiving stolen property;

— Violating the Drug Free Workplace Act[14] for which the contractor is responsible (false certification of compliance; failure to comply with certification; a large number of drug convictions by employees "as to indicate that the contractor has failed to make a good faith effort to provide a drug free workplace.")

— Affixing a "Made in America" inscription to a product that was not made in America;

— Committing an unfair trade practice;

---

8. FAR § 9.404; see Charts 1 and 2 *supra*, §§ 280–81 *supra*.

9. FAR § 9.404(a)(1).

10. FAR § 9.404(b).

11. A procurement program "refers to agency acquisition by contract of goods, services and construction." AMERICAN BAR ASSOCIATION (ABA) COMM. ON DEBARMENT AND SUSPENSION, SECTION OF PUBLIC CONTRACT LAW, THE PRACTITIONER'S GUIDE TO SUSPENSION AND DEBARMENT iv (2d ed.1996) [hereinafter ABA, PRACTITIONER'S GUIDE].

12. A nonprocurement program is "[a]ny Federal assistance program, including grants, cooperative agreements, scholarships, fellowships, assistance contracts, loans, loan guarantees, subsidies, insurance, and similar assistance transactions." *Id.* at iii.

13. ABA, PRACTITIONER'S GUIDE *supra* note 11 at 55–56, *citing* FAR § 9.405 and Common Rule .200 and .225.

14. 41 U.S.C. §§ 701–707.

— Committing "any other offense indicating a lack of business integrity or business honesty that seriously and directly affects the present responsibility of a Government contractor or subcontractor."[15]

The above grounds must be proven by "adequate evidence" before a party may be suspended. "Adequate evidence" is "information sufficient to support the reasonable belief that a particular act or omission has occurred."[16] In evaluating the adequacy of the evidence, the hearing officer is to consider "how much information is available, how credible it is given the circumstances, whether or not important allegations are corroborated, and what inferences can reasonably be drawn as a result."[17] Indictment for any of the causes listed for suspension constitutes adequate evidence.[18]

The grounds for debarment are similar and include the following:

— Conviction of or civil judgment for:

    — "Commission of fraud or a criminal offense in connection with ... obtaining, ... attempting to obtain, ... or performing a public contract or subcontract;"

    — "Violation of federal or state antitrust statutes relating to the submission of offers;"

    — Intentionally affixing a "Made in America" label to products which were not made in America;

    — "Commission of any other offense indicating a lack of business integrity or business honesty that seriously and directly affects the present responsibility of a Government contractor or subcontractor."

— Proof, by a preponderance of the evidence, that the contractor has committed:

    — "Violation of the terms of a Government contract or subcontract so serious at to justify debarment" (such as failure to follow the terms of the contract or a history of failure to perform);

    — Violations of the Drug–Free Workplace Act of 1988 for which the contractor is responsible (false certification of compliance with the Act); failure to comply; a large number of drug convictions by employees "as to indicate that the contractor has failed to make a good faith effort to provide a drug-free workplace."

    — "Any other cause of so serious or compelling a nature that it affects the present responsibility of a Government contractor or subcontractor."[19]

---

15.   FAR § 9.407–2(a).   **18.**   FAR § 9.407–2(b).

16.   FAR § 9.403.   **19.**   FAR § 9.406–2.

17.   FAR § 9.407–1.

FAR defines "preponderance of the evidence,"[20] as "proof by information that, compared with that opposing it, leads to the conclusion that the fact at issue is more probably true than not."[21] A conviction or civil judgment on the above grounds is considered proof by a preponderance of the evidence.[22]

E. PROCEEDINGS

There are two types of proceedings possible in suspension and debarment cases. As required by the FAR, these proceedings are "as informal as is practicable, consistent with principles of fundamental fairness."[23] In the first type of proceeding, whether the issue is suspension or debarment, the contractor (now respondent) is given the opportunity to present matters in opposition to the suspension or debarment. This presentation may be in writing or in person, by the contractor or by a designated representative.[24]

When suspension is sought, the second proceeding is available only to those whose suspension is *not* based upon an indictment *and* the hearing officer found, in the first proceeding, that the contractor raised a "genuine dispute over facts material to the suspension." However, even in such a situation, the contractor is not entitled to the second proceeding if there is a determination made "on the basis of the Department of Justice advice" that further legal proceedings would prejudice "substantial interests of the Government."[25]

When debarment is sought, the second proceeding is available only to those whose debarment is *not* based on a conviction or civil judgment *and* the hearing officer found, in the first proceeding, that the contractor raised a "genuine dispute over facts material to the suspension."[26]

After the second proceeding, the hearing officer will issue written findings of fact.[27]

F. IMPOSITION OF SUSPENSION OF DEBARMENT

Even if the hearing officer finds that grounds exist for suspension or debarment, neither is required. The hearing officer is to consider whether the contractor has:

— instituted "effective standards of conduct and internal control systems" that were in effect at the time of the wrongdoing or before any government investigation of the wrongdoing;

— timely disclosed the wrongdoing to the appropriate government agency;

20. FAR § 9.406–3(d)(3).

21. FAR § 9.403.

22. FAR § 9.406–3(d)(3).

23. FAR § 9.406–3(b).

24. FAR § 9.406–3(b)(1).

25. FAR § 9.407–3(b)(2).

26. FAR § 9.406–3(b)(2).

27. FAR §§ 9.406–3(d)(2)(i) and 9.407–3(d)(2); Common Rule .314(b) and .413(b).

— conducted an internal investigation of the allegations;

— fully cooperated with the government during the investigation;

— paid or has agreed to pay all damages, restitution, administrative and investigative costs and criminal, civil and administrative liability;

— taken "appropriate disciplinary action" against responsible individual;

— "implemented or agreed to implement remedial measures," review and control procedures and ethics training programs;

— eliminated the circumstances that led to the wrongdoing; and

— recognized the seriousness of the wrongdoing, and implemented programs to prevent recurrence.[28]

If the decision is made to suspend, the period of suspension "shall be for a temporary period pending the completion of investigation and any ensuing legal proceedings, unless sooner terminated by the suspending official...."[29] If the decision is made to debar, the period of debarment is to be "commensurate with the seriousness of the causes(s)."[30] Generally, debarment does not exceed three years, but debarments for violations of the Drug–Free Workplace Act may be for a period of five years.[31]

Once debarred, suspended or proposed for debarment, contractors are "excluded from receiving contracts, and agencies shall not solicit offers form, award contracts to, or consent to subcontracts with these contractors." Such contractors are also excluded from conducting business with the Government as agents or representatives of other contractors.[32] These is an exception, however: if the acquiring agency's head finds there is a "compelling reason" not to enforce the exclusion, a contractor will be exempted. This exception is granted rarely.[33]

G. REVIEW

In rare cases the General Services Administration (GSA) will review protests of suspension or debarment:

When a protestor alleges that it has been improperly suspended or debarred during the pendency of a procurement in which it was competing, [the GSA] will review the matter to ensure that the

---

28. FAR § 9.406–1(a); FAR § 9.407–1(b)(2).

29. There is a caveat: "If legal proceedings are not initiated within 12 months after the date of the suspension notice, the suspension shall be terminated unless as Assistant Attorney General requests its extension, which case it may be extended for an additional 6 months." FAR § 9.407–4.

30. FAR § 9.406–4.

31. FAR § 9.406–4.

32. FAR § 9.405.

33. Telephone Interview with Donald J. Suda, Special Assistant for Contractor Integrity, General Services Administration (Nov. 20, 1996); Telephone Interview with HHS Office of the Secretary (Dec. 2, 1996); Telephone Interview with Richard Finnegan, Associate General Counsel, Defense Logistics Agency Office of General Counsel (Dec. 3, 1996).

agency has not acted arbitrarily to avoid making an award loan offer or otherwise entitle to award, and also to ensure that minimum standards of due process have been met.[34]

Once a contractor has been suspended or debarred by the agency it may need to exhaust all administrative remedies before seeking judicial review.[35] As the Supreme Court noted in *Darby v. Cisneros*,[36] exhaustion of an agency appeal process is not required unless a statute or regulation specifically requires it: "[W]here the APA [Administrative Procedure Act[37]] applies, an appeal to a 'superior agency authority' is a prerequisite to judicial review only when expressly required by statute or . . . agency rule."[38] The exhaustion requirement will vary from agency to agency. For example, the Department of Agriculture explicitly requires that a debarred or suspended contractor appeal the debarring official's decision directly to the Department of Agriculture Board of Contract Appeals,[39] whereas the Department of Housing and Urban Development does not require administrative review of a debarring official's decision before judicial review is sought.[40] Judicial appeals from debarment and suspension generally are brought as suits for a declaratory judgment that the agency's effort to impose debarment or suspension violates the Administrative Procedure Act, and seek injunctive relief against the agency.[41]

Either a District Court or the Court of Claims has jurisdiction to hear an appeal from the agency action of suspension or debarment. United States District Courts have jurisdiction over appeals where arbitrary or capricious conduct is alleged.[42] In these instances, the scope of the court's review is limited to determining whether the agency action was "rational, based on relevant factors, and within the agency's statutory authority."[43] The Court of Federal Claims has jurisdiction over actions based on contract and thus has jurisdiction where a contractor challenges a suspension or debarment imposed prior to the award of a contract. The courts are split on whether this jurisdiction is exclusive.[44]

34. In the Matter of SDA Inc., B–253355; B–253522; B–253577, B–253577.293–2CPD (Comptroller General of the U.S., Aug. 24, 1993); In the Matter of Far West Meats, B–2333464.2; B–2334690, 68 Comp. Gen. 488 (Comptroller General of the U.S., June 9, 1989).

35. Darby v. Cisneros, 509 U.S. 137, 113 S.Ct. 2539, 125 L.Ed.2d 113 (1993).

36. 509 U.S. 137, 113 S.Ct. 2539, 125 L.Ed.2d 113 (1993).

37. 5 U.S.C. §§ 551, 704.

38. *Id.* at 154.

39. 7 C.F.R. § 3017.515 (1996).

40. 24 C.F.R. § 24.314(c)(1996).

41. *See, e.g.*, Darby v. Cisneros, 509 U.S. 137, 113 S.Ct. 2539, 125 L.Ed.2d 113 (1993).

42. Administrative Procedure Act, 5 U.S.C. § 706(2)(A);

Supreme Court: Chrysler Corp. v. Brown, 441 U.S. 281, 318, 99 S.Ct. 1705, 1726, 60 L.Ed.2d 208 (1979).

First Circuit: In re Smith & Wesson, 757 F.2d 431, 433–34 (1st Cir.1985).

See ABA PRACTITIONER'S GUIDE *supra* § 33.5 note 11 at 160.

43. Shane Meat v. Department of Defense, 800 F.2d 334, 336 (3d Cir.1986) (*quoting* Frisby v. United States Department of Housing and Urban Development, 755 F.2d 1052, 1055 (3d Cir.1985)).

44. *Cf.* Coco Brothers Inc. v. Pierce, 741 F.2d 675, 677–78 (3d Cir.1984) (holding that Court of Claims has exclusive jurisdiction to hear suit by unsuccessful bidder for construction of an apartment building on grounds that the bidders' proposal provided for inadequate storage space).

The Court of Appeals for the District of Columbia holds that it is; the First Circuit holds that this jurisdiction is not exclusive, allowing parties seeking to challenge debarment or suspension to proceed either District Court or the Court of Claims.[45]

H. MODIFICATION OF THE SUSPENSION OF DEBARMENT

A debarred or suspended entity may obtain modification of the debarment or suspension with newly discovered evidence; reversal of the conviction or civil judgment upon the debarment was based; evidence of a bona fide change in ownership or management; eliminating other causes for which the debarment was imposed or other reasons the debarring official deems appropriate.[46] When their debarment period expires, contractors are automatically removed from the GSA List.[47] The debarred contractor need not petition for reinstatement nor prove that it has cured its prior problems and become a "responsible" contractor.

I. COLLATERAL EFFECTS OF SUSPENSION AND DEBARMENT

After suspension or debarment, a contractor cannot be awarded new contracts. A contractor may continue working on contracts in existence at the time of the debarment or suspension "unless the acquiring agency ... directs otherwise."[48]

The most obvious side effect of suspension or debarment is the "reciprocal" effect of procurement suspension or debarment in the nonprocurement area.[49] In addition, for those entities that do international business, suspension or debarment may have substantial ramifications such as loss of import and export licenses granted by the State Department,[50] or automatic ineligibility for loan guarantees or insurance programs offered by the Export–Import Bank of the United States[51] or by the Overseas Private Investment Corporation; automatic ineligibility to participate in contracts financed through the United States Foreign Military Sales Program or the Foreign Military Financing Program.[52] Suspended or debarred entities may also lose their ability to perform

45. *First Circuit*: *Smith & Wesson*, 757 F.2d at 433–34.

Cf.:

D.C. *Circuit*: *Opal Manufacturing Co. v. U.M.C. Industries, Inc.*, 553 F.Supp. 131, 132–33 (D.D.C.1982) (held that Court of Claims had exclusive jurisdiction to hear dispute by one firm alleging that another firm misappropriated information to use in preparing a bid to supply the United States Postal Service with postage stamp vending machines).

46. FAR § 9.406–4(c); 7 C.F.R. § 3017.320(c) (1996).

47. *Debarment and Reinstatement of Federal Contractors: An Interim Report*, 102nd Cong. 2d Sess. 10 (1992).

48. FAR § 9.405–1.

49. 60 Fed.Reg. 33037.

50. 22 C.F.R. §§ 122.4(a)(1), 126.7(a)(5), 127.1(c)(2) (1996).

51. Application for Short–Term Single–Buyer Policy, Part IV, Par. 25, EIB–92–64 (11/94) OMB #3048–0009, Expirary Date 3/31/96.

52. ABA Practitioner's Guide, *supra* § 33.5 note 11 at 101.

work requiring security clearances;[53] act as a surety for bonds; qualify for a mortgage financed by the Federal Housing Administration (FHA) or the Veterans Administration (VA), even commercial lenders. Publicly traded companies may have to disclose the fact of suspension or debarment, if such fact is deemed to be "material" and the company has a duty to disclose such information under the Securities Exchange Act of 1934.[54] Many states and municipalities will exclude contractors who have been debarred or suspended from doing business with the state or municipality.[55] Lastly, debarred or suspended entities may lose industry certifications. Such decertification would prevent an entity from entering into contracts with private companies as well as governmental agencies.[56]

§ 33.6 Case Study: Suspension and Exclusion by the Department of Health and Human Services for Health Care Providers[1]

Agencies are free to supplement FAR.[2] The Department of Health and Human Services (HHS) has done so for health care providers that bill for services rendered to Medicare patients. The result is that in addition to possible suspension debarment under FAR, on grounds listed in FAR, Medicare providers are also subject to suspension and exclusion under HHS regulations on grounds listed in HHS regulations.

A. BACKGROUND

In 1965, when Medicare and Medicaid were created, the Secretary of Health, Education and Welfare was given minimal power to suspend or exclude providers who failed to comply with the law,[3] with the result that an "excluded" provider is ineligible to receive any payment under Medicare or any state health care program.[4] The grounds for excluding providers were expanded in 1977 to require suspension or exclusion of practitioners "convicted of a criminal offense related to such individual's

---

53. DOD 5220.22–R.

54. Rule 10b–5, 17 C.F.R. § 240.10b–5 (1996); ABA, PRACTITIONER'S GUIDE *supra* § 33.5 note 11 at 105.

55. *See, e.g.,* Ariz.Rev.Stat.Ann. § 41–2613 (West 1992); Cal.Pub.Cont.Code § 4477 (West 1994), Fla.Stat.Ann. § 287.133(3)(e)(1)(West 1995), Ga.Code Ann. § 50–25–5 (West 1994).

56. ABA, PRACTITIONER'S GUIDE *supra* § 33.5 note 11 at 118.

§ 33.6

1. For a fuller discussion of this remedy, see PAMELA H. BUCY, HEALTH CARE FRAUD: CRIMINAL, CIVIL AND ADMINISTRATIVE LAW § 5.01 (1996).

2. FAR § 1.301(a)(1).

3. The Social Security Act of 1965, which created the Medicare and Medicaid programs, provided that:

"The Secretary could terminate an agreement [to participate in Medicare or Medicaid] only after reasonable notice and only if the provider (a) does not comply with the provisions of the agreement or of the law and regulations, (b) is no longer eligible to participate, or (c) fails to provide data needed to determine what benefit amounts are payable or refuses access to financial records...."

S.REP.NO. 404, 89th Cong., 1st Sess. (1965), *reprinted in* 1965 U.S.C.C.A.N. 1943.

4. This includes Medicaid, the Maternal and Child Health Block Grant Program and the Social Services Block Grant Program.

involvement in medicare or medicaid...." In 1980, the grounds for exclusion were broadened further to cover more health professionals such as administrators of health care facilities.[5] In 1983, the Secretary of Health and Human Services delegated to the IG the responsibility to detect, prosecute and punish fraudulent acts under Medicare and Medicaid.[6] This includes authority to suspend and exclude providers and to impose civil monetary penalties.[7] The exclusion remedy was expanded substantially in 1987 when the Medicare and Medicaid Patient and Program Protection Act (MMPPPA) was enacted.[8] This Act mandated exclusion from Medicare and state health care programs of individuals who committed certain egregious acts, such as committing crimes of patient abuse or fraud. The MMPPPA also expanded grounds for exclusion.[9] In 1996, the Health Insurance Accountability and Portability Act (HIPAA) expanded, again, the grounds for exclusion and added requirements to existing grounds.[10]

B. GROUNDS FOR EXCLUSION

There are two major categories of exclusions, mandatory and permissive. The Secretary of HHS (Secretary), through its designee, the Inspector General (IG), must impose exclusion if a provider has committed any of the grounds set forth for mandatory exclusion. The Secretary retains some discretion in determining the time period for which a provider is excluded on the mandatory grounds. While the provider must be excluded for at least 5 years, the Secretary may extend the exclusion beyond the 5 years.

The Secretary retains more discretion if the provider has engaged in any of the types of conduct that trigger permissive exclusion. With permissive exclusions, the Secretary determines whether exclusion is appropriate at all. If the Secretary finds that exclusion is appropriate, the Secretary determines the length of the exclusion, up to five years. Significantly, the Secretary retains the discretion to determine whether the provider's conduct qualifies as mandatory or permissive exclusion.

As will be seen, a conviction may provide the grounds for mandatory or permissive exclusion. The statute broadly defines the term "conviction" for purposes of both mandatory and permissive exclusions.

5. Omnibus Reconciliation Act of 1980, Pub.L.N. 96–499, 1980 U.S.C.C.A.N. (94 Stat.) 5526.

6. Greene v. Sullivan, 731 F.Supp. 835, 837 (E.D.Tenn.1990).

7. Travers v. Sullivan, 801 F.Supp. 394, 399 (E.D.Wash.1992), aff'd, 20 F.3d 993 (9th Cir.1994) (citing S.Report No. 109, 100th Cong., 1st Sess. 5 (1987), reprinted in 1987 U.S.C.C.A.N. 682, 695).

8. Became effective September 1, 1987. 57 Fed.Reg. 3298 (1992). One of the major reasons for the expansion in 1987

was concern that patients needed greater protection from health care providers who had lost their professional license in one state but were able to move to another state, obtain a license and continue to practice. Id. at 684.

9. S.Rep.No. 109, reprinted in 1987 U.S.C.C.A.N. 682, 695.

10. HIPAA, Pub.L. 104–191, §§ 211–214; 42 U.S.C. § 1320a–7(a) and (b), as amended.

i. Mandatory Exclusion

There are four grounds that trigger mandatory exclusion:

— Conviction of a "criminal offense related to the delivery of an item or service under Medicare or a State health care program, including the performance of management or administrative services relating to the delivery of times or services under any such program. . . ."[11]

— Conviction, "under Federal or State law, of a criminal offense related to the neglect or abuse of a patient, in connection with the delivery of a health care item or service, including any offense that the [IG] concludes entailed, or resulted in, neglect or abuse of patients."[12]

— Conviction "under Federal or State law, in connection with the delivery of a health care item or service or with respect to any act or omission in a health care program . . . operated or financed in whole or part by any Federal, State or local government agency, of a criminal offense consisting of a felony relating to fraud, theft, embezzlement, breach of fiduciary responsibility or other financial misconduct."[13]

— Conviction "under Federal or State law, of a criminal offense consisting of a felony relating to the unlawful manufacture, distribution, prescription, or dispensing of a controlled substance."[14]

ii. Permissive Exclusion

If one is going to be excluded as a Medicare or State health care provider, there are two advantages to qualifying for a permissive, rather than mandatory, exclusion: the Secretary has greater discretion not to impose exclusion at all or, if exclusion is imposed, the period of exclusion may be shorter.

There are two types of permissive exclusions. The first type is "derivative," which are exclusions based on action by a court, licensing board or other agency. Derivative grounds for permissive exclusion include convictions, license revocation or suspension actions, and exclusions or suspensions from a Federal or State health care program. The second type of permissive exclusion is "non-derivative." In these exclusions, the Secretary must make a prima facie showing of improper, qualifying behavior. Non-derivative grounds include submission of claims for excessive charges or unnecessary services, failure to furnish medical-

---

11. 42 U.S.C. § 1320a–7(a)(1). 42 C.F.R. § 1001.101(a).

12. 42 U.S.C. § 1320a–7(a)(2); 42 C.F.R. § 1001.101. The conviction of neglect or abuse need not relate to persons receiving Medicare or Medicaid health care benefits. Westin v. Shalala, 845 F.Supp. 1446, 1451–52 (D.Kan.1994).

13. 42 U.S.C. § 1320a–7(a)(3) as amended by HIPAA, Pub.L. 104–191, § 211.

14. 42 U.S.C. § 1320a–7(a)(4) as amended by HIPAA, Pub.L. 104–191, § 211.

ly necessary services, engaging in fraud or kickbacks, and failure to disclose or supply information.[15]

a. Derivative grounds

Convictions on three types of charges render a provider eligible for permissive exclusion: fraud, obstruction of an investigation, and illegal possession or distribution of controlled substances.

Fraud. A provider qualifies for permissive exclusion if convicted under state or federal law of a misdemeanor offense relating to:

> fraud, theft, embezzlement, breach of fiduciary responsibility, or other financial misconduct [i]n connection with the delivery of any health care item or service ... or [w]ith respect to any act or omission in a health program or any program ... operated or financed in whole or part by any Federal, State or local government agency.[16]

Obstruction of Justice. The Secretary may exclude a provider who has been convicted, under Federal or State law, for interfering with or obstructing any investigation of a criminal offense involving the delivery of health care items or services, patient neglect or abuse, or any financial offense involving governmental programs.[17] The convictions included in this exclusion are perjury, witness tampering and obstruction of justice.[18]

Controlled Substances. The Secretary may exclude an individual or entity convicted, under Federal or State law, of a "criminal offense relating to the unlawful manufacture, distribution, prescription or dispensing of a controlled substance."

License Revocation or Suspension. The Secretary may exclude a provider whose license to provide health care services has been revoked or suspended "for reasons bearing on the individual's or entity's professional competence, professional performance or financial integrity."[19] This exclusion is not intended to apply if a provider loses his or her license because technical violations such as failure to pay dues and not relating to the quality of care provided.[20]

15. 57 Fed.Reg. 3298, 3299 (1992).

16. 42 C.F.R. § 1001.201; 42 U.S.C. § 1320a–7(b)(1).

17. 42 C.F.R. § 1001.301 (1995) refers to "interference with or obstruction of any investigation into any criminal offense described in §§ 1001.101 or 1001.201." Section 1001.101 lists the convictions requiring mandatory exclusion (an offense "related to the delivery of an item or service under Medicare or a State health care program" or an "offense related to the neglect or abuse of a patient.") Section 1001.201 refers to "an offense relating to fraud, theft, embezzlement, breach of fiduciary responsi-

bility, or other financial misconduct [i]n connection with the delivery of any health care item or service, or with respect to any act or omission in a program operated by, or financed in whole or in part by, any Federal, State or local government agency."

18. 42 C.F.R. § 1001.401; 42 U.S.C. § 1320a–7(b)(3).

19. 42 C.F.R. § 1001.501(a)(1); 42 U.S.C. § 1320a–7(b)(4).

20. 55 Fed.Reg. 12205, 12207 (1990); S.Rep.No. 109, 100th Cong., 1st Sess. (1987), *reprinted in* 1987 U.S.C.C.A.N. 682, 688.

Exclusion or Suspension under Federal or State Health Care Program. The Secretary may exclude providers who have been suspended or excluded, or otherwise sanctioned under any State health care program or under any federal program involving health care services, including the Department of Defense or Department of Veterans Affairs.[21]

b. Non–derivative grounds

Exclusion for Filing Excessive Charges or Supplying Unnecessary Services or Substandard Services. This is the first of the "non-derivative" grounds for permissive exclusion. Rather than basing exclusion on action taken by another agency or organization, the IG must make factual determinations to exclude a provider on a "non-derivative" ground.

Failure to Furnish Medically Necessary Items and Services. The Secretary may exclude certain providers which have failed "substantially" to provide medically necessary items or services.[22] This exclusion applies only to certain providers: health maintenance organizations (HMO),[23] competitive medical plans (CMP) with a risk-sharing contract,[24] or primary care case management plans[25] approved under Medicare or Medicaid.[26]

Exclusion for False or Improper Claims. The Secretary may exclude a provider who has committed acts that subject one to civil monetary penalties (CMP).[27] It is not necessary that a CMP actually be imposed or that CMP proceeding be commenced.[28] Exclusion may be imposed instead of or in conjunction with a CMP or criminal proceed-

---

21. 42 C.F.R. § 1001.601; 42 U.S.C. § 1320a–7(b)(5).

22. 42 C.F.R. § 1001.801(a)(2); 42 U.S.C. § 1320a–7(b)(6)(C).

23. 42 U.S.C. § 1396(m) (Section 1903(m) of the Social Security Act): A "health maintenance organization" is a "public or private organization, organized under the laws of any State" that meets the requirements of 42 U.S.C. § 1396a(w) (regarding maintenance of written policies and procedures) or 42 U.S.C. § 139a(a) (regarding State plans for medical assistance) and

"(i) makes services it provides to individuals eligible for benefits ... accessible to such individuals, within the area served by the organization, to the same extent as such services are made accessible to individuals (eligible for medical assistance under the State plan) not enrolled with the organization, and

(ii) has made adequate provision against the risk of insolvency...."

24. 42 U.S.C. § 1395mm (Section 1876 of the Social Security Act): "To qualify for a risk sharing contract, a health maintenance organization or competitive medicare plan must be organized under the laws of a state; provide specified health care services to its enrolled members; assume financial risk 'on a prospective basis' for health care services rendered to its members; and, make adequate provision against the risk of insolvency."

25. 42 U.S.C. § 1396n(b)(1) (Section 1915(b)(1) of the Social Security Act) provides that the Secretary may waive certain requirements for State plans for medical assistance as may be necessary for a state to implement a "primary care case-management system" which restricts the provider from whom an individual eligible for such services can obtain medical care services.

26. 42 C.F.R. 1001.801(a); S.Rep.No. 109, *reprinted in* 1987 U.S.C.C.A.N. 682, 689.

27. See 42 U.S.C. § 1320a–7a.

28. 42 C.F.R. § 1001.901(a).

ing.[29] The IG cannot impose exclusion on grounds against which a provider successfully defends itself in a prior CMP proceeding.[30]

Exclusion for Fraud and Kickbacks. The Secretary excludes a provider if the Secretary determines that the provider has committed acts prohibited by Section 1128B(b) of the Social Security Act,[31] (knowing and willful filing of false claims or the solicitation, offer, payment or receipt of remunerations for referrals.)

Exclusion of Entities Owned or Controlled by a Sanctioned Person. The Secretary may exclude entities "owned or controlled by individuals who have been convicted, had CMPs or assessments imposed against them, or have been excluded from any programs...."[32]

Failure to Disclose or Provide Certain Information. The Secretary may exclude any entity that does not fully, accurately and completely disclose ownership information required by law.[33]

Failure to Grant Immediate Access. Pursuant to the Inspector General Act,[34] the Inspector General is entitled access to "all records, reports, audits, reviews, documents, papers ... or other material ..."which relate to Medicare, Medicaid or other state health care programs.[35] The Secretary may exclude providers which fail to grant "immediate access" upon "reasonable request" to agency representatives although the grounds for exclusion for such failure vary, depending upon the circumstances under which access was requested.[36]

Exclusions for Failure to Comply With a Corrective Action Plan. The Secretary is authorized to review the admissions or practice patterns of hospitals reimbursed by prospective payment ("DRGs") to ensure that hospitals are not unnecessarily admitting patients or admitting individuals through unnecessary multiple admissions.[37] If the Secretary finds deficiencies in the hospital's admissions or practice patterns, the Secretary may require the hospital to adopt corrective action to remedy the deficiencies.[38] If the hospital fails "substantially" to comply

---

29. 57 Fed. Reg. 3298, 3308 (1992).

30. 57 Fed. Reg. 3298, 3308 (1992).

31. 42 U.S.C. § 1320a–7b.

32. 55 Fed.Reg. 12205, 12209 (1990); 42 C.F.R. § 1001.1001; 42 U.S.C. § 1320a–7(b)(8).

33. 42 C.F.R. § 1001.1101(a); 42 U.S.C. § 1320a–7(b)(9)(-)(11). Section 1124 of the Social Security Act, 42 U.S.C. § 1320a–3, (1994) requires disclosure of ownership and related information; Section 1124A of the Social Security Act, 42 U.S.C. § 1320a–3a, requires disclosure of ownership information of some Part B providers; Section 1126 of the Social Security Act, 42 U.S.C. § 1320a–5, requires disclosure by institutions and organizations of owners, officers and managing employees convicted of program related offenses; 42 C.F.R. § 455, subpart B, requires disclosure of ownership and control information by providers and fiscal agents; 42 C.F.R. § 420, subpart C, requires disclosure of ownership and control information by providers, Part B suppliers, intermediaries and carriers.

34. The Inspector General Act of 1978, Pub.L.No. 94–452, 92 Stat. 1101 (1978) (codified as amended at 5 U.S.C. Appendix (1994)).

35. *Id.* at § 6(a)(1).

36. 42 C.F.R. § 1001.1301; 42 U.S.C. § 1320a–7(b)(12).

37. Social Security Act § 1886(f)(2)(B), 42 U.S.C. § 1395ww(f)(2)(B).

38. *Id.*

with the corrective plan, the Secretary may exclude the hospital from Medicare, Medicaid and other state health care programs.[39]

Exclusion for Default of Health Education Loan or Scholarship Obligations. The Secretary may exclude any individual whom the Public Health Service determines has defaulted on repayments of scholarships or loans made or secured in part by the Secretary.[40] Congress emphasized that "exclusion is a remedy of last resort for collecting outstanding loan obligations."[41]

Exclusions for Violations of the Limitations on Physician Charges. The Secretary may exclude a physician who knowingly, willfully and repeatedly charges more than is permitted under Medicare. Beginning January 1, 1991 physician services are reimbursed through a "limiting charge" formula.[42]

Exclusion for Billing for Services of Assistant At Surgery During Cataract Operations. The Secretary may exclude a physician who billed Medicare for the services of an assistant surgeon during cataract surgery without obtaining prior approval.[43] The prohibition against such assistants arose after congressional investigations found that the treatment of cataracts was a major source of fraud. Congress determined that fifty cents of every dollar spent on cataract surgery is lost to fraud, waste, or abuse.[44] One of the major recommendations made by the Inspector General of HHS to help eliminate this fraud, waste and abuse was to eliminate Medicare payments for assistant surgeons for all outpatient surgery unless preapproved by a PRO or Medicare carrier.[45]

Individuals Who Retain Ownership or Leadership in Sanctioned Entities. The Secretary may exclude individuals who retain a direct or indirect ownership or leadership position in sanctioned entities and "knows or should know" of the entity's sanctioned status.[46] The term "should know" is defined as acting in deliberate disregard of truth of falsity of information or in reckless disregard of the truth or falsity of information.[47]

39. 42 C.F.R. § 1001.1401(a) (1995); 42 U.S.C. § 1320a–7(b)(13).

40. 42 C.F.R.§ 1001.1501 (1995); 42 U.S.C. § 1320a–7(b)(14).

41. S.Rep.No. 109, 100th Cong., 1st Sess. (1987), *reprinted in* 1987 U.S.C.C.A.N. 682, 692.

42. Social Security Act § 1848, 42 U.S.C. § 1395w–4(g)(2). For services rendered between January 1, 1987 to December 31, 1990, a Medicare provider was permitted to charge no more than the physician's actual charges for a set 30–month period. Social Security Act § 1842(j)(1)(C), 42 U.S.C. § 1395(j)(1)(C). After December 31, 1990, Medicare provid-ers are permitted to charge only set amounts, known as Resource–Based Relative Value Scale (RBRVS).

43. 42 C.F.R. § 1001.1701(a).

44. *Medicare Reimbursement for Cataract Surgery: Hearings Before the Subcommittee on Health of the Committee on Ways and Means*, 99th Cong., 1st Sess. 8 (1985) (statement of Claude Pepper).

45. *Id.* at 66 (Executive Summary).

46. 42 U.S.C. § 1320a–7(b)(15) as amended by HIPAA, Pub.L. 104–191, § 213.

47. 42 U.S.C. § 1320a–7a(i)(7).

§ 33.7 Procedure for Imposing Exclusion

There are seven potential steps in imposing exclusion of health care providers: (1) Notice of intent to exclude, (2) Opportunity to present written information or, in some cases, oral argument, (3) Exclusion takes effect, (4) Hearing before an Administrative Law Judge (ALJ), (5) Appeal within Health and Human Services (HHS) to the Appellate Division of the Departmental Appeals Board (DAB), (6) Review by a federal District Court, and perhaps by higher federal courts, (7) Reinstatement of the provider after the period of exclusion is completed. These procedures have been upheld as constitutional.[1] Depending on the grounds for the exclusion the procedure may vary. In particular, if a provider is excluded on permissive grounds for engaging in kickbacks of submitting false claims, Step 2, above, does not occur. Instead, steps 3 and 4 are reversed, with the result that the provider is entitled to a hearing before an ALJ before the exclusion takes effect.

If the Secretary proposes to exclude a provider, it must notify the provider in writing, informing the provider of the intent to exclude, the basis for exclusion, and the potential effect of the exclusion.[2]

There are four variations in the exclusion procedure after the notice, depending on the grounds for which a provider is to be excluded. In the first variation, the provider is given an opportunity to present written material before the exclusion goes into effect. If the OIG determines that exclusion is nevertheless appropriate, the exclusion goes into effect immediately. The provider becomes entitled to a hearing before an ALJ only *after* the exclusion has gone into effect. With the second variation, the provider is given the opportunity to present oral argument as well as written material to a representative of the Secretary before the exclusion goes into effect but the provider gets a hearing before an ALJ only *after* the exclusion has gone into effect. In the third variation, the provider does not get to submit anything before the exclusion goes into effect: the grounds for the exclusion make it self-executing. The courts have held that imposing exclusion prior to given a provider a hearing does not violate due process.[3] In the fourth variation, the provider is entitled to an ALJ hearing prior to the exclusion going into effect. This procedure, of allowing only some providers the opportunity for an ALJ hearing prior to exclusion going into effect, conforms with congressional intent and due process.

In the exclusion cases, the parties to the hearing are the "petitioner" and the Inspector General (IG) of Health and Human Services. To obtain a hearing before the ALJ the provider must file a written request

---

§ 33.7

1. *Third Circuit*: Ritter v. Cohen, 797 F.2d 119, 124 (3d Cir.1986).

Fourth Circuit: Varandani v. Bowen, 824 F.2d 307, 313 (4th Cir.1987).

Eighth Circuit: Thorbus v. Bowen, 848 F.2d 901, 903–04 (8th Cir.1988).

Ninth Circuit: Cassim v. Bowen, 824 F.2d 791, 797 (9th Cir.1987).

Tenth Circuit: Koerpel v. Heckler, 797 F.2d 858, 866 (10th Cir.1986).

2. 42 C.F.R. § 1001.2001–1001.2002.

3. Barrett v. Department of Health and Human Services, 14 F.3d 26, 27 (8th Cir.1994).

for a hearing within 60 days after the date of the Notice of Exclusion; otherwise the exclusion goes into effect.[4] The ALJ may dismiss a case, in whole or part, by summary judgment, if there is no disputed issue of material fact.[5]

The parties are entitled to be represented by an attorney at the hearing and at pre-trial conferences; conduct discovery; stipulate to facts or law; present evidence and witnesses; cross-examine witnesses; present oral arguments, as permitted by the ALJ; and submit written briefs after the hearing.

§ 33.8 Professional Licenses and Credentials: Revocation and Other Disciplinary Actions

A defendant's criminal conviction may also have an impact on her professional license or ability to conduct business. Professionals such as physicians, attorneys, accountants, architects, and many others must maintain professional licenses granted by the various states to practice their profession. In addition, some individuals must hold other credentials to engage in their chosen business. Stock brokers, commodities brokers, practitioners before the SEC, financial institutions and their executives, all must maintain certain qualifications to conduct their professional affairs.

It is difficult to predict exactly what impact a conviction will have on a defendant's professional license in part because professional licenses are variously granted and monitored by the fifty states. According to the United States Supreme Court, "The state interests implicated in this [licensing] case are particularly strong. In addition to its general interest in protecting consumers and regulating commercial transactions, the State bears a special responsibility for maintaining standards among the licensed professions."[1]

Professional licenses are deemed to be property rights and are entitled to constitutional protection, including the right to due process before suspension or revocation.[2] State codes provide the circumstances under which licenses granted by the state may be suspended, revoked, or otherwise sanctioned. Historically, the discipline imposed for licensing infractions was of two extremes: severe (suspension or revocation), or minimal (letter of reprimand). More recently, state codes have been amended to provide a greater variety of sanctions, such as mandatory participation in a substance abuse program, or conditional practice in the profession.

---

4. The date of the receipt of the notice letter will be presumed to be 5 days after the date of such notice unless there is a reasonable showing to the contrary. 42 C.F.R. § 1005.2(c) (1995).

5. 42 C.F.R. § 1005.4(b)(12).

§ 33.8

1. Ohralik v. Ohio State Bar Ass'n, 436 U.S. 447, 460, 98 S.Ct. 1912, 56 L.Ed.2d 444 (1978).

2. Greene v. McElroy, 360 U.S. 474, 492, 79 S.Ct. 1400, 1411, 3 L.Ed.2d 1377 (1959).

Although the grounds for imposing licensure discipline vary considerably from state to state, and from profession to profession, a felony conviction will cause revocation of almost any professional license.[3]

§ 33.9 Bibliography

AMERICAN BAR ASS'N, (ABA) COMM. ON DEBARMENT AND SUSPENSION; SECTION OF PUBLIC CONTRACT LAW, THE PRACTITIONER'S GUIDE TO SUSPENSION AND DEBARMENT (2d 1996).

BUCY, PAMELA H., HEALTH CARE FRAUD: CRIMINAL, CIVIL AND ADMINISTRATIVE LAW (1996).

Debarment and Reinstatement of Federal Contractors: An Interim Report, 37th Report by the House Comm. On Gov't Operations, 102nd Cong. 2d Sess. (1992).

Hearings: Debarment and Reinstatement of Federal Contractors: An Interim Report, 102nd Cong., 2d Sess. 2 (1992); *Reform of Government-wide Debarment and Suspension Procedures: Report by the Subcomm. on Oversight of Gov't Management*, Senate Comm. of Gov't. Affairs, 97th Cong. 1st Sess. 3 (1981).

Medicare Reimbursement for Cataract Surgery: Hearings Before the Subcommittee on Health of the Committee on Ways and Means, 99th Cong., 1st Sess. 8 (1985) (statement of Claude Pepper).

Reform of Government-wide Debarment and Suspension Procedures: A Report Prepared by the Subcomm. on Oversight of Gov't Management of the Senate Comm. on Gov't Affairs, 3 (1981).

Shannon, Brian D., *The Government–Wide Debarment and Suspension Regulations After a Decade—A Constitutional Framework—Yet, Some Issues Remain in Transition*, 21 PUB. CONT. L.J. 370 (1992).

UNITED STATES DEPARTMENT OF COMMERCE, ECONOMICS AND STATISTICS ADMINISTRATION; BUREAU OF THE CENSUS FOR THE OFFICE OF MANAGEMENT AND BUDGET, CONSOLIDATED FEDERAL FUNDS REPORT: FISCAL YEAR 1995.

UNITED STATES DEPARTMENT OF JUSTICE, U.S. ATTORNEYS MANUAL.

UNITED STATES GENERAL SERVICES ADMINISTRATION, OFFICE OF ACQUISITION POLICY (GSA–OAP), LISTS OF PARTIES EXCLUDED FROM FEDERAL PROCUREMENT OR NONPROCUREMENT PROGRAMS.

---

3.   PAMELA H. BUCY, HEALTH CARE FRAUD: CRIMINAL, CIVIL AND ADMINISTRATIVE LAW § 5.05 (1996).

*

TABLE OF CASES

673

675

TABLE OF CASES

677

TABLE OF CASES

TABLE OF CASES

706

TABLE OF CASES

TABLE OF CASES

TABLE OF CASES

TABLE OF CASES

TABLE OF CASES

735

738

TABLE OF CASES

TABLE OF CASES

TABLE OF CASES

TABLE OF CASES

TABLE OF STATUTES

TABLE OF STATUTES

768

TABLE OF STATUTES

TABLE OF STATUTES

TABLE OF STATUTES

TABLE OF STATUTES

TABLE OF STATUTES

TABLE OF STATUTES

TABLE OF STATUTES

WEST'S ANNOTATED INDIANA CODE

Sec.	This Work Sec.	Note
35–41–4–5	32.1	4

MONTANA CODE ANNOTATED

Sec.	This Work Sec.	Note
42–34.102(1)	31.3	6

NEW JERSEY STATUTES ANNOTATED

Sec.	This Work Sec.	Note
2C:1–11	32.1	4

NEW YORK, MCKINNEY'S PENAL LAW

Sec.	This Work Sec.	Note
155.05(2)(d)	17.3	1

RHODE ISLAND GENERAL LAWS

Sec.	This Work Sec.	Note
11–52–6	8.11	3

WEST'S REVISED CODE OF WASHINGTON ANNOTATED

Sec.	This Work Sec.	Note
10.43.040	32.1	4

MODEL PENAL CODE

Sec.	This Work Sec.	Note
2.07(1)(a)	5.3	2
2.07(1)(b)	5.3	3
2.07(1)(c)	5.3	1
2.07(5)	5.4	
2.07(5)	5.4	13
2.07(5)	5.4	14

FEDERAL REGISTER

Vol.	This Work Sec.	Note
47, p. 28854	33.2	7
50, p. 13	10.15	34
50, p. 13, 463	10.15	33
50, p. 463	10.15	35
55, p. 12205	33.6	20
55, p. 12205	33.6	32
55, p. 12207	33.6	20
55, p. 12209	33.6	32
57, p. 3298	14.7	1
57, p. 3298	33.6	8
57, p. 3298	33.6	15
57, p. 3298	33.6	29
57, p. 3298	33.6	30
57, p. 3299	33.6	15
57, p. 3308	33.6	29
57, p. 3308	33.6	30
59, p. 37534	11.5	76
60, p. 33037	33.5	49
60, pp. 33037–33066	33.2	8
62, p. 14, paras. 3249–3252	18.4	14
62, p. 98, para. 27890 (proposed)	18.8	5
62, p. 98, paras. 27890–27917	18.17	5
62, p. 98, para. 27900	18.8	5
62, p. 98, para. 27909	18.8	5

POPULAR NAME ACTS

INVESTMENT COMPANY ACT OF 1940

Sec.	This Work Sec.	Note
2(a)(36)	22.2	

SECURITIES EXCHANGE ACT OF 1934

Sec.	This Work Sec.	Note
3(a)(10)	22.2	

REVISED UNIFORM SECURITIES ACT

Sec.	This Work Sec.	Note
401(1)	22.2	4

TABLE OF RULES

TABLE OF RULES

TABLE OF RULES

*

INDEX

References are to Sections

INDEX

801

803

INDEX

INDEX

INDEX

INDEX

INDEX

INDEX

INDEX

INDEX

INDEX

†